Programming Microsoft® Visual Basic® 2005: The Language

Francesco Balena
(Code Architects)

PUBLISHED BY
Microsoft Press
A Division of Microsoft Corporation
One Microsoft Way
Redmond, Washington 98052-6399

Library of Congress Control Number 2005936844

Printed and bound in the United States of America.

1 2 3 4 5 6 7 8 9   QWT   9 8 7 6

Distributed in Canada by H.B. Fenn and Company Ltd.

A CIP catalogue record for this book is available from the British Library.

Microsoft Press books are available through booksellers and distributors worldwide. For further information about international editions, contact your local Microsoft Corporation office or contact Microsoft Press International directly at fax (425) 936-7329. Visit our Web site at *www.microsoft.com/ learning/*. Send comments to *mspinput@microsoft.com*.

Acquisitions Editor: Ben Ryan
Project Editor: Kathleen Atkins
Technical Reviewer: Jack Beaudry
Copy Editor: Christina Palaia
Indexer: Lynn Armstrong

Body Part No. X11-53584

Contents at a Glance

Table of Contents

Part II **Object-Oriented Programming**

Part III   Working with the .NET Framework

Part IV   Advanced Topics

Acknowledgments

First of all, I am glad to have the opportunity to thank my friend Giuseppe Dimauro, for helping me better understand the many secrets behind the Microsoft Windows and .NET Framework platforms. Even more important, in these six months Giuseppe had to run Code Architects, the software and consulting company that we founded a few years ago, virtually by himself. I am happy I can finally go back to the fight!

Enrico Sabbadin is a true expert in *n*-tier enterprise applications, COM+, and security, and I feel very lucky he could review all the chapters while I was writing them. He provided many valuable suggestions.

I'd like to thank Marco Bellinaso and Alberto Falossi, two pillars of the Code Architects team. While I was busy on this book, Marco did a marvelous job with our U.S. Web site (*http://www.dotnet2themax.com*) and Alberto did the same with our Italian Web site (*http://www.dotnet2themax.it*).

Next come all the wonderful people at Microsoft Press. Kathleen Atkins has taken care of all my books, and she is so marvelous that I can't even think of writing a book with another editor. Jack Beaudry helped in finding typos and mistakes in code, whereas Christina Palaia did the same with my prose. English isn't my mother tongue, so you can imagine what kind of job she had to face.

This book would be very different—or might have never been printed at all—if it weren't for Ben Ryan, my acquisitions editor, who accepted my proposal and offered many suggestions on how to improve the original structure.

Finally, my family.

Living with a full-time coder and writer isn't easy. Only a special woman like my wife, Adriana, can do it in such a delightful way. And only a special boy like my son, Andrea, has permission to break into my room to talk about his favorite movie or to ask for help with his homework.

I can't thank both of you enough for always reminding me that the most important things in life can't be rendered as a sequence of bytes, regardless of the programming language you're using.

Introduction

Finding a reference book on Microsoft Visual Basic 2005 is easy. By the time this book reaches the bookstores, you'll find plenty of Visual Basic books on the shelves. Why should you buy this one? What makes this book different? When I began to write this book, I asked myself similar questions. How can a book compete with Microsoft Visual Studio manuals and all the samples and tips you can find on the Internet? To answer this question I need to take a short historical detour.

Where Visual Basic is coming from and heading to

I have been teaching Visual Basic since the early 1990s, well before it became Visual Basic .NET, and I taught (and wrote about) Microsoft QuickBasic before then. I have seen this language evolve from the time that you were practically compelled to use GoTo statements to make things work up to today's phenomenal object-oriented features. Everything has changed in these 20 years, except one thing: developers have always underutilized—or even misused—this language.

For instance, Microsoft Visual Basic 4 was the first version to offer the ability to define classes, yet very few developers actually used classes in their applications. The few who did, however, were able to catch the Microsoft .NET Framework wave easier than their colleagues were and could deliver more powerful Visual Basic .NET applications in less time. Another example: Microsoft Visual Basic 6 developers were able to access a database through ActiveX Data Objects (ADO) using client-side recordsets in disconnected mode, but many preferred to ignore this feature and continued to work with easier-to-use but less scalable server-side cursors. (And they had serious problems when writing large client/server applications.)

Versions 2002 and 2003 of Visual Basic .NET are *very* powerful development platforms, yet I see that many developers are missing their full potential. For example, features such as threading, reflection, and custom attributes can really revolutionize the way you write applications, but only a minority of programmers leverage them. The gap between what the language offers and what most developers actually use has always been large, but it is going to become larger with Visual Basic 2005, which offers great new features such as generics, custom events, operator overloading, and many other object-oriented enhancements.

Becoming a better developer

The bottom line is: developers don't need yet another reference manual. Instead—better, in addition to a reference—they need to understand how the old and the new features can be used to create more efficient, robust, reusable, and secure code. In the programming world, you can often achieve the same result with two or more equivalent techniques, but each one has its specific pros and cons, and often selecting the right approach can have far-reaching consequences on the end result. You need more than a mere reference book to gain the knowledge needed to detect these subtle differences.

A common misunderstanding in the programming community is that all you need to write great applications is familiarity with the .NET Framework and related technologies, such as Windows Forms and ASP.NET. Granted, you do need to learn these technologies to create real-world programs, but that familiarity isn't a surrogate for in-depth knowledge of low-level mechanisms that enable you to reduce memory and resource consumption, adopt effective optimization techniques, or leverage inheritance to write more concise and reusable code. I have seen too many applications that have a great user interface, yet perform very slowly and aren't structured in an orderly manner. Maintaining and evolving these applications are nightmares and cost much more in time and money than if they had been written with a solid understanding of the .NET Framework basics in mind.

Another facet of programming that many developers tend to overlook is the quest for thorough knowledge of the tool you spend most of your time with: Visual Studio. I find it quite ironic that most developers can argue for hours about which language can be more efficient or productive, yet they fail to leverage Visual Studio to its full potential, for example, by learning how to write macros, templates, and code snippets, or how to customize the IDE to fit their needs or programming style.

Not the usual programming language reference

For all these reasons, I decided that I wanted to write something different from the typical language reference, something that would cover all the language features *and* show real-world cases when these features can be used profitably. The problem with this approach is that it tends to take a lot of space. Clearly, a book on this premise would be remarkably thicker than a standard reference book, and it would take me much longer to write.

If this book would cover the entire Visual Basic potential—including both the language features and higher-level technologies such as Windows Forms and ASP.NET—it would have exceeded the number of pages that Microsoft Press can bind in a book. And it would have hit the streets too many months after the Visual Basic 2005 release.

In the end, I saw that the only realistic solution to this issue was focusing on the language and most of the .NET Framework foundation classes—memory management, serialization, threading, reflection, PInvoke, and COM Interop—and leaving out important topics such as Windows Forms, ASP.NET Web Forms and Web Services, and ADO.NET. It was a painful decision, but now that the book is completed, I am very glad I took this route. This is a book I have had in mind for years, and I finally had the opportunity to write it.

Note As of this writing, I am planning to write at least one other book in the *Programming Microsoft Visual Basic 2005* series, but I haven't finalized the agreement with the publisher, and thus I can't be more precise about the topics I'll cover in a forthcoming book(s). If you want to learn more, read my Weblog or subscribe to my Web site's newsletter. (Information on how to do this is provided later in this introduction.)

Live updates and feedback

Even though I have been working with Visual Basic, C#, and the .NET Framework for so many years, I do continue to learn something new almost every day. You can learn more about my discoveries by visiting my Web site, where I maintain the home page for this and all my other books, at this URL:

http://www.dotnet2themax.com

You can also subscribe to the site's newsletter and receive information about new articles and code snippets available online. Or you can read my English Weblog (see Figure I-1) where I post updates about this book, comments from readers, plans for future Microsoft Press books, and so forth:

http://www.dotnet2themax.com/blogs/fbalena

> **Tip** Select the Books category to read all posts related to this and other forthcoming books. Writing this book has been a challenge. I think (and hope) I did a good job, but I surely look forward to hearing your comments, reactions, and suggestions for improvements. You can leave a comment at my Weblog or write me at *fbalena@dotnet2themax.com* or *fbalena@codearchitects.com*.

Figure I-1 My Weblog

Who Is This Book For?

The short answer is that this book is for all Visual Basic 2005 developers.

A more articulated answer is that this book is addressed to the following people:

- Developers who have been writing applications with versions 2002 and 2003 of Visual Basic .NET and want to learn all the new features in Visual Basic 2005 as quickly as possible

- Visual Basic 6 programmers who are facing the daunting task of converting their skills and their applications to Visual Basic 2005 and the .NET Framework

- Programmers who are already familiar with another programming language—for example, C, C#, C++, Java, or Borland Delphi—and who want to learn quickly how to write Visual Basic 2005 applications

- Expert Visual Basic developers who want to learn more about advanced .NET Framework programming techniques, such as memory optimization, object serialization, and threading

- Programmers of any expertise level who want to write robust and maintainable applications by leveraging object-oriented features of Visual Basic and other .NET Framework techniques, such as reflection and custom attributes

Of course, not all the chapters in this book will require the same degree of attention from each of the preceding groups. For example, Visual Basic novices will spend most of their time digesting the first half of the book, whereas expert programmers will find the second half more intriguing. Developers coming from edition 2003 of Visual Basic .NET will probably focus on chapters that are interspersed here and there in the book, for example, Chapter 4 ("Using Visual Studio 2005"), Chapter 5 ("Debugging Visual Basic Applications"), Chapter 11 ("Generics"), and Chapter 16 ("The My Namespace").

 Visual Basic 6 developers switching to Visual Studio 2005 should carefully read the sections marked with this icon. In these sections, I focus on the important differences between these two languages as well as subtle issues you might face when migrating a Visual Basic 6 application to the .NET Framework.

 Sections marked with this icon describe features that have been added in version 2005 of the Visual Basic language or in version 2.0 of the .NET Framework. Notice that some features are so important that I devote an entire chapter to them, in which case this icon appears only at the top of the chapter. Otherwise, some really minor improvements are mentioned in text without being described in a section of their own.

Organization of This Book

Programming Microsoft Visual Basic 2005: The Language is broadly organized in four parts.

The first three chapters of Part I cover the language basics. If you aren't new to Visual Basic, you might skip them, even though you might find some interesting tips here and there. If you are switching from Visual Basic 6 or Visual Basic .NET 2003, you can simply stop at the Visual Basic 6 and New icons, as described in the previous section. Regardless of your familiarity with Visual Basic, however, I recommend that you read Chapters 4 and 5 carefully because they explain the many new features of the Visual Studio IDE and illustrate concepts that are used in subsequent chapters.

Part II is devoted to object-oriented features of the Visual Basic language. Again, if you are already familiar with Visual Basic .NET, you might want to spend more time on the sections marked with the New icon, but I suggest you read Chapter 7, "Delegates and Events," and Chapter 9, "Object Lifetime," because they illustrate advanced techniques that can improve your skills remarkably. Chapter 11 is a must-read for learning more about the most intriguing and important new features of version 2.0 of the .NET Framework.

Part III is about basic types in the .NET Framework. Chapter 16, "The My Namespace," contains an in-depth description of this new Visual Basic feature, but you'll surely find a lot of useful information in all the chapters in this part. For example, Chapter 13, "Arrays and Collections," shows you how to work wonders with .NET Framework complex data structures (including generics collection). My favorite chapter is Chapter 14, "Regular Expressions," where I describe all I've learned about this exciting (and very useful) .NET Framework feature.

Part IV covers advanced programming topics, such as threading, serialization, PInvoke, and COM Interop. These features can make your applications more powerful, but failing to use them properly can introduce many hard-to-find bugs; thus, read these chapters carefully. Chapter 18, "Reflection," and Chapter 19, "Custom Attributes," are actually one very long chapter split into two: in the former, I offer a very complete reference on reflection, whereas in the latter I offer a few real-world (and quite complex) examples of the wonders custom attributes can do for you.

System Requirements

You need the following hardware and software to build and run the code samples for this book:

- Microsoft Windows XP with Service Pack 2, Microsoft Windows Server 2003 with Service Pack 1, or Microsoft Windows 2000 with Service Pack 4

- Microsoft Visual Studio 2005 Standard Edition or Microsoft Visual Studio 2005 Professional Edition. (A few sections in Chapters 4 and 5 assume that you have installed the Developer Edition of Visual Studio Team System.)

- 1-GHz Pentium or compatible processor

- 384 MB RAM (512 MB or more recommended)

- Video (800 × 600 or higher resolution) monitor with at least 256 colors (1,024 × 768 High Color 16-bit recommended)

- Microsoft Mouse or compatible pointing device

Technology Updates

As technologies related to this book are updated, links to additional information will be added to the Microsoft Press Technology Updates Web page. Visit this page periodically for updates on Visual Studio 2005 and other technologies:

http://www.microsoft.com/mspress/updates/

Code Samples

All of the code samples discussed in this book can be downloaded from the book's companion content page at the following address:

http://www.microsoft.com/mspress/companion/0-7356-2183-7/

Support for This Book

Every effort has been made to ensure the accuracy of the information in this book and the companion content. Microsoft Press provides support for books and companion content at the following Web site:

http://www.microsoft.com/learning/support/books/

I provide support for this book, including an errata page and updated code samples, at my Web site:

http://www.dotnet2themax.com/

and through my Weblog:

http://www.dotnet2themax.com/blogs/fbalena

Questions and Comments

If you have comments, questions, or ideas regarding the book or the companion content, or if you have questions that are not answered by visiting the preceding sites, please send them to Microsoft Press by e-mail:

mspinput@microsoft.com

Or by postal mail:

Microsoft Press
Attn: *Programming Microsoft Visual Basic 2005* Editor
One Microsoft Way
Redmond, WA 98052-6399

Please note that Microsoft software product support is not offered through the preceding addresses.

Part I
The Basics

Chapter 1
Introducing the Microsoft .NET Framework

In this chapter:

In the first two editions of this book—which cover versions 2002 and 2003 of the Visual Basic .NET language—I used this first chapter about the .NET Framework to explain why Microsoft decided to invest so much money and energy in this new programming platform and why it would cause a quiet revolution in the way you write Windows and Web applications.

Three years and a half have passed since the .NET Framework launch, however, and for this edition of the book I realize that such an introduction would be almost superfluous, given that much has been written about the .NET Framework in the meantime. After all, odds are that you are reading this book because you have already used Visual Basic .NET or that, at the very least, you read enough about the .NET initiative that you don't need yet another introductory chapter.

On the other hand, one of my goals is to make this book as consistent and complete as possible, so I need to introduce a few concepts that will be explained more in detail later in this book. In the end, I decided to compile a sort of glossary that you can read quickly to find your way in the .NET maze. If you aren't new to the .NET Framework, you can safely skip this section or just give it a quick read.

Unlike a traditional glossary, though, these terms are arranged in a logical order rather than in alphabetical order. Each term represents an important concept that often relies on terms that have been introduced previously.

A .NET Glossary

Assembly   A .NET application can consist of one or more assemblies. Each assembly is usually an individual EXE or DLL executable file. An assembly can also include other files, such as .html, .gif, or other nonexecutable files. Assemblies are the units of versioning in the sense that all the files in an assembly have the same version number. The assembly is also the smallest unit of logical deployment because you never deploy a subset of the files that make up the assembly. Typically, an application uses several external assemblies, including those belonging to the .NET Framework itself.

An assembly can include either one executable file or one executable file plus other data files, but single-file assemblies are by far the most common kind of assemblies. Visual Studio 2005 can create only single-file assemblies and you need to manually run the command-line compiler and linker to create multifile assemblies.

Common Language Runtime (CLR)   The .NET Framework uses a layered architecture, at the bottom of which sits the Windows API, as you see in Figure 1-1. The .NET Framework offers an object-oriented view of the operating system's functions but doesn't replace them, so most calls into the .NET Framework are ultimately resolved as calls into one of the Windows kernel DLLs. The CLR is the first layer that belongs to the .NET Framework. This layer is responsible for .NET base services, such as memory management, garbage collection, structured exception handling, and multithreading. You might think of the CLR as the supervisor of all .NET applications: You never directly interact with the CLR, but all your applications are controlled by it.

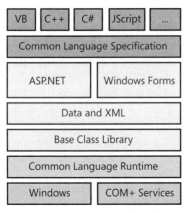

Figure 1-1   The layers in the .NET Framework

Managed and Unmanaged Code   .NET applications are said to execute as managed code because they run under the control of the CLR and are prevented from executing nonsecure code that might crash the machine or compromise your data. For example, the CLR might prevent an application from accessing the file system or the system registry if the application has been launched from an Internet location that isn't fully trusted (see later in this glossary). By contrast, non-.NET applications, such as Visual Basic 6 applications, are said to execute as unmanaged code, or native code. Of all the languages from Microsoft, only C++ can produce both managed and unmanaged code, but even C++ developers should resort to unmanaged code only if strictly necessary—for example, for doing low-level operations or for performance reasons—because only managed code gets all the benefits of the .NET platform.

Classes and Types   In .NET parlance, the type concept is more generic than the class concept. More precisely, the .NET Framework defines thousands of types; all the .NET types can be classified in two broad categories: reference types (or classes) and value types. The vast majority of .NET types are classes, so in most cases you can use the two terms interchangeably. Read the "Reference Types and Value Types" section in Chapter 2 for more details.

Base Common Library (BCL)   The .NET Framework consists of several thousands of types, grouped in about 30 assemblies. These types allow you to perform nearly all conceivable tasks, including displaying windows, reading files, and sending HTML text to a browser across the Internet. The BCL is the portion of the .NET Framework that defines all the basic data types, such as System.Object (the root of the .NET object hierarchy), numeric and date types, the String type, arrays, and collections. The BCL also contains types for managing .NET core features, such as file I/O, threading, serialization, and security. The majority of the types belonging to the BCL are compiled in the mscorlib.dll and System.dll assemblies.

.NET Languages   Most of the functionality that was embedded in traditional languages such as Visual Basic 6 is now part of the .NET Framework and is exposed as .NET types. All .NET languages can use these types, and therefore all languages have the same capabilities. For example, even though Visual Basic 2005 and Visual C# 2.0 have different syntax and different keywords, they are roughly equivalent, and both of them let you tap the full power of the .NET Framework.

In addition, all .NET Framework languages compile to IL code (see next item), which in turn is eventually compiled into native code. For this reason, you won't see any noticeable difference in performance among different languages. An exception to this rule of thumb is that a C# application that uses pointer and unsafe code can run significantly faster then the equivalent Visual Basic application. On the other hand, C# developers are strongly discouraged from using unsafe code, because the assembly is unverifiable and it might not run because of Code Access Security limitations (see later in this glossary).

Intermediate Language (IL)   Unlike traditional programming languages, .NET compilers don't produce native code that can be directly fed to and executed by the CPU. Instead, they produce the so-called IL code, which is a sort of machine language for a virtual processor that doesn't correspond to any CPU available today. While the IL code is lower level than most modern programming languages, it's higher level than pure assembly language. IL is a stack-oriented language that doesn't directly address CPU registers and is aware of high-level concepts such as strings, exceptions, and object creation.

ILDASM   Visual Studio 2005 comes with a tool named ILDASM, or IL Disassembler. (You can find it in the C:\Program Files\Microsoft Visual Studio 8\SDK\v2.0\Bin folder, for a default installation of Visual Studio.) As its name implies, this utility enables you to see the IL code stored inside a .NET assembly by letting you simply drag the .exe or .dll file from Windows Explorer to the ILDASM main window. (See Figure 1-2.) Enable the Show Source Lines option in the View menu to have ILDASM display the original source code that produced the assembly being analyzed. (You see the actual Visual Basic code only if the executable has a companion .pdb file with symbolic information.) I will use ILDASM often in this book to show what happens behind the scenes and comment the code that the Visual Basic compiler produces.

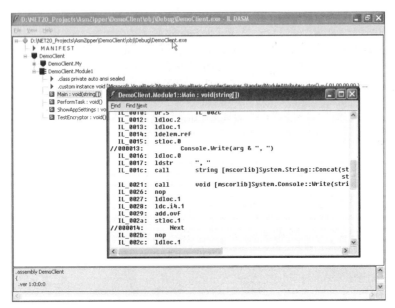

Figure 1-2 The ILDASM tool

Just-in-Time (JIT) Compiler Because no CPU can execute IL code, the CLR must convert it to native code while the program is running by launching the JIT compiler and passing it the address of entry point method (typically, the Sub Main procedure in a Visual Basic application). When the main procedure invokes other methods, the .NET runtime uses the JIT compiler to transform the IL code inside these methods into native code and then executes the native code. This on-the-fly compilation is done only once per method in the application's lifetime because the native code is kept in memory and reused when that specific method is called again.

Metadata and the Manifest In addition to IL code, an assembly includes a set of tables that contain the so-called metadata—that is, information about which types are compiled in the assembly, what are their methods, which assemblies this assembly depends on, and so forth. In the .NET Framework world, metadata is as important as the actual executable code because the CLR uses the metadata in many occasions. The most important set of metadata tables is known as the *assembly manifest*.

The great thing about metadata is that you can extend it by means of *custom attributes*, which offer a standard way to include additional metadata information in an assembly that doesn't depend on a specific programming language or compiler.

Reflection Reflection is a set of types that enable a .NET Framework application to read and use the metadata stored in an assembly. Many portions of the .NET Framework are heavily based on reflection, including the ability to serialize the current value of an object to a file or send objects to an application running on a different computer. I cover reflection exhaustively in Chapter 18.

Native Image Generator (NGen) The .NET Framework comes with the NGen utility, which allows you to *precompile* a .NET application into native code. Notice that precompiling an application doesn't necessarily buy you better performance and, in some cases, it might even produce slower code. The NGen utility is most effective with client-side applications—for example, Windows Forms applications—because it reduces the startup time, but it's less useful with server-side applications, such as Web Forms and Web Services projects, where startup time isn't critical. Notice that you can't use the NGen utility to prevent an assembly from being decompiled (see next term), because an assembly precompiled by NGen still requires the presence of the original assembly that contains readable IL code. You can read more about the NGen utility in Chapter 17.

Decompilers   A few utilities on the market enable you to analyze a compiled .NET assembly and rebuild the original C# or Visual Basic source code. In my opinion, the best tool in this category is Reflector (*http://www.aisto.com/roeder/dotnet/*), which is distributed as freeware and offers you the option to decompile into both Visual Basic and C# code. The decompilation process works so well that you might use this tool as a cross-language conversion tool: compile a piece of Visual Basic source code and then decompile it as C#, or vice versa. Another popular decompiler is Anakrino (*http://www.saurik.com/net/exemplar/*), also distributed as freeware.

Obfuscators   Because it's so easy to peek into a .NET assembly, many companies are very concerned about protecting their software from a decompiler. Unfortunately, you can't really protect an assembly from decompilation. However, you can obfuscate an assembly by renaming all type and member names into meaningless strings. Malicious users who decompile your assembly would read just a list of nonsense sequences of characters. They would still be able to understand what your code does, but this job would take much longer and you can hope they would desist.

Visual Studio 2005 comes with PreEmptive Solutions's Dotfuscator Community Edition, which is more than adequate for most obfuscating tasks. (You can run this utility from the Tools menu, see Figure 1-3.) If you are looking for a more powerful product, you should consider purchasing the Professional Edition of this product or another full-featured obfuscator such as Demeanor (*www.wiseowl.com*). Visit *http://www.howtoselectguides.com/dotnet/obfuscators/* to read more about obfuscators and their features (as well as other freeware and commercial programming tools).

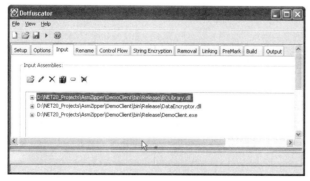

Figure 1-3   The PreEmptive Solutions's Dotfuscator Community Edition tool

Global Assembly Cache (GAC)   .NET Framework assemblies can be subdivided in two categories: private assemblies and public assemblies. Private assemblies are stored in the same folder as the application's main folder and can be used only by that application (or by other assemblies in the same folder). Shared assemblies are usually stored in the Global Assembly Cache (GAC) and can be used by all the .NET applications running on the local computer.

The GAC is an area of the hard disk (located under the C:\Windows\Assembly directory) where the .NET Framework stores all the assemblies that can be shared among all the .NET applications running on the local computer. For example, all the assemblies that are part of the .NET Framework itself are stored in the GAC. Multiple versions of the same assembly can coexist in the GAC.

Versioning   Versioning is the problem of installing a new version of a component on a computer without affecting the correct functioning of other applications that use a different version of the same component. Versioning has plagued Visual Basic 6 and COM developers for years, but the .NET Framework has solved it in a very elegant way. First, you can avoid versioning issues by using private assemblies: each application can use a different version of a private assembly because private assemblies aren't shared with other .NET applications. Second, you can install a shared assembly in the GAC because the GAC can safely contain multiple versions of the same assembly. Each application compiled against version X.Y of a given component continues to work correctly even if the user installs a newer (or older) version of the same component.

.NET Framework versioning is more flexible than COM versioning. In fact, a developer or a system administrator can use a configuration file to redirect a request for a given component to another version of the same component. The component author can release a new version that fixes a few bugs or that's more efficient and thus indirectly improve the robustness and speed of all the applications that use that component without introducing version incompatibility problems.

Versioning even extends to the .NET Framework itself. When a new version of the .NET Framework becomes available, you can install it on a computer without removing previous versions of the framework, and applications using the previous versions will continue to work. (See Figure 1-4.)

XCOPY Deployment   If a .NET application uses only private assemblies, you can install it by simply copying its folder (including any child folders) from your development machine to your customer's machine. This mechanism is known as XCOPY deployment. This feature *doesn't* imply that you should use this simple installation method instead of a full-featured installation procedure. You typically need a full-featured installation to create shortcuts on the Start menu and enable the end user to select which portions of the applications will be installed. Even considering these ancillary tasks, however, installing a .NET application is much simpler than installing a similar COM application because fewer things can go wrong.

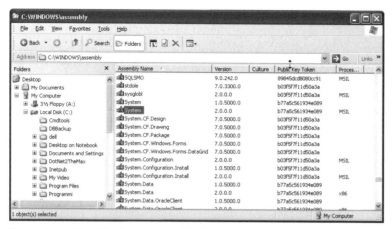

Figure 1-4   The Windows\Assembly directory of a computer on which both versions 1.1 and 2.0 of the .NET Framework have been installed.

Configuration Files   .NET applications store their settings in configuration files, which are located in the same directory as the application's main assembly. A configuration file's name is formed by appending the .config extension to the assembly's name. For example, the myapp.exe application uses the myapp.exe.config configuration file. Being stored in the application's folder, configuration files are installed correctly when you deliver the application using XCOPY deployment.

A configuration file uses XML syntax to store hierarchical data and therefore is more flexible than, say, .ini files. ASP.NET applications can use additional configuration files, one for each subdirectory containing a portion of the application; each of these secondary configuration files affect the settings of the corresponding portion of the application. A special machine.config file affects all the .NET applications running on a given computer.

Inheritance   The .NET Framework is designed around the concept of inheritance. All the objects in the .NET Framework form a hierarchy with a single root, the System.Object class, from which all the other .NET types derive. These types provide functionality in almost any conceivable area, including the user interface, data access, Internet programming, XML processing, security, and cross-machine communication.

Programming under .NET often means extending one of these types. For example, you can create a text box control that accepts only numbers by deriving a new class from the System.Windows.Forms.TextBox class and adding all the necessary code that rejects invalid entries. Classes that don't inherit from a specific .NET class implicitly inherit from System.Object and therefore benefit in other ways from being part of the .NET object hierarchy. Notice that .NET supports only single inheritance (which means that a class can't inherit from two or more classes).

Common Type Specifications (CTS)   This set of specifications dictate how a type exposes fields, properties, methods, and events; it also defines how a type can inherit from another type and possibly override its members. Because all .NET languages recognize these specifications, they can exchange data, use types written in a different language, and even inherit from them. For example, you can inherit a Visual Basic 2005 class from a C# class, and you can write a C# class that implements an interface defined in Visual Basic.

Common Language Specifications (CLS)   This set of specifications dictate the minimum features that a programming language must have to be qualified as a .NET language. For example, all .NET languages must be able to deal with primitive types such as strings, integers, and zero-based arrays, and must be able to process a .NET exception that is thrown when an error occurs. A few types in the .NET Framework don't comply with the CLS—for example, jagged arrays and arrays with a lower index other than 0. If your application exposes such non-CLS-compliant objects to the outside world, it might be unusable by other applications, depending on the .NET language used to develop them.

AppDomains   Traditionally, a Windows application runs in a distinct Win32 process. Each process is isolated from other process by means of hardware features of the CPU so that a process can't accidentally corrupt memory and data belonging to other programs. In the .NET Framework world, however, applications run in an application domain, or AppDomain. There can be one or more AppDomains running in the same Win32 process, but an assembly in a given AppDomain can't affect assemblies in other AppDomains, even if all AppDomains are in the same Win32 process. (See Figure 1-5.) AppDomain isolation is achieved at the software level because all .NET compiles produce safe code that can't access arbitrary locations of memory. Using a single process containing multiple AppDomains consumes fewer resources than splitting the application in multiple processes and makes the communication among assemblies in distinct AppDomain easier and more efficient.

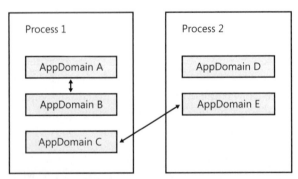

Figure 1-5   A Win32 process can host multiple AppDomains. AppDomains running in the same process can communicate more efficiently than AppDomains in different processes.

Console Applications   Console applications are .NET programs that read their input data and display their output in the console window. They are useful for creating simple utilities that you can invoke from batch files but are rarely a suitable choice for commercial applications. On the other hand, console applications are very concise and for this reason most of the code samples in this book are designed to run as console applications.

Windows Forms   Windows Forms is the portion of the .NET Framework that allows you to create traditional Win32 applications running on stand-alone computers or computers that act as clients in a large client-server application. It contrasts with Web Forms applications, which are .NET programs that run on a server and send their output as HTML text to browsers running on client computers (see later in this glossary).

Creating a Windows Forms project is similar to creating a Visual Basic 6 project: you drop one or more controls on the form's surface, assign the properties in the Properties window, and write the code that must run when the control triggers an event. In this book, I occasionally show Windows Forms applications samples to illustrate programming techniques that can't be demonstrated by means of console projects.

ClickOnce Applications   ClickOnce is a new feature of the .NET Framework version 2.0. In a nutshell, a ClickOnce project generates a Windows Forms application that can be launched from a remote computer, either on the local intranet or the Internet. ClickOnce applications have a great advantage over regular Windows Forms applications: ease of deployment. The end user needs only to click a hyperlink in the browser to either launch the remote application or install it on the local machine, depending on how the ClickOnce project was compiled. ClickOnce programs can run as partially trusted applications that are subject to Code Access Security restrictions (see later in this glossary).

GDI+   All the .NET Framework types that are related to creating images and graphics are gathered in GDI+. You can use GDI+ features both in Windows Forms applications and in ASP.NET applications. For example, you might create a histogram graph on the server and send it to the client in an HTML page with a Web Forms application, or send it to a remote client via a Web service.

ADO.NET   ADO.NET is the portion of the .NET Framework that enables you to work with databases and is therefore the .NET counterpart of the ActiveX Data Objects (ADO) technology. In spite of their similar names, ADO and ADO.NET are very different. Whereas classic ADO covers virtually all the database techniques available—including server-side and client-side cursors, disconnected resultsets, and batch updates—ADO.NET focuses mainly on disconnected resultsets (called DataSets in ADO.NET terminology) and offers no support for server-side cursors. The DataSet object is much more powerful than the ADO Recordset object and can store data coming from multiple tables, in the same database or different databases. You can create relationships among different data tables, and you can import or export both the data and the metadata as XML.

ASP.NET   ASP.NET is the portion of the .NET Framework that enables you to create Internet and intranet applications. ASP.NET applications can be divided in two categories: Web Forms applications and Web Services applications (see next two terms). Both application kinds share the ASP.NET infrastructure and use the same services—for example, caching and security services.

ASP.NET enables you to create powerful and flexible applications in a fraction of the time you needed with pre-.NET technologies such as Active Server Pages (ASP). This portion of the .NET Framework has been remarkably extended and improved in version 2.0. I don't cover ASP.NET applications in this book.

Web Forms   ASP.NET Web Forms projects create Internet and intranet applications that produce a user interface and that appear to run inside a browser. More precisely, Web Forms applications run inside Microsoft Internet Information Services (IIS) and produce HTML text that is sent to the client's browser. Thanks to the provision of many user controls—including complex controls such as grids, calendars, and tree views—you can write Web Forms applications using the same event-driven approach you use for Windows Forms applications.

Web Services   Web Services projects enable you to create components that run on a remote computer that is accessible through the Internet. Unlike Web Forms applications, a Web Service application doesn't produce HTML text: instead, client applications communicate with a Web service by sending a request encoded in an XML grammar known as Simple Object Access Protocol (SOAP). The ASP.NET infrastructure captures the request, invokes the object running inside IIS, encodes the return value back to SOAP, and sends it back to the client.

The great thing about Web Service projects is that Visual Studio automatically generates a *proxy class* for the client. The code in the client application uses this proxy class and invokes its methods as it would do with a standard object, but the proxy class transparently converts these calls into SOAP calls across the wire. The neat result is that you can work with a remote component as if it were a local object.

Visit *http://msdn.microsoft.com/webservices/webservices/building/wse/default.aspx* for more information about the Web Services Enhancements (WSE) library, which extends the standard Web Services technology with features such as security and transactions.

Remoting   Remoting is a technology that enables a .NET Framework application to invoke a method of an object defined in another application that runs in a different AppDomain, a different process on the same computer, or a different computer across the LAN or the Internet, using a transportation channel such as TCP or HTTP. Remoting is extremely efficient because data is exchanged in binary format (as opposed to Web Services, which exchange data in XML textual format).

Serviced Components   Serviced components are .NET Framework objects that can interoperate with Component Services (COM+) applications. Web services, remoting, and serviced components are the three .NET Framework technologies that allow you to run code on a remote computer, but each of them has its own advantages and defects. Web services enable you to communicate even with non-Windows platforms but are relatively inefficient. Remoting is the most efficient of the group, but can work only with other .NET Framework applications. Serviced components are midway between these extremes because they can interact with other Windows applications—not necessarily .NET Framework applications—and fully support COM+ transactions and security.

Platform Invoke and COM Interop   The CLR enables a .NET Framework application to interact with legacy, non-.NET applications. Two main kinds of interactions are supported: Platform Invoke (also known as *PInvoke*) and COM Interop. The former enables you to invoke a function compiled in a "classic" DLL, typically written in C, C++, or Borland Delphi. For example, thanks to Platform Invoke you can invoke methods in the Windows API.

COM Interop enables you to both call and be called by a COM component, including components written in Visual Basic 6. COM Interop is a critical feature when you are migrating a legacy application into a .NET Framework language because it enables you to migrate one piece of the application at the time and still be able to interact with older pieces.

Code Access Security (CAS)   Managed code always runs under the supervision of the CLR. At each call into the .NET Framework, the CLR checks that the calling code satisfies the Code Access Security rules and has the right to perform the requested operation. These rights depend on the identity of the assembly and on the location from which it is being executed. More specifically, only assemblies that are loaded from the local hard disk are granted all permissions. (Such assemblies are said to be *fully trusted*.) Applications launched from a network share or from an intranet location are prevented from doing potentially dangerous operations, such as reading and writing files. Applications running from the Internet are given few or no permissions, depending on whether the origin URL is considered to be a trusted site. (Assemblies with limited permissions are said to run in a *partially trusted* security context.)

Code running in a partially trusted context doesn't have access to the local file system, which can be a serious problem if the application needs to save data between sessions—for example, user's preferences. For this reason, the .NET Framework can manage a small portion of the local hard disk as if it were completely isolated by other folders. This portion is known as *isolated storage* and can be accessed even by applications running from an intranet location or an Internet site.

Chapter 2

Basic Language Concepts

Microsoft Visual Basic 2005 is a rich programming language that uses the entire spectrum of object-oriented programming (OOP) features plus many extensions peculiar to the Microsoft .NET environment. The problem in writing a book about this language is that all these features are tightly related to one another, so it's virtually impossible to examine each feature one at a time without also describing the others. For example, even though I won't discuss classes and inheritance until later in the book, in this chapter I need to provide at least an overview of how they work.

The code samples in this chapter assume that you have created a Console project and will take their input from and display their result in the command-line window (the black window where you can enter commands for the operating system). You can create a Console project by choosing New Project on the File menu and selecting Console Application in the New Project dialog box. I use a console window rather than a regular form, which surely makes my demos less appealing but enables me to focus on the code rather than the user interface, which isn't the topic of this chapter.

Modules, Classes, and Namespaces

The starting point in our explorations of the Visual Basic language is modules because modules provide a simple way to test small snippets of code. In real-world applications, modules are used far less frequently than regular classes (which I cover later in this chapter), but they are perfect to illustrate some important concepts.

Like classes and forms, modules are defined in source files that have a .vb extension. This can be disorienting if you are switching from Microsoft Visual Basic 6, where you can count at least six different file extensions (.frm for forms, .bas for modules, .cls for classes, and so forth). The rationale for using the same extension for all files is that there aren't significant differences among modules, classes, and forms in the .NET world. As a matter of fact, you can even have two modules or two classes in the same source file, and you can mix modules, classes, and forms in the same file. In theory, you can even have multiple forms in the same file, but in this case Microsoft Visual Studio can display only one of these forms at design time. In practice, you'll never want to have more than one form (or another class that has an associated designer) in the same source file.

Modules

You typically use a module to create a container for variables, procedures, and functions used elsewhere in the application and, in some cases, to provide a method that works as the entry point for the application. Syntactically speaking, a module block is delimited by the Module and End Module keywords and can contain private or public constants, fields, properties, and methods.

```
Module MathFunctions
    ' A public constant
    Public Const DoublePI As Double = 6.28318530717958
    ' Two private arrays
    Private names() As String
    Dim values() As Double

    ' A public function that returns the factorial of a number
    Public Function Factorial(ByVal n As Integer) As Double
        Dim res As Double
        res = 1
        For i As Integer = 1 To n
            res = res * i
        Next
        Return res
    End Function
End Module
```

The Public keyword makes the DoublePI constant and the Factorial method accessible to the entire application; I could have omitted the Public keyword in the Factorial function because methods are always public unless otherwise stated. Adding an explicit scope keyword is recommended to improve readability, though. (Scope keywords are covered in depth in the section titled "Scope" in Chapter 8, "Inheritance.")

The Main Method

The Main method is the entry point for all console applications and, optionally, for Microsoft Windows Forms applications. In its simplest form, the Main method is a Sub procedure that takes no arguments:

```
Module Main
    Sub Main()
        Dim res As Double = Factorial(10)
        Console.WriteLine(res)
    End Sub
End Module
```

A problem can occur if your application has two or more modules containing the Main method. In this case, you can tell Visual Basic which module is the right one by selecting the startup object on the Application page of the My Project designer. (See Figure 2-1.) If only one module in the project contains a Main method, you can just select the Sub Main element from the combo box and let Visual Studio find the containing module for you.

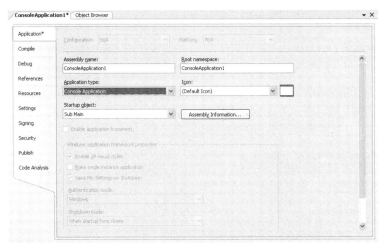

Figure 2-1   The Application page, which you display by double-clicking My Project in the Solution Explorer window. Options in the lower half of the page become active only in Windows Forms projects.

By default, Windows Forms projects don't need a Main method because you can designate a form as a startup object. Unlike previous versions of Visual Studio, you can even implement features such as splash screens and Windows XP visual styles with a few mouse clicks and without writing a single line of code. However, in some cases, you might want to be more in control of what happens when the application is launched or refuses to run if certain preconditions aren't met. In these cases, you should display the Application page of the My Project designer, ensure that the Enable Application Framework check box is clear, select the Sub Main element in the Startup Object combo box, and write a custom Main method:

```
Module Main
    Sub Main()
        InitializeAllVariables()
        Application.Run(New MainForm)
    End Sub
End Module
```

The Main method can take arguments and even return a value, two features that are especially useful when writing utilities meant to be launched from the command prompt. To process command-line arguments, you declare a Main method that takes an array of strings:

```
' Display the sum of numbers passed on the command line.
Sub Main(ByVal args() As String)
    Dim res As Double
    For i As Integer = 0 To UBound(args)
        res = res + CDbl(args(i))
    Next
    Console.WriteLine(res)
End Sub
```

You can debug an application that takes command-line arguments from inside Visual Studio by entering the command line on the Debug page of the My Project designer. Notice that a sequence of characters enclosed within double quotes is correctly considered a single argument on the command line.

Utilities and applications that are designed to run from inside a batch file often return an error code, which the batch file can test by means of an IF ERRORLEVEL statement. In this case, you just need to implement the Main method as a Function that returns an Integer, as in the following:

```
' Display the sum of numbers passed on the command line,
' return ERRORLEVEL=1 if any error.
Function Main(ByVal args() As String) As Integer
   Try
      Dim res As Double
      For i As Integer = 0 To UBound(args)
         res = res + CDbl(args(i))
      Next
      Console.WriteLine(res)
      Return 0
   Catch ex As Exception
      Console.WriteLine("One or more arguments are not valid numbers")
      Return 1
   End Try
End Function
```

Notice the use of the Try...Catch block to create a region of code that is protected against unanticipated errors; if one of the elements in the *args* array can't be converted to a number, the Try block terminates immediately and the Catch block executes instead. (Try...Catch blocks are covered in detail in Chapter 3, "Control Flow and Error Handling.")

The Sub New Method

In addition to regular methods, a module can include a special procedure named Sub New. This procedure is guaranteed to run before any other piece of code in the module and can therefore be used to initialize public and private fields used by other methods in the module. For example, you might optimize the Factorial method by calculating all possible values in advance:

```
Module MathFunctions
   Private factResults(169) As Double

   Sub New()
      factResults(0) = 1
      For i As Integer = 1 To 169
         factResults(i) = factResults(i - 1) * i
      Next
   End Sub

   Public Function Factorial(ByVal n As Integer) As Double
      ' Throw an exception if outside the range [0,169].
      Return factResults(n)
   End Function
End Module
```

The Sub New procedure runs before the main application accesses a procedure or a variable in the module, but not if the application accesses a constant because constants are resolved at compile time and their numeric or string value is burned into the compiled code.

Classes

Everything is an object in the .NET Framework, including primitive data types such as integers, floating-point numbers, date and time values, strings, arrays, you name it. Even errors (known as exceptions in .NET parlance) are objects, as are processes, threads, and so forth. Forms and controls are objects, too, of course.

In this object-oriented world, the job of a developer is somewhat different from what it has been for decades. Instead of writing code that manipulates data—the main tenet of the procedural approach—a .NET programmer is expected to define new objects from scratch or objects that extend and improve the ones that the .NET Framework already provides. To define the way an object is shaped and behaves programmers must write a class.

In a first approximation, you can think of a class as the combination of some data related to a real-world entity and a set of methods that enables the programmer to manipulate that data:

```
Public Class Person
    Public FirstName As String              ' A field
    Public LastName As String               ' A field

    Public Function CompleteName() As String   ' A method
        Return FirstName & " " & LastName
    End Function
End Class
```

Microsoft guidelines mandate that names of classes and public members follow the Pascal-Case naming convention; that is, use uppercase style for the initial character of each word, whereas private fields, method arguments, and local variables follow the camelCase naming convention (first word is lowercase, all subsequent words are initial capped, as in firstName).

Using the Person class elsewhere in the application is straightforward. You instantiate a class, that is, create an object typed after that class, by means of the New operator:

```
Dim pers As New Person()
pers.FirstName = "John"
pers.LastName = "Doe"
Console.WriteLine(pers.CompleteName)    ' => John Doe
```

Properties, Methods, and Constructors

You can make a class more robust by avoiding public fields and using public properties that wrap private fields and protect them from invalid assignments. Here's how you can replace the FirstName and LastName fields with two public properties with the same name, so that an exception is thrown if an empty string is passed to them:

```
Private m_FirstName As String
```

```
Public Property FirstName() As String
    Get
        Return m_FirstName
    End Get
    Set(ByVal value As String)
        If value = "" Then
            Throw New ArgumentException("FirstName can't be an empty string")
        End If
        m_FirstName = value
    End Set
End Property

Private m_LastName As String

Public Property LastName() As String
    Get
        Return m_LastName
    End Get
    Set(ByVal value As String)
        If value = "" Then
            Throw New ArgumentException("LastName can't be an empty string")
        End If
        m_LastName = value
    End Set
End Property
```

(Exception handling and the Throw Keyword are covered in more detail in the next chapter.) An important feature of Visual Basic classes is *method overloading*, that is, the ability to expose multiple methods with the same name but different argument signatures:

```
Public Class Person
    ...
    ' An example of method overloading
    Public Function CompleteName() As String
        Return FirstName & " " & LastName
    End Function

    Public Function CompleteName(ByVal title As String) As String
        Return title & " " & FirstName & " " & LastName
    End Function
End Class
```

(I describe method overloading in more detail in Chapter 6, "Class Fundamentals.") Another way to make a class more robust and easier to use at the same time is by providing one or more constructors. Constructors are special procedures, named Sub New, that are invoked when a client creates an instance of the class. By specifying one or more arguments, you can force clients to pass specific values when the class is instantiated:

```
' An example of a constructor
Sub New(ByVal firstName As String, ByVal lastName As String)
    Me.FirstName = firstName
    Me.LastName = lastName
End Sub
```

Constructors can be overloaded, and it's possible for a class to have multiple constructors, provided that they have a different set of parameters. Typically, a constructor assigns an incoming value to the property with the same name and not directly to the underlying field so that invalid values (empty strings in this specific case) cause the property to throw an exception that is returned to the client. If a class exposes one or more constructors with arguments, clients must pass these arguments when creating an instance of the class:

```
' In the main application
Dim pers As New Person("John", "Doe")
```

It's interesting to note that all classes have a constructor, regardless of whether you define one. In fact, if you omit a Sub New procedure, the Visual Basic compiler creates a parameterless constructor automatically, known as a *default constructor*. You can easily prove this point by browsing the class with ILDASM. If it weren't for this hidden constructor, code in the main application couldn't instantiate the class. At a minimum, the default constructor contains the code that delegates to the constructor of the base class (System.Object, if the class doesn't inherit from another base class).

Inheritance Basics

As I mentioned before, you can also create new classes by inheriting (or deriving) from a class that is already defined, either in the same application or in another assembly. You can also derive from classes in the .NET Framework, which is actually a very common action. (For example, all the Web pages you write are classes that inherit from the Page class defined in the System.Web.dll assembly.) When you derive a class from another class, the derived class inherits all the fields, properties, methods, and events (but not constructors) of the base class.

Inheritance is often used to implement the is-a relation that exists between two entities in the real world. For example, consider the task of defining an Employee class. An employee is a person and has a first name, a last name, and a complete name; therefore, you can derive the Employee class from the Person class and, if necessary, add other fields and properties that are peculiar to employees. The following code assumes that the Person class has no explicit constructor:

```
Public Class Employee
   Inherits Person

   Public BirthDate As Date              ' A new field

   Function ReverseName() As String      ' A new method
      Return LastName & ", " & FirstName
   End Function
End Class
```

If the base class has only constructors that take one or more arguments, the derived class also needs to expose its own constructor. (The reason for this requirement will become apparent in Chapter 8, "Inheritance.") Often constructors in derived classes delegate the actual execution to a constructor in the base class by means of the MyBase keyword. Assuming that the

Person class has a constructor that takes a first and last name, a constructor in the Employee class might look like this:

```
' In the Employee class
Sub New(ByVal firstName As String, ByVal lastName As String)
   ' Delegate to the constructor in the Person class.
   MyBase.New(firstName, lastName)
End Sub
```

The main application can use all the members of the Employee class without discerning between those defined in the class itself and those inherited from Person:

```
' In the main application
Dim empl As New Employee("John", "Doe")
Console.WriteLine(empl.CompleteName)      ' => John Doe
Console.WriteLine(empl.ReverseName)       ' => Doe, John
```

You can create multiple levels of inheritance. For example, you might define a third class, named PartTimeEmployee, that derives from Employee (and therefore inherits indirectly from Person). All the classes you can define derive, either directly or indirectly, from a class named System.Object defined in the mscorlib.dll assembly. You can make this inheritance relation by defining the Person class as follows:

```
Public Class Person
    Inherits System.Object
    ...
End Class
```

The compiler would produce exactly the same code it generates when the Inherits clause is missing. The System.Object class defines a few methods that are therefore inherited by all the other .NET classes, for example, the ToString method. Unless this method is redefined, it returns the complete name of the class to which an object belongs:

```
' (This code assumes that the project's namespace is ConsoleApplication1.)
Dim empl As New Employee("John", "Doe")
Console.WriteLine(empl.ToString())      ' => ConsoleApplication1.Employee
```

The Person class can redefine (or override) the ToString method to provide a more descriptive description of the object's current state by means of the Overrides keyword:

```
Public Class Person

    Public Overrides Function ToString() As String
       Return FirstName & " " & LastName
    End Function
End Class
```

Incidentally, the Write and WriteLine methods of the Console objects automatically invoke the ToString method when you pass an object reference:

```
Dim empl As New Employee("John", "Doe")
Console.WriteLine(empl)            ' => John Doe
```

These methods also support placeholders that are replaced with the values of the arguments that follow the format string:

```
Console.WriteLine("First name={0}, Last name={1}", empl.FirstName, empl.LastName)
```

The Debug.Write and Debug.WriteLine methods can take an object reference and implicitly invoke the object's ToString method, but these methods don't support placeholders:

```
Debug.WriteLine(empl)             ' => ConsoleApplication1.Employee
```

Your classes inherit more from System.Object than is visible. For example, they inherit the ability to be allocated in memory and deallocated when they aren't used any longer. In practice they inherit the behavior that makes them behave as standard .NET classes.

Inheritance is used everywhere in the .NET Framework. For example, a .NET form is nothing but a class that inherits from the System.Windows.Forms.Form class:

```
Public Class Form1
    Inherits System.Windows.Forms.Form
    …
End Class
```

Partial Classes

In Visual Basic 2005, you can use the so-called partial classes to split the definition of a class into two or more Class blocks, each one belonging to a different source file. Visual Studio uses partial classes to keep the code you manually write inside a form class—for example, to handle control events—separated from the code that it generates automatically when you place new controls on the form's surface and set its properties in the Properties window:

```
' (In the Form1.Designer.vb file)
Partial Public Class Form1
    Inherits System.Windows.Forms.Form

    …
    ' (The code that Visual Studio generates automatically goes here.)
    …
End Class

' (In the Form1.vb file)
Public Class Form1

    …
    ' (The code that you write manually goes here.)
    …
End Class
```

(Notice that the code in the Form1.vb file doesn't need the Inherits keyword because this keyword is already present in the Form1.Designer.vb file.) Keeping the two portions of the same classes in different files prevents accidental changes to the automatically generated code, which would easily make the form unusable at design time (as it happens frequently in Visual Basic .NET 2003). To make accidental changes even more unlikely, by default the

Form1.Designer.vb file doesn't appear in the project unless you click the Show All Files button in the Solution Explorer toolbar (see Figure 2-2). You can read more about partial classes in Chapter 6.

Figure 2-2   Source files containing automatically generated code, which appear in the Solution Explorer only if you select the Show All Files option on the toolbar

Static Members

Classes can expose two different types of members: instance members and static members. The simplest way to describe the difference between them is as follows: instance members belong to objects instantiated from the class; static members belong to the class itself. Static members are marked with the Shared keyword; if this keyword is missing, the member is an instance member.

The Person class exposes only instance members, which means that there will be a different value of the FirstName and LastName members for each distinct Employee object instantiated from the class. This makes sense because each employee has his or her own name. Now, let's say that you want to keep track of how many Person objects you've created so far and store this value in a field named InstanceCount. It's apparent that this value isn't a property of individual objects; rather, it's related to the Person class itself and should therefore be marked with the Shared keyword:

```
' (In the Person class)
Public Shared InstanceCount As Integer     ' A static field

Sub New(ByVal firstName As String, ByVal lastName As String)
   Me.FirstName = firstName
   Me.LastName = lastName
   InstanceCount = InstanceCount + 1      ' Keep track of the new instance.
End Sub
```

The main application can access a public shared member either by prefixing it with the name of the class or by means of an instance variable (as if the member were a regular instance member):

```
' First technique: using the class name as a prefix
Console.WriteLine(Person.InstanceCount)    ' => 0
```

```
' Second technique: using an existing instance variable
Dim pers As New Person("John", "Doe")
Console.WriteLine(pers.InstanceCount)        ' => 1
```

The compiler produces exactly the same code in both cases, but the first technique has a couple of advantages: it makes it evident that you are using a static member and it can also be used if you have no instance variable on hand (possibly because you haven't created an instance of that class yet). By default, Visual Basic 2005 emits a warning when compiling a piece of code that uses the second technique. You can turn off this warning or have the compiler emit an error instead of a warning by means of the Instance Variable Accesses Shared Member option on the Compile page of the My Project designer (see Figure 2-3).

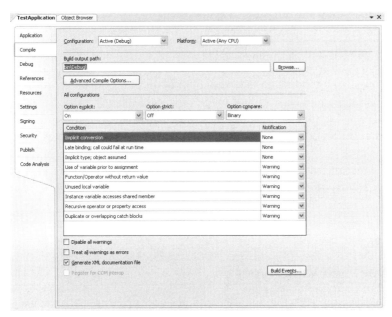

Figure 2-3   The Compile page of the My Project designer

Static members are tightly related to modules because a module is nothing but a class that can't be instantiated and whose members are implicitly static. As a matter of fact, you can access members in a module by prefixing the name of the module itself, exactly as you do with static members exposed by a regular class:

```
Console.WriteLine(MathFunctions.Factorial(10))
```

By disassembling a module using ILDASM you can see that all its members are marked with an icon containing an *S* (for *static*), as shown in Figure 2-4. If the module has a Sub New procedure, it appears in the ILDASM window as .cctor, which stands for *class constructor* (another way of saying "static constructor"). The .NET runtime executes a static constructor the first time your application references a class. To ensure that the main application can't instantiate a module, the Visual Basic compiler omits creating an instance constructor for a module and emits a compilation error if the module contains a Sub New procedure with one or more arguments.

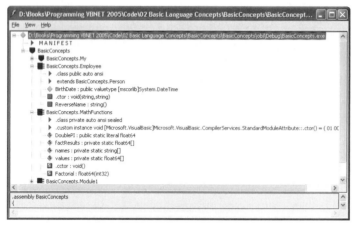

Figure 2-4   Disassembling a module using ILDASM

ILDASM also shows that a module has a special StandardModule attribute (attributes are discussed later in this chapter). This attribute enables the *static imports* feature, which enables a Visual Basic application optionally to omit the module name when referencing one of its members. (See the section titled "The Imports Statement" later in this chapter for an explanation of how this feature works.) Notice that only Visual Basic applications honor this attribute and can benefit from this feature: if you make a Visual Basic module available to developers working in other languages, they must explicitly use the module name as a prefix when referencing one of the module's members. For this reason, it's essential that you assign names to your modules that are more meaningful than the standard Module1 name that Visual Studio assigns by default.

Reference Types and Value Types

You can group all the data types that the .NET Framework supports—both the native types and the types you create—in two broad categories: reference types and value types. In a nutshell, reference types behave like objects, whereas value types behave like scalar or numeric types. You need to understand the differences between the two, or you might introduce subtle bugs into your code.

In the .NET Framework, everything is an object, and most data types are reference types. When you declare a variable of a reference type, you're allocating a pointer variable (a 32-bit integer value on 32-bit Microsoft Windows platforms) that contains the address of the actual object. The object itself is stored in a memory area called the *managed heap* and lives under the supervision of the common language runtime (CLR), whereas the pointer variable can be stored elsewhere (for example, on the stack if it's a dynamic variable declared inside a procedure).

When all the pointer variables that point to a given object go out of scope or are explicitly set to Nothing, the object undergoes a process known as garbage collection, and the memory it uses in the heap is freed. Unlike Visual Basic 6 and Component Object Model (COM) objects, the memory allocated for .NET objects isn't released immediately after all the pointer variables are destroyed because garbage collection occurs only when the .NET runtime runs out of memory in the managed heap. This phenomenon is also known as *nondeterministic finalization*, and I talk about it in greater detail in Chapter 9.

Value types inherit from System.ValueType, which in turn inherits from System.Object but redefines its methods. Value types aren't allocated in the managed heap, and the corresponding variable *holds* the value rather than *points* to it. The actual location in which a value type is stored depends on its scope: for example, local value type variables are allocated on the stack. All .NET numeric types are value types, and all the types you define with a Structure or an Enum block are also value types. (I explain Structures in the next section and Enums later in this chapter.) Strings and arrays in the .NET Framework are reference types, as are all the objects you define with a Class...End Class block. If you're in doubt as to whether a .NET type is a class or a structure, just read the documentation or view the type in the object browser (which displays different icons for classes and structures).

You'll learn more about value types in Chapter 6, but you need at least these basics to understand a few topics in this and the next chapter. In general, value types are faster than similar reference types for two reasons: there is no need to dereference a pointer to get to the actual data, and, more important, the .NET Framework doesn't need to allocate and then release memory in the managed heap. If a value type variable is held on the stack (as shown in the following graphic), the variable is automatically destroyed and no time-consuming cleanup operation is needed when you exit the procedure.

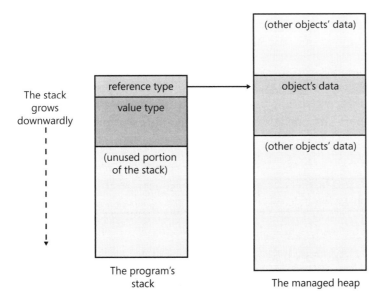

You must pay attention to whether you're dealing with a reference or a value type for two reasons. First and foremost, the assignment operation works differently in the two cases. When you assign a reference type to a variable, you're actually assigning the pointer and therefore the target variable is now pointing to the original value. No data is duplicated, and you can modify the original data through both the original and the new variable:

```
' Person is a class defined in the current application.
Dim p1 As New Person
p1.FirstName = "Francesco"
' Assign to another Person variable.
Dim p2 As Person
p2 = p1
' You can modify the original object through the new variable.
p2.FirstName = "Joe"
Console.WriteLine(p1.FirstName)     ' => Joe
```

An important detail: the .NET String class is a reference type, as the following code snippet demonstrates:

```
Dim s1 As String, s2 As String
s1 = "Francesco"
s2 = s1
' Prove that the two variables point to the same String object.
Console.WriteLine(s2 Is s1)              ' => True
```

Conversely, when you assign a value type—such as a numeric data type—to a variable of the same type, a copy of the original data is assigned, and therefore the original data and the new variable are completely unrelated.

The second reason for paying attention to the nature of the data you process—reference type or value type—concerns performance. As I've explained, value types are usually faster. In addition, sometimes a value type is converted to a reference type and back without your being aware of this internal conversion that silently slows down your code.

To refine this explanation, whenever you pass a value type to a method that takes an Object argument, the value is converted to a reference type: the .NET runtime allocates a block of memory in the managed heap, copies the value in that area, and passes the method a pointer to that memory location. This operation is known as *boxing*. For example, you have a hidden boxing operation when you pass a number to the Debug.Write method because that method can take only an Object or a String argument.

The simplest example of a boxing operation occurs when you assign a value type—an integer, for example—to an Object variable:

```
Dim i As Integer, o As Object
i = 1234
' The next statement causes the following sequence of operations:
' (1) a block of memory is allocated in the heap;
' (2) the original integer value is copied in that memory block;
' (3) the address of the block is assigned to the Object variable.
o = i
```

As you might guess, boxing a value is a time-consuming activity. Likewise, you waste CPU time when you reassign a boxed value back to a variable of a value type—an operation known as *unboxing*:

```
' …(Continuing the previous example)…
Dim i2 As Integer
' The next statement causes the following sequence of operations:
' (1) the pointer in the o variable is used to locate the data;
' (2) the integer is copied into the target variable;
' (3) the heap memory used by the o variable is garbage collected
'     (eventually, some time after the o variable is set to Nothing).
' (Next statement doesn't compile if Option Strict is On.)
i2 = o
```

Note that the previous code snippet works only if Option Strict is disabled; if Option Strict is On, you must rewrite the last statement this way:

```
i2 = CInt(o)
```

Here's the bottom line: use value types rather than reference types if you have a choice. For example, use Char variables instead of String variables if you're working with one-character strings. And enable Option Strict at the application level so that an unboxing operation can't go unnoticed. (Read the section titled "The Option Strict Directive," later in this chapter for more information.)

There's more to reference types, value types, boxing, and unboxing, as you'll learn in the next section and in Chapter 6.

Structures

Now that you know the difference between reference type and value types, you might wonder if and how you can create a custom value type. The answer is simple: you just use a Structure...End Structure block instead of a Class...End Class block. Fields inside a structure must be prefixed with an accessibility (visibility) qualifier, as in this code:

```
Public Structure PersonStruct
   Dim FirstName As String          ' Dim means Public here.
   Dim LastName As String
   Public Address As String
   Private SSN As String
End Structure
```

The declaration of the structure's data members can't use the As New declaration syntax. As comments in the preceding example suggest, the default accessibility level for structures—that is, the visibility level implied by a Dim keyword—is Public (unlike classes, where the default level is Private). Visual Basic unifies the syntax of classes and structures, and structures support most of the functionality of classes, including methods and properties:

```
Public Structure PersonStruct
   Dim FirstName As String
   Dim LastName As String
```

```
    Public Address As String
    Private SSN As String

    Function CompleteName() As String
        Return FirstName & " " & LastName
    End Function
End Structure
```

Unlike classes, structures are value types rather than reference types. Among other things, this means that Visual Basic automatically initializes a structure when you declare a variable of that type; in other words, the following statements are equivalent:

```
Dim p As PersonStruct
Dim p As New PersonStruct                      ' Verbose syntax
```

Each structure implicitly defines a parameterless constructor, which initializes each member of the structure to its default value (0 for numeric members, null string for String members, and Nothing for object members). It's illegal to define an explicit parameterless constructor or a destructor for the structure. But you can define a New constructor method with arguments, as follows:

```
Public Structure PersonStruct
    Dim FirstName As String
    Dim LastName As String
    Public Address As String
    Private SSN As String

    ' A constructor for this structure
    Sub New(ByVal firstName As String, ByVal lastName As String)
        ' Note how you can use the Me keyword to reduce ambiguity.
        Me.FirstName = firstName
        Me.LastName = lastName
    End Function
    …
End Structure
```

A consequence of the value type nature of Structure variables is that the actual data is copied when you assign a structure variable to a variable, whereas only a pointer to data is copied when you assign a reference value to a variable. Also note that the equality operator isn't supported for structures. This code summarizes the differences between classes and structures:

```
' This code assumes you have a Person class, with the same members
' as the PersonStruct structure.

' Creation is similar, but structures don't require New.
Dim aPersonObject As New Person
Dim aPersonStruct As PersonStruct          ' New is optional.

' Assignment to members is identical.
aPersonObject.FirstName = "John"
aPersonObject.LastName = "Doe"
aPersonStruct.FirstName = "John"
aPersonStruct.LastName = "Doe"
```

```
' Method and property invocation is also identical.
Console.WriteLine(aPersonObject.CompleteName())        ' => John Doe
Console.WriteLine(aPersonStruct.CompleteName())        ' => John Doe

' Assignment to a variable of the same type has different effects.
Dim aPersonObject2 As Person
aPersonObject2 = aPersonObject
' Classes are reference types; hence, the new variable receives
' a pointer to the original object.
aPersonObject2.FirstName = "Ann"
' The original object has been affected.
Console.WriteLine(aPersonObject.FirstName)     ' => Ann

Dim aPersonStruct2 As PersonStruct
aPersonStruct2 = aPersonStruct
' Structures are value types; hence, the new variable receives
' a copy of the original structure.
aPersonStruct2.FirstName = "Ann"
' The original structure hasn't been affected.
Console.WriteLine(aPersonStruct.FirstName)     ' => John
```

A few other features of classes aren't supported by structures in Visual Basic. For example, structures implicitly inherit all the methods of the Object class, but they can't explicitly inherit from another structure, nor can they be inherited from. For this reason the Inherits keyword is forbidden inside a structure.

A structure takes fewer bytes than the corresponding class. A reference type has a fixed overhead of 8 bytes, and its size is always rounded to the next multiple of 4; therefore, it takes at least 12 bytes. By comparison, a structure takes only the bytes taken by its members, rounded to the next multiple of 4. In general, you should opt for a value type if the sum of the size of its elements is 16 bytes or fewer.

Also, you can often reduce the memory footprint of a structure by arranging its elements. Structure elements are automatically aligned to addresses that are multiples of 4, except Char, Short, and UShort values (which are aligned to even addresses) and Byte and SByte (which aren't aligned at all). Thus, the following structure takes as many as 24 bytes:

```
Public Structure TestStruct
    Dim byte1 As Byte        ' Offset 0
    Dim int1 As Integer      ' Offset 4 (requires 3 padding bytes)
    Dim byte2 As Byte        ' Offset 8
    Dim int2 As Integer      ' Offset 12 (requires 3 padding bytes)
    Dim char1 As Char        ' Offset 16
    Dim int3 As Integer      ' Offset 20 (requires 2 padding bytes)
End Structure
```

By rearranging the elements in a different order you can shrink it to 16 bytes:

```
Public Structure TestStruct
    Dim byte1 As Byte        ' Offset 0
    Dim byte2 As Byte        ' Offset 1
    Dim char1 As Char        ' Offset 2
    Dim int1 As Integer      ' Offset 4
```

```
    Dim int2 As Integer        ' offset 8
    Dim int3 As Integer        ' offset 12
End Structure
```

In general you don't need this sort of manual optimization with classes because the Visual Basic compiler is able to arrange their elements automatically. You can achieve the same behavior with structures by labeling them with the StructLayout attribute (in the System.Runtime.InteropServices namespace) as follows:

```
<StructLayout(LayoutKind.Auto)> _
Public Structure TestStruct
    …
End Structure
```

Of course, you shouldn't use this attribute if you're going to pass the structure to unmanaged code—for example, a Windows API method—which expects to find the structure's elements in a well-defined order.

Namespaces

Modules and classes live in namespaces. The thousands of classes defined in the .NET Framework are grouped in namespaces, the most important of which is the System namespace that gathers the basic type classes, such as Integer, String, Array, and the Object class, from which all other .NET classes inherit. Except for the System namespace, all other namespaces in the .NET Framework are nested and their names include a dot to separate their portions. For example, the System.IO namespace includes classes that you use to work with files, such as FileStream, StreamReader, and StreamWriter, and the System.Windows.Forms namespace contains classes used in the user interface of Windows programs, such as TextBox, ComboBox, and ListBox.

References to .NET Assemblies

Before you can create or just use any object defined in the .NET Framework you must add a reference to the assembly that contains it. When you create a new Visual Basic project, Visual Studio automatically adds a reference to the most important .NET assemblies, such as System.Data.dll (containing the classes used to work with databases) and System.Xml.dll (containing the classes used to work with XML). Depending on the type of the project, other DLLs can be referenced, for example, System.Windows.Forms.dll and System.Drawing.dll in the case of Windows Forms projects. Notice that the mscorlib.dll never appears in the References folder: it is always referenced by all Visual Basic projects, and you can remove it from the list because all .NET applications require this reference and wouldn't work without it.

To use a class defined in an assembly that isn't currently referenced by the current project you must add a reference manually. You can use the Add Reference command that you find on the Project menu and on the context menu that appears if you right-click the project element in the Solution Explorer window. The Add Reference dialog box enables you to select one or more .NET assemblies as well as COM DLLs (see Figure 2-5); the tab labeled Projects enables you to add a reference to a DLL created by another project in the same solution; the tab named Browse enables you to select DLLs that don't belong to the .NET Framework. You can see the list of current references by opening the References folder in the Solution Explorer, as shown in Figure 2-6. (This folder appears only if the Show All Files option is enabled.)

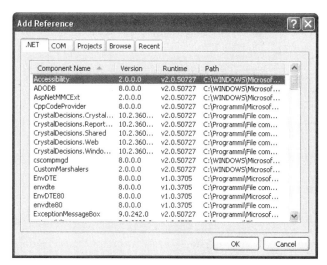

Figure 2-5   The Add Reference dialog box

Figure 2-6   The References folder in the Solution Explorer window

In general, a project can reference one or more DLLs that it doesn't actually use without causing any problem. If for any reason you want to discard unused references, just click the Unused References button on the References page of the My Project designer, which parses your project and brings up a dialog box that lists all the unused references and enables you to remove them. (See Figure 2-7.)

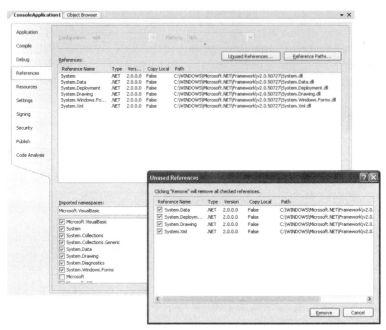

Figure 2-7   The References page of the My Project designer (left) and the Unused References dialog box (right)

The Imports Statement

The complete name of a .NET class includes its containing namespace, a bit like the complete name of a file includes its parent directory. As you can imagine, using the complete name of a class makes your code quite verbose and reduces its readability:

```
Dim bmp As System.Drawing.Bitmap              ' A bitmap
Dim ctrl As System.Windows.Forms.Control      ' A control
Dim comp As System.ComponentModel.Component   ' A component
```

You can simplify your code by adding one or more Imports statements at the top of the current source file; if a namespace appears as an argument of an Imports keyword, you can omit the namespace portion when declaring the variable and make your code more concise and readable:

```
' (At the top of the source file)
Imports System.Drawing
Imports System.Windows.Forms
Imports System.ComponentModel

' (Elsewhere in the same source file)
Dim bmp As Bitmap       ' Same as System.Drawing.Bitmap
Dim ctrl As Control     ' Same as System.Windows.Forms.Control
Dim comp As Component   ' Same as System.ComponentModel.Component
```

You can save some typing even if you don't have an Imports statement that exactly matches the namespace of the element you want to reference. For example, the following Imports statement for the System namespace enables you to make most of your external references more concise because many important objects are in the System namespace or in a namespace nested in System:

```
Imports System
…
Dim bmp As Drawing.Bitmap      ' Same as System.Drawing.Bitmap
```

Imports statements must always include the complete namespace you're importing. You can't use a previous Imports to shorten another Imports statement:

```
' *** This code doesn't compile.
Imports System
Imports Drawing      ' Meant to replace Imports System.Drawing
```

You can run into problems if you have distinct Imports statements referring to namespaces that contain classes with the same name. For example, say that both the Animals.Mammals namespace and the Computers.Accessories namespace contain a class named Mouse. In this situation, the following code won't compile because the Mouse reference is ambiguous:

```
' *** This code doesn't compile.
Imports Animals.Mammals
Imports Computers.Accessories
…
Dim m As Mouse
```

Even in this case, you can use the Imports statement to reduce your labor by specifying an alias for one of the conflicting namespaces:

```
Imports Animals.Mammals
Imports Acc = Computers.Accessories
…
Dim m As Mouse         ' Same as Animals.Mammals.Mouse
Dim m2 As Acc.Mouse    ' Same as Computers.Accessories.Mouse
```

Visual Basic lets you specify the name of a *class* in an Imports statement, a feature that enables you to access the static members of a class without prefixing them with the class name. Consider this class, defined in the ModulesDemo root namespace:

```
Public Class NumericConstants
   Public Const Zero As Integer = 0
   Public Const One As Integer = 1
End Class
```

Your application can then access the two constants as if they were globally defined:

```
' This statement imports a class, not a namespace.
Imports ModulesDemo.NumericConstants
…
Dim value As Integer
value = One               ' Assigns 1.
```

Incidentally, this feature is used by the Visual Basic compiler behind the scenes to honor the so-called *static imports* when accessing members of a module (see the section titled "Static Members" earlier in this chapter). In other words, the compiler behaves as if at the top of all source files there is one invisible Imports statement for each module defined in the application.

Projectwide Imports

Most Visual Basic projects rely heavily on a few namespaces in the .NET Framework, such as the System namespace, which contains all the basic data types, and the Microsoft.VisualBasic namespace, which contains all the Visual Basic statements, functions, and constants. Repeatedly importing these namespaces into all the files of a project is surely a nuisance. Fortunately, you don't have to do that because in Visual Basic applications you can define a number of projectwide imports on the References page of the My Project designer simply by selecting one or more elements in the Imported Namespace list near the bottom of the window (see Figure 2-7). Or you can add a projectwide Imports for one of the namespaces defined in the current project by clicking the Add User Import button after typing the namespace name in the Imported Namespaces box.

Namespace Blocks

All the classes and modules in your Visual Basic project belong to the default namespace defined in the Root Namespace field on the Application page of the My Project designer. (See Figure 2-1.) The root namespace is initially equal to the name of the project, but you can change it if you wish. Changing the root namespace is especially important when creating a DLL assembly that exposes one or more classes to other .NET applications. In this case, Microsoft naming guidelines recommend that you use a two-part name, with the first part equal to the name of your company and the second part describing what the classes in the namespace do. For example, a collection of classes related to reporting and authored by my own company should be gathered in a root namespace named CodeArchitects.Reporting and should be compiled to a DLL named CodeArchitects.Reporting.dll.

You should never place any of your classes in the System namespace or one of its child namespaces because this namespace is reserved for the classes in the .NET Framework. Even Microsoft follows this guideline quite scrupulously; in fact, the mscorlib assembly includes a namespace named Microsoft.Win32 and contains classes that work with the Windows registry. The rationale behind this decision is that the .NET Framework might be ported to non-Windows platforms that lack the registry.

You can also create explicit Namespace...End Namespace blocks anywhere in your source files. For example, you can define the HumanBeings namespace as a container for the Person class defined previously:

```
Namespace HumanBeings
    Public Class Person
       ...
    End Class
End Namespace
```

If a piece of code references a class or procedure in another namespace, it must include the complete namespace of the referenced element, as you see here:

```
' Use the Person class from another namespace.
Dim p As New HumanBeings.Person
```

Of course, you can use the Imports keyword also for simplifying references to classes defined elsewhere in the same project, but remember that all the source files in a Visual Basic project implicitly live in the root namespace and this root namespace must appear in the Imports statement:

```
' This code assumes that the root namespace is CodeArchitects.Reporting.
Imports CodeArchitects.Reporting.HumanBeings
…
Dim p As New Person
```

A Namespace block can contain only six kinds of entities: Module, Class, Structure, Interface, Enum, and Delegate. These six kinds of units are collectively known as types. A type is a concept that is more general than the concept of a class, as you'll learn later in this chapter. I've already shown you the Module, Class, and Structure blocks. Enum blocks are described in the section titled "Constants and Enums" later in this chapter (and in more depth in Chapter 12, ".NET Basic Types"). I cover Delegate types in Chapter 7, "Delegates and Events," and Interface blocks in Chapter 10, "Interfaces."

Remember that namespaces contain types and you can't define variable declarations or procedures directly inside a Namespace block. For example, the following code snippet won't compile:

```
Namespace MyNamespace
    Function MyFunction()
        …
    End Function
End Namespace
```

Interestingly, you can have multiple Namespace blocks with the same name in a project, in the same or a different source file. This feature lets you keep the logical organization of your source code entities completely distinct from the physical structure. For example, you can have a file that contains multiple namespaces, or you can have all the elements of a namespace scattered in different source files. (In fact, all the source files in your project belong to the root namespace defined on the Application page of the My Project designer.)

It's important to consider that the namespace is a programming language concept, but neither namespace nor Imports statements actually exist at the intermediate language (IL) level. You can easily prove this by disassembling a Visual Basic project and checking that all IL instructions reference .NET Framework classes using their complete name, regardless of whether you used an Imports statement to make your source code shorter.

Nested Namespaces

I already mentioned that namespaces can be nested; in fact, most of the classes in the .NET Framework live in nested namespaces, such as the System.Collections namespace (which contains collection-like types) and the System.IO namespace (used for all types related to file handling). There is no theoretical limit to nesting namespaces, and namespaces nested at three or more levels are quite common in the .NET Framework, so you can see, for example, System.Xml.Schema or System.Windows.Forms.ComponentModule.Com2Interop.

You can create nested namespaces in your Visual Basic .NET projects simply by nesting Namespace...End Namespace blocks. For example, the following code defines the Animals .Mammals.Dog, Animals.Mammals.Cat, and Animals.Reptiles.Lizard classes:

```
Namespace Animals
    Namespace Mammals
        Class Dog
            …
        End Class

        Class Cat
            …
        End Class
    End Namespace

    Namespace Reptiles
        Class Lizard
            …
        End Class
    End Namespace
End Namespace
```

The scope rules for referencing classes and functions in other namespaces can be easily extended to nested namespaces. For example, the code inside the Dog class can directly reference the Cat class, but it needs to go through the Reptiles namespace to reach the Lizard class:

```
Class Dog
    Dim aCat As New Cat()
    Dim aLizard As New Reptiles.Lizard
    …
End Class
```

In general, I don't recommend nested Namespace blocks because they lead to code that is deeply indented and therefore reduce the number of characters that are visible in the code editor. You can reduce the indent space by using a single Namespace block with a namespace name that contains a dot character, as in this code:

```
Namespace Animals.Mammals
    Class Dog
        …
    Class Cat
        …
End Namespace

Namespace Animals.Reptiles
    Class Lizard
        …
End Namespace
```

The Global Keyword

A potential problem with namespaces arises when the same name appears at different levels of the hierarchy. For example, let's say that you have a namespace named System under the root namespace named after your company:

```
Namespace System
    Public Class TestClass
        Dim appDom As System.AppDomain     ' *** Compilation error!
        ...
    End Class
End Namespace
```

The previous code raises a compilation error because any reference to the System namespace from inside the TestClass is actually a reference to your user-defined System namespace, not the .NET Framework namespace. Granted, using System as a namespace name is something you should avoid and in practice this situation is quite unlikely, but you can't rule it out completely.

To cope with this problem, Visual Basic 2005 introduces the Global keyword, which forces a namespace reference to resolve its argument starting from root namespaces, as in this example:

```
' This code is guaranteed to reference the .NET System.AppDomain class.
Dim bmp As Global.System.AppDomain
```

In practice, the Global keyword is going to be used mainly by code generator wizards and add-ins to ensure that the generated code works correctly regardless of the namespace you paste it into.

Attributes

The attribute is a new concept in programming and is used virtually everywhere in the .NET Framework, so I decided to introduce attributes in this chapter. The underlying idea is that— regardless of the language you're using—some aspects of your application can't be expressed with plain executable statements. For example, each language previous to .NET offers its own way to define project-level properties, such as the application name and version, and languages such as C++ use pragmas to affect how the compiler behaves. Before the .NET Framework, there wasn't any consistency in how this information was associated with code; each language has its own way, and different types of information often require different techniques, even within the same language. Worse, you can't extend these techniques and define custom types of information for your own purposes.

.NET attributes can solve all these problems and offer a streamlined, standardized way to associate additional information with specific pieces of code. In practice, attributes let you extend the *metadata* associated with an assembly, a class, or a method. Different languages use a slightly different syntax for attributes, but there's a unified mechanism, called *reflection*, for retrieving all the attributes associated with a piece of code. Even better, attributes are themselves a data type, and you can create your own custom attribute by simply creating a new class that inherits from System.Attribute (see Chapter 19, "Custom Attributes").

You can consider attributes to be annotations that you intersperse throughout your code. You can apply attributes to nearly every programming entity that Visual Basic supports, including classes, modules, structures, properties, methods, and enumeration blocks. Not all attributes can be applied to all entities, but the general syntax you use for inserting an attribute is consistent within each .NET language. For example, all Visual Basic attributes require an identical syntax, which differs from C# syntax.

Under Visual Basic, you enclose an attribute in angle brackets (< >) and insert it immediately before the item to which it refers. For example, you can apply System.ComponentModel .DescriptionAttribute to a class as follows:

```
<System.ComponentModel.DescriptionAttribute("Person")> Public Class Person
    ...
End Class
```

You can simplify attribute syntax in many ways. First, attributes are .NET classes; thus, you can shorten an attribute name by using a suitable Imports statement. Second, .NET guidelines dictate that the names of all attribute classes end with Attribute, but most .NET compilers, including Visual Basic and C#, let you drop the Attribute suffix from the name. Finally, you can break long lines using the underscore character to make code more readable. After applying these three rules, our initial example becomes:

```
Imports System.ComponentModel

<Description("Person")> _
Public Class Person
    ...
End Class
```

Attributes are rather peculiar .NET classes. They support properties and methods, but you can't reference them in code as you do with regular classes. In fact, you assign one or more properties only when you create the attribute, and those properties don't change during the application's lifetime.

The preceding code snippet is actually a call to the constructor method of the Description attribute, which takes the value of the Description property as an argument. Once this property has been set, it isn't changed or queried, at least not by the application that uses the attribute. The properties of specific attributes can be queried, however, by an external application, such as the compiler or the .NET Framework, by using reflection, as you'll read in Chapter 18, "Reflection." Because of their nature, attribute classes rarely have methods other than the constructor method.

An attribute's constructor method takes zero or more arguments. It can also take optional named arguments. Named arguments enable you to set additional properties not required in the constructor and are passed to the attribute constructor in the form *name:=value*.

For example, WebMethodAttribute requires optional named arguments because it exposes more properties than those you can set through its constructor:

```
' A method that is exposed as an XML Web Service.
' First argument is required, second and third arguments are optional.
<WebMethod(True, Description:="Add operation", CacheDuration:=60)> _
Function Add(ByVal n1 As Double, ByVal n2 As Double) As Double
   Return n1 + n2
End Function
```

Most attributes are closely related to specific features of the .NET runtime. Thus, it makes more sense to discuss specific attributes only in the chapter where I explain those features. For example, I'll cover some attributes that are recognized by the Visual Basic compiler in Chapter 4, "Using Visual Studio 2005."

You can apply multiple attributes to the same code entity by enclosing all of them between angle brackets:

```
' Mark the Person class as serializable and adds a description for it.
<Serializable(), Description("The Person type")> _
Public Class Person
   ...
End Class
```

 A minor improvement in Visual Basic 2005 enables you to enclose each attribute in its own pair of angle brackets, as in this code:

```
<Serializable()> _
<Description("The Person type")> _
Public Class Person
   ...
End Class
```

Another new Visual Basic 2005 feature enables you to set a few class-level attributes without writing code. Just move the caret to the first line in a class definition and press the F4 key to open the Properties window, as shown in Figure 2-8. Unfortunately, only three class attributes can be set in this way: ComClass, ComVisible, and Serializable.

Figure 2-8   Setting class-level attributes in the Properties window

As I mentioned previously, attributes can be applied to virtually any code entity. The general rule is that the attribute immediately precedes the entity to which it refers. For example, here's how you can apply the NonSerialized attribute to a class-level field:

```
<NonSerialized()> Private m_FileName As String
```

The .NET Framework also supports attributes at the assembly level. These attributes can't really precede anything—because they are inside the assembly's source code—thus, you must mark them with a special prefix:

```
<Assembly: AssemblyCopyright("Copyright © Code Architects 2005")>
```

You can read more about assembly-level attributes in Chapter 17, "Assemblies and Resources."

Variables

Visual Basic programs declare and use their variables in ways that are similar to other languages as well as previous language versions. If you're porting your code from Visual Basic 6, however, you need to be aware of some subtle differences to fully exploit the potential of .NET and not be trapped in subtle conversion issues.

Declarations and Assignments

You can declare a variable using the Dim, Private, Public, or Static keyword:

- You use Dim inside a procedure to declare a local (dynamic) variable, which is visible only inside that procedure.

- You use Dim or Private outside procedure blocks—but inside a Class or Module block—to create variables that can be accessed from anywhere inside that class or module but not from elsewhere in the project. (A variable declared using Dim inside a Structure has Public scope, however.)

- You use Public inside a Module block to create global variables—that is, variables that exist for the entire program's lifetime and that can be accessed from anywhere in the current project.

- You use Public inside a Class block to create a public field for that class.

- You use the Static keyword to declare static variables inside a procedure. (Note that you can't use the Static keyword in a procedure declaration to make all the variables in the procedure Static as you can in Visual Basic 6.)

The following piece of code demonstrates the five types of variables:

```
Module MyModule
    ' This global variable is visible to the entire application.
    Public myGlobalVar As String
    ' These variables are visible only inside the current module.
```

```
Private myModuleVar As String
Dim myModuleVar2 As String

Sub MyProcedure()
    ' This private variable is visible only inside this procedure.
    Dim myPrivateVar As String
    ' This static variable maintains its value between
    ' consecutive calls to this procedure.
    Static counter As Integer
    ...
End Sub
End Module
```

Unassigned and Unused Variables

Visual Basic 2005 emits a compilation warning if you declare a local variable that you don't use anywhere in the current method. Even though such unused variables don't usually hurt execution speed or memory footprint, their presence might be a symptom of a more serious programming mistake. You can suppress this warning, if you wish, or transform it into a compilation error by modifying the Unused Local Variable setting in the Compile page of the My Project designer (see Figure 2-3).

The Visual Basic 2005 compiler can also help you to avoid NullReferenceException errors, which occur when you declare and use a variable without initializing it, as in this code:

```
Dim s As String
' Next line causes the following compiler warning: Variable 's' is used before it
' has been assigned a value. A null reference exception could result at run time.
Console.WriteLine(s.ToString)
```

By default, these uninitialized variables cause a compiler warning, but you can also make the compiler emit an error or ignore these variables completely by changing the Use Of Variable Prior To Assignment option on the Compile page of the My Project designer. This option affects only object, string, and array variables because these variables are implicitly initialized to Nothing when they are created and might therefore cause the NullReferenceException error. Conversely, this option doesn't affect numeric values, which are implicitly initialized to zero and can be safely used in expressions. In general, this option is related to reference types and has no effect with value types. (For more details, see the section titled "Reference Types and Value Types" earlier in this chapter.)

Visual Basic uses a code flow analysis engine to understand whether a reference to a variable might cause a NullReferenceException error. Consider this code:

```
Dim s As String
If x > 0 Then
    s = "*"
End If
Console.WriteLine(s.Length)      ' Causes a warning to be emitted.
```

The last statement in the previous code does emit the warning because the compiler has no way of determining whether the If condition will evaluate to True at run time. On the other hand, the warning disappears if all the possible execution paths assign a value to the variable in question:

```
Dim s As String
If x > 0 Then
    s = "*"
Else
    s = "+"
End If
Console.WriteLine(s.Length)     ' No warning is emitted.
```

Unfortunately, the code analysis engine is far from perfect. For example, no warning is emitted if we explicitly assign Nothing to a variable and use it immediately afterward:

```
Dim s As String
s = Nothing
' No warning is emitted, even if a null reference exception is guaranteed.
Console.WriteLine(s.Length)
```

The Option Explicit and Option Compare Directives

Visual Basic derives from the BASIC language, more precisely from the Microsoft version of BASIC named QuickBasic. These older versions didn't force you to declare all the variables used in a program, and this capability has been retained in most recent versions of the language, including Visual Basic 2005, even though by default variable declarations are mandatory.

You can control this feature by means of Option Explicit directives at the top of a source file or through projectwide Option Explicit settings. Here's an example of the former technique:

```
' Force explicit declaration of all the variables in the module.
Option Explicit On
Option Explicit               ' The On clause can be omitted.

' Make variable declarations optional in the current module.
Option Explicit Off
```

By default all variables must be declared with an explicit As clause; however, you can omit the As clause if you set the Implicit Type; Object Assumed setting (on the Compile page of the My Project designer) to None or Warning. In this case, the variable is assumed to be of type Object:

```
Dim obj             ' Type Object is assumed.
```

Needless to say, it's recommended that all variables are declared with their types and you shouldn't change the default behavior if you don't have a good reason to do so. (In my opinion, this option shouldn't have ever been added to Visual Basic.)

Visual Basic supports another Option directive, named Option Compare, which enables you to control how string comparisons are carried out within the current source code file.

```
' Make string comparisons in the module work in a case-sensitive way.
Option Compare Binary

' Make string comparisons in the module work in a case-insensitive way.
Option Compare Text
```

You don't have to add an Option Explicit and an Option Compare directive at the top of each source file because it's much easier to define these behaviors at the project level, on the Compile page of the My Project designer (see Figure 2-3). Notice that Option directives in source files override those defined at the project level.

The Option Strict Directive

One historical defect of Visual Basic was the lack of control over conversions between different types. For example, in Visual Basic 6 the following code is perfectly legal:

```
Dim s As Single, d As Double
d = 1 / 3
s = d
```

The problem with the preceding code is that when you assign a Double variable or expression to a Single variable, you're going to lose precision and might even incur an overflow error. This type of conversion is also known as *narrowing* conversion. Other examples of narrowing conversions are from Long to Integer or to Byte, or from Double to Long. A conversion in the opposite direction—for example, from Single to Double—is known as *widening* conversion and is always allowed because you can't lose precision or cause overflow errors.

Visual Basic 2005 supports the Option Strict compiler directive, which you can set to On to disable implicit narrowing conversions. For example, the following code doesn't compile:

```
' At the top of the source file
Option Strict On   ' Same as Option Strict
…
' Later in the same source file...
Dim d As Double = 1.123
Dim s As Single
s = d              ' Narrowing conversion raises a compilation error.
```

You can omit the On keyword because Option Strict is sufficient to activate this feature. You don't need to include this directive in all your modules because you can set a projectwide setting on the Compile page of the My Project designer (see Figure 2-3). Option Strict directives in source files override settings at the project level.

By default, Option Strict is set to Off at the project level, presumably to facilitate importing Visual Basic 6 projects. However, I strongly suggest that you turn it on—at least for all new projects—so that you can take advantage of this new feature. You'll spend more time writing code because you have to convert values manually to the target type, but this extra effort pays off nicely at debug time because you don't have to worry about subtle conversion bugs. The easiest way to ensure that Option Strict is automatically enforced for all new projects is to enforce this option on the VB Defaults page under the Projects And Solution category of the Options dialog box, which you can reach from the Tools menu. (See Figure 2-9.)

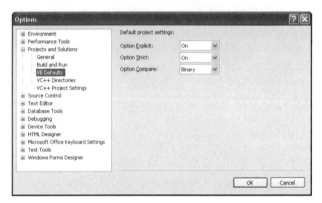

Figure 2-9   The VB Defaults page of the Options dialog box

If Option Strict is On for the entire project, you can turn it off locally by inserting the following statement at the top of individual source files:

```
Option Strict Off
```

When Option Strict is Off, you can implicitly convert from strings to dates, from string to Boolean values, and from string to numeric values, as you did in Visual Basic 6. If Option Strict is On, you must explicitly state your intention by using a conversion operator, such as CInt, CLng, or CSng:

```
' This code works regardless of the current Option Strict setting.
Dim d As Double = 1.123
Dim s As Single = CSng(d)
```

(I cover conversion operators later in this chapter.) The Option Strict On statement implicitly forces you to declare all your variables; in other words Option Strict On implies Option Explicit On. If Option Strict is On, any undeclared variable raises a compilation error. Another side effect of the Option Strict option is to disallow late binding operations:

```
' If Option Strict is On, the following code doesn't compile.
Dim o As Object
o = New Form1()
o.Show                          ' Late binding method call
```

You must disable Option Strict to assign a Boolean value to a Short, Integer, or Long variable. This behavior might be disconcerting at first because a Boolean variable can hold only the values 0 and –1, so an assignment of this kind is never a narrowing conversion, and you might not see the need for setting Option Strict to Off:

```
Dim s As Short, b As Boolean
' This line doesn't compile if Option Strict is On.
s = b
' This line always compiles. (Note the CShort conversion function.)
s = CShort(b)
```

You must use the CChar conversion operator when you're converting a string to a Char variable because such an assignment is correctly considered a narrowing conversion. The Option Strict On statement has other effects on what your code can do:

- You can't use the integer division operator backslash (\\) with floating-point numbers because this operator silently converts its operands to Long (a narrowing conversion).

- The caret (^) operator always returns a Double value, so you can't assign its result to anything other than a Double variable unless you use a conversion operator.

- Because implicit conversions from integer types to Boolean are forbidden, you can't use an integer variable by itself in an If expression as a concise way to determine whether it's equal to 0:

```
' This statement doesn't work if Option Strict is On.
Dim number As Integer
If number Then Console.WriteLine("The number isn't equal to zero.")
' The preferred syntax under Visual Basic 2005
If number <> 0 Then Console.WriteLine("The number isn't equal to zero.")
```

 Visual Basic 2005 also offers the ability to keep Option Strict disabled and yet emit a warning for each occurrence of narrowing conversion and late-binding method invocation by means of the Implicit Type and Late Binding options on the Compile page of the My Project designer (see Figure 2-3). These options are quite valuable when migrating a Visual Basic 6 application to the .NET environment because they enable you to compile your legacy code while drawing your attention to problematic statements.

Multiple Variable Declarations

You can declare multiple variables in the same Dim, Private, or Public statement:

```
Dim qty As Long, weight As Single, address As String
```

You can use a single As clause if the variables declared in a single line of the same type:

```
' Declare three Long variables.
Dim x, y, z As Long
```

Developers switching to .NET from Visual Basic 6 should pay attention to this syntax. In version 2005 of the language, variables declared with a single As are of the same type (Long in the previous code snippet). By comparison, under Visual Basic 6, the same statement declares one Long variable and two Variant variables (or whatever was the default type established by a Defxxx statement). The current behavior makes Visual Basic more consistent with other languages, such as C# and C++. Visual Basic 6 developers should also note that Visual Basic 2005 doesn't support Defxxx statements—for example, DefInt A-Z or DefLng A-Z.

A final note on multiple variable declarations in the same statement: although valid, I don't recommend this declaration style because it prevents you from commenting each variable.

This declaration style is undoubtedly clearer:

```
Dim qty As Long           ' Number of products
Dim weight As Single      ' Total weight of all products
Dim address As String     ' Shipping address
```

In addition to providing more readable code, this style lets you use initializers, as explained in the next section.

Initializers

You can declare and initialize a local variable or a class-level field in one statement. This feature enables you to simplify your code and improve its readability:

```
' Three examples of variable initializers
Dim width As Single = 1000
Dim firstName As String = "Francesco"
Dim startDate As Date = Now()
```

As the last statement shows, the value being assigned doesn't have to be constant. You can initialize a variable only if it's the sole variable declared in the Dim, Public, or Private statement:

```
' *** This line doesn't compile.
Dim x, y, z As Long = 1
```

Initializers are especially useful for class-level variables and global variables because they offer a simple way to provide a default value for fields and properties:

```
Public Class Person
    Public Country As String = "USA"
End Class
```

Initializers also work with variables holding object references. For example, the following statements declare and create an ADO.NET DataSet object:

```
Imports System.Data
...
Dim ds As DataSet
ds = New DataSet()
```

You can make your code more concise as follows:

```
Dim ds As DataSet = New DataSet()
```

Even better, Visual Basic supports a special syntax that lets you get rid of the repeated class name:

```
Dim ds As New DataSet()
```

Except for the pair of parentheses at the end (which are optional), the preceding statement looks like a Visual Basic 6 declaration, but don't let the resemblance confuse you. Under previous language versions, the As New syntax creates an auto-instancing object variable: the compiler generates code that checks such a variable before each reference to it and automatically creates an object of the corresponding type if the variable is found to be Nothing. As a result, no object is ever created if the variable is never referenced during the execution path. Under Visual Basic 2005, the preceding statement is simply a special form of a variable initializer and an object is always created when the Dim statement is executed. Visual Basic 2005 doesn't support any syntax form that corresponds to the Visual Basic 6 auto-instancing variables.

Initializers also support object constructors that take parameters. (I cover constructors in Chapter 6.) For example, the constructor for the DataSet object supports a string argument to which you pass the name of the DataSet object itself:

```
Dim ds As New DataSet("Publishers")
```

A trip to ILDASM reveals that initializers used on class fields are rendered as plain assignments in the implicit or explicit constructor that all classes have. In other words, the following code

```
Public Class Person
    Private UserName As String = "Joe"
    Public Country As String = "USA"
End Class
```

is compiled as it if were written as follows:

```
Public Class Person
    Private UserName As String
    Public Country As String

    Public Sub New()
        UserName = "Joe"
        Country = "USA"
    End Sub
End Class
```

This detail becomes of interest if the class has more constructors, as you'll see in Chapter 6. Structures don't have a default parameterless constructor, and for this reason you can't use initializers to assign a value to fields in a structure.

Object Assignments

Visual Basic 6 developers should note that the Set keyword is no longer needed to assign an object reference to an object variable, and in fact the Set keyword isn't valid in variable assignments. To understand the reason for this change, you must consider that the Set keyword was necessary under previous versions of the language only to solve the ambiguity caused by default properties, for example, the Text property of TextBox objects:

```
' This is Visual Basic 6 code.
Dim tb As TextBox
tb = Text1            ' Assign the Text1.Text to tb.Text.
Set tb = Text1        ' Assign a reference to Text1 to tb.
```

Visual Basic 2005 solves this ambiguity in a different, more radical way: default members are not supported under .NET, period. In other words, neither .NET Framework classes nor classes that you define in your code can expose a default property or method. So you don't need a special keyword to deal with those default values in assignments, and you assign scalar values and object references in the same way:

```
' In Visual Basic 2005, this is always an object assignment.
Dim tb As TextBox
tb = Text1
' You can also use initializers.
Dim tb2 As TextBox = Text1
```

Whereas the equal sign works for object assignments, you must still use the Is operator to test whether two object variables point to the same object in memory.

There is one exception to the rule that states that classes can't have a default member: a property or method can be the default member for its class if it accepts one or more arguments. Take the Collection object as an example:

```
Dim col As New Collection()
' Add two elements.
col.Add("Francesco", "FirstName")
col.Add("Balena", "LastName")

' The following statements are equivalent. (Item is the default member.)
Console.WriteLine(col.Item(1))           ' => Francesco
Console.WriteLine(col(1))                ' => Francesco
' The following statements are equivalent. (Item is the default member.)
Console.WriteLine(col.Item("LastName"))  ' => Balena
Console.WriteLine(col("LastName"))       ' => Balena
```

The reason for this exception to the general rule is that the presence of arguments makes the syntax unambiguous:

```
' This statement can only mean you're accessing the default Item method.
Dim o As Object = col(1)
' This can only mean you are storing a reference to the Collection in the o2 variable
Dim o2 As Object = col
```

Block-Scoped Variables

If a Dim statement appears inside an If...End If, Select Case...End Select, For...Next, Do...Loop, or While...End While block of code, the variable being declared is a block variable:

```
If x = 0 Then
   Dim y As Integer        ' A block variable
   …
End If
```

Block variables can be used only inside the block in which they're defined:

```
' *** This code doesn't compile.
If x = 0 Then
```

```
    Dim y As Integer     ' A block variable
    …
End If
x = y                    ' y isn't accessible from outside the For block.
```

Block variables improve the readability of your code because they make clear where a variable is used and where it can't be used. A method can contain two or more block variables with the same name (and possibly different type), provided that they are defined in nonoverlapping blocks of code:

```
If x = 0 Then
    Dim y As Integer     ' A block variable
    …
End If
Do
    Dim y As Long        ' Another block variable
    …
Loop
```

Visual Basic raises a compilation error if two variables with the same name are defined in nested blocks, for example, at the top of the method and in a For loop contained in the same method:

```
' *** This code doesn't compile.
Dim y As Integer         ' Method-level variable
If x = 0 Then
    Dim y As Integer     ' Block variable with same name
    …
End If
```

It's OK to have a block variable with the same name as a variable declared outside the procedure at the class level or globally in the application.

One important detail about block variables: although their scope is the block in which they are declared, their lifetime coincides with the procedure's lifetime. In other words, if you reenter the same block, the variable isn't initialized again and contains the value it had the last time the block was exited. For example, consider this code:

```
For i As Integer = 1 To 2
    Dim y As Long
    For j As Integer = 1 To 2
        y = y + 1
        Console.WriteLine(y)
    Next
Next
```

After you run the preceding code, the console window displays the values 1 2 3 4. If this behavior isn't exactly what you meant to achieve, you must reinitialize the variable inside the block by using an explicit assignment or by using an initializer:

```
For i As Integer = 1 To 2
    Dim y As Long = 0
    …
Next
```

Controlling Variables in For Loops

The For and For Each loops let you define their controlling variable as a block variable, using this syntax:

```
For i As Integer = 1 To 10
    ...
Next
```

This syntax was introduced in Visual Basic .NET 2003 and is relatively unknown among Visual Basic developers because many books and online articles continue to use the old syntax:

```
Dim i As Integer
For i = 1 To 10
    ...
Next
```

The new syntax is preferred in all cases because it prevents you from accidentally reusing the value of the controlling variable when the loop is exited, which is considered a programming mistake and a potential source of bugs. (What is the value of the i variable when exiting the previous loop? Is it 10 or 11? What if the loop was exited beforehand?)

Data Types

Visual Basic 2005 supports most of the data types available under previous versions of Visual Basic, including Single, Double, and String, plus a few new ones. If you are moving to the .NET Framework from Visual Basic 6, however, you should be aware of many under-the-cover details because they might introduce bugs when porting your existing applications to Visual Basic 2005.

First and foremost, the Variant type isn't supported any longer. The .NET data type closest to Variant is the System.Object type. Also, the size of all integer types has changed, and the Currency data type isn't supported any longer. Let's have a closer look at each data type.

The Object Data Type

The Object type is the one-size-fits-all data type under Visual Basic 2005 in that it can contain any type and therefore is significantly different from the Object data type that you find in Visual Basic 6. Object variables can be assigned values of any type because everything is an object in the .NET Framework, including integer and string values. As you will see in greater detail in Chapter 8, a variable can always be assigned a value whose type inherits from the variable's type. Therefore, the following statements are legal under Visual Basic 2005:

```
Dim o As Object, s As String
s = "ABCDE"
o = 123          ' Assign an integer to an Object variable.
o = s            ' Assign a string to an Object variable.
```

Integer Data Types

Visual Basic Long variables hold 64-bit signed integer values, Integer variables hold 32-bit values, Short variables hold 16-bit signed integers, and Byte variables hold 8-bit unsigned integers. If you are porting code from Visual Basic 6, you need to adjust the integer data type for existing variables. For example, let's see how you can convert a group of variable declarations from Visual Basic 6 to Visual Basic 2005:

```
' A Visual Basic 6 group of variable declarations
Dim b As Byte
Dim i As Integer
Dim l As Long

' The corresponding Visual Basic 2005 code fragment
Dim b As Byte
Dim i As Short
Dim l As Integer
```

Most of the time, you can keep Integer and Long variables when you're converting a legacy application to Visual Basic 2005, and the resulting code will work as it did previously. However, 64-bit integer operations map to multiple assembly opcodes on 32-bit processors, so unnecessarily using Long can negatively affect performance.

Visual Studio 2005 comes with a very handy utility, which you can reach by selecting the Upgrade Visual Basic 6 Code command on the Tools menu (see Figure 2-10). This command opens a dialog box where you can type or paste Visual Basic 6 code. If this code uses external COM libraries, you should add a reference to such libraries in the References tab (see Figure 2-7). You can then click the Upgrade button to have this code converted to Visual Basic 2005 and pasted in the code window. Although you can't use this utility to convert entire applications, it is very useful for short code snippets and is a valuable learning tool as well because you can use it to see quickly how most Visual Basic 6 statements can be converted to Visual Basic 2005.

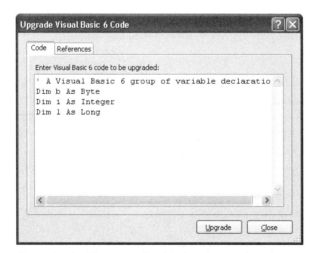

Figure 2-10   The Upgrade Visual Basic 6 tool

In general, you should always use 32-bit values because they are as fast (or slightly faster) than 16-bit values and often considerably faster than 64-bit values, especially in multiplications and divisions. If you are dealing with large arrays of 16-bit values, you might wish to use Short values to save memory. And, of course, you are forced to use Short or Long values when calling a Windows API method that requires integers of that specific size.

By default, all the integer constants you use in your application are considered to be 32-bit numbers, even if they might be rendered as 16-bit values. If desired, you can specify the size of your constants by appending an S (for Short), L (for Long), or I (Integer, seldom needed being the default size), as in this code:

```
Dim x As Short = 1234
x = x And 255S                ' Specifies a 16-bit constant
```

Numeric constants can also be expressed in hexadecimal format, which is often useful when working with bit-coded values:

```
' Clear the last four bits in a number.
x = x And &HFFF0
```

Visual Basic also supports the octal representation of integer values, even though this syntax is rarely useful:

```
' Clear the last four bits in a number.
x = x And &O177760
```

Unsigned Integer Types

Visual Basic 2005 introduces four new integer types: ULong (64-bit unsigned integers), UInteger (32-bit unsigned integers), UShort (16-bit unsigned integers), and SByte (8-bit signed integers):

```
Dim ul As ULong         ' Unsigned 64-bit integer
Dim ui As UInteger      ' Unsigned 32-bit integer
Dim us As UShort        ' Unsigned 16-bit integer
Dim sb As SByte         ' Signed 8-bit integer
```

These types are usually referred to as *unsigned integer types* even if one of them actually contains signed values. More correctly, these types are collectively known as non-CLS-compliant integer types because they aren't compliant with the Common Language Specifications (CLS) and aren't supported by all .NET languages. For this reason, you shouldn't use these types in public methods exposed by public classes visible outside the current assembly because these methods can't be invoked by all possible clients. At the very minimum, you should provide alternative methods that have arguments or return values that are fully CLS-compliant.

The simplest technique to ensure that you don't accidentally expose non-CLS-compliant types to the outside is adding a CLSCompliant attribute to the AssemblyInfo.vb source file:

```
<Assembly: CLSCompliant(True)>
```

Unlike Visual Basic .NET 2003, which ignores this attribute, the current version of Visual Basic fully honors it and emits a compilation warning if the assembly is marked as CLS-compliant and a non-CLS-compliant data type appears in the signature of a public member of a public class:

```
<Assembly: CLSCompliant(True)>

Public Class Person
   ' Next statement causes a compilation warning.
   Public Age As UInteger
End Class
```

You can avoid the warning in a variety of ways: you can change the scope of the member or its containing class, or you can explicitly mark either the class or the member with another CLSCompliant attribute:

```
Public Class Person
   <CLSCompliant(False)> _
   Public Age As UInteger
End Class
```

In practice unsigned integers are rarely necessary in most applications. One case in which they can prove useful is when you invoke a Windows API method by using PInvoke. I recommend that you don't use unsigned integers without a specific reason for doing so.

You can specify that an integer constant is to be compiled as an unsigned integer value by appending one of the following suffixes: US (for UShort), UI (for UInteger), or UL (for ULong). For example, you always need this suffix when specifying a hex constant whose leftmost bit is set:

```
' Clear the least significant word in a 32-bit unsigned integer.
Dim x As UInteger = y And &HFFFF0000UI
```

The Boolean Data Type

As its name suggests, the Boolean data type is used to store true/false values. The Boolean type takes 32 bits (4 bytes) to store a piece of information that might be stored in a bit, so large Boolean arrays take a lot memory and tax the performance of your application. Another peculiarity of this data type: whereas in the .NET run time the True value is rendered as 1, Visual Basic uses the value −1 for better compatibility with previous versions of the language. The True value is automatically converted to 1 when passed from Visual Basic to other languages, so language interoperability shouldn't be seriously affected by this decision.

Most Visual Basic programs don't depend on how True values are rendered because you typically use Boolean values from comparison operators in If and Do expressions, as in this code:

```
' The expression (x < 100) creates a temporary Boolean value.
If x < 100 Then x = x + 1
```

The internal value of True becomes important when you use comparison operators inside assignment statements. For example, a seasoned Visual Basic 6 developer might replace the preceding statement with the following one, which is more concise even though not necessarily faster:

```
' Increment x if it is less than 100.
x = x - (x < 100)
```

The preceding expression works correctly under Visual Basic 2005 as well. However, you must convert the Boolean expression to an Integer explicitly if Option Strict is On.

```
' (This works also when Option Strict is On.)
x = x - CInt(x < 100)
```

In general, however, it is recommended that you never rely on the numeric value of a Boolean value because code of this sort is quite obscure to less experienced developers or developers working with other programming languages.

Floating-Point Types

Visual Basic 2005 supports two floating-point types: Single and Double, which take, respectively, 4 and 8 bytes in memory:

```
Dim s As Single
Dim d As Double
```

As counterintuitive as it might sound, you should use Double variables instead of Single variables if you care about performance because they don't require any conversion when stored in and read from the CPU floating-point registers. You should use Single values only to save memory when creating large arrays of floating-point values, of course only if you are satisfied with their lower precision and range. (See Table 2-1 in the section titled "Mapping .NET Data Types" later in this chapter for a comparison of the range offered by all the Visual Basic types.)

As for integers, you can specify that a numeric constant be a single- or a double-precision value by using the proper suffix: an exclamation point (!) for Single values, and a number sign (#) for Double values:

```
Dim s As Single = 123.0!
Dim d As Double = s * 456.0#
```

The Decimal Data Type

When it is essential that a series of math operations isn't subjected to rounding or truncating (as is the case of currency amounts), you should use Decimal variables. This data type replaces the Currency type available in Visual Basic 6 (and other COM-based languages) and offers wider range and better precision. Indirect evidence that the Decimal type is meant to replace the Currency type shows up in the trailing at (@) symbol (once reserved for Currency values) that you now use to tell the compiler that you're actually working with a Decimal value:

```
Dim d As Decimal
…
' Make it clear that you're adding a Decimal constant.
d = d + 123.45@
```

The Decimal type holds a number in fixed-point format and is useful for preventing rounding and truncating problems; it can hold values in the range of + or −79,228,162,514,264,337,593, 543,950,335 with no decimal point or + or −7.9228162514264337593543950335 with 28 places to the right of the decimal. The smallest nonzero number that you can represent with this data type is + or −0.0000000000000000000000000001.

When selecting the best data type for your purposes and rounding errors aren't an issue, consider that Decimal values are extremely fast when addition and subtraction are involved, but their performance is much worse when multiplication and division are performed. By comparison, Double variables are slightly slower at addition and subtraction, but perform much better in all other math operations.

The String Data Type

In theory a String variable can hold more than 2 billion characters, but of course such a long string is fatal to your application. You can append new characters using either the ampersand (&) operator or the plus (+) operator, but for readability's sake the former operator is recommended (the plus operator is supported mostly for historical reasons):

```
' Two operators for appending characters to a string
Dim s As String = "ABC"
s = s & "D"              ' & operator (preferred)
s = s + "D"              ' + operator (also supported)
```

A declared string that hasn't been assigned yet holds the Nothing value or, more precisely, doesn't point to any sequence of characters in memory. There is a subtle distinction between a *null string* variable (a string variable pointing nowhere) and an *empty string* variable (a string variable pointing to a zero-length sequence of characters). You see the difference in this piece of code:

```
Dim s As String = ""
Console.WriteLine(s.Length)      ' => 0
Dim t As String                  ' (Initialized to Nothing)
Console.WriteLine(t.Length)      ' Causes a NullReferenceException error.
```

When you check a string argument inside a method you should always account for the Nothing case and behave accordingly, as in this code:

```
Sub MyProc(ByVal s As String)
   ' Deal with null strings as if they were empty strings.
   If s Is Nothing Then s = ""
   …
End Sub
```

Likewise, when authoring a Function that returns a string, you should return an empty string instead of a null string, a decision that simplifies the code that uses the function. If this isn't possible, at least clearly document that your method can return the Nothing value so that developers using your routine can take the appropriate precautions when testing the return value.

Unlike some other languages, most notably C#, Visual Basic doesn't offer a way to embed unprintable characters in a string, for example, tab and newline characters. The Microsoft .VisualBasic.dll library includes a class named ControlChars, which exposes constants such as Tab, NewLine, NullChar (the "zero" character), Cr (carriage return), Lf (line feed), and CrLf (carriage return and line feed). You must use string concatenation to include these characters in a string:

```
Dim s As String = "First line" & ControlChars.NewLine _
   & "Second line" & ControlChars.NewLine _
   & "Third line"
```

This coding style is clearly a nuisance and I believe that Microsoft should provide a simpler way to embed unprintable characters in a string, as is possible in Microsoft Visual C#. However, keep in mind that performance isn't affected by these ampersand operators because the Visual Basic compiler recognizes that all the involved strings are constant and therefore concatenates them at compile time. For this optimization to take place, however, it is essential that all the concatenations occur on the same logical line. If you split the code into separate statements, the concatenations will occur at run time and they will negatively impact the application's performance:

```
' Nonoptimized way to concatenate string constants
Dim s As String = "First line" & ControlChars.NewLine
s = s & "Second line" & ControlChars.NewLine
s = s & "Third line"
```

You'll learn a lot more about strings in Chapter 12, where I dissect all the properties and methods of the System.String class. For now, let me just hint at the Chars property, which enables you to extract one character from a string. This property is similar to, but faster than, the Mid function:

```
' Character indexes are zero-based.
Dim firstChar As Char = s.Chars(0)
```

Fixed-length strings aren't supported by Visual Basic 2005; therefore, this statement doesn't compile:

```
Dim s As String * 30          ' *** Invalid under Visual Basic 2005
```

To help you port Visual Basic 6 code that uses fixed-length strings, Microsoft has provided the FixedLengthString class in the Microsoft.VisualBasic.Compatibility.VB6 namespace. See the language manuals for more details on this class.

The Char Data Type

A Char variable can hold a single Unicode character and therefore takes 2 bytes. When assigning a literal character to a Char variable, you should use a trailing c to indicate that the literal character must be converted to a Char before the assignment:

```
Dim ch As Char = "A"c          ' Note the trailing "c" character.

' *** The following line raises a compilation error.
ch = "ABC"c                    ' More than one character
```

You can explicitly ask for a conversion from String to Char data type using the new CChar function:

```
ch = CChar(Mid("Francesco", 3, 1))
```

The CChar function is mandatory in conversions from String to Char when Option Strict is On. You can use the Chr or ChrW function to convert a Unicode code to a character, as in this code snippet:

```
ch = ChrW(65)        ' This is the "A" character.
```

ChrW is slightly more efficient than Chr because the former simply returns the Unicode character with the specified numeric code, whereas the latter must determine internally whether the current thread is using a single-byte character set (SBCS) or a double-byte character set (DBCS), must account for the current culture, and then perform the conversion accordingly.

In case you're wondering why you should use the more limited Char variable instead of a full-featured String value, the answer is simple: better performance. The reasons for this, however, will be clear only when I discuss garbage collection in Chapter 9, "Object Lifetime."

The Date Data Type

The Date type can be used to store both date and time values. For compatibility with non-.NET versions of Visual Basic, you can use date/time constants by enclosing them in number sign (#) characters, as you see here:

```
' March 3, 2005, at noon
Dim d As Date = #3/21/2005 12:00 PM#
```

You can also use the global functions Now (current date and time) and Today (current date):

```
Dim d As Date = Today
```

Because Date is a primitive type, you can also use comparison operators:

```
If Today <= #12/31/2005# Then
   ' We aren't in year 2006 yet.
End If
```

There is a lot more to learn about the Date data type, as you'll see in Chapter 12.

Constants and Enums

Visual Basic classes can contain both private and public constants; public constants are seen from outside the class as read-only fields. If Option Explicit is enabled, constants require an explicit type declaration:

```
' This statement works only if Option Strict is Off.
Public Const DefaultPassword = "mypwd"
' This statement works always and is the recommended syntax.
Public Const DefaultPassword As String = "mypwd"
```

When defining a group of related integer constants, you should define an enumerated type by means of an Enum...End Enum block. Enums are a special kind of type and they can appear anywhere in a source file, at the namespace level, or inside another module or class (in the latter case the Enum is nested in the class or module):

```
Public Enum Shape
    Triangle          ' This takes a zero value.
    Square            ' 1
    Rectangle         ' 2
    Circle            ' 3
    Unknown = -999    ' (Values don't need to be sorted.)
End Enum

' A variable that can be assigned an Enum type
Dim aShape As Shape = Shape.Square
```

By default, the constant values defined in an Enum block are 32-bit signed integers. However, you can add an explicit As clause to the Enum declaration and choose among all available signed and unsigned integer types.

```
' 16 bits are enough for this Enum, so we can use Short.
Public Enum Shape As Short
    ...
End Enum
```

For example, you might need to use Long or ULong when defining bit-coded values that require more than 32 bits; or you might opt for Short, UShort, Byte, or SByte if you expect to create large arrays of these values. In all other cases, you should use the Integer type (or omit the As clause) because it matches the 32-bit registers in Intel CPUs and delivers better performance.

You can't omit the name of the Enum when you're using an enumerated constant:

```
' *** The following line doesn't compile because you
'     must use the complete name Shape.Square.
Dim aShape As Shape = Square
```

If no explicit value is provided, the first member inside the Enum block is assigned the value 0, the second member is assigned the value 1, and so on. Even though Enum values are internally stored as integers, by default you aren't allowed to assign a number to an Enum variable if Option Strict is On, and you must convert the number to the proper Enum type before assigning it an Enum variable:

```
aShape = CType(1, Shape)
```

Mapping .NET Data Types

Each Visual Basic primitive type corresponds to a native .NET Framework data type. In other words, there is absolutely no distinction between, say, the Visual Basic string and the .NET string. More precisely, the type names I've used so far—Integer, Long, Single, String, Date, and so forth—are nothing but aliases for the corresponding .NET type, as summarized in Table 2-1 (taken from the .NET Framework Developer's Guide). The correspondence is perfect, and you can even declare your variables using the .NET data type if you prefer:

```
' Declare a String and a Date the .NET way.
Dim s As System.String      ' Equivalent to As String
Dim d As System.DateTime    ' Equivalent to As Date
```

Table 2-1   Data Types Supported Under Visual Basic 2005 and Their Corresponding .NET Framework Types

Visual Basic Type	.NET Runtime Type	Storage Size	Value Range
Boolean	System.Boolean	4 bytes	True or False.
Byte	System.Byte	1 byte	0 to 255 (unsigned).
Char	System.Char	2 bytes	0 to 65,535 (unsigned).
Date	System.DateTime	8 bytes	January 1, 1 C.E. to December 31, 9999.
Decimal	System.Decimal	12 bytes	±79,228,162,514,264,337,593,543,950, 335 with no decimal point; ±7.9228162514264337593543950335 with 28 places to the right of the decimal; smallest nonzero number is ±0.0000000000000000000000000001.
Double	System.Double	8 bytes	−1.79769313486231E308 to −4.94065645841247E-324 for negative values; 4.94065645841247E-324 to 1.79769313486232E308 for positive values.
Integer	System.Int32	4 bytes	−2,147,483,648 to 2,147,483,647.
Long	System.Int64	8 bytes	−9,223,372,036,854,775,808 to 9,223,372,036,854,775,807.
Object	System.Object	4 bytes	Any type can be stored in a variable of type Object.
SByte	System.SByte	1 byte	−128 to 127.
Single	System.Single	4 bytes	−3.402823E38 to −1.401298E-45 for negative values; 1.401298E-45 to 3.402823E38 for positive values.

Table 2-1   Data Types Supported Under Visual Basic 2005 and Their Corresponding .NET Framework Types *(Continued)*

Visual Basic Type	.NET Runtime Type	Storage Size	Value Range
String	System.String	10 bytes + (2 × string length)	0 to approximately 2 billion Unicode characters.
UInteger	System.UInt32	4 bytes	0 to 4,294,967,295 (unsigned).
ULong	System.Int64	8 bytes	0 to 18,446,744,073,709,551,615 (unsigned).
UShort	System.UInt16	2 bytes	0 to 65,535 (unsigned).
User-Defined Type (Structure block)	(Inherits from System.ValueType)	Sum of the size of its members	Each member of the structure has a range determined by its data type and is independent of the ranges of the other members.

Operators

Visual Basic 2005 supports a full gamut of operators. The effect of most is quite obvious, as in the case of math operators, whereas others might be a bit more obscure. Many of them, however, might support some features that aren't obvious even for experienced developers.

Math Operators

Visual Basic supports five operators for the four math operations. In fact, you can perform division with two operators: the forward slash (/) operator and the backslash (\) operator. I have seen many developers get confused and use the wrong operator, thus unwittingly slowing down code or, worse, delivering bogus results.

The backslash (\) operator should be used only with integer operands; it is extremely fast and truncates its result. If operands aren't integers, this operator attempts to convert them and then proceeds with the division (or throws an exception if the conversion isn't possible):

```
Dim x As Integer = 20
Console.WriteLine(x \ 3)        ' => 6  (truncates)
```

Conversely, the forward slash (/) operator should be used only with floating-point operands. If you need to truncate the result of division, use the Int function (but not the CInt or CLng operators because these operators round the result):

```
Dim y As Double = 20
Console.WriteLine(Int(y / 3))        ' => 6
```

If both operands are Single, the forward slash (/) operator performs a single-precision division and returns a Single value; otherwise, it performs double-precision division and returns a Double value. This detail can be important to realize to reduce the number of time-consuming hidden conversions. As an example of what I mean, consider this code:

```
Dim d As Double = 123
Dim s As Single = 456
```

```
' Next statement converts s to Double, performs a double-precision
' division, and finally converts the result back to a Single.
Dim res As Single = s / d
```

You can avoid one of the two hidden conversions by performing an explicit conversion yourself:

```
Dim res As Single = s / CSng(d)
```

Some informal benchmarks show that the second approach delivers code that is nearly 20 times faster than the first approach. The difference in absolute time is negligible if the operation is performed only a few times, but it becomes significant in a time-critical loop. Interestingly, you can ensure that you use the right division operator and that you don't have hidden Double-to-Single conversions by simply enabling the Option Strict feature.

An informal benchmark shows that floating-point division—both on Single and Double values—is about three times slower than multiplication. This means that, for example, multiplying by 0.5 is faster than dividing by 2 and that, in general, you can achieve faster code by replacing a division by N with a multiplication by the reciprocal of N.

```
' Divide all the elements of an array by 125.
' (This code assumes that arr is an initialized Double array.)
Dim factor As Double = 1 / 125
For i As Integer = 0 To arr.Length - 1
   arr(i) = arr(i) * factor
Next
```

The Mod operator can be applied to integer operands to evaluate the remainder of an integer division. When the dividend is negative, this operator returns a negative remainder:

```
Console.WriteLine(17 Mod 5)        ' => 2
Console.WriteLine(-17 Mod 5)       ' => -2
```

You shouldn't use the Mod operator with floating-point operands because it would introduce a hidden conversion from Single or Double to integer. To calculate the remainder of a floating-point division use the IEEERemainder static method of the System.Math class:

```
Dim y As Double = 20.5
Console.WriteLine(Math.IEEERemainder(y, 3))     ' => 2.5
```

The caret (^) operator raises a number to a power, but it always converts its operands to Double and returns a Double value. You can easily prove that by means of the ILDASM tool, which shows that this operator is translated into a call to the Pow method of the System.Math class. The following statement causes as many as three hidden conversions:

```
Dim x As Integer = 10 ^ 5
```

You can speed up exponentiation operations with a small integer exponent by replacing the exponent with a series of multiplications and possibly using temporary results:

```
' Raising a number to the fifth power
Dim num as Double = 123.45
```

```
Dim result As Double = num ^ 5

' Optimized version
Dim num as Double = 123.45
Dim result As Double = num * num * num * num * num

' Slightly faster, relies on n^5 being equal to (n^2)^2*n.
Dim num as Double = 123.45
Dim num2 As Double = num * num
Dim result As Double = num2 * num2 * num
```

Depending on the value of the exponent, a series of multiplications can be four or five times faster than the caret (^) operator (or a call to Math.Pow) and up to 50 times faster when the base number is an integer. You can even define two optimized methods to raise integer or floating-point numbers to an integer exponent by performing as few multiplications as possible:

```
Public Function Pow(ByVal number As Long, ByVal exponent As Integer) As Long
    Dim result As Long = 1
    Do While exponent > 0
       If (exponent Mod 2) = 1 Then result = result * number
       number = number * number
       exponent = exponent >> 1
    Loop
    Return result
End Function

Public Function Pow(ByVal number As Double, ByVal exponent As Integer) As Double
    Dim result As Double = 1
    Do While exponent > 0
       If (exponent Mod 2) = 1 Then result = result * number
       number = number * number
       exponent = exponent >> 1
    Loop
    Return result
End Function
```

See the section titled "Shift Operators" later in this chapter for more details about the shift right (>>) operator.

String Operators

The main string operator is &, which performs string concatenation. As I explained earlier in this chapter, the Visual Basic compiler is able to perform string concatenation at compile time; therefore, you can freely use the & operator to concatenate string literals and constants in the ControlChars class without any memory or CPU overhead because the result is evaluated at compile time:

```
' This string concatenation is evaluated at compile time.
Dim s As String = "First" & ControlChars.Tab & "Second"
```

The + operator can also perform string concatenation, but it's clearly more ambiguous and I suggest that you don't use it.

Visual Basic also includes a very handy string operator, the Like operator, which is often useful when parsing a string with complex searches. The syntax of this rarely used operator is the following:

```
result = text Like pattern
```

where *text* is the string being parsed and *pattern* is a string made up of special characters that define the search condition. The most used special characters are ? (any single character), * (zero or more characters), and # (any single digit). Here are a few examples:

```
' The Like operator is affected by the current Option Compare setting.
Option Compare Text         ' Enforce case-insensitive comparisons.
' Check that a string consists of "AB" followed by three digits.
If value Like "AB###" Then ok = True    ' e.g., "AB123"
' Check that a string starts with "ABC" and ends with "XYZ" chars.
If value Like "ABC*XYZ" Then ok = True  ' e.g., "ABCDEFGHIVWXYZ"
' Check that a string starts with "1", ends with "X", and includes 5 chars.
If value Like "1???X" Then ok = True    ' e.g., "1234X" or "1uvwx"
```

You can also specify which characters you want to include (or exclude) in the search by inserting a list enclosed in a pair of square brackets:

```
' One of the letters A,B,C followed by three digits
If value Like "[A-C]###" Then ok = True         ' e.g., "A123" or "c456"
' Three letters, the first one must be a vowel
If value Like "[AEIOU][A-Z][A-Z]" Then ok = True  ' e.g., "IVB" or "OOP"
' At least three characters, the first one can't be a digit
' Note: a leading exclamation point (!) excludes a range.
If value Like "[!0-9]??*" Then ok = True         ' e.g., "K12BC" or "ABHIL"
```

You can combine the Like and the Not operators to check whether a string contains only characters from a given subset or that you don't have consecutive characters of a given type:

```
' Only alphabetical characters
If Not (value Like "*[!A-Za-z]*") Then ok = True
' Only digits
If Not (value Like "*[!0-9]*") Then ok = True
' Any character, but no consecutive punctuation symbols
If Not (value Like "*[:;.,][:;.,]*") Then ok = True
```

In Chapter 14, "Regular Expressions," you'll learn that you can always replace a Like operator with a suitable regular expression because the latter offers many more options. However, the Like operator still has a place in the Visual Basic developer's toolbox, both because it's simpler and because in some cases it is more efficient than regular expressions are. Let's consider a simple test that checks whether a string has nine characters, starts with uppercase A, and ends with four digits. Here's a code snippet that uses the Stopwatch object (in the System.Diagnostics namespace) to time 1 million of such tests:

```
Imports System.Text.RegularExpressions
…
Dim s As String = "ABCDE1234"
```

```
Dim count As Integer = 0

Dim sw As New Stopwatch
sw.Start()
For i As Integer = 1 To 1000000
    If s Like "A????####" Then count = count + 1
Next
Console.WriteLine(sw.ElapsedMilliseconds)

sw = New Stopwatch
sw.Start()
Dim re As New Regex("^A....\d\d\d\d$")
For i As Integer = 1 To 1000000
    If re.IsMatch(s) Then count = count + 1
Next
Console.WriteLine(sw.ElapsedMilliseconds)
```

On my computer, the loop that uses the Like operator is about five times faster than the loop based on the Regex object when the project is compiled in Release mode. (By using a compiled regular expression the gap is narrower and the Like operator is only twice as fast, but in that case you must account for the time spent in compiling the Regex object.) Therefore, don't overlook the capability of the Like operator to perform complex string tests in a simple and effective way.

On the other hand, if you really care about performance, don't forget that manually testing individual characters of a string can be *much* faster than both the Like operator and the Regex object. Here's how you can perform the same test using the Length and Chars properties of the String class coupled with the AndAlso operator and the IsDigit static method of the System.Char class:

```
For i As Integer = 1 To 1000000
    If s.Length = 9 AndAlso s.Chars(0) = "A"c _
        AndAlso Char.IsDigit(s.Chars(5)) _
        AndAlso Char.IsDigit(s.Chars(6)) _
        AndAlso Char.IsDigit(s.Chars(7)) _
        AndAlso Char.IsDigit(s.Chars(8)) Then count = count + 1
Next
```

In spite of its apparent complexity, this code is about 4 times faster than the corresponding Like operator, nearly 12 times faster than the solution based on compiled regular expressions, and about 25 times faster than the solution based on standard, noncompiled regular expressions. The bottom line: never take anything for granted when deciding which solution is faster, especially when strings are involved.

Object Operators

Visual Basic supports six operators that can be used with object variables: Is, IsNot, TypeOf...Is, CType, DirectCast, and TryCast. In this section, I describe the first three of the group; see following sections for the remaining ones.

The Is operator is the simplest of the group: it simply checks that two object variables are pointing to the same instance in memory:

```
Dim s1 As String = "ABCDE"
Dim s2 As String = s1
Dim s3 As String = "12345"
Console.WriteLine(s1 = s2)        ' => True
Console.WriteLine(s1 = s3)        ' => False
```

An important note: keep in mind that Visual Basic strings are objects; therefore, when you assign a string to a string variable you're just assigning the 32-bit address in memory where characters are stored, but you aren't copying any character. This is a key difference from Visual Basic 6. The Is operator is often used to check whether an object variable hasn't been assigned anything yet:

```
' Initialize a string variable if necessary.
If s1 Is Nothing Then s1 = "ABCDE"
' Check that a string isn't null before accessing its properties.
If Not s1 Is Nothing Then Console.WriteLine(s1.Length)
```

Ensuring that an object variable isn't Nothing is such a common operation that Visual Basic 2005 has introduced the new IsNot operator, which can replace the awkward Not...Is Nothing test in the last statement of the previous code snippet:

```
' The new IsNot operator
If s1 IsNot Nothing Then Console.WriteLine(s1.Length)
```

The last object operator I cover in this section is TypeOf...Is, which you can use to test whether an object variable is of a given type:

```
' This code displays a message in the console window.
Dim obj As New Person
If TypeOf obj Is Person Then Console.WriteLine("It's a Person object")
```

The TypeOf...Is operator also returns True if the object is of a class that inherits from the specified type or if the object implements the interface specified after the Is keyword:

```
' Assuming that the Employee class inherits from Person,
' this code displays a message in the console window.
Dim obj As New Employee()
If TypeOf obj Is Person Then Console.WriteLine("It's a Person object")

' Assuming that the Employee class implements the IDisposable interface,
' this code displays a message in the console window.
If TypeOf obj Is IDisposable Then Console.WriteLine("It's a disposable object")
```

You can't use the IsNot operator to check whether an object variable isn't of the specified class or interface; thus, you need to prefix the entire expression with the Not operator:

```
If Not TypeOf obj Is IDisposable Then _
    Console.WriteLine("It isn't a disposable object")
```

CType and Conversion Operators

 Visual Basic supports the following conversion operators: CBool, CByte, CSByte, CShort, CUShort, CInt, CUInt, CLng, CULng, CSng, CDbl, CDec, CStr, CDate, CObj. As you can imagine, the CSByte, CUShort, CUInt, and CLng operators are new to Visual Basic 2005, the first version that supports non-CLS-compliant integer types. Notice that these keywords designate operators rather than functions because in some cases they are translated to native CPU opcodes rather than function calls.

As you know, the Option Strict On statement prevents the programmer from carelessly inserting code that might fail at run time because of a failed conversion. When a conversion might fail, you must make your intention clear by means of an explicit conversion operator:

```
Dim l As Long = 1234
Dim i As Integer = CInt(l)
```

You should use an explicit conversion operator whenever a narrowing conversion appears in code. Most narrowing conversions are quite obvious, for example, when you assign a Long to an Integer (as in previous code) or a Double value to a Single variable. The need for a narrowing conversion is dubious in some other cases, though:

- You need an explicit CBool operator to convert any integer or floating-point value to either False (if zero) or True (if nonzero).

- You don't need an explicit conversion to convert a signed or unsigned integer to Decimal, but must use a CDec operator to convert a Single or Double value to Decimal.

- You always need an explicit operator when converting from a signed integer type to an unsigned one; for example, you need a CUInt operator when converting from Short to UInteger, even if you are moving from a 16-bit value to a 32-bit value.

- You always need an explicit operator when converting from an unsigned integer type to a signed type of the same width or narrower. For example, you need a CInt operator when converting either a UInteger or a ULong to Integer, but not when converting a UShort to Integer.

The CStr operator is seldom used because you can convert any .NET value to a string by invoking the ToString method that all objects inherit from System.Object:

```
Dim number As Double = 12345.678
Dim s As String = number.ToString()
```

In general, the ToString method is to be preferred to the CStr operator because it lets you format the result according to a standard or a custom format:

```
s = number.ToString("G2")          ' General format, two decimal digits
s = number.ToString("##,###.000") ' Custom format
```

Similarly, you should avoid the CDate operator in favor of the Date.Parse method, which offers much more flexibility. (You can read more about the ToString method and date parsing in Chapter 12.)

The CObj operator is often overlooked when listing conversion operators on the assumption that you never need to explicitly convert a variable to the Object data type because such a conversion of the widening type doesn't require an explicit operator. This is correct, yet there is one case when you do need this operator, namely, when you want to invoke the ToString method (or another method inherited from System.Object) and all you have is an interface variable:

```
Sub DisposeObject(ByVal o As IDisposable)
    Debug.WriteLine("Disposing of " & CObj(o).ToString())
    o.Dispose()
End Sub
```

You need an explicit conversion operator also when unboxing a value held in an object variable:

```
' obj is an Object variable containing a boxed 16-bit integer or
' any other value that can be converted to a Short value.
Dim s As Short = CShort(obj)
```

A problem you must solve: how can you unbox a value type other than a primitive type? For example, let's say that you have boxed an instance of the PersonStruct structure defined in the section titled "Structures" earlier in this chapter. In this case you can use the CType operator:

```
Dim aPerson As PersonStruct
Dim obj As Object = aPerson                                    ' Boxing
…
Dim person2 As PersonStruct = CType(obj, PersonStruct)    ' Unboxing
```

Note that the second argument of the CType operator is the name of the target type and isn't enclosed in quotes. CType can be considered the universal conversion operator in that it can replace all the conversion operators discussed so far:

```
' obj is an Object variable containing an Integer.
Dim i As Integer = CType(obj, Integer)
```

If the argument can't be directly cast to the target type, CType attempts to convert it. For example, the following statement successfully converts a string to an integer, even if it requires dropping the fractional portion of the original number embedded in the string:

```
Dim res As Integer = CType("123.45", Integer)    ' => 123
```

If the argument cannot be converted to the target type, CType throws an InvalidCastException error.

The DirectCast Operator

The DirectCast keyword offers yet another way to cast a type to a different type. This keyword has the same syntax as CType but differs from the latter in a few important details. First, CType always attempts to convert the argument to the target type and is therefore able to convert a string into a numeric type (if the string actually contains a number, of course); DirectCast works only if the source argument can be cast to the target type and throws an InvalidCastException object otherwise. (DirectCast is unable to perform widening conversions even from Short to Integer or Single to Double.)

Second, DirectCast is slightly faster than CType, so you should use the former when you want to cast rather than convert a value. In practice, however, the speed difference between these operators is negligible. Summarizing, you can use the DirectCast keyword on three occasions:

- When unboxing either a primitive value type (such as a number or a date) or a custom value type you've defined with a Structure...End Structure block

- When casting a variable of a base class to a variable of a derived class—for example, a Person variable to an Employee variable or an Object variable to another reference type

- When casting an object variable to an interface variable

The TryCast Operator

You often use the DirectCast operator only after checking that the source variable is of a given type or that it implements a given interface:

```
If TypeOf obj Is Person Then
   Dim pers As Person = DirectCast(obj, Person)
   ' Use the pers variable here.
   …
End If
```

The only problem with this approach is performance because the code tests the type of the object stored in the obj variable twice, once in the TypeOf...Is operator and once in the Direct-Cast operator. You can generate faster code by leveraging the new Visual Basic 2005 TryCast operator. This operator has the same syntax as DirectCast, except it returns Nothing if the cast fails. Here's how you can rewrite the previous code snippet with this new operator:

```
Dim pers As Person = TryCast(obj, Person)
If pers IsNot Nothing Then
   ' Use the pers variable here.
   …
End If
```

The approach based on TryCast is about 20 percent faster than the code that uses DirectCast. It isn't an impressive result, but it's a good optimization technique that has no noticeable drawbacks, so I recommend that you use it when possible.

Comparison Operators

All Visual Basic primitive data types support the six comparison operators, namely, the equal sign (=), greater than or less than (<>), less than sign (<), less than or equal to sign (<=), greater than sign (>), and greater than or equal to sign (>=). You can consider them as binary operators that take two operands of the same type and return either False or True. If the two operands aren't of the same type, one of them is promoted to the operand with higher precision: for example, when a Short and an Integer value are compared, the Short operand is converted to Integer before performing the comparison; similarly, a Single operand can be converted to Double, and so forth. If no conversion is possible, either a compilation or a runtime error occurs (see more details in the section titled "The Option Strict Directive" earlier in this chapter).

You should pay attention when comparing floating-point values that are the result of a series of calculations because the combination of rounding and truncating errors can make the comparison invalid. Consider the following code:

```
Dim d As Double
For i As Integer = 1 To 10
   d = d + 0.1
Next
Console.WriteLine(d)          ' => 1       (as expected)
Console.WriteLine(d = 1)      ' => False  (how is it possible?)
```

The result from the previous code snippet seems nonsensical because the value of d is 1 and therefore we could expect that the comparison would return True. The truth is, adding 0.1 ten times actually adds a number that is slightly less than 1 because of the unavoidable rounding errors. You can easily prove this point by adding this statement to the previous code snippet:

```
Console.WriteLine(1 - d)      ' => 1.11022302462516E-16
```

These rounding errors aren't a peculiarity of the Visual Basic language; similar problems plague all programming languages, even though different languages might return different results after a series of calculations. All numerical operations are performed using binary math; therefore, the only fractional numbers that can be added or subtracted without introducing rounding errors are those that can be expressed as negative powers of two. For example, you can add 0.125 (equal to one-eighth or 2^{-3}) as many times as you wish without any problem.

Bitwise Operators

Visual Basic supports four bitwise operators: Not, And, Or, and Xor. These operators can be used only on signed and unsigned integers and combine the individual bits in their operands. These operators can be used to test or change one or more bits in a number:

```
' Test the rightmost (least significant) bit.
Dim number As Integer = 12345
If (number And 1) = 1 Then Console.WriteLine("Number is odd.")

' Clear the last eight bits (two equivalent ways).
number = number And &HFFFFFF00
number = number And Not 255

' Set the last four bits.
number = number Or 15

' Flip the most significant bit.
number = number Xor &H10000000
```

Not surprisingly, these operators are most useful with bit-coded values, that is, integer values that pack multiple pieces of information in their individual bits (or groups of bits), as is often the case with numbers passed to Windows API methods or values used to communicate with hardware devices. However, if you are familiar with binary math you can often use these operators to simplify or optimize operations and tests on regular integers. Here are a few examples:

```
' Round down to the nearest even number.
If (number Mod 2) = 1 Then number = number - 1
' Alternative way (just clears the least significant bit)
number = number And Not 1

' Round up to the nearest odd number.
If (number Mod 2) = 0 Then number = number + 1
' Alternative way (just sets the least significant bit)
number = number Or 1

' Test whether all the numbers in a group are zero.
If a = 0 And b = 0 And c = 0 Then ok = True
' Alternative way (relies on the fact that the result of Or is zero
' only if both its operands are zero)
If (a Or b Or c) = 0 Then ok = True

' Test whether all numbers in a group are positive.
If a >= 0 And b >= 0 And c >= 0 Then ok = True
' Alternative way (relies on the fact the sign bit of the result of Or
' is zero only if the sign bit of all its operands is also zero)
If (a Or b Or c) >= 0 Then ok = True

' Test whether all numbers in a group are negative.
If a < 0 And b < 0 And c < 0 Then ok = True
' Alternative way (relies on the fact the sign bit of the result of And
' is set only if the sign bit of all its operands is also set)
If (a And b And c) < 0 Then ok = True

' Test whether two numbers have the same sign.
If (a >= 0 And b >= 0) Or (a < 0 And b < 0) Then ok = True
' Alternative way (relies on the fact that the sign bit of the result from
' a Xor operator is zero if operands have same sign)
If (a Xor b) >= 0 Then ok = True
```

If you are a Visual Basic 6 developer, you have surely used And and Or operators to combine Boolean expressions in If statements. Visual Basic 2005 still supports these operators when used in this fashion, but it is recommended that you switch to the newer AndAlso and OrElse logical operators, which are illustrated next.

Logical Operators and Short-Circuit Evaluation

Visual Basic 2005 supports two logical operators, AndAlso and OrElse, that shouldn't be confused with their bitwise counterparts. Logical operators expect that their operands be Boolean, not integers. The most important feature of logical operators is short circuiting, which enables you to avoid the unnecessary evaluation of Boolean subexpressions if they wouldn't affect the value of the main expression. More precisely, if the first operand of an AndAlso operator is False, Visual Basic skips the evaluation of the remainder of the expression because the result can't be other than False. Similarly, if the first operand of an OrElse operator is True, Visual Basic skips the remainder of the expression and assigns True to the result. Let's see a simple example that uses the And operator to (inefficiently) combine two Boolean subexpressions:

```
If n1 > 0 And n1 < n2 ^ 2 Then ok = True
```

If the n1 variable is 0 or negative, the entire expression can only be False, whether the subexpression following the And operator evaluates to True or False. The And and Or operators don't do short circuiting; thus, Visual Basic always evaluate the entire If expression and incurs an unnecessary performance hit. The AndAlso operator enables you to produce better code:

```
If n1 > 0 AndAlso n1 < n2 ^ 2 Then ok = True
```

This expression is equivalent to the following, more verbose, code:

```
' "Manual" short-circuit evaluation
If n1 > 0 Then
    If n1 < n2 ^ 2 Then ok = True
End If
```

You can have short-circuit evaluation in situations in which you use the Or operator:

```
If n1 < 0 Or n1 > n2 ^ 2 Then ok = True
```

In this case, if the n1 variable is less than zero, the entire expression is surely True, so the subexpression following the Or might be sidestepped. You can enforce this smarter behavior with the OrElse operator:

```
If n1 < 0 OrElse n1 > n2 ^ 2 Then ok = True
```

These new operators also work inside complex Boolean expressions:

```
Dim n1, n2, n3 As Integer            ' All variables are 0.
' The expression following the OrElse operator isn't evaluated
' because the test on n1 and n2 is sufficient.
If n1 = 0 AndAlso (n2 = 0 OrElse n3 = 0) Then ok = True
```

Short-circuit evaluation helps you avoid some types of runtime errors without writing much code. For example, you can use the following approach to read an array element only if the index is in the valid range:

```
' This never throws an exception, even if the index is out of range.
If i >= 0 AndAlso i <= UBound(arr) AndAlso arr(i) > 0 Then
    ' arr(i) exists and is positive.
End If
```

Here's another example:

```
' AndAlso ensures that a division by zero error never occurs.
If n1 <> 0 AndAlso n2 \ n1 = n3 Then ok = True
```

The AndAlso operator helps you avoid errors when you check the property of an object variable that might be Nothing:

```
' Set ok to True if obj.Value is defined and nonnegative.
If obj IsNot Nothing AndAlso obj.Value >= 0 Then ok = True
```

Short-circuit evaluation can speed up your applications, but you must account for subtle bugs that might slip into your code. This is especially true when the subexpression contains user-defined functions that can modify the value of a field or alter the program's behavior. Consider this code:

```
' Is n2 incremented or not?
If n1 = 0 AndAlso Increment(n2) > 10 Then ok = True
...
Function Increment(ByRef value As Integer) As Integer
    value = value + 1
    Return value
End Function
```

Unless you're familiar with short-circuit evaluation you might not immediately realize that the n2 variable is incremented only if the n1 variable is 0. You can make your code more readable by using nested If statements—in other words, by writing what you might call manual short-circuiting code:

```
' Is n2 incremented or not?
If n1 = 0 Then
    If Increment(n2) > 10 Then ok = True
End If
```

Shift Operators

Visual Basic 2005 supports two binary operators for bit shifting. The double less than (<<) operator shifts its first operand to the left by the number of bits specified by its second operand:

```
Console.WriteLine(34 << 2)     ' => 136
```

Similarly, the double greater than (>>) operator shifts its first operand to the right by the number of bits specified by its second operand:

```
Console.WriteLine(34 >> 2)     ' => 8
```

If you aren't familiar with bit operations, these operators might look quite unpredictable, if not completely useless. To understand how they perform, you must convert the left-hand operator to its binary representation. For example, the binary representation of 134 is 00100010: if you shift this number two digits to the left, you get 10001000 (the binary equivalent of 134), whereas you get 00001000 (that is, 8) if you shift it two digits to the right (notice that the rightmost 1 digit is "pushed out" of the number and is lost, without any error).

The shift operators take only integer values as their left-hand operand, whereas the right-hand operand must be a 32-bit integer or a value that can be converted to the Integer type. When shifting a signed integer to the right, the sign bit is retained, which means that shifting a negative value to the right produces another negative value:

```
Dim i As Short = -8      ' -8 decimal = 11111111 11111000 binary
Console.Write(i >> 2)    ' -2 decimal = 11111111 11111110 binary
```

This type of right shifting is known as arithmetical shifting to differentiate it from the logical shifting (that does the shifting without regard for the sign bit). Visual Basic does logical shifting only when the left-hand operand is a ULong, UInteger, UShort, or Byte value because there is no sign bit in this case. With other data types, to perform right shifting without sign extension you must mask the result with an And operator:

```
' Notice the "S" suffix to force a Short hex constant.
Console.Write(i >> 2 And &H4FFFS)   ' 20478 decimal = 00111111 11111110 binary
```

If the second operand is a variable and you don't know in advance the number of bits by which the number is going to be shifted, you should use the shift right operator twice, as in:

```
' Logical shift of I to the right for N times
' (Assumes that I is Short and N is more than zero.)
Console.Write(i >> n And (&H7FFFS >> n - 1))
```

The shift operators have the lowest priority among Visual Basic operators, so you don't need to enclose the n − 1 expression in parentheses in the previous expression, but you need to enclose (&H7FFFS >> n − 1) inside parentheses to have the shift right operator be evaluated before the And operator. Notice that you should use the &H7FFFFFFF mask for Integer operands and the &H7FFFFFFFFFFFFFFF mask for Long operands.

Be aware that Visual Basic uses only the least significant bits of the second operand in an attempt to not perform too many time-consuming shift operations. For example, it ANDs the right-hand operand with 7 (binary 00000111) when shifting Byte or SByte values, 15 (binary 00001111) when shifting Short or UShort values, 31 (binary 00011111) when shifting Integer or UInteger values, and 63 (binary 00111111) when shifting Long or ULong values. This behavior can cause unexpected results. For example, you might not be prepared for this result:

```
Console.Write(2 << 33)         ' => You expect 0, but it is 4.
```

The reason is that the second operand (33, binary 0010001) is ANDed with 31 (binary 00011111), which gives 00000001; therefore, the number is shifted to the left by just one bit.

You often need to do bit shifting when you are interacting with hardware devices that require bit-coded values or when you call Windows API functions that take or return integers containing packed values. The shift left operator can be useful to perform multiplications by a power of 2. For example, shifting a value to the left by 5 bits is the same as multiplying it by 32, except that you can ignore overflow errors. Similarly, shifting a value 2 bits to the right is the same as dividing it by 4, and it also works with negative numbers because Visual Basic does arithmetic shifts.

If the operand is a Long or ULong, a shift operation is more than 25 times faster than the equivalent multiplication or division because it maps to a single CPU opcode instead of many. Shifting 16- or 32-bit values isn't significantly faster than multiplying or dividing them because in both cases only one CPU opcode is needed.

The shift left operator becomes useful to set, clear, toggle, or test an individual bit in an integer value, as the following routines demonstrate:

```
' (All these routines assume that N is in the range 0-31.)
' Set the Nth bit of a value.
Function BitSet(ByVal value As Integer, ByVal n As Integer) As Integer
   Return value Or (1 << n)
End Function

' Clear the Nth bit of a value.
Function BitClear(ByVal value As Integer, ByVal n As Integer) As Integer
   Return value And Not (1 << n)
End Function

' Toggle the Nth bit of a value.
Function BitToggle(ByVal value As Integer, ByVal n As Integer) As Integer
   Return value Xor (1 << n)
End Function

' Test the Nth bit of a value.
Function BitTest(ByVal value As Integer, ByVal n As Integer) As Boolean
   Return CBool(value And (1 << n))
End Function
```

With a little additional effort, you can also rotate integer values to the left or to the right without using a loop:

```
' Rotate an integer value N bits to the left. (N in the 0-31 range)
Function RotateLeft(ByVal value As Integer, ByVal n As Integer) As Integer
   Return (value << n) Or ((value >> 32 - n) And Not (-1 << n))
End Function

' Rotate an integer value N bits to the right. (N in the 0-31 range)
Function RotateRight(ByVal value As Integer, ByVal n As Integer) As Integer
   Return ((value >> n) And Not (-1 << 32 - n)) Or (value << 32 - n)
End Function
```

You can use the shift right operator to count the number of bits in a number:

```
Dim bitcount As Integer = 0
Do Until n = 0
```

```
   bitcount += (n And 1)
   n >>= 1
Loop
```

However, the following routine is slightly more efficient because its execution time is proportional to the number of 1 numerals in the number:

```
Function BitCount(ByVal n As Integer) As Integer
   Do Until n = 0
      BitCount += 1
      n = n And (n - 1)        ' Clear the most significant bit.
   Loop
End Function
```

(Understanding how the previous routines work is left as an exercise for you, the reader.) The .NET Framework offers the BitVector32 class for easy manipulation of bit-coded integers and the BitArray class for dealing with arrays of bits. I cover these classes in Chapter 13, "Arrays and Collections."

Shorthand for Common Operations

Visual Basic supports a variation of the standard assignment operation, which you can use when you're performing a math or string operation on a variable and are going to store the result in the variable itself. This shorthand is especially useful when you're incrementing or decrementing a variable or when you append a string to a string variable:

```
Dim x As Long = 9
Dim y As Double = 6.8
Dim s As String
x += 1             ' Increment x by 1 (same as x = x + 1).
y -= 2             ' Decrement y by 2 (same as y = y - 2).
x *= 2             ' Double x (same as x = x * 2).
x \= 10            ' Divide x by 10 (same as x = x \ 10).
y /= 4             ' Divide y by 4 (same as y = y / 4).
y ^= 3             ' Raise y to the 3rd power (same as y = y ^ 3).
s &= "ABC"         ' Append to a string (same as s = s & "ABC").
x <<= 2            ' Shift x two bits to the left (same as x = x << 2).
x >>= 1            ' Shift x one bit to the right (same as x = x >> 1).
```

If Option Strict is On, you can use neither the backslash-equals (\=) operator with floating-point variables (because the backslash operator converts its operands to Long) nor the caret-equals (^=) operator with anything but a Double variable (because the caret operator returns a Double value).

In addition to making your code more concise, in some cases this notation can make your code faster, too. This is the case when the left-hand operator is a property exposed by another object because the shortened notation reduces the total number of dots in the expression:

```
' These statements are equivalent, but the second *might* be slightly faster.
txtName.Text = txtName.Text & " Jr."
txtName.Text &= " Jr."
```

Notice the conditional verb in the comment: in many cases the JIT compiler can optimize dot operations, in which case the two notations perform equally well. However, the shortened notation is never slower than the standard notation; thus, I usually recommend using it when possible.

The GetType Operator

The .NET Framework has a great and important feature named reflection, which enables you to explore (or reflect on) all the methods and properties exposed by a given class. This is possible because each .NET class, either defined in the .NET Framework or in your own applications, corresponds to an instance of the System.Type class. For example, if your application uses 20 different classes, the .NET Framework creates 20 different instances of the System.Type class, and each instance represents one of the classes that your application uses. By invoking methods of these System.Type instances you can enumerate the members that the corresponding class exposes. I'll cover reflection in depth in Chapter 18, but for now it is important for you to understand how you can achieve a reference to a System.Type object that represents one of the types in your application.

You can get a reference to a System.Type object in many ways, two of which are most commonly used: the GetType method and the GetType operator. All objects expose the GetType method (because it is defined in the System.Object class), so you can obtain the System.Type object corresponding to the System.String type as follows:

```
Dim aString As String = "123"
Dim ty As Type = aString.GetType()
' Display the full .NET name of the string type.
Console.WriteLine(ty.FullName)                    ' => System.String
' Enumerate all the public instance methods of the String type.
For Each mi As System.Reflection.MethodInfo In ty.GetMethods()
   Console.WriteLine(mi.Name)
Next
```

However, you don't always have an object on which you can invoke the GetType method. In cases like these you can use the Visual Basic GetType operator (not to be confused with the method of the same name). For example, see how you can list all methods of the System.String type without having to create a string variable first:

```
Dim ty As Type = GetType(String)
' (Remainder of code as in previous snippet...)
…
```

The GetType operator is useful for testing the actual type of a parameter passed to a procedure. Read the comments in the following code to understand the difference between the TypeOf...Is operator and the GetType operator:

```
Sub CompareObjects(ByVal o1 As Object, ByVal o2 As Object)
   ' (Following code assumes that neither o1 nor o2 is Nothing.)
   If TypeOf o1 Is Person Then
      ' First argument is a Person or an object that derives from Person.
   End If
```

```
    If o1.GetType() Is GetType(Person) Then
      ' First argument is a Person object.
    End If
    If o1.GetType() Is o2.GetType() Then
      ' Both arguments are of the same type.
    End If
    …
End Sub
```

Arrays

All Visual Basic arrays are zero based:

```
' This statement declares an array of 11 elements.
Dim arr(10) As Integer
```

As you see in the preceding code example, the value that you pass to a Dim statement represents the highest index in the array, not the number of elements in the array, a detail that tends to confuse all developers working in other languages. For this reason, Visual Basic 2005 allows you to specify the To keyword, even though the value to its left can only be zero:

```
' Another way to declare a 11-element array
Dim arr(0 To 10) As Integer
```

Arrays can be exposed as public members of a class. This means that the following code—which would raise a compiler error under Visual Basic 6—is legal under Visual Basic 2005:

```
Public Class Person
    ' Provide up to 4 lines for address.
    Public Address(4) As String
    …
End Class
```

The ReDim Statement

You can declare an array with the Dim statement and actually allocate memory for it with a subsequent ReDim statement. You can't have a ReDim statement without a Dim statement for a given array. Because ReDim can never declare the type of an array, it doesn't support the As clause:

```
' Declare the array.
Dim arr() As Integer
…
' Create the array.
ReDim arr(100)           ' Note that no As clause is used here.
```

The ReDim statement can change the number of elements in an array but can't change the rank of the array itself, that is, the number of its dimensions (or the number of its indexes, if you prefer). You indicate the rank of an array in a Dim statement by inserting the appropriate number of commas inside the parentheses:

```
' Declare a two-dimensional array.
Dim arr2(,) As String
```

```
' Declare a three-dimensional array.
Dim arr3(,,) As String
…
' Create the arrays.
ReDim arr2(10, 10)
ReDim arr3(10, 10, 10)
```

You can re-create the array as many times as you need, provided you don't change the rank of the array. You can also use ReDim Preserve if you want to keep values already in the array. As in Visual Basic 6 and previous versions, ReDim Preserve lets you change only the number of elements in the last dimension:

```
' …(Continuing the previous code snippet)…
ReDim Preserve arr2(10, 20)
ReDim Preserve arr3(10, 10, 20)

'*** The following statements raise an
'    ArrayTypeMismatchException exception at run time.
ReDim Preserve arr2(20, 10)
ReDim Preserve arr3(10, 20, 20)
```

Array Initializers

You can initialize the values in an array by using a special form of initializer consisting of a comma-delimited list of values enclosed by curly braces:

```
' Declare and create an array of five integers.
Dim arr() As Integer = {0, 1, 2, 3, 4}
```

You must omit the number of elements in the Dim statement if you use an initializer. When creating multidimensional arrays, however, you must indicate the rank of the array and must use nested blocks of curly braces:

```
' Declare and create a two-dimensional array of strings
' with two rows and four columns.
Dim arr2(,) As String = { {"00", "01", "02", "03"}, _
                          {"10", "11", "12", "13"} }
```

Copying Arrays

In Visual Basic 6 you can assign one array to another:

```
' In Visual Basic 6, this line copies arr1 elements to arr2.
arr2() = arr1()
```

Visual Basic 2005 also supports array assignment, but the result is different from what you might expect because the .NET array is a reference type. See what a difference the reference nature of an array can make:

```
' *** Visual Basic 2005 code
Dim arr1() As Integer = {0, 111, 222, 333}
' Create another reference to the array.
```

```
Dim arr2() As Integer = arr1
' Modify the array through the second variable.
arr2(1) = 9999
' Check that the original array has been modified.
Console.WriteLine(arr1(1))             ' => 9999
```

You can actually copy an array—that is, create a new array whose elements are a copy of the elements in the original array—by means of the Clone method that the System.Array class exposes. This method creates a copy of the original array and returns a reference to that copy. Let's rewrite the previous example to use the Clone method:

```
' This code assumes that Option Strict is Off.
Dim arr3() As Integer = {0, 111, 222, 333}
' Create a copy (clone) of the array.
' (This code assumes that Option Strict is Off.)
Dim arr4() As Integer = arr3.Clone()
' Modify an element in the new array.
arr4(1) = 9999
' Check that the original array hasn't been affected.
Console.WriteLine(arr3(1))             ' => 111
```

If Option Strict is On, the preceding code fragment doesn't compile because the Clone method returns an Object value and the assignment results in a narrowing conversion. Note the empty pair of parentheses that you must use in the second argument of the CType or DirectCast operator when converting to an array of types:

```
' (This code works regardless of the current Option Strict setting.)
arr4 = DirectCast(arr3.Clone(), Integer())
```

In general, if you're converting a value to an array, the second argument of the CType or DirectCast operator must specify the rank of the target array, which you can do by using zero or more commas inside the pair of parentheses:

```
Dim arr5(,) As Integer = {{0, 1, 2, 3}, {0, 10, 20, 30}}
' Create a copy of the two-dimensional array.
Dim arr6(,) As Integer = DirectCast(arr5.Clone(), Integer(,))
```

If Option Strict is Off, you can also assign an array to an Object variable and access the array's element through late binding:

```
' …(Continuing the preceding code fragment)…
' (This code assumes that Option Strict is Off.)
Dim o As Object = arr5
Console.WriteLine(o(1, 1))             ' => 10
```

Surprisingly, if you have an array of object elements (as opposed to value types, such as numbers and structures), you can even assign the array to an Object array. For example, because the String type is a reference type, the following code runs flawlessly:

```
Dim strArr() As String = {"00", "11", "22", "33", "44"}
Dim objArr() As Object = strArr
Console.WriteLine(objArr(2))               ' => 22
```

This is a particular case of a more general rule, which states that you can assign an array of type X to an array of type Y if the X type derives from Y. Because all classes inherit from Object, you can always assign an array of reference types to an Object array. (You don't need Option Strict to be Off for this assignment to succeed.) Again, this kind of assignment works only if X is a reference type. For example, it works with strings and with classes you define but fails with numeric arrays and arrays of user-defined Structure types.

The Array object exposes many other intriguing methods, as you will learn in Chapter 13.

Alternative Syntaxes for Arrays

Visual Basic supports an alternative, undocumented syntax for declaring arrays in which the pair of parentheses follows the type name rather than the array name:

```
Dim arr As Integer()
Dim arr2 As Integer() = {1, 2, 3}
```

This syntax makes Visual Basic .NET more similar to C#, but there are other advantages as well. For example, you can reassign an array without a ReDim keyword:

```
arr2 = New Integer() {1, 2, 3, 4}
```

This syntax becomes handy when you need to create an array of values and pass it to a method because it saves you the declaration of an array variable for the sole purpose of passing it as an argument:

```
' Create an array on the fly and pass it as a method argument.
MyObject.MyMethod(New Integer() {1, 2, 3, 4})
```

Notice that you can't specify the number of elements between the two parentheses: the only way to create an array with a given number of elements is to specify all its elements between curly braces.

Empty Arrays

Visual Basic .NET enables you create two types of "empty" arrays: uninitialized arrays and arrays that contain zero elements. An uninitialized array is just an array variable set to Nothing, whereas a zero-element array is a non-Nothing variable that points to an array that has no elements. Here is the (undocumented) method for creating zero-element arrays:

```
Dim arr(-1) As Integer          ' Or whatever type you need…
```

If you have a routine that returns an array, you can decide whether you want to return Nothing or a zero-element array when an empty array should be returned. In general, returning a zero-element array makes for a more linear code in the caller. Consider this routine, which returns all the indices of a given substring in a longer string:

```
Function Matches(ByVal Text As String, ByVal Search As String) As Integer()
    ' Return Nothing if Search isn't found in Text.
```

```
   If InStr(Text, Search) = 0 Then Return Nothing
   ' Else return an array containing the indices of all occurrences.
   Dim res() As Integer
   ...
   Return res
End Function
```

The caller of the preceding routine must discern the Nothing case from the regular case:

```
Dim res() As Integer = Matches(aLongString, "abc")
If res Is Nothing Then
    Console.WriteLine("Found 0 matches")
Else
    Console.WriteLine("Found {0} matches", UBound(res) + 1)
End If
```

Now, consider what happens if you modify the Matches routine as follows:

```
' Return a zero-length array if Search isn't found in Text.
Dim res(-1) As Integer
If InStr(Text, Search) = 0 Then Return res
```

Now the caller requires less code because it doesn't have to check for Nothing first:

```
Dim res() As Integer = Matches(aLongString, "abc")
Console.WriteLine("Found {0} matches", UBound(res) + 1)
```

After this first exposure to how modules, classes, and variables are declared and used, you're ready for more details on the language and how you can control execution flow under Visual Basic.

Chapter 3

Control Flow and Error Handling

Even with the many changes in the core language syntax in recent years, Microsoft Visual Basic 2005 code still looks like code written in language versions previous to the Microsoft .NET Framework. Most of the differences are in the details, which means that sometimes you must dig far into the language specifications to find what's new in Visual Basic.

If you are switching to Visual Basic 2005 directly from Microsoft Visual Basic 6, you must be aware of many syntax differences, though, especially in statements that have to do with flow control, such as procedure definitions and execution flow statements, which I cover in the first part of this chapter. The last portion of this chapter explains what exceptions are and the .NET way of handling errors.

Note To avoid long lines, code samples in this chapter assume that the following Imports statements are used at the file or project level:

```
Imports System.Drawing
Imports System.IO
```

Execution Flow Control

Visual Basic 2005 is a mature and complete language that offers a full range of statements for controlling execution flow, such as the If, For, For Each, and Do loops. Fortunately, most of the old-style instructions, such as the GoSub statement, were dropped in the transition from Visual Basic 6 to the .NET version. The dreaded Goto statement has survived, but new statements added to the 2005 edition make it virtually superfluous.

Conditional and Loop Statements

All programming languages must provide one or more ways to execute some statements out of the sequence in which they appear in the listing. Apart from calls to Sub and Function procedures, it is possible to gather all the basic control flow statements in two groups: branch statements and loop statements.

If...Then...Else

The main branch statement is the If...Else...ElseIf...End If block. Visual Basic supports several flavors of this statement, including single-line and multiline versions:

```
' Single line version, without Else clause
If x > 0 Then y = x
' Single line version, with Else clause
If x > 0 Then y = x Else y = 0
' Same as above, but with multiple statements separated by colons
If x > 0 Then y = x: x = 0 Else y = 0

' Multiline versions of the preceding code (more readable)
If x > 0 Then
    y = x
    x = 0
Else
    y = 0
End If

' An example of If…ElseIf..Else block
If x > 0 Then
    y = x
ElseIf x < 0 Then
    y = x * x
Else                    ' X is surely 0, no need to actually test it.
    x = -1
End If
```

Often an If expression combines multiple Boolean subexpressions by means of AndAlso, OrElse, and Not operators. Read Chapter 2, "Basic Language Concepts," for several examples of these operators and the feature known as *short-circuit evaluation*.

Select Case

The Select Case statement is less versatile than the If block is in that it can test only one expression against a list of values. Each Case block can include multiple tests and you can also use the To keyword to specify value ranges:

```
' Test the first character in the firstName variable.
Dim ch As Char = firstName.Chars(0)
Select Case ch
   Case "0"c To "9"c
      ' It's a digit.
   Case "A"c To "Z"c, "a"c To "z"c
      ' It's a letter.
   Case "."c, ","c, " "c, ";"c, ":"c, "?"c
      ' It's a space or a punctuation mark.
   Case Else
      ' It's something else.
End Select
```

You can also use comparison operators in Case blocks; they must be preceded by the Is keyword:

```
Case Is < "0"c, Is > "9"c
   ' It isn't a digit.
```

You can't test object references, not even against the Nothing constant value. The Exit Select keyword enables you to abandon the Select structure before control flow reaches the end of the current Case block:

```
Case "."c, ","c, " "c, ";"c, ":"c, "?"c
   ' Process all punctuation marks here.
   …
   ' Exit now if the character is a space.
   If ch = " "c Then Exit Select
   ' Continue with remaining punctuation marks.
   …
```

The most effective optimization technique with Select Case block is to move the most frequent cases toward the top of the structure. For example, in the previous code sample, you might decide to test whether the character is a letter before testing whether it is a digit. This change can slightly speed up your code if you are parsing text that is expected to contain more words than numbers.

Some explorations with ILDASM show that the Visual Basic compiler can optimize Select Case blocks quite effectively. If the value being tested is an integer or a Char and the values in Case clauses are consecutive, the Select Case block is compiled using a switch IL opcode, which in turn is translated into a jump table at the native code level. Jump tables are very efficient and their execution time doesn't depend on the position of the corresponding Case clause. If values aren't consecutive or if you use a To keyword with too broad a range, the Visual Basic compiler translates the Select Case block into a series of If…ElseIf blocks. This series of If statements can be slower or faster than a jump table, depending on the statistic distribution of values being tested. Putting the more frequent cases near the top of the Select Case block never has any drawbacks and can optimize your code in some cases.

For…Next

You use the For…Next loop to execute a block of code a known number of times. Here's its syntax:

```
For counter [As DataType] = startValue To endValue [Step increment]
    ' Statements to be executed in the loop…
Next
```

The Step clause is optional and enables you to count backward or with increments other than one. I recommend that you always use the As clause to declare the variable inside the loop (as opposed to declaring it before the loop, which is permitted for backward compatibility with

Visual Basic .NET 2002 and earlier versions). This syntax prevents you from reusing the value in the variable when the loop exits, as I explained in the section titled "Controlling Variables in For Loops" in Chapter 2.

You can exit the loop before the controlling variable reaches its upper limit with an Exit For keyword:

```
' Find the first zero element in an array of integers.
For i As Integer = 0 To UBound(arr)
   If arr(i) = 0 Then
      Console.WriteLine("Found at position {0}", i)
      Exit For
   End If
Next
```

 Visual Basic 2005 introduces the new Continue For keyword, which enables you to jump to the next iteration without having to use an If...End If block to skip the remaining statements in the current iteration:

```
' Process only nonzero elements in an array.
For i As Integer = 0 To UBound(arr)
   If arr(i) = 0 Then Continue For
   ' These statements are processed only if arr(i) <> 0.
   ...
Next
```

The controlling variable can be of any numeric type, but in practice you should always use Integer variables, or Long if you need a larger range. When used as controlling variables, Integer or Long variables are always faster than Single, Double, or Decimal controlling variables by a factor of 10 times or more (or even 100, in the case of Decimal control variables). In addition, because of rounding errors, you cannot be completely sure that a floating-point variable is incremented correctly when the increment is a fractional quantity, and you might end up with fewer or more iterations than expected. Consider this code:

```
Dim count As Integer
For d As Single = 0 To 1 Step 0.1
   count = count + 1
Next
Console.WriteLine(count)            ' Displays "10" but should be "11"
```

If you need to increment a floating-point quantity, the safest and most efficient technique is shown in the following code snippet:

```
Dim Total As Single
' Scale start and end values by a factor of 10,
' so that you can use integers to control the loop.
For count As Integer = 0 To 10
   ' Do what you want with the Total variable, then increment it
   ' to be ready for the next iteration of the loop.
   Total += 0.1
Next
```

For Each

The For Each loop enables you to visit all the elements of an array or a collection (more precisely, all the elements of an object that implements the IEnumerable interface, as I explain in Chapter 13, "Arrays and Collections"). The controlling variable can be of any type:

```
Dim arr() As Integer = {1, 2, 3}
For Each i As Integer In arr
   Console.WriteLine(i)
Next
```

When you are working with arrays, regular For...Next loops are usually faster than and preferable to For Each...Next loops, whereas the latter type of loop is usually faster when you are working with collections. By coupling For Each loops with the ability to create arrays on the fly, you can execute a block of statements with values for a controlling variable that aren't necessarily in sequence:

```
' Check whether the value in number is prime. (Number must be <1,000.)
Dim isPrime As Boolean = True
For Each var As Integer In New Integer() {2, 3, 5, 7, 11, 13, 17, 19, 23, 29, 31}
   If (number Mod var) = 0 Then isPrime = False: Exit For
Next
```

As with For...Next loops, you can use the new Continue For keyword to jump to the next iteration of the loop and skip all the statements from the current position to the Next keyword.

Do...Loop

The Do...Loop structure is more flexible than the For...Next loop in that you can place the termination test either at the beginning or at the end of the loop. (In the latter case, the loop is always executed at least once.) You can use either the While clause (repeat while the test condition is true) or the Until clause (repeat while the test condition is false):

```
' Example of a Do loop with test condition on its top
' This loop is never executed if x <= 0.
Do While x > 0
   y = y + 1
   x = x \ 2
Loop

' Example of a Do loop with test condition on its bottom
' This loop is always executed at least once, even if x <= 0.
Do
   y = y + 1
   x = x \ 2
Loop Until x <= 0

' Endless loop–requires an Exit Do statement to get out.
Do
   ...
Loop
```

You can exit a Do loop at any moment by executing an Exit Do statement, and then skip to the next iteration by using the Continue Do statement (new in Visual Basic 2005):

```
Do
    y = y + 1
    x = x \ 2
    ' Skip the remainder of the loop if x is even.
    If (x Mod 2) = 0 Then Continue Do
    ...
Loop Until x <= 0
```

In general, there is no point in using a Do...Loop block if you can reach the same result with a For...Next block, but there is one interesting exception. Let's say that you have two nested For...Next blocks and you'd like to exit both of them from inside the innermost loop:

```
For i As Integer = 1 To 10
    For j As Integer = 1 to 20
        ' If the Evaluate function returns zero, you want to exit both loops,
        ' but this code doesn't work as desired.
        If Evaluate(i, j) = 0 Then Exit For
        ...
    Next
Next
```

The Exit For statement can exit only the innermost For block, thus the previous code snippet doesn't work as you'd like it to. The solution is to use two different kinds of loops, as in this code:

```
For i As Integer = 1 To 10
    Dim j As Integer = 1
    Do While j <= 10
        ' Exits the outermost loop
        If Evaluate(i, j) = 0 Then Exit For
        ...
        ' Prepare for next iteration.
        j += 1
    Loop
Next
```

You can apply the same technique even to three nested loops if you use the While loop, which I describe in the next section. Interestingly, you can't apply this technique to C# because its break statement doesn't let you to specify which kind of loop or block you wish to exit.

Rarely Used and Obsolete Statements

You can use the While loop to iterate over a group of statements:

```
While x > 0
    ...
End While
```

Keep in mind that this kind of loop is supported mostly for backward-compatibility reasons because it can be replaced by a more flexible Do While loop (which can have the test at the bottom of the loop or no test at all). Visual Basic also supports the Exit While and the Continue While statements to exit a While loop prematurely and to skip to the next iteration, respectively. Except for this short description, I won't be using the While loop anywhere else in this book.

Finally, we have the GoTo statement, which enables you to jump to any label in the current method:

```
GoTo ContinueFromHere
...
ContinueFromHere:
```

In practice, you *never* need to use a GoTo statement, especially now that Visual Basic supports the Continue statement and lets you skip over a bunch of statements in a loop without having to define nested If statements. For example, let's say that you are migrating a legacy application that contains this code:

```
If x > 0 Then Goto SkipAction
...
If y > 0 Then Goto Skip Action
...
If z > 0 Then Goto SkipAction
' This is the action to be skipped.
...
SkipAction:
```

Even if this code doesn't appear inside a loop, you can wrap it in a Do...Loop block that is executed only once so that you can use an Exit Do statement to skip the statements that you don't want to execute:

```
Do
    If x > 0 Then Exit Do
    ...
    If y > 0 Then Exit Do
    ...
    If z > 0 Then Exit Do
    ' This is the action to be skipped.
    ...
Loop While False
```

Procedures

Visual Basic supports Sub and Function procedures (or *methods*, in object-oriented parlance), which can have Private, Public, Friend, Protected, and Protected Friend scopes. (I explain the latter two scope keywords in Chapter 8, "Inheritance.") If no scope keyword is provided, by default Public is assumed. A procedure marked as Function can return a value, whereas a Sub procedure can't. However, the caller can decide to ignore the return value of a Function and treat it as if it were a Sub:

```
' If PrintReport is a Function returning a Boolean, both these statements are valid.
Dim ok As Boolean = PrintReport()
PrintReport()
```

A procedure's definition can include ByVal and ByRef parameters, Optional parameters, and ParamArray arguments. You must take into account a few important differences when porting a Visual Basic 6 legacy application to avoid subtle bugs and when building an application from scratch to avoid unnecessary performance hits.

Under Visual Basic 2005 the list of arguments being passed to a procedure must be enclosed in brackets, whether you're calling a Sub or a Function procedure. The Call keyword is optional and in practice you'll rarely use it:

```
Sub ProcOne()
    ProcTwo(123, "abc")
    ' You can also use the Call keyword.
    Call ProcTwo(456, "def")
End Sub

Sub ProcTwo(ByVal qty As Integer, ByVal msg As String)
    ...
End Sub
```

Conveniently, the Visual Studio editor puts a pair of parentheses around the argument list if you forget to add them yourself. If Option Strict is On, you can't rely on implicit narrowing conversions when you're passing arguments to a procedure. For example, when passing a Single or Double variable to an Integer parameter, you must make the conversion explicit by using the CInt operator; when passing a value to a string parameter, you should use the CStr operator or the ToString method that all .NET types expose:

```
Dim qty As Double = 1.23
Dim msg As Date = Now
ProcTwo(CInt(d), msg.ToString())
```

ByVal and ByRef Arguments

A procedure parameter can be declared with the ByVal or ByRef keyword, or with no keyword at all. If ByVal is used (or if no keyword is specified), Visual Basic passes arguments by value. To ensure that no ambiguity exists, Visual Studio 2005 automatically inserts a ByVal keyword when typing code in its editor. When you call such a procedure, a *copy* of the argument is made and is passed to the procedure; if the procedure modifies the corresponding parameter, the original value isn't affected.

Conversely, if you pass a variable to a ByRef parameter, any change in the parameter is reflected in the variable. If a procedure defines a ByRef parameter, you can still pass a variable by value by enclosing the value in a pair of parentheses, as in this code:

```
' PerformTask takes a by-reference integer argument.
Dim x As Integer = 123
PerformTask((x))                    ' Pass x by value, not by reference.
```

Often developers are confused about the effect of the ByVal and ByRef keywords when passing an object reference to a procedure because they mistakenly assume that ByVal causes *a copy of the object* to be passed to the callee, which isn't correct. Instead, the ByVal keyword creates a copy of the object reference, that is, the 32-bit address of the object in memory; thus, the called procedure receives another reference that points to the same area in memory. The procedure is therefore capable of affecting the original object, as this code demonstrates:

```
' The Person class exposes FirstName and LastName properties.
Sub ProcOne()
    Dim pers As New Person()
    pers.FirstName = "Francesco"
    ' Call the procedure, pass a copy of the object reference.
    ProcTwo(pers)
    ' Prove that the original object was modified.
    Console.WriteLine(pers.FirstName)         ' => FRANCESCO
End Sub

Sub ProcTwo(ByVal p As Person)
    ' Convert first name to uppercase. (ToUpper is a method of System.String.)
    p.FirstName = p.FirstName.ToUpper()
End Sub
```

This behavior raises two interesting questions. First, how can you pass an object reference to a procedure and be sure that the callee can't modify the original object? The answer is simple: you must create a copy of the object yourself before passing it to the procedure. Creating a copy of the object means creating a new object and correctly initializing all its properties. This operation can require a lot of code if the object exposes many properties, but fortunately there is a shortcut, as you'll learn in Chapter 10, "Interfaces."

Second, if the callee can modify the passed object's properties even if ByVal is used, what is the difference between ByVal and ByRef when applied to object arguments? The answer to this second question is: you need to pass an object pointer with ByRef if the callee is meant to modify the pointer itself (as opposed to one or more properties of the object). Here's an example of such a case:

```
Sub ClearPerson(ByRef p As Person)
    ' We need this test to avoid NullReferenceException errors.
    If p IsNot Nothing Then
        Debug.WriteLine("Clearing Person " & p.FirstName & " " & p.LastName)
        p = Nothing
    End If
End Sub
```

You can see a similar behavior when you pass an array to a ByVal or ByRef parameter. Remember that Visual Basic arrays are reference types—in other words, array variables point to the actual memory area in the managed heap where array items are stored. So you're passing a 4-byte pointer whether you're passing the array by value or by reference. In all cases, all changes to array elements inside the called procedure are reflected in the original array:

```
Sub TestArrayByVal()
    Dim arr() As Integer = {0, 1, 2, 3, 4}
    ' Pass the array by value to a procedure.
```

```
   ArrayProc(arr)
   ' Prove that the array element has been modified.
   Console.WriteLine(arr(3))              ' => 300
End Sub

' A procedure that modifies its array argument's elements
Sub ArrayProc(ByVal arr() As Integer)
   For i As Integer = 0 To UBound(arr)
      arr(i) = arr(i) * 100
   Next
End Sub
```

Passing an array using ByRef or ByVal makes a difference if you use a ReDim statement inside the called procedure. In this case, the original array is affected if you pass it to a ByRef argument, but it isn't modified if you pass it to a ByVal argument. To show how this works, let's build a procedure that takes two array arguments with different passing mechanisms:

```
Sub TestArrayByRef()
   Dim byvalArray(10) As Integer
   Dim byrefArray(10) As Integer
   ArrayProc2(byvalArray, byrefArray)
   ' Check which array has been affected by the ReDim statement.
   Console.WriteLine(UBound(byvalArray))    ' => 10 (not modified)
   Console.WriteLine(UBound(byrefArray))    ' => 100 (modified)
End Sub

Sub ArrayProc2(ByVal arr() As Integer, ByRef arr2() As Integer)
   ' Change the size of both arrays.
   Redim arr(100)
   Redim arr2(100)
End Sub
```

Notice that array parameters must specify the rank of the incoming array. For example, the following procedure takes a two-dimensional Long array and a three-dimensional String array:

```
Sub MyProc(ByVal arr(,) As Long, ByVal arr2(, ,) As String)
   ...
End Sub
```

The default behavior under Visual Basic 6 and previous versions was to pass arguments by reference. This means that if you're manually porting a legacy application, you must add the ByRef keyword for all those arguments that don't have the explicit ByVal keyword. For example, the following Visual Basic procedure

```
Sub MyProc(x As Integer, ByVal y As Long)
   ...
End Sub
```

must be translated as follows. (Note the change in data type as well.)

```
Sub MyProc(ByRef x As Short, ByVal y As Integer)
   ...
End Sub
```

In my experience, Visual Basic 6 developers often mindlessly omit the ByVal keyword but don't really mean to pass all the arguments by reference. When porting code from Visual Basic 6, you should reconsider whether the variable should actually be passed by reference. In most cases, an argument that should be passed by value can also be passed by reference without causing any apparent problems if the callee doesn't modify it. However, if you use an implicit ByRef where ByVal should be explicitly used in Visual Basic 6, you're creating a potential source of subtle bugs and you're also preventing the compiler from best optimizing the resulting code. If you then migrate the code to Visual Basic 2005—for example, by importing the project in Visual Studio 2005—the inefficiency and the possibility of introducing bugs persist.

The Optional Keyword

You can define optional parameters by using the Optional keyword. However, you must always provide an explicit default value for each optional parameter, even though the default value is 0, a null string, or Nothing:

```
Sub MyProc(Optional ByVal n As Integer = -1, _
   Optional ByVal p As Person = Nothing, Optional ByVal s As String = "")
   …
End Sub
```

Elsewhere in your application you can call the MyProc method and omit any optional argument, as in these statements:

```
MyProc(1)            ' Second and third arguments are omitted.
MyProc(, , "abc")    ' First and second arguments are omitted.
```

This is what happens behind the scenes when your code calls the MyProc method: if an argument is omitted, the Visual Basic compiler checks the procedure definition and creates an invisible argument that is equal to the default value defined for the corresponding parameter. In other words, the following two statements produce *exactly* the same IL and the same native code:

```
MyProc(1)
MyProc(1, Nothing, "")
```

An important consequence of this detail: there is no way for the called procedure to determine with absolute certainty whether an argument was omitted or the caller had passed its default value. (Visual Basic 6 provides the IsMissing function for these purposes, but this function didn't survive the transition to .NET.) The best you can do is check whether the argument is equal to its default value:

```
' (Inside the MyProc method)
If n = -1 Then
   ' The n argument has been omitted (presumably).
End If
```

You can use −1 as a special value if the argument shouldn't take negative values; or you can use the largest negative or positive number for that numeric type, which corresponds to the MinValue or MaxValue property that all numeric classes expose:

```
Sub MyProc(Optional ByVal x As Long = Long.MinValue)
   If x = Long.MinValue Then
      ' The x argument has been omitted (presumably).
   End If
   …
End Sub
```

If the optional argument is a Single or a Double, you can also use the special NaN (Not-a-Number) value for its default:

```
Sub MyProc(Optional ByVal x As Double = Double.NaN)
   If Double.IsNaN(x) Then
      ' The x argument has been omitted (presumably).
   End If
End Sub
```

The NaN value is assigned to a floating-point number when you perform operations that don't return a real number, such as when you pass a negative argument to the Log or Sqrt function. So there's a small chance that you could mistakenly pass it to a procedure, as in the following code:

```
' This statement passes MyProc the NaN value,
' which is mistakenly taken as a missing argument.
MyProc(Math.Sqrt(-1))
```

Optional arguments are a great Visual Basic feature because they enable you to simplify the syntax of the calling code without making the structure of the called procedure more complex. However, it is recommended that you use Optional arguments only for methods that aren't visible to other .NET assemblies because this feature isn't Common Language Specifications (CLS)–compliant and is ignored by most other .NET languages. For example, a C# developer must pass all the arguments when calling a method with optional parameters.

The ability to omit optional arguments is extremely valuable when interacting with Microsoft Office COM libraries, which expose tons of methods with optional arguments. This is one of the few areas where Visual Basic has a neat advantage over other .NET programming languages.

Even if you are sure that a public method will be used only by other assemblies written in Visual Basic, you should use the Optional keyword with extreme care because it might create subtle versioning issues. As I just explained, an optional parameter causes the caller code to generate a hidden argument whose value is equal to the parameter's default value. If you later change the default value in the procedure and you forget to recompile all its clients, existing clients will pass the wrong value to the procedure.

The bottom line: use Optional parameters only for methods that aren't visible to other assemblies. To implement public procedures that can take a variable number of arguments you should use the ParamArray keyword (see next section) or method overloading (see Chapter 6, "Class Fundamentals").

ParamArray Arguments

You can create procedures that take any number of optional arguments by using the ParamArray keyword. You can define arrays of arguments of any specific type:

```
Function Sum(ParamArray ByVal args() As Integer) As Integer
   Dim result As Integer = 0
   For index As Integer = 0 To UBound(args)
      result += args(index)
   Next
   Return result
End Function
```

Three details are worth mentioning. First, ParamArray arguments are always passed by value; therefore, assignments to them inside the procedure don't affect the original variable seen by the caller. Second, you can never omit a parameter to a procedure that expects a ParamArray:

```
' *** This statement doesn't compile.
Result = Sum(1, , 3)
```

Finally, you can always pass a real array to a method that expects a ParamArray argument, as in this code:

```
Dim arr() As Integer = {1, 2, 3}
Result = Sum(arr)
```

Interestingly, the ParamArray parameter is an array in all aspects, and you can apply to it all the methods defined for arrays in the .NET Framework. Consider the following function that uses the Array.Sort static method to return the minimum value among all the arguments passed to it:

```
Function MinValue(ParamArray ByVal args() As Integer) As Integer
   ' Sort the array, and then return its first element.
   ' (Concise code, even though not very efficient)
   Array.Sort(args)
   Return args(0)
End Function
```

Exiting a Method

You can exit a method by means of three different keywords: Exit Sub, Exit Function, and Return. Functions can return a value by assigning the value to the function's name (as you do in Visual Basic 6) or by using the Return statement:

```
' Two ways to return a value
Function DoubleIt(ByVal x As Long) As Long
   DoubleIt = x * 2
```

```
End Function

Function DoubleIt(ByVal x As Long) As Long
    Return x * 2
End Function
```

The Return statement is especially handy when a function has multiple exit points because it saves you from having to write an explicit Exit Function statement. A Return keyword without arguments exits a Sub procedure immediately, but it doesn't offer any advantage over the Exit Sub keyword. You can use the Return keyword to return arrays, as you can see in this code:

```
' Return an array containing Integers in the range 0 to n - 1.
Function InitializeArray(ByVal n As Integer) As Integer()
    Dim res(n - 1) As Integer
    For i As Integer = 0 To n - 1
        res(i) = i
    Next
    Return res
End Function
```

A reason to prefer the new Return statement to the alternative syntax is that you can then change the function name without also having to modify all the occurrences of the function name inside the procedure. It's a little detail that can save you some time during the refining phase. Also, Microsoft documentation states that the compiler can optimize code better if the Return keyword is used, so it's one more reason to use this keyword instead of assigning the return value to the variable named after the function.

Good programming practices dictate that methods should have a single exit point. Among the many benefits, this programming guideline enables you later to add diagnostic statements that display the value being returned to the caller with minimal impact on existing code. So I recommend that you don't abuse the use of the Return keyword inside your methods. It's preferable to declare a variable meant to store the return value (I typically use a variable named result for this purpose) and then return it at the end of the method.

By default, the Visual Basic 2005 compiler emits a warning if a function doesn't return a value. This means that, unless you disable the Function/Operator Without Return Value option (on the Compile page of the My Project designer), you can't omit a return value from a Boolean, numeric, or object function to have the function return False, zero, or Nothing, respectively. I suggest that you keep this option enabled because it is a great aid in detecting programming mistakes.

Recursive Methods

A Visual Basic method can be *recursive*, which means that it can invoke itself. Recursion adds a lot of flexibility to your programming style and often enables you to solve complex tasks in an elegant and concise manner. For example, here's an example of a recursive function that is mentioned by virtually all programming textbooks:

```
Function Factorial(ByVal n As Integer) As Double
    If n < 0 Then
```

```
      Throw New ArgumentException("Invalid argument")
    ElseIf n <= 1 Then
      Return 1
    Else
      Return n * Factorial(n - 1)        ' Tail recursion
    End If
End Function
```

Recursion is often used in procedures that explore a tree structure, such as the directory tree in a hard disk:

```
Sub DisplayDirTree(ByVal path As String)
    Console.WriteLine(path)
    For Each dirName As String In Directory.GetDirectories(path)
        DisplayDirTree(dirName)
    Next
End Sub
```

The two recursive examples shown so far are quite popular and have become "classic" examples of recursion. The following procedure is much less common and a bit more useful: it returns the textual representation of an integer number (for example, "One Hundred Twelve" for 112) and demonstrates how concise your code can be, thanks to recursion techniques:

```
Function NumberToText(ByVal n As Integer) As String
    Select Case n
      Case 0
         Return ""
      Case 1 To 19
         Dim arr() As String = {"One", "Two", "Three", "Four", "Five", "Six", _
            "Seven", "Eight", "Nine", "Ten", "Eleven", "Twelve", "Thirteen", _
            "Fourteen", "Fifteen", "Sixteen", "Seventeen", "Eighteen", "Nineteen"}
         Return arr(n - 1) & " "
      Case 20 To 99
         Dim arr() As String = {"Twenty", "Thirty", "Forty", "Fifty", "Sixty", _
            "Seventy", "Eighty", "Ninety"}
         Return arr(n \ 10 - 2) & " " & NumberToText(n Mod 10)
      Case 100 To 199
         Return "One Hundred " & NumberToText(n Mod 100)
      Case 200 To 999
         Return NumberToText(n \ 100) & "Hundreds " & NumberToText(n Mod 100)
      Case 100 To 1999
         Return "One Thousand " & NumberToText(n Mod 1000)
      Case 2000 To 999999
         Return NumberToText(n \ 1000) & "Thousands " & NumberToText(n Mod 1000)
      Case 1000000 To 1999999
         Return "One Million " & NumberToText(n Mod 1000000)
      Case 1000000 To 999999999
         Return NumberToText(n \ 1000000) & "Millions " & NumberToText(n Mod 1000000)
      Case 1000000000 To 1999999999
         Return "One Billion " & NumberToText(n Mod 1000000000)
      Case Else
         Return NumberToText(n \ 1000000000) & "Billions " _
            & NumberToText(n Mod 1000000000)
    End Select
End Function
```

Commands, Functions, and Constants

In an effort to make the transition from Visual Basic 6 to Visual Basic 2005 as smooth as possible, Microsoft has gathered most of the Visual Basic 6 commands and functions in the Microsoft.VisualBasic.dll assembly. All Visual Basic applications automatically reference this library and the reference can't be dropped. This library contains several classes and modules, and Visual Basic code can freely use them (and the methods they expose) thanks to a project-wide Imports statement that imports the Microsoft.VisualBasic namespace, where all the classes and modules reside.

In this section, I summarize which Visual Basic 6 commands and functions are available to Visual Basic 2005, which have been dropped, and which require a different syntax. If you aren't a Visual Basic 6 developer, you can skip this part and jump to the section titled "Error Handling" later in this chapter.

Visual Basic developers switching to the .NET platform are often puzzled about whether they should use the old Visual Basic commands or should stick to the new .NET syntax. My suggestion is to adopt the .NET syntax as soon as you feel comfortable with the new language and to avoid using methods and classes in the Microsoft.VisualBasic namespace if possible. In general, native .NET methods offer more flexibility and better performance. Just as important, if you are familiar with .NET types and methods, you can later switch to C# or another .NET language with minimal effort.

String Constants and Functions

Visual Basic 6 string constants, such as vbCrLf and vbTab, are supported as fields of the Microsoft.VisualBasic.Constants class (together with all the other Visual Basic 6 constants). This class is marked as a global class by using the StandardModule attribute, so you don't have to include the name of the class in your code, as you'd do if it were a regular class:

```
' vbCrLf is a field of the Microsoft.VisualBasic.Constants class.
Dim separator As String = vbCrLf
```

Note that the vbNullString constant is no longer necessary because you can simply use Nothing to specify a null string (as opposed to an empty string), but it is still supported for backward compatibility.

Alternatively, you can use the fields exposed by the Microsoft.VisualBasic.ControlChars class. Because this class isn't declared globally, you must include the name of the class itself (unless you use an Imports statement to import the entire class). The names of constants in this class are the same as in Visual Basic 6 except that they don't have the vb prefix:

```
' A more .NET-oriented syntax
Dim separator As String = ControlChars.CrLf
```

The ControlChars class contains the following constants: Back, Cr, CrLf, FormFeed, NewLine, NullChar, Quote, Tab, and VerticalTab.

The Microsoft.VisualBasic.Strings class exposes most of the Visual Basic string functions, including Asc, Chr, ChrW, Filter, Format, FormatCurrency, FormatDateTime, FormatNumber, FormatPercent, InStr, InStrRev, Join, LCase, Left, Len, LTrim, Mid, Replace, Right, RTrim, Space, Split, StrComp, StrReverse, Trim, and UCase. Functions that support multiple syntax forms—such as InStr and Mid—have been conveniently overloaded and all the usual syntax forms are supported. (Read Chapter 6 for more details about overloading.) These methods are globally defined, so you don't have to include the complete class name to invoke them, though you do need to specify the complete names of the constants that are related to them:

```
' Compare two strings in case-insensitive mode.
If StrComp(s1, s2, CompareMethod.Text) = 0 Then res = "Equal"
```

Visual Basic .NET doesn't support the dollar sign ($)–terminated version of string functions, such as Left$ or Space$.

Math Functions

Most math functions you need in your applications are implemented in the System.Math class. Therefore, they aren't part of the Visual Basic library, though they closely resemble the functions you had in previous versions of this language. You can classify the math functions in these groups:

- **Constants**   E, PI

- **Arithmetic functions**   Abs, BigMul, Ceiling, DivRem, Exp, Floor, IEEERemainder, Log, Log10, Max, Min, Pow, Round, Sign, Sqrt, Truncate

- **Trig and inverse trig functions**   Sin, Cos, Tan, Asin, Acos, Atan, Atan2

- **Hyperbolic trig functions**   Sinh, Cosh, Tanh

Unless you import the System.Math class, you must specify the complete class name when calling one of its methods. The calling syntax of functions that were supported under Visual Basic 6–possibly under a different name, such as Sqrt, Sign, and Atan–hasn't changed. The Log function supports one argument (natural logarithms) or two arguments (logarithms in any base):

```
' The natural logarithm of 10
Dim result As Double = Math.Log(10)        ' => 2.30258509299405
' Two ways to evaluate the decimal logarithm of 1,000
result = Math.Log(1000, 10)                ' => 3
result = Math.Log10(1000)                  ' => 3
```

The Min and Max methods do what their names suggest and are conveniently overloaded to work with any numeric type:

```
result = Math.Min(1.5, 0.7)                ' => 0.7
result = Math.Max(99, 87)                  ' => 99
```

The Floor method returns the integer less than or equal to the argument, whereas Ceiling returns the integer greater than or equal to the argument. The Truncate method (new in .NET

Framework version 2.0) simply discards any fractional portion and therefore behaves differently from Ceiling if the argument is negative:

```
result = Math.Ceiling(2.5)               ' => 3
result = Math.Floor(-1.5)                ' => -2
result = Math.Truncate(-1.5)             ' => -1
```

The Round method has been enhanced in .NET Framework 2.0 to support an enumerated MidpointRounding argument, which specifies what happens when the fractional portion of the number being rounded is exactly 0.5:

```
' Round the argument to the nearest value that is away from zero.
result = Math.Round(2.5, 0, MidpointRounding.AwayFromZero)   ' => 3
' Round the argument to the nearest even value.
result = Math.Round(2.5, 0, MidpointRounding.ToEven)         ' => 2
```

Atan2 returns the angle formed by an object of a given height y at a given distance x; it's similar to Atan, but it returns an unambiguous value for all four quadrants. The DivRem method performs an integer division and returns the remainder in the third argument:

```
Dim remainder As Long
Dim result As Long = Math.DivRem(20, 3, remainder)
Console.WriteLine("Result={0}, Remainder={1}", result, remainder)
```

The IEEERemainder function returns the remainder of a division operation; it's therefore similar to the Mod operator but works with floating-point numbers:

```
Console.WriteLine(Math.IEEERemainder(2, 1.5))   ' => 0.5
```

Date and Time Functions

The DateAndTime class includes several date and time functions, among which are DateAdd, DateDiff, DatePart, DateSerial, DateValue, Year, Month, Day, Hour, Minute, Second, MonthName, Weekday, WeekdayName, TimeSerial, and TimeValue. This class also exposes two read-only properties, Now and Timer. In general, the syntax hasn't changed from Visual Basic 6 except for the DateAdd, DateDiff, and DatePart functions, which now can take an enumerated constant instead of a string constant:

```
' Get the date two weeks from now.
newDate = DateAdd(DateInterval.WeekOfYear, 2, Now())
' The Visual Basic 6 syntax is still supported.
newDate = DateAdd("w", 2,  Now())
```

You have two new properties, namely, Today and TimeOfDay, that retrieve or set the current date and time and that replace the Time and Date properties, respectively:

```
' Reset system time to midnight.
TimeOfDay = #12:00:00 AM#
' Evaluate days left until December 31 of current year.
days = DateDiff(DateInterval.Day, Today, DateSerial(Year(Today), 12, 31))
```

The MonthName and WeekdayName functions support an extra Boolean argument to retrieve the abbreviated month or day name:

```
Console.WriteLine(MonthName(1, True))        ' => Jan
```

Interaction Commands and Functions

The Microsoft.VisualBasic.Interaction class exposes many useful commands and methods that were available in Visual Basic 6, including AppActivate, Beep, CallByName, Choose, Command, Environ, IIf, InputBox, MsgBox, Partition, Shell, and Switch. These methods are globally defined, so you don't have to include the class name when you use them:

```
MsgBox("Goodbye", MsgBoxStyle.Information)
```

The Shell function expands the Visual Basic 6 version and supports an additional argument that enables you to specify whether to wait until the shelled program terminates with an optional timeout:

```
' Run Notepad.exe, and wait until the user terminates it.
Shell("notepad", AppWinStyle.NormalFocus, True)

' Run Notepad, and then wait max 10 seconds.
Dim taskID As Long = Shell("notepad", AppWinStyle.NormalFocus, True, 10000)
If taskID = 0 Then
   Console.WriteLine("Notepad has been closed within 10 seconds.")
Else
   Console.WriteLine("Notepad is still running after 10 seconds.")
End If
```

Finally, I recommend that you never use the IIf function in time-critical loops because a plain If...Then...Else block is always faster:

```
' Two ways to achieve the same result, but the latter is preferable because
' it saves you *two* function calls, one to IIf and one to GetResult.
result = IIf(n < 10, GetResult(n), GetResult(n - 1))
If n < 10 Then result = GetResult(n) Else result = GetResult(n - 1)
```

Other Commands, Functions, and Objects

The FileSystem class includes all the usual Visual Basic file commands and functions, including ChDir, ChDrive, CurDir, Dir, FileCopy, FileDateTime, FileLen, GetAttr, Kill, MkDir, RmDir, and SetAttr. There are no relevant differences from their counterparts under previous versions of the language, except that the new FileOpen, FileClose, FileGet, FilePut, PrintLine, InputLine, and InputString commands supersede the Open#, Close#, Get#, Put#, Print#, LineInput#, and Input statements (whose nonstandard syntax can't be supported in Visual Basic 2005):

```
' Read a text file.
Dim handle As Integer = FreeFile()
' Open a file for input.
```

```
FileOpen(handle, "C:\autoexec.bat", OpenMode.Input, OpenAccess. Read)
' Read the entire file in one operation.
Dim fileText As String = InputString(handle, CInt(LOF(handle)))
' Close the file.
FileClose(handle)
```

In most cases, however, you should avoid these file-related functions in the Microsoft.Visual-Basic namespace and use other objects offered by the .NET Framework because you'll write more flexible code that way. See Chapter 15, "Files, Directories, and Streams," for more details about .NET file and directory classes.

The Conversion class provides support for functions such as Fix, Hex, Int, Oct, Str, and Val, which have the same syntax and meaning as they did under Visual Basic 6. This class also includes the ErrorToString function, which converts an error code to a description. The Error-ToString function is similar to Err.Description, but you don't need to have an actual error to retrieve the description associated with an error code:

```
' Display the description associated with error code 9.
Console.WriteLine(ErrorToString(9))    ' => Subscript out of range.
```

The Information class gathers miscellaneous functions, such as Erl, Err, IsArray, IsDate, IsError, IsNothing, IsNumeric, LBound, UBound, and TypeName. The IsEmpty and IsNull functions aren't supported because they made sense only with Variant arguments, which in turn aren't supported. However, the .NET Framework supports the DBNull data type (which represents a null value coming from a database field), and the Information type conveniently exposes an IsDBNull function, which has therefore more or less the same meaning as IsNull.

Error Handling

In the .NET world, errors in the regular execution flow are known as *exceptions*. Exceptions offer a way of raising and handling error conditions that is unified among all the .NET programming languages.

Throwing Exceptions

The main problem with dealing with errors in languages prior to .NET is that no one agrees on a single best approach. For example, functions in most Windows system DLLs written in C report errors through a return value and do that in a very confusing way. (In some cases, 0 means success and 1 means error, while in other cases the meanings are reversed.) COM components return an error code by means of a 32-bit HRESULT value, and Visual Basic applications raise errors using a COM-compliant mechanism behind the scenes. Other languages, such as C++ and Java, can use an error-handling mechanism based on exceptions.

To enable cross-language interoperability, the .NET Framework has standardized on a single method of raising and trapping errors based on exceptions. You can think of exceptions as unexpected conditions that occur during execution of your application or while code is running inside the .NET Framework itself. When this situation occurs, the code is said to *throw* an exception object that some other code is expected to *catch*.

An exception can be caught by code in the same procedure in which the error occurs. If it isn't, the exception is thrown to the caller, and it's up to the caller to remedy the error and possibly retry the operation that caused the problem. If the caller doesn't catch the exception, the exception is automatically thrown to the caller's caller, and so forth. The exception "bubbles up" the call chain until it finds a calling procedure that's willing to catch it. (You'll see in a moment what catching an exception means in practice.)

By default, if no procedure in the call chain catches the exception, the user is notified by means of an error dialog box, such as the one in Figure 3-1. By modifying the DbgJITDebugLaunchSetting value under the HKEY_LOCAL_MACHINE\Software\Microsoft\.NETFramework registry key, you can change how the common language runtime behaves when an uncaught exception is thrown. If the four least significant bits of this value are 0, the .NET Framework displays the dialog box; setting them to 1 always terminates the application, whereas setting them to 2 always runs the debugger listed in the DgbManagedDebugger value of the same registry key.

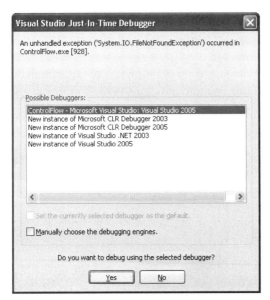

Figure 3-1 The dialog box that appears when an unhandled exception is thrown and one or more .NET debuggers are installed on the computer

The phrase *throwing an exception* is appropriate because an exception object is actually passed back to the caller when an exception occurs. The code that catches the exception can examine the exception object's properties, invoke its methods, and take any step it deems necessary—such as informing the user or silently canceling the operation that caused the problem.

Alternatively, the code can throw the exception object again—possibly after adjusting one or more of its properties—or it can throw a completely different exception object. The object being thrown back and forth exposes properties, such as Message (the error's description), Source (a string that tells where the error occurred), and HelpLink (the address of a Help page that describes how to recover from the error). The next section describes these properties in greater detail.

Visual Basic 6 developers will probably think that all this sounds familiar. In fact, even though the inner details are different, .NET exceptions work and behave in much the same way as the Visual Basic 6 error-handling mechanism. The exception object resembles the Err object (with different names for its properties); throwing an exception works surprisingly like raising an error; the bubbling up behavior is the one Visual Basic 6 uses when notifying procedures of errors if those procedures don't have an active error handler. This is known ground for Visual Basic 6 developers.

The Exception Object

The Exception object is defined in the .NET Framework, and its complete name is System .Exception. Neither the .NET runtime nor your own applications usually throw this raw exception object, though, but use one of the exception types that derive from it. You should become familiar with the exceptions that the .NET Framework exposes, some of which are depicted in Figure 3-2. For example, math operations can throw an ArithmeticException, an OverflowException, or a DivideByZeroException object, while many math functions can throw an ArgumentOutOfRangeException object. For a complete list of exception objects, just use the Search command in the Object Browser and look for the Exception substring, or use the Exceptions command from the Debug menu.

Microsoft developers intended the SystemException and the ApplicationException classes to offer a simple way to discern between .NET Framework exceptions and application-specific exceptions when handling an exception thrown at your program, and Microsoft recommends that you derive your custom exception types from ApplicationException. Unfortunately, as you can see in Figure 3-2, a few .NET exceptions derive directly from System.Exception or from System.ApplicationException. In practice, therefore, the recommendation doesn't provide a measurable advantage, and there isn't any reason for catching either the System-Exception or the ApplicationException object.

Let's have a look at the most important properties and methods that all these exception objects have in common. All these properties are read-only except Source and HelpLink.

The Message property is the descriptive text for the exception and is therefore similar to the Err.Description property in Visual Basic 6. For example, the Message property of a DivideByZeroException returns the string "Attempted to divide by zero."

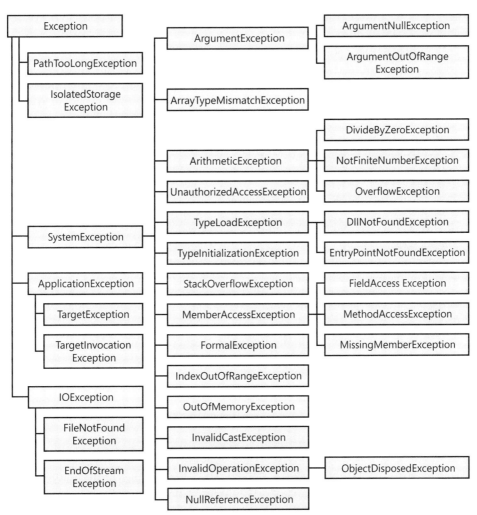

Figure 3-2   The hierarchy of the most important exception objects in the .NET Framework

The Exception object inherits the ToString method from System.Object, and it returns the same error message that would be displayed to the user in a dialog box. This is similar to the Message property, but it also includes the name of the module. If debug information is embedded in the executable, the return value includes the name of the procedure and the exact line number where the error occurred:

```
System.DivideByZeroException: Attempted to divide by zero.
at MyApplication.Form1.TestProc in C:\MyApplication\Form1.vb:line 70
```

The TargetSite property returns the name and signature of the procedure in which the exception was first thrown, expressed in C# syntax:

```
Int32 DivideNumber(Int32 x, Int32 y)
```

The StackTrace property returns a string that describes the stack path from the place the exception was originally thrown—that is, where the error occurred—to the place the error was caught. For example, say that your TestProc procedure calls the EvalResult procedure, which in turns calls the DivideNumber function, and assume that the latter two procedures don't catch exceptions. If the innermost DivideNumber function throws a DivideByZeroException, the value of the StackTrace property as read in the TestProc procedure looks like the following code:

```
at MyApplication.Form1.DivideNumber(Int32 x, I nt32 y)
    in C:\MyApplication\Form1.vb:line 91
at MyApplication.Form1.EvalResult() in
    C:\MyApplication\Form1.vb:line 87
at MyApplication.Form1.TestProc() in
    C:\MyApplication\Form1.vb:line 77
```

You get this detailed information only if the executable embeds debug information; if you compiled the program in Release mode, you won't see the name of the source file or the line number. It goes without saying that the StackTrace property is your best friend when you're trying to figure out what actually happens when your code throws an exception.

The Source property sets or returns the name of the component in which the exception was thrown and is therefore similar to the Err.Source property in Visual Basic 6. For exceptions thrown in the current application, this property returns a null string.

The HelpLink property sets or returns a Uniform Resource Name (URN) or Uniform Resource Locator (URL) to the Help file associated with the exception object, as you see here:

```
file://C:/MyApplication/manual.html#ErrorNum42
```

The Throw Keyword

Under Visual Basic 6 and previous versions, you can raise an error using the Err.Raise method. The Err object is still supported under Visual Basic, so code based on its Raise method will continue to work as before. However, you should throw your exceptions using the Throw command to comply with the exception mechanism and make your code compatible with components written in other .NET languages.

The Throw keyword takes only one argument: the exception object being thrown. Unless you already have an exception object (as happens when you are inside a Catch block; see the next section), you must create such an object and set its properties as required. In most cases, you can create an exception object and throw it in one statement:

```
' This statement broadly corresponds to
'    Err.Raise 53, , "File not found."
Throw New FileNotFoundException()
```

When you're creating the exception object, you can specify a more precise message by passing an argument to the exception object's constructor:

```
Throw New FileNotFoundException("Initialization file not found")
```

An exception class can expose multiple constructors, each one enabling a different set of properties to be initialized. For example, the constructor of the ArgumentException object can take a message or a message plus the name of the argument:

```
Sub ProcessFile(ByVal fileName As String, ByVal firstByte As Integer)
    If fileName = "" Then
        Throw New ArgumentException("Null or empty string", "fileName")
    ElseIf firstByte < 0 Then
        Throw New ArgumentException("Negative values are invalid", "firstByte")
    End If
    …
End Sub
```

Although it's recommended that you throw exceptions to emphasize exceptional events as well as programming mistakes (as in the previous code example), you should avoid throwing exceptions unnecessarily, as explained in the next section.

Performance Tips

Throwing exceptions adds overhead to your applications, so you should throw exceptions sparingly in time-critical sections of your code. In many cases, you can avoid throwing an exception by checking values before attempting an operation. For example, you can check that the divisor operand of a division operation is nonzero, that arguments you pass to methods in the .NET Framework are in the valid range, that a file or database connection is open before attempting to operate on it.

When authoring your own classes and methods, you should never use exceptions as a mechanism to return special values from a method and you should reserve them for truly rare cases. Most methods in the .NET runtime adhere to this practice. For example, the Close method of the FileStream object (and other file-related objects) as well as of the ADO.NET Connection object don't throw an exception if the file or the connection is already closed, on the assumption that, after all, at the end of the method call the file or the connection is in the intended state. (Of course, an exception *is* thrown if you attempt to read from or write to a closed stream or connection.)

Here's a good rule of thumb you can follow in your own classes: don't throw exceptions for relatively common errors, such as end-of-file or timeout conditions; instead, return a special value to the caller. For example, the Math.Log and Math.Sqrt methods return the special NaN (Not-a-Number) value when you pass them a negative number, and you might adopt a similar approach. Just remember to mention the exact behavior in your documentation.

When authoring your own classes, you can provide clients with a read-only property that enables them to understand whether a call to a method would result in an exception being thrown. For example, you can expose an EOF property that returns True when you're at the end of a data file or a bit-coded State property that tells which operations are allowed on the object. (This is the pattern used by the ADO.NET Connection object.)

Here's another performance tip that has to do with exceptions. By default, Visual Basic checks the overflow flag after each operation on integers so that it can throw an exception if the result is outside the valid range. If you're sure that this can't happen in your application, you can improve application performance by selecting the Remove Integer Overflow Checks check box in the Advanced Compiler Settings dialog box that you display by clicking the Advanced Compile Options button on the Compile page of the My Project designer (see Figure 3-3). In my informal benchmarks, after enabling this option I saw that operations on Integer variables ran from two to three times faster; multiplication and division on Long variables also ran about twice as fast, whereas speed improvement is less pronounced with addition and subtraction involving Long values.

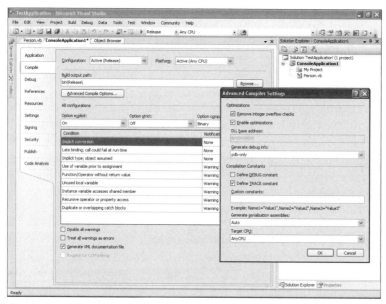

Figure 3-3   The Advanced Compiler Settings dialog box, which you display by clicking the Advanced Compile Options button on the Compile page of the My Project designer

The Try...Catch...Finally Statement

So far, you've seen how the exception-throwing mechanism works and what information an exception object carries. Now you're ready to fully appreciate the power and flexibility of the new Try...Catch...Finally block.

The Catch Keyword

Whenever you execute code that might throw an exception, you should enclose it in a Try...End Try block. The portion of code between the Try keyword and the first Catch keyword is guarded against exceptions, and if an exception is thrown, Visual Basic passes the control to the first Catch block, where you can examine the properties of the exception object and decide how to react to the error. Here's a simple example:

```
Try
   x = x \ y
   ' If y is 0, the following statement is never executed.
   y = CInt(10 ^ x)
Catch ex As Exception
   Console.WriteLine("ERROR: {0}", ex.Message)
End Try
```

As soon as an error occurs—or an exception is thrown, to comply with the .NET terminology— the program jumps to the Catch block, executes that code block, and then jumps to the first statement after the End Try keyword.

You can have multiple Catch blocks, each one filtering a specific type of exception:

```
Try
   x = x \ y
   y = CInt(10 ^ x)
Catch ex As DivideByZeroException
   ' Deal here with divide-by-zero exceptions.
   …
Catch ex As OverflowException
   ' Deal here with overflow exceptions.
   …
Catch ex As Exception
   ' Deal here with all other exceptions.
   …
End Try
```

Visual Basic compares the type of exception object being thrown with the expressions in Catch clauses in the order in which they appear, and it executes the first one that matches. Exception types are tested as if an Is operator were used; therefore, inheritance relationships are honored. It's usually a good idea to have a final Catch expression that matches the System.Exception object because this code is guaranteed to execute if no previous Catch expression matches the exception. A Catch clause for the System.Exception object always matches any exception because all exception objects inherit from System.Exception. (This last Catch clause is conceptually similar to the Else clause in a Select Case block.)

Because all Catch expressions are evaluated in the order in which they appear, you should test for most specific exceptions first, followed by less specific ones. The test for the System.Exception object, if present, should be in the last Catch block because it matches any exception; consequently, no Catch block following it can ever execute. More generally, you should never catch an exception object after catching the exception from which it inherits. For example, the Catch block for a DivideByZeroException object should never follow the Catch block for a less specific ArithmeticException object.

The Duplicate Or Overlapping Catch Blocks option on the Compile page of the My Project designer enables you to get a compilation warning or error when the Catch clauses in a Try block are in an order that would make one of them unreachable.

The As expression in the Catch block is optional. You can drop it if you don't need to examine the exception object's properties to make a decision, but in general you don't gain anything by omitting it.

You can exit from a Try...End Try structure at any time by calling the Exit Try statement, which can appear inside the Try block or any Catch block.

The .NET runtime defines a few exceptions that occur in really exceptional (and catastrophic) circumstances—namely, StackOverflowException, OutOfMemoryException, and Execution-EngineException. A common trait among these exceptions is that they can occur at any time because they aren't really caused by your application. Although you can catch them, in practice you should never do anything else but terminate the application with a suitable error message because these exceptions usually leave the application in an unstable state.

The Finally Keyword

You often need to execute a piece of cleanup code when an exception is thrown. For example, you want to close a file if an error occurs while the code is processing that file, and you want to release a lock on a database table if an error occurs while the application is processing records in that table. In cases like these, you need a Try block with a Finally clause. The code between the Finally keyword and the End Try keyword is always guaranteed to run, whether or not the code in the Try block throws an exception. The Finally block runs even if the code in a Catch block throws an exception, if the Try...End Try block is exited because of an Exit Try statement, or if the method itself is exited because of a Return statement.

Here's an example of a block of code that changes the current directory and ensures that the original directory is restored before exiting the Try...End Try structure:

```
Dim curdir As String
Try
    ' Remember the current directory, and then change it.
    curdir = Environment.CurrentDirectory
    Environment.CurrentDirectory = "c:\data"
    …
Catch ex As Exception
    ' Deal here with errors.
    …
Finally
    ' In all cases, restore the current directory.
    Environment.CurrentDirectory = curdir
End Try
```

It's legal to have a Try...Finally...End Try block without a Catch block. Such code might be appropriate when you want the caller to catch and process all the errors that have occurred in the current procedure, but at the same time you have some cleanup code that must execute no matter what. A Finally block might also be useful to provide a common block of cleanup code for a procedure that has multiple Exit Sub, Exit Function, or Return statements scattered in code:

```
Function TestFunction() As Integer
   Dim x, y As Integer
   Try
      …
      If x > 0 Then Return 1
      …
      If y = 0 Then Return 2
      …
      Return 3
   Finally
      ' This code runs whichever exit path the code takes.
      Console.Write("Value being returned is {0}", TestFunction)
   End Try
End Function
```

The preceding code snippet demonstrates that the code in the Finally block is able to inspect (and modify) the value being returned to the caller by the function. As the previous code snippet demonstrates, this technique also works if the return value was assigned using a Return statement, as opposed to being assigned to the local variable named after the function.

Finally, note that if the code in the Finally block throws an exception, the Finally block is immediately exited and the exception is thrown to the caller. Therefore, you should always check that no error can occur while the Finally code is being processed; if you can't guarantee this, you should use a nested Try…End Try structure inside the Finally block.

The When Keyword

The Catch clause supports an optional When expression, which lets you specify an additional condition that must evaluate to True for the Catch block to be selected. This feature enables you to define more specific exception filters. Look at this code:

```
Dim x, y, z, res As Integer          ' All variables are 0.
Try
   ' You can see different behaviors by commenting out or changing
   ' the order of the following statements.
   …
   res = y \ x
   …
   res = x \ y
   …
   res = x \ z
Catch ex As DivideByZeroException When (x = 0)
   Console.WriteLine("Division error: x is 0.")
Catch ex As DivideByZeroException When (y = 0)
   Console.WriteLine("Division error: y is 0.")
Catch ex As DivideByZeroException
```

```
    Console.WriteLine("Division error: no information on variables")
Catch ex As Exception
    Console.WriteLine("An error has occurred.")
End Try
```

In general, you can achieve the same behavior by using an If...ElseIf block inside a Catch block, but the When clause makes for better organization of your error-handling code. For example, if no combination of Catch and When clauses matches the current exception, execution flow will go to the last Catch block so you don't have to duplicate any code whatsoever.

The When clause can also reference the exception object's properties, so you can partition your exceptions in subcategories and have a distinct Catch block for each one of them. For example, the following code parses the Message property to extract the name of the file that hasn't been found:

```
Try
    ' Comment out next statement to see the behavior
    ' when another file is missing.
    Dim fs1 As New FileStream("c:\myapp.ini", FileMode.Open)
    Dim fs2 As New FileStream("c:\user.dat", FileMode.Open)
    ...
Catch ex As FileNotFoundException When InStr(ex.Message, "'c:\myapp.ini'") > = 0
    ' The ini file is missing.
    Console.WriteLine("Can't initialize: MyApp.ini file not found")
Catch ex As FileNotFoundException When InStr(ex.Message, "'c:\myapp.ini'") < 0
    ' Another file is missing: extract the filename from the Message property.
    Dim filename As String = Split(ex.Message, "'")(1)
    Console.WriteLine("The following file is missing: " & filename)
End Try
```

An explanation is in order: the Message property of the FileNotFoundException object returns a string in the following format:

```
Could not find file '<filename>'.
```

Therefore, you can use the InStr function (or the String.Contains method) to test whether a file you're looking for is embedded in this string. Just remember to enclose the searched-for filename in single quotation marks.

You can take advantage of the When keyword in other ways as well. For example, you might have a local variable that tracks the progress status of the procedure so that you can take different actions depending on where the error occurred. The following code should render the idea:

```
Dim currentStep As Integer
Try
    currentStep = 1                 ' Initialize the program.
    ...
    currentStep = 2                 ' Open the data file.
    ...
    currentStep = 3                 ' Process the file's contents.
    ...
```

```
    currentStep = 4              ' …And so on…
    …
Catch ex As Exception When currentStep = 1
    Console.WriteLine("An error occurred in the initialization step.")
Catch ex As FileNotFoundException When currentStep = 2
    Console.WriteLine("The data file wasn't found.")
Catch ex As Exception When currentStep = 2
    Console.WriteLine("An error occurred while opening the data file.")
Catch ex As Exception When currentStep = 3
    Console.WriteLine("An error occurred while processing data.")
' Add other Catch blocks here.
    …
End Try
```

Note that it's acceptable to have the first block catch the generic Exception object because the When condition makes the test succeed only if the error occurred in the first (initialization) step of the procedure. When sorting Catch blocks related to the same step, you should catch more specific exception objects first (as when currentStep is 2 in the preceding code).

You can also use the When keyword in an unorthodox way to solve one of the recurring problems in error logging and reporting. Let's say that you want to create a log of all the exceptions in your application, including those that are caught in a Catch clause. Apparently, the best solution is to create a generic error log routine and invoke it from inside each and every Catch block in your code, a boring and error-prone task because a typical Try block is followed by many Catch blocks. Thanks to the When keyword, you can achieve the same effect by adding just one single line of code for each Try block, shown here in bold:

```
Try
    ' Do something.
    …
Catch ex As Exception When LogException(ex)
    ' (No code here)
Catch ex As FileNotFoundException
    …
Catch ex As DivideByZeroException
    …
Catch ex As Exception
    …
End Try
```

LogException is a function that is defined elsewhere in the application (for example, in a module); it does the actual logging and always returns False:

```
Public Function LogException(ByVal ex As Exception) As Boolean
    Debug.WriteLine(ex.Message)
    Return False
End Function
```

The Catch clause immediately after the Try block matches all exceptions, so Visual Basic always evaluates the When clause to see whether its expression returns True. At this point the

LogException function is invoked, giving you an opportunity to log the exception. This function returns False; therefore, Visual Basic ignores this Catch block and passes to the ones that follow it, where the exception is actually processed.

Notice that the When keyword is specific to Visual Basic. Most other .NET languages, including C#, lack a similar capability.

When and Finally Keywords in Nested Try Blocks

You should be aware of a rather surprising behavior of the When keyword when used in a Try block that wraps another Try...Finally block that has no Catch clause. Consider the following code:

```
Dim fs As FileStream

Sub TestNestedTryWhen()
    Try
        Try
            fs = New FileStream("c:\data.txt", FileMode.Open)
            ' Process the file here.
            ...
        Finally
            Console.WriteLine("Inside inner Finally block")
            ' Close the file stream.
            fs.Close()
        End Try
    Catch ex As Exception When CheckException(ex)
        Console.WriteLine("Inside outer Catch block")
    End Try
End Sub

Function CheckException(ByVal ex As Exception) As Boolean
    Console.WriteLine("Inside CheckException function")
    Return True
End Function
```

If an error occurs in the innermost Try block, for example, after opening the file and while processing it, the order of execution of the various blocks is different from what you might expect. In fact, this is what appears in the Console window if an error occurs:

```
Inside CheckException function
Inside inner Finally block
Inside CheckException function
Inside outer Catch block
```

In other words, the When expression in all outer Try blocks is always evaluated before any inner Finally block and is also evaluated a second time before entering the outer Catch block. Even more surprisingly, this behavior occurs even if the two Try blocks reside in different procedures, for example, with the outer Try block in a method that invokes another method containing the inner Try block. (This description holds true even if the two methods belong to different classes compiled in distinct assemblies.) In most cases, this underdocumented behavior has no significant impact on the way you write your code, except for at least a couple of cases.

The first case has to do with resource allocation. In the previous example, the CheckException method might mistakenly close the FileStream object and make the stream unavailable from inside the main procedure. The second case is a bit more subtle and is related to security: if the code in the innermost Try block is impersonating a more privileged user (for example, by calling the LogonAsUser Windows API method), the code in the CheckException method runs under the more privileged account.

If you write an assembly that impersonates another user (or uses other ways to escalate its privileges), a smart hacker might take advantage of this behavior by calling your method and forcing an exception. If the call to your method is placed in a Try block that has a Catch...When clause, the hacker can have his or her code executed under the higher privileges. Fortunately, the solution to this potential security hole is quite simple: either ensure that your Try block includes one or more Catch sections or nest your dangerous code in two Try blocks rather than one, as in this code:

```
Try
   Try
      ' Impersonate a more privileged user here.
      …
   Finally
      ' Revert to original user.
   End Try
Catch
   Throw            ' Rethrow the exception to callers.
End Try
```

Rethrowing the Exception

The Throw statement is especially useful when you want to catch a subset of all the possible exceptions and delegate the remaining ones to the caller. This is a common programming pattern: each portion of the code deals with the errors it knows how to fix and leaves the others to the calling code. As I have explained previously, if no Catch expression matches the current exception, the exception is automatically thrown to the caller. But it's a good practice to do the throwing explicitly so that you make it clear that you aren't just a lazy or distracted programmer:

```
Try
   ' Do some math operations here.
   …
Catch ex As DivideByZeroException
   …
Catch ex As OverflowException
   …
Catch ex As Exception
   ' Explicitly throw this unhandled exception to the caller.
   Throw
End Try
```

The Throw statement without an argument rethrows the current exception object and must appear in a Catch clause to be valid. The only other significant difference from the version that takes an argument is that the latter also resets the StackTrace property of the exception object (as if a brand-new exception were created), so the version without an argument is preferable for rethrowing the same exception when you want to let the caller routine determine exactly where the exception occurred.

In some cases, you want to rethrow a different kind of exception object, for several reasons. You might want to hide the exact nature of the problem that has occurred or hide the details in the error message that exposes sensitive data to malicious hackers (for example, the name of the file where you store passwords and other security-related information).

Another common reason to rethrow a different exception object is to translate into more meaningful exceptions errors that would have no meaning to callers. For example, a method that performs complex calculations might fail for many different causes: an initialization file isn't found, a database connection can't be opened, a remote Web service can't be invoked, a math operation fails, and so forth. You might want to map all these exceptions to one or two distinct exception objects to simplify the job of developers calling your methods. When rethrowing a different exception, it is good practice to specify the original exception as the *inner exception* of the new exception, as in this code:

```
Try
    ' Do some math operations here.
    …
Catch ex As DivideByZeroException
    ' Throw a different exception object, but pass the original
    ' exception in the InnerException property.
    Throw New ArgumentException("Invalid arguments", ex)
' Other Catch blocks here…
    …
End Try
```

The caller of the preceding code can test the inner exception with this code:

```
Catch ex As ArgumentException
    Console.WriteLine("An ArgumentException error has occurred.")
    If ex.InnerException IsNot Nothing Then
        Console.WriteLine("Inner exception: " & ex.InnerException.Message)
    End If
```

The vast majority of .NET exception classes expose one or more constructors that take an exception object and assign it the InnerException read-only property that all exceptions inherit from System.Exception. A few exception types don't let you pass an inner exception to their constructor—for example, the ThreadAbortException—but this isn't a limitation because you should never want to throw these exceptions. Interestingly, version 1.1 of the .NET Framework contains several exception types without this capability, but nearly all of them have been extended to support inner exceptions in the transition to version 2.0.

Old-Style Error Handlers

The Visual Basic Err.Raise method and the Throw command are partially compatible. You can use a Try...End Try block to catch an error raised with the Err.Raise method, and you can use an On Error Resume Next statement and the Err object to neutralize and inspect an exception object created by the Throw command. The old and the new error-trapping mechanisms don't always coexist well, though, and there are some limitations, the most important of which is that you can't have an On Error Resume Next statement and a Try...End Try block in the same procedure.

To assist you in porting existing applications from Visual Basic 6 to the .NET Framework, the Err object has been extended with the new GetException method, which returns the exception object that corresponds to the current error. If you have a Visual Basic 6 procedure containing error-handling code that can't be easily ported to the new syntax, you can use the GetException method to correctly throw an exception object to the caller, where the exception can be processed using a Try block as usual:

```
Sub TestGetExceptionMethod()
   Try
      OldStyleErrorHandlerProc()
   Catch ex As DivideByZeroException
      Console.WriteLine("A DivideByZeroException has been caught.")
   End Try
End Sub


' This procedure traps an error using an old-style On Error Goto
' and returns it to the caller as an exception.
Sub OldStyleErrorHandlerProc()
   On Error Goto ErrorHandler
   Dim x, y As Integer          ' Cause a division-by-zero error.
   y = 1 \ x
   Exit Sub
ErrorHandler:
   ' Add cleanup code here as necessary.
   …
   ' Then report the error to the caller as an exception object.
   Throw Err.GetException()
End Sub
```

Backward compatibility with the Visual Basic 6 way of dealing with errors doesn't come free, though. If you use either On Error Goto or On Error Resume Next, the compiler generates additional IL code after each statement. This additional code can make the procedure run up to five times slower than a procedure without error trapping runs. By comparison, the Try...Catch...Finally statement adds a fixed overhead (the code that sets up the exception handler), which tends to be negligible for procedures of several statements. For this reason, it is OK to use the On Error statement when efficiency isn't an issue (for example, when working with the user interface), but you shouldn't use it in time-critical routines.

The Using...End Using Statement

 As I mentioned in the section titled "The Finally Keyword" earlier in this chapter, virtually all computer resources require that you adopt the classical allocate-use-release pattern. For example, you allocate an array, use it, and then destroy it; you open a database connection, use it, and then close it; you create a Graphical Device Interface (GDI) brush, use it, and then release it, and so forth.

The .NET Framework is capable without your help of dealing with resources that take only memory (such as arrays), as you can read in Chapter 9. For most other types of resources—files, database connections, windows, GDI+ objects, and so forth—it is essential that you give the .NET Framework a hand and release these resources explicitly. Failing to do so might add noticeable overhead to your applications or, worse, introduce serious bugs in your code.

This pattern is so common that the .NET Framework defines the IDisposable interface, which contains a single method named Dispose. All the .NET types that wrap a system resource requiring an explicit release or deallocation step (in practice, any system resource other than memory) implement this interface. For example, this is how you allocate and release a GDI+ brush:

```
Dim br As New SolidBrush(Color.Red)
' Use the brush here.
…
' Destroy it as soon as you don't need it any longer.
br.Dispose()
```

Some .NET types, most notably those that work with files and database connections, implement the IDisposable interface privately and have a public Close method that maps to the private Dispose method. For example, consider this reusable routine that returns the contents of a text file:

```
' Read the entire contents of a text file in one operation.
Public Function ReadTextFile(ByVal fileName As String) As String
   Dim sr As New StreamReader(fileName)
   Dim result As String = sr.ReadToEnd()
   sr.Close()
   Return result
End Function
```

(I provide the ReadTextFile procedure for illustration purposes only because a .NET Framework version 2.0 application can perform this job more easily by means of the new File.Read-AllText static method.)

The problem with the previous routine is unanticipated exceptions. If an error occurs while processing the file (in general, while using the resource), the current method might be exited before you have an opportunity to close the file (in general, dispose of the resource). In this specific case, the error might be caused by a bad sector or by a removable disk that is extracted before the end of the file has been reached. As you learned earlier in this chapter, you can avoid this problem by using a Try...Finally block:

```
Public Function ReadTextFile(ByVal fileName As String) As String
   Dim sr As StreamReader = Nothing
   Try
      sr = New StreamReader(fileName)
      Return sr.ReadToEnd()
   Finally
      sr.Close()
   End Try
End Function
```

This code correctly returns all exceptions to the caller, but, unlike the original version, the file is always closed before exiting the method, at the expense of a more complex structure.

The good news is that Visual Basic 2005 has a new Using statement that can automatically release one or more IDisposable objects without explicit action on your part. This is how you can rewrite the previous code to take advantage of this new feature:

```
Public Function ReadTextFile(ByVal fileName As String) As String
   Using sr As New StreamReader(fileName)
      Return sr.ReadToEnd()
   End Using
End Function
```

Behind the scenes, the Visual Basic compiler translates a Using block into a Try...Finally block, exactly as you'd do manually. Once again, notice that any exception will be reported to callers; if you want to both release your objects in an orderly way and catch exceptions, you need a complete Try...Catch...Finally block, and there is no point in using a Using block.

The argument of a Using block can only be an object that implements the IDisposable interface. This object is read-only inside the loop, thus you can't accidentally or purposely set it to Nothing (an assignment that would make the hidden Dispose call fail with a NullReference-Exception). You must either use the As New clause to create the object at the top of the Using block or invoke a method that returns a disposable object, as in this code:

```
Using sr As StreamReader = GetStreamReader()
...
```

When dealing with two or more disposable objects, you can nest Using blocks, as you'd expect. If the objects have exactly the same scope, however, you can simply specify both of them in the same Using block and let the Visual Basic compiler create two nested Try...Finally blocks for you:

```
' Copy a text file, converting to lowercase in the process.
Sub CopyFileToLowercase(ByVal inFile As String, ByVal outFile As String)
   Using sr As New StreamReader(inFile), sw As New StreamWriter(outFile)
      sw.Write(sr.ReadToEnd().ToLower())
   End Using
End Sub
```

Oddly, Visual Basic 2005 doesn't offer an Exit Using statement. If you use a disposable resource but might need to leave the code block before its natural termination, you should use a regular Try block and an Exit Try keyword.

Custom Exception Objects

Sometimes a method must report an error condition that doesn't match any of the predefined .NET exception objects. In Visual Basic 6, you can generate custom errors by passing custom error numbers to the Err.Raise method, as in this code:

```
Err.Raise 1001, , "Initialization File Not Found"
```

The .NET equivalent of this action is to define and throw an instance of a user-defined exception class. By definition, an *exception class* is a type that derives from System.Exception. More precisely, Microsoft guidelines suggest that user-defined exception types derive from System.ApplicationException (as opposed to .NET runtime exceptions, which derive from System.SystemException) and that their names have the "Exception" suffix.

All the properties of an exception object should be read-only and the caller should be able to initialize them only by means of one or more constructors. Here's an example of a custom UnableToLoadIniFileException class that has a default (but overridable) error message and that lets callers initialize the InnerException property:

```
Public Class UnableToLoadIniFileException
    Inherits System.ApplicationException

    Private Const Default_Message As String = "Unable to load initialization file"

    ' Constructors with fewer parameters delegate to the constructor with more parameters.
    Public Sub New()
       Me.New(Default_Message, Nothing)
    End Sub

    Public Sub New(ByVal message As String)
       Me.New(message, Nothing)
    End Sub

    Public Sub New(ByVal innerException As Exception)
       Me.New(Default_Message, innerException)
    End Sub

    ' The most complete constructor calls the base type's constructor.
    Public Sub New(ByVal message As String, ByVal innerException As Exception)
       MyBase.New(message, innerException)
    End Sub
End Class
```

You can use the UnableToLoadIniFileException class in a Throw command and in a Catch block:

```
' The caller code
Sub TestCustomException()
```

```
   Try
      LoadIniFile()
   Catch ex As UnableToLoadIniFileException
      Console.WriteLine(ex.Message)    ' => Unable to load...
   Catch ex As Exception
      ' Deal with other errors here.
   End Try
End Sub

' The routine that opens the ini file
Sub LoadIniFile()
   Try
      ' Try to open the ini file.
      …
   Catch ex As Exception
      ' Whatever caused the error, throw a more specific exception.
      ' (We use the default message but initialize the inner exception.)
      Throw New UnableToLoadIniFileException(ex)
   End Try
End Sub
```

Custom exception objects have many uses other than reporting a custom error message. For example, they can include custom methods that attempt to resolve the error condition. For instance, you might devise a DriveNotReadyException class that uses a method named Show-Message, which displays an error message and asks the user to insert a disk in the drive and retry the operation. Putting this code inside the exception class makes its reuse much easier.

One last note about custom exceptions: if your custom exception object can be thrown across different assemblies, possibly in different processes, you should make the exception class serializable. Read Chapter 21, "Serialization," for more details about serialization.

Chapter 4
Using Visual Studio 2005

If you have used Microsoft Visual Studio .NET 2003 or earlier versions, you'll feel immediately comfortable with Microsoft Visual Studio 2005. However, even experienced developers will be surprised by the many new features and improvements in the new version of Visual Studio.

Working with Projects and Solutions

As in all previous versions of Visual Studio, you open an existing project or a solution or create a new project or solution by means of the Open and New submenus on the File top-level menu. But even for these simple operations Visual Studio offers a few interesting new capabilities.

In Visual Studio 2005, you don't have to physically create a project or a solution. This feature is similar to the default behavior Microsoft Visual Basic 6 developers are accustomed to and is quite convenient when you just need to test some code. You enable this feature by clearing the Save New Projects When Created check box on the General page under the Project And Solutions node in the Options dialog box. Other options on the same page enable you to select a different location for projects and item templates and to hide the solution node in the Solution Explorer window if the solution contains only one project.

Another new command in Visual Studio 2005, available on the New submenu of the File upper level menu, allows you to create a project that gathers all the source files in a folder. This command is especially useful if you collect .vb source files from multiple sources and want to create an application that includes all of them.

Project and File Templates

When you create a new project, you can select among the many templates that Visual Studio offers. Visual Studio 2005 offers several project templates that weren't available in previous versions, including starter kit projects such as the Screen Saver Starter Kit and My Movie Collection Starter Kit and projects for working with Microsoft Office Excel and Word. New options in this dialog box allows you to define different names for the project and its parent solution, and you can also decide not to create a separate directory for the solution, which is a good choice if the solution contains only one project (see Figure 4-1).

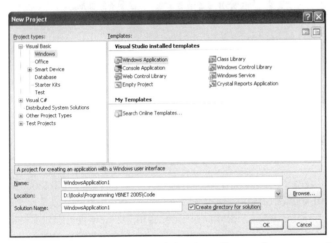

Figure 4-1   The New Project dialog box. (Test projects are available if you have installed the Visual Studio 2005 Team Edition for Software Developers.)

Another new welcome feature lets you create a project from existing code and, even better, create an ASP.NET project from a location on the local file system, without having to create an IIS Web site. To see this feature in action, select the Web Site command from the New submenu of the File menu: this action brings up the New Web Site dialog box. The Location combo box at the bottom of this dialog box shows the three options that you have when creating the new site: File System, HTTP, and FTP. (See Figure 4-2.)

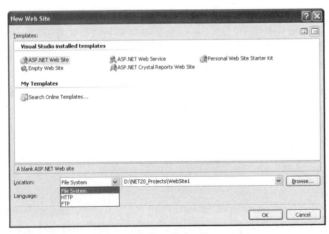

Figure 4-2   The New Web Site dialog box

Both the New Project and New Web Site dialog boxes include the Search Online Templates item, which opens Microsoft Document Explorer Help where you can search for articles, code snippets, sample applications, and additional starter kits provided by MSDN Online or developer communities such as Codezone. (See Figure 4-3.) You can filter your searches by keywords, programming languages, resource type, and technology (.NET, Win32, ASP.NET, Microsoft SQL Server, and so on).

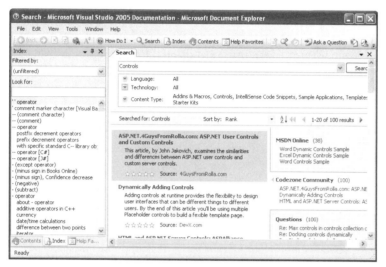

Figure 4-3   Searching online for code snippets and additional starter kits

You add a new file to the current project by selecting one of the commands on the Project menu. The actual content of this menu depends on the type of the current project: if you don't see the file type you're interested in, just select the Add New Item command (or use the Ctrl+Shift+A keyboard shortcut) and select the file type from the template gallery that appears. Visual Studio 2005 comes with several new ready-to-use templates, such as Dialog, Splash Screen, About Box, Explorer, and Login Form.

Just as important, you can add your own template and search for more templates online. All the items in the project template gallery and the file template gallery are taken from the directory specified on the General page under the Project And Solutions node in the Options dialog box, so you can have Visual Studio read the templates from a different folder if you wish. This feature can be useful to point to a remote folder so that all the developers in your company can share the same group of templates.

The Solution Explorer Window

All the files in the current solution appear in the Solution Explorer window, one of the Visual Studio windows that is used most often. It is therefore important that you become familiar with its capabilities, including some that aren't immediately obvious.

For example, you can drag any kind of file from Windows Explorer to the Solution Explorer window, including text files, Microsoft Word files, and Microsoft Excel files. This ability is valuable for keeping all the documents related to the project in the same physical location, including the draft documentation, the list of features to add, or the list of bugs to fix. Or you can add one or more data files and have these files automatically copied in the output directory when the project is compiled. You achieve this behavior by right-clicking the file, selecting the Properties command (or pressing the F4 key), and then selecting the Copy Always or Copy If Newer value for the Copy To Output Directory attribute. (See Figure 4-4.) This option is new in Visual Studio 2005 and is preferable to copying the file to the output directory manually because the location of the output directory depends on the current project configuration.

Figure 4-4   Copying a data file to the output directory. (This option isn't available in ASP.NET projects.)

You can open any file visible in the Solution Explorer simply by double-clicking it. Alternatively, you can use the Open With command from the context menu to use a different editor, for example, Notepad. Visual Studio also provides a few internal editors that can be useful at times, such as the HTML Editor, the XML Editor, and the Binary Editor. You can even add your favorite editors to this list. (See Figure 4-5.)

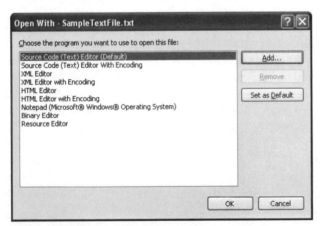

Figure 4-5   The Open With dialog box

When you add an existing file to the current project, the file is physically copied from its current location into the project's folder. All the changes you make to the file are therefore made on the local copy, not in the original file. However, Visual Studio also gives you the ability to link a file, rather than copy it. To link a file, select the Add Existing Item command on the Project menu (or use the Shift+Alt+A keyboard shortcut), navigate to the file, and then select the Add As Link command from the drop-down menu that appears when you click the arrow to the right of the Add button. (See Figure 4-6.) After you link a file to the project, you can edit it as usual, except that the original file is modified rather than a local copy.

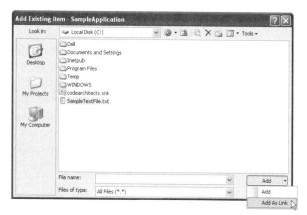

Figure 4-6   The Add As Link option of the Add Existing Item dialog box. (This option isn't available for ASP.NET projects.)

The ability to link a file proves to be very useful when you need to share a given file among multiple projects, for example, a module that contains helper functions used in most of your projects. You can't, however, use this method to share one instance of the AssemblyInfo.vb file among multiple projects to ensure that all of them have the same version number, as you could do in previous Visual Studio editions, because this file is expected to be located in the My Project folder and you can't add a linked file to this folder.

When dealing with complex projects, it is recommended that you organize your source files in project folders. For example, you can gather all your controls in a folder named Controls, your data objects in a folder named DataObjects, and so forth. Each project folder corresponds to a physical directory under the project's main folder. You create a project folder by right-clicking the solution item or another folder in the Solution Explorer window, and then selecting the New Folder command on the Add submenu. If you add a new file while the folder node is selected, the new file is created in the selected folder. Or you can move existing files to a given folder by simply dragging them inside the Solution Explorer window. Notice, however, that the action of dragging a file between different projects of the same solution copies the file instead of moving it.

The My Project Designer

When you create a new project, Visual Studio 2005 creates a directory named My Project under the main project's folder and creates an item in the Solution Explorer window also named My Project. When you double-click this item, the My Project designer appears. You can control all the major aspects of a Visual Basic project from inside the pages of this designer. In previous chapters, I describe some of the options you can find on these pages; thus, here I focus on the ones I haven't covered yet.

Assembly Attributes

All Visual Basic projects include a file named AssemblyInfo.vb in the My Project folder. This file contains several project attributes, for example, its name, its version, and the name of its publisher. You don't see this file in the Solution Explorer window unless you click the Show All Files button on the toolbar. Fortunately, unlike in previous versions of Visual Studio, in most cases you don't need to directly work with this source file because it's simpler to type this information in the Assembly Information dialog box that you can open by clicking the button with same name on the General page of the My Project designer. (See Figure 4-7.)

Figure 4-7   The Assembly Information dialog box

Build Events

Visual Basic 2005 lets you define prebuild and postbuild events. Thanks to such events, you can define the operating system commands or external executables that are launched before and after the compilation of a given project. You can decide whether the postbuild command is launched in any case, only if the build is successful, or only if the build actually modifies the output file. (See left portion of Figure 4-8.) By clicking the Edit Pre-Build or Edit Post-Build button, you display a simple editor that lets you edit each command and insert placeholders that will be replaced by common values such as the project name or location, the output (or target) file or directory, and so forth. (See right portion of Figure 4-8.)

Figure 4-8   The Build Events dialog box (left) and the Post-Build Event Command Line dialog box (right)

Build events are quite useful to automate some repetitive tasks. For example, you might use a postbuild event to copy one or more "clean" data files to the program's output directory, to rename the output executable, or to copy it to a different location. Or you might back up the entire project to a safe location after a successful build by using the following postbuild command line:

```
XCOPY "$(ProjectDir)*.*" "c:\projectbackups\$(ProjectName)" /s /d /i /k /r /y
```

Remember to enclose all file paths in double quotation marks; if you fail to do so, a file path containing spaces is considered as two or more distinct arguments. Also, it is essential that the command doesn't prompt the end user for input because such an event would make Visual Studio hang. (For this reason, the preceding command line includes the /Y option, which suppresses the prompt that asks whether an existing file should be overwritten.)

The build process stops immediately if the command you run returns an error code. If the error occurs in a prebuild command, the build step isn't even started; if the error occurs in a postbuild event, you will find the output from the compilation but the executable file isn't run. You can use a DIR command to check whether a directory or a file exists and skip the compilation step if this isn't the case.

For more complex tasks, you can use batch files containing multiple commands, conditions, and environment variables such as USERNAME and COMPUTERNAME. Remember that you can extract lines from your source files with the FIND command and that you can easily create small utilities that do anything that isn't already available as a Microsoft Windows command. For example, compile this simple console application into an executable named Logger.exe.

```
Sub Main(ByVal args() As String)
   Console.Write(Now.ToString(" yy/MM/dd hh:mm:ss "))
   Console.Write(Environment.UserName & " (" & Environment.MachineName & "): ")
   Console.WriteLine(Join(args))
End Sub
```

This code displays information on current date, time, user, and machine, followed by anything you pass to it as a command line. It goes to the standard output stream, but you can redirect it by means of the > and >> symbols. When launched in a prebuild event, this utility can be useful in keeping a trace of when each project is compiled. The following command line assumes that you have copied the Logger.exe file in a directory included in the system path:

```
logger Start compiling $(ProjectName) >> c:\compilelog.txt
```

By using a similar command for the postbuild event, you can time how long the build process takes.

References to Other Assemblies

Visual Studio 2005 makes it simple to deal with references to an external assembly. You can add a new reference by means of a command on the Project menu, a command on the context menu that appears if you right-click the project item inside the Solution Explorer window, or by clicking the Add button on the References page of the My Project designer (see Figure 4-9). Other options on this page let you automatically detect which libraries aren't used in the current project (the Unused References button) and import a namespace at the project level by simply selecting a check box in the Imported Namespaces list box.

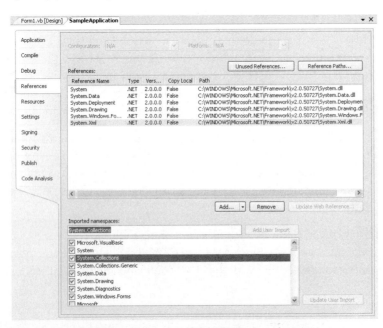

Figure 4-9   The References page of the My Project designer

Static Code Analysis

If you have installed Visual Studio 2005 Team Edition, you'll see one more page in the My Project designer, the Code Analysis page. The commands on this page enable you to perform a static code analysis on the current project. In a nutshell, code analysis looks at the compiled executable and applies a set of rules that check whether some design guidelines and programming best practices have been followed. These guidelines range from member naming rules to performance, security, and maintainability rules. (See Figure 4-10.)

Figure 4-10   The Code Analysis page of the My Project designer

You can run code analysis using the Run Code Analysis command on the Build menu, or you can have it launched at the end of the build process by selecting the Enable Code Analysis check box on the Code Analysis page. On this page, you can browse all groups of rules and the individual rules in each group. You can disable an entire group or any number of individual lines by clearing the check box on the left, and you can double-click the Status column to have a rule or a group of rules emit an error rather than a warning when they aren't satisfied.

All warnings and errors appear in the Error List window. (See Figure 4-11.) You can right-click a specific error or warning message to suppress it; suppressed messages appear in strikethrough style and won't appear again when you run the code analysis tool.

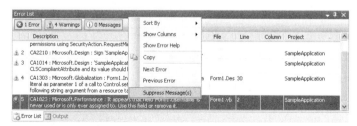

Figure 4-11   The results of a code analysis session appearing in the Error List window

When you suppress a message from inside the Error List window, Visual Studio marks the code element with a SuppressMessage attribute, which is defined in the System.Diagnostics. CodeAnalysis namespace. You should leave these attributes in your source code, and, even better, you might apply them yourself when you know in advance that a code element is correct as is even if it doesn't meet the code analysis guidelines. In its simplest form, this attribute takes two arguments: the rule category and the rule name. The rule name can be either in the short form (the rule id, such as CA1823) or the long form, as in this example:

```
<System.Diagnostics.CodeAnalysis.SuppressMessage( _
"Microsoft.Performance", "CA1823:AvoidUnusedPrivateFields")> _
Private UserName As String
```

Other optional arguments are the target (an identifier that specifies the target on which the message is being suppressed) and the justification (a text that explains why you're suppressing the message). Notice that, depending on the kind of message, you might need to apply the SuppressMessage attribute at the assembly level.

Multiple-Project Solutions

Visual Studio lets you create solutions that contain two or more projects. This feature is useful, for example, when you work with Windows Forms or ASP.NET applications using one or more classes that are stored in separate DLLs.

By default, when you create a new project, Visual Studio also creates a solution and stores the project's files in a folder that is contained in the solution's folder. By default the solution and the project have the same name, and the resulting directory structure can be quite confusing—for example, the MyApp project folder would be located in a path like C:\MyProjects\MyApp\MyApp—therefore, you should opt for a solution name that differs from the project name. Even better, clear the Create Directory For Solution check box in the New Project dialog box if you know that your solution will never have more than one project.

Alternatively, if you know in advance that you're going to work with a multiple-project solution, you can start with a blank solution and then add all the projects you need. You create a blank solution by selecting the Project command from the New submenu of the File menu (as when creating a new project), and then select the Blank Solution item on the Visual Studio Solutions page under the Other Project Types node.

A few Visual Studio features are especially important when dealing with multiple projects. All these commands can be reached from either the Project menu or the Solution Explorer context menu. To begin with, you decide which project runs when you press F5 (or invoke the Start command from the Debug menu) by right-clicking the project item and selecting the Set As StartUp Project command. The startup project appears in bold type. Typically, when you're testing one or more DLLs, the startup project is the client application that references and uses the DLLs. You can decide what exactly happens when you run the solution by means of the Build And Run page of the Projects And Solutions section of the Options dialog box, which you display from the Tools menu. (See Figure 4-12.)

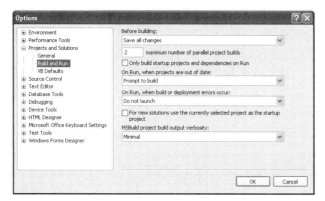

Figure 4-12   Setting project and solution behavior in the Options dialog box

The build order is very important when you're compiling multiple projects. Visual Studio is usually able to determine the correct build order—first the components, then the client application that uses them—but in some cases the IDE gets confused, especially if you remove and re-add projects to the solution. You can check the build order that Visual Studio follows in the Project Dependencies dialog box, which you open by right-clicking any project item and selecting either the Project Dependencies or the Project Build Order command. (See Figure 4-13.)

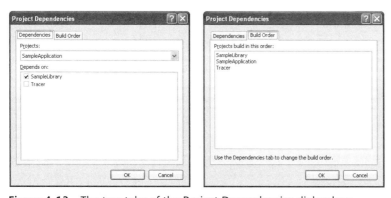

Figure 4-13   The two tabs of the Project Dependencies dialog box

When you compile the solution, by default Visual Studio recompiles all the projects, but this can be a waste of time if you are focusing on just one project—for example, only the client that uses a DLL—and you haven't changed the source code of the others. To reduce compilation time, you have a few choices:

■   Right-click a project in the Solution Explorer window and select the Build menu command to compile only that project and the projects on which the selected project depends.

■   Select a project in the Solution Explorer window and then select the Unload Project command from the Project top-level menu or from the Solution Explorer context menu. This action makes the project temporarily unavailable within the solution, so it won't be compiled during the build process. You can later reinclude the project in the solution by selecting the Reload Project command.

- Create a custom solution configuration in which one or more projects aren't part of the build process. (I explain solution configurations in the next section.)

- Select the Start New Instance command from the Debug submenu of the context menu that appears when you right-click a project in the Solution Explorer window. Another option on the same menu lets you single-step into any project in the solution.

Also new in Visual Studio 2005 is the ability to run the project that is currently selected in the Solution Explorer window by means of the F5 key (or the Start command on the Debug top-level menu) as opposed to the project that was designated as the startup project. To enable this feature, right-click the solution element (in the Solution Explorer window), select the Set Startup Projects command, switch to the Startup Project page under the Common Properties node, and select the Current Selection radio button. (See Figure 4-14.) You can even have multiple startup projects, a feature that becomes useful when you are working on two Windows Forms applications that must run together and must communicate with each other, for example, by means of .NET Remoting.

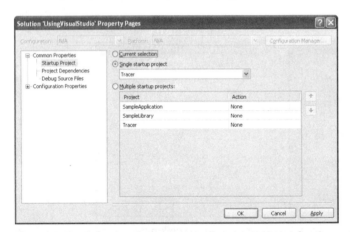

Figure 4-14   Selecting the startup project (or projects) for the current solution

The Configuration Manager

When Visual Studio creates a new project, it also creates two project configurations: Debug and Release. As its name suggests, the former is designed to debug the application: it defines the DEBUG compilation constants and disables optimizations. By contrast, the Release configuration doesn't emit any .pdb file containing information for symbolic debugging and produces more optimized code.

Project Configurations

You can change these settings by selecting a different project configuration in the combo box near the top left corner of the Compile, Debug, and Code Analysis pages of the My Project designer. (The settings you enforce on remaining pages don't depend on the current configuration.) For example, on the Compile page you might select the Release configuration from the combo box and then select the Treat All Warnings As Errors option so that any warning makes the compilation fail but only when the project is compiled in Release mode. Or you can select the All Configuration element in the combo box to apply your settings to all configurations so you don't have to select similar settings individually for multiple configurations.

You can create a custom project configuration if the standard ones don't fit your needs. For example, say that you need to debug the application with all code optimizations enabled to solve a bug that manifests only when optimizations are turned on. You can enable optimizations in the Advanced Compiler Settings dialog box when the Debug configuration is active, or, better, you can define a new project configuration named DebugOpt that produces debug information and enables optimizations.

To create a custom project configuration, select the Configuration Manager command on the Build menu or on the context menu that appears when you right-click the solution node in the Solution Explorer. (See Figure 4-15.) Select the <New...> item in the Active Solution Configuration combo box and type a name in the dialog box that appears. In this particular example, you should select Debug in the Copy Settings From combo box because the new configuration is very similar to the Debug standard configuration. Ensure that the Create New Project Configurations check box is selected, and then close both the New Solution Configuration dialog box and the Configuration Manager window. Switching to the Compile page of the My Project designer shows that DebugOpt is now the active project configuration, so you can click the Advanced Compile Options button to display the window where you can enable all compiler optimizations. (See Figure 4-16.)

After completing this step, you can easily debug your application with or without code optimizations enabled, simply by selecting an item in the Solution Configurations combo box on the Visual Studio standard toolbar. (See Figure 4-17.)

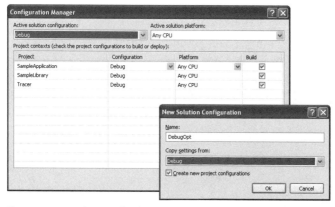

Figure 4-15   The Configuration Manager main window (left) and the dialog box that lets you define a new solution and project configuration (right)

Figure 4-16   The Advanced Compiler Settings dialog box

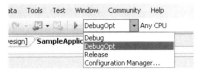

Figure 4-17   Selecting the active solution configuration from the Visual Studio main toolbar

Solution Configurations

In general, you want to compile the current solution in Debug mode when debugging and testing it, whereas you compile it in Release mode before deploying it. This holds true both for simple solutions containing a single project and for solutions that include multiple projects. However, during the debugging and refining phase of a multiproject solution, you might need to compile some projects in Debug mode, others in Release mode, and yet others in some custom configuration that you've defined for them. Solution configurations let you define whether and how each project is compiled when the solution is rebuilt.

In the Configuration Manager, you select a configuration in the Active Solution Configuration combo box and then decide the project configuration to be used for each constituent project. By clearing the check box in the Build column, you can exclude a project from the compilation step in a particular solution configuration. (This feature saves you a lot of time if you've thoroughly tested one of the projects in the solution.) Other options in the Active Solution Configuration combo box let you rename or remove a solution configuration or create a new one.

Compilation Constants

In addition to using different compiler settings, you can use project configurations to include or exclude portions of code by means of #If directives that test one or more compilation constants. Microsoft Visual Basic defines the following compiler constants:

■   **CONFIG**   The current solution configuration (e.g., "Release").

- **DEBUG and TRACE**   True if the corresponding symbol has been defined in the Advanced Compile Settings dialog box.

- **TARGET**   The type of the executable being created; can be "exe" (for console applications), "winexe" (for Windows Forms applications), and "library" (for class libraries and ASP.NET applications).

- **PLATFORM**   The type of CPU you're compiling for; in most cases, its value will be "AnyCPU."

- **VBC_VER**   The Visual Basic version, in *major.minor* format; for Visual Basic 2005, this constant is always equal to the "8.0" string.

- **CODE_ANALYSIS**   True if Code Analysis has been enabled for this project.

- **_MyType**   The value of this constant depends on the type of current project and can take values such as Console or WindowsForms. For more information, read the section titled "Using Compilation Constants" at the end of Chapter 16, "The My Namespace."

(The last four constants are new in Visual Basic 2005.) Here's how you can use these constants in #If and #ElseIf directives:

```
#If CONFIG = "DebugOpt" Then
   ...
#ElseIf TRACE Then
   ...
#End If
```

You can define other compiler constants in addition to the standard ones. These user-defined constants can be local to a source file or global to the entire project. File-scoped constants are defined by means of #Const directives, as in this code:

```
#Const INCLUDE_TESTS = True
...
#If INCLUDE_TESTS Then
    ' Insert code that performs tests here.
   ...
#End If
```

The problem with #Const directives is that you must actually edit each source code file where the directives appear if you need to change their value. This problem can be solved by defining global compilation constants in the Custom Constants box of the Advanced Compiler Settings dialog box. (See Figure 4-16.) All the settings in this dialog box depend on the current project configuration, and thus you can change the value of one or more global compilation constants simply by switching to a different configuration. User-defined compiler constants can take Boolean, numeric, or string values; use the comma to separate multiple constants, as in this code:

```
APPVERSION="1.10",DEMO=True
```

You can test multiple constants in a single #If statement by means of the standard And, Or, AndAlso, OrElse, and Not logical operators:

```
#If APPVERSION = "1.10" And DEMO = True Then
    ...
#End if
```

Compiler-Related Attributes

You can use a few attributes to affect the behavior of and the outcome of running the Visual Basic compiler and/or the JIT compiler. By learning how to use these attributes you can have better control over the IL and native code produced for your project.

The Conditional Attribute

#If directives aren't the only way you have to include or exclude a piece of code in the executable file. As a matter of fact, the #If directives have a serious flaw, which becomes apparent in this code:

```
#If LOG Then
    Sub LogMsg(ByVal MsgText As String)
        Console.WriteLine(MsgText)
    End Sub
#End If

    Sub Main()
        LogMsg("Program is starting")
        ...
        LogMsg("Program is ending")
    End Sub
```

You could exclude the LogMsg procedure from the compiled code by setting the LOG constant to a zero value, but you would get many compile errors if you did so because all the calls to that procedure would be unresolved. The only way to deal with this problem (short of adding one #If statement for each call to LogMsg) is to exclude just the body of the procedure:

```
    Sub LogMsg(ByVal MsgText As String)
#If TRACE Then
        Console.WriteLine(MsgText)
#End If
    End Sub
```

This solution is unsatisfactory, however, because of the overhead of all the calls to the empty LogMsg procedure. Visual Basic (and all .NET languages, such as C#) offers a much cleaner solution based on the Conditional attribute:

```
<Conditional("TRACE")> _
Sub LogMsg(ByVal MsgText As String)
    Console.WriteLine(MsgText)
End Sub
```

The argument of the Conditional attribute can be any global standard or user-defined constant. (You can't use constants defined by means of the #Const directive, though.) The procedure marked with the Conditional attribute is always included in the compiled application; however, calls to it are included only if the specified compilation constant has been defined and has a nonzero value. Otherwise, these calls are discarded. This practice produces the most efficient code without forcing you to add too many directives to your listing.

Because the compiler can drop all the calls to the target method—LogMsg, in the preceding example—the Conditional attribute works only with procedures that don't return a value and is ignored when applied to Function procedures. If you want to use the Conditional attribute with a procedure that returns a value to the caller, you must return the value through a ByRef argument.

The Conditional attribute allows multiple definitions, so you can specify a number of Conditional attributes for the same method. If you do so, calls to the method are included in the compiled application if any of the mentioned compilation constants have a nonzero value:

```
<Conditional("TRACE"), Conditional("LOG")> _
Sub LogMsg(ByVal MsgText As String)
   Console.WriteLine(MsgText)
End Sub
```

The Obsolete Attribute

Let's say that you inherited an important project and your job is to improve its performance by rewriting some of it. Consider the following procedure:

```
Sub BubbleSort(arr() As String)
   ...
End Sub
```

BubbleSort isn't very efficient, so you create a new sort routine based on a more efficient sort algorithm (or just use the Array.Sort method) and start replacing all calls to BubbleSort. You don't want to perform a straight find-and-replace operation, however, because you want to double-check each call. In the end, the BubbleSort routine will be deleted, but you can't do it right now because some portions of the application won't compile. The framework offers a simple solution to this recurring situation in the form of the Obsolete attribute. The constructor method for this attribute can take no arguments, one argument (the warning message), or two arguments (the message and a Boolean value that indicates whether the message is to be considered a compilation error):

```
' Mark BubbleSort as obsolete.
<Obsolete("Replace BubbleSort with ShellSort")> _
Sub BubbleSort(arr() As String)
   ...
```

The following variant additionally causes the BubbleSort routine to appear as a compilation error:

```
' Mark BubbleSort as obsolete; emit a compilation error.
<Obsolete("Replace BubbleSort with ShellSort", True)> _
Sub BubbleSort(arr() As String)
    …
```

The MethodImpl Attribute

You can apply the System.Runtime.CompilerServices.MethodImpl attribute to a method to affect how the method is JIT-compiled by the .NET runtime. This attribute takes a MethodImplOptions enumerated value, but most of the accepted values are reserved for use by the compiler. The only two values you can use are Synchronized and NoInlining: the former specifies the JIT compiler should generate code that prevents two or more threads from accessing the method at the same time, the latter that the JIT compiler shouldn't inline the method. I cover the Synchronized option in more detail in Chapter 20, "Threads," so for now let's focus on the NoInlining option.

Method inlining is an advanced and quite effective optimization technique that allows the JIT compiler to move the code in the body of a nonvirtual method directly into the caller's procedure. To understand how it works, consider this simple code:

```
Sub Main()
    Try
        Dim res As Integer = Eval(20, 10)
        Console.WriteLine(res)
    Catch ex As Exception
        Console.WriteLine(ex.ToString())
    End Try
End Sub

Function Eval(ByVal n1 As Integer, ByVal n2 As Integer) As Integer
    Return n1 \ n2
End Function
```

If you compile with optimizations enabled, most likely the JIT compiler will inline the Add method and move its code straight into the first method. In other words, it's as if you'd written this code in the Main method:

```
    Try
        Dim res As Integer = 20 \ 10
        Console.WriteLine(res)
```

This code is faster than the original because it saves a call and a return opcode at the native-code level. The shorter the code in the called method is, the more effective this optimization is. For this reason, the JIT compiler applies this optimization only under certain circumstances, most notably when the method is short (32 IL bytes or fewer); doesn't include conditional statements, loops, or Try blocks; and doesn't receive a structure as an argument.

The simplest technique to verify whether a method has been inlined is to place a breakpoint at the first statement in the method body and recompile with optimizations enabled and the

Generate Debug Info option set to Full (in the Advanced Compiler Settings dialog box). If the method has been inlined, the breakpoint is ignored, as is any attempt to single-step into the called method.

Although this optimization is usually a good thing, in some (admittedly rare) cases you might need to disable it for a specific method. This is necessary, for example, when you need to compile with optimizations enabled but with the same need to single-step into the called method. Another case is when the called procedure can throw an exception and you want to inspect the StackTrace of the resulting exception object. To see what I mean, just change the call statement as follows:

```
Dim res As Integer = Eval(20, 0)
```

This statement causes a DivideByZeroException, but the error message that appears in the console window shows that the error occurred in Main, not in the Eval method, because the call to the Eval function has been inlined. If the code in the Main method makes any decision based on where the exception occurred, the inlining optimization technique might raise a problem and you should disable it by means of a MethodImpl attribute:

```
Imports System.Runtime.CompilerServices
...
<MethodImpl(MethodImplOptions.NoInlining)> _
Function Eval(ByVal n1 As Integer, ByVal n2 As Integer) As Integer
    Return n1 \ n2
End Function
```

If you run the program after applying this attribute, you'll see that the error message correctly reports where the error has occurred.

A final note about inlining: the JIT compiler can inline only nonvirtual methods, that is, methods not marked with the Overridable keyword. If a method is overridable, there is no point in disabling inlining with a MethodImpl attribute. Read Chapter 8, "Inheritance," for more information about virtual methods and the Overridable keyword.

Writing Code

You'll probably spend more time in the code editor than in any other Visual Studio window or using any tool, so you should learn as much as you can about its features and capabilities.

The Code Editor

Visual Studio 2005 inherits many editing features of previous editions, including smart indenting; automatic insertion of the End keyword for If, Select, For, Do, and other language constructs; block outlining, that is, the ability to collapse classes, procedures, and other code blocks by clicking the plus symbol that appears to their right; and user-defined collapsible regions by means of the #Region keyword. Other features from the 2003 version are less known and it's worthwhile to summarize them here together with some new features.

■ **Change tracking**   By default all the lines that you edit are marked with a yellow stripe near the editor's left border. (See Figure 4-18.) If you then save the current file, those yellow stripes become green. (These stripes survive through compilations, but disappear if you close and then reopen the source file.) This feature is on by default, but you can disable the Track Changes option on the General page under the Text Editor node in the Options dialog box.

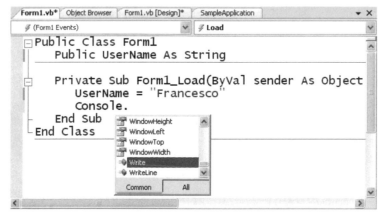

Figure 4-18   The change tracking and filtered IntelliSense features

■ **Filtered IntelliSense**   When you type the name of a variable or field and then press the period key, Visual Studio 2005 displays the list of available members divided in two panes: Common and All. (See Figure 4-18.) As you might expect, the Common pane contains only a subset of all the members that the object exposes. Interestingly, if you type or select a member from the All pane, this member appears in the Common pane the next time you ask for IntelliSense on the same object.

■ **AutoRecover**   Source files are automatically saved every 5 minutes, and the backup files are kept for a week; you can disable this feature or change these default values on the AutoRecover page under the Environment node in the Options dialog box. Backup files are named ~Autosave.*filename* in the My Documents\Visual Studio\Backup Files*projectname* folder. If the file hasn't been saved yet and has no name, a random name is used for the backup file.

■ **Tab groups and splittable windows**   You can split a code window by dragging the small gray rectangle that appears above the scrollbar near the right border so that you can work on two sections of the same source file. Or you can divide all the open windows in two horizontal or vertical tab groups by right-clicking the little tab containing the file's name and selecting the appropriate menu command, or more simply by dragging the window's tab to the right or bottom border of the window reserved for tabbed documents.

■ **Code editor tab context menu**   Commands in the context menu for the tab enable you to close all windows except the current window, open Windows Explorer to display the folder that contains the file, copy the file's full path to the Clipboard (useful for opening it with an external editor), and create a new horizontal or vertical tab group. (See Figure 4-19.)

Figure 4-19   The context menu of the editor tab

- **Clipboard ring**   The editor remembers the 15 pieces of text copied to the Clipboard most recently, and you can paste any one of them in a cyclic fashion by clicking Cycle Clipboard Ring on the Edit menu (or by using the Ctrl+Shift+V keyboard shortcut). For a more persistent way to remember text, simply drag a piece of code text to any tab in the tool box.

- **Box mode selection**   You can select a rectangular portion of code by pressing the Alt key while you drag the mouse or press an arrow key.

- **Code navigation**   You can jump to the definition of a symbol (a class, a variable, and so forth) by highlighting it and then pressing the F12 key or by right-clicking it and selecting the Go To Definition command from the context menu. Then you can go back to where you were previously by clicking the Navigate Backward button on the standard toolbar or by using the Ctrl+Hyphen keyboard command.

- **IDE Navigator**   As in previous versions of Visual Studio, you can navigate through all the tabs in the editor to access the various source files that are currently open by means of the Ctrl+Tab (to navigate forward) and Ctrl+Shift+Tab (navigate backward) shortcuts. In addition to their standard behavior, in Visual Studio 2005 these shortcuts display the IDE Navigator window, which lets you navigate to any open document and to any open active tool window by using the arrow keys. (See Figure 4-20.) Less guesswork and more productivity.

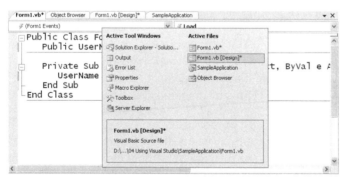

Figure 4-20   The IDE Navigator window

- **Full-screen editing**   You can enlarge the editor window by activating the full-screen editing feature by using the Shift+Alt+Enter keyboard shortcut (or selecting the Full Screen command in the View window). This command hides all toolbars and most tool windows. You can restore the standard window size by reissuing the command.

■ **Line numbers**   This feature is very handy when you're locating errors or discussing a code snippet with other developers. You can activate line numbers by opening the Options dialog box, navigating to the Basic page under the Text Editor node, and selecting the Line Numbers option. (See Figure 4-21.) Clicking Go To on the Edit menu lets you jump to a line by its given number. (This command works even if line numbers aren't visible.)

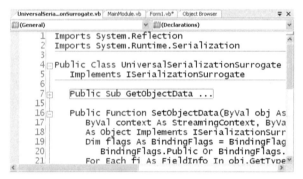

Figure 4-21   The code editor with line numbers enabled (note that line numbers account for collapsed regions of code)

■ **Line wrapping**   You can activate this feature while browsing a piece of code with very long lines. Point to Advanced on the Edit menu and select Word Wrap or press Ctrl+E, Ctrl+W to toggle this feature on and off.

■ **Parameter Copy and Paste**   Here's a tiny hidden new IntelliSense feature in Visual Studio 2005. As you know, when you type the name of a method and then the open parenthesis, the code editor displays a little yellow window containing the syntax of the method. By using the Ctrl+Shift+Alt+P shortcut, the method syntax is pasted into the editor window. It is then simple to remove the As clauses and change the parameter names to the appropriate values.

■ **Other editing commands**   You can convert a string to uppercase or lowercase, for example, and you can show or hide white spaces by means of commands on the Advanced submenu of the Edit menu. Remember that you can also move the selected code to another location simply by dragging it, or you can copy it by dragging it while pressing the Ctrl key.

The following commands don't appear on any menu: Ctrl+L moves the current line to the Clipboard; Ctrl+Shift+L deletes the current line without copying it to the Clipboard; Alt+Shift+T transposes the current line with the one below it. Finally, Ctrl+C copies the selected text to the Clipboard (as you'd expect), but it also copies the entire line if no text is currently selected.

XML Comments

A great new feature in Visual Basic 2005 is the ability to document your classes, methods, and members by means of standard XML comments. To see why this feature is so important, enter the following code:

```
Function ShowReport(ByVal user As String, ByVal condensed As Boolean) As Boolean
    ' This is just an example. Leave it blank.
End Function
```

Next, place the caret in the line that precedes the function declaration and type three apostrophes. (Alternatively, you can select the Insert Comment command from the context menu.) Visual Studio automatically creates the template for your XML comments:

```
''' <summary>
'''
''' </summary>
''' <param name="user"></param>
''' <param name="condensed"></param>
''' <returns></returns>
''' <remarks></remarks>
Function ShowReport(ByVal user As String, ByVal condensed As Boolean) As Boolean
    …
```

Filling the space between XML tags is up to you, of course. For example, you might insert this description:

```
''' <summary>
''' Show a report of all actions performed so far.
''' </summary>
''' <param name="user">Name of the user asking for the report.</param>
''' <param name="condensed">If True, a shorter report is produced.</param>
''' <returns>True if the report is created successfully, False otherwise.</returns>
''' <remarks>Don't invoke this method if no user has logged on yet.</remarks>
```

Finally, display the Compile page in the My Project designer, ensure that the Generate XML Documentation File option is selected, and compile the project. When this option is enabled, Visual Studio 2005 generates an XML file named after the executable file (e.g., MyApplication.xml for an executable named MyApplication.exe) in a standard format that is recognized by the Object Browser and that also appears in the IntelliSense little yellow window. (See Figure 4-22.)

XML comments are also recognized by tools that are able to produce a program's documentation automatically, such as the free NDoc utility (*http://ndoc.sourceforge.net*).

You can use a few other tags in addition to those that Visual Studio generates for you. Conveniently, IntelliSense is active when you type inside such comments, so you don't have to memorize all the options you have. One of the most important is the <exception> tag, which documents which exceptions the method can throw:

```
''' <exception cref="AccessViolationException">
''' The user hasn't enough privileges to run the report.
''' </exception>
```

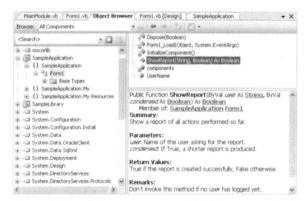

Figure 4-22 XML comments compiled in an XML file that is used by the Object Browser to better describe code elements

For more information about tags in XML comments, search for "XML documentation" in the Visual Studio Help.

Search and Replace

Visual Studio 2005 supports several kinds of search and replace commands, all of which are available on the Find And Replace submenu of the Edit menu. The Quick Find and Quick Replace commands can be applied to code in the current procedure, in the current document, in the current project, or in any document that is currently open in the editor. For actions with a broader range, you can use the Find In Files and Replace In Files commands, which allow you to specify a group of one or more folders; you can assign this group a name so that you can quickly recall it in future searches. The fifth command on the Find And Replace submenu, Find Symbol, lets you quickly search all the occurrences of a given code symbol and display its results in a dedicated tool window.

Unlike previous versions of Visual Studio, the five search and replace menu commands, as well as their shortcuts, bring you to the same dialog box even though the exact layout depends on the specific command; therefore, you can opt for a different command without closing the dialog box.

Member Definitions

Both at design time and in break mode you can quickly jump to the definition of a variable, property, method, event, or class definition by simply right-clicking its name and pressing the F12 key (or selecting the Go To Definition command from the context menu in the editor window). If the member isn't defined in a project that is currently loaded in the solution (as is the case with .NET Framework types), you are brought to the member's definition in the object browser. Once you've browsed the member definition, you can quickly go back to your previous position in code by typing Ctrl+Hyphen or by clicking the Navigate Backward icon on the standard toolbar.

Find All References

The Find All References command appears on the editor's context menu if you have selected a code element such as a field, variable, property, or type. Unlike lexicographic searches, which might include false positives in their results, the Find All References command correctly finds all places where the code element is referenced. (See Figure 4-23.) The search is always performed on all the source files in the solution and you can't exclude any of them. (This implies that the results of a search for a control include all the lines in the partial class that initializes all the form's properties.)

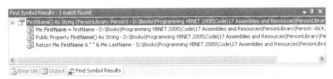

Figure 4-23   The Find Symbol Results tool window

Incremental Search

You don't need to bring up the Find dialog box for simple searches: just press Ctrl+I, start typing what you're looking for, and the caret will move to the first word that starts with the characters you've typed so far. When you type Ctrl+I again, the caret moves to the next occurrence. Use the Ctrl+Shift+I shortcut to move backward in your search. Incremental searches don't search for hidden text and inherit case-sensitivity from the most recent Find command.

Regular Expressions

You activate regular expression searches by selecting the Use option and selecting either Wildcards or Regular Expressions from the combo box immediately below the check box. The Wildcards option is the simpler of the two and enables you to use special characters in the Find What field only: ? (any single character), # (any single digit), * (zero or more characters, except newline characters), [...] (any character in the specified range), and [!...] (any character not in the specified range).

For more complex searches, you can enable the Regular Expressions option, which supports special sequences both in the Find What and the Replace With boxes. These special sequences often have the same meaning as those you can use with the System.Text.Regular-Expressions.Regex type, but their syntax is different. Most notably, most sequences in Visual Studio have a colon character as a prefix. You can gather the sequences in the following groups:

- **Character sequences**   . (dot: any character except the newline), **:a** (alphanumeric character), **:c** (alphabetical character), **:d** (digit), **:h** (hexadecimal digit), **:b** (tab or space), **\n** (newline), **\t** (tab), **:Lu** (uppercase character), **:Ll** (lowercase character), **:Ps** (open punctuation, such as open braces and brackets), **:Pe** (close punctuation, such as close braces and brackets), **:Pi** (initial double quotation marks), **:Pf** (final double quotation marks), **[aeiou]** (any character in the group), **[^aeiou]** (any character not in the group), **[A-Z]** (any character in the range), **[^A-Z]** (any character not in the range). You can use the backslash (****) to escape a character that would otherwise have a special meaning (for example, **\[** matches the open bracket).

- **String sequences**   **:w** (word), **:i** (identifier), **:z** (integer number), **:n** (floating number), **:q** (quoted string).

- **Positional clauses**   **^** (beginning of line), **$** (end of line), **<** (beginning of word), **>** (end of word).

- **Grouping and quantifiers**   **(xxx|yyy)** (either the *xxx* expression or the *yyy* expression), ***** (zero or more occurrences), **+** (one or more occurrences), **^N** (exactly *N* occurrences), **@** (zero or more occurrences, matching as few characters as possible), **#** (one or more occurrences, matching as few characters as possible).

- **Tagging clauses**   **{expr}** (assigns a numbered tag to the expression between braces), **\N** (matches the Nth tagged expression), **\0** (only in Replace box: replaces with the text in the Find What box).

Regular expressions are a complex matter and I don't have enough space to show all these clauses in action. However, I do show a few examples to give you a taste of how powerful they are, even though I omit a detailed description of how they work. After reading Chapter 14, "Regular Expressions," you might wish to come back to this section and apply those concepts to the search and replace feature in Visual Studio.

- **:i = :q** searches for string assignments.

- **(Dim|Private|Public) :i As String** searches for declarations of individual String variables.

- **<(:Lu(:Ll)*)+>** searches for any identifier in PascalCase (such as IniFileNotFound), whereas **<((:Ll)+:Lu(:Ll)*)+>** searches for identifiers in camel case (such as firstName). The **Dim <(:Lu(:Ll)*)+> As** sequence searches for local variables names in PascalCase, which therefore violate Microsoft naming guidelines (according to which local variables should be camelCase, as in firstName).

- **^:b*'.+\n** matches a line containing a comment and also matches the ending newline; **(^:b*'.+\n)+** matches a comment split over one or more lines. If you type the string **'-----\n\0'-----\n** in the Replace With box, you can easily insert a dashed line before and after a multiline comment.

- **{<:z>}(.|\n)+\1** highlights a block of code that begins and ends with the same integer constant; this search can be useful for finding recurring numeric values that might be replaced with a Const declaration. By replacing **:z** with **:n** you can search for floating-point constants; by using the **{:q}(.|\n)#\1** regular expression you can search for quoted strings that appear twice in the source file.

- The **Dim** {:i} **As** (.|\n)#<\1> sequence highlights the code between the declaration of a variable and its first use in code so that you can decide whether you should declare the variable closer to where it is used for the first time.

You can get a partial list of supported regular expressions by clicking the button to the right of the Find What box. One of the commands on this menu takes you to the Help page that describes this feature in greater detail. (See Figure 4-24.)

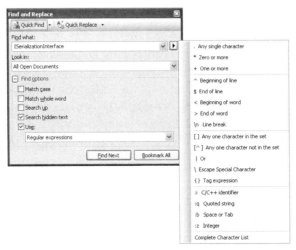

Figure 4-24   The Find dialog box with its pop-up menu to help the developer with regular expression syntax

Search Keyboard Shortcuts

A few shortcuts can help you in performing quick searches without opening the Find dialog box. You can search again for the text that was searched for most recently by pressing the F3 key; the Shift+F3 shortcut does a backward search. Also, you can start a forward search for the text that is currently selected by pressing the Ctrl+F3 shortcut; the Ctrl+Shift+F3 shortcut starts a backward search. As I already mentioned, you can use Ctrl+I and Ctrl+Shift+I to perform incremental searches.

The Find Combo Box

The Visual Studio standard toolbar offers yet another way to perform a search without opening the Find dialog box. Just click the Find combo box (or activate it by means of the Ctrl+D shortcut), type the text you're searching for, and then press Enter. Notice that the focus remains in the combo box, so you can press Enter again to move to the next occurrence.

This combo box has a few other properties that aren't immediately obvious:

- You can perform a backward search by pressing Shift+Enter.

- You can move to any line in the current document by typing the line number and pressing Ctrl+G.

- You can display Help on a given keyword or topic by typing a string and pressing the F1 key.

Unlike searches in the standard Find dialog box, the items in the Find combo box are preserved between Visual Studio sessions.

Bookmarks

Bookmarks enable you to move quickly to a specific position in the source code of the current document or project. You create a bookmark of the current position in the code window by pressing Ctrl+K, Ctrl+K; move to the next bookmark using the Ctrl+K, Ctrl+N shortcut; or move to the previous bookmark by pressing Ctrl+K, Ctrl+P. All the bookmark commands are also available on the Bookmarks submenu of the Edit menu or by means of buttons on the text editor toolbar. Bookmarks are automatically saved and reloaded with each solution.

 Visual Studio 2005 supports several new features related to bookmarks. First, by default the move to next and previous bookmark commands can bring you to a bookmark in a different file, and a new pair of commands work only inside the current document (which was the only behavior available in Visual Studio 2003). Also, you can disable a bookmark without having to remove it completely.

You now have a new Bookmarks window, which you can display by using the Ctrl+K, Ctrl+W shortcut or by selecting Bookmarks Window on the View menu. (See Figure 4-25.) You can quickly jump to a specific bookmark by double-clicking it or assigning it a descriptive name. You can enable and disable individual bookmarks by selecting the check box in each row or by using a button on the Bookmarks window toolbar to disable and reenable all bookmarks. As you might expect, disabled bookmarks are skipped over when navigating to the next or previous bookmark.

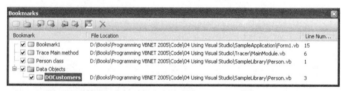

Figure 4-25   The Bookmarks window

Another button on the Bookmarks window toolbar enables you to create folders of bookmarks, and you can move a bookmark to a different folder by dragging the azure icon to the right of the check box in each row. Bookmark folders are useful for two reasons: you can disable and reenable all the bookmarks in a folder with a single mouse click, and you can decide to navigate through only the bookmarks in a folder. You can use the Ctrl+Shift+K, Ctrl+Shift+P shortcut to move to the previous bookmark in the same folder and Ctrl+Shift+K, Ctrl+Shift+N shortcut to move to the next bookmark in the same folder.

Finally, it is possible to create a bookmark that appears in the Task List window rather than in the Bookmarks window. (See next section for more details.)

The Error List and Task List Windows

The Task List window in Visual Studio 2003 was used to list both compiler-generated errors and warnings and user-defined tasks. More correctly, Visual Studio 2005 uses two different windows for these different types of information.

The Error List window displays compiler errors, warnings, and informative messages, and you can toggle on or off the display of messages of each different type by clicking the corresponding icon on the window toolbar. As you might expect, you can jump to the piece of source code that caused the compiler message (when the error is associated with a specific location in code) by double-clicking an item in this window. (See Figure 4-26.)

Figure 4-26   The Error List window

In previous versions of Visual Studio, an unsuccessful build displays an error message that asks whether you want to continue and run the last version of the executable that compiled correctly. Visual Studio 2005 lets you decide the exact behavior (launch old version, display prompt, or do nothing). You can select this and other options on the Build And Run page under the Projects And Solutions node of the Options dialog box. (See Figure 4-12.)

You use the Task List window to annotate pieces of information of three distinct kinds: user-defined tasks, shortcuts to code locations, and user comments. You decide the kind of items you want to work with at any given time by selecting an item in the combo box on the window's toolbar. (See Figure 4-27.) You can jump to the corresponding statement in code by double-clicking the Task List item. Once you have created two or more tasks, you can sort them by their priority, description, file, or line number. Each kind of task fulfills a different need and is added in a different manner:

- **User comments**   You can add a TODO user comment in the Task List by typing the following comment anywhere in the code window:

  ```
  ' TODO: text of the comment
  ```

  (See top portion of Figure 4-27.) You can also use other markers, such as HACK and UNDONE, and you can define your own markers or alter the priority of predefined markers on the Task List page of the Options dialog box. For example, you might define a custom comment named OPTIMIZE for portions of code that you haven't fine-tuned yet, or TODOC for procedures that need to be documented better.

■ **User-defined tasks**   You can create a new user-defined task by clicking the icon to the right of the combo box on the window's toolbar. You can add a description and a priority to each task and set its completion state by clicking the check box that appears in each row to insert a check mark. (See bottom portion of Figure 4-27.)

■ **Shortcuts to code**   You can create a shortcut to the current location in the code editor by using the Ctrl+K, Ctrl+H shortcut or the Add Task List Shortcut command on the Bookmarks submenu of the Edit menu. The description in the Task List window defaults to the code statement, but you can change it if you prefer and you can assign a priority to each task.

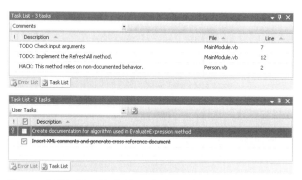

Figure 4-27   The Task List window, showing user comments (top) or user-defined tasks (bottom)

Code Snippets

Code snippets is a new Visual Studio feature that lets you quickly insert short pieces of code in the editor. You can think of code snippets as a sort of smart paste command in that the snippet can include placeholders that you can then overwrite after pasting. Visual Studio 2005 comes loaded with dozens of predefined code snippets, for both Visual Basic and C#. They include anything from one-liners to entire ready-to-use methods or even classes.

Inserting a Code Snippet

Inserting a code snippet couldn't be simpler: place the caret where you want to insert the snippet, and either type the question mark (?) character and then press the Tab key or select the Insert Snippets command from the context menu. In either case, Visual Studio displays a list of folders containing all the installed snippets, and you can navigate the list by double-clicking each element or by using the arrow keys and the Tab key until you find what you're looking for.

The majority of installed snippets have one or more variable elements, and you're expected to overwrite them with meaningful values. For example, Figure 4-28 shows the code snippet inserted when you select the Define A Property item in the Properties And Procedures subfolder of the Common Code Patterns category: the items newPropertyValue, NewProperty, and Integer are highlighted in green and you are expected to overwrite them with the actual values for the specific case. As you can imagine, if you rename the variable, the property, or the return type, other occurrences of the same item will be renamed as well. You can use the Tab key and Shift+Tab to move between all the replaceable portions of a code snippet.

```
Public Class Person

    Private newPropertyValue As Integer
    Public Property NewProperty() As Integer
        Get
            Return newPropertyValue
        End Get
        Set(ByVal value As Integer)
            newPropertyValue = value
        End Set
    End Property
End Property
```

Figure 4-28   Inserting a code snippet

Most code snippets have a shortcut assigned to them. Unlike keyboard shortcuts, a code snippet shortcut is a string of text that can't contain special keys or characters. Visual Studio displays the shortcut assigned to each code snippet in a tooltip to the right of the window containing the snippet list. For example, the shortcut assigned to the Define A Property snippet is Property. By typing a shortcut and then pressing the Tab key, you can insert a code snippet quickly, without having to navigate to the corresponding item in the folder list. Needless to say, code snippets and their shortcuts offer a tremendous productivity bonus.

Managing Code Snippets

You can list all the code snippets installed with Visual Studio by means of the Code Snippet Manager dialog box, which you open by selecting it from the Tools menu or by typing Ctrl+K, Ctrl+B. (See Figure 4-29.)

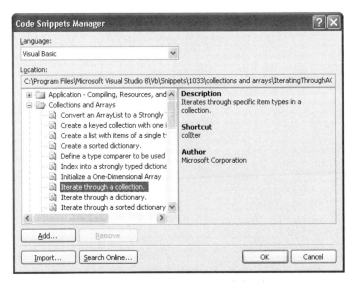

Figure 4-29   The Code Snippet Manager dialog box

Visual Basic code snippets are usually stored in XML files that have a .snippet or .vbsnippet extension, even though this isn't a strict requirement. The Location box in this dialog box shows the complete path of a code snippet file; for example, the code snippet highlighted in Figure 4-29 is stored in the IteratingThroughACollectionUsingForEach.snippet file in the C:\Program Files\Microsoft Visual Studio 8\Vb\Snippets\1033\collections and arrays folder. You can copy this path to the Clipboard, and then use the Add Existing Item command from the Project menu to edit the file with the XML Editor included in Visual Studio. Editing a snippet file lets you control the code that Visual Studio generates and adapt it to your programming style.

The Code Snippet Manager enables you to browse installed code snippets as well as specify additional folders that contain snippet files and import code snippets from an existing file. In the next section, I show you how to create a new code snippet and import it into Visual Studio.

Creating a Code Snippet

In this example, I show you how to create a new code snippet that defines a public constructor that takes an argument and assigns its value to a private field. Using Notepad or the Visual Studio XML editor, create a file named ConstructorWithOneArgument.snippet that contains the following text:

```xml
<?xml version="1.0" encoding="UTF-8"?>
<CodeSnippets xmlns="http://schemas.microsoft.com/VisualStudio/2005/CodeSnippet">
  <CodeSnippet Format="1.0.0">
    <Header>
      <Title>Sub New that assigns one field.</Title>
      <Author>Francesco Balena / Code Architects Srl</Author>
      <Description>Defines a constructor that assigns a private field.</Description>
      <Shortcut>newarg</Shortcut>
      <HelpUrl></HelpUrl>
    </Header>
    <Snippet>
      <Declarations>
        <Literal>
          <ID>FieldName</ID>
          <ToolTip>Replace with field name.</ToolTip>
          <Default>ID</Default>
        </Literal>
        <Literal>
          <ID>FieldType</ID>
          <ToolTip>Replace with the field type.</ToolTip>
          <Default>String</Default>
        </Literal>
      </Declarations>
      <Code Language="VB" Kind="method decl">
      <![CDATA[' Declare the field assigned by the constructor.
Private $FieldName$ As $FieldType$

Public Sub New(ByVal $FieldName$ As $FieldType)
   Me.$FieldName$ = $FieldName$
End Sub]]></Code>
    </Snippet>
  </CodeSnippet>
</CodeSnippets>
```

When you create a code snippet file, you must adhere to an XML schema that Microsoft has defined for files of this type. Each code snippet file must contain a <CodeSnippets> root tag, which can contain one or more <CodeSnippet> tags. (A single file can define multiple code snippets.) In turn, each <CodeSnippet> must contain a <Header> tag and a <Snippet> tag. The <Header> contains other tags that define the snippet's title, author, description, shortcut, and Help URL; all the tags except <Title> are optional, but you'll surely want to include at least the shortcut and the description.

The <Snippet> tag can contain a <Declarations> block, which, in turn, contains one or more <Literal> tags, each one defining a placeholder in the code snippet. The <ID> tag specifies the unique name used in code to identify the placeholder (for example, $FieldName$ for the literal named FieldName); the <Tooltip> tag defines the text that appears in the tooltip when the mouse is on the placeholder; <Default> is the proposed value for the placeholder.

You should use the <Object> tag instead of the <Literal> tag as a placeholder for an object that isn't defined inside the code snippet, for example, a control on a form. Object elements support the same child tags as literal elements, plus a <Type> section that specifies the object's type:

```
<Object>
  <ID>connection</ID>
  <Type>SqlConnection</Type>
  <ToolTip>Replace with the SqlConnection name.</ToolTip>
  <Default>SqlConnection1</Default>
</Object>
```

The <Code> tag is mandatory and must include a few attributes that help Visual Studio filter out which code snippets should be displayed in the list that appears in the code editor. For Visual Basic snippets, the Language attribute must be equal to the "VB" string. The Kind attribute specifies what sort of code the snippet produces and, indirectly, where the code can be inserted. The "method decl" value for this attribute means that the snippet produces a method declaration, "method body" is for snippets that produce code inside a method, and "type decl" means that the snippet generates the source code for a type; leaving this attribute empty or omitting it means that the code can be generated anywhere in a source file.

As you might expect, the <Code> section contains the actual code that Visual Studio generates. The code should be enclosed in a CDATA block, so you can use characters such as < and & (which would otherwise be invalid in a block of XML text) without having to escape them. As I mentioned before, placeholder names must be embedded between dollar signs ($); however, you can change the delimiter character by adding an attribute to the <Code> tag, as in this code:

```
<Code Language="VB" Delimiter="#">
```

You can insert inside the <Snippet> block a few other tags that don't appear in the previous example. The <References> tag can contain one or more <Reference> tags, each one defining an assembly that must be included in the project's references for the snippet to work correctly. Similarly, the <Imports> tag can contain one or more <Import> tags, each one defining a namespace that the snippet assumes is imported. If necessary, Visual Studio automatically adds a suitable Imports statement at the top of the current source file. Here's a code snippet example that requires the System.Web assembly be referenced by the current project and that imports the System.Web.Services and System.Web.Services.Protocols namespaces if necessary:

```
<Snippet>
   <References>
     <Reference>
       <Assembly>System.Web </Assembly>
     </Reference>
   </References>
   <Imports>
     <Import>
       <Namespace>System.Web.Services</Namespace>
     </Import>
     <Import>
       <Namespace>System.Web.Services.Protocols</Namespace>
     </Import>
   </Imports>
   ...
</Snippet>
```

The companion code on the Web site for this book includes a tool that lists all the code snippets installed with Visual Basic together with their shortcuts, a feature that is lacking in Visual Studio. The exploration of snippets coming from Microsoft reveals a few pearls that can make your typing faster—for example, these:

- **If, IfElse, IfElseIf**   Build an If block, an If...Else block, and an If...ElseIf...Else block.

- **TryC, TryF, TryCF**   Build a Try block with a Catch block, a Finally block, or both.

- **Property, PropRead**   Build a Property...End Property block (writeable or read-only) that wraps a private variable.

Note   If you plan to create your own code snippets, have a look at Snippy, a free Windows application that enables you to edit these XML files in a visual manner. You can download a copy of this tool at *http://www.gotdotnet.com/codegallery/codegallery.aspx?id=b0813ae7-466a-43c2-b2ad-f87e4ee6bc39.*

Refactoring Code

Refactoring is a term that stands for the ability to reorganize your source code to make it more readable, modular, and therefore maintainable. Visual Studio 2005 comes with great (and somewhat astonishing) features in the refactoring area, in the form of a built-in Rename command and an external tool named Refactor!.

The Rename Command

The Rename command lets you rename a class member and automatically change all the references to it in the same project. Using the new command is simple: right-click a member name (either in the method declaration or in a method call), select the Rename command from the context menu, type the new member name in the dialog box that appears, and then click OK to confirm changes. You can use this command with private or public fields, properties, and methods and with local variables inside methods. The scope of changes (current procedure, current class, or the entire project) depends on the scope of the member being selected.

In most cases, however, you don't even need to invoke the Rename command explicitly. In fact, when you modify the name of a class, method, or variable in the code editor, Visual Studio displays a smart tag that enables you to rename all the occurrences of that class, method, or variable elsewhere in code. (See Figure 4-30.)

Figure 4-30   The Rename smart tag

The Refactor! Tool

In addition to the rename command, you can expand Visual Studio refactoring capabilities by installing Refactor! for Visual Basic 2005, a free utility by Developer Express that you can download from *http://www.devexpress.com/vbrefactor/*. Here's a short list of the commands that Refactor! makes available:

- **Reorder Parameters**   Changes the order of parameters in a method signature and updates all statements calling that method.

- **Encapsulate Field**   Converts a field into a property and replaces all occurrences of the field in the current type.

- **Extract Method and Extract Property**   Make a separate method or read-only property, respectively, out of a group of existing statements, which is automatically replaced by a call to the new method. (See Figure 4-31.)

- **Create Overload**   Creates an overload of an existing method and allows you to exclude one or more parameters.

- **Move Declaration Near Reference**   Moves the declaration of a variable just before the first reference to that variable.

- **Move Initialization To Declaration**   Combines the declaration of a variable and its first assignment in a single statement.

Figure 4-31   The Refactor! Extract Method command

- **Split Initialization From Declaration**   Splits a variable initializer into two separate statements (declaration and assignment).

- **Introduce Local**   Creates a new local variable initialized to the selected expression and optionally replaces other occurrences of the expression with a reference to the newly created variable.

- **Flatten Conditional**   Transforms an If block that brackets all the statements of a method into an If block with reversed condition whose Then block contains a Return statement that exits the method. (See Figure 4-32.)

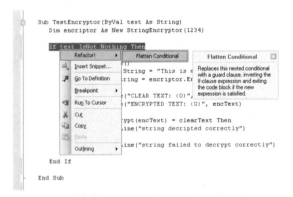

Figure 4-32   The Refactor! Flatten Conditional command

Refactor! commands can be invoked by one of the following three methods: context menu (see Figure 4-32), shortcut (Ctrl+`), or smart tags. For example, if you select a piece of code, Refactor! displays a smart tag that makes the Extract Method command available. (See Figure 4-31.) All commands are clearly explained by tooltips, and the Refactor! Help is integrated with Visual Studio Help, so you can get more information just by pressing the F1 key.

If you register your copy of Refactor! at the Developer Express Web site, you'll be able to access even more refactorings.

Miscellaneous New and Old Features

In this section, I have gathered the description of a few new features that don't fit well in any topic discussed so far, as well as several customization capabilities that have been inherited from Visual Studio 2003 but that, in my opinion, have been overlooked by most developers.

Working with Tool Windows

Moving a tool window—such as the Properties window and the Solution Explorer window—is always a minor but tricky problem with the 2002 and 2003 editions of Visual Studio because you never know how to dock the window in a single pane. As I learned, the secret is to grab a tool window by its title bar and move the mouse cursor *over the title bar of the target window.* (Just moving on the client area of another tool window doesn't make the windows stick together.)

This trick is still valid under Visual Studio 2005, but in general moving a tool window and having it stick to other dockable tool windows is much simpler now because when you drag a tool window, a set of arrowed icons appears on the screen, each one pointing to a different pane that contains other tool windows. When you move the mouse cursor over one of these icons, Visual Studio highlights the screen portion where the dragged window would be docked. If you release the mouse button when the cursor is over the icon in the center of the cross, the window being dragged becomes a tabbed document. (See Figure 4-33.)

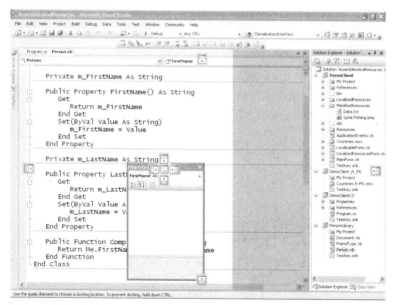

Figure 4-33   Docking a tool window

The context menu that appears when you right-click a window title bar shows the five states a window can be in: floating, dockable, tabbed document, autohide, and hide. It is therefore quite easy to move a window to and away from the larger section in the center that contains tabbed documents.

Importing and Exporting Settings

If you work on two or more computers, you'll appreciate a new feature of Visual Studio 2005: the ability to export all the current settings and later import them in the same or a different instance of the environment. The set of settings that you can export and import includes general settings (options related to the individual Visual Studio windows, such as the Object Browser), Help and Favorites settings, the settings you enforce from the Options dialog box, and all options related to Visual Studio Team Edition (only if you installed Visual Studio 2005 Team Edition, of course).

By default, any time you exit Visual Studio, your settings are stored in a file named currentsettings.vssettings in the folder named C:\Documents and Settings*username*\My Documents\ Visual Studio 2005\Settings. You can change this default location on the Import And Export Settings page under the Environment node in the Options dialog box. Changing this location can be useful if you have installed Visual Studio on several computers in your LAN and want to use the same settings regardless of which machine you log on to.

To actually export or import a group of configuration settings, you select the Import And Export Settings command from the Tools menu, which starts a wizard that lets you export all or a subset of current settings, import settings from an existing .vssettings file, or reset all settings to those contained in a .vssettings file. The main difference between the import and the reset commands is that the former lets you select which groups of settings should be imported.

If you select the import or reset action, you are given an opportunity to save current settings before proceeding so that you can easily restore current settings should you need to do so. In the next step, you select which file contains the settings you want to enforce. (See top portion of Figure 4-34.) Visual Studio keeps track of all the .vssettings files it has created, but you can use the Browse button to locate a file stored elsewhere. In addition to the settings you've created, Visual Studio offers a few predefined groups of settings that can help certain categories of developers feel comfortable in the IDE, for example, settings for Visual Basic 6 or Microsoft Visual C++ developers.

If you selected the import or the export command (but not the reset command), you'll be asked to select which settings should actually be imported or exported. (See bottom portion of Figure 4-34.) Finally, clicking the Finish button completes the wizard and runs the requested action.

Note   You can start Visual Studio 2005 using all default settings by running the devenv.exe file from the command line and specifying the /ResetSettings switch.

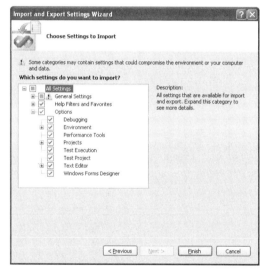

Figure 4-34   Two steps of the Import And Export Settings Wizard, which let you select the file to import (top) and the individual settings that should be imported or exported (bottom)

Project and Item Templates

A *project template* is a predefined Visual Studio project that contains customizable portions and that appears in the gallery of available project types when you add a new project to the solution. An *item template* is a customizable template for individual source files that appears in the list of available file types when you select the Add New Item command from the Project menu. Visual Studio has always supported project and item templates, and Visual Studio 2005 is no exception: it comes with a few complete template projects, such as My Movie Collection

Starter Kit and Screen Saver Starter Kit, and even more file templates, including About Box, Login Form, and Explorer Form. What makes me consider this a new feature is the fact that creating custom templates has never been so easy.

A template consists of one or more files—which can be .vb source files, .vbproj files, resource files, and data files—and one .vstemplate file. This file contains all the metadata that Visual Studio requires when the user selects the New Project or Add New Item command. Interestingly, templates are stored in compressed .zip files. If you want to modify an existing template, you must uncompress this file, apply your edits, and compress it again.

Visual Studio looks for templates in two different locations. The templates installed with Visual Studio are expected to be in the C:\Program Files\Microsoft Visual Studio 8\Common7\ IDE*TemplateDir*\Visual Basic\1033\ folder, where *TemplateDir* can be ProjectTemplates, ItemTemplates, SolutionTemplates, or Templates. (Notice that the 1033 folder is used for the English version of Visual Studio; in general, this folder matches the locale identifier, or LCID, of the localized version of the product.) Custom templates are expected to be in the Project-Templates or ItemTemplates folder under the C:\Documents and Settings*UserName*\My Documents\Visual Studio 2005\Templates directory, but you can change these default locations on the General page of the Projects And Solutions section of the Visual Studio Options dialog box. The categories you see in the Add New Project and Add New Item dialog boxes— both for installed and custom templates—reflect the folder structure of these locations on disk; therefore, you can organize both types of templates as you see fit as well as create new categories, and so on.

> **Note**   If you accidentally delete or corrupt the templates that come with Visual Studio, you can quickly restore them without reinstalling Visual Studio by navigating to the C:\Program Files\Microsoft Visual Studio 8\Common7\IDE directory and issuing the following command:
>
> ```
> DEVENV /installvstemplates
> ```

Creating a Template

You can create a template by selecting the Export Template command from the File menu. The first step of the wizard asks you to select whether you are exporting a project or an item template. In the latter case, the next two steps allow you to select which item should be exported and which references to external assemblies should be included in the template. (These steps are missing if you are exporting a project template because in that case all the items and all the references are included in the output.) In both cases, the last step of the wizard enables you to define the name, icon, description, and output location of the template being created. (See Figure 4-35.)

You should leave the Automatically Import The Template Into Visual Studio option enabled so that your template is copied in the directories where Visual Studio looks for custom templates. If you performed all the steps correctly, your template appears in the My Templates section of the New Project and Add New Item dialog boxes. (See Figure 4-36.)

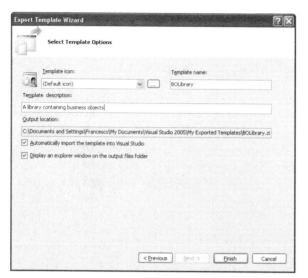

Figure 4-35   The last step of the Export Template Wizard

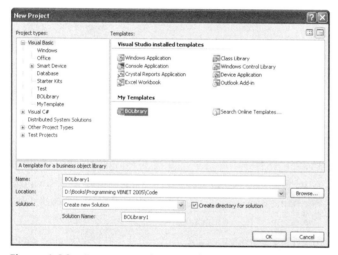

Figure 4-36   A custom project template in the New Project dialog box

Using Predefined Parameters

Before you transform a project or an item into a template, you might want to define one or more template parameters in your source code. Template parameters are enclosed in $ symbols. You might define an item template named PersonalData containing the following code:

```
' ----------------------------------------
' Author:        $username$
' Organization: $registeredorganization$
' Date/Time:     $time$
' ----------------------------------------
```

```
Public Class $safeitemname$
   Public FirstName As String
   Public LastName As String

   Public Sub New(ByVal firstName As String, ByVal lastName As String)
      Me.FirstName = firstName
      Me.LastName = lastName
   End Sub
End Class
```

See Table 4-1 for the meaning of the parameters used in the previous code snippet and all other parameters that Visual Studio 2005 supports. Here's an example of the code that the previous template might produce when I use it to create the Employee project item:

```
' ----------------------------------------
' Author:      Francesco Balena
' Organization: Code Architects
' Date/Time:   12/21/2005 15:10:17
' ----------------------------------------

Public Class Employee
   Public FirstName As String
   Public LastName As String

   Public Sub New(ByVal firstName As String, ByVal lastName As String)
      Me.FirstName = firstName
      Me.LastName = lastName
   End Sub
End Class
```

Table 4-1   Template Parameters

Name	Description
clrversion	Version of .NET Common Language Runtime (CLR).
GUID1...GUID10	A unique GUID. (A template can contain up to 10 distinct GUIDs.)
itemname	The name provided by the user in the Add New Item dialog box.
machinename	The name of the computer.
projectname	The name provided by the user in the Add New Project dialog box.
registeredorganization	The name of the company that registered the current copy of the Windows operating system.
rootnamespace	The root namespace of the current project.
safeitemname	The name of the current item, with all spaces and unsafe characters removed.
safeprojectname	The name of the current project, with all spaces and unsafe characters removed.
time	The current time, in the DD/MM/YYYY hh:mm:ss format.
userdomain	The current user domain.
username	The current user name.
year	The current year, as a four-digit number.

You can define your own template parameters, too. The first way to do so is by adding a new <CustomParameters> section in the .vstemplate file:

```
<TemplateContent>
    ...
    <CustomParameters>
        <CustomParameter Name="$propertyname$" Value="ID"/>
        <CustomParameter Name="$propertytype$" Value="String">
    </CustomParameters>
</TemplateContent>
```

The limit of this approach is that the parameter is most likely a constant because you can't change its value dynamically. Remember that you must extract the .vstemplate file from the .zip file located in the directory where Visual Studio looks for project or item templates, add your parameters, and reinclude the .vstemplate file in the .zip file.

The second technique for defining custom template parameters is based on custom wizards. A Visual Studio wizard is a class that implements the Microsoft.VisualStudio.TemplateWizard .IWizard interface and that Visual Studio instantiates when reading the .vstemplate file. You can read more in MSDN documentation.

Accessing Online Contents

 The Start page in Visual Studio 2005 shows many improvements over previous editions. Not only does it give you access to recent projects and most common Help topics, it also opens up an RSS channel to download programming-related news from MSDN. You can even select a different channel and decide how often the start page is updated by changing the settings on the Startup page under the Environment node in the Options dialog box.

Visual Studio 2005 also features a brand-new Community top-level menu. This menu enables you to access the Codezone Community's home page, ask a question and check the status of pending questions, and so forth. In my opinion, the most compelling feature of this menu is the ability to search for and download samples, code snippets, project and file templates, controls, and starter kits made available by Microsoft, user groups, and developer communities of all sorts. By using a single search, you can query the local and online MSDN archives, the Codezone Community, and the Q&A archives.

Customization Features

Visual Studio offers many ways to customize its appearance and its behavior without writing a macro or installing an add-in. Virtually all the available options are reachable from the Options dialog box, the Customize dialog box, or the External Tools dialog box.

The Options Dialog Box

Most of the options for customizing the IDE are located in the Options dialog box that you reach from the Tools menu. This dialog box is organized as a tree of pages. For example, the General page under the Environment tree node exposes the option to work with a multiple-document interface (MDI) instead of with tabbed documents. Although the MDI appearance can be more familiar to developers coming from Visual Basic 6, you should be aware that tabbed documents offer much more flexibility, and in this book I always assume that you are using the tabbed document user interface.

The Fonts And Colors page has been vastly extended in Visual Studio 2005 and now it allows you to control the style used for virtually all the windows in the IDE, not just the text editor and a few others (as was the case in previous versions). A few of the entries in the topmost combo box are especially interesting. For example, you can affect the font style for all the tool windows in one shot by selecting the item labeled [All Text Tool Windows], whereas the [Watch, Locals, And Autos Tool Windows] item affects the three windows where Visual Studio displays the value of variables and fields during debugging. The Printer item lets you print your listings with a style that is different from the one used for the code editor.

The Keyboard page is one of the most useful pages in the Options dialog box. (See Figure 4-37.) Here you can assign a shortcut key to any command defined in Visual Studio as well as to any macro you've created. All the commands that are associated with a menu are typically in the form *menuname.commandname*; so, for example, you can restrict the commands in the list to those belonging to the Tools menu by typing **tools.** in the Show Commands Containing text box. Once the command is selected, click the Press Shortcut Key box and type the key combination that you want to assign to the command or macro.

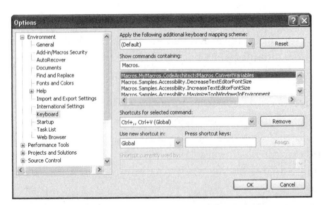

Figure 4-37   Filtering commands by typing the first characters of the command name on the Keyboard page of the Options dialog box

A frequent problem in assigning a shortcut is that most of them are already used by Visual Studio. If the combination you've pressed is currently assigned to another command, a message appears in the Shortcut Currently Used By box. Only a few combinations aren't assigned, for example, Ctrl+<, Ctrl+0, those in the range of Ctrl+5 to Ctrl+9, and those consisting of the Alt key followed by a digit. Fortunately, a shortcut can consist of two keys, and thus the number of commands to which you can assign a shortcut is higher than what you might deduce from this short description. For example, I use the Ctrl+< key sequence as the prefix for all my keyboard shortcuts, which reduces the need to memorize complex key sequences.

Personalized Toolbars and Menus

Visual Studio 2005 comes with more than 30 toolbars, even though only a few are displayed by default. You can display and hide any of these toolbars by right-clicking the menu bar or any visible toolbar and selecting or clearing items in the list. For more thorough changes, select the Customize command on the Tools menu, which opens the Customize dialog box. After you've created a new toolbar in the Toolbars tab, you can start dropping commands on it by dragging commands that appear in the rightmost pane of the Commands tab of the same dialog box. (See Figure 4-38.) You can then change the icon and other properties of the new command by right-clicking it and selecting from the context menu, and you can drag the new command elsewhere on the same or a different toolbar. Customization isn't limited to toolbars—you can customize any menu using the same technique.

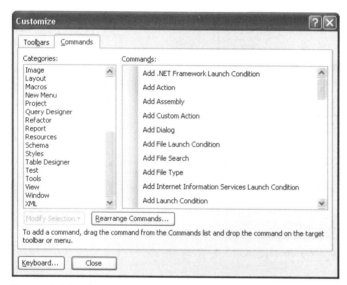

Figure 4-38   The Commands tab of the Customize dialog box

A hidden feature of the Customize dialog box lets you customize even the context menus that appear in the text editor and most other IDE windows. Switch to the Toolbars tab and select the Shortcut Menus item from the list. You'll see that many new menus have appeared in the main Visual Studio window under the standard toolbar, with each menu representing a context menu in the IDE. While these menus are still visible, switch to the Commands tab and customize the menus as usual. When you close the Customize dialog box, the shortcut menus disappear from the main window.

External Tools

The External Tools command on the Tools menu gives you a great way to launch external programs quickly from within the IDE. (See Figure 4-39.) To add a new tool to the list of those provided with Visual Studio, click the Add button, type the name of the tool in the Title box, type the complete path of the executable in the Command box, and type any argument you want to pass to the tool in the Arguments box. The Arguments box supports a few placeholders that are automatically replaced with values related to the current project or solution: $(TargetPath) is the complete path of the output file produced by the compiler, $(ProjectDir) is the folder containing the project files, and so forth. (You can get the list of all supported placeholders by clicking the arrow button to the right of this box.) Alternatively, you can select the Prompt For Arguments check box and have Visual Studio ask for arguments before launching the program. If you are running a command-line utility, you'll probably want to select the Use Output Window option to suppress the creation of a separate console window and to gather the results from the external program in the Visual Studio Output window.

Figure 4-39   Adding ILDASM as an external tool

One of the most useful external tools you might want to add to the Tools menu is the ILDASM disassembler, so I use it as an example to show you how to work with this dialog box. After clicking the Add button, type **ILDA&SM this app** in the Title box and enter the complete path to Ildasm.exe in the Command box. (By default, this tool is in the C:\Program Files\Microsoft Visual Studio 8\SDK\v2.0\Bin folder.) The ampersand (&) character in the title enables you to run ILDASM quickly by pressing Alt+T (to open the Tools menu) followed by the S key. Next, type the following string in the Arguments box:

```
/SOURCE "$(TargetPath)"
```

This command instructs ILDASM to disassemble the executable file produced by the current project (the one currently selected in the Solution Explorer) and to display the original source code together with the IL code produced by the compiler. (Source code is displayed only if you have compiled the project in Debug mode.) Remember to enclose all file paths in double quotation marks—otherwise, a space in the project path causes an invalid argument to be passed to the external utility.

Here are other useful commands that you can add to the Tools menu:

- Explorer.exe with an argument equal to $(TargetDir) displays the executable's folder in Windows Explorer. (No need to specify the complete path because Explorer.exe is on the system path.)

- Xcopy.exe with the following argument:

```
*.* "c:\Backup_Projects\$(TargetName)" /s /d /i /k /r /y
```

and an initial directory equal to $(ProjectDir) backs up the current project to a folder named C:\Backup_Projects*exename*, where *exename* is the executable created when compiling the current project. This name is usually, but not always, equal to the name of the current project: we must use it because there is no placeholder that corresponds to the project name.

- Cmd.exe with the following argument:

```
/K ""C:\Program Files\Microsoft Visual Studio 8\Common7\Tools\vsvars32.bat""
```

(notice the double quotation marks), and $(TargetDir) in the Initial Directory box opens the Visual Studio command prompt on the folder that contains the executable produced by the compiler. (You should clear the Use Output Window option for this command to work correctly.)

Macros and Commands

One of the most exciting features of the Visual Studio IDE is its ability to record and play macros to automate repetitive editing actions. Even better, you can browse the actual macro code and edit it, or create new macros from scratch.

Recording and Running a Macro

You record a macro by pointing to Macro on the Tools menu and clicking the Record TemporaryMacro command (or by using the Ctrl+Shift+R keyboard shortcut), and then using the mouse or typing in the code editor. The macro recorder records key presses, menu commands, find and replace commands, window activations, and select actions in the Solution Explorer.

When you have completed your action, stop recording by pressing Ctrl+Shift+R again, or just click the Stop Recording button on the Recorder toolbar that has appeared in the meantime. You can also cancel the recording without saving by clicking the Cancel Recording button on this toolbar. If you didn't cancel the macro recording, a new macro named TemporaryMacro is created. You can play all the actions in this macro by pointing to Macros on the Tools menu and clicking Run TemporaryMacro or by using the Ctrl+Shift+P keyboard shortcut.

Each time you record a new macro, the macro named TemporaryMacro is overwritten, so you should rename it as something else if you want to save the macro you've just recorded. Do so by pointing to Macros on the Tools menu and clicking Macro Explorer to open the Macro Explorer, which you can see in Figure 4-40. (You can also open the Macro Explorer window by using the Alt+F8 shortcut.) Then right-click TemporaryMacro, click Rename on the shortcut menu, and change the macro's name.

Figure 4-40   The Macro Explorer

Let me show an actual (and useful) example of a macro that you can create by simply recording your actions in the IDE: an automatic way to embed the selected text into the Try section of a Try...Catch...Finally structure. Let's begin by typing a couple of statements in the code editor:

```
Console.Write("Hello ")
Console.WriteLine("World")
```

Select both lines and ensure that the entire lines are highlighted, start the recording by pressing Ctrl+Shift+R, and then carefully perform the following actions:

1. Press Ctrl+X to cut the selected text to the Clipboard.

2. Type **Try** in the code editor, and then press Enter; Visual Studio creates the Try...Catch...End Try block for you.

3. While the caret is on the blank line following the Try statement, press Ctrl+V to paste the original piece of code.

4. Press the Down arrow key twice, and then press Enter to create a blank line after the Catch block.

5. Type **Finally** and press Enter again.

6. Press the Ctrl+K, Ctrl+D key combination to format the current document.

You can now press Ctrl+Shift+R to complete the recording of the macro. To ensure that you made no mistakes, select a different piece of code and use the Ctrl+Shift+P keyboard shortcut to see whether the code is correctly wrapped in a Try...Catch...Finally block. If everything is

OK, switch to the Macro Explorer window and rename the TemporaryMacro item with a more meaningful name, such as WrapInTryCatchFinally.

You can run a nontemporary macro in three ways:

- Double-click it in the Macro Explorer (or right-click it and select Run on the context menu).

- Type its name in the Command window in command mode. This action works because your new macro has, in effect, become a Visual Studio command.

- Assign it a keyboard shortcut. You can do this on the Keyboard page of the Options dialog box. See the section titled "The Options Dialog Box" earlier in this chapter for more details.

Editing a Macro

Recording a temporary macro isn't the only way you can create a macro. As a matter of fact, you can create more powerful macros by writing their code directly, even though this task usually requires a better understanding of the Visual Studio IDE object model. In this section, I provide a couple of examples of what you can achieve with this advanced technique.

First, open the Microsoft Visual Studio Macro IDE by using the Alt+F11 shortcut or selecting the Macro IDE command from the Macros submenu of the Tools menu. (See Figure 4-41.) The Macro IDE is a sort of reduced version of Visual Studio itself: it has a Project Explorer window, a Class View window, an Object Browser, and so forth. Its menu commands are a subset of the "real" Visual Studio, so you already know how to use them. For example, you can use the Project menu to add new classes and modules to the current macro project (even though you can't add forms). According to C# developers, the most severe limitation is that Visual Studio macros can be written only in Visual Basic, but this isn't a problem for us, right?

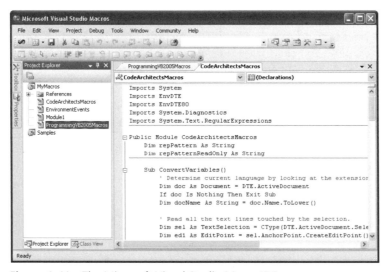

Figure 4-41   The Microsoft Visual Studio Macro IDE

Use the Add Module command on the Project menu to add a module named Programming-VB2005Macros, and then add the following code inside this new module:

```
Public Module ProgrammingVB2005Macros
    Sub WrapInIfThenElse()
        ' Retrieve the selected text, append a newline character if necessary.
        Dim sel As TextSelection = DirectCast(DTE.ActiveDocument.Selection, TextSelection)
        If sel Is Nothing Then Exit Sub
        ' Open an undo context.
        DTE.UndoContext.Open("WrapInIfThenElse")
        ' Retrieve the selected text, append a new line if necessary.
        Dim selText As String = sel.Text
        If Not selText.EndsWith(ControlChars.NewLine) Then selText &= ControlChars.NewLine
        ' Embed the selected text in an If…Then…Else block.
        Dim newText As String = String.Format("If condition Then{0}{1}Else{0}{0}End If{0}", _
            ControlChars.NewLine, selText)
        ' Replace the selection with the new text and format the document.
        sel.Text = newText
        DTE.ExecuteCommand("Edit.FormatDocument")
        ' Close the undo context.
        DTE.UndoContext.Close()
    End Sub
End Module
```

The remarks in the listing should help you understand what each line of code does. The only obscure statements maybe are the ones that open and close the undo context: by bracketing one or more editing actions between UndoContext.Open and UndoContext.Close methods, you can later undo all those actions with a single Undo command from inside the code editor. In this particular example, you might believe that the macro performs a single editing action (that is, the assignment to the Text property of the Selection object); however, Visual Studio interprets this assignment as multiple insertions of individual lines, and therefore an undo context is necessary if you want to provide the developer using your macro with the ability to undo its effects with a single key press.

Once you understand these simple concepts it's easy to create other macros that wrap the current selection in a For, For Each, or Do loop. Remember that, by default, Option Strict is Off inside the Macro IDE. You can turn it on either by adding an explicit Option Strict On statement at the top of the current source file or by enabling the Option Strict On By Default option on the Build page of the Properties window of the current macro project. Keep in mind, however, that the macro recorder assumes that Option Strict is Off, so be prepared to add a good amount of CType and DirectCast statements if you turn it on.

A macro can ask questions by means of message boxes and enable users to enter additional values by means of InputBox statements. The following macro guides the developer through the creation of a property procedure whose Set block can optionally check incoming values. You might use a code snippet for this specific task, but the macro approach is more versatile in that it lets the developer interactively decide whether specific portions of code should be included in the result:

```
Sub CreateProperty()
    Dim propName As String = InputBox("Enter the name of the property")
```

```
    If propName = "" Then Exit Sub
    Dim propType As String = InputBox("Enter the property type", , "String")
    If propType = "" Then Exit Sub
    Dim res As MsgBoxResult = MsgBox("Do you want to check incoming values?", _
        MsgBoxStyle.YesNo Or MsgBoxStyle.Question)
    Dim doCheck As String = (res = MsgBoxResult.Yes).ToString()
    CreateProperty(propName, propType, doCheck)
End Sub

' Macro with arguments
Sub CreateProperty(ByVal propName As String, Optional ByVal propType As String = "String", _
        Optional ByVal doCheck As String = "True")
    DTE.UndoContext.Open("CreateProperty " & propName)
    Dim varName As String = "m_" & propName
    Dim pattern As String = "Private {3} As {2}{0}{0}" _
        & "Public Property {1} As {2}{0}" _
        & "Get{0}Return {3}{0}End Get{0}Set(Byval value As {2}){0}"
    If CBool(doCheck) Then
        pattern &= "If value is Nothing Then{0}" _
            & "Throw New ArgumentException(){0}End If{0}"
    End If
    pattern &= "{3} = value{0}End Set{0}End Property{0}"
    Dim newText As String = String.Format(pattern, ControlChars.NewLine, _
        propName, propType, varName)
    DTE.ActiveDocument.Selection.Insert(newText)
    DTE.ExecuteCommand("Edit.FormatDocument")
    DTE.UndoContext.Close()
End Sub
```

(Note: the code produced by this macro must be manually edited if the property being generated is a value type because the comparison with Nothing fails in that case.)

As you see, you can use method overloading even with macros. The first version (without any arguments) asks the user for any value related to the task at hand; then it invokes the version that takes arguments. You might wonder why the latter version takes only string arguments and why the last two arguments are marked as optional. The reason for this arrangement will become apparent in the next section.

Only macros without arguments appear in the Macro Explorer window and can be assigned to a shortcut; thus, only the former macro can be invoked interactively from the Visual Studio IDE, short of invoking it from the Command window. (See next section.) For now, go back to the Visual Studio code editor, place the caret inside a type but outside any method, and then double-click the CreateProperty item in the Macro Explorer to check that everything works as expected.

Note You can debug a macro by setting a breakpoint on its first statement and double-clicking it in the Macro Explorer. There is also a way to test a macro from inside the Macro IDE: simply place the caret at the top of the macro procedure and press F5.

Using the Command Window

All the commands defined in Visual Studio can be executed by typing their name in the Command window. (See Figure 4-42.) If a command corresponds to a menu selection, its name usually reflects the path to the command; for example, the File.AddExistingProject command opens the Add Existing Project dialog box. Some commands can even take arguments and carry out the action without displaying any user interface; thus, for example, you can perform a case-sensitive search that uses a regular expression and that marks up all the found occurrences by using this command:

```
Edit.Find "As (Integer|String)" /markall /regex /case
```

The great thing about the Command window is that it supports IntelliSense, both for command names and for command options. To see the list of supported options, just type the forward slash (/).

Figure 4-42 The Command window

Command names are usually rather long, so typing them is tedious work even with help from IntelliSense. Fortunately, Visual Studio enables you to alias a command with a shorter name by means of the Alias command. Here's how you might alias the previous command with the name findintstr:

```
alias findintstr Edit.Find "As (Integer|String)" /markall /regex /case
```

Aliased names can include alphanumeric characters and symbols. For example, the ? is the default alias for the Debug.Print command, and in fact you can use the command ? to perform simple math operations in the Command window. You can list all the aliases currently assigned to Visual Studio commands by typing the Alias command without any argument.

Here's the scoop: all the macros you've created by recording your actions in the code editor or by editing text in the Macro IDE are first-class Visual Studio commands. For example, you can execute the CreateProperty macro in the ProgrammingVB2005Macros module by typing this string in the Command window:

```
Macros.MyMacros.ProgrammingVB2005Macros.CreateProperty
```

It makes sense to alias this long command into a simpler one, for example, crprop:

```
alias crprop Macros.MyMacros.ProgrammingVB2005Macros.CreateProperty
```

Unlike macros invoked from the Macro Explorer window or assigned to a keyboard shortcut, you can pass arguments to macros run from the Command window, provided that the macro takes only string arguments. This restriction explains the weird syntax I used when defining the second overload of the CreateProperty procedure in the previous section.Thanks to the alias you assigned to the CreateProperty macro, you can create a property procedure from inside the Command window by typing something like this:

```
crprop Quantity Integer True
```

Thanks to the optional arguments defined for the CreateProperty procedure, you can drop the third argument:

```
crprop Quantity Integer
```

In some cases, you can even drop the second argument because this argument defaults to "String":

```
crprop UserName
```

As you can see, by coupling commands, macros with arguments, and the ability to create shorter aliases, you can extend the power of Visual Studio almost infinitely.

One final note: you can execute any Visual Studio commands, both built-in commands and macro commands, from inside the Find combo box on the standard toolbar by typing a greater than sign (>) followed by the command name, as in:

```
>crprop UserName
```

Handling Macro Events

The code in a macro can even run without users explicitly launching it because a macro can react to events raised by the Visual Studio IDE. Each macro project has a module named EnvironmentEvents, where you can add the code that reacts to the IDE events. Open this module and use the combo boxes at the top of the editor window to browse all the IDE events. Visual Studio raises events for virtually any action that occurs in its IDE, including when a new solution, project, or source file is created, deleted, or renamed; when the project enters run mode, break mode, or design mode; when a window is opened, activated, moved, or closed; when the current selection changes; when a task is added to, modified, or removed from the Task List window.

 The IDE object model has been vastly improved in Visual Studio 2005, and its macros can trap more IDE events than those available in previous editions. The most important new events are the BeforeKeyPress and AfterKeyPress events exposed by the TextDocumentKeyPressEvents object. These events enable you to trap keys being pressed in the code editor so that you can discard or change them as you see fit. For example, the following macro automatically types a closing parenthesis, bracket, or brace when the user types the corresponding opening punctuation mark:

```
Private Sub TextDocumentKeyPressEvents_AfterKeyPress(ByVal Keypress As String, _
    ByVal Selection As EnvDTE.TextSelection, ByVal InStatementCompletion As Boolean) _
    Handles TextDocumentKeyPressEvents.AfterKeyPress
    ' If the key is among those we're looking for, replace the current selection
    ' with the close parenthesis, and then move the caret one position to the
    ' left so that it is left between the open and close parentheses.
    If Keypress = "(" Then
        Selection.Text = ")"
        Selection.CharLeft()
    ElseIf Keypress = "{" Then
        Selection.Text = "}"
        Selection.CharLeft()
    ElseIf Keypress = "[" Then
        Selection.Text = "]"
        Selection.CharLeft()
    End If
End Sub
```

A final note: you can't debug a macro event handler simply by setting a breakpoint in the Macro IDE and performing the action that causes the event to be raised (in the previous example, pressing a key in the code editor). For breakpoints to be recognized, you must run the macro project by pressing the F5 key, and then switch to the Visual Studio IDE and perform the action that raises the event.

Working with Macro Projects

Macro projects can be saved in two distinct formats: in binary format (the default, with the .vbmacros extension) or as Unicode text. The former format is usually preferable because the macro project loads faster, but the latter format is preferable if you need to edit the project with a standard text editor outside Visual Studio. When saving as Unicode text, the project is saved in a file with the .vsmproj extension and all the classes and modules that belong to the project are saved in separate files with the standard .vb extension in the same directory as the project file. You can also export individual classes and modules to Unicode by means of the Export command on the File menu of the Macro IDE without having to save the entire project as Unicode.

Oddly, you set the save format and the project path in the Macro Explorer window, not in the Macro IDE. Select the macro project, and then press F4 to display the Properties window. (See Figure 4-43.) The properties to be changed are Storage Format and Path, respectively. The Security property enables you to decide whether any event handler can execute when you load this project; in general, disabling event handlers for macro projects you receive from untrusted sources is a good idea. This option is also useful for disabling macro code in events that can prevent the Visual Studio IDE from working correctly.

Figure 4-43   Properties of a macro project

For better security you can prevent *all* macro projects from running. You can achieve this by clearing the Allow Macros To Run check box on the Add-in/Macros Security page under the Environment node in the Options dialog box.

Leveraging Macro Samples

Visual Studio 2005 comes with several useful macros already in the box. You can explore them by opening the Samples project that you find in the Macro Explorer, and of course you can study their source code in the Macro IDE. Some macros are just code examples, others perform tasks that are useful only in a few, specific cases; but several macros can really save you a lot of valuable time. These are my favorite ones:

- SaveView (in the Utilities module) asks for a name and saves the current window layout in a configuration with that name; LoadView reloads a window configuration with the name entered by the user. (These commands are so useful that they should be included on the Visual Studio standard toolbar.)

- TurnOnLineNumbers (in the Utilities module) enables line numbers in the code editor for all supported languages; TurnOffLineNumbers disables this feature.

- FillCommentParagraph (in the VSEditor module) reformats contiguous comment lines so that they aren't wider than a specified number of columns.

- InsertTime, InsertDate, and InsertTimeDate (in the VSEditor module) paste the current date and/or time in code; these are useful when you add a comment that states when a given piece of code was created or last edited.

- IncreaseTextEditorFontSize and DecreaseTextEditorFontSize (in the Accessibility module) change the size of the font used for the code editor.

I illustrate a few more macro examples in the section titled "Macros for Debugging" in Chapter 5, "Debugging Visual Basic Applications."

Chapter 5
Debugging Visual Basic Applications

The test and debug phase is a fundamental aspect of the job of writing software. Even if your application runs without any fatal exception, you can't consider it complete until you test and debug it thoroughly. I have divided this chapter into two portions: in the first part, I describe the many tools that Microsoft Visual Studio offers to help you in debugging your applications; in the second part, I focus on code techniques you can employ to ease testing and debugging by means of tracing and benchmarking statements.

Note   To avoid long lines, code samples in this chapter assume that the following Imports statements are used at the file or project level:

```
Imports System.Drawing
Imports System.IO
Imports System.Runtime.Serialization.Formatters.Binary
Imports System.Reflection
Imports System.Threading
Imports System.Windows.Forms
Imports Microsoft.VisualStudio.DebuggerVisualizers
```

Debugging Techniques

Microsoft Visual Studio 2005 offers many more debugging features than earlier versions do, but it's difficult to focus on the new features exclusively. For this reason, in this chapter I describe all the noteworthy features of Visual Studio, even though I spend a little more time on the brand-new ones.

Breakpoints and Tracepoints

To debug a portion of code, you typically set a breakpoint on one of its statements. You can set a breakpoint anywhere in your source code by placing the caret on a statement and pressing the F9 key, which corresponds to the Toggle Breakpoint command on the Debug menu, or simply by clicking in the gray margin area to the left of the code editor. In either case, a red circular icon appears in the left margin and the entire statement is painted with a red background. By repeating the same action you can delete an existing breakpoint. (You can also set a breakpoint by using the Ctrl+B shortcut, which opens the New Breakpoint dialog box.)

A standard breakpoint stops the application just before executing the statement where the breakpoint is placed, assuming that the program is running in Debug mode or, more precisely, in any build configuration that produces debug symbols. (If the compiler doesn't produce the .pdb file containing debug symbols, the debugger can't work correctly.) You can change this default behavior by right-clicking the red icon in the left margin and selecting one of the commands in the context menu that appears (see Figure 5-1).

Figure 5-1   All the commands that are available for a breakpoint

For example, you can temporarily disable an existing breakpoint if you want to ignore it but don't want to lose all its current settings; you can transform it into a conditional breakpoint, which stops the execution only if an expression becomes true or changes its value. The Hit Count menu command is especially useful when you debug loops because it enables you to specify that the breakpoint will be hit only when the hit count is equal to, is higher than, or is a multiple of an integer value that you specify. Finally, the Filter menu command lets you leverage a feature that is new in Visual Studio 2005: the ability to define per-thread and per-process breakpoints. (See Chapter 20, "Threads," for more details about debugging multi-threaded applications.)

Tracepoints

The When Hit command lets you create a *tracepoint*, a special breakpoint that can display a message in the Debug window or even execute a Visual Studio macro, but that doesn't necessarily suspend the execution (see Figure 5-2). As its name implies, a tracepoint is especially useful to create a log of the statements that the application executes and create a trace of all the methods invoked before the actual problem manifested. You can achieve the same effect with more traditional Debug.WriteLine statements, except tracepoints don't require that you edit the source code, can be combined with Boolean and hit count conditions, and can be disabled and enabled again with a single mouse click.

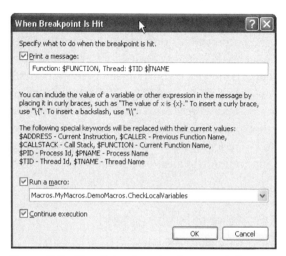

Figure 5-2 The dialog box that lets you define a tracepoint

The message displayed in the Debug window can include special placeholders that are replaced by specific values when the tracepoint is reached: $FUNCTION is the current method's name; $TID is the thread ID; $TNAME is the thread name; $PID is the process ID; $PNAME is the process name; $CALLER is the name of the method that called the current method; $CALLSTACK is the list of all the callers; $ADDRESS is the memory address of the native IL opcode where the breakpoint is located. You can include the value of one or more local variable and class fields by enclosing their names inside a pair of braces, and you can even access properties of an object, as in this message:

```
Total = {total}, Person name = {pers.LastName}. \{Called by $CALLER.\}
```

The backslash works as an escape character; therefore, you can use \{, \}, and \\ to insert an open brace, a close brace, and a backslash in the message, respectively.

Instead of, or in addition to, displaying a message, a tracepoint can execute a Visual Studio macro. To enable this feature, you simply ensure that the Run A Macro check box is selected and select a macro from the combo box below it. Only macros that take no parameters can be selected, so it looks like this feature isn't very useful. Fortunately, the code in the macro can learn virtually anything about the running program, including the value of a local variable, a class field, or a property:

```
' Insert this code in a macro referenced by a tracepoint.
Sub CheckLocalVariables()
    ' Retrieve the value of a local variable and a property.
    ' (These statements fail if no members named X or Name are accessible
    ' from the method in the main program where the tracepoint is defined.)
    Dim X As Integer = DTE.Debugger.GetExpression("X").Value
    Dim Name As String = DTE.Debugger.GetExpression("Name").Value
```

```
' Use the retrieved values here.
   ...
End Sub
```

A macro can determine the location of the tracepoint from which it was invoked by means of the DTE.Debugger.CurrentStackFrame property. This property returns an EnvDTE.Stack-Frame object that exposes properties such as Language ("Basic" for Visual Basic applications), Module (the path of the executable being debugged), FunctionName (the name of the current method, including the name of the enclosing type), ReturnType (a string describing the type of the value returned by the method, or "void" if it's a Sub procedure), Arguments (the collection of arguments passed to the method), and Locals (the collection of all the local variables and arguments defined in the method). Here's a macro that uses these properties to prepare a detailed report of the state of the application when the tracepoint was encountered:

```
' Insert this code in a macro referenced by a tracepoint.
Sub DumpMethodValues()
   Dim frame As EnvDTE.StackFrame = DTE.Debugger.CurrentStackFrame
   ' Display name of current method.
   Debug.WriteLine("Method: " & frame.FunctionName & " [returns" & frame.ReturnType & "]")
   ' Display values of arguments and local variables.
   For Each expr As EnvDTE.Expression In frame.Locals
      Debug.WriteLine("   " & expr.Name & " = " & expr.Value)
   Next
End Sub
```

Notice that the previous macro displays its results in the Output window of the Macro IDE, not the Output window of the main Visual Studio 2005 environment. In a real-world implementation, you might prefer to output the result to a log file.

The Breakpoints Window

You can view and operate over all the breakpoints in your solution by means of the Breakpoints window, which you can open by using the Ctrl+Alt+B shortcut or by selecting the Breakpoints command on the Windows submenu of the Debug menu (see Figure 5-3). You can disable a given breakpoint by clearing the check box in the leftmost column and changing all the breakpoint properties (or delete the breakpoint itself) by right-clicking the corresponding item in this window. Also, buttons on the window's toolbar let you disable or delete all existing breakpoints and define which information is displayed in the window.

Figure 5-3   The Breakpoints dockable window

Single Stepping

When you are in break mode, the statement that is about to execute (the "next" statement) is highlighted with a yellow background, at least in the default Visual Studio color scheme. You can execute one single statement or small block of statements at a time by using one of the following commands from the Debug window or the code editor's context menu:

- **Step Into (F11)**   Executes the next statement; if the statement is a method call, it steps into the called method.

- **Step Over (F10)**   Executes the next statement; if the statement is a method call, it executes the entire method without stepping into it.

- **Step Out (Shift+F11)**   Executes all the statements that follow the current statement until the current method is exited.

- **Run To Cursor (Ctrl+F10)**   Executes all the statements that follow the current statement until execution hits the statement where the caret is (or the statement that you've right-clicked, if you selected the Run To Cursor command from the context menu).

- **Set Next Statement**   Makes the statement where the caret is (or the statement you've right-clicked if you've selected this command from the context menu) the first statement that will be executed when you restart execution by pressing F5 or by using one of the single-stepping commands. You can also set the next statement by clicking the yellow arrow that marks the current statement and dragging it elsewhere in the same method.

- **Show Next Statement**   Brings the next statement into view. You can press the asterisk (*) key on the numeric keypad while holding down the Alt key to run this command.

Edit and Continue

The first new Visual Studio 2005 feature isn't really a new feature, at least for developers who have worked with Microsoft Visual Basic 6. I am talking about edit and continue, that is, the ability to modify code while in break mode and restart the debugging session from there.

As is the case under Visual Basic 6, Visual Studio 2005 doesn't accept all type of edits while in break mode. More specifically, you can add or remove statements in the current method or in other methods, but you can't declare new fields, add or remove methods, or change the signature of an existing class member. If you make a change that prevents Visual Studio from restarting, your code is highlighted with a purple wavy underline and a task is displayed in the Task List. When this happens, you must terminate and restart the application if you want to retain your code edits.

You can enable or disable the edit-and-continue feature and define its exact behavior by choosing from the many options on the Edit And Continue page under the Debugging node in the Options dialog box.

Just My Code Debugging

Just My Code debugging is a new Visual Studio 2005 feature that enables you to focus on code that you've written and ignore other code, for example, system calls or code that was generated automatically by Visual Studio. This is what you usually want to do, especially if you don't want to be involved in low-level native code debugging. A feature similar to Just My Code debugging was available in previous editions of Visual Studio, but the 2005 edition offers more control of this feature because you can also use attributes to define which methods in your code should be excluded from debugging. The Just My Code feature is affected by three attributes from the System.Diagnostics namespace.

- **DebuggerNonUserCode attribute**   Tells the debugger that the method or the type it is applied to shouldn't be considered as "my code" and should be stepped over during debugging.

```
<DebuggerNonUserCode()> _
Public Class Fraction
   ' No member in this class can be debugged.
   …
End Class
```

- **DebuggerHidden attribute**   Tells the debugger that a code member should never be debugged, regardless of whether the Enable Just My Code option (on the General page under the Debugging node of the Options dialog box) is turned off. You can apply this attribute only to methods, not to types.

```
<DebuggerHidden()> _
Public Sub PerformTask()
   ' This method can't be debugged, even if Just My Code debugging is off.
   …
End Sub
```

- **DebuggerStepThrough attribute**   Tells the debugger to step through, rather than into, the code it is applied to. This attribute is used for the InitializeComponent method in forms.

Windows for Debugging

Visual Studio offers as many as four different types of dockable tool windows (and one modal window) that you can use to display the value of fields and local variable values. You can open these windows by means of commands on the Windows submenu of the Debug menu or by typing the shortcut that appears to the right of the window name in the following list. (Notice that the shortcut for the first three windows requires two distinct key presses.)

- **Locals window (Ctrl+Alt+V, L)**   This window displays all the local variables defined in the current method. You can edit the value of a variable by double-clicking it or by selecting the Edit Value command from the context menu. (See Figure 5-4.) You can expand object values and show their properties by clicking the plus sign (+). The Hexadecimal

Display command on the context menu turns on and off hexadecimal display of values. (This command affects all the windows illustrated in this section.)

- **Autos window (Ctrl+Alt+V, A)**   This window displays all the variables used in the current statement, in the three statements preceding the current statement, and the three statements following the current statement. You can double-click an item to change its value, as you can for the Locals window.

- **Watch window (Ctrl+Alt+W, 1)**   You can add any scalar or object variable to this window by right-clicking its name and selecting the Add Watch command from the context menu, or more simply by dragging the variable from the code editor into the Watch window. There are four Watch windows, so you can keep four different sets of variables under control. You can display a variable in a Watch window other than the first Watch window by dragging the variable name from the code editor into the Watch window or by double-clicking the last (empty) line of the Watch window and typing the variable's name. You can even enter an expression such as **number+1** or **name.Length**.

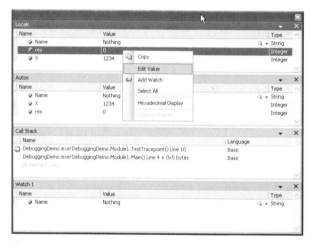

Figure 5-4   The Locals, Autos, Call Stack, and Watch tool windows

- **Call Stack window (Ctrl+Alt+C)**   This window lets you have a look at all the procedures that called the one that contains the next statement to be executed. By right-clicking each element in this window, you display a context menu that lets you set a breakpoint on the corresponding source code statement, or you can issue a Run To Cursor command. Other options on the context menu let you decide which information must be shown in the Call Stack window.

- **QuickWatch window (Shift+F9)**   This window displays the value of the scalar variable (or all the properties of the object variable) the cursor was on when you selected the QuickWatch command from the editor's context menu or used the Shift+F9 shortcut. If a property is itself an object, you can expand it as you can do in the Watch window. Unlike the previous windows, however, the QuickWatch window is modal and you have to close it to continue your debugging session.

- **Command window (Ctrl+Alt+A)**   You can display the value of a variable or an expression in the Command window by prefixing it with a question mark (?). When applied to an object variable, the ? command displays all the properties of that object.

A new feature of Visual Studio 2005 is the ability to test functions from within the Command window at design time without having to run your application. Just keep in mind that you can test only functions (but not Sub methods) in modules and that you must prefix the function name with the question mark (?), as in this code:

```
? Calculate(12, 34)
```

Data Tips and Visualizers

One of the problems that makes debugging under Microsoft Visual Studio .NET 2003 and earlier versions more difficult than it should be is the high number of open windows you need to keep the value of key variables under control. Although the Locals, Auto, and Watch windows are still available under Visual Studio 2005, a new feature is likely to quickly win the developer's heart: data tips.

Data Tips Basics

When the application is in break mode, you can display the value of a variable just by hovering the pointer on it, as you do under Visual Studio .NET 2003. The new release, however, adds the ability to browse all the public and private properties of any object (and its child objects, too). This is a great bonus when you're debugging code that works with objects other than primitive types such as numbers and strings (see Figure 5-5).

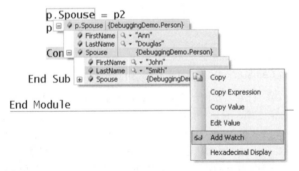

Figure 5-5   A data tip window

If the data tip is displaying an object, you can display its fields and properties by simply moving the pointer over the + symbol (no clicks are necessary); you can then collapse a node by clicking the minus sign (–) or moving the cursor away from it. If there are more than 15 items, a scroll bar appears to the right: you can scroll through the data tip window by pressing the Page Up/Page Down keys, by using the mouse wheel, or by moving the pointer over the scroll bar arrows (again, no clicks are necessary).

Unlike earlier editions of Visual Studio, a Visual Studio 2005 data tip even enables you to edit the value of a variable or an object's property by clicking a value and typing its new value, and then pressing the Enter key (or the Esc key to cancel the edit). Or you can select the Edit Value command from the data tip's context menu. Regardless of the method you adopt, the new value is immediately applied and all other debug windows are updated. Other commands in the context menu enable you to copy the value or the entire expression, display numbers as hexadecimal values, and add an item to the Watch window directly.

Here's a nice undocumented feature of the data tip window: you can make the window temporarily transparent and see the code beneath it by keeping the Ctrl key pressed.

Customizing the Data Tip Window with the DebuggerDisplay Attribute

Visual Basic gives you some degree of control over how an object is displayed in a data tip, at least for objects instantiated from a type you've defined. The customization mechanism is based on the DebuggerDisplay attribute in the System.Diagnostics namespace. You apply this attribute at the class level, and pass it a string argument that can contain property and field names enclosed in braces, as in the following code:

```
<DebuggerDisplay("Value = {Numerator} / {Denominator}")> _
Public Class Fraction
    Private m_Numerator As Integer
    Private m_Denominator As Integer

    Public Property Numerator() As Integer
        Get
            Return m_Numerator
        End Get
        Set(ByVal value As Integer)
            m_Denominator = value
        End Set
    End Property

    Public Property Denominator() As Integer
        Get
            Return m_Denominator
        End Get
        Set(ByVal value As Integer)
            m_Denominator = value
        End Set
    End Property
End Class
```

Interestingly, this attribute also affects the way an object is rendered in the Watch window.

Note   Microsoft .NET Framework version 2.0 also defines the DebuggerBrowsable attribute, which is meant to control whether a member is displayed in the data tip. C# 2.0 supports this attribute, but Visual Basic 2005 doesn't.

Visualizers

Another new great debugging feature in Visual Studio 2005 is the ability to display complex data in a custom way. For example, say that you have a string variable holding XML code: wouldn't it be cool if you could display this string in hierarchical format? This is exactly what visualizers do.

When a string value appears in a data tip window (or in another window that displays member values, such as the Watch, Locals, and Auto windows), a magnifying lens icon appears to the right of the value. If you click this icon, you can select one of the following visualizers: Text Visualizer, XML Visualizer, and HTML Visualizer (see Figure 5-6). The Text Visualizer doesn't change the way the string is displayed, but is quite handy for long string values and even supports word wrapping. You can't modify a value through a visualizer defined for the String type, though.

The great thing about visualizers is that you can even create your own visualizer with relatively little effort.

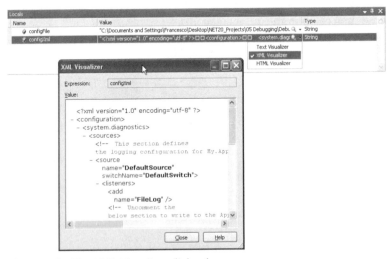

Figure 5-6   The XML Visualizer dialog box

Writing a Custom Visualizer

Writing a custom visualizer is very simple, even though it requires that you follow a series of steps carefully. In this section, I explain how to create an additional visualizer for the String object, which interprets a string as a filename and enables you to browse the file's properties and textual contents.

First, create a new Class Library project, call it Visualizers (or whatever you like), rename the default Class1.vb file to FileVisualizer.vb, and type the following code in the renamed source file:

```
Imports Microsoft.VisualStudio.DebuggerVisualizers
```

```
<Assembly: DebuggerVisualizer(GetType(FileVisualizer), GetType(VisualizerObjectSource), _
    Target:=GetType(String), Description:="File visualizer")>
```

```
Public Class FileVisualizer
   Inherits DialogDebuggerVisualizer

   Protected Overrides Sub Show(ByVal windowService As IDialogVisualizerService, _
         ByVal objectProvider As IVisualizerObjectProvider)
      Dim obj As Object = objectProvider.GetObject()

      ' Display the file in the form. (See the book's companion code for
      ' the complete source code of the FileVisualizerForm type.)
      Dim frm As New FileVisualizerForm()
      frm.FileName = obj.ToString()
      frm.ShowDialog()
   End Sub

   ' Static method to test the visualizer
   Public Shared Sub Test(ByVal obj As Object)
      Dim host As New VisualizerDevelopmentHost(obj, GetType(FileVisualizer))
      host.ShowVisualizer()
   End Sub
End Class
```

Three points are worth noticing here:

- All visualizers use types defined in the Microsoft.VisualStudio.DebuggerVisualizers DLL; therefore, you must add a reference to this assembly for this code to compile correctly.

- You need an assembly-level DebuggerVisualizer attribute that informs Visual Studio that this DLL contains a visualizer for the String type and specifies its description. The second (mandatory) argument for this attribute is usually GetType(VisualizerObjectSource), but in some cases you must write your own visualizer object source type. (More on this shortly.)

- The visualizer type (FileVisualizer, in this case) inherits from the DialogDebuggerVisualizer type and overrides the Show method. This method receives an IVisualizerObjectProvider argument; by invoking the GetObject method of this argument you can get a reference to the object to be visualized.

For your convenience, a visualizer type can also expose a static Test method, which enables you to test the visualizer before installing it. For example, to test the FileVisualizer, create a console application, add a reference to the Visualizers.dll, and run this code:

```
Dim filename As String = "C:\Windows\win.ini"   ' (Or any file you like)
Visualizers.FileVisualizer.Test(filename)
```

The code in the Show method assigns the string to the FileName property exposed by the FileVisualizerForm class. This form uses this property to create a FileInfo object and display its properties and contents. (See Figure 5-7.) The code inside the form itself doesn't pose any special challenge, and thus I omit it here for brevity, but you can browse it in the companion code for this book.

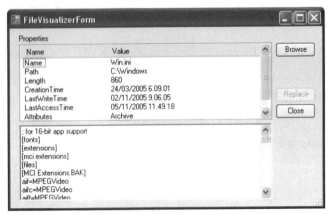

Figure 5-7   The custom file visualizer displays a file's properties and contents and even enables you to browse other files.

As the last step in installing the visualizer, you must copy the visualizer.dll file in a special directory for Visual Studio to recognize it. You have two options:

- Copy the DLL to the C:\Documents and Settings*username*\My Documents\Visual Studio 2005\Visualizers directory to make the visualizer available to a specific user.

- Copy the DLL to the C:\Program Files\Microsoft Visual Studio 8\Common7\Packages\ Debugger\Visualizers directory to make the visualizer available to all users.

Here's a tip: use a postbuild event to copy the latest version of the visualizer DLL to the selected directory automatically at the end of every successful compilation. For example, this is the command for making the visualizer available to all users:

```
CMD /k COPY "$(TargetPath)"
    "C:\Program Files\Microsoft Visual Studio 8\Common7\Packages\Debugger\Visualizers"
```

Interestingly, you don't need to reboot Visual Studio to have it realize that new visualizers are available.

In most cases, a visualizer can even *replace* the object being visualized with a different instance. Unfortunately, you can't replace a string or a StringBuilder value, but this ability is available with most other types. For example, you can easily improve the FileVisualizer class to visualize FileInfo objects in addition to string values. (Additions are in bold type.)

```
<Assembly: DebuggerVisualizer(GetType(FileVisualizer), GetType(VisualizerObjectSource), _
    Target:=GetType(String), Description:="File visualizer")>
<Assembly: DebuggerVisualizer(GetType(FileVisualizer), GetType(VisualizerObjectSource), _
    Target:=GetType(FileInfo), Description:="FileInfo visualizer")>


Public Class FileVisualizer
  Inherits DialogDebuggerVisualizer

  Protected Overrides Sub Show(ByVal windowService As IDialogVisualizerService, _
      ByVal objectProvider As IVisualizerObjectProvider)
    Dim obj As Object = objectProvider.GetObject()
```

```
        ' Display the file in the form.
        Dim frm As New FileVisualizerForm
        If TypeOf obj Is String Then
            ' This is a string containing a filename.
            frm.FileName = obj.ToString()
            frm.ShowDialog()
        ElseIf TypeOf obj Is FileInfo Then
            frm.FileName = DirectCast(obj, FileInfo).FullName
            If frm.ShowDialog() = Windows.Forms.DialogResult.OK Then
                ' Replace the FileInfo if user clicked the Replace button.
                Dim newFileInfo As New FileInfo(frm.FileName)
                objectProvider.ReplaceObject(newFileInfo)
            End If
        End If
    End Sub
    ...
End Class
```

As you can see, replacing an object is just a matter of calling the ReplaceObject method of the IVisualizerObjectProvider argument passed to the Show method.

The last detail you need to learn before you can create full-featured visualizers is how you can deal with complex objects that need to be marshaled (that is, transferred) from the project being debugged to your visualizer class. For more complex objects, you can't simply grab the object reference passed to you by Visual Studio and display its properties because these properties are actually pointers to internal structures that aren't marshaled with the object.

For example, let's say that you are writing a visualizer for the System.Drawing.Image type. By using the default VisualizerObjectSource type, Visual Studio knows how to marshal most properties of the Bitmap object, but not the actual pixels that make up the image. Therefore, you need a custom visualizer object source object that does the marshaling manually. Such a custom visualizer is a type that inherits from VisualizerObjectSource and redefines its GetData method:

```
Public Class VisualizerImageSource
    Inherits VisualizerObjectSource

    Public Overrides Sub GetData(ByVal target As Object, ByVal outgoingData As Stream)
        Dim bf As New BinaryFormatter
        bf.Serialize(outgoingData, target)
    End Sub
End Class
```

You can now specify your VisualizerImageSource class in the DebuggerVisualizer attribute that decorates the actual visualizer class.

```
<Assembly: DebuggerVisualizer(GetType(ImageVisualizer), GetType(VisualizerImageSource), _
    Target:=GetType(Image), Description:="Image visualizer")>

Public Class ImageVisualizer
    Inherits DialogDebuggerVisualizer

    Protected Overrides Sub Show(ByVal windowService As IDialogVisualizerService, _
        ByVal objectProvider As IVisualizerObjectProvider)
```

```
        ' Retrieve the object to be visualized; exit if wrong type.
        Dim img As Image = TryCast(objectProvider.GetObject(), Image)
        If img Is Nothing Then Return
        ' Display the image in the form.
        Dim frm As New ImageVisualizerForm
        frm.VisibleImage = img
        If frm.ShowDialog() = Windows.Forms.DialogResult.OK Then
            ' Replace the original value if the user selected a different image.
            objectProvider.ReplaceObject(frm.VisibleImage)
        End If
    End Sub
End Class
```

Figure 5-8 displays the custom image visualizer. As usual, you can browse the complete project in this book's companion code.

Figure 5-8   The custom image visualizer, which lets you copy and paste the image, select a different image from disk, and return a different bitmap object to the project being debugged

Dealing with Exceptions

The most evident symptom that your program isn't working correctly is that it throws more exceptions than you expect. But even if the application doesn't throw any exceptions, you can't really be too relaxed because an exception thrown by a procedure might be caught and hidden by another method up in the call stack. It is therefore essential that you learn how to deal with exceptions correctly from inside Visual Studio.

The Exceptions Dialog Box

The Visual Studio debugger offers complete control over what happens when an application throws an exception or calls a .NET method that throws an exception. You set all the relevant options from inside the Exceptions dialog box (see Figure 5-9), which you open by selecting Exceptions on the Debug menu or by using the Ctrl+Alt+E shortcut. This dialog box lists all the exception types defined in the .NET Framework CLR grouped by their namespace, together with other exceptions that Visual Basic developers won't see often, such as Win32 exceptions and Native Run-Time Checks. In most cases, you apply your decision to the Common Language Runtime Exceptions node so that your settings are valid for all the .NET exceptions. If necessary, however, you can establish a distinct behavior for each namespace or individual exception type. Unfortunately, you can't set the breaking behavior for all the exceptions that derive from a given base exception type (an option that would probably be more useful).

For each exception or group of exceptions, you can decide whether to break when the exception is thrown or when the exception isn't handled by a suitable Catch block. Activating the debugger for exceptions as soon as they are thrown, even if the application is going to handle them, can be useful to debug the error handlers in your code or to catch exceptions that would go unnoticed otherwise. For example, you can activate this option if a procedure performs much too slowly and you suspect that the reason is the high number of exceptions it has to deal with. When the debugger catches one such exception, the error message specifies that it is a *first-chance exception.*

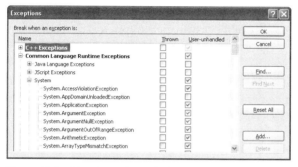

Figure 5-9   The Exceptions dialog box

The Exception Assistant Dialog Box

When an exception occurs, Visual Studio 2005 displays the Exception Assistant dialog box, which describes the problem and offers a solution if possible. (See Figure 5-10.) This dialog box lets you edit the offending line, display more details on the exception and copy these details to the Clipboard, and search for more help online. If you decide to edit the source code or close the dialog box for some other reason, you can open it again by using the Shift+Alt+F10 shortcut or in break mode by clicking the smart tag that appears on the statement that caused the exception.

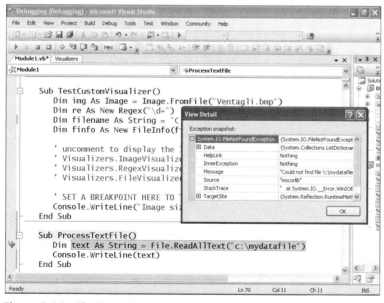

Figure 5-10   The Exception Assistant dialog box

The Exception Assistant feature is a great help during debug and test sessions, but you can disable it by displaying the Options dialog box (from the Tools menu) and clearing the Use The Exception Assistant option on the General page under the Debugging node.

Exception-Related Performance Counters

You can recall from Chapter 3, "Control Flow and Error Handling," that the more exceptions your code throws, the slower the application runs, so you should avoid throwing exceptions unnecessarily. A common problem, however, is that in some cases your code might be throwing exceptions without you being aware of it because the exception is caught and handled by a Try...Catch statement. You can diagnose this problem by having Visual Studio catch first-chance exceptions, as I explained earlier, but trapping each and every exception doesn't give you the big picture about how frequently these exceptions are thrown. In such circumstances, you might wish to use the operating system Performance utility to monitor a few performance counters that the CLR updates when an exception occurs.

Run the Performance utility from the Administrative Tools menu (which you can reach from the Start menu), press Ctrl+E (or click the leftmost button on the toolbar) to create a new counter set, and then press Ctrl+I (or click the plus-shaped button) to add counters to the set (see Figure 5-11). In the dialog box that appears, select the .NET CLR Exceptions performance object, select one or more applications in the rightmost list (or use _Globals to monitor all .NET applications currently running), and then select the following items in the leftmost list:

- # Of Exceps Thrown (the total number of exceptions thrown since the start of the application)

- # Of Exceps Thrown / Sec (the number of exceptions thrown per second)

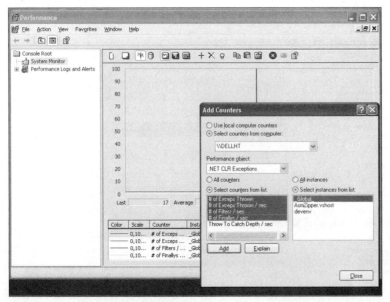

Figure 5-11   The Performance tool

Finally, click the Add button to start the monitoring and run your application as usual. If you see these counters going high, you might have found a spot where your application throws (and catches) exceptions: these are the operations you should analyze more closely to solve your performance issues.

Tracing and Benchmarking

The Visual Studio integrated debugging features are powerful enough to help you find and fix most bugs and logic errors, but in some cases you need to insert tracing statements in your code to understand why the application is misbehaving. This is especially useful when the problems occur only in compiled applications already deployed at your customer's site. The .NET Framework offers three classes that simplify this task, the Debug, Trace, and Trace-Source classes, all of which reside in the System.Diagnostics namespace. This namespace is imported at the project level by all Visual Basic projects, so you don't need to specify the complete class names in your code.

The Debug and Trace Classes

The Debug and Trace classes expose methods for sending a message to the Output window in Visual Studio or to another output device. These classes are singleton types and all their methods are static. (See the section titled "Shared Methods" in Chapter 6, "Class Fundamentals," for a description of singleton types.) Both these statements display a string in the Output window in Visual Studio:

```
Debug.WriteLine("Program has started")
Trace.WriteLine("Program has started")
```

The Write method works similarly except that it doesn't append a newline character:

```
Debug.Write("These two strings ")
Debug.WriteLine("appear on the same line.")
```

 NET Framework 2.0 adds the support for format placeholders in the message being output with the new Debug.Print method:

```
Debug.Print("Name={0}, Weight={1:N2}", "Joe", 123.4)
   ' => Name=Joe, Weight=123.40  (followed by a newline character)
```

The Debug and Trace classes are identical and expose the same methods. The only difference between them is that calls to methods of the Debug class are included in the compiled application only if the DEBUG compilation constant is defined, whereas calls to methods of the Trace class are included only if the TRACE compilation constant is defined. By default, the Debug project configuration defines both these compilation constants, whereas the Release project configuration defines only the TRACE constant. Thus, by default, output from the Trace class is included in all compiled applications, whereas output from the Debug class is discarded in applications compiled in Release mode. Thanks to this arrangement, you can include or exclude Debug messages simply by making a different solution configuration active.

The Debug and Trace classes offer many ways to control how trace messages are sent to the Output window. For example, the WriteIf and WriteLineIf methods emit the trace string only if the expression passed to the first argument is True:

```
Debug.WriteLineIf(x < 0, "Warning: x is negative")
```

The Fail method stops the application and displays a message box that lets the user abort the program, debug it, or just ignore the error. (See Figure 5-12.)

```
' You can specify a message and a detailed message.
Trace.Fail("An error has occurred", "File app.ini not found")
```

Figure 5-12   The effect of a Trace.Fail method

The Assert method is similar to Fail, with a few key differences. First, it displays the message box only if its first argument is False:

```
' You can omit the detailed message or both messages.
Trace.Assert(obj IsNot Nothing, "Unable to continue", "obj is Nothing")
```

Second, and more important, you can use a configuration file to control whether the message box is displayed and even specify a text log file that must receive all error messages. I explain .NET configuration files in detail in Chapter 17, "Assemblies and Resources"; for now let's see how you can disable message boxes coming from Assert methods and redirect them to a text file.

Select the Add New Item command from the Project menu, select the Application Configuration File element from the gallery of available items, and name the file being created app.config. Visual Studio creates an XML file that already contains some useful entries; for the task I'm discussing here, though, you should delete the contents that Visual Studio has created for you and type this text instead:

```
<configuration>
   <system.diagnostics>
      <trace autoflush="false" indentsize="3" />
      <assert assertuienabled="false" logfilename=".\ErrorLog.txt"/>
   </system.diagnostics>
</configuration>
```

When you build the current project, Visual Studio copies this configuration file to the directory with the application executable, renames the file to match the name of the EXE file, and adds the .config extension so that .NET recognizes it as the configuration file for the application. (For example, it creates a file named MyApp.exe.config for the MyApp.exe application.)

You can now run the executable again and you'll see no message boxes on the screen because all Assert messages are logged to the ErrorLog.txt file. The autoflush attribute should be false when the application is outputting to a file, so the output isn't flushed to the file at each Assert method. You can also control this feature through code by using the AutoFlush property of the Debug or Trace class.

You can control the indentation level of the output by means of the Indent and Unindent methods. These methods help you make clear how your routines are nested:

```
Sub MyProc()
    Debug.WriteLine("Entering MyProc")
    Debug.Indent()
    Debug.WriteLine("Inside MyProc")
    Debug.Unindent()
    Debug.WriteLine("Exiting MyProc")
End Sub
```

The preceding debugging code produces this output:

```
Entering MyProc
    Inside MyProc
Exiting MyProc
```

You can control the number of spaces in the indentation by means of the IndentSize property or with the indentsize attribute in the configuration file. The Debug and Trace classes have several other intriguing features, such as the ability to support trace switches and listeners that let you affect trace behavior simply by changing a few entries in the application's configuration file.

You might wonder where the output from the Trace type goes when the project isn't running under a debugger. The easiest way to display these messages is to run a utility that can display strings passed to the OutputDebugString Windows API function (the function that both the Debug and Trace classes invoke behind the scenes), for example, Mark Russinovich's Debug-View, which you can download from *http://www.sysinternals.com*. Among its many great features, DebugView is also able to gather trace information from any computer on the LAN. (See Figure 5-13.)

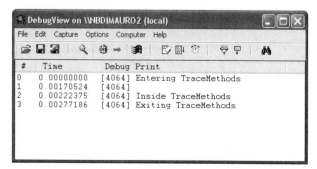

Figure 5-13   The DebugView utility from *http://www.sysinternals.com*

Trace Switches

You don't always need to generate trace information when your application is running and, even if you do, you don't usually want to keep track of all possible events that have happened during your application's lifetime. For example, you might want to record serious errors always, but you'd like to generate informative messages only if your customers complain about how the application behaves.

The .NET Framework also offers a couple of classes that help you in limiting the number of messages sent to the trace device. The BooleanSwitch class can be used when the trace message should be either sent or not sent, in a yes-or-no fashion. The TraceSwitch class allows more granular control over how messages are output by defining the following five tracing levels: Off (0, no messages), Error (1, only serious error messages), Warning (2, warnings and error messages), Info (3, informational messages, warnings, and error messages), Verbose (4, all messages).

You can create trace switches near the beginning of your application. Their constructor takes a display name, a description string, and an optional initial value:

```
' Create a BooleanSwitch, set its Enabled property set to "1" (enabled).
Dim bsProfile As New BooleanSwitch("bsProfile", _
    "Define whether profile information is displayed", "1")
' Create a TraceSwitch, set its Level property set to "2" (warnings).
Dim tsDiagnostic As New TraceSwitch("tsDiagnostic", _
    "Set the threshold level for visible diagnostic messages")
```

Even if you can assign an initial value to a BooleanSwitch or TraceSwitch object in code, the whole purpose of using these switches is the ability to define these values in the application's configuration file so that the user (possibly guided by your technical support team) can modify them before restarting the program, without your having to recompile the application. To set the values, you just have to add one or more entries in the <switches> section, as the following example illustrates:

```
<configuration>
  <system.diagnostics>
    <switches>
      <!-- Enable/disable profiling messages(0=disable, 1=enable) -->
      <add name="bsProfile" value="1"/>
      <!-- Set the threadshold for diagnostic messages
          (0=none, 1=errors, 2=warnings, 3=info, 4=verbose) -->
      <add name="tsDiagnostic" value="4" />
    </switches>
  </system.diagnostics>
</configuration>
```

The comments before each <add> section are optional, but they can be handy for letting users know how to achieve a given behavior. The values in the configuration file are read when the trace switch object is created, and it is mandatory that the first argument in the constructor matches the name attribute in the configuration file. When using a configuration file, you should refrain from assigning the Enabled and Level properties in code because you would overwrite the settings found in the file.

Once you've successfully initialized a trace switch, you can use it to make decisions related to tracing. Typically, you will use the BooleanSwitch Enabled property in the first argument of a WriteIf or WriteLineIf method of the Debug or Trace class, but you can also use it in If statements to include or exclude a block of code:

```
' Display this information only if level is verbose enough.
Trace.WriteLineIf(tsDiagnostic.Level >= 3, "Starting the application at "  & Now.ToString())

If bsProfile.Enabled Then
   ' Add code for benchmarking here.
   ...
End If
```

The simplest way to use a TraceSwitch in a WriteIf or WriteLineIf method is by making use of its TraceError, TraceWarning, TraceInfo, and TraceVerbose properties, which return True if the switch's Level property allows the output of the corresponding type of messages:

```
' Display this message only if warnings are allowed.
Trace.WriteLineIf(tsDiagnostic.TraceWarning, "INI file not found. Using default values.")
```

Trace Listeners

The feature of the Debug and Trace classes that makes them superior to custom trace techniques is their ability to add trace listeners to their output. (This ability is also exposed by the TraceSource type, which I'll address shortly.) The mechanism is simple and powerful: the Listeners property holds a collection of listener objects that are notified whenever the application emits a trace message. You can send the trace output virtually anywhere by adding new elements to the Listeners collection. For example, you might define a custom listener class that sends your tech support an e-mail when something catastrophic occurs. All versions of the .NET Framework ship with the following listener classes:

- **DefaultTraceListener**   Sends output to the Output window or any debugger able to trap strings sent by the OutputDebugString Windows API function. This listener is added by default to the Listeners collection, so you don't have to do anything special to use it. (You can use the Listeners.Clear method to remove it.)

- **TextWriterTraceListener**   Can send its output to any .NET stream. (Streams are described in Chapter 15, "Files, Directories, and Streams.")

- **EventLogTraceListener**   Sends its output to the system log.

The following listeners have been added in .NET Framework 2.0:

- **ConsoleTraceListener**   Sends its output to the console window, to either the standard output stream or the standard error stream, depending on whether you pass False or True to its constructor.

- **DelimitedListTraceListener**   Inherits from and behaves like TextWriterTraceListener, except it uses a delimiter character to separate the trace items in each line of text. (The default delimiter is the semicolon character.)

- **XmlWriterTextListener**   Inherits from TextWriterTraceListener but outputs its data as XML text.

- **FileLogTraceListener**   Sends its output to a log file. (Unlike all other listener types, the FileLogTraceListener belongs to the Microsoft.VisualBasic namespace.)

The following example shows how you can add one or more elements to the Listeners collection to achieve a variety of results:

```
' Send trace output to the console window standard output stream.
Trace.Listeners.Add(New ConsoleTraceListener(False))

' Send trace output to a text file.
Dim sw As New StreamWriter("trace.txt")
Trace.Listeners.Add(New TextWriterTraceListener(sw))
…
' Close the stream before exiting the program.
sw.Close()

' Send trace output to the Application log on the local machine,
' using a source named TracingDemo.
Dim ev As New EventLog("Application", ".", "TracingDemo")
Trace.Listeners.Add(New EventLogTraceListener("TracingDemo"))
…
' Close the event log before exiting the program.
ev.Close()
```

As it happens with trace switches, you typically initialize listeners through configuration files, rather than in code. Here's an example that shows how you can send trace output to a text file and to the console window. (Note that you must set the autoflush attribute to True when outputting to files.)

```
<configuration>
  <system.diagnostics>
    <trace autoflush="true" indentsize="4">
      <listeners>
        <add name="FileListener" initializeData=".\trace.txt"
            type="System.Diagnostics.TextWriterTraceListener" />
        <add name="ConsoleListener"
            type="System.Diagnostics.ConsoleTraceListener" />
      </listeners>
    </trace>
  </system.diagnostics>
</configuration>
```

The TraceListener class has been expanded in .NET Framework 2.0 with several new members, which have been inherited by all the trace listener types. First and foremost, you can now send a message to the trace channel by means of the new TraceError, TraceWarning, and TraceInformation methods and use the TraceOutputOptions bit-coded property to automatically include system- or process-related information in the output message, such as date and time, time stamp, thread ID, process ID, and the contents of the call stack:

```
Dim listener As New ConsoleTraceListener()
listener.TraceOutputOptions = TraceOptions.DateTime Or TraceOptions.ProcessId
Trace.Listeners.Add(listener)
Trace.TraceInformation("Application ended")
```

Another important new feature is the ability to create trace filters. A *trace filter* is a class that inherits from the System.Diagnostics.TraceFilter abstract class and overrides its ShouldTrace method to decide whether a given message should be traced or not. For example, consider this custom class that displays only trace messages output from a specific thread:

```
Public Class TraceFilterByThreadID
   Inherits TraceFilter

   Dim threadId As Integer

   Sub New(ByVal threadId As Integer)
     ' Remember the thread ID passed to the constructor.
     Me.threadId = threadId
   End Sub

   Public Overrides Function ShouldTrace(ByVal cache As TraceEventCache, _
      ByVal source As String, ByVal eventType As  TraceEventType, ByVal id As Integer, _
      ByVal formatOrMessage As String, ByVal args() As Object, ByVal data1 As Object, _
      ByVal data() As Object) As Boolean
      ' Return true only if thread ID is the one passed to the constructor.
      Return (cache.ThreadId = Me.threadId)
   End Function
End Class
```

Here's how you can use this class to display only trace messages coming from the application's main thread:

```
Dim twtl As New TextWriterTraceListener("trace2.txt")
twtl.Filter = New TraceFilterByThreadID(Thread.CurrentThread.ManagedThreadId)
Trace.Listeners.Add(twtl)
```

(Read Chapter 20 for more information about threads.)

Refreshing the Trace Settings

Trace settings are read from the configuration file only when the application is launched; changes that you make to this file are ignored until the next time the application runs. This can become an issue with server-side applications, such as ASP.NET applications or Microsoft Windows services. You can force the application to apply the most current trace settings by invoking the Trace.Refresh method. For example, you might use a FileSystemWatcher component (which I cover in Chapter 15) to monitor any change to the configuration file and invoke the Trace.Refresh method when the file is modified. (For more information, read the section titled "The Visual Studio Hosting Process" later in this chapter.)

The TraceSource Class

Although the Trace and Debug classes are quite versatile and flexible, at the end of the day you'll find that you need to write a lot of code to use them in a real application: you must define one or more trace switches and assign them to global variables (so that they can be referenced from anywhere in the project), you must use these switches in virtually every trace statement, and so forth. Another common tracing problem is accounting for different groups of trace statements, for example, when you have a set of trace statements related to profiling that outputs to a file and another set of statements that are related to critical errors and that outputs messages to the event log. You can't solve this problem easily because you have only one single Trace object with a fixed set of listeners and you must use the same tracing level for all the listeners. The TraceSource type has been added to version 2.0 of the .NET Framework to spare you most of these repetitive and tedious tasks.

Unlike the Trace object, which is a singleton and doesn't need to be instantiated, you have to create a TraceSource object and assign it to a global variable (or at least a variable that is accessible from the methods that need to emit trace messages) before you can use its TraceEvent, TraceData, and TraceInformation methods:

```
' Create a TraceSource named ProfileTracer that initially traces warnings and errors.
Dim tracer As New TraceSource("ProfileTracer")
tracer.Switch.Level = SourceLevels.Warning Or SourceLevels.Error
' Prepare to send trace messages to file.
Dim twtl As New TextWriterTraceListener(".\profiletraceinfo.txt")
tracer.Listeners.Add(twtl)
' When tracing to a file you must set the Trace.AutoFlush property. (See note.)
Trace.AutoFlush = True
...
' Trace an error message, with an ID event equal to 100.
tracer.TraceEvent(TraceEventType.Error, 100, "Out of range")
' Trace the value of an object (not shown in this short demo).
tracer.TraceData(TraceEventType.Warning Or TraceEventType.Information, 100, obj)
' Send a simple trace message. Same as:
'    TraceEvent(TraceEventType.Information, 0, "Benchmark end")
tracer.TraceInformation("Benchmark end")
```

Note When sending trace information to a file, you must either set the Trace.AutoFlush property to True or ensure that you invoke the TraceSource.Close method before exiting the program. If you fail to do so, the most recent trace messages in the cache aren't correctly flushed to the file.

The TraceSource object offer more granularity than the standard Trace object does. For example, its Switch property exposes a SourceSwitch object whose Level property takes a SourceLevels enumerated value. This value is conceptually similar to the TraceLevel value you use with TraceSwitch objects, except it is bit-coded and therefore it lets you specify any combination of message types. The SourceLevels enumerated value exposes the new Critical and

ActivityTracing values; the latter is useful for tracing when the application is launched, stopped, or suspended.

The TraceEvent and TraceData methods take a TraceEventType enumerated value that specifies which kind of message is being emitted. Again, this is a bit-coded value, so you can specify multiple categories (even though this is rarely necessary) or combine the Critical, Error, Warning, Information, or Verbose values with activity-related values such as Start, Stop, Suspend, and Resume:

```
tracer.TraceEvent(TraceEventType.Information Or TraceEventType.Start, _
    100, "Application starts")
```

The second argument in the preceding statement is the event ID, a user-defined integer that identifies which kind of event is being generated. For example, you might use an ID equal to 10 for tracing exceptions handled in the same procedure, 11 for unhandled exceptions, 12 for clean-up code, and so forth.

The third (optional) argument to the TraceEvent method is the message string, or it can be a format string followed by one or more arguments, similarly to what you do with the Console.WriteLine method:

```
tracer.TraceEvent(TraceEventType.Information, 10, "Exception {0} occurred at {1}", _
    ex.Message, ex.StackTrace)
```

The TraceData method takes one or more objects in lieu of the message string; the purpose of this method, in fact, is to record the value that one or more variables had in a given moment during your application's lifetime.

As happens with the Trace object, you can control the behavior of a TraceSource by adding entries to the configuration file. Unlike the Trace object, however, a program can use multiple TraceSource instances; therefore, the configuration file must include a <sources> tag that contains one or more <source> blocks, where each <source> block controls a TraceSource object with a given name. In the simplest case, you use a switchValue attribute to specify the trace level and include one or more <listener> blocks to specify all the listeners associated to a given TraceSource object:

```
<configuration>
    <system.diagnostics>
        <sources>
            <source name="ProfileTracer" switchValue="Verbose">
                <listeners>
                    <add name="FileListener" initializeData=".\trace.txt"
                        type="System.Diagnostics.TextWriterTraceListener" />
                    <add name="ConsoleListener"
                        type="System.Diagnostics.ConsoleTraceListener" />
                </listeners>
            </source>
        </sources>
    </system.diagnostics>
</configuration>
```

It is essential that the name attribute in the <source> tag exactly matches the name you have assigned in code to the TraceSource object. Also, it is very important that you don't assign a value to the TraceSource.Switch property in code; otherwise, you'd overwrite the value read from the configuration file. If you have recorded all your preferences in the configuration file, you can set up your TraceSource object with just a single statement:

```
Dim tracer As New TraceSource("ProfileTracer")
' We need the following statement only because we send output to a file.
Trace.AutoFlush = True
```

In a more complex scenario, you might want to define switches and listeners that are shared among multiple TraceSource objects. For example, consider this code:

```
Dim tracer As New TraceSource("ProfileTracer")
Dim actTracer As New TraceSource("ActivityTracer")
Trace.AutoFlush = True
…
actTracer.TraceEvent(TraceEventType.Start, 0)
tracer.TraceEvent(TraceEventType.Error, 100, "It's an error")
tracer.TraceEvent(TraceEventType.Warning, 100, "It's a warning")
actTracer.TraceEvent(TraceEventType.Stop, 0)
```

Let's say that you want to control both TraceSource objects with a single switch and that the ProfileTracer object should output to both the console and the trace.txt file, whereas the ActivityTracer object should output only to the file. Here's how you can shape your configuration file to keep all these settings in a single location:

```
<configuration>
   <system.diagnostics>
      <sources>
         <source name="ProfileTracer" switchName="GlobalSwitch" >
            <listeners>
               <add name="FileListener" />
               <add name="ConsoleListener" />
            </listeners>
         </source>
         <source name="ActivityTracer" switchName="GlobalSwitch">
            <listeners>
               <add name="FileListener" />
            </listeners>
         </source>
      </sources>

      <switches>
         <add name="GlobalSwitch" value="ActivityTracing,Error,Warning" />
      </switches>

      <sharedListeners>
         <add name="FileListener" initializeData=".\trace.txt"
            type="System.Diagnostics.TextWriterTraceListener" />
         <add name="ConsoleListener"
            type="System.Diagnostics.ConsoleTraceListener" />
```

```
      </sharedListeners>
   </system.diagnostics>
</configuration>
```

There are several details to notice. First, switches shared among multiple TraceSource objects are defined in the <switches> block, whereas shared listeners are in the <sharedListeners> block. The XML code inside individual <source> tags is similar to the example before this one, except you now use the switchName attribute (instead of the switchValue attribute) to reference a shared switch and you reference listeners by name. Also, notice how you can specify a bit-coded value for the GlobalSwitch switch by assigning a comma-delimited string to the value attribute in the <add> tag.

> **Note**   Visual Basic creates a default TraceSource object named DefaultSource, which you can use through the My.Application.Log object, as explained in the next section. Read the section titled "The My.Application Object" in Chapter 16, "The My Namespace," for more information.

The My.Application.Log Object

The My.Application namespace exposes a Log object (of type Microsoft.VisualBasic.Logging. Log) that simplifies tracing even further. This object exposes only two relevant methods: WriteEntry and WriteException. The former is similar to the TraceSource.TraceEvent method (even though the order of argument is different):

```
My.Application.Log.WriteEntry("File not found", TraceEventType.Error, 100)
```

As its name suggests, the WriteException method lets you keep track of all the details of an exception in a simple way:

```
Try
   …
Catch ex As Exception
   ' Log the exception, and then handle it.
   My.Application.Log.WriteException(ex)
   …
End Try
```

You can use the TraceSource object exposed by the Log object to access other features of the My.Application.Log object, for example, to programmatically change the tracing level:

```
My.Application.Log.TraceSource.Switch.Level = SourceLevels.Critical
```

When you create a new project item using the Application Configuration File template, Visual Studio 2005 generates a file that already contains all the entries for controlling the output of the My.Application.Log object. By default, this object outputs all informational messages to a FileLogTraceListener object, but you can easily send output to the system log as well simply by uncommenting a couple of portions in the XML file. All the things I discussed about

controlling TraceSource objects by means of entries in the configuration file are valid for the
My.Application.Log object as well.

The StopWatch Type

.NET Framework 2.0 has added a simple but effective type that enables you to benchmark a
piece of code with very little effort on your part: the Stopwatch class (in the System.Diagnostics
namespace). Using this class is simple:

```
' Create the StopWatch and start counting elapsed time.
Dim sw As New StopWatch()
sw.Start()
' Place the code to be benchmarked here.
…
' Stop counting the elapsed time and display the number of elapsed seconds.
sw.Stop()
Console.WriteLine("Time elapsed: {0}", sw.Elapsed)
```

You can create a Stopwatch object and start it with a single statement:

```
Dim sw As StopWatch = Stopwatch.StartNew()
```

You can query the Elapsed, ElapsedMilliseconds, and ElapsedTicks properties to retrieve the
elapsed time in seconds, milliseconds, and ticks, respectively. This type provides the highest
time resolution that is possible on a given machine, and a *tick* is equal to the smallest fraction
of a second that the Stopwatch can measure. (You can use the Frequency read-only static
field to determine how many ticks are in a second for the specific machine.)

You can use a Stopwatch object to measure the cumulative time spent running multiple and
disjointed regions of code simply by starting and stopping the clock as many times as you
wish. Or you can use the Reset method to reset the internal tick counter to zero.

Unit Testing

The Developer Edition of Microsoft Visual Studio Team System comes with a great new feature called *unit testing*. In a nutshell, the idea behind unit testing is that you write a set of test
methods, each one dedicated to testing one of the methods or the classes of your main application. Visual Studio then can run all or a subset of your test methods and report which ones
were successful and which ones failed. By creating a set of unit tests and running it periodically to check your code as you evolve and extend it, you can ensure that your edits don't
introduce bugs in areas that you've already checked.

Unit testing isn't a new concept in absolute terms. For example, Visual Studio .NET 2003
users can exploit unit-testing techniques by means of free tools such as NUnit (*http://
www.nunit.org*). If you've adopted unit-testing techniques before, you'll find yourself immediately comfortable with these new additions to Visual Studio and you'll surely appreciate the
convenience of having these tools integrated in the IDE.

> **Note** Unit testing, performance tools, and code coverage tools are available only in Visual Studio 2005 Team Edition for Software Developers. You can check which edition of Visual Studio Team Suite, if any, is installed on your computer by looking at the About Microsoft Visual Studio dialog box. If you don't see the Test top-level menu in Visual Studio, you can't use any of the features described in this section. Visual Studio Team Edition for Software Developers contains many features in addition to those I cover in this book.

To show how unit testing works in practice, create a Console project named MathWorkbench and add a Triangle.vb file containing the following code:

```
Public Class Triangle
    Dim a, b, c As Double

    Public Sub New(ByVal sideA As Double, ByVal sideB As Double, ByVal sideC As Double)
        a = sideA: b = sideB: c = sideC
        ' Check that such a triangle can actually be built.
        If a < Math.Abs(b - c) OrElse b < Math.Abs(a - c) OrElse c < Math.Abs(a - c) Then
            Throw New ArgumentException("Invalid triangle")
        End If
    End Sub

    Public Function GetPerimeter() As Double
        Return a + b + c
    End Function

    Public Function GetArea() As Double
        ' Use Heron's formula to calculate the area.
        ' WARNING: the following statement contains a typo!
        '          (Both asterisks should be replaced with a plus sign.)
        Dim halfP As Double = (a * b * c) / 2
        Return Math.Sqrt(halfP * (halfP - a) * (halfP - b) * (halfP - c))
    End Function
End Class
```

As the remarks in code indicate, the GetArea method is bugged. We will use unit testing to find it.

Creating a Test Project

The first step in performing unit testing is the creation of a test project. A test project is similar to a standard project containing code written in Visual Basic or another .NET language in that it appears in the Solution Explorer window and contains one or more source files, which in turn contain one or more classes. As you'll see in a moment, what makes these classes special is that they are flagged with a custom attribute.

You can create a test project in several ways: for example, you can select the Test Project template from the Add New Project dialog box that you can reach from the Add submenu of the File menu; or you can use the New Test command on the Test menu, which opens a dialog box that lets you create several types of test modules (in addition to the unit test modules I describe in this section). In either case, you should create a test project using a name that resembles the name of the project containing the code being tested (for example, MathWorkbenchTest) so that it's clear which projects in the Solution Explorer are test projects. (See Figure 5-14.)

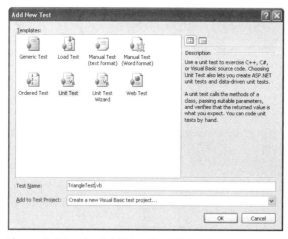

Figure 5-14 The Add New Test dialog box

All new test projects contain the AuthoringTests.txt file (a text file with instructions) and the UnitTest1.vb file (an empty test class where you can place your test methods); you can change the name of the latter file in the Add New Test dialog box. Delete these files if you wish because we don't use manual tests in this example and we're about to ask Visual Studio to generate all the test methods for us.

You can also notice that Visual Studio has added a new folder in the Solution Explorer named Solution Items, which in turn contains two items: *solutionname*.vsmdi and localtestrun .testrunconfig. As you'll see later in this section, the latter file is where details of the test process are stored.

Right-click the Class Triangle statement and select the Create Unit Tests command from the context menu. This action opens the Create Unit Tests dialog box (see Figure 5-15); in the upper portion of this dialog box you select which classes and methods you want to test, whereas the Output Project combo box near the bottom edge lets you specify to which test project the testing code will be added. (Other options in the combo box let you create a new project.) The Settings button displays a dialog box from which you can control some features of the code that will be generated; for this example, you can just accept all the default settings.

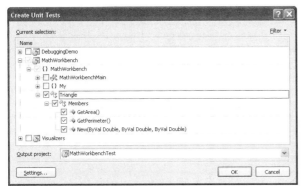

Figure 5-15   The Create Unit Tests dialog box

Ensure that the Triangle class and its three members are selected, and then click OK. Visual Studio will add a new file named TriangleTest.vb to the test project; if this file already exists, Visual Studio merges the generated code with the existing contents. To save space, here I have trimmed XML commands and a few other statements that aren't relevant to our discussion:

```
Imports MathWorkbench
Imports Microsoft.VisualStudio.TestTools.UnitTesting

  <TestMethod()> _
  Public Sub GetAreaTest()
     Dim sideA As Double 'TODO: Initialize to an appropriate value
     Dim sideB As Double 'TODO: Initialize to an appropriate value
     Dim sideC As Double 'TODO: Initialize to an appropriate value
     Dim target As Triangle = New Triangle(sideA, sideB, sideC)

     Dim expected As Double
     Dim actual As Double
     actual = target.GetArea
     Assert.AreEqual(expected, actual, _
        "MathWorkbench.Triangle.GetArea did not return the expected value.")
     Assert.Inconclusive("Verify the correctness of this test method.")
  End Sub

  <TestMethod()> _
  Public Sub GetPerimeterTest()
     Dim sideA As Double 'TODO: Initialize to an appropriate value
     Dim sideB As Double 'TODO: Initialize to an appropriate value
     Dim sideC As Double 'TODO: Initialize to an appropriate value
     Dim target As Triangle = New Triangle(sideA, sideB, sideC)
     Dim expected As Double
     Dim actual As Double
     actual = target.GetPerimeter
     Assert.AreEqual(expected, actual, _
        "MathWorkbench.Triangle.GetPerimeter did not return the expected value.")
     Assert.Inconclusive("Verify the correctness of this test method.")
  End Sub
```

```
<TestMethod()> _
Public Sub ConstructorTest()
    Dim sideA As Double 'TODO: Initialize to an appropriate value
    Dim sideB As Double 'TODO: Initialize to an appropriate value
    Dim sideC As Double 'TODO: Initialize to an appropriate value
    Dim target As Triangle = New Triangle(sideA, sideB, sideC)

    'TODO: Implement code to verify target
    Assert.Inconclusive("TODO: Implement code to verify target")
  End Sub
End Class
```

There are several interesting details to notice:

■   The test project references two other assemblies: the executable that must be tested (MathWorkbench.exe in this example) and the Microsoft.VisualStudio.Quality-Tools.UnitTestFramework.dll library, which contains several types that can be used from inside test methods.

■   The TriangleTest class is marked with the TestClass attribute; this attribute makes the class visible to the unit test subsystem in Visual Studio.

■   Each individual test method is marked with the TestMethod attribute; Visual Studio will execute all the methods marked with this attribute (and contained in classes marked with the TestClass attribute) when running the test.

■   The Initialize and Cleanup methods are marked with the TestInitialize and TestCleanup attributes; Visual Studio will invoke these two methods before and after each method marked with TestMethod, respectively; thus, you can use these methods for code that is common to all tests in the test class.

■   Visual Studio has created a lot of statements inside the individual test methods, for example, to instantiate a Triangle object that will be used for tests, plus several TODO comments that point to the pieces of code that we're expected to modify manually. All the test methods end with a call to the Assert.Inconclusive method, which is a sort of reminder for you: until you modify the source code in the method, the unit-testing mechanism can't learn anything from the outcome of the method.

The Assert object exposes many methods you can use in test methods. The AreEqual and AreNotEqual methods check the equality of two values; the IsTrue and IsFalse methods check the result of a Boolean condition; the AreSame and AreNotSame methods check whether two object references point to the same object (similar to the Visual Basic Is operator); the IsNull and IsNotNull methods check whether an object reference is Nothing; the IsInstanceOfType and IsNotInstanceOfType methods check that the value returned by the procedure being tested is of a given type:

```
' A few examples of the methods exposed by the Assert type
Assert.IsNull(actual, "The method didn't return Nothing")
Assert.IsTrue(actual >= 0, "The method returned a negative value.")
Assert.IsInstanceOfType(actual, GetType(String), "The method didn't return a string")
```

The Fail method unconditionally makes the test fail; this method is useful to check compound conditions:

```
If actual < -10 AndAlso actual > 10 Then
   Assert.Fail("The method returned a value outside the range [-10,10]")
End If
```

Running the Test Project

Let's add some code to the GetPerimeterTest and GetAreaTest methods. For example, we can check that a triangle with sides that are 30, 40, and 50 units long has a perimeter of 120 units and an area of 600 units:

```
<TestMethod()> _
Public Sub GetAreaTest()
   Dim sideA As Double = 30
   Dim sideB As Double = 40
   Dim sideC As Double = 50
   Dim target As Triangle = New Triangle(sideA, sideB, sideC)
   Dim expected As Double = 600
   Dim actual As Double
   actual = target.GetArea
   Assert.AreEqual(expected, actual, _
      "MathWorkbench.Triangle.GetArea did not return the expected value.")
End Sub

<TestMethod()> _
Public Sub GetPerimeterTest()
   Dim sideA As Double = 30
   Dim sideB As Double = 40
   Dim sideC As Double = 50
   Dim target As Triangle = New Triangle(sideA, sideB, sideC)
   Dim expected As Double = 120
   Dim actual As Double
   actual = target.GetPerimeter
   Assert.AreEqual(expected, actual, _
      "MathWorkbench.Triangle.GetPerimeter did not return the expected value.")
End Sub
```

Notice that you should delete the call to the Assert.Inconclusive method because you now have a complete test method that you can run to see whether the MathWorkbench project behaves correctly.

Select the Test Manager command from the Windows submenu of the Test top-level menu to display the window from which you can decide which tests you want to run. (See Figure 5-16.) This window enables you to list and organize all the tests defined in the current solution, as well as run all of them or just a subset. You can create a subset of tests by right-clicking the Lists Of Tests node and selecting the Create New Test List command from the context menu; then you can drag items in the right pane under a different list. Or you can click the All Loaded Test item to display all the tests in a linear list.

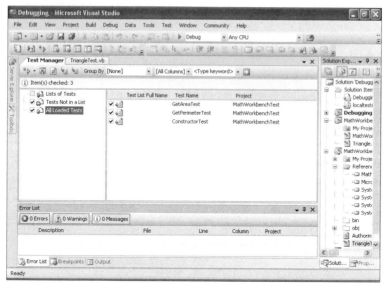

Figure 5-16   The Test Manager window

Select all the tests you want to run, and then click the Run Checked Tests button on the Test Manager toolbar. Visual Studio displays a new window named Test Results (see Figure 5-17); in this window, you can see how the test process progresses, with each individual test going through the Pending, In Progress, and Passed (or Failed, or Inconclusive) states. In our example, the GetPerimeterTest method should pass, the GetAreaTest method should fail (because of the intentional bug in the original code), and the ConstructorTest method should be flagged as inconclusive because we haven't edited the code generated by Visual Studio.

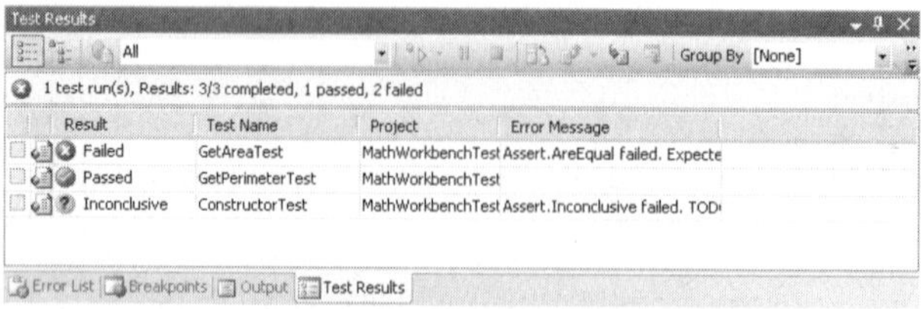

Figure 5-17   The Test Results tool window

A quick look at the GetArea method (and at the comment that I conveniently added to draw your attention to its bug) enables you to fix the problem. After changing all the asterisks to plus signs, you should be able to rerun the test–for all methods or just for the GetArea procedure–and you should get rid of the Failed icon.

You can display more details on individual tests by selecting an element and clicking the Run Details button in the Test Results window. Other buttons on this toolbar let you restrict the output to only the tests in a list or group tests by one of their attributes (for example, by the outcome of the test), or display additional columns that are hidden by default (for example, duration). You can also export all or selected results to a .trx file and reimport them in a subsequent session.

During the test phase of a project, you don't always need to run all the methods you've defined in the test project. More often than not, you might want to run just one or two test methods. For this sort of task you should use the Test View window, which you display by means of the Test View command on the Windows submenu of the Test menu. (See Figure 5-18.) By default, this window displays all the tests defined in the current solution, but you can easily filter them by their name or one of the attributes associated with them (see the section titled "Attributes for Unit Testing" later in this chapter). You can then select one or more elements by clicking them while holding down the Shift key and run all the selected tests by clicking the Run button on the window's toolbar.

Notice that both the Test Manager window and the Test View window have a toolbar button that enables you to run the unit test methods in either Release or Debug mode. (These two options are also available as commands on the Test top-level menu.) By default test methods run in Release mode, but you might need to switch to Debug mode if you suspect that the test methods themselves have some bugs.

Figure 5-18   The Test View tool window

Attributes for Unit Testing

In the ConstructorTest method, you want to check that an invalid set of arguments raises an exception. You can achieve this result by placing the creation of such an invalid triangle in a Try block to ensure that you receive the exception you expect, but there is a better way based on the ExpectedException attribute:

```
<TestMethod(), ExpectedException(GetType(ArgumentException), "Invalid triangle")> _
Public Sub ConstructorTest()
    ' An invalid triangle
    Dim sideA As Double = 100
    Dim sideB As Double = 30
    Dim sideC As Double = 50
    Dim target As Triangle = New Triangle(sideA, sideB, sideC)
End Sub
```

The first argument of the ExpectedException attribute uses the GetType operator to pass the type of the exception. The second argument is optional and is equal to the message of the exception object you expect to be thrown by the method being tested.

The Microsoft.VisualStudio.TestTools.UnitTesting.Framework namespace contains many other attributes that can be used in test projects to mark methods that Visual Studio calls before or after each test or set of tests.

- Use the TestInitialize attribute to mark the method that you want to execute before each individual test; use the TestCleanup attribute to mark the method that must execute after each test.

- Use the ClassInitialize and ClassCleanup attributes to mark the method that runs before and after, respectively, all the tests defined in the current class.

- Use the AssemblyInitialize and AssemblyCleanup attributes to mark the method that runs before and after, respectively, all the tests defined in the current test project.

These attributes can be used only with Sub methods that take no arguments, with the exception of the ClassInitialize attribute, which must be applied to a method that takes a TestContext object. The TestContext object exposes many properties that can be useful inside test methods, as I show in the next section; thus, you should save it in a class-level static field:

```
Shared TestContext As TestContext

<ClassInitialize()> _
Public Shared Sub MyClassInitialize(ByVal context As TestContext)
    ' This method runs before any of the tests defined in the current class.
    ' Save the TestContext object for later.
    TestContext = context
End Sub

<ClassCleanup()> _
Public Shared Sub MyClassCleanup()
    ' This method runs after all the tests defined in the current class.
End Sub
```

Other attributes defined in the Microsoft.VisualStudio.TestTools.UnitTesting.Framework namespace can be used to add details to individual test methods. For example, the Description attribute describes what a test does, the Owner attribute specifies the programmer who is responsible for a given test, the Priority attribute lets you indicate a priority for the test, and the Ignore attribute lets you temporarily exclude a test method from the test project without having to physically delete it or comment it. (Tests marked with this attribute are unavailable in the Test Manager window.) Here is an example:

```
<TestMethod(),Priority(5), _
    Description("Check that the perimeter is evaluated correctly")> _
Public Sub GetPerimeterTest2()
    ' Another test for the GetPerimeter method
    ...
End Sub
```

Conveniently, you can set and display these attributes directly from inside the Test Manager window by selecting a test item and pressing the F4 key or selecting the Properties command from the context menu. Just type a new value in the Properties window and Visual Studio will update the set of attributes of the corresponding test method. You can also view the attributes you're most interested in by means of the Add/Remove Columns button in the Test Manager window. (See Figure 5-19.) Other commands on the Test Manager (and the Test View) toolbar enable you to filter or group test items by their attributes.

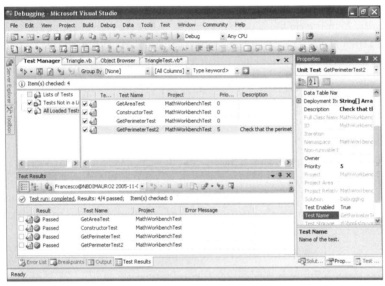

Figure 5-19   Displaying properties of a test method in the Properties window and the Test Manager window

Finally, you can associate a test method with a piece of information for which no attribute exists by means of the TestProperty attribute, which takes a (name, value) pair:

```
<TestMethod(), TestProperty("DateCreated", "03/12/2005")> _
Public Sub GetAreaTest()
    …
```

You need reflection techniques to programmatically process properties associated with a test method by means of the TestProperty attribute. (Read Chapter 18, "Reflection.")

Loading Tests from a Database

In the examples shown so far, you've used a single test method to test a procedure in the main project. In a real-world case, you should define several tests for each procedure, each test checking the result when a different set of arguments is passed. For example, you should check the behavior of a method when you pass negative or very large numbers, empty strings, or null object references. As you can imagine, writing many similar test methods for each procedure in the main application quickly becomes a nuisance. Fortunately, you can set up a test method that executes the test once for each row in a database table, where each row contains both the value of the arguments to be passed to the method and the expected return value.

You can create the database containing test values and fill it right from inside Visual Studio by following this procedure:

1. Display the Server Explorer window by using the command with the same name on the View menu.

2. Right-click the Data Connection element and select the Create New SQL Server Database command; in the dialog box that appears, select the server name (or use a dot (.) to point to the local Microsoft SQL Server), type **MathWorkbenchTest** in the New Database Name box, and then click OK to create the database.

3. In the Server Explorer window, expand the node that has been created for the new database, right-click the Tables folder, and select the Add New Table command from the context menu. This action opens a new tabbed window where you're expected to define all the columns in the new table.

4. Define the following five columns: SideA, SideB, SideC, Perimeter, Area. All these columns should be of type real and shouldn't allow nulls. Click the Close button to close the tabbed window and type **TriangleData** when Visual Studio asks for the name of the table being created. (Notice that this table has no primary key, but this isn't an issue in test databases because their tables are typically accessed sequentially.)

5. Go back to the Server Explorer, right-click the new TriangleData element, and select the Show Table Data command from the context menu. This action opens another tabbed window, where you're expected to enter one or more rows to be inserted in the new table.

6. Enter a few rows in the table, for example:

    ```
    30, 40, 50, 120, 600
    60, 50, 50, 160, 1200
    5, 12, 13, 30, 30
    ```

7. Close the tabbed window to save the new rows in the table.

8. Right-click the connection element in the Server Explorer and select the Properties command (or press the F4 key); this action displays the connection properties. You can now select the value of the Connection String property and copy it to the Clipboard so that you can easily paste in the code portion that you're about to create.

Switch to the code editor and add these new methods to the TriangleTest class:

```
<TestMethod()> _
<DataSource("System.Data.SqlClient", _
    "Data Source=.;Initial Catalog=MathWorkbenchTest;Integrated Security=True", _
    "TriangleData", DataAccessMethod.Sequential)> _
Public Sub GetPerimeterTestDB()
```

```vb
      Dim sideA As Double = CDbl(TestContext.DataRow("SideA"))
      Dim sideB As Double = CDbl(TestContext.DataRow("SideB"))
      Dim sideC As Double = CDbl(TestContext.DataRow("SideC"))
      Dim target As Triangle = New Triangle(sideA, sideB, sideC)
      Dim expected As Double = CDbl(TestContext.DataRow("Perimeter"))
      Dim actual As Double = target.GetPerimeter
      Assert.AreEqual(expected, actual, _
         "MathLibrary.Triangle.GetPerimeter did not return the expected value.")
   End Sub

   <TestMethod()> _
   <DataSource("System.Data.SqlClient", _
      "Data Source=.;Initial Catalog=MathWorkbenchTest;Integrated Security=True", _
      "TriangleData", DataAccessMethod.Sequential)> _
   Public Sub GetAreaTestDB()
      Dim sideA As Double = CDbl(TestContext.DataRow("SideA"))
      Dim sideB As Double = CDbl(TestContext.DataRow("SideB"))
      Dim sideC As Double = CDbl(TestContext.DataRow("SideC"))
      Dim target As Triangle = New Triangle(sideA, sideB, sideC)
      Dim expected As Double = CDbl(TestContext.DataRow("Area"))
      Dim actual As Double = target.GetArea
      Assert.AreEqual(expected, actual, _
         "MathLibrary.Triangle.GetArea did not return the expected value.")
   End Sub
```

The first thing to notice in this code is the new DataSource attribute, which tells Visual Studio which ADO.NET provider must be used to read the data, the database's connection string, the table name, and the access method (you can use sequential or random access). The second important detail is how the code uses the TestContext object—which was saved in the MyClassInitialize method, as explained in the previous section—and its DataRow property to retrieve individual column values in each row of the TriangleData table. Notice that the code does *not* include an explicit loop statement: Visual Studio is in charge of reading each line in the database table and invoking these test methods for each set of possible arguments and expected values.

Next, switch to the Test View window, select only the GetPerimeterTestDB and GetArea-TestDB elements, click the Run Tests button, and see how the test goes in the Test Results window. If even just one of the rows in the TriangleData table makes the test fail, the entire test is considered as failed. You can then discover which set of arguments made the test fail by looking at test details (use the Run Details button on the Test Results window's toolbar).

One short note before we move on to another topic: when testing Double values, as in the preceding code, you shouldn't use the Assert.AreSame method because rounding errors in floating-point math can make the test fail even if it shouldn't. A better approach is to check whether the difference between the expected and the actual values is smaller than a threshold that you specify:

```vb
If Math.Abs(actual - expected) > 1.0E-20 Then
   Assert.Fail("MathLibrary.Triangle.GetPerimeter did not return the expected value.")
End If
```

The TestContext Type

The code you place inside test methods can use the TestContext object to retrieve several important pieces of information about the test itself. For example, in a previous section, I showed how to use the TestContext.DataRow property to access fields in the database table. Other properties that are commonly used are DataConnection (the ADO.NET Connection object being used by the test subsystem) and TestName (the name of the test under examination). The latter property becomes especially useful when used from inside the methods marked with the TestInitialize and TestCleanup attributes. As you might recall, these methods are executed before and after each test method in the current type.

To show an actual example of how the TestContext object can be invaluable in serious test activity, let's modify our TriangleTest class so that it logs all the failed tests in the GetPerimeterTestDB and GetAreaTestDB methods:

```
Dim sw As StreamWriter
Dim failedTests As Integer

<TestInitialize()> _
Public Sub Initialize()
    ' Create a log file for each test whose name ends with "DB" suffix.
    If TestContext.TestName.EndsWith("DB") Then
        Dim fileName As String = "c:\" & TestContext.TestName & ".log"
        sw = New StreamWriter(fileName)
        failedTests = 0
    End If
End Sub

<TestCleanup()> _
Public Sub Cleanup()
    ' Append the number of failed tests and close the StreamWriter.
    If sw IsNot Nothing Then
        sw.WriteLine("Tests failed: " & failedTests.ToString())
        sw.Close()
        ' If we omit the next line, non-
DB tests would mistakenly attempt to log their results.
        sw = Nothing
    End If
End Sub
```

The code in the Initialize method ensures that the code inside tests with names that end with "DB" can use a StreamWriter object to output their results to a log file. For example, this is how you can exploit this log file inside the GetPerimeterTestDB test method:

```
' Compare expected and actual values at the end of GetPerimeterTestDB procedure.
If Math.Abs(expected - actual) > 1.0E-20 Then
    ' Output the comma-delimited list of arguments, expected and actual results.
    Dim text As String = String.Format("{0},{1},{2},{3},{4}", sideA, sideB, sideC, expected,
actual)
    sw.WriteLine(text)
    failedTests += 1
    Assert.Fail("MathLibrary.Triangle.GetPerimeter did not return the expected value.")
End If
```

You can also export test results by means of the Export Results command from the Test Results window, which creates an XML file that you can later import into Visual Studio for further analysis. However, creating a custom file gives you extra flexibility, for example, to create data in comma- or tab-delimited format and be able to import test results in other applications, such as Microsoft Office Excel.

Private Accessors

In all the examples discussed so far, the code in the test project invokes public members of the type being tested in the main project, and because the type itself is public it is possible to perform such cross-project (or, more correctly, cross-assembly) calls. What happens if you want to test members with Private or Friend scope in a public type, or any member in a type that isn't public at all? The answer comes in the form of private accessors. To see how private accessors work, go back to the main project and define a new Square class:

```
Class Square
    Dim side As Double

    Sub New(ByVal side As Double)
        If side <= 0 Then
            Throw New ArgumentException("Negative or zero value for side")
        End If
        Me.side = side
    End Sub

    Function GetPerimeter() As Double
        Return side * 4
    End Function
End Class
```

The Square class isn't marked with a Public scope; therefore, it has an implicit Friend scope and can't be accessed directly from the test project. To make it accessible you must create a private accessor.

In the code editor, right-click the class definition, select the Create Private Accessor submenu from the context menu, and finally select the MathWorkbenchTest item. (On the Create Private Accessor submenu you find the list of all the test projects defined in the current solution.) Visual Studio adds a module named VSCodeGenAccessors.vb to the selected test project and generates the code of an auxiliary type named MathWorkbench_SquareAccessor. This type works as a sort of bridge—more correctly, as a *proxy type*—between the code in the test project and the real Square class and uses reflection to access private members without the usual restrictions.

You can now create tests for the Square class as usual because Visual Studio can automatically generate the code that uses the MathWorkbench_SquareAccessor type instead of the real Square class. Once you understand the mechanism, you can even extend the accessor class with additional properties and methods and use these new members from inside test methods.

Finally, note that Visual Studio can generate private accessors automatically when you select the Create Tests command for a private type or a type that has one or more private members. I have explained the Create Private Accessor command here because it reflects the actual sequence of actions that the code generator follows behind the scenes, but in practice you'll rarely need to invoke this command manually.

Code Coverage

Obviously, a unit test session can be considered decisive only if it tests each and every statement in the main project. With projects containing hundreds of methods, and with methods containing many If and Select Case blocks, it's easy to overlook some code paths that deliver incorrect results. This is where code coverage comes to the rescue: when you enable code coverage, Visual Studio keeps track of all the statements that have been executed in a test session and is able to highlight those that haven't.

You enable code coverage by selecting the Edit Test Run Configurations submenu on the Test top-level menu and then selecting the Local Test Run (localtestrun.testrunconfig) element, which displays the dialog box shown in Figure 5-20. In this simple example, you have only one test configuration, but in real-world scenarios you can (and should) create multiple test-run configurations, each one testing a portion of your code or each one with a different set of properties (for example, with and without code coverage). You can select which test-run configuration should execute by means of another submenu on the Test menu.

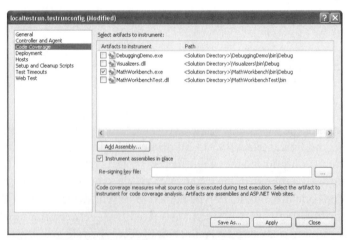

Figure 5-20   The dialog box where you can enable code coverage

Switch to the Code Coverage page and ensure that the MathWorkbench.exe file in the *SolutionDirectory*\MathWorkbench\bin\Debug path is selected in the Select Artifacts To Instrument list. Click the Close button and confirm that you want to save changes in the localtestrun.testrunconfig file, and then switch to the Test Manager window and run all tests again. It is essential that you select the Run Checked Tests command, rather than the

Debug Checked Tests, because code coverage doesn't work if you run the test project itself in Debug mode.

When the tests have been completed, click the Show Code Coverage Results button on the Test Results window's toolbar or select the Code Coverage Results element from the Windows submenu of the Test top-level menu. The Code Coverage Results tool window contains a tree-like view of the project being tested, so you can navigate to the members of the Triangle and Square classes and check how much of their code has not been covered by the test process (as a percentage of the total number of statements). (See Figure 5-21.) In this particular example, you should find that the Square class's constructor hasn't been tested completely. (Constructors appear in the tree view with the .ctor name.)

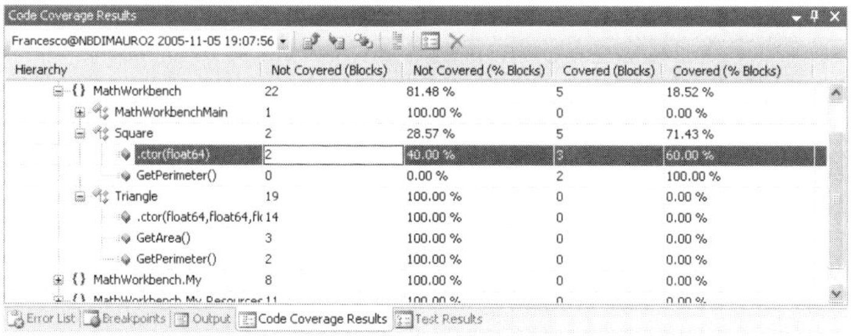

Hierarchy	Not Covered (Blocks)	Not Covered (% Blocks)	Covered (Blocks)	Covered (% Blocks)
⊟ { } MathWorkbench	22	81.48 %	5	18.52 %
⊞ ⚛ MathWorkbenchMain	1	100.00 %	0	0.00 %
⊟ ⚛ Square	2	28.57 %	5	71.43 %
⚬ .ctor(float64)	2	40.00 %	3	60.00 %
⚬ GetPerimeter()	0	0.00 %	2	100.00 %
⊟ ⚛ Triangle	19	100.00 %	0	0.00 %
⚬ .ctor(float64,float64,fk	14	100.00 %	0	0.00 %
⚬ GetArea()	3	100.00 %	0	0.00 %
⚬ GetPerimeter()	2	100.00 %	0	0.00 %
⊞ { } MathWorkbench.My	8	100.00 %	0	0.00 %
⊞ { } MathWorkbench.My.Resources	11	100.00 %	0	0.00 %

Figure 5-21   The Code Coverage Results tool window

To visualize which portion of code hasn't been tested yet, double-click the .ctor element. This action will display the Square.vb source file with its statements colored in light blue (statements that have been tested), red (statements that haven't), and light red (areas that have been tested only partially). This simple color scheme makes it immediately evident that you haven't yet tested the case when the constructor throws an exception when it receives a negative value for the *side* argument. (See Figure 5-22.)

You can turn the colored section off and on by means of the Show Code Coverage Coloring button on the Code Coverage Results window's toolbar. This button is also available on the Test toolbar that you can display by right-clicking any Visual Studio toolbar. You can also change the colors used to mark tested and untested statements in the Options dialog box on the Font And Colors page. Select the Text Editor element in the Show Settings For combo box, and locate the Coverage Not Touched Areas, Coverage Partially Touched Areas, and Coverage Touched Areas in the Display Items list.

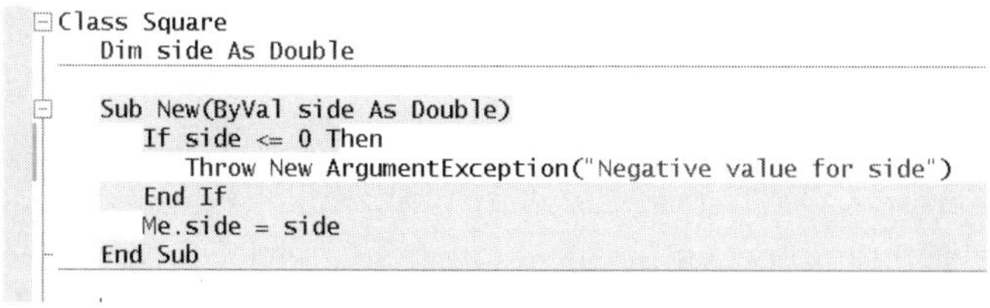

```vb
Class Square
    Dim side As Double

    Sub New(ByVal side As Double)
        If side <= 0 Then
            Throw New ArgumentException("Negative value for side")
        End If
        Me.side = side
    End Sub
```

Figure 5-22   Color highlighting of code coverage

Performance Tools

Performance tools is a feature of the Visual Studio 2005 Team Edition for Software Developers that enables you to spot bottlenecks in your code. It can work in two basic modes: sampling or instrumentation.

In sampling mode, Visual Studio samples your running code when a system event occurs and records which method is executing in that moment. At the end of the test run, Visual Studio can display a report with the list of methods that took a higher percentage of the total execution time. Four system events are considered: clock cycles (periodic samples), page faults (for applications slowed down by memory accesses and garbage collections), system calls (for problems related to slow I/O), and CPU performance counters (for low-level performance problems).

In instrumentation mode, Visual Studio adds statements to your source code so that it is possible to track exactly how many times each method was executed, for how long it ran, and so forth. In general, instrumentation mode can provide more precise results, but it can slow your code remarkably. In some cases, the extra statements can interfere with benchmark results. In both sampling and instrumentation modes, you should use performance tools on the Release build of your application (with all optimizations enabled), but you should also produce a symbol (.pdb) file. Of course, you never ship an instrumented file to your customers.

To run a performance session you must create a performance session by means of the New Performance Session command on the Performance Tools submenu of the Tools menu. This command displays the Performance Explorer tool window, which now contains an empty Performance Session element. (See left portion of Figure 5-23.)

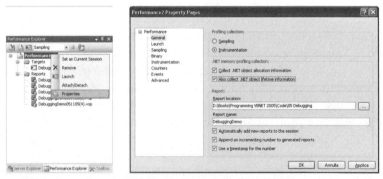

Figure 5-23 The Performance Explorer window (left) and the Properties window that enables you to change all the settings for a given performance session (right)

Right-click this element and select the Properties command, which opens a dialog box that enables you to select between sampling and instrumentation as well as set all the options related to profiling. For the most complete reports, select both options in the .NET Memory

Profiling Collection panel. (See right portion of Figure 5-23.) Finally, right-click the Targets element and select the Add Target Project command; then select which project(s) you want to profile.

You're now ready to start the performance session by clicking the Launch button on the Performance Explorer's toolbar. Visual Studio runs your application and then displays a multi-tabbed report that includes tons of useful information, including the following:

- A summary of the function that allocated more memory, types that allocated more memory, and types that allocated more instances (see left portion of Figure 5-24)

- Number of bytes allocated by each method

- Which functions call or are called by each method (in both a list format and tree view format)

- How many instances of each type have been created and how much memory these instances consumed (see right portion of Figure 5-24)

- Detailed information related to garbage collection, for example, how many objects were promoted to Gen 1 or Gen 2 (Read the section titled "Generations" in Chapter 9, "Object Lifetime," for more information about generations.)

Each time you launch a performance session, a new report is generated. All the reports generated for a given session are available under the Reports folder of the Performance Explorer window. You can rename or delete them, or export them to XML or comma-delimited (CVS) format.

Figure 5-24 Two tabs of a summary produced at the end of a performance session

You can create additional performance session items, all of which appear in the Performance Explorer window. Each session can profile the same or a different set of projects, possibly with different profiling settings—for example, sampling and instrumentation. You can have only one current session, though, and this is the session that runs when you click the Launch button. You can use the Set As Current Session command on the Performance Explorer's context menu to make another session the current session (see left portion of Figure 5-23). The Attach/Detach command, on the same menu, enables you to attach the profiler to any running application.

More Debugging and Testing Techniques

In this last section, I have collected a few debugging and testing techniques that don't fit neatly elsewhere in the chapter. In some cases, these techniques use .NET Framework objects that I haven't introduced yet or Visual Studio IDE features that I don't explain in depth anywhere in the book. You should consider these techniques more as hints to what you can do when debugging and testing your applications rather than an exhaustive description of available techniques.

The Debugger Object

In some cases, you might want to break execution by means of statements burnt into the source code rather than use Visual Studio breakpoints. This approach might be necessary, for example, if you want to break the application when a system event occurs or when the break condition is too complex as can be described in the Breakpoint dialog box. In such cases, you can use the Debugger class in the System.Diagnostics namespace, which has a Break static method that generates the same effect as the Break All command from the Debug menu:

```
For i As Integer = 0 to 100
   ' Break when the index variable is a multiple of 2, 3, or 5.
   If i Mod 2 = 0 OrElse i Mod 3 = 0 OrElse i Mod 5 = 0 Then Debugger.Break()
   ...
Next
```

The Debugger.IsAttached read-only property lets you test whether the application is running inside a debugger. Testing this property is similar to testing the DEBUG symbol in an #If directive, except the DEBUG compilation constant is always True if the application has been compiled in Debug mode (even if it isn't currently running under a debugger), whereas the IsAttached property returns True only if the application is being debugged, even if no debug symbols were produced at compilation time:

```
If Debugger.IsAttached Then
   Console.WriteLine("This application can't run under a debugger.")
   Return
End If
```

You can also use this property to implement behaviors when an exception occurs, as in this:

```
Catch e As OverflowException When Debugger.IsAttached
   ' Deal with overflows that occur when running under a debugger.
```

The StackTrace Object

The code you place inside a method can learn which method called it (and which called its caller, and so on) by means of the StackTrace type in the System.Diagnostics namespace. As its name implies, the StackTrace object keeps track of all the procedures that are pending waiting for the current one to complete.

You can create the StackTrace object in many ways. In its simplest form, you pass no arguments to its constructor and you get the complete stack image as a collection of StackFrame objects, which you can enumerate by their index:

```
Dim st As New StackTrace()
' Enumerate all the stack frame objects.
' (The frame at index 0 corresponds to the current routine.)
For i As Integer = 0 To st.FrameCount - 1
   ' Get the ith stack frame and print the method name.
   Dim sf As StackFrame = st.GetFrame(i)
   Console.WriteLine(sf.GetMethod.Name)
Next
```

Another occasion for creating a StackTrace object is when an exception is caught. In this case, you can pass the exception object to the first argument of the StackTrace constructor so that the StackTrace object contains the stack state at the time the exception was thrown, rather than when you create the StackTrace object itself. The following code creates a chain of calling procedures, with the innermost procedure causing an exception that's trapped in the outermost one:

```
Sub TestStackFrameFromException()
   Try
      ' This causes an exception.
      TestStackFrameFromException_1(1)
   Catch e As Exception
      DisplayExceptionInfo(e)
   End Try
End Sub

Sub TestStackFrameFromException_1(ByVal x As Integer)
   TestStackFrameFromException_2("abc")
End Sub

Sub TestStackFrameFromException_2(ByVal x As String)
   TestStackFrameFromException_3()
End Function

Sub TestStackFrameFromException_3()
   ' Cause an exception (null reference).
   Dim o As Object = Nothing
   Console.Write(o.ToString)
End Sub
```

DisplayExceptionInfo is a reusable routine that displays error information:

```
Sub DisplayExceptionInfo(ByVal e As Exception)
   ' Display the error message.
   Console.WriteLine(e.Message)
   Dim res As String = ""
   Dim st As New StackTrace(e, True)
   For i As Integer = 0 To st.FrameCount - 1
      ' Get the ith stack frame and the corresponding method.
      Dim sf As StackFrame = st.GetFrame(i)
```

```
        Dim mi As MemberInfo = sf.GetMethod
        ' Append the type and method name.
        res &= mi.DeclaringType.FullName & "." & mi.Name & " ("
        ' Append information about the position in the source file
        ' (but only if Debug information is available).
        If sf.GetFileName <> "" Then
            res &= String.Format("{0}, Line {1}, Col {2},", _
                sf.GetFileName, sf.GetFileLineNumber, sf.GetFileColumnNumber)
        End If
        ' Append information about offset in MSIL code, if available.
        If sf.GetILOffset <> StackFrame.OFFSET_UNKNOWN Then
            res &= String.Format("IL offset {0},", sf.GetILOffset)
        End If
        ' Append information about offset in native code and display.
        res &= " native offset " & sf.GetNativeOffset & ")"
        Console.WriteLine(res)
    Next
End Sub
```

The code inside the DisplayExceptionInfo procedure shows how you can use other methods of the StackFrame object, such as GetFileName (the name of the source file), GetFileLineNumber and GetFileColumnNumber (the position in the source file), GetILOffset (offset in IL code from the top of the module), and GetNativeOffset (offset in JIT-compiled native code). By using all these pieces of information, the DisplayExceptionInfo routine can provide a more informative error report than you usually get inside the IDE. For example, you can use the value returned by the GetILOffset to launch ILDASM and see the individual MSIL opcode that threw the exception. Note that the source code's filename, line, and column are available only if the program was compiled with debugging information. If you compiled the executable for Release configuration, these properties return a null string or zero.

Because the GetMethod method of the StackFrame object returns a MethodInfo object, you can leverage reflection to learn more about that procedure, including its argument signature, which is useful when there are overloaded versions of the same procedure or any custom attribute associated with it. (See Chapter 18 for more information about reflection.)

Here's another case when the StackTrace object can be useful. Let's say that you discover that a given method A delivers incorrect results, but only when it's being called by another method B, either directly or not. Here's a reusable method that solves this problem:

```
Public Function CheckCaller(ByVal methodName As String, _
        Optional ByVal typeName As String = Nothing, _
        Optional ByVal immediateOnly As Boolean = False) As Boolean
    ' Create a stack trace, skipping both current method and the method that invoked it.
    Dim st As New StackTrace(2)
    For i As Integer = 0 To st.FrameCount - 1
        ' Retrieve the MethodInfo object describing the calling method.
        Dim sf As StackFrame = st.GetFrame(i)
        Dim mi As MethodInfo = sf.GetMethod()
        ' Exit if method name matches. If typeName was provided, check it as well.
        If mi.Name = methodName AndAlso (typeName Is Nothing OrElse mi.ReflectedType.FullName = _
         typeName) Then Return True
```

```
      ' Exit and return False if only the immediate caller had to be checked.
      If immediateOnly Then Exit For
   Next
   Return False
End Function
```

Here's how you can use the CheckCaller method:

```
Sub OpenFile(ByVal fileName As String)
    ' Break if called directly by the PrintReport method in the MyApp.DataReport type.
    If CheckCaller("PrintReport", "MyApp.DataReport", True) Then Debugger.Break()
    …
    ' Break if called by the EvalData method (in any type),
    ' regardless of whether it's the direct caller.
    If CheckCaller("EvalData ") Then Debugger.Break()
End Sub
```

The CheckCaller method is also useful in other situations. Let's say that you have the follow-ing handler for the TextChanged event of the txtName control:

```
Private Sub txtName_TextChanged(ByVal sender As Object, ByVal e As EventArgs) _
      Handles txtName.TextChanged
    …
    ' Oops: this causes a recursive call to this method!
    txtName.Text = txtName.Text & " "
    …
End Sub
```

You can prevent the recursive call by defining a class-level Boolean field, as follows:

```
Dim runningTextChanged As Boolean

Private Sub txtName_TextChanged(ByVal sender As Object, ByVal e As EventArgs) _
      Handles txtName.TextChanged
    ' Exit if this is a recursive call.
    If runningTextChanged Then Exit Sub
    Try
       runningTextChanged = True
       …
       ' Oops: this causes a recursive call to this method!
       txtName.Text = txtName.Text & " "
       …
    Finally
       ' Use a Try…Finally to ensure that the flag is reset before exiting.
       runningTextChanged = False
    End Try
End Sub
```

You'll probably agree that it's a lot of code for just a simple task. In fact, you can simplify it sig-nificantly with the CheckCaller method:

```
    ' (Inside the txtName_TextChanged method…)
    ' Exit if this is a recursive call.
    If CheckCaller("txtName_TextChanged") Then Exit Sub
```

One last note about visiting the stack with the StackTrace object: some methods might not appear in the list because they've been inlined by the JIT compiler. If your program depends on the contents of the StackTrace object, you should disable inlining optimization by marking the method in question with the MethodImpl(MethodImplOptions.NoInlining) attribute. See the section titled "The MethodImpl Attribute" in Chapter 4, "Using Visual Studio 2005," for more information.

The Debug-in-Zone Feature

 By default, the .NET Framework considers all the applications that aren't launched from the local hard disk—such as applications originating from a network drive, from the intranet, or from the Internet—as partially trusted applications. *Partially trusted* applications are subject to the limitations of code access security (CAS), which prevents them, for example, from reading or writing the file system, accessing the registry, reading most environment variables, and so forth.

Debugging such applications is tricky in previous versions of Visual Studio. The best approach is to change the project's output path to have the executable file be created on a network drive (or on a local drive mapped to a drive letter such as Z) so that you can see how it behaves when it runs from a partially trusted location. This approach is simple but has several drawbacks: it works well to debug intranet applications, but is of no use to debug assemblies meant to be run from the Internet.

Fortunately, the new Debug-in-Zone feature of Visual Studio 2005 solves all these problems and makes the debugging of a partially trusted application a breeze. This new feature was introduced to help the creation of ClickOnce applications, but it works well with any Windows Forms or console application meant to be run from a location other than the local hard disk.

To see this feature in action, click the Security tab of the My Project designer, select the Enable ClickOnce Security Settings option, and then select the This Is A Partial Trust Application radio button (see left portion of Figure 5-25). Next, you can select an element in the Zone Your Application Will Be Installed From combo box, for example, the Local Intranet. Finally, click the Advanced button and ensure that the Debug This Application With The Selected Permission Set check box is selected in the Advanced Security Settings dialog box (see right portion of Figure 5-25).

To test this feature, place this code in the Sub Main procedure:

```
' Read the names of files in the root directory of C drive.
Dim files() As String = Directory.GetFiles("c:\")
```

When you type the dot after the name of the Directory class, you'll get a clue that the Debug-in-Zone feature is enabled because IntelliSense shows as unavailable all the members of this class that aren't permitted by CAS (see Figure 5-26). If you run the code, you'll get a SecurityException. One of the options in the Exception helper dialog box allows you to add the required permission (FileIOPermission, in this case), but the new permission won't be used until you restart the application.

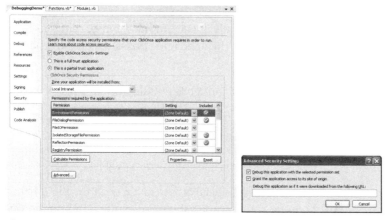

Figure 5-25   The Security page of the My Project designer (left) and the Advanced Security Settings dialog box (right)

Figure 5-26   IntelliSense grays out type members that can't be invoked when the application runs in the selected zone.

The Permissions Required By The Application area lists all the permissions recognized by the .NET Framework and contains a green icon to the right of those that are granted to your application because of the zone it originates from. If the default intranet or Internet settings aren't granular enough for your needs, you can select a zone and manually include or exclude the permissions you'd like to be assigned to your assembly.

Alternatively, you can click the Calculate Permissions button to have Visual Studio determine which permissions your application requires. The permission calculator analyzes the compiled assembly, looks for any call into the .NET Framework that might require a permission, and then adds the necessary permissions to the list. At the end of the process, you'll see these additional permissions highlighted by a yellow icon in the list.

A note is in order: the permission calculator might fail to omit permissions that are required—for example, those related to methods that you invoke through reflection—and might mistakenly include permissions used by methods that are never invoked in your executable, so you should take its results with a grain of salt.

The Visual Studio Hosting Process

Console and Windows Forms applications that you debug from inside Visual Studio 2005 don't actually run as separate processes; instead, they are hosted inside a process named *ProgramName*.vshost.exe that is automatically created in the same directory as the main executable file. This special process makes the debugging phase easier and faster, but it might introduce minor issues during debugging.

For example, if you query the name of the configuration file from inside a process in Debug mode you'll see a different name:

```
' This code assumes the application is named TestApp.
Dim configFile As String = AppDomain.CurrentDomain.SetupInformation.ConfigurationFile
Console.WriteLine(configFile)        ' => C:\TestApp\Bin\Debug\TestApp.vshost.exe.config
```

If the solution contains an app.config file, Visual Studio copies it in the bin directory twice, with the names TestApp.exe.config and TestApp.vshost.exe.config. The application reads its settings from the latter file, but some .NET methods—most notably the Trace.Refresh method—implicitly reference the former one. Therefore, if you modify the configuration file while the application is running, ensure that you edit the one from where the application being debugged reads its settings. (Or modify both files if you are in doubt.)

If the application is expected to read or modify the standard configuration file, as opposed to the version with vshost in its name, you should filter the name of the file as follows:

```
configFile = configFile.Replace(".vshost.exe.config", ".exe.config")
```

Finally, you can disable the Visual Studio host process and still be able to debug the application by clearing the Enable The Visual Studio Hosting Process check box on the Debug page of the My Project designer.

Macros for Debugging

In the section titled "Tracepoints" earlier in this chapter, you saw how you can execute a macro when execution reaches a specific statement and how the macro can read and display information about the current method, its arguments, and local variables. You don't have to use a tracepoint to execute a macro in Debug mode, though, and in fact you can easily create macros that automate many other recurring debugging tasks. For example, consider the following macro:

```
Sub ClearLocalVariables()
   Dim frame As EnvDTE.StackFrame = DTE.Debugger.CurrentStackFrame
   For Each expr As EnvDTE.Expression In frame.Locals
      ' Check whether this item is an argument or a local variable.
      Dim isArgument As Boolean = False
      For Each arg As Expression In frame.Arguments
        If arg.Name = expr.Name Then isArgument = True: Exit For
      Next
      ' If it is a local variable, reset it to its default value.
```

```
      If Not isArgument Then
        Select Case expr.Type
          Case "Integer", "Short", "Long", "Single", "Double", "Decimal"
            expr.Value = 0
          Case "Char"
            expr.Value = Chr(0)
          Case "Boolean"
            expr.Value = False
          Case Else
            ' Treat any other type as an object, but be prepared for exceptions.
            Try
              ' Assigning the Value property doesn't work in this case.
              DTE.Debugger.ExecuteStatement(expr.Name & " = Nothing")
            Catch ex As System.Exception
              ' Ignore exceptions.
            End Try
        End Select
      End If
  Next
End Sub
```

The ClearLocalVariables macro turns very useful when you are debugging a method and you use the Set Next Statement command to restart execution from the first statement in the method itself. In such a case, you want to clear all local variables to their default values (zero for numbers, Nothing for strings and objects, and so on), and this is exactly what this macro does.

In writing this macro, I had to solve a couple of minor problems. First, the Locals collection of the EnvDTE.StackFrame type includes both local variables and arguments passed to the current method; therefore, the only way to determine whether an item of this collection is a local variable is to compare it to all the members in the Arguments collection. Second, a macro can change the value of any numeric local variable simply by assigning a value to its Value property, but this method doesn't work with strings and object variables: to set their value to Nothing the macro uses an ExecuteStatement method of the Debugger object. You'd better protect this statement with a Try...Catch block in case the Select Case in the macro fails to recognize a value type. (For example, this happens with structures and with Date local variables.)

Macros can even execute debugging commands such as Step Over, Step Into, and Step Out, and you can place these commands in a loop to execute them repeatedly for a given number of times or while a given condition holds true. For example, consider this frequent debugging task: you are inside a method that you don't need to debug, but you'd like to break execution when either the current method exits or it calls another method. In this case, the Step Out command would be of no use because you'd miss all calls to other methods. In Visual Studio 2005, you can use this simple macro:

```
Sub StepIntoOrOut()
    Try
        Dim funcName As String = DTE.Debugger.CurrentStackFrame.FunctionName
        Do
            ' Single-step tracing
```

```
            DTE.Debugger.StepInto()
              ' Loop until execution leaves current function.
          Loop While DTE.Debugger.CurrentStackFrame.FunctionName = funcName
      Catch
          ' Exit whenever an error occurs.
      End Try
End Sub
```

For the best results you should assign this macro to a keyboard shortcut, for example, Ctrl+Shift+F11, which resembles the shortcut associated with the Step Out command (Shift+F11) and isn't assigned to any command in Visual Studio's default keyboard configuration.

Testing Different Configuration Files

Despite the many new features Visual Studio 2005 includes, it still lacks one facility that turns out to be quite useful when working with multiple-project configurations: the option to use a different .config file for each possible project configuration. This option is handy, for example, when each project configuration uses a different level of tracing or when you are testing versions that differ for values stored in the configuration file, such as connection strings, computer names, and so forth. In this section, I show you how you can solve this issue by means of a macro that traps the OnBuildProjConfigDone event of the BuildEvents object. (See the section titled "Handling Macro Events" in Chapter 4 for more information.)

Open the EnvironmentEvents module in the MyMacros default macro project, and then add the following Imports statements at the top of the source file:

```
Imports System.IO
Imports System.Collections
```

Next, add the following code inside the EnvironmentEvents module after the block of code that has been generated automatically:

```
Private Sub BuildEvents_OnBuildProjConfigDone( _
       ByVal Project As String, ByVal ProjectConfig As String, _
       ByVal Platform As String, ByVal SolutionConfig As String, _
       ByVal Success As Boolean) Handles BuildEvents.OnBuildProjConfigDone
    Dim prj As Project = DTE.Solution.Projects.Item(Project)
    Dim prjDir As String = Path.GetDirectoryName(prj.FileName)
    ' This macro works only with the active configuration.
    Dim cnf As Configuration = prj.ConfigurationManager.ActiveConfiguration
    ' Get a reference to the right .config file.
    Dim sourceFile As String = Path.Combine(prjDir, cnf.ConfigurationName & ".config")
    ' If not found, look for a file named Default.config.
    If Not File.Exists(sourceFile) Then sourceFile = Path.Combine(prjDir, "Default.config")
    If File.Exists(sourceFile) Then
        ' Evaluate the directory for output files.
        Dim outDir As String = cnf.Properties.Item("OutputPath").Value
        ' If relative filename, convert to absolute path.
        If Not Path.IsPathRooted(outDir) Then outDir = Path.Combine(prjDir, outDir)
        ' Derive the name of the output configuration file.
```

```
      Dim configFile As String = outDir & _
      prj.Properties.Item("OutputFileName").Value & ".config"
      ' Copy the file, renaming it in the process.
      Try
          File.Copy(sourceFile, configFile, True)
      Catch ex As System.Exception
          Debug.WriteLine(String.Format("Unable to copy config file {0} to {1}", _
             sourceFile, configFile))
      End Try
   End If
End Sub
```

When the current project is compiled, this macro looks for a file named after the current con-figuration and with a .config extension, for example, Debug.config or Release.config. If found, the macro renames this file so that it will be recognized by the executable (for example: MyApp.exe.config) and copies it to the output directory—that is, where the executable file is generated. When the application runs, it will therefore use the proper configuration file. If no file named after the current configuration exists, the macro looks for a file named Default.config. If neither file exists, the macro does absolutely nothing.

After you've created this macro, you can add one or more .config files to the solution and rename each of them after the project configuration that should use that configuration file, for example, Release.config. If most project configurations use the same configuration file, you should create a file named Default.config and store all common settings there; the macro will use this file when a more specific configuration file is missing. (Note that this macro works for Console and Windows Forms projects, but doesn't work for ASP.NET projects.)

Part II
Object-Oriented Programming

Chapter 6
Class Fundamentals

If you are switching to Microsoft .NET Framework programming from Microsoft Visual Basic 6 or another language with little or no support for object-oriented programming (OOP), you'll be overwhelmed by the large number of OOP features of Microsoft Visual Basic 2005. In practice, you can't do any sort of programming under .NET without massive use of objects and concepts, such as inheritance or interfaces, because the .NET Framework is built on these cornerstones. For this reason, you must fully understand all the OOP concepts in Visual Basic. In this chapter, I review a few of the basic concepts that I introduced in Chapter 2, "Basic Language Concepts," but I show more examples and illustrate several important coding techniques.

Developers who have already worked with previous versions of Visual Basic .NET will surely find themselves quite comfortable with Visual Basic 2005; nevertheless, I recommend that they don't skip this chapter because the new version of the language has several important OOP additions that can make programming more effective.

Note To avoid long lines, code samples in this chapter assume that the following Imports statements are used at the file or project level:

```
Imports System.IO
Imports System.Xml.Serialization
```

Fields

A class can contain both public and private fields, which look like variables declared directly inside the Class block.

```
Public Class Person
   ' Fields visible from outside the class
   Public FirstName As String
   Public LastName As String
   ' Fields that can be used only from inside the class
   Dim m_BirthDate As Date
   Dim m_LoginDate As Date
   Private EmailUserName As String
   Private EmailEnabled As Boolean = True      ' Field initializer
End Class
```

Microsoft guidelines dictate that field names use PascalCase when they contain multiple words (for example, FirstName) and never use a prefix to indicate the field's data type (the so-called Hungarian naming convention). For example, you shouldn't use the prefix str for a string variable, int for an Integer variable, or lng for a Long variable. (However, it is generally accepted that control names use a prefix that reflects their type, for example, txt for TextBox controls.) You can use all the syntax variations that you would use with plain variables, including initializers and multiple declarations on the same line, even though the latter practice degrades code readability and is therefore discouraged.

Fields can have any of the scope keywords allowed by Visual Basic: Private, Friend, Protected, Protected Friend, and Public. A field with Friend visibility can be accessed by any other code in the same project but not by code in other assemblies. (I cover Protected and Protected Friend scope qualifiers in Chapter 8, "Inheritance"):

```
' Inside the Person class
Friend EmailPassword As String
```

A minor language inconsistency is that the Dim statement defines a private field inside a Class block, whereas it declares a public field when it appears in a Structure block. From outside the class, nonprivate fields appear as plain properties and can be used as such:

```
' A block of code that uses the Person class
Dim aPerson As New Person
aPerson.FirstName = "Francesco"
aPerson.LastName = "Balena"
```

You can also declare arrays and constants as public fields:

```
Public Const DefaultPassword As String = "mypwd"
' You can define up to four addresses for this person,
' from Address(0) to Address(3).
Public Address(3) As String
```

You can access a public array field as you would access any property with an index:

```
aPerson.Address(0) = "1234 North Street"
```

> **Note**   Even though a class field can be flagged with any of the five scope keywords supported by Visual Basic, good programming rules dictate that all fields in a class should have private scope. If their value is to be made visible to code outside the class, you should implement a public property that wraps them. The only accepted exception to this rule is shared read-only fields. (See the section titled "Shared Fields" later in this chapter.)

You can declare fields and variables anywhere in a class, not just at its beginning. For example, you can declare a private variable immediately before or after the property that encapsulates it, or you can move all your variables to just before the End Class statement. If you've selected the Show Procedure Line Separators check box (on the VB Specific page of the Basic folder, under the Text Editor node of the Options dialog box), a line separator appears immediately before the Property statement.

All .NET versions of Visual Basic differ from Visual Basic 6 in the way fields are passed to methods that take ByRef arguments. In Visual Basic 6, all fields are wrapped in a pair of hidden Get and Set property procedures; therefore, when you pass a field to a procedure, you're actually passing the result of a procedure call. For this reason, the callee can never modify the value of the original field. Conversely, in all .NET editions of Visual Basic, a field behaves exactly like a variable when passed to a ByRef parameter, and as such it can be modified by the procedure being called. This apparently minor difference can be the cause of significant problems when you port a Visual Basic 6 application to Visual Basic 2005. Say you have the following Visual Basic 6 routine:

```
' Raise to the fourth power.
Function Power4(x As Double) As Double
    ' This is slightly faster than x^4.
    x = x * x
    Power4 = x * x
End Sub
```

As you might recall, Visual Basic 6 parameters lacking an explicit ByVal keyword are passed by reference. The preceding code contains a logic error because the Power4 function unnecessarily modifies an argument passed to it, but you don't see any malfunctioning unless the Visual Basic 6 program passes a variable (as opposed to a class field) to the Power4 function. However, the problem manifests itself when you migrate this code to Visual Basic 2005 because in this new version class fields *are* modified when passed to the Power4 method. For this reason, you should pay close attention when migrating a Visual Basic 6 procedure that takes ByRef arguments (including when the ByRef keyword is omitted) and ask yourself whether this passing style is really what the original author actually meant.

Finally, if the value of a class field is meant to remain constant during the object's lifetime, you should flag the field with the ReadOnly keyword.

```
Public ReadOnly CreationDate As Date = Now
```

Read-only fields can be initialized only by means of initializers (as in the previous statement) or from inside constructor methods. (Read the section titled "Constructors" later in this chapter.) Any attempt to assign such a value elsewhere in the class results in a compilation error. Notice that you can use the ReadOnly keyword by itself to create a private class field; thus, you have at least three ways to declare a read-only private field, even though you should opt for the more verbose syntax if you care about readability:

```
Private ReadOnly CreateTime As Date      ' This is the recommended syntax.
Dim ReadOnly CreateTime As Date          ' Dim should be used only for local variables.
ReadOnly CreateTime As Date              ' The variable scope isn't clear.
```

Before we move to another topic, let me draw your attention to a simple optimization technique related to class fields. When repeatedly accessing the same public or private field, you can make your code run faster by assigning the field to a local variable and using the variable in expressions. For example, consider this code:

```
Class Test
    Public publicField As Integer

    Sub RunBenchmark()
        Dim sw As New Stopwatch()
        sw.Start()
        For i As Integer = 1 To 1000000000
            publicField += 1
        Next
        sw.Stop()
        Console.WriteLine("Public field: {0} msecs", sw.ElapsedMilliseconds)

        Dim localVar As Integer
        sw = New Stopwatch()
        sw.Start()
        For i As Integer = 1 To 1000000000
            localVar += 1
        Next
        sw.Stop()
        Console.WriteLine("Local variable: {0} msecs", sw.ElapsedMilliseconds)

        Console.WriteLine("Total = {0}", publicField + localVar)
    End Sub
End Class
```

On my computer, the loop that uses the local variable is 50 percent faster than the loop that uses the public field when you compile in Release mode with optimizations enabled, which is a good result if you consider how easily this optimization technique can be applied. The reason for the performance improvement has to do with threading: fields can be accessed by other threads using the same instance of the class, whereas local variables can be used only by the current thread. Therefore, the Just-In-Time (JIT) compiler can safely produce code that stores local variables in faster CPU registers, whereas this optimization technique (known as *variable enregistration*) can't be applied to fields, which must be accessed by their address in memory.

Methods

I have covered methods in depth in the section titled "Procedures" in Chapter 3, "Control Flow and Error Handling"; therefore, here I focus mainly on features that were introduced in the .NET version of Visual Basic. Methods can be implemented as Sub or Function procedures, depending on whether they return a value and can take ByVal, ByRef, and Optional parameters.

```
' Add to the Person class.
Function CompleteName(Optional ByVal title As String = "") As String
   CompleteName = ""
   ' Use the title if provided.
   If title <> "" Then CompleteName = title & " "
   ' Append first and last name.
   CompleteName &= FirstName & " " & LastName
End Function
```

Microsoft guidelines dictate that you use PascalCase for the names of methods (for example, ClearAll) and that you use the "verb+object" syntax rather than the "object+verb" syntax (for example, PrintDocument rather than DocumentPrint). Parameters should use camelCase (for example, mainAddress) and never use a prefix that indicates their data type. Another interesting suggestion from Microsoft is that you should never define a parameter that has as its only purpose "reserved for future use" because newer versions of the class can overload a method (see the next section) to support additional arguments without breaking backward compatibility with existing code.

Overloading

Visual Basic 2005 lets you overload a method. *Method overloading* means that you can provide multiple methods with the same name but different parameter signatures, where a method's *signature* is defined as the list of its parameters and its return value; parameter names don't affect the signature, but their types and whether they are passed by ByRef or ByVal do. As far as overloading is concerned, the return type of a method isn't part of its signature; therefore, two methods with the same name must differ by more than the type of their return value.

Before explaining how you implement overloaded methods, I think it makes sense to illustrate why overloading can be useful. Suppose you're creating a collection-like class and include an Item method that provides access to the collection's elements through either a numeric or a string argument. If you couldn't count on method overloading—as is the case in Visual Basic 6—the best you could do is define a method that takes an Object parameter:

```
Function Item(ByVal index As Object) As String
   If TypeOf index Is Integer Then
      ' Access an element through its numeric index.
      …
   ElseIf TypeOf index Is String Then
      ' Access an element through its string key.
      …
   Else
      ' Raise a runtime error otherwise.
```

```
    Throw New ArgumentException()
  End If
End Function
```

Overloading enables you to implement a cleaner and more efficient solution. You define multiple procedures with the same name and different syntax:

```
Function Item(ByVal index As Integer) As String
   ' Access an element through its numeric index.
   …
End Function

Function Item(ByVal key As String) As String
   ' Access an element through its string key.
   …
End Function
```

You can optionally mark an overloaded method with the Overloads keyword, as follows:

```
Overloads Function Item(ByVal index As Integer) As String
   …
End Function
```

The Overloads keyword is optional, but if you use it for one overloaded method, you must use it for all of them. In general, I don't recommend using the Overloads keyword because it doesn't bring any advantage and doesn't improve code readability; for example, C# doesn't support any special word to mark overloaded methods.

The approach based on overloading rather than on generic Object parameters is more efficient because the compiler decides which version of the Item function is called, and no test is necessary at run time:

```
' This statement calls the first overloaded version.
result = myObj.Item(1)
' This statement calls the second overloaded version.
result = myObj.Item("foo")
```

Just as important, the compiler can flag invalid arguments, so you don't have to trap arguments of invalid type:

```
' *** The following code doesn't compile.
Dim value As Double = 1.23
result = myObj.Item(value)
```

Conveniently, IntelliSense correctly recognizes overloaded methods and displays a list of all the supported syntax forms. You can visit all of them using the Up and Down arrow keys:

```
myObj.Item(
```
▲ 1 of 2 ▼ Item (**index As Integer**) As String

Method overloading enables you to get rid of optional arguments, even though this decision requires that you create a distinct overloaded version for each possible optional argument. As I explain in Chapter 3, the problem with optional arguments is that a few .NET languages—most notably, C#—don't recognize them. C# developers calling a Visual Basic method must pass all the arguments; thus, providing overloaded versions with fewer parameters can help them write more readable code.

Overloading and Coercion

When the argument types don't exactly match the parameter signature of any available method, the compiler attempts to match them through widening coercion exclusively. (See the section titled "The Option Strict Directive" in Chapter 2 to review the difference between widening and narrowing coercion.) For example, assume that you have two overloaded Sum functions:

```
Function Sum(ByVal n1 As Long, ByVal n2 As Long) As Long
    Return n1 + n2
End Function
Function Sum(ByVal n1 As Single, ByVal n2 As Single) As Single
    Return n1 + n2
End Function
```

Now consider what happens when you invoke the Sum function with Integer arguments:

```
Dim intValue As Short = 1234
' This statement invokes the version with Long parameters.
Console.WriteLine(Sum(intValue, 1))              ' => 1235
```

In this case, both arguments are 16-bit integers, but Visual Basic correctly promotes them to Long and calls the first version of the Sum function. Here's another example:

```
' This statement invokes the floating-point version.
Console.WriteLine(Sum(intValue, 1.25!))          ' => 1235.25
```

In this case, Visual Basic realizes that only the second version can be invoked without losing precision. Finally, consider this third example:

```
Dim dblValue As Double = 1234
' *** The next statement raises a compiler error.
Console.WriteLine(Sum(dblValue, 1.25))
```

In this last case, you can't call either Sum function without the risk of losing precision or throwing an out-of-range exception at run time, so Visual Basic refuses to compile this piece of code.

Ambiguous Cases

Visual Basic must be able to resolve a method call at compile time. Therefore, two overloaded procedures of the same method must differ in more respects than simply an optional argument. For example, the following third variant of the Sum function can't compile because it differs from the second form only by an optional argument:

```
Function Sum(ByVal n1 As Single, Optional ByVal n2 As Single = 1) As Single
    Return n1 + n2
End Function
```

The compiler shows what's wrong by issuing the following message:

```
'Public Function Sum(n1 As Single, n2 As Single) As Single' and
'Public Function Sum(n1 As Single, [n2 As Single = 1.0]) As Single'
cannot overload each other because they differ only by optional parameters.
```

A corollary of this concept is that you can't create overloaded variations of a function that differ only in the type of the returned value, as I already explained earlier. For example, you can't overload a ClearValue function that returns either a null string or a null integer:

```
' *** This code doesn't compile.
Function ClearValue() As String
    ClearValue = ""
End Function
Function ClearValue() As Long
    ClearValue = 0
End Function
```

You can work around this limitation by returning a value by means of a ByRef argument; the type of the argument determines which version of the procedure is actually called:

```
' This code compiles correctly.
Sub ClearValue(ByRef arg As String)
    arg = ""
End Sub
Sub ClearValue(ByRef arg As Long)
    arg = 0
End Sub
' You should add versions for other numeric types.
...
```

Finally, remember that you can also overload class properties and that overloading isn't limited to classes; you can overload Sub and Function procedures defined in Module and Structure blocks, too.

Properties

Properties can be considered smarter fields in that they can be assigned to or read from (like a field), yet when this happens some code in the class executes, and therefore the author of the class can process the value being assigned or returned. You can implement a property by means of a Property...End Property block, which defines the property's name, its type, and its argument signature:

```
Public Property BirthDate() As Date
    ' Implementation of BirthDate property goes here.
    ...
End Property
```

Notice that a Property block can be flagged with a scope keyword, as methods can; if no keyword is used, properties are public by default. It is advisable that you use the Public keyword explicitly, though, because it makes your intention clearer.

Inside the Property block, you write a Get...End Get block, which defines which value the property returns, and a Set...End Set block, which defines how values are assigned to the property. In most cases, a property simply maps to a Private field, so the code for these two blocks often looks like this:

```
' You can define variables anywhere in a class or module.
Dim m_BirthDate As Date

Public Property BirthDate() As Date
   Get
      Return m_BirthDate
   End Get
   Set(ByVal value As Date)
      m_BirthDate = value
   End Set
End Property
```

The Set...End Set block always receives an argument named value, which stands for the value being assigned to the property itself. This argument must be of the same type as the type defined in the Property statement and must be declared using ByVal. If you happen to have a field named value or Value at the class level, you can distinguish between the field and the value argument by prefixing the field with the Me keyword or, more simply, by renaming the parameter:

```
' A class that has a Value field
Class ValueClass
   Private Value As Double

   ' A property that uses the Value field
   Public Property DoubleValue() As Double
      Get
         Return Me.Value * 2
      End Get
      Set(ByVal newValue As Double)
         Me.Value = newValue / 2
      End Set
   End Property
End Class
```

Note that Me.Value is a legal syntax in Visual Basic 2005, even if the Value field is private. Under Visual Basic 6, only public variables could be accessed through the Me keyword, but this restriction has been lifted.

Interestingly, you can pass a property to a ByRef parameter of a procedure, and any change to the argument is reflected in the property. The same happens when you increment or decrement a property using the += and -= operators, as this code shows:

```
Sub TestByRefProperty
   Dim vc As New ValueClass
   vc.DoubleValue = 100
   ClearValue(vc.DoubleValue)
```

```
    ' Show that the method actually changed the property.
    Console.WriteLine(vc.DoubleValue)              ' => 0

    vc.DoubleValue += 10
    ' Show that the property was actually incremented.
    Console.WriteLine(vc.DoubleValue)              ' => 10
End Sub

Sub ClearValue(ByRef Value As Double)
    Value = 0
End Sub
```

Visual Basic property syntax is the same whether the property returns a simple value or an object. After all, everything is an object in the .NET Framework. For example, the following Spouse property can return a Person object that represents the wife or husband of the current Person object:

```
Private m_Spouse As Person

Public Property Spouse() As Person
    Get
        Return m_Spouse
    End Get
    Set(ByVal Value As Person)
        m_Spouse = Value
    End Set
End Property
```

As you see, this syntax is no different from that of a regular property that returns a string or a numeric value.

Read-Only and Write-Only Properties

You define read-only properties by using the ReadOnly keyword and omitting the Set...End Set block:

```
' The Age property is read-only.
Public ReadOnly Property Age() As Integer
    Get
        Return Year(Now) - Year(m_BirthDate)     ' Simplistic age calculation
    End Get
End Property
```

Similarly, you can create a write-only property by omitting the Get...End Get block and using the WriteOnly keyword in the Property block:

```
' LoginDate is a write-only property.
Public WriteOnly Property LoginDate() As Date
    Set(ByVal Value As Date)
        m_LoginDate = Value
    End Set
End Property
```

> **Note**   I have covered the WriteOnly keyword only for the sake of completeness. Write-only properties are unnatural for most developers and should be avoided in real applications. When you author a class that provides a way to assign a value but doesn't offer a way to read it back, use a method instead. For example, define a SetPassword method that takes a string instead of a write-only Password property.

Attempts to write read-only properties, as well as attempts to read write-only properties, are trapped at compile time. You can determine whether a property of a .NET class is read-write or read-only by looking at it in the Object Browser.

Read-only properties especially are commonly used to expose arrays and collections to the outside. Consider the following property:

```
' The ArrayList type exposes methods such as Add, Remove, etc.
Private m_Notes As New ArrayList()

Public ReadOnly Property Notes() As ArrayList
    Get
        Return m_Notes
    End Get
End Property
```

Even if the property is read-only, clients can both read and write elements in the collection and can even add or remove them:

```
' (From outside the Person class…)
Dim aPerson As New Person
aPerson.Notes.Add("wife's name is Ann.")
aPerson.Notes.Add("Has two kids, John and Mary.")
Console.WriteLine(aPerson.Notes(0))      ' => wife's name is Ann.
```

Although this behavior might be disconcerting at first, you can explain it if you consider that the Notes property returns a reference to an ArrayList object. Once the client code has such a reference, it can access all the methods and properties in the ArrayList class, including Add and the default Item property. For this reason, it is seldom necessary to expose private arrays and collections as writeable properties.

When you work with object values, properties enable you to implement an optimization technique known as *late instantiation* (or *lazy instantiation*). In practice, the creation of the object is deferred until the property is actually requested from the outside. For example, the Notes property I just illustrated uses a private ArrayList object that is always created when the Person object is instantiated. This object takes memory and resources even if no notes are ever added to this specific instance of the Person class. Now consider this code:

```
Private m_Notes As ArrayList

Public ReadOnly Property Notes() As ArrayList
    Get
```

```
       ' Create the ArrayList at the first request.
       If m_Notes Is Nothing Then m_Notes = New ArrayList
       Return m_Notes
    End Get
End Property
```

This edit doesn't affect the code outside the class in any way, but the creation of the ArrayList object occurs only if this property is actually invoked. If this property is never used, no memory is allocated. On the other hand, consider that calling this property is now slightly slower than the speed of the original version because of the If statement, so you must weigh whether this optimization technique is worth the effort. Even though it's hard to derive a rule that is valid in all cases, I've seen that lazy instantiation often delivers a good result, especially when you create thousands of objects of a given type and when the property that wraps the private field is rarely used.

A minor issue with lazy instantiation is that the code that uses the property might accidentally create the inner object just by "touching" the property. For example, the very action of testing whether a Person object has any notes associated with it creates the inner ArrayList object, thus nullifying the optimization technique. In these cases, you should add one more read-only property that enables the client to perform the test without adding this hidden overhead:

```
Public ReadOnly Property HasNotes() As Boolean
    Get
        Return m_Notes IsNot Nothing AndAlso m_Notes.Count > 0
    End Get
End Property
```

At times it's hard to decide whether a class should expose a value to the outside as a read-only property (for example, AvailableColors) or a Function (for example, GetAvailableColors). As you might expect, the decision is mainly a matter of coding style; however, here's a short checklist that can help you make a reasonable decision:

   a. Use a read-only property when returning the value of a private field or when returning the result of a simple calculation based on private fields.

   b. Use a method when producing the result requires complex calculations or has an observable side effect.

   c. Use a method when the read operation might throw an exception.

   d. Use a method when performing a conversion.

   e. Use a method when returning an array.

   f. Use a method when invoking it twice might deliver different results.

Furthermore, in general you should use a property when the member behaves like a field; otherwise, use a method. Keep in mind that most programmers assume that they can read properties as easily as they read fields; this operation should execute quickly, have no side effects, and not throw exceptions. For these reasons, properties should be implemented in such a way that clients can assign them in any order without changing the final result. If you can't guarantee this behavior, consider exposing a method for setting a group of properties in one operation and make the corresponding values available as read-only properties.

Different Scope for Get and Set Blocks

Visual Basic 2005 introduces an important feature to the language: the ability to define different visibility for the Get and Set blocks. This capability is essential when you're defining a property that must be read-only from outside the assembly and writeable from other classes in the same assembly. Here's the Visual Basic 2005 implementation of such a property:

```
Private m_ID As Integer

Public Property ID() As Integer
   Get
      Return m_ID
   End Get
   Friend Set(ByVal value As Integer)
      If value <= 0 Then Throw New ArgumentException("Negative values are invalid")
      m_ID = value
   End Set
End Property
```

Only one of the Get or Set blocks can be decorated with a scope keyword such as Friend or Private, and such a keyword must indicate a scope that is more restrictive than the scope keyword used in the property declaration. In practice, you never need to make the Get block more restrictive than the Set block. In most cases, you'll use the Public keyword at the property level and the Friend or Private keyword for the Set block.

Another common combination is having the Friend keyword at the property level and marking the Set block with the Private keyword. This arrangement defines a property that can be read from anywhere in the current project but can be assigned only from inside the current class:

```
Private m_UserName As String

Friend Property UserName() As String
   Get
      Return m_UserName
   End Get
   Private Set(ByVal value As String)
      If value = "" Then Throw New ArgumentException("Empty strings are invalid")
      m_UserName = value
   End Set
End Property
```

You might argue that code in the class might assign the m_UserName field directly, thus you can reach a similar effect with a property marked as ReadOnly that has no Set block. Nevertheless, I recommend that you use a property with a Private Set block and that you access m_UserName only from inside the UserName property because only this coding style ensures that all invalid values are rejected. Similarly, accessing the member variable from inside the Get block enables you to implement a lazy instantiation technique, as I explained earlier in this chapter. Unfortunately, Visual Basic offers no way to prevent code in the class from accessing a field directly; therefore, in general you must exert self-discipline and ensure that you access a private field only from inside the property that wraps it.

Properties with Arguments

You can define properties that take one or more arguments in a straightforward way:

```
' (Add to the Person class...)
Dim m_Addresses(3) As String        ' Up to four distinct lines for address

' The Addresses property takes an Integer argument.
Public Property Addresses(ByVal index As Integer) As String
   Get
      Return m_Addresses (index)
   End Get
   Set(ByVal value As String)
      m_Addresses(index) = value
   End Set
End Property
```

As you would expect, you get an IndexOutOfRangeException runtime error if the Index argument is less than 0 or greater than the last valid index of the array. You can provide a more descriptive description by trapping invalid index values and throwing the exception yourself:

```
Public Property Addresses(ByVal index As Integer) As String
   Get
      If index < 0 Or index > UBound(m_Addresses) Then
         Throw New IndexOutOfRangeException("Invalid address index.")
      End If
      Return m_Addresses(index)
   End Get
   Set(ByVal value As String)
      If index < 0 Or index > UBound(m_Addresses) Then
         Throw New IndexOutOfRangeException("Invalid address index.")
      End If
      m_Addresses(index) = value
   End Set
End Property
```

Note that you can overload properties as you would overload methods. Because overloaded members must have a different signature, at least one of the overloads must be a property with arguments.

Default Properties

A type can expose one default property, that is, a property whose name can be omitted when accessing it, as it happens with the Item property of the Collection type or the Chars property of the String type. As I explain in the section titled "Object Assignments" in Chapter 2, Visual Basic supports default properties only if the property takes one or more arguments because assignments aren't ambiguous in this case. Declaring a property with arguments that also works as the default property requires that you use the Default keyword:

```
Default Public Property Addresses(ByVal index As Integer) As String
    …
End Property
```

Now you can omit the property's name when using it:

```
' Set a note for a person.
Dim aPerson As New Person
aPerson.FirstName = "Joe"
' Prove that Addresses is the default property.
aPerson(0) = "1234 Z Street"
aPerson(1) = "San Bernardino, CA 94324"

' Display all the lines that make up the address.
For i As Integer = 0 To 3
    Console.WriteLine(aPerson(i))
Next
```

Constructors

A constructor is a method that runs when a new instance of the class is created. In Visual Basic, the constructor method is always named Sub New:

```
Class Person
    Private CreateTime As Date

    Public Sub New()
        ' Display a diagnostic message.
        Console.WriteLine("A new instance of Person is being created.")
        ' Remember when this instance was created.
        CreateTime = Now
        ' Perform other initialization chores.
        …
    End Sub
End Class
```

When the constructor runs, all the fields with initializers have already been initialized, so if you access such fields from within the constructor, you will find the value assigned to them by the initializer:

```
Class Person
    Public Citizenship As String = "American"

    Public Sub New()
        ' Prove that the field has already been initialized.
        Console.WriteLine(Citizenship)        ' => American
    End Sub
End Class
```

A constructor can, and often does, take arguments. Typically, you use arguments to define which values the calling code must pass to create an object correctly. For example, you can force the calling code to pass the first and last names when the caller creates an Employee object:

```
Public Class Employee
    Public FirstName As String
    Public LastName As String

    Public Sub New(ByVal firstName As String, ByVal lastName As String)
        ' You can resolve the argument vs. field ambiguity using the Me keyword.
        Me.FirstName = firstName
        Me.LastName = lastName
    End Sub
End Class
```

The Employee class must be instantiated in this way:

```
Dim empl As Employee
empl = New Employee("Joe", "Healy")
```

You can also use a shortened syntax:

```
Dim empl As New Employee("Joe", "Healy")
```

The great thing about constructors is that they can force clients to create objects in a valid state. To achieve this goal, however, you have to ensure that only valid arguments are passed to the constructor:

```
'(A new version of the Employee constructor…)
Public Sub New(ByVal firstName As String, ByVal lastName As String)
    If firstName = "" Or lastName = "" Then
        Throw New ArgumentException()
    End If
    Me.FirstName = firstName
    Me.LastName = lastName
End Sub
```

For a cleaner and more robust design, you should morph all your fields into properties and validate their values in Set…End Set blocks. Once you have these properties in place, the constructor method can simply assign the received argument to the corresponding property. If the property procedure throws an exception, the exception will be reported to the caller as if it were thrown from inside the New procedure.

```
'(A more robust version of Employee…)
Public Sub New(ByVal firstName As String, ByVal lastName As String)
    ' Delegate validation to Property procedures.
    Me.FirstName = firstName
    Me.LastName = lastName
End Sub

Private m_FirstName As String
```

```
Public Property FirstName() As String
   Get
      Return m_FirstName
   End Get
   Set(ByVal Value As String)
      If Value = "" Then Throw New ArgumentException("Invalid FirstName value")
      m_FirstName = Value
   End Set
End Property

Private m_LastName As String

Public Property LastName() As String
   Get
      Return m_LastName
   End Get
   Set(ByVal Value As String)
      If Value = "" Then Throw New ArgumentException("Invalid LastName value")
      m_LastName = Value
   End Set
End Property
```

This coding pattern, which puts all the validation code inside the Property Set block, ensures the best results in terms of robustness and code maintenance because the Set block is the only portion of the class that has to be updated when new validation requirements arise.

Not counting assignments made through initializers, a constructor procedure is the only place from inside a class where you can assign a value to read-only fields. For example, the CreateTime field is logically a read-only field and should be declared as such:

```
' This read-only field can be assigned only from inside a constructor method.
Private ReadOnly CreateTime As Date

Public Sub New()
   CreateTime = Now
End Sub
```

As I just mentioned, you can also initialize a read-only field by using an initializer, so for simpler cases you don't really need to make the assignment from inside the constructor:

```
Private ReadOnly CreateTime As Date = Now
```

If you use the ILDASM tool to disassemble this code, you'll notice that an initializer is actually rendered as a regular assignment placed inside the constructor; therefore, the two approaches are perfectly equivalent. However, explicitly assigning a read-only field from inside the constructor can produce slightly less code when the class has multiple constructors.

Overloaded Constructors

Like all methods, the Sub New method can be overloaded. In practice, this means that you can provide users with many ways to instantiate objects, which improves the usability of your classes. For example, you might have a Product class that can be instantiated by passing the product name and an optional product numeric code:

```
Public Class Product
   Public Sub New(ByVal name As String)
      Me.Name = name
   End Sub

   Public Sub New(ByVal name As String, ByVal id As Integer)
      Me.Name = name
      Me.Id = id
   End Sub

   ' (Implementation of Name and Id properties is omitted.)
End Class
```

Note that you can't use the Overloads keyword with constructors. The preceding code can be simplified if you call the first constructor from inside the second one, or vice versa. In general, I prefer to have simpler constructors call the more complete ones:

```
Public Sub New(ByVal name As String)
   ' Call the other constructor, pass default value for second argument.
   Me.New(name, 0)
End Sub
```

(It is essential that the Me.New call is the first executable statement in the constructor method; otherwise, Visual Basic flags it as a compiler error.) The advantage of this approach is that all the initialization code is kept in a single procedure and you don't have to worry about subtle bugs caused by multiple constructors performing slightly different initialization chores.

In some cases, a class exposes two or more constructors, but you can't use delegation. For example, suppose that you have a Customer class that exposes two constructors, one taking the customer's name and the other taking the customer's ID. Clearly, one of these constructors can't delegate to the other. However, you can define a private constructor and put all the common code there.

```
Public Class Customer
   Public Sub New(ByVal name As String)
      Me.New()           ' Delegate to the private constructor.
      …
   End Sub

   Public Sub New(ByVal ID As Integer)
      Me.New()           ' Delegate to the private constructor.
      …
   End Sub

   Private Sub New()
      ' Put all the common initialization code here.
      …
   End Sub
End Class
```

Shared Members

Visual Basic classes support shared fields, properties, and methods. Shared members are also known as *static members* in other object-oriented languages, and in this book I use the two terms interchangeably. The main difference between regular members (also known as *instance members*) and shared members is that the latter members belong to the type, not to individual instances of the class. This distinction is especially evident with shared fields and properties, as you'll learn shortly.

Shared Methods

You can use the Shared keyword to mark a method as static, which makes the method callable without you needing to instantiate an object of that class. For example, consider the Triangle class I use to illustrate unit testing in Chapter 5, "Debugging Visual Basic Applications":

```
Public Class Triangle
    Dim a, b, c As Double

    Public Sub New(ByVal sideA As Double, ByVal sideB As Double, ByVal sideC As Double)
        a = sideA: b = sideB: c = sideC
        ' Check that such a triangle can actually be built.
        If a < Math.Abs(b - c) OrElse b < Math.Abs(a - c) OrElse c < Math.Abs(a - c) Then
            Throw New ArgumentException("Invalid triangle")
        End If
    End Sub

    Public Function GetPerimeter() As Double
        Return a + b + c
    End Function

    Public Function GetArea() As Double
        ' Use Heron's formula to calculate the area.
        Dim halfP As Double = (a + b + c) / 2
        Return Math.Sqrt(halfP * (halfP - a) * (halfP - b) * (halfP - c))
    End Function
End Class
```

This class does its job, but in some cases you might want to evaluate the perimeter or the area of a triangle without having to instantiate a Triangle object. Here's how you can solve this problem by means of two static methods:

```
Public Shared Function GetPerimeter(ByVal a As Double, ByVal b As Double, _
        ByVal c As Double) As Double
    Return a + b + c
End Function

Public Shared Function GetArea(ByVal a As Double, ByVal b As Double, _
        ByVal c As Double) As Double
    Dim halfP As Double = (a + b + c) / 2
    Return Math.Sqrt(halfP * (halfP - a) * (halfP - b) * (halfP - c))
End Function
```

Code inside a static method can access other static members but can't access instance fields, properties, and methods. This is a reasonable limitation in that the code in the static method wouldn't know which specific object should provide the instance data. Because static methods can be invoked before you create an instance of a given class, there might be no running object at all.

You can access a static method from outside the class in two ways: through an instance variable (as for all methods) and through the name of the class. The latter method is usually preferable because you don't need to instantiate a Triangle object:

```
Console.WriteLine(Triangle.GetPerimeter(3, 4, 5))    ' => 12
Console.WriteLine(Triangle.GetArea(3, 4, 5))         ' => 6
```

When you type the name of a class and press the Period key, IntelliSense correctly omits instance members and displays only the list of all the static fields, properties, and methods:

```
Dim result as Double = Triangle.|
```
```
  GetArea
  GetPerimeter
  Common        All
```

In general, accessing a shared member through an instance variable isn't recommended because it makes your code ambiguous. Visual Basic 2005 adds a new compiler warning that flags the statements in code where this technique is applied. You can control this feature by means of the Instance Variable Accesses Shared Member option on the Compile page of the My Project designer.

You don't even need to prefix static method names with the class name if you use a proper Imports statement, such as this one:

```
' This statement assumes that Triangle is defined in the MyProject namespace.
Imports MyProject.Triangle
...
' Invoke the GetArea shared method without specifying the class name.
Console.WriteLine(GetArea(3, 4, 5))                  ' => 6
```

In general, two types of classes contain static members exclusively. One is a class that works as a container for library functions, such as the System.Math type or the Triangle class shown previously. The other case is when you have a type for which only one instance can exist. An example of the latter type is the System.Console class, which contains only static methods and can't be instantiated; the class itself maps to the one and only console window the application manages. Such classes are known as *singletons*. The .NET Framework contains several other examples of singletons, for example, System.Environment (the operating system environment), System.Diagnostics.Debug (the Debug window), and System.Windows.Forms .Application (the running Microsoft Windows Forms application).

If a class contains only static methods—be it a function library or a singleton—there's no point in instantiating it. You can make a class noncreatable simply by adding a Private constructor whose only purpose is to suppress the automatic generation of the Public constructor that the Visual Basic compiler would perform if no constructor were provided:

```
' A class that contains only static members
Class HelperFunctions
    …
    Private Sub New()
        ' This private constructor contains no code. Its only purpose
        ' is to prevent clients from instantiating this class.
    End Sub
End Class
```

As I explain in Chapter 2, a class that contains only static members is functionally equivalent to a module. As a matter of fact, a Visual Basic module is nothing but a class that can't be instantiated and whose members are implicitly marked with the Shared keyword. As an added convenience, you can omit the name of the module when you access a module's member from a Visual Basic application—be it the same application where the module is defined or another application. This feature is known as *static imports* because it is equivalent to having a suitable Imports statement at the top of each file in your application. However, keep in mind that if you access the module from any language other than Visual Basic, you must specify the module name when you access its static members because only Visual Basic recognizes the special attribute that is used to mark modules.

A class or a module can contain a special static method named Sub Main. This procedure can be used as the entry point of the entire application. Simply select the class name in the Startup Object combo box on the Application page of the My Project designer. For this option to be available, ensure that the Enable Application Framework option is disabled. (This option can be enabled only in Windows Forms projects.)

Shared Fields

Shared or static fields are variables that can be accessed (that is, shared) by all the instances of a given class. You declare a static field as you would define any regular field, except that you prefix the variable name with the Shared keyword:

```
Public Class Invoice
    ' This variable holds the number of instances created so far.
    Shared InstanceCount As Integer

    Sub New()
        ' Increment the number of created instances.
        InstanceCount += 1
    End Sub
End Class
```

The default scope for static fields is Private, but you can create static fields that are visible from outside the class by using the Public or Friend keyword:

```
' This shared variable is visible from inside the current assembly.
Friend Shared InstanceCount As Integer
```

Static members are useful for many purposes. For example, you can use the InstanceCount shared variable to implement a read-only ID property that returns a unique number for each instance of this particular class during the application's lifetime:

```
Public Class Invoice
    ' This variable holds the number of instances created so far.
    Private Shared InstanceCount As Integer

    Public Sub New()
        ' Increment number of created instances.
        InstanceCount += 1
        ' Use the current count as the ID for this instance.
        m_Id = InstanceCount
    End Sub

    ' A unique ID for this instance
    Private ReadOnly m_Id As Long

    Public ReadOnly Property ID() As Long
        Get
            Return m_ID
        End Get
    End Property
End Class
```

Programming guidelines dictate that a class shouldn't expose public fields, and this rule applies to both instance and static fields. A field should always be wrapped by a property; therefore, a static field should be wrapped by a static property. However, it is relatively common to find examples of public static fields marked as read-only in the .NET Framework. ReadOnly static fields are logically equivalent to class-level Const statements, with an important difference: constants are assigned at compile time, whereas a ReadOnly static field is assigned at run time either by means of an initializer or from inside the shared constructor. (Read on to learn more about shared constructors.)

```
Public Shared ReadOnly StartExecutionTime As Date = Now
```

Static read-only fields with public scope are typically used to expose constant values that are related to the entire type. For example, consider the DBNull type, which represents the null values that you can read from a database. This type has no methods or properties, it just has a public, shared, and read-only field named Value, which in turns return an instance of the type itself:

```
' Store a "null" value in an object variable.
Dim obj As Object = DBNull.Value
…
' Two ways to test whether an object variable contains a "null" value.
If TypeOf obj Is DBNull Then Console.WriteLine("null value")
If obj Is DBNull.Value Then Console.WriteLine("null value")
```

Shared Properties

A static property is nothing but a Property procedure marked with the Shared keyword. In most cases, a static property is a wrapper for a private static field. For example, the Invoice class shown in the previous section might be extended by adding a NextInvoiceID read-only static property so that an application might know which ID will be assigned to the next invoice object without having to create it:

```
Public Class Invoice
    …
    Public Shared ReadOnly Property NextInvoiceID() As Long
        Get
            Return InstanceCount + 1
        End Get
    End Property
End Class
```

Read-only shared properties are often used to expose singleton objects. In the section titled "Shared Methods" earlier in this chapter, I explain that most singleton objects in the .NET Framework are implemented as individual types that expose static methods exclusively. In some cases, however, it is required that the singleton object expose regular (that is, instance) members; for example, this is the case with objects that must be marked with the Serializable attribute because the serialization infrastructure recognizes only instance fields. (Read Chapter 21, "Serialization," for more information about serialization.)

Here's a practical example of a technique that I used in several real applications. I gather all the global variables in a class named something like Globals or ProjectData that I can persist to an XML file stored on disk. To leverage the XML serialization mechanism offered by the .NET Framework, these global variables must be implemented as instance fields, but at the same time the class must be exposed as a singleton so that it can be accessed from anywhere in the application. Here's how you can build such a class:

```
' This code requires a reference to the System.Xml.dll assembly.

' (Classes must be public to use XML serialization.)
Public Class Globals
    ' This singleton instance is created when the application is created.
    Private Shared m_Value As New Globals

    ' This static read-only property returns the singleton instance.
    Public Shared ReadOnly Property Value() As Globals
        Get
            Return m_Value
        End Get
    End Property

    ' Load the singleton instance from file.
    Public Shared Sub Load(ByVal fileName As String)
        ' Deserialize the content of this file into the singleton object.
        Using fs As New FileStream(fileName, FileMode.Open)
            Dim xser As New XmlSerializer(GetType(Globals))
            m_Value = DirectCast(xser.Deserialize(fs), Globals)
        End Using
    End Sub
```

```
    ' Save the singleton instance to file.
    Public Shared Sub Save(ByVal fileName As String)
        ' Serialize the singleton object to the file.
        Using fs As New FileStream(fileName, FileMode.Create)
            Dim xser As New XmlSerializer(GetType(Globals))
            xser.Serialize(fs, m_Value)
        End Using
    End Sub

    ' Instance fields (the global variables)
    Public UserName As String
    Public Documents() As String
    Public UseSimplifiedMenus As Boolean = True
    Public UseSpellChecker As Boolean = True
End Class
```

Using the Globals class is straightforward because you must simply invoke the Load static method after the application starts and the Save static method before the application terminates. All the global variables can be accessed as properties of the Globals.Value object, as follows:

```
Globals.Value.UserName = "Francesco"
' Assign two items to the Documents array.
Globals.Value.Documents = New String(){"c:\doc1.txt", "c:\doc2.txt"}
' Save current global variables on disk.
Globals.Save("c:\myapp\globals.xml")
```

Interestingly, the very first time a given user runs the application, the XML file doesn't exist, thus the singleton Globals object will contain the default values for global variables you've defined by means of initializers.

Visual Basic 2005 comes with a very powerful mechanism for saving and retrieving user settings, which is conceptually similar to the one I illustrate in this section. You can read more about it in Chapter 16, "The My Namespace." However, the technique I just illustrated is more generic and flexible than the built-in Visual Basic mechanism is and can be used in many circumstances in which the built-in approach wouldn't work. For one, the built-in technique can store only one set of values for each user, and you can't manage multiple sets of preferences for a given user, merge current options with other users, move options to other computers, and so forth.

Shared Constructors

If you define a parameterless Shared Sub New method in a class, this procedure is called automatically just before the first instance of that class is instantiated. This special constructor is known as a *static constructor* or *type constructor*.

Typically, you use such a static constructor to initialize static fields correctly, when the initialization step can't be implemented by means of a simple initializer. For example, if all the instances of a type need to write to a unique log file, you might prefer to open the file once in the static constructor instead of from inside each instance.

The Shared Sub New procedure runs before the Sub New procedure for the first object instantiated for the class. Static constructors are implicitly Private (unlike other static methods, which are Public by default) and can't be declared using the Public or Friend scope qualifier. Static constructors are the only places where you can assign a Shared ReadOnly field:

```
Public Shared ReadOnly InitialDir As String

Shared Sub New()
   ' Remember the directory that's current when the first
   ' instance of this type is created.
   InitialDir = Directory.GetCurrentDirectory()
End Sub
```

The Globals class shown in the previous section provides another example of when a static constructor can be useful. As you might recall, applications using the Globals type should invoke its Load static method to ensure that the singleton object is correctly initialized from the XML file. Typically, this is the very first operation you should perform on this type, so it makes sense to invoke it from inside its static constructor:

```
' (Add to Globals type…)
Shared Sub New()
   ' Load the default set of variables when the application starts.
   Load("c:\myapp\defaultdata.xml")
End Sub
```

Note that there isn't such a thing as a static destructor method. However, a type might intercept the ProcessExit event of the AppDomain object, which fires when the current application is about to terminate, and perform some work in the handler for that event. For example, the Globals type might use this approach to save the current state of variables when the application exits:

```
Shared Sub New()
   ' Load the default set of variables when the application starts.
   Load("c:\myapp\defaultdata.xml")
   ' Prepare to receive an event when the application exits.
   AddHandler AppDomain.CurrentDomain.ProcessExit, AddressOf ProcessExit
End Sub

Private Shared Sub ProcessExit(ByVal sender As Object, ByVal e As EventArgs)
   ' Save current state of variables when the application exits.
   Save("c:\myapp\defaultdata.xml")
End Sub
```

See the section titled "The AddHandler Keyword" in Chapter 7, "Delegates and Events," for more information about the AddHandler keyword.

Shared Factory Methods

Before I move to another topic, I wish to illustrate another common situation in which static members can become very useful: the implementation of factory methods. A *factory method* is a method that creates an object and returns it to the caller. For example, the OleDbConnection object exposes the CreateCommand instance method, which creates and returns an OleDbCommand object; the OleDbCommand object exposes the ExecuteReader method, which returns an OleDbDataReader object. Instance factory methods are often associated with collections, as is the case of the TreeView.Nodes collection that exposes an Add method, which in turn creates a TreeNode object and adds it to the collection as a single operation. You recognize an instance factory method because, in general, this method returns an object of a type that depends on the type inside which the method is defined: the OleDbCommand object requires a parent OleDbConnection object, the OleDbDataReader object is generated from an OleDbCommand object and has no constructor of its own, a TreeNode object is always associated with the Nodes collection of a TreeView, and so forth.

All the factory methods I've listed so far are instance methods, but static factory methods are quite common too and are used when a type exposes a method that creates an instance of the type itself. You might wonder why you should use a static factory method rather than a regular instance constructor; after all, both techniques can create an object. But there is an important difference: when the constructor runs, the object has already been created, whereas a factory method can execute code *before* creating the object. This apparently minor difference has far-reaching implications. For example, if a constructor fails with an exception, the object has already been created and takes memory from the managed heap; if a factory method finds that one or more arguments are invalid, it can fail with an exception before any memory is allocated for the new object.

To see why a factory method can be useful, let's consider the following class, which enables you to read a text document and associate an ID with it:

```
Public Class TextDocument
    ' A collection of all the TextDocument objects generated so far
    Private Shared docs As New Hashtable()

    ' The public static factory method
    Public Shared Function Create(ByVal id As Long, ByVal path As String) As TextDocument
        ' Check that we haven't issued a document with this ID yet.
        If docs.Contains(id) Then Throw New ArgumentException("ID already used.")
        ' Create and return an instance with given ID.
        Return New TextDocument(id, path)
    End Function

    ' The private constructor
    Private Sub New(ByVal id As Long, ByVal path As String)
        Me.ID = id
        Me.Path = path
        Me.Text = File.ReadAllText(path)
        ' Store the current instance in the static Hashtable.
        docs.Add(id, Me)
    End Sub

    ' These should be read-only properties in a real application.
    Public ReadOnly ID As Long
    Public ReadOnly Path As String
    Public ReadOnly Text As String
End Class
```

As you can see, the constructor stores all the instances created so far in a static Hashtable. (A Hashtable is a collection of objects that can be indexed by a key; in this specific case, the key is the ID assigned to each TextDocument.) The Create static method can therefore check whether the ID passed to it has already been used and creates a new instance only if this isn't the case; otherwise, no instance is created and an exception is thrown.

Factory methods are even more useful when you define an immutable object. By definition, an *immutable object* is an object that can't be changed after its instantiation. For example, the TextDocument just introduced is an immutable object because it exposes only fields marked with the ReadOnly keyword. The .NET Framework exposes several examples of immutable objects, the most important of which is the System.String type. (More on this topic in Chapter 12, ".NET Basic Types.")

If an object is immutable, you might consider the following optimization technique: if the code using the object asks to instantiate an object with exactly the same arguments used in a previous call, the factory method might return a reference to an object that is already instantiated rather than create a new instance. For example, say that you have this code:

```
Dim td1 As TextDocument = TextDocument.Create(11, "c:\data.txt")
…
' (Later in the same application…)
' This code throws an exception, but is it what you really mean?
Dim td2 As TextDocument = TextDocument.Create(11, "c:\data.txt")
```

What should the second call to Create return? In the implementation of TextDocument shown previously, the second call throws an exception because the ID isn't unique; however, you might argue that, after all, the program is asking for exactly the same document it had requested before, so it's reasonable that it should receive a pointer to the *same* object. Surprisingly, you need to change only the code in the static factory method to implement the new behavior:

```
Public Shared Function Create(ByVal id As Long, ByVal path As String) As TextDocument
    ' The next statement returns Nothing if no element with this ID is in the Hashtable.
   Dim doc As TextDocument = DirectCast(docs(id), TextDocument)
   If doc IsNot Nothing Then
      ' If both ID and path match, return the previous instance.
      If doc.Path = path Then Return doc
      ' Otherwise, we have a document with the same ID and a different path.
      Throw New ArgumentException("ID already used.")
   End If
   ' Return an instance with given ID.
   Return New TextDocument(id, path)
End Function
```

The TextDocument class now implements a sort of cache containing all the objects created so far. The new version is more efficient because, if the user asks again for the same file, the hard disk isn't accessed at all:

```
Dim td1 As TextDocument = TextDocument.Create(11, "c:\data.txt")
Dim td2 As TextDocument = TextDocument.Create(11, "c:\data.txt")
```

```
' Prove that we get a reference to the *same* instance.
Console.WriteLine(td1 Is td2)                          ' => True
```

You might argue that, if two variables point to the same object, a piece of code in the application might change one or more properties of the object and indirectly negatively affect other portions of the same application (that use another object variable to point to the same instance). This is where the concept of immutable object comes into play: the TextDocument type doesn't expose a member that enables you to change the state of the object after initialization and therefore an instance of this class can be shared safely among different clients. This detail is essential when you use a factory method to implement a caching technique such as the one I've described in this section.

Partial Classes

I briefly hinted at partial types in Chapter 2, but it's now due time for an in-depth description. As you might recall from that earlier chapter, partial types are a new Visual Basic 2005 feature that, in a nutshell, enables you to split the implementation of a class in two or more source files. For this trick to work, at least one of the class declarations must be marked with the Partial keyword:

```
' (In file Employee_1.vb…)
Public Partial Class Employee
    Public Sub New(ByVal firstName As String, ByVal lastName As String)
        Me.FirstName = firstName
        Me.LastName = lastName
    End Sub
End Class

' (In file Employee_2.vb…)
Public Class Employee
    Public FirstName As String
    Public LastName As String
End Class
```

Code in one portion of the type can freely reference members defined in another portion, as is the case with the FirstName and LastName fields in Employee_2.vb assigned from inside the constructor in Employee_2.vb. Conveniently, IntelliSense in Microsoft Visual Studio 2005 has been extended to display all the members in a type, regardless of where those members are defined.

Note   You can use the Partial keyword only with classes. Partial modules, interfaces, and Enum types aren't supported.

Partial types are a feature of Visual Studio and the Visual Basic compiler, not the .NET Framework. If you look at the IL code generated by compiling the two portions of the Employee class, you won't see any clue that the class was originally split in two portions. Partial types have been introduced in Visual Studio 2005 to provide better support for designers in the IDE, most notably the Microsoft Windows Forms designer, the Web Form designer, and the DataSet designer. All the designers in Visual Studio generate a partial type and store this partial type in a file that is normally hidden in the Solution Explorer window.

To see how this feature works in practice, create a Windows Form in Visual Studio named Form1, drop a Button control onto its surface, and then switch to the Solution Explorer window, click the Show All Files button on the toolbar, expand the form element, and you'll see a file named Form1.Designer.vb. This is the (abridged) code you can find in this file:

```
<Global.Microsoft.VisualBasic.CompilerServices.DesignerGenerated()> _
Partial Public Class Form1
   Inherits System.Windows.Forms.Form

   'Form overrides dispose to clean up the component list.
   <System.Diagnostics.DebuggerNonUserCode()> _
   Protected Overloads Overrides Sub Dispose(ByVal disposing As Boolean)
      …
   End Sub

   <System.Diagnostics.DebuggerStepThrough()> _
   Private Sub InitializeComponent()
      Me.Button1 = New System.Windows.Forms.Button
      Me.SuspendLayout()
      …
      ' (Code that initializes all controls is omitted for brevity.)
      …
      Me.ResumeLayout(False)
   End Sub

   Friend WithEvents Button1 As System.Windows.Forms.Button
End Class
```

Visual Studio regenerates the entire file whenever you change anything on the Form's surface, yet this action never affects the code you've typed in the "standard" Form1.vb file. This approach is much better than the code regions used in Visual Studio 2003: there is absolutely no risk of accidentally overwriting the code that Visual Studio has generated, and you don't have to account for this code when you perform search and replace commands in the Form1.vb file.

Partial classes are even more useful with typed DataSet classes. In fact, Visual Studio 2005 enables you to extend a typed DataSet with your own methods and event handlers, an accomplishment that is absolutely out of reach in earlier versions of Visual Studio because your custom code would be overwritten as soon as the DataSet definition changed. (In Visual Studio .NET 2003, you can extend a DataSet only by means of inheritance.)

Even if the primary reason of existence of partial types is to better support Visual Studio designers, you can surely take advantage of these types in other ways. For example, you can split the implementation of a large class among different developers. And of course you can leverage partial classes if you generate pieces of source code automatically by means of a macro or a wizard.

Because all the portions of a partial type must be reassembled by the Visual Basic compiler, you can't use the Partial keyword to extend a type that has been compiled in a different assembly. Also, all the portions in which the type has been split must not contain pieces of code that contrast with each other. For example, consider the portion of the Form1 class defined in the visible Form1.vb file:

```
Public Class Form1
    ...
End Class
```

This code need not include an Inherits keyword because the code in Form1.Designer.vb already declares that the class derives from System.Windows.Forms.Form. If you wish, you can add an Inherits keyword in the user portion of this class as well, as long as it doesn't contrast with the Visual Studio–generated portion:

```
Public Class Form1
    Inherits System.Windows.Forms.Form
    ...
End Class
```

What you *can't* do, however, is specify a different base class for this type because it would contrast with what is declared in Form1.Designer.vb. The same concept applies to the scope keyword: for the code in Form1.vb you can either use an explicit Public keyword or omit it—in which case, Public is taken from the code in Form1.Designer.vb—but you can't specify a contrasting scope, such as Friend. Similarly, you can't use contrasting keywords such as NotInheritable and MustInherit for the same type. (See Chapter 8 for a description of these keywords.)

One last note: when the Visual Basic compiler puts the various pieces of a partial type together, it does not merge the Imports statements at the top of the file. In other words, each source file must have its own set of Imports statements.

Operator Overloading

 Visual Basic 2005 gives you the ability to redefine the way standard operators such as addition (+) and multiplication (*) work on your types. In other words, you can create types that look like primitive types, much like numeric types or the Date type.

The Operator Keyword

A type can redefine one or more operators by means of static Function methods marked with the new Operator keyword. To illustrate how this keyword works, let's define a type that represents a Fraction that has a numerator and a denominator:

```
Public Structure Fraction
    ' Read-only fields
    Private num As Long
    Private den As Long
```

```vb
    ' Read-only properties
    Public ReadOnly Property Numerator() As Long
       Get
           Return num
       End Get
    End Property

    Public ReadOnly Property Denominator() As Long
       Get
           Return den
       End Get
    End Property

    Sub New(ByVal numerator As Long, ByVal denominator As Long)
       ' Normalize the numerator and denominator.
       If numerator = 0 Then
           denominator = 1
       ElseIf denominator < 0 Then
           numerator = -numerator
           denominator = -denominator
       End If
       Dim div As Long = GCD(numerator, denominator)
       num = numerator \ div
       den = denominator \ div
    End Sub

    ' The greatest common divisor of two numbers (helper method)
    Private Function GCD(ByVal n1 As Long, ByVal n2 As Long) As Long
       n1 = Math.Abs(n1)
       n2 = Math.Abs(n2)
       Do
           ' Ensure that n1 > n2
           If n1 < n2 Then
               Dim tmp As Long = n1
               n1 = n2
               n2 = tmp
           End If
           n1 = n1 Mod n2
       Loop While n1 <> 0
       Return n2
    End Function

    ' Override ToString to provide a textual representation of the fraction.
    Public Overrides Function ToString() As String
       If num = 0 OrElse den = 1 Then
           Return num.ToString()
       Else
           Return String.Format("{0}/{1}", num, den)
       End If
    End Function
End Structure
```

Notice that the Fraction type is a value type and is *immutable* in the sense that once you've created an instance of the class you can't change its Numerator or Denominator properties. Also note that the fraction is stored in normalized format, where the numerator and denominator numbers are prime to each other:

```
' Prove that a fraction is always stored in normalized (simplified) format.
Dim f As New Fraction(2, 10)
Console.WriteLine(f)              ' => 1/5
```

Next, let's define how addition, subtraction, multiplication, and division work with the Fraction type:

```
' (Add to the Fraction type.)
Public Shared Operator +(ByVal f1 As Fraction, ByVal f2 As Fraction) As Fraction
    ' a/b + c/d = (a*d + b*c) / (b*d)
    Return New Fraction(f1.num * f2.den + f2.num * f1.den, f1.den * f2.den)
End Operator

Public Shared Operator -(ByVal f1 As Fraction, ByVal f2 As Fraction) As Fraction
    ' a/b - c/d = (a*d - b*c) / (b*d)
    Return New Fraction(f1.num * f2.den - f2.num * f1.den, f1.den * f2.den)
End Operator

Public Shared Operator *(ByVal f1 As Fraction, ByVal f2 As Fraction) As Fraction
    ' a/b * c/d = (a*c) / (b*d)
    Return New Fraction(f1.num * f2.num, f1.den * f2.den)
End Operator

Public Shared Operator /(ByVal f1 As Fraction, ByVal f2 As Fraction) As Fraction
    ' Dividing is like multiplying by the reciprocal of second operand.
    Return New Fraction(f1.num * f2.den, f1.den * f2.num)
End Operator
```

Notice that all the methods are marked with the Shared and Operator keywords; they take two Fraction operands with the ByVal keyword and return another instance of the Fraction type. The following code snippet tests the new operators:

```
Dim f1 As New Fraction(2, 5)
Dim f2 As New Fraction(1, 10)
Console.WriteLine(f1 + f2)       ' => 1/2
Console.WriteLine(f1 - f2)       ' => 3/10
Console.WriteLine(f1 * f2)       ' => 1/25
Console.WriteLine(f1 / f2)       ' => 4
```

Overloadable Operators

Visual Basic enables you to overload all the operators defined for the language, plus a few special ones, but you can't define new operators. Here's the complete list of overloadable operators:

- **Unary operators**   +, −, Not, IsTrue, IsFalse, CType
- **Binary operators**   +, −, *, /, \, &, ^, >>, <<, Mod, Like
- **Binary comparison and logical operators**   =, <>, >, >=, <, <=, And, Or, Xor

Notice that compound assignment operators, such as += and *=, are missing from the list of overloadable operators; however, if you overload the base operator (such as + and *), these compound operators are automatically overloaded as well.

You must abide by these two rules:

- The operand of a unary operator must be of the same type as the type that contains the method. (The only exception to this rule is the CType operator; see next section.)

- At least one operand of the binary operator you're overloading must be of the type that contains the method.

There is no constraint on the return value: it can be of the same type as the containing type or as any other .NET type. Here's an example of how you can redefine the unary minus for the Fraction type:

```
Public Shared Operator -(ByVal f As Fraction) As Fraction
   Return New Fraction(-f.num, f.den)
End Operator
```

As an example of an operator that takes operands of a different type, the Fraction type might overload the + operator to support addition between a Fraction and an Integer. Notice, however, that the commutative property of the addition isn't recognized automatically and you must provide two versions:

```
Public Shared Operator +(ByVal f As Fraction, ByVal n As Integer) As Fraction
   Return New Fraction(f.num + n * f.den, f.den)
End Operator

Public Shared Operator +(ByVal n As Integer, ByVal f As Fraction) As Fraction
   ' Delegate to the other overload.
   Return f + n
End Operator
```

Even if it isn't a syntactical requirement, you should never modify any property of either instance passed as operands because both unary and binary operators aren't expected to modify their arguments. Even better, you should consider using operator overloading only with *immutable* types. Finally, even though you can overload operators in any kind of type, recommended design rules suggest that you use this feature only with value types (that is, structures) because operators can be ambiguous when used with reference types. To understand the rationale behind these recommendations, consider the following statement:

```
Dim fr As New Fraction(1, 10)
fr += 1
```

If Fraction were a reference type and weren't immutable, many developers might mistakenly believe that the += adds one unit to the instance named fr because this is how a reference type would behave. But we know that the overloaded + operator returns a *different* instance of the Fraction type and the previous code doesn't change the value of the Fraction object; instead, it creates a new instance and assigns it to the same variable.

Some operators must be redefined in pairs. For example, if you overload the equality (=) operator, you must also overload the inequality (<>) operator. Similarly, the less than (<) and greater than (>) operators must be redefined together, as must the less than or equal to (<=) and greater than or equal to (>=) operators. Fortunately, comparison operators can be implemented easily because you can define three of them by negating the value returned by the other three:

```
Public Shared Operator =(ByVal f1 As Fraction, ByVal f2 As Fraction) As Boolean
    ' This code relies on the denominator always being 1 if numerator is zero.
    Return f1.num = f2.num AndAlso f1.den = f2.den
End Operator

Public Shared Operator <(ByVal f1 As Fraction, ByVal f2 As Fraction) As Boolean
    Return f1.num * f2.den < f1.den * f2.num
End Operator

Public Shared Operator >(ByVal f1 As Fraction, ByVal f2 As Fraction) As Boolean
    Return f1.num * f2.den > f1.den * f2.num
End Operator

Public Shared Operator <>(ByVal f1 As Fraction, ByVal f2 As Fraction) As Boolean
    Return Not (f1 = f2)
End Operator

Public Shared Operator <=(ByVal f1 As Fraction, ByVal f2 As Fraction) As Boolean
    Return Not (f1 > f2)
End Operator

Public Shared Operator >=(ByVal f1 As Fraction, ByVal f2 As Fraction) As Boolean
    Return Not (f1 < f2)
End Operator
```

If you overload the equality operator, Microsoft guidelines recommend that you also override both the instance and the static versions the Equals method so that the two methods return consistent results:

```
Public Overloads Function Equals(ByVal f As Fraction) As Boolean
    Return (f = Me)
End Function

Public Overloads Shared Function Equals(ByVal f1 As Fraction, _
        ByVal f2 As Fraction) As Boolean
    Return (f1 = f2)
End Function
```

Also, when redefining the Equals method you should also override the GetHashCode method. See Chapter 8 for more details on method overriding.

The IsTrue unary operator is expected to return the True Boolean value if its only argument must evaluate to True when used in the test expression of a If, ElseIf, Do Until, or Do While block. If you define IsTrue, you must also define the IsFalse operator. For example, let's suppose that you want to allow the use of fractional values in If expressions, as in the following:

```
Dim f As New Fraction(1, 10)
If f Then Console.WriteLine("Fraction isn't null")
```

Here's the code that extends the Fraction class to support this new feature:

```
Public Shared Operator IsTrue(ByVal f As Fraction) As Boolean
    Return f.num <> 0
End Operator

Public Shared Operator IsFalse(ByVal f As Fraction) As Boolean
    Return f.num = 0
End Operator
```

You might have noticed that AndAlso and OrElse aren't in the list of overloadable operators. However, if you overload both the And operator and the IsFalse operator, you indirectly overload the AndAlso operator. Likewise, if you overload both the Or and the IsTrue operators, you indirectly overload the OrElse operator.

Overloading the CType Operator

The CType unary operator is special in that it enables you to define how the instances of a given type can be converted to and from other types. For example, you might define how Fraction values can be converted to and from Long values using this code:

```
Public Shared Narrowing Operator CType(ByVal f As Fraction) As Long
    Return f.num \ f.den
End Operator

Public Shared Widening Operator CType(ByVal n As Long) As Fraction
    Return New Fraction(n, 1)
End Operator
```

Conversions can be either of the widening or the narrowing type. As you might recall from Chapter 2, a widening conversion is a conversion that can't fail or produce an overflow, underflow, or loss of precision. For this reason, the Visual Basic language never requires that you specify a conversion operator when you perform a widening conversion, such as when you convert an Integer to a Long. Conversely, a narrowing conversion might fail, and for this reason it requires an explicit conversion operator. This is how you can use the conversions defined previously:

```
' Conversions from Long to Fraction don't require an explicit operator.
Dim f As Fraction = 123

' Conversions from Fraction to Long do require an explicit operator
' (if Option Strict is On).
Dim f2 As New Fraction(12, 5)
' Both n1 and n2 are assigned the value 2 (= 12 \ 5).
' Note that both CType and CLng operators are supported.
Dim n1 As Long = CType(f2, Long)
Dim n2 As Long = CLng(f2)
```

While I am on the topic of conversions, when designing a type that is supposed to behave like a primitive type you should consider the opportunity to expose an overload of the CType operator that converts from a string and that provides the opposite kind of transformation than the ToString does:

```
Public Shared Narrowing Operator CType(ByVal value As String) As Fraction
    Dim parts() As String = value.Split("/"c)
    If parts.Length = 1 Then
        Return New Fraction(CLng(parts(0)), 1)
    ElseIf parts.Length = 2 Then
        Return New Fraction(CLng(parts(0)), CLng(parts(1)))
    Else
        Throw New ArgumentException("Invalid format")
    End If
End Operator
```

In addition to exposing this conversion as a CType overload, it is customary that you expose it also under the name of Parse:

```
Public Shared Function Parse(ByVal value As String) As Fraction
    Return CType(value, Fraction)
End Function
```

You can help developers using your type even further if you provide a method named Try-Parse, which works like the method with same name that most .NET primitive types expose. This method should return True if the conversion is possible and, if this is the case, return the converted value in the second argument passed with ByRef:

```
Public Shared Function TryParse(ByVal value As String, ByRef f As Fraction) As Boolean
    Dim parts() As String = value.Split("/"c)
    If parts.Length = 1 Then
        f = New Fraction(CLng(parts(0)), 1)
        Return True
    ElseIf parts.Length = 2 Then
        f = New Fraction(CLng(parts(0)), CLng(parts(1)))
        Return True
    Else
        Return False
    End If
End Function
```

The new TryParse method enables you to redefine one of the overloads of the CType in the following simplified form:

```
Public Shared Narrowing Operator CType(ByVal value As String) As Fraction
    Dim f As Fraction
    If TryParse(value, f) Then
        Return f
    Else
        Throw New ArgumentException("Invalid format")
    End If
End Operator
```

Interoperability with Other Languages

Only a few .NET languages support operator overloading. This detail can become a problem if you are building a class library that you want to publish and make available to other .NET developers who work with a language that doesn't support operator overloading.

The ILDASM tool can help you to understand what actually happens when you compile a type that overloads one or more operators. For each overloaded operator, the Visual Basic compiler creates a static method whose name has the op_ prefix, for example, op_Addition, op_Multiply, op_Equality, and op_BitwiseAnd. In addition, these methods are marked with a specialname IL keyword, which makes it clear that the method is the definition of an overloaded operator.

When you compile a Visual Basic 2005 or C# program that uses the type, the compiler automatically transforms all operators into calls to these special op_ methods. Thus, strictly speaking, these aren't operators but rather method calls. As a matter of fact, you can invoke one of these special methods directly if you know its name:

```
' Another way to perform fraction addition
Dim f1 As New Fraction(1, 4)
Dim f2 As New Fraction(1, 3)
Dim result As Fraction = Fraction.op_Addition(f1, f2)
```

Performing an operation such as an addition in this contorted way is quite unnatural, so at the very minimum you should expose a set of static methods with more meaningful names. Microsoft guidelines provide a list of alternative, recommended names for these methods, as shown in Table 6-1. For example, the Fraction type should expose methods such as Add, Subtract, Multiply, and Divide. These methods can just delegate to the procedures you've already written:

```
Public Shared Function Add(ByVal f1 As Fraction, ByVal f2 As Fraction) As Fraction
    Return f1 + f2
End Function
...
```

Table 6-1 Suggested Names for Methods Alternative to Operator Overloads

Operator	Special op_ method	Alternative method
– (unary)	op_UnaryNegation	Negate
+ (unary)	op_UnaryPlus	Plus
+ (binary)	op_Addition	Add
– (binary)	op_Subtraction	Subtract
*	op_Multiply	Multiply
/	op_Division	Divide
\	op_IntegerDivision	Divide
Mod	op_Modulus	Mod
Like	op_Like	Like
And	op_BitwiseAnd	BitwiseAnd

Table 6-1   Suggested Names for Methods Alternative to Operator Overloads *(Continued)*

Operator	Special op_ method	Alternative method
Or	op_BitwiseOr	BitwiseOr
Xor	op_ExclusiveOr	Xor
Not	op_OnesComplement	OnesComplement
>>	op_RightShift	RightShift
<<	op_LeftShift	LeftShift
=	op_Equality	Equals
<>	op_Inequality	Compare
<	op_LessThan	Compare
<=	op_LessThanOrEqual	Compare
>	op_GreaterThan	Compare
>=	op_GreaterThanOrEqual	Compare
CType (Widening)	op_Implicit	To*Xxx* or From*Xxx*
CType (Narrowing)	op_Explicit	To*Xxx* or From*Xxx*

Some alternative methods listed in the rightmost column of Table 6-1 are reserved Visual Basic keywords, and thus you must enclose their names in a pair of brackets:

```
Public Shared Function [Mod](ByVal f1 As Fraction, ByVal f2 As Fraction) As Fraction
    ...
End Function
```

All the comparison operands can be indirectly rendered by means of a static Compare method, which returns –1, 0, or 1 depending on whether the first operand is less than, equal to, or greater than the second operand. Here's how this method might be implemented for the Fraction type:

```
Public Shared Function Compare(ByVal f1 As Fraction, ByVal f2 As Fraction) _
    As Integer
    Return Math.Sign(f1.num * f2.den - f1.den * f2.num)
End Function
```

The last two entries in Table 6-1 refer to methods that convert to and from the type you're defining. The *Xxx* placeholder in the name should be replaced by the official .NET Framework name of the type you're converting to or from. For example, a method that converts a Fraction instance into a Long should be named ToInt64, whereas the method that does the conversion in the opposite direction should be called FromInt64:

```
Public Shared Function ToInt64(ByVal f As Fraction) As Long
    Return CType(f, Long)
End Function
```

```
Public Shared Function FromInt64(ByVal value As Long) As Fraction
    Return CType(value, Fraction)
End Function
```

Managing Types with Visual Studio

Visual Studio comes with a few tools that can help you browse all the types in your application, create new ones, and test them.

The Class View Window

The Class View window has been part of Visual Studio since its 2002 edition. In a nutshell, this window is a reduced version of the Object Browser window and displays the list of all the types defined in your project, grouped by namespaces and sorted alphabetically, by object type, or by object scope. You can open this window by means of a command on the View menu or by using the Ctrl+Shift+C shortcut.

The Class View window enables you to search types and filter them by their access type (public, protected, and so on). By default, the Class View window displays both the types defined in your project and the .NET Framework types that your project references, but you can exclude the latter ones if you wish by clearing the Show Project References option on the Class View Settings menu. (You can display this menu by clicking the fourth button on the window's toolbar.)

The most useful feature of the Class View window is its ability to create folders where you can drag types. For example, you can create a folder named Common Types and drag there all the types that you use most frequently so that you can find all of them in one place. (See Figure 6-1.)

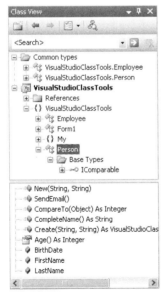

Figure 6-1   The Class View window

Although the Class View window continues to be a useful tool, its importance decreases in Visual Studio 2005 because a new tool with more features fulfills the same needs: the Class Designer window.

The Class Designer Tool

Unlike the Class View window, of which there is just one instance in the entire Visual Studio IDE, you can create as many Class Designer items as you need by selecting the Add New Item command in the Project display and selecting the Class Diagram element in the template gallery. Or you can right-click an item in the Solution Explorer window and select the View Class Diagram command.

Each class diagram hosts the graphical representation of one or more types in your project. An arrowed line joins a type to its base type, as is the case of the Employee and Person types in Figure 6-2. When the Class Designer window is active, you can display details on individual members in the Class Detail window, display their properties in the Properties window, and create new elements by dragging them from the Toolbox. The context menu that appears when you right-click the window's background enables you to add new types, export the diagram as an image (in .bmp, .gif, .jpg, and a few other formats), and change the format used for members (only the name, name and type, or full signature). The context menu that appears when you right-click an element in the diagram enables you to add new members, copy the element's image to the Clipboard, show all the base types or all the types that inherit from the current type, and more.

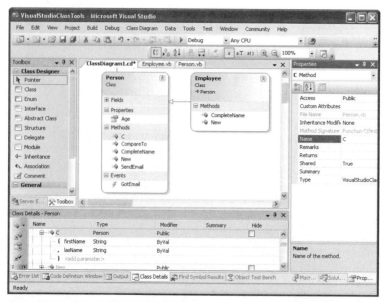

Figure 6-2   The Class Designer window

Even if it isn't apparent immediately, the Class Designer tool has a "live" connection to the underlying code in your project. If you change the name of a class in the designer, the class is renamed in the source code as well, and vice versa. Even more interesting, you can add new fields, properties, methods, and events in the Class Designer and these new members are automatically created in source code, even though they don't contain any functioning statements.

One of the many options on the Class Designer context menu enables you to display the Class Detail window, which displays details of all the class members and enables you to change their name or visibility, and add new ones. For example, you can click the plus sign (+) to the left of a method to see the list of the method's arguments, change their type and ByVal/ByRef modifier, delete them, or add new ones. Once again, your changes are immediately reflected in the source code.

I find that the Class Diagram tool is especially useful for adding XML comments to all types and their members. You simply need to select a type or one of its methods, press the F4 key to display the Properties window, and enter your comments in the Summary and Remarks elements. Other options in this window enable you to add a comment to the return value of methods, add custom attributes associated with a member, change a member's visibility keyword, change from instance to static member (or vice versa), assign an initial value to a field, and so forth.

When the Class Designer window is active you can find a new set of elements in the Toolbox window. These elements enable you to create new types, associate types, and add comments to the diagram itself. (These comments are saved in the diagram and don't generate XML comments in the source code.) To give you an idea of how you can use the Toolbox with the Class Diagram, let's suppose you have a Person and an Employee type in the diagram, as shown in Figure 6-2, and let's further suppose that you want to add a relationship between these two classes by means of the Employee.Spouse property that points to a Person object. All you have to do to implement such a property is select the Association element in the Toolbox window, and then drag a line that goes from the Employee type to the Person type. This action adds a property named Person to the Employee type, and thus you simply need to rename it as Spouse. By default this property is rendered as an association, but you can display it as a regular property by right-clicking the line that joins the two types and selecting the Show As Property command.

The last feature of the Class Designer window is really outstanding. Right-click a type and select the Create Instance command from the context menu; then select one of the constructors that the type exposes. This action opens a dialog box similar to the one shown in Figure 6-3, where you can type the arguments to be passed to the constructor and assign a name to the object that is going to be created.

```
Create Instance                              [?][X]

Constructor Prototype:
 New Employee  ( ByVal firstName As String ,
                 ByVal lastName As String  )


 Name:     ann

 Parameters:
 | Parameter     | Value    |
 | firstName     | "Ann"    | ▼
 | lastName      | "Beebe"  | ▼



                        [   OK   ]   [ Cancel ]
```

Figure 6-3   The Create Instance dialog box

The Object Test Bench Window

Once you have created a design-time instance of a type from inside the Class Designer window, you can manipulate it from inside the Object Test Bench window, which you can display by means of a command on the Other Windows submenu of the View top-level menu. (See Figure 6-4.) The Object Test Bench window enables you to play with your objects and see their behavior at design time without writing a single line of code.

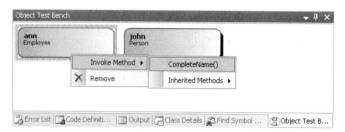

Figure 6-4   The Object Test Workbench window

Of course, you aren't limited to just one instance, and you can create as many objects as you wish. You can then right-click these objects to execute their instance methods: if the method returns a value, you can assign a name to the returned object, which is therefore added to the Object Test Bench window, and so on. You can move the mouse over an object to display all of the object's fields and properties in a data tip, and you can even modify these items as you would do in a debug session. (See the section titled "Data Tips and Visualizers" in Chapter 5.)

The Object Test Bench has a few limitations, too. For example, you can't assign object properties, invoke methods that take a generic type or an array as an argument, invoke methods that overload an operator, or pass an expression as an argument. Even with these limitations, the Object Test Bench is a great step in the right direction and can prove quite useful when you're designing your object hierarchies.

Chapter 7
Delegates and Events

I've been teaching object-oriented programming (OOP) for several years now to students and developers of all levels of expertise, and I have come to realize that some OOP topics are more difficult to grasp than are others. For example, inheritance is relatively simple and intuitive—even if the underlying low-level details aren't—whereas it takes longer to fully understand concepts such as delegates and events and, above all, to appreciate the potential benefits they bring to programming. For this reason, I decided to devote an entire chapter to these less intuitive topics, which are closely related to one another.

Note   To avoid long lines, code samples in this chapter assume that the following Imports statements are used at the file or project level:

```
Imports System.ComponentModel
Imports System.IO
Imports System.Windows.Forms
```

Delegates

A delegate is an object that enables you to invoke a method indirectly. Developers with a C, C++, or Delphi background might find a resemblance between delegates and function pointers, but there is an important difference between these two concepts. Traditional function pointers can point anywhere in memory; thus, you must be very careful when handling them: if you use the wrong address or you pass the wrong number or type of argument, your application will crash. By comparison, delegates are *type safe*: when you define a delegate, you specify the signature of the methods it can point to—that is, the specific set of expected arguments and the type of its return value—thus, there is no danger of crashing the application when you invoke the method. Another, less important difference between delegates and function pointers is that the latter can point only to static methods, whereas delegates can point to both static and instance methods.

Delegates play a central role in the Microsoft .NET architecture. For example, .NET events are internally implemented through delegates, as are asynchronous operations and many other features of .NET base classes. Even if you aren't going to use these features in your applications, delegates can be useful in themselves because they enable you to implement programming techniques that would otherwise be impossible to use.

Delegate Declaration

You must define a delegate before you can use it. The following line declares a delegate named DisplayMessage, which points to a procedure that takes a string argument:

```
' In the declaration section of a module or a class
Delegate Sub DisplayMessage(ByVal msg As String)
```

In my opinion, it's quite confusing that a delegate declaration looks like the declaration of a procedure because it hides the fact that the declaration is actually the declaration of a delegate *type*. Behind the scenes, in fact, Microsoft Visual Basic creates a new class named DisplayMessage that inherits from the System.MulticastDelegate class, as you can easily see by using the ILDASM tool or the object browser in Microsoft Visual Studio. An indirect confirmation of the fact that delegates are .NET types is that you can enter the previous statement directly at the namespace level, outside any class.

Once you have defined the DisplayMessage delegate class, you can declare a variable of the new class and then create an instance of the delegate:

```
Dim deleg As DisplayMessage
deleg = New DisplayMessage(AddressOf WriteToDebugWindow)
```

where WriteToDebugWindow is a procedure that *must* have the same signature as the DisplayMessage delegate:

```
' Display a string in the Debug window.
Sub WriteToDebugWindow(ByVal msgText As String)
   Debug.WriteLine(msgText)
End Sub
```

As I explained previously, delegates are type safe: their constructor takes the address of either a static or an instance method and the compiler can check that the target method complies with the delegate declaration (in this case, it's a Sub that takes one string argument). Delegates are immutable types: once they've been created there's no way you can have them point to another method, so it is guaranteed that a delegate variable continues to be valid until it is set to Nothing or goes out of scope.

Delegate Invocation

Finally, you're ready to call the WriteToDebugWindow procedure through the deleg variable, using the delegate's Invoke method.

```
' This statement displays the "FooBar" string in the Debug window.
deleg.Invoke("FooBar")
```

It's a long trip to just display a message, so you might wonder why delegates are so important in the .NET architecture and why you should use them. Alas, Visual Basic developers aren't accustomed to function pointers and the degree of flexibility they can introduce in a program. To give you an example of such flexibility, let's define another procedure that follows the DisplayMessage syntax:

```
' Display a string in a pop-up message box.
Sub PopupMsg(ByVal msgText As String)
   MsgBox(msgText)
End Sub
```

Now you can decide that all the messages in your program should be displayed in message boxes instead of inside the Debug window. You need only replace the statement that creates the delegate variable to do so:

```
deleg = New DisplayMessage(AddressOf PopupMsg)
```

All the existing deleg.Invoke statements scattered in the source code will work flawlessly, but will display their output in a message box.

Microsoft Visual Basic 6 developers might have noticed the use of the AddressOf operator. This operator has the same syntax that it had in Visual Basic 6, but in general, it can't be applied to the same situations for which you used it in Visual Basic 6. The Microsoft Visual Basic 2005 keyword creates a Delegate object pointing to a given procedure, and in fact, you can usually assign the result of AddressOf to a Delegate variable without having to create a Delegate object of the proper type explicitly:

```
deleg = AddressOf PopupMsg
```

When you use this shortened syntax, the compiler checks that the target procedure has an argument signature compatible with the Delegate variable being assigned. In this chapter, I use the more verbose syntax based on the New operator when I want to emphasize the class of the Delegate object being created, but you should be aware that both syntax forms are legal and that they are equally efficient and robust.

Delegates work as described for any static method—that is, Sub and Function procedures in modules and static methods in classes. For example, here's a complete example that uses a delegate to invoke a static method in a class:

```
Module MainModule
    ' Declare a delegate class.
    Delegate Function AskYesNoQuestion(ByVal msg As String) As Boolean

    Sub Main()
        ' A delegate variable that points to a shared function.
        Dim question As New AskYesNoQuestion(AddressOf MessageDisplayer.AskYesNo)

        ' Call the shared method. (Note that Invoke is omitted.)
        If question("Do you want to save?") Then
```

```
                ' Save whatever needs to be saved here.
                ...
          End If
      End Sub
End Module

Public Class MessageDisplayer
    ' Show a message box; return True if user clicks Yes.
    Public Shared Function AskYesNo(ByVal msgText As String) As Boolean
        ' Display the message.
        Dim answer As MsgBoxResult = _
            MsgBox(msgText, MsgBoxStyle.YesNo Or MsgBoxStyle.Question)
        ' Return True if the user answers yes.
        Return (answer = MsgBoxResult.Yes)
    End Function
End Class
```

Using delegates with instance methods is also straightforward. The only remarkable difference is in the argument to the AddressOf operator, which must include a reference to a specific instance of the class, as in this line of code:

```
deleg = AddressOf obj.MethodName
```

Here's a complete example that invokes an instance method of the MessageDisplayer class through a delegate:

```
Module MainModule
    Delegate Function AskQuestion(ByVal DefaultAnswer As Boolean) As Boolean

    Sub Main()
        ' Create an instance of the class, and initialize its properties.
        Dim msgdisp As New MessageDisplayer()
        msgdisp.MsgText = "Do you want to save?"
        msgdisp.MsgTitle = "File has been modified"
        ' Create the delegate to the instance method.
        ' (Note the object reference in the AddressOf clause.)
        Dim question As New AskQuestion(AddressOf msgdisp.YesOrNo)

        ' Call the instance method through the delegate.
        If question(False) Then
            ' Save whatever needs to be saved here.
        End If
    End Sub
End Module

Public Class MessageDisplayer
    Public MsgText As String
    Public MsgTitle As String

    ' Display a message box, and return True if the user selects Yes.
    Function YesOrNo(ByVal DefaultAnswer As Boolean) As Boolean
        ' This is a yes/no question.
        Dim style As MsgBoxStyle = MsgBoxStyle.YesNo Or MsgBoxStyle.Question
        ' Select the default button for this message box.
```

```
      If DefaultAnswer Then
         style = style Or MsgBoxStyle.DefaultButton1        ' Yes button
      Else
         style = style Or MsgBoxStyle.DefaultButton2        ' No button
      End If
      ' Display the message box, and return True if the user replies Yes.
      Return (MsgBox(MsgText, style, MsgTitle) = MsgBoxResult.Yes)
   End Function
End Class
```

Notice that you can have a delegate point only to methods; you can neither execute a constructor nor access a property through a delegate. If the method is overloaded, the Visual Basic compiler correctly chooses the overload that has a signature matching the delegate declaration.

When you work with delegates, you must pay attention to optional arguments. To begin with, the delegate declaration can include neither Optional nor ParamArray arguments. The procedure pointed to by the delegate can include Optional arguments, but the Optional and ParamArray keywords are ignored when matching the method's signature with the delegate's signature and you can't omit optional arguments when invoking the procedure through a delegate. Likewise, a delegate that takes an array argument can point to a procedure that takes a ParamArray argument of the same type, but when you invoke the procedure through the delegate you must pass an actual array.

Other Members of the Delegate Type

All delegate classes ultimately derive from System.Delegate; therefore, they inherit all the properties and methods defined in this base class. Invoke is the default member for delegate types; therefore, you can omit the method name when calling it. In the end, invoking a procedure through a delegate variable looks like a regular call to a method:

```
If question("Do you want to save?") Then
```

Omitting the Invoke method works even if the delegate is pointing to a procedure that takes no arguments, and this is an exception to the general rule that only methods and properties with arguments can become the default member of a class.

The two delegate properties you're likely to find useful are Target and Method. The Target property simply returns a reference to the object that is the target of the delegate. In the previous example, you might access a property of the MessageDisplayer object by using the following code:

```
' The Target method returns an Object, so you need an explicit
' cast if Option Strict is On.
Console.WriteLine(CType(question.Target, MessageDisplayer).MsgText)
```

If the delegate is pointing to a static method, the Target property returns a reference to the System.Type object that represents the class. In this case, you need to use reflection methods to extract information about the class itself.

The other useful delegate property is Method, which returns a System.Reflection.MethodInfo object that describes the method being called, its attributes, and so on. For example, you can learn the name of the target method as follows:

```
Console.WriteLine(log.Method.Name)
```

For more information about reflection and the System.Type class, see Chapter 18, "Reflection."

Callback Methods and Code Reuse

The ability for a procedure to call back its caller can augment the reuse potential of your code. For example, many Microsoft Windows API functions, such as EnumWindows and Enum-Fonts, use callback methods: you pass them the address of a procedure in your application that must be invoked for each window or font being enumerated. Your procedure can then display these elements in a list box, store them in an array, or even stop enumeration if you've found the window or the font you were interested in. In other words, the algorithm that lists all the fonts or windows in the system is provided by the Windows kernel, but your code determines how to process each element in the list.

Delegates offer a clean, efficient, and safe way to implement the same programming technique in your Visual Basic applications. For example, consider the following routine that displays all the folder names in a directory tree:

```
Sub DisplayDirectoryTree(ByVal path As String)
   For Each dirName As String In Directory.GetDirectories(path)
      ' Display name of this directory.
      Console.WriteLine(dirName)
      ' Call this routine recursively to display all subfolders.
      DisplayDirectoryTree(dirName)
   Next
End Sub
```

The problem with this naive implementation is that it can hardly be reused as is in another project. For example, you have to create another, slightly different version of the Display-DirectoryTree method if you want to display directory names in a list box rather than in the Console window or if you want to process these names in any other way.

Among their many other benefits, delegates enable you to create code that can be reused much more easily. All you have to do is extend the procedure to take a delegate argument, which in turn points to a callback routine that decides what to do with the name of individual folders:

```
' The delegate that defines the syntax of the function whose address
' can be passed to TraverseDirectoryTree
Delegate Sub TraverseDirectoryTreeCallback(ByVal dirName As String)

' A reusable routine that visits all the folders in a directory tree
' and calls back the caller by passing the name of each folder
Sub TraverseDirectoryTree(ByVal path As String, _
```

```
      ByVal cbk As TraverseDirectoryTreeCallback)
   For Each dirName As String In Directory.GetDirectories(path)
      ' Do the actual job by invoking the callback procedure.
      cbk.Invoke(dirName)
      ' Call this routine recursively to process subfolders.
      TraverseDirectoryTree(dirName, cbk)
   Next
End Sub
```

Using this procedure is straightforward:

```
Sub TestTraverseDirectoryTree ()
   ' Print the name of all the directories under c:\WINDOWS.
   TraverseDirectoryTree("C:\WINDOWS", AddressOf DisplayDirName)
End Sub

' A routine that complies with the TraverseDirectoryTreeCallback syntax
Sub DisplayDirName(ByVal path As String)
   Console.WriteLine(path)
End Function
```

You might wonder why this approach is superior to simply defining a method that returns all the folder names in an array or a collection so that the client application can use these names as it sees fit. As a matter of fact, such a method has been added to version 2.0 of the .NET Framework, so you can write the following code:

```
Sub TestListSubfolders()
   Dim dirs() As String = Directory.GetDirectories( _
      "C:\WINDOWS", "*.*", SearchOption.AllDirectories)
   For Each dirName As String In dirs
      ' Do whatever you wish with items in the returned ArrayList.
      Console.WriteLine(dirName)
   Next
End Sub
```

The problem in using the Directory.GetDirectories method to gather all the names and then process all of them in the loop is performance: if the returned array contains thousands of items, it would take a lot of time and memory to create it. During this time, the application freezes and ignores input from the end user. Also, often the client application is interested in just a subset of all results; for example, it might be interested in locating a directory named BackupFiles. What is the point in exploring all the subdirectories on your hard disk if the directory you're looking for is near the beginning of the result list?

For this reason, a method that takes a delegate to a callback method often offers a way to stop enumerations. In the next example, I define the TraverseDirectoryTreeCallback2 delegate as a function that returns a Boolean value. An improved implementation of the TraverseDirectory-Tree method might quit enumeration if the return value from the callback function is True:

```
' A delegate that defines the syntax of the function whose address
' can be passed to TraverseDirectoryTree2
Delegate Function TraverseDirectoryTreeCallback2(ByVal dirName As String) As Boolean
```

```
Function TraverseDirectoryTree2(ByVal path As String, _
      ByVal cbk As TraverseDirectoryTreeCallback2) As Boolean
   For Each dirName As String In Directory.GetDirectories(path)
      ' Invoke the callback function; exit if it canceled enumeration.
      Dim canceled As Boolean = cbk.Invoke(dirName)
      If canceled Then Return True
      ' Call this routine recursively; exit if enumeration was canceled.
      canceled = TraverseDirectoryTree2(dirName, cbk)
      If canceled Then Return True
   Next
End Function
```

The main application can now stop iteration at any point by using the appropriate callback method. For example, the following callback method would stop enumeration when a folder named printers is found:

```
Function DisplayDirName2(ByVal path As String) As Boolean
   Console.WriteLine(path)
   If path.EndsWith("\printers") Then Return True
End Function
```

Delegate Multicasting

You can get extra flexibility by using multicast delegates, which can dispatch a call to more than just one procedure. You can create a multicast delegate by taking two delegates of the same type and combining them to create a new delegate that invokes the two procedures to which the original delegate objects point.

You combine two delegates into a multicast delegate by using the Combine static method of the System.Delegate class and then assigning the result to a delegate variable of the same type. This target variable can be one of the two original delegate variables or a third delegate variable of the proper type:

```
' Notice that you can have a delegate point to methods defined in the .NET Framework.
Dim cbk As New TraverseDirectoryTreeCallback(AddressOf Console.WriteLine)
Dim cbk2 As New TraverseDirectoryTreeCallback(AddressOf Debug.WriteLine)

' Combine them into a multicast delegate; assign back to first variable.
cbk = [Delegate].Combine(cbk, cbk2)
```

Delegate is a reserved Visual Basic keyword; thus, you need to enclose it in square brackets to reference the Delegate type. However, you can avoid using square brackets by typing the complete class name:

```
cbk = System.Delegate.Combine(cbk, cbk2)
```

You can make your code more concise by creating the second delegate on the fly:

```
cbk = [Delegate].Combine(cbk, _
   New TraverseDirectoryTreeCallback(AddressOf Debug.WriteLine))
```

There's one problem, however. If the Option Strict option is On, Visual Basic prevents you from assigning the result of the Combine method (which returns a generic delegate) to a variable of a different type. So you must cast explicitly, using the CType or DirectCast function:

```
' We need this statement if Option Strict is On.
cbk = DirectCast([Delegate].Combine(cbk, _
   New TraverseDirectoryTreeCallback(AddressOf Debug.WriteLine)), _
   TraverseDirectoryTreeCallback)
```

The following code is a variant of the one you saw previously. In this case, the names of directories being scanned by the TraverseDirectoryTree method appear both in the Console window and in the Debug window:

```
Dim cbk As New TraverseDirectoryTreeCallback(AddressOf Console.WriteLine)
cbk = DirectCast([Delegate].Combine(cbk, _
   New TraverseDirectoryTreeCallback(AddressOf Debug.WriteLine)), _
   TraverseDirectoryTreeCallback)
TraverseDirectoryTree("C:\WINDOWS", cbk)
```

The preceding code creates two distinct delegate objects and then combines them. Keeping the two delegates in separate variables makes it easier to remove them (using the Remove static method) from the list that the multicast delegate maintains internally. The Remove method returns a multicast delegate that points to all the procedures originally in the delegate, minus the one being removed:

```
' Change the cbk delegate so that it doesn't display to the Debug window.
cbk = DirectCast([Delegate].Remove(cbk, cbk2), TraverseDirectoryTreeCallback)
' This method displays only a log message on the console.
TraverseDirectoryTree("C:\WINDOWS", cbk)
```

If you don't have a reference to the original delegate that was combined in the multicast delegate, you can create a new delegate that points to the proper method and then pass it to the Remove method. This action is rather counterintuitive because you create a *new* delegate only to remove an *existing* delegate from a multicast delegate, but it works well nevertheless:

```
' Another way to remove the delegate that displays to the Debug window
cbk = DirectCast([Delegate].Remove(cbk, _
   New TraverseDirectoryTreeCallback(AddressOf Debug.WriteLine), _
   TraverseDirectoryTreeCallback)
```

You can list all the individual delegate objects in a multicast delegate by using the GetInvocationList method, which returns an array of delegate objects. For example, the following code prints the name of the target for each delegate that has been combined in a multicast delegate:

```
' Get the list of individual delegates in a multicast delegate.
Dim delegates() As [Delegate] = cbk.GetInvocationList()
' List the names of all the target methods.
For Each d As [Delegate] In delegates
   Console.WriteLine(d.Method.Name)
Next
```

A multicast delegate can point to either a Sub or a Function, but the first case is by far more common because when you invoke multiple functions through a delegate, the return value of all target methods but the last one is lost. However, if you happen to have a multicast delegate that points to a Function, you can use the GetInvocationList method to invoke each target method manually and explore its return value. You'll see an example of this technique in the following section devoted to events.

Events

Events are part of the interface that a type exposes to the world, together with fields, properties, methods, and constructors. However, events are different from the others by an important detail: when a field is read, a property is written, or a method is invoked, it's the code using the object that takes the initiative. But roles are reversed when the client subscribes to an event: the object plays an active role and decides when the event fires.

In this section, I take a slightly unusual approach. Instead of starting by showing you how to define an event in a type, first I'll focus on how you can handle events raised by objects, more precisely by controls in a Windows Forms application. Later I explain how you can implement a class that exposes and raises events.

Handling Events by Using the Handles Keyword

To see how you can handle events raised by controls, create a new Windows Forms project and drop one Button and three TextBox controls on the surface of the Form1 class that Visual Studio has created for you. Next, rename the Button as btnOK and the TextBox controls as txtFirstName, txtLastName, and txtCity. The next task is to create the method that handles the Click event raised when the user clicks the button. Visual Studio gives you at least three ways to do it, the third of which has been introduced in the 2005 release.

The first technique can be used only when the event is the default event for the control, as is the case with the Click event for the Button control. In this case you can create a handler for the event by simply double-clicking the button at design time: the source code window opens and Visual Studio creates the following template:

```
' (Notice that I added an underscore to wrap the procedure declaration.)
Private Sub btnOK_Click(ByVal sender As Object, ByVal e As EventArgs) _
      Handles btnOK.Click

End Sub
```

It's important to notice that Visual Studio creates a procedure named *objectname_eventname*, but the association with the object and the event isn't based on this naming convention, as it was under Visual Basic 6 and earlier versions. Instead, the association is established by means of the Handles keyword that follows the method signature. In other words, you can rename the routine as you prefer, but it will still handle the Click event raised by the btnOK control.

Conveniently, if you change the name of the control, Visual Studio 2005 changes the Handles clause accordingly, a new feature that can save you a lot of precious time.

Delete the code that Visual Studio has generated and try the second technique, which is more generic and works for all the events, not just the default event for the control. In this case, you select the control from the leftmost combo box near the top border of the code window, and then select the event from the combo box on the right. Visual Studio creates an event handler identical to the one created previously. For example, you can use the Click event handler to close the current Form:

```
Private Sub btnOK_Click(ByVal sender As Object, ByVal e As EventArgs) _
      Handles btnOK.Click
   Me.Close()
End Sub
```

In virtually all the events in the .NET Framework, the first argument passed to the event handler is a reference to the object that is raising the event, whereas the second argument is an object whose properties bring additional information about the event itself. If no additional information is associated with the event, as is the case with the Click event, the second argument is a bare System.EventArgs object that has no properties and that in practice is never referenced from inside the event handler. Otherwise, the second argument is an object of a type that derives from System.EventArgs. For example, the handler of a KeyPress event receives a System.Windows.Forms.KeyPressEventArgs object, which in turn exposes the KeyChar and the Handled properties:

```
Private Sub txtFirstName_KeyPress(ByVal sender As Object, ByVal e As KeyPressEventArgs) _
      Handles txtFirstName.KeyPress
   ' Ignore spaces typed by the user. (This is obtained by telling
   ' the .NET Framework that we handled this key.)
   If e.KeyChar = " "c Then e.Handled = True
End Sub
```

The Handles keyword supports multiple arguments, which means that a given event handler can handle events raised by multiple controls (or multiple events raised by the same control, even though this latter case occurs less frequently). To see when such a feature might be useful, consider the following handlers, which change the background color of the control that has the input focus:

```
Private Sub Control_Enter(ByVal sender As Object, ByVal e As EventArgs) _
      Handles txtFirstName.Enter, txtLastName.Enter,  txtCity.Enter
   Dim ctrl As Control = DirectCast(sender, Control)
   ' Change the background color when this control gets the focus.
   ctrl.BackColor = Color.Yellow
End Sub

Private Sub Control_Leave(ByVal sender As Object, ByVal e As EventArgs) _
      Handles txtFirstName.Leave, txtLastName.Leave, txtCity.Leave
   Dim ctrl As Control = DirectCast(sender, Control)
   ' Restore the default background color when the control loses the focus.
   ctrl.BackColor = SystemColors.Window
End Sub
```

Microsoft Visual Studio .NET 2003 and earlier versions couldn't directly generate the skeleton for methods that handle multiple events or for methods with an arbitrary name, that is, a name not in the *objectname_eventname* format. Visual Studio 2005 overcomes this limitation by providing a new Events tab in the Properties window, as shown in Figure 7-1. To generate the template for Control_Enter, select the txtFirstName control, press the F4 key to display the Properties window, click the Events button on the window's toolbar, select the Enter item, type **Control_Enter**, and then press Enter. Visual Studio then generates the Control_Enter procedure with the Handles txtFirstName.Enter event. Next, select the txtLastName control on the form's surface and repeat the same sequence, but this time click the down arrow near the Enter item and select the Control_Enter method. (The options that appear in this drop-down list are all and only the methods in the current form whose signatures match the signature of the selected event.) Repeat once again the series of actions for the txtCity control.

You might follow the same approach for the Leave event, but when you know in advance that multiple controls share the same event handler, you can take a shorter path. Select the three controls on the form's surface, switch to the Events tab of the Properties window, select the Leave event, type the **Control_Leave** string, and press Enter.

Figure 7-1   The Event tab in the Properties window, which displays all the events that the currently selected control exposes

The WithEvents Keyword

You can use the Handles clause to handle events raised by an object only if the object has been declared at the class level with a WithEvents keyword. This holds true even for controls, as you can see by opening the Form1.Designer.vb source file that Visual Studio 2005 has created for you and looking for the following declarations:

```
Friend WithEvents btnOK As System.Windows.Forms.Button
Friend WithEvents txtFirstName As System.Windows.Forms.TextBox
Friend WithEvents txtLastName As System.Windows.Forms.TextBox
Friend WithEvents txtCity As System.Windows.Forms.TextBox
```

(Click the Show All Files button in the Solution Explorer window and expand the Form1 node to see the Form1.Designer.vb file.)

When you work with objects other than controls, you can't rely on Visual Studio to generate a variable flagged with the WithEvents keyword, so you must declare the variable yourself. The following code example uses a System.Windows.Form.Timer object to schedule the launch of an external program after a given number of milliseconds:

```
Public Class AppScheduler
    Private WithEvents Timer As New System.Windows.Forms.Timer
    Private exePath As String
    Private arguments As String

    Public Sub New(ByVal exePath As String, ByVal arguments As String, _
            ByVal milliseconds As Integer)
        ' Remember application's path and arguments for later.
        Me.exePath = exePath
        Me.arguments = arguments
        ' Activate the timer.
        Me.Timer.Interval = milliseconds
        Me.Timer.Enabled = True
    End Sub

    Private Sub Timer_Tick(ByVal sender As Object, ByVal e As EventArgs) Handles Timer.Tick
        ' Prevent the timer from firing again.
        Me.Timer.Enabled = False
        ' Run the application.
        Process.Start(exePath, arguments)
    End Sub
End Class
```

Here's how you can use the AppScheduler class to load a text file into Notepad after 5 seconds:

```
Dim sched As New AppScheduler("Notepad.exe", "c:\data.txt", 5000)
```

Handling Events in a Separate Class

Another case when the manual definition of a WithEvents variable pointing to a control is necessary is inside auxiliary classes that handle control events for you. I explain this interesting technique by using a complete and useful example.

Most developers are so accustomed to handling control events from inside the form class that they don't take into account the possibility of placing the event handler in a different place. I demonstrate how this change of perspective can help you reduce the amount of code you need to write and maintain. For example, consider the common task of validating key presses in a TextBox control. You typically implement this feature by handling the KeyPress event:

```
' Accept only digit keys in TextBox1 control.
Private Sub TextBox1_KeyPress(ByVal sender As Object, ByVal e As KeyPressEventArgs) _
        Handles TextBox1.KeyPress
```

```
' Discard any key press not in the list of valid characters.
Dim validChars As String = "0123456789"
If validChars.IndexOf(e.KeyChar) < 0 Then e.Handled = True
End Sub
```

This approach works well, but it isn't practical when you have dozens of TextBox controls on the Form's surface because it would force you to clutter your source code with many similar handlers. You can reduce this clutter by having one method handle events from many controls, but only if they share the list of valid characters. In the most general case, you need one handler for each control, which is obviously a nuisance. You can elegantly solve this issue by placing the handler outside the Form. Consider the following wrapper class:

```
Public Class TextBoxWrapper
  ' The control being wrapped
  Private WithEvents TextBox As TextBox
  ' The list of valid characters
  Private ValidChars As String

  Public Sub New(ByVal textBox As TextBox, ByVal validChars As String)
    Me.TextBox = textBox
    Me.ValidChars = validChars
  End Sub

  Private Sub TextBox_KeyPress(ByVal sender As Object, ByVal e As KeyPressEventArgs) _
      Handles TextBox.KeyPress
    ' Discard any key press not in the list of valid characters.
    If ValidChars.IndexOf(e.KeyChar) < 0 Then e.Handled = True
  End Sub
End Class
```

Notice that the WithEvents variable enables the TextBoxWrapper class to handle events raised by the TextBox passed as an argument to the constructor. Here's how the code inside a form can leverage this feature:

```
Dim qtyWrapper, phoneWrapper, idWrapper As TextBoxWrapper

Private Sub Form1_Load(ByVal sender As System.Object, ByVal e As EventArgs) _
    Handles MyBase.Load
  ' txtQty is a numeric field that can hold only positive numbers.
  qtyWrapper = New TextBoxWrapper(txtQty, "0123456789")
  ' txtPhone can contain digits and a few symbols.
  phoneWrapper = New TextBoxWrapper(txtPhone, "-0123456789()")
  ' txtID can contain only hexadecimal characters.
  idWrapper = New TextBoxWrapper(txtID, "0123456789ABCDEFabcdef")
End Sub
```

As you can see, you can reuse the code in the TextBoxWrapper class for all the TextBox controls in your application, which is surely more convenient than writing the same code in each and every form that makes up the program. Notice that it's essential that you define the qty-Wrapper, phoneWrapper, and idWrapper variables at the form level, so that they live as long as the form is active. If you use local variables, these objects would go out of scope when the Form1_Load method ends, and the wrapper would eventually be destroyed at the first garbage collection.

Also, notice that you can't use initializers to create valid instances of these TextBoxWrapper objects, as in this code:

```
' *** This code doesn't work.
Dim qtyWrapper As New TextBoxWrapper(txtQty, "0123456789")
```

Initializers don't work in this case because they are executed before the form's constructor, when the TextBox variable passed as an argument (txtQty, in this case) hasn't been assigned yet and is still Nothing.

Events and Delegates Behind the Scenes

You can fully tap the power of .NET events if you recognize that they are handled internally by means of delegates. More precisely, a class that can raise an event defines a private delegate field that points to all the clients who subscribed to the event. When the event fires, the .NET event infrastructure calls the Invoke method of the corresponding delegate field, which in turn causes all the clients to be notified of the event.

As an indirect confirmation of this fact, you can use the object browser to see that for each event defined in the .NET Framework there is a corresponding delegate. For example, all the events that take a simple EventArgs object in the second argument are managed internally by means of the System.EventHandler delegate. The KeyPress event exposed by most Windows Forms controls is handled by means of the KeyPressEventHandler delegate, which points to a Sub method that takes an Object as the first argument and a KeyPressEventArgs instance as the second argument.

Apparently, when you assign a non-null object reference to a WithEvents field, no code executes; therefore, you might ask yourself the following question: When does the application register for events coming from an object referenced by a WithEvents field? When you use the ILDASM tool to take a closer look, it reveals the trick: all the class-level variables that you mark with the WithEvents keyword are actually rendered by the Visual Basic compiler as properties, not fields. (See Figure 7-2.) These properties wrap a private variable named _objectname, for example, _btnOK for the control named btnOK. The following pseudocode illustrates what happens inside the btnOK property:

```
' This is the private, hidden reference to the control.
Private _btnOK As Button

' This is what your Visual Basic code thinks is the control reference.
Public Property btnOK() As Button
   Get
      Return _btnOK
   End Get
   Set(ByVal value As Button)
```

```
        If _btnOK IsNot Nothing Then
            ' Unregister events for the control currently pointed to by _Button1.
            ...
        End If
        ' Remember the new value.
        _btnOK = value
        If _btnOK IsNot Nothing Then
            ' Register events for the control now pointed to by _Button1.
            ...
        End If
    End Set
End Property
```

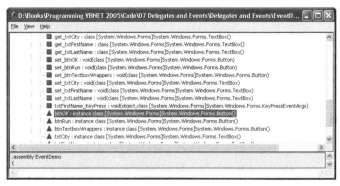

Figure 7-2   WithEvents variable implementation, as seen from inside ILDASM

As you can see, a lot of activity goes on whenever you access a control variable on a form or, more generally, an object variable declared using the WithEvents keyword. Not surprisingly, this hidden code can affect performance, both when you assign a value to these variables and (to a lesser degree) when you read their value.

Knowing what happens behind the scenes can help you reduce this overhead when you access the variable from inside a piece of time-critical code. Here are two simple techniques you can employ with minimal effort:

■ When you repeatedly read the value of a WithEvents field, for example, inside a time-critical loop that executes hundreds of times, you can assign the field value to a local variable and use that variable inside the loop.

■ When you assign a value to a WithEvents field, first ensure that you aren't assigning the same value that is already stored in the field, so that you'll never unnecessarily execute the code in the Set portion of the hidden property.

Interestingly, IntelliSense hides the _objectname_ variable, but you can reach it anyway. For example, if you have a txtFirstName control defined on the form, the following code compiles and executes correctly:

```
' Bypass the visible property and access the control directly.
_txtFirstName.Text = "Francesco"
```

I don't recommend that you access the hidden _objectname_ variable directly in real applications, though, because this is an undocumented implementation detail that might change in future versions (even though this isn't likely to happen because this hidden variable has retained its name since Visual Basic 2002). In general, bypassing the hidden property delivers a very small increase in performance only inside loops that are repeated many times: if you need to optimize such a loop, just assign the control to a local variable and use the variable inside the loop, as suggested previously.

The AddHandler Keyword

The WithEvents keyword is easy to use and hides all the low-level details involved in event handling, but it doesn't give you maximum power and flexibility. For example, you can't use the WithEvents keyword with local variables or when you don't know in advance how many controls you want to handle. Another problem with the WithEvents keyword is that it only works with instance events and isn't able to handle static events, such as those raised by the System.Console or the System.Windows.Forms.Application object. For these tasks, you need a more versatile solution, based on the AddHandler operator.

The AddHandler operator enables you to subscribe for a given event at run time. Its first argument is the *object.event* combination; its second argument is the delegate that points to the routine that will handle the event. For example, the following statement registers a handle for the Enter event of the txtFirstName control:

```
AddHandler txtFirstName.Enter, New EventHandler(AddressOf Control_Enter)
```

where the Control_Enter must be a Sub method that complies with the EventHandler delegate's signature. Notice that AddHandler is an operator, not a method call, and therefore it doesn't require a pair of parentheses around its arguments. Visual Basic is able to infer the type of delegate automatically, so you can simplify the previous statement as follows:

```
AddHandler txtFirstName.Enter, AddressOf Control_Enter
```

The counterpart of the AddHandler keyword is RemoveHandler, which unsubscribes from an event:

```
RemoveHandler txtFirstName.Enter, AddressOf Control_Enter
```

These two operators enable you to subscribe to an event at the top of a method and unsubscribe from it just before the method exits. For example, assume that you have dropped a Timer control on a form's surface; this timer is usually disabled and you want to enable it only during the execution of some methods. However, each method requires that a different action be performed when the timer becomes active. You might have a Select Case block inside the Timer's Tick event, but the AddHandler keyword provides a more elegant solution:

```
Sub FirstLongTask()
    ' Subscribe to the Tick event and enable the timer.
    AddHandler Timer1.Tick, AddressOf FirstLongTask_BackgroundActivity
```

```
    Timer1.Enabled = True
    ' Perform the task here. (Remember to call Application.DoEvents
    ' every now and then to give the timer a chance to tick.)
    ...
    ' Disable the timer and remove the event subscription.
    Timer1.Enabled = False
    RemoveHandler Timer1.Tick, AddressOf FirstLongTask_BackgroundActivity
End Sub

Private Sub FirstLongTask_BackgroundActivity(ByVal sender As Object, e As EventArgs)
    ' Code to be executed in background while FirstLongTask runs
    ...
End Sub

Sub SecondLongTask()
    ' Similar to FirstLongTask, but runs different code in the background
    AddHandler Timer1.Tick, AddressOf SecondLongTask_BackgroundActivity
    ...
    RemoveHandler Timer1.Tick, AddressOf SecondLongTask_BackgroundActivity
End Sub

Private Sub SecondLongTask_BackgroundActivity(ByVal sender As Object, e As EventArgs)
    ' Code to be executed in background while SecondLongTask runs
    ...
End Sub
```

As I mentioned previously, the AddHandler keyword enables you to handle static events, too, something that you can't do with WithEvents fields. For example, the System.Windows.Forms. Application object—which is a singleton object and exposes only static members—raises the Idle event when the program becomes idle after a series of user interface actions, such as key presses and mouse movements. You can write a handler for this event to update the user interface, for example, to show the number of characters currently contained in a TextBox. Because it is a singleton object, you can't assign the Application object to a WithEvents variable; therefore, you must register for this event by using the AddHandler keyword when the form loads:

```
Private Sub Form1_Load(ByVal sender As Object, ByVal e As EventArgs) Handles MyBase.Load
    AddHandler Application.Idle, AddressOf Application_Idle
End Sub

Private Sub Application_Idle(ByVal sender As Object, ByVal e As EventArgs)
    ' Update the user interface here.
    lblCharCount.Text = txtField.TextLength.ToString()
End Sub
```

Notice that you can't count on Visual Studio to create the skeleton of the handlers of static events.

Trapping Events from Arrays and Collections

The AddHandler command enables you to overcome one of the most serious limitations of the WithEvents keyword: the inability to trap events from an array or a collection of objects. By using the AddHandler command you can register the same handler for all the objects in the array or collection. The code in the event handler can identify which element in the array or collection raised the event by testing the first argument passed to the handler.

This technique is often used to create a centralized event handler that serves the events for all the controls on a form. For example, say that all the controls on a form have a short description associated with them; for simplicity's sake, this description is stored in the Tag property. You'd like to display the description on a control on a status bar when the mouse cursor pauses over the control, that is, when the control raises a MouseEnter event; the status bar should be cleared when the control raises a MouseLeave event. Understandably, you don't want to create a pair of handlers for each and every control on the form, especially if the form contains dozens of fields. The solution is quite easy when you use the AddHandler keyword:

```
Private Sub Form1_Load(ByVal sender As Object, ByVal e As EventArgs) Handles MyBase.Load
    ' Registers two events for each control on the Form.
    For Each ctrl As Control In GetChildControls(Me)
        AddHandler ctrl.MouseEnter, AddressOf Control_MouseEnter
        AddHandler ctrl.MouseLeave, AddressOf Control_MouseLeave
    Next
End Sub


' This code assumes that the form contains a StatusStrip control, which
' in turn contains a ToolStripStatusLabel control.

Private Sub Control_MouseEnter(ByVal sender As Object, ByVal e As EventArgs)
    Dim ctrl As Control = DirectCast(sender, Control)
    If Not ctrl.Tag Is Nothing Then ToolStripStatusLabel1.Text = ctrl.Tag.ToString()
End Sub

Private Sub Control_MouseLeave(ByVal sender As Object, ByVal e As EventArgs)
    ToolStripStatusLabel1.Text = ""
End Sub
```

The GetChildControls helper method is a recursive function that returns all the controls on a form, including those contained in another container control (for example, a Panel control) rather than directly on the form's surface:

```
' Return the list of all the controls contained in another control.
Function GetChildControls(ByVal parent As Control) As ArrayList
    Dim result As New ArrayList()
    For Each ctrl As Control In parent.Controls
        ' Add this control to the result.
        result.Add(ctrl)
        ' Recursively call this method to add all child controls as well.
        result.AddRange(GetChildControls(ctrl))
    Next
    Return result
End Function
```

Figure 7-3 shows the effect you can achieve when running the previous code.

Figure 7-3   The demo application showing how to display a Help message in a status bar when the mouse moves over a control

It is a good rule to always remove handlers created by means of the AddHandler keyword before unloading the Form:

```
Private Sub Form1_FormClosing(ByVal sender As Object, ByVal e As FormClosingEventArgs) _
      Handles Me.FormClosing
   ' Unregisters the events for all the controls on the Form.
   For Each ctrl As Control In GetChildControls(Me)
      RemoveHandler ctrl.MouseEnter, AddressOf Control_MouseEnter
      RemoveHandler ctrl.MouseLeave, AddressOf Control_MouseLeave
   Next
End Sub
```

In some cases, omitting the call to RemoveHandler doesn't cause any problems. More specifically, this is true if the object raising the event and the object serving the event are destroyed at the same time. For example, if you use AddHandler inside a form to handle events raised by a control on that same form (as in the previous example), you can safely omit RemoveHandler when the form closes because the event source (the control) and the object containing the event handler (the Form object) are both destroyed at that time.

In other cases, however, forgetting to remove an event handler can have nasty consequences. For example, say that you use AddHandler in one form (let's call it FormA) to trap events raised by another form (FormB). As you know, events are implemented by delegates; therefore, FormB has a hidden delegate that references FormA. If you neglect to call RemoveHandler when FormA closes, the hidden reference inside FormB keeps the FormA object alive. In this scenario, not only does FormA continue to consume memory and resources, it might also affect your application in other ways—for example, if it contains a timer that periodically fires an event.

Exposing Events

Now that you know all you need to know about handling events, it's time to turn your attention to how you can implement a class that exposes one or more events by means of the Event and the RaiseEvent keywords.

The Event keyword supports two syntaxes: you can specify the signature of the event explicitly, or you can define the event in terms of a delegate. The following example illustrates the former technique in a class that raises the NameChanged event when its Name property is assigned a new value:

```
Public Class User
   ' Define the event.
   Public Event NameChanged(ByVal sender As Object, ByVal e As EventArgs)

   Private m_Name As String

   Public Property Name() As String
      Get
         Return m_Name
      End Get
      Set(ByVal value As String)
         If m_Name <> value Then
            m_Name = value
            ' Raise the event (only if the property has actually changed).
            RaiseEvent NameChanged(Me, EventArgs.Empty)
         End If
      End Set
   End Property
End Class
```

You can use the EventArgs.Empty static field to provide a neutral EventArgs instance, a technique that saves you the instantiation of a new EventArgs object. You can test the NameChanged event by means of a WithEvents variable or the AddHandler keyword:

```
Dim WithEvents user As New User()

Sub TestNameChangedEvent()
   ' This assignment causes the NameChanged event to be raised.
   user.Name = "Joe"
End Sub

Private Sub User_NameChanged(ByVal sender As Object, ByVal e As EventArgs) _
      Handles user.NameChanged
   Console.WriteLine("Name property has changed")
End Sub
```

Events are internally implemented by means of delegates, so you might wonder what delegate class is used for the NameChanged event and where it is defined. Because this event uses the standard (object, EventArgs) signature, you might believe that the Visual Basic compiler automatically defines it by means of the System.EventHandler delegate, but unfortunately the compiler isn't that smart. By disassembling this class using ILDASM (see Figure 7-4), you'll notice that Visual Basic generated as many as four hidden members that are related to the NameChanged event:

- A delegate type named NameChangedEventHandler
- A class-level field named NameChangedEvent, whose type is NameChangedEventHandler

■ Two hidden methods named add_NameChanged and remove_NameChanged, which take a NameChangedEventHandler object as an argument (these are the methods indirectly invoked by the AddHandler and RemoveHandler operators)

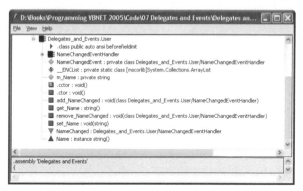

Figure 7-4   The hidden delegate class generated by the Visual Basic compiler

The mechanism that Visual Basic uses to automatically generate a hidden delegate for each public event is quite inefficient. If you have 10 events with the same signature as NameChanged, the compiler unnecessarily creates 10 delegate types, with different names but the same syntax. These delegate types pollute your namespace, increase your application's memory footprint, and slightly slow down execution (because the .NET runtime must initialize a type the first time it's referenced).

Even if performance isn't an issue, these hidden delegates reduce the usability of your code and can confuse developers working with other .NET languages. For example, C# developers can define events exclusively by means of delegates, so they might wonder why they should use a custom NameChangedEventHandler delegate that is exactly identical to the more commonly known EventHandler delegate.

To leverage the power of events fully, reduce the overhead in your application, and make your classes look better to other developers you should use the alternative syntax for the Event keyword, which enables you to define an event in terms of a specific delegate. All you need to do is change the event declaration in the User class, without touching any other portion of code inside or outside the class:

```
' (Replace the Event statement in the User class with the next statement.)
Public Event NameChanged As EventHandler
```

Another trip to ILDASM can prove that the hidden NameChangedEventHandler delegate type has gone, together with all the usability and performance issues that it causes. You'll learn shortly that this alternative syntax has other advantages.

Guidelines for Event Syntax

I explained earlier that virtually all the events exposed by .NET objects have only two arguments: an Object argument named sender, which represents the object that's raising the event; and an argument named e, which exposes the event's arguments through its fields or properties. The type of the second argument should be System.EventArgs or a class that inherits from System.EventArgs. The name of such a class should end with EventArgs.

This syntax enables a caller to set up a single event handler that serves multiple objects, or even arrays or collections of objects. If an event procedure can handle events from multiple objects, the sender argument is the only way for a client to learn which specific object raised the event. Abiding by this naming convention requires only a little extra code today, but it might simplify your job a great deal tomorrow. Also, it makes your objects appear similar to native .NET objects, thus simplifying the life of programmers who use your objects.

The .NET Framework exposes several types that derive from EventArgs and their corresponding delegate types. For example, the System.ComponentModel.CancelEventArgs class derives from EventArgs and adds a Cancel writable property. This class, together with its CancelEventHandler delegate, enables you to define a cancelable action. For example, see how you can expand the User class with a Login method that can be canceled by clients who have subscribed to the BeforeLogin event:

```
Public Class User
   Public Event BeforeLogin As CancelEventHandler
   Public Event AfterLogin As EventHandler

   Public Sub Login()
      ' Ask clients whether logging in is OK.
      Dim e As New CancelEventArgs()
      RaiseEvent BeforeLogin(Me, e)
      If e.Cancel Then Exit Sub

      ' Perform the login here…
      …
      ' Let clients know that the user has logged in.
      RaiseEvent AfterLogin(Me, EventArgs.Empty)
   End Sub
   …
End Class
```

When you define a new event, you might be lucky enough to find an EventArgs-derived class that already exposes the properties you need; in most cases, however, you must roll up your sleeves and define a custom class yourself. For example, say that you want to raise an event named NameChanging before the Name property is actually changed; the corresponding NameChangingEventArgs type should expose the ProposedValue read-only property (the name that is about to be assigned to the Name property) and the Cancel writable property (to enable clients to cancel the assignment). The simplest way to define such a class is by inheriting it from CancelEventArgs (which already provides the Cancel property):

```
Public Class NameChangingEventArgs
   Inherits CancelEventArgs

   Public Sub New(ByVal proposedValue As String)
      m_ProposedValue = proposedValue
   End Sub
```

```
    Private m_ProposedValue As String

    Public ReadOnly Property ProposedValue() As String
       Get
          Return m_ProposedValue
       End Get
    End Property
End Class
```

```
' The delegate that defines the event
Public Delegate Sub NameChangingEventHandler(ByVal sender As Object, _
    ByVal e As NameChangingEventArgs)
```

You need only a few minor changes in the User class to support the new event. (Added statements are in bold type.)

```
Public Class User
    Public Event NameChanging As NameChangingEventHandler
       …
    Public Property Name() As String
       Get
          Return m_Name
       End Get
       Set(ByVal value As String)
          If m_Name <> value Then
             ' Ask clients whether it's OK to assign the new value.
             Dim e As New NameChangingEventArgs(value)
             RaiseEvent NameChanging(Me, e)
             If e.Cancel Then Exit Property
             ' Proceed with assignment.
             m_Name = value
             ' Raise the NameChanged event (only if the property has actually changed).
             RaiseEvent NameChanged(Me, EventArgs.Empty)
          End If
       End Set
    End Property
```

A client can leverage the new event to reject invalid assignments to the Name property as follows:

```
' (Inside the client that uses the User object.)
Dim WithEvents user As New User()

Private Sub User_NameChanging(ByVal sender As Object, _
      ByVal e As NameChangingEventArgs) Handles user.NameChanging
    ' Accept only names that contain alphabetical characters; reject all others.
    If e.ProposedValue Like "*[!A-Za-z]*" Then e.Cancel = True
End Sub
```

In Chapter 11, "Generics," I explain how you can simplify the definition of EventArgs-derived classes (and their delegate companions) by means of generics.

Custom Events

 Visual Basic 2005 introduces the notion of custom events, which put you in full control of how your events behave. From a syntactical point of view, a custom event is a block that contains three methods, which contain the code that runs when a client subscribes to the event, when a client unsubscribes from the event, and when the code inside the class raises the event by means of a RaiseEvent keyword, respectively.

To show you how custom events are implemented and used, I replace the BeforeLogin event in the User class with a custom event. Delete the existing definition for this event and type this line in its place:

```
Public Custom Event BeforeLogin As CancelEventHandler
```

When you press Enter, Visual Studio will create the three-part template of the custom event. Here's a possible implementation of the event:

```
' The private delegate variable
Private m_BeforeLogin As CancelEventHandler

' The custom event
Public Custom Event BeforeLogin As CancelEventHandler
   ' Add an event handler to the list of subscribers.
   AddHandler(ByVal value As CancelEventHandler)
      m_BeforeLogin = DirectCast([Delegate].Combine(m_BeforeLogin, value), CancelEventHandler)
   End AddHandler

   ' Remove an event handler from the list of subscribers.
   RemoveHandler(ByVal value As CancelEventHandler)
      m_BeforeLogin = DirectCast([Delegate].Remove(m_BeforeLogin, value), CancelEventHandler)
   End RemoveHandler

   ' Raise the events, but only if there are any subscribers.
   RaiseEvent(ByVal sender As Object, ByVal e As CancelEventArgs)
      If m_BeforeLogin IsNot Nothing Then
         m_BeforeLogin.Invoke(sender, e)
      End If
   End RaiseEvent
End Event
```

In case you're curious, the ILDASM tool can reveal that a custom event generates three different methods: add_BeforeLogin, remove_BeforeLogin, and raise_BeforeLogin. The correspondence of these methods with the three parts of the custom event is evident.

This simple implementation of a custom event has a small advantage over the standard implementation: the actual event is raised only if there is at least one subscriber for it. However, you can optimize the code inside the class even further by checking the m_BeforeLogin delegate variable before executing the RaiseEvent keyword inside the Login method. This technique saves you from unnecessarily creating a CancelEventArgs object when there are no clients who have subscribed to the BeforeLogin event:

```
Public Sub Login()
   ' Ask clients whether logging in is OK, but only if there is at least one subscriber.
   If m_BeforeLogin IsNot Nothing Then
      Dim e As New CancelEventArgs()
      RaiseEvent BeforeLogin(Me, e)
      If e.Cancel Then Exit Sub
   End If
   …
End Sub
```

Custom events are especially important with cancelable events. When such an event has multiple subscribers, all of them are notified of the event even though the first subscriber sets the Cancel property to True. Clearly, this behavior adds overhead that might be avoided. Worse, if the second subscriber mistakenly resets the Cancel property to False, the instance that is raising the event won't cancel the action. This bug would be very difficult to spot, but a custom event enables you to avoid it:

```
' (Inside the BeforeLogin custom event...)
RaiseEvent(ByVal sender As Object, ByVal e As CancelEventArgs)
    If m_BeforeLogin IsNot Nothing Then
        For Each handler As CancelEventHandler In m_BeforeLogin.GetInvocationList()
            handler.Invoke(sender, e)
            If e.Cancel Then Exit For
        Next
    End If
End RaiseEvent
```

Custom events enable you to reduce slightly the memory footprint of a class that exposes many events. The majority of Windows Forms controls, for example, expose dozens of events, but a typical application subscribes to very few of them, if any. Thus, you might end up allocating a lot of memory for events that are never really used. The .NET Framework offers the System.ComponentModel.EventHandlerList class, which works as a repository for the events to which clients have subscribed. This class has been available since .NET Framework 1.0, but you can't use it in Visual Basic .NET 2002 and 2003 because these versions don't support custom events. The following code shows how a class can use this feature to implement only one event, but of course the more events you implement in this way, the more memory you save:

```
Public Class User2
    ' The collection of event handlers
    Private events As New EventHandlerList()

    Public Custom Event AfterLogin As EventHandler
        AddHandler(ByVal value As EventHandler)
            events.AddHandler("AfterLogin", value)
        End AddHandler
        RemoveHandler(ByVal value As EventHandler)
            events.RemoveHandler("AfterLogin", value)
        End RemoveHandler
        RaiseEvent(ByVal sender As Object, ByVal e As EventArgs)
            ' Raise the event if any client has subscribed to it.
            Dim deleg As EventHandler = TryCast(events("AfterLogin"), EventHandler)
            If deleg IsNot Nothing Then deleg.Invoke(sender, e)
        End RaiseEvent
    End Event
End Class
```

Custom events are useful in a few other cases. For example, the code in the RaiseEvent procedure might change the order in which clients are notified of the event according to their priority. In Chapter 21, "Serialization," you'll learn how custom events are important in serializable objects.

Chapter 8
Inheritance

I have already touched on the topic of inheritance in Chapter 2, "Basic Language Concepts," where I explain that inheritance is the ability to derive a new class (the *derived* or *inherited* class) from a simpler class (the *base* class). The derived class inherits all the fields, properties, methods, and events of the base class, can modify the behavior of any of those properties and methods by overriding them, and can define additional members.

Inheritance is especially effective for rendering an *is-a* relationship between two classes. For example, you can create a Bird class from the Animal class because a bird *is an* animal and therefore inherits the characteristics and behaviors of the generic animal, such as the ability to move, sleep, feed itself, and so on. You can then extend the Bird class with new properties and methods, such as the Fly and LayEgg methods. Once the Bird class is in place, you can use it as the base class for a new Falcon class, and so on. A more business-oriented example of inheritance is an Employee class that derives from the Person class, an example that we will use often in the following sections.

A few programming languages earlier than Microsoft .NET Framework, such as Microsoft Visual C++, support multiple-class inheritance, thanks to which a class can derive from more than one base class. All .NET languages, however, support only single-class inheritance.

Note To avoid long lines, code samples in this chapter assume that the following Imports statements are used at the file or project level:

```
Imports System.ComponentModel
Imports System.Drawing
Imports System.IO
Imports System.Windows.Forms
```

Inheritance Basics

To see how inheritance works in Microsoft Visual Basic, let's start by defining a simple Person base class:

```
Public Class Person
   ' Fields visible from outside the class
   Public FirstName As String
   Public LastName As String

   Public Function CompleteName() As String
      Return FirstName & " " & LastName
   End Function
End Class
```

All you need to inherit an Employee class from Person is to add an Inherits clause immediately after the Class statement:

```
' The Employee class inherits from Person.
Public Class Employee
   Inherits Person

End Class
```

Or you can use the following syntax to convince your C++ and C# colleagues that Visual Basic is a first-class object-oriented language:

```
' A more C#-like syntax
Class Employee: Inherits Person

End Class
```

The great thing about inheritance in .NET is that you can inherit from any object, including objects for which you don't have the source code, because all the plumbing code is provided by the .NET Framework. The only exception to this rule occurs when the author of the class you want to derive from has marked the class as *sealed*, which means that no other class can inherit from it. (You'll find more information about sealed classes later in this chapter.)

The derived class inherits all the Public and Friend fields, properties, methods, and events of the base class. Inheriting a field can be a problem, though, because a derived class becomes dependent on that field, and the author of the base class can't change the implementation of that field—for example, to make it a calculated value—without breaking the derived class. For this reason, it's recommended that types meant to work as base classes include only Private fields wrapped by a Public property so that you can change the internal implementation of the property without any impact on derived classes.

Note   To save space and code, some of the examples in this as well as subsequent chapters use a field where a property would be more appropriate: in other words, do as I say, not as I do.

The derived class inherits also all the shared members of the base class. For this reason, all types expose the Equals and ReferenceEquals static methods that they inherit from System.Object.

You can extend the derived class with new fields, properties, and methods simply by adding these new members anywhere in the class block:

```
Class Employee
   Inherits Person

   ' Two new public fields
   Public BaseSalary As Single
   Public HoursWorked As Integer
   ' A new private field
   Private m_HourlySalary As Single

   ' A new property
   Property HourlySalary() As Single
     Get
       Return m_HourlySalary
     End Get
     Set(ByVal Value As Single)
       m_HourlySalary = Value
     End Set
   End Property

   ' A new method
   Function GetSalary() As Single
       Return BaseSalary + m_HourlySalary * HoursWorked
   End Function
End Class
```

Using the Derived Class

You can use the derived class without even knowing that it derives from another class. However, being aware of the inheritance relationship between two classes helps you write more flexible code. For example, inheritance rules state that you can always assign a derived object to a base class variable. In our example, the rule guarantees that you can always assign an Employee object to a Person variable:

```
Dim e As New Employee
e.FirstName = "John"
e.LastName = "Evans"
' This assignment always works.
Dim p As Person = e
' This proves that p points to the Employee object.
Console.WriteLine(p.CompleteName)   '=> John Evans
```

The compiler knows that Person is the base class for Employee, and it therefore knows that all the properties and methods that you can invoke through the p variable are exposed by the Employee object as well. As a result, a call to such a method can never fail. This sort of assignment works also when the derived class inherits from the base class indirectly. *Indirect inheritance* means that there are intermediate classes along the inheritance path, such as when you have a PartTimeEmployee class that derives from Employee, which in turn derives from Person.

Another consequence of this rule is that you can assign any object reference to an Object variable because all .NET classes derive from System.Object either directly or indirectly:

```
' This assignment *always* works, regardless of the type of sourceObj.
Dim o As Object = sourceObj
```

Assignments in the opposite direction don't always succeed, though. Consider this code:

```
' (This code assumes that Option Strict is Off.)
Dim p As Person
' Sometimes p points to an Employee object, sometimes to a Person object.
If Rnd < .5 Then
    p = New Employee()
Else
    p = New Person()
End If
' This assignment fails with an InvalidCastException if Rnd was >=.5.
Dim e As Employee = p
```

The compiler can't determine whether the reference assigned to the e variable points to an Employee or a Person object, and the assignment fails at run time in the latter case. For this reason, this assignment is accepted by the compiler only if Option Strict is Off. To have the compiler accept the assignment even when Option Strict is On you must perform an explicit cast to the destination type, using the CType or the DirectCast operator. However, if the cast operation isn't valid–for example, you are trying to assign a Person object to an Employee variable–you get an InvalidCastException at run time:

```
' This statement works also when Option Strict is On.
Dim e As Employee = DirectCast(p, Employee)
```

Inheriting from a base class implicitly adds a degree of polymorphism to your code. In this context, polymorphism means that you can use the same variable to invoke members of objects of different types:

```
Dim p As Person
' Sometimes P points to an Employee object, sometimes to a Person object.
If Rnd < .5 Then
    p = New Employee()
Else
    p = New Person()
End If
' In either case, this polymorphic code uses early binding.
Console.WriteLine(p.FirstName & " " & p.LastName)
```

Even if a base class variable stores a reference to a derived object, you can't use the variable to access methods that are defined only in the derived class. For example, the following code doesn't compile:

```
' *** This code doesn't compile because you're trying to access
'       a method defined in the Employee class through a Person variable.
p.BaseSalary = 10000
```

As an exception to this rule, you can access—more precisely, you can try to access—any member in any class by using an Object variable and late binding as long as Option Strict is set to Off:

```
' *** This code requires that Option Strict be Off.
Dim o As Object = New Employee()
' The following statement uses late binding.
o.BaseSalary = 10000
```

Overriding Members in the Base Class

The derived class can modify the behavior of one or more properties and methods in the base class. Visual Basic requires that you slightly modify your code in both the base class and the derived class to implement this new behavior. For example, you have to prefix the CompleteName method in the Person class with the Overridable keyword to tell the compiler that the method can be overridden:

```
' …(In the Person (base) class)…
Public Overridable Function CompleteName() As String
    Return FirstName & " " & LastName
End Function
```

You must use the Overrides keyword to redefine the behavior of this method in the derived class:

```
' …(In the Employee derived class)…
Public Overrides Function CompleteName() As String
    Return LastName & ", " & FirstName
End Function
```

Another common term for such a method is *virtual* method (which, in fact, is the C# keyword that corresponds to Overridable).

Previous versions of Microsoft Visual Studio enabled you to generate the template of an overridden method by means of the combo box controls near the top of the code editor. Microsoft Visual Studio 2005 introduces a new shortcut for this common action: type the keyword **Overrides** and select an item from the list of overridable methods that Visual Studio displays. (See Figure 8-1). This technique has an advantage over the old method: the code is generated where the caret is located (and not at the bottom of the class, as it happened in Microsoft Visual Studio .NET 2003). Just as important, the generated template already contains a call to the base type's method:

```
Public Overrides Function CompleteName() As String
    Return MyBase.CompleteName()
End Function
```

(Read on for more information about the MyBase keyword.)

Visual Basic also supports the NotOverridable keyword, which explicitly states that a method can't be overridden; however, there's no point in using this keyword by itself because by default a method can't be overridden. In fact, you can use this keyword only in conjunction with the Overrides keyword, as I explain in the following section.

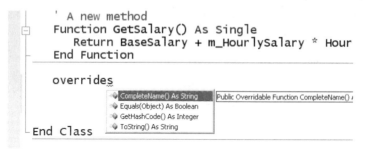

```
      ' A new method
      Function GetSalary() As Single
          Return BaseSalary + m_HourlySalary * Hour
      End Function

      overrides
```

```
  End Class
```

Figure 8-1 The list of overridable methods that appears when you type the Overrides keyword. (The list doesn't include methods that have already been overridden.)

When you override a property in the base class, you can redefine its internal implementation, but you can't alter the ReadOnly or WriteOnly qualifiers. For example, if the base class exposes a property marked as ReadOnly, you can't make it writable by overriding it in the derived class. Similarly, you can't define a read-write property that overrides a WriteOnly property in the base class. Along the same lines, if you're overriding a default member in the base class, the method in the derived class must be the default member in the derived class and requires the Default keyword.

Notice that you can't override fields, constants, events, and static members defined in the base class. The section titled "Redefining Events" later in this chapter shows how you can redefine the behavior of events in derived classes.

Override Variations

By default, a method marked with the Overrides keyword is itself overridable, so you never need both the Overrides and Overridable keywords in the same procedure definition, even though using both is legal. You do need the NotOverridable keyword to explicitly tell the compiler that an overridden method isn't overridable in derived classes:

```
' This procedure overrides a procedure in the base class, but this  procedure
' can't be overridden in any class that inherits from the current class.
Public NotOverridable Overrides Sub MyProc()
    …
End Sub
```

When adding a member with the same name but a different signature, you need neither the Overrides keyword in the derived class nor the Overridable keyword in the base class. For example, if the Employee class contains a CompleteName method with one argument, it doesn't override the parameterless method with the same name in the Person class. Therefore, no Overridable or Overrides keyword is necessary. Oddly enough, however, the method in the derived class does require the Overloads keyword if you want to avoid a compiler warning:

```
' …(In the Person (base) class)…
' Note: no Overridable keyword
```

```
Public Function CompleteName() As String
   Return FirstName & " " & LastName
End Function

' …(In the Employee (derived) class)…
' Note: no Overrides keyword, but Overloads is required to avoid a warning.
Public Overloads Function CompleteName(ByVal title As String) As String
   Return title & " " & LastName & ", " & FirstName
End Function
```

The general rule is therefore as follows: you don't need the Overloads keyword when a class defines multiple members with identical names, but you need the Overloads keyword in the derived class when the derived class exposes a new member with the same name but a different signature.

The compiler can generate more efficient code when calling nonoverridable methods instead of overridable (virtual) methods, so you might want to avoid using the Overridable keyword if you can. For example, the JIT compiler can inline regular methods but not virtual methods. (I explain inlining in the section titled "The MethodImpl Attribute" in Chapter 4, "Using Visual Studio 2005.") In addition, allocating an object that contains virtual methods takes slightly longer than the allocation of an object that has no virtual methods does. An informal benchmark shows that an overridable method can be twice or three times as slow as a non-overridable one, even though the difference in absolute terms is small and you need a loop with millions of iterations to make it apparent. The bottom line is: remember that calling a nonvirtual method can be slightly faster, but don't base your decision of whether a method should be overridable on performance considerations.

While we're talking about performance, remember that calling a virtual method on a value type forces the compiler to deal with it as a reference type, which causes the object to be boxed in the heap and therefore degrades the overall execution speed. For example, this happens when you call the ToString method on a value type such as a structure, as you can see by looking at the IL code produced by such a call.

The MyBase Keyword

The MyBase keyword is useful when you want to reference a field, property, or method of the base object. If a member hasn't been overridden in the derived class, the expressions Me.*membername* and MyBase.*membername* refer to the same member and execute the same code. However, when *membername* has been overridden in the inherited class, you need the MyBase keyword to access the member as defined in the base class. Consider the following method:

```
' …(In the Person base class)…
Public Overridable Function CompleteName() As String
   Return FirstName & " " & LastName
End Function
```

Now, let's assume that the Employee class overrides this method to prefix the complete name with the employee's title. Here's a not-so-smart implementation of this method:

```
' …(In the Employee derived class)…
Public Title As String = ""

Public Overrides Function CompleteName() As String
    Dim result As String = FirstName & " " & LastName
    If Title <> "" Then result = Title & " " & result
    Return result
End Function
```

The preceding solution isn't optimal because it doesn't reuse any code in the base class. In this particular case, the code in the base class is just a string concatenation operation, but in a real class it might be dozens or hundreds of statements. Worse, if you later change or improve the implementation of the CompleteName function in the base class, you must dutifully apply these changes to all the classes that inherit from Person. The MyBase keyword lets you implement a better solution:

```
Public Overrides Function CompleteName() As String
    Dim result As String = MyBase.CompleteName()
    If Title <> "" Then result = Title & " " & result
    Return result
End Function
```

Constructors in Derived Classes

Even though you declare constructor procedures with the Sub keyword, they aren't ordinary methods and aren't inherited from the base class in the way all other methods are. It's up to you to provide the derived class with one or more constructors if you want the derived class to be creatable using the same syntax as the base class.

If the base class has a Sub New procedure that takes no arguments, you don't strictly need to define an explicit constructor for the derived class. The same happens if you have a class with no explicit constructor because in that case the Visual Basic compiler creates a hidden constructor for you behind the scenes. As a matter of fact, all the preceding examples show that you can create an instance of the Employee class without defining a constructor for it:

```
Dim e As Employee = New Employee()
```

Things are different when the base class doesn't include either an explicit or an implicit parameterless constructor. In this case, the derived class must contain a constructor method, and the first executable line of this method must be a call to the base class's constructor. Say that the Person2 class has the following constructor method:

```
Public Class Person2
    Sub New(ByVal firstName As String, ByVal lastName As String)
        Me.FirstName = firstName
        Me.LastName = lastName
    End Sub
```

```
    ' …(other properties and methods as in Person class)…
      …
End Class
```

The derived Employee2 class must therefore contain the following code:

```
Public Class Employee2
   Inherits Person2

   Sub New(ByVal firstName As String, ByVal lastName As String)
      ' The first statement *must* be a call to the constructor in the base class.
      MyBase.New(firstName, lastName)
      ' You can continue with the initialization step here.
      …
   End Sub
End Class
```

The constructor in the derived class can have a different argument signature from the constructor in the base class, but in all cases the first executable statement must be a call to the base class's constructor:

```
Public Title As String                     ' A new field

Sub New(ByVal firstName As String, ByVal lastName As String, ByVal title As String)
   MyBase.New(firstName, lastName)
   Me.Title = title
End Sub
```

The MyClass Keyword

You can easily miss a subtle but important detail of inheritance: when a client calls a nonoverridden method of an inherited class, the method is the one defined in the base class, but it runs in the context of the derived class.

The simplest way to explain this concept is through an example, once again based on the Person-Employee pair. Let's define a Person3 base class exposing a TitledName method that returns the complete name of the person, prefixed with his or her title if one has been specified:

```
Public Enum Gender
   NotSpecified
   Male
   Female
End Enum

Class Person3
   ' (In a real-world class, these would be properties.)
   Public FirstName As String
   Public LastName As String
   Public Gender As Gender = Gender.NotSpecified

   Dim m_Title As String
   Public Overridable Property Title() As String
```

```
         Get
            Return m_Title
         End Get
         Set(ByVal Value As String)
            m_Title = Value
         End Set
      End Property

      ' Prefix the name with a title if one has been specified.
      Public Function TitledName() As String
         If Title <> "" Then
            Return Title & " " & FirstName & " " & LastName
         Else
            Return FirstName & " " & LastName
         End If
      End Function

      ' …(other members as in Person2)…
   End Class
```

The derived Employee3 class doesn't override the TitledName method, but it does override the Title property, so it's never an empty string:

```
Class Employee3
   Inherits Person3

   ' Override Title to provide a title if none has been assigned.
   Public Overrides Property Title() As String
      Get
         If MyBase.Title <> "" Then
            Return MyBase.Title
         ElseIf Gender = Gender.Male Then
            Return "Mr."
         ElseIf Gender = Gender.Female Then
            Return "Ms."
         Else
            Return ""
         End If
      End Get
      Set(ByVal Value As String)
         MyBase.Title = Value
      End Set
   End Property

   ' …(other members as in Employee2)…
End Class
```

Because the derived class doesn't override the TitledName property, the version in the base class is used. However, that code runs in the context of the derived class. Therefore, it uses the overridden version of the Title property, the one defined in Employee3 instead of the one defined in Person3:

```
Dim e As New Employee3("John", "Evans")
e.Gender = Gender.Male
' The TitledName method defined in Person3 uses the overridden
' version of Title property defined in Employee3.
Console.WriteLine(e.TitledName)           ' => Mr. John Evans
```

A simple way to anticipate the effect of inheritance is to pretend that all the nonoverridden routines in the base class have been pasted inside the derived class. So, if they reference another property or method, they call the version of the member that's defined in the derived class—not the original one defined in the base class.

However, sometimes you want a piece of code in the base class to use the nonoverridden version of the properties and methods it references. Let's use another example to clarify this concept. Let's say that a person can vote only if he or she is 18 years old, so the Person3 class contains this code:

```
Class Person3
    Public BirthDate As Date

    ' Age is defined as the number of whole years passed from BirthDate.
    Public Overridable ReadOnly Property Age() As Integer
        Get
            Age = Now.Year - BirthDate.Year
            If Now.DayOfYear < BirthDate.DayOfYear Then Age -= 1
        End Get
    End Property

    Public ReadOnly Property CanVote() As Boolean
        Get
            Return (Age >= 18)
        End Get
    End Property
End Class
```

The Employee3 class uses a looser definition of the age concept and overrides the Age property with a simpler version that returns the difference between the current year and the year when the employee was born:

```
Class Employee3
    ' Age is defined as difference between the current year and birth year.
    Public Overrides ReadOnly Property Age() As Integer
        Get
            Age = Now.Year - BirthDate.Year
        End Get
    End Property
End Class
```

Do you see the problem? The CanVote property of an Employee3 object is inherited as is from the Person3 class but incorrectly uses the Age property defined in the Employee3 class rather than the original version in the base class. To see what kind of bogus result this logical error can cause, run this code:

```
' Create a person and an employee.
Dim p As New Person3("John", "Evans")
Dim e As New Employee3("Robert", "Zare")
' They are born on the same day.
p.BirthDate = #12/31/1988#
e.BirthDate = #12/31/1988#
' (Assuming that you run this code in the year 2006…)
```

```
' The person can't vote yet (correct).
Console.WriteLine(p.CanVote)                        ' => False
' The employee is allowed to vote (incorrect).
Console.WriteLine(e.CanVote)                        ' => True
```

Once you understand where the problem is, its solution is simple: you use the MyClass key-word to ensure that a method in a base class always uses the properties and methods in that base class (as opposed to their overridden version in the inherited class). Here's how to fix the problem in our example:

```
' …(In the Person3 class)…
Public ReadOnly Property CanVote() As Boolean
   Get
      ' Always use the nonoverridden version of the Age property.
      Return (MyClass.Age >= 18)
   End Get
End Property
```

In addition to solving this logical problem—and the serious bugs that might ensue—the MyClass keyword can offer a slight performance improvement as well. As you can recall from the section titled "Override Variations" earlier in this chapter, invoking an overridden method is slightly less efficient than invoking a regular, nonvirtual method is. However, if you use MyClass to invoke a virtual method defined in the same class as the call statement, the target method is treated as a nonvirtual method and the call can be optimized.

You can easily prove this fact by disassembling the program with the ILDASM utility. Calls to a virtual method are usually rendered by means of the callvirt IL opcode, but when you use the MyClass keyword in the call, the Visual Basic compiler generates a standard call IL opcode, the same opcode used to render invocations to nonvirtual methods.

Member Shadowing

.NET lets you inherit from a class in a compiled DLL for which you neither have nor control the source code. This raises an interesting question: what happens if you add a method or a property to the inherited class and then the author of the base class releases a new version that exposes a member with the same name?

Visual Basic copes with this situation in such a way that the application that uses the derived class isn't broken by changes in the base class. If the derived class has a member with the same name as a member in the new version of the base class, you get a compilation warning, but you are still able to compile the application that uses the derived class. In this case, the mem-ber in the derived class is said to *shadow* the member with the same name in the base class. Visual Basic offers three different syntax forms of shadowing:

- A member in the derived class shadows all the members in the base class with the same name, regardless of their parameter signatures. In this case, you get a compilation warn-ing that doesn't prevent successful compilation (unless you select the Treat All Warn-ings As Errors check box on the Compile page of the My Project designer).

■ A member in the derived class marked with the Shadows keyword hides all the members in the base class with the same name, regardless of their signatures. The effect is exactly the same as in the preceding case, except you don't get any compilation warning: in other words, you use the Shadows keyword to let the compiler know that you are intentionally shadowing one or more members in the base class.

■ A member in the derived class marked with the Overloads keyword shadows only the member in the base class that has the same name and same argument signature. (Note that you can't apply the Shadows and Overloads keywords to the same member.)

Shadowing can be confusing, so it's best to look at a concrete example:

```
Class AAA
   Sub DoSomething()
      Console.WriteLine("AAA.DoSomething")
   End Sub
   Sub DoSomething(ByVal msg As String)
      Console.WriteLine("AAA.DoSomething({0})", msg)
   End Sub

   Sub DoSomething2()
      Console.WriteLine("AAA.DoSomething2")
   End Sub
   Sub DoSomething2(ByVal msg As String)
      Console.WriteLine("AAA.DoSomething2({0})", msg)
   End Sub
End Class

Class BBB
   Inherits AAA

   Overloads Sub DoSomething()
      Console.WriteLine("BBB.DoSomething")
   End Sub
   Shadows Sub DoSomething2()
      Console.WriteLine("BBB.DoSomething2")
   End Sub
End Class
```

The following routine calls the methods in the two classes:

```
Dim b As New BBB()
b.DoSomething()           ' => BBB.DoSomething
b.DoSomething("abc")      ' => AAA.DoSomething(abc)
b.DoSomething2()          ' => BBB.DoSomething2
```

As the remarks explain, the DoSomething procedure in class BBB shadows the procedure DoSomething with zero arguments in class AAA, but the procedure that takes one argument isn't shadowed and can be accessed as usual. This behavior contrasts with the DoSomething2 procedure in class BBB, which is declared with the Shadows keyword and therefore hides both procedures with the same name in class AAA. For this reason, the following statement raises a compilation error:

```
' *** This statement doesn't compile.
b.DoSomething2("abc")
```

If you drop the Shadows keyword in class BBB, the overall effect is the same, the only difference being that the call to DoSomething2 causes a compilation warning.

You've just seen that you can shadow a property or a method even if the procedure isn't marked as overridable in the base class. In practice, member shadowing makes it impossible for a developer to prevent a method from being overridden, at least from a logical point of view. To illustrate this concept, let's say that by omitting the Overridable keyword, the author of the Person3 class makes the Address property not overridable:

```
Class Person3
    ...
    Dim m_Address As String

    Property Address() As String
        Get
            Return m_Address
        End Get
        Set(ByVal Value As String)
            m_Address = Value
        End Set
    End Property
End Class
```

The author of the Employee3 class can still override the Address property—for example, to reject null string assignments—by using the Shadows keyword (to suppress compilation warnings) and manually delegating to the base class using the MyBase.Address expression:

```
Class Employee3
    Inherits Person3
    ...
    Shadows Property Address() As String
        Get
            Return MyBase.Address
        End Get
        Set(ByVal Value As String)
            If Value = "" Then Throw New ArgumentException()
            MyBase.Address = Value
        End Set
    End Property
End Class
```

In other words, you can't prevent a class member from being overridden, at least from a logical point of view. This raises a question: what is the point of using the Overridable keyword, then?

The point is, you see a different behavior when you access the member through a base class variable, depending on whether you override the member in the standard way or you shadow it, either implicitly or explicitly using the Shadows keyword. When a member has been over-ridden with Overrides, you always access the member in the derived class, even if you're referencing it through a base class variable. When a member has been shadowed (with or without the Shadows keyword), no inheritance relationship exists between the two members and, therefore, you access the member in the base class if you're using a base class variable. An example makes this concept clearer:

```
Dim e As New Employee3("Joe", "Evans")
' CORRECT: This statement raises an ArgumentException
' because of the code in the Employee class.
e.Address = ""

' Access the same object through a base class variable.
Dim p As Person3 = e
' WRONG: This raises no runtime error because the Address property procedure
' in the base class is actually executed.
p.Address = ""
```

If the Address property were redefined using the Overrides keyword, the last statement would invoke the Address property procedure in the derived class, not in the base class, and the code in the derived class would reject the incorrect assignment.

Because the redefined method in the derived class is related to the original method in the base class, the two members can have different scope qualifiers, which isn't allowed if the method in the derived class overrides the method in the base class. For example, you can have a Public method in the derived class that shadows (and possibly delegates to) a Friend method in the base class. However, keep in mind that a Private member in the derived class does not shadow a member in the base class. In other words, the Shadows keyword has no effect on Private members.

One last detail on shadowing: you can't shadow a method that is defined as MustOverridable in the base class; in this case, the compiler expects a method marked with the Overrides keyword and flags the derived class as incomplete.

Redefining Static Members

You can use neither the Overridable nor the Overrides keyword with static members because static members can't be overridden. Either they're inherited as they are or they must be shadowed and redefined from scratch in the derived class.

You cannot use the MyBase variable to invoke static methods defined in the base class if you're redefining them in the derived class because the MyBase keyword is forbidden in static methods. For example, say that you have a Person class with the following static method:

```
' …(In the Person3 base class)…
Public Father As Person
Public Mother As Person
```

```
Public Shared Function AreBrothers(ByVal p1 As Person3, ByVal p2 As Person3) As Boolean
    Return (p1.Father Is p2.Father) Or (p1.Mother Is p2.Mother)
End Function
```

Let's now say that you have an Employee3 class that inherits from Person3 and you want to redefine the AreBrothers method so that two Employee objects can be considered brothers if they have one parent in common and the same family name. The following code builds on the AreBrother shared method in the Person class so that if you later change the definition in the Person class, the Employee class automatically uses the new definition:

```
' ...(In the Employee3 derived class)...
Public Shared Shadows Function AreBrothers(ByVal e1 As Employee3, _
        ByVal e2 As Employee3) As Boolean
    Return Person3.AreBrothers(e1, e2) And (e1.LastName = e2.LastName)
End Function
```

Unfortunately, no keyword lets you reference static members in the base class in a generic way (similar to what the MyBase keyword does with instance members of the base class). You have to hard-code the name of the base class inside the source code of the derived class when calling a static method of the base class.

Sealed and Virtual Classes

Visual Basic provides a few additional keywords that let you decide whether other developers can or must inherit from your class and whether they have to override some of its members.

The NotInheritable Keyword

For security (or other) reasons, you might want to ensure that no one extends a class you created. You can achieve this by simply marking the class with the NotInheritable keyword:

```
' Ensure that no one can inherit from the Employee class.
Public NotInheritable Class Employee
    ...
End Class
```

Classes that can't be inherited from are called *sealed* classes. In general, you rarely need to seal a class, but good candidates for the NotInheritable keyword are utility classes that expose only static members. As you might expect, you can't use the Overridable keyword inside a sealed class.

A good use for the NotInheritable keyword is when you are defining an *immutable* type, that is, a type whose properties are read-only and can't be modified after the object has been instantiated. If such a class is inheritable, a derived class might violate the immutability by defining one or more writable properties. The most common immutable .NET type is the System.String type, which is in fact sealed.

The MustInherit Keyword

A situation that arises more frequently is that you want to prevent users from using your class as is and instead force them to inherit from it. In this case, the class is called an *abstract* class. You can use an abstract class to derive new classes and you can define a variable typed after the abstract class, but you can't instantiate it directly.

You make a class abstract by flagging it with the MustInherit keyword. You typically use this keyword when a class is meant to define a behavior or an archetypal object that never concretely exists. A typical example is the Animal class, which should be defined as abstract because you never instantiate a *generic* animal; rather, you create a *specific* animal—a cat, a dog, and so on, which derives some of its properties from the abstract Animal class.

Here's a more business-oriented example: your application deals with different types of documents—invoices, orders, payrolls, and so on—and all of them have some behaviors in common in that they can be stored, printed, displayed, or attached to an e-mail message. It makes sense to gather this common behavior in a Document class, but at the same time you want to be sure that no one mistakenly creates a generic Document object. After all, you never say, "I am creating a document." Rather, you say, "I am creating an invoice, an order, and so on."

```
Public MustInherit Class Document
    ' Contents in RTF format
    Private m_RTFText As String

    Public Overridable Property RTFText() As String
        Get
            Return m_RTFText
        End Get
        Set(ByVal Value As String)
            m_RTFText = Value
        End Set
    End Property

    ' Save RTF contents to file.
    Public Overridable Sub SaveToFile(ByVal fileName As String)
        …
    End Sub

    ' Load RTF contents from file.
    Public Overridable Sub LoadFromFile(ByVal fileName As String)
        …
    End Sub

    ' Print the RTF contents.
    Public Overridable Sub Print()
        …
    End Sub
End Class
```

Now you can define other classes that inherit their behavior from the Document abstract class:

```
Class PurchaseOrder
    Inherits Document

    ' Redefines how a PO is printed.
    Public Overrides Sub Print()
        ...
    End Sub
End Class
```

Note that you must explicitly use the Overridable keyword in the base class and the Overrides keyword in the inherited class, even if the base class is marked with MustInherit, because the base class can contain nonoverridable members as well.

The MustOverride Keyword

In general, users of an abstract class aren't forced to override its properties and methods. After all, the main benefit in defining a virtual class is that derived classes can reuse the code in the base class. Sometimes, however, you really want to force inherited classes to provide a custom version of a given method. For example, consider this Shape abstract class, which defines a few properties and methods that all geometrical shapes have in common:

```
Public MustInherit Class Shape
    ' Position on the X-Y plane
    Public X, Y As Single

    ' Move the object on the X-Y plane.
    Public Sub Offset(ByVal deltaX As Single, ByVal deltaY As Single)
        X = X + deltaX
        Y = Y + deltaY
        ' Redraw the shape at the new position.
        Display()
    End Sub

    Public Sub Display()
        ' No implementation here
    End Sub
End Class
```

The Shape abstract class must include the Display method—otherwise, the code in the Offset procedure won't compile—even though that method can't have any implementation because actual drawing statements depend on the specific class that will be inherited from Shape. Alas, the author of the derived class might forget to override the Display method, and no shape will ever be displayed.

In cases like this, you should use the MustOverride keyword to make it clear that the method is abstract and must be overridden in derived classes. When using the MustOverride keyword, you specify only the method's signature and must omit the End Property, End Sub, or End Function keyword:

```
Public MustInherit Class Shape
   ' …(Other members as in previous example)…
   …
   Public MustOverride Sub Display()
End Class
```

If a class has one or more abstract methods, the class itself is abstract and must be marked with the MustInherit keyword. The following Square class inherits from Shape and overrides the Display method:

```
Public Class Square
   Inherits Shape

   Public Side As Single

   Public Overrides Sub Display()
      ' Add here the statements that draw the square.
      …
   End Sub
End Class
```

Scope

Visual Basic accepts five scope qualifiers. I have already covered three of these in previous chapters: Public, Friend, and Private. (These were the same qualifiers available to Microsoft Visual Basic 6 developers.) The remaining two, Protected and Protected Friend, are related to inheritance, which explains why I deferred their description until now. Before diving into a thorough discussion of scope, though, you must learn about one more Visual Basic feature: nested classes.

Nested Classes

Visual Basic 2005 lets you nest class definitions:

```
Class Outer
   …
   Class Inner
      …
   End Class
End Class
```

The code inside the Outer class can always create and use instances of the Inner class, regardless of the scope qualifier used for the Inner class. Unlike top-level classes, a nested class can be marked with the Private scope qualifier, in which case it is available only from inside the outer class. If the nested class is declared using a scope qualifier other than Private, the nested class is visible to the outside of the Outer class, using the usual dot syntax:

```
Dim obj As New Outer.Inner()
```

Nested classes serve a variety of purposes. For example, they're useful for organizing all your classes in groups of related classes and for creating namespaces that help resolve name ambiguity, similar to what you do with Namespace . . . End Namespace blocks.

A common use for nested classes is to encapsulate one or more auxiliary classes inside the class that uses them and to avoid making them visible to other parts of the application. In this case, the inner class should be marked with the Private scope qualifier. For example, you might create a DoubleLinkedList class that internally uses the ListItem class to store the value of each element, the pointer to the previous and next element, and so forth. The ListItem class isn't meant to be visible from the outside, so it's marked as private. As a consequence, you can't have any nonprivate member in the outer class return a reference to the inner, private class:

```
Public Class DoubleLinkedList
    ' These members must be private because they refer to private type.
    Private FirstItem As ListItem
    Private LastItem As ListItem

    ' This class isn't visible from outside the DoubleLinkedList class.
    Private Class ListItem
        Public Value As Object
        Public NextItem As ListItem
        Public PreviousItem As ListItem
    End Class
End Class
```

(Notice that this example is for illustrative purposes only. Microsoft .NET Framework version 2.0 already includes a generic class named LinkedList, which I cover in Chapter 13, "Arrays and Collections," that implements a double-linked list.)

Nested classes have one peculiar feature: they can access private members in their container class if they're provided with a reference to an object of that container class:

```
Private Class ListItem
    Private list As DoubleLinkedList
    ' The constructor takes a reference to the outer DoubleLinkedList object.
    Public Sub New(ByVal list As DoubleLinkedList)
        Me.list = list
    End Sub

    ' This method references a private member in the outer class.
    Public Function IsFirstItem() As Boolean
        Return (Me Is list.FirstItem)
    End Function
    …
End Class
```

You don't need an object reference to access a shared member in the outer class.

 In Visual Basic 2005, an outer class cannot inherit from a class nested inside it. This is a major change from Microsoft Visual Basic .NET 2003 and will prevent projects that use this feature from being recompiled under the current version of Visual Basic.

Public, Friend, and Private Scope Qualifiers

You're already familiar with three of the five scope keywords in Visual Basic.

■ The Public scope qualifier makes a class or one of its members visible outside the current assembly. Note that .NET Framework 2.0 assemblies can reference a public class in another assembly even if the other assembly is compiled as an .exe file.

■ The Friend scope qualifier makes a class or one of its members visible to the current assembly. Because assemblies are usually made of just one project, for most practical purposes this keyword means that the member is visible only from inside the current project. You can use the Friend keyword to make a nested class visible from outside its container without making it Public and visible from outside the project. Note that Friend is the default scope for classes: to make a Visual Basic class visible outside the assembly that contains it, you must explicitly flag the class with the Public keyword.

■ The Private scope makes a class or a member usable only inside its container class. You can use the Private keyword with classes only if the class is nested; otherwise, you get a compilation error. A private class is usable only inside the class in which it's defined, and this includes any other nested class defined in the same container.

Few restrictions apply to using and mixing these scope keywords at the class and at the member level. For example, you can have a Private class that exposes a Public method; however, a Public method in a Public class can't expose a Protected or Private member because Visual Basic wouldn't know how to make it available outside the current assembly. Similarly, you can't inherit a Friend class from a Private class and you can't have a Public class that inherits from a Friend or Private class. The reason is that all the members in the base class should be visible to clients of the inherited class, so the scope of members in the base class can't be more limited than the scope of members in the derived class.

You can't use scope qualifiers to alter the scope of an overridden method. If a base class contains a Public method, for example, you can't override it with a Private or Friend method in the derived class. This rule ensures that if a base class variable points to an object from the derived class you can still use the variable to invoke all the overridden methods in the derived class.

The Protected Scope Qualifier

The Protected scope qualifier makes a member or a nested class visible inside the current class, as well as visible to all classes derived by the current class. Put another way, protected members are private members that are visible also from derived classes. In general, a class author defines one or more members as Protected to provide inheritors with a way to modify the usual behavior of the class, but without letting regular clients do the same. For example, consider this Report class that prints a document with a header and a footer:

```
Public Class Report
    Public Sub Print()
```

```
    ' Print the header.
    ...
    ' Print the body of the document.
    ...
    ' Print the footer.
    ...
  End Sub
End Class
```

This is an example of how you should *never* write a class that is meant to be inherited from. Here's a better version, which splits the three basic steps into their own Protected methods:

```
Public Class Report
   Public Sub Print()
      OnPrintHeader()
      OnPrintBody()
      OnPrintFooter()
   End Sub

   Protected Overridable Sub OnPrintHeader()
      ...
   End Sub
   Protected Overridable Sub OnPrintBody()
      ...
   End Sub
   Protected Overridable Sub OnPrintFooter()
      ...
   End Sub
End Class
```

Because you usually provide Protected members so that inheritors can customize the base class behavior, these members are often marked with the Overridable keyword as well. For this very reason, you should rarely use the Protected keyword with fields (which can't be overridden).

Thanks to its three protected and overridable members, you can easily create new classes that reuse most of the code in the base Report class. For example, here's a Report2 class that displays no header and adds totals before the standard footer text:

```
Public Class Report2
   Inherits Report

   Protected Overrides Sub OnPrintHeader()
      ' Print no header.
   End Sub

   Protected Overrides Sub OnPrintFooter()
      ' Print all totals here.
      ...
      ' Print the standard footer.
      MyBase.OnPrintFooter()
   End Sub
End Class
```

This pattern based on protected and overridable members is applied extensively in the .NET Framework. For example, the System.Windows.Forms.Form class exposes tons of On*Xxxx* methods, so all the forms you define in your program (which derive from the base Form class) can control each and every minor detail of the form's appearance and behavior.

The Protected Friend Scope Qualifier

The fifth and last scope qualifier available in Visual Basic is Protected Friend, which combines the features of the Friend and Protected keywords and therefore defines a member or a nested class that's visible to the entire assembly and to all inherited classes. This keyword seems to be redundant—you might think that Friend also comprises inherited classes—until you consider that .NET allows you to inherit classes from other assemblies.

In the Report sample class introduced in the previous section, you might flag the three On*Xxxx* methods with the Protected Friend Overridable keywords. This change in source code would enable other classes in the same assembly to individually print the header, the body, or the footer of the document, without providing clients outside the assembly with this capability.

Using Scope Qualifiers with Constructors

It's interesting to see what happens when you apply a scope qualifier other than Public to a constructor in a Public class. Using a Friend constructor makes the class creatable from inside the assembly but not from outside it, while leaving the class usable outside the current assembly. Incidentally, this is the closest equivalent of PublicNotCreatable classes in Visual Basic 6:

```
Public Class Widget
    ' This class can be created only from inside the current assembly.
    Friend Sub New()
        …
    End Sub
End Class
```

Obviously, clients outside the current assembly must have a way of receiving an instance of the Widget class somehow—for example, by calling a Public method of another class. A class whose methods are used to create instances of another class is called a *factory class*.

You can define a Private Sub New method if you want to prevent clients—inside and outside the assembly—from creating an instance of the class. This approach can be useful when the class contains only static members, so there's no point in creating an instance of it:

```
Public Class Triangle
    ' This private constructor prevents clients from creating an instance of this class.
    Private Sub New()
        ' No implementation code here.
    End Sub
```

```
' Add here all the static members of this class.
Public Shared Function GetArea( … ) As Double
    …
End Function
…
End Class
```

Another use for Private constructors arises when you want clients to create instances through a static factory method, rather than with the usual New keyword. For more information about factory methods, see the section titled "Shared Factory Methods" in Chapter 6, "Class Fundamentals."

The scope of the constructor has a far-reaching and somewhat surprising effect on the inheritance mechanism. To begin with, a class that has only Private constructors can't be used as a base class, even if it isn't flagged with the NotInheritable keyword. In fact, the first statement in the constructor of the derived class must invoke the base class constructor, but any attempt to call MyBase.New will fail because the Sub New procedure isn't visible outside the base class.

Along the same lines, a Public class whose constructor has a Friend scope can be used as a base class only if the derived class is defined in the same assembly. Any attempt to inherit that class from outside the assembly would fail because the inherited class can't call a constructor with a Friend scope. To let clients outside the current assembly instantiate the base class, you can add a static public factory method that returns a new instance of the class:

```
' This class is visible from outside the assembly but can't
' be used as a base class for classes outside the assembly.
Public Class Widget
    ' This constructor can be called only from inside the current assembly.
    Friend Sub New()
        …
    End Sub

    ' A pseudoconstructor method for clients located outside the current assembly.
    Public Shared Function CreateWidget() As Widget
        Return New Widget()
    End Function
End Class
```

Even if clients outside the current assembly don't use the Widget class directly, you still have to mark it as Public (rather than Friend or Private) if you use Widget as the base class for other Public classes in the current assembly, as I explained in the preceding section.

If the constructor has Protected scope, the class can be used as a base class because the constructor of the derived class can always access this constructor, but the class can't be instantiated from either inside or outside the current assembly. Finally, if the constructor has Protected Friend scope, the class can be used as a base class but can be instantiated only from inside the assembly in which it resides and from inside derived classes.

Understanding from where you can instantiate a class, and from where you can use it as a base class, is complicated by the fact that nested classes can access Private and Protected constructors. Table 8-1 can help you determine the effect of the scope of the constructor and the class itself.

Table 8-1   The Effect of Class Scope and Constructor Scope on a Class's Ability to Be Instantiated or Used as a Base Class

Class Scope[1]	Constructor Scope	Types That Can Instantiate This Class	Types That Can Inherit from This Class
Private	Private	Nested types	Nested types
	Protected	Nested types and inherited classes	Private types defined in the same container
	Friend, Protected Friend, Public	Types defined in the same container	Private types defined in the same container
Protected	Private	Nested types	Nested types
	Protected	Nested types and inherited classes	Private/Protected types defined in the same container
	Friend, Protected Friend, Public	Types defined in the same container and inherited classes	Private/Protected types defined in the same container
Friend, Protected Friend	Private	Nested types	Nested types
	Protected	Types defined in the same container and inherited classes	Types defined in current assembly
	Friend, Protected Friend, Public	Types defined in current assembly	Types defined in current assembly
Public	Private	Nested types	Nested types
	Protected	Nested types and inherited classes	All types, inside or outside current assembly
	Friend	Types defined in current assembly	Types defined in current assembly
	Protected Friend	Types defined in current assembly and inherited classes	All types, inside or outside current assembly
	Public	All types, inside or outside current assembly	All types, inside or outside current assembly

[1] Note that you can have Private, Protected, and Protected Friend classes only inside a container type.

Redefining Events

You can't override events in the same way you override properties and methods, and in fact, you can't use the Overrides keyword on events. (However, you can use the Shadows keyword on events.)

Even if you can't directly override an event, you often want to redefine what happens when the base class raises an event. For example, the inherited class might need to perform some additional processing when an event is fired from inside the base class, or it might need to suppress some or all of the events that the base class raises. These two tasks require two different approaches.

If the derived class only needs to get a notification that an event is being raised from inside the base class, you simply need to add Handles MyBase.EventName to the event handler routine. A common example of this technique is when you trap form events in a class that inherits from System.Windows.Forms.Form:

```
Public Class Form1
   Inherits System.Windows.Forms.Form

   Private Sub Form1_Load(ByVal sender As Object, ByVal e As EventArgs) _
      Handles MyBase.Load
      ' Code for the Form.Load event here.
   End Sub
End Class
```

Visual Studio makes it simple to generate the template for such event handlers. Just select the (ClassName Events) item in the leftmost combo box above the code editor window, and then select an event in the rightmost combo box.

This programming technique doesn't require that you change the base class in any way, but it has a serious shortcoming. The derived class has no control over the event itself, and it can't modify its arguments or prevent it from firing. To solve this problem, you must change the way the base class fires events—in other words, you must build the base class with inheritance in mind. Instead of using the RaiseEvent statement whenever you want to raise an event in the base class, you call an overridable method, which by convention is named OnEventname. I'll illustrate this concept by means of an enhanced version of the User type that I used in Chapter 7, "Delegates and Events" (new or modified statements are in bold type):

```
Public Class User
   ' Define the event.
   Public Event NameChanged As EventHandler

   Private m_Name As String

   Public Property Name() As String
      Get
         Return m_Name
      End Get
```

```
        Set(ByVal value As String)
            If m_Name <> value Then
                m_Name = value
                ' Raise the event (only if the property has actually changed).
                OnNameChanged(EventArgs.Empty)
            End If
        End Set
    End Property

    Protected Overridable Sub OnNameChanged(ByVal e As EventArgs)
        RaiseEvent NameChanged(Me, e)
    End Sub
End Class
```

Here's a type that derives from User and redefines the NameChanged event and suppresses it if the new name is an empty string:

```
Public Class PowerUser
    Inherits User

    Protected Overrides Sub OnNameChanged(ByVal e As EventArgs)
        ' Raise the event only if the new name is a nonempty string.
        If Me.Name <> "" Then MyBase.OnNameChanged(e)
    End Sub
End Class
```

Notice that the derived class can't directly use the RaiseEvent statement to raise one of its own events if the event is defined in the base class. The only way to indirectly raise the event is by calling the OnNameChanged method in the base class, as shown in the preceding code. For consistency, On*Xxx* methods should take an EventArgs-derived argument, even if it is an empty (and useless) EventArgs object as in this case.

Visual Inheritance

Because a form is just an object, you shouldn't be surprised to learn that you can inherit a form from another form. Form inheritance isn't different from regular inheritance, and everything you learned about inheritance so far holds true for forms as well. However, the form is a peculiar object in that it exposes a user interface, and this detail has some interesting implications. Before diving into technical details, let's see what form inheritance is good for.

Inheriting a new form from a base form enables you to reuse the user interface, the code, and the functionality in the base form. For example, you can create a DialogBoxBase that contains a Label, the OK and Cancel buttons, and some code for the Click events raised by these buttons. If you then inherit a new form from DialogBoxBase, you inherit both the user interface and the behavior of the base form. You can redefine the text of the Label, resize the form, and move the buttons accordingly (if you assigned their Anchor property correctly), and of course you can add new controls.

The great thing about inheritance is that you can later add new functionality or user interface elements to the DialogBoxBase form, for example, a Help button and the logo of your company. When you recompile the project, the new button and the logo will be part of all the forms that inherit from DialogBoxBase. Even better, inheritance works across assemblies; therefore, you can create a DLL containing the base forms you use more frequently and share this DLL among all your applications.

A Base Form Example

To see in practice how form inheritance works, let's create a new class library project named BaseForms and, inside this project, a form named DialogBoxBase. (See Figure 8-2.) The DialogBoxBase form contains a Label control, a TextBox control that is anchored to the top, left, and right borders (so that it expands and shrinks when the form is resized), and two Button controls that are anchored to the top and right borders.

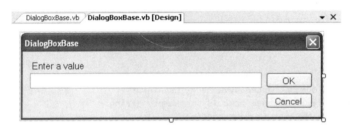

Figure 8-2   The DialogBoxBase form

When creating a base form, you should use a Protected scope for its controls so that they can be accessed and manipulated from inside inherited forms. By default, Visual Studio creates Visual Basic forms with controls that have Friend scope, but you can change a control's visibility by switching to the Properties window and assigning a different value to the Modifiers property.

The point in creating the DialogBoxBase class is simplifying the creation of forms that return the value typed by the user in the TextBox control. Because a Protected control isn't visible outside the class, the base form must expose the TextBox control's contents as a property, as in this code:

```
Property InputValue() As String
    Get
        Return txtValue.Text
    End Get
    Set(ByVal Value As String)
        txtValue.Text = Value
    End Set
End Property
```

Because an inherited class can access all the Protected elements in the base class, a form that inherits from DialogBoxBase can trap events raised by the controls on DialogBaseForm class. For example, a derived form might use the following code to enable the OK button only if the txtValue field contains at least one character:

```
Private Sub txtValue_TextChanged(ByVal sender As Object, _
    ByVal e As EventArgs) Handles txtValue.TextChanged
```

```
        Me.btnOK.Enabled = (txtValue.Text <> "")
End Sub
```

Just trapping an event from a control in the base form isn't enough in some cases, though. For example, let's say that the inherited form should close only if the string entered by the user matches a value in a database. Creating a btnOk_Click event handler doesn't work in this case because the form class would fire both Click events–in the base class and in the derived class–and the code in the derived class couldn't prevent the code in the Click event in Dialog-BoxBase from closing the form. In this case, you need to override the default behavior in the base class, using the technique I illustrated in the section titled "Redefining Events" earlier in this chapter.

All events in the base class should delegate their job to an *OnXxxx* overridable method with Protected scope. For example, the btnOk_Click event procedure should call the OnOkClick procedure, the btnCancel_Click event procedure should call the OnCancelClick procedure, and so on:

```
Public Class DialogBoxBase
    ...
    Private Sub btnOK_Click(ByVal sender As Object, ByVal e As EventArgs) _
        Handles btnOK.Click
      OnOkClick(e)
    End Sub

    Private Sub btnCancel_Click(ByVal sender As Object, ByVal e As EventArgs) _
        Handles btnCancel.Click
      OnCancelClick(e)
    End Sub

    Protected Overridable Sub OnOkClick(ByVal e As EventArgs)
      ' Close this form, return OK.
      Me.DialogResult = DialogResult.OK
    End Sub

    Protected Overridable Sub OnCancelClick(ByVal e As EventArgs)
      ' Close this form, return Cancel.
      Me.DialogResult = DialogResult.Cancel
    End Sub
End Class
```

Compile the BaseForms project before proceeding, both to ensure that everything is OK and because a form must be compiled at least once before you can inherit from it.

An Inherited Form Example

Create a new Windows Forms project named DemoClient, make it the startup project for the solution, and add a reference to the BaseForms project. Next, select the Add New Item command from the Project menu, click the Inherited Form template, type **MyDialogBox** as the name of the new form, and click the Add button. This action opens the Inheritance Picker dialog box (shown in Figure 8-3), where you can select the base form (DialogBoxBase, in our example).

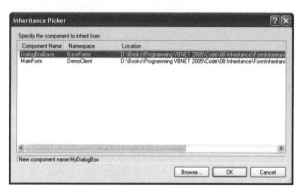

Figure 8-3   The Inheritance Picker dialog box

You can modify the properties of the new MyDialogBox form as you see fit, as well as the properties of all the controls that aren't marked as Private or Friend in the base form. The only limitation is that you can't change the Modifiers and the Name properties of any inherited control, which is quite reasonable because you can't change the name or the scope of a member inherited from a base class. Of course, you can add new controls as well, for example, a PictureBox and a CheckBox control. (See Figure 8-4.)

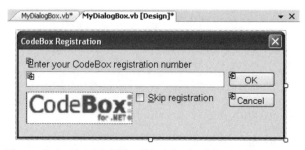

Figure 8-4   The MyDialogBox inherited form

The inherited form can override the OnOkClick protected method to refuse to be closed if the value isn't valid for the specific task. For example, in the MyDialogBox form you might want to reject the OK action if the typed value isn't a 16-character string or contains characters that aren't hexadecimal digits:

```
Protected Overrides Sub OnOkClick(ByVal e As EventArgs)
    If Not chkSkipRegistration.Checked AndAlso _
        (txtValue.Text.Length <> 16 OrElse txtValue.Text Like "*[!0-9a-fA-f]*") Then
        ' Display an error message.
        MessageBox.Show("Invalid serial number", "Error", MessageBoxButtons.OK, _
            MessageBoxIcon.Error)
    Else
        ' Perform the default action (closes the form).
        MyBase.OnOkClick(e)
    End If
End Sub
```

Adding Properties, Methods, and Events to the Base Form

You can add properties, methods, and events to the base form as you'd do with any base class. Properties in base forms, though, are peculiar because they show up in the Properties window when you open an inherited form. This feature adds a lot of power and flexibility because it allows you to change the appearance and the behavior of your derived forms without writing a single line of code.

To show this concept in action, switch to the BaseForms project and create a new form named DataEntryFormBase. This form doesn't contain any controls, just code. This code will iterate over the form's Controls collection to process all the controls that have been added to the inherited form. In this example, I show you how you can automatically change the foreground and background colors of the control that has the focus. The code that performs this action is conceptually similar to the one I show in the section titled "Trapping Events from Arrays and Collections" in Chapter 7:

```
Public Class DataEntryFormBase
    Protected Overrides Sub OnLoad(ByVal e As System.EventArgs)
        MyBase.OnLoad(e)
        ' Register events for input controls when the form loads.
        For Each ctrl As Control In GetChildControls(Me)
            If ctrl.BackColor.Equals(SystemColors.Window) Then
                AddHandler ctrl.Enter, AddressOf Control_Enter
                AddHandler ctrl.Leave, AddressOf Control_Leave
            End If
        Next
    End Sub

    ' Temporary storage for control's colors
    Private saveForeColor As Color = SystemColors.WindowText
    Private saveBackColor As Color = SystemColors.Window

    ' Change colors when the control gets the focus.
    Private Sub Control_Enter(ByVal sender As Object, ByVal e As EventArgs)
        Dim ctrl As Control = DirectCast(sender, Control)
        ctrl.ForeColor = FocusForeColor
        ctrl.BackColor = FocusBackColor
    End Sub

    ' Restore original colors when the control loses the focus.
    Private Sub Control_Leave(ByVal sender As Object, ByVal e As EventArgs)
        Dim ctrl As Control = DirectCast(sender, Control)
        ctrl.ForeColor = saveForeColor
        ctrl.BackColor = saveBackColor
    End Sub

    ' Return the list of all the controls contained in another control.
    Private Function GetChildControls(ByVal parent As Control) As ArrayList
        Dim result As New ArrayList()
        For Each ctrl As Control In parent.Controls
            ' Add this control to the result.
            result.Add(ctrl)
            ' Recursively call this method to add all child controls as well.
```

```
            result.AddRange(GetChildControls(ctrl))
      Next
      Return result
   End Function

   ...
End Class
```

The actual foreground and background colors assigned to focused controls are read from a pair of public properties, also defined in the DataEntryFormBase class:

```
Private m_FocusForeColor As Color
Private m_FocusBackColor As Color
<Description("The foreground color of focused controls.")> _
<Category("Appearance")> _
Public Property FocusForeColor() As Color
   Get
      Return m_FocusForeColor
   End Get
   Set(ByVal Value As Color)
      m_FocusForeColor = Value
   End Set
End Property

<Description("The background color of focused controls.")> _
<Category("Appearance")> _
Public Property FocusBackColor() As Color
   Get
      Return m_FocusBackColor
   End Get
   Set(ByVal Value As Color)
      m_FocusBackColor = Value
   End Set
End Property
```

The Description and Category attributes are used when the property is displayed in the Properties window. (See Figure 8-5.)

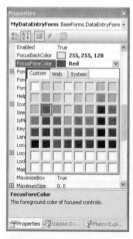

Figure 8-5 Public properties in the base form appearing in the Properties window when you open an inherited form. Notice the description of the current property, near the bottom border.

Recompile the BaseForms project, switch to the DemoClient project, and inherit a new form named MyDataEntryForm from DataEntryFormBase. Then, add a few controls on the new form, run the project, and see what happens when you move the focus from one control to another. Try with an assortment of controls—TextBox, ComboBox, ListBox, CheckBox, Buttons, and so on—to check that only controls with a white background are affected by this new behavior. (See Figure 8-6.)

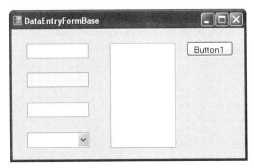

Figure 8-6 Forms that inherit from DataEntryFormBase automatically changing the color of the focused control

A base form can also expose custom events. For example, the following code uses Windows subclassing to intercept the WM_APPACTIVATE message that the operating system sends to all top-level windows when the application gets or loses the input focus. The Form object raises the Activated and Deactivated events when the form gains or loses the input focus, respectively, but these events don't carry any information that enables you to understand whether the user has switched to or from another application or another form in the current application. You can distinguish these two cases by having the base form expose the AppActivated and AppDeactivate custom events.

```
Public Class DataEntryFormBase

    ...
    ' Public events
    Public Event AppActivated As EventHandler
    Public Event AppDeactivate As EventHandler

    ' The operating system calls this method when a message is sent to the form's window.
    Protected Overrides Sub WndProc(ByRef m As Message)
        Const WM_ACTIVATEAPP As Integer = &H1C
        ' Let the base form process this message.
        MyBase.WndProc(m)
        ' Process only the WM_ACTIVATEAPP message.
        If m.Msg = WM_ACTIVATEAPP Then
            If m.WParam.ToInt32 <> 0 Then
                OnAppActivated(EventArgs.Empty)
            Else
                OnAppDeactivate(EventArgs.Empty)
            End If
        End If
    End Sub
```

```
' The OnXxxx protected methods that actually raise the event
Protected Sub OnAppActivated(ByVal e As EventArgs)
   RaiseEvent AppActivated(Me, e)
End Sub

Protected Sub OnAppDeactivate(ByVal e As EventArgs)
   RaiseEvent AppDeactivate(Me, e)
End Sub
End Class
```

A derived form might trap these events to change the appearance of all forms of an inactive application and restore the original appearance when the application gets the input focus again.

```
Public Class MyDataEntryForm
   Private Sub MyDataEntryForm_AppActivated(ByVal sender As Object, _
         ByVal e As EventArgs) Handles Me.AppActivated
      For Each frm As Form In My.Application.OpenForms
         frm.BackColor = SystemColors.Control
      Next
   End Sub

   Private Sub MyDataEntryForm_AppDeactivate(ByVal sender As Object, _
         ByVal e As EventArgs) Handles Me.AppDeactivate
      For Each frm As Form In My.Application.OpenForms
         frm.BackColor = Color.DarkGray
      Next
   End Sub
End Class
```

One last note about form inheritance. When you interact with an inherited form at design time inside Visual Studio, your actions can trigger an event in the base form. For example, when you display the inherited form, a Form_Load event fires in the base form. In most cases, but not always, running the code inside the event handler can be inappropriate at design time. For example, running the code that resizes and moves controls might be OK, whereas accessing a database to read initial values for those controls is rarely useful. You can detect whether you're at design time or run time by testing the DesignMode property:

```
' (The base form class)
Public Class DataEntryFormBase
   Private Sub DataEntryFormBase_Load(ByVal sender As Object, _
         ByVal e As EventArgs) Handles Me.Load
      ' Exit if running in design mode.
      If Me.DesignMode Then Exit Sub
      …
End Sub
```

Chapter 9

Object Lifetime

An important facet of Microsoft .NET programming is understanding how the Common Language Runtime (CLR) allocates and releases memory, and above all how objects are destroyed at the end of their life cycle. In this chapter, you'll learn how you can improve your applications' performance remarkably.

Note   To avoid long lines, code samples in this chapter assume that the following Imports statement is used at the file or project level:

```
Imports System.IO
```

The Need for Garbage Collection

Microsoft Visual Basic classes don't have destructor methods. In other words, no method or event in the class fires when the instance is destroyed. This is one of the most controversial features of the framework and was discussed for months in forums and newsgroups while the .NET Framework was in beta version.

COM and the Reference Counter

Before exploring the .NET way of dealing with object destruction, let's see how Microsoft Visual Basic 6 objects (and COM objects in general) behave in this respect. All COM objects maintain a memory location known as the *reference counter*. An object's reference counter is set to 1 when the object is created and a reference to it is assigned to a variable; the object's reference counter is incremented by 1 when a reference to the object is assigned to another variable. Finally, the object's reference counter is decremented when a variable that points to the object is set to Nothing. This mechanism is hidden from Visual Basic 6 developers and is implemented behind the scenes through the AddRef and Release methods of the IUnknown interface, an interface that all COM objects must expose. More specifically, Visual Basic 6 calls the AddRef method for you when you assign an object reference to a variable with the Set keyword. It calls the Release method when you set an object variable to Nothing.

At any given moment, a COM object's reference counter contains the number of variables that are pointing to that specific object. When the Release method is called, the object checks whether the reference counter is going to be decreased from 1 to 0, in which case the object knows it is no longer required and can destroy itself. (If the object is written in Visual Basic 6, a Class_Terminate event fires at this point.) In a sense, a COM object is responsible for its own life. An erroneous implementation of the AddNew or Release method or an unbalanced number of calls to these methods can be responsible for memory and resource leakage, a serious potential shortcoming in COM applications. (This isn't an issue in Visual Basic applications because this language manages the reference counter automatically, but it can be a source of bugs in languages that require that developers call AddRef and Release methods manually.) Besides, managing the reference counter and frequently calling the AddRef and Release methods can be a time-consuming process, which has a negative impact on the application's performance.

Even more important, it frequently happens that two COM objects keep themselves alive, such as when you have two Person objects that point to each other through their Spouse property. Unless you take some special steps to account for this situation, these objects will be released only when the application terminates, even if the application cleared all the variables pointing to them. This is the notorious *circular reference* problem and is the most frequent cause of memory leakage, even in relatively simple COM applications.

When Microsoft designed the .NET Framework, the designers decided to get rid of reference counting overhead and all the problems associated with it. .NET objects have no reference counter, and there is no counterpart for the AddRef and Release methods. Creating an object requires that a block of memory be allocated from the managed heap, an area in memory that holds all objects. (I introduce the heap in the section titled "Reference Types and Value Types" in Chapter 2, "Basic Language Concepts.") Assigning an object reference requires storing a 32-bit address in a variable (under 32-bit Microsoft Windows platforms, at least), whereas clearing an object variable requires storing 0 in it. These operations are extremely fast because they involve no method calls.

However, the .NET approach raises an issue that doesn't exist under COM: how can the .NET Framework determine when an object isn't used by the application and can be safely destroyed to free the memory that that object uses in the heap?

The Garbage Collection Process

The .NET Framework memory management relies on a sophisticated process known as *garbage collection*. When an application tries to allocate memory for a new object and the heap has insufficient free memory, the .NET Framework starts the garbage collection process, which is carried out by an internal object known as the *garbage collector*. Many technical articles use the acronym GC to indicate both garbage collection and the garbage collector; strictly speaking, System.GC stands for garbage collector, even though in most cases it can indicate both terms.

The garbage collector visits all the objects in the heap and marks those objects that are pointed to by any variable in the application. (These variables are known as *roots* because they're at the top of the application's object graph.) The garbage collection process is quite sophisticated and recognizes objects referenced indirectly from other objects, such as when you have a Person object that references other Person instances through its Children property. After marking all the objects that can be reached from the application's code, the garbage collector can safely release the remaining (unmarked) objects because they're guaranteed to be unreachable by the application.

Next, the garbage collector compacts the heap and makes the resulting block of free memory available to new objects. Interestingly, this mechanism indirectly resolves the circular reference problem because the garbage collector doesn't mark unreachable objects and therefore correctly releases memory associated with objects pointed to by other objects in a circular reference fashion but not used by the main program.

In most real-world applications, the .NET way of dealing with object lifetime is significantly more efficient than the COM way is—and this is an all-important advantage because everything is an object in the .NET architecture. On the other hand, the garbage collection mechanism introduces a new problem that COM developers don't have: *nondeterministic finalization*. A COM object always knows when its reference counter goes from 1 to 0, so it knows when the main application doesn't need it any longer. When that time arrives, a Visual Basic 6 object fires the Class_Terminate event and the code inside the event handler can execute the necessary cleanup chores, such as closing any open files and releasing Win32 resources (pens, brushes, device contexts, and kernel objects). Conversely, a .NET object is actually released sometime after the last variable pointing to it is set to Nothing. If the application doesn't create many objects, a .NET object might be collected only when the program terminates. Because of the way .NET garbage collection works, there's no way to provide a .NET class with an event equivalent to Class_Terminate, regardless of the language used to implement the class. For this reason, it's often necessary to distinguish between the *logical* destruction of an object (when the application clears the last variable pointing to the object) and its *physical* destruction (when the object is actually removed from memory).

If memory is the only resource an object uses, deferred destruction is never a problem. After all, if the application requires more memory, a garbage collection fires and a block of new memory is eventually made available. However, if the object allocates other types of resources—files, database connections, serial or parallel ports, internal Windows objects—you want to make such releases as soon as possible so that another application can use the resources. In some cases, the problem isn't just a shortage of resources. For example, if the object opens a window to display the value of its properties, you surely want that window to be closed as soon as the object is logically destroyed so that a user can't look at outdated information. Thus, the problem is: how can you run your cleanup code when your .NET object is destroyed?

This question has no definitive answer. A partial solution comes in the form of two special methods: Finalize and Dispose.

The Finalize Method

The Finalize method is a special method that the garbage collector calls just before releasing the memory allocated to the object, that is, when the object is physically destroyed. It works more or less the same way the Class_Terminate event under Visual Basic 6 (or the destructor method in C++) works except that it can be called several seconds (or even minutes or hours) after the application has logically killed the object by setting the last variable pointing to the object to Nothing (or by letting the variable go out of scope, which has the same effect). Because all .NET objects inherit the Finalize method from the System.Object class, this method must be declared using the Overrides and Protected keywords:

```
' (Add this to a Person class with usual FirstName and LastName properties.)
Protected Overrides Sub Finalize()
    Debug.WriteLine("Person object is being destroyed.")
End Sub
```

The following application shows that the Finalize method isn't called immediately when all variables pointing to the object are set to Nothing:

```
Sub Main()
    Debug.WriteLine("About to create a Person object.")
    Dim aPerson As New Person("John", "Evans")
    Debug.WriteLine("About to set the Person object to Nothing.")
    aPerson = Nothing
    Debug.WriteLine("About to terminate the application.")
End Sub
```

These are the messages that you'll see in the Debug window (interspersed among other diagnostic text):

```
About to create a Person object.
About to set the Person object to Nothing
About to terminate the application.
Person object is being destroyed.
```

The sequence of messages makes it apparent that the Person object isn't destroyed when the aPerson variable is set to Nothing—as would happen in Visual Basic 6—but only sometime later, when the application itself terminates.

Here's one important .NET programming guideline: never access any external object from a Finalize procedure because the external object might have been destroyed already. In fact, the object is being collected because it can't be reached from the main application, so a reference to another object isn't going to keep that object alive. The garbage collector can reclaim unreachable objects in any order, so the other object might be finalized before the current one. One of the few objects that can be safely accessed from a Finalize method is the base object of the current object, using the MyBase keyword.

In general, it is safe to invoke static methods from inside the Finalize method, except when the application is shutting down. In the latter case, in fact, the .NET Framework might have already destroyed the System.Type object corresponding to the type that exposes the static method. For example, you shouldn't use the Console.WriteLine method because the Console object might be gone. The Debug object is one of the few objects that is guaranteed to stay alive until the very end, however, and that's why the previous code example uses Debug .WriteLine instead of Console.WriteLine. You can discern the two cases by querying the Environment.HasShutdownStarted method:

```
Protected Overrides Sub Finalize()
    If Not Environment.HasShutdownStarted Then
        ' It is safe to access static methods of other types.
        …
    End If
End Sub
```

As I mentioned earlier, you can control the garbage collector by means of the System.GC type, which exposes only static members. For example, you can force a collection by means of its Collect method:

```
Sub Main()
    Debug.WriteLine("About to create a Person object.")
    Dim aPerson As New Person("John", "Evans")
    aPerson = Nothing
    Debug.WriteLine("About to fire a garbage collection.")
    GC.Collect()
    GC.WaitForPendingFinalizers()
    Debug.WriteLine("About to terminate the application.")
End Sub
```

The WaitForPendingFinalizers method stops the current thread until all objects are correctly finalized; this action is necessary because the garbage collection process might run on a different thread. The sequence of messages in the Debug window is now different:

```
About to create a Person object.
About to fire a garbage collection.
Person object is being destroyed.
About to terminate the application.
```

However, calling the GC.Collect method to cause an *induced garbage collection* is usually a bad idea. If you run a garbage collection frequently, you're missing one of the most promising performance optimizations that the .NET Framework offers. The preceding code example, which uses the GC.Collect method only to fire the object's Finalize method, illustrates what you should *never* do in a real .NET application. In a server-side application—such as an ASP.NET application—this rule has virtually no exceptions.

In a Windows Forms application, you can invoke the GC.Collect method, but only when the application is idle—for example, while it waits for user input—and only if you see that unexpected (that is, not explicitly requested) garbage collections are slowing the program noticeably during time-critical operations. For example, unexpected garbage collections might be an issue when your application is in charge of controlling hardware devices that require a short response time. By inducing a garbage collection when the program is idle, you decrease the probability that a standard garbage collection slows the regular execution of your application.

Objects that expose the Finalize method aren't immediately reclaimed and usually require *at least* another garbage collection before they are swept out of the heap. The reason for this behavior is that the code in the Finalize method might assign the current object (using the Me keyword) to a global variable, an advanced technique known as *object resurrection* (discussed later in this chapter). If the object were garbage collected at this point, the reference in the global variable would become invalid; the CLR can't detect this special case until the subsequent garbage collection and must wait until then to definitively release the object's memory. If you consider also that the creation of objects with a Finalize method requires a few more CPU cycles, you see that object finalization doesn't come for free. In general, you should implement the Finalize method only if you have a very good reason to do so.

The Dispose Method

Because .NET objects don't have real destructors, well-designed classes should expose a method to let well-behaved clients manually release any resource such as files, database connections, and system objects as soon as they don't need those objects any longer—that is, just before setting the reference to Nothing—rather than waiting for the subsequent garbage collection.

Classes that want to provide this feature should implement the IDisposable interface, which exposes only the Dispose method. I explain how to use disposable objects in the section titled "The Using...End Using Statement" in Chapter 3, "Control Flow and Error Handling," so here I focus on how to implement this interface in a class you design.

```
Public Class Widget
    Implements IDisposable

    Public Sub Dispose() Implements IDisposable.Dispose
        ' Close files and release other resources here.
        …
    End Sub
End Class
```

(The Implements keyword is described in Chapter 10, "Interfaces.") The Dispose method is marked as Public, and so you can invoke it directly. This is the usage pattern for an IDisposable object:

```
' Create the object.
Dim obj As New Widget()
' Use the object.
…
' Ask the object to release resource before setting it to Nothing.
obj.Dispose
obj = Nothing
```

Or you can use the Using statement, a new feature of Microsoft Visual Basic 2005:

```
' Create the object.
Using obj As New Widget()
   ' Use the object.
   ...
   ' The object is disposed of and set to Nothing here.
End Using
```

The Using statement ensures that the Dispose method is called even if the code throws an exception, but it doesn't catch the exception. If you need to handle exceptions thrown while using the object, you must give up the convenience of the Using statement and use a regular Try . . . Catch . . . Finally block:

```
Dim obj As Widget
Try
   ' Create and use the object.
   obj = New Widget
   ...
Catch ex As Exception
   ...
Finally
   ' Ensure that the Dispose method is always invoked.
   Obj.Dispose()
End Try
```

Many stream- and connection-related objects in the .NET Framework, such as FileStream and all ADO.NET connection objects, have a public Close method that delegates to the private Dispose method. If you had to implement such types in Visual Basic, you would write code such as this:

```
Public Class CustomStream
   Implements IDisposable

   Private Sub Dispose() Implements IDisposable.Dispose
      ' Close the stream here.
      ...
   End Sub

   Public Sub Close()
      Dispose()
   End Sub
End Class
```

Interestingly, the Using statement works correctly with objects that implement a private Dispose method because behind the scenes it casts the object reference to an IDisposable variable. In some cases, you might need to have an explicit cast to this interface, as in the following generic cleanup routine:

```
' Set an object to Nothing and call its Dispose method if possible.
Sub ClearObject(ByRef obj As Object)
```

```
    If TypeOf obj Is IDisposable Then
       ' You need an explicit cast. (It also works with private Dispose methods.)
       DirectCast(obj, IDisposable).Dispose
    End If
    ' Next statement works because the object is passed by reference.
    obj = Nothing
End Sub
```

.NET programming guidelines dictate that the Dispose method of an object should invoke the Dispose method of all the inner objects that the current object owns and that are hidden from the client code, and then it should call the base class's Dispose method (if the base class implements IDisposable). For example, if the Widget object has created a System.Timers .Timer object, the Widget.Dispose method should call the Timer.Dispose method. This suggestion and the fact that an object can be shared by multiple clients might cause a Dispose method to be called multiple times, and in fact a Dispose method shouldn't raise any errors when called more than once, even though all calls after the first one should be ignored. You can avoid releasing resources multiple times by using a class-level variable:

```
Private disposed As Boolean

Public Sub Dispose() Implements IDisposable.Dispose
    If disposed Then Exit Sub
    ' Ensure that further calls are ignored.
    disposed = True
    ' Close files and release other resources here.
    …
End Sub
```

.NET programming guidelines also dictate that calling any method other than Dispose on an object that has already been disposed of should throw the special ObjectDisposedException. If you have implemented the class-level disposed field, implementing this guideline is trivial:

```
Public Sub AnotherMethod()
    ' Throw an exception if a client attempts to use a disposed object.
    If disposed Then Throw New ObjectDisposedException("Widget")
    …
End Sub
```

Combining the Dispose and Finalize Methods

Typically, you can allocate a resource other than memory in one of two ways: by invoking a piece of unmanaged code (for example, a Windows API function) or by creating an instance of a .NET class that wraps the resource. You need to understand this difference because the way you allocate a resource affects the decision about implementing the Dispose or the Finalize method.

You need to implement the IDisposable interface if a method in your type allocates resources other than memory, regardless of whether the resources are allocated directly (through a call to unmanaged code) or indirectly (through an object in the .NET Framework). Conversely, you need to implement the Finalize method only if your object allocates an unmanaged resource directly. Notice, however, that implementing IDisposable or the Finalize method is strictly mandatory only if your code stores a reference to the resource in a class-level field: if a method allocates a resource and releases it before exiting, for example, by means of a Using statement, there's no need to implement either IDisposable or Finalize. In general, therefore, you must account for four different cases:

- **Neither the Dispose nor the Finalize method**   Your object uses only memory or other resources that don't require explicit deallocation, or the object releases any unmanaged resource before exiting the method that has allocated it. This is by far the most frequent case.

- **Dispose method only**   Your object allocates resources other than memory through other .NET objects, and you want to provide clients with a method to release those resources as soon as possible. This is the second most frequent case.

- **Both the Dispose and the Finalize methods**   Your object directly allocates a resource (typically by calling a method in an unmanaged DLL) that requires explicit deallocation or cleanup. You do such explicit deallocation in the Finalize method, but provide the Dispose method as well to provide clients with the ability to release the resource before your object's finalization.

- **Finalize method only**   You don't have any resource to release, but you need to perform a given action when your object is finalized. This is the least likely case, and in practice it is useful only in a few uncommon scenarios.

The first case is simple, and I have already showed how to implement the second case, so we can focus on the third case and see how the Dispose and Finalize methods can cooperate with each other. Here's an example of a ClipboardWrapper object that opens and closes the system Clipboard:

```
Public Class ClipboardWrapper
   Implements IDisposable

   Private Declare Function OpenClipboard Lib "user32" _
      Alias "OpenClipboard" (ByVal hwnd As Integer) As Integer
   Private Declare Function CloseClipboard Lib "user32" _
      Alias "CloseClipboard" () As Integer

   ' Remember whether the Clipboard is currently open.
   Dim isOpen As Boolean

   ' Open the Clipboard and associate it with a window.
   Public Sub Open(ByVal hWnd As Integer)
      ' OpenClipboard returns 0 if any error.
      If OpenClipboard(hWnd) = 0 Then Throw New Exception("Unable to open clipboard")
      isOpen = True
   End Sub

   ' Close the Clipboard—ignore the command if not open.
   Public Sub Close()
```

```
        If isOpen Then CloseClipboard()
        isOpen = False
    End Sub

    Private Sub Dispose() Implements IDisposable.Dispose
        Close()
    End Sub

    Protected Overrides Sub Finalize()
        Close()
    End Sub
End Class
```

What the OpenClipboard and CloseClipboard methods do isn't important in this context because I just selected two of the simplest Windows API procedures that allocate and release a system resource. What really matters in this example is that an application that opens the Clipboard and associates it with a window must also release the Clipboard as soon as possible because the Clipboard is a system-wide resource and no other window can access it in the meantime. (A real-world class would surely expose other useful methods to manipulate the Clipboard, but I want to keep this example as simple as possible.)

It's a good practice to have both the Dispose and the Finalize methods call the cleanup routine that performs the actual release operation (the Close method, in this example) so that you don't duplicate the code. Such a method can be public, as in this case, or it can be a private helper method. You also need a class-level variable (isOpen in the preceding code) to ensure that cleanup code doesn't run twice, once when the client invokes Dispose and once when the garbage collector calls the Finalize method. The same variable also ensures that nothing happens if clients call the Close or Dispose method multiple times.

A Better Dispose-Finalize Pattern

A problem with the technique just illustrated is that the garbage collector calls the Finalize method even if the client has already called the Dispose or Close method. As I explained previously, the Finalize method affects performance negatively because an additional garbage collection is required to destroy the object completely. Fortunately, you can control whether the Finalize method is invoked by using the GC.SuppressFinalize method. Using this method is straightforward. You typically call it from inside the Dispose method so that the garbage collector knows that it shouldn't call the Finalize method during the subsequent garbage collection.

Another problem that you might need to solve in a class that is more sophisticated than is the ClipboardWrapper demo shown earlier is that the cleanup code might access other objects referenced by the current object—for example, a control on a form—but you should never perform such access if the cleanup code runs in the finalization phase because those other objects might have been finalized already. You can resolve this issue by moving the actual cleanup code to an overloaded version of the Dispose method. This method takes a Boolean argument that specifies whether the object is being disposed of or finalized and avoids accessing external objects in the latter case. Here's a new version of the ClipboardWrapper class that uses this pattern to resolve these issues:

```
Public Class ClipboardWrapper2
    Implements IDisposable

    Private Declare Function OpenClipboard Lib "user32" _
        Alias "OpenClipboard" (ByVal hwnd As Integer) As Integer
    Private Declare Function CloseClipboard Lib "user32" _
        Alias "CloseClipboard" () As Integer

    ' Remember whether the Clipboard is currently open.
    Dim isOpen As Boolean
    ' Remember whether the object has already been disposed of.
    ' (Protected makes it available to derived classes.)
    Protected disposed As Boolean

    Public Sub New()
        ' Don't invoke Finalize unless the Open method is actually invoked.
        GC.SuppressFinalize(Me)
    End Sub

    ' Open the Clipboard and associate it with a window.
    Public Sub Open(ByVal hWnd As Integer)
        ' OpenClipboard returns 0 if any error.
        If OpenClipboard(hWnd) = 0 Then Throw New Exception("Unable to open Clipboard")
        isOpen = True
        ' Register the Finalize method, in case clients forget to call Close or Dispose.
        GC.ReRegisterForFinalize(Me)
    End Sub

    Public Sub Close()
        Dispose()                    ' Delegate to private Dispose method.
    End Sub

    Private Sub Dispose() Implements System.IDisposable.Dispose
        Dispose(True)
        ' Remember that the object has been disposed.
        disposed = True
        ' Tell .NET not to call the Finalize method.
        GC.SuppressFinalize(Me)
    End Sub

    Protected Overrides Sub Finalize()
        Dispose(False)
    End Sub

    Protected Overridable Sub Dispose(ByVal disposing As Boolean)
        ' Exit if the object has already been disposed of.
        If disposed Then Exit Sub

        If disposing Then
            ' The object is being disposed of, not finalized. It is safe to access other
            ' objects (other than the base object) only from inside this block.
            …
        End If
```

```
        ' Perform cleanup chores that must be executed in either case.
        CloseClipboard()
        isOpen = False
    End Sub
End Class
```

Notice that the constructor method invokes GC.SuppressFinalize, which tells the CLR not to invoke the Finalize method; this call accounts for the case when a client creates a ClipboardWrapper2 object but never calls its Open method. The Finalize method is registered again by means of a call to the GC.ReRegisterForFinalize method in the Open method.

Finalization issues can become even more problematic if you consider that the Finalize method also runs if the object threw an exception in its constructor method. This means that the code in the Finalize method might access members that haven't been initialized correctly; thus, your finalization code should avoid accessing instance members if there is any chance that an error occurred in the constructor. Even better, the constructor method should use a Try...Catch block to trap errors, release any allocated resource, and then call GC.Suppress-Finalize(Me) to prevent the standard finalization code from running on uninitialized members.

Note   Visual Studio 2005 enables you to implement the IDisposable interface very quickly. In fact, whenever you type the Implements IDisposable statement and press Enter, Microsoft Visual Studio creates a lot of code for you:

```
Public Class Widget
    Implements IDisposable

    Private disposedValue As Boolean = False      ' To detect redundant calls

    Protected Overridable Sub Dispose(ByVal disposing As Boolean)
        If Not Me.disposedValue Then
            If disposing Then
                ' TODO: free unmanaged resources when explicitly called
            End If
            ' TODO: free shared unmanaged resources
        End If
        Me.disposedValue = True
    End Sub

    Public Sub Dispose() Implements IDisposable.Dispose
        ' Do not change this code. Put cleanup code in Dispose(ByVal disposing As Boolean)
        ' method above.
        Dispose(True)
        GC.SuppressFinalize(Me)
    End Sub
End Class
```

Notice that no Finalize method is created automatically. This is the correct approach, because—as I emphasized previously—only types that create unmanaged resources need the Finalize method. Most disposable objects do not.

Finalizers in Derived Classes

I already explained that a well-written class that allocates and uses unmanaged resources (ODBC database connections, file and Windows object handles, and so on) should implement both a Finalize method and the IDisposable.Dispose method. If your application inherits from such a class, you must check whether your inherited class allocates any additional unmanaged resources. If not, you don't have to write any extra code because the derived class will inherit the base class implementation of both the Finalize and the Dispose methods. However, if the inherited class does allocate and use additional unmanaged resources, you should override the implementation of these methods, correctly release the unmanaged resources that the inherited class uses, and then call the corresponding method in the base class.

In the previous section, I illustrated a technique for correctly implementing these methods in a class, based on an overloaded Dispose method that contains the code for both the IDisposable.Dispose and the Finalize methods. As it happens, this overloaded Dispose method has a Protected scope, so in practice you can correctly implement the Dispose-Finalize pattern in derived classes by simply overriding one method:

```
Public Class ClipboardWrapperEx
    Inherits ClipboardWrapper2

    ' Insert regular methods here, some of which might allocate additional
    ' unmanaged resources.
    …
    ' The only method we need to override to implement the Dispose-Finalize
    ' pattern for this class.
    Protected Overloads Overrides Sub Dispose(ByVal disposing As Boolean)
        ' Exit now if the object has already been disposed of.
        ' (The disposed variable is declared as Protected in the base class.)
        If disposed Then Exit Sub

        Try
            If disposing Then
                ' The object is being disposed of, not finalized. It is safe to access other
                ' objects (other than the base object) only from inside this block.
                …
            End If

            ' Perform cleanup chores that must be executed in either case.
            …
        Finally
            ' Call the base class's Dispose method in all cases.
            MyBase.Dispose(disposing)
        End Try
    End Sub
End Class
```

If there is any chance that the code in the Dispose method might throw an exception, you should wrap it in a Try block and invoke the base class's Dispose method from the Finally block, as the previous code does. Failing to do so might result in the base class being prevented from releasing its own resources, which is something you should absolutely avoid for obvious reasons.

A Simplified Approach to Finalization

Authoring a class that correctly implements the Dispose and Finalize methods isn't exactly a trivial task, as you've seen in previous sections. However, in most cases, you can take a shortcut and dramatically simplify the structure of your code by sticking to the following two guidelines. First, you wrap each unmanaged resource that requires finalization with a class whose only member is a field holding the handle of the unmanaged resource. Second, you nest this wrapper class inside another class that implements the Dispose method (but not the Finalize method). The nested class is marked as Private; therefore, it can be accessed only by the class that encloses it.

To see in practice what these guidelines mean, consider the following sample code:

```
Public Class WinResource
   Implements IDisposable

   ' A private field that points to the wrapper of the unmanaged resource
   Private wrapper As UnmanagedResourceWrapper = Nothing
   ' True if the object has been disposed of
   Private disposed As Boolean = False

   Public Sub New(ByVal someData As String)
      ' Allocate the unmanaged resource here.
      wrapper = New UnmanagedResourceWrapper(someData)
   End Sub

   ' A public method that clients call to work with the unmanaged resource
   Public Sub DoSomething()
      ' Throw an exception if the object has already been disposed of.
      If disposed Then
         Throw New ObjectDisposedException("")
      End If

      ' This code can pass the wrapper.Handle value to API calls.
   End Sub

   Public Sub Dispose() Implements IDisposable.Dispose
      ' Avoid issues when multiple threads call Dispose at the same time.
      SyncLock Me
         ' Do nothing if already disposed of.
         If disposed Then Return
         ' Dispose of all the disposable objects used by this instance,
         ' including the one that wraps the unmanaged resource.
         ' ...
         wrapper.Dispose()
         ' Remember this object has been disposed of.
         disposed = True
```

```
      End SyncLock
   End Sub


   ' The nested private class that allocates and releases the unmanaged resource
   Private NotInheritable Class UnmanagedResourceWrapper
      Implements IDisposable
      ' An invalid handle value that the wrapper class can use to check
      ' whether the handle is valid
      Public Shared ReadOnly InvalidHandle As New IntPtr(-1)

      ' A public field, but accessible only from inside the WinResource class
      Public Handle As IntPtr = InvalidHandle

      ' The constructor allocates the unmanaged resource (e.g., a file).
      Public Sub New(ByVal someData As String)
         ' This is just a demo.…
         Me.Handle = New IntPtr(12345)
      End Sub

      Public Sub Dispose() Implements IDisposable.Dispose
         ' Exit now if this object didn't complete its constructor correctly.
         If Me.Handle = InvalidHandle Then Return

         ' Release the unmanaged resource, e.g., CloseHandle(Handle).
         …
         ' Invalidate the handle and tell the CLR not to call the Finalize method.
         Me.Handle = InvalidHandle
         GC.SuppressFinalize(Me)
      End Sub

      Protected Overrides Sub Finalize()
         Dispose()
      End Sub
   End Class
End Class
```

It's essential that the UnmanagedResourceWrapper class doesn't contain any fields, except the handle of the unmanaged resource, or any methods, except those listed. If the unmanaged resource should interact with other resources, the code that implements this interaction should be located in the WinResource class. The WinResource class must coordinate all the resources (managed and unmanaged) that it has allocated and must release them in its Dispose method.

Let's now discuss the advantages of these guidelines. First, and foremost, if the client code omits invoking the WinResource.Dispose method, all the memory used by the WinResource object will be cleared anyway at the first garbage collection. The inner UnmanagedResource-Wrapper object has a Finalize method and therefore will be released only during a subsequent garbage collection, but this object consumes very little memory, and therefore this isn't a serious issue.

Second, the inner UnmanagedResourceWrapper is private and sealed; therefore, you don't need to write any complex code that takes derived classes into account. (However, you can inherit from WinResource, if you need to.) Being private, code outside the WinResource class can't get a reference to the UnmanagedResourceWrapper object and can't resurrect it.

Third, the UnmanagedResourceWrapper has only one field, and this field is a value type; therefore, the code in the Dispose or Finalize method can't mistakenly access any reference type. (As you might recall, a reference type might already be disposed of when it's accessed during the finalization stage.) Because there is just one handle to account for, you don't have to write code that deals with errors in the UnmanagedResourceWrapper constructor. If the constructor fails, the value of the Handle field continues to be equal to the InvalidHandle constant; the Dispose method can detect this condition and skip the cleanup code.

Finally, the UnmanagedResourceWrapper class is so simple and generic that you can often copy and paste its code (with minor edits) inside other types that must manage unmanaged resources. When it is nested inside another class, you don't even need to worry about name collisions.

> **Note**   Version 2.0 of the .NET Framework introduces the SafeHandle abstract class, which makes it simpler to author classes that use unmanaged resources. Basically, a SafeHandle object is a wrapper for a Windows handle and is vaguely similar to the UnmanagedResource-Wrapper in the previous example but with many additional features, such as the protection from a kind of attack known as *handle recycle attacks*. You can find more information in MSDN documentation and a few articles from the Base Class Library (BCL) Team, such as *https://blogs.msdn.com/bclteam/archive/2005/03/15/396335.aspx* and *http://blogs.msdn.com/cbrumme/archive/2004/02/20/77460.aspx*.

Advanced Techniques

As I promised at the beginning of this chapter, you can boost your application's performance if you understand the garbage collection process more thoroughly. In the remaining sections, you'll learn about generations, weak references, resurrections, and how these techniques can help you write better .NET software.

Generations

If the garbage collector had to visit all the objects referenced by an application, the garbage collection process might impose a severe overhead. Fortunately, some recurring patterns in object creation make it possible for the garbage collector to use heuristics that can significantly reduce the total execution time.

It has been observed that, from a statistical point of view, objects created early in the program's lifetime tend to stay alive longer than objects created later in a program do. Here's how you can intuitively justify this theory: objects created early are usually assigned to global variables and will be set to Nothing only when the application ends, whereas objects created inside a class constructor method are usually released when the object is set to Nothing. Finally, objects created inside a procedure are often destroyed when the procedure exits (unless they have been assigned to a variable defined outside the procedure, for example, an array or a collection).

The garbage collector has a simple way of determining how "old" an object is. Each object maintains a counter telling how many garbage collections that object has survived. The value of this counter is the object's *generation*. The higher this number is, the smaller the chances are that the object is collected during the next garbage collection.

The current version of the CLR supports only three distinct generation values. The generation value of an object that has never undergone a garbage collection is 0; if the object survives a garbage collection, its generation becomes 1; if it survives a second garbage collection, its generation becomes 2. Any subsequent garbage collection leaves the generation counter at 2 (or destroys the object). For example, an object that has a Finalize method always survives to the first garbage collection and is promoted to generation 1 because, as I explained earlier, the CLR can't sweep it out of the heap when the garbage collection occurs.

The CLR uses the generation counter to optimize the garbage collection process—for example, by moving the generation-2 objects toward the beginning of the heap, where they are likely to stay until the program terminates; they are followed by generation-1 objects and finally by generation-0 objects. This algorithm has proven to speed up the garbage collection process because it reduces the fragmentation of the managed heap.

You can learn the current generation of any object by passing it to the GC.GetGeneration method. The following code should give you a taste of how this method works:

```
Dim s As String = "dummy string"
' This is a generation-0 object.
Console.WriteLine(GC.GetGeneration(s))          ' => 0
' Make it survive a first garbage collection.
GC.Collect(): GC.WaitForPendingFinalizers()
Console.WriteLine(GC.GetGeneration(s))          ' => 1
' Make it survive a second garbage collection.
GC.Collect(): GC.WaitForPendingFinalizers()
Console.WriteLine(GC.GetGeneration(s))          ' => 2
' Subsequent garbage collections don't increment the generation counter.
GC.Collect(): GC.WaitForPendingFinalizers()
Console.WriteLine(GC.GetGeneration(s))          ' => 2
```

The GC.Collect method is overloaded to take a generation value as an argument, which results in the garbage collection of all the objects whose generation is lower than or equal to that value:

```
' Reclaim memory for unused generation-0 objects.
GC.Collect(0)
```

In general, the preceding statement is faster than running a complete garbage collection. To understand why, let's examine the three steps the garbage collection process consists of:

1. The garbage collector marks root objects and in general, all the objects directly or indirectly reachable from the application.

2. The heap is compacted, and all the marked (reachable) objects are moved toward the beginning of the managed heap to create a block of free memory near the end of the heap. Objects are sorted in the heap depending on their generation, with generation-2 objects near the beginning of the heap and generation-0 objects near the end of the heap, just before the free memory block. (To avoid time-consuming memory move operations, objects larger than approximately 85 KB are allocated in a separate heap that's never compacted.)

3. Root object variables in the main application are updated to point to the new positions of objects in the managed heap.

You speed up the second step (fewer objects must be moved in the heap) as well as the third step (because only a subset of all variables are updated) when you collect only generation-0 objects. Under certain conditions, even the first step is completed in less time, but this optimization technique might seem counterintuitive and requires an additional explanation.

Let's say that the garbage collector reaches a generation-1 object while traversing the object graph. Let's call this object A. In general, the collector can't simply ignore the portion of the object graph that has object A as its root because this object might point to one or more generation-0 objects that need to be marked. (For example, this might happen if object A is an array that contains objects created later in the program's lifetime.) However, the CLR can detect whether fields of object A have been modified since the previous garbage collection. If it turns out that object A hasn't been written to in the meantime, it means that object A can point only to generation-1 and generation-2 objects, so there is no reason for the collector to analyze that portion of the object graph because it was analyzed during the previous garbage collection and can't point to any generation-0 objects. (Of course, a similar reasoning applies when you use the GC.Collect(1) statement to collect only generation-0 and generation-1 objects.)

The CLR often attempts to collect only generation-0 objects to improve overall performance; if the garbage collection is successful in freeing enough memory, no further steps are taken. Otherwise, the CLR attempts to collect generation-0 and generation-1 objects; if this second attempt fails to free enough memory, it collects all three generations. This means that older-generation objects might live undisturbed in the heap a long time after the application logically killed them. The exact details of the type of garbage collection the CLR performs each time are vastly undocumented and might change over time.

You can determine how many garbage collections of a given generation have occurred by querying the new CollectionCount method of the GC type:

```
' Determine how many 2-gen collections have occurred so far.
Dim count As Integer = GC.CollectionCount(2)
```

Garbage Collection and Performance

Before moving to a different topic, I want to show you how efficient .NET is at managing memory. Let's again run a code snippet similar to the one I showed in the section titled "The Finalize Method" earlier in this chapter, but comment out the statement that explicitly sets the Person object to Nothing:

```
' Compile this code with optimizations enabled.
Sub Main()
   Console.WriteLine("About to create a Person object.")
   Dim aPerson As New Person("John", "Evans")
   ' aPerson = Nothing
   ' After this point, aPerson is a candidate for garbage collection.
   Console.WriteLine("About to fire a garbage collection.")
   GC.Collect()
   GC.WaitForPendingFinalizers()
   Console.WriteLine("About to terminate the application")
End Sub
```

You might expect that the Person object is kept alive until the method exits. However, if optimizations are enabled and you run the application in Release mode, the JIT compiler is smart enough to detect that the object isn't used after the call to its constructor, so it marks it as a candidate for garbage collection. As a result, the code behaves exactly as if you explicitly set the variable to Nothing after the last statement that references it. In other words, setting a variable to Nothing as soon as you are done with an object doesn't necessarily make your code more efficient because the JIT compiler can apply this optimization technique automatically.

In one special case, however, explicitly setting a variable to Nothing can affect performance positively. This happens when you destroy an object in the middle of a loop. In this case, the Visual Basic compiler can't automatically detect whether the variable is going to be used during subsequent iterations of the loop, and therefore the garbage collector can't automatically reclaim the memory used by the object. By clearing the object variable explicitly, you can help the garbage collector understand that the object can be reclaimed.

```
' Use the aPerson object inside the loop.
For i As Integer = 1 To 100
   If i <= 50 Then
      ' Use the object only in the first 50 iterations.
      Console.WriteLine(aPerson.FirstName)
      ' Explicitly set the variable to Nothing after its last use.
      If i = 50 Then aPerson = Nothing
   Else
      ' Do something else here, but don't use the aPerson variable.
      …
   End If
Next
```

The fact that an object can be destroyed any time after the last time you reference it in code, and well before its reference goes out of scope, can have a surprisingly dangerous effect if the object wraps an unmanaged resource that is freed in the object's Finalize method. Say that you have authored a type named WinFile, which opens a file using the OpenFile API method and closes the file in the Finalize method:

```
Sub TestWinFile()
    Dim wfile As New WinFile("c:\data.txt")
    Dim handle As Integer = wfile.Handle
    ' Process the file by passing the handle to native Windows methods.
    ...
    ' (The file is automatically closed in WinFile's Finalize.)
End Sub
```

The problem here is that the garbage collector might collect the WinFile object and indirectly fire its Finalize method, which in turn would close the file before the procedure has completed its tasks. You might believe that adding a reference to the WinFile object at the end of the procedure would do the trick, but you'd be wrong. Consider this code:

```
Sub TestWinFile()
    ...
    ' A failed attempt to keep the object alive until the end of the method
    DoNothingProc(wfile)
End Sub

Sub DoNothingProc(ByVal obj As Object)
    ' No code here
End Sub
```

Surprisingly, the Visual Basic compiler is smart enough to realize that the DoNothingProc doesn't really use the object reference, and therefore passing the object to this procedure won't keep the WinFile object alive. The only method that is guaranteed to work in this case is the GC.KeepAlive method, whose name says it all:

```
Sub TestWinFile()
    ...
    ' Keep the object alive until the end of the method.
    GC.KeepAlive(wfile)
End Sub
```

In practice, however, you should never need the GC.KeepAlive method. In fact, if you authored the WinFile type correctly, it should expose the IDisposable interface, and therefore the actual code should look like this:

```
Sub TestWinFile()
    Using wfile As New WinFile("c:\data.txt")
        Dim handle As Integer = wfile.Handle
        ' Process the file by passing the handle to native Windows methods.
        ...
    End Using
End Sub
```

The GC object in .NET Framework version 2.0 has two new methods that enable you to let the garbage collector know that an unmanaged object consuming a lot of memory has been allocated or released so that the collector can fine-tune its performance and optimize its scheduling. You should invoke the AddMemoryPressure method to inform the garbage collector that the specified number of bytes has been allocated in the unmanaged memory; after releasing the object, you should invoke the RemoveMemoryPressure method to notify the CLR that an unmanaged object has been released and that the specified amount of memory is available again.

```
' Allocate an unmanaged object that takes approximately 1 MB of memory.
Dim obj As New UnmanagedResource()
GC.AddMemoryPressure(1048576)          ' = 2^20
...
' Release the object here.
obj = Nothing
GC.RemoveMemoryPressure(1048576)
```

Even though .NET garbage collection is quite efficient, it can be a major source of overhead. In fact, not counting file and database operations, garbage collection is among the slowest activities that can take place during your application's lifetime; thus, it's your responsibility to keep the number of collections to a minimum. If you suspect that an application is running slowly because of too frequent garbage collections, use the Performance utility to monitor the following performance counters of the .NET CLR Memory object, as shown in Figure 9-1:

- \# Gen 0 Collections, \# Gen 1 Collections, \# Gen 2 Collections (the number of garbage collections fired by the CLR)

- % Time In GC (the percentage of CPU time spent performing garbage collections)

- Gen 0 Heap Size, Gen 1 Heap Size, Gen 2 Heap Size, Large Object Heap Size (the size of the four heaps used by the garbage collector)

- \# Bytes In All Heaps (the sum of the four heaps used by the application, that is, Generation-0, Generation-1, Generation-2, and Large Object heaps)

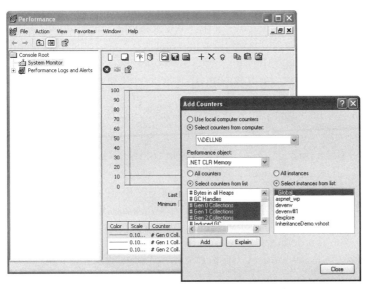

Figure 9-1 Using the Performance utility to monitor .NET memory performance counters

If the value of the first two sets of counters is suspiciously high, you can conclude that garbage collections are killing your application's performance and should browse your source code looking for the causes of the higher-than-usual activity of the managed heap. I have compiled a list of issues you should pay attention to and which counters can help you solve your performance problem:

   a.   Consider whether you can reduce the usage of the managed heap by defining structures instead of sealed classes. Structures defined as local variables are allocated on the stack and don't take space in the managed heap. On the other hand, the assignment of a structure to an Object variable causes the structure to be boxed, which takes memory from the heap and adds overhead, so you should take this detail into account when opting for a structure. Also, don't use a structure if your type implements one or more interfaces because invoking a method through an interface variable forces the boxing of the structure.

   b.   Use Char variables instead of String variables if possible because Char is a value type and Char objects don't take space in the managed heap. More important, attempt to reduce the number of temporary strings used in expressions. When many concatenation operations are involved, use a StringBuilder object. (I cover the StringBuilder type in Chapter 12, ".NET Basic Types.")

   c.   Allocate disposable objects inside Using blocks; if a Using block can't be used, allocate the disposable object inside a Try...Catch block and invoke the Dispose method from inside the Finally clause.

   d.   Allocate long-lasting objects earlier and assign them to global variables. This technique ensures that these objects will be moved near the beginning of the managed heap when the application starts and won't move from there during the application's lifetime. You can detect whether you have many objects that are candidates for this treatment by monitoring the Protected Memory From Gen 0 and Protected Memory From Gen 1 performance counters.

   e.   Avoid creating objects larger than about 85 KB if possible. These objects are stored in a separate area known as a large objects heap; moving these large objects in memory would add too much overhead, and therefore .NET never compacts this heap. As a result, the large object heap might become fragmented. An example of such a large object is an array of Double numbers (8 bytes each) with more than about 10,880 elements. You can detect whether you have many large objects by looking at the Large Object Heap Size performance counter.

   f.   As a rule, never fire a garbage collection by means of the GC.Collect method. In client applications, such as a Console or a Windows Forms application, you might start a collection only after an intensive user-interface action, for example, after loading or saving a file, so that the user won't perceive the extra overhead. Never use the GC.Collect method from inside a server-side application, such as an ASP.NET application or a COM+ library. You can detect whether you have too many GC.Collect methods in your code by monitoring the # Induced GC performance counter.

g. Never implement the Finalize method without a good reason to do so. If you do need a Finalize method, adopt the recommended pattern described earlier in this chapter. You can detect whether your finalizable objects can be the cause of a performance problem by looking at the Finalization Survivors performance counter.

h. If you must implement the Finalize method, ensure that the object doesn't take a significant amount of managed memory in addition to unmanaged resources. You can achieve this by wrapping the unmanaged resource in a nested class, as described in the section titled "A Simplified Approach to Finalization" earlier in this chapter.

Weak Object References

The .NET Framework provides a special type of object reference that doesn't keep an object alive: the *weak reference*. A weakly referenced object can be reclaimed during a garbage collection and must be re-created afterward if you want to use it again. Typical candidates for this technique are objects that take a lot of memory but whose state can be re-created with relatively little effort. For example, consider a class whose main purpose is to provide an optimized cache for the contents of text files. Traditionally, whenever you cache a large amount of data you must decide how much memory you set aside for the cache, but reserving too much memory for the cache might make the overall performance worse.

You don't have this dilemma if you use weak references. You can store as much data in the cache as you wish because you know that the system will automatically reclaim that memory when it needs it. Here's the complete source code for the CachedFile class:

```
Public Class CachedFile
   ' The name of the file cached
   Public ReadOnly Filename As String
   ' A weak reference to the string that contains the text
   Dim wrText As WeakReference

   ' The constructor takes the name of the file to read.
   Public Sub New(ByVal filename As String)
      Me.Filename = filename
   End Sub

   ' Read the contents of the file.
   Private Function ReadFile() As String
      Dim text As String = File.ReadAllText(Filename)
      ' Create a weak reference to this string.
      wrText = New WeakReference(text)
      Return text
   End Function

   ' Return the textual content of the file.
   Public Function GetText() As String
      Dim text As Object = Nothing
      ' Retrieve the target of the weak reference.
      If wrText IsNot Nothing Then text = wrText.Target
      If text IsNot Nothing Then
```

```
              ' If nonnull, the data is still in the cache.
              Return text.ToString()
           Else
              ' Otherwise, read it and put it in the cache again.
              Return ReadFile()
           End If
      End Function
End Class
```

There are two points of interest in this class. First, the ReadFile passes the value to be returned to the caller (the text variable) to the constructor of the WeakReference class and therefore creates a weak reference to the string. The second point of interest is in the GetText method, where the code queries the WeakReference.Target property. If this property returns a non-Nothing value, it means the weak reference hasn't been broken and still points to the original, cached string. Otherwise, the ReadFile method is invoked so that the file contents are read from disk and cached once again before being returned to the caller. Using the CachedFile type is easy:

```
' Read and cache the contents of the "c:\alargefile.txt" file.
Dim cf As New CachedFile("c:\alargefile.txt")
Console.WriteLine(cf.GetText())
…
' Uncomment next line to force a garbage collection.
' GC.Collect(): GC.WaitForPendingFinalizers()
…
' Read the contents again sometime later.
' (No disk access is performed, unless a garbage collection has occurred in the meantime.)
Console.WriteLine(cf.GetText())
```

By tracing into the CachedFile class, you can easily prove that in most cases the file contents can be retrieved through the weak reference and that the disk isn't accessed again. By uncommenting the statement in the middle of the previous code snippet, however, you force a garbage collection, in which case the internal WeakReference object won't keep the String object alive and the code in the class will read the file again. The key point in this technique is that the client code doesn't know whether the cached data is used or a disk access is required. It just uses the CachedFile object as an optimized building block for dealing with large text files.

Remember that you create a weak reference by passing your object to the constructor of a System.WeakReference object. However, if the object is also pointed to by a regular, nonweak reference, it will survive any intervening garbage collection. In our example, this means that the code using the CachedFile class should not store the return value of the GetText method in a string variable because that would prevent the string from being garbage collected until that variable is explicitly set to Nothing or goes out of scope:

```
' The wrong way of using the CachedFile class
Dim cf As New CachedFile("c:\alargefile.txt")
Dim text As String = cf.GetText()
' The text string will survive any garbage collection.
```

Object Resurrection

Weak references are fine to create a cache of objects that are frequently used and that can be re-created in a relatively short time. The technique I illustrate in this section offers a slightly different solution to the same problem.

Earlier in this chapter, I briefly described the technique known as *object resurrection* through which an object being finalized can store a reference to itself in a variable defined outside the current instance so that this new reference keeps the object alive. Object resurrection is likely to be useful only in unusual scenarios, such as when you're implementing a pool of objects whose creation and destruction are time-consuming. For example, let's consider the following sample class, which implements an array containing a sequence of random Double values:

```
Public Class RandomArray
   ' This array stores the elements.
   Public ReadOnly Values() As Double

   ' The constructor creates the random array.
   Sub New(ByVal length As Integer)
      ReDim Values(length - 1)
      Dim rand As New Random()
      ' This is a time-consuming operation.
      For i As Integer = 0 To length - 1
         Values(i) = rand.NextDouble()
      Next
   End Sub
End Class
```

(Notice that you'll typically apply resurrection to objects that are far more complicated than this one and that use unmanaged resources as well. I am using RandomArray only for illustration purposes.)

If the main application creates and destroys thousands of RandomArray objects, it makes sense to implement a mechanism by which a RandomArray object is returned to an internal pool when the application doesn't need it any longer; if the application later requests another RandomArray object with the same number of elements, the object is taken from the pool instead of going through the relatively slow initialization process.

The internal pool is implemented as a static ArrayList object. To ensure that the application uses a pooled object, if available, the RandomArray class has a private constructor and a static public factory method named Create. Also, the class implements the Finalize method to ensure that the instance is correctly returned to the pool when the application has finished with it. Here's the new version of the class:

```
Public Class RandomArray
   ' This array stores the elements.
   Public ReadOnly Values() As Double

   ' The constructor creates the random array.
```

```
      Private Sub New(ByVal length As Integer)
         ReDim Values(length - 1)
         Dim rand As New Random()
         ' This is a time-consuming operation.
         For i As Integer = 0 To length - 1
            Values(i) = rand.NextDouble()
         Next
      End Sub

      Protected Overrides Sub Finalize()
         ' Resurrect the object by putting it into the pool.
         Pool.Add(Me)
      End Sub

      ' The pool of objects
      Private Shared Pool As New ArrayList()

      ' The factory method
      Public Shared Function Create(ByVal length As Integer) As RandomArray
         ' Check whether there is an element in the pool with the
         ' requested number of elements.
         For i As Integer = 0 To Pool.Count - 1
            Dim ra As RandomArray = DirectCast(Pool(i), RandomArray)
            If ra.Values.Length = length Then
               ' Remove the element from the pool.
               Pool.RemoveAt(i)
               ' Reregister for finalization, in case no Dispose method is invoked.
               GC.ReRegisterForFinalize(ra)
               Return ra
            End If
         Next
         ' If no suitable element in the pool, create a new element.
         Return New RandomArray(length)
      End Function
   End Class
```

The key point in the previous code is the GC.ReRegisterForFinalize method call in the Create method. Without this call, the object handed to the application wouldn't execute the Finalize method and therefore it would miss the chance of being returned to the pool when the application logically destroys the object. (The companion code includes a better version of the RandomArray type that implements IDisposable to let the client application explicitly return an instance to the pool.)

Here's a piece of code that uses the RandomArray object:

```
' Create and use a few RandomArray objects.
Dim ra1 As RandomArray = RandomArray.Create(10000)
Dim ra2 As RandomArray = RandomArray.Create(20000)
Dim ra3 As RandomArray = RandomArray.Create(30000)
...
' Clear some of them.
```

```
ra2 = Nothing
ra3 = Nothing
' Simulate a garbage collection, which moves the two cleared objects to the pool.
GC.Collect(): GC.WaitForPendingFinalizers()

' Create a few more objects, which will be taken from the pool.
Dim ra4 As RandomArray = RandomArray.Create(20000)
Dim ra5 As RandomArray = RandomArray.Create(30000)
```

A pooled object might improve performance in other ways, for example, by creating a few instances in advance so that no initialization time is spent when the application asks for them. Object pooling can be useful in cases when performance isn't the main issue—for example, when you have a threshold for the number of objects that can be created.

Garbage Collection on Multi-CPU Computers

When the .NET runtime is executing on a workstation, it's important that the user interface work as smoothly as possible, even at the cost of some loss of overall performance. On the other hand, performance becomes the top priority when an enterprise-level .NET application runs on a server machine. To account for these differences, the .NET Framework comes with two types of garbage collectors: the workstation version and the multi-CPU server version.

When running on a single-CPU machine, the collector always works in workstation mode. In this mode, the collector runs on a concurrent thread to minimize pauses, but the additional thread-switching activity can slow the application as a whole. When the workstation version is used on a multi-CPU system, you have the option of running the garbage collector in concurrent mode: in this case, the GC thread runs on a separate CPU to minimize pauses. You activate concurrent mode by adding an entry to the configuration file:

```
<configuration>
   <runtime>
      <gcConcurrent enabled="true" />
   </runtime>
</configuration>
```

When the server version is used, objects are allocated from multiple heaps; the program freezes during a garbage collection, and each CPU works concurrently to compact one of the heaps. This technique improves overall performance and scales well when you install additional CPUs. The server version can be used only on multi-CPU systems or on systems equipped with a hyperthreaded CPU.

In previous versions of the .NET Framework, the server and the workstation versions of the garbage collector resided in different DLLs (mscorsvr.dll and mscorwks.dll) and you explicitly had to select a different DLL to enable the server version. In .NET Framework 2.0, the two versions have been merged in the mscorwks.dll, and you enable the server version by adding an entry to the configuration file:

```
<configuration>
   <runtime>
      <gcServer enabled="true" />
   </runtime>
</configuration>
```

Also new in .NET Framework 2.0 is the System.Runtime.GCSettings type, which exposes a static property that enables you to detect whether the server version of the garbage collector is used:

```
If System.Runtime.GCSettings.IsServerGC Then
   Console.WriteLine("The server version of the garbage collector is used.")
End If
```

Chapter 10
Interfaces

Understanding interfaces is important for two reasons. First, the Microsoft .NET Framework defines many important interfaces and you should learn how to fully exploit their potential, either by invoking their methods or by implementing them in your own types. Second, you can often streamline the structure of your applications by defining your own interfaces. As a matter of fact, interfaces are one of the pillars on which the design of a .NET application can be based, together with other concepts such as inheritance and custom attributes. Nevertheless, many developers fail to grasp the importance of interfaces and don't leverage their full potential.

In this chapter, I start showing how you can define a custom interface and implement it, and then I offer an overview of the most important interfaces defined in the .NET Framework and provide several code examples that illustrate how to use them in your applications.

Note To avoid long lines, code samples in this chapter assume that the following Imports statements are used at the file or project level:

```
Imports System.Data
Imports System.IO
Imports System.Runtime.Serialization
Imports System.Windows.Forms
```

Defining and Implementing Interfaces

Broadly speaking, an interface is a set of members that a class exposes. For example, all the public members of a class are said to belong to its main *class interface*, but a class can also expose other groups of properties and methods that don't have public visibility. In this section, I show how you can define these groups of members, how to implement them in multiple classes, and, above all, what the benefits in doing so are.

The Interface . . . End Interface Statement

An interface defines only the *signature* of properties and methods (member name, number and type of each parameter, and type of return value), while a class can implement that interface by providing actual code for those properties and methods as necessary. The code in each property or method can differ from class to class, provided the semantics of each method is preserved. The fact that each class can implement the same property or method in a different way is the basis for polymorphic behavior.

You define an interface in Microsoft Visual Basic by means of the Interface...End Interface block:

```
Interface IAddin
    Readonly Property Id() As Long
    Property State() As Boolean
    Function OnConnection(ByVal environment As String) As Boolean
    Sub OnDisconnection()
End Interface
```

Visual Basic interface blocks can't contain executable code, and you can include only method and property signatures. The ReadOnly and WriteOnly keywords enable you to specify whether a property can be read from and written to, but you can't specify a different scope visibility for the Get and Set procedures. An interface can't include variables, and properties and methods can't take scope qualifiers because all of them are implicitly Public. An interface can also include public events, even though in general this happens rarely and isn't recommended.

Interfaces have a scope, whether or not you declare it explicitly. As for classes, modules, and structures, the default scope for interfaces is Friend, and a Public class can't expose a Public member that returns a nonpublic interface type:

```
Public Class MyComponent
    ' *** Next statement raises a compilation error because a Public
    '       class can't expose a Friend type as a Public member.
    Public addin As IAddin
End Class
```

The preceding code snippet works only if the IAddin interface is explicitly declared as Public:

```
Public Interface IAddin
    ' …(All members as in the original definition)...
End Interface
```

Interfaces with a scope other than Public or Friend can be nested inside another type, as is also the case with classes and structures. Surprisingly, you can also define a type—a class, a structure, an enum, or another interface—inside an Interface...End Interface block. However, the nested type doesn't really belong to the interface and placing it inside the interface means only that you need an additional dot to reach the nested type. For example, consider this interface:

```
Interface IGetRange
    Function GetRange() As Range

    Class Range
        Public StartValue, EndValue As Double
    End Class
End Interface
```

In this case, having the Range class defined inside the interface might make sense to ensure that there is no name conflict with any other class with the same name. Here's a routine that receives an interface argument and retrieves a Range object:

```
Sub UseTheRangeClass(ByVal igr As IGetRange)
   Dim range As IGetRange.Range = igr.GetRange()
   …
End Sub
```

Microsoft guidelines dictate that all interface names start with the *I* character, that they not include the underscore character, and that they use Pascal casing when the name contains multiple words.

Implementing the Interface

You tell Visual Basic that a class exposes an interface by means of the Implements keyword:

```
Class MyAddin
   Implements IAddin
   …
End Class
```

When you press the Enter key at the end of the Implements statement, Microsoft Visual Studio creates the template of the interface implementation for you, a feature that is a tremendous time-saver:

```
Class MyAddin
   Implements IAddin

   Public ReadOnly Property Id() As Long Implements IAddin.Id
      Get

      End Get
   End Property

   Public Function OnConnection(ByVal environment As String) As Boolean _
      Implements IAddin.OnConnection

   End Function

   Public Sub OnDisconnection() Implements IAddin.OnDisconnection

   End Sub

   Public Property State() As Boolean Implements IAddin.State
      Get

      End Get
      Set(ByVal value As Boolean)

      End Set
   End Property
End Class
```

The syntax for implementing individual properties and methods reuses the Implements keyword to tell the compiler which procedure in your class implements a given member in the interface. The code Visual Studio generates uses Public scope for all the procedures so that those procedures can be invoked directly from clients of the MyAddin class, but working this way isn't a requirement. As a matter of fact, you can use the Private or another scope keyword, specify an explicit scope qualifier, or even use other keywords, such as Overridable:

```
Class MyAddin
    Implements IAddin

    Protected Overridable Function OnConnection(ByVal Environment As String) As Boolean _
        Implements IAddin.OnConnection

    End Function
    …
End Class
```

Speaking of scope, notice that Visual Basic enforces no constraint related to the scope of the interface that a class can implement. For example, you can have a Public class that implements a Private interface, a Private class that implements a Public interface, or any other combination of the supported scope qualifiers. However, only clients that have access to the interface's definition can access that interface's members through an interface variable. For example, if a class exposes an interface declared with Friend scope, only clients inside the same assembly can access that interface through an interface variable. Unless the individual procedures that implement the interface's members are declared with Public scope, there is no way for a client outside the current assembly to invoke those procedures.

The Implements keyword, used to mark a method as an interface method, supports multiple arguments, so you can have methods from multiple interfaces that map to the same procedure. The following example shows that methods in the interfaces and methods in the class that implements the interface can have different names:

```
' Another interface with just one property
Interface IHostEnvironment
    ReadOnly Property HashCode() As Long
End Interface

' This new version of the class implements two interfaces.
Class MyAddin
    ' You can have two distinct Implements statements if you prefer.
    Implements IAddin, IHostEnvironment

    ' This procedure implements two read-only properties from distinct interfaces.
    Public ReadOnly Property Id() As Long Implements IAddin.ID, IHostEnvironment.HashCode
        Get
            …
        End Get
    End Property

    ' …(Other implemented methods have been omitted.)...
End Class
```

A variant of this technique enables you to map multiple methods from one interface to the same procedure in the class. Mapping multiple methods to the same procedure works only if all the methods have the same argument signature and a return value of the same type.

Accessing the Interface

You can access the interface members of a type in two ways: either directly (by means of a variable typed after the class) or by means of an interface variable. In the former case, you access the method as if it were a regular member, and the scope of the method must be compatible with the location of the client; for example, a Friend method can be accessed only by a client in the same assembly.

In the latter case, you access the interface that a class implements by assigning the object to a variable typed after the interface:

```
' An instance of the class
Dim addin As New MyAddin()
' Cast to an interface variable.
Dim iadd As IAddin = addin
' Now you can access all the methods and properties in the interface.
iadd.State = True
```

If you're calling just one or two methods in the interface, you might find it convenient to do the cast operation on the fly with a CType or a DirectCast operator:

```
' Cast to the interface type and invoke a method in one operation.
' (These two statements are equivalent.)
CType(addin, IAddin).OnConnection("MyHost")
DirectCast(addin, IAddin).OnConnection("MyHost")
```

You can also use a With . . . End With block:

```
' Create a hidden, temporary interface variable.
With DirectCast(addin, IAddin)
   .OnConnection("MyHost")
   .State = True
End With
```

You can access any member regardless of its scope if you are accessing it by means of an interface variable. For example, you can invoke a Private method if it is part of the interface implementation. On the other hand, if a member of an interface is implemented through a Public procedure, you don't need to cast the object to a different type, and you can access the interface's member through a standard variable pointing to the object. For example, classes that implement the IDisposable interface usually expose a Public Sub Dispose method, which can therefore be accessed through a standard object variable.

Even a structure can implement an interface. However, keep two points in mind when you access an interface implemented in a structure. First, you can't use the DirectCast operator because it requires that its first argument be a reference type. Second, and more important, the structure is automatically and silently boxed before one of its interface members can be accessed, so you pay a hidden performance penalty every time you access an interface method through an interface variable. (You pay the same performance penalty when you access a method that the structure inherits from System.Object, such as ToString and GetHashCode.)

Interfaces and Inheritance

An interface can inherit from another interface. An inherited interface contains all the members that it defines, plus all members in the base interface. This feature is especially useful when you're creating a new, extended version of an interface:

```
Public Interface IAddin2
    Inherits IAddin
    Property Description() As String
End Interface
```

The .NET Framework offers many examples of inherited interfaces. For example, the ICollection interface inherits from IEnumerable and is the base type for both the IList and the IDictionary interfaces.

A derived interface can't redefine any member in the base interface, so you can't use the Overridable or Overrides keyword inside an interface definition. If the derived interface contains a member with the same name as a member in the base interface, the member in the derived interface shadows the member in the base interface. In this case, you get a compilation warning that you can suppress by using the Shadows keyword in the derived interface. In all cases, however, the class that implements the interface must implement both the member in the base class and the member in the derived class with the same name, which can become quite confusing. For this reason, you should avoid defining a derived interface that contains a member with the same name as a member in its base interface, even though Visual Basic allows you to do so.

A derived class automatically inherits all the interfaces (and their implementation) defined in the base type, whether they're implemented through public or private methods. You must not include any Implements statement in the derived class.

```
' This class inherits all the interfaces defined in the MyAddin class.
Class AnotherAddin
    Inherits MyAddin
End Class

' Client code
Dim addin2 As New AnotherAddin
' Prove that the inherited class exposes the IAddin interface.
DirectCast(addin2, IAddin).State = True
```

The derived class can override the implementation of interface methods defined in the base class as long as methods in the base class aren't Private and have been defined using the Overridable keyword. The code in the derived class must not use the Implements keyword in the method declaration.

```
Class AnotherAddin
    Inherits MyAddin
```

```
Protected Overrides Function OnConnection(ByVal environment As String) As Boolean
    …
End Function
End Class
```

As I showed in the section titled "Finalizers in Derived Classes" in Chapter 9, "Object Life-time," if the base class implements the IDisposable interface, .NET programming guidelines dictate that you override the Dispose method, perform your cleanup chores, and finally call the Dispose method in the base class:

```
' Assuming that the MyAddin base class implements IDisposable
' and that the Dispose method is marked as Overridable

Class AnotherAddin
    Inherits MyAddin

    Public Overrides Sub Dispose()
        ' Clean up code for the AnotherAddin class (omitted).
        …
        ' Complete the cleanup step by calling the base class's Dispose method.
        MyBase.Dispose()
    End Function
End Class
```

Interface Reimplementation

In Microsoft Visual Basic 2003, a derived class can override an interface method only if the method is explicitly declared with the Overridable keyword. This limitation seems quite reasonable, but over the years it has proved to be a serious problem for advanced Visual Basic developers willing to extend the types defined in the .NET Framework, the large majority of which implement interface methods without marking them as virtual (Overridable, in Visual Basic parlance).

To understand why the Visual Basic behavior was a problem, consider the following scenario: you inherit the MyDataTable type from the ADO.NET DataTable object and add a new field named AuthorName. The standard DataTable object implements the ISerializable interface and its GetObjectData method, which the .NET runtime invokes when the object is to be serialized in a file or sent across the wire using .NET remoting. (I cover the ISerializable interface in Chapter 21, "Serialization.") Of course, you need to serialize the new AuthorName field together with the other table data, so you'd like to override the ISerializable.GetObjectData method, invoke the GetObjectData method in the base class, and then serialize the extra field:

```
Class MyDataTable
    Inherits DataTable

    Public AuthorName As String          ' The new field

    ' *** This method causes a compilation error in Visual Basic .NET 2002,
    '     Visual Basic .NET 2003, and Visual Basic 2005.
    Public Overrides Sub GetObjectData(ByVal info As SerializationInfo, _
```

```
         ByVal context As StreamingContext)
       ...
    End Sub
End Class
```

Unfortunately, this code causes a compilation error in all versions of Visual Basic, including Visual Basic 2005, because GetObjectData isn't defined as virtual in the base DataTable class. Visual Basic versions earlier than Visual Basic 2005 don't permit you to use the Implements keyword on either the method or the class, so you're stuck. The truth is, this single issue has prevented Visual Basic programmers from developing more complex controls and components, which in fact must be authored in C# (which doesn't suffer from this limitation).

This limitation has been lifted in Visual Basic 2005, which supports a new feature called *interface reimplementation*: you can use the Implements keyword at the class level to implement an interface defined in the base class, and you can use it at the method level to define a new implementation of a given interface member:

```
Class MyDataTable
    Inherits DataTable
    Implements ISerializable

    Public AuthorName As String              ' The new field

    ' This method is invoked when an instance is serialized.
    Public Overrides Sub GetObjectData(ByVal info As SerializationInfo, _
       ByVal context As StreamingContext) Implements ISerializable.GetObjectData
        ' Let the base class serialize its own data.
        MyBase.GetObjectData(info, context)
        ' Next, serialize the new field.
        info.AddValue("AuthorName", Me.AuthorName)
    End Sub

    ' This special constructor is invoked when an instance is deserialized.
    Private Sub New(ByVal info As SerializationInfo, ByVal context As StreamingContext)
        ' Ask the base class to deserialize its own data.
        MyBase.New(info, context)
        ' Next, deserialize the new field.
        Me.AuthorName = info.GetString("AuthorName")
    End Sub
End Class
```

When you compile this code, Visual Basic emits the following compiler warning to draw your attention to the fact that method reimplementation is assumed, but the project is compiled nevertheless.

```
'System.Runtime.Serialization.ISerializable.GetObjectData' is already implemented
by the base class 'System.Data.DataTable'. Re-implementation of sub assumed.
```

Read Chapter 21 for more information about the ISerialization interface and the special constructor that it requires to deserialize a serialized instance.

Interfaces and Polymorphism

So far, I have shown how you can define an interface and how you can implement it in other classes, but I haven't explained exactly *why* you should use interfaces in the first place. In general, you author an interface to define a group of methods and properties that, taken together, implement a specific feature or set of features.

To illustrate the power of interfaces, we need a complex example, for instance, an IDataRow-Persistable interface that contains the methods that enable an object to load and save its state to a row in a DataTable:

```
Public Interface IDataRowPersistable
   ReadOnly Property PrimaryKey() As Object
   Sub Save(ByVal row As DataRow)
   Sub Load(ByVal row As DataRow)
End Interface
```

As you can see, the interface is absolutely generic and can be used by any object that requires this capability. For example, a Student class might implement it as follows:

```
Public Class Student
   Implements IDataRowPersistable

   ' These should be properties in a real-world class.
   Public FirstName As String
   Public LastName As String
   Public BirthDate As Date
   ' The primary key for this object is private.
   Private ID As Guid = Guid.Empty

   ' Two constructors
   Public Sub New(ByVal firstName As String, ByVal lastName As String, _
         ByVal birthDate As Date)
      Me.FirstName = firstName
      Me.LastName = lastName
      Me.BirthDate = birthDate
   End Sub

   Public Sub New()
   End Sub

   ' Return the primary key of this object.
   Public ReadOnly Property PrimaryKey() As Object _
         Implements IDataRowPersistable.PrimaryKey
      Get
         ' Generate the ID only when needed.
         If Me.ID.Equals(Guid.Empty) Then Me.ID = Guid.NewGuid()
         Return Me.ID
      End Get
   End Property

   Public Sub Load(ByVal row As DataRow) Implements IDataRowPersistable.Load
      Me.ID = CType(row("ID"), Guid)
      Me.FirstName = CStr(row("FirstName"))
```

```
        Me.LastName = CStr(row("LastName"))
        Me.BirthDate = CDate(row("BirthDate"))
    End Sub

    Public Sub Save(ByVal row As DataRow) Implements IDataRowPersistable.Save
        ' Save the ID only if the primary key field is null.
        If DBNull.Value.Equals(row("ID")) Then row("ID") = Me.ID
        row("FirstName") = Me.FirstName
        row("LastName") = Me.LastName
        row("BirthDate") = Me.BirthDate
    End Sub
End Class
```

Here's an example of how a program might use the IDataRowPersistable interface to save an array of Student objects into a DataTable and load it back:

```
' Define a DataTable with four fields.
Dim table As New DataTable()
' Create the ID column and make it the primary key for this table.
Dim idCol As DataColumn = table.Columns.Add("ID", GetType(Guid))
table.PrimaryKey = New DataColumn() {idCol}
table.Columns.Add("FirstName", GetType(String))
table.Columns.Add("LastName", GetType(String))
table.Columns.Add("BirthDate", GetType(Date))

' Save an array of Student objects into the DataTable.
Dim students() As Student = {New Student ("John", "Doe", #1/2/1965#), _
    New Student("Ann", "Doe", #8/17/1972#), _
    New Student("Robert", "Smith", #11/1/1973#)}
SaveObjects(table, students)
…
' Initialize an array of Studentobjects and load it from the DataTable.
Dim studArray(table.Rows.Count - 1) As Student
For i As Integer = 0 To studArray.Length - 1
    studArray(i) = New Student()
Next
LoadObjects(table, studArray)
```

This is the source code for the methods that move an array of IDataRowPersistable objects to and from a DataTable:

```
Sub SaveObjects(ByVal table As DataTable, ByVal array() As IDataRowPersistable)
    ' Retrieve the primary key name. (Multiple column keys aren't supported.)
    Dim pkName As String = table.PrimaryKey(0).ColumnName
    ' Create a DataView sorted on the primary key.
    Dim dataView As New DataView(table)
    dataView.Sort = pkName

    For Each obj As IDataRowPersistable In array
        ' Search for the corresponding DataRow in the table.
        Dim row As DataRow
        Dim rowIndex As Integer = dataView.Find(obj.PrimaryKey)

        If rowIndex >= 0 Then
            ' If found, get a reference to the corresponding DataRow.
            row = table.Rows(rowIndex)
```

```
        Else
           ' If not found, this is a new object.
           row = table.NewRow()
        End If
        ' Ask the object to save itself.
        obj.Save(row)
        ' Add to the DataTable if it was a new row.
        If rowIndex < 0 Then table.Rows.Add(row)
    Next
End Sub

Sub LoadObjects(ByVal table As DataTable, ByVal array() As IDataRowPersistable)
    ' Load each object with data from a DataRow.
    For i As Integer = 0 To table.Rows.Count - 1
        Dim row As DataRow = table.Rows(i)
        array(i).Load(row)
    Next
End Sub
```

If you look carefully at the source code of the SaveObjects and LoadObjects methods, you won't see any reference to the Student type. In fact, these methods are absolutely generic and work with any type that implements the IDataRowPersistable interface. Thanks to this interface, you created a piece of *polymorphic code* that you can reuse with many other types. For example, you might define an Employee type that implements the IDataRowPersistable interface and can still reuse much of the code that moves data to and from a DataTable (except you need a DataTable with a different schema).

Sometimes it's difficult to understand whether a given set of features should be implemented by means of an interface or by inheriting from a base class. In general, inheriting from a base class is better in terms of code conciseness because you can implement common functionality right in the base class. However, inheritance wouldn't help much in the case just shown because each derived class would need to override the methods of the IDataRowPersistable interface to account for the different name and type of their members.

In other cases, you can't leverage inheritance because the types already have a base class. For example, all Microsoft Windows Forms controls inherit from the System.Windows.Forms. Control base class, so if you had defined a given functionality by means of a base class, you couldn't use it with a Windows control because .NET doesn't support multiple inheritance.

In real-world applications, you can often mix interfaces and reflection techniques to make your code even more generic and reusable. For example, in Chapter 21 you'll see how you can use reflection to implement the ISerializable interface with code that works well regardless of the type being serialized or deserialized.

Using .NET Interfaces

The .NET Framework defines and consumes dozens of different interfaces, and expert Visual Basic developers should learn how to use them profitably. In this section, you'll see how a few such system-wide interfaces can make your life simpler.

The IComparable Interface

In the section titled "ParamArray Arguments" in Chapter 3, you saw that the System.Array class exposes the Sort static method, which enables you to sort an array of simple data types, such as numbers or strings. However, the Sort method can't directly sort more complex objects, such as Person, because it doesn't know how two Person objects compare with each other.

Implementing the IComparable interface makes your objects sortable by means of the Sort method exposed by the Array and ArrayList types. This interface exposes only one method, CompareTo, which receives an object and is expected to return –1, 0, or 1, depending on whether the object on which CompareTo is called is less than, equal to, or greater than the object passed as an argument. Let's see how you can define a Person class that's sortable on its ReverseName property:

```
Public Class Person
   Implements IComparable

   ' Public fields (should be properties in a real-world class)
   Public FirstName As String
   Public LastName As String

   ' A simple constructor
   Sub New(ByVal firstName As String, ByVal lastName As String)
     Me.FirstName = firstName
     Me.LastName = lastName
   End Sub

   ' A property that returns the name in the format "Evans, John"
   ReadOnly Property ReverseName() As String
      Get
          Return LastName & ", " & FirstName
      End Get
   End Property

   ' This private procedure adds sorting capabilities to the class.
   Private Function CompareTo(ByVal obj As Object) As Integer _
         Implements IComparable.CompareTo
      ' Any non-Nothing object is greater than Nothing.
      If obj Is Nothing Then Return 1
      ' Cast to a specific Person; error if argument is of a different type.
      Dim other As Person = DirectCast(obj, Person)
      ' The String.Compare static method does exactly what we need.
      ' (True means that the comparison is case-insensitive.)
      Return String.Compare(Me.ReverseName, other.ReverseName, True)
   End Function
End Class
```

Here's the client code that demonstrates how the IComparable interface works:

```
Dim persons() As Person = { New Person("John", "Smith"), _
   New Person("Robert", "Zare"), New Person("John", "Fredericksen") }
Array.Sort(persons)
' Display all the elements in sorted order.
```

```
For Each p As Person In persons
    Console.WriteLine(p.ReverseName)
Next
```

Notice that the implementation of CompareTo is less than optimal because it creates a lot of temporary strings (the results of calls to ReverseName), which can significantly slow down your application. Here's an implementation that's less concise and less linear, but faster:

```
Private Function CompareTo(ByVal obj As Object) As Integer _
        Implements IComparable.CompareTo
    ' Any non-Nothing object is greater than Nothing.
    If obj Is Nothing Then Return 1
    ' Cast to a specific Person object; error if the argument is of a different type.
    Dim other As Person = DirectCast(obj, Person)
    ' Compare LastName first.
    Dim result As Integer = String.Compare(Me.LastName, other.LastName, True)
    If result = 0 Then
       ' Compare FirstName only if the two persons have same last name.
       result = String.Compare(Me.FirstName, other.FirstName, True)
    End If
    Return result
End Function
```

The IComparer Interface

The IComparable interface is all you need when your objects can be compared in only one way. Most real-world objects, however, can be compared and sorted on different fields or field combinations; in such cases you can use a variation of the Array.Sort method that takes an IComparer interface as its second argument. The IComparer interface exposes only one method, Compare, which receives two object references and returns −1, 0, or 1 depending on whether the first object is less than, equal to, or greater than the second object.

A class that can be sorted on different field combinations might expose two or more nested classes that implement the IComparer interface, one class for each possible sort method. For example, you might want to sort the Person class on either the (LastName, FirstName) or (FirstName, LastName) field combination; these combinations correspond to the Reverse-Name and CompleteName read-only properties in the code that follows. Here's a new version of the class that supports these features:

```
Public Class Person
   ' (Definition of FirstName, LastName, ReverseName, and constructor omitted)
   ...
   ' A property that returns a name in the format "John Evans"
   ReadOnly Property CompleteName() As String
      Get
         Return FirstName & " " & LastName
      End Get
   End Property

   ' First auxiliary class, to sort on CompleteName
   Class ComparerByName
      Implements IComparer
```

```
         Function Compare(ByVal o1 As Object, ByVal o2 As Object) _
            As Integer Implements IComparer.Compare
            ' Two null objects are equal.
            If (o1 Is Nothing) And (o2 Is Nothing) Then Return 0
            ' Any non-null object is greater than a null object.
            If (o1 Is Nothing) Then Return 1
            If (o2 Is Nothing) Then Return -1
            ' Cast both objects to Person, and do the comparison.
            ' (Throws an exception if arguments aren't Person objects.)
            Dim p1 As Person = DirectCast(o1, Person)
            Dim p2 As Person = DirectCast(o2, Person)
            Return String.Compare(p1.CompleteName, p2.CompleteName, True)
         End Function
      End Class

      ' Second auxiliary class, to sort on ReverseName
      Class ComparerByReverseName
         Implements IComparer

         Function Compare(ByVal o1 As Object, ByVal o2 As Object) _
            As Integer Implements IComparer.Compare
            ' Two null objects are equal.
            If (o1 Is Nothing) And (o2 Is Nothing) Then Return 0
            ' Any non-null object is greater than a null object.
            If (o1 Is Nothing) Then Return 1
            If (o2 Is Nothing) Then Return -1
            ' Save code by casting to Person objects on the fly.
            Return String.Compare(DirectCast(o1, Person).ReverseName, _
               DirectCast(o2, Person).ReverseName, True)
         End Function
      End Class
End Class
```

In a real-world class, you should avoid all the temporary strings created by calls to Complete-Name and ReverseName properties and compare the LastName and FirstName properties individually, as described at the end of the section titled "The IComparable Interface" earlier in this chapter. Using the two auxiliary classes is straightforward:

```
Dim persons() As Person = { New Person("John", "Frum"), _
   New Person("Robert", "Zare"), New Person("John", "Evans") }
' Sort the array on name.
Array.Sort(persons, New Person.ComparerByName())
' Sort the array on reversed name.
Array.Sort(persons, New Person.ComparerByReverseName())
```

Your type can also provide one or more static read-only fields that can save the clients from instantiating an IComparer object:

```
Public Class Person
   …
   Public Shared ReadOnly NameComparer As New ComparerByName()
   Public Shared ReadOnly ReverseNameComparer As New ComparerByReverseName()
End Class
```

The client code becomes

```
' Sort the array on name.
Array.Sort(persons, Person.NameComparer)
' Sort the array on reversed name.
Array.Sort(persons, Person.ReverseNameComparer)
```

 String comparisons are based on the current locale, or more precisely on the value of Thread.CurrentCulture. Case-insensitive comparisons are different from what Microsoft Visual Basic 6 developers might expect, however, because they are never based on ASCII values of individual characters. For example, under Visual Basic 2005, all the variations of the character *A* (uppercase, lowercase, or accented) come before the character *B*. If you're migrating Visual Basic code that relies on ASCII code sorting for case-insensitive string comparisons, you should use the StringComparer.Ordinal read-only method, as follows:

```
' arr is a string array.
Array.Sort(Of String)(arr, StringComparer.Ordinal)
```

The StringComparer type exposes other static read-only properties, each one returning a different IComparer object that implements a different type of comparison. For example, the StringComparer.CurrentCultureIgnoreCase returns an IComparer object that compares strings in case-insensitive mode according to the current culture, whereas the Invariant-CultureIgnoreCase does the same kind of comparison but according to the invariant culture. Read the section titled "Comparing and Searching Strings" in Chapter 12, ".NET Basic Types," for more details.

Quite oddly, the .NET Framework doesn't allow you to sort an array in descending order; thus, the best you can do is sort the array as usual and then call the Array.Reverse method. A more efficient way to achieve this result would be to include a *reverse comparer*, that is, a comparer class that returns the negated result of the comparison. Instead of creating several reverse comparers, you're better off defining an adapter class that takes an IComparer object, uses it to do the comparison, but returns the negated result. The following ReverseComparer type implements this concept and, as an added touch, attempts to use the IComparable interface of either argument passed to the Compare method if the client didn't pass any IComparer object when instantiating the ReverseComparer object:

```
Public Class ReverseComparer
   Implements IComparer

   Private icomp As IComparer

   Public Sub New(Optional ByVal icomp As IComparer = Nothing)
      Me.icomp = icomp
   End Sub

   Function Compare(ByVal x As Object, ByVal y As Object) As Integer _
         Implements IComparer.Compare
      If icomp IsNot Nothing Then
         ' Use the passed IComparer object if possible; notice arguments in reverse order.
         Return icomp.Compare(y, x)
```

```
        ElseIf x IsNot Nothing AndAlso TypeOf x Is IComparable Then
            ' Use x's IComparable interface, negate result to get the reverse effect.
            Return -DirectCast(x, IComparable).CompareTo(y)
        ElseIf y IsNot Nothing AndAlso TypeOf y Is IComparable Then
            ' Use y's IComparable interface. (No need to negate the result)
            Return DirectCast(y, IComparable).CompareTo(x)
        Else
            Throw New ArgumentException("Neither argument is IComparable")
        End If
    End Function
End Class
```

Using the ReverseComparer is simple. Here's how you can sort a string array in reverse order, both in case-sensitive and case-insensitive modes:

```
Dim arr() As String = {"a", "f", "q", "b", "z", "k"}
' Reverse sort of a string array in case-sensitive mode
Array.Sort(arr, New ReverseComparer())
' Reverse sort of a string array in case-insensitive mode
Array.Sort(arr, New ReverseComparer(StringComparer.CurrentCultureIgnoreCase))
```

The ICloneable Interface

Everything is an object under the .NET Framework. One consequence of this arrangement is that when you assign a variable to another variable, you get two variables pointing to the same object, rather than two distinct copies of the data. (In this discussion, I assume you're working with reference types, not value types.) Typically, you get a copy of the data by invoking a special method that the class exposes. In the .NET world, a class should implement the ICloneable interface and expose its only method, Clone, to let the outside world know that it can create a copy of its instances. Several objects in the framework implement this interface, including Array, ArrayList, BitArray, Font, Icon, Queue, and Stack. Most of the time, implementing the ICloneable interface is straightforward:

```
Public Class Employee
    Implements ICloneable

    Public FirstName As String
    Public LastName As String
    Public Boss As Employee

    Sub New(ByVal firstName As String, ByVal lastName As String)
        Me.FirstName = firstName
        Me.LastName = lastName
    End Sub

    ' The only method of the ICloneable interface
    Public Function Clone() As Object Implements ICloneable.Clone
        ' Create a new Employee with same property values.
        Dim em As New Employee(FirstName, LastName)
        ' Properties not accepted in the constructors must be copied manually.
        em.Boss = Me.Boss
        Return em
    End Function
End Class
```

The System.Object class, from which all other classes derive, defines the MemberwiseClone protected method, which helps you clone an object without having to copy every property manually. See how you can use this method to simplify the implementation of the Clone method in the Employee class:

```
Public Function Clone() As Object Implements ICloneable.Clone
    Return Me.MemberwiseClone()
End Function
```

The ICloneable interface is never called by the .NET runtime, and its only purpose is to provide a standardized way to let other developers know that your class supports cloning by means of a well-established syntax:

```
' Define an employee and his boss.
Dim john As New Employee("John", "Evans")
Dim robert As New Employee("Robert", "Zare")
john.Boss = robert

' Clone it. The Clone method returns a generic object, so you need a cast.
Dim john2 As Employee = DirectCast(john.Clone(), Employee)
' Prove that all properties were copied.
Console.WriteLine("{0} {1}, whose boss is {2} {3}", _
    john2.FirstName, john2.LastName, john2.Boss.FirstName, john2.Boss.LastName)
    ' => John Evans, whose boss is Robert Zare
```

Shallow Copies and Deep Copies

You can perform two kinds of copy operations on an object. A *shallow copy* creates a copy of only the object in question. It doesn't make copies of secondary objects (or *child objects*) referenced by it. In contrast, a *deep copy* operation clones all secondary objects as well. The following code snippet makes this difference clear:

```
' Define an employee and his boss.
Dim john As New Employee("John", "Evans")
Dim robert As New Employee("Robert", "Zare")
john.Boss = Robert

' Clone it, and prove that the Employee object was cloned into a
' distinct instance, but his boss wasn't.
Dim john2 As Employee = DirectCast(john.Clone(), Employee)
Console.WriteLine(john Is john2)              ' => False
Console.WriteLine(john.Boss Is john2.Boss)    ' => True
```

You can see the difference between shallow and deep copy with arrays. Say that you have an array containing 100 references to Employee instances. A shallow copy of this array would create only one new object, that is, another array whose elements point to the same 100 Employee instances as the original array. A deep copy would create *at least* 101 objects, that, is a copy of the array and one copy for each of the 100 Employee objects (possibly plus other child objects of these Employee instances).

When shallow copying isn't enough and you really need to create a clone of the entire object graph that has the object at its root, you can't rely on the MemberwiseClone method alone; you must manually copy properties of each object. Here's a new Employee2 class that correctly clones the entire object graph:

```
Public Class Employee2
   Implements ICloneable

   Public Boss As Employee2
   ' ...(other fields and constructor as in Employee)...

   Public Function Clone() As Object Implements ICloneable.Clone
      ' Start with a shallow copy of this object.
      ' (This copies all nonobject properties in one operation.)
      Dim em As Employee2 = DirectCast(Me.MemberwiseClone(), Employee2)
      ' Manually copy the Boss property, reusing its Clone method.
      If em.Boss IsNot Nothing Then em.Boss = DirectCast(Me.Boss.Clone(), Employee2)
      Return em
   End Function
End Class
```

This new version of the Clone method is still concise because it uses the MemberwiseClone method to copy all nonobject values, and it builds on the Clone method for the secondary objects (only Boss, in this case). This approach also works if the employee's boss has a boss.

However, most real-world object graphs are more complex than this example, and exposing a Clone method that works correctly isn't a trivial task. For example, if the Employee2 class had a Colleagues property (a collection holding other Employee2 objects), the ensuing circular references would cause the Clone method to enter a recursion that would end with a stack overflow error. Fortunately, the .NET Framework offers a clean solution to this problem, as you can read about in the section titled "Deep Object Cloning" in Chapter 21.

One last note: the semantics of the ICloneable interface doesn't specify whether the Clone method should return a shallow copy or a deep copy of the object; thus, you are free to choose the behavior that fits your needs. However, it is essential that you clearly document this detail in the documentation that comes with your class.

A Strongly Typed Clone Method

The ICloneable interface is generic and must work with any .NET type, so its Clone method returns an Object value. As shown in previous examples, this involves a hidden boxing and unboxing sequence and forces you to use a DirectCast function to assign the cloned object to a strongly typed variable. Is there a way to avoid this overhead?

The answer is yes, and the technique is surprisingly simple. You define a public, strongly typed Clone method in the main class interface of your object and have a private IClone-able.Clone method point to it. Here's a new Employee3 class that uses this technique:

```
Public Class Employee3
   Implements ICloneable
```

```
      Public Boss As Employee3
      ' ...(other fields and constructor as in Employee)...

      ' The only method of the ICloneable interface (private)
      Private Function CloneMe() As Object Implements ICloneable.Clone
         ' Reuses the code in the strongly typed Clone method.
         Return Clone
      End Function

      ' The strongly typed Clone method (public)
      Public Function Clone() As Employee3
         ' Start creating a shallow copy of this object.
         ' (This copies all nonobject properties in one operation.)
         Clone = DirectCast(Me.MemberwiseClone(), Employee3)
         ' Manually copy the Boss property, reusing its Clone method.
         If Clone.Boss IsNot Nothing Then Clone.Boss = Me.Boss.Clone()
      End Function
End Class
```

The client code isn't cluttered with CType or DirectCast functions or slowed down by hidden unboxing operations:

```
Dim john2 As Employee3 = john.Clone()
```

You make your code more robust by using a strongly typed Clone method because the compiler can flag incorrect assignments that would otherwise throw an exception at run time. Note that you can still access the original, weakly typed Clone method by means of an ICloneable variable or by using a CType or DirectCast operator, as in this line of code:

```
Dim c As Object = DirectCast(john, ICloneable).Clone
```

The IDisposable Interface

I have already covered the IDisposable interface in Chapter 8 and mentioned it again earlier in this chapter, so I won't repeat here why types that use other disposable objects should use this interface. In this section, however, I want to show how you can leverage this interface together with the Using statement to implement an interesting behavior. Consider the following class:

```
Public Class CurrentDirectory
   Implements IDisposable

   Dim oldPath As String

   Public Sub New(ByVal newPath As String)
      ' Remember the current directory, and then change it.
      oldPath = Directory.GetCurrentDirectory()
      Directory.SetCurrentDirectory(newPath)
   End Sub

   Public Sub Restore() Implements IDisposable.Dispose
      ' Restore the original current directory.
      Directory.SetCurrentDirectory(oldPath)
   End Sub
End Class
```

This simple class enables you to write the following code:

```
Using dc As New CurrentDirectory("c:\temp")
    ' Current directory is now c:\temp.
    …
    ' The next statement restores the original current directory.
End Using
```

It's as if the IDisposable interface, together with the Using statement, enables you to "schedule" an operation for execution at the end of a block of code. Interestingly, you can even nest these blocks and you can avoid using an explicit variable to point to the IDisposable class because your code doesn't access any of its methods:

```
Using New CurrentDirectory("c:\temp")
    ' Current directory is now c:\temp.
    …
    Using New CurrentDirectory("c:\windows")
        ' Current directory is now c:\windows.
        …
        ' The next statement restores c:\temp as the current directory.
    End Using
    …
    ' The next statement restores the original current directory.
End Using
```

You can extend this concept further and create other types of disposable classes like Current-Directory. For example, the following MouseCursor class enables you to set a mouse cursor for a given Windows Forms control or Form and automatically restore it at the end of a code block:

```
Public Class MouseCursor
    Implements IDisposable

    Dim control As Control
    Dim oldCursor As Cursor

    Public Sub New(ByVal ctrl As Control, ByVal newCursor As Cursor)
        ' Remember control and old cursor, and then enforce new cursor.
        control = ctrl
        oldCursor = ctrl.Cursor
        control.Cursor = newCursor
    End Sub

    Public Sub Restore() Implements IDisposable.Dispose
        ' Restore the original cursor.
        control.Cursor = oldCursor
    End Sub
End Class
```

Using this class is much easier than manually setting and restoring the mouse cursor during a lengthy operation:

```
' This code must run inside a form class.
Using New MouseCursor(Me, Cursors.WaitCursor)
```

```
   ' Perform the lengthy operation here.
   …
   ' Next statement restores the original mouse cursor.
End Using
```

Writing Collection Classes

When Visual Basic compiles a For Each statement, it checks that the object following the In keyword supports the IEnumerable interface. When the For Each statement is executed, the code generated by the compiler invokes the only method in this interface, GetEnumerator. This function must return an object that supports the IEnumerator interface, which in turn exposes the following three members: MoveNext, Current, and Reset. The MoveNext method is called at each iteration: it should return True if a new value is available and False if there are no more elements. The Current read-only property returns the value to be used in the current iteration of the loop. The Reset method resets the internal pointer so that the next returned value is the first one in a new series. (The Reset method is currently unused by the code the Visual Basic compiler generates.)

> **Note**   I'll cover collections in more depth in Chapter 13. In this section, I will quickly review the many ways the .NET Framework provides you with for creating a custom collection and then I'll focus on collection classes that implement the IEnumerable interface directly.

Using Abstract Collection Types

You can define a class that supports iteration in a For Each loop by inheriting from one of the many base types provided by the .NET Framework, for example, the CollectionBase, ReadOnlyCollectionBase, and DictionaryBase abstract classes defined in System.Collections. For example, the following type enables you to iterate over all the lines of a text file; it doesn't allow you to add to or remove items from the collection of text lines; therefore, it inherits from the ReadOnlyCollectionBase type:

```
Public Class TextLineCollection
   Inherits ReadOnlyCollectionBase

   Sub New(ByVal path As String)
      ' Load the inner list with text lines in the specified file.
      Using sr As New StreamReader(path)
         Do Until sr.Peek < 0
            Me.InnerList.Add(sr.ReadLine)
         Loop
      End Using
   End Sub

   Default ReadOnly Property Item(ByVal index As Integer) As String
      Get
         Return Me.InnerList(index).ToString
      End Get
   End Property
End Class
```

Here's how you can use the TextLineCollection class:

```
Dim lines As New TextLineCollection("c:\myfile.txt")
' Display the last line.
Console.WriteLine(lines(lines.Count - 1))
' Display all lines in a For Each loop.
For Each s As String In lines
   Console.WriteLine(s)
Next
```

In this specific example, the Item property is marked ReadOnly because a client isn't supposed to change individual lines once the collection has been initialized. But don't confuse this ReadOnly attribute with the fact that the collection inherits from ReadOnlyCollection-Base. When applied to a collection, read-only means that the collection has a fixed size, not that individual elements aren't writable.

Using Generics

Visual Basic 2005 supports generics, so you can implement a collection type with less code than you need under previous language versions. For example, this is all the code that you need to implement a collection object of Person objects:

```
Public Class PersonCollection
   Inherits List(Of Person)
End Class
```

The PersonCollection class is strongly typed and exposes all the members you'd expect from a collection, including Add, Insert, Remove, RemoveAt, Count, and many others; unlike a weakly typed collection, though, you can add only Person instances to this collection:

```
Dim col As New PersonCollection
col.Add(New Person("John", "Evans"))      ' This statement works fine.
col.Add("a string")                       ' *** This statement doesn't compile.
```

Of course, the PersonCollection class supports the For Each loop:

```
For Each p As Person in col
   Console.WriteLine(p.CompleteName)
Next
```

You can learn more about generics in Chapter 11.

Implementing the IEnumerable and IEnumerator Interfaces

So far, I've illustrated how you can create a collection class by inheriting from the abstract classes or the generic classes that the .NET Framework defines. All these classes provide a default implementation of IEnumerable, the interface that is implicitly queried for when the collection appears in a For Each loop. However, nothing prevents you from implementing this interface directly, a technique that requires a lot more code but provides the greatest flexibility.

To illustrate these interfaces in action with a specific example, I created a TextFileReader class that enables you to iterate over all the lines in a text file within a For Each loop. This result is similar to what I achieved earlier in this chapter with the TextFileCollection class, which works well but isn't efficient and takes a lot of extra memory when you're reading long files because you need an array to store all the parsed lines. In contrast, the TextFileReader object uses no additional memory because text lines are read from the file one at a time:

```
Public Class TextFileReader
   Implements IEnumerable

   Dim path As String

   Sub New(ByVal path As String)
      Me.path = path                ' Remember for later.
   End Sub

   Private Function GetEnumerator() As IEnumerator Implements IEnumerable.GetEnumerator
      ' Return an instance of the inner enumerator.
      Return New FileReaderEnumerator(path)
   End Function
End Class
```

The GetEnumerator function returns a FileReaderEnumerator object. You can implement this class as a nested type inside FileReader. Interestingly, if the enumerator object in a For Each loop exposes the IDisposable interface, the Visual Basic and C# compilers automatically invoke the Dispose method when the loop terminates normally or exits because of an Exit For statement. The FileReaderEnumerator class takes advantage of this detail to ensure that the stream is correctly closed as soon as it is no longer necessary.

```
' The private enumerator (nested inside TextFileReader)
Private Class FileReaderEnumerator
   Implements IEnumerator, IDisposable

   Dim sr As StreamReader           ' The Stream reader
   Dim currLine As String           ' The text line just read

   Sub New(ByVal path As String)
      sr = New StreamReader(path)
   End Sub

   ' The IEnumerator interface (three methods)

   Public Function MoveNext() As Boolean Implements IEnumerator.MoveNext
      If sr.Peek >= 0 Then
         ' If not at end of file, read the next line.
         currLine = sr.ReadLine()
         Return True
      Else
```

```
            ' Else, return False to stop enumeration.
            Return False
        End If
    End Function

    Public ReadOnly Property Current() As Object Implements IEnumerator.Current
        Get
            ' Return the line read by MoveNext.
            Return currLine
        End Get
    End Property

    Public Sub Reset() Implements IEnumerator.Reset
        ' This method is never called and can be empty.
    End Sub

    Public Sub Dispose() Implements IDisposable.Dispose
        ' Close the stream when this object is disposed.
        sr.Close()
    End Sub
End Class
```

Here's how a client can read one line at a time from a text file:

```
For Each s As String In New TextFileReader("c:\myfile.txt")
    Console.WriteLine(s)
Next
```

Note that you might make the code a bit more concise by having TextFileReader implement both the IEnumerable and the IEnumerator interfaces. In general, however, keep the enumerator in a distinct class for better design and to help make your code readable.

Reusable Enumerable Adapters

A limitation of the For Each loop is that you can iterate over all the elements of a collection only in one direction, from the elements with lower indexes toward elements with higher indexes. It looks like you need a traditional, less elegant For loop to go in the opposite direction. However, now that you know the subtleties of the IEnumerable interface, you can create an adapter type that implements the IEnumerable interface and that wraps another IEnumerable object:

```
Public Class ReverseIterator
    Implements IEnumerable

    Private al As New ArrayList()

    Public Sub New(ByVal ienum As IEnumerable)
        ' Read all the elements into the inner ArrayList.
        For Each o As Object In ienum
            al.Add(o)
        Next
        ' Reverse the element order.
        al.Reverse()
```

```
      End Sub

   ' Return the GetEnumerator of the inner ArrayList.
   Public Function GetEnumerator() As IEnumerator Implements IEnumerable.GetEnumerator
      Return al.GetEnumerator()
   End Function
End Class
```

Here's how you can use this adapter to iterate over the elements of a string array in reverse direction:

```
Dim arr() As String = {"one", "two", "three", "four", "five", "six"}
For Each s As String In New ReverseIterator(arr)
   Console.Write("{0} ", s)            ' => six five four three two one
Next
```

This technique enables you to write code that is more elegant but far less efficient that a plain For with a negative step. In fact, the ReverseIterator type has to read all the elements of the array into an ArrayList object, reverse it, and pass the inner IEnumerator object back to the Visual Basic program, which will traverse all the elements a second time.

Here's another example, which reuses the TextFileReader type to display all the lines in a text file in reverse order:

```
For Each s As String In New ReverseIterator(New TextFileReader("c:\myfile.txt"))
   Console.WriteLine(s)
Next
```

You can use the same principles to create other adapter classes. For example, the following RandomIterator class enables you to visit all the elements of an IEnumerable object in random order:

```
Public Class RandomIterator
   Implements IEnumerable

   Private al As New ArrayList()

   Public Sub New(ByVal ienum As IEnumerable)
      ' Read all the elements into the inner ArrayList.
      For Each o As Object In ienum
         al.Add(o)
      Next
      ' Shuffle the ArrayList.
      Dim rand As New Random(CInt(DateTime.Now.Ticks And &H7FFFFFFF))
      For i As Integer = al.Count - 1 To 1 Step -1
         ' Swap Ith element with an element whose index is in the range [0, i].
         Dim j As Integer = rand.Next(0, i)
         Dim tmp As Object = al(i)
         al(i) = al(j)
         al(j) = tmp
      Next
   End Sub
```

```
    ' Return the GetEnumerator of the inner ArrayList.
    Public Function GetEnumerator() As IEnumerator Implements IEnumerable.GetEnumerator
        Return al.GetEnumerator()
    End Function
End Class
```

The following code shows how you can apply the RandomIterator type to display the numbers in the range 0 to 9 in random order:

```
Dim arr() As Integer = {0, 1, 2, 3, 4, 5, 6, 7, 8, 9}
For Each n As Integer In New RandomIterator(arr)
    Console.Write("{0} ", n)
Next
```

You can provide even more flexibility if you take the burden to create an adapter for both the IEnumerable object and its inner IEnumerator object. The following type enables you to both skip an initial number of elements and step over a given number of elements. The code isn't exactly simple, but what you've learned so far and the remarks in the code should suffice for you to understand how the mechanism works:

```
Public Class StepIterator
    Implements IEnumerable

    Private ienum As IEnumerator
    Private stepValue As Integer
    Private skipValue As Integer

    ' The constructor does nothing but remember values for later.
    Public Sub New(ByVal iEnumerable As IEnumerable, ByVal stepValue As Integer, _
            Optional ByVal skipValue As Integer = 0)
        Me.ienum = iEnumerable.GetEnumerator()
        Me.stepValue = stepValue
        Me.skipValue = skipValue
    End Sub

    ' Pass an instance of the inner enumerator.
    Public Function GetEnumerator() As IEnumerator Implements IEnumerable.GetEnumerator
        Return New StepEnumerator(ienum, stepValue, skipValue)
    End Function

    ' The private enumerator object
    Private Class StepEnumerator
        Implements IEnumerator

        Private ienum As IEnumerator
        Private stepValue As Integer
        Private skipValue As Integer
        Private firstIteration As Boolean = True

        ' The constructor remembers values for later.
        Public Sub New(ByVal ienum As IEnumerator, ByVal stepValue As Integer, _
                ByVal skipValue As Integer)
            Me.ienum = ienum
            Me.stepValue = stepValue
```

```
        Me.skipValue = skipValue
    End Sub


    ' MoveNext method calls the method of the original object to skip desired
    ' number of elements at the first iteration and at subsequent iterations.
    Public Function MoveNext() As Boolean Implements IEnumerator.MoveNext
        If firstIteration Then
            firstIteration = False
            ' Note that you must call MoveNext at least once at the first iteration.
            For i As Integer = 1 To skipValue + 1
                If Not ienum.MoveNext Then Return False
            Next
        Else
            ' Skip the desired number of iterations.
            For i As Integer = 1 To stepValue
                If Not ienum.MoveNext Then Return False
            Next
        End If
        ' Tell the application that there is a current value.
        Return True
    End Function


    ' Current and Reset members delegate to the original IEnumerator object.
    Public ReadOnly Property Current() As Object Implements IEnumerator.Current
        Get
            Return ienum.Current
        End Get
    End Property

    Public Sub Reset() Implements System.Collections.IEnumerator.Reset
        ienum.Reset()
    End Sub
    End Class
End Class
```

The StepIterator class solves two of the most annoying limitations of the For Each loop by adding the ability to start with an element other than the first element and the ability to visit every Nth element in the collection. For example, see how you can visit all the elements of a collection with even indexes:

```
Dim arr() As Integer = {0, 1, 2, 3, 4, 5, 6, 7, 8, 9}
For Each n As Integer In New StepIterator(arr, 2, 0)
    Console.Write("{0} ", n)                ' => 0 2 4 6 8
Next
```

and the elements with odd indexes:

```
For Each n As Integer In New StepIterator(arr, 2, 1)
    Console.Write("{0} ", n)                ' => 1 3 5 7 9
Next
```

Here's another example. Say that you have a text file containing data in comma- or tab-delimited format, one record per line, but you need to skip over the very first line because this line contains the column headers (an arrangement that is typical of data files in this format). You can use the StepIterator together with the TextFileReader type to accomplish this task in a very elegant manner:

```
For Each s As String In New StepIterator(New TextFileReader("c:\myfile.txt"), 1, 1)
   Console.WriteLine(s)
Next
```

Notice that the StepIterator class doesn't suffer from the performance issue that affected the ReverseIterator and RandomIterator types because it doesn't have to read all the elements of the inner IEnumerable object in advance.

Chapter 11
Generics

Unless you are absolutely new to Microsoft .NET programming—or you're a .NET developer who has lived on a desert island for the last two years—you should have heard about generics and the fact that they are the most important addition to Microsoft Visual Basic and other .NET languages. In this chapter, I show that generics are indeed a very important new feature of your favorite language and illustrate several examples of what generics can do to make your code faster, more concise, and more elegant.

In a nutshell, generics give you the ability to define a class that takes a type as an argument. Depending on the type argument, the generic definition generates a different concrete class. In this sense, generics add a degree of polymorphism, much like other techniques based on inheritance, interfaces, or late binding. But you'll soon discover that generics are much, much more powerful.

Before we dive into the topic, bear in mind that generics aren't a completely new concept in the programming world. In fact, .NET generics are similar to C++ templates, so you might already be familiar with the underlying concepts if you've worked in that language before. However, .NET generics have several features and advantages that C++ templates don't, for example, constraints.

Note To avoid long lines, code samples in this chapter assume that the following Imports statements are used at the file or project level:

```
Imports System.Collections
Imports System.Collections.Generic
```

The Need for Generics

Let's start with a classic example that shows why generics can be so useful. Let's consider the ArrayList type, defined in the System.Collections namespace. I cover this and other collection-like types in Chapter 13, "Arrays and Collections," but for now it will suffice to see how you can define such a collection and add elements to it:

```
' This collection will contain only integer numbers.
Dim col As New ArrayList()
col.Add(11): col.Add(13): col.Add(19)
For Each n As Integer in col
   Console.WriteLine(n)
Next
' Reading an element requires a CType or CInt operator (if Option Strict is On).
Dim element As Integer = CType(col(0), Integer)
```

As simple as it is, this code has a couple of serious problems, one related to robustness and the other related to performance. The former problem is quite simple to demonstrate: the ArrayList was designed to store values of any kind, hence it stores its value internally inside System.Object slots. This means that a developer using the ArrayList can accidentally or purposely add an element that isn't an integer, an action that would make the For Each loop fail at run time:

```
' Adding a string to the collection doesn't raise any compile-time error…
col.Add("abc")
' …but it makes the following statement fail at run time.
For Each n As Integer in col
   Console.WriteLine(n)
Next
```

Also, the latter problem depends on the ArrayList using System.Object variables internally and manifests itself when you use the ArrayList to store value-typed elements, such as numbers, enumerated values, DataTime values, and any user-defined structure. In fact, when you store a value-typed element in an Object variable, the element must be boxed. As you can recall from the section titled "Reference Types and Value Types" in Chapter 2, "Basic Language Concepts," a box operation takes both CPU cycles and memory from the managed heap, and therefore it should be avoided if possible.

The Traditional Solution

Under previous versions of the .NET Framework you can solve the former problem and make the code more robust by defining a new class that inherits from the CollectionBase type, also in the System.Collections namespace. This type is one of the many abstract types provided in the .NET Framework with the purpose of enabling developers to define their own strong-typed collection classes. Here's a very simple implementation of a custom collection class that can store only integers:

```
Public Class IntegerCollection
   Inherits CollectionBase

   Public Sub Add(ByVal item As Integer)
      Me.List.Add(item)
   End Sub
```

```
   Public Sub Remove(ByVal item As Integer)
      Me.List.Remove(item)
   End Sub

   Default Public Property Item(ByVal index As Integer) As Integer
      Get
         Return CType(Me.List(index), Integer)
      End Get
      Set(ByVal Value As Integer)
         Me.List(index) = Value
      End Set
   End Property
End Class
```

The code is quite simple: each method of your IntegerCollection class takes or returns an Integer value and delegates to a method with the same name as the inner IList object named List. In spite of its simplicity, this solution isn't exactly concise: a real-world class that exposes common methods such as Sort, Find, or Reverse (and all their overloads) would take about a hundred lines. Worse, you'd need a distinct class for each different type of strong-typed collection in your application; for example, a DoubleCollection class to hold Double values, a DateTimeCollection class for DateTime values, and so forth. Granted, you can easily generate these collections by taking a template and performing a search-and-replace operation, but for sure you can think of many other, more pleasant ways to spend your time.

All the code you put in the IntegerCollection class makes the application more robust and slightly less verbose because any attempt to store a noninteger value in the collection is trapped at compile time. Also, reading an element doesn't require a CType operator any longer:

```
' This is the only statement that must be changed from the previous example.
Dim col As New IntegerCollection
...
' Reading an element doesn't require any conversion operator.
Dim element As Integer = col(0)
' Adding anything but an integer raises a compile-time error.
col.Add("abc")                    ' *** This statement doesn't compile.
```

However, the IntegerCollection type doesn't resolve the problem related to performance because integer values are still boxed when they are stored in the inner collection. In fact, this approach makes performance slightly worse because each call to a method in the IntegerCollection class must be routed to the method of the inner List collection.

The Generics-Based Solution

The .NET Framework comes with a new namespace named System.Collections.Generic, which contains several generic collections that can be specialized to contain only values of a given type. For example, see how you can define a collection containing only integer values by means of the new List type:

```
 ' This collection will contain only integer numbers.
Dim col As New List(Of Integer)
```

```
col.Add(11): col.Add(13): col.Add(19)
For Each n As Integer in col
    Console.WriteLine(n)
Next
' Reading an element doesn't require any conversion operator.
Dim element As Integer = col(0)
```

The new Of keyword specifies that the generic List type must be specialized to work with elements of Integer type, and only with that type of element. In fact, assuming that Option Strict is On, any attempt to add elements of a different type raises a compile-time error:

```
' Adding a string causes a compile-time error.
col.Add("abc")                   ' *** This statement doesn't compile.
```

Even if this isn't apparent when looking at the code, the solution based on generics also solves the performance problem because the List(Of Integer) collection stores its elements in Integer slots—in general, in the variables typed after the type specified by the Of clause—and therefore no boxing occurs anywhere.

You can easily prove this point by compiling the following sample code:

```
Dim al As New ArrayList
al.Add(9)
Dim list As New List(Of Integer)
list.Add(9)
```

Here's the corresponding IL code generated by the Visual Basic compiler:

```
//000004:        Dim al As New ArrayList
  IL_0001:  newobj      instance void

[mscorlib]System.Collections.ArrayList::.ctor()
  IL_0006:  stloc.0
//000005:          al.Add(9)
  IL_0007:  ldloc.0
  IL_0008:  ldc.i4.s    9
  IL_000a:  box         [mscorlib]System.Int32
  IL_000f:  callvirt    instance int32
            [mscorlib]System.Collections.ArrayList::Add(object)
  IL_0014:  pop

//000006:        Dim list As New List(Of Integer)
  IL_0015:  newobj      instance void class
            [mscorlib]System.Collections.Generic.List`1<int32>::.ctor()
  IL_001a:  stloc.1
//000007:          list.Add(9)
  IL_001b:  ldloc.1
  IL_001c:  ldc.i4.s    9
  IL_001e:  callvirt    instance void class
            [mscorlib]System.Collections.Generic.List`1<int32>::Add(!0)
```

It isn't essential that you understand the meaning of each IL statement here; the key point is that it requires a box IL opcode (in bold type) to prepare the integer value for being passed to the Add method of the ArrayList object, whereas no such opcode is used when calling the Add method of the List(Of Integer) object.

Because of the missing box operation, adding value-typed items to a generic collection is remarkably faster than is adding the same items to a nongeneric collection, even though the difference can go unnoticed until the repeated box operations cause a garbage collection. In an informal benchmark, adding one million integers to a List object is about six times faster than adding them to an ArrayList is.

You can extract elements from a generic collection and assign them to a strong-typed variable without having to convert them and without causing an unbox operation. This additional optimization can make your read operations faster by a factor of about 30 percent. This speed improvement isn't as impressive as the one that results when you add items, but on the other hand, it occurs even with small collections that don't stress the garbage collector.

The .NET Framework exposes many generic types in addition to the List object just shown: the Dictionary(Of K,V) and SortedDictionary(Of K,V) generic collections enable you to create strong-typed hash tables; the Stack(Of T), Queue(Of T), and LinkedList(Of T) are useful for creating more robust and efficient versions of other common data structures. I cover these and other generic types later in this chapter and in Chapter 13.

Another important note: the type argument you pass when defining a generic instance can be any .NET type, including another generic or nongeneric collection. You can even pass a type that represents an array:

```
' A collection of generic dictionaries
Dim list As New List(Of Dictionary(Of String, Integer))
' A collection of arrays of Integers
Dim arrays As New List(Of Integer())
' Add an array to the collection.
Dim arr() As Integer = {1, 3, 5, 7, 9}
arrays.Add(arr)
' Display the second element of the first array, and then modify it.
Console.WriteLine(arrays(0)(1))           ' => 3
arrays(0)(1) = 999
```

Authoring Generic Types

In addition to using generic types defined in the .NET Framework, Microsoft Visual Basic 2005 also enables you to create your own generic types. As you'll see in a moment, the syntax for doing so is quite intuitive, even though you must account for some nonobvious details.

Generic Parameters

Let's begin with a very simple task: create a strong-typed collection that doesn't allow you to remove or modify an element after you've added it to the collection. The .NET Framework exposes many collection-like types, but none of them has exactly these features. The simplest thing to do is author a generic type named ReadOnlyList and reuse it to store elements of any sort. For simplicity's sake, the ReadOnlyList type uses a private array whose max number of elements must be defined when you instantiate a new collection:

```
Public Class ReadOnlyList(Of T)
    Dim values() As T
    ' The constructor takes the maximum number of elements.
    Public Sub New(ByVal elementCount As Integer)
        ReDim values(elementCount - 1)
    End Sub

    ' The Count read-only property
    Private m_Count As Integer

    Public ReadOnly Property Count() As Integer
        Get
            Return m_Count
        End Get
    End Property

    ' Add a new element to the collection; error if too many elements.
    Public Sub Add(ByVal value As T)
        values(m_Count) = value
        m_Count += 1
    End Sub

    ' Return the Nth element; error if index is out of range.
    Default Public ReadOnly Property Item(ByVal index As Integer) As T
        Get
            If index < 0 OrElse index >= m_Count Then _
                Throw New ArgumentException("Index out of range")
            Return values(index)
        End Get
    End Property
End Class
```

The key point in the preceding code is the declaration of the generic parameter in the first line by means of the Of keyword:

```
Public Class ReadOnlyList(Of T)
```

Once you have defined the generic parameter, you can reuse it anywhere in the class (as well as in any nested class) as if it were a regular type name. For example, the generic parameter T appears in the declaration of the inner values array and in the signature of the Add and Item members (in bold type). You can use the ReadOnlyList generic type as you'd use the List generic type, except that you must provide the maximum number of elements and you can't remove or modify any element after you've added it:

```
' This read-only list can contain up to 1,000 integer values.
Dim roList As New ReadOnlyList(Of Integer)(1000)
roList.Add(123)
Console.WriteLine(roList(0))                         ' => 123
' *** Next statement causes a compilation error: "Property Item is readonly."
roList(0) = 234
```

When you work with generics, you need a way to distinguish a generic type such as List(Of T), which contains one or more type parameters, from a generic type such as List(Of Integer), where the type parameter has been replaced (or *bound*) to a specific type. A type of the former kind is known as *generic type definition*, *open generic type*, or *unbound generic type*, whereas a type of the latter type is known as *bound generic type*.

Interestingly, the T generic parameter can be reused to define or instantiate other generic types. For example, you can simplify the ReadOnlyList class by using a private List(Of T) object instead of an array; incidentally, this change relieves you of the requirement of passing the maximum number of elements to the constructor:

```
Public Class ReadOnlyList2(Of T)
   Dim values As List(Of T)

   ' The constructor can take the maximum number of elements. (Default value is 16.)
   Public Sub New(Optional ByVal elementCount As Integer = 16)
      values = New List(Of T)(elementCount)
   End Sub

   ' The Count read-only property
   Public ReadOnly Property Count() As Integer
      Get
         Return values.Count
      End Get
   End Property

   ' Add a new element to the collection.
   Public Sub Add(ByVal value As T)
      values.Add(value)
   End Sub

   ' Return the Nth element; error if index is out of range.
   Default Public ReadOnly Property Item(ByVal index As Integer) As T
      Get
         Return values(index)
      End Get
   End Property
End Class
```

The first problem you face when working with generics is that you can't really make any assumption on the type that will be passed to the generic type parameter. For example, the Add method receives an element of the generic type T, but it can't invoke any method on this element except those inherited from System.Object. For the same reason, you can't use any operator on an element of type T, including math and comparison operators, the Is operator, and the IsNot operator. For example, the simplest way to test a value against Nothing is by means of the Object.Equals static method:

```
   Public Sub Add(ByVal value As T)
      ' Add only nonnull elements to the collection.
      If Not Object.Equals(value, Nothing) Then values.Add(value)
   End Sub
```

(Notice that value types can't be equal to Nothing; therefore, the Then statement is always executed if you pass a value type.) Because of these limitations and the inability to invoke methods in the type referenced by the parameter T, generics are best used as *containers* for objects that don't have an active role. Later in this chapter, you'll learn how you can use constraints to be able to invoke members on contained objects.

Multiple Generic Parameters

A generic class can also take multiple generic parameters. For example, consider the following Relation type, a simple class that enables you to create a one-to-one relation between two instances of a given type:

```
Public Class Relation(Of T1, T2)
   Public ReadOnly Object1 As T1
   Public ReadOnly Object2 As T2

   Public Sub New(ByVal obj1 As T1, ByVal obj2 As T2)
      Me.Object1 = obj1
      Me.Object2 = obj2
   End Sub
End Class
```

In spite of its simplicity, the Relation class can be quite useful to expand your object hierarchy with new features. For example, let's say that you have defined a Person class (which holds personal data about an individual) and a Company type (which holds information about a company). The Relation type enables you to indicate for which company a given person works:

```
Dim ca As New Company("Code Architects")
Dim john As New Person("John", "Evans")
Dim relJohnCa As New Relation(Of Person, Company)(john, ca)
Dim ann As New Person("Ann", "Beebe")
Dim relAnnCa As New Relation(Of Person, Company)(ann, ca)
```

In a real program, you typically deal with many persons and many companies, so you'd be better off creating a strong-typed list that can contain Relation objects. This can be achieved by using nested Of keywords:

```
Dim relations As New List(Of Relation(Of Person, Company))
relations.Add(relJohnCa)
relations.Add(relAnnCa)
```

The ability to nest Of keywords is a very powerful technique that extends the power of generics remarkably. For example, the following code extracts all the persons who work for a given company:

```
Function GetEmployees(ByVal relations As List(Of Relation(Of Person, Company)), _
      ByVal company As Company) As List(Of Person)
   Dim result As New List(Of Person)
   For Each rel As Relation(Of Person, Company) In relations
```

```
      If rel.Object2 Is company Then result.Add(rel.Object1)
   Next
   Return result
End Function
```

You might continue the previous example by extracting all the employees of the Code Architects company, as follows:

```
For Each p As Person In GetEmployees(relations, ca)
   Console.WriteLine(p.FirstName & " " & p.LastName)
Next
```

As you can see, using nested Of keywords can make your code quite contorted and nearly unreadable. The following section shows how you can simplify things.

Generic Methods

You can also use the Of keyword in the definition of a method. Consider the following procedure, which you can place inside a module:

```
' Exchange two arguments passed by address.
Public Sub Swap(Of T)(ByRef x As T, ByRef y As T)
   Dim tmp As T = x
   x = y
   y = tmp
End Sub
```

You can call the Swap method by passing two variables of the same type:

```
Dim n1 As Integer = 123
Dim n2 As Integer = 456
Swap(Of Integer)(n1, n2)
Console.WriteLine("n1={0}, n2={1}", n1, n2)     ' => n1=456, n2=123
```

It's remarkable that in most cases the Visual Basic compiler doesn't even require the Of keyword in the method invocation:

```
' The following statement works correctly.
Swap(n1, n2)
```

At times you do need to specify the Of clause when invoking a generic method. Consider the following definition:

```
Sub DoSomething(Of T)(ByVal x As T, ByVal y As T)
   ...
End Sub
```

The following client code works correctly even if no Of keyword is used because the compiler can determine the generic parameter to be passed behind the scenes by looking at the type of the first argument passed to the method:

```
DoSomething(123, 456)          ' Same as DoSomething(Of Integer)
DoSomething(123.56, 456.78)    ' Same as DoSomething(Of Double)
```

However, you have a problem when the two arguments have a different type. For example, this code:

```
Dim l As Long = 456
Dim n As Integer = 123
DoSomething(l, n)
```

fails to compile with the following error message:

```
Type argument inference failed for type parameter 'T' of 'Public Sub DoSomething(Of T)
(x As T, y As T)'. Type argument inferred from the argument passed to parameter 'y'
conflicts with the type argument inferred from the argument passed to parameter 'x'.
```

This error message is a bit surprising because if the compiler looks at the first value passed to the method and infers that type T stands for Long, it should be able to automatically convert the second argument from Integer to Long. However, it is evident that in this case the Visual Basic compiler isn't able to perform even a widening conversion automatically.

You can get rid of the compilation error in two ways: either by manually converting the second argument to the same type as the first one or by specifying the Of clause in the method call:

```
' Both these statements work correctly.
DoSomething(l, CLng(n))
DoSomething(Of Long)(l, n)
```

Finally notice that only generic methods are supported; there is no such thing as a generic property, field, or event. In other words, Visual Basic refuses to compile this code:

```
Property Value(Of T)() As T
    …
End Property
```

However, you can have a property that reuses a generic parameter defined in the enclosing class:

```
Public Class Item(Of T)
    Property Value() As T
        …
    End Property
End Class
```

Setting the Default Value

One interesting detail about Visual Basic generics is that you can deal with reference types and value types in the same way. To see what I mean, let's extend the implementation of the ReadOnlyList class with the ability to clear all the elements that are currently stored in the collection:

```
' (Inside the ReadOnlyList class…)
Public Sub Reset()
    ' Reset all existing elements to the type's default value.
```

```
      For i As Integer = 0 To Me.Count - 1
         values(i) = Nothing
      Next
   End Sub
```

The purpose of the Reset method is to assign the type's default value to each element; if the ReadOnlyList class stores strings or other kinds of objects, the default value is Nothing. However, if the ReadOnlyList class stores numbers or other value types, assigning the Nothing value should throw an exception at run time because you can't store Nothing in a value type variable, right?

Wrong. When Nothing is assigned to a variable typed after a generic parameter—as is the case of the values array in preceding code—the assignment is guaranteed not to fail even if the generic argument designates a value type. In this case, the default value for that type—that is, zero for numeric types, a null globally unique identifier (GUID) for the System.Guid type, and so forth—is assigned instead.

Even if it isn't immediately apparent, this feature enables you to test whether a given element matches the default value for the type. Here's an example:

```
Function IsDefaultValue(Of T)(ByVal value As T) As Boolean
   Dim defValue As T = Nothing
   Return Object.Equals(value, defValue)
End Function
```

Generic Interfaces

You can use generics with classes, structures, interfaces, and delegates (but not with modules and enum types). Generic structures work exactly the same way as generic classes do, but generic interfaces need some additional clarifications. The following code defines a generic interface and a class that implements that interface:

```
Interface IAdder(Of T)
   Function Add(ByVal n1 As T, ByVal n2 As T) As T
End Interface

Class Adder
   Implements IAdder(Of Integer)

   Public Function Add(ByVal n1 As Integer, ByVal n2 As Integer) As Integer _
         Implements IAdder(Of Integer).Add
      Return n1 + n2
   End Function
End Class
```

It is legal to implement multiple versions of the same generic interface, as in this code:

```
Class Adder
   Implements IAdder(Of Integer), IAdder(Of Double)

   Public Function Add(ByVal n1 As Integer, ByVal n2 As Integer) As Integer _
         Implements IAdder(Of Integer).Add
```

```
        Return n1 + n2
    End Function

    Public Function Add(ByVal n1 As Double, ByVal n2 As Double) As Double _
        Implements IAdder(Of Double).Add
        Return n1 + n2
    End Function
End Class
```

The most important difference between a standard interface and a generic interface is that the latter can avoid a box operation when method arguments are of a value type. For example, before generics were introduced the only way you could define a universal IAdder interface was to use Object arguments, as in the following:

```
Interface IAdder
    Function Add(ByVal n1 As Object, ByVal n2 As Object) As Object
End Interface
```

Implementing such an interface in a class would require that both the arguments and the return value—all of which are numbers, and therefore value types—be boxed and unboxed. By comparison, no boxing occurs when you implement the IAdder(Of T) interface if T is a value type.

The .NET Framework defines several generic interfaces, most of which are the generic version of weakly typed interfaces. These are the most important ones:

- IComparable(Of T), the strong-typed version of IComparable

- IComparer(Of T), the strong-typed version of IComparer

- IEquatable(Of T), which exposes an Equals method that takes an argument of a specific type

- IEnumerable(Of T) and IEnumerator(Of T), which allow a class to support For Each loops

- ICollection(Of T), which represents a collection of elements of type T

- IList(Of T), which represents a series of elements of type T

- IDictionary(Of K, V), which represents a dictionary of elements of type V indexed by keys of type K.

If the type that implements the interface is itself a generic type, the generic parameter can appear in the Of clause of the Implements statement, as in the following code:

```
Public Class TestComparer(Of T)
    Implements IComparer(Of T)
    Public Function Compare(ByVal x As T, ByVal y As T) As Integer _
        Implements IComparer(Of T).Compare
        ...
    End Function
End Class
```

In practice, however, implementing generic interfaces in this way is difficult and sometimes impossible. For example, there is no simple way to implement correctly the Compare method in the previous code snippet because the code inside the method can't make any assumption about how two elements of type T can be compared to each other and can't use comparison operators with them. (You can sometimes work around this limitation by enforcing a constraint on the generic parameter, as you'll learn in a following section.)

Interestingly, many primitive .NET types have been expanded to implement the IEquatable(Of T) and IComparable(Of T) interfaces. For example, you can now invoke the strong-typed versions of the Equals and IComparable interfaces for all numeric types:

```
Sub TestInteger(ByVal value As Integer)
    ' These statements box their value in .NET Framework 1.1, but not in .NET Framework 2.0.
    If value.Equals(0) Then Console.WriteLine("It's zero")
    If value.CompareTo(0) > 0 Then Console.WriteLine("It's positive")
End Sub
```

You can't use the generic parameter as a direct argument of the Implements keyword. In other words, the following statements don't compile:

```
Public Class TestClass(Of T)
    Implements T
    …
End Class
```

> **Note** A few generic interfaces inherit from the corresponding nongeneric one. For example, IEnumerable(Of T) inherits from IEnumerable; therefore, a class that implements the generic interface must implement both the IEnumerable(Of T).GetEnumerator method and the IEnumerator.GetEnumerator. Similarly, the IEnumerator(Of T) interface inherits from IEnumerator; therefore, a class that implements IEnumerator(Of T) must expose all three members of IEnumerator plus the strongly typed version of the Current property. (For more information about the IEnumerator interface, read Chapter 10, "Interfaces.")

Generics and Overloading

You can define generic types that have the same name but different numbers of generic parameters. For example, the following classes can coexist in the same namespace:

```
Public Class MyType
    …
End Class

Public Class MyType(Of T)
    …
End Class

Public Class MyType(Of T, K)
    …
End Class
```

This feature is similar to method overloading in the sense that the compiler chooses the type with the number of generic parameters that matches the number of generic arguments passed by the calling code:

```
Dim t1 As MyType                    ' An instance of the first class
Dim t2 As MyType(Of Long)           ' An instance of the second class
Dim t3 As MyType(Of Long, Double)   ' An instance of the third class
```

Similarly, you can define multiple methods with the same name and different sets of generic parameters. In this case, however, the rules are slightly more complicated and you must be aware of a few subtleties. Let's consider the following methods:

```
Sub DoTask(Of T, P)(ByVal x As T, ByVal y As P)
   Console.WriteLine("First version")
End Sub

Sub DoTask(Of T)(ByVal x As T, ByVal y As String)
   Console.WriteLine("Second version")
End Sub

Sub DoTask(Of T)(ByVal x As T, ByVal y As T)
   Console.WriteLine("Third version")
End Sub
```

In most cases, the Visual Basic compiler is smart enough to generate code that invokes the most specific version, even if you omit the Of clause in the method call:

```
DoTask(123, 456.78)      ' Calls DoTask(Of Integer, Double)
DoTask(123, "abc")       ' Calls DoTask(Of Integer, String)
```

However, if you attempt to pass two arguments of the same type, for example, two integers, the compiler complains and explains that overload resolution failed because no method is specific to the arguments being passed:

```
' *** Next statement raises a compilation error.
DoTask(123, 123)
```

To solve the problem you must give the compiler a hint about which version you want to be invoked:

```
' Next statement compiles correctly and invokes the third version of the method.
DoTask(Of Integer)(123, 123)
```

Generics and Inheritance

Earlier in this chapter, I stated that you can use a generic parameter anywhere in a class, as if it were a regular type name. Well, that description wasn't exactly accurate because a few exceptions exist:

- You can't use a generic parameter in the Inherits clause; in other words, you can't inherit from a type passed as a generic parameter.

- You can't use a generic parameter to reference an interface in the Implements clause, as I explain at the end of the section titled "Generic Interfaces" earlier in this chapter.

- You can't use a generic parameter in an attribute declaration.

- You can't use a generic parameter in a Declare statement or a method that is marked with the DllImport attribute, that is, in a method that runs unmanaged code.

The first limitation implies that you can't inherit a type from another type defined by means of a generic parameter:

```
' *** The following code doesn't compile.
Public Class TestClass(Of T)
   Inherits T
   …
End Class
```

Nothing prevents you, however, from using a generic type in the Inherits clause, which is in fact a rather common case. For example, the following two classes are based on the Relation type defined in an earlier section:

```
Public Class PersonCompanyRelation
   Inherits Relation(Of Person, Company)

   Public Sub New(ByVal person As Person, ByVal company As Company)
      MyBase.New(person, company)
   End Sub
End Class

Public Class PersonCompanyRelationList
   Inherits List(Of PersonCompanyRelation)
End Class
```

Thanks to these two classes, the client code that puts Person and Company objects in relation to each other can be simplified as follows:

```
Dim ca As New Company("Code Architects")
Dim john As New Person("John", "Evans")
Dim ann As New Person("Ann", "Beebe")

Dim relations As New PersonCompanyRelationList
Dim relJohnCa As New PersonCompanyRelation(john, ca)
relations.Add(relJohnCa)
relations.Add(New PersonCompanyRelation(ann, ca))
```

The GetEmployees method has a simpler and more readable declaration as well:

```
Function GetEmployees(ByVal relations As PersonCompanyRelationList, _
      ByVal company As Company) As List(Of Person)
   Dim result As New List(Of Person)
   For Each rel As Relation(Of Person, Company) In relations
      If rel.Object2 Is company Then result.Add(rel.Object1)
   Next
   Return result
End Function
```

The practice of defining and using a standard class that inherits from and wraps a generic type has several advantages:

- The structure and the syntax of client code are simpler.

- The client code can be written even in .NET languages that don't support generics, or even in unmanaged code.

Generics are fully CLS-compliant; therefore, all major .NET languages support them and you can freely expose them as parameters or return values of public methods. Even so, however, you might decide not to expose a generic type to the outside of your assembly to keep it fully interoperable with all .NET languages as well as with unmanaged clients.

Generics and the TypeOf . . . Is Operator

In general, a bound generic type can be used whenever you can use a regular type, as in this code:

```
If TypeOf obj Is List(Of String) Then
    Dim list As List(Of String) = DirectCast(obj, List(Of String))
End If
```

This rule holds true only for bound generic types, which represent real types, and isn't valid for open generic types, which represent a type definition rather than a real type. For example, the following code isn't valid (unless it appears inside a generic type that takes the T parameter):

```
' *** This code causes the following compile error: Type T is not defined.
If TypeOf obj Is List(Of T) Then
    ' obj is an open list type, such as List(Of Integer) or List(Of String).
End If
```

The previous test is rarely useful, because—even if it were a valid Visual Basic statement—you couldn't cast an object instance to a generic List(Of T) variable. As a matter of fact, you can't define such a variable:

```
' *** This statement causes two compile errors: Type T is not defined.
Dim list as List(Of T) = DirectCast(obj, List(Of T))
```

Let's see which options you have. If you simply must determine whether an object is an instance of a bound generic type, you can use this code:

```
If obj IsNot Nothing AndAlso obj.GetType().IsGenericType Then
    ' obj is an instance of a generic type.
End If
```

However, if you need to check whether an object is an instance of a generic bound type that derives from a given open generic definition, such as a type of the form List(Of T), you must use a different approach, one based on reflection. The FullName of a generic type definition consists of the complete name of the generic class, followed by an inverse quote character, and then the number of type parameters. For example, the full name of the List(Of T) generic type definition is this:

```
System.Collections.Generic.List`1
```

The FullName of a bound generic type is obtained by concatenating the complete name of the type arguments (enclosed between square brackets) to the previous string. For example, the full name of the List(Of Integer) type is

```
System.Collections.Generic.List`1[[System.Int32, mscorlib, Version=2.0.0.0,
   Culture=neutral, PublicKeyToken=b77a5c561934e089]]
```

Armed with this knowledge, you can test whether an object instance is a bound generic type of a List(Of T) using this code:

```
If obj IsNot Nothing AndAlso obj.GetType().FullName.StartsWith( _
      "System.Collections.Generic.List`1") Then
   ' obj is a generic type of the form List(Of T).
End If
```

However, notice that the previous test isn't perfectly equivalent to the TypeOf operator, which also tests whether the first argument is an instance of any type derived from the type specified in the second argument. If you must perform this sort of test, you must adopt a technique based on reflection:

```
' Test whether obj is a List(Of T) or derives from a List(Of T) type.
If obj IsNot Nothing Then
   Dim type As Type = obj.GetType()
   Do
      If type.FullName.StartsWith("System.Collections.Generic.List`1") Then
         Console.WriteLine("TypeOf obj Is List(Of T) is true!")
         Exit Do
      End If
      type = type.BaseType
   Loop Until type Is Nothing
End If
```

You can read more about reflection, the GetType operator, and the methods of the System.Type class in Chapter 18, "Reflection."

Testing and Converting Generic Values

A common problem with generics is that no evident way exists to convert a generic value into a more specific type. For example, consider this code:

```
Sub TestMethod(Of T)(ByVal value As T)
   If TypeOf value Is Integer Then         ' *** Compilation error
      Dim n As Integer = CInt(value)       ' *** Compilation error
      ...
   End If
End Sub
```

The comments highlight the two statements that cause a compilation error. The first error occurs because the first argument of TypeOf must be a reference type, but the compiler has no clue about the generic T type; the second error occurs because the compiler knows nothing about the T type and can't guarantee that the CInt operator can convert an instance of T into an integer.

In cases like this, the simplest solution is to convert the argument to Object and then deal with it as you would normally:

```
Sub CheckArguments(Of T)(ByVal value As T)
   Dim obj As Object = CObj(value)
   If TypeOf obj Is Integer Then
      Dim n As Integer = CInt(obj)
      …
   End If
End Sub
```

The problem with this approach is that it causes the value to be boxed if T is a value type. If you don't need to extract its value and want simply to test its type, you can save a box operation by means of a reflection-based technique:

```
   If value IsNot Nothing AndAlso value.GetType() Is GetType(Integer) Then
      …
   End If
```

Generic Constraints

Consider the following generic method, which returns the highest value among its arguments:

```
Public Function Max(Of T)(ByVal ParamArray values() As T) As T
   Dim result As T = values(0)
   For i As Integer = 1 To UBound(values)
      ' *** The next statement causes the following compilation error:
      '     "Operator '>' is not defined for types 'T' and 'T'."
      If values(i) > result Then result = values(i)
   Next
   Return result
End Function
```

As the remark in the preceding code indicates, the greater than sign (>) causes a compilation error because the compiler can't be sure that client code calls the method only with arguments that support this operator. This problem occurs quite frequently when you are working with generics, but you can work around it by enforcing a constraint for the T type. For example, you can require that the method be called only with types that support the IComparable interface:

```
Public Function Max(Of T As IComparable)(ByVal ParamArray values() As T) As T
   …
End Function
```

Because T surely exposes the IComparable interface, the code in the method can safely invoke the CompareTo method to calculate the highest value in the array:

```
Public Function Max(Of T As IComparable)(ByVal ParamArray values() As T) As T
   Dim result As T = values(0)
   For i As Integer = 1 To UBound(values)
      If result.CompareTo(values(i)) < 0 Then result = values(i)
   Next
   Return result
End Function
```

Here's a piece of client code that uses the Max function:

```
' No need to specify the Of clause in calling the method.
Console.WriteLine(Max(12, 23, 6, -1))                          ' => 23
```

Visual Basic 2005 supports five types of constraints:

- **Interface constraint**   The type argument must implement the specified interface.
- **Inheritance constraint**   The type argument must derive from the specified base class.
- **Class constraint**   The type argument must be a reference type.
- **Structure constraint**   The type argument must be a value type.
- **New constraint**   The type argument must expose a public parameterless (default) constructor.

Notice that you can't define a constraint specifying that a type must expose a constructor with a given signature; the New constraint ensures that one of the public constructors of the type has no arguments.

You can read more about these constraint types in the following sections.

The Interface Constraint

This kind of constraint is often used with the IComparable interface, as in the code example just shown. For instance, here's an interesting recursive method that returns the median value in a list. (The median of a list of N elements is the value that is greater than $N/2$ elements and less than the remaining $N/2$ elements.)

```
Function MedianValue(Of T As IComparable)(ByVal list As List(Of T), _
      Optional ByVal position As Integer = -1) As T
   ' Provide a default value for second argument.
   If position < 0 Then position = list.Count \ 2

   ' If the list has just one element, we've found its median.
   Dim guess As T = list(0)
   If list.Count = 1 Then Return guess
   ' This list will contain values lower and higher than the current guess.
   Dim lowerList As New List(Of T)
   Dim higherList As New List(Of T)

   For i As Integer = 1 To list.Count - 1
      Dim value As T = list(i)
      If guess.CompareTo(value) <= 0 Then
         ' The value is higher than or equal to the current guess.
         higherList.Add(value)
      Else
         ' The value is lower than the current guess.
         lowerList.Add(value)
      End If
   Next
```

```
   If lowerList.Count > position Then
      ' The median value must be in the lower-than list.
      Return MedianValue(lowerList, position)
   ElseIf lowerList.Count < position Then
      ' The median value must be in the higher-than list.
      Return MedianValue(higherList, position - lowerList.Count - 1)
   Else
      ' The guess is correct.
      Return guess
   End If
End Function
```

Of course, you can evaluate the median value of an array by sorting the array and then picking the element at index $N/2$, but MedianValue is typically faster because it saves you the sort step.

You can retrieve other interesting values in a list by passing a second argument to the Median-Value method. For example, by passing the value 0, the method returns the lowest value in the list; by passing the value 1, the method returns the second lowest value in the list; by passing the value $N - 1$, the method returns the highest value in a list of N elements; by passing the value $N - 2$, the method returns the second highest value in the list, and so forth.

You can specify a generic interface as a constraint. For example, you can improve the Median-Value as follows:

```
Function MedianValue(Of T As IComparable(Of T))(ByVal list As List(Of T), _
   Optional ByVal position As Integer = -1) As T
   …
End Function
```

The advantage of using a generic interface instead of a weakly typed interface is that no boxing occurs when the new version of the MedianValue method invokes the CompareTo method of the interface:

```
   ' In the new version of MedianValue, this statement causes no boxing.
   If guess.CompareTo(value) <= 0 Then
```

All numeric types in the .NET Framework implement the IComparable(Of T) and IEquatable(Of T) interfaces; thus, the new version of the MedianValue method can work with all the integer and floating-point numeric types. If you define a new numeric data type, it is strongly recommended that you implement the IComparable(Of T) and IEquatable(Of T) generic interfaces.

You can use the interface constraint with any interface, not just IComparable. For example, a constraint for the ISerializable interface ensures that the generic type or method can be used only with types that can be serialized and deserialized from a file or a database field. (Read Chapter 21, "Serialization," for more information about the ISerializable interface.) In the remainder of this chapter, I provide other examples of interface constraints.

The Inheritance Constraint

The inheritance constraint tells the Visual Basic compiler that a generic argument can only be a type that derives from the specified class. The syntax is similar to the interface constraint:

```
' This generic class can be used only with types that derive
' from System.Windows.Forms.Control.
Public Class ControlCollection(Of T As System.Windows.Forms.Control)
   Inherits List(Of T)
   ...
End Class
```

Because of the inheritance constraint, you can use the ControlCollection class to create a collection of Button or TextBox controls, but not Person or Company objects. In addition to improved robustness, the inheritance constraint gives you the ability to invoke any Public member of the type specified by the constraint. For example, the code in the ControlCollection class can safely access members of the Control type, such as the Text and ForeColor properties. Unfortunately, the presence of the inheritance constraint doesn't suffice to enable you to invoke the constructor of the class because classes that derive from the same base type can define a different set of constructors and even have no constructors at all. (See the section titled "The New Constraint" later in this chapter for more details.)

A few generics defined in the .NET Framework use the inheritance constraint. For example, the System.EventHandler(Of T) generic type is a delegate that can be used to define an event and mandates that the T type inherits from System.EventArgs. If EventHandler(Of T) were defined in Visual Basic, it would look like this:

```
Public Delegate Sub EventHandler(Of T As EventArgs)(ByVal sender As Object, ByVal e As T)
```

(You can see this type in action in the section titled "Generics and Events" later in this chapter.) There are a few restrictions for the type that follows the As clause in an inheritance constraint. For obvious reasons, the type can't be sealed (NotInheritable in Visual Basic) and therefore it can't be a structure. Also, you can't use the System.Object, System.ValueType, or System.Delegate types or any delegate type.

The Class and Structure Constraints

A generic parameter can be followed by the As Class clause, to specify that the type parameter is a reference type, or by the As Structure clause, to indicate that the type parameter is a value type:

```
Public Class ObjectCollection(Of T As Class)
   ...
End Class

Public Class ValueCollection(Of T As Structure)
   ...
End Class
```

> **Note**   In theory you might have two generic types with the same name that differ only by the Class or Structure constraint applied to their generic argument because the Visual Basic compiler should be able to use one or the other depending on whether the generic argument is a class or a structure. However, the compiler isn't that smart, and the general rule still applies: a namespace can contain two generic types with the same name only if they take a different number of generic parameters.

The class constraint (but not the structure constraint) adds the ability to use the Is, IsNot, and TypeOf . . . Is operators. For example, if you apply this constraint to the type parameters of the Relation generic class, you can define a Contains method that uses the Is operator to check whether a given object is part of the relation:

```vb
Public Class Relation(Of T1 As Class, T2 As Class)
    Public ReadOnly Object1 As T1
    Public ReadOnly Object2 As T2

    Public Sub New(ByVal obj1 As T1, ByVal obj2 As T2)
        Me.Object1 = obj1
        Me.Object2 = obj2
    End Sub

    Public Function Contains(ByVal obj As Object) As Boolean
        Return Me.Object1 Is obj OrElse Me.Object2 Is obj
    End Function
End Class
```

Notice that you must define the Contains method so that it takes a generic Object argument. In this particular case, it doesn't really affect the quality of your code because the two objects passed to the constructor of the Relation class are reference types and therefore no box operation occurs when the Contains method is used appropriately (unless you mistakenly pass it a value-typed element that isn't part of the relation). You might believe that you can enforce a more robust code by offering two overloads for the Contains method, as in the following:

```vb
    Public Function Contains(ByVal obj As T1) As Boolean
        Return Me.Object1 Is obj
    End Function
    Public Function Contains(ByVal obj As T2) As Boolean
        Return Me.Object1 Is obj
    End Function
```

This code compiles correctly, but only as long as the client code never creates a Relation object whose two generic parameters are the same type. For example, the following code doesn't compile:

```vb
Dim john As New Person("John", "Evans")
Dim ann As New Person("Ann", "Beebe")
Dim rel As New Relation(Of Person, Person)(john, ann)
' Next statement raises the following compilation error: "Overload resolution
' failed because no accessible 'Contains' is most specific for these arguments..."
Dim found As Boolean = rel.Contains(john)
```

Here's what has happened: when the compiler replaces both T1 and T2 with the Person type, it finds that two Contains methods are using the same signature. Oddly, the compiler should flag the statement that creates the Relation object as an error because the resulting bound generic class contains two overloaded methods with the same signature. Instead, the error is emitted only if the project actually contains a call to that method. Mysteries of .NET generics …

The New Constraint

The New constraint adds the requirement that the type passed as the generic parameter has a public parameterless constructor. This constraint allows you to create instances of the specified type, so you often use it in factory methods such as the following:

```
Public Function CreateObject(Of T As New) As T
   Return New T
End Function
```

A better example shows how you can initialize an array of objects of a given type:

```
Public Function CreateArray(Of T As New)(ByVal numEls As Integer) As T()
   Dim values(numEls - 1) As T
   For i As Integer = 0 To numEls - 1
      values(i) = New T
   Next
   Return values
End Function
```

The New constraint is often used in conjunction with other constraints, as explained in the followed section.

Multiple Constraints

It is possible to enforce more than one constraint by enclosing the constraints in a pair of braces. This syntax is especially useful to combine the New constraint with the interface constraint or the inheritance constraint, or to enforce multiple interface constraints on the same generic parameter, as in this code:

```
Public Class Widget(Of T As {New, IComparable}, V As {IComparable, IConvertible})
   …
End Class
```

The following example uses a compound constraint to implement a generic type that behaves like a sortable array:

```
Public Class SortableArray(Of T, C As {New, IComparer(Of T)})
   Dim values() As T

   Public Sub New(ByVal highestIndex As Integer)
      ReDim values(highestIndex)
   End Sub

   Public Sub Sort()
      ' Sort the array using the specified comparer object.
```

```vb
        Array.Sort(values, New C)
    End Sub

    Default Public Property Item(ByVal index As Integer) As T
        Get
            Return values(index)
        End Get
        Set(ByVal value As T)
            values(index) = value
        End Set
    End Property
End Class
```

To see the SortableArray class in action you must define a suitable comparer class, which can be as simple as this one:

```vb
Public Class ReverseIntegerComparer
    Implements IComparer(Of Integer)

    Public Function Compare(ByVal x As Integer, ByVal y As Integer) As Integer _
            Implements IComparer(Of Integer).Compare
        ' Return -1 if x > y, +1 if x < y, 0 if x = y.
        Return Math.Sign(y - x)
    End Function
End Class
```

Finally, you can define a SortableArray object that contains integers and that, when sorted, arranges elements in reverse order:

```vb
' A sortable array that can contain 11 elements
Dim arr As New SortableArray(Of Integer, ReverseIntegerComparer)(10)
arr(0) = 123
...
' Sort the array (in reverse order).
arr.Sort()
```

Note   You might wonder why the Compare method uses a Math.Sign function instead of a simpler call to the CompareTo method, exposed by the IComparable interface:

```vb
Return DirectCast(y, IComparable).CompareTo(x)
```

The reason is subtle and has to do with performance. The previous statement, in fact, causes two hidden box operations: first, the *y* variable is boxed when it is cast to the IComparable interface; second, the *x* Integer value is passed to an Object argument and therefore must be boxed as well. You can avoid the second box operation by casting to the IComparable(Of Integer) interface, as in this code:

```vb
Return DirectCast(y, IComparable(Of Integer)).CompareTo(x)
```

However, you can't avoid the first box operation, caused by the DirectCast operator, which in turn is necessary because the CompareTo method is private and can be accessed only through the IComparable interface.

In this particular case you can improve performance by passing the *y – x* difference to the Math.Sign method; when you have no other solution but to use DirectCast to invoke a private interface member, you can't avoid the extra box operation.

Checking a Constraint at Run Time

As sophisticated as it is, the constraint mechanism isn't perfect. For example, it isn't possible to request that a type passed as an argument implements *either* interface A or interface B (or both), or that it *doesn't* implement an interface or inherit from a given base class, or that it is marked with a given attribute, or that it exposes a method or a constructor with a given name and signature. And you can't check that *at least* one of the type arguments (but not necessarily all of them) implement a given interface. In cases like these, you can't specify a standard constraint; instead, the best you can do is check the condition at run time.

Provided that you know how to test the condition, it's easy to check the constraint in the generic type's constructor, as in this case:

```
Public Class ClassWithRuntimeConstraint(Of T)
    Sub New()
        ' Check that the T type implements either IDisposable or ICloneable.
        ' (We need reflection to perform this test.)
        If Not GetType(IDisposable).IsAssignableFrom(GetType(T)) AndAlso _
            Not GetType(ICloneable).IsAssignableFrom(GetType(T)) Then
            Throw New ArgumentException("Invalid type argument")
        End If
        ' Continue here with the constructor…
    End Sub
End Class
```

Although this approach works, it is less than optimal because the condition is checked each time an instance of the TestClass type is created. A better approach is to place the condition in the static constructor of the type, which is executed only once during the application's lifetime:

```
    ' Check type constraint in the static type constructor.
    Shared Sub New()
        If Not GetType(IDisposable).IsAssignableFrom(GetType(T)) AndAlso _
            Not GetType(ICloneable).IsAssignableFrom(GetType(T)) Then
            Throw New ArgumentException("Invalid type argument")
        End If
    End Sub
```

Advanced Topics

Generic types are new, powerful tools in the hands of expert developers. As with all power tools, it takes some time to master them.

Nullable Types

Virtually all databases support the concept of nullable columns, namely, columns that can contain the special NULL value. Such a special value is often used as an alias for "unknown value" or "unassigned value." The use of nullable columns tends to make database-oriented applications more complicated than they need to be. For example, you can't move a value from a nullable numeric column into an Int32 or Double .NET variable without testing the value against the DBNull.Value special value. (The actual method or operation you must perform depends on the ADO.NET object you're using.)

Microsoft .NET Framework version 2.0 introduces the concept of nullable types, that is, value types that can be assigned a special null value. Notice that only value types need to be treated in this way because reference types—such as strings and arrays—can use the Nothing value as an alias for the null state.

As you probably have already guessed by now, .NET nullable types are based on generics. For example, here's how you can define a nullable Integer value:

```
' Declare an "unassigned" nullable value.
Dim n As Nullable(Of Integer)
' Assign it a value.
n = 123
' Reset it to the "unassigned" state.
n = Nothing

' You can declare and assign a nullable value in these two ways.
Dim d1 As Nullable(Of Double) = 123.45
Dim d2 As New Nullable(Of Double)(123.45)
```

The Nullable(Of T) generic type exposes two key properties, both of which are read-only. The HasValue property returns False if the element is in the unassigned state; the Value property returns the actual value if HasValue is True; otherwise, it throws an InvalidOperationException object:

```
If n.HasValue Then
   Console.WriteLine("Value is {0}.", n.Value)
Else
   Console.WriteLine("No value has been assigned yet.")
End If
```

The Nullable(Of T) type supports conversions to and from the T type. For example, you can convert a Double value to a Nullable(Of Double) value and vice versa, but the latter conversion fails if the nullable element has no value; therefore, it is considered a narrowing conversion and requires an explicit CType operator (or equivalent, such as CInt or CDbl):

```
Dim value As Double = 123.45
' This conversion can never fail.
Dim value2 As Nullable(Of Double) = value
' The conversion in the opposite direction can fail; thus, it must be explicit.
Dim value3 As Double = CDbl(value2)
```

Even though nullable types appear to be structures, they are given special treatment at the IL level and are often interchangeable with the underlying type they can contain. This special support becomes apparent in the way nullable values are boxed and unboxed. Consider this code:

```
' Create a null value and box it.
Dim n As New Nullable(Of Integer)
Dim obj As Object = n
' obj contains something, yet next statement displays True.
```

```
Console.WriteLine(obj Is Nothing)            ' => True
' You can unbox obj to a Nullable object or directly to an Integer value.
' If the Nullable object has no value, the target variable is assigned the default value.
Dim n2 As Integer = CInt(obj)                ' n2 is assigned 0.
```

Even though you can use a nullable type in most of the places where the corresponding non-nullable type can appear, you have to account for one weird limitation: you can't pass a nullable type as a generic argument that has a structure constraint. In other words, assume you have the following generic class:

```
Public Class TestClass(Of T As Structure)
    ...
End Class
```

If you now attempt to pass a nullable type to the T argument, as in this code:

```
Dim o As TestClass(Of Nullable(Of Integer))
```

you get the following error message:

```
'System.Nullable' does not satisfy the 'Structure' constraint for type
parameter 'T'. Only non-nullable 'Structure' types are allowed.
```

Math and Comparison Operators

Unfortunately, the Nullable(Of T) generic type supports neither math nor comparison operators. In other words, you can't directly add two nullable types. Instead, you must first convert them explicitly to the corresponding numeric type:

```
' This code assumes that d1 and d2 are Nullable(Of Double) elements.
If d1.HasValue AndAlso d2.HasValue Then
    Dim sum As Double = d1.Value + d2.Value
End If
```

Another solution for this issue is based on the GetValueOrDefault method, which returns either the current value (if HasValue is True) or the default value:

```
' Add to nullable numbers, using zero if the value is null.
Dim sum As Double = d1.GetValueOrDefault() + d2.GetValueOrDefault()
```

The GetValueOrDefault method can take one argument, which is used as the default value if HasValue is False:

```
' Assign the current value, or negative infinity if value is null.
Dim value As Double = d1.GetValueOrDefault(Double.NegativeInfinity)
```

You can check whether two nullable values are equal by using the Equals(Of T) method, which nullable types inherit from the IEquatable generic interface. This feature compensates for the lack of support of the equal (=) and not equal (<>) operators:

```
If d1.Equals(0) OrElse d1.Equals(d2) Then
    ' d1 is either zero or is equal to d2.
```

```
ElseIf d1.Equals(Nothing) Then
    ' This is another way to test whether a nullable type has a value.
End If
```

Alternatively, you can use the Nullable.Equals(Of T) static method:

```
If Nullable.Equals(d1, d2) Then
    ' d1 is equal to d2.
End If
```

You can also compare two nullable values by means of the Nullable.Compare static method; according to this method, a null value is always less than any nonnull value:

```
Select Case Nullable.Compare(d1, d2)
    Case -1
        Console.WriteLine("d1 is null or is less than d2")
    Case 1
        Console.WriteLine("d2 is null or is less than d1")
    Case 0
        Console.WriteLine("d1 and d2 have same value or are both null.")End Select
```

Three-Valued Boolean Logic

Three-value logic is quite common when you are dealing with Boolean expressions with operands that can take the True, False, or Unknown value. For example, SQL makes extensive use of three-value logic because it must account for nullable fields. Consider the following SQL statement:

```
SELECT * FROM Customers WHERE City="Rome" Or Country="Vatican"
```

If the City field is NULL, the City="Rome" subexpression is also NULL; however, if Country is equal to "Vatican," the second operand of the Or operator is True, which makes the entire WHERE clause True. In other words, a True operand makes the entire Or expression equal to True even if the other operand is NULL. Likewise, a False operand in an And expression makes the entire expression False, regardless of whether the other operand is known.

Given the similarities of three-value logic values with nullable types you might believe that you can implement the former ones by using the Nullable(Of Boolean) type as a base class and then overload the And, Or, Not, and Xor operators (and a few others). Unfortunately, this isn't a viable solution because the Nullable(Of T) type is a structure and can't be the base class for another type. This means that the only way you can implement three-value logic in your application is by defining a new type from scratch, as in the following code:

```
Public Structure NullableBoolean
    Private m_HasValue As Boolean
    Private m_Value As Boolean

    Sub New(ByVal value As Boolean)
        m_HasValue = True
        m_Value = value
    End Sub
```

```vb
Public ReadOnly Property HasValue() As Boolean
    Get
        Return m_HasValue
    End Get
End Property

Public ReadOnly Property Value() As Boolean
    Get
        If Not m_HasValue Then Throw New InvalidOperationException()
        Return m_Value
    End Get
End Property

Public Overrides Function ToString() As String
    If Me.HasValue Then
        Return Me.Value.ToString()
    Else
        Return "Null"
    End If
End Function

Public Shared Operator =(ByVal v1 As NullableBoolean, _
        ByVal v2 As NullableBoolean) As NullableBoolean
    If v1.HasValue AndAlso v2.HasValue Then
        Return New NullableBoolean(v1.Value = v2.Value)
    Else
        Return New NullableBoolean
    End If
End Operator

Public Shared Operator <>(ByVal v1 As NullableBoolean, _
        ByVal v2 As NullableBoolean) As NullableBoolean
    Return Not (v1 = v2)
End Operator

Public Shared Operator And(ByVal v1 As NullableBoolean, _
        ByVal v2 As NullableBoolean) As NullableBoolean
    If (v1.HasValue AndAlso v1.Value = False) OrElse _
            (v2.HasValue AndAlso v2.Value = False) Then
        Return New NullableBoolean(False)
    ElseIf v1.HasValue AndAlso v2.HasValue Then
        Return New NullableBoolean(True)
    Else
        Return New NullableBoolean()
    End If
End Operator

Public Shared Operator Or(ByVal v1 As NullableBoolean, _
        ByVal v2 As NullableBoolean) As NullableBoolean
    If (v1.HasValue AndAlso v1.Value) OrElse _
            (v2.HasValue AndAlso v2.Value) Then
        Return New NullableBoolean(True)
    ElseIf v1.HasValue AndAlso v2.HasValue Then
        Return New NullableBoolean(False)
    Else
        Return New NullableBoolean()
    End If
```

```vbnet
            End If
    End Operator

    Public Shared Operator Not(ByVal v As NullableBoolean) As NullableBoolean
        If v.HasValue Then
            Return New NullableBoolean(Not v.Value)
        Else
            Return New NullableBoolean
        End If
    End Operator

    Public Shared Operator Xor(ByVal v1 As NullableBoolean, _
            ByVal v2 As NullableBoolean) As NullableBoolean
        If v1.HasValue AndAlso v2.HasValue Then
            Return v1.Value Xor v2.Value
        Else
            Return New NullableBoolean
        End If
    End Operator

    Public Shared Operator IsTrue(ByVal v As NullableBoolean) As Boolean
        Return v.HasValue AndAlso v.Value
    End Operator

    Public Shared Operator IsFalse(ByVal v As NullableBoolean) As Boolean
        Return v.HasValue AndAlso v.Value = False
    End Operator

    Public Shared Widening Operator CType(ByVal v As Boolean) As NullableBoolean
        Return New NullableBoolean(v)
    End Operator

    Public Shared Narrowing Operator CType(ByVal v As NullableBoolean) As Boolean
        If v.HasValue Then
            Return v.Value
        Else
            Throw New InvalidOperationException("Nullable objects must have a value")
        End If
    End Operator
End Structure
```

You use the NullableBoolean type as you'd use a Nullable(Of Boolean) type, except it supports all the operators you need when working with three-value logic:

```vbnet
Dim fal As NullableBoolean = False
Dim tru As NullableBoolean = True
Dim unk As NullableBoolean              ' Null is the default state.

Console.WriteLine(fal And unk)          ' => False
Console.WriteLine(tru And unk)          ' => Null
Console.WriteLine(fal Or unk)           ' => Null
Console.WriteLine(tru Or unk)           ' => True
Console.WriteLine(fal Xor unk)          ' => Null
Console.WriteLine(tru Xor unk)          ' => Null
Console.WriteLine(fal = unk)            ' => Null
Console.WriteLine(tru <> unk)           ' => Null
```

The CType operator allows you to convert a NullableBoolean to a Boolean by means of an explicit conversion:

```
' Throws an exception if the NullableBoolean element has an unknown value.
Dim ok As Boolean = CBool(fal)
```

The IsTrue and IsFalse operators add support for the AndAlso and OrElse keywords:

```
If fal AndAlso tru Then
   ' This block isn't executed.
End If
```

Support for Math Operators

As I emphasized many times in previous sections, a generic type can't perform any math operation on objects with a type defined by using a generic parameter. In general, no operator can be used and no method can be invoked on such objects. (As a special case, you can work around the lack of support of relational operators by enforcing a constraint for either the IComparable or the IEquatable interfaces.)

In a perfect world, all .NET numeric types would support a common interface that would allow a generic type to perform math. For example, suppose that the following interface were defined in the .NET Framework:

```
Public Interface IMath(Of T)
   Function Add(ByVal n As T) As T
   Function Subtract(ByVal n As T) As T
   Function Multiply(ByVal n As T) As T
   Function Divide(ByVal n As T) As T
End Interface
```

If all the .NET Framework numeric types supported the IMath(Of T) interface—in much the same way they support the IComparable(Of T) interface—a generic type could perform the four math operations on these types with no effort. Alas, this interface is neither defined in the .NET Framework nor implemented by any .NET type, so this approach isn't viable. It's a pity, and we can only hope that Microsoft will remedy this in a future version of the .NET Framework.

To understand how you can work around this issue, consider the relation between the IComparable(Of T) and the IComparer(Of T) interfaces. If you want to compare two objects that support the IComparable(Of T) interface, you can just invoke the CompareTo method that these objects expose. However, if the objects don't expose this interface, you can define a type that supports the IComparer(Of T) interface and that is capable of comparing two objects of type T.

Along the same lines, you can work around the lack of support for math operators by defining an ICalculator(Of T) interface, and then create one or more types that implement this interface;

these types provide the ability to perform math on elements of type T. Here's the definition of the ICalculator(Of T) interface:

```
Public Interface ICalculator(Of T)
    Function Add(ByVal n1 As T, ByVal n2 As T) As T
    Function Subtract(ByVal n1 As T, ByVal n2 As T) As T
    Function Multiply(ByVal n1 As T, ByVal n2 As T) As T
    Function Divide(ByVal n1 As T, ByVal n2 As T) As T
    Function ConvertTo(ByVal n As Object) As T
End Interface
```

Next, you need to implement one or more classes that implement this interface for all the numeric types in the .NET Framework and, optionally, for any custom type in your application that supports the four operators. You can adopt two strategies: you can have one separate class for each numeric type or an individual class that implements several versions of the interface, one of each numeric type you want to support.

The following NumericCalculator class implements the ICalculator interface for the Integer and the Double types, but you can easily extend it to support all other primitive .NET numeric types. As you can see, it's a lot of code, but it's mostly a copy-and-paste job:

```
Public Class NumericCalculator
    Implements ICalculator(Of Integer)
    Implements ICalculator(Of Double)

    ' The ICalculator(Of Integer) interface
    Public Function AddInt32(ByVal n1 As Integer, ByVal n2 As Integer) As Integer _
            Implements ICalculator(Of Integer).Add
        Return n1 + n2
    End Function
    Public Function SubtractInt32(ByVal n1 As Integer, ByVal n2 As Integer) As Integer _
            Implements ICalculator(Of Integer).Subtract
        Return n1 - n2
    End Function
    Public Function MultiplyInt32(ByVal n1 As Integer, ByVal n2 As Integer) As Integer _
            Implements ICalculator(Of Integer).Multiply
        Return n1 * n2
    End Function
    Public Function DivideInt32(ByVal n1 As Integer, ByVal n2 As Integer) As Integer _
            Implements ICalculator(Of Integer).Divide
        Return n1 \ n2
    End Function
    Public Function ConvertToInt32(ByVal n As Object) As Integer _
            Implements ICalculator(Of Integer).ConvertTo
        Return CInt(n)
    End Function

    ' The ICalculator(Of Double) interface
    Public Function AddDouble(ByVal n1 As Double, ByVal n2 As Double) As Double _
            Implements ICalculator(Of Double).Add
        Return n1 + n2
    End Function
    Public Function SubtractDouble(ByVal n1 As Double, ByVal n2 As Double) As Double _
            Implements ICalculator(Of Double).Subtract
```

```
         Return n1 - n2
      End Function
      Public Function MultiplyDouble(ByVal n1 As Double, ByVal n2 As Double) As Double _
            Implements ICalculator(Of Double).Multiply
         Return n1 * n2
      End Function
      Public Function DivideDouble(ByVal n1 As Double, ByVal n2 As Double) As Double _
            Implements ICalculator(Of Double).Divide
         Return n1 / n2
      End Function
      Public Function ConvertToDouble(ByVal n As Object) As Double _
            Implements ICalculator(Of Double).ConvertTo
         Return CDbl(n)
      End Function
End Class
```

Let's now see how you can leverage the NumericCalculator class in a generic type that works as a list but is also capable of performing some basic statistical operations on its elements:

```
Public Class StatsList(Of T, C As {New, ICalculator(Of T)})
   Inherits List(Of T)

   ' The object used as a calculator
   Dim calc As New C

   ' Return the sum of all elements.
   Public Function Sum() As T
      Dim result As T
      For Each elem As T In Me
         result = calc.Add(result, elem)
      Next
      Return result
   End Function

   ' Return the average of all elements.
   Public Function Avg() As T
      Return calc.Divide(Me.Sum, calc.ConvertTo(Me.Count))
   End Function
End Class
```

Using the StatsList generic type is a breeze:

```
Dim sl As New StatsList(Of Double, NumericCalculator)
For i As Integer = 0 To 10
   sl.Add(i)
Next
Console.WriteLine("Sum = {0}", sl.Sum)          ' => Sum = 55
Console.WriteLine("Average = {0}", sl.Avg)      ' => Average = 5
```

Generics and Events

Generics can greatly simplify the structure of types that contain public events. As you might recall from Chapter 7, "Delegates and Events," all event handlers must receive two arguments: *sender* and *e*, where the latter is a System.EventArgs (if the event doesn't expose any additional property to subscribers) or an object that derives from System.EventArgs. To follow Microsoft guidelines closely, for each event that carries one or more arguments, you should define a type named *EventName*EventArgs that derives from EventArgs, the corresponding *EventName*-EventHandler delegate, and an On*EventName* overridable procedure that raises the event. It's a lot of work for just one event, and it's no surprise that most developers don't feel like writing all this code just to implement one event.

To see how the inheritance constraint can help you in streamlining the structure of events, let's suppose you are authoring an Employee class that exposes the Name and BirthDate properties and raises a *PropertyName*Changing event before either property is modified (so that subscribers can cancel the assignment) and a *PropertyName*Changed event after the property has been assigned. According to guidelines, you should define a class named NameChangingEventArgs that exposes the ProposedValue read-only string property (the value about to be assigned to the Name property) and the Cancel read-write Boolean property (which can be set to True by event subscribers to cancel the assignment). Likewise, you should define a class named BirthDateChangingEventArgs class, which exposes the same properties except that the ProposedValue property returns a Date value. Instead of defining two distinct classes, let's create a generic type named PropertyChangingEventArgs:

```
Public Class PropertyChangingEventArgs(Of T)
    ' Inheriting from CancelEventArgs adds support for the Cancel property.
    Inherits System.ComponentModel.CancelEventArgs

    Public Sub New(ByVal proposedValue As T)
       M_ProposedValue = proposedValue
    End Sub

    Private m_ProposedValue As T

    Public ReadOnly Property ProposedValue() As T
       Get
           Return m_ProposedValue
       End Get
    End Property
End Class
```

You now have two options. First, you can use the PropertyChangingEventArgs(Of String) type for the NameChanging event and the PropertyChangingEventArgs(Of Date) type for the BirthDateChanging event; in this case you'd need to edit the code slightly in the Employee class to account for these different names. Second, you can define two regular classes that inherit from the PropertyChangingEventArgs generic type:

```
Public Class NameChangingEventArgs
    Inherits PropertyChangingEventArgs(Of String)
    …
End Class

Public Class BirthDateChangingEventArgs
    Inherits PropertyChangingEventArgs(Of Date)
    …
End Class
```

In the remainder of this section, I assume that you've adopted the first approach and that all events are directly defined in terms of the PropertyChangingEventArgs(Of T) generic type.

The System.EventHandler(Of T) type is a generic delegate that can be passed any type that derives from System.EventArgs and that relieves you from defining a different delegate for each event. Thanks to this generic type and the nongeneric EventHandler type, you can define the four events in the Employee class as follows:

```
Public Class Employee
    Event NameChanging As EventHandler(Of PropertyChangingEventArgs(Of String))
    Event BirthDateChanging As EventHandler(Of PropertyChangingEventArgs(Of Date))
    Event NameChanged As EventHandler
    Event BirthDateChanged As EventHandler
    …
```

Adding support for the Name and BirthDate properties, and corresponding *XxxxChanging* and *XxxxChanged* events, is now straightforward:

```
' (Continuing previous code snippet…)
Private m_Name As String

Public Property Name() As String
    Get
        Return m_Name
    End Get
    Set(ByVal value As String)
        If m_Name <> value Then
            Dim e As New PropertyChangingEventArgs(Of String)(value)
            OnNameChanging(e)
            If e.Cancel Then Exit Property
            m_Name = value
            OnNameChanged(EventArgs.Empty)
        End If
    End Set
End Property


Private m_BirthDate As Date

Public Property BirthDate() As Date
    Get
        Return m_BirthDate
    End Get
    Set(ByVal value As Date)
        If m_BirthDate <> value Then
            Dim e As New PropertyChangingEventArgs(Of Date)(value)
            OnBirthDateChanging(e)
            If e.Cancel Then Exit Property
            m_BirthDate = value
            OnBirthDateChanged(EventArgs.Empty)
        End If
    End Set
End Property


' Protected OnXxxx methods
Protected Overridable Sub OnNameChanging(ByVal e As _
```

```
            PropertyChangingEventArgs(Of String))
         RaiseEvent NameChanging(Me, e)
      End Sub

      Protected Overridable Sub OnNameChanged(ByVal e As EventArgs)
         RaiseEvent NameChanged(Me, e)
      End Sub

      Protected Overridable Sub OnBirthDateChanging(ByVal e As _
            PropertyChangingEventArgs(Of Date))
         RaiseEvent BirthDateChanging(Me, e)
      End Sub

      Protected Overridable Sub OnBirthDateChanged(ByVal e As EventArgs)
         RaiseEvent BirthDateChanged(Me, e)
      End Sub
End Class
```

Generics can help you reduce the amount of code needed to support events in one more way. The Set blocks in the Name and BirthDate property procedures are almost identical, except for the name of the EventArgs-derived class and the On*Xxxx* methods. Even if the names of these On*Xxxx* methods are different, the syntax is similar, so you can invoke these methods through delegates. This technique enables you to move the common code into a separate module and reuse it for all the properties in all your types:

```
Public Module EventHelper
   ' Delegates declaration
   Public Delegate Sub OnPropertyChangingEventHandler(Of T) _
      (ByVal e As PropertyChangingEventArgs(Of T))
   Public Delegate Sub OnPropertyChangedEventHandler(ByVal e As EventArgs)

   Public Sub AssignProperty(Of T)(ByRef oldValue As T, ByVal proposedValue As T, _
         ByVal onChanging As OnPropertyChangingEventHandler(Of T), _
         ByVal onChanged As OnPropertyChangedEventHandler)
      ' Nothing to do if the new value is the same as the old value.
      If Object.Equals(oldValue, proposedValue) Then Exit Sub
      ' Invoke the OnChangingXXXX method; exit if subscribers canceled the assignment.
      Dim e As New PropertyChangingEventArgs(Of T)(proposedValue)
      onChanging.DynamicInvoke(e)
      If e.Cancel Then Exit Sub
      ' Proceed with assignment, and then invoke the OnChangedXXXX method.
      oldValue = proposedValue
      onChanged.DynamicInvoke(EventArgs.Empty)
   End Sub
End Module
```

Thanks to the EventHelper module you can simplify the code in the Name and BirthDate properties significantly (changes are in bold type):

```
   Private m_Name As String

   Public Property Name() As String
      Get
```

```
            Return m_Name
         End Get
         Set(ByVal value As String)
            AssignProperty(Of String)(m_Name, value, AddressOf OnNameChanging, _
               AddressOf OnNameChanged)
         End Set
   End Property

   Private m_BirthDate As Date

   Public Property BirthDate() As Date
      Get
         Return m_BirthDate
      End Get
      Set(ByVal value As Date)
         AssignProperty(Of Date)(m_BirthDate, value, AddressOf OnBirthDateChanging, _
            AddressOf OnBirthDateChanged)
      End Set
   End Property
```

Object Pools

An *object pool* is a collection of objects that have been created and initialized in advance and are ready for the application to use them. Object pools are quite common in programming. For example, ADO.NET maintains a pool of connection objects: when the application asks for a connection to a database and a connection in the pool that already points to the specific database is available, ADO.NET takes a connection from the pool instead of instantiating it from scratch. When the application asks to close the connection, the physical connection isn't actually closed and the connection object is simply returned to the pool. When the same or another application asks for a connection to the same database, the connection object is taken from the pool, thus saving several seconds.

The following ObjectPool generic type implements a simple object pool. You can use this pool to create a new instance of a given type using the CreateObject method. When you don't need the object any longer, you can simply return it to the pool by using the DestroyObject method so that the next time the CreateObject method is invoked no object is physically created:

```
Public Class ObjectPool(Of T As New)
   Dim pool As New List(Of T)

   ' Create an object, taking it from the pool if possible.
   Function CreateObject() As T
      If pool.Count = 0 Then
         Return New T
      Else
         ' Return the first object to the pool.
         Dim item As T = pool(0)
         pool.RemoveAt(0)
         Return item
      End If
   End Function
```

```
    ' Return an object to the pool.
    Public Sub DestroyObject(ByVal item As T)
        pool.Add(item)
    End Sub
End Class
```

The ObjectPool class is especially useful for types that require a significant amount of time to be instantiated; under such circumstances, the application can improve performance substantially by keeping these objects alive in the pool:

```
Dim pool As New ObjectPool(Of Employee)
' These two elements are created when the method is invoked.
Dim e1 As Employee = pool.CreateObject()
Dim e2 As Employee = pool.CreateObject()
' Return one object to the pool, and then set its reference to Nothing.
pool.DestroyObject(e1)
e1 = Nothing
' Now the pool contains one element; thus, the next statement takes it from there.
Dim e3 As Employee = pool.CreateObject()
...
```

As I already explained, no form of generic constraint enables you to specify that a type must have a constructor with a given signature; thus, you can't pass arguments when instantiating a type that appears as a generic parameter. This issue severely limits the usefulness of the ObjectPool class.

The simplest way to work around this limitation and make the ObjectPool type more versatile is to define an interface that all poolable objects must implement:

```
Public Interface IPoolable
    Sub Initialize(ByVal ParamArray propertyValues() As Object)
    Function IsEqual(ByVal ParamArray propertyValues() As Object) As Boolean
End Interface
```

For each type you should define a minimum set of properties that can distinguish individual instances of that type. For example, two Employee objects should be considered as equal when their Name and BirthDate properties have the same values; therefore, the Employee class might implement the IPoolable interface as follows:

```
Public Class Employee
    Implements IPoolable

    Public Sub Initialize(ByVal ParamArray propertyValues() As Object) _
            Implements IPoolable.Initialize
        Me.Name = CStr(propertyValues(0))
        Me.BirthDate = CDate(propertyValues(1))
    End Sub

    Public Function IsEqual(ByVal ParamArray propertyValues() As Object) As Boolean _
            Implements IPoolable.IsEqual
        Return Me.Name = CStr(propertyValues(0)) AndAlso _
            Me.BirthDate = CDate(propertyValues(1))
    End Function
```

```
' (Implementation of Name and BirthDate properties is omitted.…)
   …
End Class
```

You can now improve the ObjectPool class to take advantage of the IPoolable interface and reuse an object in the pool only if its most important properties are equal to those of the object requested by the client:

```
Public Class ObjectPoolEx(Of T As {New, IPoolable})
   Dim pool As New List(Of T)

   ' Create an object, taking it from the pool if possible.
   Function CreateObject(ByVal ParamArray propertyValues() As Object) As T
      For i As Integer = 0 To pool.Count - 1
         Dim item As T = pool(i)
         If item.IsEqual(propertyValues) Then
            ' We've found an object with the required properties.
            pool.RemoveAt(i)
            Return item
         End If
      Next
      ' Create and return a brand-new object.
      Dim obj As New T
      obj.Initialize(propertyValues)
      Return obj
   End Function

   ' Return an object to the pool.
   Public Sub DestroyObject(ByVal item As T)
      pool.Add(item)
   End Sub
End Class
```

The code that uses the ObjectPoolEx class to create a pool of Employee objects must provide an initial value for the Name and BirthDate properties:

```
Dim pool As New ObjectPoolEx(Of Employee)
' These two elements are created when the method is invoked.
Dim e1 As Employee = pool.CreateObject("Joe", #1/1/1961#)
Dim e2 As Employee = pool.CreateObject("Ann", #2/2/1962#)
' Return them to the pool and set their references to Nothing.
pool.DestroyObject(e1)
e1 = Nothing
pool.DestroyObject(e2)
e2 = Nothing
' This object can't be taken from the pool, because its
' properties don't match any of the objects in the pool.
Dim e3 As Employee = pool.CreateObject("Joe", #3/3/1963#)
' This object matches exactly one object in the pool; thus, no new instance is created.
Dim e4 As Employee = pool.CreateObject("Ann", #2/2/1962#)
```

Once again, keep in mind that object pools are convenient only if the time you spend to instantiate an object is relevant; in all other cases, using an object pool is likely to degrade your performance without buying you any other benefit.

Part III
Working with the .NET Framework

Chapter 12
.NET Basic Types

The Microsoft .NET Framework exposes hundreds of different classes to accomplish such jobs as opening files, parsing XML, and updating databases, but it is more than just a collection of useful objects. It's a well-structured object tree that also provides objects to store values, such as numbers, dates, and strings. Everything in the .NET Framework is a class, and at the top of the object hierarchy sits the System.Object class.

Note To avoid long lines, code samples in this chapter assume that the following Imports statements are used at the file or project level:

```
Imports System.Globalization
Imports System.IO
Imports System.Runtime.InteropServices
Imports System.Security
Imports System.Threading
Imports System.Text
Imports System.Windows.Forms
```

The System.Object Type

All classes inherit—directly or indirectly—from System.Object, which means that you can always assign any object to a System.Object variable and never get a compilation or runtime error when you do so:

```
' The Object Visual Basic type is a synonym for System.Object.
Dim o As Object = New AnyOtherType()
```

Incidentally, note that interfaces are the only things in the .NET Framework that do not derive from System.Object.

Public and Protected Methods

Because .NET types inherit from System.Object (see Figure 12-1), all of them expose the four instance methods that System.Object exposes, namely, the following.

- **Equals**   An overridable method that checks whether the current object has the same value as the object passed as an argument. It returns True when two object references point to the same object instance, but many classes override this method to implement a different type of equality. For example, numeric types override this method so that it returns True if the objects being compared have the same numeric value.

- **GetHashCode**   An overridable method that returns a hash code for the object. This method is used when the object is a key for collections and hash tables. Ideally, the hash code should be unique for any given object instance so that you can check that two objects are "equal" by comparing their hash codes. However, implementing a hash function that provides unique values is seldom possible, and different objects might return the same hash code, so you should *never* infer that two instances with the same hash code are equal, whatever "equal" might mean for that specific type. A class can override this method to implement a different hash algorithm to improve performance when its objects are used as keys in collections. A class that overrides the Equals method should always override the GetHashCode method as well, so that two objects considered to be equal also return the same hash code.

- **GetType**   A method that returns a value that identifies the type of the object. The returned value is typically used in reflection operations, as explained in Chapter 18, "Reflection."

- **ToString**   An overridable method that returns the complete name of the class, for example, MyNamespace.MyClass. However, most classes redefine this method so that it returns a string that better describes the value of the object. For example, basic types such as Integer, Double, and String override this method to return the object's numeric or string value. The ToString method is implicitly called when you pass an object to the Console.Write and Debug.Write methods. Interestingly, ToString is culturally aware. For example, when applied to a numeric type, it uses a comma as the decimal separator if the current culture requires it.

The System.Object class also exposes two static methods:

- **Equals**   A static member that takes two object arguments and returns True if they can be considered to be equal. It is similar to, and often used in lieu of, the instance method with the same name, which would fail if invoked on a variable reference that is Nothing.

- **ReferenceEquals**   A static method that takes two object arguments and returns True if they reference the same instance; thus, it corresponds to the Is operator in Microsoft

Visual Basic. This method is similar to the Equals method except that derived classes can't override it.

The System.Object class also exposes two protected methods. Because everything in the .NET Framework derives directly or indirectly from System.Object, all the classes you write can invoke the following methods in their base class and override them:

■ **MemberwiseClone**   A method that returns a new object of the same type and initializes the new object's fields and properties so that the new object can be considered a copy (a clone) of the current object. You've seen this method in action in section titled "The ICloneable Interface" in Chapter 10, "Interfaces."

■ **Finalize**   An overridable method that the .NET Framework calls when the object is taken by the garbage collector. (For more information about this method, see the section titled "Finalize and Dispose Methods" in Chapter 9, "Object Lifetime.")

The System class hierarchy includes all the most common and useful objects in the .NET Framework, including all the basic data types. The most important classes are depicted in Figure 12-1.

Value Types and Reference Types (Revisited)

Most basic data types (numbers, dates, and so on) in the .NET hierarchy inherit from System.ValueType and so have a common behavior. For example, System.ValueType overrides the Equals method and redefines equality so that two object references are considered equal if they have the same value (which is the way we usually compare numbers and dates), rather than if they point to the same instance. In addition, all classes deriving from System.ValueType override the GetHashCode method so that the hash code is created by taking the object's fields into account.

Classes that inherit from System.ValueType are commonly referred to as *value types*, to distinguish them from other classes, which are collectively named *reference types*. All numeric and Enum types are value types, as are types that work with dates. The .NET documentation uses the term *type* to encompass the meaning of value and reference types. I follow that convention in this book and reserve the word *class* for reference types only.

Visual Basic prevents you from explicitly inheriting from System.ValueType. The only way you can create a value type is by creating a Structure block:

```
Structure Position
   Dim X As Double
   Dim Y As Double
   ' Add here other fields, properties, methods, and interfaces.
   …
End Structure
```

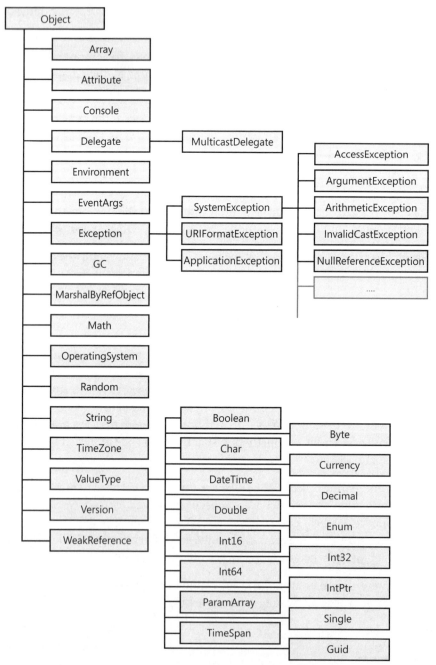

Figure 12-1   The most important classes in the System namespace

Broadly speaking, value types are more efficient than are reference types because their data isn't allocated in the managed heap and therefore isn't subject to garbage collection. More precisely, a value type declared as a local variable in a procedure is allocated on the stack; when the procedure is exited, the value is simply discarded without making any extra work for the garbage collector. (The Finalize method is ignored in structures.) This description isn't strictly accurate if the structure includes a member of a reference type, though. Consider this new version of the Position type:

```
Structure Position
   Dim X As Double
   Dim Y As Double
   Dim Description As String          ' String is a reference type.
   …
End Structure
```

The garbage collector has to reclaim the memory used for the Description string member when such a structure is destroyed. In other words, value types are significantly faster than reference types are only if they don't expose any members of a reference type.

Many technical articles explain that value types are allocated on the stack and don't take memory from the managed heap, but this description isn't 100 percent correct: if a value type is used in the definition of a reference type, it does take room in the heap, as in this case:

```
Public Class Square
   ' These two members go in the heap, in the slot allocated for the Square object.
   Public Side As Double
   Public Position As Position
   ' The pointer to the Name string is allocated in the slot for the Square
   ' object, but its characters go in *another* slot of the heap.
   Public Name As String
End Class
```

Other factors might affect your choice of a value type or a reference type. Value types are implicitly sealed and marked as NotInheritable, thus you should use a structure if your object acts like a primitive type and doesn't need to inherit special behaviors from other types, and other types don't need to derive from it. Also, structures can't be abstract and can't contain virtual methods, other than those inherited from System.Object.

A detail that might confuse many Visual Basic veterans is that the String class is a reference type, not a value type, as shown in Figure 12-1. You can easily demonstrate this point by assigning a String variable to another variable, and then testing whether both variables point to the same object:

```
Dim s1 As String = "ABCD"
Dim s2 As String = s1
' Prove that both variables point to the same object.
Console.WriteLine(s1 Is s2)      ' => True
```

.NET arrays are reference types, too, and assigning an array to an Array variable copies only the object's reference, not the array contents. The Array class exposes the Clone method to enable you to make a (shallow) copy of its elements. (See the section titled "The ICloneable Interface" in Chapter 10 for a discussion of shallow and deep copy operations.)

Boxing and Unboxing

Even if performance is your primary concern, you shouldn't always opt for value types because sometimes reference types are faster. For example, an assignment between value types involves the copy of every field in the object, whereas assigning a reference value to a variable requires only the copy of the object's address (4 bytes in 32-bit versions of the Microsoft Windows operating system).

When you pass a value type to a method that expects an Object argument, a different kind of performance hit occurs because the value must be boxed in this case. *Boxing a value* means that the compiler creates a copy of it in the managed heap and assigns the address of this copy to an Object variable or argument so that the type can then be used as a reference type. (See the section titled "Value Types and Reference Types" in Chapter 2, "Basic Language Concepts.") A boxed value doesn't maintain a link to the original value, which means you can modify either one without affecting the other.

If this boxed value is later assigned to a variable of the original (value) type, the object is said to be *unboxed* and data is copied from the managed heap into the memory allocated to the variable (for example, on the stack if it's a local variable). Not surprisingly, boxing and unboxing take CPU time and eventually require some memory to be reclaimed during a garbage collection. The bottom line: if you carry out many assignments or frequently perform operations that result in a boxing and unboxing sequence, implementing a reference type might be a wiser choice.

Boxing occurs transparently in most cases, whereas you require an explicit CType or Direct-Cast operator to convert back from an Object to a value type if Option Strict is On. You can determine whether a call causes a boxing operation by looking at the method declaration in the object browser or in the class documentation. If the method takes an argument of the type you're passing, no boxing occurs; if it takes a generic Object argument, your argument will be boxed. When you create your own methods, you might consider including overloaded variations that take arguments of different types as well as a catchall procedure that takes an Object argument.

In general, it doesn't make sense to compare the performance of a method that uses boxing with a similar method that doesn't. An informal benchmark shows that a tight loop that calls a function that requires boxing can be up to 30 times slower than a loop that doesn't use boxing. However, you must repeat the loop 10 million times to see a meaningful difference in absolute terms, so in practice you should worry about boxing only in time-critical code sections.

You might be using boxing sometimes without knowing it. First, you implicitly box a structure if you call one of the virtual methods that the structure inherits from System.Object—for example, ToString. Second, you implicitly box a structure if you call a method of an interface that the structure exposes.

As I mentioned, boxing typically occurs transparently. In rare cases, however, you must explicitly tell Visual Basic that you want to box a value by using the CObj function. This is necessary, for example, when you want to invoke the ToString method (or another method inherited from System.Object) on an interface variable, as in this code:

```
Sub DisposeIt(ByVal idisp As IDisposable)
    ' Display a diagnostic message and dispose of the object.
    ' (Explicitly box the reference to call ToString.)
    Console.WriteLine("Disposing " & CObj(idisp).ToString())
    idisp.Dispose()
End Sub
```

Sometimes Microsoft Visual Basic 2005 deals with boxed variables in a rather counterintuitive way. For example, consider the following code:

```
For i As Integer = 1 To 1000
    For j As Integer = 1 To 100000
        ' GetObject takes two Object arguments, and therefore causes
        ' the boxing of both i and j.
        GetObject(i, j)
    Next
Next
```

You might believe that you can optimize these loops by boxing the *i* variable yourself and passing the boxed value to the GetObject method, as in this code:

```
For i As Integer = 1 To 1000
    Dim obj As Object = i            ' Box i manually.
    For j As Integer = 1 To 100000
        GetObject(obj, j)            ' Only j is boxed.
    Next
Next
```

The preceding snippet is actually a bit faster under Microsoft Visual Basic .NET 2003, but—surprise!—it's remarkably *slower* than the original code under Visual Basic 2005. You need a trip to ILDASM to understand why: whenever Visual Basic passes an Object variable to a method, it calls the GetObjectValue method of the RuntimeHelpers type (in the System. Runtime.CompilerServices namespace). This call adds a hidden overhead and makes the entire snippet slower.

String Types

As discussed in Chapter 2, Visual Basic supports the String data type, which maps to the System.String class. Because System.String is a full-featured type, you can manipulate strings by means of the many methods it exposes, a technique that in general provides more flexibility and better performance than does using the functions provided by the Microsoft.VisualBasic assembly, such as Trim or Left.

To begin with, the String class exposes many overloaded constructor methods, so you can create a string in a variety of ways–for example, as a sequence of *N* same characters:

```
' A sequence of <N> characters–similar to the VB6 String function
'    (Note the c suffix to make "A" a Char rather than a String.)
Dim s As New String("A"c, 10)                    ' => AAAAAAAAAA
```

(This technique duplicates the functionality of the String function in Microsoft Visual Basic 6, which was dropped because String is now a reserved keyword.)

Properties and Methods

The only properties of the String class are Length and Chars. The former returns the number of characters in the string; the latter returns the character at a given zero-based index:

```
Dim s As String = "ABCDEFGHIJ"
Console.WriteLine(s.Length)                  ' => 10
' Note that index is always zero-based.
Console.WriteLine(s.Chars(3))                ' => D
```

Sometimes the reference nature of the String type causes behaviors you might not anticipate. For example, consider this simple code:

```
Dim s As String
Console.WriteLine(s.Length)
```

You probably expect that the second statement displays the value zero, but this statement actually throws a NullReferenceException because the String object hasn't been initialized. A simple way to avoid this problem is to make a habit of initializing all String variables explicitly, as in this code:

```
Dim s As String = ""
```

You can tap the power of the String class by invoking one of its many methods. Visual Basic 2005 strings are richer in functionality than are Visual Basic 6 strings, and they enable you to adopt a more object-oriented, concise syntax in your applications. For example, see how much simpler and more readable the operation of inserting a substring is under Visual Basic 2005:

```
Dim s As String = "ABCDEFGHIJ"
' The VB6 way of inserting a substring after the third character
s = Left(s, 3) & "1234" & Mid(s, 4)

' The VB2005 object-oriented way to perform the same operation
s = s.Insert(3, "1234")      ' => ABC1234DEFGHIJ
```

Here's another example of the compactness that you can get by using the String methods. Let's say you want to trim all the space and tab characters from the beginning of a string. With

Visual Basic 2005, you simply have to load all the characters to be trimmed in an array of Chars and pass the array to the TrimStart function:

```
Dim cArr() As Char = {" "c, ControlChars.Tab}
s = s.TrimStart(cArr)
```

(You can use the same pattern with the TrimEnd and Trim functions.) In many cases, the Visual Basic 2005 methods can deliver better performance because you can state more precisely what you're after. For example, you can determine whether a string begins or ends with a given sequence of characters by a variety of means under Visual Basic 6, but none of the available techniques is especially efficient. Visual Basic 2005 strings solve this problem elegantly with the StartsWith or EndsWith method:

```
' Check whether the string starts with "abc" and ends with "xyz."
If s.StartsWith("abc") AndAlso s.EndsWith("xyz") Then ok = True
```

You can iterate over all the characters of a string by using a For Each loop:

```
Dim s As String = "ABCDE"
For Each c As Char In s
   Console.Write(c & ".")          ' => A.B.C.D.E.
Next
```

In earlier versions of the language, iterating over all the characters of a string by means of a For Each loop was a relatively slow process because it involved the creation of an IEnumerator object (see the section titled "The IEnumerable Interface" in Chapter 10). This kind of loop is much faster in Visual Basic 2005 because the compiler automatically translates the For Each loop into the following more efficient For...Next loop:

```
' This is how Visual Basic actually compiles a For Each loop over a string.
For index As Integer = 0 To s.Length - 1
   Dim c As Char = s.Chars(index)
   …
Next
```

Comparing and Searching Strings

Many methods in the String type enable you to compare strings or search a substring inside the current string. In version 2.0 of the .NET Framework, the String type overloads both the instance and the static version of the Equals method to take an additional StringComparison enum type that specifies the locale to be used for the comparison and whether the comparison is case sensitive. In general, it is recommended that you use the static version of this method because it works well even if one or both the strings to be compared are Nothing:

```
' Compare two strings in case-sensitive mode, using Unicode values.
Dim match As Boolean = String.Equals(s1, s2)
' Compare two strings in case-insensitive mode, using the current locale.
match = String.Equals(s1, s2, StringComparison.CurrentCultureIgnoreCase)
' Compare two strings in case-sensitive mode, using the invariant locale.
```

```
match = String.Equals(s1, s2, StringComparison.InvariantCulture)
' Compare the numeric Unicode values of all the characters in the two strings.
match = String.Equals(s1, s2, StringComparison.Ordinal)
```

(Read on for more information about locales and the CultureInfo type.) In general, you should use the Ordinal and OrdinalIgnoreCase enumerated values if possible because they are more efficient. For example, these values can be fine when comparing file paths, registry keys, and XML and HTML tags.

The InvariantCulture and InvariantCultureIgnoreCase values are arguably the least useful ones and should be used in the rare cases when you compare strings that are linguistically meaningful but don't have a cultural meaning; using these values ensures that comparisons yield the same results on all machines, regardless of the culture of the current thread.

If you need to detect whether a string is less than or greater than another string, you should use the static Compare method, which can also compare substrings, in either case-sensitive or case-insensitive mode. The return value is −1, 0, or 1 depending on whether the first string is less than, equal to, or greater than the second string:

```
' Compare two strings in case-sensitive mode, using the current culture.
Dim res As Integer = String.Compare(s1, s2)
Select Case res
   Case -1: Console.WriteLine("s1 < s2")
   Case 0: Console.WriteLine("s1 = s2")
   Case 1: Console.WriteLine("s1 > s2")
End Select

' Compare the first 10 characters of two strings in case-insensitive mode.
' (Second and fourth arguments are the index of first char to compare.)
res = String.Compare(s1, 0, s2, 0, 10, True)
```

In .NET Framework 2.0, you can also pass a StringComparison enum value to specify whether you want to use the invariant locale, the current locale, or the numeric Unicode value of individual characters, and whether you want the comparison to be in case-insensitive mode:

```
' Compare two strings using the local culture in case-insensitive mode.
res = String.Compare(s1, s2, StringComparison.CurrentCultureIgnoreCase)
' Compare two substrings using the invariant culture in case-sensitive mode.
res = String.Compare(s1, 0, s2, 0, 10, StringComparison.InvariantCulture)
' Compare two strings by the numeric code of their characters.
res = String.Compare(s1, s2, StringComparison.Ordinal)
```

The StringComparer type (also new in .NET Framework 2.0) offers an alternative technique for doing string comparisons. The static properties of this type return an IComparer object able to perform a specific type of comparison on strings. For example, here's how you can perform a case-insensitive comparison according to the current culture:

```
' Compare two strings using the local culture in case-insensitive mode.
res = StringComparer.CurrentCultureIgnoreCase.Compare(s1, s2)
' Compare two strings using the invariant culture in case-sensitive mode.
res = StringComparer.InvariantCulture.Compare(s1, s2)
```

The StringComparer object has the added advantage that you can pass it to methods that take an IComparer argument, such as the Array.Sort method, but it has some shortcomings, too; for one, you can't use the StringComparer.Compare method to compare substrings.

The String type exposes also the CompareTo instance method, which compares the current string to the passed argument and returns −1, 0, or 1, exactly as the static Compare method does. However, the CompareTo method doesn't offer any of the options of the Compare method and therefore should be avoided unless you really mean to compare using the current culture's rules. In addition, because it is an instance method, you should always check that the instance isn't Nothing before invoking the method:

```
' This statement throws an exception if s1 is Nothing.
If s1.CompareTo(s2) > 0 Then Console.WriteLine("s1 > s2")
```

When comparing just the numeric Unicode value of individual characters, you can save a few CPU cycles by using the CompareOrdinal static method; in general, however, you should use this method only to test equality because it seldom makes sense to decide whether a string is greater than or less than another string based on Unicode numeric values:

```
If String.CompareOrdinal(s1, s2) = 0 Then Console.WriteLine("s1 = s2")
```

A .NET string variable is considered to be *null* if it is Nothing and is considered to be *empty* if it points to a zero-character string. In Visual Basic .NET 2003, you must test these two conditions separately, but .NET Framework 2.0 introduces the handy IsNullOrEmpty static method:

```
' These two statements are equivalent, but only the latter works in Visual Basic 2005.
Dim s As String = "ABCDE"
If s Is Nothing OrElse s.Length = 0 Then Console.WriteLine("Empty string")
If String.IsNullOrEmpty(s) Then Console.WriteLine("Empty string")
```

The simplest way to check whether a string appears inside another string is by means of the Contains method, also new in .NET Framework 2.0:

```
' The Contains method works only in case-sensitive mode.
s = "ABCDEFGHI ABCDEF"
Dim found As Boolean = s.Contains("BCD")          ' => True
found = s.Contains("bcd")                         ' => False
```

You can detect the actual position of a substring inside a string by means of the IndexOf and LastIndexOf methods, which return the index of the first and last occurrence of a substring, respectively, or −1 if the search fails:

```
Dim pos As Integer = s.IndexOf("CDE")             ' => 2
pos = s.LastIndexOf("CDE")                        ' => 12
' Both IndexOf and LastIndexOf are case sensitive by default.
pos = s.IndexOf("cde")                            ' => -1
' …but they offer an overload that can specify case-insensitivity.
pos = s.LastIndexOf("cde", StringComparison.CurrentCultureIgnoreCase)
                                                  ' => 12
```

The StartsWith and EndsWith methods enable you to check quickly whether a string starts with or ends with a given substring. By default, these methods perform a case-sensitive comparison using the current culture:

```
match = s.StartsWith("ABC")                    ' => True
match = s.EndsWith("def")                      ' => False
```

In .NET Framework 2.0, these two methods have been expanded to support a StringComparison argument and can take a CultureInfo object as a third argument so that you can specify the locale to be used when comparing characters and whether the comparison is case insensitive:

```
' Both these statements assign True to the variable.
match = s.StartsWith("abc", StringComparison.CurrentCultureIgnoreCase)
match = s.EndsWith("CDE", True, CultureInfo.InvariantCulture)
```

The IndexOfAny and LastIndexOfAny methods return the first and last occurrence, respectively, of a character among those in the specified array. Both these methods can take an optional starting index in the second argument and a character count in the third argument:

```
Dim chars() As Char = {"D"c, "F"c, "I"c}
pos = s.IndexOfAny(chars)                      ' => 3
pos = s.LastIndexOfAny(chars)                  ' => 15
pos = s.IndexOfAny(chars, 6)                   ' => 8
pos = s.IndexOfAny(chars, 6, 2)                ' => -1
```

Modifying and Extracting Strings

The simplest way to create a new string from an existing string is by means of the Substring method, which extracts a substring starting at a given index and with the specified number of arguments. This method corresponds therefore to the Mid function in the Microsoft. VisualBasic library, and you can also use it to simulate the Right function:

```
Dim s As String = "ABCDEFGHI ABCDEF"
' Extract the substring after the 11th character. Same as Mid(s, 11)
Dim result As String = s.Substring(10)         ' => ABCDEF
' Extract 4 characters after the 11th character. Same as Mid(s, 11, 4)
result = s.Substring(10, 4)                    ' => ABCD
' Extract the last 4 characters. Same as Right(s, 4)
result = s.Substring(s.Length - 4)             ' => CDEF
```

The Insert method returns the new string created by inserting a substring at the specified index, whereas the Remove method removes a given number of characters, starting at the specified index:

```
result = s.Insert(4, "-123-")                  ' => ABCD-123-EFGHI ABCDEF
result = s.Remove(4, 3)                        ' => ABCDHI ABCDEF
```

In .NET Framework 2.0, the Remove method has been overloaded with a version that takes only the start index; you can use this new version as a surrogate for the "classic" Left function:

```
' Extract the first 4 characters. Same as Left(s, 4)
result = s.Remove(4)                           ' => ABCD
```

I already hinted at the TrimStart method previously. This method, together with the TrimEnd and Trim methods, enables you to discard spaces and other characters that are found at the left side, the right side, or both sides of a string. By default these methods trim white-space characters (that is, spaces, tabs, and newlines), but you can pass one or more arguments to specify which characters have to be trimmed:

```
Dim t As String = "  001234.560   "
result = t.Trim()                        ' => "001234.560"
result = t.TrimStart(" "c, "0"c)         ' => "1234.560   "
result = t.TrimEnd(" "c, "0"c)           ' => "  001234.56"
result = t.Trim(" "c, "0"c)              ' => "1234.56"
```

The opposite operation of trimming is padding. You can pad a string with a given character, either to the left or the right, to bring the string to the specified length, by means of the PadLeft and PadRight methods. The most obvious reason for using these methods is to align strings and numbers:

```
' Right-align a number in a field that is 8-char wide.
Dim number As Integer = 1234
result = number.ToString().PadLeft(8)       ' => "    1234"
```

As their name suggests, the ToLower and ToUpper methods return a new string obtained by converting all the characters of a string to lowercase or uppercase. Version 2.0 of the .NET Framework also provides the new ToLowerInvariant and ToUpperInvariant methods, which convert a string by using the casing rules of the invariant culture:

```
' Convert the s string to lowercase, using the current culture's rules.
result = s.ToLower()
' Convert the s string to uppercase, using the invariant culture's rules.
result = s.ToUpperInvariant()
```

Microsoft guidelines suggest that you use the ToUpperInvariant method when preparing a normalized string for comparison in case-insensitive mode because this is the way the Compare method works internally when you use the StringComparison.InvariantCulture-IgnoreCase. As odd as it may sound, under certain cultures converting two strings to uppercase and then comparing them might deliver a different result from the one you receive if you convert them to lowercase before the comparison.

The Replace method replaces all the occurrences of a single character or a substring with another character or a substring. All the searches are performed in case-sensitive mode:

```
Dim k As String = "ABCDEFGHI ABCDEF"
result = k.Replace("BCDE", "--")            ' => A--FGHI A--F
```

Working with String and Char Arrays

A few methods take or return an array of String or Char elements. For example, the ToCharArray method returns an array containing all the characters in the string. You typically use this method when processing the characters separately is more efficient than extracting them from the string is. For example, consider the problem of checking whether two strings contain the same characters, regardless of their order (in other words, whether one string is the anagram of the other).

```
Dim s1 As String = "file"
Dim s2 As String = "life"
' Transform both strings to an array of characters.
Dim chars1() As Char = s1.ToCharArray()
Dim chars2() As Char = s2.ToCharArray()
' Sort both arrays.
Array.Sort(chars1)
Array.Sort(chars2)
' Build two new strings from the sorted arrays, and compare them.
Dim sorted1 As New String(chars1)
Dim sorted2 As New String(chars2)
' Compare them. (You can use case-insensitive comparison, if necessary.)
Dim match As Boolean = (String.Compare(sorted1, sorted2) = 0)      ' => True
```

You can split a string into an array of substrings by using the Split method, which takes a list of separators and an optional maximum number of elements in the result array. This method has been improved in .NET Framework 2.0 and it now has the ability to process separators of any length and to optionally drop empty elements in the result array:

```
Dim x As String = "Hey, Visual Basic Rocks!"
Dim arr() As String = x.Split(" "c, ","c, "."c)
' The result contains the words "Hey", "", "Visual", "Basic", "Rocks!"
Dim numOfWords As Integer = arr.Length          ' => 5
' Same as before, but no more than 100 elements, and drop empty items.
Dim separators() As Char = {" "c, ","c, "."c}
Dim arr2() As String = x.Split(separators, 100, StringSplitOptions.RemoveEmptyEntries)
' The result contains the words "Hey", "Visual", "Basic", "Rocks!"
numOfWords = arr2.Length                         ' => 4
```

The new ability of using multicharacter strings as a separator is quite useful when you need to retrieve the individual lines of a string containing pairs of carriage return–line feeds (CR-LF):

```
' Count the number of nonempty lines in a text file.
Dim crlfs() As String = {ControlChars.CrLf}
Dim lines() As String = File.ReadAllText("c:\data.txt").Split(crlfs, StringSplitOptions.None)
Dim numOfLines As Integer = lines.Length
```

You can perform the opposite operation, that is, concatenating all the elements of a string array, by using the Join static method. This method optionally takes the initial index and the maximum number of elements to be considered.

```
' (Continuing the previous example…)
' Reassemble the string by adding CR-LF pairs, but skip the first array element.
Dim newText As String = String.Join(ControlChars.CrLf, lines, 1, lines.Length - 1)
```

The Missing Methods

In spite of the large number of methods exposed by the String type, at times you must write your own function to accomplish recurring tasks. For example, there is no built-in method similar to PadLeft or PadRight but capable of centering a string in a field of a given size. Here's the code that performs this task:

```
Function PadCenter(ByVal s As String, ByVal width As Integer, _
      Optional ByVal padChar As Char = " "c, _
      Optional ByVal truncate As Boolean = False) As String
   Dim diff As Integer = width - s.Length
   If diff = 0 OrElse (diff < 0 AndAlso Not truncate) Then
      ' Return the string as is.
      Return s
   ElseIf diff < 0 Then
      ' Truncate the string.
      Return s.Substring(0, width)
   Else
      ' Half of the extra chars go to the left, the remaining ones go to the right.
      Return s.PadLeft(width - diff \ 2, padChar).PadRight(width, padChar)
   End If
End Function
```

The Microsoft.VisualBasic library contains a few functions that don't have a corresponding method in the String type. For example, there is no native .NET method similar to StrReverse, which reverses the characters in a string. Here's the remedy, in the form of a custom method that also enables you to reverse only a portion of the string:

```
Function StringReverse(ByVal s As String, Optional ByVal startIndex As Integer = 0,_
      Optional ByVal count As Integer = -1) As String
   Dim chars() As Char = s.ToCharArray()
   If count < 0 Then count = s.Length - startIndex
   Array.Reverse(chars, startIndex, count)
   Return New String(chars)
End Function
```

Occasionally, you might need to duplicate a string a given number of times. The Microsoft.VisualBasic library offers the StrDup function, but this function works only with one-character strings. Here's a better method based on the CopyTo method that enables you to duplicate a string of any length:

```
Function StringDuplicate(ByVal s As String, ByVal count As Integer) As String
   ' Prepare a character array of given length.
   Dim chars(s.Length * count - 1) As Char
   ' Copy the string into the array multiple times.
   For i As Integer = 0 To count - 1
      s.CopyTo(0, chars, i * s.Length, s.Length)
   Next
   Return New String(chars)
End Function
```

Or you can use the following one-liner, which builds a string of spaces whose length is equal to the number of repetitions and then replaces each space with the string to be repeated:

```
' Repeat the Text string a number of times equal to Count.
Dim dupstring As String = New String(" "c, Count).Replace(" ", Text)
```

You can use the IndexOf method in a loop to count the number of occurrences of a substring:

```
Function CountSubstrings(ByVal source As String, ByVal search As String) As Integer
    Dim count As Integer = -1
    Dim index As Integer = -1
    Do
        count += 1
        index = source.IndexOf(search, index + 1)
    Loop Until index < 0
    Return count
End Function
```

You can also calculate the number of occurrences of a substring with the following technique, which is more concise but slightly less efficient than is the previous method because it creates two temporary strings:

```
count = source.Replace(search, search & "*").Length - source.Length
```

String Optimizations

An important detail to keep in mind is that a String object is *immutable*: once you create a string, its contents can never change. In fact, all the methods shown so far don't modify the original String; rather, they return another String object that you might or might not assign to the same String variable. Understanding this detail enables you to avoid a common programming mistake:

```
Dim s As String = "abcde"
' You *might* believe that next statement changes the string…
s.ToUpper()
' …but it isn't the case because the result wasn't assigned back to s.
Console.WriteLine(s)                   ' => abcde
' This is the correct way to invoke string methods.
s = s.ToUpper()
```

If you do assign the result to the same variable, the original string becomes unreachable from the application (unless there are other variables pointing to it) and will eventually be disposed of by the garbage collector. Because String values are immutable, the compiler can optimize the resulting code in ways that wouldn't be possible otherwise. For example, consider this code fragment:

```
Dim s1 As String = "1234" & "5678"
Dim s2 As String = "12345678"
Console.WriteLine(s1 Is s2)                    ' => True
```

The compiler computes the concatenation (&) operator at compile time and realizes that both variables contain the same sequence of characters, so it can allocate only one block of memory for the string and have the two variables pointing to it. Because the string is immutable, a new object is created behind the scenes as soon as you attempt to modify the characters in that string:

```
' …(Continuing the previous code fragment)…
' Attempt to modify the S1 string using the Mid statement.
Mid(s1, 2, 1) = "x"
' Prove that a new string was created behind the scenes.
Console.WriteLine(s1 Is s2)                       ' => False
```

Because of this behavior, you never really need to invoke the Clone method to explicitly create a copy of the string. Simply use the string as you would normally, and the compiler creates a copy for you if and when necessary.

The CLR can optimize string management by maintaining an internal pool of string values known as an *intern pool* for each .NET application. If the value being assigned to a string variable coincides with one of the strings already in the intern pool, no additional memory is created and the variable receives the address of the string value in the pool. As shown earlier, the compiler is capable of using the intern pool to optimize string initialization and have two string variables pointing to the same String object in memory. This optimization step isn't performed at run time, though, because the search in the pool takes time and in most cases it would fail, adding overhead to the application without bringing any benefit.

```
' Prove that no optimization is performed at run time.
s1 = "1234"
s1 &= "5678"
s2 = "12345678"
' These two variables point to different String objects.
Console.WriteLine(s1 Is s2)                       ' => False
```

You can optimize string management by using the Intern static method. This method searches a string value in the intern pool and returns a reference to the pool element that contains the value if the value is already in the pool. If the search fails, the string is added to the pool and a reference to it is returned. Notice how you can "manually" optimize the preceding code snippet by using the String.Intern method:

```
s1 = "ABCD"
s1 &= "EFGH"
' Move S1 to the intern pool.
s1 = String.Intern(s1)
' Assign S2 a string constant (that we know is in the pool).
s2 = "ABCDEFGH"
' These two variables point to the same String object.
Console.WriteLine(s1 Is s2)                       ' => True
```

This optimization technique makes sense only if you're working with long strings that appear in multiple portions of the applications. Another good time to use this technique is when you have many instances of a server-side component that contain similar string variables, such as a database connection string. Even if these strings don't change during the program's lifetime, they're usually read from a file, and, therefore, the compiler can't optimize their memory allocation automatically. Using the Intern method, you can help your application produce a smaller memory footprint. You can also use the IsInterned static method to check whether a string is in the intern pool (in which case the string itself is returned) or not (in which case the method returns Nothing):

```
' Continuing previous example…
If Not String.IsInterned(s1) Is Nothing Then
   ' This block is executed because s1 is in the intern pool.
End If
```

Here's another simple performance tip: try to gather multiple string concatenations in the same statement instead of spreading them across separate lines. The Visual Basic compiler can optimize multiple concatenation operations only if they're in the same statement.

The CultureInfo Type

The System.Globalization.CultureInfo class defines an object that you can inspect to determine some key properties of any installed languages. You can also use the object as an argument in many methods of the String and other types. The class exposes the Current-Culture static property, which returns the CultureInfo object for the current language:

```
' Get information about the current locale.
Dim ci As CultureInfo = CultureInfo.CurrentCulture
' Assuming that the current language is Italian, we get:
Console.WriteLine(ci.Name)                          ' => it
Console.WriteLine(ci.EnglishName)                   ' => Italian
Console.WriteLine(ci.NativeName)                    ' => italiano
Console.WriteLine(ci.LCID)                          ' => 16
Console.WriteLine(ci.TwoLetterISOLanguageName)      ' => it
Console.WriteLine(ci.ThreeLetterISOLanguageName)    ' => ita
Console.WriteLine(ci.ThreeLetterWindowsLanguageName) ' => ITA
```

You can get additional information about the locale through the TextInfo object, exposed by the property with the same name:

```
Dim ti As TextInfo = ci.TextInfo
Console.WriteLine(ti.ANSICodePage)                  ' => 1252
Console.WriteLine(ti.EBCDICCodePage)                ' => 20280
Console.WriteLine(ti.OEMCodePage)                   ' => 850
Console.WriteLine(ti.ListSeparator)                 ' => ;
```

The CultureInfo object exposes two properties, NumberFormat and DateTimeFormat, which return information about how numbers and dates are formatted according to a given locale. For example, consider this code:

```
' How do you spell "Sunday" in German?
' First create a CultureInfo object for German/Germany.
```

```
' (Note that you must pass a string in the form "locale-COUNTRY" if
' a given language is spoken in multiple countries.)
Dim ciDe As New CultureInfo("de-DE")
' Next get the corresponding DateTimeFormatInfo object.
Dim dtfi As DateTimeFormatInfo = ciDe.DateTimeFormat
' Here's the answer.
Console.WriteLine(dtfi.GetDayName(DayOfWeek.Sunday))    ' => Sonntag
```

You'll find the "locale-COUNTRY" strings in many places of the .NET Framework. The GetCultures static method returns an array of all the installed cultures, so you can inspect all the languages that your operating system supports:

```
' Get info on all the installed cultures.
Dim ciArr() As CultureInfo = CultureInfo.GetCultures(CultureTypes.AllCultures)
' Print abbreviation and English name of each culture.
For Each c As CultureInfo In ciArr
   Console.WriteLine("{0} ({1})", c.Name, c.EnglishName)
Next
```

 The GetCultureInfo static method, new in version 2.0, enables you to retrieve a cached, read-only version of a CultureInfo object. When you repeatedly use this method to ask for the same culture, the same cached CultureInfo object is returned, thus saving instantiation time:

```
Dim ci1 As CultureInfo = CultureInfo.GetCultureInfo("it-IT")
Dim ci2 As CultureInfo = CultureInfo.GetCultureInfo("it-IT")
' Prove that the second call returned a cached object.
Console.WriteLine(ci1 Is ci2)                         ' => True
```

The auxiliary TextInfo object permits you to convert a string to uppercase, lowercase, or title case (for example, "These Are Four Words") for a given language:

```
' Create a CultureInfo object for Canadian French. (Use a cached object if possible.)
Dim ciFr As CultureInfo = CultureInfo.GetCultureInfo("fr-CA")
' Convert a string to title case using Canadian French rules.
s = ciFr.TextInfo.ToTitleCase(s)
```

Most of the string methods whose result depends on the locale accept a CultureInfo object as an argument, namely, Compare, StartsWith, EndsWith, ToLower, and ToUpper. (This feature is new to .NET Framework 2.0 for the last four methods.) Let's see how you can pass this object to the String.Compare method so that you can compare strings according to the collation rules defined by a given language. One overloaded version of the Compare method takes four arguments: the two strings to be compared, a Boolean value that indicates whether the comparison is case insensitive, and a CultureInfo object that specifies the language to be used:

```
' Compare two strings in case-insensitive mode according to rules of Italian language.
Dim s1 As String = "cioè"
Dim s2 As String = "CIOÈ"
' You can create a CultureInfo object on the fly.
If String.Compare(s1, s2, True, New CultureInfo("it")) = 0 Then
   Console.WriteLine("s1 = s2")
End If
```

Here also is an overloaded version that compares two substrings:

```
If String.Compare(s1, 1, s2, 1, 4, True, New CultureInfo("it")) = 1 Then
   Console.WriteLine("s1's first four chars are greater than s2's")
End If
```

If you don't pass any CultureInfo object to the Compare method, the comparison is performed using the locale associated with the current thread. You can change this locale value by assigning a CultureInfo object to the CurrentCulture property of the current thread, as follows:

```
' Use Italian culture for all string operations and comparisons.
Thread.CurrentThread.CurrentCulture = New CultureInfo("it-IT")
```

You can also compare values according to an invariant culture so that the order in which your results are evaluated is the same regardless of the locale of the current thread. In this case, you can pass the return value of the CultureInfo.InvariantCulture static property:

```
If String.Compare(s1, s2, True, CultureInfo.InvariantCulture) = 0 Then …
```

.NET Framework 2.0 offers the new StringComparison enumerated type that enables you to perform comparisons and equality tests in using the current culture, the invariant culture, and the numeric values of individual characters, both in case-sensitive and case-insensitive ways. For more details and examples, read the section titled "Comparing and Searching Strings" earlier in this chapter.

The Encoding Class

All .NET strings store their characters in Unicode format, so sometimes you might need to convert them to and from other formats—for example, ASCII or the UCS Transformation Format 7 (UTF-7) or UTF-8 variants of the Unicode format. You can do this with the Encoding class in the System.Text namespace.

The first thing to do when converting a .NET Unicode string to or from another format is create the proper encoding object. The Encoding class opportunely exposes the most common encoding objects through the following static properties: ASCII, Unicode (little-endian byte order), BigEndianUnicode, UTF7, UTF8, UTF32, and Default (the system's current ANSI code page). Here's an example of how you can convert a Unicode string to a sequence of bytes that represent the same string in ASCII format:

```
Dim text As String = "A Unicode string with accented vowels: àèéìòù"
Dim uni As Encoding = Encoding.Unicode
Dim uniBytes() As Byte = uni.GetBytes(text)
Dim ascii As Encoding = Encoding.ASCII
Dim asciiBytes() As Byte = Encoding.Convert(uni, ascii, uniBytes)

' Convert the ASCII bytes back to a string.
Dim asciiText As String = ascii.GetChars(asciiBytes)
Console.WriteLine(asciiText)   ' => A Unicode string with accented vowels: ?????
```

You can also create other Encoding objects with the GetEncoding static method, which takes either a code page number or code page name and throws a NotSupportedException if the code page isn't supported:

```
' Get the encoding object for code page 1252.
Dim enc As Encoding = Encoding.GetEncoding(1252)
```

The GetEncodings method (new in .NET Framework 2.0) returns an array of EncodingInfo objects, which provide information on all the Encoding objects and code pages installed on the computer:

```
For Each ei As EncodingInfo In Encoding.GetEncodings
   Console.WriteLine("Name={0}, DisplayName={1}, CodePage={2}", _
      ei.Name, ei.DisplayName, ei.CodePage)
Next
```

The GetChars method expects that the byte array you feed it contains an integer number of characters. (For example, it must end with the second byte of a two-byte character.) This requirement can be a problem when you read the byte array from a file or from another type of stream, and you're working with a string format that allows one, two, or three bytes per character. In such cases, you should use a Decoder object, which remembers the state between consecutive calls. For more information, read the MSDN documentation.

Formatting Numeric Values

The Format static method of the String class enables you to format a string and include one or more numeric or date values in it, in a way similar to the Console.Write method. The string being formatted can contain placeholders for arguments, in the format {N} where N is an index that starts at 0:

```
' Print the value of a string variable.
Dim xyz As String = "foobar"
Dim msg As String
msg = String.Format("The value of {0} variable is {1}.", "XYZ", xyz)
   ' => The value of XYZ variable is foobar.
```

If the argument is numeric, you can add a colon after the argument index and then a character that indicates what kind of formatting you're requesting. The available characters are G (general), N (number), C (currency), D (decimal), E (scientific), F (fixed-point), P (percent), R (round-trip), and X (hexadecimal):

```
' Format a Currency according to current locale.
msg = String.Format("Total is {0:C}, balance is {1:C}", 123.45, -67)
   ' => Total is $123.45, balance is ($67.00)
```

The number format uses commas—or to put it more precisely, the thousands separator defined by the current locale—to group digits:

```
msg = String.Format("Total is {0:N}", 123456.78)   ' => Total is 123,456.78
```

You can append an integer after the N character to round or extend the number of digits after the decimal point:

```
msg = String.Format("Total is {0:N4}", 123456.785555)    ' => Total is 123,456.7856
```

The decimal format works with integer values only and throws a FormatException if you pass a noninteger argument; you can specify a length that, if longer than the result, causes one or more leading zeros to be added:

```
msg = String.Format("Total is {0:D8}", 123456)             ' => Total is 00123456
```

The fixed-point format is useful with decimal values, and you can indicate how many decimal digits should be displayed (two if you omit the length):

```
msg = String.Format("Total is {0:F3}", 123.45678)          ' => Total is 123.457
```

The scientific (or exponential) format displays numbers as *n.mmmE+eeee*, and you can control how many decimal digits are used in the mantissa portion:

```
msg = String.Format("Total is {0:E}", 123456.789)   ' => Total is 1.234568E+005
msg = String.Format("Total is {0:E3}", 123456.789)  ' => Total is 1.235E+005
```

The general format converts to either fixed-point or exponential format, depending on which format delivers the most compact result:

```
msg = String.Format("Total is {0:G}", 123456)    ' => Total is 123456
msg = String.Format("Total is {0:G4}", 123456)   ' => Total is 1.235E+05
```

The percent format converts a number to a percentage with two decimal digits by default, using the format specified for the current culture:

```
msg = String.Format("Percentage is {0:P}", 0.123)    ' => Total is 12.30 %
```

The round-trip format converts a number to a string containing all significant digits so that the string can be converted back to a number later without any loss of precision:

```
' The number of digits you pass after the "R" character is ignored.
msg = String.Format("Value of PI is {0:R}", Math.PI)
   ' => Value of PI is 3.1415926535897931
```

Finally, the hexadecimal format converts numbers to hexadecimal strings. If you specify a length, the number is padded with leading zeros if necessary:

```
msg = String.Format("Total is {0:X8}", 65535)    ' => Total is 0000FFFF
```

You can build custom format strings by using a few special characters, whose meaning is summarized in Table 12-1. Here are a few examples:

```
msg = String.Format("Total is {0:##,###.00}", 1234.567)    ' => Total is 1,234.57
msg = String.Format("Percentage is {0:##.000%}", .3456)    ' => Percentage is 34.560%
```

```
' An example of prescaler
msg = String.Format("Length in {0:###,.00 }", 12344)      ' => Total is 12.34

' Two examples of exponential format
msg = String.Format("Total is {0:#.#####E+00}", 1234567) ' => Total is 1.23457E+06
msg = String.Format("Total is {0:#.#####E0}", 1234567)    ' => Total is 1.23457E6

' Two examples with separate sections
msg = String.Format("Total is {0:##;<##>}", -123)         ' => Total is <123>
msg = String.Format("Total is {0:#;(#);zero}", 1234567)   ' => Total is 1234567
```

In some cases, you can use two or three sections to avoid If or Select Case logic. For example, you can replace the following code:

```
If n1 > n2 Then
   msg = "n1 is greater than n2"
ElseIf n1 < n2 Then
   msg = "n1 is less than n2"
Else
   msg = "n1 is equal to n2"
End If
```

with the more concise but somewhat more cryptic code:

```
msg = String.Format("n1 is {0:greater than;less than;equal to} n2", n1 - n2)
```

A little-known feature of the String.Format method—as well as all the methods that use it internally, such as the Console.Write method—is that it enables you to specify the width of a field and decide to align the value to the right or the left:

```
' Build a table of numbers, their square, and their square root.
' This prints the header of the table.
Console.WriteLine("{0,-5} | {1,7} | {2,10:N2}", "N", "N^2", "Sqrt(N)")
For n As Integer = 1 To 100
   ' N is left-aligned in a field 5-char wide,
   ' N^2 is right-aligned in a field 7-char wide, and Sqrt(N) is displayed with
   ' 2 decimal digits and is right-aligned in a field 10-char wide.
   Console.WriteLine("{0,-5} | {1,7} | {2,10:N2}", n, n ^ 2, Math.Sqrt(n))
Next
```

You specify the field width after the comma symbol; use a positive width for right-aligned values and a negative width for left-aligned values. If you want to provide a predefined format, use a colon as a separator after the width value. As shown in the previous example, field widths are also supported with numeric, string, and date values.

Finally, you can insert literal braces by doubling them in the format string:

```
Console.WriteLine(" {{{0}}}", 123)            ' => {123}
```

Table 12-1   Special Formatting Characters in Custom Formatting Strings

Format	Description
#	Placeholder for a digit or a space.
0	Placeholder for a digit or a zero.
.	Decimal separator.
,	Thousands separator; if used immediately before the decimal separator, it works as a prescaler. (For each comma in this position, the value is divided by 1,000 before formatting.)
%	Displays the number as a percentage value.
E+000	Displays the number in exponential format, that is, with an E followed by the sign of the exponent, and then a number of exponent digits equal to the number of zeros after the plus sign.
E-000	Like the previous exponent symbol, but the exponent sign is displayed only if negative.
;	Section separator. The format string can contain one, two, or three sections. If there are two sections, the first applies to positive and zero values, and the second applies to negative values. If there are three sections, they are used for positive, negative, and zero values, respectively.
\char	Escape character, to insert characters that otherwise would be taken as special characters (for example, \; to insert a semicolon and \\ to insert a backslash).
'...' "..."	A group of literal characters. You can add a sequence of literal characters by enclosing them in single or double quotation marks.
Other	Any other character is taken literally and inserted in the result string as is.

Formatting Date Values

The String.Format method also supports date and time values with both standard and custom formats. Table 12-2 summarizes all the standard date and time formats and makes it easy to find the format you're looking for at a glance.

```
Dim aDate As Date = #5/17/2005 3:54 PM#
msg = String.Format("Event Date Time is {0:f}", aDate)
' => Event Date Time is Tuesday, May 17, 2005 3:54 PM
```

If you can't find a standard date and time format that suits your needs, you can create a custom format by putting together the special characters listed in Table 12-3:

```
msg = String.Format("Current year is {0:yyyy}", Now) ' => Current year is 2005
```

The default date separator (/) and default time separator (:) formatting characters are particularly elusive because they're replaced by the default date and time separator defined for the current locale. In some cases—most notably when formatting dates for a structured query language (SQL) SELECT or INSERT command—you want to be sure that a given separator is used on all occasions. In this case, you must use the backslash escape character to force a specific separator:

```
' Format a date in the format mm/dd/yyyy, regardless of current locale.
msg = String.Format("{0:MM\/dd\/yyyy}", aDate)    ' => 05/17/2005
```

Table 12-2   **Standard Formats for Date and Time Values**[1]

Format	Description	Pattern	Example
d	ShortDatePattern	MM/dd/yyyy	1/6/2005
D	LongDatePattern	dddd, MMMM dd, yyyy	Thursday, January 06, 2005
f	Full date and time (long date and short time)	dddd, MMMM dd, yyyy HH:mm	Thursday, January 06, 2005 3:54 PM
F	FullDateTimePattern (long date and long time)	dddd, MMMM dd, yyyy HH:mm:ss	Thursday, January 06, 2005 3:54:20 PM
g	general (short date and short time)	MM/dd/yyyy HH:mm	1/6/2005 3:54 PM
G	General (short date and long time)	MM/dd/yyyy HH:mm:ss	1/6/2005 3:54:20 PM
M,m	MonthDayPattern	MMMM dd	January 06
Y,y	YearMonthPattern	MMMM, yyyy	January, 2005
t	ShortTimePattern	HH:mm	3:54 PM
T	LongTimePattern	HH:mm:ss	3:54:20 PM
s	SortableDateTime Pattern (conforms to ISO 8601) using current culture	yyyy-MM-dd HH:mm:ss	2005-01-06T15:54:20
u	UniversalSortable DateTimePattern (conforms to ISO 8601), unaffected by current culture	yyyy-MM-dd HH:mm:ss	2002-01-06 20:54:20Z
U	UniversalSortable DateTimePattern	dddd, MMMM dd, yyyy HH:mm:ss	Thursday, January 06, 2005 5:54:20 PM
R,r	RFC1123Pattern	ddd, dd MMM yyyy HH':'mm':'ss 'GMT'	Thu, 06 Jan 2005 15:54:20 GMT
O,o	RoundtripKind (useful to restore all properties when parsing)	yyyy-MM-dd HH:mm:ss.fffffffK	2005-01-06T15:54: 20.0000000-08:00

[1]   Notice that formats U, u, R, and r use Universal (Greenwich) Time, regardless of the local time zone, so example values for these formats are 5 hours ahead of example values for other formats (which assume local time to be U.S. Eastern time). The Pattern column specifies the corresponding custom format string made up of the characters listed in Table 12-3.

Table 12-3   **Character Sequences That Can Be Used in Custom Date and Time Formats**

Format	Description
d	Day of month (one or two digits as required).
dd	Day of month (always two digits, with a leading zero if required).
ddd	Day of week (three-character abbreviation).

Table 12-3   Character Sequences That Can Be Used in Custom Date and Time Formats *(Continued)*

Format	Description
dddd	Day of week (full name).
M	Month number (one or two digits as required).
MM	Month number (always two digits, with a leading zero if required).
MMM	Month name (three-character abbreviation).
MMMM	Month name (full name).
y	Year (last one or two digits, no leading zero).
yy	Year (last two digits).
yyyy	Year (four digits).
H	Hour in 24-hour format (one or two digits as required).
HH	Hour in 24-hour format (always two digits, with a leading zero if required).
h	Hour in 12-hour format (one or two digits as required).
hh	Hour in 12-hour format.
m	Minutes (one or two digits as required).
mm	Minutes (always two digits, with a leading zero if required).
s	Seconds (one or two digits as required).
ss	Seconds.
t	The first character in the AM/PM designator.
f	Second fractions, represented in one digit. (*ff* means second fractions in two digits, *fff* in three digits, and so on up to 7 fs in a row.)
F	Second fractions, represented in an optional digit. Similar to f, except it can be used with DateTime.ParseExact without throwing an exception if there are fewer digits than expected. (New in .NET Framework 2.0.).
tt	The AM/PM designator.
z	Time zone offset, hour only (one or two digits as required).
zz	Time zone offset, hour only (always two digits, with a leading zero if required).
zzz	Time zone offset, hour and minute (hour and minute values always have two digits, with a leading zero if required).
K	The Z character if the Kind property of the DateTime value is Utc; the time zone offset (e.g., "-8:00") if the Kind property is Local; an empty character if the Kind property is Unspecified. (New in .NET Framework 2.0.).
/	Default date separator.
:	Default time separator.
\char	Escape character, to include literal characters that would be otherwise considered special characters.
%format	Includes a predefined date/time format in the result string.
'...' "..."	A group of literal characters. You can add a sequence of literal characters by enclosing them in single or double quotation marks.
other	Any other character is taken literally and inserted in the result string as is.

The Char Type

The Char class represents a single character. There isn't much to say about this data type, other than it exposes a number of useful static methods that enable you to test whether a single character meets a given criterion. All these methods are overloaded and take either a single Char, or a String plus an index in the string. For example, you check whether a character is a digit as follows:

```
' Check an individual Char value.
Dim ok As Boolean = Char.IsDigit("1"c)          ' => True
' Check the Nth character in a string.
ok = Char.IsDigit("A123", 0)                    ' => False
```

This is the list of the most useful static methods that test single characters: IsControl, IsDigit, IsLetter, IsLetterOrDigit, IsLower, IsNumber, IsPunctuation, IsSeparator, IsSymbol, IsUpper, and IsWhiteSpace.

You can convert a character to uppercase and lowercase with the ToUpper and ToLower static methods. By default these methods work according to the current thread's locale, but you can pass them an optional CultureInfo object, or you can use the culture-invariant versions ToUpperInvariant and ToLowerInvariant:

```
Dim newChar As Char = Char.ToUpper("a"c)                    ' => A
newChar = Char.ToLower("H"c, New CultureInfo("it-IT"))      ' => h
Dim loChar As Char = Char.ToLowerInvariant("G"c)           ' => g
```

You can convert a string into a Char by means of the CChar operator or the Char.Parse method. Or you can use the new TryParse static method (added in .NET Framework 2.0) to check whether the conversion is possible and perform it in one operation:

```
If Char.TryParse("a", newChar) Then
    ' newChar contains the a character.
End If
```

The Char class doesn't directly expose the methods to convert a character into its Unicode value and back. If you don't want to use the Asc, AscW, Chr, and ChrW methods in the Microsoft.VisualBasic.Strings module, you can resort to a pair of static methods in the System.Convert type:

```
' Get the Unicode value of a character (same as Asc, AscW).
Dim uni As Short = Convert.ToInt16("A"c)
' Convert back to a character.
Dim ch As Char = Convert.ToChar(uni)
```

I cover the Convert class in more detail later in this chapter.

The StringBuilder Type

As you know, a String object is immutable, and its value never changes after the string has been created. This means that any time you apply a method that changes its value, you're actually creating a new String object. For example, the following statement:

```
s = s.Insert(3, "1234")
```

doesn't modify the original string in memory. Instead, the Insert method creates a new String object, which is then assigned to the S object variable. The original string object in memory is eventually reclaimed during the next garbage collection unless another variable points to it. The superior memory allocation scheme of .NET ensures that this mechanism adds a relatively low overhead; nevertheless, too many allocate and release operations can degrade your application's performance. The System.Text.StringBuilder object offers a solution to this problem.

You can think of a StringBuilder object as a buffer that can contain a string with the ability to grow from zero characters to the buffer's current capacity. Until you exceed that capacity, the string is assembled in the buffer and no memory is allocated or released. If the string becomes longer than the current capacity, the StringBuilder object transparently creates a larger buffer. The default buffer initially contains 16 characters, but you can change this by assigning a different capacity in the StringBuilder constructor or by assigning a value to the Capacity property:

```
' Create a StringBuilder object with initial capacity of 1,000 characters.
Dim sb As New StringBuilder(1000)
```

You can process the string held in the StringBuilder object with several methods, most of which have the same name as and work similarly to methods exposed by the String class—for example, the Insert, Remove, and Replace methods. The most common way to build a string inside a StringBuilder object is by means of its Append method, which takes an argument of any type and appends it to the current internal string:

```
' Create a comma-delimited list of the first 100 integers.
For n As Integer = 1 To 100
    ' Note that two Append methods are faster than a single Append,
    ' whose argument is the concatenation of N and ",".
    sb.Append(n)
    sb.Append(",")
Next
' Insert a string at the beginning of the buffer.
sb.Insert(0, "List of numbers: ")
Console.WriteLine(sb)    ' => List of numbers: 1,2,3,4,5,6,…
```

The Length property returns the current length of the internal string:

```
' Continuing previous example…
Console.WriteLine("Length is {0}.", sb.Length)    ' => Length is 309.
```

There's also an AppendFormat method, which enables you to specify a format string, much like the String.Format method, and an AppendLine method (new in .NET Framework 2.0), which appends a string and the default line terminator:

```
For n As Integer = 1 To 100
   sb.AppendLine(CStr(n))
Next
```

The following procedure compares how quickly the String and StringBuilder classes perform a large number of string concatenations:

```
Dim s As String = ""
Const TIMES As Integer = 10000

Dim sw As New Stopwatch()
sw.Start()
For i As Integer = 1 To TIMES
   s &= CStr(i) & ","
Next
sw.Stop()
Console.WriteLine("Regular string: {0} milliseconds",  sw.ElapsedMilliseconds)

sw = New Stopwatch()
sw.Start()
Dim sb As New StringBuilder(TIMES * 4)
For i As Integer = 1 To TIMES
   ' Notice how you can merge two Append methods.
   sb.Append(i).Append(",")
Next
sw.Stop()
Console.WriteLine("StringBuilder: {0} milliseconds.", sw.ElapsedMilliseconds)
```

The results of this benchmark can really be astonishing because they show that the String-Builder object can be more than 100 times faster than the regular String class is. The actual ratio depends on how many iterations you have and how long the involved strings are. For example, when TIMES is set to 20,000 on my computer, the standard string takes 5 seconds to complete the loop, whereas the StringBuilder type takes only 8 milliseconds!

The SecureString Type

The way .NET strings are implemented has some serious implications related to security. In fact, if you store confidential information in a string—for example, a password or a credit card number—another process that can read your application's address space can also read your data. Although getting access to a process's address space isn't really a trivial task, consider that some portions of your address space are often saved in the operating system's swap file, where reading them is much easier.

The fact that strings are immutable means that you can't really clear a string after using it. Worse, because a string is subject to garbage collection, there might be several copies of it in memory, which in turn increases the probability that one of them goes in the swap file. A .NET

Framework version 1.1 application that wants to ensure the highest degree of confidentiality should stay clear of standard strings and use some other technique, for example, an encrypted Char or Byte array, which is decrypted only one instant before using the string and cleared immediately afterward.

Version 2.0 of the .NET Framework makes this process easier with the introduction of the SecureString type, in the System.Security namespace. Basically, a SecureString instance is an array of characters that is encrypted using the Data Protection API (DPAPI). Unlike the standard string, and similarly to the StringBuilder type, the SecureString type is mutable: you build it one character at a time by means of the AppendChar method, similar to what you do with the StringBuilder type, and you can also insert, remove, and modify individual characters by means of the InsertAt, SetAt, and RemoveAt methods. Optionally, you can make the string immutable by invoking the MakeReadOnly method. Finally, to reduce the number of copies that float in memory, SecureString instances are *pinned*, which means that they can't be moved around by the garbage collector.

The SecureString type is so secure that it exposes neither a method to initialize it from a string nor a method that returns its contents as clear text: the former task requires a series of calls to AppendChar, the latter can be performed with the help of the Marshal type, as I'll explain shortly. A SecureString isn't serializable and therefore you can't even save to file for later retrieval. And of course you can't initialize it from a string burnt into your code, which would defy the intended purpose of this type. What are your options for correctly initializing a SecureString object, then?

A first option is to store the password as clear text in an access control list (ACL)–protected file and read it one char at a time. This option isn't bulletproof, though, and in some cases it can't be applied anyway because the confidential data is entered by the user at run time.

Another option—actually the only option that you can adopt when the user enters the confidential data at run time—is to have the user enter the text one character at a time, and then encrypt it on the fly. The following code snippet shows how you can fake a password-protected TextBox control in a Windows Forms application that never stores its contents in a regular string:

```
Dim password As New SecureString()

Private Sub txtPassword_KeyPress(ByVal sender As Object, ByVal e As KeyPressEventArgs) _
      Handles txtPassword.KeyPress
   Select Case Asc(e.KeyChar)
      Case 8
         ' Backspace: remove the char from the secure string.
         If txtPassword.SelectionStart > 0 Then
            password.RemoveAt(txtPassword.SelectionStart - 1)
         End If
      Case Is >= 32
         ' Delete current selection.
         If txtPassword.SelectionLength > 0 Then
```

```
            For i As Integer = txtPassword.SelectionStart + _
                txtPassword.SelectionLength - 1 To txtPassword.SelectionStart Step -1
                password.RemoveAt(i)
            Next
        End If
        ' Regular character: insert it in the secure string.
        If txtPassword.SelectionStart = txtPassword.SelectionLength Then
            password.AppendChar(e.KeyChar)
        Else
            password.InsertAt(txtPassword.SelectionStart, e.KeyChar)
        End If
        ' Display (and store) an asterisk in the text box.
        e.KeyChar = "*"c
    End Select
End Sub
```

As I mentioned before, the SecureString object doesn't expose any method that returns its contents as clear text. Instead, you must use a couple of methods of the Marshal type, in the System.Runtime.InteropServices namespace:

```
' Convert the password into an unmanaged BSTR.
Dim ptr As IntPtr = Marshal.SecureStringToBSTR(password)
' For demo purposes, convert the BSTR into a regular string and use it.
Dim pw As String = Marshal.PtrToStringBSTR(ptr)
…
' Clear the unmanaged BSTR used for the password.
Marshal.ZeroFreeBSTR(ptr)
```

Of course, the previous code isn't really secure because at one point you have assigned the password to a regular string. In some cases, this is unavoidable, but at least this approach ensures that the clear text string exists for a shorter amount of time. An alternative, better approach is to have the unmanaged Basic string (BSTR) processed by a piece of unmanaged code.

You really see the benefits of this technique when you use a member that accepts a Secure-String instance, for example, the Password property of the ProcessStartInfo type:

```
' Run Notepad under a different user account.
Dim psi As New ProcessStartInfo("notepad.exe")
psi.UseShellExecute = False
psi.UserName = "Francesco"
psi.Password = password
Process.Start(psi)
```

Numeric Types

I illustrated most of the operations you can perform on numbers in Chapter 2, "Basic Language Concepts." In this section, I complete the discussion showing you the members exposed by the basic numeric classes, particularly the methods related to parsing and formatting.

As you know, Short, Integer, and Long types are just aliases for the Int16, Int32, and Int64 .NET classes. By recognizing their true nature and by using their methods and properties, you can better exploit these types. This section applies to all the numeric types in the .NET Framework, such as Boolean, Byte, SByte, Short (Int16), Integer (Int32), Long (Int64), UShort (UInt16), UInteger (UInt32), ULong (UInt64), Single, Double, and Decimal.

Properties and Methods

All numeric types—and all .NET classes, for that matter—expose the ToString method, which converts their numeric value to a string. This method is especially useful when you're appending the number value to another string:

```
Dim myValue As Double = 123.45
Dim res As String = "The final value is " & myValue.ToString()
```

The ToString method is culturally aware and by default uses the culture associated with the current thread. For example, it uses a comma as a decimal separator if the current thread's culture is Italian or German. Numeric types overload the ToString method to take either a format string or a custom formatter object. (For more detail, refer to the section titled "Formatting Numeric Values" earlier in this chapter.)

```
' Convert an integer to hexadecimal.
Console.WriteLine(1234.ToString("X"))        ' => 4D2
' Display PI with 6 digits (in all).
Dim d As Double = Math.PI
Console.WriteLine(d.ToString("G6"))          ' => 3.14159
```

You can use the CompareTo method to compare a number with another numeric value of the same type. This method returns 1, 0, or –1, depending on whether the current instance is greater than, equal to, or less than the value passed as an argument:

```
Dim sngValue As Single = 1.23
' Compare the Single variable sngValue with 1.
' Note that you must force the argument to Single.
Select Case sngValue.CompareTo(CSng(1))
   Case 1: Console.WriteLine("sngValue is > 1")
   Case 0: Console.WriteLine("sngValue is = 1")
   Case -1: Console.WriteLine("sngValue is < 1")
End Select
```

The argument must be the same type as the value to which you're applying the CompareTo method, so you must convert it if necessary. You can use a conversion function, such as the CSng function in the preceding code, or append a conversion character, such as ! for Single, I for Integer, and so on:

```
' ...(Another way to write the previous code snippet)...
Select Case sngValue.CompareTo(1.0!)
...
```

All the numeric classes expose the MinValue and MaxValue static fields, which return the smallest and greatest value that you can express with the corresponding type:

```
' Display the greatest value you can store in a Double variable.
Console.WriteLine(Double.MaxValue)      ' => 1.79769313486232E+308
```

The numeric classes that support floating-point values—namely, Single and Double classes—expose a few additional read-only static properties. The Epsilon property returns the smallest positive (nonzero) number that can be stored in a variable of that type:

```
Console.WriteLine(Single.Epsilon)      ' => 1.401298E-45
Console.WriteLine(Double.Epsilon)      ' => 4.94065645841247E-324
```

The NegativeInfinity and PositiveInfinity fields return a constant that represents an infinite value, whereas the NaN field returns a constant that represents the Not-a-Number value (NaN is the value you obtain, for example, when evaluating the square root of a negative number). In some cases, you can use infinite values in expressions:

```
' Any number divided by infinity gives 0.
Console.WriteLine(1 / Double.PositiveInfinity)      ' => 0
```

The Single and Double classes also expose static methods that enable you to test whether they contain special values, such as IsInfinity, IsNegativeInfinity, IsPositiveInfinity, and IsNaN.

Formatting Numbers

All the numeric classes support an overloaded form of the ToString method that enables you to apply a format string:

```
Dim intValue As Integer = 12345
Console.WriteLine(intValue.ToString("##,##0.00"))  ' => 12,345.00
```

The method uses the current locale to interpret the formatting string. For example, in the preceding code it uses the comma as the thousands separator and the period as the decimal separator if running on a U.S. system, but reverses the two separators on an Italian system. You can also pass a CultureInfo object to format a number for a given culture:

```
Dim ci As New CultureInfo("it-IT")
Console.WriteLine(intValue.ToString("##,##0.00", ci))      ' => 12.345,00
```

The previous statement works because the ToString takes an IFormatProvider object to format the current value, and the CultureInfo object exposes this interface. In this section, I show you how you can take advantage of another .NET object that implements this interface, the NumberFormatInfo object.

The NumberFormatInfo class exposes many properties that determine how a numeric value is formatted, such as NumberDecimalSeparator (the decimal separator character), Number-GroupSeparator (the thousands separator character), NumberDecimalDigits (number of decimal digits), CurrencySymbol (the character used for currency), and many others. The simplest way to create a valid NumberFormatInfo object is by means of the CurrentInfo shared method of the NumberFormatInfo class; the returned value is a read-only Number-FormatInfo object based on the current locale:

```
Dim nfi As NumberFormatInfo = NumberFormatInfo.CurrentInfo
```

(You can also use the InvariantInfo property, which returns a NumberFormatInfo object that is culturally independent.)

The problem with the preceding code is that the returned NumberFormatInfo object is read-only, so you can't modify any of its properties. This object is therefore virtually useless because the ToString method implicitly uses the current locale anyway when formatting a value. The solution is to create a clone of the default NumberFormatInfo object and then modify its properties, as in the following snippet:

```
' Format a number with current locale formatting options, but use a comma
' for the decimal separator and a space for the thousands separator.
' (You need DirectCast because the Clone method returns an Object.)
Dim nfi As NumberFormatInfo = _
    DirectCast(NumberFormatInfo.CurrentInfo.Clone, NumberFormatInfo)
' The nfi object is writable, so you can change its properties.
nfi.NumberDecimalSeparator = ","
nfi.NumberGroupSeparator = " "
' You can now format a value with the custom NumberFormatInfo object.
Dim sngValue As Single = 12345.5
Console.WriteLine(sngValue.ToString("##,##0.00", nfi)) ' => 12 345,50
```

For the complete list of NumberFormatInfo properties and methods, see the MSDN documentation.

Parsing Strings into Numbers

All numeric types support the Parse static method, which parses the string passed as an argument and returns the corresponding numeric value. The simplest form of the Parse method takes one string argument:

```
' Next line assigns 1234 to the variable.
Dim shoValue As Short = Short.Parse("1234")
```

An overloaded form of the Parse method takes a NumberStyle enumerated value as its second argument. NumberStyle is a bit-coded value that specifies which portions of the number are allowed in the string being parsed. Valid NumberStyle values are AllowLeadingWhite (1), AllowTrailingWhite (2), AllowLeadingSign (4), AllowTrailingSign (8), AllowParentheses (16), AllowDecimalPoint (32), AllowThousand (64), AllowExponent (128), AllowCurrencySymbol (256), and AllowHexSpecifier (512). You can specify which portions of the strings are valid by using the Or bitwise operator on these values, or you can use some predefined compound values, such as Any (511, allows everything), Integer (7, allows trailing sign and leading/trailing white), Number (111, like Integer but allows thousands separator and decimal point), Float (167, like Integer but allows decimal separator and exponent), and Currency (383, allows everything except exponent).

The following example extracts a Double from a string and recognizes white spaces and all the supported formats:

```
Dim dblValue As Double = Double.Parse(" 1,234.56E6  ", NumberStyles.Any)
    ' dblValue is assigned the value 1234560000.
```

You can be more specific about what is valid and what isn't:

```
Dim style As NumberStyles = NumberStyles.AllowDecimalPoint _
    Or NumberStyles.AllowLeadingSign
' This works and assigns -123.45 to sngValue.
Dim sngValue As Single = Single.Parse("-123.45", style)
' This throws a FormatException because of the thousands separator.
sngValue = Single.Parse("12,345.67", style)
```

A third overloaded form of the Parse method takes any IFormatProvider object; thus, you can pass it a CultureInfo object:

```
' Parse a string according to Italian rules.
sngValue = Single.Parse("12.345,67", New CultureInfo("it-IT"))
```

 All the numeric types in .NET Framework 2.0 expose a new method named TryParse, which allows you to avoid time-consuming exceptions if a string doesn't contain a number in a valid format. (This method is available in .NET Framework 1.1 only for the Double type.) The TryParse method takes a variable by reference in its second argument and returns True if the parsing operation is successful:

```
Dim intValue As Integer
If Integer.TryParse("12345", intValue) Then
    ' intValue contains the result of the parse operation.
Else
    ' The string doesn't contain an integer value in a valid format.
End If
```

A second overload of the TryParse method takes a NumberStyles enumerated value and an IFormatProvider object in its second and third arguments:

```
Dim style As NumberStyles = NumberStyles.AllowDecimalPoint _
    Or NumberStyles.AllowLeadingSign
Dim aValue As Single
If Single.TryParse("-12.345,67", style, New CultureInfo("it-IT"), aValue) Then
    …
End If
```

The Convert Type

The System.Convert class exposes several static methods that help in converting to and from the many data types available in .NET. In their simplest form, these methods can convert any base type to another type and are therefore equivalent to the conversion functions that Visual Basic offers:

```
' Convert the string "123.45" to a Double (same as CDbl function).
Dim dblValue As Double = Convert.ToDouble("123.45")
```

The Convert class exposes many To*Xxxx* methods, one for each base type: ToBoolean, ToByte, ToChar, ToDateTime, ToDecimal, ToDouble, ToInt16, ToInt32, ToInt64, ToSByte, ToSingle, ToString, ToUInt16, ToUInt32, and ToUInt64:

```
' Convert a Double value to an integer (same as CInt function).
Dim intValue As Integer = Convert.ToInt32(dblValue)
```

The To*Xxxx* methods that return an integer type—namely, ToByte, ToSByte, ToInt16, ToInt32, ToInt64, ToUInt16, ToUInt32, and ToUInt64—expose an overload that takes a string and a base and convert a string holding a number in that base. The base can only be 2, 8, 10, or 16:

```
' Convert from a string holding a binary representation of a number.
Dim result As Integer = Convert.ToInt32("11011", 2)        ' => 27
' Convert from an octal number.
result = Convert.ToInt32("777", 8)                         ' => 511
' Convert from an hexadecimal number.
result = Convert.ToInt32("AC", 16)                         ' => 172
```

You can perform the conversion in the opposite direction—that is, from an integer into the string representation of a number in a different base—by means of overloads of the ToString method:

```
' Determine the binary representation of a number.
Dim text As String = Convert.ToString(27, 2)               ' => 11011
' Determine the hexadecimal representation of a number. (Note: result is lowercase.)
text = Convert.ToString(172, 16)                           ' => ac
```

The Convert class exposes two methods that make conversions to and from Base64-encoded strings a breeze. (This is the format used for Multipurpose Internet Mail Extensions (MIME) e-mail attachments.) The ToBase64String method takes an array of bytes and encodes it as a Base64 string. The FromBase64String method does the conversion in the opposite direction:

```
' An array of 16 bytes (two identical sequences of 8 bytes)
Dim b1() As Byte = {12, 45, 213, 88, 11, 220, 34, 0, _
    12, 45, 213, 88, 11, 220, 34, 0}
' Convert it to a Base64 string.
Dim s64 As String = Convert.ToBase64String(b1)
Console.WriteLine(s64)
' Convert it back to an array of bytes, and display it.
Dim b2() As Byte = Convert.FromBase64String(s64)
For Each b As Byte in b2
   Console.Write("{0} ", b)
Next
```

A new option in .NET Framework 2.0 enables you to insert a line separator automatically every 76 characters in the value returned by a ToBase64String method:

```
s64 = Convert.ToBase64String(b1, Base64FormattingOptions.InsertLineBreaks)
```

In addition, the Convert class exposes the ToBase64CharArray and FromBase64CharArray methods, which convert a Byte array to and from a Char array instead of a String. Finally, the class also exposes a generic ChangeType method that can convert (or at least, attempt to convert) a value to any other type. You must use the Visual Basic GetType operator to create the System.Type object to pass in the method's second argument:

```
' Convert a value to Double.
Console.WriteLine(Convert.ChangeType(value, GetType(Double)))
```

Random Number Generator

Visual Basic 2005 still supports the time-honored Randomize statement and Rnd function for backward compatibility with Visual Basic 6, but serious .NET developers should use the System.Random class instead. You can set the seed for random number generation in this class's constructor method:

```
' The argument must be a 32-bit integer.
Dim rand As New Random(12345)
```

When you pass a given seed number, you always get the same random sequence. To get different sequences each time you run the application, you can have the seed depend on the current time:

```
' You need these conversions because the Ticks property
' returns a 64-bit value that must be truncated to a 32-bit integer.
rand = New Random(CInt(Date.Now.Ticks And Integer.MaxValue))
```

Once you have an initialized Random object, you can extract random positive 32-bit integer values each time you query its Next method:

```
For i As Integer = 1 To 10
   Console.WriteLine(rand.Next)
Next
```

You can also pass one or two arguments to keep the return value in the desired range:

```
' Get a value in the range 0 to 1000.
Dim intValue As Integer = rand.Next(1000)
' Get a value in the range 100 to 1,000.
intValue = rand.Next(100, 1000)
```

The NextDouble method is similar to the Rnd function in the Microsoft.VisualBasic library in that it returns a random floating-point number between 0 and 1:

```
Dim dblValue As Double = rand.NextDouble()
```

Finally, you can fill a Byte array with random values with the NextBytes method:

```
' Get an array of 100 random byte values.
Dim buffer(100) As Byte
rand.NextBytes(buffer)
```

> **Note**   Although the Random type is OK in most kinds of applications, for example, when developing card games, the values it generates are easily reproducible and aren't random enough to be used in cryptography. For a more robust random value generator, you should use the RNGCryptoServiceProvider class, in the System.Security.Cryptography namespace.

The DateTime Type

System.DateTime is the main .NET class for working with date and time values. Not only does it offer a place to store data values, it also exposes many useful methods that can replace all the Visual Basic–specific date and time functions. For backward compatibility with Visual Basic 6, Visual Basic 2005 lets you use the Date type as a synonym for the System.DateTime type. In this section, I use the Date class name most of the time, but keep in mind that you can always replace it with System.DateTime or just DateTime (because of the projectwide Imports System statement).

You can initialize a Date value in a number of ways:

```
' Create a Date value by providing year, month, and day values.
Dim dt As Date = New Date(2005, 1, 6)          ' January 6, 2005

' Provide also hour, minute, and second values.
dt = New Date(2005, 1, 6, 18, 30, 20)          ' January 6, 2005 6:30:20 PM

' Add millisecond value (half a second in this example).
dt = New Date(2005, 1, 6, 18, 30, 20, 500)

' Create a time value from ticks (10 million ticks = 1 second).
Dim ticks As Long = 20000000                   ' 2 seconds
' This is considered the time elapsed from Jan. 1 of year 1.
dt = New Date(ticks)                           ' 1/1/0001 12:00:02 AM
```

Because Date and System.DateTime are synonyms, the following statements are perfectly equivalent:

```
dt = New DateTime(2005, 1, 6)
dt = New Date(2005, 1, 6)
```

You can use the Now and Today static properties:

```
' The Now property returns the system date and time.
dt = Date.Now                  ' For example, October 17, 2005 3:54:20 PM
' The Today property returns the system date only.
dt = Date.Today                ' For example, October 17, 2005 12:00:00 AM
```

The UtcNow static property returns the current time expressed as a Universal Time Coordinate (UTC) value and enables you to compare time values originated in different time zones; this property ignores the Daylight Saving Time if currently active for the current time zone:

```
dt = Date.UtcNow
```

Once you have an initialized Date value, you can retrieve individual portions by using one of its read-only properties, namely, Date (the date portion), TimeOfDay (the time portion), Year, Month, Day, DayOfYear, DayOfWeek, Hour, Minute, Second, Millisecond, and Ticks:

```
' Is today the first day of the current month?
If Date.Today.Day = 1 Then Console.WriteLine("First day of month")
' How many days have passed since January 1?
Console.WriteLine(Date.Today.DayOfYear)
' Get current time - note that ticks are included.
Console.WriteLine(Date.Now.TimeOfDay)      ' => 10:39:28.3063680
```

The TimeOfDay property is peculiar in that it returns a TimeSpan object, which represents a difference between dates. Although this class is distinct from the Date class, it shares many of the Date class properties and methods and nearly always works together with Date values, as you'll see shortly.

A note for the curious programmer: a DateTime value is stored as the number of ticks (1 tick = 100 nanoseconds) elapsed since January 1, 0001; this storage format can work for any date between 1/1/0001 and 12/12/9999. In .NET Framework 2.0, this tick value takes 62 bits, and the remaining 2 bits are used to preserve the information whether the date/time is in Daylight Saving Time and whether the date/time is relative to the current time zone (the default) or is expressed as a UTC value.

Adding and Subtracting Dates

The DateTime class exposes several instance methods that enable you to add and subtract a number of years, months, days, hours, minutes, or seconds to or from a Date value. The names of these methods leave no doubt about their function: AddYears, AddMonths, AddDays, AddHours, AddMinutes, AddSeconds, AddMilliseconds, AddTicks. You can add an integer value when you're using AddYears and AddMonths and a decimal value in all other cases. In all cases, you can pass a negative argument to subtract rather than add a value:

```
' Tomorrow's date
dt = Date.Today.AddDays(1)
' Yesterday's date
dt = Date.Today.AddDays(-1)
' What time will it be 2 hours and 30 minutes from now?
dt = Date.Now.AddHours(2.5)

' A CPU-intensive way to pause for 5 seconds.
Dim endTime As Date = Date.Now.AddSeconds(5)
Do: Loop Until Date.Now > endTime
```

The Add method takes a TimeSpan object as an argument. Before you can use it, you must learn to create a TimeSpan object, choosing one of its overloaded constructor methods:

```
' One Long value is interpreted as a Ticks value.
Dim ts As TimeSpan = New TimeSpan(13500000)        ' 1.35 seconds
' Three integer values are interpreted as hours, minutes, seconds.
ts = New TimeSpan(0, 32, 20)                        ' 32 minutes, 20 seconds
```

```
' Four integer values are interpreted as days, hours, minutes, seconds.
ts = New TimeSpan(1, 12, 0, 0)                    ' 1 day and a half
' (Note that arguments aren't checked for out-of-range errors; therefore,
'  the next statement delivers the same result as the previous one.)
ts = New TimeSpan(0, 36, 0, 0)                    ' 1 day and a half
' A fifth argument is interpreted as a millisecond value.
ts = New TimeSpan(0, 0, 1, 30, 500)               ' 90 seconds and a half
```

Now you're ready to add an arbitrary date or time interval to a DateTime value:

```
' What will be the time 2 days, 10 hours, and 30 minutes from now?
dt = Date.Now.Add(New TimeSpan(2, 10, 30, 0))
```

The DateTime class also exposes a Subtract instance method that works in a similar way:

```
' What was the time 1 day, 12 hours, and 20 minutes ago?
dt = Date.Now.Subtract(New TimeSpan(1, 12, 20, 0))
```

The Subtract method is overloaded to take another Date object as an argument, in which case it returns the TimeSpan object that represents the difference between the two dates:

```
' How many days, hours, minutes, and seconds have elapsed
' since the beginning of the third millennium?
Dim startDate As New Date(2001, 1, 1)
Dim diff As TimeSpan = Date.Now.Subtract(startDate)
```

Once you have a TimeSpan object, you can extract the information buried in it by using one of its many properties, whose names are self-explanatory: Days, Hours, Minutes, Seconds, Milliseconds, Ticks, TotalDays, TotalHours, TotalMinutes, TotalSeconds, and TotalMilliseconds. The TimeSpan class also exposes methods such as Add, Subtract, Negate, and CompareTo.

The CompareTo method enables you to determine whether a Date value is greater or less than another Date value:

```
' Is current date later than October 30, 2005?
Select Case Date.Today.CompareTo(New Date(2005, 10, 30))
   Case 1    ' Later than Oct. 30, 2005
   Case -1   ' Earlier than Oct. 30, 2005
   Case 0    ' Today is Oct. 30, 2005.
End Select
```

And you can use comparison operators if you don't need three-state logic:

```
If Date.Today > New Date(2005, 10, 30) Then …
```

By default, DateTime values are relative to the current time zone and you should never compare values coming from different time zones, unless they are in UTC format (see the section titled "Working with Time Zones" later in this chapter). Also, when evaluating the difference between two dates in the same time zone, you might get a wrong result if a transition to or from Daylight Saving Time has occurred between the two dates. This is one more reason to use dates in UTC format.

The IsDaylightSavingTime method (new in .NET Framework 2.0) enables you to detect whether Daylight Saving Time is active for the current time zone:

```
If Date.Now.IsDaylightSavingTime() Then Console.Write("Daylight Saving Time is active")
```

Finally, the Date class exposes two static methods that can be handy in many applications:

```
' Test for a leap year.
Console.WriteLine(Date.IsLeapYear(2000))          ' => True
' Retrieve the number of days in a given month.
Console.WriteLine(Date.DaysInMonth(2000, 2))      ' => 29
```

In spite of the abundance of date and time methods, the DateTime type doesn't offer a simple way to calculate the whole number of years or months elapsed between two dates. For example, you can't calculate the age of a person using this statement:

```
Dim age As Integer = Date.Now.Year - aPerson.BirthDate.Year
```

because the result would be one unit greater than the correct value if the person hasn't celebrated her birthday in the current year. I have prepared a couple of reusable routines that provide the missing functionality:

```
' Return the whole number of years between two dates.
Function YearDiff(ByVal startDate As Date, ByVal endDate As Date) As Integer
   Dim result As Integer = endDate.Year - startDate.Year
   If endDate.Month < startDate.Month OrElse (endDate.Month = startDate.Month _
      AndAlso endDate.Day < startDate.Day) Then result -= 1
   Return result
End Function

' Return the whole number of months between two dates.
Function MonthDiff(ByVal startDate As Date, ByVal endDate As Date) As Integer
   Dim result As Integer = endDate.Year * 12 + endDate.Month - _
      (startDate.Year * 12 + startDate.Month)
   If endDate.Month = startDate.Month AndAlso endDate.Day < startDate.Day Then result -= 1
   Return result
End Function
```

Formatting Dates

The DateTime type overrides the ToString method to accept a standard date format among those specified in Table 12-2 or a user-defined format created by assembling the characters listed in Table 12-3:

```
' This is January 6, 2005 6:30:20.500 PM–U.S. Eastern Time.
Dim dt As Date = New Date(2005, 1, 6, 18, 30, 20, 500)

' Display a date using the LongDatePattern standard format.
Dim dateText As String = dt.ToString("D")      ' => Thursday, January 06, 2005
' Display a date using a custom format.
dateText = dt.ToString("d-MMM-yyyy")           ' => 6-Jan-2005
```

You can format a Date value in other ways by using some peculiar methods that only this type exposes:

```
Console.WriteLine(dt.ToShortDateString())       ' => 1/6/2005
Console.WriteLine(dt.ToLongDateString())        ' => Thursday, January 06, 2005
Console.WriteLine(dt.ToShortTimeString())       ' => 6:30 PM
Console.WriteLine(dt.ToLongTimeString())        ' => 6:30:20 PM
Console.WriteLine(dt.ToFileTime())              ' => 127495062205000000
Console.WriteLine(dt.ToOADate())                ' => 38358.7710706019
' The next two results vary depending on the time zone you're in.
Console.WriteLine(dt.ToUniversalTime())         ' => 1/7/2005 12:30:20 PM
Console.WriteLine(dt.ToLocalTime())             ' => 1/6/2005 12:30:20 PM
```

A few of these formats might require additional explanation:

- The ToFileTime method returns an unsigned 8-byte value representing the date and time as the number of 100-nanosecond intervals that have elapsed since 1/1/1601 12:00 A.M. The DateTime type also supports the ToFileTimeUtc method, which ignores the local time zone.

- The ToOADate method converts to an OLE Automation–compatible value. (This is a Double value similar to the Date values used in Visual Basic 6.)

- The ToUniversalTime method considers the Date value a local time and converts it to UTC format.

- The ToLocalTime method considers the Date value a UTC value and converts it to a local time.

The Date class exposes two static methods, FromOADate and FromFileTime, to parse an OLE Automation date value or a date formatted as a file time.

Parsing Dates

The operation complementary to date formatting is date parsing. The Date class provides a Parse static method for parsing jobs of any degree of complexity:

```
Dim dt As Date = Date.Parse("2005/1/6 12:30:20")
```

The flexibility of this method becomes apparent when you pass an IFormatProvider object as a second argument to it—for example, a CultureInfo object or a DateTimeFormatInfo object. The DateTimeFormatInfo object is conceptually similar to the NumberFormatInfo object described earlier in this chapter (see the section titled "Formatting Numbers" earlier in this chapter), except it holds information about separators and formats allowed in date and time values:

```
' Get a writable copy of the current locale's DateTimeFormatInfo object.
Dim dtfi As DateTimeFormatInfo
dtfi = CType(DateTimeFormatInfo.CurrentInfo.Clone, DateTimeFormatInfo)
' Change date and time separators.
dtfi.DateSeparator = "-"
dtfi.TimeSeparator = "."
```

```
' Now we're ready to parse a date formatted in a nonstandard way.
dt = Date.Parse("2005-1-6 12.30.20", dtfi)
```

Many non-U.S. developers will appreciate the ability to parse dates in formats other than month/day/year. In this case, you have to assign a correctly formatted pattern to the DateTimeFormatInfo object's ShortDatePattern, LongDatePattern, ShortTimePattern, LongTimePattern, or FullDateTimePattern property before doing the parse:

```
' Prepare to parse (dd/mm/yy) dates, in short or long format.
dtfi.ShortDatePattern = "d/M/yyyy"
dtfi.LongDatePattern = "dddd, dd MMMM, yyyy"

' Both these statements assign the date "January 6, 2005."
dt = Date.Parse("6-1-2005 12.30.44", dtfi)
dt = Date.Parse("Thursday, 6 January, 2005", dtfi)
```

You can use the DateTimeFormatInfo object to retrieve standard or abbreviated names for weekdays and months, according to the current locale or any locale:

```
' Display the abbreviated names of months.
For Each s As String In DateTimeFormatInfo.CurrentInfo.AbbreviatedMonthNames
   Console.WriteLine(s)
Next
```

Even more interesting, you can set weekday and month names with arbitrary strings if you have a writable DateTimeFormatInfo object, and then you can use the object to parse a date written in any language, including invented ones. (Yes, including Klingon!)

Another way to parse strings in formats other than month/day/year is to use the ParseExact static method. In this case, you pass the format string as the second argument, and you can pass Nothing to the third argument if you don't need a DateTimeFormatInfo object to further qualify the string being parsed:

```
' This statements assigns the date "January 6, 2005."
dt = Date.ParseExact("6-1-2005", "d-M-yyyy", Nothing)
```

The second argument can be any of the supported DateTime format listed in Table 12-2. In .NET Framework 2.0, the new format F has been added to support the ParseExact method when there are a variable number of fractional digits.

Both the Parse and ParseExact methods throw an exception if the input string doesn't comply with the expected format. As you know, exceptions can add a lot of overhead to your applications and you should try to avoid them if possible. Version 2.0 of the .NET Framework extends the DateTime class with the TryParse and the TryParseExact methods, which return True if the parsing succeeds and store the result of the parsing in a DateTime variable passed a second argument:

```
Dim aDate As Date
If Date.TryParse("January 6, 2005", aDate) Then
   ' aDate contains the parsed date.
End If
```

Another overload of the TryParse method takes an IFormatProvider object (for example, a CultureInfo instance) and a DateTimeStyles bit-coded value; the latter argument enables you to specify whether leading or trailing spaces are accepted and whether local or universal time is assumed:

```
Dim ci As New CultureInfo("en-US")
If Date.TryParse(" 6/1/2005 14:26 ", ci, DateTimeStyles.AllowWhiteSpaces Or _
    DateTimeStyles.AssumeUniversal, aDate) Then
    ' aDate contains the parsed date.
End If
```

If you specify the DateTimesStyles.AssumeUniversal enumerated value (new in .NET Framework 2.0), the parsed time is assumed to be in UTC format and is automatically converted to the local time zone. By default, date values are assumed to be relative to the current time zone.

Working with Time Zones

DateTime values in version 1.1 of the .NET Framework have a serious limitation: they are always expected to store a local time, rather than a normalized UTC time. This assumption causes a few hard-to-solve issues, the most serious of which is a problem that manifests itself when a date value is serialized in one time zone and deserialized in a different zone, using either the SoapFormatter or the XmlSerializer object. These two objects, in fact, store information about the time zone together with the actual date value: when the object is deserialized in a different time zone, the time portion of the date is automatically adjusted to reflect the new geographical location.

In most cases, this behavior is correct, but at times it causes the application to malfunction. Let's say that a person is born in Italy on January 1, 1970, at 2 A.M.; if this date value is serialized as XML and sent to a computer in New York—for example, by using a Web service or by saving the information in a file that is later transferred using FTP or HTTP—the person would appear to be born on December 31, 1969, at 8 P.M. As you can see, the issue with dates in .NET Framework 1.1 originates from the fact that you can't specify whether a value stored in a DateTime variable is to be considered relative to the current time zone or an absolute UTC value.

This problem has been solved quite effectively in .NET Framework 2.0 by the addition of a new Kind property to the DateTime type. This property is a DateTimeKind enumerated value that can be Local, Utc, or Unspecified. For backward compatibility with .NET Framework 1.1 applications, by default a DateTime value has a Kind property set to DateTimeKind.Local, unless you specify a different value in the constructor:

```
' February 14, 2005 at 12:00 AM, UTC value
Dim aDate As New Date(2005, 2, 14, 12, 0, 0, DateTimeKind.Utc)
' Test the Kind property.
Console.WriteLine(aDate.Kind.ToString)          ' Utc
```

The Kind property is read-only, but you can use the SpecifyKind static method to create a different DateTime value if you want to pass from local to UTC time or vice versa:

```
' Next statement changes the Kind property (but doesn't change the date/time value!).
Dim newDate As Date = Date.SpecifyKind(aDate, DateTimeKind.Utc)
```

An important note: the Kind property is accounted for only when serializing and deserializing a date value and is ignored when doing comparisons.

In .NET Framework 1.1, DateTime values are serialized as 64-bit numbers by means of the Ticks property. In .NET Framework 2.0, however, when saving a DateTime value to a file or a database field, you should save the new Kind property as well; otherwise, the deserialization mechanism would suffer from the same problems you see in .NET Framework 1.1. The simplest way to do so is by means of the new ToBinary instance method (which converts the DateTime object to a 64-bit value) and the new FromBinary static method (which converts a 64-bit value to a DateTime value):

```
' Convert to a Long value.
Dim lngValue As Long = aDate.ToBinary()
…
' Convert back from a Long to a Date value.
Dim newDate As Date = Date.FromBinary(lngValue)
```

You can also serialize a DateTime value as text. In this case, you should use the ToString method with the o format (new in .NET Framework 2.0). This format serializes all the information related to a date, including the Kind property and the time zone (if the date isn't in UTC format), and you can read it back by means of a ParseExact method if you specify the new DateTimeStyles.RoundtripKind enumerated value:

```
' Serialize a date in UTC format.
Dim text As String = aDate.ToString("o", CultureInfo.InvariantCulture)
…
' Deserialize it into a new DateTime value.
newDate = Date.ParseExact(text, "o", CultureInfo.InvariantCulture, _
    DateTimeStyles.RoundtripKind)
```

The TimeZone Type

The .NET Framework supports time zone information through the System.TimeZone object, which you can use to retrieve information about the time zone set in Windows regional settings:

```
' Get the TimeZone object for the current time zone.
Dim tz As TimeZone = TimeZone.CurrentTimeZone
' Display name of time zone, without and with Daylight Saving Time.
' (I got these results by running this code in Italy.)
Console.WriteLine(tz.StandardName)  ' => W. Europe Standard Time
Console.WriteLine(tz.DaylightName)  ' => W. Europe Daylight Time
```

The most interesting piece of information here is the offset from UTC format, which you retrieve by means of the GetUTCOffset method. You must pass a date argument to this method because the offset depends on whether Daylight Saving Time is in effect. The returned value is in ticks:

```
' Display the time offset of W. Europe time zone in March 2005,
' when no Daylight Saving Time is active.
Console.WriteLine(tz.GetUTCOffset(New Date(2005, 3, 1)))   ' => 01:00:00
' Display the time offset of W. Europe time zone in July,
' when Daylight Saving Time is active.
Console.WriteLine(tz.GetUTCOffset(New Date(2005, 7, 1)))   ' => 02:00:00
```

The IsDaylightSavingTime method returns True if Daylight Saving Time is in effect:

```
' No Daylight Saving Time in March
Console.WriteLine(tz.IsDaylightSavingTime(New Date(2005, 3, 1)))
' => False
```

Finally, you can determine when Daylight Saving Time starts and ends in a given year by retrieving an array of DaylightTime objects with the TimeZone's GetDaylightChanges method:

```
' Retrieve the DaylightTime object for year 2005.
Dim dlc As DaylightTime = tz.GetDaylightChanges(2005)
' Note that you might get different start and end dates if you
' run this code in a country other than the United States.
Console.WriteLine("Starts at {0}, Ends at {1}, Delta is {2} minutes", _
   dlc.Start, dlc.End, dlc.Delta.TotalMinutes)
   ' => Starts at 3/27/2005 2:00:00 A.M., ends at 10/30/
2005 3:00:00 A.M., Delta is 60 minutes.
```

The Guid Type

The System.Guid type exposes several static and instance methods that can help you work with globally unique identifiers (GUIDs), that is, those 128-bit numbers that serve to uniquely identify elements and that are ubiquitous in Windows programming. The NewGuid static method is useful for generating a new unique identifier:

```
' Create a new GUID.
Dim guid1 As Guid = Guid.NewGuid()
' By definition, you'll surely get a different output here.
Console.WriteLine(guid1.ToString)        '=> 3f5f1d42-2d92-474d-a2a4-1e707c7e2a37
```

If you already have a GUID—for example, a GUID you have read from a database field—you can initialize a Guid variable by passing the GUID representation as a string or as an array of bytes to the type's constructor:

```
' Initialize from a string.
Dim guid2 As New Guid("45FA3B49-3D66-AB33-BB21-1E3B447A6621")
```

There are only two more things you can do with a Guid object: you can convert it to a Byte array with the ToByteArray method, and you can compare two Guid values for equality using the Equals method (inherited from System.Object):

```
' Convert to an array of bytes.
Dim bytes() As Byte = guid1.ToByteArray
For Each b As Byte In bytes
   Console.Write("{0} ", b)
      ' => 239 1 161 57 143 200 172 70 185 64 222 29 59 15 190 205
Next

' Compare two GUIDs.
If Not guid1.Equals(guid2) Then
   Console.WriteLine("GUIDs are different.")
End If
```

Enums

I briefly covered enumerated values in Chapter 2. Now I complete the description of Enum blocks by mentioning all the methods you can apply to them.

Any Enum you define in your application derives from System.Enum, which in turn inherits from System.ValueType. Ultimately, therefore, user-defined Enums are value types, but they are special in that you can't define additional properties, methods, or events. All the methods they expose are inherited from System.Enum. (It's illegal to explicitly inherit a class from System.Enum in Visual Basic.)

All the examples in this section refer to the following Enum block:

```
' This Enum defines the data type accepted for a value entered by the end user.
Enum DataEntry As Integer            ' As Integer is optional.
   IntegerNumber
   FloatingNumber
   CharString
   DateTime
End Enum
```

By default, the first enumerated type is assigned the value 0. You can change this initial value if you want, but you aren't encouraged to do so. In fact, it is advisable that 0 be a valid value for any Enum blocks you define; otherwise, a noninitialized Enum variable would contain an invalid value.

The .NET documentation defines a few guidelines for Enum values:

■ Use names without the Enum suffix; use singular names for regular Enum types and plural for bit-coded Enum types.

■ Use PascalCase for the name of both the Enum and its members. (An exception is constants from the Windows application API, which are usually all uppercase.)

- Use 32-bit integers unless you need a larger range, which normally happens only if you have a bit-coded Enum with more than 32 possible values.

- Don't use Enums for open sets, that is, sets that you might need to expand in the future (for example, operating system versions).

Displaying and Parsing Enum Values

The Enum class overrides the ToString method to return the value as a readable string format. This method is useful when you want to expose a (nonlocalized) string to the end user:

```
Dim de As DataEntry = DataEntry.DateTime
' Display the numeric value.
Console.WriteLine(de)                    ' => 3
' Display the symbolic value.
Console.WriteLine(de.ToString)           ' => DateTime
```

Or you can use the capability to pass a format character to an overloaded version of the ToString method. The only supported format characters are G, g (general), X, x (hexadecimal), F, f (fixed-point), and D, d (decimal):

```
' General and fixed formats display the Enum name.
Console.WriteLine(de.ToString("F"))      ' => DateTime
' Decimal format displays Enum value.
Console.WriteLine(de.ToString("D"))      ' => 3
' Hexadecimal format displays eight hex digits.
Console.WriteLine(de.ToString("X"))      ' => 00000003
```

The opposite of ToString is the Parse shared method, which takes a string and converts it to the corresponding enumerated value:

```
' This statement works only if Option Strict is Off.
de = [Enum].Parse(GetType(DataEntry), "CharString")
```

Two things are worth noticing in the preceding code. First, the Parse method takes a Type argument, so you typically use the GetType operator. Second, Parse is a static method and you must use Enum as a prefix; Enum is a reserved Visual Basic word, so you must either enclose it in brackets or use its complete System.Enum name.

Being inherited from the generic Enum class, the Parse method returns a generic object, so you have to set Option Strict to Off (as in the previous snippet) or use an explicit cast to assign it to a specific enumerated variable:

```
' You can use the GetType method (inherited from System.Object)
' to get the Type object required by the Parse method.
de = CType([Enum].Parse(GetType(DataEntry), "CharString"), DataEntry)
```

The Parse method throws an ArgumentException if the name doesn't correspond to a defined enumerated value. Names are compared in a case-sensitive way, but you can pass a True optional argument if you don't want to take the string case into account:

```
' *** This statement throws an exception.
Console.WriteLine([Enum].Parse(de.GetType, "charstring"))
' This works well because case-insensitive comparison is used.
Console.WriteLine([Enum].Parse(de.GetType, "charstring", True))
```

Other Enum Methods

The GetUnderlyingType static method returns the base type for an enumerated class:

```
Console.WriteLine([Enum].GetUnderlyingType(de.GetType))    ' => System.Int32
```

The IsDefined method enables you to check whether a numeric value is acceptable as an enumerated value of a given class:

```
If [Enum].IsDefined(GetType(DataEntry), 3) Then
   ' 3 is a valid value for the DataEntry class.
   de = CType(3, DataEntry)
End If
```

The IsDefined method is useful because the CType operator doesn't check whether the value being converted is in the valid range for the target enumerated type. In other words, the following statement doesn't throw an exception:

```
' This code produces an invalid result, yet it doesn't throw an exception.
de = CType(123, DataEntry)
```

Another way to check whether a numeric value is acceptable for an Enum object is by using the GetName method, which returns the name of the enumerated value or returns Nothing if the value is invalid:

```
If [Enum].GetName(GetType(DataEntry), 3) IsNot Nothing Then
   de = CType(3, DataEntry)
End If
```

You can quickly list all the values of an enumerated type with the GetNames and GetValues methods. The former returns a String array holding the individual names (sorted by the corresponding values); the latter returns an Object array that holds the numeric values:

```
' List all the values in DataEntry.
Dim names() As String = [Enum].GetNames(GetType(DataEntry))
Dim values As Array = [Enum].GetValues(GetType(DataEntry))
For i As Integer = 0 To names.Length - 1
   Console.WriteLine("{0} = {1}", names(i), CInt(values.GetValue(i)))
Next
```

Here's the output of the preceding code snippet:

```
IntegerNumber = 0
FloatingNumber = 1
CharString = 2
DateTime = 3
```

Bit-Coded Values

The .NET Framework supports a special Flags attribute that you can use to specify that an Enum object represents a bit-coded value. For example, let's create a new class named ValidDataEntry class, which enables the developer to specify two or more valid data types for values entered by an end user:

```
<Flags()> Enum ValidDataEntry
    None = 0                    ' Always define an Enum value equal to 0.
    IntegerNumber = 1
    FloatingNumber = 2
    CharString = 4
    DateTime = 8
End Enum
```

The FlagAttribute class doesn't expose any property, and its constructor takes no arguments: the presence of this attribute is sufficient to label this Enum type as bit-coded.

Bit-coded enumerated types behave exactly like regular Enum values do except their ToString method recognizes the Flags attribute. When an enumerated type is composed of two or more flag values, this method returns the list of all the corresponding values, separated by commas:

```
Dim vde As ValidDataEntry = ValidDataEntry.IntegerNumber Or ValidDataEntry.DateTime
Console.WriteLine(vde.ToString)          ' => IntegerNumber, DateTime
```

If no bit is set, the ToString method returns the name of the enumerated value corresponding to the zero value:

```
Dim vde2 As ValidDataEntry
Console.WriteLine(vde2.ToString)      ' => None
```

If the value doesn't correspond to a valid combination of bits, the Format method returns the number unchanged:

```
vde = CType(123, ValidDataEntry)
Console.WriteLine(vde.ToString)        ' => 123
```

The Parse method is also affected by the Flags attribute:

```
vde = CType([Enum].Parse( _
    vde.GetType(), "IntegerNumber, FloatingNumber"), ValidDataEntry)
Console.WriteLine(CInt(vde))           ' => 3
```

Chapter 13
Arrays and Collections

The Microsoft .NET Framework doesn't merely include classes for managing system objects, such as files, directories, processes, and threads. It also exposes objects, such as complex data structures (queues, stacks, lists, and hash tables), that help developers organize information and solve recurring problems. Many real-world applications use arrays and collections, and the .NET Framework support for arrays and collection-like objects is really outstanding. It can take you a while to become familiar with the many possibilities that the .NET runtime offers, but this effort pays off nicely at coding time.

Arrays and collections have become even richer and more powerful in Microsoft .NET Framework version 2.0 with the introduction of generics, both because many types have been extended with generic methods and because you can create strong-typed collections much more easily in this new version of the framework.

Note To avoid long lines, code samples in this chapter assume that the following Imports statements are used at the file or project level:

```
Imports System.Collections.Specialized
Imports System.Collections.Generic
Imports System.Collections.ObjectModel
Imports System.IO
Imports System.Text.RegularExpressions
```

The Array Type

By default, .NET arrays have a zero-based index. One-dimensional arrays with a zero lower index are known as *SZArrays* or *vectors* and are the fastest type of arrays available to developers. .NET also supports arrays with a different lower index, but they aren't CLS-compliant, aren't very efficient, and aren't recommended. In practice, you never need an array with a different lower index, and I won't cover them in this book.

The Array class constructor has a Protected scope, so you can't directly use the New keyword with this class. This isn't a problem because you create an array using the standard Microsoft Visual Basic syntax and you can even use initializers, as described in Chapter 2, "Basic Language Concepts":

```
' An array initialized with the powers of 2
Dim intArr() As Integer = {1, 2, 4, 8, 16, 32, 64, 128, 256, 512}
' Noninitialized two-dimensional array
Dim lngArr(10, 20) As Long
' An empty array
Dim dblArr() As Double
```

You can also create an array and initialize it on the fly, which is sometimes useful for passing an argument or assigning a property that takes an array without having to create a temporary array. To see why this feature can be useful, consider the following code:

```
' Create a temporary array.
Dim tmp() As Integer = {2, 5, 9, 13}
' The obj.ValueArray property takes an array of Integers.
obj.ValueArray = tmp
' Clear the temporary variable.
tmp = Nothing
```

The ability to create and initialize an array in a single statement can make the code more concise, even though the syntax you need isn't exactly intuitive:

```
obj.ValueArray = New Integer() {2, 5, 9, 13}
```

You get an error if you access a null array, which is an array variable that hasn't been initialized yet. Because the array is an object, you can test it using a plain Is operator and use ReDim on the array if necessary:

```
If dblArr Is Nothing Then ReDim dblArr(100)        ' Note: no As clause in ReDims
```

You can query an array for its rank (that is, the number of dimensions) by using its Rank property, and you can query the total number of its elements by means of its Length property:

```
' …(Continuing the first example in this chapter)…
Dim res As Long = lngArr.Rank                  ' => 2
' lngArr has 11*21 elements.
res = lngArr.Length                            ' => 231
```

Starting with version 1.1, the .NET Framework supports 64-bit array indexes, so an array index can also be a Long value. To support these huge arrays, the Array class has been expanded with a LongLength property that returns the number of elements as a Long value.

The GetLength method returns the number of elements along a given dimension, whereas GetLowerBound and GetUpperBound return the lowest and highest indexes along the specified dimension. Unlike the argument that you pass to the LBound and UBound functions in the Microsoft.VisualBasic library, the dimension number is zero-based, not one-based:

```
' …(Continuing previous example)…
res = lngArr.GetLength(0)                      ' => 11, same as UBound(1)-1
```

```
res = lngArr.GetLowerBound(1)              ' => 0, same as LBound(2)
res = lngArr.GetUpperBound(1)              ' => 20, same as UBound(2)-1
```

You can visit all the elements of an array using a single For Each loop and a strongly typed variable. This technique also works with multidimensional arrays, so you can process all the elements in a two-dimensional array with just one loop:

```
Dim strArr(,) As String = {{"00", "01", "02"}, {"10", "11", "12"}}
For Each s As String In strArr
    Console.Write(s & ",")      ' => 00,01,02,10,11,12
Next
```

Notice that a For Each loop on a multidimensional array visits array elements in a row-wise order (all the elements in the first row, and then all the elements in the second row, and so on); in Microsoft Visual Basic 6 and earlier versions, this loop worked in column-wise order.

The Array class supports the ICloneable interface, so you can create a shallow copy of an array using the Clone instance method. (See the section titled "The ICloneable Interface" in Chapter 10, "Interfaces," for a discussion about shallow and deep copy operations.)

```
' This works if Option Strict is Off.
Dim anotherArray(,) As String= strArr.Clone()

' This is the required syntax if Option Strict is On.
Dim anotherArray(,) As String = DirectCast(strArr.Clone, String(,))
```

The CopyTo method enables you to copy a one-dimensional array to another one-dimensional array; you decide the starting index in the destination array:

```
' Create and initialize an array (10 elements).
Dim sourceArr() As Integer = {1, 2, 3, 5, 7, 11, 13, 17, 19, 23}
' Create the destination array (must be same size or larger).
Dim destArr(19) As Integer
' Copy the source array into the second half of the destination array.
sourceArr.CopyTo(destArr, 10)
```

Sorting Elements

The Array class offers several static methods for processing arrays quickly and easily. In Chapter 3, "Control Flow and Error handling," you read about the Array.Sort method, and in Chapter 10 you learned that you can sort arrays of objects using an arbitrary group of keys by means of the IComparable and IComparer interfaces. But the Array.Sort method is even more flexible than anything you've seen so far. For example, it can sort just a portion of an array:

```
' Sort only elements [10,100] of the targetArray.
' Second argument is starting index; last argument is length of the subarray.
Array.Sort(targetArray, 10, 91)
```

You can also sort an array of values using another array that holds the sorting keys, which enables you to sort arrays of structures or objects even if they don't implement the ICompara-ble interface. To see how this overloaded version of the Sort method works, let's start defining a structure:

```
Structure Employee
    Public FirstName As String
    Public LastName As String
    Public HireDate As Date

    Sub New(ByVal firstName As String, ByVal lastName As String, ByVal hireDate As Date)
        Me.FirstName = firstName
        Me.LastName = lastName
        Me.HireDate = hireDate
    End Sub

    ' A function to display an element's properties easily
    Function Description() As String
        Return String.Format("{0} {1} (hired on {2})", FirstName, LastName, _
            HireDate.ToShortDateString())
    End Function
End Structure
```

The following code creates a main array of Employee structures, creates an auxiliary key array that holds the hiring date of each employee, and finally sorts the main array using the auxil-iary array:

```
' Create a test array.
Dim employees() As Employee = { New Employee("John", "Evans", #3/1/2001#), _
    New Employee("Robert", "Zare", #8/12/2000#), _
    New Employee("Ann", "Beebe", #11/1/1999#)}
' Create a parallel array of hiring dates.
Dim hireDates(employees.Length - 1) As Date
For i As Integer = 0 To employees.Length - 1
    hireDates(i) = employees(i).HireDate
Next
' Sort the array of Employees using HireDates to provide the keys.
Array.Sort(hireDates, employees)
' Prove that the array is sorted on the HireDate field.
For Each em As Employee in employees
    Console.WriteLine(em.Description)
Next
```

Interestingly, the key array is sorted as well, so you don't need to initialize it again when you add another element to the main array:

```
' Add a fourth employee.
ReDim Preserve employees(3)
employees(3) = New Employee("Chris", "Cannon", #5/9/2000#)
' Extend the key array as well—no need to reinitialize it.
ReDim Preserve hireDates(3)
hireDates(3) = employees(3).HireDate
' Re-sort the new, larger array.
Array.Sort(hireDates, employees)
```

An overloaded version of the Sort method enables you to sort a portion of an array of values for which you provide an array of keys. This is especially useful when you start with a large array that you fill only partially:

```
' Create a test array with a lot of room.
Dim employees(1000) As Employee
' Initialize only its first four elements.
…
' Sort only the portion actually used.
Array.Sort(hireDates, employees, 0, 4)
```

All the versions of the Array.Sort method that you've seen so far can take an additional IComparer object, which dictates how the array elements or keys are to be compared with one another. (See the section titled "The IComparer Interface" in Chapter 10.)

The Array.Reverse method reverses the order of elements in an array or in a portion of an array, so you can apply it immediately after a Sort method to sort in descending order:

```
' Sort an array of Integers in reverse order.
Array.Sort(intArray)
Array.Reverse(intArray)
```

You pass the initial index and number of elements to reverse only a portion of an array:

```
' Reverse only the first 10 elements in intArray.
Array.Reverse(intArray, 0, 10)
```

You have a special case when you reverse only two elements, which is the same as swapping two consecutive elements, a frequent operation when you're working with arrays:

```
' Swap elements at indexes 5 and 6.
Array.Reverse(intArray, 5, 2)
```

Clearing, Copying, and Moving Elements

You can clear a portion of an array by using the Clear method, without a For loop:

```
' Clear elements [10,100] of an array.
Array.Clear(arr, 10, 91)
```

The Array.Copy method enables you to copy elements from a one-dimensional array to another. There are two overloaded versions for this method. The first version copies a given number of elements from the source array to the destination array:

```
Dim intArr() As Integer = {1, 2, 3, 4, 5, 6, 7, 8, 9, 10}
Dim intArr2(20) As Integer
' Copy the entire source array into the first half of the target array.
Array.Copy(intArr, intArr2, 10)
For i As Integer = 0 To 20
   Console.Write("{0} ", intArr2(i))
      ' => 1 2 3 4 5 6 7 8 9 10 0 0 0 0 0 0 0 0 0 0 0
Next
```

The second version lets you decide the starting index in the source array, the starting index in the destination array (that is, the index of the first element that will be overwritten), and the number of elements to copy:

```
' Copy elements at indexes 5-9 to the end of intArr2.
Array.Copy(intArr, 5, intArr2, 15, 5)
' This is the first element that has been copied.
Console.WriteLine(intArr2(15))                          ' => 6
```

You get an exception of type ArgumentOutOfRangeException if you provide wrong values for the indexes or the destination array isn't large enough, and you get an exception of type RankException if either array has two or more dimensions.

The Copy method works correctly even when source and destination arrays have elements of different types, in which case it attempts to cast each individual source element to the corresponding element in the destination array. The actual behavior depends on many factors, though, such as whether the source or the destination is a value type or a reference type. For example, you can always copy from any array to an Object array, from an Integer array to a Long array, and from a Single array to a Double array because they are widening conversions and can't fail. Copy throws an exception of type TypeMismatchException when you attempt a narrowing conversion between arrays of value types, even though individual elements in the source array might be successfully converted to the destination type:

```
Dim intArr3() As Integer = {1, 2, 3, 4, 5, 6, 7, 8, 9, 10}
' This Copy operation succeeds even if array types are different.
Dim lngArr3(20) As Long
Array.Copy(intArr3, lngArr3, 10)
' This Copy operation fails with ArrayTypeMismatchException.
'    (But you can carry it out with an explicit For loop.)
Dim shoArr3(20) As Short
Array.Copy(intArr3, shoArr3, 10)
```

Conversely, if you copy from and to an array of reference type, the Array.Copy method attempts the copy operation for each element; if an InvalidCastException object is thrown for an element, the method copies neither that element nor any of the values after the one that raised the error. This behavior can cause a problem because your code now has an array that is only partially filled.

 The ConstrainedCopy method, new in .NET Framework 2.0, solves the issue I just mentioned, sort of. If an exception occurs when using this method, all changes to the destination array are undone in an orderly manner, so you can never end up with an array that has been copied or converted only partially. However, the ConstrainedCopy method can't really replace the Copy method in the previous code snippet because it requires that no form of boxing, unboxing, casting, widening conversion, or narrowing conversion occurs. In practice, you should use the ConstrainedCopy method only in critical regions where an unexpected exception, including a .NET internal error, might compromise your data.

The Array.Copy method can even copy a portion of an array over itself. In this case, the Copy method performs a "smart copy" in the sense that elements are copied correctly in ascending order when you're copying to a lower index and in reverse order when you're copying to a higher index. So you can use the Copy method to delete one or more elements and fill the hole that would result by shifting all subsequent elements one or more positions toward lower indexes:

```
Dim lngArr4() As Long = {1, 2, 3, 4, 5, 6, 7, 8, 9, 10}
' Delete element at index 4.
Array.Copy(lngArr4, 5, lngArr4, 4, 5)
' Complete the delete operation by clearing the last element.
Array.Clear(lngArr4, lngArr4.Length - 1, 1)
' Now the array contains: {1, 2, 3, 4, 6, 7, 8, 9, 10, 0}
```

You can use this code as the basis for a reusable routine that works with any type of array:

```
Sub ArrayDeleteElement(ByVal arr As Array, ByVal index As Integer)
   ' This method works only with one-dimensional arrays.
   If arr.Rank <> 1 Then Throw New ArgumentException("Invalid rank")
   ' Shift elements from arr(index+1) to arr(index).
   Array.Copy(arr, index + 1, arr, index, UBound(arr) - Index)
   ' Clear the last element.
   Array.Clear(arr, arr.Length - 1, 1)
End Sub
```

Inserting an element is also easy, and again you can create a routine that works with arrays of any type:

```
Sub ArrayInsertElement(ByVal arr As Array, ByVal index As Integer, _
      Optional ByVal newValue As Object = Nothing)
   ' This method works only with one-dimensional arrays.
   If arr.Rank <> 1 Then Throw New ArgumentException("Invalid rank")
   ' Shift elements from arr(index) to arr(index+1) to make room.
   Array.Copy(arr, index, arr, index + 1, arr.Length - index - 1)
   ' Assign the element using the SetValue method.
   arr.SetValue(newValue, index)
End Sub
```

The Array class exposes the SetValue and GetValue methods to assign and read elements. You don't normally use these methods in regular programming, but they turn out to be useful in routines that work with any type of array. You can also use the generics to make your code even more concise, more robust, and faster:

```
Sub ArrayDeleteElement(Of T)(ByVal arr() As T, ByVal index As Integer)
   Array.Copy(arr, index + 1, arr, index, UBound(arr) - Index)
   arr(index) = Nothing
End Sub

Sub ArrayInsertElement(Of T)(ByVal arr() As T, ByVal index As Integer, _
      ByVal newValue As T = Nothing)
   Array.Copy(arr, index, arr, index + 1, arr.Length - index - 1)
   arr(index) = newValue
End Sub
```

(See the section titled "Generic Methods" in Chapter 11, "Generics," for more information about generic methods.) You can also use Copy with multidimensional arrays, in which case the array is treated as if it were a one-dimensional array with all the rows laid down in memory one after the other. This method works only if the source and destination arrays have the same rank, even if they can have a different number of rows and columns. This feature provides us with the ability to implement a better ReDim Preserve. As you may recall from Chapter 2, the ReDim Preserve statement can change only the rightmost dimension of a multidimensional array. See how you can work around this limitation with the Array.Copy method:

```
Dim arr(,) As Integer = {{1, 2}, {3, 4}, {5, 6}}
' We want to "redim preserve" this array so that its size becomes (rows, columns).
' Create a temporary array with as many rows as required, but same number of columns.
Dim tmpArr(rows, arr.GetUpperBound(1)) As Integer
' Next statement copies all elements from old array into the temporary one.
Array.Copy(arr, tmpArr, Math.Min(arr.Length, tmpArr.Length))
' Add or remove columns as desired.
ReDim Preserve tmpArr(rows, columns)
' Replace the old array with the temporary one.
arr = tmpArr
```

The previous code requires two memory allocations—the first one when you create the new array, the second one caused by the ReDim Preserve command—which makes its performance less than optimal. In fact, and quite surprisingly, the previous code is slower than the solution that copies each element from the old array into the new one. Here's a more efficient, generic method that works with arrays of any type:

```
Function RedimPreserve(Of T)(ByVal arr(,) As T, ByVal rows As Integer, _
      ByVal cols As Integer) As T(,)
   Dim newArr(rows, cols) As T
   For r As Integer = 0 To Math.Min(arr.GetUpperBound(0), rows)
      For c As Integer = 0 To Math.Min(arr.GetUpperBound(1), cols)
         newArr(r, c) = arr(r, c)
      Next
   Next
   Return newArr
End Function
```

You can do some interesting tricks with the Buffer type, which exposes static methods that perform byte-by-byte operations on one-dimensional arrays. For example, you can quickly copy the bits of a Char array into a Short array to peek at the Unicode value of the individual Char elements:

```
Dim chars() As Char = {"A"c, "B"c, "C"c, "D"c}
Dim codes(3) As UShort
' Syntax is: BlockCopy(sourceArray, sourceIndex, destArray, destIndex, byteCount)
Buffer.BlockCopy(chars, 0, codes, 0, 8)
For Each code As UShort In codes
   Console.Write("{0} ", code)                 ' => 65 66 67 68
Next
```

The elements in the two arrays don't need to be the same size; thus, for example, you can inspect the individual bytes of a Long array as follows:

```
Dim values() As Double = {123, 456, 789}     ' 3 Doubles = 24 bytes
Dim bytes(23) As Byte
Buffer.BlockCopy(values, 0, bytes, 0, 24)
```

Other methods of the Buffer type allow you to read and write individual bytes inside an array. For security reasons, the Buffer class works only with arrays of primitive types, such as Boolean, Char, and all numeric types. Arrays of other types cause an exception of type ArgumentException to be thrown.

Searching Values

The IndexOf method searches an array for a value and returns the index of the first element that matches or −1 if the search fails:

```
Dim strArr() As String = {"Robert", "Joe", "Ann", "Chris", "Joe"}
Dim index As Integer = Array.IndexOf(strArr, "Ann")        ' => 2
' Note that string searches are case sensitive.
index = Array.IndexOf(strArr, "ANN")                       ' => -1
```

You can also specify a starting index and an optional ending index; if an ending index is omitted, the search continues until the end of the array. You can use the following approach to find all the values in the array with a given value:

```
' Search for all the occurrences of the "Joe" string.
index = Array.IndexOf(strArr, "Joe")
Do Until index < 0
   Console.WriteLine("Found at index {0}", index)
   ' Search next occurrence.
   index = Array.IndexOf(strArr, "Joe", index + 1)
Loop
```

The LastIndexOf method is similar to IndexOf except that it returns the index of the last occurrence of the value. Because the search is backward, you must pass a start index equal to the end index:

```
' A revised version of the search loop, which searches
' from higher indexes toward the beginning of the array.
index = Array.LastIndexOf(strArr, "Joe", strArr.Length - 1)
Do Until index < 0
   Console.WriteLine("Found at index {0}", index)
   index = Array.LastIndexOf(strArr, "Joe", index - 1)
Loop
```

The IndexOf and LastIndexOf methods perform a linear search, so their performance degrades linearly with larger arrays. You deliver much faster code if the array is sorted and you use the BinarySearch method:

```
' Binary search on a sorted array
Dim strArr2() As String = {"Ann", "Chris", "Joe", "Robert", "Sam"}
index = Array.BinarySearch(strArr2, "Chris")               ' => 1
```

If the binary search fails, the method returns a negative value that's the bitwise complement of the index of the first element that's larger than the value being searched for. This feature enables you to determine where the value should be inserted in the sorted array:

```
index = Array.BinarySearch(strArr2, "David")
If index >= 0 Then
    Console.WriteLine("Found at index {0}", index)
Else
    ' Negate the result to get the index for the insertion point.
    index = Not index
    Console.WriteLine("Not Found. Insert at index {0}", index)
        ' => Not found. Insert at index 2.
End If
```

You can pass a start index and the length of the portion of the array in which you want to perform the search, which is useful when you're working with an array that's only partially filled:

```
index = Array.BinarySearch(strArr2, 0, 3, "Chris")          ' => 1
```

Finally, both syntax forms for the BinarySearch method support an IComparer object at the end of the argument list; this argument lets you determine how array elements are to be compared. In practice, you can use the same IComparer object that you passed to the Sort method when you sorted the array.

Jagged Arrays

Visual Basic also supports arrays of arrays, that is, arrays whose elements are arrays. This is a familiar concept to most C++ programmers, but it might be new to many Visual Basic programmers.

Arrays of arrays—also known as *jagged arrays*—are especially useful when you have a two-dimensional matrix with rows that don't have the same length. You can render this structure by using a standard two-dimensional array, but you'd have to size it to accommodate the row with the highest number of elements, which would result in wasted space. The arrays of arrays concept isn't limited to two dimensions only, and you might need three-dimensional or four-dimensional jagged arrays. Here is an example of a "triangular" matrix of strings:

```
"a00"
"a10"   "a11"
"a20"   "a21"   "a22"
"a30"   "a31"   "a32"   "a33"
```

Even though Visual Basic supports arrays of arrays natively, I can't consider the syntax to be intuitive. The next code snippet shows how you can initialize the preceding structure and then process it by expanding its rows:

```
' Initialize an array of arrays.
Dim arr()() As String = {New String() {"a00"}, _
    New String() {"a10", "a11"}, _
    New String() {"a20", "a21", "a22"}, _
    New String() {"a30", "a31", "a32", "a33"}}
```

```
' Show how you can reference an element.
Dim elem As String = arr(3)(1)                    ' => a31
' Assign an entire row.
arr(0) = New String() {"a00", "a01", "a02"}
' Read an element just added.
elem = arr(0)(2)                                  ' => a02

' Expand one of the rows.
ReDim Preserve arr(1)(3)
' Assign the new elements. (Currently they are Nothing.)
arr(1)(2) = "a12"
arr(1)(3) = "a13"
' Read back one of them.
elem = arr(1)(2)                                  ' => a12
```

An obvious advantage of jagged arrays is that they take less memory than regular multidimensional arrays do. Even more interesting, the JIT compiler produces code that is up to five or six times faster when accessing a jagged array than when accessing a multidimensional array. However, keep in mind that jagged arrays aren't CLS-compliant; thus, they shouldn't appear as arguments or return values in public methods.

A great way to take advantage of the higher speed of jagged arrays while continuing to use the standard array syntax and hiding implementation details at the same time is by defining a generic type that wraps an array of arrays:

```
Public Class Matrix(Of T)
   Private values()() As T

   Sub New(ByVal rowMax As Integer, ByVal colMax As Integer)
      ReDim values(rowMax)
      For i As Integer = 0 To rowMax
         Dim row(colMax) As T
         values(i) = row
      Next
   End Sub

   Default Public Property Item(ByVal row As Integer, ByVal col As Integer) As T
      Get
         Return values(row)(col)
      End Get
      Set(ByVal value As T)
         values(row)(col) = value
      End Set
   End Property
End Class
```

Using the Matrix class is almost identical to using a two-dimensional array; the only difference is in the way you create an instance of the array:

```
Dim mat As New Matrix(Of Double)(100, 200)
mat(10, 1) = 123.45
Console.WriteLine(mat(10, 1))                     ' => 123.45
```

Because of the way the CLR optimizes jagged arrays, the Matrix class is two to three times faster than a standard two-dimensional array is, while preserving the latter's standard syntax. Can you ask for more?

Generic Methods

In version 2.0 of the .NET Framework, the Array type has been extended with several generic methods. In general, these methods offer better type safety and, in most cases, better performance. For example, consider the following code:

```
' (Visual Basic .NET 2003 code)
' Create an array with a nonzero value in the last element.
Dim arr(100000) As Short
arr(100000) = -1
' Search for the nonzero element.
Dim index As Integer = Array.IndexOf(arr, -1)
```

The standard IndexOf method must work with arrays of all kinds; thus, the search it performs isn't optimized for Integer arrays. More specifically, the second argument must be boxed when you pass a value type, as in this case. To solve these issues, the Array class in .NET Framework 2.0 supports the IndexOf(Of T) generic method:

```
index = Array.IndexOf(Of Short)(arr, -1)
```

The generic method appears to be from 15 to 100 times faster than the standard method is, depending on how many repetitions you execute. (Remember that each time you call the standard method, a boxing operation takes place and a temporary object is created behind the scenes.) Even with a few repetitions, the generic approach is clearly to be preferred, especially when you consider that it simply requires adding an Of clause to existing Visual Basic .NET 2003 code. Notice that there is no performance gain in using this method with a reference type, for example, a String array.

Interestingly, the Visual Basic 2005 compiler automatically selects the generic version of a method, if possible—therefore, most of your Visual Basic .NET 2003 code will gain better performance if you simply recompile it under the current Microsoft Visual Studio version. This behavior is a consequence of the fact that you can drop the Of clause in generic methods if no ambiguity ensues, as I explained in the section titled "Generic Methods" in Chapter 11. More specifically, the compiler selects the generic version of the second argument if it matches perfectly the type of the array passed in the first argument. For example, consider this code:

```
Dim arr(100000) As Integer
arr(100000) = -1
' Next statement is compiled using the IndexOf(Of Integer) generic method.
index = Array.IndexOf(arr, -1)

Dim search As Short = -1
' Next statement is compiled using the standard IndexOf, and boxing occurs.
index = Array.IndexOf(arr, search)
```

This undocumented behavior can lead to a serious loss of performance in some cases. For example, consider this code:

```
Dim lngArr(100000) As Long
lngArr(100000) = -1
index = Array.IndexOf(lngArr, -1)
```

Quite surprisingly, the last statement in this code snippet is compiled using a standard IndexOf method instead of the more efficient IndexOf(Of Long) method as you might expect. The reason: the −1 argument is considered a 32-bit value and therefore doesn't match the Long array passed in the first argument. You therefore must either explicitly use the generic method or force the type of the second argument, as follows:

```
' Two techniques to force the compiler to use the generic method
index = Array.IndexOf(Of Long)(lngArr, -1)
index = Array.IndexOf(lngArr, -1L)
```

If you think that this is just a syntax detail and that you shouldn't care about which method is actually chosen by the compiler, well, think again. If you force the compiler to select the IndexOf(Of Long) method instead of the IndexOf standard method, your code can run *almost two orders of magnitude faster*! The actual ratio depends on how many times you invoke the method and becomes apparent when this number is high enough to fire one or more garbage collections.

> **Note** The code examples in the remaining portion of this chapter use the generic syntax to emphasize the generic nature of methods, even if in most cases the Of clause might be dropped. Although there aren't any established guidelines in this field, I recommend that you use an explicit Of clause in all cases, both to make your code more readable and to force the compiler to use the generic version when a standard version of the same method is available.

A few other generic methods that mirror existing methods have been added, including Binary-Search, LastIndexOf, and Sort. The generic sort method can take one or two generic parameters, depending on whether you pass a parallel array of keys:

```
' Sort an array of integers.
Array.Sort(Of Integer)(arr)
' Sort an array of integers using a parallel array of string keys.
Dim keys() As String
' Fill the array of keys.
…
' Sort the integer array using the parallel key array.
Array.Sort(Of String, Integer)(keys, arr)
```

The Resize(Of T) method performs the same operation as the ReDim Preserve statement; it was added to the .NET Framework primarily because other languages, including C#, didn't have such a handy keyword:

```
Dim arr() As Integer = {0, 1, 2, 3, 4}
…
```

```
' Extend the array to contain 10 elements, but preserve existing ones.
' Same as ReDim Preserve arr(10)
Array.Resize(Of Integer)(arr, 10)
```

There is no Resize method to resize a two-dimensional array, but it's easy to create one by reusing a technique I showed in the section titled "Clearing, Copying, and Moving Elements" earlier in this chapter:

```
Sub Resize(Of T)(ByRef arr(,) As T, ByVal rows As Integer, ByVal columns As Integer)
    If rows <= 0 OrElse columns <= 0 Then Throw New ArgumentException("Invalid new size")
    ' Create a temporary array with as many rows as required, but same number of columns.
    Dim tmpArr(rows - 1, arr.GetLength(1) - 1) As T
    ' Next statement copies the old array into the temporary one.
    Array.Copy(arr, tmpArr, Math.Min(arr.Length, tmpArr.Length))
    ' Add or remove columns as desired.
    ReDim Preserve tmpArr(rows - 1, columns - 1)
    ' Replace old array with the temporary one.
    arr = tmpArr
End Sub
```

All the remaining generic methods in the Array class take a delegate as an argument and enable you to perform a given operation without writing an explicit For or For Each loop. These methods are especially useful in C# because that language supports *anonymous methods* (a type of method that you can inline where a delegate is expected, in the middle of another method), but they can be used in Visual Basic as well. Most of these methods take a Predicate(Of T) delegate; predicate delegates point to a function that takes an argument of type T and return a Boolean value, which is typically the result of a test condition on the argument. For example, let's define this simple function that returns True if a number is positive and divisible by 10:

```
Function IsMultipleOfTen(ByVal n As Integer) As Boolean
    Return n > 0 AndAlso (n Mod 10) = 0
End Function
```

Next, let's write a piece of code that uses this function to find the first element in an array that satisfies this condition:

```
Dim arr() As Integer = {1, 3, 60, 4, 30, 66, -10, 79, 10, -4}
Dim result As Integer = 0
For i As Integer = 0 To arr.Length - 1
    If IsMultipleOfTen(arr(i)) Then
        result = arr(i)
        Exit For
    End If
Next
If result = 0 Then
    Console.WriteLine("Not found")
Else
    Console.WriteLine("Result = {0}", result)       ' => Result = 60
End If
```

You'll probably agree that it's a lot of code for such a simple task, especially considering that the code that tests divisibility is stored in a separate function. Now, see how elegant the code becomes when we use the Find(Of T) generic method to get rid of the For loop:

```
Dim res As Integer = Array.Find(Of Integer)(arr, AddressOf IsMultipleOfTen)
```

There is also a FindLast(Of T) generic method that, as its name implies, returns the last element in the array that matches the condition:

```
res = Array.FindLast(Of Integer)(arr, AddressOf IsMultipleOfTen)
```

Of course, the power of generics ensures that you can also use a similarly concise approach when looking for an element in a string array, a Double array, or an array of any type. If you simply want to check whether an element matching the condition exists, but you aren't interested in its value, you can use the new Exists generic method:

```
If Array.Exists(Of Integer)(arr, AddressOf IsMultipleOfTen) Then
    ' The array contains at least one positive multiple of 10.
End If
```

A limitation of the Find and FindLast methods is that they always return the default value of the type T if no match is found: Nothing for strings and other reference types, zero for numbers, and so forth. In the preceding example, you know that the result—if found—is strictly positive, so a result equal to zero means that no match was found. If the zero or Nothing value might be a valid match, however, you must opt for a different approach, based on the FindIndex(Of T) generic method:

```
Dim index As Integer = Array.FindIndex(Of Integer)(arr, AddressOf IsMultipleOfTen)
If index < 0 Then
    Console.WriteLine("Element not found")
Else
    Console.WriteLine("Element {0} found at index {1}", arr(index), index)
        ' => Element 60 found at index 2
End If
```

As you might expect, there is also a FindLastIndex(Of T) method that returns the last element that satisfies the condition:

```
index = Array.FindLastIndex(Of Integer)(arr, AddressOf IsMultipleOfTen)  ' => 8
```

Unlike the Find and FindLast methods, both the FindIndex and FindLastIndex methods expose two overloads that enable you to indicate the starting index and the number of elements to be searched. If you are interested in gathering all the elements that match the condition, you might therefore use these methods in a loop, until they return −1, as in the following code:

```
Dim index As Integer = -1
Dim al As New ArrayList()     ' Can replace with List(Of Integer) for better performance.
```

```
Do
    ' Find the next match; exit the loop if not found.
    index = Array.FindIndex(Of Integer)(arr, index + 1, AddressOf IsMultipleOfTen)
    If index < 0 Then Exit Do
    ' Remember the match in an ArrayList.
    al.Add(arr(index))
Loop
' Convert the ArrayList to a strong-typed array.
Dim matches() As Integer = CType(al.ToArray(GetType(Integer)), Integer())
Console.WriteLine("Found {0} matches", matches.Length)     ' => Found 3 matches
```

Once again, you'll surely appreciate the conciseness that the FindAll(Of T) method gives you:

```
' This statement is equivalent to the previous code snippet.
Dim matches() As Integer = Array.FindAll(Of Integer)(arr, AddressOf IsMultipleOfTen)
```

The TrueForAll(Of T) generic method enables you to quickly check whether all the elements in the array match the condition:

```
If Array.TrueForAll(Of Integer)(arr, AddressOf IsMultipleOfTen) Then
    ' All elements in the array are positive multiples of 10.
Else
    ' There is at least one element that isn't a positive multiple of 10.
End If
```

Note that there isn't a FalseForAll(Of T) generic method; therefore, you can't use this approach to check whether *none* of the elements in the array satisfies the condition expressed by the predicate function. Instead, you must create a different method that tests the inverse condition and use a predicate that points to this new method in a TrueForAll method. Alternatively, you can create an adapter class exposing a predicate method that automatically reverses the meaning of another predicate method:

```
Public Class ReversePredicate(Of T)
    Dim predicate As Predicate(Of T)

    Public Sub New(ByVal predicate As Predicate(Of T))
        Me.predicate = predicate
    End Sub

    Public Function Reverse(ByVal obj As T) As Boolean
        Return Not predicate(obj)
    End Function
End Class
```

Here's how you can use the ReversePredicate class with the IsMultipleOfTen predicate:

```
' Implement the missing FalseForAll method by means of the ReversePredicate type.
Dim revPred As New ReversePredicate(Of Integer)(AddressOf IsMultipleOfTen)
If Array.TrueForAll(Of Integer)(arr, AddressOf revPred.Reverse) Then
    Console.WriteLine("No elements in the array are positive multiples of ten.")
Else
    Console.WriteLine("There is at least one element that is a positive multiple of ten.")
End If
```

The ConvertAll(Of T, U) generic method provides a very powerful way to convert all the elements in an array into values of the same or different type. For example, consider the following conversion function:

```
Function ConvertToHex(ByVal n As Integer) As String
   Return Convert.ToString(n, 16)
End Function
```

Here's how you can quickly create an array of strings that contains the hexadecimal equivalent of the elements in the Integer array:

```
Dim hexValues() As String = Array.ConvertAll(Of Integer, String) _
   (arr, AddressOf ConvertToHex)
```

The second argument for the ConvertAll(Of T, U) method must be a delegate that points to a function that takes an argument of type T and returns a value of type U. In some cases, you don't even need to define a separate function because you can use a static method already defined in the .NET Framework. For example, here's how you can convert a numeric array into a string array:

```
Dim arrStr() As String = Array.ConvertAll(Of Integer, String) _
   (arr, AddressOf Convert.ToString)
```

Many math transformations can be achieved by passing a delegate that points to one of the static methods of the Math type, for example, to round or truncate a Double or a Decimal value to an integer. You can use any of such methods, provided that the method takes only one argument.

The Microsoft.VisualBasic namespace provides many static methods that you can use for this purpose. For example, you don't really need the ConvertToHex function because you can use the Hex method exposed by the Conversion module:

```
' (Notice that you can also drop the Conversion prefix.)
hexValues = Array.ConvertAll(Of Integer, String) (arr, AddressOf Conversion.Hex)
```

The next example converts all the elements of a string array to uppercase:

```
arrStr = Array.ConvertAll(Of String, String) (arrStr, AddressOf UCase)
```

By using other methods in the Microsoft.VisualBasic.String module you can convert all the elements of a string array to lowercase, trim their leading or trailing spaces (or both), or reverse them.

The ForEach method, the last generic method in this overview, enables you to execute a given action or method for each element in the array; its second argument is an Action(Of T) delegate, which must point to a Sub procedure that takes an argument of type T. Here's an example that outputs all the elements of an array to the console window, without an explicit loop:

```
Array.ForEach(Of String)(arrStr, AddressOf Console.WriteLine)
```

Please notice that I am providing these examples mainly as a demonstration of the power of generic methods in the Array type. I am not suggesting that you should always prefer these methods to simpler (and more readable) For or For Each loops, but it's good to have a choice.

The System.Collections Namespace

The System.Collections namespace exposes many classes that can work as data containers, such as collections and dictionaries. You can learn the features of all these objects individually, but a smarter approach is to learn about the underlying interfaces that these classes might implement.

The ICollection, IList, and IDictionary Interfaces

All the collection classes in the .NET Framework implement the ICollection interface, which inherits from IEnumerable and defines an object that supports enumeration through a For Each loop. The ICollection interface exposes a read-only Count property and a CopyTo method, which copies the elements from the collection object to an array.

The ICollection interface defines the minimum features that a collection-like object should have. The .NET Framework exposes two more interfaces whose methods add power and flexibility to the object: IList and IDictionary.

Many classes in the .NET Framework implement the IList interface. This interface inherits from ICollection, and therefore from IEnumerable, and represents a collection of objects that can be individually indexed. All the implementations of the IList interface fall into three categories: read-only (the collection's elements can't be modified or deleted, nor can new elements be inserted), fixed size (existing items can be modified, but elements can't be added or removed), and variable size (items can be modified, added, and removed).

The IList interface exposes several members, in addition to the Count property and the CopyTo method inherited from IEnumerable. The names of these methods are quite self-explanatory: Add appends an element to the end of the collection; Insert adds a value between two existing elements; Remove deletes an element given its value; RemoveAt deletes an element at a given index; Clear removes all the elements in one operation. You can access an element at a given index by means of the Item property and check whether an element with a given value exists with the Contains method (which returns a Boolean) or the IndexOf method (which returns the index where the element is found, or −1 if the element isn't found). You'll see all these methods and properties in action when I discuss the ArrayList type.

The IDictionary interface defines a collection-like object that contains one or more (key, value) pairs, where the key can be any object (not just a string, as in Visual Basic 6 collections). As for the IList interface, implementations of the IDictionary interface can be read-only, fixed size, or variable size.

The IDictionary interface inherits the Count and CopyTo members from ICollection and extends it using the following methods: Add(key, value) adds a new element to the collection and associates it with a key; Remove removes an element with a given key; Clear removes all elements; Contains checks whether an element with a given key exists. You can access items in an IDictionary object with the Item(key) property; the Keys and Values read-only properties return an array containing all the keys and all the values in the collection.

For a class that implements the ICollection, IList, or IDictionary interface it isn't mandatory that you expose all the interface's properties and methods as Public members. For example, the Array class implements IList, but the Add, Insert, and Remove members don't appear in the Array class interface because arrays have a fixed size. You get an exception if you invoke these methods after casting an array reference to an IList variable.

A trait that all the classes in System.Collections have in common except the BitArray and BitVector32 types is that they store Object values. This means that you can store any type of value inside them and even store instances of different types inside the same collection. In some cases, this feature is useful, but when used with value types these collections cause a lot of boxing activity and their performance is less than optimal. Also, you often need to cast values to a typed variable when you unbox collection elements. As you read in Chapter 11, you should use a strong-typed generic collection to achieve type safety and more efficient code.

The ArrayList Type

You can think of the ArrayList class as a hybrid of the Array and Collection objects in that it enables you to work with a set of values as if it were an array and a collection at the same time. For example, you can address elements by their indexes, sort and reverse them, and search a value sequentially or by means of a binary search as you do with arrays; you can append elements, insert them in a given position, or remove them as you do with collections.

The ArrayList object has an initial capacity—in practice, the number of slots in the internal structure that holds the actual values—but you don't need to worry about that because an ArrayList is automatically expanded as needed, as are all collections. However, you can optimize your code by choosing an initial capability that offers a good compromise between used memory and the overhead that occurs whenever the ArrayList object has to expand:

```
' Create an ArrayList with default initial capacity of 4 elements.
Dim al As New ArrayList()
' Create an ArrayList with initial capacity of 1000 elements.
Dim al2 As New ArrayList(1000)
```

(Notice that the initial capacity was 16 in .NET version 1.1 but has changed to 4 in version 2.0.) The ArrayList constructor can take an ICollection object and initialize its elements accordingly. You can pass another ArrayList or just a regular array:

```
' Create an array on the fly and pass it to the ArrayList constructor.
Dim al3 As New ArrayList(New String(){"one", "two", "three"})
```

You can modify the capacity at any moment to enlarge the internal array or shrink it by assigning a value to the Capacity property. However, you can't make it smaller than the current number of elements actually stored in the array (which corresponds to the value returned by the Count property):

```
' Make the ArrayList take only the memory that it strictly needs.
al.Capacity = al.Count
' Another way to achieve the same result
al.TrimToSize()
```

When the current capacity is exceeded, the ArrayList object doubles its capacity automatically. You can't control the growth factor of an ArrayList, so you should set the Capacity property to a suitable value to avoid time-consuming memory allocations.

Another way to create an ArrayList object is by means of its static Repeat method, which enables you to specify an initial value for the specified number of elements:

```
' Create an ArrayList with 100 elements equal to an empty string.
Dim al4 As ArrayList = ArrayList.Repeat("", 100)
```

The ArrayList class fully implements the IList interface. You add elements to an ArrayList object by using the Add method (which appends the new element after the last item) or the Insert method (which inserts the new element at the specified index). You remove a specific object by passing it to the Remove method, remove the element at a given index by using the RemoveAt method, or remove all elements with the Clear method:

```
' Be sure that you start with an empty ArrayList.
al.Clear()
' Append the elements "Joe" and "Ann" at the end of the ArrayList.
al.Add("Joe")
al.Add("Ann")
' Insert "Robert" item at the beginning of the list. (Index is zero-based.)
al.Insert(0, "Robert")
' Remove "Joe" from the list.
al.Remove("Joe")
' Remove the first element of the list ("Robert" in this case).
al.RemoveAt(0)
```

The Remove method removes only the first occurrence of a given object, so you need a loop to remove all the elements with a given value. You can't simply iterate through the loop until you get an error, however, because the Remove method doesn't throw an exception if the element isn't found. Therefore, you must use one of these two approaches:

```
' Using the Contains method is concise but not very efficient.
Do While al.Contains("element to remove")
    al.Remove("element to remove")
Loop
```

```
' A more efficient technique: loop until the Count property becomes constant.
Dim saveCount As Integer
```

```
Do
   saveCount = al.Count
   al.Remove("element to remove")
Loop While al.Count < saveCount
```

You can read and write any ArrayList element using the Item property. This property is the default member, so you can omit it and deal with this object as if it were a standard zero-based array:

```
al(0) = "first element"
```

Just remember that an element in an ArrayList object is created only when you call the Add method, so you can't reference an element whose index is equal to or higher than the Array-List's Count property. As with collections, the preferred way to iterate over all elements is through the For Each loop, even though you can surely use a standard For loop:

```
' These two loops are equivalent.
For Each o As Object In al
   Console.WriteLine(o)
Next

For i As Integer = 0 To al.Count - 1
   Console.WriteLine(al(i))
Next
```

The ArrayList class exposes methods that allow you to manipulate ranges of elements in one operation. The AddRange method appends to the current ArrayList object all the elements contained in another object that implements the ICollection interface. Many .NET classes other than those described in this chapter implement ICollection, such as the collection of all the items in a ListBox control and the collection of nodes in a TreeView control. The following routine takes two ArrayList objects and returns a third ArrayList that contains all the items from both arguments:

```
Function ArrayListJoin(ByVal al1 As ArrayList, ByVal al2 As ArrayList) As ArrayList
   ' Note how we avoid time-consuming reallocations.
   Dim res As New ArrayList(al1.Count + al2.count)
   ' Append the items in the two ArrayList arguments.
   res.AddRange(al1)
   res.AddRange(al2)
   Return res
End Function
```

The InsertRange method works in a similar way but lets you insert multiple elements at any index in the current ArrayList object:

```
' Insert all the items of al2 at the beginning of al.
al.InsertRange(0, al2)
' RemoveRange deletes multiple elements in the al object:
' Delete the last four elements (assumes there are at least four elements).
al.RemoveRange(al.Count - 4, 4)
```

Adding or removing elements from the beginning or the middle of an ArrayList is an expensive operation because all the elements with higher indexes must be shifted accordingly. In general, the Add method is faster than the Insert method and should be used if possible.

You can read or write a group of contiguous elements by means of the GetRange and SetRange methods. The former takes an initial index and a count and returns a new ArrayList that contains only the elements in the selected range; the latter takes an initial index and an ICollection object:

```
' Display only the first 10 elements to the console window.
For Each o As Object In al.GetRange(0, 10)
    Console.WriteLine(o)
Next
' Copy the first 20 elements from al to al2.
al2.SetRange(0, al.GetRange(0, 20))
```

You can quickly extract all the items in the ArrayList object by using the ToArray method or the CopyTo method. Both of them support one-dimensional target arrays of any compatible type, but the latter also allows you to extract a subset of ArrayList:

```
' Extract elements to an Object array (never throws an exception).
Dim objArr() As Object = al.ToArray()
' Extract elements to a String array (might throw an InvalidCastException).
Dim strArr() As String = DirectCast(al.ToArray(GetType(String)), String())

' Same as above but uses the CopyTo method.
' (Note that the target array must be large enough.)
Dim strArr2(al.Count) As String
al.CopyTo(strArr2)
' Copy only items [1,2], starting at element 4 in the target array.
Dim strArr3() As String = {"0", "1", "2", "3", "4", "5", "6", "7", "8", "9"}
' Syntax is: CopyTo(sourceIndex, target, destIndex, count).
al.CopyTo(0, strArr3, 4, 2)
```

The ArrayList class supports other useful methods, such as Sort, Reverse, BinarySearch, Contains, IndexOf, LastIndexOf, and Reverse. I described most of these methods in the section devoted to arrays, so I won't repeat their description here.

The TrimToSize method deserves a special mention. As I explained previously, the ArrayList automatically doubles its capacity whenever it needs room for a new element. After many insertions (and deletions) you might end up with an ArrayList that contains many unused slots; if you don't plan to add more elements to the ArrayList, you can reclaim the unused space by means of the TrimToSize method:

```
al.TrimToSize()
```

The last feature of the ArrayList class that's worth mentioning is its Adapter and ReadOnly static methods. The Adapter method takes an IList-derived object as its only argument and creates an ArrayList wrapper around that object. In other words, instead of creating a copy of the argument, the Adapter method creates an ArrayList object that "contains" the original collection. All the changes you make on the outer ArrayList object are duplicated in the original collection, and vice versa. You might want to use the Adapter method because the ArrayList class implements several methods—Reverse, Sort, BinarySearch, ToArray, IndexOf, and LastIndexOf, just to name a few—that are missing in a simpler IList object. The following code sample demonstrates how you can use this technique to reverse (or sort, and so on) all the items in a ListBox control:

```
' Create a wrapper around the ListBox.Items (IList) collection.
Dim lbAdapter As ArrayList = ArrayList.Adapter(ListBox1.Items)
' Reverse their order.
lbAdapter.Reverse()
```

If you don't plan to reuse the ArrayList wrapper, you can make this code even more concise:

```
ArrayList.Adapter(ListBox1.Items).Reverse()
```

The ReadOnly static method is similar to Adapter, except it returns an ArrayList that you can't modify in any way, including adding, removing, or assigning elements. This method can be useful when you want to pass your ArrayList to a method you didn't write yourself and you want to be sure that the method doesn't mistakenly modify the ArrayList or its elements.

The Hashtable Type

The Hashtable class implements the IDictionary interface, and it behaves much like the Scripting.Dictionary object you might have used in Visual Basic 6. (The Dictionary object can be found in the Microsoft Scripting Runtime library.) All objects based on the IDictionary interface manage two internal series of data—values and keys—and you can use a key to retrieve the corresponding value. The actual implementation of the interface depends on the specific type. For example, the Hashtable type uses an internal hash table, a well-known data structure that has been studied for decades by computer scientists and has been thoroughly described in countless books on algorithms.

When a (key, value) pair is added to a Hashtable object, the position of an element in the internal array is based on the numeric hash code of the key. When you later search for that key, the key's hash code is used again to locate the associated value as quickly as possible, without sequentially visiting all the elements in the hash table. Collection objects in Visual Basic 6 use a similar mechanism, except that the key's hash code is derived from the characters in the key and the key must necessarily be a string. Conversely, the .NET Hashtable class lets you use any object as a key. Behind the scenes, the Hashtable object uses the key's GetHashCode, a method that all objects inherit from System.Object.

Depending on how the hash code is evaluated, it frequently happens that multiple keys map to the same slot (or *bucket*) in the hash table. In this case, you have a *collision*. The .NET Hashtable object uses double hashing to minimize collisions, but it can't avoid collisions completely. Never fear—collisions are automatically dealt with transparently for the programmer, but you can get optimal performance by selecting an adequate initial capacity for the hash table. A larger table doesn't speed up searches remarkably, but it makes insertions faster.

You can also get better performance by selecting a correct load factor when you create a Hashtable object. This number determines the maximum ratio between values and buckets before the hash table is automatically expanded. The smaller this value is, the more memory is allocated to the internal table and the fewer collisions occur when you're inserting or searching for a value. The default load factor is 1.0, which in most cases delivers a good-enough performance, but you can set a smaller load factor when you create the Hashtable if you're willing to trade memory for better performance. You can initialize a Hashtable object in many ways:

```
' Default load factor and initial capacity
Dim ht As New Hashtable()
' Default load factor and specified initial capacity
Dim ht2 As New Hashtable(1000)
' Specified initial capability and custom load factor
Dim ht3 As New Hashtable(1000, 0.8)
```

You can also initialize the Hashtable by loading it with the elements contained in any other object that implements the IDictionary interface (such as another Hashtable or a SortedList object). This technique is especially useful when you want to change the load factor of an existing hash table:

```
' Decrease the load factor of the current Hashtable.
ht = New HashTable(ht, 0.5)
```

Other, more sophisticated variants of the constructor let you pass an IComparer object to compare keys in a customized fashion, an IHashCodeProvider object to supply a custom algorithm for calculating hash codes of keys, or an IEqualityComparer object if you want to change the way keys are compared with each other. (More on this later.)

Once you've created a Hashtable, you can add a key and value pair, read or modify the value associated with a given key through the Item property, and remove an item with the Remove method:

```
' Syntax for Add method is Add(key, value).
ht.Add("Joe", 12000)
ht.Add("Ann", 13000)
' Referencing a new key creates an element.
ht.Item("Robert") = 15000
' Item is the default member, so you can omit its name.
ht("Chris") = 11000
Console.Write(ht("Joe"))      ' => 12000
' The Item property lets you overwrite an existing element.
' (You need CInt or CType if Option Strict is On.)
ht("Ann") = CInt(ht("Ann")) + 1000
' By default keys are compared in case-insensitive mode,
' so the following statement creates a *new* element.
ht("ann") = 15000
' Reading a nonexistent element doesn't create it.
```

```
Console.WriteLine(ht("Lee"))          ' Doesn't display anything

' Remove an element given its key.
ht.Remove("Chris")
' How many elements are now in the Hashtable?
Console.WriteLine(ht.Count)           ' => 4

' Adding an element that already exists throws an exception.
ht.Add("Joe", 11500)                  ' Throws ArgumentException.
```

As I explained earlier, you can use virtually anything as a key, including a numeric value. When you're using numbers as keys, a Hashtable looks deceptively similar to an array:

```
ht(1) = 123
ht(2) = 345
```

But never forget that the expression between parentheses is just a key and not an index; thus, the ht(2) element isn't necessarily stored "after" the ht(1) element. As a matter of fact, the elements in a Hashtable object aren't stored in a particular order, and you should never write code that assumes that they are. This is the main difference between the Hashtable object and the SortedList object (which is described next).

The Hashtable object implements the IEnumerable interface, so you can iterate over all its elements with a For Each loop. Each element of a Hashtable is a DictionaryEntry object, which exposes a Key and a Value property:

```
For Each de As DictionaryEntry In ht
   Console.WriteLine("ht('{0}') = {1}", de.Key, de.Value)
Next
```

The Hashtable's Keys and Values properties return an ICollection-based object that contains all the keys and all the values, respectively, so you can assign them to any object that implements the ICollection interface. Or you can use these properties directly in a For Each loop:

```
' Display all the keys in the Hashtable.
For Each o As Object In ht.Keys      ' Or use ht.Values for all the values.
   Console.WriteLine(o)
Next
```

An important detail: the ICollection objects returned by the Keys and Values properties are "live" objects that continue to be linked to the Hashtable and reflect any additions and deletions performed subsequently, as this code demonstrates:

```
ht.Clear()
Dim values As ICollection = ht.Values
ht.Add("Chris", 11000)
' Prove that the collection continues to be linked to the Hashtable.
Console.WriteLine(values.Count)           ' => 1
```

By default, keys are compared in a case-sensitive way, so Joe, JOE, and joe are considered distinct keys. You can create case-insensitive instances of the Hashtable class through one of its many constructors, or you can use the CreateCaseInsensitiveHashtable static method of the System.Collections.Specialized.CollectionsUtil, as follows:

```
Dim ht4 As Hashtable = CollectionsUtil.CreateCaseInsensitiveHashtable()
```

Another way to implement a Hashtable that deals with keys in a nonstandard fashion is by providing an IEqualityComparer object to override the default comparison algorithm. For example, say that you want to create a Hashtable where all keys are Double (or convertible to Double) but are automatically rounded to the second decimal digit so that, for example, the keys 1.123 and 1.199 resolve to the same element in the Hashtable. You might perform the rounding each time you add or retrieve an element in the table, but the approach based on the IEqualityComparer interface is more elegant because it moves the responsibility into the Hashtable and away from the client:

```
Public Class FloatingPointKeyComparer
    Implements IEqualityComparer

    Dim digits As Integer

    Sub New(ByVal digits As Integer)
        Me.digits = digits
    End Sub

    Public Shadows Function Equals(ByVal x As Object, ByVal y As Object) As Boolean _
            Implements IEqualityComparer.Equals
        Dim d1 As Double = Math.Round(CDbl(x), digits)
        Dim d2 As Double = Math.Round(CDbl(y), digits)
        Return d1 = d2
    End Function

    Public Shadows Function GetHashCode(ByVal obj As Object) As Integer _
            Implements IEqualityComparer.GetHashCode
        Dim d As Double = Math.Round(CDbl(obj), digits)
        Return d.GetHashCode()
    End Function
End Class
```

The FloatingPointKeyComparer's constructor takes the number of digits used when rounding keys, so you can use it for any precision. The following example illustrates how to use it for keys rounded to the second decimal digit.

```
ht = New Hashtable(New FloatingPointKeyComparer(2))
ht.Add(1.123, "first")
ht.Add(1.456, "second")
' Prove that keys that round to the same Double number resolve to same item.
Console.WriteLine(ht(1.119))                ' => first
```

The SortedList Type

The SortedList object is arguably the most versatile nongeneric collection-like object in the .NET Framework. It implements the IDictionary interface, like the Hashtable object, and also keeps its elements sorted. Alas, you pay for all this power in terms of performance, so you should use the SortedList object only when your programming logic requires an object with all this flexibility.

The SortedList object manages two internal arrays, one for the values and one for the companion keys. These arrays have an initial capacity, but they automatically grow when the need arises. Entries are kept sorted by their key, and you can even provide an IComparer object to affect how complex values (a Person object, for example) are compared and sorted. The SortedList class provides several constructor methods:

```
' A SortedList with default capacity (16 entries)
Dim sl As New SortedList()
' A SortedList with specified initial capacity
Dim sl2 As New SortedList(1000)

' A SortedList can be initialized with all the elements in an IDictionary.
Dim ht As New Hashtable()
ht.Add("Robert", 100)
ht.Add("Ann", 200)
ht.Add("Joe", 300)
Dim sl3 As New SortedList(ht)
```

As soon as you add new elements to the SortedList, they're immediately sorted by their key. Like the Hashtable class, a SortedList contains DictionaryEntry elements:

```
For Each de As DictionaryEntry In sl3
   Console.WriteLine("sl3('{0}') = {1}", de.Key, de.Value)
Next
```

Here's the result that appears in the console window:

```
sl3('Ann') = 200
sl3('Joe') = 300
sl3('Robert') = 100
```

Keys are sorted according to the order implied by their IComparable interface, so numbers and strings are always sorted in ascending order. If you want a different order, you must create an object that implements the IComparer interface. For example, you can use the following class to invert the natural string ordering:

```
Public Class ReverseStringComparer
   Implements IComparer

   Function Compare(ByVal x As Object, ByVal y As Object) As Integer _
        Implements IComparer.Compare
     ' Just change the sign of the String.Compare result.
     Return -String.Compare(x.ToString, y.ToString)
   End Function
End Class
```

You can pass an instance of this object to one of the two overloaded constructors that take an IComparer object:

```
' A SortedList that sorts elements through a custom IComparer
Dim s14 As New SortedList(New ReverseStringComparer())

' A SortedList that loads all its elements from a Hashtable and
' sorts them with a custom IComparer object.
Dim s15 As New SortedList(ht, New ReverseStringComparer)
```

Here are the elements of the resulting SortedList object:

```
s15('Robert') = 100
s15('Joe') = 300
s15('Ann') = 200
```

The SortedList class compares keys in case-sensitive mode, with lowercase characters coming before their uppercase versions (for example, Ann comes before ANN, which in turn comes before Bob). If you want to compare keys without taking case into account, you can create a case-insensitive SortedList object using the auxiliary CollectionsUtil object in the System.Collections.Specialized namespace:

```
Dim s16 As SortedList = CollectionsUtil.CreateCaseInsensitiveSortedList()
```

In this case, trying to add two elements whose keys differ only in case throws an ArgumentException object.

You are already familiar with the majority of the members exposed by the SortedList type because they are exposed also by the Hashtable or ArrayList types: Capacity, Count, Keys, Values, Clear, Contains, CopyTo, Remove, RemoveAt, TrimToSize. The meaning of other methods should be self-explanatory: ContainsKey returns True if the SortedList contains a given key and is a synonym for Contains; ContainsValue returns True if the SortedList contains a given value; GetKey and GetByIndex return the key or the value at a given index; SetByIndex changes the value of an element at a given index; IndexOfKey and IndexOfValue return the index of a given key or value, or −1 if the key or the value isn't in the SortedList. All these methods work as intended, so I won't provide any code examples for them.

A couple of methods require further explanation, though: GetKeyList and GetValueList. These methods are similar to the Keys and Values properties, except they return an IList object rather than an ICollection object and therefore you can directly access an element at a given index. As for the Keys and Values properties, the returned object reflects any change in the SortedList.

```
s1 = New SortedList()
' Get a live reference to key and value collections.
Dim alKeys As IList = s1.GetKeyList()
Dim alValues As IList = s1.GetValueList()
' Add some values, out of order.
s1.Add(3, "three")
```

```
sl.Add(2, "two")
sl.Add(1, "one")
' Display values in sorted order.
For i As Integer = 0 To sl.Count - 1
   Console.WriteLine("{0} = ""{1}""", alKeys(i), alValues(i))
Next
' Any attempt to modify the IList object throws an exception.
alValues.Insert(0, "four")          ' Throws NotSupportedException error.
```

As I said before, the SortedList class is the most powerful collection-like object, but it's also the most demanding in terms of resources and CPU time. To see what kind of overhead you can expect when using a SortedList object, I created a routine that adds 100,000 elements to an ArrayList object, a Hashtable object, and a SortedList object. The results were pretty interesting: the ArrayList object was about 4 times faster than the Hashtable object, which in turn was from 8 to 100 times faster than the SortedList object. Even though you can't take these ratios as reliable in all circumstances, they clearly show that you should never use a more powerful data structure if you don't really need its features.

In general, you should never use a SortedList if you can get along with a different data structure, unless you really need to keep elements sorted *always*. In most practical cases, however, you just need to sort elements after you've read them, so you can load them into a Hashtable and, when loading has completed, pass the Hashtable to the SortedList's constructor. To illustrate this concept and show how these types can cooperate with each other, I have prepared a short program that parses a long text string (for example, the contents of a text file) into individual words and loads them into an ArrayList; then it finds unique words by loading each word in a Hashtable and finally displays the sorted list of words in alphabetical order, together with the number of occurrences of that word:

```
' Read the contents of a text file. (Change file path as needed.)
Dim filetext As String = File.ReadAllText("c:\document.txt")
' Use regular expressions to parse individual words, put them in an ArrayList.
Dim alWords As New ArrayList()
For Each m As Match In Regex.Matches(filetext, "\w+")
   alWords.Add(m.Value)
Next
Console.WriteLine("Found {0} words.", alWords.Count)

' Create a case-insensitive Hashtable.
Dim htWords As Hashtable = CollectionsUtil.CreateCaseInsensitiveHashtable()
' Process each word in the ArrayList.
For Each word As String In alWords
   ' Search this word in the Hashtable.
   Dim elem As Object = htWords(word)
   If elem Is Nothing Then
      ' Not found: this is the first occurrence.
      htWords(word) = 1
   Else
      ' Found: increment occurrence count.
      htWords(word) = CInt(elem) + 1
   End If
Next
```

```
' Sort all elements alphabetically.
Dim slWords As New SortedList(htWords)
' Display words and their occurrence count.
For Each de As DictionaryEntry In slWords
    Console.WriteLine("{0} ({1} occurrences)", de.Key, de.Value)
Next
```

Read Chapter 14 for more information about regular expressions.

Other Collections

Although the ArrayList, Hashtable, and SortedList types are collections you might need in your applications most frequently, the System.Collections namespace contains several other useful types. In this roundup section, I cover the Stack, Queue, BitArray, and BitVector32 types.

The Stack Type

The System.Collections.Stack type implements a last in, first out (LIFO) data structure, namely, a structure into which you can push objects and later pop them out. The last object pushed in is also the first one being popped out. The three basic methods of a Stack object are Push, Pop, and Peek; the Count property returns the number of elements currently in the stack:

```
Dim st As New Stack()
' Push three values onto the stack.
st.Push(10)
st.Push(20)
st.Push(30)
' Pop the value on top of the stack, and display its value.
Console.WriteLine(st.Pop())                 ' => 30
' Read the value on top of the stack without popping it.
Console.WriteLine(st.Peek())                ' => 20
' Now pop it.
Console.WriteLine(st.Pop())                 ' => 20
' Determine how many elements are now in the stack.
Console.WriteLine(st.Count)                 ' => 1
' Pop the only value still on the stack.
Console.WriteLine(st.Pop())                 ' => 10
' Check that the stack is now empty.
Console.WriteLine(st.Count)                 ' => 0
```

The only other methods that can prove useful are Contains, which returns True if a given value is currently on the stack; ToArray, which returns the contents of the stack as an array of the specified type; and Clear, which removes all the elements from the stack:

```
' Is the value 10 somewhere on the stack?
If st.Contains(10) Then Console.Write("Found")
' Extract all the items to an array.
Dim values() As Object = st.ToArray()
' Clear the stack.
st.Clear()
```

The Stack object supports the IEnumerable interface, so you can iterate over its elements without popping them by means of a For Each loop:

```
For Each o As Object In st
    Console.WriteLine(o)
Next
```

The Queue Type

A first in, first out (FIFO) structure, also known as a *queue* or *circular buffer*, is often used to solve recurring programming problems. You need a queue structure when a portion of an application inserts elements at one end of a buffer and another piece of code extracts the first available element at the other end. This situation occurs whenever you have a series of elements that you must process sequentially but you can't process immediately.

You can render a queue in Visual Basic by leveraging the System.Collections.Queue object. Queue objects have an initial capacity, but the internal buffer is automatically extended if the need arises. You create a Queue object by specifying its capacity and a growth factor, both of which are optional:

```
' A queue with initial capacity of 200 elements; a growth factor equal to 1.5
' (when new room is needed, the capacity will become 300, then 450, 675, etc.)
Dim qu1 As New Queue(200, 1.5)
' A queue with 100 elements and a default growth factor of 2
Dim qu2 As New Queue(100)
' A queue with 32 initial elements and a default growth factor of 2
Dim qu3 As New Queue()
```

The key methods of a Queue object are Enqueue, Peek, and Dequeue. Check the output of the following code snippet, and compare it with the behavior of the Stack object:

```
Dim qu As New Queue(100)
' Insert three values in the queue.
qu.Enqueue(10)
qu.Enqueue(20)
qu.Enqueue(30)
' Extract the first value, and display it.
Console.WriteLine(qu.Dequeue())              ' => 10
' Read the next value, but don't extract it.
Console.WriteLine(qu.Peek())                 ' => 20
' Extract it.
Console.WriteLine(qu.Dequeue())              ' => 20
' Check how many items are still in the queue.
Console.WriteLine(qu.Count)                  ' => 1
' Extract the last element, and check that the queue is now empty.
Console.WriteLine(qu.Dequeue())              ' => 30
Console.WriteLine(qu.Count)                  ' => 0
```

The Queue object also supports the Contains method, which checks whether an element is in the queue, and the Clear method, which clears the queue's contents. The Queue class implements IEnumerable and can be used in a For Each loop.

The BitArray Type

A BitArray object can hold a large number of Boolean values in a compact format, using a single bit for each element. This class implements IEnumerable (and thus supports For Each), ICollection, and ICloneable. You can create a BitArray object in many ways:

```
' Provide the number of elements (all initialized to False).
Dim ba As New BitArray(1024)
' Provide the number of elements, and initialize them to a value.
Dim ba2 As New BitArray(1024, True)

' Initialize the BitArray from an array of Boolean, Byte, or Integer.
Dim boolArr(1023) As Boolean
' Initialize the boolArr array here.
...
Dim ba3 As New BitArray(boolArr)

' Initialize the BitArray from another BitArray object.
Dim ba4 As New BitArray(ba)
```

You can retrieve the number of elements in a BitArray by using either the Count property or the Length property. The Get method reads and the Set method modifies the element at the specified index:

```
' Set element at index 9, and read it back.
ba.Set(9, True)
Console.WriteLine(ba.Get(9))              ' => True
```

The CopyTo method can move all elements back to an array of Booleans, or it can perform a bitwise copy of the BitArray to a zero-based Byte or Integer array:

```
' Bitwise copy to an array of Integers
Dim intArr(31) As Integer                ' 32 elements * 32 bits each = 1024 bits
' Second argument is the index in which the copy begins in target array.
ba.CopyTo(intArr, 0)
' Check that bit 9 of first element in intArr is set.
Console.WriteLine(intArr(0))             ' => 512
```

The Not method complements all the bits in the BitArray object:

```
ba.Not()                                 ' No arguments
```

The And, Or, and Xor methods let you perform the corresponding operation on pairs of Boolean values stored in two BitArray objects:

```
' Perform an AND operation of all the bits in the first BitArray
' with the complement of all the bits in the second BitArray.
ba.And(ba2.Not)
```

Finally, you can set or reset all the bits in a BitArray class using the SetAll method:

```
' Set all the bits to True.
ba.SetAll(True)
```

The BitArray type doesn't expose any methods that let you quickly determine how many True (or False) elements are in the array. You can take advantage of the IEnumerator support of this class and use a For Each loop:

```
Dim bitCount As Integer = 0
For Each b As Boolean In ba
   If b Then bitCount += 1
Next
Console.WriteLine("Found {0} True values.", bitCount)
```

The BitVector32 Type

The BitVector32 class (in the System.Collections.Specialized namespace) is similar to the BitArray class in that it can hold a packed array of Boolean values, one per bit, but it's limited to 32 elements. However, a BitVector32 object can store a set of small integers that takes up to 32 consecutive bits and is therefore useful with bit-coded fields, such as those that you deal with when passing data to and from hardware devices.

```
Dim bv As New BitVector32()
' Set one element and read it back.
bv(1) = True
Console.WriteLine(bv(1))                ' => True
```

You can also pass a 32-bit integer to the constructor to initialize all the elements in one pass:

```
' Initialize all elements to True.
bv = New BitVector32(-1)
```

To define a BitVector32 that is subdivided into sections that are longer than 1 bit, you must create one or more BitVector32.Section objects and use them when you later read and write individual elements. You define a section by means of the BitVector32.CreateSection static method, which takes the highest integer you want to store in that section and (for all sections after the first one) the previous section. Here's a complete example:

```
bv = New BitVector32()
' Create three sections, of 4, 5, and 6 bits each.
Dim se1 As BitVector32.Section = BitVector32.CreateSection(15)
Dim se2 As BitVector32.Section = BitVector32.CreateSection(31, se1)
Dim se3 As BitVector32.Section = BitVector32.CreateSection(63, se2)

' Assign a given value to each section.
bv(se1) = 10
bv(se2) = 20
bv(se3) = 40
' Read values back.
Console.WriteLine(bv(se1))         ' => 10
Console.WriteLine(bv(se2))         ' => 20
Console.WriteLine(bv(se3))         ' => 40
```

The Data property sets or returns the internal 32-bit integer; you can use this property to save the bit-coded value into a database field or to pass it to a hardware device:

```
' Read the entire field as a 32-bit value.
Console.WriteLine(bv.Data)                       ' => 20810
Console.WriteLine(bv.Data.ToString("X"))         ' => 514A
```

Abstract Types for Strong-Typed Collections

As I have emphasized many times in earlier sections, all the types in the System.Collections namespace—with the exception of BitArray and BitVector32—are weakly typed collections that can contain objects of any kind. This feature makes them more flexible but less robust because any attempt to assign an object of the "wrong" type can't be flagged as an error by the compiler. You can overcome this limitation by creating a strong-typed collection class.

In Visual Basic .NET 2003, you can implement custom strong-typed collection types by inheriting from one of the abstract base classes that the .NET Framework offers, namely:

- **CollectionBase**   For strong-typed IList-based collections, that is, types that are functionally similar to ArrayList but capable of accepting objects of a specific type only.

- **ReadOnlyCollectionBase**   Like CollectionBase, except that the collection has a fixed size and you can't add elements to or remove elements from it after it has been instantiated. (Individual items can be either read-only or writable, depending on how you implement the collection.)

- **DictionaryBase**   For strong-typed IDictionary-based collections, that is, types that are functionally similar to Hashtable but capable of accepting objects of a specific type only.

- **NameObjectCollectionBase**   (In the System.Collections.Specialized namespace) for strong-typed collections whose elements can be accessed by either their index or the key associated with them. (You can think of these collections as a hybrid between the Array-List and the Hashtable types.)

The importance of these base collection types has decreased in Visual Basic 2005 because generics permit you to implement strong-typed collections in a much simpler and more efficient manner. However, in some scenarios you might need to use these base types in .NET Framework 2.0 as well, for example, when implementing a collection that must accept objects of two or more distinct types and these types don't share a common base class or interface. Another case when generics aren't very helpful is when you need to implement the IEnumerable interface directly, as I show in Chapter 10.

The CollectionBase Type

For the sake of illustration I will show how you can inherit from CollectionBase to create an ArrayList-like collection that can host only Person objects. Consider the following definition of a Person:

```
Public Class Person
    ' These should be properties in a real-world application.
```

```
    Public FirstName As String
    Public LastName As String
    Public Spouse As Person
    Public ReadOnly Children As New ArrayList

    Public Sub New(ByVal firstName As String, ByVal lastName As String)
       Me.FirstName = firstName
       Me.LastName = lastName
    End Sub

    Public Function ReverseName() As String
       Return LastName & ", " & FirstName
    End Function
End Class
```

As you might notice, the Spouse member enables you to create a one-to-one relationship between two Person objects, whereas the Children member can implement a one-to-many relationship. The problem is, the Children collection is weakly typed; thus, a client program might mistakenly add to it an object of the wrong type without the compiler being able to spot the problem. You can solve this issue by creating a class that inherits from CollectionBase and that exposes a few strong-typed members that take or return Person objects:

```
Public Class PersonCollection
    Inherits CollectionBase

    Public Sub Add(ByVal item As Person)
       Me.List.Add(item)
    End Sub

    Public Sub Remove(ByVal item As Person)
       Me.List.Remove(item)
    End Sub

    Default Public Property Item(ByVal index As Integer) As Person
       Get
          Return DirectCast(Me.List(index), Person)
       End Get
       Set(ByVal Value As Person)
          Me.List(index) = Value
       End Set
    End Property
End Class
```

The PersonCollection type inherits most of its public members from its base class, including Count, Clear, and RemoveAt; these are the members with signatures that don't mention the type of the specific objects you want to store in the collection (Person, in this case). Your job is to provide only the remaining members, which do nothing but delegate to the inner IList object by means of the protected List property.

To make the collection behave exactly as an ArrayList you need to implement additional members, including Sort, IndexOf, and BinarySearch. These methods aren't exposed by the protected List property, but you can reach them by using the InnerList protected member (which returns the inner ArrayList):

```
Public Sub Sort()
    Me.InnerList.Sort()
End Sub
```

When you've completed the PersonCollection type, you can replace the declaration of the Children member in the Person class to implement the one-to-many relationship in a more robust manner:

```
' (In the Person class…)
Public ReadOnly Children As New PersonCollection()

' (In the client application…)
Dim john As New Person("John", "Evans")
john.Children.Add(New Person("Robert", "Zare"))     ' This works.
' The next statement doesn't even compile if Option Strict is On.
john.Children.Add(New Object())                     ' Compilation error!
```

Quite surprisingly, however, the PersonCollection isn't very robust because an application can still add non-Person objects to it by accessing its IList interface:

```
' These statements raise neither a compiler warning nor a runtime error!
DirectCast(john.Children, IList).Item(0) = New Object()
DirectCast(john.Children, IList).Add(New Object())
```

Unfortunately, there is no way to tell the compiler to reject the preceding statement, but at least you can throw an exception at run time by checking the type of objects being assigned or added in the OnValidate protected method:

```
' (In the PersonCollection class…)
Protected Overrides Sub OnValidate(ByVal value As Object)
    If Not TypeOf value Is Person Then Throw New ArgumentException("Invalid item")
End Sub
```

The CollectionBase abstract class exposes other protected methods that can be overridden to execute a piece of custom code just before or after an operation is performed on the collection: OnClear and OnClearComplete methods run before and after a Clear method; OnInsert and OnInsertComplete methods run when an item is added to the collection; OnRemove and OnRemoveComplete run when an item is removed from the collection; OnSet and OnSet-Complete run when an item is assigned; OnGet runs when an item is read. For example, you might need to override these methods when the collection must notify another object when its contents change.

The ReadOnlyCollectionBase Type

The main difference between the CollectionBase type and the ReadOnlyCollectionBase type is that the latter doesn't expose any public member that would let clients add or remove items, such as Clear and RemoveAt. For a fixed-sized collection, you shouldn't expose methods such as Add and Remove, so in most cases your only responsibility is to implement the Item property. If you mark this property with the ReadOnly key, clients can't even assign a new value to the collection's elements:

```
Public Class ReadOnlyPersonCollection
    Inherits ReadOnlyCollectionBase

    Public Sub New()
        ' Initialize the inner collection here.
        …
    End Sub

    Default Public ReadOnly Property Item(ByVal index As Integer) As Person
        Get
            Return DirectCast(Me.List(index), Person)
        End Get
    End Property
End Class
```

The DictionaryBase Type

The technique to create a strong-typed dictionary is similar to what I've just showed for the CollectionBase type, except you inherit from DictionaryBase. This base class enables you to access an inner IDictionary object by means of the Dictionary protected member. Here's a PersonDictionary class that behaves much like the Hashtable object but can contain only Person objects that are indexed by a string key:

```
Public Class PersonDictionary
    Inherits DictionaryBase

    Public Sub Add(ByVal key As String, ByVal item As Person)
        Me.Dictionary.Add(key, item)
    End Sub

    Public Sub Remove(ByVal key As String)
        Me.Dictionary.Remove(key)
    End Sub

    Default Public Property Item(ByVal key As String) As Person
        Get
            Return DirectCast(Me.Dictionary(key), Person)
        End Get
        Set(ByVal Value As Person)
            Me.Dictionary(key) = Value
        End Set
    End Property

    Protected Overrides Sub OnValidate(ByVal key As Object, ByVal value As Object)
        If Not TypeOf key Is String Then Throw New ArgumentException("Invalid key")
        If Not TypeOf value Is Person Then Throw New ArgumentException("Invalid item")
    End Sub
End Class
```

The NameObjectCollectionBase Type

As I mentioned previously, you can inherit from the NameObjectCollectionBase type to implement a strong-typed collection that can refer to its elements by either a key or a numeric index. This type uses an internal Hashtable structure, but it doesn't expose it to inheritors. Instead, your public methods must perform their operation by delegating to a protected Base*Xxxx* method, such as BaseAdd or BaseGet. Here's a complete example of a strong-typed collection based on the NameObjectCollectionBase abstract class:

```
Public Class PersonCollection2
   Inherits NameObjectCollectionBase

   Sub Add(ByVal key As String, ByVal p As Person)
      Me.BaseAdd(key, p)
   End Sub

   Sub Clear()
      Me.BaseClear()
   End Sub

   ' The Remove method that takes a string key
   Sub Remove(ByVal key As String)
      Me.Remove(key)
   End Sub

   ' The Remove method that takes a numeric index
   Sub Remove(ByVal index As Integer)
      Me.Remove(index)
   End Sub

   ' The Item property that takes a string key
   Default Property Item(ByVal key As String) As Person
      Get
         Return DirectCast(Me.BaseGet(key), Person)
      End Get
      Set(ByVal Value As Person)
         Me.BaseSet(key, Value)
      End Set
   End Property

   ' The Item property that takes a numeric index
   Default Property Item(ByVal index As Integer) As Person
      Get
         Return DirectCast(Me.BaseGet(index), Person)
      End Get
      Set(ByVal Value As Person)
         Me.BaseSet(index, Value)
      End Set
   End Property
End Class
```

Generic Collections

In Chapter 11, you saw how you can implement your own generic types. However, in most cases you don't really need to go that far because you can simply use one of the many types defined in the System.Collections.Generic namespace, which contains both generic collection types and generic interfaces. You can use the generic collections both directly in your applications or inherit from them to extend them with additional methods. In either case, generics can make your programming much, much simpler.

For example, going back to the example in the section titled "The CollectionBase Type" earlier in this chapter, you can have the Person class expose a strong-typed collection of other Persons as easily as this code:

```
Public Class Person
   Public ReadOnly Children As New List(Of Person)
   ...
End Class
```

On the other hand, if you are migrating code from Visual Basic .NET 2003 and don't want to break existing clients, you can use a different approach and replace the existing version of the PersonCollection strong-typed collection with this code:

```
Public Class PersonCollection
   Inherits List(Of Person)
   ' … and that's it!
End Class
```

Not only is the implementation of PersonCollection simpler, it is also more complete because it exposes all the methods you expect to find in an ArrayList, such as Sort and Reverse. Just as important, if the element type is a value type—such as a numeric type or a structure—the generic-based implementation is also far more efficient because values are never passed to an Object argument and therefore are never boxed.

The List Generic Type

If you are familiar with the ArrayList type, you already know how to use most of the functionality exposed by the List(Of T) type and its members: Add, Clear, Insert, Remove, RemoveAt, RemoveAll, IndexOf, LastIndexOf, Reverse, Sort, and BinarySearch. You can perform operations on multiple items by means of the GetRange, AddRange, InsertRange, and RemoveRange methods. The GetRange method returns another List(Of T) object, so you can assign its result in a strongly typed fashion:

```
' Copy elements between two strong-typed collections.
Dim persons As New List(Of Person)
persons.Add(New Person("John", "Evans"))
...
' Create a new collection and initialize it with five elements from first collection.
Dim persons2 As New List(Of Person)(persons.GetRange(0, 5))
```

```
' Add elements 10-14 from first collection.
persons2.AddRange(persons.GetRange(10, 5))
```

A List(Of T) collection can contain any object that derives from T; for example, a Person collection can also contain Employee objects if the Employee class derives from Person.

Interestingly, the AddRange and InsertRange methods take any object that implements the IEnumerable(Of T) interface; thus, you can pass them either another List object or a strong-typed array:

```
Dim arr() As Person = {New Person("Robert", "Evans"), _
   New Person("Ann", "Beebe")}
' Insert these elements at the beginning of the collection.
persons.InsertRange(0, persons)
```

Because the arguments must implement the IEnumerable(Of T) interface, you can't pass them an Object array or a weakly typed ArrayList, even if you know for sure that the array or the ArrayList contains only objects of type T. In this case, you must write an explicit For Each loop:

```
' Add all the Person objects stored in an ArrayList.
For Each p As Person In myArrayList
   persons.Add(p)
Next
```

The Remove method doesn't throw an exception if the specified element isn't in the collection; instead, it returns True if the element was successfully removed, False if the element wasn't found:

```
If persons.Remove(aPerson) Then
   Console.WriteLine("The specified person was in the list and has been removed.")
End If
```

The TrimExcess method allows you to reclaim the memory allocated to unused slots:

```
persons.TrimExcess()
```

This method does nothing if the list currently uses 90 percent or more of its current capability. The rationale behind this behavior is that trimming a list is an expensive operation and there is no point in performing it if the expected advantage is negligible.

Alternatively, you can assign the Capacity property directly. By default, the initial capacity is 4, unless you pass a different value to the constructor, but this value might change in future versions of the .NET Framework:

```
persons.Capacity = persons.Count
```

Some generic methods of the List type might puzzle you initially. For example, the Sort method works as expected if the element type supports the IComparable interface; however, you can't provide an IComparer object to it to sort according to a user-defined order, as you'd do with a weak-typed ArrayList. Instead, you must define a class that implements the strong-typed IComparer(Of Person) interface. For example, the following class can work as a strong-typed comparer for the Person class:

```
Public Class PersonComparer
   Implements IComparer(Of Person)

   Public Function Compare(ByVal x As Person, ByVal y As Person) As Integer _
         Implements IComparer(Of Person).Compare
      Return x.ReverseName.CompareTo(y.ReverseName)
   End Function
End Class
```

You can then use the PersonComparer class with the Sort method:

```
' Sort a collection of persons according to the ReverseName property.
persons.Sort(New PersonComparer())
```

(You can also use the same PersonComparer class with BinarySearch for superfast searches in a sorted collection.) A welcome addition to the Sort method in ArrayList is the ability to pass a delegate of type Comparison(Of T), which points to a function that compares two T objects and returns an integer that specifies which is greater. This feature means that you don't need to define a distinct comparer class for each possible kind of sort you want to implement:

```
' This function can be used to sort in the descending direction.
Function ComparePersonsDesc(ByVal p1 As Person, ByVal p2 As Person) As Integer
   ' Notice that the order of arguments is reversed.
   Return p2.ReverseName.CompareTo(p1.ReverseName)
End Function

' Elsewhere in the program…
Sub SortPersonList()
   Dim persons As New List(Of Person)
   …
   persons.Sort(AddressOf ComparePersonsDesc)
End Sub
```

In addition to all the methods you can find in the ArrayList, the List type exposes all the new generic methods that have been added to the Array class in .NET Framework 2.0 and that expect a delegate as an argument, namely, ConvertAll, Exists, Find, FindAll, FindIndex, FindLastIndex, ForEach, and TrueForAll. For example, the TrueForAll method takes a Predicate(Of T) delegate, which must point to a function that tests a T object and returns a Boolean, so you can pass it the address of the String.IsNullOrEmpty static method to check whether all the elements of a List(Of String) object are null or empty:

```
Dim list As New List(Of String)
' Fill the list and process its elements…
…
If list.TrueForAll(AddressOf String.IsNullOrEmpty) Then
   Console.WriteLine("All elements are null or empty strings.")
End If
```

You can also use the instance Equals method that the String type and most numeric types expose to check whether all elements are equal to a specific value:

```
Dim testValue As String = "ABC"
If list.TrueForAll(AddressOf testValue.Equals) Then
    Console.WriteLine("All elements are equal to 'ABC'")
End If
```

Generic methods based on delegates often enable you to create unbelievably concise code, as in this example:

```
' Create two strong-typed collections of Double values.
Dim list1 As New List(Of Double)(New Double() {1, 2, 3, 4, 5, 6, 7, 8, 9})
Dim list2 As New List(Of Double)(New Double() {0, 9, 12, 3, 6})
' Check whether the second collection is a subset of the first one.
Dim isSubset As Boolean = list2.TrueForAll(AddressOf list1.Contains)   ' => False

' One statement to find all the elements in list2 that are contained in list1
Dim list3 As List(Of Double) = list2.FindAll(AddressOf list1.Contains)
' Remove from list1 and list2 the elements that they have in common.
list1.RemoveAll(AddressOf list3.Contains)
list2.RemoveAll(AddressOf list3.Contains)

' Display the elements in the three lists.
list1.ForEach(AddressOf Console.WriteLine)       ' => 1 2 4 5 7 8
list2.ForEach(AddressOf Console.WriteLine)       ' => 0 12
list3.ForEach(AddressOf Console.WriteLine)       ' => 9 3 6
```

The only method left to discuss is AsReadOnly. This method takes no arguments and returns a System.Collections.ObjectModel.ReadOnlyCollection(Of T) object, which, as its name suggests, is similar to the List type except you can neither add or remove objects nor modify existing items. Interestingly, the value returned by AsReadOnly is an adapter of the original list; thus, the elements in the returned list reflect any insertions and deletions performed on the original list. This feature enables you to pass a read-only reference to an external procedure that can read the most recent data added to the list but can't modify the list in any way:

```
' Get a read-only wrapper of the original list.
Dim roList As ReadOnlyCollection(Of Double) = list1.AsReadOnly()
Console.WriteLine(roList.Count = list1.Count)        ' => True
' Prove that roList reflects all the operations on the original list.
list1.Add(123)
Console.WriteLine(roList.Count = list1.Count)        ' => True
```

The Dictionary Generic Type

The Dictionary(Of TKey,TValue) type is the generic counterpart of the Hashtable type because it can store (key, value) pairs in a strong-typed fashion. For example, here's a dictionary that can contain Person objects and index them by a string key (the person's complete name):

```
Dim dictPersons As New Dictionary(Of String, Person)
dictPersons.Add("John Evans", New Person("John", "Evans"))
dictPersons.Add("Robert Zare", New Person("Robert", "Zare"))
```

The constructor of this generic class can take a capacity (the initial number of slots in the inner table), an object that implements the IDictionary(Of TKey,TValue) generic interface (such as another generic dictionary), an IEqualityComparer(Of T) object, or a few combinations of these three values. (In .NET Framework 2.0, the default capacity is just three elements, but might change in future versions of the .NET Framework.)

The constructor that takes an IEqualityComparer(Of T) object enables you to control how keys are compared. I demonstrated how to use the nongeneric IEqualityComparer interface in the section titled "The Hashtable Type" earlier in this chapter, so you should have no problem understanding how its generic counterpart works. The following class normalizes a person's name to the format "LastName,FirstName" and compares these strings in case-insensitive fashion:

```
Public Class NameEqualityComparer
   Implements IEqualityComparer(Of String)

   Public Shadows Function Equals(ByVal x As String, ByVal y As String) As Boolean _
         Implements IEqualityComparer(Of String).Equals
      Return String.Equals(NormalizedName(x), NormalizedName(y))
   End Function

   Public Shadows Function GetHashCode(ByVal obj As String) As Integer _
         Implements IEqualityComparer(Of String).GetHashCode
      Return NormalizedName(obj).GetHashCode()
   End Function

   ' Helper method that returns a person name in uppercase and in the
   ' (LastName,FirstName) format, without any spaces.
   Private Function NormalizedName(ByVal name As String) As String
      ' If there is a comma, assume that name is already in (last,first) format.
      If name.IndexOf(","c) < 0 Then
         ' Find first and last names.
         Dim separators() As Char = {" "c}
         Dim parts() As String = name.Split(separators, 2, _
            StringSplitOptions.RemoveEmptyEntries)
         ' Invert the two portions.
         name = parts(1) & "," & parts(0)
      End If
      ' Delete spaces, if any.
      If name.IndexOf(" "c) >= 0 Then name = name.Replace(" ", "")
      ' Convert to uppercase and return.
      Return name.ToUpper()
   End Function
End Class
```

You can use the NameEqualityComparer type to manage a dictionary of Persons whose elements can be retrieved by providing a name in several different formats:

```
dictPersons = New Dictionary(Of String, Person)(New NameEqualityComparer())
dictPersons.Add("John Evans", New Person("Joe", "Evans"))
dictPersons.Add("Robert Zare", New Person("Robert", "Zare"))
' Prove that the last element can be retrieved by providing a key in
' either the (last,first) format or the (first last) format, that spaces
```

```
' are ignored, and that character casing isn't significant.
Dim name As String
name = dictPersons("robert zare").ReverseName        ' => Zare, Robert
name = dictPersons("ZARE, robert").ReverseName       ' => Zare, Robert
```

If necessary, you can retrieve a reference to the IEqualityComparer object by means of the dictionary's Comparer read-only property.

Unlike the Remove method in the Hashtable type, but similar to the Remove method in the List generic type, the Remove method of the Dictionary generic class returns True if the object was actually removed and False if no object with that key was found; therefore, you don't need to search the element before trying to remove it:

```
If dictPersons.Remove("john evans") Then
    Console.WriteLine("Element John Evans has been removed")
Else
    Console.WriteLine("Element John Evans hasn't been found")
End If
```

When a Dictionary object is used in a For Each loop, at each iteration you get an instance of the KeyValuePair(Of TKey,TValue) generic type, which enables you to access the dictionary elements in a strong-type fashion:

```
For Each kvp As KeyValuePair(Of String, Person) In dictPersons
    ' You can reference a member of the Person class in strong-typed mode.
    Console.WriteLine("Key={0} FirstName={1}", kvp.Key, kvp.Value.FirstName)
Next
```

The TryGetValue method is conceptually similar to the TryCast operator: you pass a key and an object (which is taken by reference); if an element with that key is found, its value is assigned to the object and the method returns True. You can therefore test the presence of an element and retrieve it with a single operation by using this code:

```
Dim p As Person = Nothing
If dictPersons.TryGetValue("ann beebe", p) Then
    ' The variable p contains a reference to the found element.
    Console.WriteLine("Found {0}", p.ReverseName)
Else
    Console.WriteLine("Not found")
End If
```

The remaining members of the Dictionary type are quite straightforward: the Keys and Values read-only properties, the Clear method, the ContainsKey and ContainsValue methods. They work exactly as do the methods with the same names of the Hashtable object (except that they are strong-typed) and I won't repeat their descriptions here.

The LinkedList Generic Type

Linked lists are data structures with elements that aren't stored in contiguous memory locations; you can visit all the elements of these lists because each element has a pointer to the next element (simple linked list) or to both the next and the previous elements (doubly linked list). Elements in such a structure are called *nodes* and cannot be referenced by means of an index or a key. You can reach a node only by following the chain of pointers, either starting at the first element and moving forward or starting at the last element and moving backward. Because there is no key, elements can have duplicate values. See Figure 13-1 for the .NET implementation of the double linked list data structure.

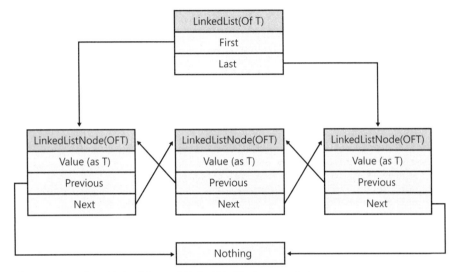

Figure 13-1   The LinkedList and LinkedListNode generic types

The LinkedList(Of T) type implements a strong-typed doubly linked list. Each node in a LinkedList structure is implemented as a LinkedListNode(Of T) object and exposes only four properties: Value (an object of type T), List (the list this node belongs to), and Previous and Next (pointers to the previous and next node in the list). You can create a node by passing an object of type T to its constructor or by means of one of the methods in the parent LinkedList object, as you'll see in a moment. Two nodes in the list are special in that they represent the first and last nodes in the linked list. (These nodes are often called the *head* and the *tail* of the linked list.) You can get a reference to these nodes by means of the First and Last properties of the LinkedList type.

Enough theory for now. Let's see how to create and use a strong-typed generic linked list that can contain one or more Person objects. The remarks in code will help you to understand what happens inside the list:

```
Dim lnkList As New LinkedList(Of Person)
' An empty linked list has no first or last node.
Console.WriteLine(lnkList.First Is Nothing)       ' => True
Console.WriteLine(lnkList.Last Is Nothing)        ' => True
```

The LinkedList type exposes four methods for adding a new node: AddFirst, AddLast, AddBefore, and AddAfter. All these methods have two overloads: the first overload takes an object of type T, wraps it into a LinkedListNode(Of T) object, inserts the node in the list, and returns it to the caller; the second overload takes a LinkedListNode(Of T) object and inserts it in the list at the desired position, but doesn't return anything. In most cases, you can write more concise code by using the former syntax and discarding the return value:

```
' Add the first node of the list.
Dim p1 As New Person("John", "Evans")
lnkList.AddFirst(p1)
' When the list contains only one node, the first and last nodes coincide.
Console.WriteLine(lnkList.First Is lnkList.Last)         ' => True
```

Now the list isn't empty and you can add new elements using existing nodes as a reference for the AddBefore or AddAfter methods:

```
' Add a new node after the list head.
lnkList.AddAfter(lnkList.First, New Person("Ann", "Beebe"))
' The new node has become the list's tail node.
Console.WriteLine(lnkList.Last.Value.ReverseName)       ' => Doe, Ann
' Add a new node immediately before the list tail.
lnkList.AddBefore(lnkList.Last, New Person("Robert", "Zare"))
' Add a new node after the current list tail (it becomes the new tail).
lnkList.AddLast(New Person("James", "Hamilton"))
' Now the list contains four elements.
Console.WriteLine(lnkList.Count)                        ' => 4
```

You can iterate over all the elements in a linked list in a couple of ways. First, you can use a traditional For Each loop:

```
For Each p As Person In lnkList
    Console.Write("{0} ", p.FirstName)       ' => Joe Robert Ann James
Next
```

Second, you can take advantage of the nature of the doubly linked list by following the chain of node pointers. This technique gives you more flexibility because you can traverse the list in both directions.

```
' Visit all nodes in reverse order.
Dim node As LinkedListNode(Of Person) = lnkList.Last
Do Until node Is Nothing
    Console.WriteLine(node.Value.ReverseName)
    node = node.Previous
Loop
```

```
' Change last name from Evans to Hamilton.
node = lnkList.First
Do Until node Is Nothing
    If node.Value.LastName = "Evans" Then node.Value.LastName = "Hamilton"
    node = node.Next
Loop
```

Another good reason you might traverse the linked list manually is because you gain the ability to insert and delete nodes during the process. (Either operation would throw an exception if performed from inside a For Each loop.) Before I show how to perform this operation, let's take a step backward for a moment.

As I have already mentioned, the first thing to do on a freshly created LinkedList instance is create its first node (which also becomes its last node). This operation introduces an asymmetry between the first element added to the list and all the elements after it because adding the first element requires a different piece of code. This asymmetry makes programming a bit more complicated.

You can avoid the asymmetry and simplify programming by assuming that the first node in the linked list is a special node that contains no meaningful value:

```
Dim aList As New LinkedList(Of Person)
aList.AddFirst(New LinkedListNode(Of Person)(Nothing))
' You can now add all nodes with a plain AddLast method.
aList.AddLast(New Person("Joe", "Evans"))
aList.AddLast(New Person("Ann", "Beebe"))
aList.AddLast(New Person("Robert", "Zare"))
```

You must take the "dummy" first node into account when iterating over all the elements:

```
' We are sure that the first node exists; thus, the next statement can never throw.
Dim aNode As LinkedListNode(Of Person) = aList.First.Next
Do Until aNode Is Nothing
   Console.WriteLine(aNode.Value.ReverseName)
   aNode = aNode.Next
Loop
```

The first empty node simplifies programming remarkably because you don't need to take any special case into account. For example, here's a loop that removes all the persons that match a given criterion:

```
aNode = aList.First.Next
Do Until aNode Is Nothing
   ' Remove this node if the last name is Evans.
   If aNode.Value.LastName = "Evans" Then
      ' Backtrack to previous node and remove the node that was current.
      ' (We can be sure that the previous node exists.)
      aNode = aNode.Previous
      aList.Remove(aNode.Next)
   End If
   aNode = aNode.Next
Loop
```

The LinkedList type also exposes the RemoveFirst and RemoveLast methods to remove the list's head and tail nodes, respectively. There is also an overload of the Remove method that takes an object of type T and returns True if the object was found and removed, False otherwise.

A last note about the technique based on the dummy first node: remember to take this dummy node into account when you display the number of elements in the list:

```
Console.WriteLine("The list contains {0} persons", aList.Count - 1)
```

The only methods I haven't covered yet are Find and FindLast, which take an object of type T and return the LinkedListNode(Of T) object that holds that object, or Nothing if the search fails. Keep in mind, however, that searching a node is a relatively slow operation because these methods have to start at one of the list's ends and traverse each element until they find a match.

Other Generic Collections

The System.Collections.Generic namespace contains a few other generic collections, namely:

- **Stack(Of T)**   The strong-typed version of the Stack collection class
- **Queue(Of T)**   The strong-typed version of the Queue collection class
- **SortedDictionary(Of TKey, TValue)**   The strong-typed version of the SortedList, which uses keys of type TKey associated with values of type TValue

The SortedDictionary type exposes many of the methods of the Dictionary type, but it also keeps all its elements in sorted order. To keep elements sorted, the constructor can take an object that implements the IComparer(Of TKey) generic interface. For example, suppose that your sorted list uses a filename as a key and you want to sort the elements according to file extension. First, define a comparer class that implements the IComparer(Of String) interface:

```
Public Class FileExtensionComparer
   Implements IComparer(Of String)

   Public Function Compare(ByVal x As String, ByVal y As String) As Integer _
        Implements IComparer(Of String).Compare
      ' Compare the extensions of filenames in case-insensitive mode.
      Dim res As Integer = String.Compare(Path.GetExtension(x), Path.GetExtension(y), True)
      If res = 0 Then
         ' If extensions are equal, compare the entire filenames.
         res = String.Compare(Path.GetFileName(x), Path.GetFileName(y), True)
      End If
      Return res
   End Function
End Class
```

You can then define a sorted dictionary that contains the text associated with a series of text files and keeps the entries sorted on the file extensions:

```
Dim fileDict As New SortedDictionary(Of String, String)(New FileExtensionComparer())
' Load some elements.
fileDict.Add("c:\foo.txt", File.ReadAllText("foo.txt"))
fileDict.Add("c:\data.txt", File.ReadAllText("data.txt"))
fileDict.Add("c:\data.doc", File.ReadAllText("data.doc"))
' Check that files have been sorted on their extensions.
For Each kvp As KeyValuePair(Of String, String) In fileDict
   Console.Write("{0}, ", kvp.Key)     ' => c:\data.doc, c:\data.txt, c:\foo.txt,
Next
```

Like the method with the same name of the Dictionary type, the TryGetValue method allows you to check whether an element with a given key exists and read it with a single operation:

```
Dim text As String = Nothing
If fileDict.TryGetValue("foo.txt", text) Then
   ' The text variable contains the value of the "foo.txt" element.
End If
```

Even if elements in a SortedDictionary can be accessed in order, you can't reference them by their index. If you need to read the key or the value of the Nth element, you must first copy the Keys or Values collection to a regular array:

```
' Display the value for the first item.
Dim values(fileDict.Count - 1) As String
fileDict.Values.CopyTo(values, 0)
Console.WriteLine(values(0))
```

A Notable Example

I won't cover the Stack(Of T) and Queue(Of T) generic types: if you are familiar with their weak-typed counterparts, you already know how to use them. However, I do provide an example that demonstrates that these classes can help you write sophisticated algorithms in an efficient manner and with very little code. More precisely, I show you how to implement a complete Reverse Polish Notation (RPN) expression evaluator.

First a little background, for those new to RPN. An RPN expression is a sequence of operands and math operators in postfix notation. For example, the RPN expression "12 34 +" is equivalent to 12 + 34, whereas the expression "12 34 + 56 78 - *" is equivalent to (12 + 34) * (56 − 78). The RPN notation was used in programmable calculators in the 1980s and in programming languages such as Forth, but it is useful in many cases even today. (For example, a compiler must translate an expression to RPN to generate the actual IL or native code.) The beauty of the RPN notation is that you never need to assign a priority to operators and therefore you never need to use parentheses even for the most complex expressions. In fact, the rules for evaluating an RPN expression are quite simple:

1. Extract the tokens from the RPN expression one at a time.

2. If the token is a number, push it onto the stack.

3. If the token is an operator, pop as many numbers off the stack as required by the operator, execute the operation, and push the result onto the stack again.

4. When there are no more tokens, if the stack contains exactly one element, this is the result of the expression, else the expression is unbalanced.

Thanks to the String.Split method and the Stack(Of T) generic type, implementing this algorithm requires very few lines of code:

```
Public Function EvalRPN(ByVal expression As String) As Double
   Dim stack As New Stack(Of Double)
   ' Split the string expression into tokens.
```

```
        Dim operands() As String = expression.ToLower().Split(New Char() {" "c}, _
            StringSplitOptions.RemoveEmptyEntries)
        For Each op As String In operands
            Select Case op
                Case "+"
                    stack.Push(stack.Pop() + stack.Pop())
                Case "-"
                    stack.Push(-stack.Pop() + stack.Pop())
                Case "*"
                    stack.Push(stack.Pop() * stack.Pop())
                Case "/"
                    Dim tmp As Double = stack.Pop()
                    stack.Push(stack.Pop() / tmp)
                Case "sqrt"
                    stack.Push(Math.Sqrt(stack.Pop()))
                Case Else
                    ' Assume this token is a number, throw if the parse operation fails.
                    stack.Push(Double.Parse(op))
            End Select
        Next
        ' Throw if stack is unbalanced.
        If stack.Count <> 1 Then Throw New ArgumentException("Unbalanced expression")
        Return stack.Pop()
End Function
```

Here are a few usage examples:

```
Dim res As Double = EvalRPN("12 34 + 56 78 - *")   ' => -1012
res = EvalRPN("123 456 + 2 /")                      ' => 289.5
res = EvalRpn("123 456 + 2 ")                       ' => Exception: Unbalanced expression
res = EvalRpn("123 456 + 2 / *")                    ' => Exception: Stack empty
```

The System.Collections.ObjectModel Namespace

Previously, I showed that you can inherit from a generic type and implement either a standard class or another generic type. For example, the following code implements a typed collection of Person objects:

```
Public Class PersonCollection
    Inherits List(Of Person)
End Class
```

The next code defines a new generic type that is similar to a sorted dictionary except it allows you to retrieve keys and values by their numeric index, thus solving one of the limitations of the SortedDictionary generic type:

```
Public Class IndexableDictionary(Of TKey, TValue)
    Inherits SortedDictionary(Of TKey, TValue)

    ' Retrieve a key by its index.
    Function GetKey(ByVal index As Integer) As TKey
        ' Retrieve the Nth key.
        Dim keys(Me.Count - 1) As TKey
```

```
      Me.Keys.CopyTo(keys, 0)
      Return keys(index)
   End Function

   Default Public Overloads Property Item(ByVal index As Integer) As TValue
      Get
         Return Me(GetKey(index))
      End Get
      Set(ByVal value As TValue)
         Me(GetKey(index)) = value
      End Set
   End Property
End Class
```

(Notice that the IndexableDictionary class has suboptimal performance because finding the key with a given index is a relatively slow operation.) Here's how you can use the Indexable-Dictionary type:

```
Dim idPersons As New IndexableDictionary(Of String, Person)
idPersons.Add("Zare, Robert", New Person("Robert", "Zare"))
idPersons.Add("Beebe, Ann", New Person("Ann", "Beebe"))
Console.WriteLine(idPersons(0).ReverseName)          ' => Beebe, Ann
```

Even if inheriting from concrete types such as List and Dictionary is OK in most cases, sometimes you can write better inherited classes by deriving from one of the abstract generic types defined in the System.Collections.ObjectModel namespace:

- **Collection(Of T)**   Provides a base class for generic collections that can be extended by adding or removing elements

- **ReadOnlyCollection(Of T)**   Provides a base class for generic read-only collections

- **KeyedCollection(Of TKey,TValue)**   Provides a base class for generic dictionaries

The main difference between regular generic types and the preceding abstract types is that the latter expose several protected methods that you can override to get more control of what happens when an element is modified or added to or removed from the collection. For example, the Collection(Of T) class exposes the following protected methods: ClearItems, InsertItem, RemoveItem, and SetItems, plus an Items protected property that lets you access the inner collection of items.

Here's an example of a collection that can store a set of IComparable objects and that exposes an additional pair of read-only properties that returns the minimum and maximum values in the collection:

```
Public Class MinMaxCollection(Of T As IComparable)
   Inherits Collection(Of T)

   Private min As T, max As T
   Private upToDate As Boolean

   Public ReadOnly Property MinValue() As T
```

```vb
        Get
            If Not upToDate Then UpdateValues()
            Return min
        End Get
    End Property

    Public ReadOnly Property MaxValue() As T
        Get
            If Not upToDate Then UpdateValues()
            Return max
        End Get
    End Property

    Protected Overrides Sub InsertItem(ByVal index As Integer, ByVal item As T)
        MyBase.InsertItem(index, item)
        If Me.Count = 1 Then
            UpdateValues()
        ElseIf upToDate Then
            ' If values are up-to-date, adjusting the min/max value is simple.
            If min.CompareTo(item) > 0 Then min = item
            If max.CompareTo(item) < 0 Then max = item
        End If
    End Sub

    Protected Overrides Sub SetItem(ByVal index As Integer, ByVal item As T)
        MyBase.SetItem(index, item)
        If min.CompareTo(item) = 0 OrElse max.CompareTo(item) = 0 Then upToDate = False
    End Sub

    Protected Overrides Sub RemoveItem(ByVal index As Integer)
        Dim item As T = Me(index)        ' Remember value before removing it.
        MyBase.RemoveItem(index)
        If min.CompareTo(item) = 0 OrElse max.CompareTo(item) = 0 Then upToDate = False
    End Sub

    Protected Overrides Sub ClearItems()
        MyBase.ClearItems()
        upToDate = False
    End Sub

    Private Sub UpdateValues()
        If Me.Count = 0 Then
            ' Assign default value of T if collection is empty.
            min = Nothing : max = Nothing
        Else
            ' Else evaluate the min/max value.
            min = Me(0): max = Me(0)
            For Each item As T In Me
                If min.CompareTo(item) > 0 Then min = item
                If max.CompareTo(item) < 0 Then max = item
            Next
        End If
        ' Signal that min/max values are now up-to-date.
        upToDate = True
    End Sub
End Class
```

The noteworthy aspect of the MinMaxCollection is that it keeps an up-to-date value of the MinValue and MaxValue properties if possible, as long as the client program just adds new elements. If the client changes or removes an element that is currently the minimum or the maximum value, the upToDate variable is set to False so that the MinValue and MaxValue properties are recalculated the next time they are requested. This algorithm is quite optimized, yet it's generic enough to be used with any numeric type (more precisely: any type that supports the IComparable interface):

```
Dim col As New MinMaxCollection(Of Double)
' MinValue and MaxValue are always updated during these insertions.
col.Add(123): col.Add(456): col.Add(789): col.Add(-33)
' This removal doesn't touch MinValue and MaxValue.
col.Remove(456)
Console.WriteLine("Min={0}, Max={1}", col.MinValue, col.MaxValue)  ' => Min=-33, Max=789
' This statement does affect MinValue and therefore sets upToDate=False.
col.Remove(-33)
' The next call to MinValue causes the properties to be recalculated.
Console.WriteLine("Min={0}, Max={1}", col.MinValue, col.MaxValue) ' => Min=123, Max=789
```

The KeyedCollection(Of TKey,TValue) generic type is conceptually similar to Collection(Of T), but it can be used to implement custom dictionaries, either generic or not. In addition to the ClearItems, InsertItem, RemoveItem, and SetItem methods, the KeyedCollection type exposes the protected overridable GetKeyForItem method, which takes an object of type T and returns its key.

The ReadOnlyCollection(Of T) abstract class is similar to Collection(Of T), except that it doesn't expose any method for changing, adding, or removing elements after the collection has been created. (It is therefore the strong-typed counterpart of the ReadOnlyCollectionBase nongeneric abstract class.) Because the only operation that is supported after creation is enumeration, this base class doesn't expose any overridable protected methods.

Chapter 14
Regular Expressions

Regular expressions are a standard way to search for and optionally replace occurrences of substrings and text patterns. If you aren't familiar with regular expressions, just think of the wildcard characters you use at the command prompt to indicate a group of files (as in *.txt) or the special characters you can use with the Like operator in Microsoft Visual Basic (see Chapter 2, "Basic Language Concepts") or in SQL queries:

```
SELECT name, city FROM customers WHERE name LIKE "A%"
```

Many computer scientists have thoroughly researched regular expressions, and a few programming languages—most notably Perl and Awk—are heavily based on regular expressions. In spite of their usefulness in virtually every text-oriented task (including parsing log files and extracting information from HTML files), regular expressions are relatively rarely used by Microsoft Windows programmers, probably because they are based on a rather obscure syntax.

You can regard regular expressions as a highly specific programming language, and you know that all languages take time to learn and have idiosyncrasies. But when you see how much time regular expressions can save you—and I am talking about both coding time and CPU time—you'll probably agree that the effort you expend learning their contorted syntax is well worth it.

This isn't the first time I mention regular expressions in this book. For example, I mentioned regular expressions in the section titled "String Constants and Functions" in Chapter 3, where I compare the Like operator to regular expressions, and in Chapter 4, where I introduce Microsoft Visual Studio 2005 searches based on regular expressions. However, Visual Studio uses a notation that differs from the one I explain in this chapter, so you can't apply the actual patterns you'll learn in this chapter to searches in the code editor, even though all basic concepts are the same.

> **Note**   To avoid long lines, code samples in this chapter assume that the following Imports statements are used at the file or project level:
>
> ```
> Imports System.Globalization
> Imports System.IO
> Imports System.Text
> Imports System.Text.RegularExpressions
> ```

Regular Expression Overview

The Microsoft .NET Framework comes with a very powerful regular expression engine that's accessible from any .NET language, so you can leverage the parsing power of languages such as Perl without having to switch away from your favorite language.

The Fundamentals

Regex is the most important class in this group, and any regular expression code instantiates at least an object of this class (or uses one of the Regex static methods). This object represents an immutable regular expression. You instantiate this object by passing to it the search pattern, written using the special regular expression language, which I describe later:

```
' This regular expression defines any group of two characters
' consisting of a vowel followed by a digit (\d).
Dim re As New Regex("[aeiou]\d")
```

The Matches method of the Regex object applies the regular expression to the string passed as an argument; it returns a MatchCollection object, a read-only collection that represents all the nonoverlapping matches:

```
Dim re As New Regex("[aeiou]\d")
' This source string contains three groups that match the Regex.
Dim text As String = "a1 = a1 & e2"
' Get the collection of matches.
Dim mc As MatchCollection = re.Matches(text)
' How many occurrences did we find?
Console.WriteLine(mc.Count)                        ' => 3
```

You can also pass to the Matches method a second argument, which is interpreted as the index where the search begins.

The MatchCollection object contains individual Match objects, which expose properties such as Value (the matching string that was found), Index (the position of the matching string in the source string), and Length (the length of the matching string, which is useful when the regular expression can match strings of different lengths):

```
' …(Continuing the previous example)…
For Each m As Match In mc
   ' Display text and position of this match.
   Console.WriteLine("'{0}' at position {1}" , m.Value, m.Index)
Next
```

The preceding code displays these lines in the console window:

```
'a1' at position 0
'a1' at position 5
'e2' at position 10
```

The Regex object is also capable of modifying a source string by searching for a given regular expression and replacing it with something else:

```
Dim text As String = "a1 = a1 & e2"
' Search for the "a" character followed by a digit.
Dim re2 As New Regex("a\d")
' Drop the digit that follows the "a" character.
Dim res As String = re2.Replace(text, "a")        ' => a = a & e2
```

The Regex class also exposes static versions of the Match, Matches, and Replace methods. You can use these static methods when you don't want to instantiate a Regex object explicitly:

```
' This code snippet is equivalent to the previous one, but it doesn't
' instantiate a Regex object.
res = Regex.Replace(text, "a\d", "a")
```

The best way to learn regular expressions is, not surprisingly, through practice. To help you in this process, I have created a RegexTester application that enables you to test any regular expression against any source string or text file. (See Figure 14-1.) This application has been a valuable tool for me in exploring regular expression intricacies, and I routinely use it whenever I have a doubt about how a construct works.

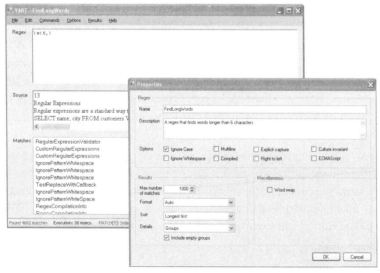

Figure 14-1   The RegexTester application, enabling you to experiment with all the most important methods and options of the Regex object

The Regular Expression Language

Table 14-1 lists all the constructs that are legal as regular expression patterns, grouped in the following categories:

- **Character escapes**   Used to match single characters. You need them to deal with non-printable characters (such as the newline and the tab characters) and to provide escaped versions for the characters that have a special meaning inside regular expression patterns. Together with substitutions, these are the only sequences that can appear in a replacement pattern.

- **Character classes**   Offer a means to match one character from a group that you specify between brackets, as in [aeiou]. You don't need to escape special characters when they appear in brackets except in the cases of the dash and the closing bracket, which are the only characters that have special meaning inside brackets. For example, [()[\]{}] matches opening and closing parentheses, brackets, and braces. (Notice that the] character is escaped, but the [character isn't.)

- **Atomic zero–width assertions**   Specify where the matching string should be but don't consume characters. For example, the abc$ regular expression matches any abc word immediately before the end of a line without also matching the end of the line.

- **Quantifiers**   Specify that a subexpression must be repeated a given number of times. A particular quantifier applies to the character, character class, or group that immediately precedes it. For example, \w+ matches all the words with one or more characters, whereas \w{3,} matches all the words with at least three characters. Quantifiers can be divided in two categories: greedy and lazy. A *greedy* quantifier, such as * and +, always matches as many characters as possible, whereas a *lazy* quantifier, such as *? and +?, attempts to match as few characters as possible.

- **Grouping constructors**   Can capture and name groups of subexpressions as well as increase the efficiency of regular expressions with noncapturing look-ahead and look-behind modifiers. For example, (abc)+ matches repeated sequences of the "abc" string; (?<total>\d+) matches a group of one or more consecutive digits and assigns it the name total, which can be used later inside the same regular expression pattern or for substitution purposes.

- **Substitutions**   Can be used only inside a replacement pattern and, together with character escapes, are the only constructs that can be used inside replacement patterns. For example, when the sequence ${total} appears in a replacement pattern, it inserts the value of the group named total. Parentheses have no special meanings in replacement patterns, so you don't need to escape them.

- **Backreference constructs**   Enable you to reference a previous group of characters in the regular expression pattern by using its group number or name. You can use these constructs as a way to say "match the same thing again." For example, (?<value>\d+)=\k<value> matches identical numbers separated by an = symbol, as in the "123=123" sequence.

- **Alternating constructs**   Provide a way to specify alternatives; for example, the sequence "I (am|have)" can match both the "I am" and "I have" strings.

- **Miscellaneous constructs**   Include constructs that allow you to modify one or more regular expression options in the middle of the pattern. For example, A(?i)BC matches all the variants of the ABC word that begin with uppercase A (such as Abc, ABc, AbC, and ABC). See Table 14-2 for a description of all the regular expression options.

Table 14-1   The Regular Expression Language

Category	Sequence	Description
Character escapes	any character	Characters other than .$^{[(|)*+?\ match themselves.
	\a	The bell alarm character (same as \x07).
	\b	The backspace (same as \x08), but only when used between brackets or in a replacement pattern. Otherwise, it matches a word boundary.
	\t	The tab character (same as \x09).
	\r	The carriage return (same as \x0D).
	\v	The vertical tab character (same as \x0B).
	\f	The form-feed character (same as \x0C).
	\n	The newline character (same as \x0A).
	\e	The escape character (same as \x1B).
	\040	An ASCII character expressed in octal notation (must have up to three octal digits). For example, \040 is a space.
	\x20	An ASCII character expressed in hexadecimal notation (must have exactly two digits). For example, \x20 is a space.
	\cC	An ASCII control character. For example, \cC is control+C.
	\u0020	A Unicode character in hexadecimal notation (must have exactly four digits). For example, \u0020 is a space.
	*	When the backslash is followed by a character in a way that doesn't form an escape sequence, it matches the character. For example, * matches the * character.
Character classes	.	The dot character matches any character except the newline character. It matches any character, including newline, if you're using the Singleline option.
	[aeiou]	Any character in the list between the opening and closing brackets; [aeiou] matches any vowel.
	[^aeiou]	Any character except those in the list between the opening and closing brackets; [^aeiou] matches any nonvowel.
	[a-zA-Z]	The - (dash) character enables you to specify ranges of characters: [a-zA-Z] matches any lowercase or uppercase character; [^0-9] matches any nondigit character. Notice, however, that accented letters aren't matched.

Table 14-1   The Regular Expression Language *(Continued)*

Category	Sequence	Description
	[a-z-[aeiou]]	Character class subtraction: when a pair of brackets is nested in another pair of brackets and is preceded by a minus sign, the regular expression matches all the characters in the outer pair except those in the inner pair. For example, [a-z-[aeiou]] matches any lowercase character that isn't a vowel. (Support for character class subtractions has been added in .NET Framework version 2.0.)
	\w	A word character, which is an alphanumeric character or the underscore character; same as [a-zA-Z_0-9] but also matches accented letters and other alphabetical symbols.
	\W	A nonword character; same as [^a-zA-Z_0-9] but also excludes accented letters and other alphabetical symbols.
	\s	A white-space character, which is a space, a tab, a form-feed, a newline, a carriage return, or a vertical-feed character; same as [\f\n\r\t\v].
	\S	A character other than a white-space character; same as [^ \f\n\r\t\v].
	\d	A decimal digit; same as [0-9].
	\D	A nondigit character; same as [^0-9].
	\p{name}	A character included in the named character class specified by {name}; supported names are Unicode groups and block ranges, for example, Ll, Nd, or Z.
	\P{name}	A character not included in groups and block ranges specified in {name}.
Atomic zero–width assertions	^	The beginning of the string (or the beginning of the line if you're using the Multiline option).
	$	The end of the string (or the end of the line if you're using the Multiline option).
	\A	The beginning of a string (like ^ but ignores the Multiline option).
	\Z	The end of the string or the position before the newline character at the end of the string (like $ but ignores the Multiline option).
	\z	Exactly the end of the string, whether or not there's a newline character (ignores the Multiline option).
	\G	The position at which the current search started—usually one character after the point at which the previous search ended.
	\b	The word boundary between \w (alphanumeric) and \W (non-alphanumeric) characters. It indicates the first and last characters of a word delimited by spaces or other punctuation symbols.
	\B	Not on a word boundary.

Table 14-1 The Regular Expression Language *(Continued)*

Category	Sequence	Description
Quantifiers	*	Zero or more matches; for example, \bA\w* matches a word that begins with A and is followed by zero or more alpha-numeric characters; same as {0,}.
	+	One or more matches; for example, \b[aeiou]+\b matches a word composed only of vowels; same as {1,}.
	?	Zero or one match; for example, \b[aeiou]\d?\b matches a word that starts with a vowel and is followed by zero or one digits; same as {0,1}.
	{N}	Exactly N matches; for example, [aeiou]{4} matches four consecutive vowels.
	{N,}	At least N matches; for example, \d{3,} matches groups of three or more digits.
	{N,M}	Between N and M matches; for example, \d{3,5} matches groups of three, four, or five digits.
	*?	Lazy *; the first match that consumes as few repeats as possible.
	+?	Lazy +; the first match that consumes as few repeats as possible, but at least one.
	??	Lazy ?; zero repeats if possible, or one.
	{N}?	Lazy {N}; equivalent to {N}.
	{N,}?	Lazy {N,}; as few repeats as possible, but at least N.
	{N,M}?	Lazy {N,M}; as few repeats as possible, but between N and M.
Grouping constructs	(substr)	Captures the matched substring. These captures are numbered automatically, based on the order of the left parenthesis, starting at 1. The zeroth capturing group is the text matched by the whole regular expression pattern.
	(?<name>expr) (?'name'expr)	Captures the subexpression and assigns it a name. The name must not contain any punctuation symbols.
	(?:expr)	Noncapturing group, that is, a group that doesn't appear in the Groups collection of the Match object.
	(?imnsx-imnsx: expr)	Enables or disables the options specified in the subexpression. For example, (?i-s) uses case-insensitive searches and disables single-line mode (see Table 14-2 for information about regular expression options).
	(?=expr)	Zero-width positive look-ahead assertion; continues match only if the subexpression matches at this position on the right. For example, \w+(?=,) matches a word followed by a comma, without matching the comma.
	(?!expr)	Zero-width negative look-ahead assertion; continues match only if the subexpression doesn't match at this position on the right. For example, \w+\b(?![,:;]) matches a word that isn't followed by a comma, a colon, or a semicolon.

Table 14-1 The Regular Expression Language *(Continued)*

Category	Sequence	Description
	(?<=expr)	Zero-width positive look-behind assertion; continues match only if the subexpression matches at this position on the left. For example, (?<=[,;])\w+ matches a word that follows a comma or semicolon, without matching the comma or semicolon. This construct doesn't backtrack.
	(?<!expr>	Zero-width negative look-behind assertion; continues match only if the subexpression doesn't match at this position on the left. For example, (?<!,)\b\w+ matches a word that doesn't follow a comma.
	(?>expr)	Nonbacktracking subexpression; the subexpression is fully matched once, and it doesn't participate in backtracking. The subexpression matches only strings that would be matched by the subexpression alone.
	(?<name1-name2>expr) (?'name1-name2'expr)	Balancing group definition. Deletes the definition of the previously defined group name2 and stores in group name1 the interval between the previously defined name2 group and the current group. If no group name2 is defined, the match backtracks. Because deleting the last definition of name2 reveals the previous definition of name2, this construct allows the stack of captures for group name2 to be used as a counter for keeping track of nested constructs such as parentheses.
Substitution	$N	Substitutes the last substring matched by group number N ($0 replaces the entire match).
	${name}	Substitutes the last substring matched by a (?<name>) group.
	$&	Substitutes the entire match (same as $0).
	$_	Substitutes the entire source string.
	$`	Substitutes the portion of the source string up to the match.
	$'	Substitutes the portion of the source string that follows the match.
	$+	Substitutes the last captured group.
	$$	A single dollar symbol (only when it appears in a substitution pattern).
Back reference constructs	\N \NN	Back reference to a previous group. For example, (\w)\1 finds doubled word characters, such as ss in expression. A backslash followed by a single digit is always considered a back reference (and throws a parsing exception if such a numbered reference is missing); a backslash followed by two digits is considered a numbered back reference if there's a corresponding numbered reference; otherwise, it's considered an octal code. In case of ambiguity, use the \k<name> construct.
	\k<name> \k'name'	Named back reference. (?<char>\w)\d\k<char> matches a word character followed by a digit and then by the same word character, as in the "B2B" string.
Alternating constructs	|	Either/or. For example, vb|c#|java. Leftmost successful match wins.

Table 14-1   The Regular Expression Language *(Continued)*

Category	Sequence	Description
	(?(expr)yes|no)	Matches the yes part if the expression matches at this point; otherwise, matches the no part. The expression is turned into a zero-width assertion. If the expression is the name of a named group or a capturing group number, the alternation is interpreted as a capture test (see next case).
	(?(name)yes|no)	Matches the yes part if the named capture string has a match; otherwise, matches the no part. The no part can be omitted. If the given name doesn't correspond to the name or number of a capturing group used in this expression, the alternation is interpreted as an expression test (see previous case).
Miscella-neous constructs	(?imnsx-imnsx)	Enables or disables one or more regular expression options. For example, it allows case sensitivity to be turned on or off in the middle of a pattern. Option changes are effective until the closing parenthesis (see also the corresponding grouping construct, which is a cleaner form).
	(?# comment)	Inline comment inserted within a regular expression. The text that follows the # sign and continues until the first closing) character is ignored.
	#	X-mode comment; the text that follows an unescaped # until the end of line is ignored. This construct requires that the x option or the RegexOptions.IgnorePatternWhiteSpace enumerated option be activated.

Regular Expression Options

The Match, Matches, and Replace static methods of the Regex object support an optional argument, which lets you specify one or more options to be applied to the regular expression search (see Table 14-2). For example, the following code searches for all occurrences of the "abc" word, regardless of its case:

```
Dim source As String = "ABC Abc abc"
Dim mc As MatchCollection = Regex.Matches(source, "abc")
Console.WriteLine(mc.Count)                    ' => 1
mc = Regex.Matches(source, "abc", RegexOptions.IgnoreCase)
Console.WriteLine(mc.Count)                    ' => 3
```

By default, the Regex class transforms the regular expression into a sequence of opcodes, which are then interpreted when the pattern is applied to a specific source string. If you specify the RegexOptions.Compiled option, however, the regular expression is compiled into IL rather than regular expression opcodes. This feature enables the Just-In-Time (JIT) compiler to convert the expression to native CPU instructions, which clearly deliver better performance:

```
' Create a compiled regular expression that searches
' words that start with uppercase or lowercase A.
Dim reComp As New Regex("\Aw+", RegexOptions.IgnoreCase Or RegexOptions.Compiled)
```

The extra performance that the Compiled option can buy you varies depending on the specific regular expression, but you can reasonably expect a twofold increase in speed in most cases. However, the extra compilation step adds some overhead, so you should use this option only if you plan to use the regular expression multiple times. Another factor that you should take into account when using the RegexOptions.Compiled option is that the compiled IL code isn't unloaded when the Regex object is reclaimed by the garbage collector—it continues to take memory until the application terminates. So you should preferably limit the number of compiled regular expressions. Also, consider that the Regex class caches all regular expression opcodes in memory, so a regular expression isn't generally reparsed each time it's used. The caching mechanism also works when you use static methods and don't explicitly create Regex instances.

The RegexOptions.IgnorePatternWhitespace option tells the Regex object to ignore spaces, tabs, and newline characters in the pattern and to enable #-prefixed remarks. You see the usefulness of this option when you want to format the pattern with a more meaningful layout and to explain what each of its portions does:

```
' Match a string optionally enclosed in single or double quotation marks.
Dim pattern As String = _
    "\s*           # ignore leading spaces" + ControlChars.CrLf & _
    "(             # two cases: quoted or unquoted string" + ControlChars.CrLf & _
    "(?<quote>     # case 1: define a group named 'quote' '" + ControlChars.CrLf & _
    "['""])        # the group is a single or a double quote" + ControlChars.CrLf & _
    ".*?           # a sequence of characters (lazy matching)" + ControlChars.CrLf & _
    "\k<quote>     # followed by the same quote char" + ControlChars.CrLf & _
    "|             # end of case 1" + ControlChars.CrLf & _
    "[^'""]+       # case 2: a string without quotes" + ControlChars.CrLf & _
    ")             # end of case 2" + ControlChars.CrLf & _
    "\s*           # ignore trailing spaces"
Dim re As New Regex(pattern, RegexOptions.IgnorePatternWhitespace)
...
```

Because spaces are ignored, to match the space character you must use either the [ ] character class or the \x20 character escape (or another equivalent escape sequence) when the Ignore-PatternWhitespace option is used.

The RegexOptions.Multiline option enables multiline mode, which is especially useful when you're parsing text files instead of plain strings. This option modifies the meaning and the behavior of the ^ and $ assertions so that they match the start and end of each line of text, respectively, rather than the start or end of the whole string. Thanks to this option, you need only a handful of statements to create a grep-like utility that displays how many occurrences of the regular expression passed in the first argument are found in the files indicated by the second argument:

```
' Compile this application and create FileGrep.Exe executable.
Sub Main(ByVal args() As String)
    ' Show syntax if too few arguments.
    If args.Length <> 2 Then
        Console.WriteLine("Syntax: FILEGREP ""regex"" filespec")
```

```
        Exit Sub
    End If

    Dim pattern As String = args(0)
    Dim filespec As String = args(1)
    ' Create the regular expression (throws if pattern is invalid).
    Dim filePattern As New Regex(pattern, RegexOptions.IgnoreCase Or RegexOptions.Multiline)

    ' Apply the regular expression to each file in specified or current directory.
    Dim dirname As String = Path.GetDirectoryName(filespec)
    If dirname.Length = 0 Then dirname = Directory.GetCurrentDirectory
    Dim search As String = Path.GetFileName(filespec)
    For Each fname As String In Directory.GetFiles(dirname, search)
        ' Read file contents and apply the regular expression to it.
        Dim text As String = File.ReadAllText(fname)
        Dim mc As MatchCollection = filePattern.Matches(text)
        ' Display filename if one or more matches.
        If mc.Count > 0 Then
            Console.WriteLine("{0} [{1} matches]", fname, mc.Count)
        End If
    Next
End Sub
```

For example, you can use the FileGrep utility to find all .vb source files in the current directory that contain the definition of a public ArrayList variable:

```
FileGrep "^\s*Public\s+\w+\s+As\s+(New\s+)?ArrayList" *.vb
```

(For simplicity's sake, the regular expression doesn't account for variants of the basic syntax, such as the presence of the ReadOnly keyword or of the complete System.Collections.ArrayList class name.) It's easy to modify this code to display details about all occurrences or to extend the search to an entire directory tree.

> **Note**   The Windows operating system includes a little-known command-line utility named FindStr, which supports searches with regular expressions and recursion over subdirectories, case-insensitive matches, display of lines that do *not* include the pattern, and so forth. Learn more by typing FindStr /? at the command prompt.

Another way to specify a regular expression option is by means of the (?imnsx-imnsx) construct, which lets you enable or disable one or more options from the current position to the end of the pattern string. The following code snippet finds all Dim, Private, and Public variable declarations at the beginning of individual text lines. Note that the regular expression options are specified inside the pattern string instead of as an argument of the Regex.Matches method:

```
' The pattern matches from the keyword to the end of the line.
Dim pattern As String = "(?im)^\s+(dim|public|private) \w+ As .+(?=\r\n)"
Dim source As String = File.ReadAllText("Module1.vb")
Dim mc As MatchCollection = Regex.Matches(source, pattern)
```

Table 14-2   Regular Expression Options[1]

RegexOptions enum Value	Option	Description
None		No option.
IgnoreCase	i	Case insensitivity match.
Singleline	s	Singleline mode; changes the behavior of the . (dot) character so that it matches any character (instead of any character but the newline character).
Multiline	m	Multiline mode; changes the behavior of ^ and $ so that they match the beginning and end of individual lines, respectively, instead of the whole string.
ExplicitCapture	n	Captures only explicitly named or numbered groups of the form (?<name>) so that naked parentheses act as noncapturing groups without your having to use the (?:) construct.
IgnorePatternWhitespace	x	Ignores unescaped white space from the pattern and enables comments marked with #. Significant spaces in the pattern must be specified as [ ] or \x20.
CultureInvariant		Uses the culture implied by CultureInfo.InvariantCulture, instead of the locale assigned to the current thread.
Compiled		Compiles the regular expression and generates IL code; this option generates faster code at the expense of longer startup time.
ECMAScript		Enables ECMAScript-compliant behavior. This flag can be used only in conjunction with the IgnoreCase, Multiline, and Compiled flags.
RightToLeft		Specifies that the search is from right to left instead of from left to right. If a starting index is specified, it should point to the end of the string.

[1]   These regular expression options can be specified when you create the Regex object. If a character is provided in the middle column, they can be specified also from inside a (?) construct. All these options are turned off by default.

Regular Expression Types

Now that I have illustrated the fundamentals of regular expressions, it's time to examine all the types in the System.Text.RegularExpressions namespace.

The Regex Type

As you've seen in the preceding section, the Regex type provides two overloaded constructors—one that takes only the pattern and another that also takes a bit-coded value that specifies the required regular expression options:

```
' This Regex object can search the word "dim" in a case-insensitive way.
Dim re As New Regex("\bdim\b", RegexOptions.IgnoreCase)
```

The Regex class exposes only two properties, both of which are read-only. The Options property returns the second argument passed to the object constructor, while the RightToLeft property returns True if you specified the RightToLeft option. (The regular expression matches from right to left.) No property returns the regular expression pattern, but you can use the ToString method for this purpose.

Searching for Substrings

The Matches method searches the regular expression inside the string provided as an argument and returns a MatchCollection object that contains zero or more Match objects, one for each nonintersecting match. The Matches method is overloaded to take an optional starting index:

```
' Get the collection that contains all the matches.
Dim mc As MatchCollection = re.Matches(source)

' Print all the matches after the 100th character in the source string.
For Each m As Match In re.Matches(source, 100)
    Console.WriteLine(m.ToString)
Next
```

You can change the behavior of the Matches method (as well as the Match method, described later) by using a \G assertion to disable scanning. In this case, the match must be found exactly where the scan begins. This point is either at the index specified as an argument (or the first character if this argument is omitted) or immediately after the point where the previous match terminates. In other words, the \G assertion finds only *consecutive* matches:

```
' Finds consecutive groups of space-delimited numbers.
Dim re As New Regex("\G\s*\d+")
' Note that search stops at the first non-numeric group.
Console.WriteLine(re.Matches("12 34 56 ab 78").Count)      ' => 3
```

Sometimes, you don't really want to list all the occurrences of the pattern when determining whether the pattern is contained in the source string would suffice. For example, this is usually the case when you are checking that a value typed by the end user complies with the expected format (for example, it's a phone number or a social security number in a valid format). If that's your interest, the IsMatch method is more efficient than the Matches method is because it stops the scan as soon as the first match is found. You pass to this method the input string and an optional start index:

```
' Check whether the input string is a date in the format mm-dd-yy or
' mm-dd-yyyy. (The source string can use slashes as date separators and
' can contain leading or trailing white spaces.)
Dim re2 As New Regex("^\s*\d{1,2}(/|-)\d{1,2}\1(\d{4}|\d{2})\s*$")
If re2.IsMatch(" 12/10/2001  ") Then
    Console.WriteLine("The date is formatted correctly.")
    ' (We don't check whether month and day values are in valid range.)
End If
```

The regular expression pattern in the preceding code requires an explanation:

1. The ^ and $ characters mean that the source string must contain one date value and nothing else. These characters must be used to check whether the source string *matches* the pattern, rather than *contains* it.

2. The \s* subexpression at the beginning and end of the string means that we accept leading and trailing white spaces.

3. The \d{1,2} subexpression means that the month and day numbers can have one or two digits, whereas the (\d{4}|\d{2}) subexpression means that the year number can have four or two digits. The four-digit case must be tested first; otherwise, only the first two digits are matched.

4. The (/|-) subexpression means that we take either the slash or the dash as the date separator between the month and day numbers.

5. The \1 subexpression means that the separator between day and year numbers must be the same separator used between month and day numbers.

The Matches method has an undocumented feature that becomes very handy when parsing very long strings. When you use the return value of this method in a For Each loop—as I did in the majority of examples shown so far—this method performs a sort of lazy evaluation: instead of processing the entire string, it stops the parsing process as soon as the first Match object can be returned to the calling program. When the Next statement is reached and the next iteration of the loop begins, it restarts the parsing process where it had left previously, and so forth. If you exit the loop with an Exit For statement, the remainder of the string is never parsed, which can be very convenient if you are looking for a specific match and don't need to list all of them. You can easily prove this feature with this code:

```
' Prepare to search for the "A" character.
Dim re As New Regex("A")
' Create a very long string with a match at its beginning and its end.
Dim text As String = "A" & New String(" "c, 1000000) & "A"

Dim sw As New Stopwatch()
sw.Start()
For Each m As Match In re.Matches(text)
   ' Show how long it took to find this match.
   Console.WriteLine("Elapsed {0} milliseconds", sw.ElapsedMilliseconds)
Next
sw.Stop()
```

The output in the console window proves that the first Match object was returned almost instantaneously, whereas it took some millions of CPU cycles to locate the character at the end of the string:

```
Elapsed 0 milliseconds
Elapsed 80 milliseconds
```

Keep in mind that this lazy evaluation feature of the Matches method is disabled if you query other members of the returned MatchCollection object, for example, the Count property. It's quite obvious that the only way to count the occurrences of the pattern is to process the entire input string.

In some special cases you might want to have even more control on the parsing process, for example, to skip portions of the string that aren't of interest for your purposes. In these cases, you can use the Match method, which returns only the first Match object and lets you iterate over the remaining matches using the Match.NextMatch method, as this example demonstrates:

```
' Search all the dates in a source string.
Dim source As String = " 12-2-1999  10/23/2001 4/5/2001 "
Dim re As New Regex("\s*\d{1,2}(/|-)\d{1,2}\1(\d{4}|\d{2})")
' Find the first match.
Dim m As Match = re.Match(source)
' Enter the following loop only if the search was successful.
Do While m.Success
    ' Display the match, but discard leading and trailing spaces.
    Console.WriteLine(m.ToString.Trim())
    ' Find the next match; exit if not successful.
    m = m.NextMatch()
Loop
```

The Split method is similar to the String.Split method except it defines the delimiter by using a regular expression rather than a single character. For example, the following code prints all the elements in a comma-delimited list of numbers, ignoring leading and trailing white-space characters:

```
Dim source As String = "123, 456,,789"
Dim re As New Regex("\s*,\s*")
For Each s As String In re.Split(source)
    ' Note that the third element is a null string.
    Console.Write(s & "-")                    ' => 123-456--789-
Next
```

(You can modify the pattern to \s*[,]+\s* to discard empty elements.) The Split method supports several overloaded variations, which let you define the maximum count of elements to be extracted and a starting index (if there are more elements than the given limit, the last element contains the remainder of the string):

```
' Split max 5 items.
Dim arr() As String = re.Split(source, 5)
' Split max 5 items, starting at the 100th character.
Dim arr2() As String = re.Split(source, 5, 100)
```

The Replace Method

The Regex.Replace method lets you selectively replace portions of the source string. This method requires that you create numbered or named groups of characters in the pattern and then use those groups in the replacement pattern. The following code example takes a string that contains one or more dates in the mm-dd-yy format (including variations with a / separator or a four-digit year number) and converts them to the dd-mm-yy format while preserving the original date separator:

```
Dim source As String = "12-2-1999  10/23/2001  4/5/2001 "
Dim pattern As String = _
    "\b(?<mm>\d{1,2})(?<sep>(/|-))(?<dd>\d{1,2})\k<sep>(?<yy>(\d{4}|\d{2}))\b"
Dim re As New Regex(pattern)
Console.WriteLine(re.Replace(source, "${dd}${sep}${mm}${sep}${yy}"))
    ' => 2-12-1999  23/10/2001  5/4/2001
```

The pattern string is similar to the one shown previously, with an important difference: it defines four groups—named mm, dd, yy, and sep—that are later rearranged in the replacement string. The \b assertion at the beginning and end of the pattern ensures that the date is a word of its own.

The Replace method supports other overloaded variants. For example, you can pass two additional numeric arguments, which are interpreted as the maximum number of substitutions and the starting index:

```
' Expand all "ms" abbreviations to "Microsoft" (regardless of their case).
Dim text As String = "Welcome to ms Ms ms MS"
Dim re2 As New Regex("\bMS\b", RegexOptions.IgnoreCase)
' Replace up to two occurrences, starting at the 12th character.
Console.WriteLine(re2.Replace(text, "Microsoft", 2, 12))
    ' => Welcome to ms Microsoft Microsoft MS
```

If the replacement operation does something more sophisticated than simply delete or change the order of named groups, you can use an overloaded version of the Replace function that takes a delegate argument pointing to a filter function you've defined elsewhere in the application. This feature gives you tremendous flexibility, as the following code demonstrates:

```
Sub TestReplaceWithCallback()
    ' This pattern defines two integers separated by a plus sign.
    Dim re As New Regex("\d+\s*\+\s*\d+")
    Dim source As String = "a = 100 + 234: b = 200+345"
    ' Replace all sum operations with their results.
    Console.WriteLine(re.Replace(source, AddressOf DoSum))
        ' => a = 334: b = 545
End Sub

' The callback method
Private Function DoSum(ByVal m As Match) As String
    ' Parse the two operands.
    Dim args() As String = m.Value.Split("+"c)
    Dim n1 As Long = CLng(args(0))
    Dim n2 As Long = CLng(args(1))
    ' Return their sum, as a string.
    Return (n1 + n2).ToString()
End Function
```

The delegate must point to a function that takes a Match object and returns a String object. The code inside this function can query the Match object properties to learn more about the match. For example, you can use the Index property to peek at what immediately precedes or follows in the source string so that you can make a more informed decision.

Callback functions are especially useful to convert individual matches to uppercase, lowercase, or proper case:

```
Private Function ConvertToUpperCase(ByVal m As Match) As String
    Return m.Value.ToUpper()
End Function

Private Function ConvertToLowerCase(ByVal m As Match) As String
    Return m.Value.ToLower()
End Function

Private Function ConvertToProperCase(ByVal m As Match) As String
    ' We must convert to lowercase first, to ensure that ToTitleCase works as intended.
    Return CultureInfo.CurrentCulture.TextInfo.ToTitleCase(m.Value.ToLower())
End Function
```

Here's an example:

```
' Convert country names in the text string to uppercase.
Dim text As String = "I visited italy, france, and then GERMANY."
Dim re2 As New Regex("\b(Usa|France|Germany|Italy|Great Britain)\b", _
    RegexOptions.IgnoreCase)
text = re2.Replace(text, AddressOf ConvertToProperCase)
Console.WriteLine(text)      ' => I visited Italy, France, and then Germany.
```

Static Methods

All the methods shown so far are also available as static methods; therefore, in many cases you don't need to create a Regex object explicitly. You generally pass the regular expression pattern to the static method as a second argument after the source string. For example, you can split a string into individual words as follows:

```
' \W means "any nonalphanumeric character."
Dim words() As String = Regex.Split("Split these words", "\W+")
```

The Regex class also exposes a few static methods that have no instance method counterpart. The Escape method takes a string and converts the special characters .$^{[(|)*+?\ to their equivalent escaped sequence. This method is especially useful when you let the end user enter the search pattern:

```
Console.WriteLine(Regex.Escape("(x)"))      ' => \(x\)

' Check whether the character sequence the end user entered in
' the txtChars TextBox control is contained in the source string.
If Regex.IsMatch(source, Regex.Escape(txtChars.Text)) Then ...
```

The Unescape static method converts a string that contains escaped sequences back into its unescaped equivalent. This method can be useful even if you don't use regular expressions; for example, to build strings that contain carriage returns, line feeds, and other nonprintable chapters by using a C#-like syntax and without having to concatenate string constants and subexpressions based on the Chr function:

```
s = Regex.Unescape("First line\r\nSecond line ends with null char\x00")
```

The CompileToAssembly Method

When you use the RegexOptions.Compiled value in the Regex constructor, you can expect a slight delay for the regular expression to be compiled to IL. In most cases, this delay is negligible, but you can avoid it if you want by using the CompileToAssembly static method to precompile one or more regular expressions. The result of this precompilation is a separate assembly that contains one Regex-derived type for each regular expression you've precompiled. The following code shows how you can use the CompileToAssembly method to create an assembly that contains two precompiled regular expressions:

```
' The namespace for both compiled regex types in this sample
Dim nsName As String = "CustomRegex"
' The first regular expression compiles to a type named RegexWords.
' (The last argument means that the type is public.)
Dim rci1 As New RegexCompilationInfo("\w+", RegexOptions.Compiled, _
    "RegexWords", nsName, True)
' The second regular expression compiles to a type named RegexIntegers.
Dim rci2 As New RegexCompilationInfo("\d+", RegexOptions.Compiled, _
    "RegexIntegers", nsName, True)
' Create the array that defines all compiled regular expressions.
Dim regexInfo() As RegexCompilationInfo = {rci1, rci2}

' Compile these types to an assembly named "CustomRegularExpressions".
Dim an As New System.Reflection.AssemblyName
an.Name = "CustomRegularExpressions"
Regex.CompileToAssembly(regexInfo, an)
```

The preceding code creates an assembly named CustomRegularExpressions.Dll in the same directory as the current application's executable. You can add a reference to this assembly from any Visual Studio 2005 project and use the two RegexWords and RegexIntegers types, or you can load these types using reflection (see Chapter 18). In the former case, you can use a strongly typed variable:

```
Dim reWords As New CustomRegex.RegexWords
For Each m As Match In reWords.Matches("A string containing five words")
    Console.WriteLine(m.Value)
Next
```

The MatchCollection and Match Types

The MatchCollection class represents a set of matches. It has no constructor because you can create a MatchCollection object only by using the Regex.Matches method.

The Match class represents a single match. You can obtain an instance of this class either by iterating on a MatchCollection object or directly by means of the Match method of the Regex class. The Match object is immutable and has no public constructor.

The main properties of the Match class are Value, Length, and Index, which return the matched string, its length, and the index at which it appears in the source string. The ToString method returns the same string as the Value property does. I already showed you how to use the IsSuccess property of the Match class and its NextMatch method to iterate over all the matches in a string.

You must pay special attention when the search pattern matches an empty string, for example, \d* (which matches zero or more digits). When you apply such a pattern to a string, you typically get one or more empty matches, as you can see here:

```
Dim re As New Regex("\d*")
For Each m As Match In re.Matches("1a23bc456de789")
   ' The output from this loop shows that some matches are empty.
   Console.Write(m.Value & ",")   ' => 1,,23,,,456,,,789,,
Next
```

As I explained earlier, a search generally starts where the previous search ends. However, the rule is different when the engine finds an empty match because it advances by one character before repeating the search. You would get trapped in an endless loop if the engine didn't behave this way.

If the pattern contains one or more groups, you can access the corresponding Group object by means of the Match object's Groups collection, which you can index by the group number or group name. I discuss the Group object shortly, but you can already see how you can use the Groups collection to extract the variable names and values in a series of assignments:

```
Dim source As String = "a = 123: b=456"
Dim re2 As New Regex("(\s*)(?<name>\w+)\s*=\s*(?<value>\d+)")
For Each m As Match In re2.Matches(source)
   Console.WriteLine("Variable: {0}, Value: {1}", _
      m.Groups("name").Value, m.Groups("value").Value)
Next
```

This is the result displayed in the console window:

```
Variable: a, Value: 123
Variable: b, Value: 456
```

The Result method takes a replace pattern and returns the string that would result if the match were replaced by that pattern:

```
' This code produces exactly the same result as the preceding snippet.
For Each m As Match In re2.Matches(source)
   Console.WriteLine(m.Result("Variable: ${name}, Value: ${value}"))
Next
```

The Group Type

The Group class represents a single group in a Match object and exposes a few properties whose meanings should be evident. The properties are Value (the text associated with the group), Index (its position in the source string), Length (the group's length), and Success

(True if the group has been matched). This code sample is similar to the preceding example, but it also displays the index in the source string where each matched variable was found:

```
Dim text As String = "a = 123: b=456"
Dim re As New Regex("(\s*)(?<name>\w+)\s*=\s*(?<value>\d+)")
For Each m As Match In re.Matches(text)
    Dim g As Group = m.Groups("name")
    ' Get information on variable name and value.
    Console.Write("Variable '{0}' found at index {1}", g.Value, g.Index)
    Console.WriteLine(", value is {0}", m.Groups("value").Value)
Next
```

This is the result displayed in the console window:

```
Variable 'a' found at index 0, value is 123
Variable 'b' found at index 9, value is 456
```

The following example is more complex but also more useful. It shows how you can parse <A> tags in an HTML file and display the anchor text (the text that appears underlined on an HTML page) and the URL it points to. As you can see, it's just a matter of a few lines of code:

```
Dim re As New Regex("<A\s+HREF\s*=\s*("".+?""|.+?)>(.+?)</A>", RegexOptions.IgnoreCase)
' Load the contents of an HTML file.
Dim text As String = File.ReadAllText("test.htm")
' Display all occurrences.
Dim m As Match = re.Match(text)
Do While m.Success
    Console.WriteLine("{0} => {1}", m.Groups(2).Value, m.Groups(1).Value)
    m = m.NextMatch()
Loop
```

To understand how the preceding code works, you must keep in mind that the <A> tag is followed by one or more spaces and then by an HREF attribute, which is followed by an equal sign and then the URL, which can be enclosed in quotation marks. All the text that follows the closing angle bracket up to the ending tag </A> is the anchor text. The regular expression uses the .+? lazy quantifier so as not to match too many characters and miss the delimiting quotation mark or closing angle bracket.

The regular expression defined in the preceding code defines two unnamed groups—the URL and the anchor text—so displaying details for all the <A> tags in the HTML file is just a matter of looping over all the matches. The regular expression syntax is complicated by the fact that quotation mark characters must be doubled when they appear in a Visual Basic string constant.

A few methods in the Regex class can be useful to get information about the groups that the parser finds in the regular expression. The GetGroupNames method returns an array with the names of all groups; the GroupNameFromNumber returns the name of the group with a given index; and the GroupNumberFromName returns the index of a group with a given name. See the MSDN documentation for more information.

The CaptureCollection and Capture Types

The search pattern can include one or more capturing groups, which are named or unnamed subexpressions enclosed in parentheses. Capturing groups can be nested and can capture multiple substrings of the source strings because of quantifiers. For example, when you apply the (\w)+ pattern to the "abc" string, you get one match for the entire string and three captured substrings, one for each character.

Fortunately, in most cases you don't need to work with captures because analyzing the source string at the match and group levels is often sufficient. You can access the collection of capture substrings through the Captures method of either the Match or the Group object. This method returns a CaptureCollection object that in turn contains one or more Capture objects. Individual Capture objects enable you to determine where individual captured substrings appear in the source string. The following code displays all the captured strings in the "abc def" string:

```
Dim text As String = "abc def"
Dim re As New Regex("(\w)+")
' Get the name or numbers of all the groups.
Dim groups() As String = re.GetGroupNames()

' Iterate over all matches.
For Each m As Match In re.Matches(text)
   ' Display information on this match.
   Console.WriteLine("Match '{0}' at index {1}", m.Value, m.Index)
   ' Iterate over the groups in each match.
   For Each s As String In groups
      ' Get a reference to the corresponding group.
      Dim g As Group = m.Groups(s)
      ' Get the capture collection for this group.
      Dim cc As CaptureCollection = g.Captures
      ' Display the number of captures.
      Console.WriteLine("  Found {0} capture(s) for group {1}", cc.Count, s)
      ' Display information on each capture.
      For Each c As Capture In cc
         Console.WriteLine("    '{0}' at index {1}", c.Value, c.Index)
      Next
   Next
Next
```

The text that follows is the result produced in the console window. (Notice that group 0 always refers to the match expression itself.)

```
Match 'abc' at index 0
  Found 1 capture(s) for group 0
    'abc' at index 0
  Found 3 capture(s) for group 1
    'a' at index 0
    'b' at index 1
    'c' at index 2
Match 'def' at index 4
```

```
Found 1 capture(s) for group 0
  'def' at index 4
Found 3 capture(s) for group 1
  'd' at index 4
  'e' at index 5
  'f' at index 6
```

Regular Expressions at Work

Most of the examples so far have showed many possible applications of regular expressions, yet they just scratch the surface of the power of regular expressions. In this last section, I illustrate more examples and provide hints of how to make the most of this powerful feature of the .NET Framework.

Common Regex Patterns

For your convenience, I have prepared a list of recurring patterns, which you can often use as is in your code (see Table 14-3). To help you find the pattern that suits your needs, the list includes some patterns that I covered earlier in this chapter as well as patterns that I discuss in following sections. You should enclose the pattern between a pair of \b sequences if you want to find individual words, or between the ^ and $ characters if you want to test whether the entire input string matches the pattern.

Table 14-3   Common Regular Expression Patterns

Sequence	Description
\d+	Positive integer.
[+-]?\d+	A positive or negative integer whose sign is optional.
[+-]?\d+(\.\d+)?	A floating-point number whose sign and decimal portion are optional.
[+-]?\d+(\.\d+)?(E[+-]?\d+)?	A floating-point number that can be optionally expressed in exponential format (e.g., 1.23E+12); the mantissa sign and the exponent sign are optional.
[0-9A-Fa-f]+	A hexadecimal number.
\w+	A sequence of alphanumeric and underscore characters; same as the [A–Za–z0–9_]+ sequence.
[A–Z]+	An all-uppercase word.
[A–Z][a–z]+	A proper name (the initial character is uppercase, and then all lowercase characters).
[A–Z][A–Za–z']+	A last name (the initial character is uppercase, and string can contain other uppercase characters and apostrophes, as in O'Brian).
[A–Za–z]{1,10}	A word of 10 characters or fewer.
[A–Za–z]{11,}	A word of 11 characters or more.
[A-Za-z_]\w*	A valid Visual Basic and C# identifier that begins with a letter or underscores and optionally continues with letters, digits, or underscores.

Table 14-3 **Common Regular Expression Patterns** *(Continued)*

Sequence	Description
(?<q>["']).*?\k<q>	A quoted string enclosed in either single or double quotation marks.
(10|11|12|0?[1–9])(?<sep>[-/])(30|31|2\d|1\d|0?[1–9])\k<sep>(\d{4}|\d{2})	A U.S. date in the mm-dd-yyyy or mm/dd/yyyy format. Month and day numbers can have a leading zero; month number must be in the range 1–12; day number must be in the range 1–31 (but invalid dates such as 2/30/2004 are matched); year number can have two or four digits and isn't validated.
(30|31|2\d|1\d|0?[1–9])(?<sep>[-/])(10|11|12|0?[1–9])\k<sep>(\d{4}|\d{2})	A European date in the dd-mm-yyyy or dd/mm/yyyy format. (See previous entry for more details.)
(2[0–3]|[01]\d|\d):[0–5]\d	A time value in the hh:mm 24-hour format; leading zero for hour value is optional.
\(\d{3}\)–\d{3}–\d{4}	A phone number such as (123)-456-7890.
\d{5}(-\d{4})?	A U.S. ZIP Code.
\d{3}-\d{2}-\d{4}	A U.S. social security number (SSN).
((\d{16}|\d{4}(-\d{4}){3})|(\d{4}(\d{4}){3}))	A 16-digit credit card number that can embed optional dashes or spaces to define four groups of four digits, for example, 1234567812345678, 1234-5678-1234-5678, or 1234 5678 1234 5678. (Needless to say, it doesn't validate whether it is a valid credit card number.)
([0–9A–Fa–f]{32}|[0–9A–Fa–f]{8}-([0–9A–Fa–f]{4}-){3}[0–9A–Fa–f]{12})	A 32-digit GUID, with or without embedded dashes, as in 00000304-0000-0000-C000-000000000046.
([A–Za–z]:)?\\?([^/:*?<>"|\\]+\\)*[^/:*?<>"|\\]+	A Windows filename, with or without a drive and a directory name.
(http|https)://([\w-]+\.)+[\w-]+(/[\w- ./?%&=]*)?	An Internet URL; you should use the regular expression in case-insensitive mode to also match prefixes such as HTTP or Https.
\w+([-+.]\w+)*@\w+([-.]\w+)*\.\w+([-.]\w+)*	An Internet e-mail address.
((25[0-5]|2[0-4]\d|1\d\d|[1-9]\d|\d)\.){3}(25[0-5]|2[0-4]\d|1\d\d|[1-9]\d|\d)	A four-part IP address, such as 192.168.0.1; the pattern verifies that each number is in the range 0–255.
([1-5]\d{4}|6[0-4]\d{3}|65[0-4]\d{2}|655[0-2]\d|6553[0-4]|\d{1,4})	A 16-bit integer that can be assigned to a UShort variable, in the range of 0 to 65,535.
(-?[12]\d{4}|-?[0-1]\d{3}|-?32[0-6]\d{2}|-?327[0-5]\d|-?3276[0-7]|-32768|-?\d{1,4})	A 16-bit integer that can be assigned to a Short variable, in the range of –32,768 to 32,767.
^(?=.*\d)(?=.*[a-z])(?=.*[A-Z])\w{8,}$	A password of at least eight alphanumeric characters that contains at least one digit, one lowercase character, and one uppercase character. Replace the \w term with [0-9A-Za-z@.] to allow some symbols so that users can use their e-mail address as a password.

You can find more regular expressions in the Visual Studio Regular Expression Editor dialog box (see Figure 14-2) or by browsing the huge regular expression library you can find at *http://www.regexlib.com*. If you are serious about regular expressions, don't miss The Regulator free utility, which you can download from *http://regex.osherove.com/*.

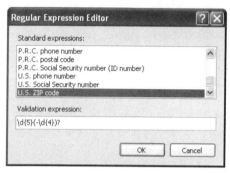

Figure 14-2   Setting the ValidationExpression property of a RegularExpressionValidator ASP.NET control by selecting one of the common regular expressions you find in the Regular Expression Editor dialog box

Searching for Words and Quoted Strings

A quite common operation with regular expressions is splitting a long string into words. Apparently, this is also the simplest task you can perform with regular expressions:

```
Dim text As String = "A word with àccéntèd vowels, and the 123 number."
Dim pattern As String
pattern = "\w+"
For Each m As Match In Regex.Matches(text, pattern)
    Console.WriteLine(m.Value)
Next
```

The problem with this oversimplified approach is that it also includes sequences of digits and underscores in the collection of results, and you might not want that. A better attempt is as follows:

```
pattern = "[A-Za-z]+"
...
```

This works better, but fails to include entire words if they contain accented characters or characters from other alphabets, such as Greek or Cyrillic. Under previous versions of the .NET Framework, you could solve this issue by using the little-used \p sequence, which allows you to specify a Unicode character class. For example, the \p{Ll} sequence matches any lowercase character, whereas the \p{Lu} sequence matches any uppercase character. The solution to the problem is therefore as follows:

```
pattern = "(\p{Lu}|\p{Ll})+"
...
```

The character class subtraction feature, introduced in .NET Framework 2.0, offers a new solution to the problem, based on the consideration that you can "subtract" the digits and the underscore from the range of characters expressed by the \w sequence:

```
pattern = "[\w-[0-9_]]+"
...
```

When extracting words, you often want to discard *noise words*, such as articles (the, a, an), conjunctions (and, or), and so forth. You might discard these words inside the For Each loop, but it's more elegant to have the regular expression get rid of them:

```
pattern = "\b(?!(the|a|an|and|or|on|of|with)\b)\w+"
text = "A fox and another animal on the lawn"
For Each m As Match In Regex.Matches(text, pattern, RegexOptions.IgnoreCase)
   Console.Write ("{0} ", m.Value)     ' => fox another animal lawn
Next
```

The \w+ in the previous pattern specifies that we are looking for a word, but the (?!...\b) expression specifies that the match must not begin with one of the noise words; the neat result is that the pattern matches all the words except those in the noise list.

Another common problem related to parsing is when you need to consider a quoted string as an individual word, such as when you parse the command passed to a command-line utility. (In this specific case, you might define a Sub Main that takes an array of strings as an argument and let the .NET Framework do the job for you, but it wouldn't work in the most general case.) The following regular expression matches an individual word or a string embedded in either single or double quotation marks:

```
' For simplicity's sake, use \w+ to match an individual word.
pattern = "(?<q>[""']).*?\k<q>|\w+"
```

Notice that the .*? does a lazy matching so that it matches any character between the quotation marks but won't match the closing quotation mark.

Sometimes you might want to extract just *unique* words, such as when you want to make a dictionary of all the words in a text file or a set of text files. A possible solution is to extract all the words and use a Hashtable object to remember the words found so far:

```
Dim text As String = "one two three two zone four three"
Dim re As New Regex("\w+")
Dim words As New Hashtable()
For Each m As Match in re.Matches(text)
   If Not words.Contains(m.Value) Then
      Console.Write("{0} ", m.Value)
      words.Add(m.Value, Nothing)
   End If
Next
```

Quite surprisingly, you can achieve the same result with a single, albeit complex, regular expression:

```
pattern = "(?<word>\b\w+\b)(?!.+\b\k<word>\b)"
For Each m As Match in Regex.Matches(text, pattern)
   Console.Write(m.Value & " ")
Next
```

The expression (?<word>\b\w+\b) matches a sequence of alphanumeric characters (\w) on a word boundary (\b) and assigns this sequence the name "word". The (?!) construct means that the word just matched must not be followed by the word already matched (the back reference \k<word>) even if there are other characters in the middle (represented by the .+ sequence). Translated into plain English, the regular expression means "match any word in the text that isn't followed by another instance of the same word" or, more simply, "match all the words that appear only once in the document or the last occurrence of a repeated word." As you can see, all the unique words are found correctly, even though their order is different from the previous example:

```
one two zone four three
```

Notice that the \b characters in the regular expression prevent partial matches ("one" doesn't match the trailing portion of "zone"). A slightly different regular expression can find the duplicated words in a document:

```
pattern = "(?<word>\b\w+\b)(?=.+\b\k<word>\b)"
```

where the (?=) construct means that the word match must be followed by another instance of itself. (Notice that this pattern finds all the duplicates; therefore, it finds two duplicates if there are three occurrences of a given word.) Although the regex-only techniques are very elegant, the look-ahead (?=) clause makes them relatively inefficient: for example, on a source text of about 1 million characters, the regex-only technique is approximately 8 times slower than the technique that uses an auxiliary Hashtable to keep track of all the words already parsed.

One last type of word search I want to explain is the *proximity search*, which is when you search two strings that must be found close to each other in the source string, with no more than N words between them. For example, given the "one two three two zone four three" source string, a proximity search for the words "one" and "four" with N equal to 4 would be successful, whereas it would fail with N equal to 3. The pattern for such a proximity search is quite simple:

```
pattern = "\bone(\w+\w+){0,4}\w+\bfour\b"
If Regex.IsMatch(text, pattern, RegexOptions.IgnoreCase) Then
   ' At least one occurrence of the words "one" and "four"
   ' with four or fewer words between them.
End If
```

You can also define a function that takes the input string, the two words, and the maximum distance between them and returns a MatchCollection object:

```
Function ProximityMatches(ByVal text As String, ByVal word1 As String, _
   ByVal word2 As String, ByVal maxDistance As Integer) As MatchCollection
```

```
    Dim pattern As String = "\b" & word1 & "(\W+\w+){0," & maxDistance.ToString() & "}\" _
        & "w+\b" & word2 & "\b"
    Dim re As New Regex(pattern, RegexOptions.IgnoreCase)
    Return re.Matches(text)
End Function
```

Thus, the previous code snippet would become

```
Dim mc As MatchCollection = ProximityMatches(text, "one", "four", 4)
If mc.Count > 0 Then
    …
End If
```

Validating Strings, Numbers, and Dates

As I explained earlier in this chapter, typically you can use a search pattern as a validation pattern by simply enclosing it in the ^ and $ symbols and using the IsMatch method instead of the Matches method. For example, the following code checks that a string—presumably the Text property of a TextBox control—contains a five-digit U.S. ZIP Code:

```
pattern = "^\d{5}$"
If Regex.IsMatch(text, pattern) Then
    ' It's a string containing five digits.
End If
```

Things become more interesting when you want to *exclude* a few combinations from the set of valid strings, which you can do with the (?!) clause. For example, the 00000 sequence isn't a valid ZIP code, and you can exclude it by using the following pattern:

```
pattern = "^(?!00000)\d{5}$"
```

You can use the (?=) look-ahead assertion to check that the input string contains all characters in a given class, regardless of their position. For example, you can use the following pattern to enforce a robust password policy and ensure that the end user types a password of at least eight characters and that it contains a combination of digits and uppercase and lowercase letters:

```
pattern = "^(?=.*\d)(?=.*[a-z])(?=.*[A-Z])\w{8,}$"
```

Let's see how this pattern works. The first (?=.*\d) clause makes the search fail at the very beginning if the portion of the input string to its right (and therefore, the entire input string) doesn't contain any digits. The (?=.*[a-z]) clause checks that the input string contains a lowercase character, and the (?=.*[A-Z]) clause does the same for uppercase characters. These three look-ahead clauses don't consume any characters, and therefore the remaining \w{8,} clause can check that the input string contains at least eight characters.

Validating a number in a given range poses a few interesting problems. In general, you might not want to use regular expressions to validate numbers or dates because the Parse and Try-Parse methods exposed by the DateTime type and all numeric types offer more flexibility and cause fewer headaches. However, in some cases, regular expressions can be a viable solution even for this task, for example, when you want to extract valid numbers and dates from a longer document.

Checking that an integer has up to the specified number of digits is a trivial problem, of course:

```
' Validate an integer in the range of 0 to 9,999; accept leading zeros.
pattern = "^\d{1,4}$"
```

The negative (?!) look-ahead clause lets you rule out a few cases, for example:

```
' Validate an integer in the range 1 to 9,999; reject leading zeros.
pattern = "^(?!0)\d{1,4}$"
...
```

```
' Validate an integer in the range 0 to 9,999; reject leading zeros.
' (Same as previous one, but accept a single zero as a special case.)
pattern = "^(0|(?!0)\d{1,4})$"
...
```

If the upper limit of the accepted range isn't a number in the form 99...999, you can still use regular expressions to do the validation, but the pattern becomes more complex. For example, the following pattern checks that a number is in the range 0 to 255 with no leading zeros:

```
pattern = "^(25[0-5]|2[0-4]\d|1\d\d|[1-9]\d|\d)$"
```

The 25[0-5] clause validates numbers in the range 250 to 255; the 2[0-4]\d clause validates numbers in the range 200 to 249; the 1\d\d clause validates numbers in the range 100 to 199; the [1-9]\d clause takes care of the numbers 10 to 99; finally, the \d clause covers the range 0 to 9. A slight modification of this pattern allows you to validate a four-part IP address, such as 192.168.0.11:

```
pattern = "^((25[0-5]|2[0-4]\d|1\d\d|[1-9]\d|\d)\.){3}" _
    & "(25[0-5]|2[0-4]\d|1\d\d|[1-9]\d|\d)$"
```

Things quickly become complicated with larger ranges:

```
' Validate an integer number in the range 0 to 65,535; leading zeros are OK.
pattern = "^([1-5]\d{4}|6[0-4]\d{3}|65[0-4]\d{2}|655[0-2]\d|6553[0-4]|\d{1,4})$"
```

Numbers that can have a leading sign require special treatment:

```
' Validate an integer in the range -32,768 to 32,767; leading zeros are OK.
pattern = "^(-?[12]\d{4}|-?3[0-1]\d{3}|-?32[0-6]\d{2}|-?327[0-5]\d|" _
    & "-?3276[0-7]|-32768|-?\d{1,4})$"
```

Notice in the previous pattern that the special case −32768 must be dealt with separately; all the remaining clauses have an optional minus sign in front of them. You can use a similar technique to validate a time value:

```
' Validate a time value in the format hh:mm; the hour number can have a leading zero.
pattern = "^(2[0-3]|[01]\d|\d):[0-5]\d$"
```

Validating a date value is much more difficult because each month has a different number of days and, above all, because the valid day range for February depends on whether the year is a leap year. Before I illustrate the complete pattern for solving this problem, let's see how we can use a regular expression to check whether a two-digit number is a multiple of 4:

```
' If the first digit is even, the second digit must be 0, 4, or 8.
' If the first digit is odd, the second digit must be 2 or 6.
pattern = "^([02468][048]|[13579][26])$"
```

Under the simplified assumption that the year number has only two digits, and therefore the date refers to a year in the current century, we can simplify the regular expression significantly because the year 2000 was a leap year, unlike 1900 and 2100. To better explain the final regular expression I have split the pattern onto four lines:

```
' This portion deals with months with 31 days.
Dim p1 As String = "(0?[13578]|10|12)/(3[01]|[012]\d|\d)/\d{2}"
' This portion deals with months with 30 days.
Dim p2 As String = "(0?[469]|11)/(30|[012]\d|\d)/\d{2}"
' This portion deals with February 29 in leap years.
Dim p3 As String = "(0?2)/29/([02468][048]|[13579][26])"
' This portion deals with other days in February.
Dim p4 As String = "(0?2)/(2[0-8]|[01]\d|\d)/\d{2}"
' Put all the patterns together.
pattern = String.Format("^({0}|{1}|{2}|{3})$", p1, p2, p3, p4)
' Check the date.
If Regex.IsMatch(text, pattern) Then
   ' Date is valid.
End If
```

If the year number can have either two or four digits, we must take into account the fact that all years divisible by 100 are not leap years, except if they are divisible by 400. (For example, 1900 isn't a leap year, but 2000 is.) This constraint makes the regular expression more complicated, but by now you should be experienced enough to understand how the following code works:

```
' This portion deals with months with 31 days.
Const s1 As String = "(0?[13578]|10|12)/(3[01]|[12]\d|0?[1-9])/(\d\d)?\d\d"
' This portion deals with months with 30 days.
Const s2 As String = "(0?[469]|11)/(30|[12]\d|0?[1-9])/(\d\d)?\d\d "
' This portion deals with days 1-28 in February in all years.
Const s3 As String = "(0?2)/(2[0-8]|[01]\d|0?[1-9])/(\d\d)?\d\d"
' This portion deals with February 29 in years divisible by 400.
Const s4 As String = "(0?2)/29/(1600|2000|2400|2800|00)"
' This portion deals with February 29 in noncentury leap years.
Const s5 As String = "(0?2)/29/(\d\d)?(0[48]|[2468][048]|[13579][26])"
' Put all the patterns together.
pattern = String.Format("^({0}|{1}|{2}|{3}|{4})$", s1, s2, s3, s4, s5)
...
```

(Notice that I might have merged the portions s4 and s5 in a single subexpression that validates all leap years, but I kept the two expressions separate for clarity's sake.) It's easy to derive a similar regular expression for dates in dd/mm/yy format and to account for separators other than the dash character.

Searching for Nested Tags

When you apply regular expressions to HTML or XML files, you must take the hierarchical natures of these files into account. For example, let's say that you want to extract the contents of <table>...</table> sections in an HTML file. You can't simply use a pattern such as this:

```
<table[\s>].*?</table>)
```

because it would return bogus results when you apply it to a text that contains nested tables, such as this:

```
<table border=1><tr><td><table>…</table></td><td>…</td></tr></table>
```

In cases like these, the balancing group definition construct shown in Table 14-1 can help because it lets you take nested tags into account. (For a great example of how you can use this construct, read *http://blogs.msdn.com/bclteam/archive/2005/03/15/396452.aspx.*) However, this construct is quite difficult to use and has some limitations, the most notable of which is that it doesn't work well if you're looking for a series of nested tags, as when you want to display all <table>, <tr>, and <td> blocks. In cases like these, you need two nested loops, as in the following code:

```vb
' Find all nested HTML tags in a file. (e.g., <table>…</table>)
Dim text As String = File.ReadAllText("test.htm")
Dim re As New Regex("<(?<tag>(table|tr|td|div|span))[\s>]", RegexOptions.IgnoreCase)
For Each m As Match In re.Matches(text)
   ' We've found an open tag. Let's look for open and close versions of this tag.
   Dim tag As String = m.Groups("tag").Value
   Dim openTags As Integer = 1
   Dim pattern2 As String = String.Format("((?<open><{0})[\s>]|(?<close>)</{0}>)", tag)
   Dim found As String = Nothing
   Dim re2 As New Regex(pattern2, RegexOptions.IgnoreCase)

   For Each m2 As Match In re2.Matches(text, m.Index + 1)
      If m2.Groups("open").Success Then
         openTags += 1
      ElseIf m2.Groups("close").Success Then
         openTags -= 1
         If openTags = 0 Then
            found = text.Substring(m.Index, m2.Index + m.Length - m.Index + 1)
            Exit For
         End If
      End If
   Next
   ' Display this match.
   If found IsNot Nothing Then
      Console.WriteLine(found)
   Else
      Console.WriteLine("Unmatched tag {0} at index {1}", tag, m.Index)
   End If
Next
```

Once you understand how this code works, you can easily modify it to match other hierarchical entities, for example, parentheses in a math expression or nested type definitions in a .vb source file.

Parsing Data Files

Even though XML has emerged as the standard technology in exchange information, many legacy applications still output data in older and simpler formats. Two such formats are fixed-width text files and delimited text files. Microsoft Visual Basic 2005 supports a new TextField-Parser object that can simplify this task remarkably (see Chapter 15, "Files, Directories, and Streams"), but you can also solve this problem with regular expressions in a very elegant manner. Let's consider a fixed-width data file such as this one:

```
John   Evans   New York
Ann    Beebe   Los Angeles
```

Each text line contains information about first name (6 characters), last name (8 characters), and city. The largest city has 9 characters, but usually we can assume that the last field takes all the characters up to the end of the current line. Reading this file requires very few lines of code:

```
Dim pattern As String = "^(?<first>.{6})(?<last>.{8})(?<city>.+)$"
Dim re As New Regex(pattern)
Using sr As New StreamReader("c:\data.txt")
   Do Until sr.EndOfStream
      Dim m As Match = re.Match(sr.ReadLine())
      Console.WriteLine("First={0}, Last={1}, City={2}", _
         m.Groups("first").Value.TrimEnd(), m.Groups("last").Value.TrimEnd(), _
         m.Groups("city").Value.TrimEnd())
   Loop
End Using
```

The expression (?<first>.{6}) creates a group named "first" that corresponds to the initial 6 characters. Likewise, (?<last>.{8}) creates a group named "last" that corresponds to the next 8 characters. Finally, (?<city>.+) creates a group for all the remaining characters on the line and names it as "city". The ^ and $ characters stand for the beginning and the end of the line, respectively.

The beauty of this approach is that it is quite easy to adapt the code to different field widths and to work with delimited fields. For example, if the fixed-width fields are separated by semi-colons, you simply modify the regular expression as follows, without touching the remaining code:

```
pattern = "^(?<first>.{6});(?<last>.{8});(?<city>.+)$"
```

Let's now adapt the parsing program to another quite common exchange format: delimited text files. In this case, each field is separated from the next one by a comma, a semicolon, a tab, or another special character. To further complicate things, such files usually allow values embedded in single or double quotation marks; in this case, you can't just use the Split method of the String type to do the parsing because your result would be bogus if a quoted value happens to include the delimiter (as in "Evans, John").

In such cases, regular expressions are a real lifesaver. In fact, you just need to use a different regular expression pattern with the same parsing code used in previous examples. Let's start with the simplified assumption that there are no quoted strings in the file, as in the following:

```
John  , Evans, New York
Ann, Beebe, Los Angeles
```

I threw in some extra white spaces to add interest to the discussion. These spaces should be ignored when you're parsing the text. Here is the regular expression that can be used to parse such a comma-delimited series of values:

```
pattern = "^\s*(?<first>.*?)\s*,\s*(?<last>.*?)\s*,\s*(?<city>.*?)\s*$"
```

You don't need to modify other portions of the parsing code I showed previously. It is essential that \s* sequences and the delimiter character (the comma, in this specific case) are placed outside the (?) construct so that they aren't included in named groups. Also notice that we use the .*? sequence to avoid matching the delimiter character or the spaces that might surround it.

Next, let's see how to parse quoted fields, such as those found in the following text file:

```
'John, P.' , "Evans" , "New York"
'Robert "Zare"', "" , "Los Angeles, CA"
```

Text fields can be surrounded by both single and double quotation marks and they can contain the comma symbol as well as the quotation mark not used as a delimiter. The regular expression that can parse this text file is more complex:

```
pattern = "^\s*(?<q1>[""'])(?<first>.*?)\k<q1>\s*," & _
   "\s*(?<q2>[""'])(?<last>.*?)\k<q2>\s*,\s*(?<q3>[""'])(?<city>.*?)\k<q3>\s*$"
```

The (?<q1>["']) subexpression matches either the single or the double leading quotation mark delimiter and assigns this group the name "q1". (The double quotation mark character is doubled because it appears in a Visual Basic string.) The \k<q1> subexpression is a back reference to whatever the q1 group found and therefore matches whichever quotation mark character was used at the beginning of the field. The q2 and q3 groups have the same role for the next two fields. Once again, you don't need to change any other statement in the parsing routine.

The previous pattern has a small defect, though. Many programs that output data in delimited format enclose a text field in quotation marks only if the field contains the delimiter character. For example, in the following data file the first and last fields in the first record are enclosed in quotation marks because they embed a comma, but the fields in the second record aren't.

```
"John, P." , Evans , "Los Angeles, CA"
Robert, Zare, New York
```

To solve this minor problem I need to introduce one of the most powerful features of regular expressions: conditional matching. Look closely at the following pattern:

```
pattern = "^\s*(?<q1>[""']?)(?<first>.*?)(?(q1)\k<q1>)\s*" & _
    ",\s*(?<q2>[""']?)(?<last>.*?)(?(q2)\k<q2>)\s*" & _
    ",\s*(?<q3>[""']?)(?<city>.*?)(?(q3)\k<q3>)\s*$"
```

The (?<q1>["']?) is similar to the pattern used in the previous example, except it has a trailing ? character; therefore, it matches an optional single or double quotation mark character. Later in the same line you find the (?(q1)\k<q1>) clause, which tests whether the q1 group is defined and, if so, matches its value. In other words, if the q1 group actually matched the single or double quotation mark character, the expression (?(q1)\k<q1>) matches it again; otherwise, the expression is ignored. The same reasoning applies to the other two fields in the record.

The (?(expr)...) clause has an optional "no" portion (see Table 14-1), so you might even match a portion of a string if a previous group has *not* been matched.

Parsing and Evaluating Expressions

A nice and somewhat surprising application of regular expressions is in expression evaluation. In the section titled "The Replace Method" earlier in this chapter, you saw how you can evaluate the result of an addition operation embedded in a string such as "12+34", thanks to the overload of the Replace method that takes a callback function. Of course, you don't have to stop at additions, and in fact you can create a complete and quite versatile expression evaluator built on a single regular expression and some support code. Creating such a regular expression isn't a trivial task, though. Let's analyze the Evaluate method a piece at a time:

```
Function Evaluate(ByVal expr As String) As Double
    ' A floating-point number, with optional leading and trailing spaces
    Const num As String = "\s*[+-]?\d+\.?\d*\b\s*"
    ' A number inside a pair of parentheses
    Const nump As String = "\s*\((?<nump>" & num & ")\)\s*"
    ' Math operations
    Const add As String = "(?<![*/^]\s*)(?<add1>" & num & ")\+(?<add2>" _
        & num & ")(?!\s*[*/^])"
    Const subt As String = "(?<![*/^]\s*)(?<sub1>" & num & ")\-(?<sub2>" _
        & num & ")(?!\s*[*/^])"
    Const mul As String = "(?<!\^\s*)(?<mul1>" & num & ")\*(?<mul2>" & num & ")(?!\s*\^)"
    Const div As String = "(?<!\^\s*)(?<div1>" & num & ")\/(?<div2>" & num & ")(?!\s*\^)"
    Const modu As String = "(?<!\^\s*)(?<mod1>" & num _
        & ")\s+mod\s+(?<mod2>" & num & ")(?!\s*\^)"
    Const pow As String = "(?<pow1>" & num & ")\^(?<pow2>" & num & ")"
    ' 1-operand and 2-operand functions
    Const fone As String = "(?<fone>(exp|log|log10|abs|sqr|sqrt|sin|cos|tan|asin|acos|atan))" _
        & "\s*\((?<fone1>" & num & ")\)"
    Const ftwo As String = "(?<ftwo>(min|max)\s*)\((?<ftwo1>" & num _
        & "),(?<ftwo2>" & num & ")\)"
```

```
' Put everything in a single regex.
Const pattern As String = "(" & fone & "|" & ftwo & "|" & modu & "|" & pow & "|" _
   & div & "|" & mul & "|" & subt & "|" & add & "|" & nump & ")"
Dim reEval As New Regex(pattern, RegexOptions.IgnoreCase)     …
```

The pattern corresponding to the num constant represents a floating-point number, optionally preceded by a plus or minus sign. Let's now consider the regular expression that defines
the addition operation: it consists of two numbers, each one forming a named group (add1
and add2); the two numbers are separated by the + symbol. Additionally, the pattern is preceded by a (?<![*/^]\s*) negative look-behind assertion, which ensures that the first operand
doesn't follow an operator with a higher priority than addition (that is, the multiplication,
division, or raising to power operator). Similarly, the second operand is followed by the
(?!\s*[*/^]) negative look-ahead assertion, which ensures that the addition isn't followed by
an operation with higher priority. The patterns for other math operations are similar, so
I won't describe them in detail. The body of the Evaluate function follows:

```
   …
' Add a space after a +/- used for additions and subtractions to ensure
' they are not mistakenly taken as the leading sign of a number.
expr = Regex.Replace(expr, "(?<=[0-9)]\s*)[+-](?=[0-9(])", "$0 ")

Dim reNumber As New Regex("^" & num & "$")
' Loop until the expression is reduced to a number.
Do Until reNumber.IsMatch(expr)
   ' Replace only the first subexpression that can be processed.
   Dim newExpr As String = reEval.Replace(expr, AddressOf PerformOperation, 1)
   ' If the expression hasn't been simplified, there must be a problem.
   If expr = newExpr Then Throw New ArgumentException("Invalid expression")
   ' Reenter the loop with the new expression.
   expr = newExpr
Loop
' Convert to a floating-point number and return.
Return Double.Parse(expr)
End Function
```

At the top of the Do loop, the reNumber regular expression checks whether the expression
contains a number: in this case, the loop is exited and the value of the number is returned to
the caller. If this isn't the case, the loop is repeated in the attempt to simplify the expression
using the reEval regular expression; if the expression doesn't change, it means that the expression can't be simplified further because it is malformed, and the method throws an exception.
If the expression has been simplified, the loop is reentered.

The PerformOperation callback method is where the actual math operations are carried out.
Detecting which operator has been matched is simple because all the groups defined by the
various operators have different names:

```
Private Function PerformOperation(ByVal m As Match) As String
   Dim result As Double
   If m.Groups("nump").Length > 0 Then
      Return m.Groups("nump").Value.Trim()
```

```
    ElseIf m.Groups("neg").Length > 0 Then
        Return "+"
    ElseIf m.Groups("add1").Length > 0 Then
        result = Double.Parse(m.Groups("add1").Value) + Double.Parse(m.Groups("add2").Value)
    ElseIf m.Groups("sub1").Length > 0 Then
        result = Double.Parse(m.Groups("sub1").Value) - Double.Parse(m.Groups("sub2").Value)
    ElseIf m.Groups("mul1").Length > 0 Then
        result = Double.Parse(m.Groups("mul1").Value) * Double.Parse(m.Groups("mul2").Value)
    ElseIf m.Groups("mod1").Length > 0 Then
        result = Math.IEEERemainder(Double.Parse(m.Groups("mod1").Value), _
            Double.Parse(m.Groups("mod2").Value))
    ElseIf m.Groups("div1").Length > 0 Then
        result = Double.Parse(m.Groups("div1").Value) / Double.Parse(m.Groups("div2").Value)
    ElseIf m.Groups("pow1").Length > 0 Then
        result = Double.Parse(m.Groups("pow1").Value) ^ Double.Parse(m.Groups("pow2").Value)
    ElseIf m.Groups("fone").Length > 0 Then
        Dim operand As Double = Double.Parse(m.Groups("fone1").Value)
        Select Case m.Groups("fone").Value.ToLower()
            Case "exp" : result = Math.Exp(operand)
            Case "log" : result = Math.Log(operand)
            Case "log10" : result = Math.Log10(operand)
            Case "abs" : result = Math.Abs(operand)
            Case "sqrt" : result = Math.Sqrt(operand)
            Case "sin" : result = Math.Sin(operand)
            Case "cos" : result = Math.Cos(operand)
            Case "tan" : result = Math.Tan(operand)
            Case "asin" : result = Math.Asin(operand)
            Case "acos" : result = Math.Acos(operand)
            Case "atan" : result = Math.Atan(operand)
        End Select
    ElseIf m.Groups("ftwo").Length > 0 Then
        Dim operand1 As Double = Double.Parse(m.Groups("ftwo1").Value)
        Dim operand2 As Double = Double.Parse(m.Groups("ftwo2").Value)
        Select Case m.Groups("ftwo").Value.ToLower()
            Case "min" : result = Math.Min(operand1, operand2)
            Case "max" : result = Math.Max(operand1, operand2)
        End Select
    End If
    Return result.ToString()
End Function
```

It's easy to create a console application or a Windows Forms program that asks the user for an expression and displays the expression value. Figure 14-3 shows such a program in action. The only interesting piece of code is the method that runs when the user clicks the Eval button:

```
Private Sub btnEval_Click(ByVal sender As Object, ByVal e As EventArgs)
    Try
        ' Read and evaluate the expression typed in the txtExpression field.
        Dim res As Double = Evaluate(txtExpression.Text)
        ' Display the result in a Label control.
        lblResult.Text = res.ToString()
    Catch ex As Exception
        lblResult.Text = "ERROR " & ex.Message
    End Try
End Sub
```

The Evaluate function and the PerformOperation helper method have a total of only 65 executable statements, yet they implement a full-fledged expression evaluator that you can easily expand to support additional operators and functions. Such conciseness is possible thanks to the power of regular expressions and, in particular, to the ability to specify look-behind and look-ahead negative assertions, which ensures that the priority of the various operators is honored.

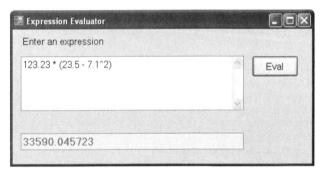

Figure 14-3   The demo application that tests the Evaluate method

Parsing Code

Developers spend a lot of time with code; thus, you might consider source files as one of the primary types of data you deal with. As such, source files are great candidates for being parsed and processed by means of regular expressions. In the following example, I illustrate a very simple console application that reads a Visual Basic source file and outputs information about the total number of lines, blank lines, comment lines, and executable lines it contains, and then it splits the file into types and their members and displays detailed information about each of them.

The Main procedure of this application is just a driver for the CodeStats class:

```
Module MainModule
   Sub Main(ByVal args() As String)
      Dim fileName As String = args(0)
      Dim code As String = File.ReadAllText(fileName)
      Dim stats As New CodeStats("FILE", fileName, code)
      Console.Write(stats.Description(0))
   End Sub
End Module
```

The CodeStats type is where the actual parse occurs. Each instance of this class has public fields to store information about line count, plus a Members collection that can contain other CodeStats instances. For example, the CodeStats object for the file contains a collection of CodeStats objects related to the types defined in the file, and CodeStats objects related to types have a collection of CodeStats objects related to type members (methods and property procedures). For the sake of simplicity, I account for neither nested types nor less common blocks such as custom events.

```vb
Public Class CodeStats
    Public Type As String
    Public Name As String
    Public TotalLines As Integer
    Public BlankLines As Integer
    Public CommentLines As Integer
    Public ExecutableLines As Integer
    ' Child elements
    Public Members As New List(Of CodeStats)()

    Dim reTotalLines As New Regex("^.*$", RegexOptions.Multiline)
    Dim reBlankLines As New Regex("^\s*$", RegexOptions.Multiline)
    Dim reCommentLines As New Regex("^\s*('|Rem ).*$", _
        RegexOptions.Multiline Or RegexOptions.IgnoreCase)
    Dim reTypes As New Regex("(Public|Friend|Private|Protected|Protected Friend)?\s*" & _
        "(Shadows|NotInheritable|MustInherit)?\s*" & _
        "(?<type>(Class|Module|Interface|Enum|Structure))" & _
        "\s+(?<name>\w+)[\w\W]+?End \k<type>", _
        RegexOptions.IgnoreCase Or RegexOptions.Multiline)
    Dim reMembers As New Regex("(Public|Friend|Private|Protected|Protected Friend)?\s*" & _
        "(Default|Shared)?\s*(ReadOnly|WriteOnly)?\s*(Overloads)?\s*" & _
        "(Shadows|Overridable|Overrides|MustOverride|NotOverridable)?\s*" & _
        "(?<type>(Function|Sub|Property))\s+(?<name>\w+)[\w\W]+?End \k<type>", _
        RegexOptions.IgnoreCase Or RegexOptions.Multiline)

    ' The constructor
    Sub New(ByVal type As String, ByVal name As String, ByVal code As String)
        Me.Type = type
        Me.Name = name
        Me.TotalLines = reTotalLines.Matches(code).Count
        Me.BlankLines = reBlankLines.Matches(code).Count
        Me.CommentLines = reCommentLines.Matches(code).Count
        Me.ExecutableLines = TotalLines - BlankLines - CommentLines

        If type = "FILE" Then
            For Each m As Match In reTypes.Matches(code)
                Members.Add(New CodeStats("TYPE", m.Groups("name").Value, m.Value))
            Next
        ElseIf type = "TYPE" Then
            For Each m As Match In reMembers.Matches(code)
                Members.Add(New CodeStats("MEMBER", m.Groups("name").Value, m.Value))
            Next
        End If
    End Sub

    Function Description(ByVal indentLevel As Integer) As String
        Dim indent As New String(" "c, indentLevel * 2)
        Dim sb As New StringBuilder
        sb.AppendFormat("{0}{1} {2}{3}", indent, Type, Name, Environment.NewLine)
        indent &= "  "
        sb.AppendFormat("{0}Total lines:    {1,6}{2}", indent, TotalLines, _
            Environment.NewLine)
        sb.AppendFormat("{0}Blank lines:    {1,6}{2,9:P1}{3}", indent, _
            BlankLines, BlankLines / TotalLines, Environment.NewLine)
        sb.AppendFormat("{0}Comment lines:  {1,6}{2,9:P1}{3}", indent, _
            CommentLines, CommentLines / TotalLines, Environment.NewLine)
```

```
        sb.AppendFormat("{0}Executable lines: {1,6}{2,9:P1}{3}", indent, _
            ExecutableLines, ExecutableLines / TotalLines, Environment.NewLine)
        sb.Append(Environment.NewLine)
        ' Ask child objects to display their description.
        For Each stats As CodeStats In Me.Members
            sb.Append(stats.Description(indentLevel + 1))
        Next
        Return sb.ToString()
    End Function
End Class
```

Interestingly, I ran this code to count lines in its own source file, so I learned that I could create an effective and useful programming utility with just 63 executable statements, which is quite a good result. (See Figure 14-4.)

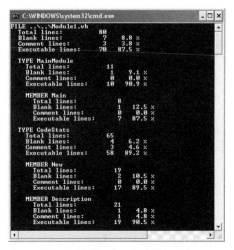

Figure 14-4 Using the CodeStats class to count how many statements its own source code contains

Playing with Regular Expressions (Literally)

By now, you should be convinced that regular expressions are too powerful to be used only for plain text searches and substitutions. In this last example, I want to prove that regular expressions can be useful when you'd never suspect that searches are involved and that you can use them simply to perform pattern matching.

Let's consider the game of poker. I won't build an entire application that plays poker (nor encourage gambling in any way...), but I will focus on a very small programming problem that is related to this game. How would you write a method that evaluates the score corresponding to a hand of five cards? You can solve this problem in a variety of ways, with numerous If and Select Case statements, but the solution offered by regular expressions can hardly be beaten as far as elegance, performance, and conciseness are concerned.

The following method accepts five strings, each one corresponding to a card in the hand and each one consisting of a character pair: the first character stands for the card value and can be a digit 1–9, or T, J, Q, or K (where T stands for Ten); the second character of the pair is the card's suit and can be C (clubs), D (diamonds), H (hearts), or S (spades). The code in the method sorts the five cards by their value, and then builds two separate strings—one containing the five values and the other containing the five suits—and tests them against suitable regular expressions, starting from the most complex and moving to the simpler ones. (Testing the regular expressions in this order is crucial; otherwise, a plain straight would be mistakenly reported as a straight flush and a pair would appear to be a full house or a four-of-a-kind.)

```
Public Function EvalPokerScore(ByVal ParamArray cards() As String) As String
   ' Sort the array and create the sequence of values and of suits.
   Array.Sort(cards)
   Dim values As String = cards(0)(0) & cards(1)(0) & cards(2)(0) & _
      cards(3)(0) & cards(4)(0)
   Dim suits As String = cards(0)(1) & cards(1)(1) & cards(2)(1) & _
      cards(3)(1) & cards(4)(1)

      ' Check each sequence in order.
      If Regex.IsMatch(values, "12345|23456|34567|45678|56789|6789T|789JT|89JQT" _
            & "|9JKQT|1JKQT") AndAlso Regex.IsMatch(suits, "(.)\1\1\1\1") Then
         ' Notice that we must account for the fact that the values T,J,Q,K
         ' don't appear in this order after being sorted alphabetically.
         Return "StraightFlush"
      ElseIf Regex.IsMatch(values, "(.)\1\1\1") Then
         Return "FourOfAKind"
      ElseIf Regex.IsMatch(values, "(.)\1\1(.)\2|(.)\3(.)\4\4") Then
         ' A full house can be either 3+2 or 2+3 cards with the same values.
         Return "FullHouse"
      ElseIf Regex.IsMatch(suits, "(.)\1\1\1\1") Then
         Return "Flush"
      ElseIf Regex.IsMatch(values, _
            "12345|23456|34567|45678|56789|6789T|789JT|89JQT|9JKQT|1JKQT") Then
         Return "Straight"
      ElseIf Regex.IsMatch(values, "(.)\1\1") Then
         Return "ThreeOfAKind"
      ElseIf Regex.IsMatch(values, "(.)\1(.)\2") Then
         Return "TwoPairs"
      ElseIf Regex.IsMatch(values, "(.)\1") Then
         Return "OnePair"
      Else
         Return "HighCard"
      End If
End Function
```

Here are a few examples of how you can call the method and the results it returns:

```
EvalPokerScore("1H", "4H", "3H", "5H", "2H")   ' => StraightFlush
EvalPokerScore("9C", "9S", "8H", "TD", "9D")   ' => ThreeOfAKind
EvalPokerScore("8C", "KC", "TC", "QC", "9C")   ' => Flush
EvalPokerScore("TC", "KC", "QD", "8D", "9H")   ' => HighCard
```

The EvalPokerScore method is so concise that you might be surprised to learn that you can simplify it further. The trick is simple and leverages the fact that patterns are just strings and can be stored in a data structure. In this case, you can use a two-dimensional array so that you can test each pattern in a For loop. (Use a pattern that always matches, such as a plain dot, if you aren't interested in matching either the values or the suits.)

```
' (Replace the sequences of If statements in previous listing with this code.)
Dim scores(,) As String = {{"12345|23456|34567|45678|56789|6789T|" _
    & "789JT|89JQT|9JKQT|1JKQT", "(.)\1\1\1\1", "StraightFlush"}, _
    {"(.)\1\1\1", ".", "FourOfAKind"}, _
    {"(.)\1\1(.)\2|(.)\3(.)\4\4", ".", "FullHouse"}, _
    {".", "(.)\1\1\1\1", "Flush"}, _
    {"12345|23456|34567|45678|56789|6789T|789JT|89JQT|9JKQT|1JKQT", ".", "Straight"}, _
    {"(.)\1\1", ".", "ThreeOfAKind"}, _
    {"(.)\1.?(.)\2", ".", "TwoPairs"}, _
    {"(.)\1", ".", "OnePair"}}
For i As Integer = 0 To scores.GetUpperBound(0)
    If Regex.IsMatch(values, scores(i, 0)) And Regex.IsMatch(suits, scores(i, 1)) Then
        Return scores(i, 2)
    End If
Next
Return "HighCard"
End Function
```

The preceding code highlights the fact that regular expressions have the ability to replace code with just data, in this case a series of If statements with strings stored in an array. In this particular example, this feature isn't especially useful (other than to make the code more concise). In many applications, however, this ability can make a big difference. For example, you can store all the validation patterns in a database or an XML file so that you can actually change the behavior of your application without even recompiling its code.

Chapter 15

Files, Directories, and Streams

The Microsoft .NET Framework offers excellent support for working with files and directories through the following classes in the System.IO namespace:

- **Path**   Contains static methods to manipulate path information.

- **Directory, File**   Contain static methods that enable you to enumerate and manipulate directories and files.

- **DirectoryInfo, FileInfo**   Represent individual directories or files and expose the methods to query and manipulate their attributes.

- **DriveInfo**   Represents an individual drive and exposes the methods to query and manipulate its attributes. (This class is new in Microsoft .NET Framework version 2.0.)

- **FileSystemWatcher**   Can notify your program when a file or a directory is created, deleted, renamed, or modified in a folder or a folder tree.

The most important new feature in version 2.0 of the .NET Framework is the support for Microsoft Windows access control lists (ACLs) at the directory and file levels. ACLs are supported in a uniform way across the Directory, File, DirectoryInfo, and FileInfo types, so I gathered a detailed description of this new feature in a separate section named "Working with Access Control Lists."

> **Note**   To avoid long lines, code samples in this chapter assume that the following Imports
> statements are used at the file or project level:
>
> ```
> Imports Microsoft.VisualBasic.FileIO
> Imports System.Globalization
> Imports System.IO
> Imports System.IO.Compression
> Imports System.Net
> Imports System.Net.Sockets
> Imports System.Security
> Imports System.Security.AccessControl
> Imports System.Security.Principal
> Imports System.Text
> ```

The Path Type

The Path class is the simplest type in the System.IO namespace. It exposes static fields and methods that can help you process file and directory paths. Four static fields return information about valid drive and filename separators; you might want to query them to prepare your programs to run on other operating systems if and when the .NET Framework is ported to platforms other than the Windows operating system:

```
Console.WriteLine(Path.AltDirectorySeparatorChar)   ' => /
Console.WriteLine(Path.DirectorySeparatorChar)      ' => \
Console.WriteLine(Path.PathSeparator)               ' => ;
Console.WriteLine(Path.VolumeSeparatorChar)         ' => :
```

The GetInvalidPathChars and GetInvalidFileNameChars methods return an array containing the characters that can't be used in paths and filenames, respectively:

```
' Note: the actual output from following methods includes unprintable characters.
Console.WriteLine(Path.GetInvalidPathChars())       ' => <>|
Console.WriteLine(Path.GetInvalidFileNameChars())   ' => <>|:*?\/
```

The GetTempPath and GetTempFileName methods take no arguments and return the location of the Windows temporary directory and the name of a temporary file, respectively:

```
Console.WriteLine(Path.GetTempPath)
   ' => C:\Documents and Settings\Francesco\Local Settings\Temp
Console.WriteLine(Path.GetTempFileName)
   ' => C:\Documents and Settings\Francesco\Local Settings\Temp\tmp1FC7.tmp
```

Other methods enable you to extract information from a file path without having to worry about whether the file or the directory exists:

```
Dim file As String = "C:\MyApp\Bin\MyApp.exe"
Console.WriteLine(Path.GetDirectoryName(file))      ' => C:\MyApp\Bin
Console.WriteLine(Path.GetFileName(file))           ' => MyApp.exe
Console.WriteLine(Path.GetExtension(file))          ' => .exe
```

```
Console.WriteLine(Path.GetFileNameWithoutExtension(file)) ' => MyApp
Console.WriteLine(Path.GetPathRoot(file))                 ' => C:\
Console.WriteLine(Path.HasExtension(file))                ' => True
Console.WriteLine(Path.IsPathRooted(file))                ' => True
```

You can use the GetDirectoryName on files and directory names; in the latter case, it returns the name of the parent directory. For example, you can use this technique to retrieve the name of the main Windows directory (which is the parent folder of the Windows System32 directory):

```
Dim winDir As String = Path.GetDirectoryName(Environment.SystemDirectory)
```

The GetFullPath method expands a relative path to an absolute path, taking the current directory into account:

```
' Next line assumes that current directory is C:\MyApp.
Console.WriteLine(Path.GetFullPath("MyApp.Exe"))          ' => C:\MyApp\MyApp.Exe
```

The GetFullPath has a nice feature: it normalizes paths that contain double dots and enables you to prevent attacks based on malformed paths. For example, let's say that you must allow access to the c:\public directory and prevent access to the c:\private folder. If you check the folder without normalizing the path, a malicious hacker might access a file in the private folder by providing a string such as c:\public\..\private*filename*.

The ChangeExtension method returns a filename with a different extension:

```
Console.WriteLine(Path.ChangeExtension("MyApp.Exe", "dat")) ' => MyApp.dat
```

Finally, the Combine method takes a path and a filename and combines them into a valid filename, adding or discarding backslash characters as required:

```
Console.WriteLine(Path.Combine("C:\MyApp", "MyApp.Dat"))    ' => C:\MyApp\MyApp.Dat
```

The Directory and File Types

The Directory and File types contain only static methods that set or return information about entries in the file system. I cover both types in one section because they share most of their methods.

Enumerating Directories and Files

Thanks to the GetDirectories and GetFiles methods of the Directory type, you need very little code to iterate over all the directories and files of a directory tree. For example, the following code displays the structure of a directory tree and (optionally) the names of files in each folder:

```
Sub DisplayDirTree(ByVal dir As String, ByVal showFiles As Boolean, _
    Optional ByVal level As Integer = 0)
    ' Display the name of this folder with correct indentation.
    Console.WriteLine(New String("-"c, level * 2) & dir)
```

```
    Try
        ' Display all files in this folder with correct indentation.
        If showFiles Then
            For Each fname As String In Directory.GetFiles(dir)
                Console.WriteLine(New String(" "c, level * 2 + 2) & fname)
            Next
        End If
        ' A recursive call to display all the subdirectories in this folder
        For Each subdir As String In Directory.GetDirectories(dir)
            DisplayDirTree(subdir, showFiles, level + 1)
        Next
    Catch
        ' Do nothing if any error (presumably "Drive not ready").
    End Try
End Sub
```

You can pass a directory name to the DisplayDirTree procedure or display the directory tree of all the drives in your system by using the GetLogicalDrives method of the Directory type:

```
' Warning: this loop is going to take a *lot* of time.
For Each rootDir As String In Directory.GetLogicalDrives()
    DisplayDirTree(rootDir, True)
Next
```

The GetFiles and GetDirectories methods can take a second argument containing wildcards to filter the result:

```
' Display all the *.txt files in C:\DOCS.
For Each fname As String In Directory.GetFiles("c:\docs", "*.txt")
    Console.WriteLine(fname)
Next
```

 A new, welcome addition to the GetFiles and GetDirectories methods is the ability to automatically search in subdirectories. For example, the following code displays all the DLLs in the c:\windows directory tree:

```
For Each file As String In Directory.GetFiles("c:\windows", "*.dll", _
        System.IO.SearchOption.AllDirectories)
    Console.WriteLine(file)
Next
```

Notice that you must fully qualify the SearchOption argument because both the System.IO and the Microsoft.VisualBasic.FileIO namespaces contain a type with this name.

Manipulating Directories and Files

As their names suggest, the SetCurrentDirectory and GetCurrentDirectory methods of the Directory type set and return the current directory:

```
' Save the current directory.
Dim currDir As String = Directory.GetCurrentDirectory
' Change the current directory to something else.
```

```
Directory.SetCurrentDirectory("C:\Temp")
...
' Restore the current directory.
Directory.SetCurrentDirectory(currDir)
```

The Directory.CreateDirectory method creates a directory and all the intermediate directories in the path if necessary:

```
' Next line works even if the C:\MyApp directory doesn't exist yet.
Directory.CreateDirectory("C:\MyApp\Data")
```

The Directory and File types have several methods in common. The Exists method checks whether a file or a directory exists, the Delete method removes it, and the Move method moves a file or an entire directory to a different folder and possibly renames it in the process:

```
If File.Exists("c:\data.txt") Then
   File.Move("c:\data.txt", "d:\data.txt")
End If
```

By default, the Directory.Delete method can remove only an empty directory, but it has an overload that enables you to remove an entire directory tree:

```
' Delete the c:\tempdir folder and all its subfolders.
Directory.Delete("c:\tempdir", True)
```

You can use the GetCreationTime, GetLastAccessTime, GetLastWriteTime, and GetAttributes static methods to display information about a file or a directory or to filter files according to their attributes:

```
' Display only read-only .txt files in the c:\docs folder.
For Each fname As String In Directory.GetFiles("c:\docs", "*.txt")
   If CBool(File.GetAttributes(fname) And FileAttributes.ReadOnly) Then
      Console.WriteLine(fname)
   End If
Next
```

The SetCreationTime, SetLastWriteTime, and SetLastAccessTime methods let you modify the date attributes of a file or directory:

```
' Change the access date and time of all files in C:\Docs.
For Each fname As String In Directory.GetFiles("C:\Docs")
   File.SetLastAccessTime(fname, Date.Now)
Next
```

You can use the SetCreationTime method to create a "touch" utility that modifies the last write time of all the files specified on its command line:

```
' Change the access date/time of all files whose names are passed on the command line.
Sub Main(ByVal args() As String)
   For Each fname As String In args
      File.SetCreationTime(fname, Date.Now)
   Next
End Sub
```

Each Get*Xxxx*Time and Set*Xxxx*Time method that reads or modifies a date attribute has a matching Get*Xxxx*TimeUtc and Set*Xxxx*TimeUtc method that works with coordinated universal time (UTC), that is, an absolute DateTime value that isn't affected by the current time zone. These methods were added in Microsoft .NET Framework version 1.1 to enable you to compare files that are scattered across the Internet. For example, you can use the File.GetLast-WriteUtc method to implement a replication program that compares the files at two Internet sites in different time zones and overwrites the older one with the newer version.

The Directory type doesn't expose a GetAttributes method, but the File.GetAttributes method works also for directories, so this limitation isn't an issue. The SetAttributes and GetAttributes methods set or return a bit-coded FileAttributes value, which is a combination of Normal (no attributes), Archive, ReadOnly, Hidden, System, Directory, Compressed, Encrypted, Temporary, NotContentIndexed, and a few other values:

```
' Display system and hidden files in C:\.
For Each fname As String In Directory.GetFiles("C:\")
   Dim attr As FileAttributes = File.GetAttributes(fname)
   ' Display the file if marked as hidden or system (or both).
   If CBool(attr And FileAttributes.Hidden) Or CBool(attr And FileAttributes.System) Then
      Console.WriteLine(fname)
   End If
Next
```

With a little bit of tweaking, you can make the If expression more concise, as follows:

```
If CBool(attr And (FileAttributes.Hidden Or FileAttributes.System)) Then
   …
```

The File type exposes a few methods that are missing in the Directory type. The Copy method can copy a file and overwrite the destination if necessary:

```
' True in the last argument means "overwrite the target file" if it exists already.
File.Copy("c:\data.bin", "c:\backup\data.bin", True)
```

Three methods of the File type are new in .NET Framework 2.0. The Replace method performs a move+copy operation as a single command: it creates a backup copy of the destination file, and then copies the source file to the destination file. An optional fourth argument, if True, tells .NET to ignore any error that might occur when merging the attributes or the ACL of the two files involved in the command:

```
' Back up the current contents of c:\data.bin into c:\data.bak, and
' then copy the contents of c:\newdata.bin into c:\data.bin.
File.Replace("c:\data.bin", "c:\newdata.bin", "c:\data.bak", True)
```

The Encrypt method encrypts a file on an NTFS file system partition so that it can be read only by the current user; the process can be reversed by running the Decrypt method:

```
' Ensure that no other user account can read a file during a lengthy operation.
Try
   File.Encrypt("c:\secretdata.txt")
   …
```

```
Finally
   ' Or just delete the file…
   File.Decrypt("c:\secretdata.txt")
End Try
```

Reading and Writing Files

 In addition to the operations illustrated in the previous section, the File object can perform atomic read and write operations on text and binary files in a very simple manner. All the methods that enable you to perform these tasks have been added in .NET Framework 2.0.

You read an entire text file by means of the ReadAllText method, and write it using the WriteAllText method:

```
' Read a text file, convert its contents to uppercase, and save it to another file.
Dim text As String = File.ReadAllText("c:\testfile.txt")
File.WriteAllText("c:\upper.txt", text.ToUpper())
```

Alternatively, you can read and write an array of strings by means of the ReadAllLines and WriteAllLines methods:

```
' Read the source file into an array of strings.
Dim lines() As String = File.ReadAllLines("c:\source.txt")
Dim count As Integer = 0
' Delete empty lines, by moving non-empty lines toward lower indices.
For i As Integer = 0 To lines.Length - 1
   If lines(i).Trim.Length > 0 Then
      lines(count) = lines(i)
      count += 1
   End If
Next
' Trim excess lines and write to destination file.
ReDim Preserve lines(count - 1)
File.WriteAllLines("c:\dest.txt", lines)
```

The AppendAllText method appends a string to an existing text file or creates a text file if the file doesn't exist yet:

```
' Append a message to a log file, creating the file if necessary.
Dim msg As String = String.Format("Application started at {0}{1}", Now, ControlChars.CrLf)
File.AppendAllText("c:\log.txt", msg)
```

The five methods shown so far have an overloaded version that accepts a System.Text.Encoding object. (See Chapter 12, ".NET Basic Types," for more details.) The ReadAllBytes and WriteAll-Bytes methods are similar, except they work with a Byte array and therefore are more useful with binary files:

```
' Very simple encryption of a binary file
Dim bytes() As Byte = File.ReadAllBytes("c:\source.dat")
' Flip every other bit in each byte.
For i As Integer = 0 To bytes.Length - 1
   bytes(i) = bytes(i) Xor CByte(&H55)
```

```
Next
' Write it to a different file.
File.WriteAllBytes("c:\dest.dat", bytes)
```

In addition to the read and write methods that process the entire file, the File type exposes methods that open the file for reading, writing, or appending data and return a FileStream object. The most flexible of these methods is the Open method, which takes a filename and up to three additional arguments:

```
Dim fs As FileStream = File.Open(FileName, FileMode, FileAccess, FileShare)
```

Let's see these arguments in more detail:

- The FileMode argument can be Append, Create, CreateNew, Open, OpenOrCreate, or Truncate. Open and Append modes fail if the file doesn't exist; Create and CreateNew fail if the file exists already. Use OpenOrCreate to open a file or to create one if it doesn't exist yet.

- The FileAccess argument specifies what the application wants to do with the file and can be Read, Write, or ReadWrite.

- The FileShare argument tells which operations other FileStreams can perform on the open file. It can be None (all operations are prohibited), ReadWrite (all operations are allowed), Read, Write, Delete (new in .NET Framework 2.0), or Inheritable (not supported directly by Win32).

The File class exposes three variants of the Open method: Create, OpenRead, and OpenWrite. Like the generic Open method, these variants return a FileStream object. There are also three specific methods for working with text files (CreateText, OpenText, and AppendText), which return a StreamReader or StreamWriter object. I explain how to use the FileStream, the StreamReader, and the StreamWriter objects later in this chapter.

The DirectoryInfo and FileInfo Types

The DirectoryInfo and FileInfo types represent individual directories and files. Both types inherit from the FileSystemInfo abstract class and therefore have several properties in common, namely, Name, FullName, Extension, Exists, Attributes, CreationTime, CreationTimeUtc, LastWriteTime, LastWriteTimeUtc, LastAccessTime, and LastAccessTimeUtc. They also have two methods in common: Delete and Refresh, where the latter ensures that all properties are up-to-date.

You can get a reference to a DirectoryInfo or FileInfo object by using its constructor method, which takes the path of a specific directory or file:

```
' Create a DirectoryInfo object that points to C:\.
Dim diRoot As New DirectoryInfo("c:\")
' Create a FileInfo object that points to c:\autoexec.bat.
Dim fiAutoexec As New FileInfo("c:\autoexec.bat")
```

Once you have a reference to a DirectoryInfo object, you can use its methods to enumerate the folder's contents and get other DirectoryInfo or FileInfo objects. (You can also apply filter criteria.)

```
' List the directories in c:\.
For Each di As DirectoryInfo In diRoot.GetDirectories()
   Console.WriteLine(di.Name)
Next

' List all the *.txt files in c:\.
For Each fi As FileInfo In diRoot.GetFiles("*.txt")
   Console.WriteLine(fi.Name)
Next
```

The DirectoryInfo.GetFileSystemInfos method returns an array of FileSystemInfo objects. Both the DirectoryInfo and FileInfo types inherit from the FileSystemInfo type, so you can write process both files and subdirectories in a folder with a single loop:

```
For Each fsi As FileSystemInfo In diRoot.GetFileSystemInfos()
   ' Use the [dir] or [file] prefix.
   Dim prefix As String = Nothing
   If CBool(fsi.Attributes And FileAttributes.Directory) Then
      prefix = "dir"
   Else
      prefix = "file"
   End If
   ' Print type, name, and creation date.
   Console.WriteLine("[{0}] {1} - {2}", prefix, fsi.Name, fsi.CreationTime)
Next
```

Most of the members of the DirectoryInfo and FileInfo types perform the same action as do the static methods with the same or similar names exposed by the Directory and File types. For example, the FileInfo.CreationTime property enables you to read and modify the creation date of a file, just like the File object's GetCreationTime and SetCreationTime methods do. Among the few exceptions is the FileInfo.Length property, which returns the length of a file:

```
' List all empty files in c:\.
For Each fi As FileInfo In diRoot.GetFiles()
   If fi.Length = 0 Then Console.WriteLine(fi.Name)
Next
```

You can get the parent directory of a file in two ways: the DirectoryName property returns the name of the directory, whereas the Directory property returns the DirectoryInfo object that represents that directory:

```
' List all the files in the same directory as the FileInfo object named fiDoc.
For Each fi As FileInfo In fiDoc.Directory.GetFiles()
   Console.WriteLine(fi.Name)
Next
```

You can create a new folder by means of the CreateSubdirectory method of the DirectoryInfo object:

```
' Create a folder named Reports in the c:\tempdocs directory.
Dim diDocs As New DirectoryInfo("c:\tempdocs")
diDocs.CreateSubdirectory("Reports")
```

Both the DirectoryInfo and the FileInfo types expose a MoveTo and a Delete method, but the DirectoryInfo.Delete method can take a Boolean argument, which, if True, causes the deletion of the entire subdirectory tree:

```
' (Continuing previous code snippet…)
' Delete the c:\tempdocs directory and its subfolders.
diDocs.Delete(True)
```

In version 2.0 of the .NET Framework, the FileInfo object has been expanded with the IsReadOnly property (True if the file is read-only) and three methods: Encrypt, Decrypt, and Replace. For more details about these methods, read the description of methods with the same names in the section titled "The Directory and File Types" earlier in the chapter:

```
' Encrypt all the writable files in the c:\private directory.
Dim diPrivate As New DirectoryInfo("c:\private")
For Each fi As FileInfo In diPrivate.GetFiles()
   If Not fi.IsReadOnly Then fi.Encrypt()
Next
```

Finally, the FileInfo object exposes six methods that open a file, namely, Open, OpenRead, OpenWrite, OpenText, CreateText, AppendText. They have the same purpose as the static methods with the same names exposed by the File type.

> **Note**   At the end of this overview of the DirectoryInfo and FileInfo objects you might wonder whether you should use the instance methods of these types rather than the static methods with the same names exposed by the Directory and File types, respectively. In most cases, there is no "correct" decision and it's mostly a matter of programming style and the specific needs that arise in a given program. For example, I find myself more comfortable with the Directory and File types, but I use the DirectoryInfo and FileInfo objects if I need to buffer the data about a directory or a file, or if I need to process files and directories in a uniform manner (as made possible by the FileSystemInfo base class). Interestingly, the FileInfo object doesn't expose some of the methods that have been added to the File type in .NET Framework 2.0, such as ReadAllText or WriteAllLines; thus, in general, using the File type gives you a little extra flexibility that is missing from the FileInfo class.

The DriveInfo Type

Previous versions of the .NET Framework expose no classes for retrieving information about existing drives, and thus you must use either PInvoke calls to the Windows API or Windows Management Instrumentation (WMI) classes. This gap has been filled in version 2.0 with the introduction of the DriveInfo type.

You can create a DriveInfo object in two ways: by passing a drive letter to its constructor or by means of the GetDrives static method, which returns an array containing information about all the installed drives:

```
' Display the volume label of drive C.
Dim driveC As New DriveInfo("c:")
Console.WriteLine(driveC.VolumeLabel)
```

When enumerating drives, it's crucial that you don't attempt to read any member before testing the IsReady property:

```
' Display name and total size of all available drives.
For Each di As DriveInfo In DriveInfo.GetDrives()
   If di.IsReady Then
      Console.WriteLine("{0}  {1:N}", di.Name, di.TotalSize)
   End If
Next
```

The DriveInfo object exposes the following properties: Name, VolumeLabel, RootDirectory (the DirectoryInfo object that represents the root folder), DriveType (an enumerated value that can be Fixed, Removable, CDRom, Ram, Network, and Unknown), DriveFormat (a string such as NTFS or FAT32), TotalSize (the capacity of the drive in bytes), Total-FreeSpace (the total number of free bytes), and AvailableFreeSpace (the number of available free bytes; can be less than TotalFreeSpace if quotas are used). All the properties are read-only, which is quite understandable (even though I'd surely like to increase the amount of free space on a drive by simply setting a property!), except for the VolumeLabel property:

```
' Change the volume label of drive D.
Dim driveD As New DriveInfo("d:")
driveD.VolumeLabel = "MyData"
```

The following loop displays in a tabular format information about all the installed drives, while skipping over the drives that aren't ready:

```
Console.WriteLine("{0,-6}{1,-10}{2,-8}{3,-16}{4,18}{5,18}", _
   "Name", "Label", "Type", "Format", "TotalSize", "TotalFreeSpace")
Console.WriteLine(New String("-"c, 78))
For Each di As DriveInfo In DriveInfo.GetDrives()
   If di.IsReady Then
      Console.WriteLine("{0,-6}{1,-10}{2,-8}{3,-16}{4,18:N0}{5,18:N0}", _
         di.Name, di.VolumeLabel, di.DriveType.ToString, di.DriveFormat, _
         di.TotalSize, di.TotalFreeSpace)
   Else
      Console.WriteLine("{0,-6}(not ready)", di.Name)
   End If
Next
```

Here's an example of what you might see in the console window:

```
Name  Label    Type    Format               TotalSize   TotalFreeSpace
--------------------------------------------------------------------------
C:\            Fixed   NTFS             20,974,428,160    8,009,039,872
D:\   DATA     Fixed   NTFS             39,028,953,088   10,244,005,888
E:\   (not ready)
```

The FileSystemWatcher Type

The FileSystemWatcher component lets you monitor a directory or a directory tree so that you get a notification when something happens inside it—for example, when a file or a subdirectory is created, deleted, or renamed or when the folder's attributes are changed. This component can be useful in many circumstances. For example, say that you're creating an application that automatically encrypts all the files stored in a given directory. Without this component, you should poll the directory at regular time intervals (typically using a Timer), but the FileSystemWatcher component makes this task easier. Another good example of how this component can be useful is when you cache a data file in memory to access its contents quickly, but need to reload it when another application modifies the data.

This component works on Microsoft Windows Millennium Edition (Me), Windows NT, Windows 2000, Windows XP, and Windows Server 2003.

Initializing a FileSystemWatcher Component

You can create a FileSystemWatcher component in either of two ways: by means of code or by dragging it from the Components tab of the Toolbox to the tray area of a Windows Forms class, a Web Forms page, or another Microsoft Visual Studio designer. There's no noticeable difference in performance or flexibility, so any method is fine. The demo application uses a component in a form's component tray area, which I have renamed fsw (see Figure 15-1), but creating it through code is equally simple:

```
' Use WithEvents to be able to trap events from this object.
Dim WithEvents fsw As New FileSystemWatcher()
```

Before you use this component, you must initialize at least its Path, IncludeSubdirectories, Filter, and NotifyFilter properties. The Path property is the name of the directory that you want to watch; notice that you're notified of changes occurring inside the directory, but not of changes to the directory's attributes (such as its Hidden or ReadOnly attribute).

The IncludeSubdirectories property should be set to False if you want to be notified of any change inside the specified directory only, or to True if you want to watch for changes in the entire directory tree whose root is the folder specified by the Path property.

The Filter property lets you specify which files you're interested in; for example, use *.* to get notifications about all the files in the directory or *.txt to watch only files with the .txt extension. The default value for this property is a null string, which means all files (same as *.*).

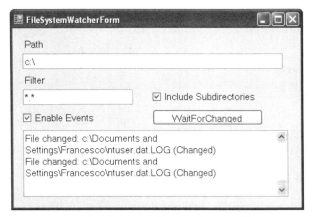

Figure 15-1   The demo application that enables you to experiment with the FileSystemWatcher component

The NotifyFilter property is a bit-coded value that specifies which kind of modifications are announced by means of the component's Changed event. This property can be a combination of one or more NotifyFilters enumerated values: Attributes, CreationTime, DirectoryName, FileName, LastAccess, LastWrite, Security, and Size. The initial value of this property is Last-Write Or FileName Or DirectoryName, so by default you don't get notifications when an attribute is changed.

Here's an example of how you can set up a FileSystemWatcher component to watch for events in the C:\Windows directory and its subdirectories:

```
Dim WithEvents fsw As New FileSystemWatcher()
…
fsw.Path = "c:\windows"
fsw.IncludeSubdirectories = True          ' Watch subdirectories.
fsw.Filter = "*.dll"                      ' Watch only DLL files.
' Add attribute changes to the list of changes that can fire events.
fsw.NotifyFilter = fsw.NotifyFilter Or NotifyFilters.Attributes
' Enable event notification.
fsw.EnableRaisingEvents = True
```

Getting Notifications

Once you've set up the component correctly, you can get a notification when something happens. You can achieve this by writing event handlers or using the WaitForChanged method.

Events

The simplest way to get a notification from the FileSystemWatcher component is by writing handlers for the component's events. However, events don't fire until you set EnableRaising-Events to True. The Created, Deleted, and Changed events receive a FileSystemEventArgs object, which exposes two important properties: Name (the name of the file that has been created, deleted, or changed) and FullPath (its complete path):

```
Private Sub fsw_Created(ByVal sender As Object, _
    ByVal e As FileSystemEventArgs) Handles fsw.Created
  Console.WriteLine("File created: {0}", e.FullPath)
End Sub

Private Sub fsw_Deleted(ByVal sender As Object, _
    ByVal e As FileSystemEventArgs) Handles fsw.Deleted
  Console.WriteLine ("File deleted: {0}", e.FullPath)
End Sub

Private Sub fsw_Changed(ByVal sender As Object, _
    ByVal e As FileSystemEventArgs) Handles fsw.Changed
  Console.WriteLine ("File changed: {0}", e.FullPath)
End Sub
```

The FileSystemEventArgs object also exposes a ChangeType enumerated property, which tells whether the event is a create, delete, or change event. You can use this property to use a single handler to manage all three events, as in this code:

```
Private Sub fsw_All(ByVal sender As Object, ByVal e As FileSystemEventArgs) _
    Handles fsw.Changed, fsw.Created, fsw.Deleted
  Console.WriteLine("File changed: {0} ({1})", e.FullPath, e.ChangeType)
End Sub
```

The Changed event receives no information about the type of change that fired the event, such as a change in the file's LastWrite date or attributes. Finally, the Renamed event receives a RenamedEventArgs object, which exposes two additional properties: OldName (the name of the file before being renamed) and OldFullPath (its complete path):

```
Private Sub fsw_Renamed(ByVal sender As Object, ByVal e As RenamedEventArgs) _
    Handles fsw.Renamed
  Console.WriteLine("File renamed: {0} => {1}", e.OldFullPath, e.FullPath)
End Sub
```

You can also have multiple FileSystemWatcher components forward their events to the same event handler. In this case, use the first argument to detect which specific component raised the event.

The FileSystemWatcher component raises one event for each file and for each action on the file. For example, if you delete 10 files, you receive 10 distinct Deleted events. If you move 10 files from one directory to another, you receive 10 Deleted events from the source directory and 10 Created events from the destination directory.

The WaitForChanged Method

If your application doesn't perform any operation other than waiting for changes in the specified path, or if you monitor file operations from a secondary thread, you can write simpler and more efficient code by using the WaitForChanged method. This method is synchronous and doesn't return until a file change is detected or the (optional) timeout expires. On return from this method the application receives a WaitForChangedResult structure, whose fields enable you to determine whether the timeout elapsed, the type of event that occurred, and the name of the involved file:

```
' Create a *new* FileSystemWatcher component with values from
' the txtPath and txtFilter controls.
Dim tmpFsw As New FileSystemWatcher(txtPath.Text, txtFilter.Text)
' Wait max 10 seconds for any file event.
Dim res As WaitForChangedResult = tmpFsw.WaitForChanged(WatcherChangeTypes.All, 10000)

' Check whether the operation timed out.
If res.TimedOut Then
    Console.WriteLine("10 seconds have elapsed without an event")
Else
    Console.WriteLine("Event: {0} ({1}), res.Name, res.ChangeType.ToString())
End If
```

The WaitForChanged method traps changes only in the directory the Path property points to and ignores the IncludeSubdirectories property. For this reason, the WaitForChangedResult structure includes a Name field but not a FullPath field. The first argument you pass to the Wait-ForChanged method lets you further restrict the kind of file operation you want to intercept:

```
' Pause the application until the c:\temp\temp.dat file is deleted.
tmpFsw = New FileSystemWatcher("c:\temp", "temp.dat")
tmpFsw.WaitForChanged(WatcherChangeTypes.Deleted)
```

Buffer Overflows

You should be aware of potential problems when too many events fire in a short time. The File-SystemWatcher component uses an internal buffer to keep track of file system actions so that events can be raised for each one of them even if the application can't serve them fast enough. By default, this internal buffer is 8 KB long and can store about 160 events. Each event takes 16 bytes, plus 2 bytes for each character in the filename. (Filenames are stored as Unicode characters.) If you anticipate a lot of file activity, you should increase the size of the buffer by setting the InternalBufferSize property to a larger value. The size should be an integer multiple of the operating system's page size (4 KB under Microsoft Windows 2000 and later versions). Alternatively, you can use the NotifyFilter property to limit the number of change operations that fire the Changed event or set IncludeSubdirectories to False if you don't need to monitor an entire directory tree. (Use multiple FileSystemWatcher components to monitor individual subdirectories if you aren't interested in monitoring all the subdirectories under a given path.)

You can't use the Filter property to prevent the internal buffer from overflowing because this property filters out files only after they've been added to the buffer. When the internal buffer overflows, you get an Error event:

```
Private Sub fsw_Error(ByVal sender As Object, ByVal e As ErrorEventArgs) _
        Handles fsw.Error
    Console.WriteLine("FileSystemWatcher error: {0}", e.GetException().Message)
End Sub
```

If you notice that your application receives this event, you should change your event handling strategy. For example, you might store all the events in a queue and have them served by another thread.

Troubleshooting

By default, the Created, Deleted, Renamed, and Changed events run in a thread taken from the system thread pool. (See Chapter 20, "Threads," for more information about the thread pool.) Because Windows Forms controls aren't thread safe, you should avoid accessing any control or the form itself from inside the FileSystemWatcher component's event handlers. If you find this limitation unacceptable, you should assign a Windows Forms control to the component's SynchronizingObject property, as in this code:

```
' Use the Form object as the synchronizing object.
fsw.SynchronizingObject = Me
```

The preceding code ensures that all event handlers run in the same thread that serves the form itself. When you create a FileSystemWatcher component using the Visual Studio 2005 designer, this property is automatically assigned the hosting form object.

Here are a few more tips about the FileSystemWatcher component and the problems you might need to solve when using it:

- The FileSystemWatcher component starts raising events when the Path property is non-empty and the EnableRaisingEvents property is True. You can also prevent the component from raising unwanted events during the initialization phase of a Windows Forms class by bracketing your setup statements between a call to the BeginInit method and a call to the EndInit method. (This is the approach used by the Visual Studio designer.)

- As I mentioned before, this component works only on Windows Me, Windows NT, Windows 2000, Windows XP, and Windows Server 2003. It raises an error when it points to a path on machines running earlier versions of the operating system. Remote machines must have one of these operating systems to work properly, but you can't monitor a remote Windows NT system from another Windows NT machine. You can use UNC-based directory names only on Windows 2000 or later systems. The FileSystemWatcher component doesn't work on CD-ROM and DVD drives because their contents can't change.

- In some cases, you might get multiple Created events, depending on how a file is created and on the application that creates it. For example, when you create a new file using Notepad, you see the following sequence of events: Created, Deleted, Created, and Changed. (The first event pair fires because Notepad checks whether the file exists by attempting to create it.)

- A change in a file can generate an extra event in its parent directory as well because the directory maintains information about the files it contains (their size, last write date, and so on).

- If the directory the Path property points to is renamed, the FileSystemWatcher component continues to work correctly. However, in this case, the Path property returns the old directory name, so you might get an error if you use it. (This happens because the component references the directory by its handle, which doesn't change if the directory is renamed.)

- If you create a directory inside the path being watched and the IncludeSubdirectories property is True, the new subdirectory is watched as well.

- When a large file is created in the directory, you might not be able to read the entire file immediately because it's still owned by the process that's writing data to it. You should protect any access to the original file with a Try block and, if an exception is thrown, attempt the operation again some milliseconds later.

- When the user deletes a file in a directory, a new file is created in the Recycle Bin directory.

Working with Access Control Lists

One of the most important new features in .NET Framework 2.0 is the support for reading and modifying Windows access control lists (ACLs) from managed code without having to call functions in the Windows API as was necessary in previous .NET versions. To support this new feature, Microsoft introduced the System.Security.AccessControl namespace, added a few types to the System.Security.Principal namespace, and, above all, added several methods to all the .NET types that represent system resources to which an ACL can be associated. Examples of such resources are files, directories, the registry, Active Directory objects, and many types in the System.Threading namespace. In this chapter, I focus on file resource exclusively, but the concepts I introduce are valid for other resource types.

Account Names and Security Identifiers

Before you can see how to manipulate file ACLs, you must become familiar with three classes in System.Security.Principal namespace. The IdentityReference is an abstract type that represents a Windows identity and is the base class for the other two classes, NTAccount and SecurityIdentifier.

The IdentityReference type has one important property, Value, which returns the textual representation of the identity. The NTAccount type overrides this property to return an account or group name, such as BUILTIN\Users or NT AUTHORITY\SYSTEM, whereas the SecurityIdentifier class overrides the property to return the textual representation of a security identifier (SID), for example, S-1-5-21-583907252-1563985344-1957994488-1003. (This representation is also known as Security Descriptor Definition Language format, or SDDL.) The following code creates an NTAccount object and translates it to the security identifier (SID) format by means of the Translate method that the NTAccount type inherits from IdentityReference:

```
Dim nta As New NTAccount("BUILTIN\Administrators")
Dim sia As SecurityIdentifier = _
   DirectCast(nta.Translate(GetType(SecurityIdentifier)), SecurityIdentifier)
```

```
Console.WriteLine("Name={0}, SID={1}", nta.Value, sia.Value)
   ' => Name=BUILTIN\Administrators, SID=S-1-5-32-544
```

The NTAccount type also exposes a constructor that takes two arguments, the domain name and the account name:

```
nta = New NTAccount("CADomain", "Francesco")
```

Interestingly, Microsoft Visual Basic 2005 supports the equal to (=) and not equal to (<>) operators to enable you to test two NTAccount or two SecurityIdentifier objects. The = operator always returns False when comparing two objects of different types; therefore, you must always convert an NTAccount to a SecurityIdentifier object (or vice versa) before comparing the objects:

```
' (Continuing previous code snippet…)
Dim isSameAccount As Boolean = (nta = sia)                  ' => False
isSameAccount = (nta.Translate(GetType(SecurityIdentifier)) = sia)  ' => True
```

The constructor of the SecurityIdentifier type is overloaded to take either a SID in textual format or a WellKnownSidType enumerated value, such as AccountGuestSid (guest users), AnonymousSid (the anonymous account), and LocalSystemSid (the Local System account):

```
' Create the SecurityIdentifier corresponding to the Administrators group.
' (Second argument must be non-Nothing for some kinds of well-known SIDs.)
Dim sia2 As New SecurityIdentifier(WellKnownSidType.BuiltinAdministratorsSid, Nothing)
Console.WriteLine(sia2.Value)                        ' => S-1-5-32-544
Dim nta2 As NTAccount = DirectCast(sia2.Translate(GetType(NTAccount)), NTAccount)
Console.WriteLine(nta2.Value)                        ' => BUILTIN\Administrators

' Here's another way to get a reference to the same account.
sia2 = New SecurityIdentifier("S-1-5-32-544")
```

You can retrieve the SecurityIdentifier object corresponding to the current Windows user as follows:

```
Dim siUser As SecurityIdentifier = WindowsIdentity.GetCurrent().User
```

Another common use of the SecurityIdentifier type is for checking whether a user is in a given group or role:

```
' Create the WindowsPrincipal corresponding to current user.
Dim wp As New WindowsPrincipal(WindowsIdentity.GetCurrent())
' Create the SecurityIdentifier for the BUILTIN\Administrator group.
Dim siAdmin As New SecurityIdentifier(WellKnownSidType.BuiltinAdministratorsSid, Nothing)
' Check whether the current user is an administrator.
Console.WriteLine("Is a power user = {0}", wp.IsInRole(siAdmin))
```

The DirectorySecurity and FileSecurity Types

The System.Security.AccessControl namespace includes nearly all the types that let you control the ACLs associated with a Windows resource, such as the FileSecurity, DirectorySecurity, and RegistrySecurity types. (Only two ACL-related types aren't in this namespace, namely,

System.DirectoryServices.ActiveDirectorySecurity and Microsoft.Iis.Metabase.MetaKeySecurity.) In this section, I focus on the FileSecurity and DirectorySecurity objects, which, not surprisingly, are very similar. In fact, both of them inherit from the FileSystemSecurity class, which, in turn, inherits from NativeObjectSecurity.

You can get a reference to a FileSecurity or DirectorySecurity object in one of the following two ways. First, you can pass a path to its constructor, together with an AccessControlSection enumerated value that specifies which security information you're interested in:

```
' Retrieve only access information related to the c:\docs folder.
Dim dirSec As New DirectorySecurity("c:\docs", AccessControlSections.Access)
' Retrieve all security information related to the c:\test.doc file.
Dim fileSec As New FileSecurity("c:\test.txt", AccessControlSections.All)
```

(Valid values for AccessControlSections are Access, Owner, Audit, Group, All, and None.) Second, you can use the GetAccessControl method exposed by the Directory, File, DirectoryInfo, and FileInfo types:

```
' (This code is equivalent to previous snippet.)
dirSec = Directory.GetAccessControl("c:\docs", AccessControlSections.Access)
fileSec = File.GetAccessControl("c:\test.txt", AccessControlSections.All)
```

The simplest operation you can perform with a FileSecurity or a DirectorySecurity object is retrieving the discretionary access control list (DACL) or system access control list (SACL) associated with the resource in SDDL format:

```
' Get access-related security information for the c:\test.txt file.
Console.WriteLine(fileSec.GetSecurityDescriptorSddlForm(AccessControlSections.Access))
    ' => D:AI(D;;DCLCRPCR;;;SY)(A;ID;FA;;;BA)…
```

> **Note**   A discretionary access control list (DACL) defines who is granted or denied access to an object. Each Windows object is associated with a DACL, which consists of a list of access control entries (ACEs); each ACE defines a trustee and specifies the access rights that are granted, denied, or audited for that trustee. If the object has no DACL, everyone can use the object; otherwise, each ACE is tested until the user (or the process that is impersonating the user) is granted the access to the object. If no ACE grants this permission, the user is prevented from using the object.
>
> A system access control list (SACL) enables administrators to log attempts to use a given object. A SACL contains one or more ACEs; each ACE specifies a trustee and the type of access (from that trustee) that causes the system to create an entry in the security event log. The entry in the log can be generated when the access succeeds, fails, or both.

An SDDL string is rarely useful, though, or at least it is hard for humans to decode. To get the ACL in readable format you can use one of the following methods: GetOwner (to retrieve the owner of the resource), GetGroup (to retrieve the primary group associated with the owner), GetAccessRules (to retrieve the collection of access rules), and GetAuditRules (to retrieve the collection of audit rules). These three methods have similar syntax.

The GetOwner and GetGroup methods return a single object that derives from Identity-Reference, therefore either an NTAccount or a SecurityIdentifier object. You specify which object you want to be returned by passing a proper System.Type object as an argument:

```
' Get the owner of the C:\Test.doc as an NTAccount object.
Dim nta3 As NTAccount = DirectCast(fileSec.GetOwner(GetType(NTAccount)), NTAccount)
' Get the primary group of the owner of C:\Test.doc as a SecurityIdentifier object.
Dim sia3 As SecurityIdentifier = DirectCast(fileSec.GetGroup( _
   GetType(SecurityIdentifier)), SecurityIdentifier)
```

Once you have an NTAccount or a SecurityIdentifier object you can query all of its properties, as shown in the previous section.

The GetAccessRules method returns a collection of AccessRule objects, where each individual member in the collection tells whether a given action is granted or denied to a given user or group of users. Similar to the GetOwner and GetGroup methods, you must pass a System.Type object that specifies whether the user name or group is expressed by means of an NTAccount object or a SecurityIdentifier object:

```
' Display the header of the result table.
Console.WriteLine("{0,-25}{1,-30}{2,-8}{3,-6}", "User", "Rights", "Access", "Inherited")
Console.WriteLine(New String("-"c, 72))
' First argument tells whether to include access rules explicitly set for the object.
' Second argument tells whether to include inherited rules.
For Each fsar As FileSystemAccessRule In fileSec.GetAccessRules(True, True, _
      GetType(NTAccount))
   Console.WriteLine("{0,-25}{1,-30}{2,-8}{3,-6}", fsar.IdentityReference.Value, _
      fsar.FileSystemRights, fsar.AccessControlType, fsar.IsInherited)
Next
```

The FileSystemAccessRule.FileSystemRights property returns a bit-coded FileSystemRights enumerated type that exposes values such as Read, Write, Modify, Delete, ReadAndExecute, FullControl, ReadAttributes, WriteAttributes, and many others. (See Table 15-1.) The FileSystemAccessRule.AccessControlType returns an enumerated value that can only be Allow or Deny. Here's the kind of output the previous code produces in the console window:

```
User                     Rights                       Access   Inherited
------------------------------------------------------------------------
BUILTIN\Administrators   FullControl                  Allow    True
NT AUTHORITY\SYSTEM      FullControl                  Allow    True
DESKTOP01\FrancescoB     Write                        Deny     False
BUILTIN\Users            ReadAndExecute, Synchronize  Allow    True
```

You can compare these results with the actual permissions set for the specific file. To do so, right-click the file in Windows Explorer, select the Properties command from the context menu, and switch to the Security tab, as shown in Figure 15-2. (If you don't see this tab, select the Folder Options command from the Tools menu in Windows Explorer, switch to the View tab, and ensure that the Use Simple File Sharing option is cleared.) Some attributes are visible in the Advanced Security Settings dialog box, which you display by clicking the Advanced button.

Figure 15-2   The Security tab of the Properties dialog box (left) and the Advanced Security Settings dialog box (right) of a file

Table 15-1   Values of the FileSystemRights Enumerated Type

Value	Description
AppendData	Specifies the right to append data to the end of a file.
ChangePermissions	Specifies the right to change the security and audit rules associated with a file or folder.
CreateDirectories	Specifies the right to create a folder. This right requires the Synchronize right. If you don't explicitly set the Synchronize right when creating a file or folder, the Synchronize right will be set automatically for you.
CreateFiles	Specifies the right to create a file. This right requires the Synchronize right. If you don't explicitly set the Synchronize right when creating a file or folder, the Synchronize right will be set automatically for you.
Delete	Specifies the right to delete a folder or file.
DeleteSubdirectoriesAnd-Files	Specifies the right to delete a folder and any files contained within that folder.
ExecuteFile	Specifies the right to run an application file.
FullControl	Specifies the right to exert full control over a folder or file and to modify access control and audit rules.
ListDirectory	Specifies the right to list the contents of a folder.
Modify	Specifies the right to read, write, list folder contents, delete folders and files, and run application files.
Read	Specifies the right to open and copy folders or files as read-only. It includes the right to read file system attributes, extended file system attributes, and access and audit rules.
ReadAndExecute	Specifies the right to open and copy folders or files as read-only and to run application files. It includes the right to read file system attributes, extended file system attributes, and access and audit rules.
ReadAttributes	Specifies the right to open and copy file system attributes from a folder or file. It doesn't include the right to read data, extended file system attributes, or access and audit rules.

Table 15-1   Values of the FileSystemRights Enumerated Type *(Continued)*

Value	Description
ReadData	Specifies the right to open and copy a file or folder. It doesn't include the right to read file system attributes, extended file system attributes, or access and audit rules.
ReadExtendedAttributes	Specifies the right to open and copy extended file system attributes from a folder or file. It doesn't include the right to read data, file system attributes, or access and audit rules.
ReadPermissions	Specifies the right to open and copy access and audit rules from a folder or file. It doesn't include the right to read data, file system attributes, and extended file system attributes.
Synchronize	Specifies the right to synchronize a file or folder. The right to create a file or folder requires this right. If you don't explicitly set this right when creating a file, the right will be set automatically for you.
TakeOwnership	Specifies the right to change the owner of a folder or file.
Traverse	Specifies the right to list the contents of a folder and to run applications contained within that folder.
Write	Specifies the right to create folders and files and to add or remove data from files. It includes the ability to write file system attributes, extended file system attributes, and access and audit rules.
WriteAttributes	Specifies the right to open and write file system attributes to a folder or file. It doesn't include the ability to write data, extended attributes, or access and audit rules.
WriteData	Specifies the right to open and write to a file or folder. It doesn't include the right to open and write file system attributes, extended file system attributes, or access and audit rules.
WriteExtendedAttributes	Specifies the right to open and write extended file system attributes to a folder or file. It doesn't include the ability to write data, attributes, or access and audit rules.

You can change security-related information as well. For example, the FileSecurity object exposes the SetOwner method for changing the owner of a file:

```
' Transfer the ownership of the c:\test.doc file to the System account.
Dim nta5 As New NTAccount("NT AUTHORITY\SYSTEM")
fileSec.SetOwner(nta5)
```

Modifying ACLs

You can do more than just change the owner of a file or directory object. In fact, you can specify exactly who can (or can't) do what, by creating or manipulating a FileSecurity or DirectorySecurity object and associating it with a file or directory. This is made possible by the SetAccessControl method exposed by the Directory, File, DirectoryInfo, and FileInfo types.

The simplest technique for changing the ACL of a file or a directory is by cloning the ACL obtained from another object, as in this code:

```
' Create a copy of the all permissions associated with c:\test.doc.
' (You can also copy just the access permissions, for example.)
Dim sddl As String = fileSec.GetSecurityDescriptorSddlForm(AccessControlSections.All)
Dim fileSec2 As New FileSecurity
fileSec2.SetSecurityDescriptorSddlForm(sddl)
' Enforce these permissions on the c:\data.txt file.
File.SetAccessControl("c:\data.txt", fileSec2)
```

For tasks that are more complex than just copying an existing ACL you create individual FileSystemAccessRule objects and pass them to the FileSecurity.AddAccessRule method:

```
' Create an access rule that grants full control to administrators.
Dim ntAcc1 As New NTAccount("BUILTIN\Administrators")
Dim fsar1 As New FileSystemAccessRule(ntAcc1, FileSystemRights.FullControl, _
    AccessControlType.Allow)
' Create another access rule that denies write permissions to ASPNET user.
Dim ntAcc2 As New NTAccount("DESKTOP01\ASPNET")
Dim fsar2 As New FileSystemAccessRule(ntAcc2, FileSystemRights.Write, _
    AccessControlType.Deny)
' Create a FileSecurity object that contains these two access rules.
Dim fsec As New FileSecurity
fsec.AddAccessRule(fsar1)
fsec.AddAccessRule(fsar2)
' Assign these permissions to the c:\data.txt file.
File.SetAccessControl("c:\data.txt", fsec)
```

An overload of the constructor lets you specify how permissions inherited from the parent object (the containing directory, in the case of the file system) should be dealt with.

```
Dim fsar3 As New FileSystemAccessRule(ntAcc2, _
    FileSystemRights.Write Or FileSystemRights.Read, _
    InheritanceFlags.ContainerInherit Or InheritanceFlags.ObjectInherit, _
    PropagationFlags.None, AccessControlType.Allow)
```

The ContainerInherit flag means that the rule is propagated to all containers that are children of the current object, whereas the ObjectInherit flag means that the rule is propagated to all objects that are children of the current object. In the case of the file system, if the current object is a folder, the ContainerInherit flag affects its subdirectories and the ObjectInherit flag affects the files contained in the folder.

The PropagationFlags.None flag means that the rule applies to both the object and its children. The other two values for this flag are InheritOnly and NoPropagateInherit. The former value means that the rule applies to child objects but not to the object itself, thus you can enforce a rule for all the files and directories in a folder without affecting the folder itself; the latter value means that rule inheritance applies for only one level, therefore the rule affects the children of an object but not its grandchildren. In practice, these two flags aren't used often.

The FileSecurity type exposes other methods that enable you to modify the set of access rules contained in the object: ModifyAccessRule changes an existing access rule; PurgeAccessRules removes all the rules associated with a given IdentityReference object; RemoveAccessRule-Specific removes a specific access rule; ResetAccessRule adds the specified access rule and removes all the matching rules in one operation. Read MSDN documentation for details about these methods.

The FileSecurity object is also capable of reading and modifying the audit rules associated with a file or directory. (Audit rules specify which file operations on a file, either successful or not, are logged by the system.) For example, the following code displays all the audit rules associated with a file:

```
Console.WriteLine("{0,-25}{1,-30}{2,-8}{3,-6}", "User", "Rights", "Outcome", "Inherited")
Console.WriteLine(New String("-"c, 72))
For Each fsar As FileSystemAuditRule In fsec.GetAuditRules(True, True, GetType(NTAccount))
    Console.WriteLine("{0,-25}{1,-30}{2,-8}{3,-6}", fsar.IdentityReference.Value, _
        fsar.FileSystemRights, fsar.AuditFlags, fsar.IsInherited)
Next
```

The AuditFlags property is an enumerated value that can be Success or Failure. Similarly to what happens with access rules, you can use the AddAuditRule method to add an audit rule to the FileSecurity object, the ModifyAuditRule method to change an existing audit rule, and so forth.

The Stream Type

The Stream abstract type represents a sequence of bytes going to or coming from a storage medium (such as a file) or a physical or virtual device (such as a parallel port, an interprocess communication pipe, or a TCP/IP socket). Streams allow you to read from and write to a backing store, which can correspond to one of several storage mediums. For example, you can have file streams, memory streams, and network streams.

Because it's an abstract class, you don't create a Stream object directly, and you rarely use a Stream variable in your code. Rather, you typically work with types that inherit from it, such as the FileStream and the NetworkStream types.

Stream Operations

The fundamental operations you can perform on streams are read, write, and seek. Not all types of streams support all these operations—for example, the NetworkStream object doesn't support seeking. You can check which operations are allowed by using the stream's CanRead, CanWrite, and CanSeek properties.

Most Stream objects perform data buffering in a transparent way. For example, data isn't immediately written to disk when you write to a file stream; instead, bytes are buffered and are eventually flushed when the stream is closed or when you issue an explicit Flush method. Buffering can improve performance remarkably. File streams are buffered, whereas memory streams aren't because there's no point in buffering a stream that maps to memory. You can use a BufferedStream object to add buffering capability to a stream object that doesn't offer it natively—for example, the NetworkStream object. Using BufferedStream in this fashion can improve performance remarkably if the application sends many small data packets rather than a few large ones.

Most of the properties of the Stream type—and of types that inherit from Stream—work as you would intuitively expect them to work:

- The Length property returns the total size of the stream, whereas the Position property determines the current position in the stream (that is, the offset of the next byte that will be read or written). You can change the stream's length using the SetLength method and change the position using the Seek method, but not all Stream types support these two methods.

- The Read method reads a number of bytes from the specified position into a Byte array, advances the stream pointer, and finally returns the number of bytes read. The ReadByte method reads and returns a single byte.

- The Write method writes a number of bytes from an array into the stream, and then advances the stream pointer. The WriteByte method writes a single byte to the stream.

- The Close method closes the stream and releases all the associated resources. The Flush method empties a buffered stream and ensures that all its contents are written to the underlying store. (It has no effect on nonbuffered streams.)

- In .NET Framework 2.0, you can use the CanTimeout read-only property to determine whether the stream supports timeouts in read and write operations; if this is the case, you can read or set these timeouts by means of the ReadTimeout and WriteTimeout properties. (These values are in milliseconds.)

Specific streams can implement additional methods and properties, such as the following:

- The FileStream class exposes the Handle property (which returns the operating system file handle) and the Lock and Unlock methods (which lock or unlock a portion of the file). When you're working with FileStream objects, the SetLength method actually trims or extends the underlying file.

- The MemoryStream class exposes the Capacity property (which returns the number of bytes allocated to the stream), the WriteTo method (which copies the entire contents to another stream), and the GetBuffer method (which returns the array of unsigned bytes from which the stream was created).

- The NetworkStream class exposes the DataAvailable property (which returns True when data is available on the stream for reading).

Stream Readers and Writers

Because the generic Stream object can read and write only individual bytes or groups of bytes, most of the time you use auxiliary stream reader and stream writer objects that let you work with more structured data, such as a line of text or a Double value. The .NET Framework offers several stream reader and writer pairs:

- The BinaryReader and BinaryWriter types can work with primitive data in binary format, such as a Single value or an encoded string.

- The StreamReader and StreamWriter types can work with strings of text, such as the text you read from or write to a text file. These types can work in conjunction with an Encoder object, which determines how characters are encoded in the stream.

- The StringReader type can read from a string; the StringWriter class can write to a String-Builder. (It can't write to a string because .NET strings are immutable.)

- TextReader and TextWriter are abstract types that define how to work with strings of text in Unicode format. TextReader is the base type for the StreamReader and StringReader types; TextWriter is the base type for the StreamWriter and StringWriter types.

- The XmlTextReader and XmlTextWriter types work with XML text.

- The ResourceReader and ResourceWriter types work with resource files.

Reading and Writing Text Files

You typically use a StreamReader object to read from a text file. You can obtain a reference to such an object in many ways:

```
' With the File.OpenText static method
Dim fileName As String = "c:\test.txt"
Dim sr As StreamReader = File.OpenText(fileName)

' With the OpenText instance method of a FileInfo object
Dim fi2 As New FileInfo(fileName)
Dim sr2 As StreamReader = fi2.OpenText

' By passing a FileStream from the Open method of the File class to
' the StreamReader's constructor method
' (This technique lets you specify mode, access, and share mode.)
Dim st3 As Stream = File.Open(fileName, _
    FileMode.Open, FileAccess.ReadWrite, FileShare.ReadWrite)
Dim sr3 As New StreamReader(st3)

' By opening a FileStream on the file and then passing it
' to the StreamReader's constructor method
Dim fs4 As New FileStream(fileName, FileMode.Open)
Dim sr4 As New StreamReader(fs4)

' By getting a FileStream from the OpenRead method of the File class
' and passing it to the StreamReader's constructor
Dim sr5 As New StreamReader(File.OpenRead(fileName))
```

```
' By passing the filename to the StreamReader's constructor
Dim sr6 As New StreamReader(fileName)

' By passing the filename and encoding
Dim sr7 As New StreamReader("c:\autoexec.bat", System.Text.Encoding.Unicode)
Dim sr8 As New StreamReader(fileName, System.Text.Encoding.ASCII)

' As before, but we let the system decide the best encoding.
Dim sr9 As New StreamReader(fileName, True)
```

The FileStream type in .NET Framework 2.0 has been expanded with new constructors to support two important new features. First, you can pass a FileSecurity object when you create a file, to specify the ACL associated with the file itself. Second, you can pass a FileOptions bit-coded value to specify additional options when opening a file. Supported values are None, SequentialScan (optimize caching for sequential access), RandomAccess (optimize caching for random access), WriteThrough (write data directly to disk, without buffering it), Encrypted (encrypt the file so that it can be read only by the same user account), Asynchronous (the file can be used for asynchronous reading and writing), and DeleteOnClose (the file is temporary and must be deleted when it's closed).

```
' Create a file for sequential reading and writing, with a 2-KB buffer;
' the file will be deleted when closed.
Dim fs10 As New FileStream("c:\test.tmp", FileMode.CreateNew, FileAccess.ReadWrite, _
   FileShare.Read, 2048, FileOptions.SequentialScan Or FileOptions.DeleteOnClose)
```

After you get a reference to a StreamReader object, you can use one of its many methods to read one or more characters or whole text lines. The Peek method returns the code of the next character in the stream without actually extracting it, or it returns the special −1 value if there are no more characters. In practice, this method is used to test an end-of-file condition:

```
' Display all the text lines in the c:\test.txt file.
Dim sr As New StreamReader("c:\test.txt")
Do Until sr.Peek = -1
   Console.WriteLine(sr.ReadLine())
Loop
sr.Close()
```

In .NET Framework 2.0 you can rewrite the previous code in a more robust and readable style by means of the new EndOfStream read-only property and the Using statement:

```
Using sr As New StreamReader("c:\test.txt")
   Do Until sr.EndOfStream
      Console.WriteLine(sr.ReadLine())
   Loop
End Using
```

You can also read one character at a time using the Read method, or you can read all the remaining characters using the ReadToEnd method:

```
' Read the entire contents of C:\test.doc in one shot.
Dim sr As New StreamReader("c:\test.txt")
Dim fileContents As String = sr.ReadToEnd()
```

If you opened the StreamReader through a Stream object, you can use the Stream object's Seek method to move the pointer or read its current position. If you did not open the StreamReader through a Stream object, you can still access the inner Stream object that the .NET runtime creates anyway, through the StreamReader's BaseStream property:

```
' ...(Continuing previous code example)...
' If the file is longer than 100 chars, process it again, one character at a
' time (admittedly a silly thing to do, but it's just a demo).
If fileContents.Length >= 100 Then
    ' Reset the stream's pointer to the beginning.
    sr.BaseStream.Seek(0, SeekOrigin.Begin)
    ' Read individual characters until EOF is reached.
    Do Until sr.EndOfStream
        ' Read method returns an integer, so convert it to Char.
        Console.Write(sr.Read().ToString())
    Loop
End If
sr.Close()
```

You use a StreamWriter object to write to a text file. As with the StreamReader object, you can create a StreamWriter object in many ways:

```
' By means of the CreateText static method of the File type
Dim fileName As String = "c:\text.dat"
Dim sw1 As StreamWriter = File.CreateText(fileName)

' By passing a FileStream from the Open method of the File class to
' the StreamWriter's constructor method
Dim st2 As Stream = File.Open(fileName, _
    FileMode.Create, FileAccess.ReadWrite, FileShare.None)
Dim sw2 As New StreamWriter(st2)

' By opening a FileStream on the file and then passing it
' to the StreamWriter's constructor
Dim fs3 As New FileStream(fileName, FileMode.Open)
Dim sw3 As New StreamWriter(fs3)

' By getting a FileStream from the OpenWrite method of the File type
' and passing it to the StreamWriter's constructor
Dim sw4 As New StreamWriter(File.OpenWrite(fileName))

' By passing the filename to the StreamWriter's constructor
Dim sw5 As New StreamWriter(fileName)
```

Other overloads of the StreamWriter's constructor allow you to specify whether the file is to be opened in append mode, the size of the buffer, and an Encoding object:

```
' Open the c:\test.dat file in append mode, be prepared to output
' ASCII characters, and use a 2-KB buffer.
Dim sw6 As New StreamWriter("c:\test.new", True, Encoding.ASCII, 2024)
```

The NewLine property (new in .NET Framework 2.0) lets you specify a nonstandard value for the line termination character:

```
' Terminate each line with a null character followed by a newline character.
sw6.NewLine = ControlChars.NullChar & ControlChars.NewLine
```

The StreamWriter class exposes the Write and WriteLine methods: the Write method can write the textual representation of any basic data type (Integer, Double, and so on); the Write-Line method works only with strings and automatically appends a newline character. Leave the AutoFlush property set to False (the default value) if you want the StreamWriter to adopt a limited form of caching; you'll probably need to issue a Flush method periodically in this case. Set this property to True for those streams or devices, such as the console window, from which the user expects immediate feedback.

The following code uses a StreamReader object to read from a file and a StreamWriter object to copy the text to another file after converting the text to uppercase:

```
Using sr As New StreamReader("c:\test.txt")
   Using sw As New StreamWriter("c:\test.new")
      Do Until sr.EndOfStream
         sw.WriteLine(sr.ReadLine.ToUpper())
      Loop
   End Using      ' This actually writes data to the file and closes it.
End Using
```

If you're working with smaller text files, you can also trade some memory for speed and do without a loop. The following code uses a single Using block, but the Visual Basic compiler correctly expands it into two nested blocks, as in the previous code snippet:

```
Using sr As New StreamReader("c:\test.txt"), sw As New StreamWriter("c:\test.new")
   sw.WriteLine(sr.ReadToEnd().ToUpper())
End Using
```

You should always close the Stream object after using it, either by means of a Using block or explicitly with a Close method. If you fail to do so, the stream keeps the file open until the next garbage collection calls the Stream's Finalize method. There are at least two reasons why you'd rather close the stream manually. First, if the file is kept open longer than strictly necessary, you can't delete or move the underlying file, nor can another application open it for reading and/or writing (depending on the access mode you specified when opening the file). The second reason is performance: the code in the Stream's Close method calls the GC.Suppress-Finalize method, so the Stream object isn't finalized and therefore the resources it uses are released earlier.

Reading and Writing Binary Files

The BinaryReader and BinaryWriter types are suitable for working with binary streams; one such stream might be associated with a file containing data in native format. In this context, *native format* means the actual bits used to store the value in memory. You can't create a

BinaryReader or BinaryWriter object directly from a filename as you can with the Stream-Reader and StreamWriter objects. Instead, you must create a Stream object explicitly and pass it to the constructor method of either the BinaryReader or the BinaryWriter class:

```
' Associate a stream with a new file opened with write access.
Dim st As Stream = File.Open("c:\values.dat", FileMode.Create, FileAccess.write)
' Create a BinaryWriter associated with the output stream.
Dim bw As New BinaryWriter(st)
```

Working with the BinaryWriter object is especially simple because its Write method is over-loaded to accept all the primitive .NET types, including signed and unsigned integers, Single, Double, and String values. The following code snippet writes 10 random Double values to a binary file:

```
' ...(Continuing previous example)...
' Save 10 Double values to the file.
Dim rand As New Random()
For i As Integer = 1 To 10
   bw.Write(rand.NextDouble())
Next
' Flush the output data to the file.
bw.Close()
```

The BinaryReader class exposes many Read*Xxxx* methods, one for each possible native data type. Unlike the StreamReader type, which exposes an EndOfStream property, the BinaryReader type requires that you use the PeekChar method to check whether other bytes are available:

```
' Read back values written in previous example.

' Associate a stream with an existing file, opened with read access.
Dim st2 As Stream = File.Open("c:\values.dat", FileMode.Open, FileAccess.Read)
' Create a BinaryReader associated with the input stream.
Using br2 As New BinaryReader(st2)
   ' Loop until data is available.
   Do Until br2.PeekChar() = -1
      ' Read the next element. (We know it's a Double.)
      Console.WriteLine(br2.ReadDouble())
   Loop
   ' Next statement closes both the BinaryReader and the underlying stream.
End Using
```

Outputting strings with a BinaryWriter requires some additional care, however. Passing a string to the Write method outputs a length-prefixed string to the stream. If you want to write only the actual characters (as happens when you're working with fixed-length strings), you must pass the Write method a Char array. The Write method is overloaded to take additional arguments that specify which portion of the array should be written.

Reading back strings requires different techniques as well, depending on how the string was written. You use the ReadString method for length-prefixed strings and the ReadChars method for fixed-length strings. You can see an example of these methods in action in the section "Memory Streams" later in this chapter.

> **Note** File streams can be opened for asynchronous read and write operations, which can speed up your code's performance significantly. You'll learn about asynchronous file operations in Chapter 20.

Working with Fixed-Length and Delimited Data Files

In Chapter 14 you saw how you can use regular expressions to read text files that use either delimited or fixed-length fields. The new TextFieldParser type (in the Microsoft .VisualBasic.FileIO namespace) offers a simpler way to accomplish the same task. As the name of its namespace suggests, this type is part of the Microsoft.VisualBasic library and doesn't "officially" belong to the .NET Framework. (C# developers can of course use this class by adding a reference to the Microsoft.VisualBasic.dll assembly.)

Using the TextFieldParser to read text files with delimited fields is a trivial procedure. You open the data file by passing the filename to the TextFieldParser constructor, together with an Encoding object, and then you assign an array of delimiters to the Delimiters property and optionally set the TrimWhiteSpace property to False if you don't want to discard leading and trailing spaces (the default value for this property is True):

```
Dim parser As New TextFieldParser("c:\data.txt", Encoding.Default)
' Field separator can be either a comma or a semicolon.
parser.Delimiters = New String() {",", ";"}
parser.TrimWhiteSpace = True
```

(Other overloads of the constructor take a Stream or a TextReader object.) Next, you need a loop that processes the file one line at a time until the EndOfData property returns True; the ReadFields method reads the next record (that is, the next line of text) and splits it into fields:

```
Do Until parser.EndOfData
   Dim fields() As String = parser.ReadFields()
   ' Process each field in current record here.
   …
Loop
parser.Close()
```

Conveniently, the TextFieldParser type correctly interprets quoted strings (even if they embed one of the delimiter characters). For example, consider the following data file:

```
"John P.", Evans, New York
Robert, Zare, "Los Angeles, CA"
```

Here's the Visual Basic code that can process it:

```
Using parser As New TextFieldParser("data.txt", Encoding.Default)
   parser.Delimiters = New String() {","}
   parser.TrimWhiteSpace = True
```

```
Do Until parser.EndOfData
   Dim fields() As String = parser.ReadFields()
   Console.WriteLine("First={0}, Last={1}, Location={2}", fields(0), fields(1), fields(2))
Loop
End Using
```

The result in the console window proves that both quotation marks and surrounding spaces have been correctly removed, and that the comma inside the quoted city name hasn't been mistakenly taken as a field separator:

```
First=John P., Last=Evans, City=New York
First=Robert, Last=Zare, City=Los Angeles, CA
```

Reading text files containing fixed-length fields with the TextFieldParser is equally simple, the only differences being that you must set the TextFieldType property to the FieldType.Fixed-Width enumerated value and assign an array of Integers to the FieldWidths property; each element of this array is interpreted as the width of the corresponding field. For example, let's say that we have the following data file:

```
John P. Evans    Dallas
Robert  Zare     Boston
```

Here's the code fragment that can read it:

```
Using parser As New TextFieldParser("data2.txt", Encoding.Default)
   parser.TextFieldType = FieldType.FixedWidth
   parser.FieldWidths = New Integer() {8, 10, 6}
   Do Until parser.EndOfData
      Dim fields() As String = parser.ReadFields()
      Console.WriteLine("First={0}, Last={1}, City={2}", fields(0), fields(1), fields(2))
   Loop
End Using
```

Keep in mind that quotation marks *aren't* automatically stripped off when reading fixed-width text files.

The PeekChars method returns a number of characters without actually reading them from the stream. This method is especially useful with data files in which the first field contains a special code that affects the format of the current line. For example, consider the following data file that contains a mix of invoice headers and invoice details:

```
IH 1    12/04/2005 John Evans
ID 12      Monitor XY       129.99
ID 4       Printer YZ       212.00
ID 3       Hard disks Z4    159.00
IH 2    12/06/2005 Robert Zare
ID 8       Monitor XY       129.99
ID 2       Notebook ABC     850.00
```

The first three characters in each line specify whether the line is an invoice header (IH) or invoice detail (ID); in the former case, the line contains the invoice number, date, and customer; in the latter case, the line contains the quantity, description, and unit price. The format of the two records is different; in this specific case they have the same number of fields, but this is just a coincidence because the number of fields might differ as well. Here's the Visual Basic code that can interpret this data file:

```
Using parser As New TextFieldParser("data3.txt", Encoding.Default)
   parser.TextFieldType = FieldType.FixedWidth
   Dim headerWidths() As Integer = {3, 4, 11, 12}
   Dim detailWidths() As Integer = {3, 6, 18, 6}
   parser.FieldWidths = headerWidths

   Do Until parser.EndOfData
      Dim code As String = parser.PeekChars(2)
      If code = "IH" Then
         parser.FieldWidths = headerWidths
         Dim fields() As String = parser.ReadFields()
         Console.WriteLine("Invoice #{0}, Date={1}, Customer={2}", fields(1), fields(2), _
            fields(3))
      ElseIf code = "ID" Then
         parser.FieldWidths = detailWidths
         Dim fields() As String = parser.ReadFields()
         Console.WriteLine("   #{0} {1} at ${2} each", fields(1), fields(2), fields(3))
      Else
         Throw New MalformedLineException("Invalid record code")
      End If
   Loop
End Using
```

The MalformedLineException type is defined in the Microsoft.VisualBasic.FileIO namespace; the TextFieldParser object throws this exception when the format of the current record doesn't match what it expects to find. When your code catches this exception, you can attempt to solve the problem by querying its ErrorLine property (the text line that caused the problem) or the ErrorLineNumber (the number of the malformed line). The line number is returned also by the LineNumber property of the MalformedLineException type. If you aren't sure about the integrity of the file being parsed, you should write code like this:

```
Do Until parser.EndOfData
   Try
      ' Process fields here.
      …
   Catch ex As MalformedLineException
      Console.WriteLine("Line #{0} is malformed. Ignored.", ex.LineNumber)
   End Try
Loop
```

Before we move to a different topic, notice that .NET Framework 2.0 doesn't offer a type that writes data files in either delimited or fixed-width format. The reason is evident: writing such files is too easy, thanks to the String.Format method and its many options, and few developers would resort to a separate class for such a simple task. For example, the following statement can output a line of text consisting of three left-aligned, fixed-length fields:

```
' sw is a StreamWriter object, p is a Person object that exposes
' the FirstName, LastName, and City properties.
sw.WriteLine(String.Format("{0,-8}{1,-10}{2,-16}", p.FirstName, p.LastName, p.City))
```

Creating a delimited file is even simpler because you just need to put double quotation marks around fields that might contain the delimiter character:

```
' Output data to a semicolon-delimited file.
sw.WriteLine(String.Format("""{0}"";""{1}"";""{2}""", p.FirstName, p.LastName, p.City))
```

Other Stream Types

Stream readers and writers aren't just for files, even though files are undoubtedly the most common kind of stream. In this last section, I cover other common types that derive from the Stream class.

Memory Streams

The MemoryStream object allows you to deal with memory as if it were a temporary file, a technique that usually delivers better performance than does using an actual file. The following code snippet shows how to write to and then read back 10 random numbers from a stream; this example is similar to a code snippet illustrated earlier in this chapter, except this code uses a memory stream instead of a file stream:

```
' Create a memory stream with initial capacity of 1 KB.
Dim st As New MemoryStream(1024)
Dim bw As New BinaryWriter(st)
Dim rand As New Random()
' Write 10 random Double values to the stream.
For i As Integer = 1 To 10
   bw.Write(rand.NextDouble())
Next

' Rewind the stream to the beginning and read back the data.
st.Seek(0, SeekOrigin.Begin)
Dim br As New BinaryReader(st)
Do Until br.PeekChar = -1
   Console.WriteLine(br.ReadDouble())
Loop

bw.Close()
br.Close()
st.Close()
```

Of course, in this particular example you might have used an array to store random values and read them back. However, the approach based on streams lets you move from a memory stream to a file-based stream by changing only one statement (the stream constructor).

This example writes three strings to a MemoryStream and then reads them back; it shows how to work with length-prefixed strings and two techniques for reading fixed-length strings:

```
Dim st As New MemoryStream(1000)
Dim bw As New BinaryWriter(st)
' The BinaryWriter.Write method outputs a length-prefixed string.
bw.Write("a length-prefixed string")
' We'll use this 1-KB buffer for both reading and writing.
Dim buffer(1023) As Char

Dim s As String = "13 Characters"        ' A fixed-length string
s.CopyTo(0, buffer, 0, s.Length)         ' Copy into the buffer.
bw.Write(buffer, 0, s.Length)            ' Output first 13 chars in buffer.
bw.Write(buffer, 0, s.Length)            ' Do it a second time.

' Rewind the stream, and prepare to read from it.
st.Seek(0, SeekOrigin.Begin)
Dim br As New BinaryReader(st)
' Reading the length-prefixed string is simple.
Console.WriteLine(br.ReadString())       ' => A length-prefixed string

' Read the fixed-length string (13 characters) into the buffer.
br.Read(buffer, 0, 13)
s = New String(buffer, 0, 13)            ' Convert to a string.
Console.WriteLine(s)                     ' => 13 Characters

' Another way to read a fixed-length string (13 characters)
' (ReadChars returns a Char array that we can pass to the string constructor.)
s = New String(br.ReadChars(13))
Console.WriteLine(s)                     ' => 13 Characters
```

String-Based Streams

If the data you want to read is already contained in a string variable, you can use a StringReader object to retrieve portions of it. For example, you can load the entire contents of a text file or a multiline text box control into a string and then extract the individual lines by using the StringReader.ReadLine method:

```
' The veryLongString variable contains the text to parse.
Dim strReader As New StringReader(veryLongString)
' Display individual lines of text.
Do Until strReader.Peek = -1
   Console.WriteLine(strReader.ReadLine())
Loop
```

Of course, you can implement the same technique in other, equivalent ways—for example, by using the Split function to get an array with all the individual lines of code—but the solution based on the StringReader object is more resource-friendly because it doesn't duplicate the data in memory. As a matter of fact, the StringReader and StringWriter types don't even create an internal Stream object to store the characters; rather they use the string itself as the backing store for the stream. (This fact explains why these two types don't expose the BaseStream property.)

You use a StringWriter object to output values to a string. However, you can't associate it with a String object because .NET strings are immutable. Instead, you have to create a StringBuilder and then associate it with a StringWriter object:

```
' Create a string with the space-separated abbreviated names of weekdays.
Dim sb As New StringBuilder()
' The StringWriter associated with the StringBuilder
Dim strWriter As New StringWriter(sb)

' Output day names to the string.
For Each d As String In DateTimeFormatInfo.CurrentInfo.AbbreviatedDayNames
    strWriter.Write(d)
    strWriter.Write(" ")         ' Append a space.
Next
Console.WriteLine(sb)            ' => Sun Mon Tue Wed Thu Fri Sat
```

Network Streams

The .NET Framework supports exchanging data over the network using Transmission Control Protocol (TCP) by means of TcpClient and TcpListener types, both in the System.Net.Sockets namespace. TCP ensures that data is either correctly received or an exception is thrown, and for this reason it is the preferred protocol when you can't afford to lose data. The applications involved in data exchange can reside on the same computer or on different computers over the LAN or connected through the Internet. The actual data sent over the wire is read from and written to a NetworkStream object, also in the System.Net.Sockets namespace.

TCP assumes you have a server application that listens to requests coming from one or more clients. The client and the server applications must agree on the port number as well as the format of the data being sent over the wire. In the following example, the client application sends the name of a text file as a string terminated with a CR-LF character. The server application receives the filename sent from the client, searches the file in a specific directory, and sends the file's contents back to the client. Because the file contents can be of any length, the server application prefixes the actual data with a line containing the length of the data so that the client can read the exact number of bytes from NetworkStream. (In a real-world application, using a length prefix is important because a single server-side send operation can translate into multiple receive operations on the client side.) Both applications terminate when the client sends an empty filename to the server.

The server application must create a TcpListener object that listens to a given port and accepts incoming requests from clients. The AcceptTcpClient method waits until a connection is made and returns the TcpClient object that represents the client making the request. The GetStream method of this TcpClient object returns a NetworkStream that the server application can use to read data from clients and send them a result.

```
' The server application
Sub Main()
    ' Listen to port 2048.
```

```
Dim localhostAddress As IPAddress = IPAddress.Loopback
Dim tcpList As New TcpListener(localhostAddress, 2048)
tcpList.Start()

Do
    ' Wait for the next client to make a request.
    Console.WriteLine("Waiting for data from clients...")
    Dim tcpCli As TcpClient = tcpList.AcceptTcpClient()
    ' Read data sent by the client (a CR-LF-separated string in this case).
    Dim ns As NetworkStream = tcpCli.GetStream()
    Dim sr As New StreamReader(ns)
    Dim receivedData As String = sr.ReadLine()

    If receivedData <> "" Then
        ' Read a file with this name from the C:\docs directory.
        Dim fileName As String = Path.Combine("c:\docs", receivedData)
        Console.WriteLine("Reading file {0}...", fileName)

        Dim resultData As String = Nothing
        Try
            resultData = File.ReadAllText(fileName)
        Catch ex As Exception
            resultData = "*** ERROR: " & ex.Message
        End Try
        SendData(ns, resultData)
    End If
    ' Release resources and close the NetworkStream.
    sr.Close()
    ns.Close()
    tcpCli.Close()
    ' Exit if the client sent an empty string.
    If receivedData = "" Then Exit Do
Loop
' Reject client requests from now on.
tcpList.Stop()
End Sub

' Send a length-prefixed string.
Sub SendData(ByVal ns As NetworkStream, ByVal data As String)
    ' Send it back to the client.
    Dim sw As New StreamWriter(ns)
    sw.WriteLine(data.Length)
    sw.Write(data)
    sw.Flush()                              ' This is VERY important.
    sw.Close()
End Sub
```

The client code must instantiate a TcpClient object that references the server application by means of the server application's URL and port number. (The port number should be in the range of 1024 to 65535.) Next, the client invokes the TcpClient.GetStream method to retrieve the NetworkStream object that can be used to send and receive data from the server.

```
' The client application
Sub Main()
    Do
        ' Ask the end user for a filename.
```

```vb
Console.Write("Enter a file name [an empty string to quit] >> ")
Dim fileName As String = Console.ReadLine()

' This code assumes a server on the local machine is listening to port 2048.
Dim tcpCli As New Sockets.TcpClient("localhost", 2048)
' Retrieve the stream that can send and receive data.
Dim ns As NetworkStream = tcpCli.GetStream()
' Send a CR-LF-terminated string to the server.
Dim sw As New StreamWriter(ns)
sw.WriteLine(fileName)
sw.Flush()                                  ' This is VERY important!

        If fileName <> "" Then
            ' Receive data from the server application and display it.
            Dim resultData As String = ReadData(ns)
            Console.WriteLine(resultData)
        End If
        ' Release resources and close the NetworkStream.
        sw.Close()
        ns.Close()
        If fileName = "" Then Exit Do
    Loop
End Sub

' Read a length-prefixed string.
Function ReadData(ByVal ns As NetworkStream) As String
    Dim sr As New StreamReader(ns)
    Dim dataLength As Integer = CInt(sr.ReadLine())
    Dim buffer(dataLength - 1) As Char
    sr.Read(buffer, 0, dataLength)
    sr.Close()
    Return New String(buffer)
End Function
```

To test this code, create a directory named c:\docs and store a few text files in it. Compile the server and the client applications as separate Console projects and run both of them. Enter the name of a file in the client application and wait for the server to send back the textual content of the file.

Alternatively, you can create a solution that contains both these projects; then, right-click the solution item in the Solution Explorer window and select the Properties command. Select the Startup Project page in the dialog box that appears, click the Multiple Startup Projects radio button, and set the Action value to Start for both the server-side and client-side projects. (See Figure 15-3.) If you now press F5 or select the Start command from the Debug menu, both projects will be launched.

The NetworkStream type exposes a few other members of interest. For example the DataAvailable property returns True if there is data waiting to be read. Network streams don't support the seek operation; thus, the CanSeek property always returns False and the Seek method throws an exception, as do the Length and Position properties.

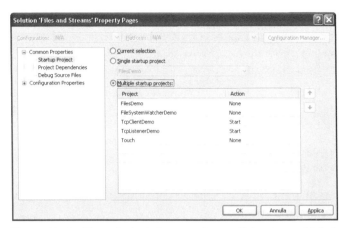

Figure 15-3   The solution's Property Pages dialog box, which lets you decide which project to run when you press the F5 key

The most important feature added in .NET Framework 2.0 is the support for timeouts through the ReadTimeout and WriteTimeout properties. By default, all read and write operations wait until data can be received or sent, but if you assign a value (in milliseconds) to these properties, any operation that doesn't complete within the specified timeout throws an IOException object.

> **Note**   As with all the applications that exchange data using TCP, these sample applications (more precisely, the server application) might open a security hole on your computer because in theory a remote client might use the application to read the contents of a file on your computer. It is therefore essential that you protect your system by using other methods (for example, a firewall) and that you terminate the server application as soon as you're done with your experiments.

Buffered Streams

Most of the stream types in the .NET Framework provide a transparent mechanism for buffering, for example, the FileStream type, whereas other types never require buffering because they already map to a block of memory, as is the case with the MemoryStream, the StringReader, and StringWriter types. The remaining stream types, for example, the NetworkStream type, don't use any internal cache mechanism; thus, writing to and reading small pieces of data from them can be extremely inefficient. In such cases, you can improve performance by using an auxiliary BufferedStream object.

Using a BufferedStream object is quite simple and amounts to using this object to "wrap" another (unbuffered) stream. For example, let's say that you have the following piece of code:

```
' Initialize the array here (omitted).
Dim arr() As String
...
```

```
' Send the array of strings to a TCP server application.
Dim tcpCli As New TcpClient("localhost", 2048)
Dim ns As NetworkStream = tcpCli.GetStream()
Dim sw As New StreamWriter(ns) For Each s As String In arr
   sw.WriteLine(s)
Next
```

You can make this code faster using a BufferedStream object by replacing the statement in bold type with these two lines:

```
Dim bufStream As New BufferedStream(ns, 8192)
Dim sw As New StreamWriter(bufStream)
```

The second argument passed to the BufferedStream's constructor is the size of the buffer; if omitted a default size of 4,096 bytes is used.

The great thing about the BufferedStream type is that it manages its internal buffer in a very smart way. If you read or write a piece of data larger than the buffer's size, the buffer isn't even used for that specific read or write operation; if you only read and write large pieces of data, the buffer isn't even allocated. You get the best performance with the BufferedStream if you perform a series of read or write operations, but don't alternate often between reads and writes.

Compressed Streams

 Two new types for compressing data have been added in version 2.0 of the .NET Framework: DeflateStream and GZipStream, both in the System.IO.Compression namespace. Both types enable you to compress and uncompress the bytes that flow through the stream; they expose a very similar interface and are virtually interchangeable; the only substantial difference is the format of their compressed output.

The DeflateStream type uses the Deflate compression algorithm, a patent-free algorithm that combines the LZ77 algorithm and Huffman coding; the main advantage of this algorithm is that data of any length can be compressed and uncompressed using an intermediate buffer of limited size. The GZipStream type uses the same Deflate algorithm, but it includes a cyclic redundancy check (CRC) value to detect data corruption.

The peculiarity of these two types is that they can work only together with another stream-based object. In fact, a DeflatedStream or GZipStream object "wraps" another stream that actually writes to the actual medium (if you are compressing data) or reads from the medium (if you are uncompressing data). Given the similarities between the two types, I show how to use just the DeflateStream type.

Compressing data is the easiest operation if you already have the data in a Byte array. For example, the following code uses the File.ReadAllBytes method to read the entire source file (that is, the uncompressed file) and compresses it into a new file:

```
Dim uncompressedFile As String = "test.txt"
Dim compressedFile As String = "test.zip"
' Read the source (uncompressed) file in the buffer.
```

```
Dim buffer() As Byte = File.ReadAllBytes(uncompressedFile)
' Open the destination (compressed) file with a FileStream object.
Dim outStream As New FileStream(compressedFile, FileMode.Create)
' Wrap a DeflateStream object around the output stream.
Dim zipStream As New DeflateStream(outStream, CompressionMode.Compress)
' write the contents of the buffer.
zipStream.Write(buffer, 0, buffer.Length)
' Flush compressed data and close all output streams.
zipStream.Flush()
zipStream.Close()
outStream.Close()
```

Things are slightly more complicated if the source file is too long to be read in memory and you must process it in chunks. The following reusable procedure adopts a more resource-savvy approach:

```
Sub CompressFile(ByVal uncompressedFile As String, ByVal compressedFile As String)
    ' Open the source (uncompressed) file, using a 4-KB input buffer.
    Using inStream As New FileStream(uncompressedFile, FileMode.Open, _
            FileAccess.Read, FileShare.None, 4096)
        ' Open the destination (compressed) file with a FileStream object.
        Using outStream As New FileStream(compressedFile, FileMode.Create)
            ' Wrap a DeflateStream object around the output stream.
            Using zipStream As New DeflateStream(outStream, CompressionMode.Compress)
                ' Prepare a 4-KB read buffer .
                Dim buffer(4095) As Byte
                Do
                    ' Read up to 4 KB from the input file; exit if no more bytes.
                    Dim readBytes As Integer = inStream.Read(buffer, 0, buffer.Length)
                    If readBytes = 0 Then Exit Do
                    ' Write the contents of the buffer to the compressed stream.
                    zipStream.Write(buffer, 0, readBytes)
                Loop
                ' Flush and close all streams.
                zipStream.Flush()
            End Using                  ' Close the DeflateStream object.
        End Using                  ' Close the output FileStream object.
    End Using                  ' Close the input FileStream object.
End Sub
```

When uncompressing a compressed file, you have no choice: you must process the incoming data in chunks. Here's the reason: when you read N compressed bytes, you don't know how many data bytes the decompress process will create. Here's a reusable method that implements all the necessary steps:

```
Sub UncompressFile(ByVal compressedFile As String, ByVal uncompressedFile As String)
    ' Open the output (uncompressed) file, use a 4-KB output buffer.
    Using outStream As New FileStream(uncompressedFile, FileMode.Create, _
            FileAccess.Write, FileShare.None, 4096)
        ' Open the source (compressed) file.
        Using inStream As New FileStream(compressedFile, FileMode.Open)
            ' Wrap the DeflateStream object around the input stream.
            Using zipStream As New DeflateStream(inStream, CompressionMode.Decompress)
                ' Prepare a 4-KB buffer.
                Dim buffer(4095) As Byte
```

```
        Do
            ' Read enough compressed bytes to fill the 4-KB buffer.
            Dim bytesRead As Integer = zipStream.Read(buffer, 0, 4096)
            ' Exit if no more bytes were read.
            If bytesRead = 0 Then Exit Do
            ' Else, write these bytes to the uncompressed file and loop.
            outStream.Write(buffer, 0, bytesRead)
        Loop
        ' Ensure that cached bytes are written correctly and close all streams.
        outStream.Flush()
      End Using          ' Close the DeflateStream object.
    End Using            ' Close the input FileStream object.
  End Using              ' Close the output FileStream object.
End Sub
```

Let's recap the rules for using the DeflateStream type correctly. When compressing data, you pass the output stream to the DeflateStream's constructor and specify CompressionMode .Compress in the second argument, and then you write the (uncompressed) bytes with the DeflateStream.Write method. Conversely, when uncompressing data, you pass the input stream to the DeflateStream's constructor and specify CompressionMode.Decompress in the second argument, and then you read (compressed) bytes with the DeflateStream.Read method.

Finally, remember that you can use the DeflateStream and GZipStream types in a chain of streams; for example, you can output data to a BufferedStream object, which cascades to a DeflateStream object, which uses a NetworkStream object to send the compressed data across the wire. You can see a use for compressed streams in the section titled "A Practical Example: Compressed Serialization" in Chapter 21, "Serialization."

Chapter 16
The My Namespace

One of the most helpful new features of Microsoft Visual Basic 2005 is the introduction of the My namespace. In a nutshell, the My namespace contains a collection of objects that provide simplified paths to many areas in the Microsoft .NET Framework, for example, to work with the file system and the printer. Put this way, the My namespace looks like yet another class library that duplicates what—in one form or another—is already in the .NET Framework. As you'll read in this chapter, however, there is more to learn about this new feature, which, incidentally, isn't available under any other .NET language from Microsoft.

In addition to reducing the amount of code you need to write, the My namespace exposes a few objects that are created dynamically as you add features to the current project. For example, each form class you add to the project is made visible through a distinct property of the My.Forms collection. Similarly, each resource or configuration setting you define in the project becomes a property of the My.Resources and My.Settings objects; such a property is of the same type as the resource or the setting—be it a string, a number, or even a complex object—thus, you can access the resource or the setting in a strong-typed fashion, use IntelliSense to discover all the resources and settings defined in the application, and avoid runtime errors caused by typos.

> **Note** To avoid long lines, code samples in this chapter assume that the following Imports statements are used at the file or project level:

```
Imports Microsoft.VisualBasic.FileIO
Imports Microsoft.VisualBasic.ApplicationServices
Imports Microsoft.Win32
Imports System.Collections.ObjectModel
Imports System.Collections.Specialized
Imports System.ComponentModel
Imports System.Configuration
Imports System.Data
Imports System.Data.OleDb
Imports System.Data.SqlClient
Imports System.Globalization
Imports System.IO
Imports System.Media
Imports System.Net
Imports System.Net.NetworkInformation
Imports System.Threading
```

Overview of the My Namespace

The My namespace is the starting point to access the following objects:

- **My.Application**   Exposes information about the current Console or Windows Forms application, such as its path, version, locale, and user authentication mode.

- **My.Computer**   Exposes several child objects that let you gather information about and use the most important features of the computer, such as its file system, audio and video subsystems, memory, keyboard, mouse, network, serial ports, printer, and so forth.

- **My.Forms**   Exposes one property for each form class defined in the current project and enables you to reference the default instance for that form without having to explicitly create one object of the form class.

- **My.Resources**   Contains one child object for each resource defined for the current project.

- **My.Settings**   Exposes one property for each configuration setting defined in the current settings; a resource can be at the application level (shared by all users) or at the user level. A user-level resource can be modified through code and saved for a subsequent session.

- **My.User**   Returns information about the currently logged on user and lets you implement a custom authentication mechanism.

- **My.WebServices**   Exposes one property for each Web service the current project has a reference to and enables you to access them without having to create a proxy object each time you need to invoke a method in the Web service.

The My.Application Object

A feature of the My namespace that might disorient you is that not all its objects are created under all types of projects. For example, the My.Forms object is available only in Windows Forms applications. The My.Application object is available in Console and Windows Forms applications, but some of its members are available only under projects of the latter type. This arrangement is possible because, at least in part, the My namespace is created dynamically by Microsoft Visual Studio as you change the properties of your project or add new forms, resources, or settings.

Some of the My.Application properties and events become available in a Windows Forms application only if you select the Enable Application Framework check box on the Application page of the My Project designer (see Figure 16-1). The Visual Basic application framework allows you to perform most of the tasks that you typically do when an application starts its execution—including applying Microsoft Windows XP visual styles, showing a splash screen, and refusing to load if another instance of the application is already running—without writing a single line of code. The application framework can't coexist with your custom initialization code in Sub Main, though, and in fact the startup object in the project must be a form when the application framework is used. (Sub Main item and module names disappear from the list of items that can be used as the startup object.)

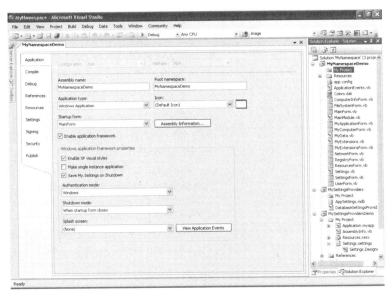

Figure 16-1   Enabling the Visual Basic application framework

Some of the properties and methods of the My.Application object are simply convenient aliases of members exposed by other objects in the .NET Framework, so it's mostly a matter of deciding whether you prefer the Visual Basic way or the standard .NET way. For example, you can determine the culture used to format numbers and dates and to retrieve UI-related resources by means of the Application.Culture and Application.UICulture, respectively, and you can change these values by means of the Application.ChangeCulture and Application.ChangeUICulture methods; or you can perform the same operations by manipulating the CurrentCulture and the CurrentUICulture properties of the current thread:

```
' Retrieve the CultureInfo for the current thread (two equivalent ways).
Dim ci1 As CultureInfo = My.Application.Culture
Dim ci2 As CultureInfo = Thread.CurrentThread.CurrentCulture
' Change it to Italian culture (two equivalent ways).
My.Application.ChangeCulture("it-IT")
Thread.CurrentThread.CurrentCulture = New CultureInfo("it-IT")


' Retrieve the CultureInfo for the current UI thread (two equivalent ways).
Dim ci3 As CultureInfo = My.Application.UICulture
Dim ci4 As CultureInfo = Thread.CurrentThread.CurrentUICulture
' Change it to Italian culture (two equivalent ways).
My.Application.ChangeUICulture("it-IT")
Thread.CurrentThread.CurrentUICulture = New CultureInfo("it-IT")
```

Similarly, the My.Application.CommandLineArgs property returns the same information available through the Environment.GetCommandLineArgs method, whereas the My.Application.GetEnvironmentVariable method is identical to Environment.GetEnvironmentVariable. See

Table 16-1 for the complete list of members of the My.Application object. (Notice that a few items in the table are related to ClickOnce applications, which I don't cover in this book.)

Table 16-1   The My.Application Object

Category	Name	Description
Properties	ApplicationContext	Returns the ApplicationContext used for the current Windows Forms application, which in turn lets you retrieve the main form.
	CommandLineArgs	Gets a ReadOnlyCollection(Of String) containing the command-line arguments for the application.
	Culture	Gets the CultureInfo object used to parse and format numbers and dates.
	Deployment	Gets the application's ClickOnce Application-Deployment object, which provides support for updating the current deployment programmatically and for on-demand download of files.
	Info	Returns an AssemblyInfo object, which in turn lets you retrieve version, path, title, description, working set, and other information on the application's assembly.
	IsNetworkDeployed	True if the application was deployed using Click-Once.
	Log	Returns the Log object, which in turn provides properties and methods for writing event and exception information to the application log's listeners.
	UICulture	Returns the CultureInfo that the current thread uses to retrieve culture-specific resources.
Properties (Windows Forms only)	MinimumSplashScreen-DisplayTime	Determines the minimum length of time, in milliseconds, that the splash screen is displayed.
	OpenForms	Returns the collection of open forms.
	SaveMySettingsOnExit	Determines whether the application saves all user settings on exit.
	SplashScreen	Determines the form to be used as the splash screen.
Methods	ChangeCulture(string)	Changes the culture used to parse and format numbers and dates.
	ChangeUICulture(string)	Changes the culture that the current thread uses to retrieve culture-specific resources.
	GetEnvironment-Variable(varname)	Returns the value of an environment variable.
Methods (Windows Forms only)	DoEvents	Processes all the Windows messages in the queue.

Table 16-1   **The My.Application Object** *(Continued)*

Category	Name	Description
	OnCreateSplashScreen (protected scope)	Executes when the application creates its splash screen.
	Run(commandargs)	Starts the Visual Basic startup/shutdown application model.
Events (Windows Forms only)	NetworkAvailability-Changed	Fires when the application gains or loses availability of the network.
	Shutdown	Fires when the application shuts down, after all forms have been closed. (It doesn't fire in case of abnormal termination.)
	Startup	Fires when the application starts up, before the startup form is created.
	StartupNextInstance	Fires when another instance of a single-instance application starts up; receives the command line of the other application.
	UnhandledException	Fires when an unhandled exception occurs; the handler for this event can decide whether the application should terminate.

The Info object is especially useful in that it returns a bunch of information that would otherwise be available only through reflection-based or other techniques. You assign most of these values in the dialog box that you reach by means of the Assembly Information button in the Application tab of the My Project designer (see Figure 16-2). This dialog box provides a visual way to edit all the assembly-level attributes that are stored in AssemblyInfo.vb in the My Project folder. (You must click the Show All Files button in the Solution Explorer window to see this file.)

Figure 16-2   The Assembly Information dialog box

Typically, you display this information in an About dialog box or use it in diagnostic reports:

```
' (txtInfo is a TextBox that will contain diagnostics information.)
With My.Application.Info
   txtInfo.AppendText("AssemblyName: " & .AssemblyName & ControlChars.CrLf)
   txtInfo.AppendText("Directory: " & .DirectoryPath & ControlChars.CrLf)
   txtInfo.AppendText(ControlChars.CrLf)

   txtInfo.AppendText("CompanyName: " & .CompanyName & ControlChars.CrLf)
   txtInfo.AppendText("Copyright:" & .Copyright & ControlChars.CrLf)
   txtInfo.AppendText("Description: " & .Description & ControlChars.CrLf)
   txtInfo.AppendText("ProductName:" & .ProductName & ControlChars.CrLf)
   txtInfo.AppendText("Title:" & .Title & ControlChars.CrLf)
   txtInfo.AppendText("Trademark: " & .Trademark & ControlChars.CrLf)
   txtInfo.AppendText("Version: " & .Version.ToString() & ControlChars.CrLf)
   txtInfo.AppendText(ControlChars.CrLf)

   txtInfo.AppendText("Working set : " & .WorkingSet.ToString() & ControlChars.CrLf)
End With
```

The My.Application.Log object offers a simple way to log trace and error information. Basically, the application framework creates a TraceSource object named DefaultSource. The WriteEntry and the WriteException methods of the Log source do nothing but invoke the TraceEvent method of this underlying object for you:

```
' These two statements are equivalent.
My.Application.Log.WriteEntry("User login", TraceEventType.Information, 101)
My.Application.Log.TraceSource.TraceEvent(TraceEventType.Information, 101, "User login")
```

Of course, you can also access the My.Application.Log.TraceSource object directly to fully leverage the potential of this object. (See Chapter 5, "Debugging and Testing," for more details about the TraceSource object and how to control its features by means of configuration files.) When you create a new Application Configuration File item in a Visual Basic project, Microsoft Visual Studio generates a file that already accounts for the TraceSource object named DefaultSource and associates it with a FileLog listener. You can perform this association simply by uncommenting a few lines in the XML file (highlighted in bold type in the following listing):

```
<?xml version="1.0" encoding="utf-8" ?>
<configuration>
  <system.diagnostics>
    <sources>
      <!-- This section defines the logging configuration for My.Application.Log -->
        <source name="DefaultSource" switchName="DefaultSwitch">
          <listeners>
            <add name="FileLog"/>
            <!-- Uncomment the below section to write to the Application Event Log -->
            <!--<add name="EventLog"/>-->
          </listeners>
        </source>
    </sources>
    <switches>
      <add name="DefaultSwitch" value="Information" />
    </switches>
```

```
  <sharedListeners>
    <add name="FileLog"
      type="Microsoft.VisualBasic.Logging.FileLogTraceListener, Microsoft.VisualBasic,
      Version=8.0.0.0, Culture=neutral, PublicKeyToken=b03f5f7f11d50a3a,
      processorArchitecture=MSIL" initializeData="FileLogWriter" />
    <!-- Uncomment the following section and replace APPLICATION_NAME with the name
      of your application to write to the Application Event Log -->
    <!--<add name="EventLog" type="System.Diagnostics.EventLogTraceListener"
      initializeData="APPLICATION_NAME"/> -->
  </sharedListeners>
 </system.diagnostics>
</configuration>
```

The simplest way to write a handler for one of the events of the My.Application object is by clicking the View Application Events button in the Application tab of the My Project designer. This action brings you to a module named ApplicationEvents.vb stored in the My Project folder. The following code provides an example of the many techniques you can implement thanks to these events:

```
Partial Friend Class MyApplication
    Private Sub MyApplication_Shutdown(ByVal sender As Object, ByVal e As EventArgs) _
        Handles Me.Shutdown
      ' Save all data when the application shuts down.
      …
    End Sub

    Private Sub MyApplication_Startup(ByVal sender As Object, _
        ByVal e As Microsoft.VisualBasic.ApplicationServices.StartupEventArgs) _
        Handles Me.Startup
      ' Refuse to activate this program from 6 P.M. to 8 A.M.
      If Now.TimeOfDay > New TimeSpan(18, 0, 0) OrElse Now.TimeOfDay < New TimeSpan(8, 0, 0)
Then
        e.Cancel = True
      End If
    End Sub

    Private Sub MyApplication_StartupNextInstance(ByVal sender As Object, ByVal _
        e As Microsoft.VisualBasic.ApplicationServices.StartupNextInstanceEventArgs) _
        Handles Me.StartupNextInstance
      If e.CommandLine.Count >= 1 Then
        Dim documentFile As String = e.CommandLine(0)
        ' Load the requested document inside the current instance.
        …
      End If
    End Sub

    Private Sub MyApplication_UnhandledException(ByVal sender As Object, ByVal _
        e As Microsoft.VisualBasic.ApplicationServices.UnhandledExceptionEventArgs) _
        Handles Me.UnhandledException
      ' Log the exception, and then ask whether the user wants to exit.
      My.Application.Log.WriteException(e.Exception)
      Dim msg As String = e.Exception.Message & ControlChars.CrLf & _
        "Do you want to exit the application?"
      If MessageBox.Show(msg, "Error!", MessageBoxButtons.YesNo, MessageBoxIcon.Error) _
          = DialogResult.Yes Then
```

```
                e.ExitApplication = True
        Else
                e.ExitApplication = False
        End If
    End Sub

    Private Sub MyApplication_NetworkAvailabilityChanged(ByVal sender As Object, _
            ByVal e As Microsoft.VisualBasic.Devices.NetworkAvailableEventArgs) _
            Handles Me.NetworkAvailabilityChanged
        If e.IsNetworkAvailable Then
            ' Connect the application to network resources.
            …
        Else
            ' Disconnect the application from network resources.
            …
        End If
    End Sub
End Class
```

If for some reason you can't or don't want to enable the Visual Basic application framework, you need to know how to simulate these events. The Startup event can be replaced by a piece of code in the Sub Main procedure. The System.Windows.Forms.Application object exposes the ApplicationExit and ThreadException events, which work similarly to the Shutdown and UnhandledException events of the My.Application object. Replacing the NetworkAvailability-Changed event requires that you trap the event with the same name exposed by the System .Net.NetworkInformation.NetworkChange object. In some cases, you might need to use this object anyway, specifically when you also need to be alerted when the network address changes:

```
Sub Main()
    AddHandler NetworkChange.NetworkAvailabilityChanged, AddressOf NetAvailabilityChanged
        AddHandler NetworkChange.NetworkAddressChanged, AddressOf NetAddressChanged
    ' Display the main form.
    Application.Run(New MainForm())
End Sub

Private Sub NetAvailabilityChanged(ByVal sender As Object, ByVal e As
NetworkAvailabilityEventArgs)
    ' The computer has been connected to or disconnected from the network.
    …
End Sub

Private Sub NetAddressChanged(ByVal sender As Object, ByVal e As EventArgs)
    ' The network address of the computer has changed.
    …
End Sub
```

Another way to get an alert when the computer goes offline and online is by trapping the NetworkAvailabilityChanged event of the My.Computer.Network object.

Unfortunately, there is no simple alternative way to detect when another instance of the current application is launched and to pass its command-line arguments to the running instance. If you need to implement single-instance applications, use of the Visual Basic application framework and the StartupNextInstance event is your best choice.

The My.Computer Object

The My.Computer object is undoubtedly the richest object in the My namespace in terms of functionality. Except for the Name property, which returns the name of the computer, all its properties return child objects that enable you to leverage the many features of the local computer: file and audio systems, memory, keyboard, mouse, network, serial ports, the Clipboard, and the system registry. I have summarized these child objects and their main members in Table 16-2. As usual, you can reach these capabilities by means of standard .NET types, but the My.Computer object offers some very convenient shortcuts.

Table 16-2   Child Objects of the My.Computer Object

Object	Member	Description
Audio	Play(string, mode)	Plays .wav data stored in a file, a stream, or a Byte array; offers the option to play in the background and loop until the Stop method is invoked.
	PlaySystemSound(sound)	Plays a system sound; the argument is a System.Media.SystemSound object that represents one of the system sounds in the Windows operating system.
	Stop	Stops a sound playing in the background.
Clipboard	Clear	Clears the contents of the Clipboard.
	ContainsAudio, ContainsFileDropList, ContainsImage	Return True if the Clipboard contains audio data, a list of drop files, or an image, respectively.
	ContainsData(format)	Returns True if the Clipboard contains data in the specified format.
	ContainsText([format])	Returns True if the Clipboard contains text; the optional format argument can be Text, UnicodeText, Rtf, Html, CommaSeparatedValue.
	GetAudioStream, GetData(string), GetFileDropList, GetImage, GetText([format])	Return the contents of the Clipboard as an audio stream, as data in arbitrary format, as a list of drop files, as an image, or as text in the specified format, respectively.
	GetDataObject	Returns an IDataObject that represents the data stored in the Clipboard.
	SetAudio(bytearr), SetAudio(stream)	Place audio data in the Clipboard.
	SetData(format, object)	Place data in arbitrary format in the Clipboard.

Table 16-2   Child Objects of the My.Computer Object *(Continued)*

Object	Member	Description
	SetDataObject(data, copy [retrytimes, retrydelay])	Place an object in the Clipboard; if the copy argument is True, data stays in the Clipboard after the application exits; the last two optional arguments enable you to specify whether an unsuccessful operation should be retried.
	SetFileDropList(filepaths)	Add a collection of filenames to the Clipboard, ready to be dropped.
	SetImage(image)	Add an image to the Clipboard in bitmap format.
	SetText(text [,format])	Add text data to the Clipboard in the specified format.
Clock	GmtTime	Returns the current local date and time on this computer, expressed as a UTC (GMT) time.
	LocalTime	Returns the current local date and time on this computer.
	TickCount	Returns the millisecond count from the computer's system timer.
FileSystem	CombinePath(path1, path2)	Combines two paths.
	CopyDirectory(source, dest [,overwrite]), CopyDirectory(source, dest [,showUi, uiCancel])	Copy a directory; the showUi argument lets you decide to display the standard Windows dialog box or just the error message; the uiCancel argument lets you decide whether an exception is thrown if the user cancels the action.
	CopyFile(source, dest [,overwrite]), CopyFile(source, dest [,showUi, uiCancel])	Copy a file. (See CopyDirectory for a description of arguments.)
	CreateDirectory(path)	Creates a new directory.
	CurrentDirectory	Gets or sets the current directory.
	DeleteDirectory(path, force), DeleteDirectory(path, showUi, recycle [,uiCancel])	Delete a folder; the force argument specifies whether the method throws an exception if the folder isn't empty; the showUi argument determines whether to display the standard Windows dialog box or just the error message; the recycle argument enables you to decide whether to send files to the recycle bin; the uiCancel argument determines whether an exception is thrown if the user cancels the action.
	DeleteFile(path), DeleteFile(path, showUi, recycle [,uiCancel])	Delete a file. (See DeleteDirectory for a description of arguments.)
	DirectoryExists(path), FileExists(path)	Return True if the specified directory or file exists.

Table 16-2   Child Objects of the My.Computer Object *(Continued)*

Object	Member	Description
	Drives	Gets a ReadOnlyCollection(Of DriveInfo) containing information on this computer's drives.
	FindInFiles(path, search, ignorecase, recurse [,wildcards])	Returns a ReadOnlyCollection(Of String) containing the names of all the files in the specified folder that contain a text string; the recurse argument lets you extend the search to subdirectories; the wildcards argument is a ParamArray that specifies which files should be searched.
	GetDriveInfo(drive), GetDirectoryInfo(path), GetFileInfo(path)	Return the DriveInfo, DirectoryInfo, or FileInfo object corresponding to the specified path.
	GetDirectories(path [,recurse, wildcards]), GetFiles(path [,recurse, wildcards])	Return a ReadOnlyCollection(Of String) containing the names of all the subdirectories and all files in the specified folder, respectively; the recurse argument lets you extend the search to subdirectories; the wildcards argument is a ParamArray that specifies which directories should be returned.
	GetName(path)	Returns the name and the extension of a file or a directory (obtained by stripping the directory portion of the name).
	GetParentPath(path)	Returns the path portion of a filename or directory name.
	GetTempFileName	Creates a uniquely named, zero-byte temporary file on disk and returns the full path of that file.
	MoveDirectory(source, dest [,overwrite]), MoveDirectory (source, dest [,showUi, uiCancel])	Move a directory to a different location. (See CopyDirectory for a description of arguments.)
	MoveFile(source, dest [,overwrite]), MoveFile (source, dest [,showUi, uiCancel])	Move a file to a different location. (See CopyDirectory for a description of arguments.)
	OpenTextFieldParser(path, widths), OpenTextFieldParser(path, delimiters)	Open a fixed-width text file and returns a FieldParser object that can be used to extract field values; widths is a ParamArray that specifies the width of each field; delimiters is a ParamArray that specifies the field delimiters.
	OpenTextFileReader(path [,enconding])	Opens a text file for reading and returns a StreamReader object.
	OpenTextFileWriter(path, append [,encoding])	Opens a text file for writing, optionally in append mode, and returns a StreamReader object.

Table 16-2   Child Objects of the My.Computer Object *(Continued)*

Object	Member	Description
	ReadAllByes(path), ReadAll-Text(path [,encoding])	Return the contents of a binary or text file, respectively.
	RenameDirectory(path, newname), RenameFile(path, newname)	Rename a directory or a file, respectively.
	SpecialDirectories	Gets an object whose properties return the path of special folders: AllUsersApplicationData, CurrentUserApplicationData, Desktop, MyDocuments, MyMusic, MyPictures, Programs, Temp.
	WriteAllBytes(path, bytearr, append)	Writes a Byte array to the specified binary file, optionally in append mode.
	WriteAllText(path, text, append [,encoding])	Writes a string to the specified text file, optionally in append mode and with a specific encoding.
Info	AvailablePhysicalMemory	Gets the total amount of free physical memory for the computer.
	AvailableVirtualMemory	Gets the total amount of free virtual address space available for the computer.
	InstalledUICulture	Gets the CultureInfo object representing the culture installed with the operating system.
	OSFullName	Gets the full operating system name, for example, "Microsoft Windows Server 2003 Standard Edition."
	OSPlatform	Gets the platform identifier for the operating system of the computer, for example, "Win32NT."
	OSVersion	Gets the version of the operating system of the computer, for example, "5.2.3790.0."
	TotalPhysicalMemory	Gets the total amount of physical memory for the computer.
	TotalVirtualMemory	Gets the total amount of virtual address space available for the computer.
Keyboard	AltKeyDown, CtrlKeyDown, ShiftKeyDown	Return True if the Alt, Ctrl, or Shift key is being pressed.
	CapsLock, NumLock, ScrollLock	Return True if the CapsLock, NumLock, or ScrollLock key is turned on.
	SendKeys(keys [,wait])	Sends one or more keystrokes to the active window, optionally waiting until the keys are processed.
Mouse	ButtonsSwapped	Returns True if the functionality of the left and right mouse buttons has been swapped.
	WheelExists	Returns True if the mouse has a scroll wheel.
	WheelScrollLines	Returns a number that indicates how much to scroll when the mouse wheel is rotated one notch.

Table 16-2 Child Objects of the My.Computer Object *(Continued)*

Object	Member	Description
Network	DownloadFile(url, destfile [[,username, password [,showUi, timeout, overwrite, cancel]])	Downloads a file from a URL; url is the remote address (can be a string or a System.Uri object); destfile is the name of the local file to be created; username and password are the credentials to be supplied if the site requires authentication (can be replaced by an ICredentials object); showUi is True to display a dialog box; timeout is the connection timeout; overwrite is True to force overwriting an existing local file; cancel specifies whether an exception is thrown if the user cancels the operation.
	IsAvailable	Returns True if the computer is connected to a network.
	NetworkAvailability-Changed	This event fires when the value of the IsAvailable property changes.
	Ping(url [,timeout])	Pings the specified server; url is the remote address (can be a string or a System.Uri object). The timeout argument is the optional connection timeout in milliseconds; returns True if the operation is successful.
	UploadFile(url, sourcefile [[,username, password [,showUi, timeout, overwrite, cancel]])	Uploads a file to a remote address; sourcefile is the name of the local file that must be uploaded. (See DownloadFile for a description of all other arguments.)
Ports	OpenSerialPort(name [baudrate, parity, databits, stopbits])	Opens a serial port with specified properties and returns a SerialPort object.
	SerialPortNames	Gets a ReadOnlyCollection(Of String) containing the names of all the serial ports installed on the computer.
Registry	ClassesRoot, CurrentConfig, CurrentUser, DynData, Local-Machine, PerformanceData, Users	Return a RegistryKey value corresponding to a HKEY_* registry hive.
	GetValue(keyname, value-name, defvalue)	Returns an object containing the value of the specified registry value, or the defvalue argument if the value is missing.
	SetValue(keyname, value-name, value)	Stores the value passed in the third argument to the specified registry value.
Screen	AltScreens	Gets an array of all displays in the system.
	BitsPerPixel	Returns the number of bits of memory associated with one pixel of data.
	Bounds	Returns a System.Drawing.Rectangle object that represents the bounds of the display.
	DeviceName	Gets the device name associated with the screen, for example, "\\.\DISPLAY1."

Table 16-2   Child Objects of the My.Computer Object *(Continued)*

Object	Member	Description
	FromPoint(point), FromControl(ctrl), FromRectangle(rect), FromHandle(intptr)	Gets the Screen object for the display that contains the specified point or the largest portion of the specified control, rectangle, or object referred to by the specified handle.
	GetBounds(point)	Gets the bounds of the display that contains the specified point.
	GetWorkingArea(point), GetWorkingArea(rect)	Get the working area closest to the specified point or rectangle. (The working area is the desktop area of the display, excluding the taskbar, docked windows, and docked toolbars.)
	Primary	Returns True if the screen is the primary screen. (The object returned by My.Computer.Screen is always the primary screen.)
	PrimaryScreen	Returns the primary screen.
	WorkingArea	Returns a System.Drawing.Rectangle object that represents the working area of the display, that is, the desktop area excluding the taskbar, docked windows, and docked toolbars.

Working with Sounds

The My.Computer.Audio object has only one feature: it allows you to play a .wav file, either synchronously or asynchronously. In the former case, the Play method waits for the completion of the action; in the latter case, the sound goes in the background and you can even loop over it until the application executes the Stop method. For example, you can keep a sound playing while a form is being displayed:

```
Private Sub Form1_Load(ByVal sender As Object, ByVal e As EventArgs) Handles Me.Load
    My.Computer.Audio.Play("c:\mybackgroundsound.wav", AudioPlayMode.BackgroundLoop)
End Sub

Private Sub Form1_FormClosed(ByVal sender As Object, _
        ByVal e As FormClosedEventArgs) Handles Me.FormClosed
    My.Computer.Audio.Stop()
End Sub
```

You aren't limited to playing sound files because you can also play audio data stored in a stream or a Byte array. (Later in this chapter, I explain how to play sounds stored as resources.) Unfortunately, you can play only standard Pulse-Coded Modulation (PCM) wave files; other forms of .wav files, as well as MP3 and WMA files, aren't supported. Another minor problem is that data can't be loaded in the background; thus, the user interface will freeze if loading a huge audio file. You can work around the latter problem by staying clear of the My.Computer.Audio object and using the System.Media.SoundPlayer object instead:

```
Dim WithEvents Player As New SoundPlayer
```

```
Private Sub Form1_Load(ByVal sender As Object, ByVal e As EventArgs) Handles Me.Load
   Player.SoundLocation = "c:\mybackgroundsound.wav"
   Player.LoadAsync()
End Sub

Private Sub Player_LoadCompleted(ByVal sender As Object, _
      ByVal e As AsyncCompletedEventArgs) Handles Player.LoadCompleted
   Player.PlayLooping()
End Sub
```

Working with the Clipboard

The My.Computer.Clipboard object offers the same methods exposed by the System.Windows.Forms.Clipboard object; thus, you can switch from one object to the other with minimal edits to source code. When working with data in a standard format—text, image, audio, or a list of files dropped from Windows Explorer—you can use the corresponding Get*Xxxx*, Set-*Xxxx*, and Contains*Xxxx* methods. These methods are self-explanatory, so I won't cover them in great detail. Just notice that the GetText, SetText, and ContainsText methods support an optional enumerated TextDataFormat value, which can be Text, UnicodeText, Rtf, Html, and CommaSeparatedValue; thus, you should write code like the following:

```
' Read text from the Clipboard in RTF format if possible, else read it
' as plain text. (rtbClipboard is a RichTextBox control.)
If My.Computer.Clipboard.ContainsText(TextDataFormat.Rtf) Then
   rtbClipboard.Rtf = My.Computer.Clipboard.GetText(TextDataFormat.Rtf)
ElseIf My.Computer.Clipboard.ContainsText(TextDataFormat.Text) Then
   rtbClipboard.Text = My.Computer.Clipboard.GetText(TextDataFormat.Text)
End If
```

When you write data in a format other than the ones listed previously, you should use the SetData method. For example, let's suppose you have defined this Widget class:

```
<Serializable()> _
Public Class Widget
   Public Name As String
End Class
```

(Notice that the object must be marked with the Serializable attribute to be successfully placed in the Clipboard.) You can then create a custom "Widget" format and save in this format:

```
Dim widget As New Widget
widget.Name = "Foobar"
My.Computer.Clipboard.SetData("Widget", widget)
```

Either the same or a different instance of this application—or any other application that has a reference to the Widget type—can retrieve a Widget object from the Clipboard as follows:

```
Dim widget As Widget = DirectCast(My.Computer.Clipboard.GetData("Widget"), Widget)
If widget Is Nothing Then
   MsgBox("No Widget object in the clipboard")
Else
   MsgBox("Found a widget object named " & widget.Name)
End If
```

The GetDataObject method returns an IDataObject object, whose members allow you to retrieve more information about the data in the Clipboard:

```
' Retrieve all the formats currently in the Clipboard; the True argument means
' that we are also interested in the format obtainable by converting the data.
Dim formats() As String = My.Computer.Clipboard.GetDataObject().GetFormats(True)
```

The SetDataObject method enables you to copy a piece of information in multiple formats to the Clipboard. Here's how to proceed:

```
Dim data As New DataObject
data.SetData("Text", "1234")              ' Also copies in UnicodeText format.
data.SetData("System.String", "1234")
data.SetData("System.Int32", 1234)
My.Computer.Clipboard.SetDataObject(data)
```

Here's how you can later retrieve the data in one of these formats:

```
Dim value As Integer = DirectCast(My.Computer.Clipboard.GetData("System.Int32"), Integer)
MsgBox(value)
```

The next code snippet shows how to copy data in comma-delimited format so that you can pass it to other applications such as Microsoft Office Excel with very little effort:

```
' Export data to a 2x4 cell range in Excel.
Dim values As String = String.Format("1,2,3,4{0}5,6,7,8{0}", Environment.NewLine)
Dim bytes As Byte() = System.Text.Encoding.UTF8.GetBytes(values)
Dim ms As New System.IO.MemoryStream(bytes)
Dim data As New DataObject()
data.SetData(DataFormats.CommaSeparatedValue, ms)
Clipboard.SetDataObject(data, True)
MsgBox("Switch to Excel and paste data where you see fit.")
```

Notice that many non-U.S. cultures use the comma as the decimal separator. When you write applications for the world market, you should separate items by means of the character returned by the ListSeparator property of the TextInfo object exposed by the CultureInfo object of the current culture, as in this code:

```
Dim values As String = String.Format("1,2,3,4{0}5,6,7,8{0}", Environment.NewLine)
values = values.Replace(",", Thread.CurrentThread.CurrentCulture.TextInfo.ListSeparator)
```

The SetDataObject method is capable of making the copied data persist in the Clipboard even after the current application has ended and can retry the copy operation the specified number of times if it doesn't succeed on the first attempt.

Working with the File System

The My.Computer.FileSystem object exposes many of the methods that are made available by the Directory, File, and Path types in the System.IO namespace. For example, you can copy, delete, move, and rename both individual files and entire directories (or directory trees), enumerate all folders and files in a directory, parse a path for the filename and folder name portions, and read or write an entire text or binary file in a single operation. The syntax of most methods is so obvious that I won't cover all of them in detail. (If you are puzzled, just review Chapter 15, "Files, Directories, and Streams.")

Hidden in the signature of a few methods, however, are some real gems that have no counterparts in the System.IO namespace. For example, the FindInFiles method lets you perform a case-sensitive or case-insensitive search in all the files in a directory or a directory tree:

```
' Retrieve the path of the My Documents special folder.
Dim myDocumentsPath As String = My.Computer.FileSystem.SpecialDirectories.MyDocuments
' Look for the string "Visual Basic" in all document files in this
' directory tree, in case-insensitive mode.
Dim files As ReadOnlyCollection(Of String) = My.Computer.FileSystem.FindInFiles( _
    myDocumentsPath, "Visual Basic", True, SearchOption.SearchAllSubDirectories)
' Show all filenames in a list box.
lstFiles.Items.Clear()
For Each file As String In files
    lstFiles.Items.Add(file)
Next
```

Even more interesting is the ability that some methods have to display a standard Windows dialog box when performing a file operation and to detect whether the user clicks the Cancel button to stop the action. (See Figure 16-3.) The following example shows how the CopyDirectory method works:

```
' Copy the c:\Data folder to the c:\Backup folder, showing the standard dialog box.
Try
    My.Computer.FileSystem.CopyDirectory("c:\Data", "c:\Backup", _
        UIOption.AllDialogs, UICancelOption.ThrowException)
Catch ex As OperationCanceledException
    ' The user canceled the operation.
    …
End Try
```

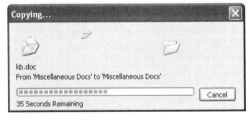

Figure 16-3   The Copying dialog box

You can have this method display only error messages, and you can decide that no exception is thrown if the user cancels the operation. (Oddly, you get an OperationCanceledException only if users cancel the command when asked whether a file should be replaced, but not if they click the Cancel button while the copy operation is progressing.) Notice that no type in the "official" .NET Framework exposes such a functionality, and in fact displaying this dialog box in Microsoft .NET Framework version 1.1 requires a call to the Windows API using PInvoke.

The CopyDirectory, CopyFile, MoveDirectory, MoveFile, DeleteDirectory, and DeleteFile methods all work in a similar manner, so I won't show an example for each one of them. The last two methods, however, have an additional option that enables you to send the deleted files to the Recycle Bin or delete them permanently:

```
' Delete the c:\tempfiles folder, displaying the standard Windows dialog box,
' sending files to the Recycle Bin, and doing nothing if user canceled the action.
My.Computer.FileSystem.DeleteDirectory("c:\tempfiles", UIOption.AllDialogs, _
    RecycleOption.SendToRecycleBin, UICancelOption.DoNothing)
```

Retrieving Information About the Computer

The Clock, Info, Keyboard, Mouse, Ports, and Screen child objects of My.Computer are basically containers for read-only properties that you can query to retrieve information about the system. For example, the following code retrieves information about the operating system and the screen:

```
' Display information in a list box named lstResults.
lstResults.Items.Clear()
With My.Computer.Info
    lstResults.Items.Add("AvailablePhysicalMemory = " & .AvailablePhysicalMemory.ToString())
    lstResults.Items.Add("AvailableVirtualMemory = " & .AvailableVirtualMemory.ToString())
    lstResults.Items.Add("InstalledUICulture = " & .InstalledUICulture.Name)
    lstResults.Items.Add("OSFullName = " & .OSFullName)
    lstResults.Items.Add("OSPlatform = " & .OSPlatform)
    lstResults.Items.Add("OSVersion = " & .OSVersion)
    lstResults.Items.Add("TotalPhysicalMemory = " & .TotalPhysicalMemory.ToString())
    lstResults.Items.Add("TotalVirtualMemory = " & .TotalVirtualMemory.ToString())
    lstResults.Items.Add("")
End With
With My.Computer.Screen
    lstResults.Items.Add("BitsPerPixel = " & .BitsPerPixel.ToString())
    lstResults.Items.Add("Width = " & .Bounds.Width.ToString())
    lstResults.Items.Add("Height = " & .Bounds.Height.ToString())
    lstResults.Items.Add("DeviceName = " & .DeviceName.ToString())
    lstResults.Items.Add("Primary = " & .Primary.ToString())
    lstResults.Items.Add("WorkingArea.Left = " & .WorkingArea.Left.ToString())
    lstResults.Items.Add("WorkingArea.Top = " & .WorkingArea.Top.ToString())
    lstResults.Items.Add("WorkingArea.Width = " & .WorkingArea.Width.ToString())
    lstResults.Items.Add("WorkingArea.Height = " & .WorkingArea.Height.ToString())
    lstResults.Items.Add("")
End With
```

Most of the information exposed by these child objects is available through other types in the .NET Framework, but the My.Computer object usually offers a more streamlined solution. For example, the ModifierKeys static property of the System.Windows.Forms.Control type returns information about which keys are currently pressed, but the AltKeyDown, ShiftKey-Down, and CtrlKeyDown properties of the My.Computer.Keyboard object work even if you don't have a Control instance on hand (for example, in Console applications).

The My.Computer.Ports object offers just a couple of members: the SerialPortNames returns a collection of strings holding the names of all the serial ports installed on the computer; the OpenSerialPort method opens a serial port and returns a System.IO.Ports.SerialPort object that you can use to interact with the port. In practice, you can perform the same operations directly by means of the SerialPort object without going through the My namespace.

Working with the Network

The My.Network object simplifies some common tasks related to the Internet. The IsAvailable property returns True if the computer is connected to a network; when the value of this property changes, the object fires a NetworkAvailabilityChanged event. As I explained earlier in this chapter, you can detect when this happens also by means of the System.Net.NetworkInformation.NetworkChange object.

The Ping method takes a computer name, a URL, or an IP address and an optional timeout, and returns a Boolean indicating whether the specified address can be pinged. In practice, you should always wrap this method in a Try...Catch block:

```
Dim found As Boolean = False
If My.Computer.Network.IsAvailable Then
    Try
        ' Attempt to ping the dotnet2themax.com site, with a 3-second timeout.
        found = My.Computer.Network.Ping("www.dotnet2themax.com", 3000)
    Catch ex As Exception
        ' Optionally display an error message here.
    End Try
End If
If found Then
    ' The site is reachable.
    …
End If
```

The DownloadFile method can be used to either download a file or, more simply, read the contents of an HTML page at a given URL. It accepts an optional user name and password, so it can be used with sites that support Basic authentication (use Nothing if credentials aren't required), can display a dialog box to show the progress of the operation, can time out after the specified interval in milliseconds (default is 100 seconds), and can automatically overwrite the local file if so desired.

```
Try
    ' The remote address must include a protocol name.
    Dim url As String = "http://www.microsoft.com"
    Dim fileName As String = "c:\Microsoft Home Page.html"
    ' True means that a progress dialog box should be displayed;
    ' False means that the local file shouldn't be overwritten;
    ' Timeout is 3 seconds.
    My.Computer.Network.DownloadFile(url, fileName, Nothing, Nothing, True, 3000, False)
Catch ex As WebException When ex.Message = "The operation has timed out"
    ' A timeout has occurred: the site isn't reachable.
    …
```

```
Catch ex As OperationCanceledException
   ' The end user canceled the operation while it was progressing.
   ...
Catch ex As IOException
   ' Unable to save the file, presumably because the target file already exists.
   ...
End Try
```

The UploadFile method is similar and takes the same set of arguments, except the second argument is the file that must be uploaded to the URL specified by the first argument.

Being based on types defined in the System.Net namespace, the My.Computer.Network object is subject to the configuration settings found in the <system.net> section of the configuration file. For example, the following settings specify the address of the proxy to be used for all Internet requests and that the proxy shouldn't be used for local addresses, for URLs in the form of *.codearchitects.com, and for IP addresses in the form of 192.168.100.*:

```
<configuration>
   <system.net>
      <defaultProxy>
         <proxy proxyaddress="http://myproxyserver:80" bypassonlocal="true"/>
         <bypasslist>
            <!-- addresses are expressed as regular expressions -->
            <add address="\w+\.codearchitects\.com />
            <add address="192\.168\.100\.\d{1,3}" />
         </bypasslist>
      </defaultProxy>
   </system.net>
</configuration>
```

Working with the Registry

The My.Computer.Registry object exposes seven read-only properties, each one returning the Microsoft.Win32.RegistryKey object corresponding to one of the registry hives, such as HKEY_CLASSES_ROOT, HKEY_CURRENT_CONFIG, and so forth. As a matter of fact, you can sidestep the My.Computer.Registry object and obtain these objects by means of the properties exposed by the Microsoft.Win32.Registry object:

```
' Two equivalent ways to get a RegistryKey object
Dim key1 As RegistryKey = My.Computer.Registry.ClassesRoot
Dim key2 As RegistryKey = Registry.ClassesRoot
```

In all code samples that follow I use the My.Computer.Registry object, but it is intended that you can work directly with the Microsoft.Win32.Registry object instead.

Each RegistryKey object has three instance properties, whose names are entirely self-explanatory: Name, SubKeyCount, and ValueCount. If SubKeyCount is higher than 0, you can use the GetSubKeyNames method to return an array of strings that contains the names of all the subkeys, and then you can use the OpenSubKey method to retrieve the RegistryKey object corresponding to each subkey. If the key doesn't exist, this method returns Nothing without throwing an exception:

```
' Check whether Microsoft Word is installed on this computer
' by searching the HKEY_CLASSES_ROOT\Word.Application key.
Dim key As RegistryKey = My.Computer.Registry.ClassesRoot.OpenSubKey("Word.Application")
If key Is Nothing Then
   Console.WriteLine("Microsoft Word isn't installed")
Else
   Console.WriteLine("Microsoft Word is installed")
   ' Always close registry keys after using them.
   key.Close
End If
```

If the ValueCount property is greater than 0, you can use the GetValueNames method to retrieve an array of all the value names under the current key, and then you can use the GetValue method to retrieve the data associated with a given value. The following reusable routine peeks in the registry to retrieve the CLSID associated with the specified COM component:

```
' Return the CLSID of a COM component, or "" if not found.
Function GetCLSID(ByVal ProgId As String) As String
   Dim guid As String = Nothing
   ' Open the key associated with the ProgID.
   Dim regProgID As RegistryKey = My.Computer.Registry.ClassesRoot.OpenSubKey(ProgId)
   If Not (regProgID Is Nothing) Then
      ' If found, open the CLSID subkey.
      Dim regClsid As RegistryKey = regProgID.OpenSubKey("CLSID")
      If Not (regClsid Is Nothing) Then
         ' If found, get its default value. Second optional argument is the
         ' string to be returned if the specified value doesn't exist.
         ' (Returns an Object that we must convert to a string.)
         guid = CStr(regClsid.GetValue(""))
         regClsid.Close()
      End If
      regProgId.Close()
   End If
   Return guid
End Function
```

```
' A usage example: get the CLSID of the ADODB.Recordset object.
Console.WriteLine(GetCLSID("ADODB.Recordset"))
    ' => {00000514-0000-0010-8000-00AA006D2EA4}
```

Remember to close any RegistryKey object that you opened using the OpenSubKey method or CreateSubKey (which I discuss shortly). You don't have to close the registry keys corresponding to the upper-level hives returned by static methods of the Registry class.

The GetValue method returns an object, which can contain a number, a string, an array of bytes, or Nothing if the value doesn't exist. If you want to distinguish a nonexistent value from a value whose associated data is a null string, you can pass a second argument, which is the data returned if the value hasn't been found:

```
' Return the data, or "<not found>" if the value isn't there.
Console.Write(regClsid.GetValue("", "<not found>")
```

The following snippet demonstrates how these classes let you implement routines that extract information from the registry with few lines of code:

```
' Display information on all the COM components installed on this computer.
Sub DisplayCOMComponents()
    ' Iterate over the subkeys of the HKEY_CLASSES_ROOT\CLSID key.
    Dim regClsid As RegistryKey = _
        My.Computer.Registry.ClassesRoot.OpenSubKey("CLSID")
    For Each clsid As String In regClsid.GetSubKeyNames
        ' Open the subkey.
        Dim regClsidKey As RegistryKey = regClsid.OpenSubKey(clsid)
        ' Get the ProgID. (This is the default value for this key.)
        Dim ProgID As String = CStr(regClsidKey.GetValue(""))
        ' Get the InProcServer32 key, which holds the DLL path.
        Dim regPath As RegistryKey = regClsidKey.OpenSubKey("InprocServer32")
        If regPath Is Nothing Then
            ' If not found, it isn't an in-process DLL server;
            ' let's see if it's an out-of-process EXE server.
            regPath = regClsidKey.OpenSubKey("LocalServer32")
        End If
        If Not (regPath Is Nothing) Then
            ' If either key has been found, retrieve its default value.
            Dim filePath As String = CStr(regPath.GetValue(""))
            ' Display all the relevant info gathered so far.
            Console.WriteLine(ProgId & " " & clsid & " -> " & filePath)
            regPath.Close()
        End If
        regClsidKey.Close()
    Next
End Sub
```

Figure 16-4 shows the output produced by a similar routine in the demo application, which displays the result in a ListBox control instead of in the console window.

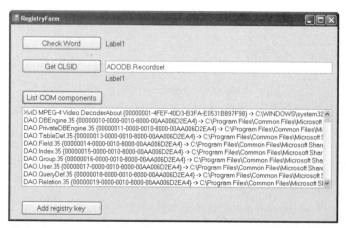

Figure 16-4   The demo application, which parses the registry and lists all installed COM components

If you already know the name of the registry value you want to read or write, you can use the GetValue and SetValue methods of the My.Computer.Registry object without going through the trouble of creating a RegistryKey object:

```
Dim keyName As String = "HKEY_CLASSES_ROOT\Word.Application\Curver"
' Second argument is the value name; use Nothing for the default value.
' Third argument is the value to be returned if the value is missing.
Dim value As String = My.Computer.Registry.GetValue(keyName, Nothing, "").ToString()
```

The RegistryKey class also lets you modify the registry by creating or deleting subkeys and values. (You can't do it directly with the My.Computer.Registry object.) When you plan to write data under a key, you must open the key for writing, which you do by passing True as the second argument to the OpenSubKey method:

```
' The following code snippets, taken together, add company/product
' keys under the HKEY_LOCALMACHINE\SOFTWARE key, as many Windows apps do.

' Open the HKEY_LOCALMACHINE\SOFTWARE key.
Dim regSoftware As RegistryKey = _
    My.Computer.Registry.LocalMachine.OpenSubKey("SOFTWARE", True)
```

The CreateSubKey method creates a registry key or opens an existing key. You don't need to specify that you're opening in writing mode:

```
' Add a key for the company name (or open it if it exists already).
Dim regCompany As RegistryKey = regSoftware.CreateSubKey("Code Architects")
' Add another key for the product name (or open it if it exists already).
Dim regProduct As RegistryKey = regCompany.CreateSubKey("FormMaximizer")
```

The SetValue method creates a new value and associates data with it. The second argument can be any data type that can be stored in the registry:

```
' Create three values under the Product key.
regProduct.SetValue("Path", "C:\FormMaximizer\Bin")  ' A string value
regProduct.SetValue("MajorVersion", 2)               ' A number
regProduct.SetValue("MinorVersion", 1)               ' A number
```

You can delete values by using the DeleteValue method and delete keys by using the Delete-SubKey method:

```
' Delete the three values just added.
regProduct.DeleteValue("Path")
regProduct.DeleteValue("MajorVersion")
regProduct.DeleteValue("MinorVersion")
' Delete the Product and Company keys after closing them.
regProduct.Close()
regCompany.DeleteSubKey("FormMaximizer")
regCompany.Close()
regSoftware.DeleteSubKey("Code Architects")
```

The RegistryKey object also exposes the DeleteSubTreeKey, which deletes an entire registry subtree. So the previous code snippet could be replaced by the following one-liner:

```
regSoftware.DeleteSubKeyTree("Code Architects")
```

> **Warning**   Writing to the registry is a dangerous activity, and you must know very well what you're doing. Otherwise, you might damage sensitive data and be forced to reinstall one or more applications or the complete operating system. At a minimum, you should back up your registry before proceeding.

The My.User Object

Despite a low number of properties and methods, which I list in Table 16-3, the My.User object is one of the most important elements in the My namespace because it lets you check the identity of the current user as well as plug in a custom authentication mechanism. By default, the Name property returns the name of the current user, if authenticated, in the format *machinename\username* or *domainname\username*:

```
If My.User.IsAuthenticated Then
    Console.WriteLine(My.User.Name)              ' => MYPC\Francesco
Else
    Console.WriteLine("User isn't authenticated")
End If
```

You can retrieve the same information by means of the Identity property of the CurrentPrincipal object. In some cases, this alternative approach can be more useful because it lets you learn which mechanism was used to authenticate the user:

```
With Thread.CurrentPrincipal.Identity
    Console.WriteLine("IsAuthenticated: " & .IsAuthenticated.ToString())
    Console.WriteLine("Name: " & .Name)
    Console.WriteLine("AuthenticationType: " & .AuthenticationType)
        ' => Can be NTLM, Basic, Forms, Passport, or a custom string.
End With
```

You can also retrieve information about the current user by means of the GetCurrent static method of the System.Security.Principal.WindowsIdentity object, assuming that the current thread isn't impersonating another user and that you haven't defined a custom Principal object.

In most cases, however, you are more interested in the user's role, such as when you want to prevent unauthorized users from performing a dangerous operation. You can specify the role to be checked by means of an enumerated value (for built-in roles) or a role name (for user-defined roles). In the latter case, you can also specify the name of a remote computer:

```
If My.User.IsInRole(BuiltInRole.Administrator) Then
    Console.WriteLine("User is an administrator.")
```

```
ElseIf My.User.IsInRole("Managers") Then
    Console.WriteLine("User is in the Managers group.")
ElseIf My.User.IsInRole("MYSERVER\Administrators") Then
    Console.WriteLine("User is an administrator of the MYSERVER computer.")
End If
```

> **Note**   By default the My.User object returns information about the current Windows user, but only if the Authentication Mode option on the Application page of the My Project designer is set to Windows. If this option is set to ApplicationDefined, the My.User object doesn't return any useful information about the current user.

Table 16-3   The My.User Object

Category	Name	Description
Properties	CurrentPrincipal	Gets or sets the current principal (for role-based security)
	IsAuthenticated	Returns True if the user has been authenticated
	Name	Returns the name of the current user
Method	InitializeWith-WindowsUser	Sets the thread's current principal to the Windows user that started the application
	IsInRole(rolename), IsInRole(builtinrole)	Returns True if the current user is in the named or built-in role passed as the argument

The My.Resources Object

Resources offer a great way to include in the assembly's executable one or more pieces of information that would otherwise be provided as separate files. For example, you can embed a text file as a resource and then read the contents in that file from inside the application without having to distribute it as a separate file.

Unlike all the My elements shown so far, and those that I cover after this section, technically speaking the My.Resources element is a namespace, not a type. (More precisely, it is a namespace that maps to a hidden type, as you'll discover in the section titled "Extending My.Resources" later in this chapter.) This hybrid between a namespace and a type is dynamically populated by Visual Studio by generating a new element each time you define a new resource on the Resources page of the My Project designer. The designer supports strings, images, icons, .wav files, and any other kind of files. For uniformity's sake, I continue to refer to My.Resources as if it were a regular type.

Adding a string resource is straightforward, as shown in Figure 16-5: you just enter a resource name, the string value, and an optional comment. For all other resource types, you can just drop a file from Windows Explorer or use one of the commands on the Add Resource menu to create a new image, icon, or text file. Interestingly, you can author new images, icons, and text files by means of editors that are built in to Visual Studio. (See Figure 16-6.)

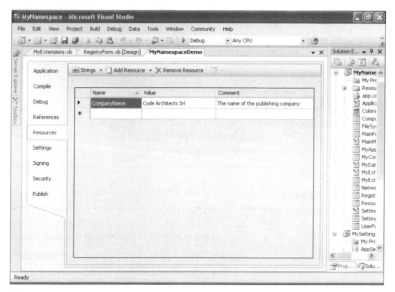

Figure 16-5   The Resources page of the My Project designer

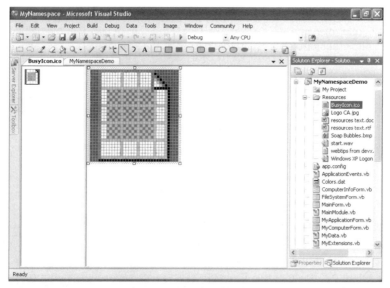

Figure 16-6   Editing a bitmap using the built-in editor

All the resources you create (other than strings) are stored in the Resources folder under the project folder. If you select a resource in the My Project designer and then switch to the Properties window, you can set a comment for the resource and use the Persistence property to decide whether the resource is linked or embedded. This property affects only how you deal with the resource from inside Visual Studio. In the former case, the resource is stored as a separate file in the project and you can edit it from inside Visual Studio; in the latter case, the resource is embedded in a .resx file and can no longer be edited directly from inside Visual Studio. Linked resources (the default option) are usually the best choice, but you might want to use embedded resources if you want to share the resource among multiple projects. Both linked and embedded resources are compiled in the executable's manifest and are accessed in the same way at run time.

Each resource must be assigned a name, and this name must be a valid Visual Basic identifier. Such a constraint ensures that the resource can be exposed as an element of the My.Resource namespace. For example, if you have defined a string resource named CompanyName, you can access it from inside the application as follows:

```
Dim company As String = My.Resources.CompanyName
```

Interestingly, you can later change the name of a resource and have Visual Studio automatically update all references in the current project. Image resources are returned as System .Drawing.Bitmap objects; thus, you can assign them to the Image property of a PictureBox control:

```
Me.PictureBox1.Image = My.Resources.CompanyLogo
```

Even more interesting, in some cases you can assign a resource to a control's property at design time and without writing a single line of code. This is possible, for example, with the Image property of PictureBox controls: switch to the Properties window, click the ellipsis button near the property name, and select the resource among those you have defined on the Resources page of the My Project designer. (See Figure 16-7.)

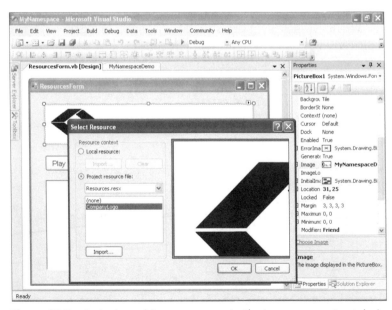

Figure 16-7   Assigning a bitmap resource to the Image property at design time

Icon resources are returned as System.Drawing.Icon objects, which you can assign to Form objects or elements in a TreeView or ListView control:

```
Me.Icon = My.Resource.MainFormIcon
```

Text files can be ASCII, Unicode, and RTF files; they are returned as strings and therefore can be assigned directly to the Text property of a TextBox control or the Rtf property of a RichTextBox control:

```
Me.RichTextBox1.Rtf = My.Resources.RegistrationHelpFile
```

When you add a file that isn't a text file, the corresponding resource is returned as a Byte array, and it's up to you to extract the information contained in the file:

```
Dim bytes() as Byte = My.Resources.CustomBinaryData
```

You can switch from binary to text representation of a file resource by modifying its FileType property in the Properties window.

Finally, audio resources are returned as System.IO.UnmanagedMemoryStream objects, which you can pass to the Play method of the My.Computer.Audio object or the System.Media .SoundPlayer object:

```
My.Computer.Audio.Play(My.Resources.ShutDownSound, AudioPlayMode.WaitToComplete)
```

The My.Resources object exposes two properties that don't correspond to any resources you've defined in the My Project designer. The ResourceManager read-only property returns the cached System.Resources.ResourceManager object that is used internally to extract the resource from the assembly; such an object is useful when it's impossible or impractical to access resources in a strongly typed fashion, as in this code:

```
' Read resources from CompanyName1 to CompanyName10.
For i As Integer = 1 To 10
   Dim resName As String = "CompanyName" & CStr(i)
   Dim company As String = My.Resources.ResourceManager.GetString(resName)
   …
Next
```

The GetResourceSet method of the ResourceManager object enables you to cycle through all the resources defined in the current assembly:

```
For Each de As DictionaryEntry In My.Resources.ResourceManager.GetResourceSet( _
      CultureInfo.CurrentUICulture, False, True)
   Console.WriteLine("{0} = {1}", de.Key, de.Value)
Next
```

The Culture property is the System.Globalization.CultureInfo object that affects which version of a locale-dependent resource is extracted. You can assign this property to retrieve resources for a locale other than the current one:

```
' From now on, use resources for the Italian culture.
My.Resources.Culture = New System.Globalization.CultureInfo("it-IT")
```

Read the "Satellite Assemblies" section in Chapter 17, "Assemblies and Resources," for more information on creating localized resources.

The My.Settings Object

As you learned in previous chapters, .NET applications store their settings in an XML configuration whose name is obtained by appending the .config extension to the executable file name (as in MyApplication.exe.config). In .NET Framework version 2.0, these configuration files have become even more flexible and powerful, thanks to the ability to store user-level settings (in addition to application-level settings) and to save these user settings when the application exits. These two features—both missing in .NET Framework 1.x—are actually related to each other: you need user-level settings (for example, preferences about color, fonts, window size and position) only if you have the ability to save these values when the user modifies them. Conversely, application-level settings (for example, the connection string to a database or the URL of a Web service) are set once and for all when the application is compiled or installed on the customer's machine, and should be modified only by the administrator or the personnel of the tech support department.

Microsoft Visual Studio 2005 automatically generates the code of the My.Settings class, which in turn exposes all the application's settings as properties. You can add one or more settings on the Settings page of the My Project designer, select its type and value, and indicate whether it's an application-level read-only setting or a user-level writeable setting. (See Figure 16-8.)

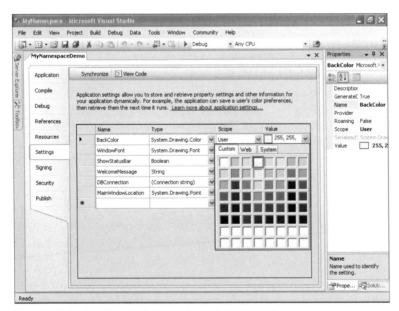

Figure 16-8   Editing settings in Visual Studio 2005

You aren't limited to settings of the String type or of another primitive .NET type, such as Int32 or Boolean. In fact, you can define a setting of any .NET type provided that the type is serializable. For example, you can create settings of type Color, Font, Point, or Size, which are great to store user preferences about your application's windows. Additionally, Visual Studio supports two special setting types for database connection strings and Web service URLs.

If you don't see the type you need in the Type list, just select the Browse element at the end of the list and select a type in the dialog box that Visual Studio displays. Notice that this dialog box doesn't display all .NET serializable types: it displays only the types for which a type UI designer exists; if this isn't the case, the value of the settings can't be edited in the Value column.

Once you have defined one or more settings, they appear as properties of the My.Settings object and you can use them in a strong-typed fashion:

```
Private Sub Form1_Load(ByVal sender As Object, ByVal e As EventArgs) Handles MyBase.Load
    ' Enforce user preferences when the form loads.
    Me.BackColor = My.Settings.BackColor
    Me.Font = My.Settings.WindowFont
End Sub
```

If the setting is at the user level, you can assign it a new value:

```
My.Settings.BackColor = Color.White
' Change the current form's font to italics.
My.Settings.WindowFont = New Font(Me.Font, FontStyle.Italics)
```

You can decide whether a user-level setting should roam when Windows roaming profiles are enabled. (Roaming users are users that can connect from any computer in a LAN and still find all their Windows preferences and settings.) To set this and a few other advanced properties of a setting, select an item on the Settings page of the My Project designer and switch to the Properties window. As it happens with the members of the My.Resources object, you can rename a setting item and Visual Studio automatically changes all occurrences in code to reflect the new name.

If the setting value is to be assigned to a property of a Windows Forms control when the parent form is displayed, you can have Visual Studio generate the code automatically, by following this procedure:

1. Select the control (or the form itself) and switch to the Properties window.

2. Expand the (ApplicationSettings) item, at the top of the property list. If the property that must be bound to the setting value isn't in the list, click the ellipses button near the (PropertyBinding) subitem.

3. Select the property from the list that appears (see Figure 16-9), click the down arrow to its right, and select one of the settings from the list, or click the New element to create a new setting.

Figure 16-9   Binding a setting to a property of a control

A small icon appears in the Properties window to the right of all the properties that are bound to application or user settings.

Quite conveniently, Visual Studio also generates the code that automatically saves a control property to a user-level setting, which makes it very easy for users to reopen a form in the same state it was in the last time they worked with it, in the same or in the previous program session. Among the many properties you can save and reload automatically are the Location and Size of each individual form of your application; even better, each user will find a form exactly where it was closed during the previous session.

> **Note**   Not all controls and not all properties on a control can be bound to a setting. More specifically, a component must implement the IBindableComponent interface and must implement a *Xxxx*Changed event for each property or implement the INotifyPropertyChanged interface to notify that a bound property's value has changed. If the component doesn't implement IBindableComponent, the property will be set when the form loads but won't be updated automatically; if the component doesn't notify when a property changes, the setting file isn't updated when the property changes. Some Windows Forms components, such as the ToolStripItem, don't support settings binding.

My.Settings Entries in Configuration Files

It is interesting to see where and how setting values are stored. The following listing is an example of a configuration file that contains one application-level and one user-level setting for an application named MyApp. (Longer entries have been rendered as multiple lines for typographical reasons.)

```
<configuration>
  <configSections>
    <sectionGroup name="userSettings"
```

```
         type="System.Configuration.UserSettingsGroup,
         System, Version=2.0.0.0, Culture=neutral, PublicKeyToken=b77a5c561934e089" >
      <section name="MyApp.My.MySettings"
          type="System.Configuration.ClientSettingsSection,
          System, Version=2.0.0.0, Culture=neutral, PublicKeyToken=b77a5c561934e089"
          allowExeDefinition="MachineToLocalUser" requirePermission="false" />
    </sectionGroup>
    <sectionGroup name="applicationSettings"
        type="System.Configuration.ApplicationSettingsGroup,
        System, Version=2.0.0.0, Culture=neutral, PublicKeyToken=b77a5c561934e089" >
      <section name="MyApp.My.MySettings"
         type="System.Configuration.ClientSettingsSection,
         System, Version=2.0.0.0, Culture=neutral, PublicKeyToken=b77a5c561934e089"
         requirePermission="false" />
    </sectionGroup>
  </configSections>

  <connectionStrings>
    <add name="MyApp.My.MySettings.DBConnection" connectionString=
        "Data Source=MAINSVR;Initial Catalog=Northwind;Integrated Security=True" />
  </connectionStrings>

  <userSettings>
    <MyApp.My.MySettings>
      <setting name="BackColor" serializeAs="String">
        <value>255, 255, 192</value>
      </setting>
      <setting name="WindowFont" serializeAs="String">
        <value>Arial Rounded MT Bold, 11.25pt</value>
      </setting>
      …
    </MyApp.My.MySettings>
  </userSettings>

  <applicationSettings>
    <MyApp.My.MySettings>
      <setting name="ShowStatusBar" serializeAs="String">
        <value>True</value>
      </setting>
      …
    </MyApp.My.MySettings>
  </applicationSettings>
</configuration>
```

The entries in the <configSections> section define the two sections that appear later in the same configuration file and the .NET types that are able to process the values these sections contain. The <userSettings> and <applicationSettings> sections are where the individual settings are defined. The <connectionStrings> section contains any connection string implicitly defined when you add a data source to the current project or when you select the (ConnectionString) type for a setting.

As you know, user-level settings can be modified by the application, and thus the entry in the application's configuration file is just the default value and doesn't necessarily reflect the current value for a given user. Here's an example of a configuration file that contains the setting values for a specific user:

```
<configuration>
   <userSettings>
      <MyApp.Settings>
         <setting name="BackColor" serializeAs="String">
            <value>180, 128, 128</value>
         </setting>
      </MyApp.Settings>
   </userSettings>
</configuration>
```

User-level settings are stored in a file named user.config in the following folder:

```
c:\Documents and Settings\Username\Local Settings\Application Data\CompanyName\
AppDomainName_Evidence_Hash\Version
```

where *CompanyName* is the value of the CompanyName attribute if available (otherwise, the element is ignored); *AppDomainName* is the FriendlyName of the current AppDomain (it usually defaults to the executable file's name); *Evidence* can be StrongName, URL, or Path and reflects the kind of evidence that identifies the assembly; *Hash* is the SHA1 hash of the evidence associated with the current AppDomain (the strong name if possible, else the URL, or the executable path); *Version* is the four-part version number of the executable. For example, the settings associated with the user named Francesco and related to version 1.1 of an application named MyApp.exe written by my company (CodeArchitects) might be stored in the following folder:

```
c:\Documents and Settings\Administrator\Local Settings\Application Data\
   CodeArchitects\MyApp.exe_StrongName_vnvevct2pj1zeypy4yebywjdwvylgr3g
```

You can discover the folder where the .NET Framework stores the settings file for the current user and the current application by querying the Application.LocalUserAppDataPath. Unfortunately, this property is read-only and you can't change the location of the settings file. (The location of the settings file is different for roaming users.) Interestingly, even if settings are stored on disk, they can be read and written to even when the application is partially trusted, as it happens with ClickOnce applications.

You can delete all the files used to store user-level settings by clicking the Synchronize button at the top of the Settings page of the My Project designer. (See Figure 16-8.)

My.Settings Properties and Methods

The My.Settings object exposes a few members in addition to those that correspond to the settings you've created in the My Project designer. The most important of these methods is Save, which saves all user-level settings:

```
My.Settings.Save()
```

Interestingly, you don't strictly need to save settings programmatically when a Windows Forms application exits because you can have the Visual Basic application framework infrastructure do it for you by simply selecting the Save My.Settings On Shutdown check box on the Application page of the My Project designer. For other types of projects, you must invoke the Save method explicitly.

The Reload method rereads all settings from the configuration file; if the setting is bound to a property, the property is also affected:

```
My.Settings.Reload()
```

The Reset method resets all settings to their default value using the data stored in the application's configuration file and ignoring any changes to user-level settings. Again, if the setting is bound to a property, the property is automatically assigned:

```
My.Settings.Reset()
```

The Item property is the default member for the My.Settings object; thus, you can retrieve the value of any property in a late-bound mode using code like this:

```
Dim backColor As Color = CType(My.Settings("BackColor"), Color)
```

The Properties collection returns information about all the defined settings and allows you to iterate over all of them:

```
For Each sp As SettingsProperty In My.Settings.Properties
   Dim desc As String = String.Format("{0} (As {1}) = {2} (Default={3})", _
      sp.Name, sp.PropertyType.FullName, My.Settings(sp.Name), sp.DefaultValue)
   Console.WriteLine(desc)
Next
```

Here's an example of what might appear in the console window after running the previous code snippet:

```
Username (As String) = Francesco (Default=unknownuser)
ShowStatusBar (As Boolean) = True (Default=False)
MainWindowLocation (As System.Drawing.Point) = Point [X=96, Y=60]
   (Default=Point [X=120, Y=100])
```

My.Settings Events

The My.Settings class also exposes four events that allow you to customize the default behavior:

- The SettingChanging event is raised before a user setting's value is changed; code in the event handler can inspect the value about to be assigned and optionally reject the assignment.

- The PropertyChanged event is raised after a user setting's value is changed.

- The SettingsLoaded event is raised when the application fills values of the My.Settings object at startup time and after a Reload or Reset method.

- The SettingsSaving event fires before the application saves user-level settings; code in the event handler can optionally cancel the save operation.

Thanks to partial classes, you can handle these events anywhere in the application, but the standard place for their handlers is in a file named Settings.vb. You can create and open this file by clicking the View Code button on the Settings page of the My Project designer.

The SettingChanging event is especially useful to reject invalid values for a given setting. For example, you might want to reject negative values for a property that indicates a position on the screen:

```
Partial Friend NotInheritable Class Settings
    Private Sub Settings_SettingChanging(ByVal sender As Object, ByVal e As _
        System.Configuration.SettingChangingEventArgs) Handles Me.SettingChanging
        Select Case e.SettingName
            Case "MainWindowLocation"
                Dim pt As Point = CType(e.NewValue, Point)
                If pt.X < 0 OrElse pt.Y < 0 Then
                    ' Cancel the assignment if either coordinate is negative.
                    e.Cancel = True
                    ' Ensure that the saved value isn't negative.
                    My.Settings.MainWindowLocation = _
                        New Point(Math.Max(pt.X, 0), Math.Max(pt.Y, 0))
                End If
            ' Test other settings here.
            …
        End Select
    End Sub
```

The PropertyChanged event is useful for notifying other portions of the application that a setting has changed. For example, if the user modifies the BackColor property, you should enforce the new value for all the forms that are currently open:

```
    ' Inside the Settings partial class…
    Private Sub Settings_PropertyChanged(ByVal sender As Object, ByVal e As _
        System.ComponentModel.PropertyChangedEventArgs) Handles Me.PropertyChanged
        If e.PropertyName = "BackColor" Then
            ' Change the BackColor property of all open forms.
            For Each frm As Form In My.Application.OpenForms
                frm.BackColor = My.Settings.BackColor
            Next
        End If
    End Sub
```

The SettingsSaving event allows you to give your user a chance to discard changes that were made during the current session:

```
    ' Inside the Settings partial class…
    Private Sub Settings_SettingsSaving(ByVal sender As Object, ByVal e As _
```

```
        System.ComponentModel.CancelEventArgs) Handles Me.SettingsSaving
        If MessageBox.Show("Do you want to save new settings?", "Exiting the Application", _
                MessageBoxButtons.YesNo, MessageBoxIcon.Question) = DialogResult.No Then
            e.Cancel = True
        End If
    End Sub
End Class
```

The My.Forms and My.WebServices Objects

The last two objects in the My namespace are My.Forms and My.WebServices, whose properties return the default instance of all the forms and all the Web service proxy classes defined in the current project. For example, if you have defined a form named MainForm in your application, you can access the default instance of such a form as follows:

```
My.Forms.MainForm.Show()
```

The obvious advantage of the My.Forms object is that you can access this default instance from anywhere in the project without having to store a reference to it in a public field of a module (or a static public field of a class, which is equivalent).

```
' Another way to define a default instance of all the forms in the project
Module Forms
    Public MainForm As New MainForm
    Public OptionsForm As New OptionsForm
End Module

...
' Elsewhere in the application…
Forms.MainForm.Show()
```

It is important to notice that the default form instance in Visual Basic 2005 behaves differently from the default form instance in Microsoft Visual Basic 6. In the earlier version of the language, you have to manually set the instance to Nothing after unloading the form to ensure that all fields are correctly reset the next time you access the form:

```
' Visual Basic 6 code
MainForm.Show()

...
' Unload the form and set it to Nothing.
Unload MainForm
Set MainForm = Nothing
```

Visual Basic 2005 doesn't require that you do any specific action when the form unloads.

The My.WebServices object is similar to My.Forms, except its properties expose a default instance of all the Web service proxy classes defined in the project. This enables you to write code like the following:

```
' Invoke the GetCoordinates method exposed by the GeoService Web service.
My.WebServices.GeoService.GetCoordinates("New York")
```

Extending and Customizing the My Namespace

An interesting feature of the My namespace is that it is a combination of types compiled in the Microsoft.VisualBasic.dll library and types that Visual Studio creates on the fly as you add elements to the current project. This little magic is made possible by partial classes, hidden modules, and a few special attributes. Because partial classes can't be split between two assemblies, the root of the My namespace actually resides inside the current project, but some of its child objects are compiled in the external DLL, whereas other are defined by source code generated in the current project.

In this section, you'll learn more about the My namespace internals and how to expand or customize the namespace with new objects or new members for existing objects. Before you get started, however, you should carefully weigh this decision. For example, you might decide that creating a traditional class library can be a better choice, especially if you want to make your extensions available to developers working in other languages. Also, keep in mind that customizing the My namespace requires that you include source code in all the projects that use the extended features, and this approach can quickly become a maintenance nightmare.

Adding Top-Level Objects

The simplest operation you can perform on the My namespace is adding a new object to the namespace at the same level as the Application, Computer, and User objects. For example, let's say that you want to add a new top-level object named Data, which exposes a few utility methods for working with ADO.NET.

There are two ways to do this, the simplest of which is defining a type in the My namespace that exposes only static methods. The following example shows how you can define a method that returns a DataTable given a connection string and an SQL query:

```
Namespace My
    Public Class Data
        Public Shared Function GetDataTable(ByVal connString As String, _
            ByVal query As String) As DataTable
            Dim dt As New DataTable
            ' Open a connection.
            Using cn As New SqlConnection(connString)
                cn.Open()
                ' Open a data reader.
                Dim cmd As New SqlCommand(query, cn)
                Using dr As SqlDataReader = cmd.ExecuteReader()
                    ' Fill the data table.
                    dt.Load(dr)
                End Using
            End Using
            Return dt
        End Function
    End Class
End Namespace
```

You can then use the new My.Data type from elsewhere in the application as follows:

```
' The connection string is stored in My.Settings.
Dim connstr As String = My.Settings.NorthwindConnectionString
Dim dt As DataTable = My.Data.GetDataTable(connstr, "SELECT * FROM Customers")
```

Defining a type with just static members doesn't fit perfectly in the My namespace infra-structure, however, and can make some programming tasks harder than they should be. For example, you can't serialize and deserialize the state of static fields and properties as easily as you do with instance members. To work around this limitation you should take a different approach.

All the top-level objects in the My namespace are defined in types with names that start with the My prefix. For example, the My.Application object is defined in a class named MyApplica-tion, My.Settings in a class named MySettings, and so forth. One hidden module named MyProject exposes a read-only property named Application (which returns an instance of the MyApplication class), another read-only property named Settings (which returns an instance of the MySettings class), and so on. You can follow the same pattern to add your My.Data object:

```
Namespace My
    <System.Diagnostics.DebuggerNonUserCodeAttribute(), _
     Microsoft.VisualBasic.HideModuleName()> _
    Public Module MyCustomTypes
        Dim m_data As MyData

        Public ReadOnly Property Data() As MyData
            Get
                ' Instantiate the object only when strictly needed.
                If m_data Is Nothing Then m_data = New MyData
                Return m_data
            End Get
        End Property
    End Module
End Namespace

Public Class MyData
    Public Function GetDataTable(ByVal connString As String, ByVal query As String) _
        As DataTable
        …
    End Function
End Class
```

The MyData class is outside the My namespace and contains only instance members. The name of the type defined inside the My namespace (MyCustomTypes, in this example) isn't important because the HideModuleName attribute tells IntelliSense to hide the name when the user types My followed by a period. (Unfortunately, you can't simply extend the hidden MyProject module because modules don't support the Partial class.)

Extending My.Application and My.Computer

The hidden MyApplication and MyComputer types are marked with the Partial keyword, and thus you can extend them with new members without too much trouble. For example, the following snippet extends My.Application with a property that returns the font used for menus and My.Computer with a property that returns the domain name:

```
Namespace My
   Partial Friend Class MyApplication
      ' The font used for menus.
      Public ReadOnly Property MenuFont() As Font
         Get
            Return SystemInformation.MenuFont
         End Get
      End Property
   End Class

   Partial Friend Class MyComputer
      ' The name of the user's domain, or the computer name if no domain is present.
      Public ReadOnly Property DomainName() As String
         Get
            Return SystemInformation.UserDomainName
         End Get
      End Property
   End Class
End Namespace
```

You can expand My.Computer with additional child objects—for example, My.Computer. Printers—but unfortunately you can't add new members to existing child objects by means of partial classes because they are defined in the Visual Basic library.

You can make the My.Application object more useful by extending it with new events. The following code takes advantage of the OnInitialize method to expose a new event named DisplaySettingsChanged, which fires when the resolution or color depth of the screen changes:

```
Namespace My
   Partial Friend Class MyApplication
      Public Event DisplaySettingsChanged As EventHandler

      Protected Overrides Function OnInitialize( _
            ByVal commandLineArgs As ReadOnlyCollection(Of String)) As Boolean
         AddHandler SystemEvents.DisplaySettingsChanged, AddressOf Events_SettingsChanged
         Return MyBase.OnInitialize(commandLineArgs)
      End Function

      Private Sub Events_SettingsChanged (ByVal sender As Object, ByVal e As EventArgs)
         OnDisplaySettingsChanged(e)
      End Sub

      Protected Overridable Sub OnDisplaySettingsChanged(ByVal e As EventArgs)
         RaiseEvent DisplaySettingsChanged(Me, e)
```

```
        End Sub
    End Class
End Namespace
```

The My.Application object exposes other protected and overridable methods you can leverage to expose new events: OnCreateSplashScreen (which fires when initialization is completed), OnStartup (raised before the Startup event), OnRun (raised just before showing the main form), OnCreateMainForm (raised when the My.Application.MainForm property is assigned), and OnShutdown (raised before the Shutdown event). To preserve this mechanism, you should raise your custom events from On*Xxxx* protected methods, as the previous code snippet does.

Extending My.Resources

Extending My.Resources requires a different approach because My.Resources is a namespace, not an object. You might need to extend My.Resources to support resource types that can't be specified directly in the My Project designer. For example, you can't define a resource of type String array directly in Visual Studio, but you can do it by adding a hidden module to the My.Resources namespace.

The following code defines a new resource named Colors, which returns an array of strings containing color names:

```
Namespace My.Resources
    <System.Diagnostics.DebuggerNonUserCodeAttribute(), _
    Microsoft.VisualBasic.HideModuleName()> _
    Friend Module MyResources

        '''<summary>
        '''   Looks up a string array containing color names.
        '''</summary>
        Friend ReadOnly Property Colors() As String()
            Get
                Return New String(){"Black", "White", "Yellow", "Red", "Green", "Blue"}
            End Get
        End Property
    End Module
End Namespace
```

Another reason for customizing the My.Resources object is because you might want to link resources that aren't stored in a resource file or embedded in the current assembly. For example, you might decide to provide the list of colors in a separate text file—so that your user can extend or customize the list as needed. Here's how you can proceed:

1. Select the Add New Item command from the Project menu and create a new text file named Colors.dat.

2. Select the Colors.dat file in the Solution Explorer, click the Properties button (at the top of the Solution Explorer window) to display the Properties window, and then change the value of the Copy To Output Directory property to Copy Always or Copy If Newer.

3. Fill the Colors.dat file with color names, one for each row.

4. Replace the Colors member of the MyResources class with this code:

```
Private m_Colors() As String

Friend ReadOnly Property Colors() As String()
    Get
        If m_Colors Is Nothing Then
            Dim separators() As String = {ControlChars.CrLf}
            m_Colors = My.Computer.FileSystem.ReadAllText("colors.dat"). _
                Split(separators, StringSplitOptions.RemoveEmptyEntries)
        End If
        Return m_Colors
    End Get
End Property
```

Notice that the Colors property reads the file once and then caches its value in a private field.

Extending My.Settings

You can add new properties to My.Settings by adopting a technique similar to the one I just explained for My.Application or My.Resources, even if some details are different. All the settings you define in the My Project designer are translated to properties of a partial class named MySettings; application-level settings generate read-only properties, whereas user-level settings generate writable properties. All the properties are marked with special attributes, as shown in the following example, which is an abridged version of the Settings.Designer.vb file that Visual Studio generates for an application-level setting, a user-level setting, and a connection string:

```
<Global.System.Runtime.CompilerServices.CompilerGeneratedAttribute(), _
    Global.System.ComponentModel.EditorBrowsableAttribute( _
    Global.System.ComponentModel.EditorBrowsableState.Advanced)> _
Partial Friend NotInheritable Class MySettings
    Inherits Global.System.Configuration.ApplicationSettingsBase

    <Global.System.Configuration.ApplicationScopedSettingAttribute(), _
     Global.System.Diagnostics.DebuggerNonUserCodeAttribute(), _
     Global.System.Configuration.DefaultSettingValueAttribute("True")> _
    Public ReadOnly Property ShowStatusBar() As Boolean
        Get
            Return CType(Me("ShowStatusBar"),Boolean)
        End Get
    End Property

    <Global.System.Configuration.UserScopedSettingAttribute(), _
     Global.System.Diagnostics.DebuggerNonUserCodeAttribute(), _
     Global.System.Configuration.DefaultSettingValueAttribute("192, 255, 255")> _
    Public Property BackColor() As Global.System.Drawing.Color
        Get
            Return CType(Me("BackColor"),Global.System.Drawing.Color)
        End Get
        Set(ByVal value As Global.System.Drawing.Color)
```

```
        Me("BackColor") = value
      End Set
  End Property


  <Global.System.Configuration.ApplicationScopedSettingAttribute(), _
    Global.System.Diagnostics.DebuggerNonUserCodeAttribute(), _
    Global.System.Configuration.SpecialSettingAttribute( _
      Global.System.Configuration.SpecialSetting.ConnectionString), _
    Global.System.Configuration.DefaultSettingValueAttribute( _
      "Data Source=MYSERVER;Initial Catalog=Northwind;Integrated Security=True")> _
  Public ReadOnly Property NorthwindConnectionString() As String
    Get
       Return CType(Me("NorthwindConnectionString"),String)
    End Get
  End Property
End Class
```

As you can see, attributes applied to properties specify the scope of the setting (application or user) and its default value; connection strings (and Web service URLs) are marked with an additional SpecialSetting attribute.

Adding New Settings

The MySettings class is marked with the Partial keyword, so you can extend it with other settings. Extending this class is required to implement settings whose type isn't directly supported by Visual Studio, for example, arrays of strings, as in this example:

```
Partial Friend Class MySettings
    <Global.System.Configuration.UserScopedSettingAttribute(), _
    Global.System.Diagnostics.DebuggerNonUserCodeAttribute(), _
    Global.System.Configuration.DefaultSettingValueAttribute(Nothing)> _
  Public Property UserNicknames() As String()
    Get
    Return CType(Me("UserNicknames"), String())
    End Get
    Set(ByVal value As String())
       Me("UserNicknames") = value
    End Set
  End Property
End Class
```

Settings that you add in this way must *not* be defined in the My Project designer; otherwise, Visual Studio would generate a property with the same name.

Using a Custom Settings Provider

In addition to defining custom settings through a partial class, you can use a different medium for storing setting values between sessions. This is made possible by the pluggable setting architecture of the .NET Framework. In other words, the code that stores setting values in configuration files isn't hard-coded in the System.Configuration.ApplicationSettingBase type (the type from which the Settings class derives); instead, the code that actually loads and saves settings is compiled in a separate class. Version 2.0 of the .NET Framework comes with only one provider class, namely, the LocalFileSettingsProvider, which is used by default for all settings, but you can create your own settings provider.

A custom settings provider can give you the flexibility that many modern applications need. For example, you can create a provider that stores application and user settings in a database on the server of a LAN (like in the example I illustrate shortly) so that administrators can change application settings without having to change the configuration file on each client machine and users can apply their settings regardless of the machine they log on to. Another example: you can use a provider that reads and writes settings through a Web service to extend setting support to WANs and the Internet. Or you might store settings in the registry of the local or a remote machine. Even if you decide to use a file to store your settings, a custom settings provider might improve the mechanism, for example, by encrypting the file or moving the file to a network share.

The following code sample shows how you can create a custom settings provider that stores user and application settings in a Microsoft Access database named AppSettings. This database should have one or more tables, each one named after one of the applications that use the provider. To test-drive the demo settings provider, create the AppSettings database, and then add a table named after your application (MySettingsProvidersDemo, in this example). This table contains the following varchar fields of adequate length: UserName, SettingName, SettingValue. For simplicity's sake, all settings are expected to be strings or types that can be converted to strings.

Fill the MySettingsProvidersDemo table with the initial values of the settings that your application uses. The UserName field should be NULL for application-level settings or should contain the name of the user in the format *machine\username* or *domain\username*. (See Figure 16-10.)

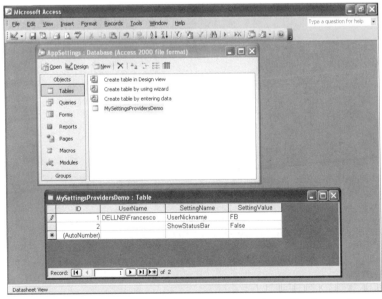

Figure 16-10   Filling a Microsoft Access table with application and user settings

Create a new Class Library project named MySettingsProviders, add a reference to the
System.Configuration.dll assembly, and include the following DatabaseSettingsProvider class.
The code assumes that the Access database resides in the c:\UserData folder; in a real appli-
cation the database location should be read from file or the registry.

```
Public Class DatabaseSettingsProvider
   Inherits SettingsProvider

   ' The connection to the database that holds application settings. (Edit as required.)
   Private connStr As String = "Provider=Microsoft.Jet.OLEDB.4.0;" _
      & "Data Source=""c:\UserData\AppSettings.mdb"";Persist Security Info=True"

   ' The name of the calling application
   Private m_ApplicationName As String = Assembly.GetExecutingAssembly().GetName().Name

   Public Overrides Property ApplicationName() As String
      Get
         Return m_ApplicationName
      End Get
      Set(ByVal value As String)
         m_ApplicationName = value
      End Set
   End Property

   ' Return the name of this settings provider.
   Public Overrides ReadOnly Property Name() As String
      Get
         Return "DatabaseSettingsProvider"
      End Get
   End Property

   Public Overrides Sub Initialize(ByVal name As String, ByVal config As NameValueCollection)
      MyBase.Initialize(Me.Name, config)
   End Sub

   ' Get the values for all settings from the database.

   Public Overrides Function GetPropertyValues(ByVal context As SettingsContext, _
         ByVal collection As SettingsPropertyCollection) As SettingsPropertyValueCollection
      ' Load a hash table with all the application- and user-level settings.
      Dim ht As New Hashtable()
      Using cn As New OleDbConnection(connStr)
         cn.Open()
         ' Find all application and current user's settings.
         Dim sql As String = String.Format( _
            "SELECT * FROM {0} WHERE UserName='{1}' OR UserName IS NULL", _
            Me.ApplicationName, My.User.Name)
         Dim cmd As New OleDbCommand(sql, cn)
         Using dr As OleDbDataReader = cmd.ExecuteReader()
            ' Assign to hash table for quick retrieval.
            Do While dr.Read
               ht.Add(dr("SettingName").ToString, dr("SettingValue"))
            Loop
```

```
            End Using
      End Using


      ' Return property values in the format expected by the caller.
      Dim values As New SettingsPropertyValueCollection()
      For Each prop As SettingsProperty In collection
          Dim propValue As New SettingsPropertyValue(prop)
          propValue.IsDirty = False
          propValue.SerializedValue = ht(prop.Name)
          values.Add(propValue)
      Next
      Return values
   End Function


   ' Update the database when settings have changed.

   Public Overrides Sub SetPropertyValues(ByVal context As SettingsContext, _
         ByVal collection As SettingsPropertyValueCollection)
      Using cn As New OleDbConnection(connStr)
          cn.Open()

          For Each propValue As SettingsPropertyValue In collection
              If propValue.IsDirty Then
                  ' Update the database with the new value. For simplicity we
                  ' use dynamic SQL and double all quotation marks in values.
                  ' A more robust implementation should use parameterized commands.
                  Dim value As String = propValue.SerializedValue.ToString().Replace("'", "")
                  Dim sql As String = String.Format("UPDATE {0} SET SettingValue='{1}'" _
                      & " WHERE UserName='{2}' AND SettingName='{3}'", _
                      Me.ApplicationName, value, My.User.Name, propValue.Name)
                  Using cmd As New OleDbCommand(sql, cn)
                      Dim rowsAffected As Integer = cmd.ExecuteNonQuery()
                      ' Insert a new row if the update command failed.
                      If rowsAffected = 0 Then
                          cmd.CommandText = String.Format( _
                              "INSERT {0} VALUES ('{1}', '{2}', '{3}')", _
                              Me.ApplicationName, My.User.Name, propValue.Name, value)
                          cmd.ExecuteNonQuery()
                      End If
                  End Using
              End If
          Next
      End Using
   End Sub
End Class
```

The structure of a settings provider is relatively simple. This class inherits from the SettingsProvider type, implements the abstract ApplicationName property, and overrides the following methods: Initialize, GetPropertyValues (where settings are read from the storage medium), and SetPropertyValues (where settings are written to the storage medium). Such linearity is a bit obfuscated in the previous example by the ADO.NET code necessary to physically load and save settings, but the remarks should be clear enough to explain how the code works.

To see the new settings provider in action, create a standard Console or Windows Forms project and add a reference to the MySettingsProviders project. Your project never actually calls into the provider class directly, but this step ensures that Visual Studio copies the provider's DLL to the main application's output directory.

Next, go to the Settings page of the My Project designer and create one or more string settings, either with application scope or with user scope, as you'd do normally. The only difference between standard settings stored in the configuration file and settings stored in the database is that for the latter ones you must switch to the Properties window and type the complete name of the provider class in the Provider property, as shown in Figure 16-11:

```
MySettingsProviders.DatabaseSettingsProvider
```

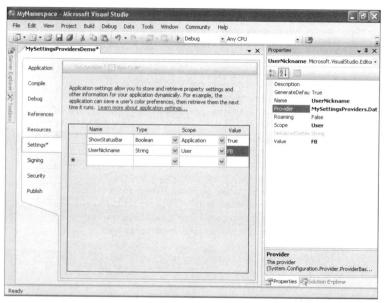

Figure 16-11 Associating a setting with a custom settings provider

Your custom settings provider can implement the IApplicationSettingsProvider interface to provide extra functionality, such as support for side-by-side execution of different versions of an application, retaining application settings when upgrading a ClickOnce application, and resetting settings to their default value. Read MSDN documentation for more details about this interface.

Using Compilation Constants

As I explained at the beginning of this chapter, not all the types in the My namespace are defined for all types of projects, and some objects—most notably, the My.Application, My.Computer, and My.User objects—expose a different set of properties depending on the type of the current type. (More correctly, these objects derive from a different base class, depending on the project type.) This behavior is implemented by defining a few compilation constants that the Visual Basic compiler queries when it assembles the My namespace.

The most important of such compilation constants is _MyType because its value affects all the other constants. The _MyType constant reflects the type of the current project and can take values such as Console, Windows, and WindowsForms. If you assign a custom value to this constant, the Visual Basic compiler won't define any class in the My namespace, so you can reshape it to fit your needs exactly by defining or omitting one of the following compilation constants:

- **_MYAPPLICATIONTYPE**   Can take one of the following string values: Windows, Console, WindowsForms; it affects the base class from which the My.Application object inherits (ApplicationBase, ConsoleApplicationBase, or WindowsFormsApplicationBase, respectively).

- **_MYCOMPUTERTYPE**   Can take one of the following string values: Windows, Web; it affects the base class from which the My.Computer object inherits (Computer or Server-Computer, respectively).

- **_MYUSERTYPE**   Can take one of the following string values: Windows, Web; it affects the base class from which the My.User object inherits (User or WebUser, respectively).

- **_MYFORMS**   Is a Boolean value that determines whether the My.Forms object is included.

- **_MYWEBSERVICES**   Is a Boolean value that determines whether the My.WebServices object is included.

For example, if you pass the following compilation constants to the Visual Basic compiler:

```
_MyType="Custom", _MYAPPLICATIONBASE="WindowsForms", _MYFORMS=True
```

the Visual Basic compiler will populate the My namespace with only the My.Application and My.Forms objects (in addition to My.Settings and My.Resources, which are always included), and you are free to redefine the remaining objects as you prefer. For example, you might redefine My.User to return an object of a different type and implement a custom authentication and authorization mechanism. You can define custom compilation constants in the Advanced Compiler Settings dialog box, which you can reach from the Compile page of the My Project designer.

Chapter 17
Assemblies and Resources

All the Microsoft Visual Basic applications you've seen so far were stand-alone executables, with all the code included in a single .exe file. Larger programs, however, are usually split into multiple executables—typically one .exe file and one or more DLLs. In this chapter, you'll see how easy creating a class library is and how you can be prepared to deal with versioning issues.

Note To avoid long lines, code samples in this chapter assume that the following Imports statements are used at the file or project level:

```
Imports System.Configuration
Imports System.Globalization
Imports System.IO
Imports System.Reflection
Imports System.Resources
Imports System.Runtime.CompilerServices
Imports System.Runtime.InteropServices
Imports System.Security.Permissions
```

Components

Creating a Microsoft .NET Framework component using Microsoft Visual Studio 2005 is embarrassingly simple. In practice, you can prototype your component by writing a class in a standard Console or Windows Forms application so that you have only one project to worry about. When the debug step is completed and your class works as expected, you can move the class to a separate DLL while continuing to use the same client code in the main application.

Creating a .NET Class Library

Let's say that you already have a DemoClient project that contains a Person class in the Person.vb source file and some client code that uses it. To move this class into a separate DLL you need to perform the following three easy steps:

1. Point to Add on the File menu and choose the New Project command to create a new project of type Class Library. Name your project PersonLibrary, if you want to match my description. Delete the default Class1.vb file that Visual Studio created.

2. In the Solution Explorer window, right-click the Person.vb file from the DemoClient project and select the Cut command; then right-click the PersonLibrary project item and select the Paste command. This sequence moves the Person.vb file across projects. (You can also drag a file with the mouse to move it to another project, but then you need to delete it manually from the project where it resided.)

3. Right-click the DemoClient project node in the Solution Explorer window and select the Add Reference command. Switch to the Projects tab in the Add Reference dialog box, select the PersonLibrary item, and click OK. (See Figure 17-1.)

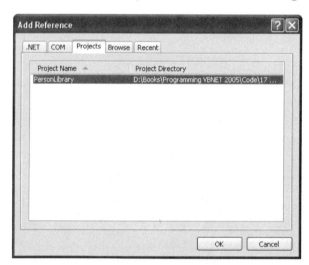

Figure 17-1   The Add Reference dialog box

The reference you just added lets the DemoClient project reference the Person class with a typed variable and create its instances with the New keyword, exactly as if the Person class was defined in that project. The only change you need to apply to your source code is an Imports statement that lets the client application find the Person class even if it moved to a different namespace:

```
Imports PersonLibrary

Module MainModule
    Sub Main()
```

```
        Dim p As New Person("John", "Evans")
        Console.WriteLine(p.CompleteName)
    End Sub
End Module
```

By default, all the assemblies that an application references are automatically copied to the application's folder at the end of each compilation. You can disable this behavior by following this procedure:

1. Click the Show All Files button on the Solution Explorer toolbar to display all the elements in the project.

2. Open the References node and select the reference you're interested in, and then press the F4 key to display the Properties window for that reference. (See Figure 17-2.)

3. Set the Copy Local property to False.

    By default this property is True for assemblies that belong to the current solution and False for all others, including assemblies from the .NET Framework.

Figure 17-2   Properties of an assembly reference

 Unlike previous editions, Visual Studio 2005 enables you to add a reference to EXE assemblies. This new feature was presumably added to let test projects reference types in a Console or Windows Forms project being tested, but it can be useful in standard applications as well. (Read the section titled "Unit Testing" in Chapter 5, "Debugging Visual Basic Applications," for more information about test projects.)

Creating Hostable Components

Strictly speaking, compiling a class in a separate DLL doesn't make it a component. In .NET parlance, a component is a class that inherits from System.ComponentModel.Component. This base class provides an implementation of the IComponent interface, which in turn is

what lets you drop an instance of the class onto a designer's surface. The System.Windows
.Forms.Timer class is a well-known example of a component. You can drop an instance of this
class on a form's surface and set its properties at design time in the Properties window.

It is advisable that you create a component by selecting the Add Components command from
the Project menu so that Visual Studio can create some additional code that makes your
component a well-behaved citizen in the .NET world. Visual Studio uses partial classes to keep
the user-accessible portion of the component's code as clean as possible. (See Figure 17-3.)

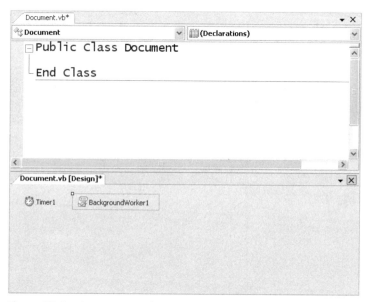

Figure 17-3   A component has a code editor and a designer surface; you can display both at the
same time by using the New Horizontal Tab Group command on the Window menu.

Visual Studio displays a component by using one of two different editors: the code editor and
the designer. If your component uses other components (for example, a timer or any object
that you can drag from the Server Explorer window), you can drop these components on the
designer's surface, much like you do with controls on a form. You don't have to worry about
the code that creates and destroys these components because Visual Studio generates this
code for you.

The main advantage of a component over a simple class is that the former can be added to the
Toolbox and dropped on a designer, and its public properties can be assigned at design time
in the Properties window. Before you can actually drop a component on a designer, you must
compile the project containing the component. Next, right-click the Toolbox and select the
Choose Items command. (This command is also available on the Tools menu.) In the Choose
Toolbox Items dialog box, click Browse, select the component's DLL, and then click OK to
add the component (more precisely, all the components in the DLL) to the Toolbox. (See
Figure 17-4.)

Unlike previous versions, Visual Studio 2005 doesn't require that you explicitly add a component to the Toolbox if the component is compiled in a project included in the same solution and referenced by the project you're working with currently.

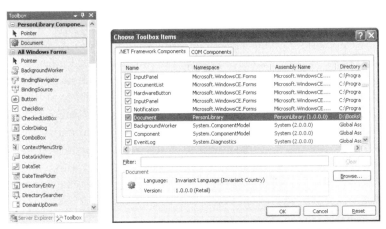

Figure 17-4   The Choose Toolbox Items dialog box (on the right) lets you add controls and components to the Toolbox tab that is currently visible (on the left). You can click on the Assembly Name column to quickly see all the components in a given assembly.

Assemblies

From a physical point of view, an assembly is just a collection of one or more executable and nonexecutable modules (examples of nonexecutable modules are resource, image, and HTML files). From a logical perspective, an assembly is the smallest unit of reuse, versioning, and deployment for .NET applications. For example, you can't assign different version numbers to the various files that make up an assembly.

When you're deciding which types should go in the same assembly, consider the following points:

- **Code reuse**   The assembly is the smallest unit of reuse, so you should keep together types that are normally used together.

- **Versioning**   The assembly is also the smallest unit of versioning, and all the modules in an assembly have the same versioning information.

- **Scoping**   The assembly scope (enforced by the Friend keyword) lets you define which types are visible from outside the module in which they're defined, but not from the outside world.

In Microsoft .NET Framework version 2.0, you can have an assembly expose its Friend types to other assemblies by means of the InternalsVisibleTo attribute, as I explain later in this chapter, even though this feature isn't fully supported in Visual Basic.

Private and Shared Assemblies

The .NET Framework supports two types of assemblies: private and shared. The latter type is also known as *strong-named* or *signed* assemblies for reasons that are explained in the next section.

A private assembly can be stored only in the main application's directory (or one of its sub-directories) and therefore can be used only by that application or another application installed in the same directory. Private assemblies are simpler to build and administer than shared assemblies are; they support XCOPY deployment and you can install a complete application simply by copying all its files and directories to the target computer's hard disk without having to register anything. (Of course, you still have to create shortcuts from the Start menu and other, similar amenities, but the concept should be clear.) In most circumstances, private assemblies are the best choice to make, even though you might end up with multiple identical copies of the same assembly in different directories. Private assemblies can help put an end to so-called DLL hell, and any developer or system administrator should be glad to trade some inexpensive disk space for more robust code.

A strong-named assembly is usually installed in a well-defined location of the hard disk, under the \Windows\Assembly directory. This location is known as the global assembly cache (GAC). The .NET Framework installs a special shell extension that lets you browse this directory with Windows Explorer and display information about all the assemblies installed in the GAC, including their version and culture. (See Figure 17-5.) You can also display more extensive version information by right-clicking an item and selecting Properties on the shortcut menu, an action that brings up the Properties dialog box for that assembly.

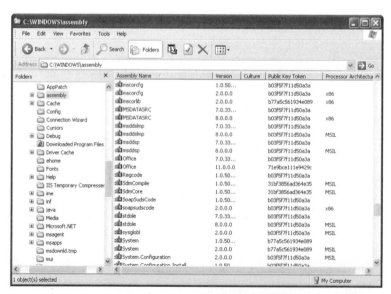

Figure 17-5   The global assembly cache as seen inside Windows Explorer

The assembly's public key token is a sort of signature of the software company that published the assembly. The public key token is a 64-bit hash value derived from the publisher's public key (which is 1,024 bits long, or 128 bytes); it isn't guaranteed to be universally unique like the public key, but it can be considered unique for most practical purposes.

What you see in Windows Explorer doesn't match the actual physical structure of the \Windows\Assembly directory. In fact, the GAC contains several directories, one for each assembly. In turn, each directory contains a subdirectory for each version of the assembly. For example, the System.dll assembly belonging to .NET Framework 2.0 is found in this directory:

```
C:\WINDOWS\assembly\GAC_MSIL\System\2.0.0.0__b77a5c561934e089
```

in which 2.0. 0.0 is the version of the assembly and b77a5c561934e089 is the Microsoft public key token.

Starting with .NET Framework 2.0, there are actually several GAC subdirectories: GAC_MSIL is for portable assemblies containing platform-independent IL code that will be JIT-compiled as needed; GAC_32 is for assemblies containing native 32-bit code, and GAC_64 is for assemblies containing native 64-bit code. If you've installed version 1.0 or 1.1 of the .NET Framework, you'll also find a directory named GAC.

This directory structure enables you to store different versions of the same assembly without any filename conflicts. You can bypass the Microsoft Windows shell extension and freely explore the real structure of the GAC by opening a command prompt window and navigating to the C:\Windows\Assembly directory. Notice, however, that the GAC structure is an implementation detail and you shouldn't rely on this structure if you want to be compatible with future versions.

You can add to and delete assemblies from the GAC only if you have administrative rights on the system, which makes .NET applications that work with strong-named assemblies in the GAC inherently more robust than those that work with private assemblies. You can add to or remove assemblies from the GAC using a utility named GACUTIL, and you can remove an assembly from the GAC by selecting Uninstall on the shortcut menu inside Windows Explorer.

There are several key differences between private and shared assemblies:

- A signed (shared) assembly supports version information, and the GAC can keep different versions of the same assembly without any conflict so that each application can continue to work with the version it was compiled against (unless the administrator opts for a different binding policy). Private assemblies can be versioned, but version information is for your reference only, and the runtime doesn't use it. A private assembly is supposed to be deployed with the application itself, so the runtime doesn't enforce any special versioning policy.

- A signed assembly in the GAC makes your applications more robust in two ways. First, when the assembly is added to the cache, an integrity check is performed on all the files in the assembly to ensure that they haven't been altered after the compilation. Second, only the system administrator can install or remove an assembly from the GAC.

- A signed assembly in the GAC is more efficient than a private assembly is because the runtime can locate it faster and it doesn't need to be verified. Moreover, if multiple applications reference the same signed assembly, the runtime can load only one instance in memory in most circumstances (which saves resources and improves load time even more).

- Two (or more) versions of a signed assembly can run in the same process. For example, an application might use version 1.0 of the AAA assembly and a BBB assembly that uses version 1.1 of the AAA assembly. This important feature is called *side-by-side execution*, and it ensures that you won't have a compatibility problem when you mix components together.

- A signed assembly can be signed with an Authenticode digital signature. The signing mechanism uses a public key encryption schema, which guarantees that a particular assembly was created by a given manufacturer and that no one tampered with it.

Signed assemblies are usually stored in the GAC, but this isn't a requirement. For example, you might deploy a signed assembly in a known directory on the hard disk, where two or more applications can find it. However, only signed assemblies in the GAC benefit from all the advantages in the preceding list. (Signed assemblies deployed in other directories do support side-by-side execution and public key signing, though.)

As a rule, you write code for private and signed assemblies in the same way because the only difference between them is an attribute in your code (or an option that you set through Visual Studio). However, the main goal in building signed assemblies is to share them among different applications, so you must take this constraint into account. For example, a shared assembly shouldn't create temporary files with fixed names and paths because calls from different clients might overwrite such files. Moreover, the .NET Framework supports side-by-side execution of shared assemblies in the same process (not just on the same machine), so a shared assembly shouldn't depend on process-wide resources.

Strong Names

The .NET runtime looks for private assemblies only inside the caller application's directory tree, so the developer is in charge of avoiding naming conflicts for the private assemblies the application references. On the other hand, shared assemblies are typically deployed in the GAC, so it's vital for the runtime to distinguish shared assemblies that have the same name but that come from different publishers.

The .NET Framework ensures that a shared assembly's name is unique at the system level by assigning the assembly a strong name. You can think of a strong name as the combination of a textual name, a version number, a culture, a public key, and a value indicating the processor architecture. When displayed in a human-readable format, a strong name looks like the following text:

```
mscorlib, Version=2.0.0.0, Culture=neutral,
PublicKeyToken=b77a5c561934e089, ProcessorArchitecture=x86
```

The public key token is displayed in lieu of the longer public key. The previous string is always known as the *display name* of the assembly to distinguish it from the assembly's name, which is the filename without the .dll extension (as in mscorlib).

 The ProcessorArchitecture value is new in .NET Framework 2.0 and is used to differentiate among versions of the same assembly that are compiled for specific processors. This value can be MSIL (processor-independent), x86 (all 32-bit processors), IA64 (Itanium 64-bit), or AMD64 (AMD 64-bit). This value helps the CLR bind the correct version of the assembly and prevents the installation of an assembly that is incompatible with the target system. Notice that you can run assemblies marked for the x86 processor architecture on 64-bit machines: in this case, the assembly runs in the Windows-on-Windows (WOW) environment that emulates the 32-bit architecture.

In most cases, you create processor-independent assemblies, but you might need to compile a platform-specific assembly if your code must behave differently on different platforms or because you use PInvoke to call a method in the Windows API and you know that the 32-bit and 64-bit versions of that method behave differently. Another reason is that you're using a COM component, which forces you to specify the x86 so that your application will run in a WOW environment on 64-bit machines.

You can create platform-specific compiled assemblies by selecting an item in the Target CPU list box of the Advanced Compiler Settings dialog box, which you reach from the Compile page of the My Project designer. (See Figure 17-6.)

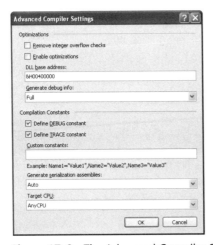

Figure 17-6   The Advanced Compiler Settings dialog box

The security mechanism is based on a public key encryption method, but you don't have to be a cryptography wizard to create assemblies with strong names.

You generate strong-named assemblies in a two-step process. First, you run the Strong Name (SN) command-line utility to create an .snk file that contains a random-generated public and private key pair. Second, you add an assembly-level attribute to tell the compiler that the public key in that .snk file must be burned into the executable file. You can perform these steps manually, but in most cases you'll use Visual Studio 2005 for both of them.

You generate a random public and private key pair from the command line by using the -k option of the SN utility, which is located in the \Program Files\Microsoft Visual Studio 8\SDK\v2.0\Bin directory:

```
sn -k mykey.snk
```

This command creates the mykey.snk file, which contains the two keys. Store this file in a safe place (and make copies of it if necessary) because from now on you should use it to sign all the strong-named assemblies produced by your company.

After creating an .snk file, you can choose from several ways to produce an assembly with a strong name. If you're compiling from the command prompt, you use the VBC program with the /keyfile option for single-file assemblies, or you use the Assembly Linker utility (AL) with the /keyfile option for assemblies made of multiple files. The preferred way to create a signed assembly, however, is by inserting an AssemblyKeyFile attribute into the application's source code (typically into the AssemblyInfo.vb file):

```
<Assembly: AssemblyKeyFile("c:\myapp\mykey.snk")>
```

The filename must be an absolute path so that it can reference the only .snk file that you use for all the strong assemblies you produce.

As I mentioned before, Visual Studio 2005 is capable of performing both these steps for you. Open the Signing page of the My Project designer, select the Sign The Assembly check box, select the <New...> element from the combo box below it, and then select a name for the .snk file that will be created and associated with the current project. (See Figure 17-7.) In most cases, however, you'll use the <Browse...> element from the combo box to point to the .snk file that contains the public and private keys of your company.

> **Note**   Visual Studio gives you the ability to protect new publishers' key files with a password, which must be at least 6 characters long. It is strongly recommended that you use this option, which in fact is enabled by default. In this case, the file being produced has a .pfx extension (Personal Information Exchange), and users will be prompted for the password when they try to use this file. A .pfx file can be added to a certificate container.

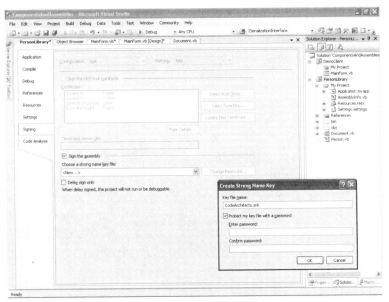

Figure 17-7 The Signing page of the My Project designer and the dialog box where you define a new .snk file

Regardless of whether you're creating a new .snk file or are pointing to an existing file, Visual Studio copies the file in the project's folder, so you can copy your source files to another computer without any problem. To support this feature, Visual Studio doesn't generate an AssemblyKeyFile attribute (which requires an absolute path); instead, it uses the /keyfile option when it invokes the VBC compiler.

The AssemblyInfo.vb file that Visual Studio automatically creates in the My Project folder contains an AssemblyVersion attribute with an argument equal to 1.0.0.0:

```
<Assembly: AssemblyVersion("1.0.0.0")>
```

The manifest section of any other assembly that references the signed assembly you've just signed will include the signed assembly's public key. When the caller assembly invokes one of the types in the signed assembly, the runtime compares the public key token in the manifest with the signed assembly's public key token so that the caller can be completely sure that the signed assembly hasn't been tampered with. (The CLR uses this 8-byte token instead of the entire public key to save space in the caller assembly manifest.) Notice that any .NET executable can reference a signed assembly, but a signed assembly can only reference other signed assemblies.

This mechanism just described ensures that the signed assembly hasn't been modified, but it doesn't ensure that the signed assembly actually comes from a specific software manufacturer. This latter issue is solved through full Authenticode signatures that can be applied to signed assemblies. These Authenticode signatures add a certificate that establishes trust. You can apply this Authenticode signature to an existing assembly by running the Signcode.exe utility.

Because strong names are a combination of a text name and a public key, they guarantee name uniqueness. If two companies use the same name for their (distinct) assemblies, their public keys are different and therefore the strong names are different as well. Name uniqueness extends to all versions of the same assembly, and the CLR ensures that—when it's opting for a given version of an assembly requested by a managed class—only assemblies coming from the same software company will be taken into account.

Installing in the GAC

The preferred way to install signed assemblies is to register them in the GAC. You can use a drag-and-drop operation or the GACUTIL command-line utility. Using a drag-and-drop operation is simple: use Windows Explorer to navigate to the \Windows\Assembly directory, and drop the DLL on the right-hand pane. (See Figure 17-5.) Running the GACUTIL utility is also straightforward and has the added benefit of being an action that you can include in an installation script:

```
gacutil /i testassembly.dll
```

You can add a command to the Tools menu in Visual Studio that runs this command on the current project by means of the External Tools command, or you can run it automatically after each successful build by means of a build event.

The /i command overwrites any assembly in the GAC with the same identity, but doesn't remove copies of the same assembly with a different version number because one of the goals of the GAC is to store multiple versions of the same assembly. Each new version that you install is added to the GAC, so you should periodically clear intermediate versions of the assembly from the GAC or run GACUTIL using the /u command to remove an outdated version of the assembly before installing a more recent one. You can list all the files in the GAC by means of the /l command.

The GACUTIL command can also specify an assembly trace reference, with the /r option. A *trace reference* maintains information about which application uses the assembly in the GAC so that the uninstall procedure for the application can determine whether it should remove the assembly GAC or should leave it there because it is being used by other applications. Applications installed with the Microsoft Installer (MSI) automatically add a trace reference and remove it when the application is uninstalled. Read MSDN documentation for more information about this option.

Adding an assembly to the GAC doesn't make your assembly visible in the Visual Studio Add Reference dialog box. This dialog box never parses the GAC and just displays assemblies located in the following two directories: C:\WINDOWS\Microsoft.NET\Framework*vx.y.zzzz* (the main .NET Framework directory) and C:\Program Files\Microsoft Visual Studio 8\ Common7\IDE\PublicAssemblies. You might save your assemblies to the latter directory to make them quickly selectable from inside Visual Studio. Even better, you can add a new registry key under the HKEY_LOCAL_MACHINE\SOFTWARE\Microsoft\.NETFramework\ AssemblyFolders key, name it MyAssemblies (or any name you like), and set the default value of this key equal to the directory that contains your assemblies (either private or shared). The next time you launch Visual Studio you'll see all the assemblies in this directory in the list of selectable ones.

By default, Visual Studio doesn't take the version number into account when referencing a strong-named assembly that isn't part of the current solution. This behavior allows you to replace the referenced assembly with a newer version without having to update the reference. The application's manifest will point to the version of the reference at compilation time. You can disable this behavior by selecting the specific reference, press the F4 key to bring up the Properties window, and set the Specific Version property to True. (See Figure 17-2.)

Assembly-Level Attributes

You can set many assembly properties directly from inside your source code by using the many attribute classes in the System.Reflection namespace. All Visual Basic projects include a file named AssemblyInfo.vb, which contains template code for all the attributes described in this section. Although you can place assembly-level attributes in any source file of your project—provided that they are outside a type definition—it is recommended that you define them in the AssemblyInfo.vb file, which is located in the My Project folder. (You must click the Show All Files button to display the contents of this folder.)

Here's the abridged version of the AssemblyInfo.vb file you can find in a newly created Visual Basic project:

```
Imports System
Imports System.Reflection
Imports System.Runtime.InteropServices

<Assembly: AssemblyTitle("WindowsApplication1")>
<Assembly: AssemblyDescription("")>
<Assembly: AssemblyCompany("Code Architects")>
<Assembly: AssemblyProduct("WindowsApplication1")>
<Assembly: AssemblyCopyright("Copyright © Code Architects 2005")>
<Assembly: AssemblyTrademark("")>
<Assembly: CLSCompliant(True)>
<Assembly: ComVisible(False)>
' The following statement will surely be different in your project.
<Assembly: Guid("9cfaf625-ac1a-4afa-bd8f-16456c995ab0")>
<Assembly: AssemblyVersion("1.0.0.0")>
<Assembly: AssemblyFileVersion("1.0.0.0")>
```

Conveniently, Visual Basic 2005 lets you change these attributes without editing the Assembly-Info.vb file directly. You simply have to display the My Project designer, select the General page, and click the Assembly Information button (see Figure 17-8).

Figure 17-8   The Assembly Information dialog box

Table 17-1 lists the most important assembly-level attributes that the runtime supports. (Attributes related to COM Interop and security aren't included.)

Table 17-1   Assembly-Level Attributes

Attribute	Description
AssemblyCompany	The company name.
AssemblyConfiguration	A custom configuration setting to be stored in the assembly's manifest.
AssemblyCopyright	The copyright string.
AssemblyCulture	The supported culture. Passing a nonempty string marks the assembly as a satellite assembly, which is an assembly that contains only resources for a given culture; don't use a nonempty string for a regular assembly.
AssemblyDelaySign	Marks the assembly for partial or delayed signing. (Takes True or False; requires either AssemblyKeyFile or AssemblyKeyName.)
AssemblyDescription	The product description string.
AssemblyFileVersion	The Win32 version number, which doesn't have to be equal to the assembly version.
AssemblyFlags	Assembly flags, which tell which degree of side-by-side support the assembly offers.
AssemblyInformation alVersion	Informational version. A string version to be used in product and marketing literature.
AssemblyKeyFile	The file that contains the public/private key to make a signed assembly (or only the public key if partial signing).
AssemblyKeyName	The key container that holds the public/private key pair.
AssemblyProduct	The name of the product.
AssemblyTitle	The title for the assembly.

Table 17-1   Assembly-Level Attributes *(Continued)*

Attribute	Description
AssemblyTrademark	The trademark string.
AssemblyVersion	The assembly version number; can use the asterisk (*) for the revision and build or just for the build number to let the CLR generate version numbers using a time-based algorithm.
CLSCompliant	The assembly is or isn't compliant with CLS guidelines.
InternalsVisibleTo	Nonpublic types in the assembly are visible to another assembly specified by the argument. (New in .NET Framework 2.0.)
NeutralResourcesLanguage	The neutral culture of the assembly.
ObfuscateAssembly	Instructs obfuscation tools to use their standard obfuscation rules for the appropriate assembly types. (New in .NET Framework 2.0.)
Obfuscation	Instructs obfuscation tools to apply obfuscation to this assembly. (New in .NET Framework 2.0.)
SatelliteContractVersion	The version of satellite assemblies, if different from version of main assembly.

The InternalsVisibleTo Attribute

Version 2.0 of the .NET Framework supports the concept of *friend assemblies*, that is, assemblies that can reference nonpublic types defined in another assembly. Friend assemblies are important because they solve a frequent issue of Microsoft .NET Framework version 1.1 assemblies. The bad news is that this attribute isn't fully supported by Visual Basic 2005.

Let's say that you have two units of code that you must compile into separate assemblies A and B—for example, because they have different security settings or because they are written in different .NET languages. (As for the second requirement, you might use the Assembly Linker tool to create an assembly that combines modules written in different languages, but in practice this is a nuisance and few developers want to take that path.) Next, suppose that assembly B (and only assembly B) needs to access a few types in assembly A. Alas, if you mark those types with the Public keyword, they will be visible to *all* assemblies.

Version 1.1 of the .NET Framework doesn't offer an elegant solution to this recurring problem. The .NET Framework 1.1 technique that gets closer is based on the StrongNameIdentity-Permission attribute, which grants access to a type only to certain assemblies:

```
' Make the ConfidentialData type visible to all assemblies with a given public key.
<StrongNameIdentityPermission(SecurityAction.RequestMinimum, _
    PublicKey:="002400683011af5799aced238935f32ab125790aa787786343440023410" & _
    "073958138838746ac86ef8732623f87978223aced6767169876acde74e59a6457be26ee0" & _
    "045467467ce68a123cdef89648292518478536964ace47852361985636487523b7e0e25b" & _
    "71ad39acef23457893574852568eac5863298de685de69124de56eded66978425008142e" & _
    "f723bfe602345459574568790b365852cdead454585c6")>
Public Class ConfidentialData

    …
End Class
```

The solution based on the StrongNameIdentityPermission attribute isn't optimal, however, because it requires that you use it to mark each and every type in assembly A that you want to expose to assembly B. (You can use the attribute at the assembly level, but in that case you'd restrict the set of assemblies that can use *any* type in assembly A, which is rarely desirable.)

The .NET Framework 2.0 solution is straightforward because you simply need to have assembly A declare that assembly B is a friend assembly:

```
<Assembly: InternalsVisibleTo("AssemblyB, PublicKey=002400683011af5799aced23…")>
```

(You can retrieve the public key token of an assembly by means of the -T option of the SN command-line utility.) If assembly B isn't strong named, you can drop the PublicKey portion from the attribute's argument:

```
<Assembly: InternalsVisibleTo("AssemblyB")>
```

Unfortunately, as I have already mentioned, this attribute is only partially supported by Visual Basic 2005. More precisely, you can apply the attribute in a Visual Basic assembly, but Visual Basic clients don't recognize it. You must write a client using C# to actually use Friend types in a Visual Basic assembly. IntelliSense recognizes this attribute and correctly displays all the Friend types in an assembly as well as members with Friend visibility when you browse them from a "friend" C# project. (See Figure 17-9.)

Keep in mind that "assembly friendship" is neither reciprocal nor transitive: if A declares that B is a friend assembly, it doesn't mean that A is also a friend assembly of B and can peek into B's private types. Likewise, even if B is friend of A and C is a friend of B, you can't conclude that C is a friend of A. Instead, you'll need a specific InternalsVisibleTo attribute in A that grants friendship to C.

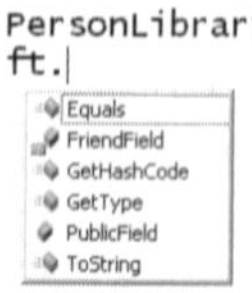

```
PersonLibrary.FriendType ft = new PersonLibrary.FriendType(
ft.|
    Equals
    FriendField
    GetHashCode
    GetType
    PublicField
    ToString
```

Figure 17-9   The InternalsVisibleTo attribute is recognized by C# client projects only

Resources and Satellite Assemblies

The .NET Framework supports the concept of satellite assemblies, which are separate DLLs that contain just the resources for a specific culture and no executable code. Satellite assemblies can be deployed separately and can extend the main application with support for additional languages without having to recompile and redeploy the application itself.

The simplest way to create a resource is by means of the My Project designer, as explained in Chapter 16, "The My Namespace." All the resources created in the My Project designer appear as strong-typed properties of the My.Resources object. In this section, you'll learn alternative ways to create resources, either localized or not.

Manifest Resources

You can embed any data file—including text files and images—in the assembly's manifest by following these simple steps.

1. Right-click the project element in the Solution Explorer window and select the New Folder command from the Add menu to create a project folder to hold your manifest resources—for example, a folder named ManifestResources. This step is optional, but it is recommended to keep manifest resources separated from other source and data files.

2. Right-click the folder you've just created and select the Add Existing Item option to add the file that must be included as a manifest resource, or simply drag the file from Windows Explorer into the Solution Explorer window. If the file is already in the project's directory, click the Show All Files button on the Solution Explorer toolbar, right-click the file icon, and select the Include In Project command.

3. Select the file in the Solution Explorer, press the F4 key (or click the Properties button on the Solution Explorer toolbar) to display the properties of that file, and then change the Build Action property from Content to Embedded Resource (see Figure 17-10).

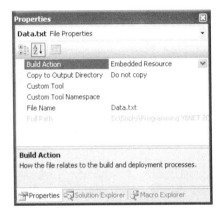

Figure 17-10   The properties of a file, which include the action to be performed at build time (can be None, Compile, Content, or Embedded Resource)

The following code shows how you can programmatically access a text file named Data.txt from inside an assembly whose default namespace is CodeArchitects.

```
Dim resFile As String = "CodeArchitects.Data.txt"
' Get a reference to the current assembly.
Dim asm As Assembly = Assembly.GetExecutingAssembly()
Dim stream As Stream = asm.GetManifestResourceStream(resFile)
' Display the contents of the embedded file.
Using reader As New StreamReader(stream)
    Dim fileText As String = reader.ReadToEnd()
    MessageBox.Show(fileText, "DATA.TXT")
End Using
```

The name of a resource is formed by the assembly's root namespace, followed by the filename and extension (without the path). An important detail: resource names are compared in case-sensitive mode. You can check the exact names of embedded resources by means of the ILDASM tool or programmatically with the Assembly.GetManifestResourceNames method, which returns a string array that contains all the files you've embedded in the assembly, as well as one .resource file for each Windows Forms class in the application.

In general, manifest resources under Visual Basic 2005 are less important than they were in previous versions because in most cases it is preferable that you access resources in a strong-typed fashion by means of the My.Resources object. However, manifest resources can still be useful, for example, when you want to access them as a stream rather than as a self-contained object. For example, a text file can be accessed and processed one line at a time without your having to load the contents of the entire file in memory.

Another minor advantage of manifest resources is that you access them by their name, in a sort of late-bound mode. For example, this mechanism lets you dynamically select a resource whose name matches (or contains) the name or the role of the current user. Also, you might build the name of the resource to be loaded by appending the current culture, which partially remedies the fact that manifest resources aren't localizable:

```
' Load a manifest resource named like CodeArchitects.Data.it-IT.txt.
Dim resFile As String = "CodeArchitects.Data." & My.Application.Culture.Name & ".txt"
```

Localized Form Resources

Visual Studio gives you the ability to create Windows Forms applications that support multiple cultures, without writing a single line of code. The magic works because Visual Studio generates all the necessary resource files behind the scenes for you.

Let's take the simple form shown in Figure 17-11 as an example. The first step in localizing a form is to set its Localizable property to True. This is a design-time property that you won't find in the Object Browser. It tells the designer's code generator that the values of the properties of the form and its controls are stored in a .resx resource file instead of being hard-coded in the source code.

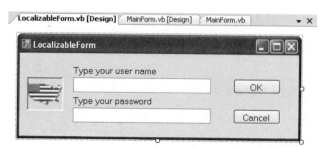

Figure 17-11 A localizable form with captions and one image, as it appears when the Language property is set to (Default)

Next, set the form's Language property to the alternative locale that you want to support. This property is available only at design time, and you can assign to it any of the locales that .NET supports. (See Figure 17-12.) The form designer continues to display the same interface as before, but you can now change all the properties of the form and its controls (including their position, size, visibility, and so on). All the values that you set from now on will be associated with the alternative locale just selected. Figure 17-13 shows how the form might look to an Italian end user. Of course, you can repeat this procedure with any language that you want to support.

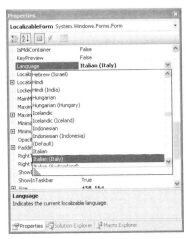

Figure 17-12   Setting the Language property to Italian

Figure 17-13   The Italian version of the original form

> **Note**   The localization process can involve more than just changing the visible strings in the user interface or strings used from code. For example, you might need to move a control to a different location or make it invisible under some localized versions. Visual Studio correctly keeps track of different values for properties such as Size, Location, and Visible under different languages. Nevertheless, you should test your form thoroughly before you make it localizable because any change you make to its user interface afterward will require more coding efforts.

The great thing about localized forms is that in most cases, you can simply forget about them. You run an application containing localized forms as you'd run a regular application. If the current user's culture matches one of the languages you have defined, the form and its controls will use the properties you've set for that language; otherwise, the default language will be used. The fallback mechanism is quite sophisticated: for example, you can create resources with both one-part and two-part locale names, for example, it (for generic Italian) and it-IT (for Italian as spoken in Italy). If the current UI locale is it-IT, the latter resource file is used; if the locale is it-CH (Swiss Italian), it falls back to the it resource file. If it is en-US or fr-FR, it falls back to the neutral language resource file.

Also, Visual Studio uses a space-saving mechanism to avoid unnecessarily large resource files. Only properties with a localized value that is different from the default value are stored in resource files. Also, if you define a localized version for the it (generic Italian), it-IT (Italian as spoken in Italy), and it-CH (Italian as spoken in Switzerland), the it-IT and it-CH resource files will contain entries only for those values for which the Italian and Swiss versions differ.

A minor problem with localized forms is that they require additional testing and debugging. The easiest way to test a localized form is to modify the culture of the UI thread, which you do by invoking the ChangeUICulture of the My.Application (which internally creates a suitable CultureInfo object and assigns it to the CurrentUICulture property of the Thread.Current-Thread object). It's essential that you perform this operation before displaying the application's user interface, for example, in the Startup event of the My.Application object:

```
' In the ApplicationEvents.vb source file
Namespace My
   Class MyApplication
      Private Sub MyApplication_Startup(ByVal sender As Object, _
            ByVal e As ApplicationServices.StartupEventArgs) Handles Me.Startup
         ' Change UI culture to Italian.
         My.Application.ChangeUICulture("it-IT")
      End Sub
   End Class
End Namespace
```

When you make a form localizable, Visual Studio creates a .resx file for each specified language, including the default one. You must click the Show All Files button on the Solution Explorer's toolbar to see these .resx files inside the Visual Studio window. (See Figure 17-14.) Each file is named after the locale to which it's bound. As I explained previously, a .resx file for a given language contains a resource item only if the resource value for that language is different from the default value.

When you compile the project, Visual Studio creates a subdirectory of the Bin directory, names this subdirectory after the locale for which the resource has been created ("it-IT" in this example), and places there a new DLL named *applicationname*.resources.dll (for example, myapp.resources.dll). You can then XCOPY the Bin directory and all its subdirectories to the end user's machine without having to deploy the .resx file. Read the section titled "Probing" later in this chapter for more information about how the CLR locates satellite DLLs.

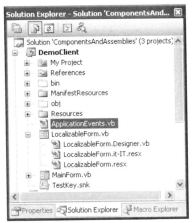

Figure 17-14   The .resx resource files as they appear in the Solution Explorer window after you click the Show All Files button

If you double-click a .resx file in the Solution Explorer, a resource editor window appears. This editor is exactly like the one you use for resources associated with the My.Resources object, so this is known ground for you. The name of each resource is in the *controlname.propertyname* format, for example, btnOK.Text, so you can review and modify localized resources quickly and easily from this editor without having to go through the form's designer. When you attempt to modify a resource value, Visual Studio prompts you to confirm your intention because you might set a wrong value and make the entire form unusable.

Localized Strong-Typed String Resources

Once you understand how Visual Studio names and uses the resource files associated with localized forms, it's easy to duplicate this behavior with your own resource files and have your localized resources appear as properties of the My.Resources object. The following technique can be used for strings that can't be assigned directly to a control's property, for example, the text you display in a message box:

1. Create a Visual Basic project containing a couple of strong-typed string resources, named MsgText and MsgTitle, and use them as the text and the title argument in a MessageBox.Show method. (You can also define other types of resources, if necessary.)

2. In the Solution Explorer window, create a project folder named Localized Resources (any name will do) that you'll use for localized resource files; this step is optional, but helps you not to pollute the root-level directory of your project.

3. Click the Show All Files button on the Solution Explorer toolbar, open the My Project folder, right-click the Resources.resx file, select the Copy command, right-click the Localized Resources folder, and then select the Paste command.

4. Rename the Resources.resx file you have created so that it matches the culture you want to support. For example, use the Resources.it-IT.resx name for Italian resources. (See Figure 17-15.)

Figure 17-15   Creating an Italian version of the Resources.resx file

5. Double-click the renamed .resx file to display the usual resource designer. Translate
    strings to the language you want to support and change other types of resources as
    needed. If a value is the same as the default value, you can just delete the item from
    the localized resource file so that .NET will use the language-neutral resource. When
    replacing a resource other than a string, you must delete the original item and then add
    a file with exactly the same name.

You can now run the application as usual, but ensure that you use the My.Application
.ChangeUICulture method in the Startup event to force the application to use the specific
locale (Italian, in this example), as I explained in the previous section. If you've performed
all steps correctly, you'll see that even strong-typed resources will now refer to the Italian
culture.

```
Me.PictureBox1.Image = My.Resources.MyPicture
MessageBox.Show(My.Resources.MsgText, My.Resources.MsgTitle)
```

Custom Resource Files

You don't strictly need to work with strong-typed resources exposed as properties of the
My.Resources object because you can access resource files directly by means of the Resource-
Manager object in the System.Configuration namespace. In some cases, this approach can be
the only practical one, such as when you have to deal with hundreds of resource names—for
example, the localized names of all the countries in the world—and you want to display them
in a string array. In this case, the strong-typed feature of the My.Resources object is of little use.
Another reason for using the ResourceManager directly is for reading a resource associated
with a different language without having to switch the UI locale.

To create a custom resource file use the Add New Item command from the Project menu,
select the Resources File template, and assign a meaningful name, such as Countries.resx.

As usual, I suggest that you put your resource files in a specific folder named Resources or something similar. Double-click the .resx file and add strings and other types of resources to it, as you see fit. For example, add the following items:

```
Country001 = "United States of America"
Country002 = "United Kingdom"
Country003 = "Italy"
```

Notice that I used resource names in the format Country*NNN* because the sample code will index them in a For loop, but you can use any meaningful name. You can now create other resource files as needed, by copying and pasting the default file in the Solution Explorer and then renaming the file to match the locale. For example, create a Countries.it-IT.resx file for country names in Italian, a Countries.fr-FR.resx for names in French, and so forth. For example, the Italian version might look like the following:

```
Country001 = "Stati Uniti d'America"
Country002 = "Regno Unito"
Country003 = "Italia"
```

Of course, your resource files can contain any kind of resources, not just strings. Next, write the code that reads all resource names into a ComboBox control:

```
' The resource filename is in the format rootnamespace.filename.
Dim resFile As String = "CodeArchitects.Countries"
' Create a resource manager that reads the resource file.
Dim manager As New ResourceManager(resFile, Assembly.GetExecutingAssembly())
cboCountries.Items.Clear()
' Read the three country names.
For i As Integer = 1 To 3
    ' Build the resource name, in the CountryNNN format.
    Dim resName As String = "Country" & i.ToString("000")
    ' Read the resource value and add it to the combo box.
    Dim resValue As String = manager.GetString(resName)
    cboCountries.Items.Add(resValue)
Next
```

(Notice that the resource filename is in the format *rootnamespace.filename* and has no extension.) The ResourceManager object exposes two other methods that let you retrieve a resource value: GetStream (new in .NET Framework 2.0) is used for streamlike resources, whereas GetObject is used for any other type of object. These two methods and the GetString method support an optional CultureInfo argument, which allows you to retrieve a resource for a specific language, even though it isn't currently associated with the UI thread. If there is no resource file for the specified locale, the ResourceManager object falls back to the default resource file:

```
' Read the name of the first country as spelled in French, if possible.
Dim ci As New CultureInfo("fr-FR")
Dim value As String = manager.GetString("Country001", ci)
```

Satellite Assemblies

An inconvenience of the techniques I have illustrated in previous sections is that all localized resource files are part of the main project, and thus you must recompile the entire application to add the support for a new language or change a resource in a language that you support already. Granted, you need to deploy only the *applicationname*.resources.dll files that contain the new or changed resources, but when you support dozens of different languages, recompiling the entire application just to change a typo in a string resource isn't practical.

In some scenarios, you might find it more convenient to compile resource files separately, using resource-only satellite projects. For example, you should compile resource files separately when you outsource the production of such files to other companies and you don't want to give out your source code together with the resource files. Follow this series of actions to create a satellite project that contains a set of localized resources:

1. Create a new Class Library project, in the same solution as the main application or in a different solution. The name of this project isn't important, but you might want to use a name formed by appending the name of the main project and the culture identifier. (In this example, you might name the project DemoClient_fr_FR because the satellite assembly will contain resources for the fr-FR culture.) Delete the Class1.vb or Class1.cs file that Visual Studio creates automatically.

2. On the Application page of the new project, change the assembly name to match the name of the main application (DemoCliente, in this example) and change the root namespace to match the root namespace of the main application. In this example, we assume that this namespace is CodeArchitects; in general, .NET guidelines dictate that it should match your company's name.

3. Ensure that version numbers in the main executable and the satellite project match perfectly and that the satellite assembly is signed with the same public key as the main application (or that both of them aren't signed).

4. On the Compile page of the My Project designer, change the Output path value to point to the subdirectory where the main application's assembly is created. For example, if the main project is stored in the C:\Projects\DemoClient folder, the output directory for both the main application and its satellite assemblies should be C:\Projects\DemoClient\bin\Debug if you compile in Debug mode, or C:\Projects\DemoClient\bin\Release if you compile in Release mode.

5. In the AssemblyInfo.vb file, add an AssemblyCulture attribute that specifies the culture of the satellite assembly.

   ```
   <Assembly: AssemblyCulture("fr-FR")>
   ```

You are now ready to add one or more .resx files to the satellite assembly. However, it is essential that all the .resx files you create embed the culture name in their name. For example, a file containing the French name of all countries should be named Countries.fr-FR.resx.

In practice, you can drag a .resx file from the main project inside the Solution Explorer window to copy it into the satellite project, and then rename and edit it.

You can now compile the satellite assembly as usual. Visual Studio 2005 recognizes the AssemblyCulture attribute and correctly creates an assembly named DemoClient.resources.dll. This assembly is created in a subdirectory named after the assembly culture, under the folder you have specified in step 2. In this folder, Visual Studio also creates the "standard" DemoClient.dll assembly. This assembly contains no code and no resources and can be deleted before deploying the application or automatically by means of a postcompilation build event.

Attributes for Satellite Assemblies

A couple of attributes become useful when you're dealing with custom resource files and satellite assemblies, in addition to the AssemblyCulture discussed in the previous section.

As explained in step 3 of the previous section, the version number of a satellite assembly must match the version number of the main executable, and thus it looks like you must redeploy all the satellite assemblies whenever you change the version number of the main application. The SatelliteContractVersion attribute is useful in cases like these because it tells the .NET runtime that the main assembly wants to load satellite assemblies of the specified version:

```
' (Add to AssemblyInfo.vb file in main assembly.)
' Use version 1.0.0.0 of satellite assemblies, even if the
' version of current executable is different.
<Assembly: SatelliteContractVersion("1.0.0.0")>
```

It goes without saying that you shouldn't change the version of a satellite DLL; otherwise, the .NET runtime will fail to load it. To keep track of different versions of these DLLs you can increment the FileVersion attribute instead.

The NeutralResourcesLanguage attribute is used in the main project to specify the language associated with the resources in the main executable. This attribute isn't mandatory, but can speed up resource lookup because it tells the .NET runtime that it doesn't need to scan any satellite assembly if the UI language happens to match the neutral resource language (a rather frequent case):

```
' Specify that neutral resources are in English.
<Assembly: NeutralResourcesLanguage("en")>
```

Visual Studio 2005 lets you enter this attribute from the Assembly Information dialog box. (See Figure 17-8.)

Version 2.0 of the .NET Framework supports a new resource model in which even neutral-language resources are stored in a satellite DLL. Although this model is slightly less robust, because a user might make the program unusable by accidentally deleting its satellite DLLs, it is also more flexible because you can then update resources in the neutral-language DLL

without redeploying the main executable. You can enforce this model by passing a second argument to the NeutralResourcesLanguage attribute:

```
' Specify that neutral resources are in English, but these resources
' are held is a satellite DLL.
<Assembly: NeutralResourcesLanguage("en", _
    UltimateResourceFallbackLocation.ResourceLocation = Satellite)>
```

The Binding Process

When the running application references a different assembly, the CLR must resolve this reference—that is, it must bind the assembly of your choice to the caller application. This portion of the CLR is known as the assembly resolver. The reference stored in the calling assembly contains the name, version, culture, and public key token of the requested assembly if the assembly is strong-named. The version is ignored and the public key is missing if the assembly is private. The process that the runtime follows to locate the correct assembly consists of several heuristic steps:

1. Checks version policy in configuration files
2. Uses the assembly if it has been loaded previously
3. Searches the assembly in the GAC
4. Searches the assembly using codebase hints if there are any
5. Probes the application's main directory tree

These five steps apply to a strong-named assembly. When you're binding a private assembly, the CLR skips step 1 because the runtime ignores version information in private assemblies. Similarly, the CLR skips steps 3 and 4 when binding private assemblies because they can't be stored in the GAC and can't be associated with codebase hints. The following sections describe each step in detail.

Version Policy in Application Configuration Files

You can change the behavior of .NET applications and assemblies by means of configuration files. This mechanism gives both developers and system administrators great flexibility in deciding how managed applications search for the assemblies they must bind to. For example, a configuration file might enable you to specify that requests for version 1.0 of a given assembly should be redirected to version 2.0 of the same assembly. The .NET Framework supports three types of configuration files: the application configuration file, the publisher configuration file, and the machine configuration file.

The application configuration file affects the behavior of a single .NET application. This file must reside in the application's directory and have the same name as the application's main executable and the .config extension. For example, the application C:\bins\sampleapp.exe should have a configuration file named C:\bins\sampleapp.exe.config.

The publisher configuration file is tied to a signed assembly and affects all the managed applications that use that assembly. Typically, publishers of .NET components provide a configuration file when they release a new version of the component that fixes a few known bugs. The statements in the publisher's configuration file will therefore redirect all requests for the old version to the new one. A component vendor should provide a publisher configuration file only if the new version is perfectly backward compatible with the assembly being redirected. Each major.minor version of an assembly can have its own publisher configuration file. An application can decide to disable this feature for some or all of the assemblies that it uses.

Finally, the machine configuration file (also known as the administrator configuration file) affects the behavior of all the managed applications running under a given version of the .NET runtime. This file is named machine.config and is located in the \Windows\Microsoft.NET\ Framework\vx.y.zzzz\Config directory (where x.y.zzzz is the .NET Framework version). The settings in this file override the settings in both the application and publisher configuration files and can't be overridden.

All three types of configuration files are standard XML files that can contain several sections. The outermost section is marked by the <configuration> tag and might contain the <runtime> section (among others), which in turn contains information about the assemblies you want to redirect. Here's an example of an application configuration file:

```
<?xml version="1.0" encoding="UTF-8" ?>
<configuration>
   <runtime>
      <assemblyBinding xmlns="urn:schemas-microsoft-com:asm.v1">
         <dependentAssembly>
            <assemblyIdentity name="myAsm" culture="neutral"
                            publicKeyToken="378b4bc89e0bb9a3" />
            <bindingRedirect oldVersion="1.0.0.0" newVersion="2.0.0.0" />
            <publisherPolicy apply="no"/>
         </dependentAssembly>
      </assemblyBinding>
   </runtime>
</configuration>
```

Remember that XML tags and attributes are case sensitive, so you must type the tags exactly as reported in the preceding example. Visual Basic developers are accustomed to case-insensitive identifiers and can easily overlook this important detail.

Each <dependentAssembly> section is related to an assembly for which you want to establish a new version policy. This section must contain an <assemblyIdentity> subsection that identifies the assembly itself, with the name, culture, and public key token attributes. You can determine the public key token of a shared assembly by browsing the GAC from Windows Explorer, by using the GACUTIL command-line utility with the -l switch, or by using the SN utility, as follows:

```
sn -T myasm.dll
```

After the mandatory <assemblyIdentity> subsection, the <dependentAssembly> section can contain the following subsections:

■   The <bindingRedirect> section redirects one version of the assembly to another. For example, the preceding configuration file redirects all requests for version 1.0.0.0 of the assembly to version 2.0.0.0. The four numbers specified in the oldVersion and newVersion attributes are in the form major.minor.revision.build. The oldVersion attribute can specify a range of versions; for example, the following setting specifies that any version from 1.0 to 1.2 should be redirected to version 1.3, regardless of revision and build numbers:

```
<bindingRedirect oldVersion="1.0.0.0-1.2.65535.65535" newVersion="1.3.0.0"/>
```

■   The <publisherPolicy> section determines whether the publisher configuration file should be applied to this assembly. If you specify a "no" value for the apply attribute, as in the preceding example, the publisher configuration file is ignored and the application is said to work in *safe mode*.

■   The <codeBase> section specifies where the assembly is located. This information is especially useful for assemblies downloaded from the Internet or for shared assemblies that haven't been installed in the GAC. (For more information, read the section titled "Codebase Hints" coming up shortly.)

By default, the publisher's policy is enabled for all assemblies. You can disable it for a specific assembly by using a <publisherPolicy> tag inside a <dependentAssembly> section (as shown in the preceding example), or you can disable it for all the assemblies that an application uses by inserting a <publisherPolicy> tag directly inside the <assemblyBinding> section:

```
<assemblyBinding xmlns="urn:schemas-microsoft-com:asm.v1">
   <publisherPolicy apply="no"/>
</assemblyBinding>
```

If you disable the publisher's policy for the entire application, you can't reenable it for individual assemblies. For this reason, the only reasonable setting for the apply attribute is the "no" value, both at the global level and at the individual assembly level.

The <assemblyBinding> section can contain a <qualifyAssembly> element, which specifies how the CLR must handle an Assembly.Load method whose argument isn't a fully qualified assembly name:

```
<assemblyBinding xmlns="urn:schemas-microsoft-com:asm.v1">
   <qualifyAssembly partialName="myasm"
      fullName="myAsm, Version=1.0.0.0, Culture=neutral,
      PublicKeyToken=378b4bc89e0bb9a3"
</assemblyBinding>
```

For more information about the Assembly.Load method, read Chapter 18, "Reflection," and MSDN documentation.

A .NET Framework 2.0 application can depend on an assembly that is platform-specific, that is, an assembly for which two (or more) versions exist, one for 32-bit and one for 64-bit platforms. If you are sure that assemblies for different platforms will always have the same version number (in other words, you always update and deploy new versions for them at the same time), you can use the guidelines described previously in this section because the .NET runtime will always bind to the correct assembly. If you can't be sure that these assemblies always have the same version, you should specify two binding policies, one for each platform you support. (In theory, you might provide two configuration files, one for each platform, but it would be contrary to the principles of XCOPY deployment.) You can do this by means of the new processorArchitecture attribute in the <assemblyIdentity> element, as in this example:

```xml
<?xml version="1.0" encoding="UTF-8" ?>
<configuration>
   <runtime>
      <assemblyBinding xmlns="urn:schemas-microsoft-com:asm.v1">
         <dependentAssembly>
            <assemblyIdentity name="myAsm" culture="neutral"
                              publicKeyToken="378b4bc89e0bb9a3"
                              processorArchitecture="x86" />
            <bindingRedirect oldVersion="1.0.0.0" newVersion="2.1.0.0" />
         </dependentAssembly>
         <dependentAssembly>
            <assemblyIdentity name="myAsm" culture="neutral"
                              publicKeyToken="378b4bc89e0bb9a3"
                              processorArchitecture="ia64" />
            <bindingRedirect oldVersion="1.0.0.0" newVersion="2.3.0.0" />
         </dependentAssembly>
      </assemblyBinding>
   </runtime>
</configuration>
```

The processorArchitecture attribute can be assigned the values msil, x86, ia64, and amd64. These values are case-sensitive. If the configuration file has two <assemblyIdentity> elements, one with the processorArchitecture attribute and one without this attribute, the former element is used if the attribute matches the current platform, whereas the latter element will be used in all other cases.

You can use the AppDomain.ApplyPolicy method (new in .NET Framework 2.0) to learn which assemblies are going to be loaded by your application. This method takes an assembly name and returns the version of an assembly that will actually be loaded after .NET has applied its binding policy:

```vb
Dim oldName As String = "myAsm, Version=1.0.0.0, Culture=neutral, " _
   & "PublicKeyToken=378b4bc89e0bb9a3"
Dim newName As String = AppDomain.CurrentDomain.ApplyPolicy(oldName)
' (Assuming the previous configuration file has been used in x86 architecture)
Console.WriteLine(newName)      ' => myAsm, Version=2.1.0.0,…
```

Previously Loaded Assemblies and GAC Searches

In the second step of the binding process, the CLR checks whether the specific assembly has been requested in previous calls. If this is the case, the CLR redirects the call to the assembly already loaded, and the binding process stops here.

The CLR uses the assembly's strong name to decide whether the assembly is already in memory. This case can occur even if the application never previously requested the assembly but another assembly in the same process did and the requested assembly can safely be shared between multiple clients. As I've already explained, the strong name is a combination of the assembly's name, version, culture, publisher's public key, and processor architecture. The filename isn't part of the identity of the assembly, so you should never assign the same identity to different files.

If the assembly hasn't been loaded already, the binding process continues by searching the GAC for an assembly with that identity. This step applies only to assemblies with strong names because private assemblies can't be stored in the GAC. First, the runtime searches the GAC folder containing platform-specific assemblies, for example, GAC_32 on a 32-bit computer; if this search fails, it searches in the GAC_MSIL folder that contains assemblies compiled as IL code.

If the assembly is found in the GAC, the binding process stops here.

Codebase Hints

Once the version of the assembly is known and the assembly isn't in the GAC, the runtime has to locate the assembly file. The runtime usually accomplishes this task by means of a search process known as *probing* (described in the next section), but the developer, the publisher of the component, or the system administrator can disable probing by adding a codebase hint to one of the three configuration files. A codebase hint is a <codeBase> tag that appears in a <dependentAssembly> section.

Codebase hints are especially useful and common in browser-based and ClickOnce scenarios to inform the CLR of the location from which a given assembly can be downloaded. For example, the following portion of the configuration file tells the runtime that versions 1.0 through 1.4 of the MathFns assembly can be downloaded from *http://www.dotnet2themax.com/asms/mathfns.dll* (this is just an example—there is no such assembly at this URL).

```
...
<assemblyBinding xmlns="urn:schemas-microsoft-com:asm.v1">
   <dependentAssembly>
      <assemblyIdentity name="mathfns" culture="en-us"
                        publicKeyToken="378b4bc89e0bb9a3" />
      <bindingRedirect oldVersion="1.0.0.0" newVersion="2.0.0.0" />
      <publisherPolicy apply="no"/>
      <codeBase version="1.0.0.0-1.4.65535.65535"
         href="http://www.dotnet2themax.com/ams/mathfns.dll"/>
```

```
      </dependentAssembly>
</assemblyBinding>
...
```

In some cases, you don't even need a codebase hint for every assembly used by an application. For example, if the MathFns assembly references the TrigFns assembly, the runtime automatically reuses the hint for MathFns and assumes that TrigFns can be downloaded from *http:// www.dotnet2themax.com/assemblies/trigfns.dll.*

You can use codebase hints to reference assemblies outside the application's main directory, provided the assembly has a strong name. Either using a codebase hint or installing the assembly in the GAC is the only valid way to reference an assembly located outside the application's main directory, and both techniques work only with assemblies with strong names. For example, you might decide to install an assembly in a separate directory if it is going to be used by multiple applications from your client (and you don't want to deploy all these applications in the same directory). In general, however, strong-named assemblies deployed to a location other than the GAC don't offer any advantages other than a simpler installation; on the con side, they load slightly more slowly than assemblies in the GAC do and aren't protected from accidental deletions.

You can also have codebase hints in the machine.config file. This feature is important when you want to make a new version available to all the applications installed on a computer but for some reason you don't want to install the component in the GAC.

If a codebase hint is provided but no assembly is found at the specified address, or the assembly is found but its identity doesn't match the identity of the assembly the runtime is looking for, the binding process stops with an error.

Probing

Probing is the process by which the runtime can locate an assembly inside the application's directory or one of its subdirectories. As I explained in the preceding section, the runtime begins probing only if no codebase hint has been provided for the assembly. Probing is a set of heuristic rules based on the assembly's name, base directory, culture, and private binpath.

The binpath is a list of directories, expressed as relative names that implicitly refer to subdirectories under the application's main directory. (Absolute paths are invalid.) The binpath is specified as a semicolon-delimited list of directories and is assigned to the privatePath attribute of the <probing> tag, inside the <assemblyBinding> section of an application configuration file:

```
...
<assemblyBinding xmlns="urn:schemas-microsoft-com:asm.v1">
  <probing privatePath="bin;bin2\subbin;utils"/>
</assemblyBinding>
...
```

The sequence of directories searched for during the probing process depends on whether the assembly in question has a culture. For assemblies without a culture, the search is performed in each location in the order listed:

1. The application's base directory

2. The subdirectory named after the assembly

3. Each directory in the binpath list

4. The subdirectory named after the assembly under each directory in the binpath list

The runtime scans these directories first looking for a DLL named after the assembly (for example, myasm.dll). If the search fails, the runtime performs the search again in all these directories, this time looking for an EXE named after the assembly (myasm.exe).

For example, let's assume that the runtime is searching for an assembly named myasm.dll and the binpath is the one defined in the previous configuration file. Here are the files that the runtime searches for (assuming that the main application directory is C:\myapp):

```
C:\myapp\myasm.dll
C:\myapp\myasm\myasm.dll
C:\myapp\bin\myasm.dll
C:\myapp\bin\subbin\myasm.dll
C:\myapp\utils\myasm.dll
C:\myapp\bin\myasm\myasm.dll
C:\myapp\bin\subbin\myasm\myasm.dll
C:\myapp\utils\myasm\myasm.dll

C:\myapp\myasm.exe
C:\myapp\myasm\myasm.exe
C:\myapp\bin\myasm.exe
C:\myapp\bin\subbin\myasm.exe
C:\myapp\utils\myasm.exe
C:\myapp\bin\myasm\myasm.exe
C:\myapp\bin\subbin\myasm\myasm.exe
C:\myapp\utils\myasm\myasm.exe
```

For assemblies with a culture, the sequence is slightly different:

1. The application's base subdirectory named after the culture

2. The subdirectory named after the assembly under the directory defined in point 1

3. The subdirectory named after the culture under each subdirectory defined in the binpath

4. The subdirectory named after the assembly under each directory defined in point 3

Again, the runtime searches these directories for a DLL named after the assembly and then for an EXE file named after the assembly. For example, let's assume that an application using the preceding configuration file is requesting an assembly named myasm and marked as Italian culture ("it-IT"). These are the places where the runtime would search for this assembly:

```
C:\myapp\it-IT\myasm.dll
C:\myapp\it-IT\myasm\myasm.dll
C:\myapp\bin\it-IT\myasm.dll
C:\myapp\bin\subbin\it-IT\myasm.dll
C:\myapp\utils\it-IT\myasm.dll
C:\myapp\bin\it-IT\myasm\myasm.dll
C:\myapp\bin\subbin\it-IT\myasm\myasm.dll
C:\myapp\utils\it-IT\myasm\myasm.dll

C:\myapp\it-IT\myasm.exe
C:\myapp\it-IT\myasm\myasm.exe
C:\myapp\bin\it-IT\myasm.exe
C:\myapp\bin\subbin\it-IT\myasm.exe
C:\myapp\utils\it-IT\myasm.exe
C:\myapp\bin\it-IT\myasm\myasm.exe
C:\myapp\bin\subbin\it-IT\myasm\myasm.exe
C:\myapp\utils\it-IT\myasm\myasm.exe
```

If even this last step fails, the runtime checks whether the assembly was part of a Windows Installer package; if this is the case, the runtime asks the Windows Installer to install the assembly. (This feature is known as *on-demand installation*.) The Windows Installer program has other important features, such as the ability to advertise the application's availability, use the Add or Remove Programs option in Control Panel, and repair the application if necessary.

The Assembly Binding Log Viewer Utility (FUSLOGVW)

You now know everything you need to know about assembly binding, although in practice you're in the dark when the runtime can't locate one or more assemblies at run time. If you are running the program under the Visual Studio 2005 debugger, you can read a log of failed binding operations in the Debug window, a piece of information that usually lets you spot and fix the problem quickly and easily.

If you have already deployed the application on the user's machine, however, you can't use the Visual Studio debugger. In such a situation, the Assembly Binding Log Viewer can be a real lifesaver. The FUSLOGVW utility is located in the C:\Program Files\Microsoft Visual Studio 8\SDK\v2.0\Bin folder: you can run it from the command line or add it to the Start menu. (See Figure 17-16.)

You can specify whether FUSLOGVW should log all binding operations, just the unsuccessful ones, or no binding operations at all in the Log Settings dialog box that you open by clicking the Settings button, and you can also enable a custom log that shows only the failed binding operations that occur in a specified directory. Notice that the logging feature is disabled by default.

The options in the Log Categories panel let you display all bind operations or hide those related to assemblies that were compiled using the NGen tool. (See later in this chapter for more information about this tool.) You can display more details on any entry in the main window by clicking the View Log button or by double-clicking the entry.

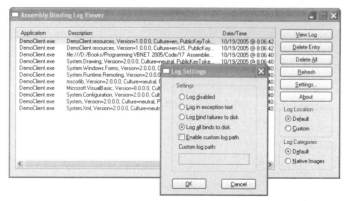

Figure 17-16   The Log Options dialog box in the FUSLOGVW utility, which lets you log all binds or just failed ones, for all assemblies or only those in the specified directory

Configuration Files

You've seen that you can affect the behavior of a specific application or the whole system by means of configuration files. In this section, I describe these files in more depth, though I leave out some major topics, such as ASP.NET settings, which are beyond the scope of this book.

Setting the Runtime Version

In general, you should always run a .NET application only on a computer where you have (or your customer has) installed the .NET Framework against which the application was compiled. Only in this case can you be sure that all calls to methods in the CLR will work as expected. However, the CLR is able to run an executable compiled under a different version of the .NET Framework. This technique is called *redirection* and can be affected by configuration files.

Let's begin with an important note: an application compiled under Visual Studio 2005 can't run under .NET Framework 1.1. The reason is that the addition of many new features, including generics, asks for a change in metadata format in a way that makes the .NET Framework 2.0 executable incompatible with the .NET Framework 1.1 runtime. This limitation implies that you need to worry only about .NET Framework 1.*x* applications running under .NET Framework 2.0.

If the .NET Framework 2.0 runtime is installed on a computer, it will always attempt to load the .NET version the application was compiled against. This means that you don't need any configuration file to run a .NET Framework 1.1 application on a system where both versions 1.1 and 2.0 of the .NET Framework are installed. (This behavior is new to .NET Framework 2.0 because in the same situation you need a configuration file under .NET Framework 1.1.)

Versions 1.1 and 2.0 of the .NET Framework (but not version 1.0) recognize multiple <supportedRuntime> tags in the configuration file, the order of which dictates which .NET Framework version should be used when more than one version is installed on the end user machine. When you want to run an application compiled under version 1.0 of the .NET Framework on a machine that has either version 1.1 or 2.0 of the .NET Framework (or both), you specify a pair of <supportedRuntime> tags, the first of which points to .NET Framework 1.1 because this version is more similar to version 1.0:

```
<?xml version="1.0"?>
<configuration>
  <startup>
    <supportedRuntime version="v1.1.4322"/>
    <supportedRuntime version="v2.0.50727"/>
  </startup>
</configuration>
```

You redirect only the runtime but don't need any <bindingRedirect> tag for the individual .NET assemblies that the application uses because .NET Framework version 1.1 or later is able to automatically redirect requests for older assemblies to the assemblies in the current version. This feature is called *unification* and works only for .NET Framework assemblies; third-party assemblies must be redirected manually by means of a <dependentAssembly> element.

Unification rules have changed in .NET Framework 2.0. Starting with this version, the runtime compares the major.minor version of the requested assembly with the major.minor version of the installed .NET Framework and will do the redirection only if the former version number is less than or equal to the latter. This new rule guarantees that a .NET Framework 1.1 application requesting, say, version 1.0.5000.0 of System.dll works well under .NET Framework 2.0 because it will be serviced with version 2.0.50727.0 of this assembly. However, if Microsoft releases a version 2.1 of the .NET Framework, an application compiled under version 2.0 asking for version 2.0.50727.0 of System.dll won't run under this new version, unless the configuration file contains one <dependentAssembly> element for each .NET assembly that must be redirected to the newer 2.1 version.

You can programmatically test which version of the .NET Framework your code is running under by invoking the GetSystemVersion method of the System.Runtime.InteropServices .RuntimeEnvironment class:

```
If RuntimeEnvironment.GetSystemVersion = "v2.0.50727" Then
    ' Running under version 2.0 of the .NET Framework
    …
End If
```

You can use this method to selectively disable the portions of your application that use features that aren't supported under the version of the .NET Framework in use.

Let me conclude this section with a warning. Even if the .NET Framework provides the ability to have an application run under different versions of the runtime, this feature comes at a high cost: you must thoroughly debug and test your code under different configurations (and possibly on different machines), which takes a lot of time and effort. Microsoft has done wonders to ensure that .NET Framework 1.1 applications work well under version 2.0 of the .NET Framework; however, version 2.0 is quite different from version 1.1 in many critical ways, so in most cases you can't expect that a program compiled under version 1.1 will run correctly under a newer version. A wiser solution might be to invest your time in recompiling the source code under the most recent version of the runtime and ensuring that your customers have that recent version installed.

The .NET Framework Configuration Tool

Although you should be familiar with the syntax of machine.config and application configuration files, most of the time you can perform your administration chores by using a Microsoft Management Console snap-in. The snap-in offers a simple user interface that lets you browse and modify files using a visual approach. This tool can be used only with Microsoft Windows NT, Windows 2000, Windows XP, and Windows Server 2003. You can launch the Microsoft .NET Framework Configuration tool from the Administrative Tools submenu of the Start menu.

To interactively change the configuration file of an application you first must add the application to the list of configured applications by right-clicking the Application element and selecting the Add command. You can then right-click the application element and select the Properties menu command to display a dialog box that enables you to change the most important settings you'd put inside an application's configuration file. (See Figure 17-17.)

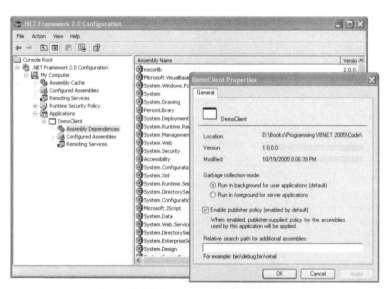

Figure 17-17 Adding an application to the list of configured applications with the .NET Framework Configuration tool

Next, expand the application element, right-click the Configured Assemblies folder, and select the Add command to add a new assembly to the list of those that this application must redirect. When you click Finish, a window like the one shown in Figure 17-18 appears. Here you specify how versions are redirected and the codebase corresponding to each version of the assembly in question. (These settings correspond to entries in the .config file for the specific assembly.)

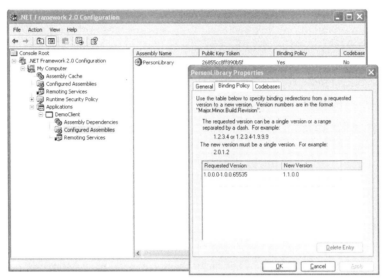

Figure 17-18   Adding an assembly to the list of configured assemblies for a specific application

The NGen Tool

You have read countless times in previous chapters that the .NET runtime compiles the IL code to native code—the process known as Just-In-Time compilation—one instant before running a method for the first time. JIT compilation has a lot of advantages, most of which derive from the exact knowledge of the runtime environment. For example, the JIT compiler can produce a sequence of opcodes that is optimized for the target CPU, can optimize away indirect method calls (which would otherwise require a vtable-lookup operation), and can make some decisions based on the available resources. Several other potential advantages aren't exploited in the current version of the .NET Framework, but might be in the future. For example, the JIT compiler might dynamically recompile a piece of code with more aggressive optimization if that code is executed very frequently.

JIT compilation has several drawbacks, too. First and foremost, the JIT compiler tends to slow the startup step of an application because it has to compile many types and methods before the user can see something on the screen. (Startup time is an issue especially for Windows Forms programs, but isn't a serious problem for server-side applications that are meant to run for days or months.) Also, the JIT compiler must perform its chores while the program is already running; thus, it typically has no time to analyze the entire application's IL code to apply global optimizations, as most traditional compilers do.

To cope with these issues, the .NET Framework includes a tool named NGen, which translates an entire assembly to native code. This step is performed only once, and therefore startup time is dramatically reduced. Unlike traditional compilers, the NGen tool doesn't allow you to compile the application on your development system and then move the native code executable to the customer's machine: an application can be compiled with NGen only after the application has been installed on the target computer and the assembly containing the IL code must be present for proper execution. This detail implies that you can't use NGen as a tool to prevent assembly decompilation. Microsoft itself uses NGen to precompile a few assemblies in the .NET Framework, most notably mscorlib.dll, which in part explains why installing the framework takes a significant amount of time.

The NGen tool compiles an application's assembly and stores its native code image in a directory known as native image cache, under the C:\Windows\Assembly folder. You don't need to do anything else because the binding process will automatically select this image instead of the IL image (which must always be available). An important warning: .NET runs the native code image only if its version corresponds to the IL image that would be run otherwise. This means that if you recompile the original assembly, you *must* compile it again with NGen; otherwise, the native code version will do nothing but take space on your hard disk. A less evident consequence is that a native code image becomes obsolete even if any of the assemblies it depends on are recompiled. For example, if you have written a custom control and you later update it, you should recompile all the applications that use that control. If you fail to do so, .NET will use the IL version and no error message will inform you of what has happened. This detail explains why NGen hasn't been very popular among .NET developers, at least until version 1.1.

The NGen version included in .NET Framework 2.0 has many new great features that makes it a much more useful tool:

- When you precompile an application (as opposed to a library DLL), NGen creates a native code image of both the application and all the assemblies it depends on.

- If the application or one of its dependencies is updated, NGen can automatically recompile both the application and all its dependencies. This is possible because .NET Framework 2.0 installs a Windows service process known as .NET Runtime Optimization Service, which checks whether an application compiled with NGen needs to be recompiled. This service works in the background when your CPU is idle, but you can force it to perform all pending tasks if you wish.

- NGen locates dependent assemblies by using the same probing logic described earlier in this chapter; this guarantees that the correct versions of these dependent assemblies are used. (In .NET Framework 1.1, there were a few discrepancies between the logic used by NGen and the one used by the CLR at run time.)

■ Assemblies compiled with NGen can be shared among application domains in a process, unlike what happened in .NET Framework 1.1. An important consequence of this improvement is that you can see the benefits of precompiled assemblies also in ASP.NET applications.

Note that you need administrative privileges to run NGen.

Using the NGen Tool

The syntax for NGen has changed in .NET Framework 2.0, even though the old syntax is still supported. According to the new syntax, you specify the command for NGen in its first argument. For example, the INSTALL command generates a native code image for the executable file passed in the second argument (known as the *root executable*) and all the assemblies it depends on:

```
NGEN INSTALL myapp.exe
```

Then NGen utility is stored in the C:\Windows\Microsoft.NET\Framework\v2.0.50727 directory, and thus the preceding command works only if you have added this directory to the system path. Here's an easy tip: add a command on the Tools menu so that you can invoke the NGen utility on the current executable directly from inside Visual Studio 2005.

If the assembly to be precompiled is in the GAC, the command syntax is slightly different and requires that you specify the assembly's strong name, as in this code:

```
NGEN INSTALL "myapp, Version=1.0.0.0, Culture=neutral,
   PublicKeyToken=ab349f12fe3a234e, ProcessorArchitecture=x86"
```

By default, NGen compiles both the main application and all its dependencies, as they appear in the assembly's manifest. This implies that assemblies that are loaded dynamically through the Assembly.Load method must be compiled separately. You can limit the number of dependent assemblies that are compiled by NGen with the /NODEPENDENCIES option:

```
NGEN INSTALL myapp.exe /NODEPENDENCIES
```

You use the UNINSTALL command to remove all the native code images related to a root executable and all its dependent assemblies (unless these assemblies are used by other applications compiled with NGen):

```
NGEN UNINSTALL MyApp.exe
```

You can also specify a strong name to have NGen look in the GAC for the root assembly. The strong name you provide might lack some elements: for example, if you omit the Culture attribute, NGen uninstalls all the assemblies with the given name, regardless of their culture. If you provide just the assembly name, all the native code images of that assembly will be removed.

The UPDATE command tells NGen to recompile all the native code images that need to be updated, that is, the images that correspond to assemblies that have been updated or that depend on assemblies that have been updated since the last time this command was invoked:

```
NGEN UPDATE
```

Depending on how many assemblies need to be refreshed, this command can take several seconds or even minutes to complete. In the next section, you'll see how to mitigate this issue by means of the new asynchronous features of NGen.

The last basic command I want to cover is DISPLAY, which simply lists all the items in the native image cache, subdivided into two sections containing only the root assemblies and all the native images:

```
NGEN DISPLAY
```

You can pass an assembly name or an assembly path, which restricts the output to that assembly and all the roots that depend on it. For example, the following command shows cache information about a specific executable:

```
NGEN DISPLAY c:\myapp.exe
```

whereas the next command displays information about System.dll and all the roots that depend on it:

```
NGEN DISPLAY System
```

As usual, you can specify a complete or a partial strong name if the assembly is stored in the GAC.

Using the NGen Service

Some NGen commands support the /QUEUE switch, which causes the command to be scheduled for later execution through the .NET Runtime Optimization Service. This service doesn't start automatically with the Windows operating system and is launched indirectly when a queued command is invoked; when there are no more commands in the queue waiting to be carried out, the service goes to sleep again. By default, this service performs its chores only when the system is idle, even though you can assign a higher priority to a specific command and you can tell the service to complete all the pending commands.

To generate a native code image asynchronously, you append the /QUEUE option to the INSTALL command:

```
NGEN INSTALL myapp.exe /QUEUE
```

The /QUEUE switch can be optionally followed by a priority, in the range of 1 to 3, where 1 is the highest priority. (The default value is 3.) A priority is sometimes necessary to ensure that an assembly is compiled before another one. Commands with priority 1 or 2 don't wait for system idle time:

```
NGEN INSTALL myapp.exe /QUEUE:1
```

You can schedule a system-wide update by applying the /QUEUE option to the UPDATE command:

```
NGEN UPDATE /QUEUE
```

You can display which commands are pending by issuing the following command:

```
NGEN QUEUE STATUS
```

The PAUSE command has two more subcommands, for pausing and restoring the activity of the background service. For example, to avoid conflicts it is recommended that you pause the service before compiling two or more assemblies in the background:

```
NGEN QUEUE PAUSE
NGEN INSTALL myapp.exe /QUEUE
NGEN INSTALL myapp2.exe /QUEUE
...
NGEN QUEUE CONTINUE
```

Finally, you can force the background service to complete all pending recompilations by means of the EXECUTEQUEUEDITEMS command, which optionally takes a priority number in the range of 1 to 3. For example, the following command forces all pending updates with priority equal to 1:

```
NGEN EXECUTEQUEUEDITEMS 1
```

If you omit the priority number, the preceding command returns only when all pending recompilations are completed.

Debugging Native Images

You must use the /DEBUG switch of the INSTALL command if you plan to debug the native code version; this option tells NGen to generate debug symbols and everything that is needed by the debugger. If you omit this switch and attempt to debug an assembly, the IL image is used instead:

```
NGEN INSTALL MyApp.exe /DEBUG
```

You can also specify an option that generates native images that can be used under a profiler:

```
NGEN INSTALL MyApp.exe /PROFILE
```

Interestingly, the native image cache can contain the versions compiled with and without this switch at the same time, so you don't have to worry about running NGen with a different setting to test the debug and the release version. You can check whether a native code image version of a DLL is used by means of the FUSLOGVW I described earlier in this chapter, which has a special log category for native images.

When you compile a DLL that will eventually be compiled with NGen, it is essential that you select a correct base address in the Advanced Compiler Settings dialog box. (See Figure 17-6.) Ideally, all the managed and native DLLs used by an application should have a different base address and their addresses should be separated enough to let the operating system load the DLLs in memory at their base address. If a DLL can't be loaded at its base address because those memory locations are already taken, the Windows operating system has to *rebase* the DLL (that is, patch the DLL in memory to change the target of all jump and call opcodes). Rebasing is a relatively slow process, but what is more important is that a rebased DLL can't be shared among processes and therefore doesn't make optimal use of memory. You can check the base address for any DLL by means of the DUMPBIN tool.

Attributes for NGen

You can control a couple of important NGen features by means of attributes in your source code.

Domain-Neutral Assemblies

A domain-neutral assembly is an assembly that can be shared among different AppDomains in a process. The assembly is JIT-compiled only once and it takes a fixed amount of memory even if used by multiple AppDomains, two features that make domain-neutral assemblies improve performance. For example, the mscorlib is always loaded as a domain-neutral assembly.

Domain-neutral assemblies have a few drawbacks, too. First, a domain-neutral assembly is never unloaded from memory, even if all the AppDomains using it have been unloaded. Second, access to static fields is slightly slower than usual because it must go through an indirection level. (Such an indirection level is needed because the CLR must ensure that each AppDomain sees its own set of static fields.)

The great news is that the NGen tool is now able to compile domain-neutral assemblies, a definite improvement over the version provided with earlier .NET versions. For example, you can compile assemblies used by Microsoft ASP.NET 2.0.

You decide whether your application can load domain-neutral assemblies by decorating its Sub Main method with a LoaderOptimization attribute:

```
<LoaderOptimization(LoaderOptimization.MultiDomain)> _
Sub Main()
    ...
End Sub
```

(This attribute is ignored when applied to any method other than Sub Main.) You have three possible values for the attribute's argument:

- **LoaderOptimization.SingleDomain**   The assembly is optimized to work with single AppDomains, and it won't load domain-neutral assemblies except mscorlib (which is always loaded in a domain-neutral mode). This is the default setting.

- **LoaderOptimization.MultiDomain**   The assembly is optimized to be shared among multiple application domains, all of which run the same application, and will load domain-neutral assemblies.

- **LoaderOptimization.MultiDomainHost**   The assembly is optimized to be shared among multiple application domains, which don't necessarily run the same application, and will load strong-named assemblies from the GAC in domain-neutral mode. This is the setting used for ASP.NET.

Remember that this attribute is just a hint for the assembly loader; depending on specific circumstances, the runtime can ignore the optimization you have requested and load the assembly using the default mode.

Hard Binding

Hard binding is an NGen feature that improves performance and reduces the amount of memory (the working set) used by a native image. Hard binding is especially useful when all or most dependent assemblies are usually loaded when the main application runs. If an application is hard bound to one or more dependent assemblies, the native images of all these assemblies are loaded when the application is launched. The downside is that the startup time can increase and make native image optimization less evident.

You can control which dependent assemblies are hard bound to an application by means of two attributes: DependencyAttribute and DefaultDependencyAttribute. You use the Dependency attribute in the main application to specify how likely a dependent assembly will be loaded:

```
' (Inside the main application...)
' The MathFunctions assembly will always be loaded.
<Assembly: Dependency("MathFunctions", LoadHint.Always)>
' The FinancialFunctions assembly will be loaded sometimes.
<Assembly: Dependency("FinancialFunctions", LoadHint.Sometimes)>
' Use the default load hint for the StringFunctions assembly.
<Assembly: Dependency("StringFunctions", LoadHint.Default)>
```

When the Dependency attribute uses the LoadHint.Default value, the actual hint is taken from the dependent assembly, where it must have been specified by means of a DefaultDependency attribute:

```
' (Inside the StringFunction assembly...)
' This assembly is likely always to be loaded by clients.
<Assembly: DefaultDependency(LoadHint.Always)>
```

Assemblies that are more likely to be loaded by the main application are also more likely to be hard bound by NGen. However, remember that the Dependency attribute provides a hint, not a command, and NGen can decide to ignore such a hint.

Part IV
Advanced Topics

Chapter 18
Reflection

Reflection is a set of classes that allow you to access and manipulate assemblies and modules and the types and the metadata that they contain. For example, you can use reflection to enumerate loaded assemblies, modules, and classes and the methods, properties, fields, and events that each type exposes. Reflection plays a fundamental role in the Microsoft .NET Framework and works as a building block for other important portions of the runtime. The runtime uses reflection in many circumstances, such as to enumerate fields when a type is being serialized or is being marshaled to another process or another machine. Microsoft Visual Basic transparently uses reflection whenever you access an object's method through late binding.

Reflection code typically uses the types in the System.Reflection namespace; the only class used by reflection outside this namespace is System.Type, which represents a type in a managed module. The .NET Framework also contains the System.Reflection.Emit namespace, which contains classes that let you create an assembly dynamically in memory. For example, the .NET Framework uses the classes in this namespace to compile a regular expression into IL code when the RegexOptions.Compiled option is specified. Because of its narrow scope, I won't cover the System.Reflection.Emit namespace in this book.

> **Note**   To avoid long lines, code samples in this chapter assume that the following Imports statements are used at the file or project level:

```
Imports System.CodeDom.Compiler
Imports System.Collections.Generic
Imports System.ComponentModel
Imports System.Diagnostics
Imports System.IO
Imports System.Reflection
Imports System.Runtime.InteropServices
```

Working with Assemblies and Modules

The types in the System.Reflection namespace form a logical hierarchy, at the top of which you find the Assembly class, as you can see in Figure 18-1. All the classes in the hierarchy shown in the figure belong to the System.Reflection namespace, except System.Type. FieldInfo, PropertyInfo, and EventInfo inherit from the MemberInfo abstract class, whereas MethodInfo and Constructor-Info inherit from the MethodBase abstract class (which in turn derives from MemberInfo).

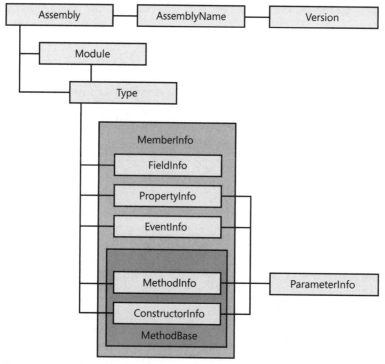

Figure 18-1   The Reflection logical hierarchy

In this section, I describe the Assembly, AssemblyName, and Module classes.

The Assembly Type

As its name implies, the Assembly type represents a .NET assembly. This type offers no construc-tor method because you never actually create an assembly, but simply get a reference to an existing assembly. There are many ways to perform this operation, as described in the following section.

Loading an Assembly

The Assembly type exposes several static methods that return a reference to an assembly, either running or not (that is, stored on disk but currently not running):

```
' Get a reference to the assembly this code is running in.
Dim asm As Assembly = Assembly.GetExecutingAssembly()
```

```
' Get a reference to the assembly a type belongs to.
asm = Assembly.GetAssembly(GetType(System.Data.DataSet))
' Another way to reach the same result.
asm = GetType(System.Data.DataSet).Assembly

' Get a reference to an assembly given its display name.
' (The argument can be the assembly's full name, which includes
'  version, culture, and public key.)
asm = Assembly.Load("mscorlib")

' Get a reference to an assembly given its filename or its full name.
asm = Assembly.LoadFrom("c:\myapp\mylib.dll")

' Another way to get a reference to an assembly given its path. (See text for notes.)
asm = Assembly.LoadFile("c:\myapp\mylib.dll")
```

Microsoft Visual Basic .NET 2003 requires that Assembly be enclosed in a pair of brackets to distinguish it from the language keyword, but this restriction has been lifted in the current version of the language. Also notice that Microsoft .NET Framework version 1.1 supports the LoadWithPartialName method, which is now obsolete and causes a compilation warning. Along the same lines, version 1.1 of these Load*Xxx* methods ignores any unknown or incorrect attribute in the display name; in the same circumstances, the Microsoft .NET Framework version 2.0 runtime throws an exception.

A few subtle differences exist among the Load, LoadFrom, and LoadFile methods, and also a few minor changes from .NET Framework 1.1 might impact the way existing applications behave, as explained in the following list. These differences have to do with how the assembly is located and the binding context in which the assembly is loaded. The *binding context* works like a cache for loaded assemblies so that the .NET runtime doesn't have to locate the same assembly again and again each time the application asks for it. (See the section titled "Previously Loaded Assemblies and GAC Searches" in Chapter 17, "Assemblies and Resources.")

■ The Load method takes the assembly name, either the short name or the fully qualified name (that includes version, culture, and public key token). If a fully qualified name is provided, this method searches the GAC first and, in general, it follows the same probing sequence that the .NET runtime applies when loading an assembly because your code references one of its types. (See Chapter 17 for details about the probing process.) Assemblies loaded with the Load method become part of the execution context; the main advantage of assemblies loaded in this context is that the .NET runtime is able to resolve their dependencies. You can enumerate assemblies in the execution context with this code:

```
For Each refAsm As Assembly In AppDomain.CurrentDomain.GetAssemblies()
    Console.WriteLine(refAsm.FullName)
Next
```

■ The LoadFrom method takes either a relative or absolute file path; if relative, the assembly is searched in the application's base directory. An assembly loaded with this method becomes part of the LoadFrom context. If an NGen image for the assembly exists, it won't be used, but if an assembly with the same identity can be found by probing or is already loaded in the LoadFrom context, the method returns that assembly instead, a behavior that can be quite confusing. When an assembly in the LoadFrom context is executed, the .NET runtime is able to locate its dependencies correctly only if they are under the application's base directory or are already loaded in the LoadFrom context.

■ The LoadFile method also takes a file path. It works similarly to LoadFrom, but the assembly is loaded in a different context, and the .NET runtime is unable to find its dependencies, unless they are already loaded in the Load context or you handle the AssemblyResolve event of the AppDomain object. (See the next section for more details about this event.)

To make things more complicated, the behavior of these methods has changed slightly in .NET Framework 2.0. First, both LoadFrom and LoadFile apply the probing policy (which they ignored in .NET Framework 1.1). Second, these methods check the identity of the assembly and load the assembly from the GAC if possible. There is a small probability that these minor changes may break your existing code, so pay attention when you are migrating your reflection-intensive applications to Microsoft Visual Basic 2005.

Another minor difference from version 1.1 is that if loading of an assembly fails once, it will continue to fail even if you remedy the error, until that AppDomain exists. In other words, you can't just trap the exception and ask the user to install the requested assembly in the GAC or in the application's base directory. Instead, you'll have to restart the application or at least load the assembly in a different AppDomain.

.NET Framework 2.0 has the ability to load an assembly for inspection purposes only, using either the ReflectionOnlyLoad or the ReflectionOnlyLoadFrom method:

```
' Load the System.Data.dll for reflection purposes.
asm = Assembly.ReflectionOnlyLoad( _
   "System.Data, Version=2.0.0.0, Culture=neutral, PublicKeyToken=b77a5c561934e089")

' Load a file for reflection purposes, given its path.
asm = Assembly.ReflectionOnlyLoadFrom("c:\myapp\mylib.dll")
```

You can enumerate members and perform most other reflection-related operations when you load an assembly in this way, but you can't instantiate a type in these assemblies and therefore you can't execute any code inside them. Unlike the LoadFrom and LoadFile methods, you are allowed to load the assembly even though Code Access Security (CAS) settings would otherwise prevent you from doing so.

Another difference from other load methods is that the ReflectionOnlyLoad and Reflection-OnlyLoadFrom methods ignore the binding policy. Thus, you can load exactly the assemblies you are pointing to—you can even inspect assemblies compiled for a different process architecture—except if you load an assembly with the same identity as one that is already loaded in the inspection context, the latter assembly is returned.

Assemblies loaded with these two methods become part of yet another context, known as the inspection context. There is exactly one inspection context in each AppDomain, and you can enumerate the assemblies it contains with this code:

```
For Each refAsm As Assembly In AppDomain.CurrentDomain.ReflectionOnlyGetAssemblies()
   Console.WriteLine(refAsm.FullName)
Next
```

The Assembly object has a new read-only property, ReflectionOnly, which returns True if the assembly is loaded in the inspection context.

AppDomain Events

When the .NET runtime successfully loads an assembly, either as the result of a JIT-compilation action or while executing an Assembly.Load*Xxxx* method, the AppDomain instance that represents the current application domain fires an AssemblyLoad event. You can use this event to determine exactly when an assembly is loaded, for example, for diagnostics purposes:

```
Sub TestAppDomainLoadAssemblyEvent()
   ' Subscribe to the AppDomain.AssemblyLoad event.
   Dim appDom As AppDomain = AppDomain.CurrentDomain
   AddHandler appDom.AssemblyLoad, AddressOf AppDomain_AssemblyLoad
   ' This statement causes the JIT compilation of DoSomethingWithXml method,
   ' which in turn loads the System.Xml.dll assembly.
   DoSomethingWithXml()
   ' Unsubscribe from the event.
   RemoveHandler appDom.AssemblyLoad, AddressOf AppDomain_AssemblyLoad
End Sub

Private Sub DoSomethingWithXml()
   ' This statement causes the loading of the System.Xml.dll assembly
   ' (assuming that no other XML-related type has been used already and that
   ' the program has been compiled in Release mode).
   Dim doc As New System.Xml.XmlDocument()
End Sub

Sub AppDomain_AssemblyLoad(ByVal sender As Object, ByVal e As AssemblyLoadEventArgs)
   Console.WriteLine("Assembly {0} is being loaded", e.LoadedAssembly.Location)
End Sub
```

Notice that methods in applications compiled in Debug mode are JIT-compiled earlier; therefore, the previous code snippet delivers the expected results only if compiled in Release mode.

When the .NET runtime isn't able to load an assembly, the current AppDomain instance fires an AssemblyResolve event. By handling this event, you can tell the CLR where the assembly is located. For example, let's suppose that you want to force an application to search for dependent assemblies—either private or shared—in a given folder. As you might recall from Chapter 17, by default weakly typed assemblies must be located in the application's folder or one of its subfolders, but the AssemblyResolve event enables you effectively to override the .NET standard binding policy. The handler for this event is peculiar: it is implemented as a

Function that returns an Assembly instance (the assembly that our code loaded manually) or Nothing if the load operation must fail:

```
Sub AppDomainAssemblyResolveEvent()
    ' Subscribe to the AppDomain.AssemblyResolve event.
    Dim appDom As AppDomain = AppDomain.CurrentDomain
    AddHandler appDom.AssemblyResolve, AddressOf AppDomain_AssemblyResolve
    ' Attempt to load an assembly that isn't in the private path.
    Dim asm As Assembly = Assembly.Load("EvaluatorLibrary")
    Console.WriteLine("Found {0} assembly at {1}", asm.FullName, asm.Location)
    ' Unsubscribe from the event.
    RemoveHandler appDom.AssemblyResolve, AddressOf AppDomain_AssemblyResolve
End Sub

Private Function AppDomain_AssemblyResolve(ByVal sender As Object, _
        ByVal e As ResolveEventArgs) As Assembly
    ' Search the assembly in a different directory.
    Dim searchDir As String = "c:\myassemblies"
    For Each dllFile As String In Directory.GetFiles(searchDir, "*.dll")
        Try
            Dim asm As Assembly = Assembly.LoadFile(dllFile)
            ' If the DLL is an assembly and its name matches, we've found it.
            If asm.GetName().Name = e.Name Then Return asm
        Catch ex As Exception
            ' Ignore DLLs that aren't valid assemblies.
        End Try
    Next
    ' If we get here, return Nothing to signal that the search failed.
    Return Nothing
End Function
```

The AssemblyResolve event lets you do wonders, if used appropriately. For example, you might load an assembly from a network share; or you might store all your assemblies in a database binary field and load them when needed, leveraging the Assembly.Load overload that takes a Byte array as an argument.

The AppDomain type also exposes the ReflectionOnlyAssemblyResolve event. As its name suggests, this event is similar to AssemblyResolve, except it fires when the resolution of an assembly fails in the reflection-only context, that is, when the ReflectionOnlyLoad or the ReflectionOnlyLoadFrom method fails. The ReflectionOnlyAssemblyResolve event also fires when the .NET runtime successfully locates the assembly you're loading for reflection-only purposes but fails to load one of the assemblies that the target assembly depends on.

Properties and Methods

Once you have a valid reference to an Assembly object, you can query its properties to learn additional information about it. For example, the FullName property returns a string that holds information about the version and the public key token (this data is the same as the string returned by the ToString method).

```
' This is the ADO.NET assembly.
asm = GetType(System.Data.DataSet).Assembly
Console.WriteLine(asm.FullName)
   ' => System.Data, Version=2.0.0.0, Culture=neutral, PublicKeyToken=b77a5c561934e089
```

The Location and CodeBase read-only properties both return the actual location of the assembly's file, so you can learn where assemblies in the GAC are actually stored, for example:

```
Console.WriteLine(asm.Location)
   ' => C:\WINDOWS\assembly\GAC_32\System.Data\2.0.0.0__ b77a5c561934e089\System.Data.dll
```

When you're not working with assemblies downloaded from the Internet, the information these properties return differs only in format:

```
' …(Continuing previous example)…
Console.WriteLine(asm.CodeBase)
   ' => file:///C:/WINDOWS/assembly/GAC_32/System.Data/2.0.0.0__
        b77a5c561934e089/System.Data.dll
```

The GlobalAssemblyCache property returns a Boolean value that tells you whether the assembly was loaded from the GAC. The ImageRuntimeVersion returns a string that describes the version of the CLR stored in the assembly's manifest (for example, v.2.0.50727). The EntryPoint property returns a MethodInfo object that describes the entry point method for the assembly, or it returns Nothing if the assembly has no entry point (for example, if it's a DLL class library). MethodInfo objects are described in the section titled "Enumerating Members" later in this chapter.

The Assembly class exposes many instance methods, the majority of which enable you to enumerate all the modules, files, and types in the assembly. For example, the GetTypes method returns an array with all the types (classes, interfaces, and so on) defined in an assembly:

```
' Enumerate all the types defined in an assembly.
For Each ty As Type In asm.GetTypes()
   Console.WriteLine(ty.FullName)
Next
```

You can also list only the public types that an assembly exports by using the GetExported-Types method.

The Assembly class overloads the GetType method inherited from System.Object so that it can take a type name and return the specified Type object.

```
' Next statement assumes that the asm variable is pointing to System.Data.dll.
Dim ty2 As Type = asm.GetType("System.Data.DataTable")
```

If the assembly doesn't contain the specified type, the GetType method returns Nothing. By passing True as its second argument, you can have this method throw a TypeLoadException if the specified type isn't found, and you can have the type name compared in a case-insensitive way by passing True as a third argument:

```
' This statement doesn't raise any exception because type name
' is compared in a case-insensitive way.
Dim ty3 As Type = asm.GetType("system.data.datatable", True, True)
```

Finally, two methods of the Assembly class return an AssemblyName object, which is described in the next section.

The AssemblyName Type

The AssemblyName class represents the object that .NET uses to hold the identity and to retrieve information about an assembly. A fully specified AssemblyName object has a name, a culture, and a version number, but the runtime can also use partially filled AssemblyName objects when searching for an assembly to be bound to caller code. Most often, you get a reference to an existing AssemblyName object by using the GetName property of the Assembly object:

```
' Get a reference to an assembly and its AssemblyName.
Dim asm As Assembly = Assembly.Load("mscorlib")
Dim an As AssemblyName = asm.GetName()
```

You can also get an array of AssemblyName objects using the GetReferencedAssemblies method:

```
' Get information on all the assemblies referenced by the current assembly.
Dim anArr() As AssemblyName
anArr = Assembly.GetExecutingAssembly.GetReferencedAssemblies()
```

Most of the properties of the AssemblyName type are self-explanatory, and some of them are also properties of the Assembly type (as is the case of the FullName and CodeBase properties):

```
Console.WriteLine(an.FullName)
   ' => mscorlib, Version=2.0.0.0, Culture=neutral, PublicKeyToken=b77a5c561934e089

' The ProcessorArchitecture property is new in .NET Framework 2.0.
' It can be MSIL, X86, IA64, Amd64, or None.
Console.WriteLine(an.ProcessorArchitecture.ToString())    ' => X86

' These properties come from the version object.
Console.WriteLine(an.Version.Major)                        ' => 2
Console.WriteLine(an.Version.Minor)                        ' => 0
Console.WriteLine(an.Version.Build)                        ' => 0
Console.WriteLine(an.Version.Revision)                     ' => 0
' You can also get the version as a single number.
Console.WriteLine(an.Version)                              ' => 2.0.0.0
```

A few methods of the AssemblyName object return a Byte array. For example, you can get the public key and the public key token by using the GetPublicKey and GetPublicKeyToken methods:

```
' Display the public key token of the assembly.
For Each b As Byte In an.GetPublicKeyToken()
   Console.Write("{0} ", b)
Next
```

The CultureInfo property gets or sets the culture supported by the assembly, or returns Nothing if the assembly is culture-neutral.

Unlike most other reflection types, the AssemblyName type has a constructor, which lets you create an AssemblyName instance from the display name of an assembly:

```
Dim an2 As New AssemblyName("mscorlib, Version=2.0.0.0, Culture=neutral, " _
    & "PublicKeyToken=b77a5c561934e089, ProcessorArchitecture=x86")
```

The Module Type

The Module class represents one of the modules in an assembly; don't confuse it with a Visual Basic Module block, which corresponds to a Type object. You can enumerate all the elements in an assembly by using the Assembly.GetModules method:

```
' Enumerate all the modules in the mscorlib assembly.
Dim asm As Assembly = Assembly.Load("mscorlib")
' (Note that Module is a reserved word in Visual Basic.)
For Each mo As [Module] In asm.GetModules()
    Console.WriteLine("{0} - {1}", mo.Name, mo.ScopeName)
Next
```

The preceding code produces only one output line:

```
mscorlib.dll - CommonLanguageRuntimeLibrary
```

The Name property returns the name of the actual DLL or EXE, whereas the ScopeName property is a readable string that represents the module. The vast majority of .NET assemblies (and all the assemblies you can build with Microsoft Visual Studio 2005 without using the Assembly Linker tool) contain only one module. This module is the one that contains the assembly manifest, and you can get a reference to it by means of the Assembly.Manifest-Module property:

```
Dim manModule As [Module] = asm.ManifestModule
```

In general, you rarely need to work with the Module type, and I won't cover it in more detail in this book.

Working with Types

The System.Type class is central to all reflection actions. It represents a managed type, a concept that encompasses classes, structures, modules, interfaces, and enums. The Type class provides all the means to enumerate a type's fields, properties, methods, and events, as well as set properties and fields and invoke methods dynamically.

An interesting detail: a Type object that represents a managed type is unique in a given App-Domain. This means that when you retrieve the Type object corresponding to a given type (for example, System.String) you always get the same instance, regardless of how you retrieve the Type object. This feature allows for the automatic synchronization of multiple static method invocations, among other benefits.

Retrieving a Type Object

The Type class itself doesn't expose any constructors because you never really create a Type object; rather, you get a reference to an existing one. You can choose from many ways to retrieve a reference to a Type object. In previous sections, you saw that you can enumerate all the types in an Assembly or a Module:

```
For Each t As Type In asm.GetTypes()
   Console.WriteLine(t.FullName)
Next
```

More often, you get a Type object using the Visual Basic GetType operator, which takes the unquoted name of a class:

```
Dim ty As Type = GetType(String)
Console.WriteLine(ty.FullName)            ' => System.String
```

If you already have an instance of the class in question, you can use the GetType method that all objects inherit from System.Object:

```
Dim d As Double = 123.45
ty = d.GetType()
Console.WriteLine(ty.FullName)            ' => System.Double
```

The Type.GetType static method takes a quoted class name, so you can build the name of the class dynamically (something you can't do with the GetType function):

```
' Note that you can't pass Type.GetType a Visual Basic synonym,
' such as Short, Integer, Long, or Date.
ty = Type.GetType("System.Int64")
Console.WriteLine(ty.FullName)            ' => System.Int64
```

The GetType method looks for the specified type in the current assembly and then in the system assembly (mscorlib.dll). Like the Assembly.GetType instance method, the Type.GetType static method returns Nothing if the specified type doesn't exist, but you can also pass True as its second argument to force a TypeLoadException in this case, and you can pass True as its third argument if you want the type name to be compared in a case-insensitive way. If the type you want to reference is neither in the caller's assembly nor in mscorlib.dll, you must append a comma and the name of the assembly in which the type resides. For example, the following code snippet shows how you get a reference to the System.Data.DataSet class, which resides in the assembly named System.Data. Because the GAC might contain many assemblies with this friendly name, you must pass the complete identity of the assembly after the first comma:

```
Dim typeName As String = "System.Data.DataSet, System.Data, " _
    & "Version=2.0.0.0, Culture=neutral, PublicKeyToken=b77a5c561934e089"
ty = Type.GetType(typeName)
```

.NET Framework 2.0 adds a variant of the previous method, which loads a type for inspection purposes only (similar to the Assembly.ReflectionOnlyLoad method):

```
' Second argument tells whether an exception is thrown if the type isn't found.
' Third argument tells whether case should be ignored in the search.
ty = Type.ReflectionOnlyGetType(typeName, False, True)
```

The TypeResolve Event

When the .NET runtime isn't able to load a type successfully, it fires the TypeResolve event of the AppDomain object that represents the current application domain. As it happens with the AssemblyResolve event, the TypeResolve event gives you the ability to override the .NET Framework's default binding policy. The following example shows how you can use this event:

```
Sub TestTypeResolveEvent()
    ' Subscribe to the AppDomain.TypeResolve event.
    Dim appDom As AppDomain = AppDomain.CurrentDomain
    AddHandler appDom.TypeResolve, AddressOf AppDomain_TypeResolve
    ' Get a reference to the Form type.
    ' (It should fail, but it doesn't because we are handling the TypeResolve event.)
    Dim ty As Type = Type.GetType("System.Windows.Forms.Form")
    ' Create a form and show it.
    Dim obj As Object = ty.InvokeMember("", BindingFlags.CreateInstance, Nothing, _
        Nothing, Nothing, Nothing)
    ty.InvokeMember("Show", BindingFlags.InvokeMethod, Nothing, obj, Nothing)
    ' Unsubscribe from the event.
    RemoveHandler appDom.TypeResolve, AddressOf AppDomain_TypeResolve
End Sub

Private Function AppDomain_TypeResolve(ByVal sender As Object, _
        ByVal e As ResolveEventArgs) As Assembly
    If e.Name = "System.Windows.Forms.Form" Then
        Dim asmFile As String = Path.Combine( _
            RuntimeEnvironment.GetRuntimeDirectory, "System.Windows.Forms.dll")
        Return Assembly.LoadFile(asmFile)
    End If
    ' Return Nothing if unable to provide an alternative.
    Return Nothing
End Function
```

The TypeResolve event fires when you fail to load a type through reflection, but it doesn't when the .NET runtime has located the assembly and the assembly doesn't contain the searched type. (If the CLR isn't able to locate the assembly, an AppDomain.AssemblyResolve event fires.) For example, the following statement doesn't cause the TypeResolve event to be fired because the CLR can locate the mscorlib.dll even though that assembly doesn't contain the definition of the Form type:

```
Dim ty2 As Type = GetType(Object).Assembly.GetType("System.Windows.Forms.Form")
```

Exploring Type Properties

All the properties of the Type object are read-only for one obvious reason: you can't change an attribute (such as name or scope) of a type defined in a compiled assembly. The names of most properties are self-explanatory, such as the Name (the type's name), FullName (the complete name, which includes the namespace), and Assembly (the Assembly object that contains the type). The IsClass, IsInterface, IsEnum, and IsValueType properties let you classify a given Type object. For example, the following code lists all the types exported by mscorlib.dll, specifying whether each is a class, an enum, a value type, or an interface:

```
Dim asm As Assembly = Assembly.Load("mscorlib")
For Each t As Type In asm.GetExportedTypes()
   If t.IsClass Then
      Console.WriteLine(t.Name & " (Class)")
   ElseIf t.IsEnum Then
      ' An enum is also a value type, so we must test IsEnum before IsValueType.
      Console.WriteLine(t.Name & " (Enum)")
   ElseIf t.IsValueType Then
      Console.WriteLine(t.Name & " (Structure)")
   ElseIf t.IsInterface Then
      Console.WriteLine(t.Name & " (Interface)")
   Else
      ' This statement is never reached because a type
      ' can't be anything other than one of the above.
   End If
Next
```

The IsPublic and IsNotPublic properties return information about the type's visibility. You should use these properties only with types that aren't nested in other types: the IsPublic property of a nested type is always False.

If the type is nested inside another type, you must use the following IsNested*Xxxx* properties to deduce the scope used to declare the type: IsNestedPublic (Public), IsNestedAssembly (Friend), IsNestedFamily (Protected), IsNestedFamORAssem (Protected Friend), IsNested-Private (Private), and IsNestedFamANDAssem (Protected and visible only from inside the assembly, a scope you can't define with Visual Basic). You can also use the DeclaringType property to get the enclosing type of a nested type; this property returns Nothing if the type isn't nested.

While we are on this subject, notice that the FullName property of a nested type includes a plus sign (+) to separate the name of the class and the name of its enclosing type, as in:

```
MyNamespace.MyEnclosingType+MyNestedType
```

A couple of properties are new in .NET Framework 2.0: IsNested returns True if the type is nested in another type (regardless of its scope), whereas IsVisible lets you determine whether the type can be accessed from outside the assembly; it returns True if the type is a Public top-level type or is a Public type nested inside a Public type.

You can get information about inheritance relationships by means of the BaseType (the base class for a type), IsAbstract (True for MustInherit classes), and IsSealed (True for NotInheritable classes) properties:

```
' (The asm variable is pointing to mscorlib…)
For Each t As Type In asm.GetExportedTypes()
   Dim text As String = t.FullName & " "
   If t.IsAbstract Then text &= "MustInherit "
   If t.IsSealed Then text &= "NotInheritable "
   ' We need this test because System.Object has no base class.
   If t.BaseType IsNot Nothing Then
      text &= "(base: " & t.BaseType.FullName & ") "
   End If
   Console.WriteLine(text)
Next
```

You can get additional information on a given type by querying a few methods, such as IsSubclassOfType (returns True if the current type is derived from the type passed as an argument), IsAssignableFrom (returns True if the type passed as an argument can be assigned to the current type), and IsInstanceOfType (returns True if the object passed as an argument is an instance of the current type). Let's recap a few of the many ways you have to test an object's type:

```
If TypeOf obj Is Person Then
   ' obj can be assigned to a Person variable (the Visual Basic way).
End If

If GetType(Person).IsAssignableFrom(obj.GetType()) Then
   ' obj can be assigned to a Person variable (the reflection way).
End If

If GetType(Person).IsInstanceOfType(obj) Then
   ' obj is a Person object.
End If

If GetType(Person) Is obj.GetType() Then
   ' obj is a Person object (but fails if obj is Nothing).
End If

If obj.GetType().IsSubclassOf(GetType(Person)) Then
   ' obj is an object that inherits from Person.
End If
```

Enumerating Members

The Type class exposes an intimidatingly large number of methods. The following methods let you enumerate type members: GetMembers, GetFields, GetProperties, GetMethods, GetEvents, GetConstructors, GetInterfaces, GetNestedTypes, and GetDefaultMembers. All these methods (note the plural names) return an array of elements that describe the members of the type represented by the current Type object. The most generic method in this group is

GetMembers, which returns an array with all the fields, properties, methods, and events that the type exposes. For example, the following code lists all the members of the System.String type:

```
Dim minfos() As MemberInfo = GetType(String).GetMembers()
For Each mi As MemberInfo In minfos
   Console.WriteLine("{0} ({1})", mi.Name, mi.MemberType)
Next
```

The GetMembers function returns an array of MemberInfo elements, where each MemberInfo represents a field, a property, a method, a constructor, an event, or a nested type (including delegates defined inside the class). MemberInfo is an abstract type from which more specific types derive—for example, FieldInfo for field members and MethodInfo for method members. The MemberInfo.MemberType enumerated property lets you discern between methods, properties, fields, and so on.

The GetMembers method returns two or more MemberInfo objects with the same name if the class exposes overloaded properties and methods. So, for example, the output from the preceding code snippet includes multiple occurrences of the Format and Concat methods. You also find multiple occurrences of the constructor method, which is always named .ctor. In the next section, I show how you can explore the argument signature of these overloaded members. Also note that the GetMembers method returns public, instance, and static members, as well as methods inherited by other objects, such as the GetHashCode method inherited from System.Object.

The GetMembers method supports an optional BindingFlags enumerated argument. This bit-coded value lets you narrow the enumeration—for example, by listing only public or instance members. The BindingFlags type is used in many reflection methods and includes many enumerated values, but in this case only a few are useful:

- The Public and NonPublic enumerated values restrict the enumeration according to the scope of the elements. (You must specify at least one of these flags to get a nonempty result.)

- The Instance and Static enumerated values restrict the enumeration to instance members and static members, respectively. (You must specify at least one of these flags to get a nonempty result.)

- The DeclaredOnly enumerated value restricts the enumeration to members declared in the current type (as opposed to members inherited from its base class).

- The FlattenHierarchy enumerated value is used to include static members up the hierarchy.

This code lists only the public, nonstatic, and noninherited members of the String class:

```
' Get all public, instance, noninherited members of String type.
Dim minfo() As MemberInfo = GetType(String).GetMembers( _
   BindingFlags.Public Or BindingFlags.Instance Or BindingFlags.DeclaredOnly)
```

The preceding code snippet produces an array that includes the ToString method, which at first glance shouldn't be in the result because it's inherited from System.Object. It's included because the String class adds an overloaded version of this method, and this overloaded method is the one that appears in the result array.

To narrow the enumeration to a given member type, you can use a more specific Get*Xxxx*s method. When you're using a Get*Xxxx*s method other than GetMembers, you can assign the result to an array of a more specific type, namely, PropertyInfo, MethodInfo, ConstructorInfo, FieldInfo, or EventInfo. (All these specific types derive from MemberInfo.) For example, this code lists only the methods of the String type:

```
For Each mi As MethodInfo In GetType(String).GetMethods()
   Console.WriteLine(mi.Name)
Next
```

The GetInterfaces or GetNestedTypes method return an array of Type elements, rather than a MemberInfo array, so the code in the loop is slightly different:

```
For Each itf As Type In GetType(String).GetInterfaces()
   Console.WriteLine(itf.FullName)
Next
```

All the Get*Xxxx*s methods—with the exception of GetDefaultMembers and GetInterfaces—can take an optional BindingFlags argument to restrict the enumeration to public or nonpublic, static or instance, and declared or inherited members. For more sophisticated searches, you can use the FindMembers method, which takes a delegate pointing to a function that filters individual members. (See MSDN documentation for additional information.)

In many cases, you don't need to enumerate a type's members because you have other ways to find out the name of the field, property, methods, or event you want to get information about. You can use the GetMember or other Get*Xxx* methods (where *Xxx* is a singular word) of the Type class—namely, GetMember, GetField, GetProperty, GetMethod, GetEvent, GetInterface, GetConstructor, and GetNestedType—to get the corresponding MemberInfo (or a more specific object):

```
' Get information about the String.Chars property.
Dim pi2 As PropertyInfo = GetType(String).GetProperty("Chars")
```

If you're querying for an overloaded property or method, you need to ask for a specific version of the member by using GetProperty or GetMethod and specifying the exact argument signature by passing an array of Type objects as its second argument:

```
' Get the MethodInfo object for the IndexOf string method with the
' following signature: IndexOf(char, startIndex, endIndex).

' Prepare the signature as an array of Type objects.
Dim argTypes() As Type = {GetType(Char), GetType(Integer), GetType(Integer)}
' Ask for the method with given name and signature.
Dim mi2 As MethodInfo = GetType(String).GetMethod("IndexOf", argTypes)
```

The method signature you pass to GetMethod must include information about whether the argument is passed by reference or is an array. Two new methods of the Type class make this task simpler than it is in .NET Framework 1.1:

```
' This code shows how you can build a reference to the following method
'      Sub TestMethod(ByRef x As Integer, ByVal arr(,) As String).
Dim argType1 As Type = GetType(Integer).MakeByRefType()
Dim argType2 As Type = GetType(String).MakeArrayType(2)
Dim arrTypes() As Type = {argType1, argType2}
Dim mi3 As MethodInfo = GetType(TestClass).GetMethod("TestMethod", arrTypes)
```

Speaking of arrays, notice that the name of array types ends with a pair of brackets:

```
Dim arrTy As Type = GetType(Integer())
Dim arrTy2 As Type = GetType(Integer(,))
Console.WriteLine(arrTy.FullName)       ' => System.Int32[]
Console.WriteLine(arrTy2.FullName)      ' => System.Int32[,]
```

Also, the name of a type that represents a ByRef argument has a trailing ampersand (&) character; therefore, you need to process the value returned by the FullName property if you want to display a type name using Visual Basic syntax:

```
Dim vbTypeName As String = _
   argType1.FullName.Replace("[", "(").Replace("]", ")").Replace("&", "")
```

Finally, your code can easily get a reference to the MethodBase that describes the method being executed by means of a static member of the MethodBase type:

```
Dim currMethod As MethodBase = MethodBase.GetCurrentMethod()
```

Exploring Type Members

After you get a reference to a MemberInfo object—or a more specific object, such as FieldInfo or PropertyInfo—you can retrieve information about the corresponding member. Because all these specific *Xxxx*Info objects derive from MemberInfo, they have some properties in common, including Name, MemberType, ReflectedType (the type used to retrieve this MemberInfo instance), and DeclaringType (the type where this member is declared). The values returned by the last two properties differ only if the member has been inherited.

The following loop displays the name of all the members exposed by the String type, together with a description of the member type. To make things more interesting, I'm suppressing constructor methods, multiple definitions for overloaded methods, and methods inherited from the base Object class:

```
' We use this ArrayList to keep track of items already displayed.
Dim al As New ArrayList()
For Each mi As MemberInfo In GetType(String).GetMembers()
   If mi.MemberType = MemberTypes.Constructor Then
      ' Ignore constructor methods.
   ElseIf Not mi.DeclaringType Is mi.ReflectedType Then
      ' Ignore inherited members.
```

```
      ElseIf Not al.Contains(mi.Name) Then
         ' If this element hasn't been listed yet, do it now.
         Console.WriteLine("{0}  ({1})", mi.Name, mi.MemberType)
         ' Add this element to the list of processed items.
         al.Add(mi.Name)
      End If
Next
```

Exploring Fields

Except for the members inherited from MemberInfo, a FieldInfo object exposes only a few properties, including FieldType (the type of the field), IsLiteral (True if the field is actually a constant), IsInitOnly (True if the field is marked as ReadOnly), IsStatic (True if the field is marked as Shared), and other Boolean properties that reflect the scope of the field, such as IsPublic, IsAssembly (Friend), IsFamily (Protected), IsFamilyOrAssembly (Protected Friend), IsFamilyAndAssembly (Protected but visible only from inside the same assembly, a scope not supported by Visual Basic), and IsPrivate:

```
' List all the nonconstant fields with Public or Friend scope in the TestClass type.
For Each fi As FieldInfo In GetType(TestClass).GetFields( _
      BindingFlags.Public Or BindingFlags.NonPublic Or BindingFlags.Instance)
   If (fi.IsPublic OrElse fi.IsAssembly) AndAlso Not fi.IsLiteral Then
      Console.WriteLine("{0} As {1}", fi.Name, fi.FieldType.Name)
   End If
Next
```

A new method in .NET Framework 2.0 allows you to extract the value of a constant:

```
' List all the public constants in the TestClass type.
For Each fi As FieldInfo In GetType(TestClass).GetFields()
   If fi.IsLiteral Then
      Console.WriteLine("{0} = {1}", fi.Name, fi.GetRawConstantValue())
   End If
Next
```

Exploring Methods

Like FieldInfo, the MethodInfo type exposes the IsStatic property and all the other scope-related properties you've just seen, plus a few additional Boolean properties: IsVirtual (the method is marked with the Overridable keyword), IsAbstract (MustOverride), and IsFinal (NotOverridable). The IsSpecialName property returns True if the method has been created by the compiler and should be dealt with in a special way, as is the case of the methods generated by properties and operators. If the method returns a value (a Function, in Visual Basic parlance), the ReturnType property returns the type of the return value; otherwise, it returns a special type whose name is System.Void. This snippet uses these properties to display information on all the methods in a class, exposed in a Visual Basic–like syntax:

```
For Each mi As MethodInfo In GetType(Array).GetMethods()
   ' Ignore special methods, such as property getters and setters.
   If mi.IsSpecialName Then Continue For
```

```
   If mi.IsFinal Then
      Console.Write("NotOverridable ")
   ElseIf mi.IsVirtual Then
      Console.Write("Overridable ")
   ElseIf mi.IsAbstract Then
      Console.Write("MustOverride ")
   End If
   Dim retTypeName As String = mi.ReturnType.FullName
   If retTypeName = "System.Void" Then
      Console.WriteLine("Sub {0}", mi.Name)
   Else
      Console.WriteLine("Function {0} As {1}", mi.Name, retTypeName)
   End If
Next
```

The ConstructorInfo type exposes the same members as the MethodInfo type (not surprisingly because both these types inherit from the MethodBase abstract class, which in turn derives from MemberInfo), with the exception of ReturnType (constructors don't have a return type).

Exploring Properties

The PropertyInfo type exposes only three interesting properties besides those inherited from MemberInfo: PropertyType (the type returned by the property), CanRead (False for write-only properties), and CanWrite (False for read-only properties). Oddly, the PropertyInfo type doesn't expose members that indicate the scope of the property or whether it's a static property. You can access this information only indirectly by means of one of the following methods: GetGetMethod (which returns the MethodInfo object corresponding to the Get method), GetSetMethod (the MethodInfo object corresponding to the Set method), or GetAccessors (an array of one or two MethodInfo objects, corresponding to the Get and/or Set accessor methods):

```
Sub ExploringProperties()
   ' Display instance and static Public properties.
   For Each pi As PropertyInfo In GetType(TestClass).GetProperties( _
         BindingFlags.Public Or BindingFlags.Instance Or BindingFlags.Static)
      ' Get either the Get or the Set accessor methods.
      Dim modifier As String = ""
      Dim mi As MethodInfo
      If pi.CanRead Then
         mi = pi.GetGetMethod()
         If Not pi.CanWrite Then modifier = "ReadOnly "
      Else
         mi = pi.GetSetMethod()
         modifier = "WriteOnly "
      End If
      ' Add the Shared qualifier if necessary.
      If mi.IsStatic Then modifier = "Shared " & modifier
      ' Display only Public and Protected properties.
      If mi.IsPublic Or mi.IsFamily Then
         Console.WriteLine("Public {0}Property {1} As {2}", modifier, pi.Name, _
```

```
            pi.PropertyType.FullName)
        End If
    Next
End Sub
```

If you need to retrieve a property accessor only to determine its scope or whether the property is static, you can use the GetAccessors method as follows:

```
' Get the first property accessor, even if it's private.
mi = pi.GetAccessors(True)(0)
```

By default the GetGetMethod, GetSetMethod, and GetAccessors methods return only public accessor methods; if the accessor method doesn't exist or isn't public, the return value is Nothing. However, these methods are overloaded to take a Boolean argument: if you pass True, they return the accessor method even if it doesn't have a public scope.

Exploring Events

Getting information about an event is complicated by the fact that the EventInfo type has no property that lets you determine the scope of the event or whether it's static. Instead, you must use GetAddMethod to return the MethodInfo object corresponding to the method that adds a new subscriber to the list of listeners for this event. (This is the method that the AddHandler keyword calls for you behind the scenes.) Typically, this method is named add_*Eventname* and is paired with the remove_*Eventname* hidden method (the method called by RemoveHandler and whose MethodInfo is returned by the GetRemoveMethod). The Visual Basic compiler creates these methods for you by default, unless you define a custom event.

You can query the MethodInfo object returned by either GetAddMethod or GetRemoveMethod to discover the event's scope, its arguments, and whether it's static:

```
' Get information on the SampleEvent event of the TestClass object.
Dim ei As EventInfo = GetType(TestClass).GetEvent("SampleEvent")
' Get a reference to the hidden add_SampleEvent method.
Dim mi2 As MethodInfo = ei.GetAddMethod()
' Test the method scope and check whether it's static.
...
```

Exploring Parameters

The one thing left to do is enumerate the parameters that a property or a method expects. Both the GetIndexParameters (of ParameterInfo) and the GetParameters (of MethodInfo) methods return an array of ParameterInfo objects, where each element describes the attributes of the arguments passed to and from the member.

A ParameterInfo object has properties with names that are self-explanatory: Name (the name of the parameter), ParameterType (the type of the parameter), Member (the MemberInfo the parameter belongs to), Position (an integer that describes where the parameter appears in the method signature), IsOptional (True for optional parameters), and DefaultValue (the default value of an optional parameter). The following code shows how to display the calling syntax for a given method:

```
Dim mi As MethodInfo = GetType(TestClass).GetMethod("MethodWithOptionalArgs")
Console.Write(mi.Name & "(")
For Each pi As ParameterInfo In mi.GetParameters()
    ' Display a comma if it isn't the first parameter.
    If pi.Position > 0 Then Console.Write(", ")
    If pi.IsOptional Then Console.Write("Optional ")
    ' Notice how you can discern between ByVal and ByRef parameters.
    Dim direction As String = "ByVal"
    If pi.ParameterType.IsByRef Then direction = "ByRef"
    ' Process the parameter type.
    Dim tyName As String = pi.ParameterType.FullName
    ' Convert [] into () and drop the & character (included if parameter is ByRef).
    tyName = tyName.Replace("[", "(").Replace("]", ")").Replace("&", "")
    Console.Write("{0} {1} As {2}", direction, pi.Name, tyName)
    ' Append the default value for optional parameters.
    If pi.IsOptional Then Console.Write(" = " & GetObjectValue(pi.DefaultValue))
Next
Console.WriteLine(")")
```

The previous code snippet uses the GetObjectValue auxiliary method, which returns the value of an object in Visual Basic syntax:

```
Function GetObjectValue(ByVal obj As Object) As String
    If obj Is Nothing Then
        Return "Nothing"
    ElseIf obj.GetType() Is GetType(String) Then
        Return """" & obj.ToString() & """"
    ElseIf obj.GetType() Is GetType(Date) Then
        Return "#" & obj.ToString() & "#"
    ElseIf obj.GetType().IsEnum Then
        ' It's an enum type.
        Return obj.GetType().Name & "." & [Enum].GetName(obj.GetType(), obj)
    Else
        ' It's something else, including a number.
        Return obj.ToString()
    End If
End Function
```

Getting the syntax for an event is more complicated because the EventInfo object doesn't expose the GetParameters method. Instead, you must use the EventHandlerType property to retrieve the Type object corresponding to the delegate that defines the event. The Invoke method of this delegate, in turn, has the same signature as the event:

```
Dim ei As EventInfo = GetType(TestClass).GetEvent("SampleEvent")
Dim delegType As Type = ei.EventHandlerType
Dim mi2 As MethodInfo = delegType.GetMethod("Invoke")
For Each pi As ParameterInfo In mi2.GetParameters()
    …
Next
```

Exploring the Method Body

Version 2.0 of the .NET Framework introduces a new feature that, although not completely implemented, surely goes in a very promising direction: the ability to peek at the IL code compiled for a given method. The entry point for this capability is the new MethodBase .GetMethodBody method, which returns a MethodBody object. In turn, a MethodBody object exposes properties that let you list the local variables, evaluate the size of the stack that the method uses, and explore the Try...Catch exception handlers defined in the inspected method.

```
' Get a reference to the method in a type.
Dim mi As MethodInfo = GetType(TestClass).GetMethod("TestMethod")
Dim mb As MethodBody = mi.GetMethodBody()
' Display the number of used stack elements.
Console.WriteLine("Stack Size = {0}", mb.MaxStackSize)

' Display index and type of local variables.
Console.WriteLine("Local variables:")
For Each lvi As LocalVariableInfo In mb.LocalVariables
   Console.WriteLine("  var[{0}] As {1}", lvi.LocalIndex, lvi.LocalType.FullName)
Next

' Display information about exception handlers.
Console.WriteLine("Exception handlers:")
For Each ehc As ExceptionHandlingClause In mb.ExceptionHandlingClauses
   Console.Write("  Type={0}, ", ehc.Flags.ToString())
   If ehc.Flags = ExceptionHandlingClauseOptions.Clause Then
      Console.Write("ex As {0}, ", ehc.CatchType.Name)
   End If
   Console.Write("Try off/len={0}/{1}, ", ehc.TryOffset, ehc.TryLength)
   Console.WriteLine("Handler off/len={0}/{1}", ehc.HandlerOffset, ehc.HandlerLength)
Next
```

The list of exception handlers doesn't differentiate between Catch and Finally clauses belonging to distinct Try blocks, but you can group them correctly by looking at elements with identical TryOffset properties. The Flags property of the ExceptionHandlingClause object helps you understand whether the clause is a filter (When block), a clause (Catch block), or a Finally block. The type of the Exception object is exposed by the CatchType property. For example, given the following method:

```
Sub TestMethod(ByRef x As Integer, ByVal arr(,) As String)
   Try
      Console.WriteLine("First Try block")
   Catch ex As NullReferenceException
      …
   Catch ex As Exception
      …
   Finally
      …
   End Try

   Try
      Console.WriteLine("Second Try block")
```

```
    Catch ex As NullReferenceException
       …
    Catch ex As OverflowException
       …
    Catch ex As Exception
       …
    End Try
End Sub
```

Here's the information that might be displayed in the console window. (The actual offset and length information varies depending on the actual executable statements in the method.)

```
Stack Size = 2
Local variables:
  var[0] As System.NullReferenceException
  var[1] As System.Exception
  var[2] As System.NullReferenceException
  var[3] As System.OverflowException
  var[4] As System.Exception
Exception handlers:
  Type=Clause, ex As NullReferenceException, Try off/len=2/14, Handler off/len=16/26
  Type=Clause, ex As Exception, Try off/len=2/14, Handler off/len =42/26
  Type=Finally, Try off/len=2/66, Handler off/len=68/12
  Type=Clause, ex As NullReferenceException, Try off/len=82/13, Handler off/len=95/26
  Type=Clause, ex As OverflowException, Try off/len=82/13, Handler off/len=121/26
  Type=Clause, ex As Exception, Try off/len=82/13, Handler off/len=147/27
```

Notice that the list of local variables is likely to include variables that you haven't declared explicitly but that are created for you by the compiler to store intermediate results, such as the Exception variables in Catch clauses or the upper limit of a For loop.

The only method of the MethodBody object of interest is GetILAsByteArray, which returns an array containing the raw IL opcodes. These opcodes are fully documented, so you might use this method to disassemble a .NET executable. As you can guess, this isn't exactly a trivial task, however.

Reflecting on Generics

 Reflection techniques in .NET Framework 2.0 fully support generic types, and you must account for them when exploring the types that an assembly exposes.

Exploring Generic Types

You can distinguish generic type definitions from regular types when enumerating all the types in an assembly by checking their IsGenericTypeDefinition method. The full name of a generic type definition contains a inverse quote character followed by the number of type arguments in the definition. Therefore, given the following code:

```
' List all the generic types in mscorlib.
Dim asm As Assembly = GetType(Object).Assembly
```

```
For Each ty As Type In asm.GetTypes()
   If ty.IsGenericTypeDefinition() Then
      Console.WriteLine(ty.FullName)
   End If
Next
```

This is the kind of results you'll see in the console window:

```
System.Collections.Generic.List`1
System.Collections.Generic.Dictionary`2
System.Action`1
…
```

The names of the generic parameters in the type definition don't appear in the type name because they aren't meaningful in the composition of a unique type name: as you might recall from Chapter 11, "Generics," you can have two generic type definitions with the same name only if the number of their generic parameters differs. The syntax based on the inverse quote character becomes important if you want to retrieve a reference to the generic type definition, as in this code:

```
Dim genType As Type = asm.GetType("System.Collections.Generic.Dictionary`2")
```

There is no built-in method or property that returns the signature of the generic type as it appears in source code, and thus you have to manually strip the inverse quote character from the name and use the GetGenericArguments method to retrieve the name of type parameters:

```
' (Continuing previous code example)
Dim typeName As String = genType.FullName
' Strip the inverse quote character.
typeName = typeName.Remove(typeName.IndexOf("`"c)) & "(Of "
' Append the name of each type parameter.
For Each tyArg As Type In genType.GetGenericArguments()
    ' The GenericParameterPosition property reflects the position where
    ' this argument appears in the signature.
    If tyArg.GenericParameterPosition > 0 Then typeName &= ","
    typeName &= tyArg.Name
Next
typeName &= ")"     ' => System.Collections.Generic.Dictionary(Of TKey,TValue)
```

Exploring Generic Methods

You must adopt a similar approach when exploring the generics methods of a type. (Remember that a method with generic arguments can appear in both a regular and a generic type.) You can check whether a method has a generic definition by means of the MethodInfo .IsGenericMethodDefinition method and explore its generic parameters by means of the MethodInfo.GetGenericArguments method. For example, the following loop displays the name of all the methods in a type using the Of clause for generic methods:

```
' List all the generic methods of the System.Array type.
For Each mi As MethodInfo In GetType(Array).GetMethods()
    If mi.IsGenericMethodDefinition Then
        Dim methodName As String = mi.Name & "(Of "
```

```
    For Each tyArg2 As Type In mi.GetGenericArguments()
        If tyArg2.GenericParameterPosition > 0 Then methodName &= ","
        methodName &= tyArg2.Name
    Next
    methodName &= ")"
    Console.WriteLine(methodName)        ' => IndexOf(Of T),…
  End If
Next
```

When you explore the parameters of a method, you must discern between regular types (e.g., System.String) and types passed as an argument to a generic type or method (e.g., T or K). This is possible because the Type class exposes a new IsGenericParameter property, which returns False in the former case and True in the latter. It is essential that you test this method before doing anything else with a Type value because some properties of a type used as a parameter in a generic class return meaningless values or might throw an exception. For example, this is the most correct way to assemble the signature of a method:

```
' (The mi variable points to a MethodInfo object.)
Dim signature As String = mi.Name & "("
For Each par As ParameterInfo In mi.GetParameters()
   If par.Position > 0 Then signature &= ", "
   signature &= par.Name & " As " & GetTypeName(par.ParameterType)
Next
signature &= ")"
Dim retType As Type = mi.ReturnType
If retType.FullName <> "System.Void" Then
   signature &= " As " & GetTypeName(retType)
End If
Console.WriteLine(signature)
   ' => TestMethod(key As K, values As V(), count As System.Int32) As T
```

where the GetTypeName function is defined as follows:

```
Function GetTypeName(ByVal type As Type) As String
   If type.IsGenericParameter Then
      Return type.Name
   Else
      Return type.FullName.Replace("[", "(").Replace("]", ")").Replace("&", "")
   End If
End Function
```

Exploring Members That Use Generic Types

A slightly different problem occurs when you are dealing with a member of a type (either a regular or generic type) and the member uses or returns a generic type that has already been bound with nongeneric arguments, as in the following case:

```
Function Convert(x As List(Of Integer)) As Dictionary(Of String, Double)
   …
End Function
```

When you reflect on the argument and the return type of the previous method, you get the following types:

```
System.Collections.Generic.List`1[[System.Int32, mscorlib, Version=2.0.0.0,
   Culture=neutral, PublicKeyToken=b77a5c561934e089]]

System.Collections.Generic.Dictionary`2[[System.String, mscorlib, Version=2.0.0.0,
   Culture=neutral, PublicKeyToken=b77a5c561934e089],
   [System.Double, mscorlib, Version=2.0.0.0, Culture=neutral,
   PublicKeyToken=b77a5c561934e089]]
```

Three details are worth noticing:

- The type name uses the inverse quote character syntax and is followed by the names of all the types that are bound to the generic type.

- Each argument consists of the type's full name followed by the display name of the assembly where the type is defined, all enclosed in a pair of square brackets.

- The entire list of argument types is enclosed in an additional pair of square brackets.

You can easily extract the name of a generic type and its argument types by parsing this full name, for example, by using a regular expression. Alternatively, you can use the IsGenericType method to check whether the type is the bound version of a generic type, and, if this is the case, you can use the GetGenericTypeDefinition method to extract the name of the original generic type and the GetGenericArguments method to extract the type of individual type arguments:

```
' (The mi variable points to a MethodInfo object.)
Dim retType As Type = mi.ReturnType
Dim typeName As String = retType.GetGenericTypeDefinition.FullName
typeName = typeName.Remove(typeName.IndexOf("`"c)) & "(Of "
Dim sep As String = ""
For Each argType As Type In retType.GetGenericArguments
   typeName &= sep & GetTypeName(argType)
   sep = ", "
Next
typeName &= ")"
Console.WriteLine(typeName)
   ' => System.Collections.Generic.Dictionary(Of System.String, System.Double)
```

In practice, you can gather all the cases that I've illustrated so far in an expanded version of the GetTypeName function (which I introduced in the previous section):

```
Function GetTypeName(ByVal type As Type) As String
   Dim typeName As String = Nothing
   If type.IsGenericTypeDefinition Then
      ' It's the type definition of an "open" generic type.
      typeName = type.FullName
      typeName = typeName.Remove(typeName.IndexOf("`"c)) & "(Of "
      For Each targ As Type In type.GetGenericArguments()
         If targ.GenericParameterPosition > 0 Then typeName &= ","
```

```
            typeName &= targ.Name
        Next
        typeName &= ")"
    ElseIf type.IsGenericParameter Then
        ' It's a parameter in an Of clause.
        typeName = type.Name
    ElseIf type.IsGenericType Then
        ' This is a generic type that has been bound to specific types.
        typeName = type.GetGenericTypeDefinition.FullName
        typeName = typeName.Remove(typeName.IndexOf("`"c)) & "(Of "
        Dim sep As String = ""
        For Each argType As Type In type.GetGenericArguments
            typeName &= sep & GetTypeName(argType)
            sep = ", "
        Next
        typeName &= ")"
    Else
        ' This is a regular type.
        typeName = type.FullName
    End If
    ' Account for array types and byref types.
    typeName = typeName.Replace("[", "(").Replace("]", ")").Replace("&", "")
    Return typeName
End Function
```

Thanks to its being recursive, this function is able to deal correctly even with contorted cases such as these:

```
Public MyList As List(Of Dictionary(Of String, Double))
Public MyDictionary As Dictionary(Of String, Dictionary(Of String, List(Of Integer)))
```

Binding a Generic Type

Sometimes you might need to bind a generic type with a set of one or more specific type arguments. This is necessary, for example, when you want to retrieve the Type object that corresponds to List(Of String) or Dictionary(Of String, Integer). The key for this operation is the Type.MakeGenericType method:

```
' Retrieve the type that corresponds to MyGenericTable(Of String, Double).
Dim typeName As String = "MyApp.MyGenericTable`2"
' Get a reference to the "open" generic type.
Dim genType As Type = Assembly.GetExecutingAssembly().GetType(typeName)
' Bind the "open" generic type to a set of arguments, and retrieve
' a reference to the MyGenericTable(Of String, Double).
Dim type As Type = genType.MakeGenericType(GetType(String), GetType(Double))
```

A bound generic type can be useful on at least a couple of occasions. First, you can use it when you need to create an instance of a specific type. (I cover object instantiation through reflection later in this chapter.) Second, you can use it when you are looking for a method with a signature that contains an argument of a specific type. Say you have the following class:

```
Public Class TestClass
    Sub TestSub(ByVal list As List(Of Integer), ByVal x As Integer)
        …
```

```
    End Sub
    Sub TestSub(ByVal list As List(Of String), ByVal x As String)
        ...
    End Sub
End Class
```

How can you build a MethodInfo object that points to the first TestMethod rather than the second one? Here's the solution:

```
' First, get a reference to the List "open" generic type.
Dim typeName As String = "System.Collections.Generic.List`1"
Dim openType As Type = GetType(Object).Assembly.GetType(typeName)
' Bind the open List type to the Integer type.
Dim boundType As Type = openType.MakeGenericType(GetType(Integer))
' Prepare the signature of the method you're interested in.
Dim argTypes() As Type = {boundType, GetType(Integer)}
' Get the reference to that specific method.
Dim method As MethodInfo = GetType(TestClass).GetMethod("TestSub", argTypes)
```

When you bind an open generic type to a set of argument types, you should ensure that generic constraints are fulfilled. Reflection enables you to extract the constraints associated with each argument by means of the GetGenericParameterConstraints method, whereas the GenericParameterAttributes property returns an enum value that provides information about the New, Class, and Structure constraints:

```
Dim genType As Type = Assembly.GetExecutingAssembly().GetType("MyApp.GenericList`1")
For Each argType As Type In genType.GetGenericArguments()
    ' Get the class and interface constraints for this argument.
    For Each constraint As Type In argType.GetGenericParameterConstraints()
        Console.WriteLine(constraint.FullName)
    Next
    ' Get the New, Class, or Structure constraints.
    Dim attrs As GenericParameterAttributes = argType.GenericParameterAttributes
    If CBool(attrs And GenericParameterAttributes.DefaultConstructorConstraint) Then
        Console.WriteLine("  New (default constructor)")
    End If
    If CBool(attrs And GenericParameterAttributes.ReferenceTypeConstraint) Then
        Console.WriteLine("  Class (reference type)")
    End If
    If CBool(attrs And GenericParameterAttributes.NotNullableValueTypeConstraint) Then
        Console.WriteLine("  Structure (nonnullable value type)")
    End If
Next
```

Reflecting on Attributes

As you might recall from Chapter 2, "Basic Language Concepts," .NET attributes provide a standard way to extend the metadata at the assembly, type, and member levels and can include additional information with a format defined by the programmer. Not surprisingly, the .NET Framework also provides the means to read this attribute-based metadata from an assembly. Because the attributes you define in your code are perfectly identical to the attributes that the .NET Framework defines for its own purposes, the mechanism for extracting either kind of attributes is the same. Therefore, even though in this section I show you how to extract .NET attributes, keep in mind that you can apply the same techniques for extracting your custom attributes. (You'll find many examples of the latter ones in Chapter 19, "Custom Attributes.")

Exploring Attributes

You can use several techniques to extract the custom attribute associated with a specific element.

First, you can use the IsDefined method exposed by the Assembly, Module, Type, Parameter-Info, and MemberInfo classes (and all the classes that inherit from MemberInfo, such as Field-Info and PropertyInfo). This method returns True if the attribute is defined for the specified element, but doesn't let you read the attribute's fields and properties. The last argument passed to the method is a Boolean value that specifies whether attributes inherited from the base class should be returned:

```
' The second argument specifies whether you also want to test
' attributes inherited from the base class.
If GetType(Person).IsDefined(GetType(SerializableAttribute), False) Then
   Console.WriteLine("The Person class is serializable")
End If
```

(See the companion code for the complete listing of the Person type.) Second, you can use the GetCustomAttributes method (note the plural) exposed by the Assembly, Module, Type, ParameterInfo, and MemberInfo classes (and all the classes that inherit from MemberInfo). This method returns an array containing all the attributes of the specified type that are associated with the specified element so that you can read their fields and properties, and you can specify whether attributes inherited from the base class should be included in the result:

```
' Display all the Conditional attributes associated with the Person.SendEmail method.
Dim mi As MethodInfo = GetType(Person).GetMethod("SendEmail")
' GetCustomAttributes returns an array of Object elements, so you need to cast.
Dim miAttrs() As ConditionalAttribute = DirectCast( _
   mi.GetCustomAttributes(GetType(ConditionalAttribute), False), ConditionalAttribute())
' Check whether the result contains at least one element.
If miAttrs.Length > 0 Then
   Console.WriteLine("SendEmail is marked with the following Conditional attribute(s):")
   ' Read the properties of individual attributes.
   For Each attr As ConditionalAttribute In miAttrs
     Console.WriteLine("   <Conditional(""{0}"")>", attr.ConditionString)
   Next
End If
```

Third, you can use an overload of the GetCustomAttributes method exposed by the Assembly, Module, Type, ParameterInfo, and MemberInfo classes (and all the classes that inherit from it) that doesn't take an attribute type as an argument. When you use this overload, the method returns an array containing all the custom attributes associated with the element:

```
' Display all the attributes associated with the Person.FirstName field.
Dim fi As FieldInfo = GetType(Person).GetField("FirstName")
Dim fiAttrs As Array = fi.GetCustomAttributes(False)
' Check whether the result contains at least one element.
```

```
If fiAttrs.Length > 0 Then
   Console.WriteLine("FirstName is marked with the following attribute(s):")
   ' Display the name of all attributes (but not their properties).
   For Each attr As Attribute In fiAttrs
      Console.WriteLine(attr.GetType().FullName)
   Next
End If
```

To further complicate your decision, you can achieve the same results shown previously by means of static methods of the System.Attribute type:

```
' Check whether the Person class is marked as serializable.
If Attribute.IsDefined(GetType(Person), GetType(SerializableAttribute)) Then
   Console.WriteLine("The Person class is serializable")
End If
```

```
' Retrieve the Conditional attributes associated with the Person.SendEmail method,
' including those inherited from the base class.
Dim mi As MethodInfo = GetType(Person).GetMethod("SendEmail")
Dim miAttrs() As ConditionalAttribute = DirectCast( _
   Attribute.GetCustomAttributes(mi, GetType(ConditionalAttribute), True), _
ConditionalAttribute())
' Check whether the result contains at least one element.
If miAttrs.Length > 0 Then
   …
End If
```

```
' Display all the attributes associated with the Person.FirstName field.
Dim fi As FieldInfo = GetType(Person).GetField("FirstName")
Dim fiAttrs As Array = Attribute.GetCustomAttributes(fi, False)
' Check whether the result contains at least one element.
If fiAttrs.Length > 0 Then
   …
End If
```

The System.Attribute class also exposes the GetCustomAttribute static method (note the singular), which returns the only attribute of the specified type:

```
' Read the Obsolete attribute associated with the Person class, if any.
Dim tyAttr As ObsoleteAttribute = DirectCast(Attribute.GetCustomAttribute( _
   GetType(Person), GetType(ObsoleteAttribute)), ObsoleteAttribute)
If tyAttr IsNot Nothing Then
   Console.WriteLine("The Person class is marked as obsolete.")
   Console.WriteLine("  IsError={0}, Message={1}", tyAttr.IsError, tyAttr.Message)
End If
```

An important note: you should never use the Attribute.GetCustomAttribute method with attributes that might appear multiple times—such as the Conditional attribute—because in that case the method might throw an AmbiguousMatchException object.

All these alternatives are quite confusing, so let me recap when each of them should be used:

- If you just need to check whether an attribute is associated with an element, use the Attribute.IsDefined static method or the IsDefined instance method exposed by the Assembly, Module, Type, ParameterInfo, and MemberInfo classes. This technique doesn't actually instantiate the attribute object in memory and is therefore the fastest of the group.

■ If you are checking whether a single-instance attribute is associated with an element and you want to read the attribute's fields and properties, use the Attribute.GetCustom-Attribute static method. (Don't use this technique with attributes that might appear multiple times—such as the Conditional attribute—because in that case the method might throw an AmbiguousMatchException object.)

■ If you are checking whether a multiple-instance attribute is associated with an element and you want to read the attribute's fields and properties, use the Attribute.GetCustom-Attributes static method or the GetCustomAttributes method exposed by the Assembly, Module, Type, ParameterInfo, and MemberInfo classes. You must use this technique when reading all the attributes associated with an element, regardless of the attribute type.

 Although all the techniques discussed in this section are available in .NET Framework 1.1 as well, there is a new important change in how you use them to query some special CLR attributes, such as Serializable, NonSerialized, DllImport, StructLayout, and FieldOffset. To improve performance and to save space in metadata tables, previous versions of the .NET Framework stored these special attributes using a format different from all other attributes. Consequently, you couldn't reflect on these attributes by using one of the techniques I just illustrated. Instead, you had to use special properties exposed by other reflection objects, for example, the IsSerialized and IsLayoutSequential properties of the Type class or the IsNonSerialized property of the FieldInfo class. A welcome addition in .NET Framework 2.0 is that you don't need to use any of these properties any longer because all the special .NET attributes can be queried by means of the IsDefined, GetCustomAttribute, and GetCustom-Attributes methods described in this section. (However, properties such as IsSerializable and IsLayoutSequential continue to be supported for backward compatibility.)

The CustomAttributeData Type

 Version 1.1 of the .NET Framework has a serious limitation related to custom attributes: you could search attributes buried in metadata, instantiate them, and read their properties, but you have no documented means for extracting the exact syntax used in code to define the attribute. For example, you can't determine whether an attribute field or property is assigned in the attribute's constructor using a standard (mandatory) argument or a named (optional) argument; if the field or property is equal to its default value (Nothing or zero), you can't determine whether it happened because the property was omitted in the attribute's construc-tor. For example, these limitations prevent a .NET developer from building a full-featured object browser.

In addition to this limitation inherited from .NET Framework 1.1, you run into another prob-lem under .NET Framework 2.0 when you want to extract custom attributes from assemblies that have been loaded for reflection-only purposes. In fact, both the GetCustomAttribute and the GetCustomAttributes methods instantiate the custom attribute and therefore would run some code inside the assembly, which is prohibited.

Both issues have been resolved by means of the new CustomAttributeData type and the auxiliary CustomAttributeTypedArgument class (which represents a positional argument in the attribute's constructor) and CustomAttributeNamedArgument class (which represents a named argument).

You create an instance of the CustomAttributeData type by means of the GetCustomAttributes static method that the type itself exposes. Each CustomAttributeData object has three properties: Constructor (the ConstructorInfo object that represents the attribute's constructor being used), ConstructorArguments (a list of CustomAttributeTypedArgument objects), and NamedArguments (a list of CustomAttributeNamedArgument objects):

```
' Retrieve the syntax used in custom attributes for the TestClass type.
Dim attrList As IList(Of CustomAttributeData) = _
   CustomAttributeData.GetCustomAttributes(GetType(TestClass))

' Iterate over all the attributes.
For Each attrData As CustomAttributeData In attrList
    ' Retrieve the attribute's type, by means of the ConstructorInfo object.
    Dim attrType As Type = attrData.Constructor.DeclaringType
    ' Start building the Visual Basic code.
    Dim attrString As String = "<" & attrType.FullName & "("
    Dim sep As String = ""

    ' Include all mandatory arguments for this constructor.
    For Each typedArg As CustomAttributeTypedArgument In attrData.ConstructorArguments
        attrString &= sep & FormatTypedArgument(typedArg)
        ' A comma is used as the separator for all elements after the first one.
        sep = ", "
    Next

    ' Include all optional arguments for this constructor.
    For Each namedArg As CustomAttributeNamedArgument In attrData.NamedArguments
        ' The TypedValue property returns a CustomAttributeTypedArgument object.
        Dim typedArg As CustomAttributeTypedArgument = namedArg.TypedValue
        ' Use the MemberInfo property to retrieve the field or property name.
        attrString &= sep & namedArg.MemberInfo.Name & ":=" & FormatTypedArgument(typedArg)
        ' A comma is used as the separator for all elements after the first one.
        sep = ", "
    Next
    ' Complete the attribute syntax and display it.
    attrString &= ")>"
    Console.WriteLine(attrString)
Next
```

The FormatTypedArgument method takes a CustomAttributeTypedArgument object and returns the corresponding Visual Basic code that can initialize it:

```
' Return a textual representation of a string, date, or numeric value.
Function FormatTypedArgument(ByVal typedArg As CustomAttributeTypedArgument) As String
    If typedArg.ArgumentType Is GetType(String) Then
        ' It's a quoted string.
        Return """" & typedArg.Value.ToString() & """"
```

```
    ElseIf typedArg.ArgumentType Is GetType(Date) Then
        ' It's a Date constant.
        Return "#" & typedArg.Value.ToString() & "#"
    ElseIf typedArg.ArgumentType.IsEnum Then
        ' It's an enum value.
        Return typedArg.ArgumentType.Name & "." & _
            [Enum].GetName(typedArg.ArgumentType, typedArg.Value)
    Else
        ' It's something else (presumably a number).
        Return typedArg.Value.ToString()
    End If
End Function
```

Creating a Custom Object Browser

All the reflection properties shown enable you to create a custom object browser that can solve problems that are out of reach for the object browser included in Visual Studio. Creating a custom object browser isn't a trivial task, though, especially if you want to implement a sophisticated user interface. For this reason, in this section I focus on a simple but useful object browser implemented as a Console application.

The sample application I discuss here is able to display all the types and members in an assembly that are marked with the Obsolete attribute. I implemented this utility to keep an updated list of members that are in beta versions of .NET Framework 2.0 but would have been removed before the release version, as well as members that were present in .NET Framework 1.1 but have been deprecated in the current version. You can pass it the path of an assembly or launch it without passing anything on the command line: in the latter case, the utility will analyze all the assemblies in the .NET Framework main directory.

The program displays its results in the console window and takes several minutes to explore all the assemblies in the .NET Framework, but you can redirect its output to a file and then load the file in a text editor to quickly search for a type or a method. Here are the core routines:

```
Imports System.IO
Imports System.Reflection
Imports System.Runtime.InteropServices

Module MainModule
    Sub Main(ByVal args() As String)
        If args.Length = 0 Then
            ShowObsoleteMembers()
        Else
            ShowObsoleteMembers(args(0))
        End If
    End Sub

    ' Process all the assemblies in the .NET Framework directory.
    Sub ShowObsoleteMembers()
        Dim path As String = RuntimeEnvironment.GetRuntimeDirectory()
        For Each asmFile As String In Directory.GetFiles(path, "*.dll")
            ShowObsoleteMembers(asmFile)
```

```vb
      Next
   End Sub

   ' Process an assembly at the specified file path.
   Sub ShowObsoleteMembers(ByVal asmFile As String)
      Try
         Dim asm As Assembly = Assembly.LoadFrom(asmFile)
         ShowObsoleteMembers(asm)
      Catch ex As Exception
         ' The file isn't a valid assembly.
      End Try
   End Sub

   ' Process all the types and members in an assembly.
   Sub ShowObsoleteMembers(ByVal asm As Assembly)
      Dim attrType As Type = GetType(ObsoleteAttribute)

      ' This header is displayed only if this assembly contains obsolete members.
      Dim asmHeader As String = String.Format("ASSEMBLY {0}{1}", _
         asm.GetName().Name, ControlChars.CrLf)

      For Each type As Type In asm.GetTypes()
         ' This header will be displayed only if the type is obsolete or
         ' contains obsolete members.
         Dim typeHeader As String = String.Format("   TYPE {0}{1}", _
            GetTypeName(type), ControlChars.CrLf)

         ' Search the Obsolete attribute at the type level.
         Dim attr As ObsoleteAttribute = DirectCast( _
            Attribute.GetCustomAttribute(type, attrType), ObsoleteAttribute)
         If attr IsNot Nothing Then
            ' This type is obsolete.
            Console.Write(asmHeader & typeHeader)
            ' Display the message attached to the attribute.
            Dim message As String = "WARNING"
            If attr.IsError Then message = "ERROR"
            Console.WriteLine("      {0}: {1}", message, attr.Message)
            ' Don't display the assembly header again.
            asmHeader = ""
         Else
            ' The type isn't obsolete; let's search for obsolete members.
            For Each mi As MemberInfo In type.GetMembers()
               attr = DirectCast(Attribute.GetCustomAttribute(mi, _
                  attrType), ObsoleteAttribute)
               If attr IsNot Nothing Then
                  ' This member is obsolete.
                  Dim memberHeader As String = String.Format("      {0} {1}", _
                     mi.MemberType.ToString().ToUpper(), GetMemberSyntax(mi))
                  Console.WriteLine(asmHeader & typeHeader & memberHeader)
                  ' Display the message attached to the attribute.
                  Dim message As String = "WARNING"
                  If attr.IsError Then message = "ERROR"
                  Console.WriteLine("         {0}: {1}", message, attr.Message)
                  ' Don't display the assembly and the type header again.
                  asmHeader = ""
                  typeHeader = ""
```

```
                End If
            Next
          End If
      Next
   End Sub
End Module
```

The main program uses a few helper routines, for example, to assemble the name of a type or the signature of a method using Visual Basic syntax. I have explained how this code works in previous sections, so I won't do it again here. I have gathered these methods in a separate module so that you can reuse them easily in other reflection-intensive projects:

```
Module ReflectionHelpers

   ' Returns the name of a type. (Supports generics and array types.)
   Function GetTypeName(ByVal type As Type) As String
      Dim typeName As String = Nothing
      Dim suffix As String = ""

      ' Account for array types.
      If type.IsArray Then
         suffix = "()"
         type = type.GetElementType()
      End If
      ' Account for byref types.
      If type.IsByRef Then type = type.GetElementType()

      If type.IsGenericTypeDefinition Then
         ' It's the type definition of an "open" generic type.
         typeName = type.FullName
         typeName = typeName.Remove(typeName.IndexOf("`"c)) & "(Of "
         For Each targ As Type In type.GetGenericArguments()
            If targ.GenericParameterPosition > 0 Then typeName &= ","
            typeName &= targ.Name
         Next
         typeName &= ")"
      ElseIf type.IsGenericParameter Then
         ' It's a parameter in an Of clause.
         typeName = type.Name
      ElseIf type.IsGenericType Then
         ' This is a generic type that has been bound to specific types.
         typeName = type.GetGenericTypeDefinition.FullName
         typeName = typeName.Remove(typeName.IndexOf("`"c)) & "(Of "
         Dim sep As String = ""
         For Each argType As Type In type.GetGenericArguments
            typeName &= sep & GetTypeName(argType)
            sep = ", "
         Next
         typeName &= ")"
      Else
         ' This is a regular type.
         typeName = type.FullName
      End If
      Return typeName & suffix
   End Function
```

```
' Return the name of a member. (Recognizes constructors and generic methods.)
Public Function GetMemberName(ByVal mi As MemberInfo) As String
    Dim memberName As String = mi.Name

    Select Case mi.MemberType
        Case MemberTypes.Constructor
            memberName = "New"
        Case MemberTypes.Method
            ' Account for generic methods.
            Dim method As MethodInfo = DirectCast(mi, MethodInfo)
            If method.IsGenericMethodDefinition() Then
                ' Include all type arguments.
                memberName &= "(Of "
                For Each ty As Type In method.GetGenericArguments()
                    If ty.GenericParameterPosition > 0 Then memberName &= ","
                    memberName &= ty.Name
                Next
                memberName &= ")"
            End If
    End Select
    Return memberName
End Function

' Returns the syntax of a member
Public Function GetMemberSyntax(ByVal member As MemberInfo) As String
    Dim memberSyntax As String = GetMemberName(member)

    Select Case member.MemberType
        Case MemberTypes.Property
            Dim pi As PropertyInfo = DirectCast(member, PropertyInfo)
            memberSyntax &= GetParametersSyntax(pi.GetGetMethod(True).GetParameters()) _
                & " As " & GetTypeName(pi.PropertyType)
        Case MemberTypes.Method
            Dim mi As MethodInfo = DirectCast(member, MethodInfo)
            memberSyntax = memberSyntax & GetParametersSyntax(mi.GetParameters())
            If mi.ReturnType.FullName <> "System.Void" Then
                memberSyntax &= " As " & GetTypeName(mi.ReturnType)
            End If
        Case MemberTypes.Constructor
            Dim ci As ConstructorInfo = DirectCast(member, ConstructorInfo)
            memberSyntax &= memberSyntax & GetParametersSyntax(ci.GetParameters)
        Case MemberTypes.Event
            Dim ei As EventInfo = DirectCast(member, EventInfo)
            Dim mi As MethodInfo = ei.EventHandlerType.GetMethod("Invoke")
            memberSyntax &= GetParametersSyntax(mi.GetParameters())
    End Select
    Return memberSyntax
End Function

' Returns the syntax of an array of parameters.
Private Function GetParametersSyntax(ByVal parInfos() As ParameterInfo) As String
    Dim paramSyntax As String = "("
    Dim sep As String = ""
    For Each pi As ParameterInfo In parInfos
        paramSyntax &= sep & GetTypeName(pi.ParameterType)
        sep = ", "
```

```
        Next
        Return paramSyntax & ")"
    End Function
End Module
```

As provided, the utility displays output in a purely textual format. It is easy, however, to change the argument of String.Format methods so that it outputs XML or HTML text, which would greatly improve the appearance of the result. (The complete demo program contains modified versions of this code that outputs HTML and XML text.)

Reflection at Run Time

So far, I've shown how to use reflection to enumerate all the types and members in an assembly, an activity that is central to applications such as object browsers or code generators. If you write mostly business applications, you might object that reflection doesn't have much to offer you, but this isn't correct. In fact, reflection also allows you to actually create objects and invoke methods in a sort of "late-bound" mode, that is, without you having to burn the type name and the method name in code. In this section, I show a series of techniques based on this capability.

Creating an Object Dynamically

Let's start by seeing how you can instantiate an object given its type name. You can choose from three ways to create a .NET object using reflection: by using the CreateInstance method of the System.Activator class, by using the InvokeMember method of the Type class, or by invoking one of the type's constructor methods.

If the type has a parameterless constructor, creating an instance is simple:

```
' Next statement assumes that the Person class is defined in
' an assembly named "MyApp".
Dim type As Type = Assembly.GetExecutingAssembly().GetType("MyApp.Person")
Dim o As Object = Activator.CreateInstance(type)
' Prove that we created a Person.
Console.WriteLine("A {0} object has been created", o.GetType().Name)
```

To call a constructor that takes one or more parameters, you must prepare an array of values:

```
' (We reuse the type variable from previous code...)
' Use the constructor that takes two arguments.
Dim args2() As Object = {"Joe", "Evans"}
' Call the constructor that matches the parameter signature.
Dim o2 As Object = Activator.CreateInstance(type, args2)
```

You can use InvokeMember to create an instance of the class and even pass arguments to its constructor, as in the following code:

```
' Prepare the array of parameters.
Dim args3() As Object = {"Joe", "Evans"}
```

```
' Constructor methods have no name and take Nothing in the second to last argument.
Dim o3 As Object = type.InvokeMember("", BindingFlags.CreateInstance, _
    Nothing, Nothing, args3)
```

Creating an object through its constructor method is a bit more convoluted, but I'll demonstrate the technique here for the sake of completeness:

```
' Prepare the argument signature as an array of types (two strings).
Dim argTypes() As Type = {GetType(String), GetType(String)}
' Get a reference to the correct constructor.
Dim ci As ConstructorInfo = type.GetConstructor(argTypes)
' Prepare the parameters.
Dim args4() As Object = {"Joe", "Evans"}
' Invoke the constructor and assign the result to a variable.
Dim o4 As Object = ci.Invoke(args4)
```

Regardless of the technique you used to create an instance of the type, you usually assign the instance you've created to an Object variable, as opposed to a strongly typed variable. (If you knew the name of the type at compile time, you wouldn't need to use reflection in the first place.) There is only one relevant exception to this rule: when you know in advance that the type being instantiated derives from a specific base class (or implements a given interface), you can cast the Object variable to a variable typed after that base class (or interface) and access all the members that the object inherits from the base class (or interface).

 The new MakeArrayType method of the Type class makes it very simple to instantiate arrays using reflection, as you can see in this code:

```
' Create an array of Double. (You can pass an integer argument to the MakeArrayType
' method to specify the rank of the array, for multidimensional arrays.
Dim arrType As Type = GetType(Double).MakeArrayType()
' The new array has 10 elements.
Dim arr As Array = DirectCast(Activator.CreateInstance(arrType, 10), Array)
' Prove that an array of 10 elements has been created.
Console.WriteLine("{0} {1} elements", arr.Length, arr.GetValue(0).GetType.Name)
```

When you work with an array created using reflection, you typically assign its elements with the SetValue method and read them back with the GetValue method:

```
' Assign the first element and read it back.
arr.SetValue(123.45, 0)
Console.WriteLine(arr.GetValue(0))          ' => 123.45
```

Accessing Members

In the most general case, after you've created an instance by using reflection, all you have is an Object variable pointing to a type and no direct way to access one of its members. The easiest operation you can perform is reading or writing a field by means of the GetValue and SetValue methods of the FieldInfo object:

```
' Create a Person object and reflect on it.
Dim type As Type = Assembly.GetExecutingAssembly().GetType("MyApp.Person")
```

```
Dim args() As Object = {"Joe", "Evans"}
Dim o As Object = Activator.CreateInstance(type, args)

' Get a reference to its FirstName field.
Dim fi As FieldInfo = type.GetField("FirstName")
' Display its current value, and then change it.
Console.WriteLine(fi.GetValue(o))          ' => Joe
fi.SetValue(o, "Robert")

' Prove that it changed, by casting to a strong-type variable.
Dim pers As Person = DirectCast(o, Person)
Console.WriteLine(pers.FirstName)          ' => Robert
```

Like FieldInfo, the PropertyInfo type exposes the GetValue and SetValue methods, but properties can take arguments, and thus these methods take an array of arguments. You must pass Nothing in the second argument if you're calling parameterless properties.

```
' (Continuing previous example…)
' This code assumes that the Person type exposes a 16-bit Age property.
' Get a reference to the PropertyInfo object.
Dim pi As PropertyInfo = type.GetProperty("Age")
' Note that the type of value must match exactly.
' (Integer constants must be converted to Short, in this case.)
pi.SetValue(pers, 35S, Nothing)
' Read it back.
Console.WriteLine(pi.GetValue(pers, Nothing))    ' => 35
```

If the property takes one or more arguments, you must pass an Object array containing one element for each argument:

```
' Get a reference to the PropertyInfo object.
Dim pi2 As PropertyInfo = type.GetProperty("Notes")
' Prepare the array of parameters.
Dim args2() As Object = {1}
' Set the property.
pi2.SetValue(o, "Tell John about the briefing", args2)
' Read it back.
Console.WriteLine(pi2.GetValue(o, args2))
```

A similar thing happens when you're invoking methods, except that you use the Invoke method instead of GetValue or SetValue:

```
' Get the MethodInfo for this method.
Dim mi As MethodInfo = type.GetMethod("SendEmail")
' Prepare an array for expected arguments.
Dim arguments() As Object = {"This is a message", 3}
' Invoke the method.
mi.Invoke(o, arguments)
```

Things are more interesting when optional arguments are involved. In this case, you pass the Type.Missing special value, as in this code:

```
' …(Initial code as above)…
' Don't pass the second argument (optional).
```

```
arguments = New Object() {"This is a message", type.Missing}
mi.Invoke(o, arguments)' Don't pass the second argument.
```

Alternatively, you can query the DefaultValue property of corresponding ParameterInfo to learn the default value for that specific argument:

```
' …(Initial code as above)…
' Retrieve the DefaultValue from the ParameterInfo object.
arguments = New Object() {"This is a message", mi.GetParameters(1).DefaultValue}
mi.Invoke(o, arguments)
```

The Invoke method traps all the exceptions thrown in the called method and converts them into TargetInvocationException; you must check the InnerException property of the caught exception to retrieve the real exception:

```
Try
    mi.Invoke(o, arguments)
Catch ex As TargetInvocationException
    Console.WriteLine(ex.InnerException.Message)
Catch ex As Exception
    Console.WriteLine(ex.Message)
End Try
```

The InvokeMember Method

In some cases, you might find it easier to set properties dynamically and invoke methods by means of the Type object's InvokeMember method. This method takes the name of the member; a flag that says whether it's a field, property, or method; the object for which the member should be invoked; and an array of Objects for the arguments if there are any. Here are a few examples:

```
' Create an instance of the Person type using InvokeMember.
Dim type As Type = Assembly.GetExecutingAssembly().GetType("MyApp.Person")
Dim arguments() As Object = {"John", "Evans"}
Dim obj As Object = type.InvokeMember("", BindingFlags.CreateInstance,_
    Nothing, Nothing, arguments)

' Set the FirstName field.
Dim args() As Object = {"Francesco"}         ' One argument
type.InvokeMember("FirstName", BindingFlags.SetField, Nothing, obj, args)
' Read the FirstName field. (Pass Nothing for the argument array.)
Dim value As Object = type.InvokeMember("FirstName", BindingFlags.GetField, _
    Nothing, obj, Nothing)

' Set the Age property, create the argument array on the fly.
type.InvokeMember("Age", BindingFlags.SetProperty, Nothing, obj, _
    New Object() {35S})

' Call the SendEMail method.
Dim args2() As Object = {"This is a message", 2}
type.InvokeMember("SendEmail", BindingFlags.InvokeMethod, Nothing, obj, args2)
```

It is very important that you pass the correct value for the BindingFlags argument. All the examples shown so far access public instance members, but you must explicitly add the NonPublic and/or Static modifiers if the member is private or static:

```
' Read the m_Age private field.
value = type.InvokeMember("m_Age", BindingFlags.GetField Or BindingFlags.NonPublic _
    Or BindingFlags.Instance, Nothing, obj, Nothing)
```

When you invoke a static member, you must pass Nothing in the second to last argument. The same rule applies when you use InvokeMember to call a constructor method because you don't yet have a valid instance in that case.

The InvokeMember method does a case-sensitive search for the member with the specified name, but it's quite forgiving when it matches the type of the arguments because it will perform any necessary conversion for you if the types don't correspond exactly. You can change this default behavior by means of the BindingFlags.IgnoreCase (for case-insensitive searches) and the BindingFlags.ExactBinding (for exact type matches) values.

InvokeMember works correctly if one or more arguments are passed by reference. For example, if the SendEmail method would take the priority in a ByRef argument, on return from the method call the args2(1) element would contain the new value assigned to that argument.

Even though InvokeMember can make your code more concise—because you don't have to get a reference to a specific FieldInfo, PropertyInfo, or MethodInfo object—it surely doesn't make your code faster. In fact, the InvokeMember method must perform two distinct operations internally: the discovery phase (looking for the member with the specified signature) and the execution phase. If you use InvokeMember to call the same method a hundred times, it will "rediscover" the same method a hundred times, which clearly adds overhead that you can avoid if you reflect on the member once and then access the member through a FieldInfo, PropertyInfo, or MethodInfo object. For this reason, you shouldn't use InvokeMember when repeatedly accessing the same member, especially in time-critical code.

Creating a Universal Comparer

As you might recall from Chapter 10, "Interfaces," you implement the IComparer interface in auxiliary classes that work as comparers for other types, whether they are .NET types or custom types you've defined. The main problem with comparer types is that you must define a distinct comparer type for each possible sort criterion. Clearly, this requirement can soon become a nuisance. Reflection gives you the opportunity to implement a *universal comparer*, a class capable of working with any type of object and any combination of fields and properties and that supports both ascending and descending sorts.

Before discussing how the UniversalComparer type works, let me show you how you can use it. You create a UniversalComparer instance by passing its constructor a string argument that resembles an ORDER BY clause in SQL.

```
Dim persons() As Person = Nothing
' Init the array here.
…
' Sort the array on the LastName and FirstName fields.
Dim comp As New UniversalComparer(Of Person)("LastName, FirstName ")
Array.Sort(Of Person)(persons, comp)
```

You can even sort in descending mode separately on each field:

```
Dim comp As New UniversalComparer(Of Person)("LastName DESC, FirstName DESC")
Array.Sort(Of Person)(persons, comp)
```

Not surprisingly, the UniversalComparer class relies heavily on reflection to perform its magic. Here's its complete source code:

```
Public Class UniversalComparer(Of T)
    Implements IComparer, IComparer(Of T)

    Private sortKeys() As SortKey

    Public Sub New(ByVal sort As String)
        Dim type As Type = GetType(T)
        ' Split the list of properties.
        Dim props() As String = sort.Split(","c)
        ' Prepare the array that holds information on sort criteria.
        ReDim sortKeys(props.Length - 1)

        ' Parse the sort string.
        For i As Integer = 0 To props.Length - 1
            ' Get the Nth member name.
            Dim memberName As String = props(i).Trim()
            If memberName.ToLower().EndsWith(" desc") Then
                ' Discard the DESC qualifier.
                sortKeys(i).Descending = True
                memberName = memberName.Remove(memberName.Length - 5).TrimEnd()
            End If
            ' Search for a field or a property with this name.
            sortKeys(i).FieldInfo = type.GetField(memberName)
            If sortKeys(i).FieldInfo Is Nothing Then
                sortKeys(i).PropertyInfo = type.GetProperty(memberName)
            End If
        Next
    End Sub

    ' Implementation of IComparer.Compare
    Public Function Compare(ByVal o1 As Object, ByVal o2 As Object) As Integer _
            Implements IComparer.Compare
        Return Compare(CType(o1, T), CType(o2, T))
    End Function
```

```vb
' Implementation of IComparer(Of T).Compare
Public Function Compare(ByVal o1 As T, ByVal o2 As T) As Integer _
        Implements IComparer(Of T).Compare
    ' Deal with simplest cases first.
    If o1 Is Nothing Then
        ' Two null objects are equal.
        If o2 Is Nothing Then Return 0
        ' A null object is less than any non-null object.
        Return -1
    ElseIf o2 Is Nothing Then
        ' Any non-null object is greater than a null object.
        Return 1
    End If

    ' Iterate over all the sort keys.
    For i As Integer = 0 To sortKeys.Length - 1
        Dim value1 As Object, value2 As Object
        Dim sortKey As SortKey = sortKeys(i)
        ' Read either the field or the property.
        If sortKey.FieldInfo IsNot Nothing Then
            value1 = sortKey.FieldInfo.GetValue(o1)
            value2 = sortKey.FieldInfo.GetValue(o2)
        Else
            value1 = sortKey.PropertyInfo.GetValue(o1, Nothing)
            value2 = sortKey.PropertyInfo.GetValue(o2, Nothing)
        End If

        Dim res As Integer
        If value1 Is Nothing And value2 Is Nothing Then
            ' Two null objects are equal.
            res = 0
        ElseIf value1 Is Nothing Then
            ' A null object is always less than a non-null object.
            res = -1
        ElseIf value2 Is Nothing Then
            ' Any object is greater than a null object.
            res = 1
        Else
            ' Compare the two values, assuming that they support IComparable.
            res = DirectCast(value1, IComparable).CompareTo(value2)
        End If

        ' If values are different, return this value to caller.
        If res <> 0 Then
            ' Negate it if sort direction is descending.
            If sortKey.Descending Then res = -res
            Return res
        End If
    Next
    ' If we get here, the two objects are equal.
    Return 0
End Function

' Nested type to store detail on sort keys
Private Structure SortKey
    Public FieldInfo As FieldInfo
```

```
        Public PropertyInfo As PropertyInfo
        ' True if sort is descending.
        Public Descending As Boolean
    End Structure
End Class
```

As the comments in the source code explain, the universal comparer supports comparisons on both fields and properties. Because this class uses reflection intensively, it isn't as fast as a more specific comparer can be, but in most cases the speed difference isn't noticeable.

Dynamic Registration of Event Handlers

Another programming technique you can implement through reflection is the dynamic registration of an event handler. For example, let's say that the Person class exposes a GotEmail event and you have an event handler in the MainModule type:

```
Public Class Person
    Event GotEmail(ByVal sender As Object, ByVal e As EventArgs)

    ...
    ' A method that fires the GotEmail event
    Sub SendEmail(ByVal text As String, Optional ByVal priority As Integer = 1)

        ...
        Dim e As New GotEmailEventArgs(text, priority)
        RaiseEvent GotEmail(Me, e)
    End Sub
End Class

Module MainModule
    Sub GotEmail_Handler(ByVal sender As Object, ByVal e As GotEmailEventArgs)
        Console.WriteLine("GotEmail event fired")
    End Sub
    ...
End Module
```

Here's the code that registers the procedure for this event, using reflection exclusively:

```
' obj and type initialized as in previous examples…
' Get a reference to the GotEmail event.
Dim ei As EventInfo = type.GetEvent("GotEmail")
' Get a reference to the delegate that defines the event.
Dim handlerType As Type = ei.EventHandlerType
' Create a delegate of this type that points to a method in this module.
Dim handler As [Delegate] = [Delegate].CreateDelegate( _
    handlerType, GetType(MainModule), "GotEmail_Handler")
' Register this handler dynamically.
ei.AddEventHandler(obj, handler)
' Call the method that fires the event, using reflection.
Dim args() as Object = {"Hello Joe", 2}
Type.InvokeMember("SendEmail", BindingFlags.InvokeMethod, Nothing, obj, args)
```

A look at the console window proves that the EventHandler procedure in the MainModule type was invoked when the code in the Person.SendEmail method raised the GotEmail event. If the event handler is an instance method, the second argument to the Delegate.CreateDelegate method must be an instance of the class that defines the method; if the event handler is a static method (as in the previous example), this argument must be a Type object corresponding to the class where the method is defined.

The previous code doesn't really add much to what you can do by registering an event by means of the AddHandler operator. But wait, there's more. To show how this technique can be so powerful, I must make a short digression on delegates.

Delegate Covariance and Contravariance in C# 2.0

.NET Framework 2.0 has enhanced delegates with two important features: covariance and contravariance. Unfortunately, however, these features are available only in C#, and therefore I am forced to illustrate these concepts in that language.

Both these features relax the requirement that a delegate object must match exactly the signature of its target method. More specifically, delegate covariance means that you can have a delegate point to a method with a return value that inherits from the return type specified by the delegate. Let's say we have the following delegate:

```
// A delegate that can point to a method that takes a TextBox and returns an object.
delegate object GetControlData(TextBox ctrl);
```

The GetControlData delegate specifies object as the return value; therefore, the covariance property tells that this delegate can point to any method that takes a TextBox control, regardless of the method's return value, because all .NET types inherit from System.Object. The only requirement is that the method actually returns something; therefore, you can't have this delegate point to a C# void method (a Sub method, in Visual Basic parlance). For example, a GetControlData delegate might point to the following method because the String type inherits from System.Object:

```
// A function that takes a TextBox control and returns a String
string GetText(TextBox ctrl)
{ return ctrl.Text; }
```

Delegate contravariance means that a delegate can point to a method with an argument that is a base class of the argument specified in the delegate's signature. For example, a GetControlData delegate might point to a method that takes one argument of the Control or Object type because both these types are base classes for the TextBox argument that appears in the delegate:

```
// A function that takes a Control and returns an Object value.
object GetTag(Control ctrl)
{ return ctrl.Tag; }
```

It's important to realize that covariance and contravariance relax the constraint that a delegate can point only to a method with a signature that doesn't exactly match the delegate's signature, but they don't make the code less robust because no type mismatch exception can occur at run time.

Delegate Covariance and Contravariance in Visual Basic 2005

Don't look for delegate covariance and contravariance in Visual Basic documentation because you won't find any information. As a matter of fact, Visual Basic 2005 doesn't support these features. Period.

Well, not exactly. Granted, Visual Basic doesn't support these features directly, but you can achieve them nevertheless. Covariance and contravariance are supported at the CLR level, and you can create a delegate that leverages both of them through reflection. Let's say you have the following delegate and the following method in a Windows Forms class:

```
Delegate Function GetControlData(ByVal ctrl As TextBox) As Object

Function GetText(ByVal ctrl As Control) As String
    Return ctrl.Text
End Function
```

You know that you can't create a GetControlData delegate that points to the GetText method directly in Visual Basic because the language supports neither covariance nor contravariance. However, you can create a MethodInfo object that points to the GetText method and then pass this object to the Delegate.CreateDelegate static method:

```
' The target method
Dim method As MethodInfo = Me.GetType().GetMethod("GetText")
' Build the delegate through reflection.
Dim deleg As GetControlData = DirectCast([Delegate].CreateDelegate( _
    GetType(GetControlData), Me, method), GetControlData)
' Show that the delegate works correctly.
Console.WriteLine(deleg(Me.TextBox1))      ' Displays the TextBox1.Text property.
```

This code is only marginally slower than the C# counterpart, but this isn't a serious issue because you typically create a delegate once and use it repeatedly.

The most interesting application of this feature is the ability to have an individual method handle all the events coming from one or more objects, provided that the event has the canonical .NET syntax (sender, e), where the second argument can be any type that derives from EventArgs. Consider the following event handler:

```
' (Inside a Form class)
Sub MyEventHandler(ByVal sender As Object, ByVal e As EventArgs)
    Console.WriteLine("An event has fired")
End Sub
```

The following code can make all the events exposed by an object point to the "universal handler":

```
' (Inside the same Form class…)
' The control we want to trap events from
Dim ctrl As Object = TextBox1
For Each ei As EventInfo In ctrl.GetType().GetEvents()
    Dim handlerType As Type = ei.EventHandlerType
```

```
      ' The universal event handler method
      Dim method As MethodInfo = Me.GetType().GetMethod("MyEventHandler")
      ' Leverage contravariance to create a delegate that points to the method.
      Dim handler As [Delegate] = [Delegate].CreateDelegate(handlerType, Me, method)
      ' Use reflection to register the event.
      ei.AddEventHandler(ctrl, handler)
   Next
   ' Prove that it works by causing a TextChanged event.
   ctrl.Text &= "*"
```

This code proves that it is technically possible to use reflection to have all the events of an object point to an individual handler, but this technique doesn't look very promising. After all, the MyEventHandler method has no means to understand which event was fired. To get that information, we need to do more.

A Universal Event Handler

What we need is an object that is able to "mediate" between the event source and the object where the event is handled. Writing this object requires some significant code, but the result is well worth the effort. The EventInterceptor class exposes only one event, ObjectEvent, defined by the ObjectEventHandler delegate:

```
Public Delegate Sub ObjectEventHandler(ByVal sender As Object, ByVal e As ObjectEventArgs)

Public Class EventInterceptor
   ' The public event
   Public Event ObjectEvent As ObjectEventHandler

   ' This is invoked from inside the EventInterceptorHandler auxiliary class.
   Protected Sub OnObjectEvent(ByVal e As ObjectEventArgs)
      RaiseEvent ObjectEvent(Me, e)
   End Sub
   …
End Class
```

The EventInterceptor class uses the nested EventInterceptorHandler type to trap events coming from the object source. More precisely, an EventInterceptorHandler instance is created for each event that the event source can raise. The EventInterceptor class supports multiple event sources; therefore, the number of EventInterceptorHandler instances can be quite high: for example, if you trap the events coming from 20 TextBox controls, the EventInterceptor object will create as many as 1,540 EventInterceptorHandler instances because each TextBox control exposes 77 events. For this reason, the AddEventSource method supports a third argument that enables you to specify which events should be intercepted:

```
   Public Sub AddEventSource(ByVal eventSource As Object, _
         ByVal includeChildren As Boolean, ByVal filterPattern As String)
      For Each ei As EventInfo In eventSource.GetType().GetEvents()
         ' Skip this event if its name doesn't match the pattern.
         If Not String.IsNullOrEmpty(filterPattern) AndAlso Not _
            Regex.IsMatch(ei.Name, "^" & filterPattern & "$") Then Continue For

         ' Get the signature of the underlying delegate.
```

```
            Dim mi As MethodInfo = ei.EventHandlerType.GetMethod("Invoke")
            Dim pars() As ParameterInfo = mi.GetParameters()
            ' Check that event signature is in the form (sender, e).
            If mi.ReturnType.FullName = "System.Void" AndAlso pars.Length = 2 _
                    AndAlso pars(0).ParameterType Is GetType(Object) AndAlso _
                    GetType(EventArgs).IsAssignableFrom(pars(1).ParameterType) Then
                ' Create an EventInterceptorHandler that handles this event.
                Dim interceptor As New EventInterceptorHandler(eventSource, ei, Me)
            End If
        Next
        ' Recurse on child controls if so required.
        If TypeOf eventSource Is Control AndAlso includeChildren Then
            For Each ctrl As Control In DirectCast(eventSource, Control).Controls
                AddEventSource(ctrl, includeChildren, filterPattern)
            Next
        End If
    End Sub
    …
End Class        ' End of EventInterceptor class
```

The EventInterceptorHandler nested class does a very simple job: it uses reflection to register its EventHandler method as a listener for the specified event coming from the specified event source. When the event is fired, the EventHandler method calls back the OnObjectEvent method in the parent EventInterceptor object, which in turn fires the ObjectEvent event:

```
Private Class EventInterceptorHandler
    ' The event being intercepted
    Public ReadOnly EventInfo As EventInfo
    ' The parent EventInterceptor
    Public ReadOnly Parent As EventInterceptor

    Public Sub New(ByVal eventSource As Object, ByVal eventInfo As EventInfo, _
            ByVal parent As EventInterceptor)
        Me.EventInfo = eventInfo
        Me.Parent = parent
        ' Create a delegate that points to the EventHandler method.
        Dim method As MethodInfo = Me.GetType().GetMethod("EventHandler")
        Dim handler As [Delegate] = _
            [Delegate].CreateDelegate(eventInfo.EventHandlerType, Me, method)
        ' Register the event.
        eventInfo.AddEventHandler(eventSource, handler)
    End Sub

    Public Sub EventHandler(ByVal sender As Object, ByVal e As EventArgs)
        ' Notify the parent EventInterceptor object.
        Dim objEv As New ObjectEventArgs(sender, EventInfo.Name, e)
        Parent.OnObjectEvent(objEv)
    End Sub
End Class
```

Here's how a Windows Forms application can use the EventInterceptor object to get a notification when any event of any control fires:

```
Dim WithEvents Interceptor As New EventInterceptor

Private Sub Form1_Load(ByVal sender As Object, ByVal e As EventArgs) Handles MyBase.Load
```

```
     Interceptor.AddEventSource(Me, True, "")
  End Sub

  Private Sub Interceptor_ObjectEvent(ByVal sender As Object, ByVal e As ObjectEventArgs) _
     Handles Interceptor.ObjectEvent
     Dim msg As String = String.Format("Event {0} from control {1}", _
        DirectCast(e.EventSource, Control).Name, e.EventName)
     Debug.WriteLine(msg)
  End Sub
```

You can limit the number of events that you receive by passing a regular expression pattern to the AddEventSource method:

```
  ' Trap only xxxChanged events.
  Interceptor.AddEventSource(Me, True, ".+Changed")
  ' Trap only mouse and keyboard events.
  Interceptor.AddEventSource(Me, True, "(Mouse|Key).+)")
```

For more information, see the source code of the complete demo program. (See Figure 18-2.)

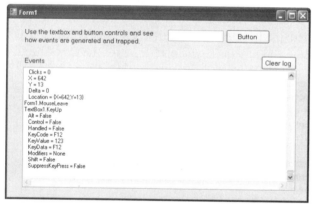

Figure 18-2　The EventInterceptor demo application

Scheduling a Sequence of Actions

Reflection allows you to implement techniques that would be very difficult (and sometimes impossible) to implement using a more traditional approach. For example, the ability to invoke methods through MethodInfo objects gives you the ability to deal with call sequences as if they were just another data type that your application processes. To see what I mean, let's say that your application must perform a series of actions—for example, file creation, registry manipulation, variable assignments—as an atomic operation. If any one of the involved actions fails, all the actions performed so far should be undone in an orderly manner: files should be deleted, registry keys should be restored, variables should be assigned their original value, and so forth.

Implementing an undo strategy in the most general case isn't a simple task, especially if some of the actions are performed only conditionally when other conditions are met. What you need is a generic solution to this problem, and you'll see how elegantly you can solve this programming task through reflection. To begin with, let's define an Action class, which represents a method—either a static or an instance method:

```
Public Class Action
    Public ReadOnly Message As String       ' Description of the action
    Public ReadOnly [Object] As Object      ' Instance on which the method is called
    Public ReadOnly Method As MethodInfo    ' The method to be invoked
    Public ReadOnly Arguments() As Object   ' Arguments for the method

    ' Second argument can be an object (for instance methods) or a Type (for static methods).
    Public Sub New(ByVal message As String, ByVal obj As Object, _
            ByVal methodName As String, ByVal ParamArray arguments() As Object)
        Me.Message = message
        Me.Arguments = arguments
        ' Determine the type this method belongs to.
        Dim type As Type = TryCast(obj, Type)
        If type Is Nothing Then
            Me.Object = obj
            type = obj.GetType()
        End If
        ' Prepare the list of argument types, to call GetMethod without any ambiguity.
        Dim argTypes(arguments.Length - 1) As Type
        For index As Integer = 0 To arguments.Length - 1
            If arguments(index) IsNot Nothing Then
                argTypes(index) = arguments(index).GetType()
            End If
        Next
        ' Retrieve the actual MethodInfo object, throw an exception if not found.
        Me.Method = type.GetMethod(methodName, argTypes)
        If Me.Method Is Nothing Then
            Throw New ArgumentException("Missing method")
        End If
    End Sub

    ' Execute this method.
    Public Sub Execute()
        Me.Method.Invoke(Me.Object, Me.Arguments)
    End Sub
End Class
```

Instead of performing a method directly, you can create an Action instance and then invoke its Execute method:

```
' Create c:\backup directory.
Dim act As New Action("Create c:\backup directory", _
    GetType(Directory), "CreateDirectory", "c:\backup")
act.Execute()
```

Of course, executing a method in this way doesn't bring any benefit. You see the power of this technique, however, if you define another type that works as a container for Action instances and that can also remember the "undo" action for each method being executed:

```
Public Class ActionSequence
    ' The parallel lists of actions and undo actions
    Private Actions As New List(Of Action)
```

```vbnet
Private UndoActions As New List(Of Action)
' This delegate must point to a method that takes a string.
Private DisplayMethod As Action(Of String)


' The constructor takes a delegate to a method that can output a message.
Public Sub New(ByVal displayMethod As Action(Of String))
    Me.DisplayMethod = displayMethod
End Sub


' Add an action and an undo action to the list.
Public Sub Add(ByVal action As Action, ByVal undoAction As Action)
    Actions.Add(action)
    UndoActions.Add(undoAction)
End Sub


' Insert an action and an undo action at a specific index in the list.
Public Sub Insert(ByVal index As Integer, ByVal action As Action, ByVal undoAction As Action)
    Actions.Insert(index, action)
    UndoActions.Insert(index, undoAction)
End Sub


' Execute all pending actions, return true if no exception occurred.
Public Function Execute(ByVal ignoreExceptions As Boolean) As Boolean
    ' This is the list of undo actions to execute in case of error.
    Dim undoSequence As New ActionSequence(Me.DisplayMethod)

    For index As Integer = 0 To Actions.Count - 1
        Dim act As Action = Actions(index)
        ' Skip over null actions.
        If act Is Nothing Then Continue For

        Try
            ' Display the message and execute the action.
            DisplayMessage(act.Message)
            act.Execute()
            ' If successful, remember the undo action. The undo action is placed
            ' in front of all others so that it will be the first to be executed in case of error.
            undoSequence.Insert(0, UndoActions(index), Nothing)
        Catch ex As TargetInvocationException
            ' Ignore exceptions if so required.
            If ignoreExceptions Then Continue For
            ' Display the error message.
            DisplayMessage("ERROR: " & ex.InnerException.Message)
            ' Perform the undo sequence. (Ignore exceptions while undoing.)
            DisplayMessage("UNDOING OPERATIONS...")
            undoSequence.Execute(True)
            ' Signal that an exception occurred.
            Return False
        End Try
    Next
    ' Signal that no exceptions occurred.
    Return True
End Function


' Report a message through the delegate passed to the constructor.
Private Sub DisplayMessage(ByVal text As String)
```

```
      If Me.DisplayMethod IsNot Nothing Then
         Me.DisplayMethod(text)
      End If
   End Sub
End Class
```

The constructor of the ActionSequence type takes an Action(Of String) object, which is a delegate to a Sub method that takes a string as an argument. This method will be used to display all the messages that are produced during the action sequence: it can point to a method such as the Console.WriteLine method (to display messages in the console window), the WriteLine method of a StreamWriter object (to write messages to a log file), the AppendText method of a TextBox control (to display messages inside a TextBox control), or a method you define in your application:

```
' Prepare to write diagnostic messages to a log file.
Dim sw As New StreamWriter("c:\logfile.txt")
Dim actionSequence As New ActionSequence(AddressOf sw.WriteLine)
...
' Close the stream when you're done with the ActionSequence object.
sw.Close()
```

The following code shows how you can schedule a sequence of actions and undo them if an exception is thrown during the process:

```
' Schedule the creation of c:\backup directory.
Dim actionSequence As New ActionSequence(AddressOf Console.WriteLine)
Dim act As New Action("Create c:\backup directory", GetType(Directory), _
   "CreateDirectory", "c:\backup")
Dim undoAct As New Action("Delete c:\backup directory", GetType(Directory), _
   "Delete", "c:\backup", True)
actionSequence.Add(act, undoAct)

' Create a readme.txt file in the c:\ root directory.
Dim contents As String = "Instructions for myapp.exe..."
act = New Action("Create the c:\myapp_readme.txt", GetType(File), _
   "WriteAllText", "c:\myapp_readme.txt", contents)
' Notice that this action has no undo action.
actionSequence.Add(act, Nothing)

' Move the readme file to the backup directory.
act = New Action("Move the c:\myapp_readme.txt to c:\backup\readme.txt", GetType(File), _
   "Move", "c:\myapp_readme.txt", "c:\backup\readme.txt")
undoAct = New Action("Move c:\backup\readme.txt to c:\myapp_readme.txt", GetType(File), _
   "Move", "c:\backup\readme.txt", "c:\myapp_readme.txt")
actionSequence.Add(act, undoAct)

' Execute the action sequence. (False means that an exception undoes all actions.)
actionSequence.Execute(False)
```

After running the previous code snippet, you should find a new c:\backup directory containing the files readme.txt and win.ini. To see how the ActionSequence type behaves in case of error, delete the c:\backup directory and intentionally cause an error in the sequence by attempting to copy a file that doesn't exist:

```
' (Insert the lines in bold type before the call to the Execute method.)
…
' Copy the c:\missing.txt file to the c:\backup directory.
act = New Action("Copy c:\missing.txt to c:\backup", GetType(File), _
    "Copy", "c:\missing.text", "c:\backup\missing.txt")
undoAct = New Action("Delete c:\backup\missing.text", GetType(File), _
    "Delete", "c:\backup\missing.text")
actionSequence.Add(act, Nothing)

' Execute the action sequence. (False means that an exception undoes all actions.)
actionSequence.Execute(False)
```

The intentional error causes the ActionSequence object to undo all the actions before the one that caused the exception, and in fact at the end of the process you won't find any c:\backup directory, as confirmed by the text that appears in the console window:

```
Create c:\backup directory
Create the c:\myapp_readme.txt
Move the c:\myapp_readme.txt to c:\backup\readme.txt
Copy c:\missing.txt to c:\backup
ERROR: Could not find file 'c:\missing.text'.
UNDOING OPERATIONS...
Move the c:\backup\readme.txt file back to c:\myapp_readme.txt
Delete c:\backup directory
```

In this example, I used the ActionSequence type to undo a sequence of actions that are hard-coded in the program, but I could have used a similar technique to implement an Undo menu command in your applications. Or I could have read the series of actions from a file instead, to implement undoable scripts.

You can expand the ActionSequence type with new features. For example, you might have the series of actions be performed on a background thread (see Chapter 20, "Threads," for more information) and specify multiple undo methods for a given action. You might add properties to the Action type to specify whether a failed method should abort the entire sequence. Also, you might extend the Action class with the ability to create new instances (that is, to call constructors in addition to regular methods) and to pass instances created in this way as arguments to other methods down in the action sequence. As usual, the only limit is your imagination.

On-the-Fly Compilation

Earlier in this chapter, I mentioned the System.Reflection.Emit namespace, which has classes that let you create an assembly on the fly. The .NET Framework uses these classes internally in a few cases—for example, when you pass the RegexOptions.Compiled option to the constructor of the Regex object (see Chapter 14, "Regular Expressions"). Using reflection emit, however, isn't exactly the easiest .NET programming task, and I'm glad I've never had to use it heavily in a real-world application.

Nevertheless, at times the ability to create an assembly out of thin air can be quite tantalizing because it opens up a number of programming techniques that are otherwise impossible. For example, consider building a routine that takes a math expression entered by the end user (as a string), evaluates it, and returns the result. In the section titled "Parsing and Evaluating Expressions" in Chapter 14, I showed how you can parse and evaluate an expression at run time, but that approach is several orders of magnitude slower than evaluating a compiled expression is and can't be used in time-critical code, such as for doing function plotting or finding the roots of a higher-degree equation (see Figure 18-3). In this case, your best option is to generate the source code of a Visual Basic program, compile it on the fly, and then instantiate one of its classes.

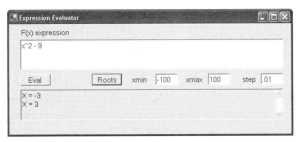

Figure 18-3 The demo application, which uses on-the-fly compilation to evaluate functions and find the roots of any equation that uses the X variable

The types that allow us to compile an assembly at run time are in the Microsoft.VisualBasic namespace (or in the Microsoft.CSharp namespace, if you want to generate and compile C# source code) and in the System.CodeDom.Compiler namespace, so you need to add proper Imports statements to your code to run the code samples that follow.

The first thing to do is generate the source code for the program to be compiled dynamically. In the expression evaluator demo application, such source code is obtained by inserting the expression that the end user enters in the txtExpression field in the middle of the Eval method of an Evaluator public class:

```
Dim source As String = String.Format( _
    "Imports Microsoft.VisualBasic{0}" _
    & "Imports System.Math{0}" _
    & "Public Class Evaluator{0}" _
    & "    Public Function Eval(ByVal x As Double) As Double{0}" _
    & "        Return {1}{0}" _
    & "    End Function{0}" _
    & "End Class{0}", _
    ControlChars.CrLf, txtExpression.Text)
```

Next, you create a CompilerParameters object (in the System.CodeDom.Compiler namespace) and set its properties; this object broadly corresponds to the options you'd pass to the VBC command-line compiler:

```
Dim params As New CompilerParameters
' Generate a DLL, not an EXE executable.
' (Not really necessary because False is the default.)
params.GenerateExecutable = False
```

```
#If DEBUG Then
    ' Include debug information.
    params.IncludeDebugInformation = True
    ' Debugging works if we generate an actual DLL and keep temporary files.
    params.TempFiles.KeepFiles = True
    params.GenerateInMemory = False
#Else
    ' Treat warnings as errors, don't keep temporary source files.
    params.TreatWarningsAsErrors = True
    params.TempFiles.KeepFiles = False
    ' Optimize the code for faster execution.
    params.CompilerOptions = "/Optimize+"
    ' Generate the assembly in memory.
    params.GenerateInMemory = True
#End If
    ' Add a reference to necessary strong-named assemblies.
    params.ReferencedAssemblies.Add("Microsoft.VisualBasic.Dll")
    params.ReferencedAssemblies.Add("System.Dll")
```

The preceding code snippet shows the typical actions you perform to prepare a Compiler-Parameters object, as well as its most important properties. The statements inside the #If block are especially interesting. You can include debug information in a dynamic assembly and debug it from inside Visual Studio by setting the IncludeDebugInformation property to True. To enable debugging, however, you must generate an actual .dll or .exe file (Generate-InMemory must be False) and must not delete temporary files at the end of the compilation process (the KeepFiles property of the TempFiles collection must be True). If debugging is correctly enabled, you can force a break in the generated assembly by inserting the following statement in the code you generate dynamically:

```
System.Diagnostics.Debugger.Break()
```

You are now ready to compile the assembly:

```
' Create the VB compiler.
Dim provider As New VBCodeProvider
Dim compRes As CompilerResults = provider.CompileAssemblyFromSource(params, source)

' Check whether we have errors.
If compRes.Errors.Count > 0 Then
    ' Gather all error messages and display them.
    Dim msg As String = ""
    For Each compErr As CompilerError In compRes.Errors
        msg &= compErr.ToString & ControlChars.CrLf
    Next
    MessageBox.Show(msg, "Compilation Failed", MessageBoxButtons.OK, MessageBoxIcon.Error)
Else
    ' Compilation was successful.
    …
End If
```

If the compilation was successful, you use the CompilerResults.CompiledAssembly property to get a reference to the created assembly. Once you have this Assembly object, you can create an instance of its Evaluator class and invoke its Eval method by using standard reflection techniques:

```
Dim asm As Assembly = compRes.CompiledAssembly
Dim evaluator As Object = asm.CreateInstance("Evaluator")
Dim evalMethod As MethodInfo = evaluator.GetType.GetMethod("Eval")
Dim args() As Object = {CDbl(123)}    ' Pass x = 123
Dim result As Object = evalMethod.Invoke(evaluator, args)
```

Notice that you can't reference the Evaluator class by a typed variable because this class (and its container assembly) doesn't exist yet when you compile the main application. For this reason, you must use reflection both to create an instance of the class and to invoke its members.

Another tricky thing to do when applying this technique is to have the dynamic assembly call back a method in a class defined in the main application by means of reflection, for example, to let the main application update a progress bar during a lengthy routine. Alternatively, you can define a public interface in a DLL and must have the class in the main application implement the interface; being defined in a DLL, the dynamic assembly can create an interface variable and therefore it can call methods in the main application through that interface.

You must be aware of another detail when you apply on-the-fly compilation in a real application: once you load the dynamically created assembly, that assembly will take memory in your process until the main application ends. In most cases, this problem isn't serious and you can just forget about it. But you can't ignore it if you plan to build many assemblies on the fly. The only solution to this problem is to create a separate AppDomain, load the dynamic assembly in that AppDomain, use the classes in the assembly, and finally unload the AppDomain when you don't need the assembly any longer. On the other hand, loading the assembly in another AppDomain means that you can't use reflection to manage its types (reflection works only with types in the same AppDomain as the caller). Please see the demo application in the companion code for a solution to this complex issue.

Performance Considerations

I have warned about the slow performance of reflection-based techniques often in this chapter. Using reflection to invoke methods is similar to using the late-binding techniques that are available in script languages such as Microsoft Visual Basic Scripting Edition (VBScript), in Visual Basic 6 when you use a Variant variable, or even in Visual Basic 2005 when you invoke a method using an Object variable and Option Strict is Off.

In general, invoking a method by using reflection is many times slower than a direct call is, and therefore you shouldn't use these techniques in time-critical portions of your application. In some scenarios, however, you need to defer the decision about which method to call until run time, and therefore a direct call is out of the question. Even then, reflection should be your last resort and should be used only if you can't solve the problem with another technique based on indirection, for example, an interface or a delegate.

If you decide to use reflection and you must invoke a method more than once or twice, you should use Type.GetMethod to get a reference to a MethodInfo object and then use the MethodInfo.Invoke method to do the actual call, rather than using the Type.InvokeMember method because the former technique requires that you perform the discovery phase only once.

Don't use the BindingFlags.IgnoreCase value with the Get*Xxxx* method (singular form), if you know the exact spelling of the member you're looking for, and specify the BindingFlags.ExactBinding value if possible because it speeds up the search. The latter flag suppresses implicit type conversions; therefore, you must supply the exact type of each argument:

```
' This code doesn't work-the GetMethod method returns Nothing.
' You must either use Integer instead of Short in the argTypes signature
' or drop the BindingFlags.ExactBinding bit in the GetMethod call.
Dim argTypes() As Type = {GetType(Char), GetType(Short)}
Dim mi As MethodInfo = GetType(String).GetMethod("IndexOf", BindingFlags.ExactBinding Or _
   BindingFlags.Public Or BindingFlags.Instance, Nothing, argTypes, Nothing)
```

 .NET Framework 2.0 improves performance in many ways. For example, in previous versions of the .NET Framework, a call to the Type.Get*Xxxx* (singular) adds a noticeable overhead because all the type's members are queried anyway, as if Type.GetMembers were called. The results from this first call are cached, so at least you pay this penalty only once, but this approach has a serious issue: if you reflect on many types, all the resulting MemberInfo objects are kept in memory and are never discarded until the application terminates.

In .NET Framework 2.0, a Type.Get*Xxxx* method (singular form) doesn't cause the exploration of the entire Type object, and therefore execution is faster and memory consumption is kept to a minimum. Also, the cache used by reflection is subject to garbage collection; therefore, type and member information is discarded unless you keep it alive by storing a reference in a Type or MemberInfo field at the class level.

An alternative technique for storing information about a large number of types and members without taxing the memory is based on the RuntimeTypeHandle and RuntimeMethodHandle classes that you can use instead of the Type and MemberInfo classes. Handle-based objects use very little memory, yet they allow you to rebuild a reference to the actual Type or MemberInfo-based object very quickly, as this code demonstrates:

```
' Store information about a method in the Person type.
Dim hType As RuntimeTypeHandle = GetType(Person).TypeHandle
Dim hMethod As RuntimeMethodHandle = GetType(Person).GetMethod("SendEmail").MethodHandle
…
' (Later in the application…)
' Rebuild the Type and MethodBase objects.
Dim ty As Type = Type.GetTypeFromHandle(hType)
Dim mb As MethodBase = MethodBase.GetMethodFromHandle(hMethod, hType)
' Use them as needed.
…
```

Security Issues

A warning about using reflection at run time is in order. As you've seen in previous sections, reflection allows you to access any type and any member, regardless of their scope. Therefore, you can use reflection even to instantiate private types, call private methods, or read private variables.

More precisely, your code can perform these operations if it is fully trusted or at least has ReflectionPermission. All the applications that run from the local hard disk have this permission, whereas applications running from the Internet don't. In general, if you don't have ReflectionPermission, you can perform only the following reflection-related techniques:

■ Enumerate assemblies and modules.

■ Enumerate public types and obtain information about them and their public members.

■ Set public fields and properties and invoke public members.

■ Access and enumerate family (Protected) members of a base class of the calling code.

■ Access and enumerate assembly (Friend) members from inside the assembly in which the calling code runs.

You see that code can access through reflection only those types and members that it can access directly anyway. For example, a piece of code can't access a private field in another type or invoke a private member in another type, even if that type is inside the same assembly as the calling code. In other words, reflection doesn't give code more power than it already has; it just adds flexibility because of the additional level of indirection that it provides.

This discussion on reflection is important for one reason: never rely on the Private scope keyword to hide confidential data from unauthorized eyes because a malicious user might create a simple application that uses reflection to read your data. If the application runs from the local hard disk, it has ReflectionPermission and can therefore access all the members of your assembly, regardless of whether it's an EXE or a DLL. (If you also consider that decompiling a .NET assembly is as easy, you see that the only way to protect confidential data is by means of cryptography.)

The ability to invoke nonpublic members can be important in some scenarios. For example, in the section titled "The ICloneable Interface" in Chapter 10, I show how a type can implement the Clone method by leveraging the MemberwiseClone protected method, but in some cases you'd like to clone an object for which you don't have any source code. Provided that your application runs in full trust mode and has ReflectionPermission, you can clone any object quite easily with reflection. Here's a reusable routine that performs a (shallow) copy of the object passed as an argument:

```
Function CloneObject(Of T)(ByVal obj As T) As T
    If obj Is Nothing Then
        ' Cloning a null object is easy.
        Return Nothing
```

```
        ElseIf TypeOf CObj(obj) Is ICloneable Then
            ' Take advantage of the ICloneable interface, if possible.
            Dim iclone As ICloneable = DirectCast(obj, ICloneable)
            Return CType(iclone.Clone(), T)
        Else
            ' Use reflection if everything else failed.
            ' (Throws if application doesn't have ReflectionPermission.)
            Dim mi As MethodInfo = obj.GetType().GetMethod("MemberwiseClone", _
                BindingFlags.ExactBinding Or BindingFlags.NonPublic Or BindingFlags.Instance)
            Return CType(mi.Invoke(obj, Nothing), T)
        End If
End Function
```

Assuming that you have a Person type—with the usual FirstName, LastName, and Spouse properties—the following code tests that the CloneObject method works correctly:

```
Dim john As New Person("John", "Evans")
Dim ann As New Person("Ann", "Beebe")
john.Spouse = ann
ann.Spouse = john
' We need no CType or DirectCast, thanks to generics.
Dim john2 As Person = CloneObject(john)
' Prove that it worked.
Console.WriteLine("{0} {1}, spouse is {2} {3}", john2.FirstName, john2.LastName, _
    john2.Spouse.FirstName, john2.Spouse.LastName)
    ' => John Evans, spouse is Ann Beebe
```

Chapter 19
Custom Attributes

In Chapter 18, "Reflection," I illustrate the power of reflection and hint at how you can use it to enumerate the Microsoft .NET Framework attributes associated with code entities, for example, to determine programmatically whether a class is serializable. In this chapter, I focus on how you can write your own custom attributes and use them to implement advanced programming techniques.

Applying .NET attributes is vaguely similar to assigning properties to a Windows Forms or Web Form control. When you assign a value to the Location and BackColor properties, you know that a piece of code in the .NET Framework will eventually read those properties and change the position and the background color of that control. Properties promote *declarative programming*, by which you state what you want to achieve and let another piece of code process the property and run the actual instructions that carry out the assignment. Similarly, when you label a type or a class member with an attribute, you declare how that type or that member should be processed and let another piece of code perform the actual action.

This description holds true with all the .NET attributes I illustrate in earlier (and later) chapters, and it's also true with the custom attributes that you author. The ability to define and apply custom attributes is among the most underestimated .NET features. That's why I devote an entire chapter to this topic.

Note To avoid long lines, code samples in this chapter assume that the following Imports statements are used at the file or project level:

```
Imports System.CodeDom.Compiler
Imports System.Collections.Generic
Imports System.IO
Imports System.Reflection
Imports System.Runtime.Serialization.Formatters.Binary
Imports System.Text
Imports System.Text.RegularExpressions
Imports System.Windows.Forms
Imports System.Xml.Serialization
```

Introducing Custom Attributes

As you learned in previous chapters, attributes are pieces of metadata that you attach to code entities—assemblies, classes, methods, or individual fields—to affect the behavior of the Microsoft Visual Basic compiler, the JIT compiler, or other portions of the .NET runtime.

Most of the time, you'll use only attributes that are defined in the .NET Framework and documented in the .NET SDK. Attributes are simply .NET classes, though, and nothing prevents you from designing your own attribute types. The main difference between your custom attributes and predefined .NET attributes is that the former ones require that you write the code that discovers and uses them.

Building a Custom Attribute Class

A custom attribute is a class that inherits from System.Attribute. Its name must end with *Attribute*, and it is marked with an AttributeUsage attribute that tells the compiler to which program entities the attribute can be applied: classes, modules, methods, and so on. A custom attribute class can contain fields, properties, and methods that accept and return values only of the following types: Boolean, Byte, Short, Integer, Long, Char, Single, Double, String, Object, System.Type, and public Enum. It can also receive and return one-dimensional arrays of one of the preceding types. A custom attribute class can have no explicit constructor at all, but it's customary to have one or more constructors that specify the mandatory arguments to be passed to the attribute.

 Note   Custom attributes must be visible to at least two assemblies: the assembly where you apply the attribute and the assembly that reads and processes the applied attributes. For this reason, custom attribute types are usually defined in DLL assemblies. For simplicity's sake, all the sample attribute types I illustrate in this chapter are gathered in a demo DLL named CustomAttributes and are contained in a namespace also named CustomAttributes. You should add a reference to this DLL in all the projects where you apply or process these custom attributes.

The following example shows a custom attribute class that lets you annotate any class or class member with the name of the author, the source code version when the member was completed, and an optional property that specifies whether the code has been completely tested.

```
' The AttributeTargets.All value means that this attribute
' can be used with any program entity.
<AttributeUsage(AttributeTargets.All)> _
Public Class VersionAttribute
    ' All attribute classes inherit from System.Attribute.
    Inherits System.Attribute

    ' The Attribute constructor takes two required values.
```

```
   Sub New(ByVal author As String, ByVal version As Single)
      m_Author = author
      m_Version = version
   End Sub


    ' Private fields
   Private m_Author As String
   Private m_Version As Single
   Private m_Tested As Boolean

   Public ReadOnly Property Author() As String
      Get
         Return m_Author
      End Get
   End Property

   Public ReadOnly Property Version() As Single
      Get
         Return m_Version
      End Get
   End Property

   Public Property Tested() As Boolean
      Get
         Return m_Tested
      End Get
      Set(ByVal Value As Boolean)
         m_Tested = Value
      End Set
   End Property
End Class
```

Microsoft guidelines dictate that all the values accepted in the attribute constructor be implemented as read-only properties, whereas arguments that can't be set through the constructor
must be implemented as read-write properties because they can be assigned only through
named parameters, as in the following code:

```
<Version("John", 1.10, Tested:=True)> _
Public Class TestVersionClass

    …
```

An attribute can expose fields, but in general encapsulating a value inside a property is preferable. Attribute classes can also include other kinds of members, but in practice this happens
infrequently: an attribute is just a repository for metadata values that are read by other programs; therefore, fields and properties are all you need most of the time. Attributes are meant
to be discovered by a piece of code running in a different assembly, and therefore these classes
typically have a Public scope.

The argument passed to the AttributeUsage attribute specifies that the VersionAttribute
attribute—or just Version, because the trailing Attribute portion of the name can be omitted—
can be used with any program entity. The argument you pass to the AttributeUsage constructor is a bit-coded value formed by adding one or more elements in this list: Assembly (1),

Module (2), Class (4), Struct (8), Enum (16), Constructor (32), Method (64), Property (128), Field (256), Event (512), Interface (1,024), Parameter (2,048), Delegate (4,096), ReturnValue (8,192), or All (16,383, the sum of all preceding values).

The AttributeUsage attribute supports two additional properties, which can be passed as named arguments in the constructor method. The AllowMultiple property specifies whether the attribute being defined—VersionAttribute, in this case—can appear multiple times inside angle brackets. The Inherited attribute tells whether a derived class inherits the attribute. The default value for both properties is False.

The Conditional attribute, which I introduced in Chapter 4, "Using Visual Studio 2005," is an example of an attribute that supports multiple instances and is also an example of an attribute that's inherited by derived classes. If the Conditional attribute were implemented in Visual Basic, its source code would be more or less as follows:

```
<AttributeUsage(AttributeTargets.Method, AllowMultiple:=True, Inherited:=True)> _
Public Class ConditionalAttribute
    Inherits System.Attribute

    Private m_ConditionString As String

    ' The constructor method
    Sub New(ByVal conditionString As String)
        Me.ConditionString = conditionString
    End Sub

    ' The only property of this attribute class
    Property ConditionString() As String
        Get
            Return m_ConditionString
        End Get
        Set(ByVal Value As String)
            m_ConditionString = Value
        End Set
    End Property
End Class
```

(Notice that the ConditionalAttribute type violates Microsoft's own guidelines because the ConditionString writable property can also be set through the constructor.)

Let's go back to the Version attribute. You can apply it to a class and its members:

```
<Version("John", 1.01)> _
Public Class TestVersionClass
    <Version("Robert", 1.01, Tested:=True)> _
    Sub MyProc()
        ...
    End Sub

    <Version("Ann", 1.02)> _
    Function MyFunction() As Long
        ...
    End Function
End Class
```

Compile the class in a Console project named TestApplication and read on to see how you can discover the attribute.

Reflecting on a Custom Attribute

As I emphasized previously, an attribute is a piece of information stored somewhere in its assembly's metadata tables, waiting for a program—let's call it the *agent*—to extract it and use it. When you apply .NET standard attributes, the agent program is the Visual Basic compiler, the JIT compiler, or the CLR; when you apply a custom attribute, you must write the agent code yourself. Such an agent code can be in the same DLL where the attribute is defined (if it's meant to be invoked from other assemblies) or in a separate EXE file (if it runs as a stand-alone program).

In our first example, the agent program can be as simple as a piece of code that scans an assembly and displays a report that lists which types have been authored by whom and which code members have been tested. Create another Console application, name it ShowVersion, add a reference to the CustomAttributes DLL, and type the following code:

```
Imports System.Reflection
Imports CustomAttributes

Module MainModule
    Sub Main(ByVal args() As String)
        ' Read the assembly whose path is passed as an argument.
        Dim asm As [Assembly] = [Assembly].LoadFile(args(0))
        ' Display the header.
        Console.WriteLine("{0,-40}{1,-12}{2,-10}{3,-6}", _
            "Member", "Author", "Version", "Tested")
        Console.WriteLine(New String("-"c, 68))

        ' Iterate over all public and private types.
        For Each type As Type In asm.GetTypes()
            ' Extract the attribute associated with the type.
            Dim attr As VersionAttribute = DirectCast(Attribute.GetCustomAttribute( _
                type, GetType(VersionAttribute)), VersionAttribute)
            If attr IsNot Nothing Then
                Console.WriteLine("{0,-40}{1,-12}{2,-10}{3,-6}",
                    type.FullName, attr.Author, attr.Version, attr.Tested)
            End If

            ' Iterate over all public and private members.
            For Each mi As MemberInfo In type.GetMembers( _
                    BindingFlags.Public Or BindingFlags.NonPublic _
                    Or BindingFlags.Instance Or BindingFlags.Static)
                ' Extract the attribute associated with each member.
                attr = DirectCast(Attribute.GetCustomAttribute(mi, _
                    GetType(VersionAttribute)), VersionAttribute)
                If attr IsNot Nothing Then
                    Console.WriteLine("    {0,-36}{1,-12}{2,-10}{3,-6}", _
                        mi.Name, attr.Author, attr.Version, attr.Tested)
                End If
```

```
        Next
      Next
    End Sub
End Module
```

(You might want to go to Chapter 18 to read about the many techniques you can adopt to reflect on a custom attribute.) Compile the application and run it, passing the path of the TestApplication.exe assembly as an argument on the command line. You should see this report in the console window:

```
Member                               Author    Version   Tested
----------------------------------------------------------------
TestApplication.TestVersionClass     John      1.01      False
    MyProc                           Robert    1.01      True
    MyFunction                       Ann       1.02      False
```

Thanks to reflection and custom attributes, you now have a report utility that lets you quickly display the author, the version, and the tested status of all the methods inside a compiled assembly. Sure, you can author a similar utility that reads special remarks in source code, but such a utility wouldn't work on compiled assemblies and, if your team works with other programming languages, you would be forced to write a different parser for each distinct language.

You can extend the ShowVersion utility to spot outdated or untested code quickly, and you can extend the VersionAttribute type with other properties, such as DateCreated and Date-Modified. You might automatically run ShowVersion at the end of your compilation process—for example, as a postbuild compilation step—to ensure that only fully tested code makes its way to your customers.

A Custom Attribute for CSV Serialization

The .NET Framework offers great support for serializing an object instance to and from XML, by means of the XmlSerializer type:

```
' Create a Person object.
Dim pers As New Person()
pers.FirstName = "John"
pers.LastName = "Evans"


' Serialize it to a file.
Dim ser As New XmlSerializer(GetType(Person))
Using fs As New FileStream("c:\person.xml", FileMode.Create)
    ser.Serialize(fs, pers)
End Using


' Read it back. (Reuses the same serializer object.)
Using fs As New FileStream("c:\person.xml", FileMode.Open)
    Dim p As Person = DirectCast(ser.Deserialize(fs), Person)
    Console.WriteLine("{0} {1}", p.FirstName, p.LastName)     ' => John Evans
End Using
```

At the end of the serialization process, the person.xml file contains the following text:

```
<?xml version="1.0"?>
<Person xmlns:xsd="http://www.w3.org/2001/XMLSchema"
        xmlns:xsi="http://www.w3.org/2001/XMLSchema-instance">
  <FirstName>John</FirstName>
  <LastName>Evans</LastName>
</Person>
```

As you can see, each property of the Person type is rendered as an XML element named after the property itself. When you import XML data produced by another program, however, you have no control over the XML schema adopted during the serialization process; to solve this potential problem, you can change the default behavior of the XmlSerializer type, for example, change the names of XML elements and decide that properties be rendered as XML attributes rather than elements, as in this XML fragment:

```
<PersonalData xmlns:xsd="http://www.w3.org/2001/XMLSchema"
        xmlns:xsi="http://www.w3.org/2001/XMLSchema-instance"
        first="John" last="Evans">
</PersonalData>
```

As you might have guessed, you can exert this degree of control on the XML serialization process by applying attributes to the members of the Person class. For example, you can produce the previous XML file by defining the Person type as follows:

```
<XmlRoot("PersonalData")> _
Public Class Person
    <XmlAttributeAttribute("first")> _
    Public FirstName As String
    <XmlAttributeAttribute("last")> _
    Public LastName As String
End Class
```

Unfortunately, not all the world out there speaks XML. This is especially true for legacy applications running on mainframes, which often exchange data in a simple comma-separated value (CSV) format. I already hinted at how you can process this sort of data file in the section titled "Working with Fixed-Length and Delimited Data Files" in Chapter 15, "Files, Directories, and Streams," where I introduced the new TextFieldParser type. In this chapter, I show you how to solve the same problem with a more powerful and elegant technique based on a CsvSerializer type and the CsvField custom attribute.

Let's start by defining the CsvFieldAttribute type, which can be applied to individual fields and properties of a class to affect how instances of that class are rendered in CSV format. This custom attribute has three properties: Index is the position of the field in the output; Quoted is a Boolean property that specifies whether the field or property's value must be enclosed in double quotation marks; Format is an optional format string, which gives you better control over how dates and numbers are written to the CSV file. The index value is mandatory; therefore, the Index property is marked as read-only and must be assigned from inside the attribute's constructor; the other two properties are optional and can be assigned by means of named arguments.

```
<AttributeUsage(AttributeTargets.Field Or AttributeTargets.Property)> _
Public Class CsvFieldAttribute
    Inherits Attribute
    Implements IComparable

    ' These would be properties in a real-world implementation.
    Public ReadOnly Index As Integer
    Public Quoted As Boolean = False
    Public Format As String = ""

    Public Sub New(ByVal index As Integer)
        Me.Index = index
    End Sub

    ' Attributes are sorted on their Index property.
    Public Function CompareTo(ByVal obj As Object) As Integer _
            Implements IComparable.CompareTo
        Return Me.Index.CompareTo(DirectCast(obj, CsvFieldAttribute).Index)
    End Function
End Class
```

Unlike most attribute types, the CsvFieldAttribute class exposes an interface, IComparable, and its Compare method. The reason for this design decision will be clear shortly. Let's now define an Employee class that uses the CsvField attribute:

```
Imports AttributeLibrary

Public Class Employee
    <CsvField(1, Quoted:=True)> _
    Public FirstName As String
    <CsvField(2, Quoted:=True)> _
    Public LastName As String
    <CsvField(3, Format:="dd/M/yyyy")> _
    Public BirthDate As Date

    Dim m_Salary As Decimal
    <CsvField(4, Format:="######.00")> _
    Public Property Salary() As Decimal
        Get
            Return m_Salary
        End Get
        Set(ByVal Value As Decimal)
            m_Salary = Value
        End Set
    End Property

    ' Constructors and other methods…
    Sub New()
    End Sub
End Class
```

The Employee class requires a default constructor for the CsvSerializer to work correctly. (The XmlSerializer has a similar requirement.) I have included an explicit parameterless constructor, in case you wish to add other constructors later.

The toughest part is writing the CsvSerializer class, which uses reflection to read the CsvField attribute associated with each field and property exposed by the type being serialized. By implementing the CsvSerializer class as a generic type you can write more concise and efficient code:

```
Public Class CsvSerializer(Of T As New)
    Private type As Type
    Private separator As String
    Private attrList As New SortedDictionary(Of CsvFieldAttribute, MemberInfo)
    Private rePattern As String

    ' Constructors
    Sub New()
        Me.New(",")
    End Sub

    Sub New(ByVal separator As String)
        Me.type = GetType(T)
        Me.separator = separator
        BuildAttrList()
    End Sub
    ...
```

The CsvSerializer class assumes that the field separator is a comma, but it offers an alternate constructor that enables you to specify a different separator, for example, the semicolon. While inside the constructor, the CsvSerializer class parses all the members of the T type and creates a list of (CsvFieldAttribute, MemberInfo) pairs to speed up the actual serialization and deserialization process. Such a list is stored in a SortedDictionary object and is sorted on the attribute's Index property. (Here's why the CsvFieldAttribute type implements the IComparable interface.) In addition to creating the sorted dictionary, the BuildAttrList procedure creates a regular expression that can parse individual lines of a data file in CSV format. I won't describe this regular expression in detail because I explain a similar technique in the section titled "Parsing Data Files" in Chapter 14, "Regular Expressions."

```
' Build the sorted list of (attribute, MemberInfo) pairs.
Private Sub BuildAttrList()
    ' Create the list of public members that are flagged with the
    ' CsvFieldAttribute, sorted on the attribute's Index property.
    For Each mi As MemberInfo In type.GetMembers()
        ' Get the attribute associated with this member.
        Dim attr As CsvFieldAttribute = DirectCast(Attribute.GetCustomAttribute( _
            mi, GetType(CsvFieldAttribute)), CsvFieldAttribute)
        If attr IsNot Nothing Then
            ' Add to the list of attributes found so far, sorted on Index property.
            attrList.Add(attr, mi)
        End If
    Next
```

```
    ' Create the regex pattern and format string output pattern.
    Dim sb As New StringBuilder()
    Dim sep As String = ""

    For Each de As KeyValuePair(Of CsvFieldAttribute, MemberInfo) In attrList
        ' Add a separator to the pattern, but only from the second iteration onward.
        If sb.Length > 0 Then sb.Append(separator)
        sb.Append(" *")
        ' Get attribute and Memberinfo for this item.
        Dim attr As CsvFieldAttribute = de.Key
        Dim mi As MemberInfo = de.Value

        ' Append to the regex for this element.
        If Not attr.Quoted Then
            sb.AppendFormat("(?<{0}>[^{1}]+)", mi.Name, separator)
        Else
            sb.AppendFormat("""(?<{0}>[^""]+)""", mi.Name)
        End If
        sb.Append(" *")
    Next
    ' Set the pattern.
    rePattern = sb.ToString()
End Sub
```

The CsvSerializer type exposes two Serialize methods, one that works with files and the
other that works with any StreamWriter object. (The former method delegates its job to the
latter.) Both methods take an ICollection(Of T) generic collection in their second argument,
so you can serialize entire arrays and collections of T instances.

Serializing an individual object is easy. The list of serializable members is already in the attr-
List dictionary and is sorted in the correct sequence, so it's just a matter of reading the corresponding field or property, outputting its value to the stream, and applying the correct format
string if one has been specified by means of the CsvField attribute:

```
' Serialize to text file.
Public Sub Serialize(ByVal fileName As String, ByVal col As ICollection(Of T))
    Using writer As New StreamWriter(fileName)
        Serialize(writer, col)
    End Using
End Sub

' Serialize to a stream.
Public Sub Serialize(ByVal writer As StreamWriter, ByVal col As ICollection(Of T))
    For Each obj As T In col
        ' This is the result string.
        Dim sb As New StringBuilder()

        For Each kvp As KeyValuePair(Of CsvFieldAttribute, MemberInfo) In attrList
            ' Append the separator (but not at the first element in the line).
            If sb.Length > 0 Then sb.Append(separator)
            ' Get attribute and MemberInfo.
            Dim attr As CsvFieldAttribute = kvp.Key
            Dim mi As MemberInfo = kvp.Value
```

```
        ' Get the value of the field or property, as an Object.
        Dim fldValue As Object = Nothing
        If TypeOf mi Is FieldInfo Then
            fldValue = DirectCast(mi, FieldInfo).GetValue(obj)
        ElseIf TypeOf mi Is PropertyInfo Then
            fldValue = DirectCast(mi, PropertyInfo).GetValue(obj, Nothing)
        End If

        ' Get the format to be used with this field/property value.
        Dim format As String = "{0}"
        If attr.Format <> "" Then format = "{0:" & attr.Format & "}"
        If attr.Quoted Then format = """" & format & """"
        ' Call the ToString, with a format argument if specified.
        sb.AppendFormat(format, fldValue)
      Next
      ' Output to the stream.
      writer.WriteLine(sb.ToString)
   Next
End Sub
```

Deserializing from a file or a stream is only marginally more difficult. The Deserialize method uses the regular expression that was built when the CsvSerializer object was instantiated, and it extracts the value of each regular expression's Group. The Deserialize methods take an optional argument that specifies whether the first line should be ignored: this feature enables you to process data files in which the first line contains a header that lists the names of fields:

```
' Deserialize a text file.
Public Function Deserialize(ByVal fileName As String, _
      Optional ByVal ignoreFieldHeader As Boolean = False) As T()
   Using reader As New StreamReader(fileName)
       Return Deserialize(reader, ignoreFieldHeader)
   End Using
End Function

' Deserialize from a stream.
Public Function Deserialize(ByVal reader As StreamReader, _
      Optional ByVal ignoreFieldHeader As Boolean = False) As T()
   ' The result collection
   Dim list As New List(Of T)
   ' Create a compiled Regex for best performance.
   Dim re As New Regex("^" & rePattern & "$", RegexOptions.Compiled)
   ' Skip the field header, if necessary.
   If ignoreFieldHeader Then reader.ReadLine()

   Do Until reader.Peek() = -1
      Dim text As String = reader.ReadLine()
      Dim m As Match = re.Match(text)
      If m.Success Then
         ' Create an instance of the target type.
         Dim obj As New T()
         ' Set individual properties.
         For Each de As KeyValuePair(Of CsvFieldAttribute, MemberInfo) In attrList
            ' Get attribute and MemberInfo.
            Dim attr As CsvFieldAttribute = de.Key
            Dim mi As MemberInfo = de.Value
```

```
         ' Retrieve the string value.
         Dim strValue As String = m.Groups(mi.Name).Value

         If TypeOf mi Is FieldInfo Then
            Dim fi As FieldInfo = DirectCast(mi, FieldInfo)
            Dim fldValue As Object = Convert.ChangeType(strValue, fi.FieldType)
            fi.SetValue(obj, fldValue)
         ElseIf TypeOf mi Is PropertyInfo Then
            Dim pi As PropertyInfo = DirectCast(mi, PropertyInfo)
            Dim propValue As Object = Convert.ChangeType(strValue, pi.PropertyType)
            pi.SetValue(obj, propValue, Nothing)
         End If
      Next
      ' Add this object to result.
      list.Add(obj)
   End If
Loop
' Return the array of instances.
Return list.ToArray()
End Function
```

Using the CsvSerializer is simple:

```
' Create and fill a sample array of Employee objects.
Dim arr(9) As Employee
…

' Serialize all the objects to a file.
Const DATAFILE As String = "employees.txt"
Dim ser As New CsvSerializer(Of Employee)
ser.Serialize(DATAFILE, arr)
…

' Deserialize them from the file back to a different array.
Dim arr2() As Employee = ser.Deserialize(DATAFILE)
```

The CsvSerializer type and its CsvField companion attribute enable you to serialize an object to the CSV format by writing very little code. You might achieve the same result by adopting a technique that isn't based on attributes, but you can hardly reach the same degree of code reusability and ease of maintenance. For example, if the order of fields in the CSV file changes, you simply need to edit one or more attributes in the Employee class without changing code elsewhere in the application and without having to worry about side effects.

> **Note**   Often you can replace, or complement, custom attributes burnt in source code with an external file that holds the same kind of information. In this particular case, you might use an XML file that contains the order of fields and the field format so that you simply need to provide a different XML file when the file format changes, without having to recompile the application. Both solutions have their pros and cons. XML files often give you more flexibility—for example, they can store hierarchical information—whereas custom attributes ensure that the metadata always travels with the code it refers to. Also, attributes are a more natural choice when the metadata doesn't change often and when, if the metadata changes, you need to recompile the code anyway. In this particular case, for example, if a new version of the CSV file has additional fields, you need to recompile the project anyway, and therefore custom attributes can be the preferred approach to store the metadata.

Building a Benchmark Tool

Microsoft Visual Studio 2005 offers many tools for testing your applications, as you learned in Chapter 5, "Debugging Visual Basic Applications." However, when it's time to write benchmarks, the .NET Framework gives you the Stopwatch type, and that's it. If you need to benchmark multiple routines, compare and sort their results, and write a little report, you have to write all the plumbing code. You *had* to, at least.

Writing a tool that automates the production of your benchmarks requires very little effort. First, you need an attribute to mark the methods that you want to benchmark. For simplicity's sake, this version uses public fields instead of properties:

```
<AttributeUsage(AttributeTargets.Method)> _
Public Class BenchmarkAttribute
    Inherits Attribute
    Implements IComparable(Of BenchmarkAttribute)

    Public Sub New(ByVal group As String)
        If group Is Nothing Then group = ""
        Me.Group = group
    End Sub

    Public ReadOnly Group As String = ""    Public Name As String = ""
    Public NormalizationFactor As Double = 1
    Public Function CompareTo(ByVal other As BenchmarkAttribute) As Integer _
            Implements System.IComparable(Of BenchmarkAttribute).CompareTo
        Dim res As Integer = Me.Group.CompareTo(other.Group)
        If res = 0 Then res = Me.Name.CompareTo(other.Name)
        Return res
    End Function
End Class
```

This class implements the IComparable(Of T) generic interface because instances of the attribute will be used as keys in a SortedList collection, as you'll see shortly. You can apply the Benchmark attribute only to a Sub or Function static method that takes no arguments, for example, methods in a Module type:

```
Public Module TestBenchmarkModule
    <Benchmark("Concatenation")> _
    Sub TestString()
        Dim s As String = ""
        For i As Integer = 1 To 10000
            s &= i.ToString()
        Next
    End Sub

    <Benchmark("Concatenation", NormalizationFactor:=100)> _
    Sub TestStringBuilder()
        Dim sb As New System.Text.StringBuilder()
        For i As Integer = 1 To 1000000
            sb.Append(i)
        Next
    End Sub
```

```
<Benchmark("Division", Name:="Integer division")> _
Function TestIntegerDivision() As Integer
    Dim res As Integer
    For i As Integer = 1 To 10000000
        res = 1000000 \ i
    Next
    Return res
End Function

<Benchmark("Division", Name:="Long division")> _
Function TestLongDivision() As Long
    Dim res As Long
    For i As Integer = 1 To 10000000
        res += 1000000 \ i
    Next
    Return res
End Function

<Benchmark("Division", Name:="Double division")> _
Function TestDoubleDivision() As Double
    Dim res As Double
    For i As Integer = 1 To 10000000
        res += 1000000 / i
    Next
    Return res
End Function
End Module
```

The only mandatory argument of the Benchmark attribute is its Group property: benchmark methods that must be compared with each other must have the same Group name, and the tool you're going to build sorts results by their group. In the previous example, two benchmark groups, Concatenation and Division, contain two and three benchmarks, respectively. A benchmark also has a name, which defaults to the method name: this name identifies the individual benchmark in the report, and thus you should select a descriptive text for this property.

To see when the NormalizeFactor property can be useful, consider the TestString method, which appends 10,000 characters to a regular string. You'd like to compare this method with TestStringBuilder, but adding just 10,000 characters to a StringBuilder takes too little time to be measured by means of a Stopwatch object. The solution is to have the TestStringBuilder method perform one million iterations and to set the NormalizeFactor property to 100 so that the benchmark code knows that the result time must be divided by 100.

The structure of the benchmark tool is also simple. It scans the assembly passed to it on the command line, looking for methods flagged with the Benchmark attribute. (Only static methods with zero arguments are considered.) It sorts all benchmarks by their Group property, and then invokes each method in each group, sorts the results, and displays a report.

```
Module BenchmarkTool
    Sub Main(ByVal args() As String)
        ' Parse the assembly whose path is passed as an argument.
        Dim asm As [Assembly] = [Assembly].LoadFile(args(0))
```

```vbnet
    ' Search all methods marked with the Benchmark attribute, sorted by their Group.
    Dim attrList As New SortedDictionary(Of BenchmarkAttribute, MethodInfo)

    ' Iterate over all public and private static methods of all types.
    For Each type As Type In asm.GetTypes()
        For Each mi As MethodInfo In type.GetMethods(BindingFlags.Public _
                Or BindingFlags.NonPublic Or BindingFlags.Static)
            ' Extract the attribute associated with each member.
            Dim attr As BenchmarkAttribute = DirectCast(Attribute.GetCustomAttribute(mi, _
                GetType(BenchmarkAttribute)), BenchmarkAttribute)
            ' This must be a Sub that takes no arguments.
            If attr IsNot Nothing AndAlso mi.GetParameters().Length = 0 Then
                ' Benchmark name defaults to method name.
                If attr.Name.Length = 0 Then attr.Name = mi.Name
                attrList.Add(attr, mi)
            End If
        Next
    Next

    Dim lastGroup As String = Nothing
    Dim timingList As New SortedDictionary(Of Long, BenchmarkAttribute)
    ' Display the report header.
    Console.WriteLine("{0,-20}{1,-30}{2,14}{3,12}", "Group", "Test", "Seconds", "Rate")
    Console.Write(New String("-"c, 78))

    ' Run all tests, sorted by their group.
    For Each kvp As KeyValuePair(Of BenchmarkAttribute, MethodInfo) In attrList
        Dim attr As BenchmarkAttribute = kvp.Key
        Dim mi As MethodInfo = kvp.Value

        ' Show a blank line if this is a new group.
        If attr.Group <> lastGroup Then
            DisplayGroupResult(timingList)
            Console.WriteLine()
            lastGroup = attr.Group
            timingList.Clear()
        End If

        ' Invoke the method.
        Dim sw As Stopwatch = Stopwatch.StartNew()
        mi.Invoke(Nothing, Nothing)
        sw.Stop()
        ' Remember total timing, taking normalization factor into account.
        timingList.Add(CLng(sw.ElapsedTicks / attr.NormalizationFactor), attr)
    Next
    ' Display result of the last group.
    DisplayGroupResult(timingList)
End Sub

' Helper routine that displays all the timings in a group
Private Sub DisplayGroupResult(ByVal timingList As SortedDictionary(Of Long, _
        BenchmarkAttribute))
    If timingList.Count = 0 Then Exit Sub
    Dim bestTime As Long = -1
    For Each kvp As KeyValuePair(Of Long, BenchmarkAttribute) In timingList
```

```
' The first timing in the sorted collection is also the best timing.
If bestTime < 0 Then bestTime = kvp.Key
Dim rate As Double = kvp.Key / bestTime
Console.WriteLine("{0,-20}{1,-30}{2,14:N4}{3,12:N2}", kvp.Value.Group, _
    kvp.Value.Name, kvp.Key / 100000000, rate)
        Next
    End Sub
End Module
```

Groups in the final report are sorted alphabetically, whereas benchmarks in each group are sorted by their timings, after normalizing them if necessary. (Faster benchmarks come first.) The rightmost column, Rate, compares each timing with the best time in its group. For example, this is the report produced on my computer by running the tool against the five benchmarks listed previously:

Group	Test	Seconds	Rate
Concatenation	TestStringBuilder	0.1435	1.00
Concatenation	TestString	17.8863	124.66
Division	Double division	3.8228	1.00
Division	Integer division	5.8769	1.54
Division	Long division	6.1644	1.61

You can improve on this first version of the benchmark tool in many ways. For example, you might save benchmark reports and automatically compare timings against a previous run of the tool to check whether some key methods of your application are performing slower than they did previously.

Writing Plug-ins for Windows Forms Applications

Most business applications must be extensible and customizable to meet specific requirements of different customers. For example, one customer might require additional fields on a data entry form; another customer might want to delete or add menu commands, and so forth. Typically, developers respond to these requirements by interspersing tons of If and Select Case statements in code, but this approach is clearly unsatisfactory and can quickly lead to maintenance insanity.

Even if customization isn't a requirement, you might want to build your applications from the ground up with extensibility in mind so that you can later release new modules that fit into the main application without forcing users to reinstall a completely new version. If your application can be extended and customized without having to recompile its source code, expert users might create their own modules, without putting your support team under pressure.

The first and most delicate step in building extensible and customizable applications is designing a plug-in infrastructure. In this section, I show you how to implement a powerful and flexible mechanism that enables you (or your users) to create plug-ins that are notified when a form in the main application is created so that each plug-in can add its own controls and menu commands or even replace the original form with a completely different form. Not surprisingly, the technique I am about to illustrate is based on custom attributes. It is a simplified version of the extension mechanism we use for Code Architects' Windows Forms applications that need to be extensible.

The PluginLibrary Project

Create a new blank solution and add a Class Library project named PluginLibrary. This project contains only two classes: FormExtenderAttribute and FormExtenderManager.

The FormExtenderAttribute Type

For simplicity's sake, the listing for the FormExtender custom attribute class uses fields instead of properties. (The companion code for this book uses property procedures that validate incoming values, though.)

```
<AttributeUsage(AttributeTargets.Class)> _
Public Class FormExtenderAttribute
   Inherits Attribute

   Public ReadOnly FormName As String
   Public ReadOnly Replace As Boolean
   Public IncludeInherited As Boolean

   Public Sub New(ByVal formName As String)
      Me.New(formName, False)
   End Sub

   Public Sub New(ByVal formName As String, ByVal Replace As Boolean)
      Me.FormName = formName
      Me.Replace = Replace
   End Sub
End Class
```

You can use the FormExtender attribute with two different kinds of classes. You can use it either with a plug-in (nonvisual) class that must be notified when a form in the main application has been created or with a plug-in form class that replaces a form in the main application. In the former case, you set the Replace argument to False (or omit it); in the latter case, you assign it the True value. In both cases, FormName is the complete name of a form in the main application that is being instantiated; if IncludeInherited is True, the plug-in works with both the specified form class and all the forms that inherit from that form class. These three properties enable you to create several plug-in flavors:

```
<FormExtender("MainApplication.MainForm")> _
Public Class MainForm_Extender
   Sub New(ByVal frm As MainForm)
      ' This plug-in class is instantiated when the MainForm is loaded.
      ...
   End Sub
End Class
```

```
<FormExtender("System.Windows.Forms.Form", IncludeInherited:=True)> _
Public Class GenericForm_Extender
    Sub New(ByVal frm As Form)
        ' This plug-in class is instantiated when any form in the main application is
        ' loaded because it specifies a generic form and sets IncludeInherited to True.
        …
    End Sub
End Class


<FormExtender("MainApplication.MainForm", True)> _
Public Class OptionForm_Replacement
    Inherits System.Windows.Forms.Form
    ' This form replaces the main application's OptionsForm class.
    …
End Class
```

Plug-in classes that don't replace a form (Replace argument is False) are instantiated immediately after the form in the main application and a reference to the form is passed to their constructor so that the plug-in has an opportunity to add one or more user interface elements. (Read on for examples.)

The FormExtenderManager Type

The FormExtenderManager class exposes three important static methods. The InitializePlugins method parses all the DLL assemblies in a directory that you specify, looks for types marked with the FormExtender attribute, and stores information about these types in a generic Dictionary for later retrieval. If the main application doesn't call this method explicitly, it will be executed anyway when any of the next two methods is invoked. (In this case, you can't specify a path, and InitializePlugins automatically looks for plug-ins in the main application's folder.)

```
Public Class FormExtenderManager
    ' All the FormExtenders known to this manager
    Private Shared extenders As Dictionary(Of String, FormExtenderInfo)

    ' Initialize the list of form extenders (two overloads).
    Public Shared Sub InitializePlugIns()
        Dim dirName As String = Path.GetDirectoryName(Application.ExecutablePath) ' & "\PlugIns"
        InitializePlugIns(dirName)
    End Sub

    Public Shared Sub InitializePlugIns(ByVal dirName As String)
        extenders = New Dictionary(Of String, FormExtenderInfo)
        ' Visit all the DLLs in this directory.
        For Each dllName As String In Directory.GetFiles(dirName, "*.dll")
            Try
                ' Attempt to load this assembly.
                Dim asm As [Assembly] = [Assembly].LoadFile(dllName)
                ParseAssembly(asm)
            Catch ex As Exception
                ' Ignore DLLs that aren't assemblies.
            End Try
        Next
    End Sub
```

The extenders Dictionary contains instances of the FormExtenderInfo nested type. This dictionary is built inside the ParseAssembly private method:

```
Private Shared Sub ParseAssembly(ByVal asm As Assembly)
   Dim attrType As Type = GetType(FormExtenderAttribute)
   ' Check all the types in the assembly.
   For Each type As Type In asm.GetTypes()
      ' Retrieve the FormExtenderAttribute.
      Dim attr As FormExtenderAttribute = DirectCast(Attribute.GetCustomAttribute( _
         type, attrType, False), FormExtenderAttribute)
      If attr IsNot Nothing Then
         ' Add to the dictionary.
         Dim info As New FormExtenderInfo
         info.FormName = attr.FormName
         info.Replace = attr.Replace
         info.IncludeInherited = attr.IncludeInherited
         info.Type = type
         extenders.Add(info.FormName, info)
      End If
   Next
End Sub

' A nested class used to hold information on extenders
Private Class FormExtenderInfo
   Public FormName As String
   Public Replace As Boolean
   Public IncludeInherited As Boolean
   Public Type As Type
End Class
```

The Create method takes a form type, creates an instance of that form type, and then notifies all plug-ins that the form has been created. However, if a plug-in class has a FormExtender attribute whose FormName property matches the form's name and whose Replace proterty is set to True, the Create method creates an instance of the plug-in form rather than the original form.

```
Public Shared Function Create(Of T As Form) As Form
   ' Initialize plug-ins if necessary.
   If extenders Is Nothing Then InitializePlugIns()
   Dim formType As Type = GetType(T)
   Dim formName As String = formType.FullName
   Dim mustNotify As Boolean = True

   ' Check whether this form appears in the dictionary.
   If extenders.ContainsKey(formName) Then
      Dim info As FormExtenderInfo = extenders(formName)
      ' If form must be replaced, instantiate the corresponding type instead.
      If info.Replace Then
         formType = info.Type
         mustNotify = False
      End If
   End If

   ' Create the form and notify the plug-in classes.
```

```
      Dim frm As Form = DirectCast(Activator.CreateInstance(formType, True), Form)
      If mustNotify Then NotifyFormCreation(frm)
      Return frm
   End Function
```

NotifyFormCreation takes a form type as an argument and instantiates all the plug-in classes that have been declared as extensions for the specified form.

```
      Public Shared Sub NotifyFormCreation(ByVal frm As Form)
         ' Initialize plug-ins if necessary.
         If extenders Is Nothing Then InitializePlugIns()
         Dim formName As String = frm.GetType().FullName
         Dim extenderType As Type = Nothing

         ' Check whether this form appears in the dictionary.
         If extenders.ContainsKey(formName) Then
            ' Don't notify forms that would replace the original one.
            If Not extenders(formName).Replace Then extenderType = extenders(formName).Type
         Else
            ' Check whether there is an extender that applies to one of the base classes.
            Dim type As Type = frm.GetType()
            Do
               type = type.BaseType
               If extenders.ContainsKey(type.FullName) Then
                  Dim info As FormExtenderInfo = extenders(type.FullName)
                  ' We can use this extender only if IncludeInherited is True.
                  If info.IncludeInherited AndAlso Not info.Replace Then
                     extenderType = info.Type
                     Exit Do
                  End If
               End If
               ' Continue until we get to the System.Windows.Forms.Form base class.
            Loop Until type Is GetType(Form)
         End If

         If extenderType IsNot Nothing Then
            ' Call the extender's constructor, passing the form instance as
            ' an argument. (It fails if such a constructor is missing.)
            Dim args() As Object = {frm}
            Activator.CreateInstance(extenderType, args)
         End If
      End Sub
   End Class    ' End of FormExtenderManager class
```

Notice that this version of the PluginLibrary supports only one plug-in for each form. A more complete implementation would manage a list of all the plug-ins that want to be notified when a given form is created. (Clearly, only one plug-in class can replace a form, though.)

The MainApplication and MainApplicationStartup Projects

Applications that are extensible through plug-ins must be built by following a couple of criteria. First, the application is actually split into two assemblies: a DLL that contains the bulk of the application, including all its forms, and a simple EXE that displays the application's main form (and therefore indirectly bootstraps the DLL). It is necessary to have all the forms in a separate DLL because plug-ins might need to inherit from one of the forms in the main application. (You can reference a type in another EXE assembly, but you can't inherit a form from a form defined in an EXE.) The second criterion requires that you instantiate a form by means the FormExtenderManager.Create method rather than the New keyword, as I explain shortly.

The Startup Project

Let's create the startup assembly first. Create a Windows Forms application, clear the Enable Application Framework check box (on the Application page of the My Project designer), and set the Startup Object option to Sub Main. Next, create a module named MainModule, and type this code:

```
' (This code assumes that you've imported the PluginLibrary namespace.)
Sub Main()
    Application.EnableVisualStyles()
    Application.Run(FormExtenderManager.Create(Of MainApplication.MainForm)())
End Sub
```

The current project requires a reference to both the PluginLibrary project and the MainApplication project, which I illustrate in the following section.

The MainApplication Project

Next, create a Class Library project named MainApplication, and add a reference to the PluginLibrary project and to any other .NET assembly you use, including the System .Windows.Forms.dll assembly. Also, the code that follows assumes that an Imports statement for the PluginLibrary namespace has been added at the file or project level where necessary.

Start adding forms to this project and the code that uses these forms as you'd do normally, with one exception: use the FormExtenderManager.Create method rather than a plain New keyword to instantiate a form. For example, the MainForm class can have a menu, as shown in Figure 19-1. The Sample Form command on the View menu should display a form named SampleForm, and thus you should display such a form using the following code:

```
Dim frm As Form = FormExtenderManager.Create(Of SampleForm)()
frm.Show()
```

Alternatively, if you are sure that a form is never replaced by a plug-in form, you can create the form normally and then use the NotifyFormCreation method to let plug-ins know that the form has been created. You can call this method from inside the overridden OnLoad method:

```
Protected Overrides Sub OnLoad(ByVal e As EventArgs)
    MyBase.OnLoad(e)
    FormExtenderManager.NotifyFormCreation(Me)
End Sub
```

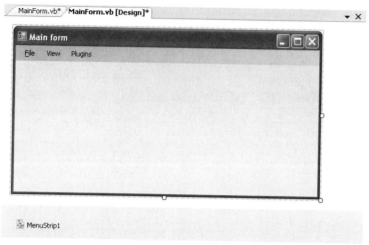

Figure 19-1   The application's main form

Creating Inheritable Forms

If the main application accesses one or more public members of a form, you can't simply replace the original form with another form defined in the plug-in DLL. For example, notice how the following code accesses the Total public property of the CalculatorForm:

```
Dim frmCalc As CalculatorForm = _
   DirectCast(FormExtenderManager.Create(Of CalculatorForm)(), CalculatorForm)
If frmCalc.ShowDialog() = Windows.Forms.DialogResult.OK Then
   ' Read the Total public property of the CalculatorForm type.
   MessageBox.Show(frmCalc.Total.ToString(), "Total", MessageBoxButtons.OK, _
      MessageBoxIcon.Information)
End If
```

The only way for a plug-in to replace the CalculatorForm type with a different form without making the previous code fail is by having the plug-in form inherit from CalculatorForm. (Because of this requirement you had to define all the application's forms in a DLL rather than in a plain EXE.) If you want to allow plug-ins to do the replacement in a simple way, you should create the CalculatorForm class with inheritance in mind. (Read the section titled "Visual Inheritance" in Chapter 8, "Inheritance," for more information about inheriting forms.) Basically, this means that you have to adhere to the following guidelines:

- In the Properties window, set the Modifiers property to Protected for all the controls on the form. (Tip: select all controls by pressing Ctrl+A and change the Modifiers property for all of them in one operation.)

- Don't put any "interesting" code inside event handlers; instead, place this code inside Public or Protected methods marked with the Overridable keyword and call these methods from inside event handlers.

For example, the CalculatorForm must update all TextBox controls on the right when the contents of any field on the left changes. (See Figure 19-2.) Here's the correct way to update these calculated fields:

```
Public Class CalculatorForm
    Public Total As Decimal

    Private Sub ValueChanged(ByVal sender As Object, ByVal e As EventArgs) Handles _
            txtUnits.TextChanged, txtUnitPrice.TextChanged, txtPercentTax.TextChanged
        CalculateTotal()
    End Sub

    Protected Overridable Sub CalculateTotal()
        Try
            Dim units As Integer = CInt(txtUnits.Text)
            Dim unitPrice As Decimal = CDec(txtUnitPrice.Text)
            Dim percentTax As Decimal = CDec(txtPercentTax.Text)
            Dim total As Decimal = units * unitPrice
            Dim tax As Decimal = total * percentTax / 100
            Dim grandTotal As Decimal = total + tax

            txtTotal.Text = total.ToString("N2")
            txtTax.Text = tax.ToString("N2")
            txtGrandTotal.Text = grandTotal.ToString("N2")
        Catch ex As Exception
            ' Clear result fields if any error.
            txtTotal.Text = ""
            txtTax.Text = ""
            txtGrandTotal.Text = ""
        End Try
    End Sub
End Class
```

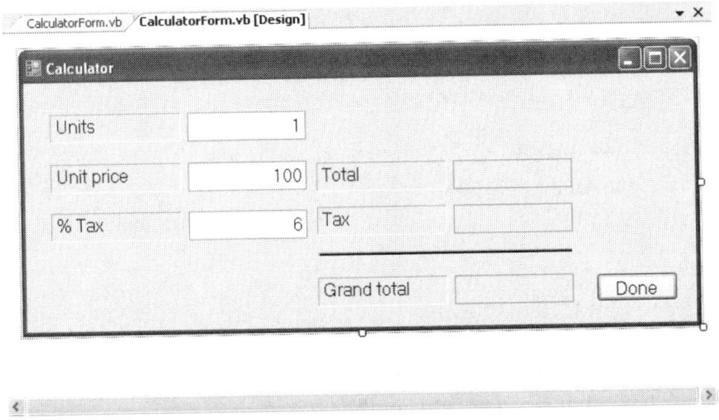

Figure 19-2   The CalculatorForm, which lets you perform simple calculations

Before proceeding, make MainApplicationStartup the startup project in the solution and run the application. You haven't defined any plug-ins so far, and thus the PluginLibrary should do absolutely nothing.

The SamplePlugin Project

You're now ready to create your first plug-in. Add a new Class Library project, name it Sample-Plugin, and add a reference to the PluginLibrary and the MainApplication projects. The sample plug-in project contains three types: SampleForm_Replacement is a form that replaces the SampleForm form; MainForm_Extender adds a menu command to the application's main form; CalculatorForm is a form that replaces the CalculatorForm class.

Replacing a Form with a Different Form

The first class is very simple indeed. Just create a form named SampleForm_Replacement, mark it with the FormExtender attribute, and add controls as you'd do in a regular form:

```
<PluginLibrary.FormExtender("MainApplication.SampleForm", True)> _
Public Class SampleForm_Replacement
    …
End Class
```

In this case, the replacement form doesn't need to have any relation with the original form because the main application never references a method, a field, or a control from outside the form class itself.

Extending a Form with User Interface Elements

The MainForm_Extender class extends the MainForm class without replacing it; thus, you must flag the MainForm_Extender class with a FormExtender attribute whose Replace property is False. The plug-in infrastructure will pass a MainForm instance to this class's constructor when the main form is loaded so that code in MainForm_Extender can add new elements to the form's Controls collection or, as in this case, to the DropDownItems collection of a StripMenu component:

```
<PluginLibrary.FormExtender("MainApplication.MainForm")> _
Public Class MainForm_Extender
    Sub New(ByVal frm As MainApplication.MainForm)
        ' Add an entry to the Plugins menu.
        Dim item As New ToolStripMenuItem("Show Date", Nothing, AddressOf MenuClick)
        frm.mnuPlugins.DropDownItems.Add(item)
    End Sub

    ' React when the menu item is clicked.
    Private Sub MenuClick(ByVal sender As Object, ByVal e As EventArgs)
        MessageBox.Show(Date.Now.ToString(), "Current Date/Time", _
            MessageBoxButtons.OK, MessageBoxIcon.Information)
    End Sub
End Class
```

Notice that the previous code assumes that the mnuPlugins ToolStripMenu object on the application's MainForm is declared as Public; otherwise, the code in the plug-in DLL can't add new elements to it.

Replacing a Form with an Inherited Form

The CalculatorForm_Replacement form both inherits from and replaces the main application's CalculatorForm type. To create this form, select the Add New Item command from the Project menu, select the Inherited Form template, click the Add button, pick the Calculator-Form element inside the Inheritance Picker dialog box, and then click OK.

Next, make the form taller and move the two bottom-most rows of fields down to make room for new controls that let you define a discount percentage. (See Figure 19-3.) Finally, add this code to make the form perform as intended:

```
<PluginLibrary.FormExtender("MainApplication.CalculatorForm", True)> _
Public Class CalculatorForm_Replacement

    Private Sub txtPercentDiscount_TextChanged(ByVal sender As Object, ByVal e As EventArgs) _
        Handles txtPercentDiscount.TextChanged
        CalculateTotal()
    End Sub

    Protected Overrides Sub CalculateTotal()
        If Not Me.Visible Then Exit Sub
        Try
            Dim units As Integer = CInt(txtUnits.Text)
            Dim unitPrice As Decimal = CDec(txtUnitPrice.Text)
            Dim percentTax As Decimal = CDec(txtPercentTax.Text)
            Dim percentDiscount As Decimal = CDec(txtPercentDiscount.Text)

            Dim total As Decimal = units * unitPrice
            Dim discount As Decimal = total * percentDiscount / 100
            Dim discountedTotal As Decimal = total - discount
            Dim tax As Decimal = discountedTotal * percentTax / 100
            Dim grandTotal As Decimal = discountedTotal + tax

            txtTotal.Text = total.ToString("N2")
            txtDiscount.Text = discount.ToString("N2")
            txtDiscountedTotal.Text = discountedTotal.ToString("N2")
            txtTax.Text = tax.ToString("N2")
            txtGrandTotal.Text = grandTotal.ToString("N2")
        Catch ex As Exception
            ' Clear result fields if an exception is thrown.
            txtTotal.Text = ""
            txtDiscount.Text = ""
            txtDiscountedTotal.Text = ""
            txtTax.Text = ""
            txtGrandTotal.Text = ""
        End Try
    End Sub
End Class
```

Notice that you need to handle the TextChange event only for the txtPercentDiscount control because the original CalculatorForm class in the main application takes care of the other input controls. When the original form invokes the CalculateTotal method, the overridden version in CalculatorForm_Replacement runs and you have an opportunity to take discount into account.

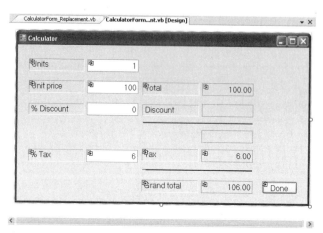

Figure 19-3   The new SamplePlugin project, which extends the CalculatorForm to account for a discount percentage

Compiling and Testing the SamplePlugin Project

By default, The FormExtenderManager.InitializePlugins method looks into the main application's folder for plug-in DLLs. In our example, this folder is the folder where the MainApplicationStartup EXE file is located; therefore, you should manually copy the Sample-Plugin.dll file into this folder whenever you recompile the SamplePlugin project. Alternatively, you can define a postcompilation build step that automates the copy operation or, even better, modify the Build Output Path setting (on the Compile page of the My Project designer) so that the SamplePlugin.dll file is compiled right in the main application's folder.

Another simple solution to this minor issue is to have MainApplicationStartup project include a reference to the SamplePlugin project. The code in the main application's project never references the plug-in project, but this reference forces Visual Studio to copy the plug-in DLL into the application's folder whenever you recompile the solution.

Once all the executables are compiled and stored in the right folders, you can run the application, check that the new user interface elements have been created, and check that they react as intended.

One final note: the PluginLibrary enables you to extend or replace any form defined in the main application, but the concepts it relies on can be applied to any kind of class, not just forms. In the last section of this chapter, you'll learn more about using custom attributes to affect the way objects are instantiated and used in your applications.

A Framework for *N*-Tiered Applications

The last example in this chapter is also the most complex code sample in the entire book. It is a completely functional, though simplified, framework that promotes the creation of data-centric applications that can be expanded, modified, and customized at will. In this section,

I refer to this framework as the CAP framework because it's a (very) stripped-down version of Code Architect Platform, a product that my company has built and refined over the years and that is the heart of many real-world data-centric applications used in Italian government agencies that serve up to ten thousand clients simultaneously. (Contact me if you need information about the real thing.)

An *n-tiered application* is an application that makes a clear distinction between objects that generate the user interface, objects that represent real-world entities (the *business objects*), and objects that take care of reading and writing data on a database or another persistent medium (the *data objects*). All the data objects used in an application make up the Data Access Layer, or DAL. Keeping the three kinds of objects completely distinct makes programming more complex, but it offers an unparalleled degree of flexibility. For example, if your *n*-tiered application has a DAL that works with Oracle, you might replace it with a DAL that is tailored for Microsoft SQL Server. If the user interface, business, and data layers are completely distinct, this change has no impact on either the user interface or the business tier.

Having distinct data and business tiers offers additional advantages. For example, in some cases you can change the structure of the database with minimal or no impact on the user interface. Even better, you can deploy the data objects on a remote computer, where they can interact with the database in a more efficient way. (In this case, the data objects must have a way of communicating with the business tier or the user interface tier by means of a remoting technique supported by .NET, such as Web Services, serviced components, or .NET remoting.) If the *n*-tiered application is designed correctly, you can change the deployment configuration of individual data and business objects to match a specific network configuration, again with minimal impact on other tiers.

The example I illustrate in this section is a simplified *n*-tiered application, which has only the user interface tier (a Windows Forms client) and the data tier. For simplicity's sake, no business tier is included. Also, in an attempt to make the code as concise as possible, DAL objects move data from the database to the application and back by means of typed DataSet objects. Some Service Oriented Architecture (SOA) purists might dislike this design choice, but—again—I wanted to simplify the code to make the important details stand out. If you don't like using DataSets in this fashion, you can modify the framework to use custom collections. This replacement is relatively simple, thanks to generic collections. (See Chapter 11, "Generics.")

Despite its simplicity, the CAP framework supports a couple of advanced features. First, the client application never instantiates a data object directly; instead, it uses a factory class named DataObjectFactory, which returns a data object that is specific for a given configuration and the specified database table. This approach enables you to use different data objects for different configurations transparently—such as "SqlServer," "Oracle," "Access," "Demo," and so forth—without changing the code in the client application. Different configurations can correspond to different databases, different application versions, different network topologies, and so on.

> **Note** In this chapter, I use the term *database table* to indicate the entity that a data object reads from and writes to. A data object can interact with sources other than database tables—for example, text or XML files, or a Web Service—therefore, you shouldn't take this term literally in this context. Think of it more as an abstract "data entity" than a physical database table.

Second, and more interesting, you can associate one or more companion objects with each data object. A *data object companion* is an object that attaches itself to a data object and can take part in commands that read or write data to the database. The job of a companion object can be as simple as logging all database operations to a trace file or as complex as filtering the data being read from or written to the database. Near the end of this chapter, I show you how to build a companion object that extends a data object with caching abilities.

The DataObjectLibrary Project

All the interfaces, custom attributes, and helper types that make up the CAP framework are gathered in the DataObjectLibrary.dll assembly. (See Figure 19-4.) This assembly must be referenced both by the client application and the DLLs that contain data objects and companion objects. In the remainder of this chapter I assume that an Imports statement for the DataObjectLibrary namespace has been added at the file or project level where necessary.

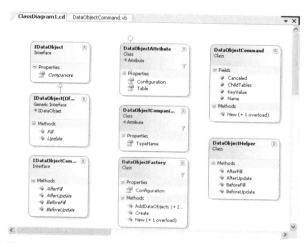

Figure 19-4 All the types in the DataObjectLibrary project, the core of the CAP framework

Interfaces

The CAP framework defines three interfaces. The IDataObject and IDataObject(Of T) interfaces define the methods that a data object must expose, whereas the IDataObjectCompanion interface defines the data commands a companion object can take part in:

```
Public Interface IDataObject
    ReadOnly Property Companions() As List(Of IDataObjectCompanion)
End Interface
```

```
Public Interface IDataObject(Of TDataSet As DataSet)
   Inherits IDataObject
   Function Fill(ByVal ds As TDataSet, ByVal command As DataObjectCommand) As TDataSet
   Function Update(ByVal ds As TDataSet, ByVal command As DataObjectCommand) As TDataSet
End Interface

Public Interface IDataObjectCompanion
   Sub BeforeFill(ByVal obj As IDataObject, ByVal ds As DataSet, _
      ByVal command As DataObjectCommand)
   Sub BeforeUpdate(ByVal obj As IDataObject, ByVal ds As DataSet, _
      ByVal command As DataObjectCommand)
   Sub AfterFill(ByVal obj As IDataObject, ByVal ds As DataSet, _
      ByVal command As DataObjectCommand)
   Sub AfterUpdate(ByVal obj As IDataObject, ByVal ds As DataSet, _
      ByVal command As DataObjectCommand)
End Interface
```

Notice that the IDataObject(Of T) interface derives from the nongeneric IDataObject interface and defines data objects that work with a strong-typed DataSet object. The role of these interfaces will be clear shortly.

Custom Attributes

The DataObjectLibrary project contains two custom attributes: DataObjectAttribute is used to mark data objects, whereas DataObjectCompanionAttribute is used to mark companion objects. Here's an abridged definition of these attributes, where I have replaced properties with fields to keep the listing as concise as possible. (See the companion code for the complete definition of these classes.)

```
<AttributeUsage(AttributeTargets.Class Or AttributeTargets.Struct, Inherited:=True)> _
Public Class DataObjectAttribute
   Inherits Attribute
   Implements IComparable(Of DataObjectAttribute)

   Public Sub New(ByVal configuration As String, ByVal table As String)
      Me.Configuration = configuration
      Me.Table = table
   End Sub

   ' The configuration in which the data object is valid
   Public ReadOnly Configuration As String
   ' The database table this data object applies to
   Public ReadOnly Table As String

   ' Support for the IComparable(Of DataObjectAttribute) interface
   Public Function CompareTo(ByVal other As DataObjectAttribute) As Integer _
         Implements System.IComparable(Of DataObjectAttribute).CompareTo
      Dim res As Integer = Me.Configuration.CompareTo(other.Configuration)
      If res = 0 Then res = Me.Table.CompareTo(other.Table)
      Return res
   End Function
End Class
```

```
<AttributeUsage(AttributeTargets.Class, AllowMultiple:=True)> _
Public Class DataObjectCompanionAttribute
   Inherits Attribute
   ' The type of the data object. Use "" for all data objects.
   Public ReadOnly TypeName As String

   Public Sub New(ByVal typeName As String)
      If typeName Is Nothing Then typeName = ""
      TypeName = typeName
   End Sub
End Class
```

The DataObjectCompanionAttribute can be applied multiple times to the same class: in other words, a companion object can serve multiple data objects.

The DataObjectFactory Type

The DataObjectFactory type is a key component of the CAP framework. Client applications use this type to instantiate the data object that corresponds to a given configuration and a given database table.

```
Public Class DataObjectFactory
   ' This dictionary holds all data objects found so far.
   Public ReadOnly DataObjects As New Dictionary(Of String, Type)
   ' This holds all validator objects for a given data object.
   Public ReadOnly DataCompanions As New Dictionary(Of String, List(Of Type))

   ' Constructors
   Sub New(ByVal configuration As String, ByVal assembly As Assembly)
      Me.Configuration = configuration
      AddDataObjects(assembly)
   End Sub

   Sub New(ByVal configuration As String, ByVal assemblyFile As String)
      Me.New(configuration, Assembly.LoadFile(assemblyFile))
   End Sub

   ' The Configuration property (read-only)
   Public ReadOnly Configuration As String
```

The AddDataObjects method is where the DataObjectFactory type parses an assembly and records all the data objects and the companion objects it finds:

```
Public Sub AddDataObjects(ByVal assembly As Assembly)
   For Each type As Type In assembly.GetTypes()
      ' Look for types marked with the DataObject attribute.
      Dim doAttr As DataObjectAttribute = DirectCast(Attribute.GetCustomAttribute( _
         type, GetType(DataObjectAttribute), False), DataObjectAttribute)
      ' Ensure that type implements IDataObject and that it's suitable for
      ' this configuration, or that current configuration is an empty string.
      If doAttr IsNot Nothing AndAlso GetType(IDataObject).IsAssignableFrom(type) _
            AndAlso (String.Compare(Me.Configuration, doAttr.Configuration, True) = 0 _
            OrElse Me.Configuration.Length = 0) Then
```

```
            ' Add to the dictionary only if not there already.
            If Not DataObjects.ContainsKey(doAttr.Table.ToLower()) Then _
                DataObjects.Add(doAttr.Table.ToLower(), type)
        End If

        ' Look for types marked with the DataObjectValidator attribute.
        ' (This attribute allows multiple instances.)
        Dim coAttrs() As DataObjectCompanionAttribute = DirectCast( _
            Attribute.GetCustomAttributes(type, GetType(DataObjectCompanionAttribute), _
            False), DataObjectCompanionAttribute())
        If coAttrs IsNot Nothing AndAlso coAttrs.Length > 0 Then
            ' Iterate over each instance of the attribute.
            For Each coAttr As DataObjectCompanionAttribute In coAttrs
                ' Create an item in the DataValidators dictionary, if necessary.
                If Not Me.DataCompanions.ContainsKey(coAttr.TypeName) Then
                    Me.DataCompanions.Add(coAttr.TypeName, New List(Of Type))
                End If
                ' Add this validator to the list.
                Me.DataCompanions(coAttr.TypeName).Add(type)
            Next
        End If
    Next
End Sub
```

The Create method is invoked by client applications when they need a data object for a specific database table:

```
Public Function Create(ByVal table As String) As IDataObject
    If Not Me.DataObjects.ContainsKey(table.ToLower()) Then
        Throw New ArgumentException("Table not found: " & table)
    End If
    ' Create an instance of the corresponding data object.
    Dim type As Type = Me.DataObjects(table.ToLower())
    Dim dataObj As IDataObject = DirectCast( _
        Activator.CreateInstance(type, True), IDataObject)

    ' Add all data companions that are associated with this specific data object.
    If Me.DataCompanions.ContainsKey(type.FullName) Then
        ' Create an instance of each validator associated with this data object
        ' and add the validator to the Validators collection.
        For Each coType As Type In Me.DataCompanions(type.FullName)
            Dim compObj As IDataObjectCompanion = DirectCast( _
                Activator.CreateInstance(coType, True), IDataObjectCompanion)
            dataObj.Companions.Add(compObj)
        Next
    End If

    ' Add data companions that are associated with all data objects.
    If Me.DataCompanions.ContainsKey("") Then
        ' Create an instance of each validator associated with this data object
        ' and add the validator to the Validators collection.
        For Each coType As Type In Me.DataCompanions("")
            Dim compObj As IDataObjectCompanion = DirectCast( _
                Activator.CreateInstance(coType, True), IDataObjectCompanion)
            dataObj.Companions.Add(compObj)
        Next
```

```
        End If
        Return dataObj
    End Function
End Class          ' End of DataObjectFactory type.
```

In practice, a client application must create an instance of the DataObjectFactory type for a given configuration and then invoke the Create method when a new data object is needed. The Create method instantiates the data object associated with the configuration/table combination, creates all the data companions that should be associated with that data object, and finally returns the data object to the client:

```
' (In a client application…)
' Prepare a list of all data objects in the application's folder.
Dim factory As New DataObjectFactory("Access", Application.StartupPath)

Sub PerformQuery()
    ' Create a data object for the Customers database table that
    ' knows how to deal with NWINDDataSet objects.
    Dim doCustomers As IDataObject(Of NWINDDataSet) = _
        DirectCast(factory.Create("Customers"), IDataObject(Of NWINDDataSet))
    …
End Sub
```

If you have your data objects spread in more than one DLL, you can call the AddDataObjects method, one for each DLL.

The DataObjectCommand Type

The DataObjectCommand type is a repository for storing information about an operation that a data object must perform. It contains only fields and one constructor.

```
Public Class DataObjectCommand
    ' The name of this command
    Public ReadOnly Name As String
    ' The list of child tables to be included in the fill/update command
    Public ReadOnly ChildTables As New List(Of String)
    ' The value of key column. (This version supports only one key column.)
    Public ReadOnly KeyValue As Object
    ' True if this command has been canceled (by a data companion)
    Public Canceled As Boolean

    Sub New(ByVal name As String, ByVal keyValue As Object, _
            ByVal ParamArray childTables() As String)
        Me.Name = name
        Me.KeyValue = keyValue
        If childTables IsNot Nothing Then Me.ChildTables.AddRange(childTables)
    End Sub
End Class
```

The DataObjectCommand type adds a lot of flexibility to the CAP framework. Thanks to this type, data objects simply need to expose two methods, Fill and Update, which can execute virtually all the operations you typically perform on a database. Each method can behave differently, depending on the values you pass through the DataObjectCommand argument. For example, the Fill method can read an entire table or just one row, depending on whether you've assigned a value to the KeyValue property, and might return the rows in child tables as well, if you have passed the name of one or more child tables.

```
' (In a client application…)
' Create a data object for the Customers database table that
' knows how to deal with NWINDDataSet objects.
Dim doCustomers As IDataObject(Of NWINDDataSet) = _
   DirectCast(factory.Create("Customers"), IDataObject(Of NWINDDataSet))
' Create a command that reads the entire Customers table (no key specified)
' and also retrieves the Orders child table.
Dim command As New DataObjectCommand("GetCustomers", Nothing, "Orders")
' Use the data object to fill a local DataSet.
doCustomers.Fill(Me.NwindDataSet1, command)
```

A crucial feature of the CAP framework is that all companion objects can inspect the Data-ObjectCommand that has been passed to the Fill or Update method, both before and after the actual data operation is performed. In the "before" phase, a companion object can set the command's Cancel property to True and indirectly prevent the command from being carried out. Later in this chapter, I show you how you can use this feature to implement a caching mechanism: in that case, the companion object fills the DataSet with data taken from the cache, and then sets the Cancel property to False to notify the data object that it doesn't have to actually extract data from the database. A common operation you can perform either in the "before read" or in the "after read" phase is setting a filter on the data being read to ensure that each user can see only the data he or she is allowed to see. You often use the "before write" phase to validate all data one instant before it is written to the database.

The DataObjectHelper Type

The last type in the CAP framework is simply a container for static helper methods. You can use this helper object to reduce the amount of code inside individual data objects.

```
Public Class DataObjectHelper
   Public Shared Function BeforeFill(ByVal obj As IDataObject, ByVal ds As DataSet, _
         ByVal command As DataObjectCommand) As Boolean
      For Each companion As IDataObjectCompanion In obj.Companions
         companion.BeforeFill(obj, ds, command)
      Next
      Return Not command.Canceled
   End Function

   Public Shared Function BeforeUpdate(ByVal obj As IDataObject, ByVal ds As DataSet, _
         ByVal command As DataObjectCommand) As Boolean
      For Each companion As IDataObjectCompanion In obj.Companions
         companion.BeforeUpdate(obj, ds, command)
      Next
      Return Not command.Canceled
   End Function
```

```
    Public Shared Function AfterFill(ByVal obj As IDataObject, ByVal ds As DataSet, _
        ByVal command As DataObjectCommand) As Boolean
      For Each companion As IDataObjectCompanion In obj.Companions
        companion.AfterFill(obj, ds, command)
      Next
      Return Not command.Canceled
    End Function

    Public Shared Function AfterUpdate(ByVal obj As IDataObject, ByVal ds As DataSet, _
        ByVal command As DataObjectCommand) As Boolean
      For Each companion As IDataObjectCompanion In obj.Companions
        companion.AfterUpdate(obj, ds, command)
      Next
      Return Not command.Canceled
    End Function
End Class
```

In practice, each method in this class notifies all the companions of a data object that a
Before*Xxxx* or After*Xxxx* step has been reached, and it returns True if no companion object
has canceled the command. Thanks to this helper class, the code in the data object can be
simplified remarkably:

```
' (Inside a data object...)
Public Function Fill(ByVal ds As NWINDDataSet, ByVal command As DataObjectCommand) _
        As NWINDDataSet Implements IDataObject(Of NWINDDataSet).Fill
    ' Notify all companion objects that the Fill command is about to be executed.
    If DataObjectHelper.BeforeFill(Me, ds, command) Then
        ' Execute the Fill command. (No companion object has canceled it.)
        ...
    End If
    ' Notify all companion objects that the Fill command has been completed.
    DataObjectHelper.AfterFill(Me, ds, command)
    Return ds
End Function

Public Function Update(ByVal ds As NWINDDataSet, ByVal command As DataObjectCommand) _
        As NWINDDataSet Implements IDataObject(Of NWINDDataSet).Update
    ' Notify all companion objects that the Update command is about to be executed.
    If DataObjectHelper.BeforeUpdate(Me, ds, command) Then
        ' Execute the Update command. (No companion object has canceled it.)
        ...
    End If
    ' Notify all companion objects that the Update command has been completed.
    DataObjectHelper.AfterUpdate(Me, ds, command)
    Return ds
End Function
```

The DataSets Project

The next step in building a data-centric application based on the CAP framework is creating
a separate DLL project where you define one or more strong-typed DataSet types. Keeping
your DataSets in a separate project is necessary because both the main application and the

various DLLs that contain data objects and companion objects must have a reference to these shared DataSet types.

The demo solution contains an assembly named DataSets, which contains one DataSet type named NWINDDataSet, which is shaped after the NWIND.MDB Microsoft Access database. (I use this database because chances are that you already have it on your computer; if not, it comes with the companion code for this book.) I am using Access only for the sake of simplicity: *n*-tiered applications typically work with enterprise-sized database engines such as SQL Server or Oracle.

The whole point in using data objects is the ability to keep the code in the main application completely separate from the data access code so that you can easily migrate this sample application to use a different database engine. For this reason, you should look at the NWINDDataSet type only as a container for data, not as a sort of in-memory database that exactly mirrors the structure of a real database. As I noted previously, a data object doesn't necessarily interact with a database and can read from and write to other data stores, such as XML files.

You can create the NWINDDataSet type in Visual Studio 2005 very simply. Select the Add New Data Source command from the Data menu to open the Data Source Configuration Wizard. In the first step, select the Database option and click Next; in the second step, click the New Connection button to create a new OLE DB connection that points to the NWIND.MDB file. When you click Next, Visual Studio asks whether you want to include the .mdb file in the project folder: answer No, because the NWINDDataSet type should have no direct relation to the database you're using, as I just emphasized. In the next step, accept that you want to save the connection string in the application's configuration file. (See Figure 19-5.) In the fourth and last steps, select which tables you want to include in the DataSet. In this demo, you can just select the Customers, Orders, and Order Details tables.

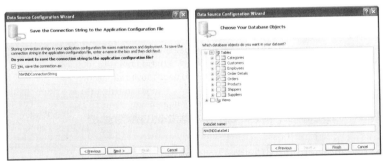

Figure 19-5 Two steps in the Data Source Configuration Wizard

When you click the Finish button, Visual Studio creates the file NWINDDataSet.xsd, which contains the schema of the new DataSet. You can double-click this file in the Solution Explorer to view the graphical representation of all the tables in the DataSet and their relations. (See Figure 19-6.) In Microsoft Visual Studio .NET 2003, you had to add table relationships by hand.

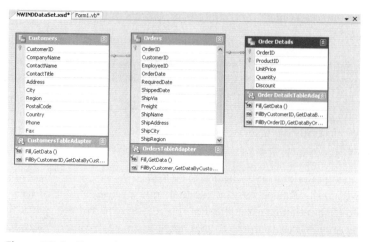

Figure 19-6 For each DataTable in the DataSet, you can define one or more custom commands, such as FillByCustomerID.

Each DataTable type in the DataSet has a companion TableAdapter object, which enables you to read data from and write data to that table by means of methods named Fill, GetData, and Update. In addition to these standard methods, you can define your own queries by right-clicking a table in the .xsd schema, pointing to Add, and selecting Query. For example, the sample code requires that you add a query named FillByCustomerID. In the first step of the TableAdapter Query Configuration Wizard, you decide whether you want to retrieve data using an SQL statement or a stored procedure; if you're using an Access database, only the first option is available. In the second step, you select which type of query you want to perform; for this demo, choose the Select Which Returns Rows option. In the next step, type the SQL statement that returns data, for example, a parameterized query that returns a single record:

```
SELECT CustomerID, CompanyName, ContactName, ContactTitle, Address, City,
    Region, PostalCode, Country, Phone, Fax FROM Customers WHERE CustomerID=?
```

(Use an argument name prefixed with the at sign (@) if you're accessing a SQL Server database.) In the fourth step, assign a name to the FillXxxx and GetDataXxxx commands you are creating (FillByCustomerID and GetDataByCustomerID, in this specific example). Finally, click the Finish button to generate the custom TableAdapter commands. (See Figure 19-7.)

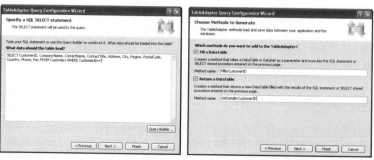

Figure 19-7 Two steps of the TableAdapter Query Configuration Wizard

Note   Although I love the power of TableAdapters and their custom commands, I can't help but notice that the Microsoft decision to generate TableAdapter types in the same assembly as the DataSet type they refer to is a rather questionable design choice that makes TableAdapters less useful in enterprise-level *n*-tiered applications. In such applications, TableAdapter objects shouldn't be located in the same assembly where the DataSet is defined because this arrangement prevents each data object from using a TableAdapter object that is specific for a given database.

In this demo program, we leave the TableAdapters as nested classes of the NWINDDataSet type. In a real application, however, you should cut the TableAdapter code from that type and paste it into the same assembly where the data objects for that specific database are located. Of course, you'll also need to update all the Imports statements to ensure that all the TableAdapter commands continue to work correctly even if they now reference a DataSet in a different assembly.

The DemoClient Project

Even if you haven't defined any data objects so far, already you can create a client application that will use them. In fact, the client application doesn't need any direct reference to the assembly that contains your data objects. More precisely, the application should *not* have such a reference because clients must be completely independent of the actual data objects. If you don't create a dependency between the client and a specific data object, you can later replace a new set of DAL objects to match a different database or network configuration.

Create a new Windows Forms project named DemoClient and ensure it has a reference to the DataObjectLibrary and DataSets projects. Open the Data section of the Toolbox, drop a DataSet component onto the form's designer, specify DataSets.NWINDDataSet as the typed DataSet, and name it NwindDataSet1. Next, drop two BindingSource components onto the form, name them bsCustomers and bsCustomerOrders, and set their properties as follows:

```
bsCustomers.DataSource = NwindDataSet1
bsCustomers.DataMember = Customers
bsCustomersOrders.DataSource = bsCustomers
bsCustomersOrders.DataMember = CustomersOrders
```

Create a very simple user interface by dropping a couple of buttons and two DataGridView controls on the main form, as shown in Figure 19-8. Set the DataSource property of the topmost DataGridView equal to bsCustomers and the DataSource property of the bottommost DataGridView equal to bsCustomersOrders. Finally, enter this code in the form's class:

```
' Look for all the data objects in the application's folder.
Dim factory As New DataObjectFactory("Access", Application.StartupPath)

Private Sub btnFill_Click(ByVal sender As Object, ByVal e As EventArgs) _
      Handles btnFill.Click
   Dim doCustomers As IDataObject(Of NWINDDataSet) = _
      DirectCast(factory.Create("Customers"), IDataObject(Of NWINDDataSet))
```

```
Dim command As New DataObjectCommand("GetCustomers", Nothing, "Orders")
doCustomers.Fill(Me.NwindDataSet1, command)
End Sub

Private Sub btnUpdate_Click(ByVal sender As Object, ByVal e As EventArgs) _
    Handles btnUpdate.Click
    Dim doCustomers As IDataObject(Of NWINDDataSet) = _
        DirectCast(factory.Create("Customers"), IDataObject(Of NWINDDataSet))
    Dim command As New DataObjectCommand("UpdateCustomers", Nothing, "Orders")
    doCustomers.Update(Me.NwindDataSet1, command)
End Sub
```

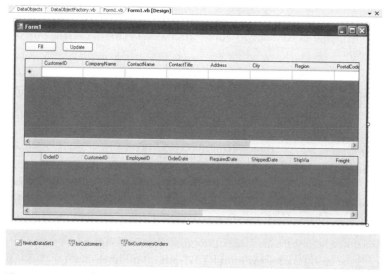

Figure 19-8 The main form of the DemoClient project

I commented on this code in the section titled "The DataObjectCommand Type" earlier in this chapter. Just notice that the client code has no direct reference to the actual data object: it uses a DataObjectFactory to get a data object that works with the specified configuration/table combination, it specifies a data command in a generic way, and finally it interacts with the data object by means of the IDataObject(Of T) generic interface.

Compile the DemoClient project to ensure that everything is in place, but don't run it yet because it won't work until you define at least one data object for the "Access" configuration.

The DataObjects Project

Create a new Class Library project named DataObjects and ensure that the output directory for this project matches the output directory of the main application. This build configuration simulates what happens in a real-world application when you deploy a DLL holding one or more data objects in the main application's folder.

The DOCustomers Type

A data object is a class that implements the IDataObject(Of T) generic interface and that is marked with the DataObject custom attribute. For example, the following data object is used under the configuration named "Access" and can access the database table named "Customers":

```
<DataObject("Access", "Customers")> _
Public Class DOCustomers
   Implements IDataObject(Of NWINDDataSet)

   ' The IDataObject interface
   Private m_Companions As New List(Of IDataObjectCompanion)

   Public ReadOnly Property Companions() As List(Of IDataObjectCompanion) _
         Implements IDataObject.Companions
      Get
         Return m_Companions
      End Get
   End Property

   ' The IDataObject(Of TDataSet) interface
   Public Function Fill(ByVal ds As NWINDDataSet, ByVal command As DataObjectCommand) _
      As NWINDDataSet Implements IDataObject(Of NWINDDataSet).Fill
      …
   End Function

   Public Function Update(ByVal ds As NWINDDataSet, ByVal command As DataObjectCommand) _
      As NWINDDataSet Implements IDataObject(Of NWINDDataSet).Update
      …
   End Function
End Class
```

The main application invokes the Fill method to read one or more database tables into the DataSet. The DOCustomer object is expected to read data from the database and fill one or more tables of the DataSet passed in the first argument. The data object learns which child tables to read, if any, by looking at the ChildTable collection of the DataObjectCommand passed in the second argument. (Corresponding statements in the following listing are in bold type.) Before actually reading any data, however, the data object notifies its companion objects that an operation is about to be performed:

```
Public Function Fill(ByVal ds As NWINDDataSet, ByVal command As DataObjectCommand) _
      As NWINDDataSet Implements IDataObject(Of NWINDDataSet).Fill
   If ds Is Nothing Then ds = New NWINDDataSet()
   If DataObjectHelper.BeforeFill(Me, ds, command) Then
      Dim taCustomers As New NWINDDataSetTableAdapters.CustomersTableAdapter
      taCustomers.Fill(ds.Customers)
      If command.ChildTables.Contains("Orders") Then
         Dim taOrders As New NWINDDataSetTableAdapters.OrdersTableAdapter
         taOrders.Fill(ds.Orders)
      End If
   End If
   DataObjectHelper.AfterFill(Me, ds, command)
   Return ds
End Function
```

You can easily enhance the DOCustomer type to support additional commands. For example, this data object might be able to read data about individual customers and their orders:

```
' (Replace the bold section of previous listing with this code.)
Dim customerId As String = ""
If command.KeyValue IsNot Nothing Then customerId = command.KeyValue.ToString()

Dim taCustomers As New NWINDDataSetTableAdapters.CustomersTableAdapter
If customerId.Length = 0 Then
   taCustomers.Fill(ds.Customers)
Else
   taCustomers.FillByCustomerID(ds.Customers, customerId)
End If

If command.ChildTables.Contains("Orders") Then
   Dim taOrders As New NWINDDataSetTableAdapters.OrdersTableAdapter
   If customerId.Length = 0 Then
      taOrders.Fill(ds.Orders)
   Else
      taOrders.FillByCustomerID(ds.Orders, customerId)
   End If
End If
```

Typically, the Update method is simpler and has fewer options. Here's an implementation of this method that writes the Customers table and, optionally, the Orders child table. This code splits in two parts the updates to the Customers table—first it inserts the new records and then it removes the deleted records—to not break the referential integrity of the records that take part in the Customers_Orders relation:

```
Public Function Update(ByVal ds As NWINDDataSet, ByVal command As DataObjectCommand) _
   As NWINDDataSet Implements IDataObject(Of NWINDDataSet).Update
   If DataObjectHelper.BeforeUpdate(Me, ds, command) Then
      Dim taCustomers As New NWINDDataSetTableAdapters.CustomersTableAdapter
      ' Send new and modified rows to the database.
      taCustomers.Update(ds.Customers.Select(Nothing, Nothing, _
         DataViewRowState.Added Or DataViewRowState.ModifiedCurrent))
      ' Update the child table, if so requested.
      If command.ChildTables.Contains("Orders") Then
         Dim taOrders As New NWINDDataSetTableAdapters.OrdersTableAdapter
         taOrders.Update(ds.Orders)
      End If
      ' Remove deleted records from the database.
      taCustomers.Update(ds.Customers.Select(Nothing, Nothing, DataViewRowState.Deleted))
   End If
   DataObjectHelper.AfterUpdate(Me, ds, command)
   Return ds
End Function
```

A more robust implementation should account for other relations that exist in the database. For example, you can't delete a row in the Orders table if you don't delete all the rows in the Order Details table that are related to that specific order. Also, a real-world data object should perform all the updates under a transaction so that all changes can be rolled back if an error occurs during the process.

At this point, you can compile the entire solution and run the DemoClient application. If you didn't make any mistakes, the application should be able to view and modify any record in the Customers and the Orders tables. Once you're sure that everything is working as expected, you can begin building a few companion objects for the DOCustomer type.

Data object companions can be located in the same assembly as the data objects they refer to or in a separate assembly. In the demo solution, I opted for the first approach to keep the number of projects as low as possible, but in most real-world cases you should put them in their own assembly.

The Tracer Companion Type

The simplest data object companion you can build is a tracer component, which displays details of all the operations being performed on data. Such a tracer component can work with any data object; thus, the first argument in the DataObjectCompanion attribute that marks it can be an empty string:

```
<DataObjectCompanion("")> _
Public Class Tracer
   Implements IDataObjectCompanion

   Public Sub BeforeFill(ByVal obj As IDataObject, ByVal ds As DataSet, _
        ByVal command As DataObjectCommand) _
        Implements IDataObjectCompanion.BeforeFill
     Console.WriteLine("[{0}] BeforeFill - Command:{1}", _
        CObj(obj).GetType().Name, command.Name)
   End Sub

   Public Sub BeforeUpdate(ByVal obj As IDataObject, ByVal ds As DataSet, _
        ByVal command As DataObjectCommand) _
        Implements IDataObjectCompanion.BeforeUpdate
     Console.WriteLine("[{0}] BeforeUpdate - Command:{1}", _
        CObj(obj).GetType().Name, command.Name)
   End Sub

   Public Sub AfterFill(ByVal obj As IDataObject, ByVal ds As DataSet, _
        ByVal command As DataObjectCommand) _
        Implements IDataObjectCompanion.AfterFill
     Console.WriteLine("[{0}] AfterFill - Command:{1}", _
         CObj(obj).GetType().Name, command.Name)
   End Sub

   Public Sub AfterUpdate(ByVal obj As IDataObject, ByVal ds As DataSet, _
        ByVal command As DataObjectCommand) _
        Implements IDataObjectCompanion.AfterUpdate
     Console.WriteLine("[{0}] AfterUpdate - Command:{1}", _
        CObj(obj).GetType().Name, command.Name)
   End Sub
End Class
```

Recompile the DataObjects.dll, run again the DemoClient, and test the read and update commands: you should see the various diagnostic messages in the Visual Studio console window. (Needless to say, a real tracer object should send its output to a debugger or a file.)

The CustomerCache Companion Type

The second companion type in the DataObjects project is far more interesting in that it enables you to cache the result of a query on a local file transparently so that the actual database isn't accessed too often. Thanks to the CAP framework's infrastructure, such a caching feature can be achieved with very little code. First, define a user-level setting named CacheFile and assign it the path to the cache file you want to create, for example, c:\CustomersCache .xml. Next, enter this code:

```vb
<DataObjectCompanion("DataObjects.DOCustomers")> _
Public Class CustomerCache
    Implements IDataObjectCompanion

    ' The location of the cache file is stored in the application's config file.
    Dim cacheFile As String = My.Settings.CacheFile

    Public Sub AfterFill(ByVal obj As IDataObject, ByVal ds As DataSet, _
        ByVal command As DataObjectCommand) _
        Implements IDataObjectCompanion.AfterFill
      If command.ChildTables.Contains("Orders") And Not command.Canceled Then
        SaveToCache(ds)
      End If
    End Sub

    Public Sub AfterUpdate(ByVal obj As IDataObject, ByVal ds As DataSet, _
        ByVal command As DataObjectCommand) _
        Implements IDataObjectCompanion.AfterUpdate
      If command.ChildTables.Contains("Orders") And Not command.Canceled Then
        SaveToCache(ds)
      End If
    End Sub

    Public Sub BeforeFill(ByVal obj As IDataObject, ByVal ds As DataSet, _
        ByVal command As DataObjectCommand) _
        Implements IDataObjectCompanion.BeforeFill
      ' If the cached file has already been saved today, use cached data.
      If File.Exists(cacheFile) AndAlso File.GetCreationTime(cacheFile).Date = Date.Today Then
        LoadFromCache(ds)
        ' Let the data objects know that the command has been canceled.
        command.Canceled = True
      End If
    End Sub

    Public Sub BeforeUpdate(ByVal obj As IDataObject, ByVal ds As DataSet, _
        ByVal command As DataObjectCommand) _
        Implements IDataObjectCompanion.BeforeUpdate
      ' Nothing to do.
    End Sub

    ' Save and load from the cache.
    Private Sub SaveToCache(ByVal ds As DataSet)
      Console.WriteLine("Dataset is being saved to {0}", cacheFile)
      ds.RemotingFormat = SerializationFormat.Binary
```

```
    Using fs As New FileStream(cacheFile, FileMode.Create)
        Dim bf As New BinaryFormatter
        bf.Serialize(fs, ds)
    End Using
End Sub

Private Sub LoadFromCache(ByVal ds As DataSet)
    Console.WriteLine("Dataset is being loaded from {0}", cacheFile)
    ds.RemotingFormat = SerializationFormat.Binary
    Using fs As New FileStream(cacheFile, FileMode.Open)
        Dim bf As New BinaryFormatter
        Dim ds2 As DataSet = DirectCast(bf.Deserialize(fs), DataSet)
        ds.Merge(ds2)
    End Using
End Sub
End Class
```

The companion object checks the creation date of the cache file in the BeforeFill method, and then, if the cache file has been created on the same day, the DataSet is filled with data taken from the local file and the command is canceled. Other companion objects can check the command's Canceled property and decide whether they should perform their intended action. For example, the Tracer companion might output a message that makes it clear that the default command has been canceled.

The CustomerFilter Companion Type

The last companion type I show is a filter that automatically removes from the DataSet all the records that the current client shouldn't see and that ensures that records being written to the database meet specific criteria. In this particular example, the CustomerFilter class displays only customers who are located in Germany (see Figure 19-9), but of course you can expand the code as you prefer:

```
<DataObjectCompanion("DataObjects.DOCustomers")> _
Public Class CustomerFilter
    Implements IDataObjectCompanion

    Public Country As String = "Germany"

    Public Sub AfterFill(ByVal obj As IDataObject, ByVal ds As DataSet, _
            ByVal command As DataObjectCommand) _
            Implements IDataObjectCompanion.AfterFill
        Dim ds2 As NWINDDataSet = DirectCast(ds, NWINDDataSet)
        ' Remove all customers not in the specified country.
        For i As Integer = ds2.Customers.Rows.Count - 1 To 0 Step -1
            If ds2.Customers(i).Country <> Country Then
                ' Remove this row from the result.
                ds2.Customers.Rows.RemoveAt(i)
            End If
        Next
    End Sub
```

```
Public Sub BeforeUpdate(ByVal obj As IDataObject, ByVal ds As DataSet, _
      ByVal command As DataObjectCommand) _
      Implements IDataObjectCompanion.BeforeUpdate
   Dim ds2 As NWINDDataSet = DirectCast(ds, NWINDDataSet)
   For Each custRow As NWINDDataSet.CustomersRow In ds2.Customers.GetChanges().Rows
      If custRow.Country <> Country Then
         Throw New Exception("Records must have Country = " & Country)
      End If
   Next
End Sub

Public Sub AfterUpdate(ByVal obj As IDataObject, ByVal ds As DataSet, _
      ByVal command As DataObjectCommand) _
      Implements IDataObjectCompanion.AfterUpdate
   ' Nothing to do.
End Sub

Public Sub BeforeFill(ByVal obj As IDataObject, ByVal ds As DataSet, _
      ByVal command As DataObjectCommand) _
      Implements IDataObjectCompanion.BeforeFill
   ' Nothing to do.
End Sub
End Class
```

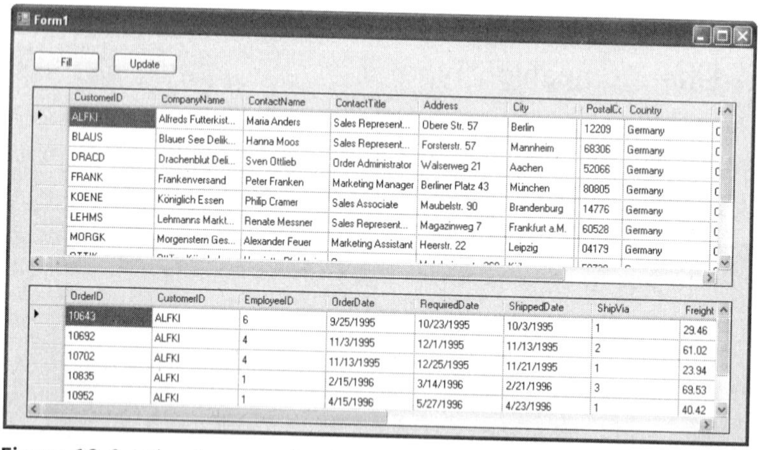

Figure 19-9   The demo application filtering customers by their country

You can improve the CustomerFilter type to support a filter based on an SQL clause that the type would use to modify the Select command. This approach would be far more efficient than reading all the data and discarding those pieces you aren't interested in is.

The GenericFilter Companion Type

The CustomerFilter type always filters in only customers that reside in Germany, which is a rather unrealistic assumption. A more useful filter class should let client applications decide which filter should be applied. In general, a companion object might require that the client application provide one or more values to its constructor. In this case, the client application should instantiate the companion object directly, initialize its properties, and then add it to the data object's Companions collection:

```
Dim doCustomers As IDataObject(Of NWINDDataSet) = _
    DirectCast(factory.Create("Customers"), IDataObject(Of NWINDDataSet))
' Add a companion filter that filters in only customers whose City is Berlin.
doCustomers.Companions.Add(New GenericFilter("Customers", "City", "Berlin"))
```

Obviously, the previous code works only if the main client has a reference to the assembly where the GenericFilter type is defined.

A companion object meant to be instantiated directly by the client application shouldn't be marked by a DataObjectCompanion attribute because this attribute would force the CAP framework to instantiate the attribute directly, and such instantiation would fail if the constructor takes one or more arguments. The following code shows how such a companion object can be implemented:

```
Public Class GenericFilter
    Implements IDataObjectCompanion

    Public ReadOnly TableName As String
    Public ReadOnly FieldName As String
    Public ReadOnly FieldValue As Object

    Public Sub New(ByVal tableName As String, ByVal fieldName As String, _
            ByVal fieldValue As Object)
        Me.TableName = tableName
        Me.FieldName = fieldName
        Me.FieldValue = fieldValue
    End Sub

    Public Sub AfterFill(ByVal obj As IDataObject, ByVal ds As DataSet, _
            ByVal command As DataObjectCommand) _
            Implements IDataObjectCompanion.AfterFill
        Dim dt As DataTable = ds.Tables(TableName)
        ' Remove all rows that don't match the condition.
        For i As Integer = dt.Rows.Count - 1 To 0 Step -1
            If Not dt.Rows(i)(FieldName).Equals(FieldValue) Then
                dt.Rows.RemoveAt(i)
            End If
        Next
    End Sub

    Public Sub BeforeUpdate(ByVal obj As IDataObject, ByVal ds As DataSet, _
            ByVal command As DataObjectCommand) _
            Implements IDataObjectCompanion.BeforeUpdate
        Dim dt As DataTable = ds.Tables(TableName)
        ' Check that all rows match the filter condition.
        For Each row As DataRow In dt.GetChanges().Rows
            If Not row(FieldName).Equals(FieldValue) Then
                Throw New Exception("Record doesn't match the filter criteria")
            End If
        Next
    End Sub
```

```
' AfterFill and AfterUpdate methods contain no statements.
    ...
End Class
```

By now you should be convinced that companion objects can add a nearly unlimited degree of flexibility to your data-centric applications. Here are a few suggestions:

- Use the BeforeUpdate method to fix values that are out of the valid range.

- Implement sophisticated security and audit rules, for example, to prevent certain users from accessing data outside the normal working hours, and log all such attempts.

- Keep a log of queries that take longer so that you can later fine-tune the application or add new indexes to the database.

- Send an e-mail to a supervisor when data with exceptionally high or low values is entered, for example, when an employee enters an order with a value higher than a given threshold.

- Build more sophisticated caching policies than those adopted by the sample Customer-Cache type.

You might also consider the opportunity to extend the CAP framework with more features. For example, the DataObjectCommand type might support additional properties to specify whether a transaction is requested or already exists, whether data pagination is requested, and so forth.

Chapter 20

Threads

If you don't look closely at the Microsoft Windows architecture, you might think that the operating system allocates CPU time to processes so that they can execute at the same time, even on single-CPU systems. The truth is, CPU time is allocated to threads, not processes. You can think of threads as independent execution paths, which can access resources such as memory. Processes, on the other hand, are passive containers for running threads, even though they have many other interesting features, such as the ability to allocate resources and provide a linear address space where you can store your variables and arrays.

Note To avoid long lines, code samples in this chapter assume that the following Imports statements are used at the file or project level:

```
Imports System.ComponentModel
Imports System.Diagnostics
Imports System.IO
Imports System.Reflection
Imports System.Runtime.CompilerServices
Imports System.Runtime.Remoting.Messaging
Imports System.Security.AccessControl
Imports System.Security.Principal
Imports System.Threading
```

Threading Fundamentals

The Windows operating system allows *preemptive multitasking*, which means a thread can be suspended at almost any time and another thread can be given CPU time. This contrasts with *cooperative multitasking*, allowed by versions of the Windows operating system through 3.1, in which each thread must explicitly ask for suspension. As you can imagine, cooperative multitasking makes the operating system more fragile because a thread crash affects the entire system.

When to Use Threads

Each thread maintains a private set of structures (the thread context) that the operating system uses to save information when the thread isn't running, including the values of CPU registers at the time when the thread was suspended and the processor was allocated to another thread. A thread also maintains its own exception handlers and a priority level. For example, you can assign higher priority to threads that manage the user interface (so that they're more responsive) and lower priority to threads for less urgent tasks, such as background printing. In all cases, the time slice allocated to each thread is relatively short, so the end user has the perception that all the threads (and all the applications) run concurrently.

The thread scheduler—that is, the portion of the operating system that schedules existing threads and preempts the running thread when its time slice expires—takes some CPU time for its own chores. Moreover, the operating system consumes some memory to keep the context of each thread, be it active or temporarily suspended. For this reason, if too many threads are active at the same time, this scheduling activity can take a significant amount of time and can degrade the overall performance, leaving less spare time to worker threads (the threads that do something useful). So, you should never create more threads than strictly necessary, or you should use threads taken from the thread pool, as I explain later in this chapter.

You might want to create additional threads to perform operations such as asynchronous file or database I/O, communication with a remote machine or a Web server, or low-priority background jobs. You make the most of multithreading when you allocate distinct threads to tasks that have different priorities or that take a lot of time to complete. Before opting for a multithreading application, you should consider available alternatives, such as using timers to schedule recurring tasks or taking advantage of the Application.Idle event in Windows Forms applications.

The main problem with threads is that they can compete for shared resources, where a resource can be as simple as a variable or as complex as a database connection or a hardware device. You must synchronize access to such resources—otherwise, you can get into trouble, for reasons that will be clear shortly. Microsoft Visual Basic provides the SyncLock construct to help you deal with these problems, and the Microsoft .NET Framework offers several synchronization objects. The key to effective multithreading is learning how to use these features properly.

Creating Threads

The System.Threading.Thread class offers all the methods and properties you need to create and manage threads. To create a new thread, you simply instantiate a new Thread object and then invoke its Start method. The Thread type's constructor requires one argument, a ThreadStart delegate object that points to the method that runs when the thread starts. In Microsoft .NET Framework version 1.1, such a method had to be a Sub without any arguments; in .NET Framework version 2.0, the method can have zero or one object argument.

The following Visual Basic application spawns a second thread that prints some messages to the console window:

```
Sub RunThread()
    ' Create a new thread and define its starting point.
    Dim t As New Thread(New ThreadStart(AddressOf RunThread_Task))
    ' Run the new thread.
    t.Start()

    ' Print some messages to the console window.
    For i As Integer = 1 to 10
        Console.WriteLine("Msg #{0} from main thread", i)
        ' Wait for 0.2 seconds.
        Thread.Sleep(200)
    Next
End Sub

Sub RunThread_Task()
    For i As Integer = 1 To 10
        Console.WriteLine("Msg #{0} from secondary thread", i)
        ' Wait for 0.2 seconds.
        Thread.Sleep(200)
    Next
End Sub
```

The console window will contain intermixed messages from both the main and the secondary threads, evidence that they are running independently. You can omit the explicit instantiation of the ThreadStart delegate because the Visual Basic compiler can infer the delegate type by looking at the signature of the target method:

```
' Create a new thread and define its starting point.
Dim t As New Thread(AddressOf RunThread_Task)
```

The Start method is asynchronous in the sense that it might return before the spawned thread has actually started its execution. A thread terminates when its main method (RunThread_Task, in this case) exits, when an unhandled exception occurs, or when the thread is programmatically killed by a Thread.Abort method. The application as a whole terminates only when all its threads terminate. You can check how many threads an application has created by using the Windows Task Manager utility, which you can run by using the Ctrl+Shift+Esc shortcut. You must use the Select Columns command on the View menu in the Processes tab and select the Thread Count check box to see this information. (See Figure 20-1.) Interestingly, this utility shows that .NET applications might have additional threads—for example, the thread that manages garbage collections and finalizers—over which you apparently have no control.

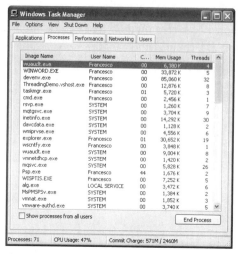

Figure 20-1 The Windows Task Manager utility

Passing Data to and from a Thread

In version 1.1 of the .NET Framework, passing data to a thread and receiving a result from it requires that you write some code because the ThreadStart delegate that the Start method takes as an argument must point to a Sub procedure without arguments. Version 2.0 fixes this serious issue by defining a new delegate named ParameterizedThreadStart, which points to a Sub that takes an Object argument.

The following code shows how the main thread can pass the other thread a value—in this case, the number of iterations of the For loop:

```
Sub RunParameterizedThread()
   Dim t As New Thread(AddressOf RunParameterizedThread_Task)
   ' Specify that we want 20 iterations.
   t.Start(20)
   ...
End Sub

Sub RunParameterizedThread_Task(ByVal obj As Object)
   For i As Integer = 1 To CInt(obj)
      Console.WriteLine("Msg #{0} from secondary thread", i)
      ' Wait for 0.2 seconds.
      Thread.Sleep(200)
   Next
End Sub
```

If you need to pass multiple arguments to the other thread, you can pass an array of values, or, even better, you can define a class that carries all the values. The latter technique makes for more readable code and is recommended if the secondary thread must return a value to the main thread, as in this case:

```
Private Class ThreadData
   ' Input values
```

```
      Public Iterations As Integer
      Public Message As String
      ' Output values
      Public CurrentIteration As Integer
      Public Done As Boolean
End Class

Sub RunThreadWithObjectArgument()
      ' Create an instance of the ThreadData class and initialize its fields.
      Dim data As New ThreadData()
      data.Iterations = 20
      data.Message = "Msg #{0} from secondary thread"

      ' Run the secondary thread.
      Dim t As New Thread(AddressOf RunThreadWithObjectArgument_Task)
      t.Start(data)
      …
End Sub

Sub RunThreadWithObjectArgument_Task(ByVal obj As Object)
      Dim data As ThreadData = DirectCast(obj, ThreadData)
      For i As Integer = 1 To data.Iterations
          Console.WriteLine(data.Message, i)
          data.CurrentIteration = i
          Thread.Sleep(200)
      Next
      ' Set the Done flag.
      data.Done = True
End Sub
```

The ThreadData instance is accessible from both threads, and therefore it can be used to exchange information in the two directions. In this specific example, the main thread can query the CurrentIteration to learn how many messages the other thread has displayed in the console window and can test the Done field to check whether the other thread has terminated its execution:

```
' (In the main thread…)
' Wait until the other thread has reached the 10th iteration.
Do Until data.CurrentIteration >= 10
    Thread.Sleep(100)
Loop
```

Unfortunately, this code might not work well in all circumstances because whenever an object can be accessed by multiple threads—as is the case with the ThreadData object—race conditions might arise. You can read more about this topic in the section titled "Storing and Sharing Data" later in this chapter.

Working with Threads

To manipulate a Windows thread, you need a reference to the corresponding Thread object. This can be a reference to a new thread or a reference to the current thread—that is, the thread that is running the code—which you get by using the Thread.CurrentThread static method.

Once you have a reference to a Thread object, you can read or set its properties or abort it using members of the Thread class.

```
' Define and start a new thread.
Dim t As New Thread(AddressOf TheTask)
t.Start()
…
' Abort the thread.
t.Abort()
```

As I explained earlier, a thread naturally terminates when it reaches the Exit or End statement of its main procedure, but it also can be aborted by another thread (or by itself) by means of the Abort method. Like the Start method, the Abort method is asynchronous in the sense that it doesn't abort the thread immediately (unless you call the method for the current thread). In fact, threads can be aborted only when they reach a safe point. In general, a *safe point* is a point in time when it's safe to perform a garbage collection—for example, when a method call returns.

The CLR has several ways to control when a thread reaches a safe point for a garbage collection. It can, for example, *hijack* the thread: when the thread is making a call to a class in the framework, the CLR pushes an extra return address (which points to a location in the CLR itself) onto the call stack. Then, when the method call completes, the CLR can take control and decide whether it's time to perform a garbage collection or to abort the thread if there's a pending Abort method.

There's another reason the Abort method doesn't immediately halt a thread. Instead of killing the thread immediately—as is the case with the ExitThread and TerminateThread Windows API functions—the Abort method causes a ThreadAbortException to be thrown in the target thread. This exception is special in that managed code can't catch it. However, if the target thread is executing inside a Try...End Try block, the code in the Finally clause is guaranteed to be executed and the thread is aborted only at the completion of the Finally clause. A thread might even detect that it's being aborted (by means of the ThreadState property, described in the next section) and might continue to run code in the Finally clause to postpone its death. (Trusted code can also cancel an Abort method using the ResetAbort method—see the SDK documentation for additional details.)

 The Thread class also exposes the Suspend and Resume methods, for suspending a thread and resuming the execution of a suspended thread. In .NET Framework 2.0, however, these methods have been deprecated. If you need to synchronize two threads, you should resort to .NET types, such as Mutex or Semaphore, which I illustrate later in this chapter. The reason the Suspend method (and, consequently, its Resume counterpart) has been deprecated is that if a thread is suspended while it is performing a critical section, while it is holding a lock, or while it is executing the static constructor of a type that is also used elsewhere in your application, your entire application might be compromised.

A thread can suspend itself temporarily by using the Thread.Sleep static method, which takes a timeout in milliseconds:

```
' Pause for half a second.
Thread.Sleep(500)
```

The Sleep method works only on the current thread. Using this method is similar to calling the Windows API Sleep function. You can use the special 0 timeout value to terminate the current time slice and relinquish control to the thread scheduler, or you can use the Timeout.Infinite value (−1) to suspend the current thread indefinitely until another thread wakes it up. You can also pass a TimeSpan object to specify the length of the timeout.

It's quite common to wait for a thread to terminate; for example, the main thread can start a worker thread and then continue to execute to the point at which it must ensure that the worker thread has completed its task. You can use the Join method to easily achieve this behavior, as you can see in the following snippet:

```
Dim t As New Thread(AddressOf TheTask)
t.Start()
' …(Do something else.)…
…
' Wait for the other thread to die.
t.Join()
```

The Join method can take an optional timeout, expressed in milliseconds or as a TimeSpan object. The method returns True if the thread died within the specified timeout; it returns False if the method returned because the timeout elapsed:

```
' Wait for the other thread to die, but print a message every second.
Do Until t.Join(1000)
   Console.WriteLine("Waiting for the other thread to die...")
Loop
```

An important note: never call Join on the running thread because this action would cause the current thread to stop forever. If you are in doubt, compare the Thread instance with the current thread before proceeding:

```
' Join a thread only if it's alive and isn't the current thread.
If t.IsAlive AndAlso t IsNot Thread.CurrentThread Then
   t.Join()
End If
```

When a thread calls Sleep on itself or Join on another thread, the calling thread enters the WaitSleepJoin state (see Table 20-1 in the following section). A thread exits this state when the timeout expires or when another thread invokes the Interrupt method on it. When the Interrupt method is called, the target thread receives a ThreadInterruptedException, which must be caught or the thread will be killed. Thus, the following is the typical code that you should write for threads that go to sleep and are waiting for another thread to wake them up:

```
Try
    ' Go to sleep for 10 seconds or until another thread
    ' calls the Interrupt method on this thread.
    Thread.Sleep(10000)
    ' We get here if the timeout elapsed and no exception is thrown.
    ...
Catch e As ThreadInterruptedException
    ' We get here if the thread has been interrupted.
    ...
End Try
```

Thread Properties

You can test whether a thread is active—that is, it has started and isn't dead yet—using the IsAlive read-only property. When it's applied to the current thread, this property always returns True, for obvious reasons.

You can also check the state of any thread—including the current one—by using the Thread-State enumerated property, whose values are summarized in Table 20-1. This is a bit-coded value because a thread can be in more than one state at any given time, so you should test individual bits with the And operator:

```
If CBool(Thread.CurrentThread.ThreadState And ThreadState.StopRequested) Then
    ' The current thread is being stopped.
End If
```

Table 20-1   The Possible Values for the ThreadState Property

State	Description
Aborted	The thread has been aborted.
AbortRequested	The thread is responding to an Abort request.
Background	The thread is running in the background. (Same as the IsBackground property.)
Running	The thread is running. (Another thread has called the Start method.)
Stopped	The thread has been stopped. (A thread can never leave this state.)
StopRequested	The thread is about to stop.
Suspended	The thread has been suspended.
SuspendRequested	The thread is responding to a Suspend request.
Unstarted	The thread has been created, but the Start method hasn't been called yet.
WaitSleepJoin	The thread has called Monitor.Wait or Thread.Join on another thread.

The IsBackground property tells whether a thread is a low-priority background thread. Interestingly, you can change the background state of a thread by assigning True or False to this property before the thread starts:

```
' Make a thread a background thread before starting it.
t.IsBackground = True
t.Start()
```

An important detail: background threads don't keep an application alive, so if your application has created one or more background threads, it should check the IsAlive property of all of them before exiting the main thread. Otherwise, those threads are mercilessly killed, regardless of what they're doing at that moment.

The Priority property offers a different way to affect a thread's priority without making it a background thread. This property sets or returns one of the ThreadPriority enumerated values, which are Normal, AboveNormal, BelowNormal, Highest, or Lowest:

```
' Supercharge the current thread.
Thread.CurrentThread.Priority = ThreadPriority.Highest
```

The Windows operating system can adjust the priority of threads automatically—for example, when an application becomes the foreground application—but changing the priority of a thread through code isn't recommended, so you should do it only for a good reason—for example, to ensure that enough CPU time is assigned to your code even if it runs in the background.

All threads have a Name property. This property is usually a null string, but you can assign it a value for the threads you create. The Name property doesn't change the behavior of a thread, but it turns useful during the debugging phase, as you'll read in the next section. For example, the thread name is reported in the message that the Microsoft Visual Studio 2005 debugger displays when a thread terminates.

The Thread class doesn't expose any property that returns the ID of the underlying Windows physical thread. The reason: a managed thread might map to a Windows fiber (a.k.a. lightweight thread); therefore, they don't have a stable thread ID. This is the case today when a .NET assembly runs inside Microsoft SQL Server and might happen under a future version of the operating system. Under the current version of the Windows operating system, you can retrieve the physical thread ID with a call to the GetCurrentThreadId Windows API function or, even better, by calling the AppDomain.GetCurrentThreadId static property:

```
Dim currThreadId As Integer = AppDomain.GetCurrentThreadId()
```

However, neither technique is recommended, and the GetCurrentThreadId method has been marked as obsolete in .NET Framework 2.0. In the new version of the framework, you can use the Thread.ManagedThreadID read-only property as a thread ID that is stable and is guaranteed not to change during the life of the thread:

```
Dim id As Integer = Thread.CurrentThread.ManagedThreadId
```

Storing and Sharing Data

Whenever you have multiple threads that share data you also need a way to synchronize access to that data. If two threads can access the same variable, you might ensure that they don't change it at the same time because the result isn't a pleasant one. Data sharing and synchronization are always two facets of the same issue.

Local, Class, and Static Variables

The scope of a variable determines whether multiple threads can share it. Threads never share local dynamic variables—that is, variables defined inside a procedure and not marked by the Static keyword—even if the threads happen to be executing inside that procedure at the same moment. The reason is simple: local variables are allocated on the stack. Each thread maintains its own private stack and keeps its own copy of all local dynamic variables, which means that you can't share data among threads using local dynamic variables. The good news is that you don't have to worry about synchronizing access to such variables.

By default, threads share all other types of variables—that is, class-level fields, module-level variables, and local Static variables. You can use these variables to make data visible to all the running threads. Unfortunately, you also have to provide a way to synchronize access to this data. Consider this simple code:

```
' The globalvar variable should never be negative.
If globalVar > 0 Then
   Console.WriteLine("About to change globalVar")
   globalVar = globalVar - 1
End If
```

If access to the globalVar variable isn't arbitrated and synchronized in some way, a thread might execute, test the value of globalVar, find that it's 1, and enter the Then code block. The first statement in this block is a call into the runtime, which gives the thread manager a chance to perform a thread switch and activate another thread. What happens if the other thread enters the same block of code? As you might expect, it finds that the globalVar variable is still 1, and the other thread (incorrectly) enters the block. As a result, the variable is decremented twice and becomes negative, which you probably don't want and which might cause an error later in the application. Logic errors of this kind are problematic because they occur in random fashion, are rarely reproducible, and therefore are very difficult to debug.

This code summarizes which variables are shared among threads:

```
Class TaskClass
    Dim Field As Integer              ' Field (shared)

    Sub TheTask()
       Dim dynamicVar As Integer      ' Dynamic variable (nonshared)
       Static staticVar As Integer    ' Static variable (shared)
       ...
    End Sub
End Class
```

Even if you decide not to explicitly create new threads in your applications, you might have to worry about arbitrating access to shared variables anyway, if your class has a Finalize method. In fact, by default the Finalize method of your objects runs on a different thread than your application's main thread does; therefore, you should ensure that either you don't access any shared variables from Finalize methods or you protect these variables by using synchronization blocks (which I explain later).

Finally, you have to worry about how variables are shared between threads if you use objects that create secondary threads and fire their events on these secondary threads, as is the case of the FileSystemWatcher component (which I describe in Chapter 15, "Files, Directories, and Streams"). This situation is especially problematic if you are calling a multithreaded object from inside a Windows Forms application because code in form objects must run in the same thread that created the form itself—or the application might crash. You can read more about this issue in the section titled "The ISynchronizeInvoke Interface," near the end of this chapter.

The ThreadStatic Attribute

To understand the kinds of problems you have to watch out for when you're working with multithreaded applications, consider this simple class:

```
Class SampleClass
  Public Shared ThreadName As String
  ...
End Class
```

Suppose that this class can be used by multiple threads but that each thread wants to store and retrieve a distinct value for the ThreadName static field. Unfortunately, being static, the ThreadName variable is shared among all the instances of the class and hence all the threads, so each thread will override the current value with its own ThreadName.

To obviate this problem, the .NET runtime supports the concept of thread-relative variables, which are static variables and fields that are shared among all class instances but not among threads. You create a thread-relative Static variable by marking the declaration of a Shared class-level field in a class with the ThreadStatic attribute:

```
' The ThreadName variable isn't shared among threads.
<ThreadStatic()> Public Shared ThreadName As String
```

Because Visual Basic modules are simply classes whose members are automatically flagged as Shared, you can also apply the ThreadStatic attribute to any module-level variable in a module. (You can't apply this attribute to fields that aren't shared, though.)

Threads and Unhandled Exceptions

When a thread—either the main thread or a secondary thread—throws an exception and your code doesn't catch it, an AppDomain.UnhandledException event is fired. The event receives an UnhandledExceptionEventArgs object, which exposes two properties, ExceptionObject and IsTerminating. The former is of course the exception being thrown, but it returns an Object value, and you must cast it to an Exception variable before you can read the usual properties such as Message and StackTrace, as the following code example demonstrates:

```
Sub TestThreadException()
    ' Prepare to trap AppDomain events.
    AddHandler AppDomain.CurrentDomain.UnhandledException, _
        AddressOf AppDomain_UnhandledException
    ' Cause an exception on a secondary thread.
    Dim t As New Thread(AddressOf TestThreadException_Task)
    t.Start()
    t.Join()
    ' This line will never be reached.
    Console.WriteLine("Application terminated normally")
End Sub

Private Sub TestThreadException_Task()
    Throw New DivideByZeroException()
End Sub

Private Sub AppDomain_UnhandledException(ByVal sender As Object, _
        ByVal e As UnhandledExceptionEventArgs)
    ' Show information about the current exception.
    Dim ex As Exception = DirectCast(e.ExceptionObject, Exception)
    Console.WriteLine(ex.Message)
End Sub
```

One important thing about this event: you can trap it correctly only when the application isn't running under the Visual Studio debugger, so you must start the program by choosing Start Without Debugging from the Debug menu or by pressing the Ctrl+F5 shortcut.

 In .NET Framework 1.1, the value of the IsTerminating property (and therefore the effect of the exception on the application's life) depends on the kind of thread being terminated. An exception on a secondary thread—for example, a thread used by the garbage collector to call the Finalize method, a thread created with the Thread class, or a thread taken from the thread pool—isn't fatal for the application (even if it might cause error messages to appear, depending on the type of the current application). Only uncaught exceptions thrown by the main thread or an unmanaged thread—for example, a thread running in a COM object called by a .NET assembly—terminate the application.

In .NET Framework 2.0, an unhandled exception on any thread will terminate the application. This is clearly a breaking change that might force you to rewrite and retest old applications being ported to the new version of the .NET Framework, but Microsoft correctly decided that letting exceptions silently kill your secondary thread was just too dangerous. You can, however, revert to the .NET Framework 1.x behavior by adding the following entry to the application's configuration file:

```
<configuration>
    <runtime>
        <legacyUnhandledExceptionPolicy enabled="1"/>
    </runtime>
</configuration>
```

Although the UnhandledException event can be useful, keep in mind that you can't catch and solve every unhandled exception using this technique. In practice, you only can save any unsaved data, log the exception somewhere (for example, in the system event log), and display a dialog box to inform the user that the application is closing. Regardless of whether you're handling the UnhandledException event, .NET applications display a message box that asks whether you want to debug the application or send Microsoft a report of the error. (See Figure 20-2.) If you decide not to debug the application, a complete error message is displayed in the command window (if there is one) and the application is terminated.

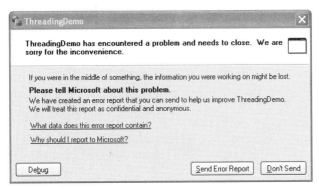

Figure 20-2   The dialog box that .NET applications display by default when an unhandled exception occurs

Debugging Threads

You can see the name of the running thread—as well as other information such as the application name and the stack frame—by activating the Debug Location toolbar inside Visual Studio 2005. (You can activate any toolbar by right-clicking any Visual Studio menu or toolbar.) This data is especially useful when you want to determine where a thread is executing when you hit a breakpoint. You can display this toolbar by right-clicking any toolbar and clicking Debug Location on the shortcut menu. (See Figure 20-3.)

Figure 20-3   The Debug Location toolbar, which displays the thread name and other information about the running process

The Thread window in Visual Studio 2005 lets you list all the running threads, the method being executed, and the name, status, and priority of each thread. You activate this window by pointing to Windows on the Debug menu and clicking Threads. (The current program must be in break mode for you to see this menu command.) The yellow arrow on the left identifies the current thread, and you can switch to another thread by right-clicking it. (See Figure 20-4.) You can also freeze a thread, which is then displayed with two vertical blue bars, and restart (thaw) it.

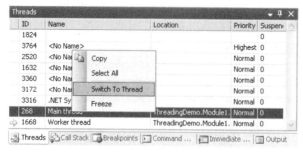

Figure 20-4   The Threads window, which lists all threads and lets you freeze and restart them

Visual Studio 2005 supports the ability to define per-process and per-thread breakpoints, which is a great bonus when debugging applications that use many threads. To make a breakpoint active only for a given thread, take note of the thread's ID (from the Threads window), right-click the red breakpoint icon in the left margin of the code editor, and select the Filter command. This command brings up the Breakpoint Filter dialog box (see Figure 20-5), where you can type an expression such as this:

```
ThreadId = 1234
```

Even better, assign the thread a name from code, and then use this name in the Breakpoint Filter dialog box as follows:

```
ThreadName = "Worker thread"
```

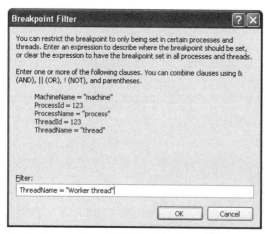

Figure 20-5   The Breakpoint Filter dialog box

The Performance utility offers a way to monitor threads and the performance bottlenecks they might create. (See Figure 20-6.) The .NET Framework has a performance object named .NET CLR LocksAndThreads that exposes several counters, the most important of which are the following:

- **# of current logical threads**   The current number of threads known to the CLR in a given application.

- **# of current physical threads**   The number of native Windows threads created and owned by the CLR.

- **# of current recognized threads**   The number of threads that were created outside the CLR (for example, in a COM component) that the runtime has recognized.

- **contention rate/sec**   Rate at which threads in the runtime fail to acquire a managed lock—for example, when reaching a SyncLock block. A high number for this counter is a symptom indicating that the application isn't well designed for multithreaded operations.

- **total # of contentions**   The total number of times threads in the CLR have failed to acquire a managed lock.

- **current queue/sec**   The average number of threads waiting to acquire a lock; a high value means that most threads spend most of their time waiting for a lock to become available.

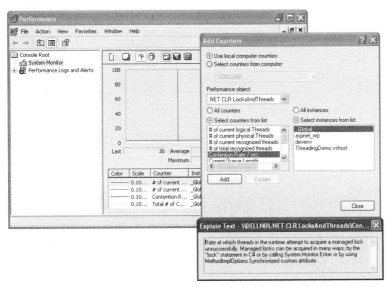

Figure 20-6   The Performance utility, which lets you see several statistics regarding CLR threads

The meaning of some of these counters—most notably, those related to contention and locks—will become evident later in this chapter.

Thread Synchronization

Now that you know how a thread can share data or prevent data from being shared, you're ready to tackle synchronization issues related to concurrent access to variables and objects accessible by multiple threads at the same time.

The SyncLock Statement

As you know, a thread can be preempted at any time, usually at the completion of a call to an object's method. The following example demonstrates what can happen when a piece of code isn't guaranteed to execute atomically:

```
Sub SynchronizationProblem()
    ' Create 10 secondary threads.
    For i As Integer = 0 To 9
        Dim t As New Thread(AddressOf SynchronizationProblem_Task)
        t.Start(i)
    Next
End Sub

Sub SynchronizationProblem_Task(ByVal obj As Object)
    Dim number As Integer = CInt(obj)
    ' Print a lot of information to the console window.
    For i As Integer = 1 To 1000
        ' Split the output line in two pieces.
        Console.Write(" ")
        Console.Write(number)
    Next
End Sub
```

A glance at the console window shows some interruptions of a thread between the Console .Write statements, which result in scrambled output. (See Figure 20-7.)

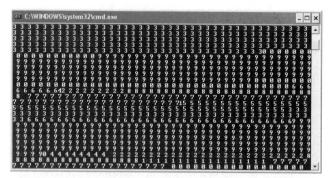

Figure 20-7   The console window clearly showing that writing a space plus the thread number isn't an atomic operation

The runtime offers no means of ensuring that a group of statements behaves as an atomic, uninterruptible operation. This would be too stiff a requirement in an operating system that must guarantee multitasking to all applications. However, most of the time you would be satisfied to have atomicity at the application level (rather than at the system level). In the preceding code, for example, it would be enough to ensure that only one thread in the current application can execute a specific block of statements at a time. You can achieve this by enclosing those statements in a SyncLock...End SyncLock block. The SyncLock block requires a variable as an argument, and this variable must satisfy the following requirements:

- It must be a variable shared by all the threads (typically, a class-level variable or a module-level variable without the ThreadStatic attribute).
- It must be a reference type, for example, a String or an Object variable. (Using a value type causes a compilation error.)
- It must not have a Nothing value. (Using a Nothing value causes a runtime error.)

Here's the code shown before, which has been revised to leverage the SyncLock block (additions are in bold type):

```
' The lock object. (Any non-Nothing reference value will do.)
Private consoleLock As New Object()

Sub SynchronizationProblem_Task(ByVal obj As Object)
   Dim number As Integer = CInt(obj)
   ' Print a lot of information to the console window.
   For i As Integer = 1 To 1000
      SyncLock consoleLock
         ' Split the output line in two pieces.
         Console.Write(" ")
         Console.Write(number)
      End SyncLock
   Next
End Sub
```

The preceding code uses the consoleLock variable to arbitrate access to the Console object, which is the only resource that all threads share in this trivial example and is therefore the only resource for which you need to provide synchronization. Real-world applications might contain many SyncLock blocks; such blocks can share the same object variable or use different variables for finer granularity. As a rule of thumb, you should have a distinct object variable for each shared resource that must be synchronized or for each group of statements that must be executed by one thread at a time.

Each SyncLock block implicitly uses a hidden Try...End Try block because Visual Basic must ensure that the lock is correctly released if an exception is thrown. (A lock release requires a Monitor.Exit method.) For this reason, jumping into a SyncLock block by using a Goto statement is illegal.

If the SyncLock block is placed inside an instance method of a class and all threads are running inside a method of that instance, you can pass Me to the SyncLock statement because this object surely satisfies all the requirements. It's accessible by all threads, it's a reference value, and it surely is non-Nothing.

```
Class TestClass
   Sub TheTask()
      SyncLock Me
         ' Only one thread at a time can access this code.
         …
      End SyncLock
   End Sub
End Class
```

> **Note**   You can use Me in this fashion only if you need to synchronize on a single resource, for example, the console window or a specific file. If you have multiple synchronization blocks that protect multiple resources, you'll typically use different variables as the argument of the SyncLock block. Even more important, you should use Me as the argument of a SyncLock block only if the class isn't visible outside the current assembly; otherwise, another application might use the same instance in a different SyncLock block and would therefore prevent your threads from executing a block of code without any real reason. In general, you should never use a public object visible to other assemblies as the argument for a SyncLock keyword.

Also notice that some code samples you can find on the Internet use the GetType operator to retrieve a Type object that is then used as a lock object to protect a static method. Using a Type object in this fashion is strongly discouraged by Microsoft and should be avoided.

When you use nested SyncLock statements to synchronize access to multiple objects, it's essential that you follow the identical nesting sequence everywhere in your application. Acquiring locks in identical order avoids deadlocks among different portions of your application. This rule of thumb also applies to those cases when code in a SyncLock block calls a method containing another SyncLock block.

```
' Always use this sequence when locking objLock1 and objLock2.
SyncLock objLock1
    SyncLock objLock2
        …
    End SyncLock
End SyncLock
```

The Thread class in .NET Framework 2.0 supports two new methods named BeginCritical-Section and EndCriticalSection. The names of these methods suggest that you can use them to mark an uninterruptible block of code, but this isn't the case. Instead, these methods have been introduced to make .NET applications more reliable in critical conditions: they tell the CLR that a block of code shouldn't suffer from unanticipated exceptions deriving from JIT compilation errors or other problems that aren't caused by the application instead. For more information, read the MSDN documentation.

Performance Considerations and Lazy Instantiation

Putting a SyncLock block around all the pieces of code that access a shared variable can be overkill and can degrade your application's performance, especially when it runs on a multi-processor computer. (Locks on multiple-CPU computers can be quite time-consuming.) If you can avoid a SyncLock block without compromising the integrity of your data, you should absolutely do it. For example, consider how you can implement the Singleton pattern using lazy instantiation in a multithreaded environment:

```
Public Class Singleton
    Private Shared m_Instance As Singleton
    Private Shared sharedLock As New Object()
```

```
      Public Shared ReadOnly Property Instance() As Singleton
         Get
            SyncLock sharedLock
               If m_Instance Is Nothing Then m_Instance = New Singleton
               Return m_Instance
            End SyncLock
         End Get
      End Property
End Class
```

(See Chapter 6, "Class Fundamentals," for an introduction to singletons.) The problem with the previous code is that most accesses to the Instance property don't need synchronization because the m_Instance private variable needs to be instantiated only the first time the property is read. Here's a better way to implement the requested behavior:

```
Class Singleton
   Private Shared m_Instance As Singleton
   Private Shared sharedLock As New Object

   Public Shared ReadOnly Property Instance() As Singleton
      Get
         If m_Instance Is Nothing Then
            SyncLock sharedLock
               If m_Instance Is Nothing Then m_Instance = New Singleton()
            End SyncLock
         End If
         Return m_Instance
      End Get
   End Property
End Class
```

Synchronized Objects

Another problem related to threading is that not every .NET object can be shared safely among threads. In other words, not all .NET objects are *thread-safe*. When you're writing a multithreaded application, you should always check the documentation to determine whether the objects and the methods you're using are thread-safe. For example, all the static methods of the Regex, Match, and Group classes are thread-safe, but their instance methods aren't and shouldn't be invoked by different threads at the same time. Some .NET objects—most notably, Windows Forms objects and controls—pose even more severe limitations in that only the thread that created them can call their methods: these objects are said to require *thread affinity*. (Read the section titled "Threading in Windows Forms Applications" later in this chapter for more information about accessing Windows Forms controls from a different thread.)

Synchronized .NET Types

Several objects that aren't thread-safe natively—including ArrayList, Hashtable, Queue, SortedList, Stack, TextReader, TextWriter, and regular expression Match and Group classes—expose a Synchronized static method, which returns a thread-safe object that's equivalent to the one you pass as an argument. Most of these classes also expose the IsSynchronized property, which returns True if you're dealing with a thread-safe instance:

```
' Create an ArrayList object, and add some values to it.
Dim al As New ArrayList()
al.Add(1): al.Add(2): al.Add(3)
' Create a synchronized, thread-safe version of this ArrayList.
Dim syncAl As ArrayList = ArrayList.Synchronized(al)
' Prove that the new object is thread-safe.
Console.WriteLine(al.IsSynchronized)        ' => False
Console.WriteLine(syncAl.IsSynchronized)    ' => True
' You can now share the syncAl object among different threads.
...
```

Keep in mind that accessing these synchronized objects is typically slower than accessing the corresponding nonsynchronized object because each method call goes through a series of internal tests. In most cases, you can write more efficient code if you use regular arrays and collections and you synchronize access to their members by means of standard SyncLock blocks.

The Synchronization Attribute

Using the System.Runtime.Remoting.Contexts.Synchronization attribute is the simplest way to provide synchronized access to an entire object so that only one thread can access its instance fields and methods. That is, any thread can use that instance of the class, but only one thread at a time can execute one of the methods. If a thread is executing code inside the class, any other thread that attempts to use that class has to wait. In other words, it's as if there were SyncLock blocks enclosing every method of that class, with all these blocks using the same lock variable.

The following code shows how you can synchronize a class using the Synchronization attribute. Also notice that the class must inherit from ContextBoundObject to be marked as a context-bound object:

```
<System.Runtime.Remoting.Contexts.Synchronization()> _
Class Display
    Inherits ContextBoundObject

    ...
End Class
```

The Synchronization attribute automatically synchronizes access to all instance fields, properties, and methods, but it doesn't provide synchronization for static members. The attribute can take an optional argument, which can be either True or False (to indicate whether reentrant calls are permitted) or one of the constants exposed by the SynchronizationAttribute class itself: NOT_SUPPORTED, SUPPORTED, REQUIRED, REQUIRES_NEW. For more information, read the MSDN documentation.

The MethodImpl Attribute

In most cases, synchronizing an entire class is overkill, and protecting just a few of its methods from concurrent accesses is often satisfactory. You can apply this sort of protection by wrapping the body of such methods in a SyncLock block. Or you can use a simpler technique based on the System.Runtime.CompilerServices.MethodImpl attribute:

```
Class MethodImplDemoClass
    ' This method can be executed by one thread at a time.
    <MethodImpl(MethodImplOptions.Synchronized)> _
    Sub SynchronizedMethod()
        ...
    End Sub
End Class
```

Applying the MethodImpl attribute for multiple methods in the class provides the same effect as wrapping the body of those methods with SyncLock blocks that use the Me instance as the lock variable. In other words, a thread calling a method marked with the MethodImpl attribute will block any other thread calling the same or a different method marked with this attribute.

Interestingly, you also can use the MethodImpl attribute for static methods. The object variable implicitly used to lock static methods is different from the object variable used for instance methods, so a thread invoking a static method marked with the MethodImpl attribute doesn't block another thread calling an instance method marked with the same attribute. (More precisely, static methods marked with the MethodImpl attribute use the System.Type object that identifies the current type.)

Volatile Read and Write Operations

When a variable is shared among multiple threads and the application runs on a multiprocessor computer, you should take another potential cause of malfunctioning into account. The problem with multiprocessor systems is that each processor has its own cache; therefore, if you write to a class field from one thread, the new value is written to the cache associated with the current CPU and isn't automatically "published" for all the CPUs to see it. A similar problem can also occur with 64-bit CPUs, which can rearrange the order of execution of a block of statements, including reads and writes from memory: such a rearrangement never has a visible effect as far as only one thread is accessing a given portion of memory, but it might cause problems when memory is accessed by multiple threads.

The .NET Framework offers two solutions to this issue: the VolatileRead and VolatileWrite pair of methods, and the MemoryBarrier method, all exposed by the Thread type.

The VolatileWrite method enables you to write a variable and ensure that the new value is automatically written in the memory shared by all processors and is not kept in a CPU register (where it would be hidden from other threads). Likewise, the VolatileRead method enables you to read a variable in a safe way because it forces all the caches in the system to be emptied before the read operation is carried out. Both methods are overloaded to take a primitive variable (numeric or Object) by reference, as in this code:

```
Class TestClass
    Private Shared sharedValue As Integer

    Function IncrementValue() As Integer
        Dim value As Integer = Thread.VolatileRead(sharedValue)
        value += 1
        Thread.VolatileWrite(sharedValue, value)
        Return value
    End Function
End Class
```

The VolatileRead and VolatileWrite methods are OK as long as a numeric or an object value is accessed, but they can't be applied when another kind of type is used. (You can't just use the overload that takes an Object variable because you can't rely on casting when a by-reference argument is involved.) This consideration leads us to the MemoryBarrier method.

The MemoryBarrier method flushes the contents of all caches and CPU registers to the main memory, and thus it ensures that variables contain the most recent data that was written to them. For example, the following code ensures that the Singleton pattern—which I illustrated in the section titled "Performance Considerations and Lazy Instantiation" earlier in this chapter—is absolutely bullet-proof even on multi-CPU systems:

```
Class Singleton
    Private Shared m_Instance As Singleton
    Private Shared sharedLock As New Object()

    Public Shared ReadOnly Property Instance() As Singleton
        Get
            If m_Instance Is Nothing Then
                SyncLock sharedLock
                    If m_Instance Is Nothing Then
                        Dim tempInstance As Singleton = New Singleton()
                        ' Ensure that writes related to instantiation are flushed.
                        Thread.MemoryBarrier()
                        m_Instance = tempInstance
                    End If
                End SyncLock
            End If
            Return m_Instance
        End Get
    End Property
End Class
```

You should place a call to MemoryBarrier just before the assignment that "publishes" a new value for all the other threads to see in the preceding example; this call ensures that the assignment to tempInstance is completed before trying the assignment to the variable that is going to be shared among threads.

The Monitor Type

The SyncLock block provides an easy-to-use method for dealing with synchronization issues, but it can be inadequate in many situations. For example, a thread can't just test a SyncLock code block and avoid being blocked if another thread is already executing the SyncLock block or another SyncLock block that is associated with the same object.

SyncLock blocks are internally implemented using Monitor objects. Interestingly, you can use a Monitor object directly and get more flexibility, although at the expense of somewhat more complex code.

You never instantiate individual Monitor objects, and in fact, all the methods I illustrate are static methods of the Monitor type. The most important method is Enter, which takes an object as an argument. This object works exactly like the argument you pass to a SyncLock block and undergoes the same constraints—it must be a non-Nothing reference variable that's shared by all the threads. If no other thread owns the lock on that object, the current thread acquires the lock and sets its internal lock counter to 1. If another thread currently owns the lock, the calling thread must wait until the other thread releases the lock and the lock becomes available. If the calling thread already owns the lock, each call to Monitor.Enter increments the internal lock counter.

The Monitor.Exit method takes the lock object as an argument and decrements its internal lock counter. If the counter reaches 0, the lock is released so that other threads can acquire it. Calls to Monitor.Enter and Monitor.Exit must be balanced, or the lock will never be released:

```
' A non-Nothing module-level object variable
Dim objLock As New Object()
…
Try
    ' Attempt to enter the protected section;
    ' wait if the lock is currently owned by another thread.
    Monitor.Enter(objLock)
    ' Do something here.
    …
Finally
    ' Release the lock.
    Monitor.Exit(objLock)
End Try
```

If the statements between Monitor.Enter and Monitor.Exit are likely to raise an exception, you should put all the code in a Try…End Try block because it's imperative that you always release the lock. If a thread calls the Interrupt method on another thread that is currently waiting inside a Monitor.Enter method, the thread receives a ThreadInterruptedException, which is another good reason for using a Try…End Try block.

The Enter and Exit methods of a Monitor object let you replace a SyncLock block but don't bring you any additional advantages. You see the extra flexibility of the Monitor class when you apply its TryEnter method. This method is similar to Enter, but the method exits and returns False if the lock can't be acquired in the specified timeout. For example, you can attempt to get the monitor lock for 10 milliseconds and then give up, without blocking the current thread indefinitely. The following code rewrites a previous example based on SyncLock, this time using the Monitor object, and also displays the failed attempts to acquire the lock:

```
Try
   Do Until Monitor.TryEnter(consoleLock, 10)
      Debug.WriteLine("Thread " + Thread.CurrentThread.Name + _
         " failed to acquire the lock")
   Loop
   ' Split the output line in pieces.
   Console.Write(" ")
   Console.Write(Thread.CurrentThread.Name)
Finally
   ' Release the lock.
   Monitor.Exit(consoleLock)
End Try
```

The Mutex Type

The Mutex type provides yet another synchronization primitive. A *mutex* is a Windows kernel object that can be owned by one thread at a time and is said to be in a *signaled* state if no thread currently owns it.

A thread requests ownership of a mutex by means of the Mutex.WaitOne static method (which doesn't return until the ownership has been successfully achieved) and releases it by means of the Mutex.ReleaseMutex static method. A thread requesting the ownership of a Mutex object that it owns already doesn't block itself, but even in that case it must call ReleaseMutex an equal number of times. This is how you can implement a synchronized section using a Mutex object:

```
' This Mutex object must be accessible to all threads.
Dim m As New Mutex()

Sub WaitOneExample()
   m.WaitOne()
   ' Enter the synchronized section.
   …
   ' Exit the synchronized section.
   m.ReleaseMutex()
End Sub
```

In a real application, you should use a Try block to protect your code from unhandled errors and place the call to ReleaseMutex in the Finally block. If you pass WaitOne an optional timeout argument, the method returns the control to the thread when the ownership is successfully achieved or the timeout expires. You can tell the difference between the two results by looking at the return value. True means ownership was acquired, and False means the timeout expired.

```
' Attempt to enter the synchronized section, but give up after 0.1 seconds.
If m.WaitOne(100, False) Then
```

```
   ' Enter the synchronized section.
   …
   ' Exit the synchronized section, and release the mutex.
   m.ReleaseMutex()
End If
```

When used in this way, the Mutex type provides a mechanism equivalent to the Monitor .TryEnter method, without offering any additional features. You see the added flexibility of the Mutex type when you consider its WaitAny and WaitAll static methods. The WaitAny method takes an array of Mutex objects and returns when it manages to acquire the ownership of one of the Mutex objects in the list (in which case, that Mutex becomes signaled) or when the optional timeout expires. The return value is the array index of the Mutex object that became signaled or the special value 258 if the timeout expired.

You typically use an array of Mutex objects when you have a limited number of resources, such as communication ports, and you want to allocate each one to a thread as soon as the resource becomes available. In this situation, a signaled Mutex object means that the corresponding resource is available, so you can use the Mutex.WaitAny method for blocking the current thread until any of the Mutex objects become signaled. (The Mutex type inherits the WaitAny method from its WaitHandle base class.) Here's the skeleton of an application that uses this approach:

```
' An array of three Mutex objects
Dim mutexes() As Mutex = {New Mutex(), New Mutex(), New Mutex()}

Sub WaitAnyExample()
   ' Wait until a resource becomes available.
   ' (Returns the index of the available resource.)
   Dim mutexNdx As Integer = Mutex.WaitAny(mutexes)
   ' Enter the synchronized section.
   ' (This code should use only the resource corresponding to mutexNdx.)
   …
   ' Exit the synchronized section, and release the resource.
   mutexes(mutexNdx).ReleaseMutex()
End Sub
```

The WaitAll static method (also inherited from the WaitHandle base class) takes an array of Mutex objects and returns the control to the application only when all of them have become signaled. This method is especially useful when you can't proceed until all the other threads have completed their jobs:

```
' Wait until all resources have been released.
Mutex.WaitAll(mutexes)
```

A minor problem of the WaitAll method is that you can't call it from the main thread of a Single Thread Apartment (STA) application, such as a Console application or a Windows Forms application. If the main thread of an STA application must stop until a group of mutexes is released, you should use the WaitAll from a separate thread and then use the Thread.Join method on that thread to stop the main thread until the WaitAll method returns.

The new SignalAndWait static method, which the Mutex type inherits from the WaitHandle base class, allows you to signal one Mutex object and wait on another Mutex object (in general, any object that inherits from WaitHandle) as an atomic operation:

```
' Signal the first mutex and wait for the second mutex to become signaled.
Mutex.SignalAndWait(mutexes(0), mutexes(1))
```

Unlike other synchronization objects covered so far, Mutex objects can be assigned a name, which brings up one of the most important features of these objects. Mutex objects that have the same name are shared among different processes. You can create an instance of a named Mutex using this syntax:

```
Dim m As New Mutex(False, "mutexname")
```

If a Mutex with that name already exists in the system, the caller gets a reference to it; otherwise, a new Mutex object is created. This mechanism lets you share Mutex objects among different applications and therefore enables these applications to synchronize their access to shared resources.

A new constructor added in .NET Framework 2.0 allows you to test whether the calling thread was granted the initial ownership of the Mutex:

```
Dim ownership As Boolean
Dim m As New Mutex(True, "mutexname", ownership)
If ownership Then
   ' This thread owns the mutex.
   …
End If
```

A common use of named mutexes is to determine whether the running application is the first (or the only) instance being loaded. If this is not the case, the application might exit immediately or wait until the other instance has completed its chores, as in this code sample:

```
Sub Main()
   Dim ownership As Boolean
   Dim m As New Mutex(True, "DemoMutex", ownership)
   If ownership Then
      Console.WriteLine("This app got the ownership of Mutex named DemoMutex")
      Console.WriteLine("Press ENTER to run another instance of this app")
      Console.ReadLine()
      Process.Start(Assembly.GetExecutingAssembly().GetName().CodeBase)
   Else
      Console.WriteLine("This app is waiting to get ownership of Mutex named DemoMutex")
      m.WaitOne()
   End If
   ' Perform the task here.
   …
   Console.WriteLine("Press ENTER to release ownership of the mutex")
   Console.ReadLine()
   m.ReleaseMutex()
End Sub
```

The OpenExisting static method, also new in .NET Framework 2.0, offers an alternative way to open a named system-wide Mutex object. Unlike the Mutex constructor, this method enables you to specify which degree of control you need to exert on the Mutex:

```
Try
   ' Request a mutex with the right to wait for it and to release it.
   Dim rights As MutexRights = MutexRights.Synchronize Or MutexRights.Modify
   Dim m As Mutex = Mutex.OpenExisting("mutexname", rights)
   ' Use the mutex here.
   …
Catch ex As WaitHandleCannotBeOpenedException
   ' The specified object doesn't exist.
Catch ex As UnauthorizedAccessException
   ' The specified object exists, but current user doesn't have the
   ' necessary access rights.
Catch ex As IOException
   ' A Win32 error has occurred.
End Try
```

The most important new feature of the Mutex type is the support for access control lists (ACLs), in the form of the System.Security.AccessControl.MutexSecurity object. You can specify an ACL when you instantiate a new Mutex object, use the GetAccessControl method to retrieve the MutexSecurity object associated with a given Mutex, and enforce a new ACL with the SetAccessControl method:

```
Dim ownership As Boolean
Dim m As New Mutex(True, "mutexname", ownership)
If Not ownership Then
   ' Determine who is the owner of the mutex.
   Dim mutexSec As MutexSecurity = m.GetAccessControl()
   Dim account As NTAccount = DirectCast(mutexSec.GetOwner(GetType(NTAccount)), _
      NTAccount)
   Console.WriteLine("Mutex is owned by {0}", account)
End If
```

Review the section titled "Working with Access Control Lists" in Chapter 15 for more information about ACLs in version 2.0 of the .NET Framework.

The Semaphore Type

The Semaphore type is new in .NET Framework 2.0 and maps on the Win32 semaphore object. Unlike all other threading objects (which are found in mscorlib), this type is implemented in System.dll.

A semaphore is used in situations when you want no more than *N* threads to execute in a given portion of code or access a given resource. A semaphore has an initial count and a maximum count, and you must pass these values to its constructor:

```
' A semaphore that has an initial count of 1 and a maximum count of 2.
Dim sem As New Semaphore(1, 2)
```

A thread can attempt to take ownership of a semaphore by calling the WaitOne method; if the current count is higher than zero, the count is decremented and the method returns immediately; otherwise, the WaitOne method waits until another thread releases the semaphore or until the optional timeout expires. A thread releases a semaphore by calling the Release method, which increases the count by 1 (or by the specified amount) and returns the *previous* count value.

```
Dim sem As New Semaphore(2, 2)
' Next statement brings count from 2 to 1.
sem.WaitOne()
…

' Next statement brings count from 1 to 2.
sem.Release()
' Next statement attempts to bring count from 2 to 3, but
' throws a SemaphoreFullException.
sem.Release()
```

You typically use a Semaphore object as follows:

```
' Initial count is initially equal to max count.
Dim sem2 As New Semaphore(2, 2)

Sub Semaphore_Example()
   ' Wait until a resource becomes available.
   sem2.WaitOne()
   ' Enter the synchronized section.
   …

   ' Exit the synchronized section, and release the resource.
   sem2.Release()
End Sub
```

(Remember to use a Try…Finally block to ensure that the semaphore is released even if the code throws an exception.) Like mutexes, semaphores can have a name and be shared among processes. When you try to create a Semaphore object that already exists, the initial and maximum count values are ignored:

```
Dim ownership As Boolean
Dim sem3 As New Semaphore(2, 2, "semaphoreName", ownership)
If ownership Then
   ' Current thread has the ownership of the semaphore.
   …
End If
```

The Semaphore object supports ACLs, which you can pass to the constructor, read with the GetAccessControl method, or modify with the SetAccessControl method. See the section titled "The Mutex Type" earlier in this chapter for more details about ACLs.

It's important for you to notice that the Mutex and the Semaphore types (as well as the AutoResetEvent, ManualResetEvent, and EventWaitHandle types that I cover in a later section) all inherit from the WaitHandle base class and therefore can be passed as arguments to the WaitAny, WaitAll, and SignalAndWait static methods of the WaitHandle type. This means that you can easily synchronize resources that are protected with any of these objects, as in this code:

```
' Wait until two mutexes, two semaphores, and one event object become signaled.
Dim waitHandles() As WaitHandle = {mutex1, mutex2, sem1, sem2, event1}
WaitHandle.WaitAll(waitHandles)
```

The ReaderWriterLock Type

Many resources in the real world can be either read from or written to. Often these resources allow either multiple read operations or a single write operation running in a given moment. For example, multiple clients can read a data file or a database table, but if the file or the table is being written to, no other read or write operation can occur on that resource. You can create a lock that implements single-writer, multiple-reader semantics by using a ReaderWriterLock object.

Using this object is straightforward. All the threads intending to use the resource should share the same instance of the ReaderWriterLock type. Before attempting an operation on the resource, a thread should call either the AcquireReaderLock or the AcquireWriterLock method, depending on the operation to be performed. These methods block the current thread until the lock of the requested type can be acquired (for example, until no other thread is holding the lock if you requested a writer lock). Finally, the thread should call the ReleaseReaderLock or ReleaseWriterLock method when the read or write operation on the resource has been completed.

The following code example creates 10 threads that perform either a read or a write operation on a shared resource (relevant statements are in bold type):

```
Dim rwl As New ReaderWriterLock()
Dim rnd As New Random()

Sub TestReaderWriterLock()
   For i As Integer = 0 To 9
      Dim t As New Thread(AddressOf ReaderWriterLock_Task)
      t.Start(i)
   Next
   …
End Sub

Sub ReaderWriterLock_Task(ByVal obj As Object)
   Dim n As Integer = CInt(obj)
   ' Perform 10 read or write operations. (Reads are more frequent.)
   For i As Integer = 1 To 10
      If rnd.NextDouble < 0.8 Then
         ' Attempt a read operation.
         rwl.AcquireReaderLock(Timeout.Infinite)
         Console.WriteLine("Thread #{0} is reading", n)
         Thread.Sleep(300)
         Console.WriteLine("Thread #{0} completed the read operation", n)
         rwl.ReleaseReaderLock()
      Else
```

```
                   ' Attempt a write operation.
                   rwl.AcquireWriterLock(Timeout.Infinite)
                   Console.WriteLine("Thread #{0} is writing", n)
                   Thread.Sleep(300)
                   Console.WriteLine("Thread #{0} completed the write operation", n)
                   rwl.ReleaseWriterLock()
               End If
       Next
   End Sub
```

If you run this code, you'll see that multiple threads can be reading at the same time and that a writing thread blocks all the other threads.

The AcquireReaderLock and AcquireWriterLock methods can take a timeout argument, expressed as a number of milliseconds or a TimeSpan value. You can test whether the lock was acquired successfully by means of the IsReaderLockHeld or IsWriterLockHeld read-only property if you passed a value other than Timeout.Infinite:

```
' Attempt to acquire a reader lock for no longer than 1 second.
rwl.AcquireWriterLock(1000)
If rwl.IsWriterLockHeld Then
   ' The thread has a writer lock on the resource.
   …
End If
```

A thread that owns a reader lock can also attempt to upgrade to a writer lock by calling the UpgradeToWriterLock method and later go back to the reader lock by calling Downgrade-FromWriterLock.

The great thing about ReaderWriterLock objects is that they are lightweight objects and can be used in large numbers without affecting performance significantly. And because the AcquireReaderLock and AcquireWriterLock methods take a timeout, a well-designed application should never suffer from deadlocks. Nevertheless, a deadlock can still occur when you have two threads and each thread is waiting for a resource that the other thread won't release until the operation completes.

The Interlocked Type

The Interlocked type provides a way to perform the simple atomic operations of incrementing and decrementing a shared variable. This class exposes only static methods (not counting members inherited from Object). Consider the following code:

```
' Increment and Decrement methods work with 32-bit and 64-bit integers.
Dim lockCounter As Integer
…
' Increment the counter and execute some code if its previous value was zero.
If Interlocked.Increment(lockCounter) = 1 Then
   …
End If
' Decrement the shared counter.
Interlocked.Decrement(lockCounter)
```

The Add method is new in .NET Framework 2.0; it allows you to increment or decrement a 32-bit or 64-bit integer by the specified quantity:

```
If Interlocked.Add(lockCounter, 2) <= 10 Then …
```

The Interlocked class exposes two additional static methods. The Exchange method lets you assign a value of your choosing to an Integer, Long, Single, Double, IntPtr, or Object variable and return its previous value, as an atomic operation. In .NET Framework 2.0, the Exchange method has been overloaded to take an object argument; therefore, in practice you can make this method work with any reference type, for example, the String type:

```
Dim s1 As String = "123"
Dim s2 As String = Interlocked.Exchange(s1, "abc")
Console.WriteLine("s1={0}, s2={1}", s1, s2)
```

The CompareExchange method works similarly, but it does the swap only if the memory location is currently equal to a specific value that you provide as an argument.

The ManualResetEvent, AutoResetEvent, and EventWaitHandle Types

The last synchronization objects I illustrate in this chapter are three classes that work in a similar way: ManualResetEvent, AutoResetEvent, and EventWaitHandle. The last type is the base class for the other two and has been added in version 2.0 of the .NET Framework. Even if the ManualResetEvent and the AutoResetEvent types haven't been made obsolete, in practice you can replace them with the new EventWaitHandle type, which actually gives you even more flexibility.

The ManualResetEvent and AutoResetEvent types are most useful when you want to temporarily stop one or more threads until another thread says it's OK to proceed. You use these objects to wake up a thread much like an event handler can execute code in an idle thread, but don't be fooled by the "event" in their names. You don't use regular event handlers with these objects.

An instance of these types can be in either a signaled or an unsignaled state. These terms don't really have any special meaning; just think of them as on or off states. You pass the initial state to their constructor, and any thread that can access the object can change the state to signaled (using the Set method) or unsignaled (using the Reset method). Other threads can use the WaitOne method to wait until the state becomes signaled or until the specified timeout expires.

```
' Create an auto reset event object in nonsignaled state.
Dim are As New AutoResetEvent(False)
' Create a manual reset event object in signaled state.
Dim mre As New ManualResetEvent(True)
```

The only difference between ManualResetEvent and AutoResetEvent objects is that the latter ones automatically reset themselves (that is, become unsignaled) immediately after a thread blocked on a WaitOne method has been restarted. In practice, an AutoResetEvent object wakes up only one of the waiting threads when the object becomes signaled, whereas a ManualResetEvent object wakes up all the waiting threads and must be manually reset to unsignaled, as its name suggests.

As I mentioned previously, you can always replace an AutoResetEvent or a ManualResetEvent object with a proper EventWaitHandle object, as follows:

```
' These statements are equivalent to the previous code example.
Dim are As New EventWaitHandle(False, EventResetMode.AutoReset)
Dim mre As New EventWaitHandle(True, EventResetMode.ManualReset)
```

Event objects are especially useful in producer–consumer situations. You might have a single producer thread that evaluates some data—or reads it from disk, a serial port, the Internet, and so on—and then calls the Set method on a shared synchronization object so that one or more consumer threads can be restarted and process the new data. You should use an AutoResetEvent object (or an EventWaitHandle object with the AutoReset option) if only one consumer thread should process such data; you should use a ManualResetEvent object (or an EventWaitHandle object with the ManualReset option) if data should be processed by all consumers.

The following example shows how you can have multiple threads (the producer threads) performing file searches on different directories at the same time but a single thread (the consumer thread) collecting their results. This example uses a shared AutoResetEvent object to wake up the consumer thread when new filenames have been added to the List(Of String) object, and it also uses the Interlocked class to manage the counter of running threads so that the main thread knows when there's no more data to consume.

```
' The shared AutoResetEvent object
Public are As New AutoResetEvent(False)
' The list where matching filenames should be added
Public fileList As New List(Of String)()
' The number of running threads
Public searchingThreads As Integer
' An object used for locking purposes
Public lockObj As New Object()

Sub TestAutoResetEvent()
    ' Search *.zip files in all the subdirectories of C.
    For Each dirname As String In Directory.GetDirectories("C:\")
        Interlocked.Increment(searchingThreads)
        ' Create a new wrapper class, pointing to a subdirectory.
        Dim sf As New FileFinder()
        sf.StartPath = dirname
        sf.SearchPattern = "*.zip"
        ' Create and run a new thread for that subdirectory only.
        Dim t As New Thread(AddressOf sf.StartSearch)
        t.Start()
    Next

    ' Remember how many results we have so far.
```

```
    Dim resCount As Integer = 0
    Do While searchingThreads > 0
        ' Wait until there are new results.
        are.WaitOne()

        SyncLock lockObj
            ' Display all new results.
            For i As Integer = resCount To fileList.Count - 1
                Console.WriteLine(fileList(i))
            Next
            ' Remember that you've displayed these filenames.
            resCount = fileList.Count
        End SyncLock
    Loop
    Console.WriteLine("")
    Console.WriteLine("Found {0} files", resCount)
End Sub
```

Each producer thread runs inside a different FileFinder object, which must be able to access the public variables defined in the preceding code.

```
Class FileFinder
    Public StartPath As String        ' The starting search path
    Public SearchPattern As String    ' The search pattern

    Sub StartSearch()
        Search(Me.StartPath)
        ' Decrease the number of running threads before exiting.
        Interlocked.Decrement(searchingThreads)
        ' Let the consumer know it should check the thread counter.
        are.Set()
    End Sub

    ' This recursive procedure does the actual job.
    Sub Search(ByVal path As String)
        ' Get all the files that match the search pattern.
        Dim files() As String = Directory.GetFiles(path, SearchPattern)
        ' If there is at least one file, let the main thread know about it.
        If files IsNot Nothing AndAlso files.Length > 0 Then
            ' Ensure found files are added as an atomic operation.
            SyncLock lockObj
                ' Add all found files.
                fileList.AddRange(files)
                ' Let the consumer thread know about the new filenames.
                are.Set()
            End SyncLock
        End If

        ' Repeat the search on all subdirectories.
        For Each dirname As String In Directory.GetDirectories(path)
            Search(dirname)
        Next
    End Sub
End Class
```

Using an EventWaitHandle in lieu of an AutoResetEvent or ManualResetEvent object gives you one important feature: the ability to create a system-wide named object that you can share with other processes. The syntax for the EventWaitHandle constructor is similar to the one exposed by the Mutex class:

```
' Create a system-wide auto reset event that is initially in the signaled state.
Dim ownership As Boolean
Dim ewh As New EventWaitHandle(True, EventResetMode.AutoReset, "eventname", ownership)
If ownership Then
    ' The event object was created by the current thread.
    ...
End If
```

You can also use the OpenExisting static method to open an existing event object.

```
' This statement throws a WaitHandleCannotBeOpenedException if the specified
' event doesn't exist, or an UnauthorizedAccessException if the current
' user doesn't have the required permissions.
ewh = EventWaitHandle.OpenExisting("eventname", EventWaitHandleRights.FullControl)
```

The second important new feature of event objects in .NET Framework 2.0 is the support for ACLs by means of the SetAccessControl and GetAccessControl methods, which take and return an instance of the EventWaitHandleSecurity type. You can use these methods in much the same way you use the SetAccessControl and GetAccessControl methods exposed by the Mutex objects and all other .NET objects that support ACLs, and thus I won't provide any code samples.

Using the Thread Pool

Creating too many threads can easily degrade system performance, especially when the additional threads spend most of their time in a sleeping state and are restarted periodically only to poll a resource or to update the display. You can often improve the performance of your code significantly by resorting to the .NET thread pool, which permits the most efficient use of thread resources. Some objects in the System.Threading namespaces, such as Timers, transparently use the thread pool (see the following sections for more details about timers).

The ThreadPool Type

The thread pool is created the first time you invoke the ThreadPool.QueueUserWorkItem method or when a timer or a registered wait operation queues a callback operation. The pool has a default limit of 25 active threads; each thread uses the default stack size and runs at the default priority. The thread pool is available in all Windows versions.

You can borrow a thread from the pool by using the ThreadPool.QueueUserWorkItem method, which requires a WaitCallback delegate and an optional object that holds the data you want to pass to the thread. The WaitCallback delegate must point to a Sub procedure that receives one Object argument (whose value is either the optional object passed to the

QueueUserWorkItem method or Nothing). The following code shows how you can use a large number of threads to call an instance method of a class:

```
For i As Integer = 1 To 20
    ' Create a new object for the next lightweight task.
    Dim task As New LightweightTask()
    ' Pass additional information to it. (Not used in this demo.)
    task.SomeData = "other data"
    ' Run the task with a thread from the pool. (Pass the counter as an argument.)
    ThreadPool.QueueUserWorkItem(AddressOf task.Execute, i)
Next
```

The next block is the LightweightTask class, which contains the code that actually runs in the thread taken from the pool:

```
Class LightweightTask
    Public SomeData As String

    ' The method that contains the interesting code
    ' (Not really interesting in this example)
    Sub Execute(ByVal state As Object)
        Console.WriteLine("Message from thread #{0}", state)
    End Sub
End Class
```

The running thread can determine whether it has been taken from the thread pool by querying the Thread.CurrentThread.IsThreadPoolThread property. You can retrieve the highest number of threads in the pool by invoking the ThreadPool.GetMaxThreads static method, and the number of the threads that are currently available by invoking the ThreadPool .GetAvailableThreads static method.

A new method in .NET Framework 2.0 enables you to change the maximum number of threads in the pool:

```
' Maximum 30 worker threads and maximum 10 asynchronous I/O threads in the pool
ThreadPool.SetMaxThreads(30, 10)
```

You might sometimes be puzzled about whether you should create a thread yourself or borrow a thread from the pool. A good heuristic rule: use the Thread class when you want to run the associated task as soon as possible or when you perform a time-consuming task that doesn't run often. In the majority of cases, you should use the thread pool for more scalable server-side tasks.

The Timer Type

The .NET Framework offers several types of timers, each one with its strengths and limitations. For example, you should use the System.Windows.Forms.Timer control inside Windows Forms applications. If your application doesn't have a user interface, you should use either the System.Threading.Timer class or the System.Timers.Timer class. These two classes are broadly equivalent in their functionality, so I describe only the first one.

The Timer class in the System.Threading namespace offers a simple way to create a timer that calls back a given procedure. You can use this class to schedule an action in the future, and this action can be performed with whatever frequency you decide, including just once. The Timer's constructor takes four arguments:

- A TimerCallback delegate pointing to the procedure that's called when the timer's timeout elapses. The callback procedure must be a Sub that takes a single Object as an argument.

- An object that will be passed to the callback procedure. This object can be an individual number or string, an array or collection (or any other object) that holds additional data required by the callback method. (This data might be necessary because one callback procedure can serve multiple timers.) Use Nothing if you don't need to pass additional data to the callback procedure.

- A TimeSpan value that specifies the due time—that is, when the timer must invoke the callback routine for the first time. This argument can be specified as a Long or UInteger value, in which case the elapsed time is measured in milliseconds. Pass Timeout.Infinite to prevent the timer from starting, or pass 0 to activate it immediately.

- A TimeSpan value that specifies the timer's period—that is, how often the timer must invoke the callback routine after the first time. This argument can be specified as a Long or UInteger value, in which case the elapsed time is measured in milliseconds. Pass –1 or Timeout.Infinite to disable periodic signaling.

The values that you pass to the Timer's constructor aren't exposed as properties. After the timer is running, you can change these values only by means of a Change method, which takes only two arguments, the due time and the period. The Timer object has no Stop method. You stop the timer by calling its Dispose method. The following example shows how to use the timer with a callback procedure:

```
Sub TestThreadingTimer()
   ' Get the first callback after one second.
   Dim dueTime As New TimeSpan(0, 0, 1)
   ' Get additional callbacks every half second.
   Dim period As New TimeSpan(0, 0, 0, 0, 500)
   ' Create the timer.
   Using t As New Timer(AddressOf TimerProc, Nothing, dueTime, period)
      ' Wait for five seconds in this demo, and then destroy the timer.
      Thread.Sleep(5000)
   End Using
End Sub


' The callback procedure
Sub TimerProc(ByVal state As Object)
   ' Display current system time in console window.
   Console.WriteLine("Callback proc called at {0}", Date.Now)
End Sub
```

The callback procedure runs on a thread taken from the thread pool, so you should arbitrate access to variables and other resources used by the main thread by using one of the synchronization features that I describe in this chapter.

Asynchronous Operations

By now, you should be familiar with the Thread class and all the synchronization issues that you have to address when you're creating multithreading applications. At times, however, you'd simply like to execute a method call without blocking the main thread. For example, you might want to perform a long math calculation on a secondary thread while the application's main thread takes care of the user interface. In this case, what you really want to do is make a single asynchronous method call, which runs on another thread while the caller thread continues its normal execution. This programming model is so common that the .NET Framework offers special support for it so that *all* methods can be called asynchronously without your having to specifically design the target method to support asynchronous calls.

This generic mechanism is based on asynchronous delegates. In addition, the framework offers more asynchronous support in many specific areas, including file I/O, XML Web services, and messages sent over Microsoft Message Queuing (MSMQ). Thanks to this unified approach, you need to learn the asynchronous programming pattern only once, and you can apply it to all these areas.

Asynchronous Delegates

I describe how delegates work in Chapter 7, "Delegates and Events," but I intentionally left out a few details that are related to asynchronous use of delegates. In this section, I show you how you can use advanced features of delegates to call a method asynchronously. Let's start by defining a method that could take a significant amount of time to complete and therefore is a good candidate for an asynchronous call:

```
' This procedure scans a directory tree for a file.
' It takes a path and a file specification and returns a list of
' filenames; it returns the number of directories that have been
' parsed in the third argument.

Function FindFiles(ByVal path As String, ByVal fileSpec As String, _
      ByRef parsedDirs As Integer) As List(Of String)
   ' Prepare the result.
   FindFiles = New List(Of String)()
   ' Get all files in this directory that match the file spec.
   FindFiles.AddRange(Directory.GetFiles(path, fileSpec))
   ' Remember that a directory has been parsed.
   parsedDirs += 1

   ' Scan subdirectories.
   For Each subdir As String In Directory.GetDirectories(path)
     ' Add all the matching files in subdirectories.
     FindFiles.AddRange(FindFiles(subdir, fileSpec, parsedDirs))
   Next
End Function
```

You call the FindFiles routine by passing a starting path, a file specification (which can contain wildcards), and an Integer variable. On returning from the function, the Integer variable holds the number of directories that have been parsed, whereas the function itself returns a List object that contains the names of the files that match the specification:

```
Dim parsedDirs As Integer
' Find *.dll files in the C:\WINDOWS directory tree.
Dim files As List(Of String) = FindFiles("c:\windows", "*.dll", parsedDirs)
For Each file As String In files
    Console.WriteLine(file)
Next
' Use the output argument.
Console.WriteLine("  {0} directories have been parsed.", parsedDirs)
```

Asynchronous Calls

The first step in implementing an asynchronous call to the FindFiles function is defining a delegate class that points to it:

```
Delegate Function FindFilesDelegate(ByVal path As String, _
    ByVal fileSpec As String, ByRef parsedDirs As Integer) As List(Of String)
```

To call the FindFiles procedure asynchronously, you create a delegate that points to the routine and use the delegate's BeginInvoke method to call the routine as you would use the delegate's Invoke method. The BeginInvoke method—which has been created for you by the Visual Basic compiler—takes the same arguments as the procedure the delegate points to, plus two additional arguments that I describe later. Unlike the Invoke method, though, BeginInvoke returns an IAsyncResult object. You can then query the IsCompleted read-only property of this IAsyncResult object to determine when the called routine has completed its execution. If this property returns True, you call the delegate's EndInvoke method to retrieve both the return value and the value of any argument that was passed by using ByRef (parsedDirs in the following procedure):

```
' Create a delegate that points to the target procedure.
Dim findFilesDeleg As New FindFilesDelegate(AddressOf FindFiles)
' Start the asynchronous call; get an IAsyncResult object.
Dim parsedDirs As Integer
Dim ar As IAsyncResult = findFilesDeleg.BeginInvoke( _
    "c:\windows", "*.dll", parsedDirs, Nothing, Nothing)

' Wait until the method completes its execution.
Do Until ar.IsCompleted
    Console.WriteLine("The main thread is waiting for FindFiles results.")
    Thread.Sleep(500)
Loop

' Now you can get the results.
Dim files As List(Of String) = findFilesDeleg.EndInvoke(parsedDirs, ar)
For Each file As String In files
    Console.WriteLine(file)
Next
Console.WriteLine("  {0} directories have been parsed.", parsedDirs)
```

You should call EndInvoke only after IAsyncResult.IsCompleted returns True; otherwise, the EndInvoke method blocks the calling thread until the called procedure completes. (And you would lose the advantage of making an asynchronous call.)

The code in the preceding procedure polls the IsCompleted property to determine when the asynchronous call has completed. A less CPU-intensive means to achieve the same result uses the IAsyncResult.AsyncWaitHandle property, which returns a WaitHandle synchronization object. You can then use the WaitOne method of this object to make the main thread wait until the asynchronous call completes:

```
ar.AsyncWaitHandle.WaitOne()
```

As you learned earlier in the section titled "The Mutex Type," the WaitHandle type exposes the WaitAny and WaitAll static methods, which are especially useful when you run multiple asynchronous operations in parallel. Both methods take an array of WaitHandle objects: the WaitAny method blocks the calling thread until any of the asynchronous operations complete, whereas the WaitAll method blocks the calling thread until all the asynchronous operations complete. Unfortunately, you can't call these two methods from a thread running in a Single Thread Apartment (STA); thus, you must create a separate thread using the Thread class and run the asynchronous operations from this new thread (unless you're already running in a thread outside an STA).

Asynchronous Callback Procedures

As I explained earlier, the BeginInvoke method takes all the arguments in the original method's signature, plus two additional arguments. The second-to-last argument is a delegate pointing to a callback procedure that's called when the asynchronous method completes its execution:

```
Dim ar As IAsyncResult = findFilesDeleg.BeginInvoke( _
    "c:\windows", "*.dll", parsedDirs, AddressOf MethodCompleted, Nothing)
```

The technique based on callback procedures offers a viable alternative to making the main thread use the IsCompleted or AsyncWaitHandle property of the IAsyncResult object to determine when it's safe to gather the return value and any ByRef arguments.

The callback procedure must follow the syntax of the AsyncCallback delegate (defined in the System namespace), which defines a Sub procedure that takes an IAsyncResult object as its only argument. The code inside the callback procedure should call the delegate's EndInvoke method to retrieve the return value and the value of any ByRef arguments. Here's a possible implementation of the callback procedure for the example seen previously:

```
Sub MethodCompleted(ByVal ar As IAsyncResult)
    Dim parsedDirs As Integer
    Dim files As List(Of String) = findFilesDeleg.EndInvoke(parsedDirs, ar)
    ' Display found files.
    ' …(Omitted, same as previous examples) …
End Sub
```

This approach poses two minor problems. First, the callback routine doesn't have any way of knowing why it has been called, so it's difficult to reuse the same callback routine for multiple asynchronous calls. This problem can be solved easily by passing one value in the last argument of the BeginInvoke method:

```
' (In the caller program...)
Dim msg As String = "DLL files in c:\windows"
Dim ar As IAsyncResult = findFilesDeleg.BeginInvoke( _
    "c:\windows", "*.dll", parsedDirs, AddressOf MethodCompleted, msg)
```

(If you need to pass two or more values, you can stuff them into an array and pass the array as the argument.) You can extract this argument by querying the AsyncState property of the IAsyncResult argument in the callback method:

```
' (In the callback method...)
Dim msg As String = DirectCast(ar.AsyncState, String)
```

Second, the callback method must have access to the delegate variable (findFilesDeleg, in this particular example); this isn't an issue when both routines belong to the same class or module (you can simply declare the delegate as a private class-level variable), but it becomes a problem when the callback routine is in another class, possibly located in a different assembly. You can solve this problem by casting the IAsyncResult value to an AsyncResult object and then querying the AsyncDelegate property of the AsyncResult object:

```
' (Inside the callback method...)
Dim deleg As FindFilesDelegate = DirectCast(DirectCast(ar, _
    AsyncResult).AsyncDelegate, FindFilesDelegate)
```

To recap, this is the code you need to write in the method that creates the asynchronous delegate:

```
' Create a delegate that points to the target procedure.
Dim findFilesDeleg As New FindFilesDelegate(AddressOf FindFiles)
' Start the async call, pass a delegate pointing to the MethodCompleted
' procedure, and get an IAsyncResult object.
Dim parsedDirs As Integer
Dim msg As String = "DLL files in c:\windows"
Dim ar As IAsyncResult = findFilesDeleg.BeginInvoke( _
    "c:\windows", "*.dll", parsedDirs, AddressOf MethodCompleted, msg)
...
```

The callback method must retrieve the data passed in the AsyncState property of the IAsyncResult object:

```
Sub MethodCompleted(ByVal ar As IAsyncResult)
    ' Extract the delegate.
    Dim deleg As FindFilesDelegate = DirectCast(DirectCast(ar, _
    AsyncResult).AsyncDelegate, FindFilesDelegate)
    ' Extract the argument.
    Dim msg As String = DirectCast(ar.AsyncState, String)
    ' Call the EndInvoke method, and display result.
```

```
   Console.WriteLine(msg)
   Dim parsedDirs As Integer
   For Each file As String In deleg.EndInvoke(parsedDirs, ar)
      Console.WriteLine(file)
   Next
   Console.WriteLine("  {0} directories have been parsed.", parsedDirs)
End Sub
```

More on Asynchronous Method Invocation

A relevant detail I haven't covered yet is how the asynchronous architecture deals with exceptions. It turns out that both the BeginInvoke and EndInvoke methods can throw an exception.

If BeginInvoke throws an exception, you know that the asynchronous call hasn't been queued and you shouldn't call the EndInvoke method. These exceptions might be thrown by the .NET asynchronous infrastructure—for example, when the target of the asynchronous call is a remote object that can't be reached.

EndInvoke can throw an exception, too; this happens either when the asynchronous method throws an exception or when the .NET asynchronous infrastructure throws an exception—for example, when the remote object can't be reached any longer. The obvious suggestion is that you should bracket EndInvoke calls inside a Try...End Try block, as you would do for any regular method call that can throw an exception.

Sometimes, however, you don't really care whether the called method actually throws an exception. This might be the case, for example, if the procedure doesn't return a value and doesn't take ByRef arguments. You can inform the .NET runtime that you aren't interested in the outcome of the method, including any exceptions it might throw, by marking the method with the System.Runtime.Remoting.Messaging.OneWay attribute:

```
<System.Runtime.Remoting.Messaging.OneWay()> _
Sub MethodThatMayThrow(ByVal anArgument As Object)
   ...
End Sub
```

You get no error if this attribute is applied to a method that includes a ByRef argument or a return value, but such argument or return value isn't returned to the calling application. Here are a few more tips about asynchronous calls:

- The effect of calling EndInvoke twice on the same IAsyncResult object is indefinite, so you should avoid performing this operation.

- Even if BeginInvoke takes a ByRef argument, the .NET asynchronous infrastructure doesn't record the address of this argument anywhere, and therefore it can't automatically update the variable when the method completes. The only way to retrieve the value of an output argument is by passing it to the EndInvoke method.

- If the called method takes a reference to an object (passed with either ByVal or ByRef), the method can assign that object's properties. The caller can see those new values even before the asynchronous method completes. If both the caller and the called method access the same object, however, you might want to provide some form of synchronization of its property procedures.

- The .NET asynchronous infrastructure provides no generic means to cancel an asynchronous method once the BeginInvoke method has been called because in many cases there's no reliable way to cancel a running operation. In general, it's up to the class's author to implement a method that cancels an asynchronous method call.

Asynchronous File Operations

The great thing about asynchronous support in .NET is that once you become familiar with its programming pattern, you can apply it to several classes that expose asynchronous operations natively—that is, without the need of an explicit asynchronous delegate to the method. In this section, I show you how to use the BeginRead, EndRead, BeginWrite, and EndWrite methods of the Stream type to perform asynchronous file I/O. All the stream-based classes, including FileStream, inherit these methods. Other .NET types expose a similar Begin/End pattern, for example, the Web services proxy classes that Visual Studio generates.

The BeginWrite method takes a Byte array that contains the data to be written to the stream, the index of the first element to write, and the number of bytes to write: these are the same arguments that the regular, synchronous Write method accepts. You also pass an AsyncCallback delegate and a state object, as you do with all the asynchronous method invocations that were shown in earlier sections. The callback routine must conclude the write operation by invoking the EndWrite method and then close the stream.

The BeginRead method has the same argument signature as BeginWrite, with the first three values defining the location at which data read from the stream will be stored. The callback routine must conclude the asynchronous read operation by invoking an EndRead method and then close the stream. The EndRead method returns the total number of bytes read; a 0 value means that there were no more bytes to read.

The following code shows an example of asynchronous write and read operations on the same file. A single callback routine serves both the write and the read operations: the type of operation is passed as a string in the last argument to BeginWrite and BeginRead. To keep the code simple, both the caller routine and the callback routine share the variable pointing to the Byte array buffer and the FileStream object. In a real-world application, you might want to pack this data into an object and pass it as the last argument to BeginWrite and BeginRead:

```
' The file being read from or written to
Const FileName As String = "C:\TESTDATA.TMP"
' The FileStream object used for both reading and writing
Dim fs As FileStream
```

```
' The buffer for file I/O
Dim buffer(1048575) As Byte

Sub TestAsyncFileOperations()
    ' Fill the buffer with random data.
    For i As Integer = 0 To UBound(buffer)
        buffer(i) = CByte(i Mod 256)
    Next

    ' Create the target file in asynchronous mode (open in asynchronous mode).
    fs = New FileStream(FileName, FileMode.Create, _
        FileAccess.Write, FileShare.None, 65536, True)
    ' Start the async write operation.
    Console.WriteLine("Starting the async write operation")
    Dim ar As IAsyncResult = fs.BeginWrite(buffer, 0, _
        buffer.Length, AddressOf AsyncFileCallback, "write")

    ' Wait a few seconds until the operation completes.
    Thread.Sleep(4000)
    ' Now read the file back.
    fs = New FileStream(FileName, FileMode.Open, _
        FileAccess.Read, FileShare.None, 65536, True)
    ' Size the receiving buffer.
    ReDim buffer(CInt(fs.Length) - 1)
    ' Start the async read operation.
    Console.WriteLine("Starting the async read operation")
    ar = fs.BeginRead(buffer, 0, buffer.Length, _
        AddressOf AsyncFileCallback, "read")
End Sub

' This is the callback procedure for both async read and write.
Sub AsyncFileCallback(ByVal ar As IAsyncResult)
    ' Get the state object (the "write" or "read" string).
    Dim opName As String = ar.AsyncState.ToString()

    ' The behavior is quite different in the two cases.
    Select Case opName
        Case "write"
            Console.WriteLine("Async write operation completed")
            ' Complete the write, and close the stream.
            fs.EndWrite(ar)
            fs.Close()
        Case "read"
            Console.WriteLine("Async read operation completed")
            ' Complete the read, and close the stream.
            Dim bytes As Integer = fs.EndRead(ar)
            Console.WriteLine("Read {0} bytes", bytes)
            fs.Close()
    End Select
End Sub
```

You get the best benefits from asynchronous file I/O if you also open the FileStream for asynchronous operations by passing True in the last argument of the object's constructor:

```
fs = New FileStream(path, mode, access, share, bufferSize, useAsync)
```

When you open a FileStream in this way, synchronous operations are slowed, but asynchronous operations are completed faster. Keep in mind that read and write operations of less then 64 KB are usually performed synchronously anyway, even if you use BeginWrite or BeginRead, and that the useAsync argument might be ignored on Windows platforms that don't support asynchronous file operations. You can test whether the FileStream was actually opened for asynchronous operation by testing its IsAsync property.

Adding Asynchronous Support to Your Types

Even though the .NET Framework enables you to invoke any method of any type asynchronously, it's a good idea to expose a pair of Begin*Xxxx*/End*Xxxx* methods for any lengthy task that your class can perform. This pattern is especially useful if you can also expose a Cancel*Xxxx* method, which allows clients to abort an asynchronous operation. (As you saw earlier, asynchronous delegates don't expose this feature because, in general, the .NET Framework can't assume that it is safe to cancel a running method without causing a corruption.)

The following example shows a TextFileReader class that exposes a Read method for reading a text file in a synchronous manner; the BeginRead and EndRead methods to perform the same operation asynchronously, and the CancelRead method to cancel an asynchronous read operation.

```
Public Class TextFileReader
    ' This private delegate matches the signature of the Read method.
    Private Delegate Function InvokeRead(ByVal fileName As String) As String

    ' True if the asynchronous operation has been canceled
    Private canceled As Boolean
    ' A delegate that points to the Read method
    Private deleg As InvokeRead
    ' The object used to control asynchronous operations
    Private ar As IAsyncResult

    ' The Read method (synchronous)
    Public Function Read(ByVal fileName As String) As String
        canceled = False
        Dim sb As New System.Text.StringBuilder()
        Using sr As New StreamReader(fileName)
            Do While sr.Peek() <> -1
                sb.Append(sr.ReadLine()).Append(ControlChars.CrLf)
                If canceled Then Return Nothing
            Loop
            Return sb.ToString()
        End Using
    End Function

    ' The following methods add support for asynchronous operations.
    Public Sub BeginRead(ByVal fileName As String)
        deleg = New InvokeRead(AddressOf Read)
        ar = deleg.BeginInvoke(fileName, Nothing, Nothing)
    End Sub
```

```
    Public Function EndRead() As String
        If canceled OrElse deleg Is Nothing Then
            Return Nothing
        Else
            Return deleg.EndInvoke(ar)
        End If
    End Function

    Public Sub CancelRead()
        ' Cause the Read method to exit prematurely.
        If Not canceled AndAlso deleg IsNot Nothing Then
            canceled = True
            deleg.EndInvoke(ar)
        End If
    End Sub
End Class
```

You can easily apply the same mechanism to other classes that expose time-consuming operations that can be split into simpler tasks.

Threading in Windows Forms Applications

All the techniques I have illustrated so far were applied in a Console application, and I had a good reason to do so. In fact, you must take into account some constraints when you implement threading in a Windows Forms project; otherwise, your application will almost surely fail at run time.

The problem with Windows Forms objects—both controls and the Form object itself—is that they must be accessed *exclusively* from the thread that created them. In fact, all the Windows Forms objects rely on the STA model because windows and controls are based on the Win32 message architecture, which is inherently apartment-threaded. This means that you can create a control or a form from any thread, but all the methods of the control must be called from that same thread.

This constraint can create a serious problem because other .NET portions use the free-threading model, and carelessly mixing the two models isn't a wise idea. Even if you don't explicitly create a thread in your code, you might experience problems any way, for example, if you access a UI element from the Finalize method of a type. (As you know, the Finalize method runs on a thread other than the main thread.)

The ISynchronizeInvoke Interface

The only members that you can call on a control object from another thread are those exposed by the ISynchronizeInvoke interface: the Invoke, BeginInvoke, and EndInvoke methods and the InvokeRequired read-only property.

The InvokeRequired property returns True if the caller can't access the control directly (that is, if the caller is running in a thread other than the thread that created the control). If this is the case, the caller should invoke the Invoke method to access any member exposed by the control. The Invoke method is synchronous, and therefore the calling thread is blocked until the UI thread completes the method. Alternatively, the calling thread can use the BeginInvoke and EndInvoke methods to perform the operation asynchronously: the pattern for using these two methods is exactly the same as the one I illustrate in the section titled "Asynchronous Delegates" earlier in this chapter. In this section, I focus on the Invoke method only, but you can easily apply these concepts to the BeginInvoke and EndInvoke methods as well.

The Invoke method takes a delegate pointing to a method (Sub or Function) and can take an Object array as a second argument if the method expects one or more arguments. The Windows Forms infrastructure ensures that the procedure pointed to by the delegate is executed in the UI thread and can therefore safely access any control on the form.

Let's see how you can use the Invoke method to access a control from a non-UI thread. The following example shows how you can visit all the directories in a directory tree from a secondary thread, while displaying the name of the directory being parsed in a Label control.

The first thing to do is to define a method that performs the intended UI operation; such a method can be as simple as this procedure:

```
' This method must run in the main UI thread.
Sub ShowMessage(ByVal msg As String)
   Me.lblMessage.Text = msg
   Me.Refresh()
End Sub
```

Next, you define a delegate type that can point to the previous method and a variable that can hold an instance of the delegate. This variable is defined at the form level so that it can be shared by all methods in the form:

```
' A delegate that can point to the ShowMessage procedure
Delegate Sub ShowMessageDelegate(ByVal msg As String)
' An instance of the delegate
Dim threadSafeDelegate As ShowMessageDelegate
```

You need a method that starts the secondary thread. Being a Windows Forms application, this method is likely to be the Click handler of a Button control:

```
' Parse the c:\windows directory when the user clicks this button.
Private Sub btnSearch_Click(ByVal sender As Object, ByVal e As EventArgs) _
      Handles btnSearch.Click
   Dim t As New Thread(AddressOf SearchFiles)
   t.Start("c:\windows")
End Sub
```

Finally, you write the code that runs in the secondary thread. It is essential, however, that this code accesses the lblMessage control only by means of a call to the ShowMessage method, and that this call occurs through the Invoke method of the Form class (or the Invoke method of any control on the form, which is perfectly equivalent). Such calls are highlighted in bold type in the following listing:

```
' (This method runs in a non-UI thread.)
Sub SearchFiles(ByVal arg As Object)
   ' Retrieve the argument.
   Dim path As String = arg.ToString()
   ' Prepare the delegate
   threadSafeDelegate = New ShowMessageDelegate(AddressOf ShowMessage)
   ' Invoke the worker procedure. (The result isn't used in this demo.)
   Dim files As List(Of String) = GetFiles(path)
   ' Show that execution has terminated.
   Dim msg As String = String.Format("Found {0} files", files.Count)
   Me.Invoke(threadSafeDelegate, msg)
End Sub

' A recursive function that retrieves all the files in a directory tree
' (This method runs in a non-UI thread.)
Function GetFiles(ByVal path As String) As List(Of String)
   ' Display a message.
   Dim msg As String = String.Format("Parsing directory {0}", path)
   Me.Invoke(threadSafeDelegate, msg)
   ' Read the files in this folder and all subfolders.
   Dim files As New List(Of String)
   For Each fi As String In Directory.GetFiles(path)
      files.Add(fi)
   Next
   For Each di As String In Directory.GetDirectories(path)
      files.AddRange(GetFiles(di))
   Next
   Return files
End Function
```

The implementation of this technique becomes more complicated if the ShowMessage method is being used by both the UI thread and a non-UI thread. For example, the GetFiles method might be called from a UI thread, in which case making the call through the Invoke method adds an overhead that might and should be avoided. In this case, you should test the Invoke-Required property first and make a regular method call if the property returns False, as in the following:

```
   ' (Inside the SearchFiles and GetFiles methods)
   If Me.InvokeRequired Then
      Me.Invoke(threadSafeDelegate, msg)
   Else
      ShowMessage(msg)
   End If
```

There is an even better approach, though: instead of testing the InvokeRequired property from each caller, you test it from inside the ShowMessage method itself:

```
' This method can run in the UI thread or in a non-UI thread.
Sub ShowMessage(ByVal msg As String)
   ' Use the Invoke method only if necessary.
```

```
If Me.InvokeRequired Then
    Me.Invoke(threadSafeDelegate, msg)
    Return
End If

Me.lblMessage.Text = msg
Me.Refresh()
End Sub
```

After this change, any piece of code that must display a message on the lblMessage control can just call the ShowMessage without having to worry about whether the code is running in the UI thread or in a secondary thread.

Note It is crucial that you don't suspend or invoke the Join method on the main UI thread in a Windows Forms application while waiting for the other thread to complete because these actions would prevent the main thread from accepting calls from the other thread through the Invoke method.

In some circumstances, a .NET application can access a control from a non-UI thread without causing any problems. For example, it might happen when accessing simple controls (such as a Label) or when performing operations that don't cause a Win32 message to be sent behind the scenes. Also, many properties can be read (but not assigned) without interacting with the underlying Windows control because the property value is stored in a field of the .NET control. It is quite possible that a few .NET Framework 1.1 applications in the real world mistakenly access a control from the wrong thread without causing any noticeable problem. More frequently, however, the application has some sort of random malfunctioning that you can't easily associate with the actual cause.

Microsoft wanted to change this behavior and ensure that these mistakes don't go unnoticed, but at the same time wanted to preserve compatibility with existing applications so that an application compiled with Microsoft Visual Studio .NET 2003 continues to work well under .NET Framework 2.0. Thus, Microsoft adopted the following strategy: Visual Studio 2005 applications that access a control from a non-UI thread cause an exception, but only if compiled in Debug mode. The rationale is that developers won't miss this exception while testing new programs and can fix the problem before releasing the final version.

The BackgroundWorker Component

Although the ISynchronizeInvoke interface enables you to avoid threading problems in Windows Forms applications, most Visual Basic developers need a simpler and less error-prone approach. For example, they need a simple way to cancel an asynchronous method call safely, something that the ISynchronizeInvoke interface doesn't provide automatically.

For this reason, Microsoft has added the BackgroundWorker component to the Toolbox. As you'll see in a moment, using this new component is a breeze and will surely simplify the creation of robust multithreaded Windows Forms application.

The BackgroundWorker component has only two interesting properties: the WorkerReportsProgress (True if the component raises the ProgressChanged event) and WorkerSupportsCancellation (True if the component supports the CancelAsync method). The default value for both properties is False, and therefore you must set them to True if you want to take full advantage of this component. (The example that follows assumes that these properties are set to True.) Using the BackgroundWorker component typically requires the following actions:

1. Create a handler for the DoWork event and fill it with the code you want to run in the secondary thread. This code runs when the RunWorkerAsync method is called. The RunWorkerAsync method accepts an argument, which is passed to the DoWork event. The code in the DoWork event handler can't directly access the controls on the form because it runs in a non-UI thread.

2. Use the ReportProgress method from inside the DoWork event handler when you need to access a UI element. This method fires the ProgressChanged event if the WorkerReportsProgress property is True; otherwise, an InvalidOperationException object is thrown. The handlers for the ProgressChanged event run in the UI thread, and therefore they can safely access the form and its controls.

3. Use the CancelAsync method of the BackgroundWorker control to immediately abort the secondary thread. This method requires that the WorkerSupportsCancellation property be True; otherwise, an InvalidOperationException object is thrown. The code in the DoWork handler should periodically check the CancellationPending property and gracefully exit when this property becomes True.

4. Write a handler for the RunWorkerCompleted event if you need to perform an action when the secondary thread has completed, either naturally or because of a call to the CancelAsync method. Handlers of this event run in the UI thread, and therefore they can access any UI element.

Typically, the code in the DoWork event handler must return a value to the main thread. Instead of assigning this value to a class-level field—a dangerous technique that might lead to race conditions—the code should assign this value to the Result property of the DoWorkEventArgs object. This value is then made available to the main UI thread by means of the Result property of the RunWorkerCompletedEventArgs object passed to the RunWorkerCompleted event.

To recap, here's the typical structure of a form that uses the BackgroundWorker component:

```
' The button that starts the asynchronous operation
Private Sub btnStart_Click(ByVal sender As Object, ByVal e As EventArgs) _
      Handles btnStart.Click
   Dim argument As Object = "abcde"              ' The argument
```

```
        BackgroundWorker1.RunWorkerAsync(argument)
        ' Disable this button, and enable the "Stop" button.
        btnStart.Enabled = False
        btnStop.Enabled = True
    End Sub


    ' The button that cancels the asynchronous operation
    Private Sub btnStop_Click(ByVal sender As Object, ByVal e As EventArgs) _
            Handles btnStop.Click
        BackgroundWorker1.RunWorkerAsync(argument)
    End Sub


    ' The code that performs the asynchronous operation
    Private Sub BackgroundWorker1_DoWork(ByVal sender As Object, _
            ByVal e As DoWorkEventArgs) Handles BackgroundWorker1.DoWork
        ' Retrieve the argument.
        Dim argument As Object = e.Argument
        Dim percentage As Integer = 0
        …
        ' The core of the asynchronous task
        Do Until BackgroundWorker1.CancellationPending
            …
            ' Report progress when it makes sense to do so.
            BackgroundWorker1.ReportProgress(percentage)
        Loop
        ' Return the result to the caller.
        e.Result = primes
    End Sub


    ' This method runs when the ReportProgress method is invoked.
    Private Sub BackgroundWorker1_ProgressChanged(ByVal sender As Object, _
        ByVal e As ProgressChangedEventArgs) Handles BackgroundWorker1.ProgressChanged
        ' It is safe to access the user interface from here.
        ' For example, show the progress on a progress bar or another control.
        ToolStripProgressBar1.Value = e.ProgressPercentage
    End Sub


    ' This method runs when the asynchronous task is completed (or canceled).
    Private Sub BackgroundWorker1_RunWorkerCompleted(ByVal sender As Object, _
            ByVal e As RunWorkerCompletedEventArgs) Handles BackgroundWorker1.RunWorkerCompleted
        ' It is safe to access the user interface from here.
        …
        ' Reset the Enabled state of the Start and Stop buttons.
        btnStart.Enabled = True
        btnStop.Enabled = False
    End Sub
```

The following completed example shows how you can use the BackgroundWorker component to search for files on an asynchronous thread. (See Figure 20-8.) This is the same
problem I solved in the section titled "The ISynchronizeInvoke Interface" earlier in this
chapter, and thus you can easily compare the two techniques.

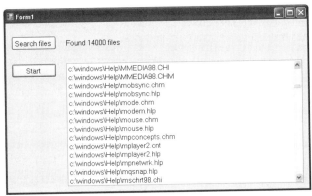

Figure 20-8   A demo application using the BackgroundWorker component to search for files in the background

The new version based on the BackgroundWorker component, however, is slightly more complex because it supports the cancellation of the asynchronous task:

```
' The result from the SearchFiles procedure
Dim files As List(Of String)
' We need this variable to avoid nested calls to ProgressChanged.
Dim callInProgress As Boolean

' The same button works as a Start and a Stop button.
Private Sub btnStart_Click(ByVal sender As Object, ByVal e As EventArgs) _
      Handles btnStart.Click
   If btnStart.Text = "Start" Then
      lstFiles.Items.Clear()
      Me.BackgroundWorker1.RunWorkerAsync("c:\windows")
      Me.btnStart.Text = "Stop"
   Else
      Me.BackgroundWorker1.CancelAsync()
   End If
End Sub

' The code that starts the asynchronous file search
Private Sub BackgroundWorker1_DoWork(ByVal sender As Object, ByVal e As DoWorkEventArgs) _
      Handles BackgroundWorker1.DoWork
   ' Retrieve the argument.
   Dim path As String = e.Argument.ToString()
   ' Invoke the worker procedure.
   files = New List(Of String)
   SearchFiles(path)
   ' Return a result to the RunWorkerCompleted event.
   Dim msg As String = String.Format("Found {0} files", files.Count)
   e.Result = msg
End Sub

' A recursive function that retrieves all the files in a directory tree.
Sub SearchFiles(ByVal path As String)
   ' Display a message.
```

```
      Dim msg As String = String.Format("Parsing directory {0}", path)
      ' Notice that we don't really use the percentage;
      ' instead, we pass the message in the UserState property.
      Me.BackgroundWorker1.ReportProgress(0, msg)

      ' Read the files in this folder and all subfolders.
      ' Exit immediately if the task has been canceled.
      For Each fi As String In Directory.GetFiles(path)
         If Me.BackgroundWorker1.CancellationPending Then Return
         files.Add(fi)
      Next
      For Each di As String In Directory.GetDirectories(path)
         If Me.BackgroundWorker1.CancellationPending Then Return
         SearchFiles(di)
      Next
   End Sub


   Private Sub BackgroundWorker1_ProgressChanged(ByVal sender As Object, _
         ByVal e As ProgressChangedEventArgs) _
         Handles BackgroundWorker1.ProgressChanged
      ' Reject nested calls.
      If callInProgress Then Return
      callInProgress = True
      ' Display the message, received in the UserState property.
      Me.lblMessage.Text = e.UserState.ToString()
      ' Display all files added since last call.
      For i As Integer = lstFiles.Items.Count To files.Count - 1
         lstFiles.Items.Add(files(i))
      Next
      Me.Refresh()
      ' Let the Windows operating system process message in the queue.
      ' If you omit this call, clicks on buttons are ignored.
      Application.DoEvents()
      callInProgress = False
   End Sub

   Private Sub BackgroundWorker1_RunWorkerCompleted(ByVal sender As Object, _
         ByVal e As RunWorkerCompletedEventArgs) _
         Handles BackgroundWorker1.RunWorkerCompleted
      ' Display the last message and reset button's caption.
      Me.lblMessage.Text = e.Result.ToString()
      btnStart.Text = "Start"
   End Sub
```

This code is quite self-explanatory, except for the handler of the ProgressChanged event. This code must contain a call to the Application.DoEvents() method; otherwise, the application can't process clicks on the Stop button (or any other UI action, for that matter). However, calls to this method might cause nested calls to the ProgressChanged procedure itself, and these additional calls might cause a StackOverflowException. For this reason, the code uses an auxiliary callInProgress Boolean field to avoid such nested calls.

Also notice that this application doesn't need to report a progress percentage to the main thread, and it uses the ReportProgress method just as a means to execute a piece of code in the UI thread. The actual message to be displayed is passed in the UserState property. If your application uses a progress bar or another indicator of progress, however, you should avoid unnecessary calls to the ReportProgress method because each call causes a thread switch and is relatively expensive in terms of processing time. In such cases, you should store the current percentage in a class field and call the method only if the percentage has actually changed:

```
Dim currentPercentage As Integer

Private Sub BackgroundWorker1_DoWork(ByVal sender As Object, ByVal e As DoWorkEventArgs) _
      Handles BackgroundWorker1.DoWork
   Const TotalSteps = 5000
   For i As Integer = 1 To TotalSteps
      …
      ' Evaluate progress percentage.
      Dim percentage As Integer = (i * 100) \ TotalSteps
      ' Report to UI thread only if percentage has changed.
      If percentage <> currentPercentage Then
         BackgroundWorker1.ReportProgress(percentage)
         currentPercentage = percentage
      End If
   Next
End Sub
```

Chapter 21
Serialization

Serialization is the act of saving (or *serializing*) an object onto a storage medium—a file, a database field, a buffer in memory—and later *deserializing* it from the storage medium to re-create an object instance that can be considered identical to the original one. Serialization is a key feature in the Microsoft .NET Framework and is transparently used by the CLR for tasks other than simply saving an object to a file—for example, for marshaling an object by value to another application. You should make an object serializable if you plan to send it to another application or save it on disk, in a database field, or in an ASP.NET Session object. For example, exception objects should be made serializable if they can be thrown from another AppDomain.

Serialization and *persistence* are often used as synonyms, so you can also say that an object is persisted and depersisted. The SDK documentation makes a distinction, however, and uses *persistence* to mean that the data is stored in a durable medium, such as a file or a database field, whereas *serialization* can be applied to objects stored in nondurable media, such as memory buffers.

Note   To avoid long lines, code samples in this chapter assume that the following Imports statements are used at the file or project level:

```
Imports System.IO
Imports System.Reflection
Imports System.Runtime.Serialization
Imports System.Runtime.Serialization.Formatters
Imports System.Runtime.Serialization.Formatters.Binary
Imports System.Runtime.Serialization.Formatters.Soap
Imports System.Security.Permissions
```

Basic Serialization

The .NET Framework knows how to serialize all basic data types, including numbers, strings, and arrays of numbers and strings, so you can save and reload these types to and from a file stream (or any other type of stream) with minimal effort. All you need to serialize and deserialize a basic object is a proper formatter object.

Formally speaking, a *formatter* is an object that implements the IFormatter interface (defined in the System.Runtime.Serialization namespace). You can create your own formatter by defining a class that implements this interface, but most of the time you can use one of the formatter objects provided by the .NET Framework:

■ The BinaryFormatter object, defined in the System.Runtime.Serialization.Formatters .Binary namespace, provides an efficient way to persist an object in a compact binary format. In practice, the actual bits in memory are persisted, so the serialization and deserialization processes are very fast.

■ The SoapFormatter object, defined in the System.Runtime.Serialization.Formatters .Soap namespace, persists data in human-readable XML format, following the Simple Object Access Protocol (SOAP) specifications. The serialization and deserialization processes are somewhat slower than they are with the BinaryFormatter object. On the other hand, data can be sent easily to another application through HTTP and displayed in a human-readable format.

The SoapFormatter type has been marked as obsolete in Microsoft .NET Framework version 2.0 and its use has been deprecated in favor of the BinaryFormatter. For this reason, our discussion will revolve mainly around the BinaryFormatter type.

The .NET Framework supports a third form of serialization, based on the XmlSerializer type and known as *XML serialization* (not to be confused with SOAP serialization). I briefly hinted at this type in the section titled "Shared Properties" in Chapter 6, "Class Fundamentals," and in the section titled "A Custom Attribute for CSV Serialization" in Chapter 19, "Custom Attributes," but I won't discuss this technique any further in this book.

Binary Serialization

The key methods that all formatter objects support are Serialize and Deserialize, whose purpose is quite evident. The Serialize method takes a Stream object as its first argument and the object to be serialized as its second argument:

```
' Create an array of integers.
Dim arr() As Integer = {1, 2, 4, 8, 16, 32, 64, 128, 256}
' Open a stream for output.
Using fs As New FileStream("c:\powers.dat", FileMode.Create)
   ' Create a binary formatter for this stream.
   Dim bf As New BinaryFormatter()
   ' Serialize the array to the file stream, and flush the stream.
   bf.Serialize(fs, arr)
End Using
```

The BinaryFormatter (and all other .NET formatters) can complete its task because the .NET Framework uses reflection to inspect any object at run time and discover, read, and assign all the object's fields and properties.

Reading back the file data and deserializing it into an object require the Deserialize function, which takes the input Stream as its only argument and returns an Object value, which must be cast to a properly typed variable:

```
Dim arr2() As Integer
' Open a file stream for input.
Using fs2 As New FileStream("c:\powers.dat", FileMode.Open)
   ' Create a binary formatter for this stream.
   Dim bf2 As New BinaryFormatter()
   ' Deserialize the contents of the file stream into an Integer array.
   ' (Deserialize returns an object that must be coerced.)
   arr2 = DirectCast(bf2.Deserialize(fs2), Integer())
End Using
```

You can indicate the reason you're creating a formatter by passing a StreamingContext object to the second argument of the formatter's constructor. The streaming context object contains information about the serialization and deserialization process and can be used by the object being serialized. For example, a formatter might opt for a compression algorithm if it's being serialized to a file. Even if you don't know whether the object you're serializing takes advantage of this additional information, specifying the streaming context is a good programming practice. Here's how you define a formatter that's used to serialize an object to a file:

```
Dim sc As New StreamingContext(StreamingContextStates.File)
Dim bf As New BinaryFormatter(Nothing, sc)
```

You can simplify the code that serializes and deserializes objects to and from files with a pair of reusable generic methods:

```
Public Sub SerializeToFile(Of T)(ByVal path As String, ByVal obj As T)
   ' Open the stream for output.
   Using fs As New FileStream(path, FileMode.Create)
      ' Create a formatter for this file stream.
      Dim bf As New BinaryFormatter(Nothing, _
         New StreamingContext(StreamingContextStates.File))
      ' Serialize the object and close the stream.
      bf.Serialize(fs, obj)
   End Using
End Sub

Public Function DeserializeFromFile(Of T)(ByVal path As String) As T
   ' Open the stream for input.
   Using fs As New FileStream(path, FileMode.Open)
      ' Create a formatter for this file stream.
      Dim bf As New BinaryFormatter(Nothing, _
         New StreamingContext(StreamingContextStates.File))
      ' Deserialize the object from the stream.
      Return DirectCast(bf.Deserialize(fs), T)
   End Using
End Function
```

Interestingly, the assembly containing the type being deserialized doesn't have to be loaded in memory. By default, the serialized stream contains information about the assembly identity (name, version, culture, and publisher's key if it is a strong-named assembly) and the assembly is searched and loaded as if you were instantiating one of its type with a standard New keyword. In some cases, the fact that the deserialization process preserves type identity can be a problem when the assembly's version changes. Read the section titled "Version-Tolerant Serialization (VTS)" later in this chapter for more information.

SOAP Serialization

You can change the serialization format to SOAP by simply using another formatter object, the SoapFormatter in the System.Runtime.Serialization.Formatters.Soap namespace, which is contained in the System.Runtime.Serialization.Formatters.Soap.dll assembly. This assembly isn't referenced by default by Microsoft Visual Basic projects, so you have to add a reference to it yourself.

```
' Create a Hashtable object, and fill it with some data.
Dim ht As New Hashtable()
ht.Add("One", 1)
ht.Add("Two", 2)
ht.Add("Three", 3)
' Create a SOAP serializer.
Dim sf As New SoapFormatter()
' Save the Hashtable to disk in SOAP format.
Using fs As New FileStream("c:\hashtable.xml", FileMode.Create)
    sf.Serialize(fs, ht)
End Using

' Reload the file contents, using the same SoapFormatter object.
Dim ht2 As Hashtable
Using fs As New FileStream("c:\hashtable.xml", FileMode.Open)
    ht2 = DirectCast(sf.Deserialize(fs), Hashtable)
End Using
' Prove that the object has been deserialized correctly.
For Each de As DictionaryEntry In ht2
    Console.WriteLine("Key={0}  Value={1}", de.Key, de.Value)
Next
```

As I noted earlier, the SoapFormatter has been marked as obsolete in .NET Framework 2.0, and thus you should always use the BinaryFormatter. However, the SOAP formatter has a feature that the binary formatter lacks: the serialized stream is made of readable XML text and you can actually browse it. For example, you can double-click the c:\hashtable.xml file from inside Windows Explorer to view its contents in a Microsoft Internet Explorer window. This ability is quite handy in the test and debug phase. Even if your applications use the BinaryFormatter object exclusively, you might find it useful to temporarily switch to the SoapFormatter object and persist the serialization stream to a file to understand why your objects aren't serialized and deserialized correctly.

Creating Serializable Types

You've seen how the CLR can serialize and deserialize basic types such as strings and arrays; thus, the next logical step is to understand how you can define a serializable object in your own code. It turns out that, in practice, the only thing you do to make a class serializable is to flag it with the Serializable attribute, whose constructor takes no arguments:

```
<Serializable()> _
Class Person
    ...
End Class
```

For this attribute to work correctly, only two conditions must be met: the base class must be serializable and all the fields in the class must be of a serializable type. If these conditions aren't fulfilled, any attempt to serialize an instance of the type results in a SerializationException error.

The first requirement isn't a problem when you inherit from System.Object because the Object class is serializable, but when you derive a class from something else you should ascertain whether your base class is serializable. The Serializable attribute isn't automatically inherited by derived classes and must be applied to them manually. (If it were inherited, all classes would automatically be serializable because they derive directly or indirectly from System.Object.)

If your type includes a public or private field whose type isn't serializable, you can take one of the following approaches: you either mark the field with the NonSerialized attribute or use custom serialization. I cover the latter technique in the section titled "Custom Serialization" later in this chapter, so let's focus on the NonSerialized attribute for now. You can apply this attribute to any public or private field:

```
<NonSerialized()> Private m_Password As String
```

In general, you should use the NonSerialized attribute for those fields that you don't want to be persisted when the object is serialized. As I explained previously, this attribute is required for fields whose type isn't serializable, for example, a field that points to a Windows Forms control (because the System.Windows.Forms.Control type isn't serializable). Another case when this attribute is virtually mandatory is when the value of a field isn't going to be valid when the object is being deserialized. Among such variables would be pointers, file handles, and handles to other operating system handles, for example, handles to windows, controls, brushes, and so forth. Other candidates for the NonSerializable attribute are fields whose value can be easily recalculated from other properties, as in the following Person class:

```
<Serializable()> _
Public Class Person
    Public ReadOnly FirstName As String
    Public ReadOnly LastName As String
    Private ReadOnly BirthDate As Date
    <NonSerialized()> Private m_Age As Integer

    ' Note that BirthDate can be set only by means of the constructor method.
    Sub New(ByVal firstName As String, ByVal lastName As String, ByVal birthDate As Date)
        Me.FirstName = firstName
        Me.LastName = lastName
        Me.BirthDate = birthDate
    End Sub
```

```
' The Age property caches its value in the m_Age private variable.
Public ReadOnly Property Age() As Integer
    Get
        ' Evaluate Age if not cached already.
        If m_Age = 0 Then
            m_Age = Now.Year - BirthDate.Year
            If BirthDate.DayOfYear > Now.DayOfYear Then m_Age -= 1
        End If
        Return m_Age
    End Get
End Property
End Class
```

The support for serializable types has been expanded to generic types in .NET Framework 2.0. For example, the following piece of code builds on the SerializeToFile and DeserializeFromFile routines described in the preceding section and shows how you can serialize and deserialize a List(Of Person) object.

```
Dim list As New List(Of Person)
list.Add(New Person("Joe", "Healy", #1/12/1960#))
list.Add(New Person("John", "Evans", #3/6/1962#))
list.Add(New Person("Ann", "Beebe", #10/4/1965#))
SerializeToFile("c:\persons.dat", list)

' Reload the file contents into another list object.
Dim list2 As List(Of Person) = DeserializeFromFile(Of List(Of Person))("c:\persons.dat")
For Each p As Person In list2
    Console.WriteLine("{0} {1} ({2})", p.FirstName, p.LastName, p.Age)
Next
```

This result appears in the console window:

```
Joe Healy (45)
John Evans (43)
Ann Beebe (40)
```

The noteworthy detail here is that, although the BirthDate field is private, the deserialization mechanism is able to restore correctly it from the input stream. (The evidence is the fact the Age property is evaluated correctly.) In other words, the deserialization mechanism is capable of ignoring scope rules. Keep this detail in mind when you define a class with a member containing sensitive information, such as passwords and credit card numbers, because this information is included in the serialized stream. If you serialize using a SoapFormatter, a malicious user can find and even modify it by simply loading the file into a text editor; if you used a BinaryFormatter, the information might not be stored in a human-readable format yet anyone with a bit of knowledge of the .NET deserialization mechanism can retrieve it.

Object Graphs

An object graph is a set of multiple objects with references to one another. You can serialize object graphs as easily as individual objects. The previous listing shows a simple form of object graph, because a List(Of Person) holds references to individual Person objects. As a result, the serialization of the List(Of Person) object indirectly causes the serialization of all the referenced Person objects. In general, the CLR can serialize all the objects that are directly or indirectly reachable from the object passed to the Serialize method. (Such an object is known as the *root object* of the graph.)

In the simplest cases, when there are no circular references between objects, each object is met exactly once during both the serialization and deserialization processes. Real-world object hierarchies are usually more complex than that, but the serialization infrastructure is capable of dealing with these cases, too. To demonstrate this point, you can add the following field to the Person class:

```
' (Add to the Person class…)
Public Spouse As Person
```

Then you can serialize and deserialize an entire object graph with this code:

```
' Create three Person objects.
Dim p1 As New Person("Joe", "Healy", #1/12/1960#)
Dim p2 As New Person("John", "Evans", #3/6/1962#)
Dim p3 As New Person("Ann", "Beebe", #10/4/1965#)
' Define the relationship between two of them.
p2.Spouse = p3
p3.Spouse = p2

' Load them into a List(Of Person) object in one operation.
Dim list As New List(Of Person)(New Person(){p1, p2, p3})
' Serialize to disk.
SerializeToFile("c:\persons.dat", list)

' Reload into another List(Of Person) object and display.
Dim list2 As List(Of Person) = DeserializeFromFile(Of List(Of Person))("c:\persons.dat")
For Each p As Person In list2
   Console.WriteLine("{0} {1} ({2})", p.FirstName, p.LastName, p.Age)
   If Not (p.Spouse Is Nothing) Then
      ' Show the spouse's name if there is one.
      Console.WriteLine("   Spouse of " & p.Spouse.FirstName)
   End If
Next
```

This new version contains a circular reference between p2 and p3 objects, so p3 can be reached from both the root object—the List(Of Person) object—and the p2.Spouse property. This circular reference might cause an endless loop, but the CLR is smart enough to understand that both references point to the same object, which is therefore persisted only once. (This is one of the most serious limitations of XML serialization.) A look at the Output window can easily prove this point:

```
Joe Healy (45)
John Evans (43)
   Spouse of Ann
Ann Beebe (40)
   Spouse of John
```

Serialization and Events

Serializable types that expose events can pose a special challenge. As you learned in Chapter 7, "Delegates and Events," events are based on delegates, which in turn are just pointers to a method, possibly defined in another type. When you serialize an object that exposes one or more events, you are actually serializing the entire object graph that includes all the objects that have subscribed to the root object's events. Such a behavior can cause two problems. First, you typically don't want to serialize these subscribers; second, and most serious, if these subscribers aren't serializable, the serialization process fails.

Here's a simple example that proves this point, based on a Widget class that raises a NameChanged event when its Name property changes:

```
<Serializable()> _
Public Class Widget
    Public Event NameChanged As EventHandler

    Private m_Name As String

    Property Name() As String
       Get
           Return m_Name
       End Get
       Set(ByVal value As String)
          If m_Name <> value Then
             m_Name = value
             RaiseEvent NameChanged(Me, EventArgs.Empty)
          End If
       End Set
    End Property
End Class
```

Create a form, drop a Button control on it, double-click the button, and type this code:

```
Sub Button_Click(ByVal sender As Object, ByVal e As EventArgs) Handles Button1.Click
    Dim w As New Widget()
    ' Create a delegate that points to the form instance.
    AddHandler w.NameChanged, AddressOf Widget_NameChanged
    SerializeToFile("c:\widget.dat", w)
End Sub

Private Sub Widget_NameChanged(ByVal sender As Object, ByVal e As EventArgs)
    Debug.WriteLine("Name has changed")
End Sub
```

When you load the form, the BinaryFormatter.Serialize method throws a SerializationException. The error is caused by the attempt to serialize the current form instance, which is pointed to by the delegate behind the NameChanged event. Alas, forms aren't serializable.

You can solve the problem by marking the delegate as NonSerialized. To do so, you must define all your events as custom events, as in the following example:

```
<Serializable()> _
Public Class Widget
```

```
<NonSerialized()> _
Dim m_NameChangedHandler As EventHandler

Public Custom Event NameChanged As EventHandler
    AddHandler(ByVal value As EventHandler)
        m_NameChangedHandler = DirectCast([Delegate].Combine(m_NameChangedHandler, value), _
            EventHandler)
    End AddHandler

    RemoveHandler(ByVal value As EventHandler)
        m_NameChangedHandler = DirectCast([Delegate].Remove(m_NameChangedHandler, value), _
            EventHandler)
    End RemoveHandler

    RaiseEvent(ByVal sender As Object, ByVal e As System.EventArgs)
        If m_NameChangedHandler IsNot Nothing Then
            m_NameChangedHandler(sender, e)
        End If
    End RaiseEvent
End Event
    …
End Class
```

Alternatively, you might implement a custom serialization mechanism and avoid persisting delegate fields. Read the section titled "The FormatterServices Helper Type" later in this chapter for more details about how you can solve this problem by means of a custom serialization technique.

Deep Object Cloning

As you might remember from the section titled "Shallow Copies and Deep Copies" in Chapter 10, "Interfaces," you can use the protected MemberwiseClone member (inherited from System .Object) to implement the ICloneable interface and its Clone method in any class you define:

```
Public Class Person
    Implements ICloneable

    ' …(variables and methods as in previous example) …

    Public Function Clone() As Object Implements ICloneable.Clone
        Return Me.MemberwiseClone()
    End Function
End Class
```

This approach to object cloning has two limitations. First, you can clone an object only if you can modify its source code because the MemberwiseClone method is protected and accessible only from inside the class itself. Second, and more important in many circumstances, the MemberwiseClone method performs a shallow copy of the object—that is, it creates a copy of the object but not of any object referenced by the object. For example, the Clone method of the preceding Person class would not also clone the Person object pointed to by the Spouse property. In other words:

```
' Define husband and wife.
Dim p1 As New Person("Joe", "Healy", #1/12/1960#)
```

```
Dim p2 As New Person("Ann", "Beebe", #10/4/1965#)
p1.Spouse = p2
p2.Spouse = p1
' Clone the husband.
Dim q1 As Person = DirectCast(p1.Clone, Person)
' The Spouse person hasn't been cloned because it's a shallow copy.
Console.WriteLine(q1.Spouse Is p1.Spouse)            ' => True
```

Thanks to object serialization's ability to work with complex object graphs, you can easily solve both problems I mentioned previously. In fact, you can create a generic method that performs a deep copy of any object passed to it. For the best performance, it uses a memory stream and a binary formatter, and specifies that the object is being serialized for cloning:

```
Function CloneObject(Of T)(ByVal obj As T) As T
   ' Create a memory stream and a formatter.
   Using ms As New MemoryStream(1000)
      Dim bf As New BinaryFormatter(Nothing, _
         New StreamingContext(StreamingContextStates.Clone))
      ' Serialize the object into the stream.
      bf.Serialize(ms, obj)
      ' Position stream pointer back to first byte.
      ms.Seek(0, SeekOrigin.Begin)
      ' Deserialize into another object.
      Return CType(bf.Deserialize(ms), T)
   End Using
End Function
```

Here's the code that drives the CloneObject routine:

```
' … (p1 and p2 are initialized as in preceding example) …
' Clone the husband. (Notice that the type T can be inferred from the argument.)
Dim q1 As Person = CloneObject(p1)
Dim q2 As Person = q1.Spouse
' Prove that properties were copied correctly.
Console.WriteLine("{0} {1}", q1.FirstName, q1.LastName)   ' => Joe Healy
Console.WriteLine("{0} {1}", q2.FirstName, q2.LastName)   ' => Joe Healy
' Prove that both objects were cloned because it's a deep copy.
Console.WriteLine(p1 Is q1)                              ' => False
Console.WriteLine(p2 Is q2)                              ' => False
```

Version-Tolerant Serialization (VTS)

In version 1.1 of the .NET Framework, you have to face a versioning problem when trying to deserialize an object into a more recent version of the same type. In fact, the Serialize method saves the complete name of the assembly where the serialized type is defined, where the complete name includes the assembly name, version, and public key token if the assembly has a strong name. (See Chapter 16, "The My Namespace," for more information about assemblies' strong names.) When the object is deserialized, version 1.1 of the CLR attempts to instantiate an object of the same type and same version. If that specific version isn't available, the CLR throws a SerializationException.

Version 2.0 of the .NET Framework solves the problem in quite a radical way by introducing *version-tolerant serialization* (VTS) and *deserialization*: the version number is ignored when deserializing an object, only the type's name is taken into account. More precisely, VTS supports the following features:

- Unexpected data is ignored. (This enables older versions of the application to deserialize objects saved by newer versions.)

- Missing optional data is tolerated. (This enables newer versions of the application to deserialize objects saved by older versions.)

The OptionalField Attribute

If the new version of a type being deserialized has a field that was missing in the version that was serialized, you should mark the field with the OptionalField attribute. For example, here's an updated Person class that exposes the new Country field:

```
Class Person
    <OptionalField()> Public Country As String
    ' Define all the other members here.
    …
End Class
```

If the deserialized stream doesn't contain the value of a field marked as optional, the field retains its default value. Optional fields are simply ignored during the deserialization process, and therefore they will retain their default value: zero if numbers, Nothing if string or objects, and so forth. You might believe that you can force a different initial value for these optional fields by using an initializer, as in the following:

```
<OptionalField()> Public Country As String = "USA"
```

However, initializers and constructors don't run at all during the deserialization process, and therefore these values are ignored. For this reason it is important that the default value be a valid value for a new instance of the class. If this isn't the case, you need to implement the IDeserializationCallback interface or use a deserialization event, as described in a later section.

The OptionalField attribute can take the VersionAdded named argument, as in the following:

```
<OptionalField(VersionAdded:=2)> _
Public Country As String
```

The integer value you pass to the VersionAdded parameter enables you to specify in which version of the class the optional field was added. As I describe in the section titled "The IDeserializationCallback Interface" later in this chapter, you can then use this version number to initialize the optional field with a value that depends on the class version.

The Binder Property

In some cases, you might want to exert more control over which specific type is used to deserialize the saved state of an object. This is possible thanks to serialization binder objects and the Binder property that all formatters expose. Let's suppose that you have moved your objects from one assembly to another, and therefore the namespace and possibly even the name of the object have changed.

The first step is defining a new type that inherits from the SerializationBinder abstract class and overrides the BindToType method. The code in this method can test the name of the type in the serialized stream and returns the Type object corresponding to the object that will actually be deserialized (or Nothing if the CLR's default behavior is OK for you). The following example assumes that you have serialized an object with version 1.0 of the assembly named BOLibrary and you want to deserialize it with the MyApp.Customer object, defined in the current assembly:

```
Public Class MySerializationBinder
    Inherits SerializationBinder

    Public Overrides Function BindToType(ByVal assemblyName As String, _
        ByVal typeName As String) As Type
        ' Read the version of the assembly.
        Dim an As New AssemblyName(assemblyName)
        If an.Name = "BOLibrary" AndAlso typeName = "BOLibrary.Customer" Then
            ' Return the CustomerEx type taken from current assembly.
            Return GetType(CustomerEx)
        Else
            ' Otherwise, tell the CLR to apply the default binding policy.
            Return Nothing
        End If
    End Function
End Class
```

Once you have defined your custom binding policy, you simply need to assign an instance of this class to the formatter's Binder property:

```
Dim bf As New BinaryFormatter()
bf.Binder = New MySerializationBinder()
' Proceed with deserialization as usual. (fs is an open stream.)
Dim obj As Object = bf.Deserialize(fs)
Dim custEx As CustomerEx = DirectCast(obj, CustomerEx)
...
```

If you force the CLR to deserialize a type that is different from the type that was originally serialized in the stream, it is essential that the old and the new type are similar enough to make the deserialization process make sense. Interestingly, the CLR doesn't throw an exception if the new type has fewer or more members than the original type does; the only condition that must be met is that members with the same name must have the same type, or at least a conversion must be possible. Keep in mind that the CLR uses reflection to discover each field in the new type and then searches for the corresponding value in the stream.

Custom Serialization

When the basic techniques I illustrated so far aren't powerful enough to solve your serialization and deserialization requirements, you should implement a custom serialization technique. You can have trouble, for example, when you want to dynamically decide which information should be persisted or when you need to execute code when the object is deserialized, possibly to recalculate values that are no longer valid.

The IDeserializationCallback Interface

The simplest case of custom serialization is to perform some custom actions when the object has been completely deserialized, for example, to initialize fields marked with the NonSerialized or the OptionalField attribute. For example, say that your Person class opens a FileStream in its constructor and all the other methods in the class rely on this FileStream object to do their chores. As you know, no standard constructor runs when the object is being deserialized, so after deserialization all methods will find the stream closed. You can solve this problem by implementing the IDeserializationCallback interface; this interface has only one method, OnDeserialization, which the .NET Framework invokes when the current object has been completely deserialized:

```
<Serializable()> _
Public Class Person2
    Implements IDeserializationCallback
    <OptionalField()> Public Country As String
    <NonSerialized()> Private logStream As FileStream
    ' Define all the other fields here.
    …
    Sub New(ByVal firstName As String, ByVal lastName As String, ByVal birthDate As Date)
        ' Initialize the FirstName, LastName, and BirthDate fields.
        …
        ' Open the file for logging.
        OpenLogFile()
    End Sub

    ' This method is called when the object has been completely deserialized.
    Private Sub OnDeserialization(ByVal sender As Object) _
        Implements IDeserializationCallback.OnDeserialization
        ' Reopen the file stream when the object is deserialized.
        OpenLogFile()
        ' Provide a default value for the Country optional field.
        If Country Is Nothing Then Country = "USA"
    End Sub

    ' Open a log file just for this instance.
    Private Sub OpenLogFile()
        Dim fileName As String = Me.FirstName & " " & Me.LastName & ".txt"
        logStream = New FileStream(fileName, FileMode.OpenOrCreate)
    End Sub
End Class
```

It is important to be aware that the .NET Framework invokes the OnDeserialization method when the entire object graph has been entirely deserialized. This means that you can rely on the fact that all the child objects of the current object have been correctly initialized when this method runs. This detail is important if the fields you must initialize depend on other fields.

As I explained in the previous section, the OptionalField attribute supports the VersionAdded named argument:

```
<OptionalField(VersionAdded:=2)> _
Public Country As String
```

Typically, you use this argument if the initial value of an optional field depends on the version of the class or some other data. For example, let's say that this value should be initialized to "USA" if VersionAdded is equal to 1; otherwise, it should be assigned an empty string. Here's the new version of the OnDeserialization method that implements this behavior:

```
' This method is called when the object has been completely deserialized.
Private Sub OnDeserialization(ByVal sender As Object) _
    Implements IDeserializationCallback.OnDeserialization
    …
    ' Only if the Country field hasn't been deserialized
    If Country Is Nothing Then
        ' Use reflection to read the OptionalField attribute.
        Dim fi As FieldInfo = Me.GetType().GetField("Country")
        Dim attr As OptionalFieldAttribute = TryCast(Attribute.GetCustomAttribute(fi, _
            GetType(OptionalFieldAttribute)), OptionalFieldAttribute)
        If attr Is Nothing Then
            ' This should never happen.
        ElseIf attr.VersionAdded = 1 Then
            Country = "USA"
        Else
            Country = ""
        End If
    End If
End Sub
```

The ISerializable Interface

The ISerializable interface allows you to be in full control of both the serialization and deserialization processes. For example, you might implement this interface if some fields should be persisted or depersisted only if specific conditions are true, or if you want to persist the fields in a nondefault format. The ISerializable interface exposes only one method, GetObjectData, which has the following syntax:

```
Protected Sub GetObjectData(ByVal info As SerializationInfo, _
    ByVal context As StreamingContext)
    …
End Sub
```

The GetObjectData method is invoked when the object is passed to the formatter's Serialize method. Its purpose is to fill the SerializationInfo object with all the information about the object being serialized. The code inside this method can examine the StreamingContext structure to retrieve additional details about the serialization process, for example, to learn whether the object is being serialized to a file or to memory.

The presence of the ISerializable interface implies the existence of a special constructor method with the following syntax:

```
Protected Sub New(ByVal info As SerializationInfo, ByVal context As StreamingContext)
   …
End Sub
```

The CLR calls this special constructor when the object is deserialized. You won't get a compilation error if you omit this constructor, but you get a runtime error when you try to deserialize the object if this constructor is missing. The scope you use for the GetObjectData and the special constructor is crucial: these procedures should have a Protected scope if the class can be inherited from because derived classes might (and usually do) invoke them. If the class is sealed, you can use a Private scope keyword. Oddly, many .NET types expose either or both these procedures as public members, but you should avoid doing so in your applications. If the special constructor has Private or Protected scope, the type must have at least another constructor with Public scope; otherwise, you won't be able to instantiate it from your code.

The SerializationInfo object acts like a dictionary object. In the GetObjectData method, you fill this dictionary with one or more values using the AddValue method:

```
Protected Sub GetObjectData(ByVal info As SerializationInfo, _
      ByVal context As StreamingContext) Implements ISerializable.GetObjectData
   ' Save all fields.
   info.AddValue("FirstName", Me.FirstName)
   info.AddValue("LastName", Me.FirstName)
   …
End Sub
```

As you might expect, the object passed to the AddValue method must be serializable; otherwise, an exception occurs. You can later retrieve values with the GetValue method, which requires the value name and type, as you see here:

```
Protected Sub New(ByVal info As SerializationInfo, ByVal context As StreamingContext)
   ' Retrieve serialized fields.
   Me.FirstName = CStr(info.GetValue("FirstValue", GetType(String)))
   Me.LastName = CStr(info.GetValue("LastValue", GetType(String)))
   …
End Sub
```

Conveniently, the SerializationInfo object exposes many other GetXxxx methods that return data in a specific format, such as GetString and GetInt32:

```
   ' A more concise way to retrieve the FirstName value
   Me.FirstName = info.GetString("FirstValue")
```

In all cases, values in the stream are converted to the requested type, or an InvalidCastException is thrown if the conversion isn't possible.

Security Implications

As you know, a formatter can access fields that would otherwise be inaccessible. For this reason, the client code that performs the serialization and deserialization steps requires special permission to do so, namely, the SecurityPermission with the SerializationFormatter flag. By default, this permission is given to fully trusted code but not to code originating from the intranet or the Internet. If your object contains sensitive information, you should protect the GetObjectData method with an attribute that demands this permission, as in the following code:

```
<SecurityPermission(SecurityAction.Demand, SerializationFormatter:=True)> _
Protected Sub GetObjectData(ByVal info As SerializationInfo, _
   ByVal context As StreamingContext)
   …
End Sub
```

Remember that, even if you save the object's state by means of the BinaryFormatter, strings stored as clear text can easily be extracted from a stream serialized on a disk file or a database field. Other data types, for example, numbers and dates, aren't human-readable but could be extracted from a serialized stream with just a little more effort. Therefore, if your type contains sensitive data, you should always implement the ISerializable interface and encrypt this data.

A Practical Example: Compressed Serialization

One of the things you can do by implementing the ISerializable interface is compress the serialized stream so that the object can be saved to smaller files or be transferred to another application using .NET remoting in less time. The following CompactArray(Of T) type behaves like a regular array, except its serialized version takes fewer bytes:

```
<Serializable()> _
Public Class CompactArray(Of T)
   Implements ISerializable

   ' Actual elements are stored in this private array.
   Private arr() As T

   ' The constructor takes the number of elements in the array.
   Sub New(ByVal numEls As Integer)
      ReDim arr(numEls - 1)
   End Sub

   ' The default Item property makes this class look like a standard array.
   Default Public Overridable Property Item(ByVal index As Integer) As T
      Get
         Return arr(index)
      End Get
      Set(ByVal value As T)
         arr(index) = value
      End Set
   End Property
```

```
' Compress data when the object is serialized.
Protected Sub GetObjectData(ByVal info As SerializationInfo, ByVal context _
      As StreamingContext) Implements ISerializable.GetObjectData
   ' Serialize the private array to a compressed stream in memory.
   Using memStream As New MemoryStream()
      Using zipStream As New DeflateStream(memStream, CompressionMode.Compress)
         Dim bf As New BinaryFormatter()
         bf.Serialize(zipStream, arr)
         zipStream.Flush()
         ' Save the contents of the compressed stream.
         Dim bytes() As Byte = memStream.GetBuffer()
         info.AddValue("bytes", bytes)
      End Using
   End Using
End Sub

' Decompress data when the object is deserialized.
Protected Sub New(ByVal info As SerializationInfo, ByVal context As StreamingContext)
   ' Retrieve the bytes and initialize a memory buffer.
   Dim bytes() As Byte = DirectCast(info.GetValue("bytes", GetType(Byte())), Byte())
   Using inStream As New MemoryStream(bytes)
      ' Wrap a DeflateStream object around the compressed buffer.
      Using zipStream As New DeflateStream(inStream, CompressionMode.Decompress)
         Dim bf As New BinaryFormatter
         arr = DirectCast(bf.Deserialize(zipStream), T())
      End Using
   End Using
End Sub
End Class
```

Read the section titled "Compressed Streams" in Chapter 15, "Files, Directories, and Streams," for more information about the DeflateStream type.

Custom Serialization and Inheritance

When you inherit from a class that implements ISerializable and the derived class adds new fields that should be serialized, you must create your own version of the GetObjectData method and the special constructor implied by this interface. For example, if you have a CompactArrayEx class that inherits from CompactArray and adds a DefaultValue property, this is the code you should write:

```
<Serializable()> _
Public Class CompactArrayEx(Of T)
   Inherits CompactArray(Of T)
   Implements ISerializable                ' Interface reimplementation!

   Public ReadOnly DefaultValue As T       ' A new field in the derived class

   Sub New(ByVal numEls As Integer, ByVal defaultValue As T)
      MyBase.New(numEls)
      Me.DefaultValue = defaultValue
   End Sub
```

```
' The GetObjectData method is reimplemented.
Protected Overloads Sub GetObjectData(ByVal info As SerializationInfo, _
       ByVal context As StreamingContext) Implements ISerializable.GetObjectData
    ' Deserialize the base class, and then deserialize any additional field.
    MyBase.GetObjectData(info, context)
    info.AddValue("DefaultValue", Me.DefaultValue)
End Sub

Protected Sub New(ByVal info As SerializationInfo, ByVal context As StreamingContext)
    ' Serialize the base class, and then serialize any additional field.
    MyBase.New(info, context)
    Me.DefaultValue = CType(info.GetValue("DefaultValue", GetType(T)), T)
End Sub
End Class
```

The CompactArrayEx leverages the interface reimplementation feature, which is new in Microsoft Visual Basic 2005 and which I cover in Chapter 10, "Interfaces." Thanks to interface reimplementation, the derived class can contain an Implements keyword related to an interface already implemented by the base class and can therefore have its own version of the GetObjectData method even if the method wasn't marked as virtual in the base class. This feature allows you to derive from an ISerializable object and redefine the serialization algorithm even if you don't have or can't modify the base class's source code.

Let me state again that you must implement the GetObjectData method only if the derived class needs to serialize additional fields; otherwise, the inherited class can rely on its base class's implementation of the ISerializable interface. However, regardless of whether the derived class exposes additional fields, in all cases you must implement the special constructor because this constructor isn't automatically inherited by the derived class. If the derived class doesn't have additional classes, the special constructor simply delegates to the base class's constructor:

```
Protected Sub New(ByVal info As SerializationInfo, ByVal context As StreamingContext)
    MyBase.New(info, context)
    ' No more code here.
End Sub
```

The FormatterServices Helper Type

The FormatterServices class exposes a few static methods that help you build code that serializes and deserializes an object. For example, the FormatterServices.GetSerializableMembers method returns an array of MemberInfo elements, one element for each class member that must be serialized (in other words, all fields except those marked with the NotSerialized attribute). The FormatterServices.GetObjectData method takes the array returned by the aforementioned method and returns an Object array holding the value of each member. The following procedure builds on these two methods and helps you serialize any object:

```
' Helper procedure meant to be called from inside ISerializable.GetObjectData method.
Public Sub GetObjectDataHelper(ByVal info As SerializationInfo, _
    ByVal context As StreamingContext, ByVal obj As Object)
```

```
   ' Get the list of serializable members.
   Dim members() As MemberInfo = FormatterServices.GetSerializableMembers(obj.GetType)
   ' Read the value of each member.
   Dim values() As Object = FormatterServices.GetObjectData(obj, members)
   ' Store values in the SerializationInfo object, using the member name as the key.
   For i As Integer = 0 To members.Length - 1
      info.AddValue(members(i).Name, values(i))
   Next
End Sub
```

The FormatterServices.PopulateObjectMembers method takes an array of MemberInfo and Object values and assigns all the serializable members of a given object. You can use this method in a generic helper routine that initializes a deserialized object:

```
' Helper procedure meant to be called from inside ISerializable's special constructor
Public Sub ISerializableConstructorHelper(ByVal info As SerializationInfo, _
      ByVal context As StreamingContext, ByVal obj As Object)
   ' Get the list of serializable members for this object.
   Dim members() As MemberInfo = FormatterServices.GetSerializableMembers(obj.GetType)
   Dim values(members.Length - 1) As Object
   ' Read the value for this member (assuming it's a field).
   For i As Integer = 0 To members.Length - 1
      ' Retrieve the type for this member.
      Dim fi As FieldInfo = TryCast(members(i), FieldInfo)
      If fi IsNot Nothing Then
         values(i) = info.GetValue(fi.Name, fi.FieldType)
      End If
   Next
   ' Assign all serializable members in one operation.
   FormatterServices.PopulateObjectMembers(obj, members, values)
End Sub
```

These two helper routines make implementation of the ISerializable interface a breeze. This is what a serializable class that uses these routines looks like:

```
<Serializable()> _
Public Class SampleClass
   Implements ISerializable

   Public Sub GetObjectData(ByVal info As SerializationInfo, _
         ByVal context As StreamingContext) Implements ISerializable.GetObjectData
      GetObjectDataHelper(info, context, Me)
   End Sub

   Protected Sub New(ByVal info As SerializationInfo, ByVal context As StreamingContext)
      ISerializableConstructorHelper(info, context, Me)
   End Sub

   ' …(The remainder of the class)…
   …
End Class
```

You can use a variation of this technique to solve the problems caused by events and delegates that point to nonserializable types, which I illustrate earlier in the section titled "Serialization and Events." Instead of invoking the standard FormatterServices.GetSerializableMembers method, you call the following helper method to discard delegate fields:

```
' Get the list of serializable members of a type, except delegates.
Function GetSerializableMembersEx(ByVal type As Type) As MemberInfo()
   Dim list As New List(Of MemberInfo)
   For Each mi As MemberInfo In FormatterServices.GetSerializableMembers(type)
      ' Add this element to the result only if it isn't a delegate.
      Dim fi As FieldInfo = TryCast(mi, FieldInfo)
      If fi IsNot Nothing And Not _
         GetType([Delegate]).IsAssignableFrom(fi.FieldType) Then
         list.Add(mi)
      End If
   Next
   Return list.ToArray()
End Function
```

In the GetDataObjectHelper and ISerializableConstructorHelper procedures, you call this new method instead of the FormatterServices.GetSerializableMembers method:

```
Sub GetObjectDataHelper(ByVal info As SerializationInfo, _
      ByVal context As StreamingContext, ByVal obj As Object)
   ' Get the list of serializable members.
   Dim members() As MemberInfo = FormatterServices.GetSerializableMembers(obj.GetType)
   …
End Sub

Public Sub ISerializableConstructorHelper(ByVal info As SerializationInfo, _
      ByVal context As StreamingContext, ByVal obj As Object)
   ' Get the list of serializable members for this object.
   Dim members() As MemberInfo = FormatterServices.GetSerializableMembers(obj.GetType)
   …
End Sub
```

You can use the new versions of the GetDataObjectHelper and ISerializableConstructorHelper procedures inside any type that exposes public events to ensure that event subscribers aren't serialized when the main object is serialized.

Serialization and Deserialization Events

 Version 2.0 of the .NET Framework adds a completely new mechanism for custom serialization and deserialization based on the following four attributes: OnSerializing, OnSerialized, OnDeserializing, and OnDeserialized. You use one of these attributes to mark a Sub procedure that takes a StreamingContext argument:

```
[OnSerializing]
Private Sub BeforeSerialization(ByVal context As StreamingContext)
   ' This code runs before the object is serialized.
End Sub

[OnSerialized]
```

```
Private Sub AfterSerialization(ByVal context As StreamingContext)
   ' This code runs after the object has been serialized.
End Sub

[OnDeserializing]
Private Sub BeforeDeserialization(ByVal context As StreamingContext)
   ' This code runs before the object is deserialized.
End Sub

[OnDeserialized]
Private Sub AfterDeserialization(ByVal context As StreamingContext)
   ' This code runs after the object has been deserialized.
End Sub
```

An important note: these attributes are honored only when the object is serialized and deserialized by means of the BinaryFormatter and are ignored when the SoapFormatter or another formatter is used. You can mark more than one method with the same attribute, but the usefulness of such a practice is questionable because in this case the CLR calls marked methods in an unpredictable order. If the object implements the IDeserializationCallback interface, the method marked with the OnDeserialized attribute runs after the IDeserializationCallback .OnDeserialization method.

Typically, you use the OnDeserialized attribute in lieu of the IDeserializationCallback interface. For example, here's a different version of the Person class that reopens the log file after deserialization is completed. (Compare with the code shown in the section titled "The IDeserializationCallback Interface" earlier in this chapter.)

```
<Serializable()> _
Public Class Person3
   ' The class doesn't implement the IDeserializationCallback interface.
   Dim logStream As FileStream

   ' This method is called when the object been deserialized completely.
   <OnDeserialized()> _
   Private Sub AfterDeserialization(ByVal context As StreamingContext)
      OpenLogFile()
   End Sub

   ' (Definition of OpenLogFile and other members omitted.…)
   …
End Class
```

The OnDeserializing attribute is especially useful for assigning an initial value to an optional field: if the field is found in the stream, the serialized value will overwrite the one you assign from code:

```
<Serializable()> _
Class Person
   <OptionalField()> Public Country As String

   ' This method is called when the object been deserialized completely.
   <OnDeserialized()> _
```

```
Private Sub BeforeDeserialization(ByVal context As StreamingContext)
    Country = "USA"
End Sub

' (Other members omitted.…)
…
End Class
```

A clear advantage of the new .NET Framework 2.0 attributes over the ISerializable interface is that you don't need to manually invoke a method in the base class, as you must do inside the GetObjectData method and the special constructor. The CLR runs methods marked with these attributes in the base class first and then it runs the methods marked with these attributes in the current class. (These attributes aren't automatically inherited.) You can't apply these attributes to static methods or instance methods marked as Overridable or MustInherit.

Although you can always use the OnDeserializing and OnDeserialized attributes to replace the IDeserializationCallback interface (provided that the object is serialized with the binary formatter), the four attributes can't really substitute for the ISerializable interface because the methods don't receive the SerializationInfo object and therefore can't manually store data in and retrieve data from it.

The IObjectReference Interface

In some cases, you might want to implement a singleton object that is also serializable. A few singleton types in the .NET Framework, such as the Console or the GC objects, expose only static members and can't be serialized; therefore, they aren't interesting in this discussion. To be serializable, a singleton object must store its state in instance fields and is typically implemented as follows:

```
<Serializable()> _
Public Class Singleton
    ' The one and only instance is created when the type is initialized.
    Public Shared ReadOnly Instance As New Singleton()

    ' One or more instance fields
    Public Id As Integer
    …

    ' Prevent clients from instantiating this type.
    Private Sub New()
    End Sub
End Class
```

Unfortunately, this naïve implementation doesn't work. For example, if you serialize this type twice and you later deserialize the two instances, they won't point to the same object. The CLR doesn't automatically recognize the singleton nature of this type.

The IObjectReference interface can help solve this problem. This interface exposes only one method, GetRealObject. If a type A implements this interface, you can pass this type as an argument to the SerializationInfo.SetType method inside the ISerializable.GetObjectData method of another type B (the singleton type). When type B is deserialized, the special constructor implied by the ISerializable interface isn't called; instead, the CLR creates an instance of type A and calls its IObjectReference.GetRealObject method, which is expected to return the deserialized object.

In the most general case, A and B are distinct types, and in fact the MSDN documentation shows an example based on the Singleton class (our type B) that uses a nested, private, and sealed class named SingletonSerializationHelper (our type A). However, you can simplify the code remarkably if you make the Singleton class implement the IObjectReference directly, as in the following example:

```
<Serializable()> _
Public Class Singleton
    Implements IObjectReference

    ' The one and only instance is created when the type is initialized.
    Public Shared ReadOnly Instance As New Singleton()

    ' One or more instance fields
    Public Id As Integer

    ' Prevent clients from instantiating this class.
    Private Sub New()
    End Sub

    Private Function GetRealObject(ByVal context As StreamingContext) As Object _
            Implements IObjectReference.GetRealObject
        Return Instance
    End Function
End Class
```

This is what happens behind the scenes: when the CLR realizes that an instance of the Singleton type is about to be deserialized, it checks whether the type implements the IObjectReference interface and, if this is the case, it invokes the GetRealObject method instead, which returns the only shared instance of the class. You can check that this implementation works correctly as follows:

```
' Get a singleton instance and serialize it.
Dim s1 As Singleton = Singleton.Instance
SerializeToFile("c:\singleton.dat", s1)
' Deserialize it into a different variable and check that they point to the object.
Dim s2 As Singleton = DeserializeFromFile(Of Singleton)("c:\singleton.dat")
Console.WriteLine(s1 Is s2)                    ' True
```

The IObjectReference interface is also useful for types that aren't strictly singleton, yet expose a static factory method instead of a regular constructor. For example, consider the following type:

```
<Serializable()> _
Public Class IdValuePair
    ' This is where all instances created so far are stored.
    Private Shared dict As New Dictionary(Of Integer, IdValuePair)
```

```
' Instance fields
Public ReadOnly Id As Integer
Public ReadOnly Value As String

' Private constructor prevents instantiation.
Private Sub New(ByVal id As Integer, ByVal value As String)
   Me.Id = id
   Me.Value = value
End Sub

' The factory method
Public Shared Function Create(ByVal id As Integer, ByVal value As String) As IdValuePair
   ' Add a new instance to the private table if necessary.
   If Not dict.ContainsKey(id) Then
      dict.Add(id, New IdValuePair(id, value))
   End If
   ' Always return an instance from the cache.
   Return dict(id)
End Function
End Class
```

Serializing and deserializing an IdValuePair object poses the same challenges that singleton objects pose because you must ensure that serialized objects with the same Id property are deserialized as a single instance. Once again, you can solve this problem by implementing the IObjectReference interface:

```
<Serializable()> _
Class IdValuePair
   Implements IObjectReference
   …
   Private Function GetRealObject(ByVal context As StreamingContext) As Object _
         Implements IObjectReference.GetRealObject
      ' The instance has been deserialized, so you can access its properties.
      Debug.WriteLine("GetRealObject method for ID=" & Me.Id.ToString())
      Return Create(Me.Id, Me.Value)
   End Function
End Class
```

A minor problem with this approach is that the GetRealObject method is invoked three times during the deserialization process, as you can see thanks to the Debug.WriteLine statement. However, these calls don't add a noticeable overhead and don't have other side effects.

The ISerializationSurrogate Interface

The ISerialization interface enables you to define a custom serialization process, but doesn't allow you to intervene in the serialization process of a *different* type, more specifically a type whose source code isn't available or modifiable. For example, you might need to take over the serialization process of a type if that type isn't serializable, or if you are serializing a type that exposes one or more fields that return nonserializable values.

This specific problem can be solved by defining a *surrogate type*, which by definition is a type that implements the ISerializationSurrogate interface. This interface has only two methods,

GetObjectData and SetObjectData, which have signatures similar to the ISerializable
.GetObjectData method and the special constructor implied by the ISerializable interface,
respectively. To see this technique in action, let's define three types that are related to each
other:

```
<Serializable()> _
Public Class PurchaseOrder
    Public Supplier As Supplier
    Public Attachment As Document
End Class

Public Class Document
    Public Number As Integer
    Public Location As String
End Class

Public Class Supplier
    Public ReadOnly ID As String
    Public ReadOnly Name As String

    Sub New(ByVal id As String, ByVal name As String)
        Me.id = id
        Me.name = name
    End Sub
End Class
```

The PurchaseOrder class is marked as serializable, but any attempt to serialize it is going to fail
because the types of its Supplier and Attachment fields are nonserializable. However, you can
work around this problem by defining two auxiliary surrogate types, one of the Document
class and one for the Supplier class:

```
Public Class DocumentSerializationSurrogate
    Implements ISerializationSurrogate

    Public Sub GetObjectData(ByVal obj As Object, ByVal info As SerializationInfo, _
            ByVal context As StreamingContext) Implements ISerializationSurrogate.GetObjectData
        ' Save the properties of the object being serialized.
        Dim instance As Document = DirectCast(obj, Document)
        info.AddValue("Number", instance.Number)
        info.AddValue("Location", instance.Location)
    End Sub

    Public Function SetObjectData(ByVal obj As Object, ByVal info As SerializationInfo, _
            ByVal context As StreamingContext, ByVal selector As ISurrogateSelector) _
            As Object Implements ISerializationSurrogate.SetObjectData
        ' Populate the (uninitialized) object passed as an argument.
        Dim instance As Document = DirectCast(obj, Document)
        instance.Number = info.GetInt32("Number")
        instance.Location = info.GetString("Location")
        ' You can return Nothing if you've populated the object passed as an argument.
        Return Nothing
    End Function
End Class
```

The surrogate for the Supplier class is similar, except that the SetObjectData method can't simply populate the uninitialized object passed in the first argument because the fields of the Supplier type are read-only and can be initialized only by calling a constructor:

```
Public Class SupplierSerializationSurrogate
    Implements ISerializationSurrogate

    Public Sub GetObjectData(ByVal obj As Object, ByVal info As SerializationInfo, _
            ByVal context As StreamingContext) Implements ISerializationSurrogate.GetObjectData
        ' Save the properties of the object being serialized.
        Dim instance As Supplier = DirectCast(obj, Supplier)
        info.AddValue("Id", instance.ID)
        info.AddValue("Name", instance.Name)
    End Sub

    Public Function SetObjectData(ByVal obj As Object, ByVal info As SerializationInfo, _
            ByVal context As StreamingContext, ByVal selector As ISurrogateSelector) _
            As Object Implements ISerializationSurrogate.SetObjectData
        ' Ignore the object passed as an argument and create a new instance.
        Dim id As String = info.GetString("Id")
        Dim name As String = info.GetString("Name")
        Return New Supplier(id, name)
    End Function
End Class
```

You're finally ready to serialize a PurchaseOrder object:

```
' Create a PurchaseOrder instance and its dependent objects.
Dim po As New PurchaseOrder
po.Supplier = New Supplier("JH", "Joe Healy")
po.Attachment = New Document()
po.Attachment.Number = 11
po.Attachment.Location = "c:\docs\description.doc"

' Create an empty instance of the standard SurrogateSelector object.
Dim surSel As New SurrogateSelector()
surSel.AddSurrogate(GetType(Document), _
    New StreamingContext(StreamingContextStates.All), _
    New DocumentSerializationSurrogate)
' Tell the SurrogateSelector how to deal with Document and Supplier objects.
surSel.AddSurrogate(GetType(Supplier), _
    New StreamingContext(StreamingContextStates.All), _
    New SupplierSerializationSurrogate)
' Create the BinaryFormatter and set its SurrogateSelector property.
Dim bf As New BinaryFormatter
bf.SurrogateSelector = surSel

' Serialize to a memory stream and deserialize into a different object.
Dim ms As New MemoryStream
bf.Serialize(ms, po)
ms.Seek(0, SeekOrigin.Begin)
Dim po2 As PurchaseOrder = DirectCast(bf.Deserialize(ms), PurchaseOrder)

' Prove that the object deserialized correctly.
```

```
Console.WriteLine(po2.Supplier.Name)          ' => Joe Healy
Console.WriteLine(po2.Attachment.Number)      ' => 11
```

The classes for which you provide a surrogate type can appear in multiple places in the object hierarchy, but you still need to define a serialization surrogate for that type only once. For example, suppose you extend the Supplier class as follows:

```
Public Class Supplier
   ...
   ' (Add after all existing members…)
   Public Description As Document
End Class
```

In this case, you must modify the SupplierSerializationSurrogate class to account for the new field, but the code that actually serializes and deserializes the PurchaseOrder object continues to work as before.

Interestingly, you can easily build a "universal" serialization surrogate that can work with simple types that expose fields that don't require any special processing. As you can guess, it's just a matter of using a bit of reflection:

```
Public Class UniversalSerializationSurrogate
   Implements ISerializationSurrogate

   Public Sub GetObjectData(ByVal obj As Object, ByVal info As SerializationInfo, _
         ByVal context As StreamingContext) Implements ISerializationSurrogate.GetObjectData
      Dim flags As BindingFlags = BindingFlags.Instance Or _
         BindingFlags.Public Or BindingFlags.Public
      For Each fi As FieldInfo In obj.GetType().GetFields(flags)
         info.AddValue(fi.Name, fi.GetValue(obj))
      Next
   End Sub

   Public Function SetObjectData(ByVal obj As Object, ByVal info As SerializationInfo, _
         ByVal context As StreamingContext, ByVal selector As ISurrogateSelector) _
         As Object Implements ISerializationSurrogate.SetObjectData
      Dim flags As BindingFlags = BindingFlags.Instance Or _
         BindingFlags.Public Or BindingFlags.Public
      For Each fi As FieldInfo In obj.GetType().GetFields(flags)
         fi.SetValue(obj, info.GetValue(fi.Name, fi.FieldType))
      Next
      Return obj
   End Function
End Class
```

Serialization surrogates are quite handy for solving recurring problems related to serialization, but they aren't a remedy in all possible circumstances. In general, surrogates are OK only with simple classes that expose fields of primitive types, such as strings or numeric types. In general, if you don't have the source code of the nonserializable type, you can't be absolutely sure that you are serializing everything correctly; therefore, you should always double-check the behavior of your application when using a surrogate with a class you didn't author yourself.

Inheriting from a Nonserializable Type

A common problem in advanced serialization scenarios occurs when you need to author a serializable type A and this class must derive from a nonserializable type B. In previous sections, you saw that type A must implement the ISerializable interface, but this step doesn't really resolve all the issues you face. In fact, to serialize and deserialize the base type correctly you must use reflection and read all its fields, including private fields in the base class. There are other problems to solve as well: for example, the (nonserializable) base type B might inherit from a serializable type C, in which case you should rely on type C's serialization code to ensure that data is saved and restored correctly.

To solve this problem once and for all, I wrote a SerializationHelpers module containing a few methods that you can invoke from types that implement the ISerializable interface and that solve most of the aforementioned issues:

```
Module SerializationHelpers
   ' Return True if a type and all its base types are serializable.
   Function TypeIsSerializable(ByVal type As Type) As Boolean
      Do Until type Is Nothing
         ' Exit now if the type isn't serializable.
         If Not type.IsSerializable Then Return False
         ' If this type implements ISerializable, we can assume it's fully serializable.
         If GetType(ISerializable).IsAssignableFrom(type) Then Return True
         ' Continue to analyze its base class.
         type = type.BaseType
      Loop
      Return True
   End Function
   …
```

The TypeIsSerializable helper method returns True if a type can use default serialization, or False if it requires custom serialization. A type can use default serialization only if it is marked as serializable and all its base types are also serializable, or if any class in the inheritance tree implements the ISerializable interface (in which case the method assumes that the type knows how to deal with its base classes, even if not all of them are serializable).

The SerializeObjectFields method is a bit more complex in that it fills a SerializationInfo object with the value of all the fields of an object, serializes the base object, and serializes all fields whose type isn't serializable by default. The key to this mechanism is using the Path.Combine method to create a hierarchy of keys in the SerializationInfo object.

If a field value is nonserializable, the SerializeObjectFields method invokes itself recursively to save all the object's fields. In addition, it saves the Type of the object referenced by the field because it can't rely on the field's type. (For example, a field whose type is Control might point to a TextBox object.) The type of such complex fields is stored separately in a SerializationInfo slot named *Type.

To further complicate matters, the SerializationInfo object doesn't provide an enumerator or a method to extract the keys it contains; therefore, for each level in the hierarchy the SerializeObjectFields method must save a list of complex fields that require special treatment; in the following code, this list is maintained in the complexFields ArrayList and is then saved in a slot named *Complex.

```
Sub SerializeObjectFields(ByVal info As SerializationInfo, ByVal key As String, _
     ByVal obj As Object, ByVal type As Type)
  If type Is Nothing Then type = obj.GetType()

  If type.BaseType IsNot GetType(Object) Then
     ' First, serialize the base class's fields.
     SerializeObjectFields(info, Path.Combine("*Base", key), obj, type.BaseType)
  End If

  ' Next, loop over all fields that are declared in this type.
  Dim complexFields As New ArrayList
  For Each fi As FieldInfo In type.GetFields(BindingFlags.Instance Or _
        BindingFlags.Public Or BindingFlags.NonPublic Or BindingFlags.DeclaredOnly)
     ' Remember the value of all serializable fields.
     If Not fi.IsNotSerialized Then
        ' Build the complete field name.
        Dim fieldKey As String = Path.Combine(key, fi.Name)
        ' Read actual field value.
        Dim value As Object = fi.GetValue(obj)

        If value Is Nothing OrElse TypeIsSerializable(value.GetType()) Then
           ' Save directory if field's type is serializable.
           info.AddValue(fieldKey, value)
        Else
           ' Remember this is a complex field.
           complexFields.Add(fi.Name)
           ' Remember its type.
           info.AddValue(Path.Combine(fieldKey, "*Type"), value.GetType())
           ' Store the object value by calling this method recursively.
           SerializeObjectFields(info, fieldKey, value, Nothing)
        End If
     End If
  Next
  ' Remember the list of simple fields.
  info.AddValue(Path.Combine(key, "*Complex"), complexFields)
End Sub
```

The DeserializeObjectFields method processes the data stored by the SerializeObjectFields procedure: it reads all the slots of a SerializationInfo object and assigns all the fields of an object passed as an argument, going deep in the inheritance hierarchy to deserialize complex objects manually one field at a time:

```
Sub DeserializeObjectFields(ByVal info As SerializationInfo, ByVal key As String, _
     ByVal obj As Object, ByVal type As Type)
  If type Is Nothing Then type = obj.GetType()
```

```
    ' First, deserialize the base class's fields.
    If type.BaseType IsNot GetType(Object) Then
        DeserializeObjectFields(info, Path.Combine("*Base", key), obj, type.BaseType)
    End If

    ' Retrieve the list of complex (nonserializable) fields.
    Dim complexFields As ArrayList = DirectCast(info.GetValue( _
        Path.Combine(key, "*Complex"), GetType(ArrayList)), ArrayList)

    ' Loop over all fields that are declared in this type.
    For Each fi As FieldInfo In type.GetFields(BindingFlags.Instance Or _
            BindingFlags.Public Or BindingFlags.NonPublic Or BindingFlags.DeclaredOnly)
        ' Read the value of all serializable fields.
        If Not fi.IsNotSerialized Then
            Dim fieldKey As String = Path.Combine(key, fi.Name)
            Dim value As Object = Nothing

            If Not complexFields.Contains(fi.Name) Then
                ' Read directly if it's a serializable type.
                value = info.GetValue(fieldKey, GetType(Object))
            Else
                ' Retrieve the type of this field.
                Dim fieldType As Type = DirectCast(info.GetValue( _
                    Path.Combine(fieldKey, "*Type"), GetType(Type)), Type)
                ' Create an uninitialized object of that type.
                value = FormatterServices.GetUninitializedObject(fieldType)
                ' Fill this instance by calling this method recursively.
                DeserializeObjectFields(info, fieldKey, value, Nothing)
            End If
            fi.SetValue(obj, value)
        End If
    Next
  End Sub
End Module      ' End of SerializationHelpers module
```

The method uses the FormatterServices.GetUninitializedObject method to create an instance of the type whose fields are all set to the default value (zero or Nothing). This method bypasses any constructor exposed by the class and is also extremely efficient. (It is the same method used by the CLR during the default deserialization step.)

Here's an example that uses the SerializationHelpers module. It shows a serializable Employee type that inherits from the nonserializable PersonalData class. To prove that the mechanism works well even in complex fields—either serializable or not—the PersonalData class has a Spouse field (of type PersonalData) and the Employee type has a Boss field (of type Employee), and both types have a private field with the same name (m_BirthDate), which apparently can be initialized only through the constructor.

```
Public Class PersonalData
    Public LastName As String
    Public FirstName As String
    Public Spouse As PersonalData
    Private m_BirthDate As Date                    ' A private field
```

```vb
    Sub New(ByVal firstName As String, ByVal lastName As String, ByVal birthDate As Date)
        Me.FirstName = firstName
        Me.LastName = lastName
        Me.m_BirthDate = birthDate
    End Sub

    Public ReadOnly Property BirthDate() As Date
        Get
            Return m_BirthDate
        End Get
    End Property
End Class

<Serializable()> _
Public Class Employee
    Inherits PersonalData
    Implements ISerializable

    Public Boss As Employee
    Private m_BirthDate As Date                 ' A private field

    Sub New(ByVal firstName As String, ByVal lastName As String, ByVal birthDate As Date)
        MyBase.New(firstName, lastName, birthDate)
        ' Also save the birth date in the private field at this hierarchy level.
        Me.m_BirthDate = birthDate
    End Sub

    Public Sub GetObjectData(ByVal info As SerializationInfo, ByVal context As StreamingContext) _
        Implements ISerializable.GetObjectData
        SerializeObjectFields(info, "", Me, Nothing)
    End Sub

    Public Sub New(ByVal info As SerializationInfo, ByVal context As StreamingContext)
        ' Unfortunately, we *must* have a call to the base class's constructor.
        MyBase.New("anyfirstname", "anylastname", New Date())
        DeserializeObjectFields(info, "", Me, Nothing)
    End Sub
End Class
```

Here's a piece of code that tests the serialization features of the Employee type:

```vb
Dim em As New Employee("Joe", "Healy", #1/12/1960#)
em.Spouse = New Employee("Ann", "Beebe", #4/6/1962#)
em.Spouse.Spouse = em
em.Boss = New Employee("Robert", "Zare", #11/7/1965#)
SerializeToFile("employee.dat", em)
Dim em2 As Employee = DeserializeFromFile(Of Employee)("employee.dat")

Console.WriteLine(em2.FirstName)              ' => Joe
Console.WriteLine(em2.Spouse.FirstName)       ' => Ann
Console.WriteLine(em2.Boss.FirstName)         ' => Robert
Console.WriteLine(em2.Boss.BirthDate)         ' => #11/7/1965#
' Check that circular references are handled correctly.
Console.WriteLine(em2.Spouse.Spouse is em2)   ' => True
```

This technique is sophisticated enough to handle circular references correctly, such as the relation that ties two Person objects through their Spouse property. It also deals correctly with object identity. For example, imagine that Joe's spouse is also his boss:

```
Dim em As New Employee("Joe", "Healy", #1/12/1960#)
em.Boss = New Employee("Ann", "Beebe", #4/6/1962#)
em.Spouse = em.Boss
' Serialize and deserialize the object graph (as in previous code example).
…
' Prove that object identity has been preserved.
Console.WriteLine(em2.Boss Is em2.Spouse)          ' => True
```

Chapter 22
PInvoke and COM Interop

The Microsoft .NET Framework is a revolution in the programming world. Managed applications are going to become the most common type of Microsoft Windows software. However, even the most enthusiastic .NET Framework fan can't reasonably expect that unmanaged code is going to disappear anytime soon, for at least three reasons. First, rewriting all existing software as managed code can be cost-prohibitive, and the advantage of having it running as a managed application might not justify migration costs. Second, many services are available today to Windows programmers only as COM components, such as Microsoft Office Word or Excel object libraries. Third, the .NET Framework encompasses many but not all features of the operating system. You still need unmanaged code to write shell extensions, work with memory mapped files, or perform cross-process window subclassing, just to mention a few Windows features not yet encapsulated in the .NET Framework.

For these and other reasons, Microsoft provides two distinct yet related mechanisms to use unmanaged code from a .NET Framework application: Platform Invoke (also known as PInvoke) and COM Interop. PInvoke technology lets .NET code call "traditional" DLLs, such as those that make up the Windows kernel or those written in C or C++, whereas COM Interop lets you reuse COM components from a .NET Framework language or call .NET Framework components from COM applications.

Despite their different purposes, these two technologies have a lot in common, and it makes sense to discuss them in the same chapter. For example, with only a few exceptions, they share the marshaling rules that dictate how data can be moved from the managed world to the unmanaged world and back. PInvoke is the simpler of the two technologies, so I cover it first. I defer COM Interop to the second part of this chapter.

> **Note** To avoid long lines, code samples in this chapter assume that the following Imports statements are used at the file or project level:
>
> ```
> Imports System.ComponentModel
> Imports System.Runtime.InteropServices
> Imports System.Reflection
> Imports System.Text
> Imports System.Threading
> Imports Microsoft.Win32
> ```

Using PInvoke

Before you can call a function in an external DLL, you must declare the function's name and syntax. Microsoft Visual Basic 2005 provides two different ways to do so: the Declare keyword and the DllImport attribute. The former provides backward compatibility with earlier versions of the language; the latter is the mechanism adopted by all .NET Framework languages. Except for the different syntax, the two approaches are broadly equivalent, with DllImport being slightly more flexible.

The Declare Keyword

Microsoft Visual Basic has supported the Declare keyword since version 1, so odds are that you are already familiar with it. A difference from Visual Basic 6 is that you can use a public Declare statement anywhere in your application, including module, form, and class blocks. Here's its complete syntax:

```
Declare [Ansi|Unicode|Auto] [Sub|Function] procedurename Lib "dllname"
[Alias "entrypoint"] ( arglist ) [As returntype]
```

where *procedurename* is the name of the procedure as seen in the Visual Basic program, *dllname* is the name of the DLL, and *entrypoint* is the name of the procedure in the DLL. (This name can be different from *procedurename* and can include characters that are invalid in Visual Basic.) In most cases, you can convert Declare statements written for Microsoft Visual Basic 6 to Visual Basic 2005 without any change other than adjusting data types (for example, translating Long to Integer).

Visual Basic 2005 supports the optional Ansi, Unicode, and Auto keywords, which dictate how strings are passed to the external DLL. Ansi specifies that strings are passed as ANSI strings (the default behavior); Unicode forces strings to be passed as Unicode; Auto causes strings to be passed as ANSI strings under Microsoft Windows 98 and Windows Millennium Edition (Me) or as Unicode strings under more recent versions of the operating system.

The following code snippet declares two functions in the Windows User32.dll and invokes them to retrieve the handle of a window titled "Untitled–Notepad," resize the window, and move the window to the upper left corner of the screen. You should launch Notepad on an empty document before trying this code.

```
' (The Ansi qualifier is optional.)
Private Declare Ansi Function FindWindow Lib "user32" Alias "FindWindowA" _
   (ByVal lpClassName As String, ByVal lpWindowName As String) As Integer
Private Declare Function MoveWindow Lib "user32" Alias "MoveWindow" _
   (ByVal hWnd As Integer, ByVal x As Integer, ByVal y As Integer, _
   ByVal nWidth As Integer, ByVal nHeight As Integer, _
   ByVal bRepaint As Integer) As Integer

Sub TestFindWindow()
   ' This works only on English and U.S. versions of the Windows operating system.
   Dim hWnd As Integer = FindWindow(Nothing, "Untitled - Notepad")
   If hWnd <> 0 Then
      MoveWindow(hWnd, 0, 0, 600, 300, 1)
   Else
      MessageBox.Show("Window not found", "Error")
   End If
End Sub
```

As this snippet demonstrates, you can use Nothing to pass a null string. In Visual Basic 6 or earlier versions, you would have passed the vbNullString constant in these circumstances. (This constant is still supported but is superfluous under Visual Basic 2005.) Remember that a null string is always different from an empty string—that is, a string that contains no characters—when calling a function in a DLL.

A Declare statement can include Optional arguments; if you omit an optional argument when calling the function, its default value is pushed on the stack anyway. If the external function receives an incorrect number of arguments, your application is likely to crash.

The DllImport Attribute

Although the Declare keyword is still supported, you should abandon it in favor of the DllImport attribute. This attribute is preferable because it offers additional options and also because it works in virtually all .NET Framework languages, including C#, so it makes your code more readable to other developers and more easily ported to other languages.

The DllImport attribute is defined in the System.Runtime.InteropServices namespace and can be applied only to static methods—namely, methods defined in a module or class methods flagged with the Shared keyword. The method marked with this attribute is used only as a blueprint for deriving the type of arguments and the type of the return value (if there is one); a compilation error occurs if the method contains executable code. In the simplest case, the DllImport attribute specifies only the name of the DLL that contains the external function:

```
Public Class WindowsFunctions
   <DllImport("user32")> _
   Public Shared Function FindWindow(ByVal lpClassName As String, _
      ByVal lpWindowName As String) As Integer
```

```
          ' No code here
      End Function


      <DllImport("user32")> _
      Shared Function MoveWindow(ByVal hWnd As Integer, ByVal x As Integer, _
          ByVal y As Integer, ByVal nWidth As Integer, ByVal nHeight As Integer, _
          ByVal bRepaint As Integer) As Integer
          ' No code here
      End Function
  End Class
```

As you can see, the .dll extension in the DLL name can be omitted. If the path is also omitted, the DLL must be in a system folder or another directory listed in the PATH environment variable.

Once you have declared an external function, you can invoke it as if it were defined in managed code:

```
Dim hWnd As Integer = WindowsFunctions.FindWindow(Nothing, "Untitled - Notepad")
If hWnd <> 0 Then
    WindowsFunctions.MoveWindow(hWnd, 0, 0, 600, 300, 1)
Else
    MessageBox.Show("Window not found", "Error")
End If
```

The DllImport attribute supports several optional arguments, which let you precisely define how the external procedure should be called and how it returns a value to the caller.

```
<DllImport("filename.dll", CharSet:=charsetoption, ExactSpelling:=bool, _
    EntryPoint:="procname", CallingConvention:=calloption, _
    SetLastError:=bool, BestFitMapping:=bool, ThrowOnUnmappableChar:=bool)> _
...
```

The CharSet argument tells how strings are passed to the external routine; it can be CharSet .Ansi (the default), CharSet.Unicode, or CharSet.Auto. This argument has the same meaning as the Ansi, Unicode, or Auto qualifier in the Declare statement. In addition, if you specify the Ansi setting and a function with that name isn't found in the DLL, Visual Basic appends the "A" character to the function name and tries again. If you specify the Unicode setting, Visual Basic appends the "W" character to the function name before searching for it; if this first search fails, Visual Basic searches for the name you've provided. Notice the subtle difference between the Ansi and Unicode settings—the latter works as described because the .NET Framework uses Unicode strings, and therefore a function that takes Unicode strings is preferable because it is more efficient than is one that doesn't.

The ExactSpelling argument is a Boolean value that determines whether the method name must match exactly the name in the DLL; if True (the default setting), the CharSet setting has no effect on the function name being searched.

The EntryPoint argument specifies the actual function name in the DLL and is therefore equivalent to the Alias clause in a Declare statement. In practice, you use this argument if the entry point name is an invalid or a reserved name in Visual Basic (such as Friend), if it duplicates a name already defined in the application, or if it's an ordinal entry point (such as "#123").

The CallingConvention argument specifies the calling convention for the entry point. Available values are WinApi (the default), CDecl, FastCall, StdCall, and ThisCall. You rarely need to specify this option.

The SetLastError argument indicates whether the called function sets the Win32 last error code. If this argument is True, the compiler emits additional code that saves the last error code; therefore, you should leave this argument False (its default value) if you know that the function you're calling doesn't set the Win32 error.

When the CLR converts Unicode strings to ANSI, each Unicode character is translated to the close-matching ANSI character, or to "?" if no close-matching character exists. This approach is usually desirable, but it might cause problems if the close-matching character is a character that might have a special meaning for the called procedure. For example, if the close-matching character is the backslash character, a string representing a path might point to the wrong place. You can disable the default behavior by setting the BestFitMapping argument to False (the default is True), and you can have the CLR throw an exception if a Unicode character in the string has no close-matching character in the ANSI set by setting the ThrowOnUnmappableChar argument to True (the default is False).

The following example shows how you can use the DllImport attribute to call a method named Friend in a DLL named myfunctions.dll, which takes Unicode strings and affects the Win32 error code:

```
' We must use an aliased name because Friend is a reserved keyword.
<DllImport("myfunctions.dll", EntryPoint:="Friend", _
    CharSet:=CharSet.Unicode, SetLastError:=True)> _
Shared Function MakeFriends(ByVal s1 As String, ByVal s2 As String) As Integer
    ' No implementation code
End Function
```

If the external routine sets the Win32 error code and you passed True to the SetLastError argument, you can read this error code when the call returns by means of either the Err.LastDllError method or the Marshal.GetLastWin32Error method:

```
Dim res As Integer = MakeFriends("first", "second")
If Err.LastDllError <> 0 Then
    ' Deal with the error here.
End If
```

You can read the last error code only once. External routines declared with the Declare keyword always set the Win32 error code; therefore, using DllImport provides a slight optimization if the external routine doesn't set the error code or if you aren't going to test it after the call.

A new assembly-level attribute enables you to specify the character set to be assumed for all the DllImport attributes that lack an explicit CharSet named argument:

```
' Change the default CharSet value from Ansi to Auto.
<Assembly: DefaultCharSet(CharSet.Auto)>
```

Marshaling Data

To invoke a function in an external DLL successfully, you must be familiar with how data is passed from Visual Basic to the external DLL, and how results are passed back to Visual Basic. This mechanism is known as *data marshaling*.

Most data types can be passed from managed to unmanaged code without much concern on your part because these data types have the same memory representation in the two worlds. These types are known as *blittable types*, a group that includes Byte, Short, Integer, Long, Single, Double, and Date types, as well as one-dimensional arrays thereof and structures that contain only blittable elements. You should pass blittable types if possible because they can cross the boundary between managed and unmanaged code very efficiently.

Nonblittable types are those that have a different representation in the two worlds, or that might have many representations in the unmanaged world, and must undergo marshaling when they cross the border between the managed and unmanaged worlds.

The most common nonblittable types are Boolean, Char, String, Decimal, and Array. The Boolean type is nonblittable because it can be 1, 2, or 4 bytes in the unmanaged world and because the True value can be represented as either 1 or −1. The Char type can be translated to either an ANSI or a Unicode character. The String type can be transformed in a variety of unmanaged formats, including null-terminated strings or length-prefixed BSTRs (each with the ANSI and Unicode variants). The Decimal type must be converted to Currency. Arrays are nonblittable because they can be translated either to SAFEARRAYS or to C-style arrays. You can determine exactly how nonblittable data is passed to or returned from managed code by means of the MarshalAs attribute, which I cover in the next section.

Many Windows API functions that are designed to send a string value back to the caller don't actually return a string in the return value; instead, they take a string buffer as an argument and fill it with zero or more characters. (The actual return value is often an integer that specifies how many characters have been placed in the buffer.)

When passing a String to such external methods, you have a problem to solve: .NET Framework strings are immutable, and you wouldn't see a different value in the string when the call returns. To see the actual returned string, you must pass a StringBuilder object instead. Here's an example of how you can define the GetClassName API function:

```
' Add these lines to the WindowsFunctions class.
<DllImport("user32")> _
Public Shared Function GetClassName(ByVal hWnd As IntPtr, ByVal buffer As StringBuilder, _
    ByVal charcount As Integer) As Integer
End Function
```

The first argument, a 32-bit integer, is declared as an IntPtr element. Using an IntPtr instead of an Integer gives you two benefits. First, you can pass the value of a form's Handle property without any conversion. Second, the IntPtr type automatically matches the size of CPU registers and works well under 64-bit versions of the Windows operating system. Here's how you can retrieve the class name of the current form:

```
Dim buffer As New StringBuilder(512)
' The last argument is the max number of characters in the buffer.
WindowsFunctions.GetClassName(Me.Handle, buffer, buffer.Capacity)
Dim classname As String = buffer.ToString()
```

The MarshalAs Attribute

The .NET Framework provides a default marshaling mechanism for each nonblittable type, but you modify the default behavior by means of the MarshalAs attribute. The following code shows how to use this attribute to let the compiler know that the (fictitious) CheckString procedure takes an ANSI null-terminated string and returns a Boolean value as a 2-byte integer that uses −1 to represent the True value:

```
<DllImport("mydll")> _
Shared Function CheckString( _
    <MarshalAs(UnmanagedType.LPWStr)> ByVal s As String) _
    As <MarshalAs(UnmanagedType.VariantBool)> Boolean
End Function
```

You can apply the MarshalAs attribute to parameters, fields, and return values. In most cases, the attribute takes only the UnmanagedType enumerated value that determines how the value is converted during the marshaling operation. Some UnmanagedType values, however, might require additional arguments, such as ArraySubType and SizeConst. See Table 22-1 for more details.

Table 22-1   UnmanagedType Enumerated Values

Value	Description
AnsiBStr	A length-prefixed ANSI character string. (Length is single byte.)
AsAny	A dynamic type that determines the type of an object at run time and marshals the object as that type. (Not valid for COM Interop.)
Bool	A 4-byte Boolean value, corresponding to the Win32 BOOL type. (0 is False; any other value is True.) This is the default way of passing Boolean values for PInvoke.
BStr	A length-prefixed double-byte Unicode character string. (The default way of passing strings for COM Interop.)
ByValArray	A fixed-length array field inside a structure. The SizeConst field must specify the number of elements in the array; the ArraySubType field can specify the UnmanagedType enumerated value that corresponds to the type of the array elements, if array elements aren't blittable.

Table 22-1   UnmanagedType Enumerated Values *(Continued)*

Value	Description
ByValTStr	A fixed-length string field in a structure. The SizeConst argument must contain the size of the buffer in bytes. The CharSet attribute in the class determines the type of the characters.
Currency	A COM Currency value. (Can be used only with Decimal values.)
I1, I2, I4, I8	A 1-byte, 2-byte, 4-byte, or 8-byte signed integer.
IDispatch	A COM IDispatch interface pointer (same as the As Object variable in Visual Basic 6).
Interface	A COM interface pointer that specifies the exact interface type or the default interface type when applied to a class. The GUID of the interface is obtained from the class metadata.
IUnknown	A COM IUnknown interface pointer. (Can be used with Object values.)
LPArray	A pointer to the first element of a C-style array. When marshaling from the .NET Framework to unmanaged code, the array length is determined at run time. When marshaling from unmanaged code to the .NET Framework, the array length is determined from the SizeConst or SizeParamIndex arguments, optionally followed by the unmanaged type of array elements if they aren't blittable.
LPStr	A single-byte, null-terminated ANSI character string. (Can be used with String and StringBuilder elements.)
LPTStr	A platform-dependent character string. ANSI on Windows 98 and Windows Me, Unicode on Microsoft Windows NT and later versions. (Not valid with COM Interop.)
LPWStr	A 2-byte, null-terminated Unicode character string.
R4, R8	A 4-byte or 8-byte floating-point number.
SafeArray	An OLE Automation SafeArray. You can use the SafeArraySubType field to define the default element type.
Struct	A Variant used to marshal a structure or a formatted reference type.
SysInt, SysUInt	A platform-independent signed or unsigned integer. Four bytes on 32-bit Windows, 8 bytes on 64-bit Windows.
U1, U2, U4, U8	A 1-byte, 2-byte, 4-byte, or 8-byte unsigned integer.
VariantBool	A 2-byte OLE Boolean value, also known as VARIANT_BOOL (–1 for True; 0 for False). This is the default way of passing Boolean values for COM Interop.
VBByRefStr	Allows Visual Basic to receive correctly the new value of a string modified in unmanaged code. (Not valid for COM Interop.)

The following code shows how you can use the MarshalAs attribute to pass a Unicode string to the Windows API function that changes the current directory. This example is for illustration purposes only; you can achieve the same result by using the CharSet.Unicode setting in the DllImport attribute.

```
<DllImport("kernel32", EntryPoint:="SetCurrentDirectoryW")> _
Function SetCurrentDirectory( _
    <MarshalAs(UnmanagedType.LPWStr)> ByVal lpPathName As String) As Integer
End Function
```

The following structure contains two string fields flagged with the MarshalAs attribute. When this structure is passed to an external procedure, the first field is translated to a null-terminated ANSI string, whereas the second field becomes a 256-character fixed-length string.

```
Structure MyStructure
   <MarshalAs(UnmanagedType.LPStr)> Public f1 As String
   <MarshalAs(UnmanagedType.ByValTStr, SizeConst:=256)> Public f2 As String
End Structure
```

Here's another example that uses the SizeConst optional argument:

```
Structure Employee
   ' Marshal the Name string as an ANSI fixed-length string of 100 chars.
   ' (We must account for the extra null character.)
   <MarshalAs(UnmanagedType.ByValTStr, SizeConst:=101)> _
   Dim Name As String
   ...
End Structure
```

The StructLayout Attribute

The .NET Framework defines a couple of attributes that let you control how the elements of a Structure block are arranged in memory and how the runtime should marshal them when they're passed to a function in an external DLL.

Fields of a structure are arranged in memory in the order in which they appear in source code, even though the compiler is free to insert padding bytes to arrange members so that 16-bit values are aligned with word boundaries, 32-bit values are aligned with double-word boundaries, and so on. This arrangement—known as an *unpacked layout*—delivers the best performance because Intel processors work faster with aligned data.

You can finely control where each member of the structure or the class is located by means of the StructLayout attribute. The allowed values for this attribute are StructLayout.Auto (the compiler can reorder elements for best performance—for example, by grouping value types together), StructLayout.Sequential (elements are laid out and properly aligned sequentially in memory), and StructLayout.Explicit.

```
<StructLayout(LayoutKind.Explicit)> _
Structure ARGBColor
   ...
End Structure
```

By default, Visual Basic 2005 uses the StructLayout.Auto setting for classes and StructLayout .Sequential for structures.

The StructLayout attribute supports three additional fields: CharSet, Pack, and Size. CharSet defines how string members in the structure are marshaled when the structure is passed to a DLL and can be Unicode, Ansi, or Auto. This argument, which defaults to Auto, has the same meaning as the DllImport argument with same name.

The Pack field defines the packing size for the structure and can be 1, 2, 4, 8 (the default), 16, 32, 64, 128, or the special value 0 that uses the default packing size for the current platform. A structure whose LayoutKind is Sequential always aligns elements to this number of bytes; if you omit the StructLayout attribute, elements align to their natural boundary (2-byte words for Short elements, 4-byte double words for Integer and Single, addresses that are multiples of 8 for Long and Double, and so forth).

The Size field determines the total length of the structure when passed to unmanaged code; you can use this argument to increase the length of a structure. (You can reach the same goal by appending dummy, unused fields to the structure.)

```
<StructLayout(LayoutKind.Sequential, CharSet:=CharSet.Unicode, Pack:=4)> _
Structure ARGBColor

    ...

End Structure
```

By default, the Visual Basic compiler is free to arrange class members in a way that optimizes memory usage and performance. This corresponds to the StructLayout.Auto setting. When passing an object—as opposed to a structure—to unmanaged code, you must apply the Struct-Layout attribute with a different setting, typically StructLayout.Explicit. Classes flagged in this way are known as *formatted classes*. PInvoke supports classes as arguments only if they are formatted classes, with only a few exceptions such as the String and StringBuilder types; conversely, COM Interop doesn't enforce any limitation in passing a reference type.

In practice, you will rarely pass a reference to an object other than String or StringBuilder as an argument to an external DLL using PInvoke. If you do, however, remember that the DLL receives a *pointer* to the data in the object. From the perspective of the called routine, an object reference passed with ByVal is similar to a structure passed with ByRef because, in both cases, the routine receives an address. If you pass an object reference to a ByRef argument, the routine receives the address of a pointer that points to the object's data.

The FieldOffset Attribute

When you opt for an explicit layout, the definition of all the fields in a structure must include a FieldOffset attribute that has an argument specifying the distance in bytes from the beginning of the structure:

```
<StructLayout(LayoutKind.Explicit)> _
Structure ARGBColor
    <FieldOffset(0)> Public Red As Byte
    <FieldOffset(1)> Public Green As Byte
    <FieldOffset(2)> Public Blue As Byte
    <FieldOffset(3)> Public Alpha As Byte
End Structure
```

The StructLayout and the FieldOffset attributes let you simulate a *union*, a language feature that many languages, such as C and C++ have had since their inception. A union is a structure in which two or more elements overlap in memory. Or, if you prefer, a union permits you to refer to the same memory location in a structure using different names. The key to unions in Visual Basic 2005 is the support for explicit structure layout. Consider the following example:

```
<StructLayout(LayoutKind.Explicit)> _
Structure RGBColor
    <FieldOffset(0)> Public Red As Byte
    <FieldOffset(1)> Public Green As Byte
    <FieldOffset(2)> Public Blue As Byte
    <FieldOffset(3)> Public Alpha As Byte
    <FieldOffset(0)> Public Value As Integer
End Structure
```

The following graphic illustrates how these elements are located in memory:

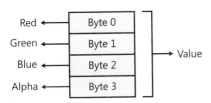

In other words, you can access the 4 bytes as a whole through the Value field or individually through the Red, Green, Blue, and Alpha fields. The following code shows how useful this feature can be:

```
' Split a color into its components.
Dim rgb As RGBColor
rgb.Value = &H112233             ' This is equal to 1122867.
Console.WriteLine("Red={0}, Green={1}, Blue={2}", rgb.Red, rgb.Green, rgb.Blue)
    ' => Red=51, Green=34, Blue=17
```

You can also combine the three RGB components into a single color:

```
rgb.Red = 51
rgb.Green = 34
rgb.Blue = 17
Console.WriteLine("RGB color = {0}", rgb.Value)     ' => 1122867
```

Unions make it possible to implement some tricky conversion routines far more efficiently than using standard math operators. Consider the following structure:

```
<StructLayout(LayoutKind.Explicit)> _
Structure IntegerTypes
    ' A 64-bit integer
    <FieldOffset(0)> Public Long0 As Long
    ' Two 32-bit integers
    <FieldOffset(0)> Public Integer0 As Integer
    <FieldOffset(4)> Public Integer1 As Integer
    ' Four 16-bit integers
    <FieldOffset(0)> Public Short0 As Short
    <FieldOffset(2)> Public Short1 As Short
```

```
   <FieldOffset(4)> Public Short2 As Short
   <FieldOffset(6)> Public Short3 As Short
   ' Eight 8-bit integers
   <FieldOffset(0)> Public Byte0 As Byte
   <FieldOffset(1)> Public Byte1 As Byte
   <FieldOffset(2)> Public Byte2 As Byte
   <FieldOffset(3)> Public Byte3 As Byte
   <FieldOffset(4)> Public Byte4 As Byte
   <FieldOffset(5)> Public Byte5 As Byte
   <FieldOffset(6)> Public Byte6 As Byte
   <FieldOffset(7)> Public Byte7 As Byte
End Structure
```

This structure takes exactly 8 bytes, but you can refer to those bytes in multiple ways. For example, you can extract the low and high bytes of a 16-bit integer:

```
Dim it As IntegerTypes
it.Short0 = 517                       ' Hex 0205
Console.WriteLine(it.Byte0)           ' => 5
Console.WriteLine(it.Byte1)           ' => 2
```

This technique works also if the structure fields are declared as Private. However, you should use it only with integer member types, such as Byte, Short, Integer, and Long; trying to interpret locations as Single or Double values often returns the special NaN (Not-a-Number) value. Trying to map a reference type (such as a String) throws an exception because the Visual Basic compiler rejects structures in which reference types overlap with other members or aren't aligned properly.

Most of the structures used by Windows API functions are unpacked and don't require any special attribute. Others, most notably those in the Shell32.dll library, might require you to define an explicit layout. One such example is the SHFILEOPSTRUCT structure that you pass as an argument to the SHFileOperation function:

```
Private Declare Ansi Function SHFileOperation Lib "shell32.dll" _
    Alias "SHFileOperationA" (ByRef lpFileOp As SHFILEOPSTRUCT) As Integer

<StructLayout(LayoutKind.Explicit)> _
Structure SHFILEOPSTRUCT
   <FieldOffset(0)> Public hwnd As IntPtr
   <FieldOffset(4)> Public wFunc As Integer
   <FieldOffset(8)> Public pFrom As String
   <FieldOffset(12)> Public pTo As String
   <FieldOffset(16)> Public fFlags As Short
   <FieldOffset(18), MarshalAs(UnmanagedType.Bool)> _
       Public fAnyOperationsAborted As Boolean
   <FieldOffset(22)> Public hNameMappings As Integer
   <FieldOffset(26)> Public lpszProgressTitle As IntPtr
       ' (It was String, only used if FOF_SIMPLEPROGRESS.)
End Structure
```

By carefully examining the previous structure, you can see that the fFlags field (a 2-byte integer) is immediately followed by a 4-byte Boolean value. If this structure were unpacked, two padding bytes would be inserted between these two fields. Unfortunately, the Shell32.dll library expects a packed structure, so we must resort to explicit layout. Notice also that the last element in the structure is defined as a string in the Windows SDK documentation, but we must use an IntPtr or an Integer in Visual Basic because strings are reference types and must be aligned to the double word.

Here's a procedure that uses the SHFileOperation API function to copy one or more files while displaying the standard Windows dialog box (shown in Figure 22-1). This API function automatically manages name collisions and allows undelete operations.

```vb
' Copy a file using the SHFileOperation API function.
' It can return 0 (OK), 1 (user canceled the operation), or 2 (error).
Function CopyFile(ByVal source As String, ByVal dest As String) As Integer
    ' Fill an SHFILEOPSTRUCT structure.
    Dim sh As SHFILEOPSTRUCT
    sh.wFunc = 2                  ' = FO_COPY, a file copy operation
    sh.hwnd = IntPtr.Zero      ' No owner window
    sh.pTo = dest
    ' Ensure source file ends with an extra null char. (See SDK docs.)
    sh.pFrom = source & ControlChars.NullChar
    sh.fFlags = &H48           ' = ALLOWUNDO Or RENAMEONCOLLISION

    ' The API functions returns nonzero if there is a problem.
    Dim res As Integer = SHFileOperation(sh)
    If res = 0 Then
        Return 0                 ' 0 means everything was OK.
    ElseIf sh.fAnyOperationsAborted Then
        Return 1                 ' 1 means user aborted the operation.
    Else
        Return 2                 ' 2 means an error has occurred.
    End If
End Function
```

Figure 22-1   The standard window that the SHFileOperation API function displays when copying files

Here's how you can use the CopyFile function to copy all the files in the C:\Docs directory to the C:\Backup directory:

```vb
Select Case CopyFile("c:\Docs\*.*", "c:\Backup")
    Case 0: MessageBox.Show("All files were copied correctly.")
    Case 1: MessageBox.Show("User canceled the operation.")
    Case 2: MessageBox.Show("An error occurred.")
End Select
```

Delegates and Callback Procedures

A method in an external DLL can take the address of a *callback procedure*. A callback procedure is a procedure in your program that the external method calls to notify your code that something has happened. For example, the EnumWindows API function enumerates all the upper top-level windows in the system and invokes a callback method for each found window. You can write code in the callback procedure that uses this information—for example, by displaying the name of the window in a ListBox control or by filling an array of structures for later processing.

Visual Basic 6 applications can call EnumWindows, EnumFonts, and other Enum*Xxxx* functions in the Windows API and pass them the address of a local callback function, using the AddressOf operator. This technique is unsafe because the application crashes if the callback routine doesn't comply with the expected syntax for arguments and return values. (You can learn about the expected syntax of Enum*Xxxx* procedures from the Windows SDK documentation.) Visual Basic 2005 enables you to call these Windows API functions in a safe way by means of delegates.

Before you can declare an external procedure that uses a callback mechanism, you must create a delegate class that defines the syntax of the callback routine:

```
' This is the syntax for an EnumWindows callback procedure.
Delegate Function EnumWindowsCBK(ByVal hwnd As Integer, _
    ByVal lParam As Integer) As Integer
```

In the definition of the API function, you specify the callback argument using the delegate type:

```
Declare Function EnumWindows Lib "user32" (ByVal lpEnumFunc As EnumWindowsCBK, _
    ByVal lParam As Integer) As Integer
```

Finally, you can write the actual callback procedure and pass its address to the external method. The delegate argument forces you to pass the address of a procedure that complies with the delegate's syntax:

```
Sub TestAPICallback()
    EnumWindows(AddressOf ListWindows, 0)
End Sub

' The second argument to the callback function is ignored in this demo.
' In a real application, it helps discern the
' reason why this procedure has been called.
Function ListWindows(ByVal hwnd As Integer, ByVal lParam As Integer) As Integer
    ' Display the handle of this top-level window.
    lstWindows.Items.Add(hwnd)
    ' Return 1 to continue enumeration.
    Return 1
End Function
```

The preceding code snippet displays the 32-bit handle of all the top-level windows in the system. The complete demo shows how you can display the handle and other pieces of information about all the open windows in the system by using the EnumWindows and EnumChildWindows API functions in a recursive fashion. (See Figure 22-2.)

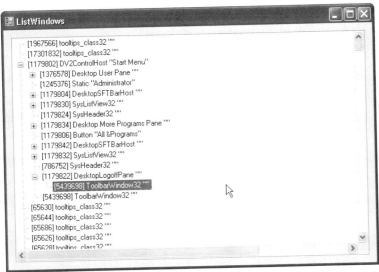

Figure 22-2   The demo program, which uses the Windows API to display the tree of all open windows

The In and Out Attributes

The .NET Framework marshaler always copies a parameter's values from managed code to the unmanaged DLL, but it copies the value back only if the parameter is passed by reference. This means that you see the new value if the callee changes the value of a ByRef parameter. At first glance, therefore, the semantics of the ByVal and ByRef keywords is also preserved when working with PInvoke. However, things aren't always so smooth, and you must be prepared to work around a few potential problems you might have with reference types.

As I explained earlier, the PInvoke marshaler can pass a reference type only if the type is a formatted class (that is, it uses an explicit layout), with String and StringBuilder types being among the few exceptions. The PInvoke marshaler copies the fields of a formatted structure to unmanaged memory instead of just passing a pointer to the managed object. (The COM Interop marshaler, however, simply passes the object pointer, as you'd expect.)

As you know, if you pass a ByVal object to a Visual Basic 2005 routine that modifies the object's fields, you see the new fields' values when the call returns. Conversely, the PInvoke marshaler doesn't copy data back to the object when you pass a reference type to an external DLL, to achieve better performance. In other words, by default, reference types are passed as input-only arguments. You can change this behavior by flagging the argument with explicit In and Out attributes, as follows:

```
' "In" is a reserved word, so you can't omit the Attribute portion.
Declare Sub TestRoutine Lib "mydll" (<InAttribute, Out> objref As Object)
```

The StringBuilder class is an exception to this rule because the PInvoke marshaler copies it back even if you pass it by value and without the Out attribute. You can omit the In attribute when passing a ByRef argument that doesn't have to be initialized.

In its quest for greater efficiency, under certain circumstances, the marshaler can decide to *pin* the passed argument, a detail that makes things a bit more complicated. When an argument is pinned, the marshaler passes the address of the original value in the managed heap rather than the address of a copy. (The word *pinning* is used because the object is pinned in memory and doesn't move even if a garbage collection occurs in the meantime.)

For example, under PInvoke, a .NET Framework string passed by value to a Unicode string argument is pinned: the callee receives the address of the internal character buffer, and no copy occurs. If the callee doesn't abide by the by-value semantics and mistakenly changes the passed string, the managed heap might be corrupted. (This happens, for example, if a longer string is assigned.)

Pinning can occur only with strings passed by value. The PInvoke marshaler always copies ByRef string arguments to a temporary buffer and then passes the address of this buffer to the external routine. When the call returns, the marshaler creates a new string with the characters found in the buffer and passes the new string back to the caller. (This double copy is necessary to preserve string immutability.)

Pinning occurs also when you pass a blittable formatted class because the marshaler can improve performance by passing a pointer to the object's memory in the managed heap. Pinning happens regardless of whether you use the Out attribute. (In other words, the Out attribute forces a copy of the value back to Visual Basic only if the argument isn't pinned.)

Arrays are reference types and can be pinned, too. More precisely, an array is pinned if its elements are blittable and you make either a PInvoke call or a COM Interop call to an object that lives in the same apartment as the caller. Arrays defined as part of a structure are dealt with as other objects, but they can be passed by value by flagging them with a MarshalAs attribute, as follows:

```
<StructLayout(LayoutKind.Sequential)> Structure MyStruct
    <MarshalAs(UnmanagedType.ByValArray, SizeConst:=64)> _
    Public s1() As Short
End Structure
```

The structure in the preceding code takes 128 bytes when it is passed by value on the stack because the MarshalAs attribute specifies that the s1 array has 64 elements. Without this attribute, the array would have been marshaled as any other object reference, and the structure would take only 4 bytes.

The Marshal Class

You've seen that you can affect the behavior of the PInvoke marshaler by means of a few attributes, but in the most intricate cases, you must resort to *manual marshaling* techniques, which require that you manually allocate and deallocate unmanaged memory and copy your data into it.

The basis for manual marshaling is the Marshal class, a container for static methods that let you do virtually anything you might need to do with unmanaged memory. I mentioned this class when I described the Marshal.GetLastWin32Error method in the section titled "The DllImport Attribute" earlier in this chapter.

The SizeOf method takes an object or a structure (or a System.Type that identifies a structure or a class) and returns the number of bytes that object or structure would take when marshaled to unmanaged code:

```
' These statements display the same value.
Console.WriteLine(Marshal.SizeOf(GetType(Person)))
Console.WriteLine(Marshal.SizeOf(New Person()))
```

The OffsetOf method takes two arguments: a System.Type that identifies either a structure or a class flagged with the StructLayout attribute, and the name of one of the type's members. The method returns the offset of the member in the unmanaged representation of the structure or class:

```
Console.WriteLine(Marshal.OffsetOf(GetType(Person), "FirstName"))
```

You can allocate three kinds of unmanaged memory with the methods of the Marshal class; each kind must be deallocated later with a different method.

The AllocHGlobal method allocates memory by invoking the GlobalAlloc API function and returns a pointer to the allocated memory. You can resize the memory block with the ReAllocHGlobal method and release it with the FreeHGlobal method:

```
' Allocates and then releases 10 KB of memory using GlobalAlloc API function.
Dim ptr As IntPtr = Marshal.AllocHGlobal(10240)
...
Marshal.FreeHGlobal(ptr)
```

Notice that memory allocated in this way isn't controlled by garbage collection. If you forget to release it, it will be freed only when the application terminates.

When working with COM, you typically use a different allocating technique based on the CoTaskMemAlloc function. You can deal with this kind of memory through the AllocCoTaskMem, ReAllocCoTaskMem, and FreeCoTaskMem shared methods:

```
' Allocates and then releases 10 KB of memory using CoTaskMemAlloc OLE function.
Dim ptr As IntPtr = Marshal.AllocCoTaskMem(10240)
...
Marshal.FreeCoTaskMem(ptr)
```

Once you have allocated a block of unmanaged memory, you usually want to store some data in it before calling an unmanaged function or read data from it when the call returns. If the memory block contains an array of numeric, Char, or DateTime elements, you can use the Copy method:

```
' Pass an array of integers to a procedure that expects a pointer.
Dim values() As Integer = {1, 3, 5, 9, 11, 13, 15}
Dim bytes As Integer = values.Length * 4
' Allocate a block of memory and copy array elements into it.
Dim ptr As IntPtr = Marshal.AllocHGlobal(bytes)
Marshal.Copy(values, 0, ptr, bytes)
' Call the external routine.
TheExternalProc(ptr)
' Copy array elements back to the array and release memory.
Marshal.Copy(ptr, values, 0, bytes)
Marshal.FreeHGlobal(ptr)
```

You often have to allocate a block of unmanaged memory and copy a .NET Framework string into it, possibly after converting the string to ANSI. You can perform this operation in a single step by using one of the following techniques: use StringToHGlobalAnsi, StringToHGlobalUni, and StringToHGlobalAuto when copying a string into a block allocated with GlobalAlloc API function; or use StringToCoTaskMemAnsi, StringToCoTaskMemUni, and StringToCoTask-MemAuto when copying a string into a block allocated with the CoTaskMemAlloc function. The last portion of the method name indicates whether the string is converted to ANSI during the copy process:

```
' Use GlobalAlloc to allocate unmanaged memory and copy a string
' after converting it to ANSI if running under Windows 98 or Windows Me.
Dim s As String = "A .NET Framework string passed to COM"
Dim ptr As IntPtr = Marshal.StringToHGlobalAuto(s)
…
Marshal.FreeHGlobal(ptr)
```

You can also allocate a BSTR—which is the standard format for a COM string—and copy a string into it with the StringToBSTR method; memory allocated in this fashion must be released with the FreeBSTR method:

```
Dim s As String = "A .NET Framework string passed to COM"
Dim ptr As IntPtr = Marshal.StringToBSTR(s)
…
Marshal.FreeBSTR(ptr)
```

 If the unmanaged string contains confidential data, this data will continue to hang in memory until it is overwritten by other information, and other programs—including viruses and Trojan horses—might read it. To reduce this risk, you might want to fill it with zeros before releasing the block by means of the ZeroFree* methods that have been added to the Marshal class in version 2.0 of the .NET Framework, for example, ZeroFreeBSTR or ZeroFreeCoTaskMemAnsi:

```
ZeroFreeBSTR(ptr)
```

Also, for added security you might decide to work with SecureString objects exclusively. (Read the section titled "The SecureString Type" in Chapter 12, ".NET Basic Types," for more information.)

The Marshal class offers methods that write individual values into a block of unmanaged memory (WriteByte, WriteInt16, WriteInt32, WriteInt64, WriteIntPtr) and that read them back (ReadByte, ReadInt16, ReadInt32, ReadInt64, ReadIntPtr). The first argument to these methods is the IntPtr value returned by an allocation method, and the second (optional) argument is an offset into the memory block:

```
' Write an integer at offset 10 in a block of unmanaged memory.
Dim oldValue As Integer = 1234
Marshal.WriteInt32(ptr, 10, oldValue)
' Call the unmanaged function.
...
' Read the integer back.
Dim newValue As Integer = Marshal.ReadInt32(ptr, 10)
```

To show what you can do in practice with the allocation methods of the Marshal class, I have prepared an enhanced version of the CopyFile procedure that I introduced in the section titled "The FieldOffset Attribute" earlier in this chapter. As you might remember, the last element of the SHFILEOPSTRUCT structure that the SHFileOperation Windows API function uses is a string field that isn't aligned to the 4-byte boundary. The lack of alignment forces us to declare this element as an IntPtr instead of a string, or the program would throw a runtime exception. This element is used to display a user-defined message in the Copy File dialog box instead of the name of the file being copied. The enhanced version of the CopyFile function takes this user-defined message as an optional argument:

```
Function CopyFile(ByVal source As String, ByVal dest As String, _
      Optional ByVal progressText As String = Nothing) As Integer
   ' Fill an SHFILEOPSTRUCT structure.
   Dim sh As SHFILEOPSTRUCT
   sh.wFunc = 2              ' = FO_COPY, a file copy operation
   sh.hwnd = IntPtr.Zero     ' No owner window
   sh.pTo = dest
   ' Ensure source filename ends with an extra null char. (See SDK docs.)
   sh.pFrom = source & ControlChars.NullChar
   sh.fFlags = &H48          ' = ALLOWUNDO Or RENAMEONCOLLISION
   If Not (progressText Is Nothing) Then
      ' Allocate an ANSI string in memory and store its pointer here.
      sh.lpszProgressTitle = Marshal.StringToHGlobalAnsi(progressText)
      sh.fFlags = sh.fFlags Or &H100    ' &H100 = SIMPLEPROGRESS
   End If
   Dim res As Integer = SHFileOperation(sh)
   If Not (progressText Is Nothing) Then
      ' Release any memory taken for the progressText string.
      Marshal.FreeHGlobal(sh.lpszProgressTitle)
      sh.lpszProgressTitle = IntPtr.Zero
   End If
   ' The API functions return nonzero if there is a problem.
```

```
    If res = 0 Then
       Return 0                  ' 0 means everything was OK.
    ElseIf sh.fAnyOperationsAborted Then
       Return 1                  ' 1 means user aborted the operation.
    Else
       Return 2                  ' 2 means an error has occurred.
    End If
End Function
```

For more details, see the demo program that comes with this book's companion code.

Calling COM Components from .NET

There are three ways to enable a .NET application to call a COM object: you can use the Microsoft Visual Studio Add Reference command, you can run the Type Library Importer utility (TlbImp), or you can code against the TypeLibConverter class. Before looking at the practical details, however, it is important for you to understand what happens behind the scenes when a Visual Basic 2005 client uses a COM object.

The Runtime Callable Wrapper

Calling a COM component from a .NET Framework application is made possible by an object named the Runtime Callable Wrapper, or RCW. (See Figure 22-3.) This object "wraps" the COM component and makes it look to .NET clients like a regular managed component. The RCW is in charge of several tasks, all of which are necessary to make the COM component appear to its clients as a .NET Framework component. Such tasks include the marshaling of data, the conversion of COM's HRESULT values to exceptions, and the management of the COM component's lifetime (which is based on reference counting instead of garbage collection).

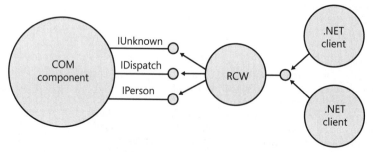

Figure 22-3   The Runtime Callable Wrapper object

The RCW consumes several important COM interfaces—including IUnknown, IDispatch, IDispatchEx, IProvideClassInfo, ISupportErrorInfo, and IErrorInfo—and hides them from .NET Framework clients. For example, a .NET Framework client can use a COM component through late binding because the RCW consumes the IDispatch interface behind the scenes to dispatch these calls to the actual object. The RCW is also responsible for object identity: there is one and only one RCW for each distinct COM object, regardless of how references to the COM object have been returned to the managed client(s). This requirement is necessary for the Is operator to work correctly with references pointing to a COM object.

The .NET Framework creates an RCW not only when a managed client explicitly instantiates a COM object, but also when a COM method returns a reference to a new object that isn't already known to the CLR because the COM Interop infrastructure always creates one distinct RCW for each COM object accessed from a managed application, regardless of whether it was created or returned by another method. The COM Interop infrastructure correctly preserves identity even in the most intricate cases. For example, when a managed client passes a .NET Framework object as an argument to a COM method and the unmanaged code later returns that object to the client, COM Interop correctly recognizes that the returned object is actually a managed object and returns a reference to that managed object, without creating an RCW.

A .NET Framework client can create a COM object in two different ways: as an early-bound object or as a late-bound object. You usually create an early-bound object by calling its constructor (with New) and assigning the result to a specific variable; you create a late-bound object by using Activator.CreateInstance and assigning the result to a generic Object variable.

The difference in how the object is created affects the type of RCW object that COM Interop creates behind the scenes. In the early binding case, the RCW is a well-defined .NET Framework type, and you can invoke its methods using the "dot" syntax, as you do with all .NET types. In the late binding case, the type of the RCW is System.__ComObject, and you can invoke the methods of the wrapped COM object only by using reflection (including reflection methods that Visual Basic transparently calls for you when Option Strict is Off and you use late-bound calls).

The CLR can early-bind a COM component only if metadata is available for it. This metadata must be available both at compile time (to generate the IL code) and at run time (to create the RCW object). The metadata for a COM component is similar to the metadata associated with standard .NET Framework types, except for a few attributes that identify that type as a COM component. In general, this metadata is extracted from the COM object's type library, implicitly as you use Visual Studio or explicitly if you use TlbImp.

Importing a COM Component with Visual Studio

The companion code that comes with this book includes a sample COM component named TestComComponent.dll. This component is written in Visual Basic 6 and exposes a Person class with the usual FirstName, LastName, and CompleteName members. Before proceeding, ensure that the component is registered in the Windows registry, using the regsvr32 tool:

```
REGSVR32 TestComComponent.dll
```

The simplest way to create metadata for a COM component is to let Visual Studio do it for you. Choose the Add Reference command from the Project menu to display the Add Reference dialog box, and then click the COM tab. It might take several seconds to fill this window the first time you run this command because Visual Studio parses the system registry and looks for all the registered COM components. When this process is completed, you see a list of components like the one shown in Figure 22-4. If the COM component you're looking for doesn't appear in this list, switch to the Browse tab and navigate to the folder where the component DLL resides.

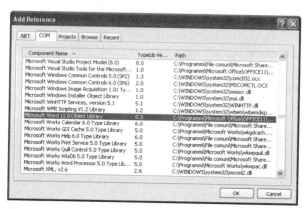

Figure 22-4   The COM tab of the Add Reference dialog box

When you click the OK button, Visual Studio parses the component's type library—which is embedded in the DLL itself in the case of a Visual Basic 6 component—and generates an assembly named Interop.TestComComponent.dll. This DLL is known as *interop assembly*. If you use ILDASM to peek into an interop assembly, you'll see that it contains a lot of metadata but very little executable code.

Using the Imported Interop Assembly

The main goal of COM Interop is to let the developer use COM objects as if they were .NET Framework components. As a matter of fact, the Visual Basic 2005 code that uses this component looks absolutely similar to the code you'd write to access a standard .NET Framework component:

```
Dim pers As New TestComComponent.Person
pers.FirstName = "John"
pers.LastName = "Evans"
Dim res As String = pers.CompleteName()
```

The preceding code snippet shows that you can use an imported COM object exactly as if it were a .NET Framework object. The only way a programmer could determine whether an object is a COM object is by using the Marshal.IsComObject method or by reflecting on the object's attributes.

On the other hand, if you know that you're dealing with an imported COM object, often you can optimize your code's behavior and avoid subtle bugs that derive from the different nature of COM and .NET Framework components. The different ways that COM and the .NET Framework manage object lifetime offers an example of what I mean.

A "true" COM component is destroyed as soon as the last variable that points to it is set to Nothing. However, a managed client has a reference to the RCW, which is a .NET object that works as a proxy for the COM component. Even if the managed client sets all the references to the COM object to Nothing, the RCW will not be picked up by the garbage collector until some time afterward. If the COM performs critical cleanup code in its destructor—such as closing a file or unlocking a record—the actual cleanup will occur later, and you might get an error when trying to access that specific file or record.

You can force the immediate release of a COM object by invoking the Marshal.ReleaseComObject method just before setting the object reference to Nothing:

```
Marshal.ReleaseComObject(pers)
pers = Nothing
```

In more advanced scenarios, you can also use the AddRef, Release, and QueryInterface methods of the Marshal class to directly access the object's IUnknown interface and manage its internal reference counter.

The ReleaseComObject method invokes the component's Release method for you and decreases the object's reference counter. If other clients are keeping a reference to the object, the object itself won't be released. In version 2.0 of the .NET Framework, you can use the new FinalReleaseComObject method, which tries to force the release by setting the reference counter to zero and returns the new value of the reference counter. By testing this return value you can detect whether the release operation was successful:

```
Dim counter As Integer = Marshal.FinalReleaseComObject(pers)
If counter = 0 Then Console.WriteLine("Object was successfully released.")
```

Importing a COM Component with TlbImp

Although the Visual Studio Add Reference dialog box offers a quick-and-dirty method to create metadata for a COM component, in some cases, you need to use the Type Library Importer command-line utility (TlbImp) provided with the .NET Framework SDK. For example, this utility is necessary when you want to perform the conversion by means of a batch or MAKE program or when you import the COM component as a strong-name assembly. (Strong name is required if you want to reference it from another strong-name assembly.) The syntax for TlbImp is simple:

```
TLBIMP source.dll [/OUT:dest.dll]
```

If the /out option is omitted, TlbImp creates a DLL with a name that matches the internal name of the type library, which might be different from its filename. For example, the type library associated with a Visual Basic 6 component is named after the project, not the DLL file (which in fact can be renamed before registering the type library). If the /out option is used, its argument affects both the name of the assembly being created and the namespace of the types inside it. For example, the following command creates a DLL named MyApp.Data.dll that contains types such as MyApp.Data.Invoice:

```
TLBIMP MyApp.dll [/OUT:MyApp.Data]
```

If the internal name of the type library matches its filename, you must use the /out switch because TlbImp correctly refuses to overwrite the source file. If the source DLL contains multiple type libraries (as is the case with the Visual Basic 6 type library, msvbvm60.dll), TlbImp extracts only the first type library, but you can append \N to the filename to extract the Nth type library. For example, the following command imports the VBRUN type library (which is the third type library embedded in msvbvm60.dll):

```
TLBIMP c:\Windows\System32\msvbvm60.dll\3 /OUT:vbrun.dll
```

As I've already mentioned, you must use TlbImp instead of the Visual Studio Add Reference command to generate interop assemblies with a strong name and a version number. Another good reason to use TlbImp is to generate classes in a namespace different from the default one. You can accomplish these tasks with the /keyfile, /asmversion, and /namespace options:

```
TLBIMP source.dll /KEYFILE:c:\codearchitects.snk /ASMVERSION:2.0.0.0
/NAMESPACE:CodeArchitects
```

Here the .snk file containing the public/private key pair has been generated previously with the option -k of the SN utility or from the Signing page of the My Project designer in Visual Studio. By default, TlbImp recursively imports all the type libraries referenced by the type library you specify. You can avoid this behavior by providing one or more /reference options pointing to other assemblies—in which case, TlbImp will attempt to solve external types in the assemblies you specify before it imports them. You can also specify the /strictref option if you want to cause an error if one or more external references could not be resolved without importing another type library:

```
TLBIMP source.dll /REFERENCE:Interop.Office.dll /STRICTREF
```

You can find additional details on TlbImp and its options in the .NET SDK documentation.

Primary Interop Assemblies

When working with COM Interop assemblies, you might bump into the following problem. Let's say that you create an interop assembly for the Microsoft Office Word type library, and you sign it to obtain a strong-name assembly. As a consequence, all the objects in this assembly have an identity that depends on your assembly's name and version and your publisher key. Let's further suppose that your program interacts with another .NET Framework application that uses Word through COM Interop and that has been authored by another company. Here's the problem: if the other company has created *another* interop assembly for Word and has signed it with *their* public key, their Word objects and your Word objects have different identities. For example, if a method in the other application returns a Word.Document object, your code throws a type mismatch exception when it attempts to store the return value to a Word.Document variable.

Microsoft has anticipated this problem and has introduced the concept of Primary Interop Assembly (PIA). A PIA is the "official" interop assembly for a COM component. It should be created by the manufacturer of the COM component itself, and it should be installed in the GAC and registered in the registry. Here's how you can create a PIA for a COM component that you've authored:

1. Use the /primary option of TlbImp to create the primary interop assembly, as follows:

    ```
    TLBIMP mylib.dll /OUT:mypia.dll /PRIMARY /KEYFILE:mycompany.snk
    ```

2. Run the AsmReg utility to add the PrimaryInteropAssembly registry key under the HKEY_CLASSES_ROOT\TypeLib\{tlbguid}\Version key related to the COM component:

    ```
    ASMREG mypia.dll
    ```

3. Run the GacUtil tool to install the interop assembly in the GAC:

    ```
    GACUITIL –i mypia.dll
    ```

4. Copy the assembly file to the C:\Program Files\Microsoft.NET\Primary Interop Assemblies folder to make it appear in Visual Studio .NET's Add Reference dialog box. (This step is optional.)

Visual Studio deals with PIAs in a special way: when you add a reference to a type library for which a PIA exists, Visual Studio doesn't import the type library as it normally would; instead, it uses the PIA installed in the system. Notice that a PIA can reference only other PIAs.

Microsoft provides the PIAs for a few important type libraries, such as adodb, Microsoft.mshtml, Microsoft.stdformat, office, and stdole. Other PIAs might be available on the Microsoft Web site.

Registration-Free COM Components

 A new feature of Visual Studio 2005 dramatically simplifies the deployment of COM components: registration-free COM components. Strictly speaking, this feature is part of the Microsoft Windows XP and Windows Server 2003 operating systems and could be exploited even without Visual Studio 2005. However, it's a new property in the IDE that makes this feature so accessible and easy to use.

A registration-free component is a COM component that resides in its client application's folder and can be accessed without having to register it in the registry with the RegSvr32 program or another similar tool. Even better, these COM components can be used only by the clients that are stored in their folder; therefore, different clients can use different versions of the same COM component. It's obvious that the deployment of these components is much simpler than usual and their setup routines can cause fewer troubles.

Defining a registration-free COM component is very simple in Visual Studio 2005: select the interop assembly in the project's reference list, press F4 to display the Properties window, and change the Isolated property from False (the default) to True, as shown in Figure 22-5. That's it!

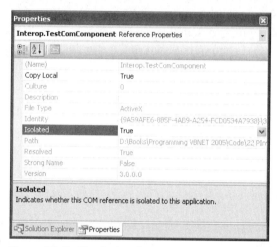

Figure 22-5   The Isolated property of an interop assembly added to the references of a project

Behind the scenes, Visual Studio generates a file named appname.exe.manifest, which contains the information that the COM infrastructure uses to locate the component. Keep in mind, however, that this manifest file is used only if COM fails to find the component in the registry. This implies that you need to unregister the component before you can test this feature. To do so, open a command-line window, navigate to the folder where the component is stored, and issue this command:

```
REGSVR32 /U TestComComponent.dll
```

You can now run the application from Windows Explorer and check that the COM component is instantiated correctly. (Running the application from inside Visual Studio would throw an exception because Visual Studio expects that the COM component is registered correctly.) You can double-check that the component runs in registration-free mode by temporarily renaming or deleting the manifest file: any attempt to run the application now throws a COM exception error.

Registration-free components are especially useful in ClickOnce scenarios, but you can leverage them in any application that uses one or more COM components. When weighing whether you should use these components, consider that you can use them only under Windows XP and Windows Server 2003 operating systems. The component must be an ActiveX DLL (not an ActiveX EXE), can't be a system component such as msxml6.dll, an Office object library, a Visual Studio plug-in, or an ActiveX control meant to be used in Microsoft Internet Explorer or in the Visual Studio Toolbox. When using third-party components, check with their vendors whether they already provide a manifest for their DLLs, and use it if available.

Late Binding and Reflection

In most real-world situations, you will import the metadata for a COM component and use it through early binding, but it's good to know that you don't strictly have to. In fact, managed code can access COM objects by using late binding and reflection techniques without having to import their type library. This technique can be useful when you use a COM object only once in a while, or when you don't know at compile time which objects your application will use.

Creating a COM component in a late-bound fashion requires that you use the Type.GetType-FromProgID or Type.GetTypeFromCLSID static methods to retrieve the Type object corresponding to the COM component with a given ProgID or CLSID. You can then pass this Type object to the Activator.CreateInstance method to create an instance of the component, which you typically assign to an Object variable. Finally, you use the Type.InvokeMember method to call a method, set a property, or read a property of the object, as you learned in Chapter 18, "Reflection."

The following code shows you how to create an ADODB.Connection object in a late-bound fashion and then query it for its Version property and open a connection to a Microsoft SQL Server database:

```
' Get the Type object for the ADODB.Connection COM component.
Dim ty As Type = Type.GetTypeFromProgID("ADODB.Connection")
' Create a Connection object through late binding.
Dim cn As Object = Activator.CreateInstance(ty)
' Use InvokeMember to retrieve the connection's Version property.
Dim version As String = CStr(ty.InvokeMember("Version", _
    BindingFlags.GetProperty, Nothing, cn, Nothing))

' Open the connection. (Open method takes one argument.)
Dim args() As Object = {"Provider=SQLOLEDB.1;Integrated Security=SSPI;" _
    & "Initial Catalog=pubs;Data Source=."}
ty.InvokeMember("Open", Reflection.BindingFlags.InvokeMethod, Nothing, cn, args)
```

When you invoke a method through late binding, you are implicitly relying on the COM object's IDispatch interface. This detail has a number of consequences. For example, the method name is case-insensitive because IDispatch works in this way, and all arguments are converted to Variant before being passed to the COM object. All COM components written with Visual Basic 6 support IDispatch and can be accessed in this fashion, but you can't use this technique with a few vtable-only components written in some other languages.

The BinderFlags value passed to InvokeMember is transparently converted to IDispatch flags. For example, BinderFlags.InvokeMethod corresponds to the DISPATCH_METHOD flag, and BinderFlags.GetProperty corresponds to DISPATCH_PROPERTYGET. BinderFlags.SetProperty might pose a problem, however, because it is translated to DISPATCH_PROPERTYPUT or DISPATCH_PROPERTYPUTREF, so it is unclear whether the property being assigned has both a Property Let and a Property Set procedure. In this case, you can precisely describe which Property procedure you're calling by using either the BinderFlags.PutDispProperty value

(DISPATCH_PROPERTYPUT, for Property Let) or the BinderFlags.PutRefDispProperty value (DISPATCH_PROPERTYPUTREF, for Property Set).

The System.Type class has a few members that are useful when working with COM objects. You can use the IsComObject read-only property to check whether a .NET type is actually a wrapper for a COM class and the GUID property to retrieve the component's GUID. The Base-Type property of a COM object created through late binding is System.__ComObject, whereas the BaseType property of an early-bound COM object is Nothing.

> **Note**   The next two sections assume that you are familiar with advanced COM programming topics, such as HRESULTs, VT_* Variant subtypes, and apartments. If you aren't familiar with these concepts, you might want to skip these sections.

COM Interop Marshaling

I covered data marshaling in the section titled "Using PInvoke" earlier in this chapter, but a few issues that concern COM Interop only are left to be discussed.

To begin with, you must learn how COM errors are returned to a managed client. The CLR checks the HRESULT 32-bit value returned from all COM methods: if the COM method returns an error, this value is negative. In this case, the CLR attempts to generate the exception that matches the returned HRESULT value. It can find the matching exception type by look-ing for a known mapping or by calling methods of the IErrorInfo interface to retrieve addi-tional information about the error, if the COM object supports this interface. If both these attempts fail, the CLR throws a generic COMException object. The ErrorCode property of this COMException object contains the original HRESULT value, so you can use it in a Select Case block to provide different recovery actions for different error codes.

Variant arguments are another common source of problems. When you import a type library, all arguments and return values of Variant type are converted to Object values by the type library import process. If you pass a value to one of these Object arguments, the CLR dynam-ically determines the internal type of the Variant that is actually passed to COM. For example, Integer values are converted to VT_I4 Variants, Boolean values to VT_BOOL Variants, Nothing values to VT_EMPTY Variants, and DBNull values to VT_NULL Variants. (The internal type of a Variant corresponds to the value returned by the VarType function under Visual Basic 6.)

However, not all COM types correspond to .NET Framework types, so you might need to resort to one of the following auxiliary classes to force the marshaler to convert your Object value to a specific VT_* type: CurrencyWrapper (VT_CY), UnknownWrapper (VT_UNKNOWN), DispatchWrapper (VT_DISPATCH), and ErrorWrapper (VT_ERROR). For example, here's how you can pass a .NET Decimal value to a Variant argument that is expected to receive a Currency value:

```
Dim cw As New CurrencyWrapper(2.5@)
obj.MyMethod(cw)
```

Objects passed to Variant arguments pose other problems, too, because the runtime must copy the Object into a brand-new Variant. If the object is passed by value and the COM method changes one or more object properties, these changes can't be seen by the managed client. A similar thing happens when a COM method returns a Variant value that contains an object: in this case, the runtime copies the Variant into a brand-new Object value, but changes to this object's properties aren't propagated to the original Variant seen by the COM component.

Changes in both directions are seen if a managed client passes an object to a ByRef Variant argument, but keep in mind that the COM method might assign a completely different type of object to the argument. Therefore, you can't assume that, when the method returns, the argument still contains the same type of object it did before the call.

The situation is even more complicated if the Variant returned from COM has the VT_BYREF bit set, which indicates that the Variant contains a 32-bit pointer to the data. (For example, a Variant that contains a VT_BYREF+VT_DISPATCH value is actually a pointer to an object.) If the Variant is passed by value, the marshaler correctly recognizes the BT_BYREF bit and is able to retrieve the object reference, but any changes to this .NET Framework object aren't propagated to the original COM object (unlike what would happen if the client were a true COM application). If the Variant is passed with the ByRef keyword, however, changes to the .NET object are correctly propagated to the original COM object, but only if the COM method hasn't changed the type of the object. If the COM method has changed the object's type, an InvalidCastException occurs on return from the method.

The bottom line: steer clear of COM objects that take and return Variant arguments, if possible. If you can't avoid them, read the documentation carefully, and use the preceding notes as a guideline for troubleshooting code that doesn't behave as expected.

Threading Issues

One more issue must be taken into account when accessing COM from a .NET Framework client. COM components live either in a Single Thread Apartment (STA) or in a Multi Thread Apartment (MTA), even though a few components can live in both apartment types. By comparison, .NET Framework applications run as free-threaded code, don't use apartments, and implement synchronization by other means (for example, synchronized regions and locks).

The CLR must initialize either an STA or an MTA before a managed client can call a COM object. The type of the apartment being initialized affects all subsequent calls: if the apartment isn't compatible with the apartment where the COM component resides, COM has to create a proxy/stub pair between them, which in turn has a serious negative effect on performance. All Visual Basic 6 components can live only in an STA; therefore, calls to these components coming from .NET Framework clients that have initialized an MTA will be slowed by an intermediate proxy/stub.

Visual Basic 2005 Console and Windows Forms applications initialize an STA by default, but other types of applications initialize an MTA by default. You can affect the apartment type that a managed thread creates by testing the current apartment type with the Thread object's GetApartmentState method and, if necessary, setting it with the SetApartmentState or TrySetApartmentState method. You must call these methods before you make the first call to COM:

```
If Thread.CurrentThread.GetApartmentState() = ApartmentState.Unknown Then
    ' Apartment hasn't been created yet.
    If Thread.CurrentThread.TrySetApartmentState(ApartmentState.STA) Then
        ' You successfully managed to set STA mode.
        …
    Else
        ' For some reason you can't use STA mode. You can decide to emit error
        ' or do whatever is more appropriate for the current application.
        …
End If
' Now you can call a Visual Basic 6 component.
Dim sc As New SampleComponent.SampleObject
```

You can't change the apartment type after the thread has initialized the apartment. Further attempts to modify the ApartmentState property are simply ignored, without raising any exception. Another way to tell the CLR which apartment type should be created is by flagging the Sub Main procedure with either the STAThread or the MTAThread attribute:

```
<STAThread()> _
Sub Main
    …
End Sub
```

> **Note** ASP.NET applications create MTA apartments by default, but you can set the Page.AspCompatMode property or the AspCompat attribute in a @Page directive to True to force the page to execute in an STA. This setting is also necessary to call COM+ objects that access built-in objects such as Request or Response either through the ObjectContext object or through the argument passed to the OnStartPage method. For this property or attribute to work correctly, however, the COM or COM+ object must be created from inside the Page_Init or Page_Load event handler, as opposed to from inside the page's constructor or by means of a field initializer. Setting this property or attribute to True degrades the page's performance, so you should weigh the tradeoff of having an ASP.NET page running in an STA vs. going through a proxy/stub when the page calls an STA-only COM object.

Calling .NET Objects from COM

When porting a large Visual Basic 6 application to .NET, you might decide to leave the bulk of the application as unmanaged code while rewriting selected components as Visual Basic 2005 classes. In this scenario, roles are reversed: unmanaged COM-based code works as the client of managed components. The COM Interop portion of the .NET Framework makes this scenario feasible.

The COM Callable Wrapper

A COM Callable Wrapper (CCW) works as a wrapper for a .NET Framework component exposed to a COM client. (See Figure 22-6.) It synthesizes any COM interface that clients expect to find, most notably IUnknown ("the mother of all COM interfaces") and IDispatch (which makes the object accessible from languages such as Microsoft Visual Basic Scripting Edition (VBScript) or through late binding in Visual Basic 6 and earlier versions). The CCW is also responsible for the object identity, so there is always at most one CCW instance for each instance of the .NET Framework component, even if multiple clients have a reference to the same object. The CCW also protects the .NET Framework object from garbage collections and morphs CLR exceptions into HRESULT codes when the method call returns to the COM client.

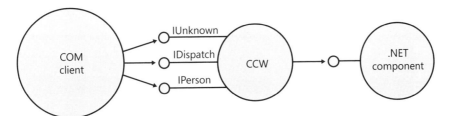

Figure 22-6   The COM Callable Wrapper object

For the .NET Framework to be able to create a suitable CCW object, you must create a type library for each component you want to expose to the COM world. Providing a type library helps COM developers code against the .NET Framework class—for example, by leveraging the Visual Basic 6 Object Browser and the IntelliSense feature—and lets the .NET Framework object expose richer information at run time. A type library is also necessary at run time to let OleAut32 marshal remote instances of the objects.

Creating a Sample .NET Component

To see in practice how you can expose a Visual Basic 2005 component to the COM world, let's create a sample class and see how a COM client can access it. Start by creating a new Class Library project, name it SampleNetComponent, and delete the default Class1.vb file.

When creating a .NET Framework class meant to be exposed to COM clients, you can save time by using the Add New Item command from the Project menu and selecting the COM Class template. Name the new component Employee, and click OK. Visual Studio creates a new class that is already decorated with some key attributes that make the class visible to COM clients. Here's an abridged version of what Visual Studio creates if you select the COM Class template:

```
<ComClass(Employee.ClassId, Employee.InterfaceId, Employee.EventsId)> _
Public Class Employee
    Public Const ClassId As String = "f1cdeea2-601b-479d-b1f4-ec9cc4905f04"
    Public Const InterfaceId As String = "452d1073-df75-443a-b3fb-a397628eb883"
    Public Const EventsId As String = "5d5ded49-1162-4f6c-93c8-74a010202072"
```

```
' A creatable COM class must have a Public Sub New with no parameters, otherwise,
' the class isn't registered in the registry and can't be created via CreateObject.
Public Sub New()
   MyBase.New()
End Sub
End Class
```

You can now add members to this class, including properties, methods, and events. .NET Framework assemblies meant to be used by COM clients are usually registered in the GAC, and for this reason, they should be signed with a strong name. In Visual Studio 2005, you can perform this action on the Signing page of the My Project designer. Next, switch to the Compile page, and ensure that the Register For COM Interop option is selected. This option forces Visual Studio to create a type library with the same name as the DLL (SampleNetComponent.tlb, in this example) and to register this type library in the system registry.

Build the project, create a DLL named SampleNetComponent.Dll, and then create another project that references and uses the Employee class. This second project can be as simple as a Console application; it serves only to verify that the class works as expected. You'll notice that all the extra attributes in the Employee class don't affect the way the class can be used by a managed client.

Now you can bring up Visual Basic 6, add a reference to this SampleNetComponent.tlb file, and use the .NET Framework class as if it were a standard COM component. (See the companion code for a demo client written in Visual Basic 6.)

Important   .NET Framework components undergo all the usual binding and probing rules, even when they are accessed by COM clients. If you don't install the assembly in the GAC, the assembly should be stored as a private assembly in the unmanaged application's directory. If the client is a Visual Basic 6 application running inside the IDE (as opposed to compiled on disk), the application's directory is C:\Program Files\Microsoft Visual Studio\VB98—namely, the directory where the VB6.EXE executable resides.

The RegAsm and TlbExp Tools

You can also use a couple of utilities in the .NET Framework SDK to export an assembly to a type library. You should become familiar with these utilities because they offer some extra flexibility that you can't achieve solely with the Visual Studio export capabilities.

The Assembly Registration Tool (RegAsm) takes the name of an assembly and registers all the classes it contains in the system registry:

```
REGASM samplenetcomponent.dll /tlb:netcomp.tlb
```

The /tlb switch is optional, but you'll want to use it so that RegAsm produces a type library that COM clients can use to reference .NET Framework objects through early binding. In practice, you can omit the /tlb switch and not create a type library for the component only if

COM clients create and use instances of the .NET class exclusively through late binding by means of the CreateObject function and Object (or Variant) variables.

You can think of RegAsm as a RegSvr32 utility that works with .NET components instead of COM components. As with the RegSvr32 utility, you can unregister a component from the registry by using the /u option:

```
REGASM samplenetcomponent.dll /u
```

The RegAsm utility supports two more useful switches. The /codebase option adds a Code-Base registry entry and should be used only if the .NET assembly isn't shared or isn't going to be registered in the GAC. (Visual Studio 2005 uses the /codebase option when exporting an assembly.)

```
REGASM samplenetcomponent.dll /codebase
```

The other option is /regfile, which doesn't register the component but creates a .reg file that you can later use to create all the necessary registry keys. (You can't use this option with /u or /tlb, and you can't duplicate its effect from inside Visual Studio.)

```
REGASM samplenetcomponent.dll /regfile:netcomp.reg
```

The .NET Framework SDK offers another tool that you can use to export a type library, the Type Library Exporter utility (TlbExp). TlbExp has the same effect as using the /tlb option with RegAsm, except the component isn't registered:

```
TLBEXP samplenetcomponent.dll /OUT:netcomp.tlb
```

If you omit the /out option, TlbExp creates a type library with the same name as the source DLL but with a .tlb extension. In practice, you'll use TlbExp far less frequently than you use RegAsm.

Conversion Details

.NET Framework assemblies embed more metadata than COM type libraries do; therefore, it is unavoidable that some information is lost in the conversion process from .NET to COM. In most cases, you don't need to care about these details, but you should keep a few things in mind. In this section, I summarize what you should be careful about.

Assembly version information consists of a four-part number, whereas type libraries support only major and minor version numbers. During the conversion process, the assembly's revision and build version numbers are discarded. If the assembly had no version information—that is, the version is 0.0.0.0—the type library is assigned version 1.0; otherwise, it couldn't be loaded correctly by a COM client.

A .NET Framework class or interface is exported to a coclass or interface with the same name. The namespace portion of the class or interface name is discarded: type libraries don't support the concept of nested classes or interfaces, and therefore the conversion "flattens" the object hierarchy. For example, a type named Animal.Mammal.Mouse is exported to a coclass named Mouse. When a name collision would result—for example, because another class is named Hardware.Peripheral.Mouse—the type is exported with its full name, but periods are replaced by underscores.

A Visual Basic class must be nonabstract (that is, not marked with the MustInherit keyword) and must expose a public parameterless constructor, either explicit or implicit, for it to be converted to a COM creatable class. (COM doesn't support constructors with arguments.) Creatable classes are assigned a ProgID equal to their complete namespace+name path. This ProgID generation process usually works flawlessly because ProgIDs can contain periods, except when the complete class name is longer than 39 characters or contains punctuation symbols other than periods. In such cases, you should specify a ProgID attribute in your Visual Basic 2005 source code. (See the next section.) Noncreatable classes are marked with the noncreatable attribute in the type library. Only creatable classes are registered by the RegAsm utility.

Any coclass generated by the conversion process is assigned a class identifier (CLSID) calculated using a hash function on the complete class name (including its namespace). This technique ensures that different classes generate different CLSIDs, and therefore each .NET Framework class is converted to a distinct COM class. This technique also ensures that the same CLSID is generated regardless of how many times the conversion process is performed. You can also assign a custom ID if you need to, as explained in the following section.

The conversion process generates one *class interface* for each .NET Framework class. Interfaces generated by the conversion process are assigned an interface identifier (IID) calculated using a hash function on the complete interface name (including its namespace) as well as the signatures of its methods. The hash function ensures that a different IID is generated if the interface name, the order of its methods, or the signature of any method changes. The generation of a new IID is necessary to comply with the immutable interface concept in COM. Notice that method names aren't taken into account by the hash function and that you can control the IID value using the Guid attribute, as explained in the next section.

Only public instance members are exposed through a class interface; static members, nondefault constructors, and members with a scope other than Public aren't exported to COM. You can selectively hide one or more public methods to COM by means of the ComVisible attribute, as I explain in the next section.

Methods preserve their name when they are exported to a class interface (or any interface, for that matter). However, Visual Basic 2005 supports method overloading, whereas COM doesn't. To let COM clients call overloaded versions of a method, TlbExp generates a distinct method for each overloaded variant and decorates the name of additional methods with an ordinal number, starting at 2, so that each method is assigned a unique name. For example, three overloaded versions of a method named MyMethod are exported as MyMethod, MyMethod_2, and MyMethod_3. There is no guarantee that numbers will always be assigned in the same order if you repeat the export process.

Marshaling data from COM to .NET works along the same general guidelines described earlier in this chapter. However, you should be careful about method signatures when working with Visual Basic 6 as a client. A Visual Basic 6 client can't call a .NET Framework method that takes a ByVal array. You should change the method signature so that the array is passed ByRef, which is the only legal way to pass array arguments in earlier Visual Basic versions.

Using Attributes to Control the Conversion

Now that you have a broad view of how the conversion from assemblies to type libraries works, let's see how you can decorate the .NET Framework class with attributes to gain control of the conversion process and solve some of the problems I mentioned in the previous section.

The ComVisible, ProgId, and Guid Attributes

By default, public assemblies, classes, and interfaces are exported and made visible to COM clients. However, you can make a specific public element invisible to COM by using the ComVisible attribute, which can be applied at the assembly, class, or member level. If applied at the assembly level, the attribute affects the visibility of all classes in the assembly, unless a class-level attribute forces a different visibility. Likewise, an attribute at the class level affects all the methods in the class that aren't flagged with a ComVisible attribute. Consider this code:

```
<Assembly: ComVisible(False)>
<ComVisible(True)> _
Public Class Person          ' This class is visible to COM.

    ...
    <ComVisible(False)> _
    Sub DoSomething()        ' This method isn't visible to COM.
        ...
    End Sub
End Class

Public Class Employee        ' This class isn't visible to COM.
    ...
End Class
```

Interestingly, if a method takes or returns a type that isn't visible to COM, the argument or the return value is exported to COM as an IUnknown value; if a method takes or returns a structure (as opposed to a class) that isn't visible to COM, the method isn't exported at all.

You can explicitly assign a ProgID to a class by using the ProgId attribute in the Visual Basic source code. For example, the following code assigns the MouseCollection class a ProgID equal to Animal.Mice:

```
<ProgID("Animal.Mice")> _
Public Class MouseCollection
    ...
End Class
```

You can also assign a specific GUID to a class or an interface by using the Guid attribute. When you apply this attribute at the assembly level, it is taken as the TLBID identifier for the entire type library:

```
' This is the TLBID for the exported type library.
<Assembly: Guid("3DC10475-92DB-4E52-A3D2-925AA4E8BA17")>

' This is the CLSID for the class.
<Guid("{E6A2200A-5869-4C89-83A1-D0FE8540020B}")> _
Public Class MouseCollection

    ...

End Class
```

The DispId Attribute

All the members of a COM IDispatch interface must be marked with a DISPID value, and these values are generated automatically in the conversion from .NET to COM. In general, you never see these DISPIDs and don't need to control their generation. The only exception worth mentioning is the special 0 value, which is reserved for the class default member.

As you might remember from your Visual Basic 6 days, most controls and objects have a default member—for example, the Text property for TextBox controls and the Caption property for Label controls. The default member of .NET classes exported to COM is the ToString method that all classes inherit from System.Object, but you can make any property or method the default class member by applying the DispId attribute, as in the following:

```
<DispId(0)> Property Name() As String

    ...

End Property
```

The ComClass and ClassInterface Attributes

You can be in control of the CLSID and the IID of the class interface generated for a .NET Framework class as well as the IID of the generated interface that handles events by means of the ComClass attribute. (Visual Studio automatically inserts this attribute when it generates a COM class, as explained in the section titled "Creating a Sample .NET Component" earlier in this chapter.) Interestingly, the ComClass attribute belongs to the Microsoft.VisualBasic namespace, unlike all other attributes related to COM Interop (which belong to the System .Runtime.InteropServices namespace).

Flagging a .NET Framework class with this Visual Basic–specific ComClass attribute has many advantages and a few disadvantages. On the pro side, classes flagged with this attribute correctly expose properties, methods, and events to both early-bound and late-bound COM clients, with very little effort on your part. On the con side, however, these classes don't expose their public fields, nor do they expose methods inherited from System.Object, including the useful ToString method.

Any public .NET Framework class can be exposed to COM, provided that its source code contains a ComVisible(True) attribute at the class or the assembly level. A class exposed to COM with a ComVisible attribute but without a ComClass attribute exports its class interface—that is, the interface that contains all the properties and methods defined in the class—as an IDispatch interface. This means that COM clients can access the class's members only by means of late binding. Late binding is slow, isn't robust, and doesn't allow you to trap events. Despite these shortcomings, Microsoft decided to make class interfaces accessible through IDispatch by default. Late binding ensures that you don't incur versioning problems:

```
' *** Visual Basic 6 code
Dim o As Object
Set o = CreateObject("SampleNetComponent.Employee")
o.MyMethod()
```

You can control which type of class interface the export process generates by means of the ClassInterface attribute. This attribute can take one of the following ClassInterfaceType enumerated values: AutoDispatch (the default—methods are accessible through late binding only), AutoDual (methods are accessible through early and late binding), None (no class interface is created and only methods in secondary interfaces can be accessed). Here's how you must decorate a class to offer support for both early binding and late binding:

```
<ClassInterface(ClassInterfaceType.AutoDual)> _
Public Class Employee
    ...
End Class
```

Clients of a class flagged with the ClassInterface attribute that specifies an AutoDual interface type can access public fields and the four instance methods that all .NET Framework classes inherit from System.Object; these two kinds of members aren't visible if you decorate the class with the ComClass attribute.

However, a class flagged with just the ClassInterface attribute doesn't make its events visible to clients. To solve this problem, I need to introduce two more attributes.

The InterfaceType and ComSourceInterfaces Attributes

Let's say that you have the following class:

```
Public Class Person
    Public Event GotEmail(ByVal msg As String)
    Public Event TodayIsMyBirthday(ByVal age As Integer)
    ...
End Class
```

As I've just explained, these events aren't automatically exposed to COM clients if the class isn't flagged with the ComClass attribute. To make events visible to COM clients when this attribute isn't used, you must define a separate interface that contains the event signature and mark the interface with an InterfaceType attribute to make it an IDispatch interface, as follows:

```
<InterfaceType(ComInterfaceType.InterfaceIsIDispatch)> _
Public Interface Person_Events
    Sub GotEmail(ByVal msg As String)
    Sub TodayIsMyBirthday(ByVal age As Integer)
End Interface
```

Next you must flag the Person class with a ComSourceInterfaces attribute that informs COM Interop that the class events are defined in the Person_Events interface:

```
<ClassInterface(ClassInterfaceType.AutoDual), _
 ComSourceInterfaces(GetType(Person_Events))> _
Public Class Person
    Public Event GotEmail(ByVal msg As String)
    Public Event TodayIsMyBirthday(ByVal age As Integer)
    …
End Class
```

After these edits, Visual Basic 6 clients can assign an instance of the Employee class to a With-Events variable and correctly trap events.

The ComRegisterFunction and ComUnregisterFunction Attributes

At times, you might need to perform a custom action when the .NET class is registered as a COM component by RegAsm (or by Visual Studio, if you have selected the Register For COM Interop option). For example, you might want to ask the end user for a password or add some keys to the registry (in addition to those added by the registration process). Accomplishing these tasks is as easy as adding a shared procedure to the class and marking it with the ComRegisterFunction attribute:

```
Const COMPANYKEY As String = "Software\CodeArchitects\MyApp"

<ComRegisterFunction()> _
Private Shared Sub Register(ByVal ty As Type)
    Dim key As RegistryKey = Registry.CurrentUser.CreateSubKey(COMPANYKEY)
    key.SetValue("InstallDate", Now.ToLongDateString)
    key.Close()
End Sub
```

If you add a registry key at installation time, you should remove it when the class is unregistered as a COM component. In this case, you create another static procedure and mark it with the ComUnregisterFunction attribute:

```
Private Shared Sub UnRegister(ByVal ty As Type)
    Registry.CurrentUser.DeleteSubKey(COMPANYKEY)
End Sub
```

Both these procedures can be private or public, provided that they are marked with the Shared keyword and take a System.Type argument; this Type value identifies the class being registered or unregistered.

Working with Exceptions

Most CLR exceptions are automatically translated into the corresponding HRESULT codes when they are marshaled back to COM clients. For example, a DivideByZeroException object is translated to an HRESULT code equal to COR_E_DIVIDEBYZERO, which a Visual Basic 6 client can trap with an On Error statement and interpret as an error that has an Err.Number code of 11.

In those rare cases when you need to return a more specific HRESULT code, you can use a couple of techniques. The first and simplest one relies on the ThrowExceptionForHR method of the Marshal class:

```
' Throw an exception that has an HRESULT of hex 80001234.
Marshal.ThrowExceptionForHR(&H80001234)
```

The second, more elegant technique consists of the definition of a custom exception class that has a constructor that assigns the desired error code to its HResult protected property:

```
Public Class CustomException
   Inherits Exception

   Sub New(ByVal message As String)
      MyBase.New(message)
      Me.HResult = &H80001234
   End Sub
End Class
```

Your Visual Basic 2005 class can then throw an exception with a given HRESULT by throwing this custom exception as it would any standard exception:

```
Throw New CustomException("File not found")
```

Writing COM-Friendly .NET Framework Components

.NET Framework components that are meant to be exposed to COM clients shouldn't use features that COM-based clients can't see. Or they should provide alternative ways for COM clients to access those features. Here's a brief summary of the dos and don'ts of COM-friendly components:

■ Only public and nonabstract classes can be exposed to COM; use ComVisible(False) for public MustInherit classes.

■ Avoid deep hierarchies in Visual Basic classes, such as nested classes or namespaces with more than two levels.

■ The class must expose an implicit or explicit parameterless constructor; constructors with parameters can't be accessed through COM Interop.

■ The class shouldn't expose shared members because they aren't visible to COM clients.

■ The class shouldn't expose overloaded members because they can create confusion when used by COM clients.

■ If the class exposes events, define them in a separate interface, and use the ComSource-Interfaces attribute to let COM Interop export them correctly.

■ For simplicity's sake, use the ComClass attribute if COM clients don't need to access fields, trap events, or invoke methods inherited from System.Object.

■ Use custom exception classes that set the HResult property for returning nonstandard error codes to COM clients.

The .NET Framework offers superb support for the transition to and from the unmanaged world, thanks to PInvoke and COM Interop. In most cases, these two worlds can communicate quite easily, but you must be familiar with the techniques I have covered in this chapter to solve some of the problems you might bump into when writing real-world applications. However, never forget that a .NET Framework application that relies on COM components inherits many of the issues that have plagued COM programming, for example, the tendency to leak memory.

Index

Symbols

& (ampersand), 57, 64, 170
&= (ampersand-equals), 77–78
<> (angle brackets), 40, 41
''' (apostrophes), 147
* (asterisk), 65, 149
*= (asterisk-equals), 77–78
@ (at symbol), 56
\ (backslash), 47, 62, 183
\= (backslash-equals), 77–78
([|]) brackets, 276, 413
^ (caret), 47, 63–64
^= (caret-equals), 77–78
(:) colon, 149
{} (curly braces), 80, 82, 419
$ (dollar sign), 101, 157, 165
(.) dot character, 32, 38
"" (double quotation marks), 131
>> (double greater than), 74–77, 132
>>= (double greater than-equals), 77–78
<< (double less than), 74–77
<<= (double less than-equals), 77–78
= (equals), 50, 70, 80, 271–272
! (exclamation point), 56, 65
/ (forward slash), 62–63, 176
/= (forward slash-equals), 77–78
> (greater than), 70, 132, 177
<= (greater than or equal to), 70
<> (greater than or less than), 70
< (less than), 70
<= (less than or equal to), 70
- (minus), 188
(number sign), 56, 59, 65, 149
() (parentheses), 75, 82, 92
. (period), 32, 38, 144
+ (plus), 57, 64, 186, 188
? (question mark), 65, 149, 176, 188
[] (square brackets), 276, 413
?+Tab key combination, 154
_ (underscore character), 40

A

abstract classes. *See also* base classes; inheritance
    deriving collection classes from base collection types, 389–390
    generic collection types, 539
    inheritance and, 323–325
    for strong-typed collections, 522–526. *See also* strong-typed collection classes

access control entries (ACEs), 601
access control lists (ACLs), 599–606
    account names and security identifiers, 599–600
    DirectorySecurity and FileSecurity types, 600–604
    modifying, 604–606
    Mutex type, 849
access, Visual Studio 2005 online, 126–127, 167. *See also* Help
accessibility. *See* scope
accessors, private, 221–222
AccessRule type, 602
account names, 599–600
Active Server Pages (ASP), 12
Active Solution Configuration combo box, 137, 138
ActiveX Data Objects (ADO), 11
Adapter method, 510
adapters, reusable enumerable, 392–396
Add As Link command, 128
Add Existing Item dialog box, 129
Add New Item command, 127, 164
Add New Test dialog box, 209–210
Add Reference dialog box, 32–33, 674, 929–930
Add Watch command, 187
AddFirst, AddLast, AddBefore, and AddAfter methods, 533
AddHandler keyword, 297–300. *See also* events
addition assignment operators, 77–78
AddMemoryPressure method, 361
AddRange method, 509, 528
AddRef method, 341
$ADDRESS placeholder, 183
AddressOf operator, 283
ADO.NET, 11
Advanced Compiler Settings dialog box, 110, 137–138, 139, 142, 681
Advanced Security Settings dialog box, 230–231, 603
AfterKeyPress event, 178
Alias command, 176
aliases, namespaces and, 35
Alt key, 145, 168
Alt+* key combination, 185
alternating constructs, regular expression, 547, 550–551
Alt+F11 key combination, 173
Alt+F8 key combination, 171
ampersand (&), 57, 64, 170
ampersand-equals (&=), 77–78
Anakrino decompiler utility, 7
And method, 520
And operator, 71–73, 75, 273
AndAlso operator, 66, 72–74, 86, 273
angle brackets (<>), 40, 41
anonymous methods, 502

Francesco Balena

Francesco Balena began his software studies in the late 1970s and had to fight for a while with huge IBM mainframes and tons of punched cards while he waited for the PC to be invented. From those good old days—when the word *megabyte* made little sense and *gigabyte* was pure blasphemy—he retained his taste for writing the most efficient and resource-aware code possible.

In more recent years, Francesco has become a contributing editor and member of the Technical Advisory Board of *Visual Studio Magazine* (formerly *Visual Basic Programmer's Journal*), for which he has written more than 80 articles and columns. He's the author of the best-sellers *Programming Microsoft Visual Basic 6.0*, *Programming Microsoft Visual Basic .NET*, and *Programming Microsoft Visual Basic .NET Version 2003*, as well as coauthor of *Applied .NET Framework Programming in Microsoft Visual Basic .NET* (with Jeffrey Richter) and *Practical Guidelines and Best Practices for Microsoft Visual Basic and Visual C# Developers* (with Giuseppe Dimauro), all from Microsoft Press. Francesco teaches Microsoft Visual Basic and C# courses in the United States and Europe and speaks at developer conferences such as VSLive!, SQL2TheMax, WinDev, and WinSummit. He is the founder of the popular .NET-2-The-Max site (*http://www.dotnet2themax.com*), where you can find articles, tips, routines, and updates as they occur for this book.

Francesco is the lead author of VBMaximizer, a best-seller add-in for Microsoft Visual Basic 6 that has won an award from readers of *Visual Studio Magazine*, and he is coauthor of CodeBox for .NET (a code repository tool) and Form Maximizer for .NET (a set of Microsoft Windows Forms controls). Since 2002, he has been the Microsoft MSDN Regional Director for Italy and is cofounder of Code Architects, an Italian company that specializes exclusively in Microsoft .NET Framework programming and training and that consults for many large software companies in Italy, including Microsoft.

Francesco lives in Bari, Italy, with his wife, Adriana and his son, Andrea, but spends a lot of his time abroad. In a previous life, he had many good times playing his alto sax with big bands and jazz combos until he found that computer programming can be just as much fun and doesn't require that he be awake and blowing until 4 A.M. each and every night. Only later did he realize that—to write code and meet deadlines—he wouldn't be going to sleep before 4 A.M. anyway, but it was too late to change his mind.

orm Maximizer.NET

m Maximizer.NET is an innovative component library that extends standard Windows Forms
trols with 35 new design-time properties, and enables you to enhance existing applications
out replacing any existing control or writing a single line of code. Here's a partial list of what
m Maximizer .NET enables you to do:

Validate user input: Force a specific data type, a valid range, a validation regex; or specify a custom expression that references other controls, form variables, and methods.

Define the state of a control: Decide when a control becomes visible, enabled, or readonly, depending on the value of other fields or the user's role.

Create calculated fields: Enter an expression in the Properties window and have the field automatically recalculated when other fields on the form change.

Change field appearance: Change the appearance of fields when they receive the input focus, fail to validate, or meet custom condition (e.g. negative numbers, empty fields).

Format data: Automatically format numbers and dates when the focus leaves the control.

Assign common tasks to buttons and menus: Load/save text files and images, show forms and common dialogs, launch applications, without writing code.

…plus auto-tabbing, multiline tooltips, field descriptions, toolbar hotkeys, centralized events, nonrectangular forms, and more.

orm Maximizer.NET works with any .NET programming language. Full C# source code is available (in Form Maximizer .NET Enterprise Edition only).

Read more about Form Maximizer .NET and download a fully functional demo version at
www.dotnet2themax.com/formmaximizer

Form Maximizer.NET and CodeWall.NET have been authored by Francesco Balena and are distributed by Code Architects Srl, Italy (www.codearchitects.com).

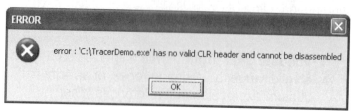
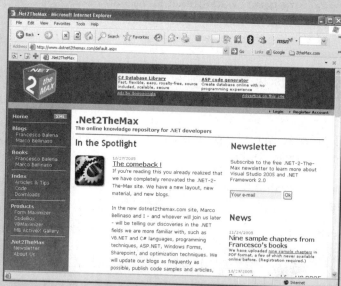

What do you think of this book? We want to hear from you!

Do you have a few minutes to participate in a brief online survey? Microsoft is interested in hearing your feedback about this publication so that we can continually improve our books and learning resources for you.

To participate in our survey, please visit:

www.microsoft.com/learning/booksurvey

And enter this book's ISBN, 0-7356-2183-7. As a thank-you to survey participants in the United States and Canada, each month we'll randomly select five respondents to win one of five $100 gift certificates from a leading online merchant.* At the conclusion of the survey, you can enter the drawing by providing your e-mail address, which will be used for prize notification *only*.

Thanks in advance for your input. Your opinion counts!

Sincerely,

Microsoft Learning

Learn More. Go Further.